Office 2000 Essentials Course

Brian Favro

Russel Stolins

Developmental Editor: Brian Favro
Marketing Director: David Gauny
Production Management, Design and Publishing Consultation: The Cowans
Copy Editing: Nick Murray
Technical Illustrations: Rappid Rabbit Design
Composition: The Cowans
Index: Bayside Indexing Service
Manufacturing Coordinator: The Cowans
Printer and Binder: Courier, Kendallville

ISBN 1-887281-83-5

Manufactured in the United States of America.

10 9 8

LABYRINTH
PUBLICATIONS®

3314 Morningside Drive, El Sobrante, California 94803
(800) 522-9746 www.labyrinth-pub.com

The authors would like to acknowledge with great appreciation the important contributions of the following individuals: Leslie Morales of City College of San Francisco for her excellent document formatting advice, Charles Barrett of San Mateo County Regional Occupational Program for his assistance with exercise development, Janet Smith of Albuquerque TVI Community College for her helpful content suggestions, Mary-Jo Wainwright of Mission Valley ROP for her testing and content recommendations, Kathy Stubbs of Santa Fe Community College for facilitating the testing of Web folders, Merlin Emrys for his outstanding Web page programming of the simulation pages, and Curt and Arlene Cowan for their patience, publishing knowledge, composition work, and excellent editorial advice.

Contents

How this Book is Organized

This book is organized along the seven primary applications taught. This organization helps you become familiar with each application program for a period of time and offers sufficient repetition so routine commands can become second-nature.

Unit One: Computer Concepts and Windows

These three lessons introduce the basics of running a computer with Windows. The unit begins with an overview of the basic concepts of computer hardware and software. Later lessons introduce essential skills of running application programs, moving and sizing program windows, and saving your work. Finally, you will learn how to use Window's online Help system and how to move and copy files on a floppy disk.

Unit Two: Internet Explorer 5.0

This lesson covers the basics of browsing the World Wide Web, including how to navigate to Web sites with Web addresses (URLs) and hyperlinks. The basics of using an Internet search engine are also covered.

Unit Three: Outlook 2000

These two lessons cover the basic features of Outlook 2000. The unit begins with the basics of sending and receiving email messages. You will learn how to compose email messages, check for incoming email and how to reply to messages that you receive from others. The unit concludes with topics on other primary features of Outlook such as the Calendar and Task list.

Unit Four: Word 2000

The Word unit consists of seven lessons that introduce word processing using Word 2000. The unit begins with basic techniques for keying and editing documents and includes business document formatting. The unit concludes with advanced topics such as desktop publishing and emailing Word documents.

Unit Five: Excel 2000

The Excel unit consists of five lessons that introduce worksheet skills using Excel 2000. The unit begins with basic techniques for constructing and formatting worksheets. The unit concludes with advanced topics such as charting and publishing workbooks on the World Wide Web.

Unit Six: Access 2000

The Access unit consists of four lessons that introduce database concepts and skills using Access 2000. This unit discusses the most important introductory database techniques including the set up and use of tables, forms, queries, and reports. The final lesson teaches you how to output data from an Access database to Excel for further analysis.

Unit Seven: PowerPoint 2000

The PowerPoint unit consists of three lessons that introduce presentation techniques using PowerPoint 2000. The unit provides all the techniques necessary to develop and deliver effective presentations. Important techniques covered include working with templates, graphics, animation, and delivering electronic slide shows.

Tips to Make Learning Easier

There are several myths, assumptions, and concerns that many new computer users share. Read this page several times during the coming weeks as you begin to master the skills of computer use.

Anyone Can Learn to Use a Computer

It doesn't take a special kind of person or a special way of thinking to master using a computer. You don't need to be a programmer in order to use a computer. In fact, most computer users will never do any programming themselves.

Mistakes Won't Damage the Computer

You can't damage the computer by pressing the wrong key or by giving the wrong command through the keyboard or with the mouse. Don't be afraid to try a command or procedure, even if you are unsure it will work. Most of the time, a computer will simply beep or display an error message, then it will let you continue working. Many programs have an Undo command that allows you to reverse your most recent commands.

Mental Overload

As you begin learning, you need to think about every action you take. You might feel a bit overwhelmed at first by the many details presented to you. However, basic tasks will become easier as you repeat them over and over; they will eventually become intuitive, and you will no longer need to think about them. This will free up your mind to learn more new tasks and features-and those will eventually become intuitive as well.

The process of learning computer skills is similar to the experience of learning to drive a new car. At first, everything feels very complex, and you must anxiously pay attention to everything that is going on around you. But after you have driven for awhile, the basics of accelerating, braking, and turning eventually become so intuitive that you no longer need to think about each individual act. Your mind and body react instinctively to traffic. The same holds true for learning the basic commands on a computer.

Today's Computer Programs are Easy to Learn

Early computer programs often had little in common with other programs. Today, there are many features, menus, and commands that are common in many programs. This makes it easier to use what you have learned from one program to learn another. So, if you've had a bad experience with computers in the past, relax. You will be pleasantly surprised by the progress you can make in a few weeks if you apply these tips.

TIP!
Ask for assistance if a command or instruction does not work for you after about three minutes of trying.

Know When to Ask a Question

Don't struggle too long with a troublesome task before asking for assistance. Once in a while, something may go wrong that you don't yet have the skill or understanding to fix. That is the time to ask for assistance. You need not struggle with a problem for 20 or 30 minutes while getting more and more frustrated. Nor should you erase whatever you were doing and start over. You can learn by watching how an instructor or lab assistant resolves a problem.

TIP!
Ask a question if an explanation or exercise in this text does not make sense after you go through it.

There Are No Dumb Questions

Although computer programs have become much easier to learn, they aren't yet totally intuitive. Any question you have is a good question to ask. In fact, chances are that several other people in the class need an answer to the same question. So go ahead and ask any questions that occur to you during class—your instructor is eager to help you learn and succeed.

The Web Site

The book has a Web site designed to support the lessons and to provide additional learning resources. The URL of the Web site is: **www.offtowork.com/oe.**

Simulations

Very realistic simulations of typical tasks such as Web searches support several of the lessons. These simulations overcome one of the most significant obstacles to a detailed Internet tutorial—stability. Since the Web is constantly changing, it is impossible to create stable exercises that use "live" Web sites. Instead, detailed exercises are based on simulations of Web sites. The exercises function from screen to screen just like the live sites do. However, the simulations are based on the *offtowork.com* Web site and will function exactly the same throughout the publication life of the book.

Index of Simulations

Simulation Name	Topic/Activity
Computer Museum	Detailed tutorial on browsing a Web site. Includes recognizing various types of hyperlinks, saving and printing Web pages.
Work with Frames	Detailed tutorial on browsing a Web site that uses frames.
Obsolete Computer Museum	Detailed tutorial on browsing a Web site with primitive browsing controls.
Standard Search	Detailed tutorial on how to perform a standard search with a search engine. Includes techniques for narrowing searches.

Lesson Support

Some lessons are supported with additional content on the Web site. For example, Lesson 1, Computer Concepts, is supported by many links on the Web to additional information on microprocessors, hardware, and software. Some of the Integration lessons require students to refer to Web pages for information, to insert a hyperlink into a document, and other activities.

Quick Reference Index and From the Keyboard

Take a moment to review the Quick Reference Index on pages xiii–xiv. Quick Reference items are generic instructions to accomplish a particular task or set of related tasks. Unlike the steps in a Hands-On exercise, these instructions will work in any situation. The Quick Reference can be very useful to you for review and can help you get things done long after the course you used this book for is over.

Also, the *From the Keyboar*d index on pages xv and xvi lists many shortcut keys you can use to execute commands. You will find additional shortcut keys listed in drop-down menus of the Microsoft Office Application. For each keystroke, you should hold down the first key listed, then tap the second key. If three keys are listed, hold down the first two keys as you tap the third key.

Quick Reference Index

ACCESS TASKS

POWERPOINT TASKS

From the Keyboard Summary Sheet

KEYSTROKES FOR ALL APPLICATIONS

Bold .... CTRL+B

Italics .... CTRL+I

Underline .... CTRL+U

Cut .... CTRL+X

Copy .... CTRL+C

Paste .... CTRL+V

Undo .... CTRL+Z

Redo .... CTRL+Y

Open .... CTRL+O

Save .... CTRL+S

Print .... CTRL+P

UNIT 1: COMPUTER CONCEPTS AND WINDOWS

Close active program window .... ALT+F4

UNIT 2: INTERNET EXPLORER 5.0

Move back one page .... ALT+←

Move forward one page .... ALT+→

Move to bottom of page .... END

Move to top of page .... HOME

Open a new browser window .... CTRL+N

Stop loading page .... ESC

UNIT 3: OUTLOOK 2000

Delete selected item .... CTRL+D

New appointment event .... CTRL+N

New email message .... CTRL+SHIFT+M

Open selected event .... CTRL+O

Open selected item .... CTRL+O

UNIT 4: WORD 2000

Align Center .... CTRL+E

Align Left .... CTRL+L

Align Right .... CTRL+R

Decrease font size one point .... CTRL+[

Delete from insertion point to beginning of word .... CTRL+BACKSPACE

Delete from insertion point to end of word .... CTRL+DELETE

Find .... CTRL+F

Go To dialog box .... CTRL+G

Hanging indent .... CTRL+T

Hanging indent—Remove .... CTRL+SHIFT+T

Increase font size one point .... CTRL+]

Insert date .... ALT+SHIFT+D

Insert page break .... CTRL+ENTER

Insert time .... ALT+SHIFT+T

Justify .... CTRL+J

Left indent .... CTRL+M

Left indent—Remove .... CTRL+SHIFT+M

Open dialog box .... CTRL+O

Repeat .... CTRL+Y

Replace .... CTRL+H

Show or hide characters .... CTRL+SHIFT+8

Start Spelling and Grammar checker F7

Thesaurus dialog box .... SHIFT+F7

UNIT 5: EXCEL 2000

Comma style .... CTRL+SHIFT+!

Currency style .... CTRL+SHIFT+$

Delete to end of line .... CTRL+SHIFT+DELETE

Format Cells dialog box .... CTRL+1

General style .... CTRL+SHIFT+~

Percent style .... CTRL+SHIFT+%

Repeat .... CTRL+Y

UNIT 6: ACCESS 2000

Delete selected objects .... DELETE

Open a selected object .... ENTER

Open a selected object in Design view .... CTRL+ENTER

UNIT 7: POWERPOINT 2000

New Slide box .... CTRL+M

Pop-up menu .... CTRL+F10

Visual Conventions

This book uses many visual and typographic cues to guide you through the lessons. This page provides examples and describes the function of each.

Typographic Cue	**What It Indicates**
Ⓐ Ⓑ Ⓒ	These characters indicate the order in which tasks should be performed in a Hands-On exercise.
`Type this text`	Anything you should type at the keyboard is printed in this typeface.
TIP!	This is an important tip which usually contains shortcuts or reminders.
Note!	This contains information that will help you understand a concept or a feature.
Warning!	Read and consider each warning before continuing with the lesson.
WEB	This is a reference to additional information about the topic on the Off-to-Work Web site is given here. The URL to the Web site for this textbook is: www.offtowork.com/oe.
Command→Command	Indicates multiple selections to be made from a menu bar. For example: **File→Save** means you should click the **File** command in the menu bar, then click the **Save** command from the drop-down menu.
From the Keyboard **From the Keyboard**	These margin notes indicate shortcut keys for executing a task described in the text. For example, CTRL+S to save your work in an application program.

Special Section	**Purpose**
Quick Reference Quick Reference	These sections contain generic procedures you can use to accomplish a task at any time. *Note: As you work through a lesson, you should not perform instructions in Quick Reference sections unless you are told to do so in a Hands-On exercise instruction.*
Hands-On Exercise	This section contains specific instructions for the exercise you are working on. You should always work through the Hands-On exercises. These exercises will guide you step-by-step through the topics. You will be told exactly what to do, which keys to press, and other steps to try out a new skill or feature.
Concepts Review	This section contains questions that help you gauge your mastery of the concepts covered in the lesson.
Skill Builders	This section contains additional exercises that provide opportunities for review.
Assessment	This section contains a test on the material covered in the lesson.

UNIT 1

Computer Concepts and Windows

The three lessons of this unit introduce you to the basics of running a computer with Windows. The unit begins with an overview of computer hardware and software. Later lessons introduce essential skills for running application programs, moving and sizing program windows, and saving your work. Finally, you will learn how to use Windows' online Help system and how to move and copy files on a floppy disk.

LESSON 1

Computer Concepts

When most people look inside a typical desktop computer, they see a bewildering array of cables, circuit boards, wires, and computer chips. However, the primary components of a computer system are easier to understand than you might expect. In this lesson you will learn about the physical components of computer systems (hardware) and the logical components (software). You will learn how a computer system's hardware and software work together to help you get work done, play games, and access the Internet. By the end of this lesson, you should be able to identify the primary components of a typical computer system and make sense of the computer specifications featured in advertisements.

In This Lesson

Case Study

Karen wants to purchase a computer system that will effectively meet her needs. Depending on the types of work she expects to perform on the computer, some features and capabilities will be more valuable than others. Here are some examples.

If she uses the system primarily for ...	She will want these types of features ...
Browsing the Internet	A basic system with a fast modem and ink-jet printer
Desktop publishing	A fast system with a large monitor and laser printer
Computer games	The latest video hardware for 3-D graphics
Video editing	A video capture card to connect to a VCR and a very large hard drive to hold video movies she is editing

TIP!

Spend your money on features and performance that make a tangible difference in your productivity and enjoyment.

Getting the Most for Your Money

The fastest, most feature-packed system is not necessarily Karen's best choice. She needs a balanced system, with all of its parts able to perform efficiently. For example, if she spends less money on the microprocessor (the computer's "brain"), she may have more money to spend on a better printer, a larger monitor (screen), and other features that could make the computer more useful for its primary tasks. The latest and fastest hardware almost always costs more than the previous generation, even though the previous generation may be just slightly slower.

Obsolescence

As Karen considers the purchase of a new computer system, she worries that it could soon become outdated. She even feels tempted to wait a few months for the next generation of technology to become available. Here are two factors she should keep in mind:

- Every computer eventually becomes obsolete—that is, unable to run the software you must use to get work done. But most new computers can keep up with developments for at least three to four years. That is enough time to benefit from your investment.
- If Karen waits several months for the next generation of computers, that is time she could have spent learning how to use the computer and becoming more productive. This time could be worth hundreds or even thousands of dollars to her. For example, it could lead to a better job or a promotion.

Learning the Basics

Before she makes her purchase decision, Karen decides to learn more about what's inside the computer itself. This has always been a mystery to her. But a friend explained that it's not really all that complicated to understand the basic components of the computer and the functions they perform.

Computer Systems

A computer system is a complex machine built with various mechanical parts, electronic circuits and program codes. All of these components must work together precisely. Later topics will explain many of these components in detail. This topic describes the most basic classifications of computer systems.

Basic Components

All the components of a computer system can be grouped into two types:

- **Hardware—**Hardware is the *physical* part of the computer system. Examples of hardware are the keyboard, the monitor, and any other physical component of the computer.
- **Software—**Software is the *logical* part of the computer system. Software consists of the programming instructions that let the computer interact with you to accomplish tasks. Software is typically stored on hard drives, CD-ROM disks, and floppy disks. Examples of software are Windows 98™ and Microsoft Word™.

Types of Computers

The first electronic computers were constructed in the 1940s. They were very large machines that filled a room with vacuum tubes and wiring. As computers have evolved, they have become smaller and faster. Two basic types of computers are:

- **Mainframe—**Mainframe computers can fit in a typical living room. They are designed to support large, corporate-level data processing. Hundreds of users can work simultaneously on a mainframe computer.
- **Personal Computers—**Personal computers (PCs), are small enough to fit on a desktop, or even inside a briefcase. A personal computer gets its computing power from a silicon chip called a *microprocessor* and is designed for operation by a single user.

Types of Personal Computers

There are three basic types of personal computer systems:

- **Desktop—**A desktop computer is designed to sit on top of your desk, or as a tower unit sitting alongside or under the desk. Desktop computers are easy to upgrade with new capabilities and devices.

- **Notebook—**Notebook computers are designed to be light enough to carry with you. They contain batteries, so they can operate without being plugged into a power outlet. This portability comes at a price. A notebook computer usually costs at least twice as much as a desktop computer with similar capabilities.

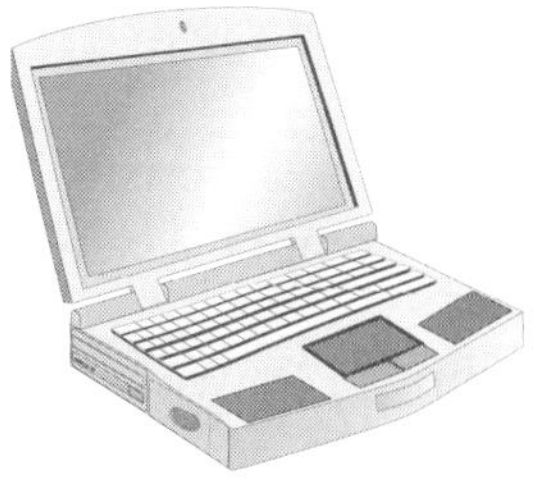

- **Network Server—**A network server usually looks similar to a desktop computer system, but runs special operating system software that provides network services to many other computers. Network servers let computer users share files and printers, send and receive email messages, and may also provide Internet and security services. Most personal computers used in business are connected to a network.

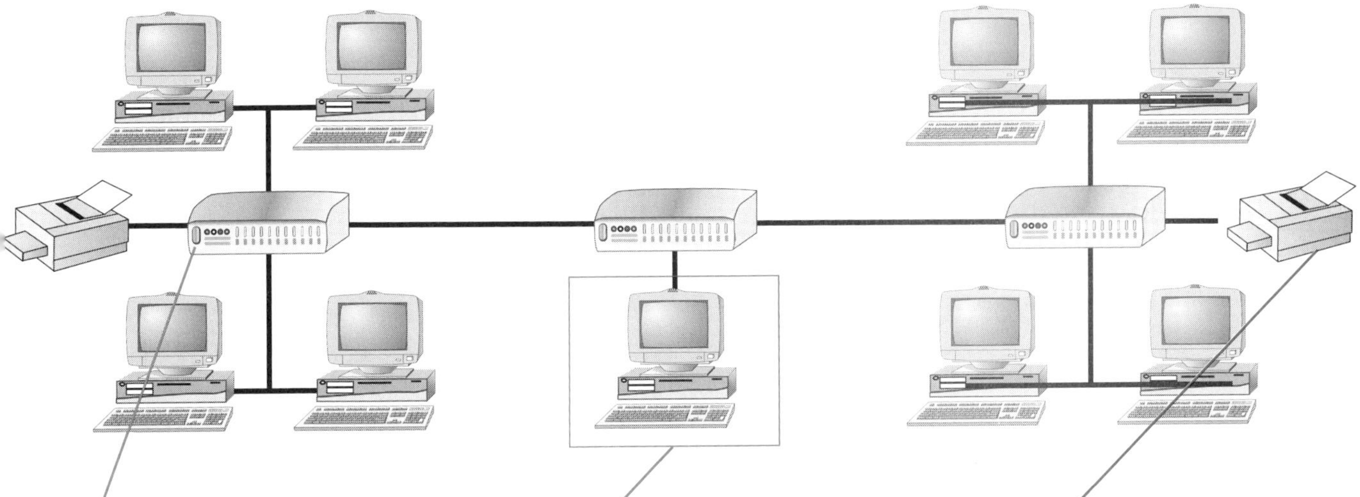

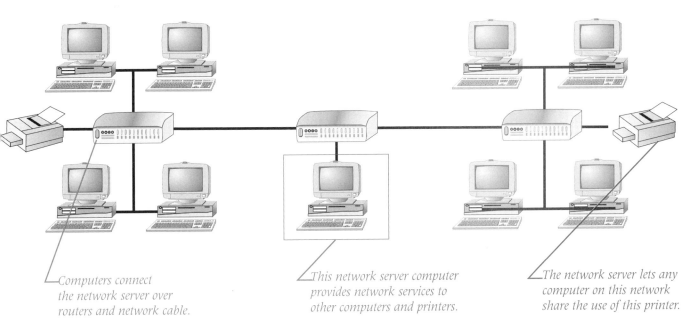

Computers connect the network server over routers and network cable.

This network server computer provides network services to other computers and printers.

The network server lets any computer on this network share the use of this printer.

Desktop Computer Components

Desktop computer hardware is divided into the following components:

- **System Unit—**This is the box that holds the most fundamental components of the computer, such as the microprocessor, random access memory, and disk drives.

The system unit

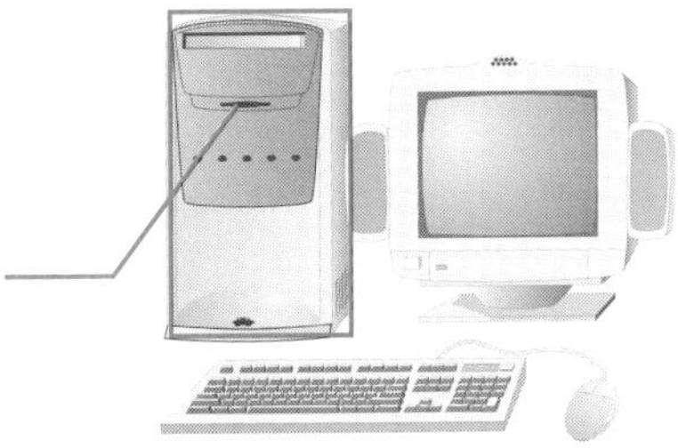

- **Peripherals—**These are the hardware components *outside* the system unit. Examples of peripherals are the keyboard, mouse, monitor, and printer.

Units of Measure

The computer industry has its own terminology to describe and measure the performance and features of computer systems. These terms are explained in various sections of this lesson:

Term	What It Measures	See page . . .
Bits	The most basic element of computer data	8
Bytes	The size of software files, the capacity of disk drives, and random access memory (RAM)	8
Megahertz (MHz)	The speed of the computer's microprocessor	10
Resolution	The sharpness of output from a printer or the dots displayed on the computer screen	17, 18, and 19

Bits and Bytes

The most basic unit of information on the computer is the bit. A bit is a single circuit in the computer system that is switched on or off. By itself, a bit doesn't hold much information. But if 8 bits are strung together in a specific order, they form a byte. This is like interpreting the dots and dashes in Morse Code. In the examples below, notice how varying the position of a single bit changes the meaning of each byte.

Letter	Morse Code	Byte (ASCII)*
A	· -	10000001
B	- - - ·	10000010
C	- · - ·	10000011

*ASCII (pronounced "ask-ee") is an internationally accepted code for representing characters in the computer. It defines byte codes for 128 different alphabetic, numeric, and symbol characters. (The name is an acronym for American Standard Code for Information Interchange.)

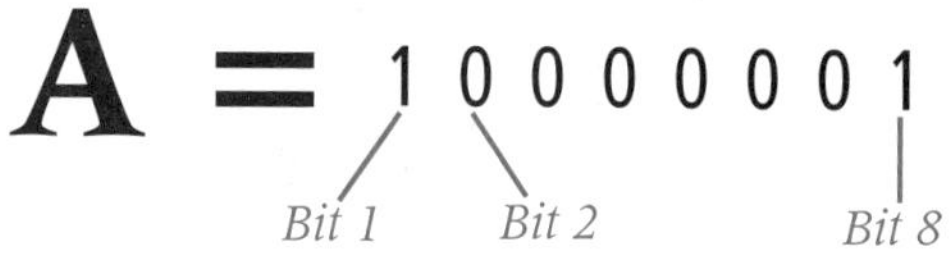
A = 1 0 0 0 0 0 0 1
Bit 1
Bit 2
Bit 8

Kilobytes and Megabytes

The table below lists the most common terms used to describe the size of software files and the capacity of random access memory, hard drives, and other storage devices explained later in this lesson.

Term	Description	Examples
Bit	A single on-off switch in a computer circuit	0 or 1
Byte	A single character of data	A, B, C, $, @, {, \
Kilobyte (KB)	Approximately one thousand bytes of data	About one single-spaced typed page of text
Megabyte (MB)	Approximately one million bytes of data	About 3 average-length novels
Gigabyte (GB)	Approximately one billion bytes of data	3,000 novels' worth of text, or about 1,500 large color pictures

NOTE! *The exact size of a kilobyte is actually 1,024 bytes. However, most people just round off those extra 24 bytes. Similarly, most people round off the extra bytes when referring to a megabyte or gigabyte.*

Inside the System Unit, Part 1

Most of a computer's processing power is determined by the components inside the system unit. Nearly all system units have an open-architecture design, with modular parts that can be snapped in and out of the system. Open architecture permits the upgrading of a computer with new features and capabilities long after it was originally built. Part 1 describes the basic processing components of the system unit:

- System board
- Microprocessor
- Random access memory (RAM)
- Disk drives

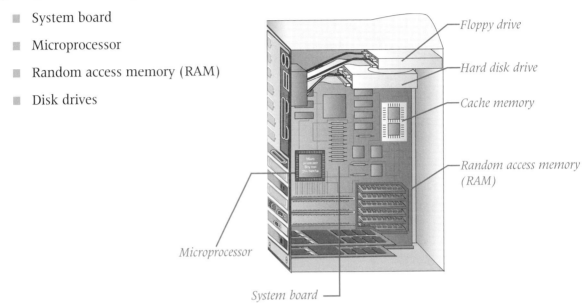

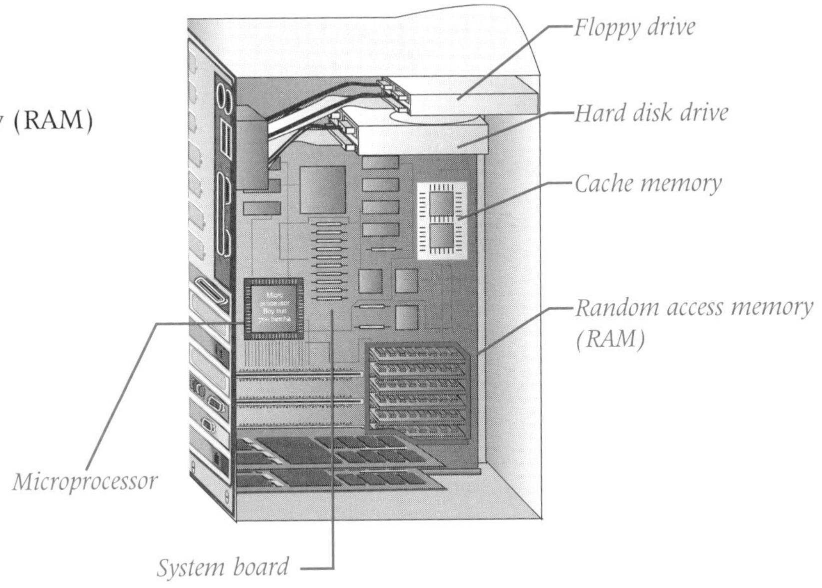
Floppy drive
Hard disk drive
Cache memory
Random access memory (RAM)
Microprocessor
System board

The System Board

The system board (also called the "motherboard") has sockets and connectors that hold the essential circuitry of the computer. System boards on newer computers may also contain additional features such as built-in sound hardware and connectors to plug in disk drives.

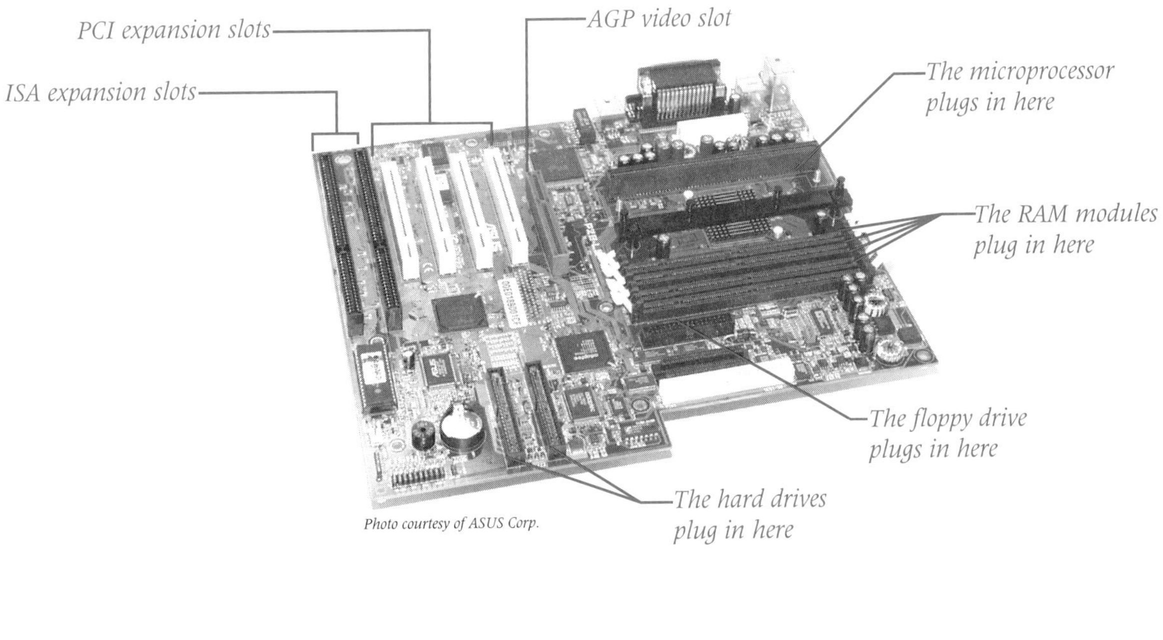
PCI expansion slots
ISA expansion slots
AGP video slot
The microprocessor plugs in here
The RAM modules plug in here
The floppy drive plugs in here
The hard drives plug in here

Photo courtesy of ASUS Corp.

WEB

See the Lesson 1 *Web page for links to more information on microprocessors.*

The Microprocessor

A microprocessor is a single silicon chip containing the complete circuitry of a computer. The microprocessor serves as the "brain" of a microcomputer. Because it determines the basic processing power of the computer, most advertisements start by telling you the make and model of the microprocessor. Intel's Celeron™ and Pentium III™ series are very popular microprocessors. Many used computers are equipped with the Intel i486 microprocessor.

intel
pentium III

Photo courtesy of Intel Corp.

One example of a microprocessor is Intel's Pentium III.

Microprocessor Performance

Several design elements combine to set the performance of a microprocessor. The internal architecture of the microprocessor, its physical dimensions (die size), and the efficiency of its most basic commands (instruction set) are examples of these design elements. The quality of other components in the computer are also critical to the performance of its microprocessor. For example, a fast microprocessor in a computer equipped with very little random access memory (or RAM, described in the next topic) may run programs more slowly than a slower microprocessor working with plenty of RAM. The most tangible factor in a microprocessor's performance is its clock speed.

Clock Speed

A microprocessor contains an internal clock which is set to a specific speed. One cycle (or one "tick" of the internal clock) is a single pulse of electrical current flowing through the microprocessor. The microprocessor carries out one action for each cycle—even if it's just looking to see if you typed something at the keyboard. The raw speed of the microprocessor is measured in megahertz (MHz), or millions of cycles per second. Early PC microprocessors ran at almost 5MHz. Most ads for microcomputers tell you the model of microprocessor and its clock speed. For example: Intel Celeron/400MHz, AMD K6-III/450MHz, and Intel Pentium III/600MHz.

Today's most powerful microprocessors run at speeds of 600MHz or more. This top speed rating keeps going up every few months. However, sheer speed doesn't always translate literally into performance. That's where benchmarks can be helpful.

WEB

Check the Lesson 1 Web page for links to Web sites about benchmarks.

Benchmarks

How can you compare one microprocessor with another? The best method is to research their ratings on a benchmark. Benchmarks are programs that measure the performance of a computer system. You can get a good idea of the relative performance of three microprocessors when you compare their benchmark test results on similarly configured systems.

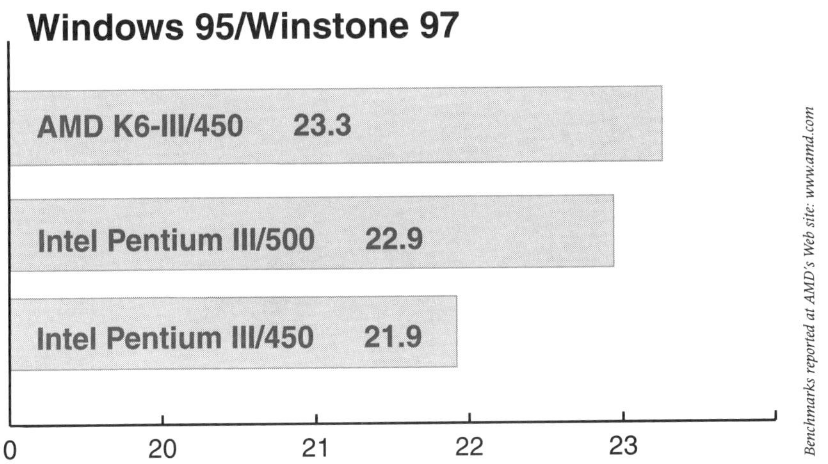

Windows 95/Winstone 97
AMD K6-III/450 23.3
Intel Pentium III/500 22.9
Intel Pentium III/450 21.9
0
20
21
22
23
Benchmarks reported at AMD's Web site: www.amd.com

According to this benchmark test, the AMD K6-III microprocessor has slightly higher performance than a similarly configured Pentium III. Since the K6 also costs less than the Pentium III, it might represent a better value for some computer users.

Cost

If you want the fastest microprocessor available, you will pay a high premium for it. The very fastest model of a microprocessor can cost up to 50% more than the models just one or two levels below it. Thus, you could pay several hundred dollars more for a microprocessor that might give you just 10% more processing speed—a speed difference you might not even be able to notice as you work with your programs. If you are purchasing your first computer and expect to run basic programs such as a word processor or a Web browser, you are probably better off buying a microprocessor that is a few notches below the top of the line but meets your needs. The money you save (perhaps $400 or more) could be spent on other parts of the computer, such as a larger monitor or a better printer.

Random Access Memory

Random access memory (RAM) is a special type of chip that temporarily stores data as it is processed. While the microprocessor is the single most important component inside the system unit box, RAM plays a critical role in the computer's operation. Everything you see on the computer screen is actually temporarily stored in your computer's RAM. Think of RAM as the *workbench* of your computer.

How RAM Works

The microprocessor never accesses software directly from the computer's disk drives. Instead, the operating system software loads software from the disk drives into RAM. Then the microprocessor reads the software from RAM for processing and places the results of processing back into RAM. The process of transferring data in and out of the microprocessor to RAM is repeated millions of times each second. The diagram below displays the sequence that one operating system, Windows, follows to run programs and process data as you work.

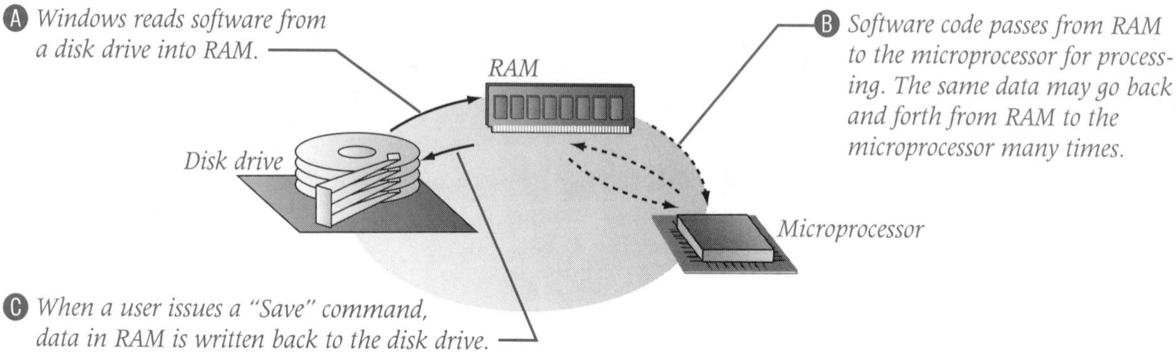
A Windows reads software from a disk drive into RAM.
B Software code passes from RAM to the microprocessor for processing. The same data may go back and forth from RAM to the microprocessor many times.
RAM
Disk drive
Microprocessor
C When a user issues a "Save" command, data in RAM is written back to the disk drive.

RAM Is Volatile Memory

The moment you switch off power to the computer, all of the data residing in RAM is erased. Because it can change so instantly, RAM is sometimes referred to as *volatile* memory. In order to safely store your work for future work sessions, you must save it to a disk drive. Since RAM temporarily stores correspondence and other work you perform on the computer, it is very important to remember to save your work before you switch off the computer.

Locations of RAM

A computer system actually has various types of RAM in several locations inside the system unit. However, when you see an advertisement describing the amount of RAM the computer is equipped with, it always refers to the main system RAM. Other types of RAM include cache RAM (see the next page) and video RAM (described on page 18).

Types of RAM Modules

TIP! *Some system boards can accept both types of RAM modules, but you should never install both types together. Doing so could damage the RAM. (The modules run at different electrical current settings.)*

RAM chips are small modules that plug into special slots in the system board. The capacity of these modules is rated in megabytes. Popular sizes are 16, 32, 64, and 128MB. There are two basic types of RAM modules:

- **SDRAM—**SDRAM modules have become the most common form of RAM on new computers. An SDRAM module is also often referred to as a DIMM (dual inline memory module).
- **EDO RAM—**EDO RAM modules are slightly less expensive than SDRAM. On Pentium systems, EDO RAM modules must always be installed in pairs. EDO RAM is also often referred to as a SIMM (single inline memory module).

An SDRAM (DIMM) module

Cache RAM

Most computers also come with another form of RAM called a cache (pronounced "cash"). This is expensive, high-speed RAM that stores the most recently used program code and data. Any time the microprocessor needs fresh data to process, it checks to see if any of the data it needs is already in the cache. The microprocessor can work with data in the cache much more quickly than if it must go to normal RAM or the hard drive to process the data. Modern microprocessors have internal (also called Level 1) cache memory built right into them, and external (Level 2) cache memory installed on the system board.

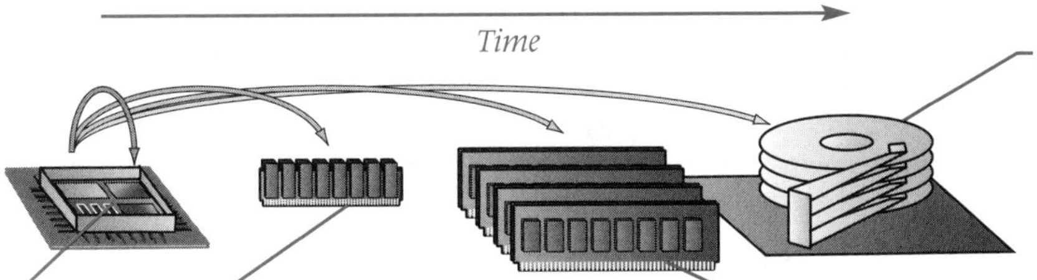
Time
A When the microprocessor loads new code for processing, it looks for the most recently used code in the Level 1 cache inside the microprocessor itself.
B If there is no code at the Level 1 cache, the microprocessor next looks at the Level 2 cache on the system board.
C System RAM is the third place searched for code.
D If the necessary code does not reside in the cache or RAM, the system must load the software code from the disk drive. This final method is much slower than any of the others.

How Much RAM Do You Need?

The system RAM in your computer is measured in megabytes. Most new computers are equipped with 32 megabytes of RAM. This is enough to run most popular programs. It is relatively easy to install additional RAM in a computer. The following points can help you determine the amount of system RAM you will want for your computer:

- The more RAM your computer has, the more programs you can run at one time.
- Sophisticated application programs for computer graphics and databases require plenty of RAM to run efficiently. See the table on page 33 for a comparison of the RAM requirements of different types of application programs.
- When you purchase application software, the amount of system RAM necessary to run the software is indicated on the package.

Disk Drives

When software is installed on a computer, it is stored on various disk drives in the system unit. Some types of disks are fixed inside the computer, and others are removable. The various disk drives are often referred to as the computer's mass-storage devices.

Listed below are the most popular types of disk drives for personal computers. Each type has capabilities that make it ideal for particular tasks.

Drive Name	Description	Typical Capacity*
Hard drive	A fixed (nonremovable) disk drive inside the system unit. Hard drives are very fast and can hold very large amounts of software, such as application programs and your user data files. When you install a new application program on the computer, it is stored on the hard drive.	500MB to 6GB
Floppy drive	A floppy drive reads data from and writes data to floppy disks (also called "floppies"). Floppy disks get their name from the flexible disk inside the plastic disk housing. This disk has a magnetic oxide coating similar to cassette tapes. Floppy drives are very slow compared to other types of drives, especially hard drives. Floppy disks are very convenient for carrying your work to another computer.	1.4KB
CD-ROM drive	A CD-ROM (Compact Disk-Read Only Memory) drive can hold large amounts of data. CD-ROM disks look similar to music CDs but store their information differently. However, most CD-ROM drives can play music CDs. CD-ROM drives are rated for their transfer speed. A 32x CD-ROM drive can transfer data 32 times faster than the very first CD-ROM drives that appeared in the late 1980s.	650MB
Recordable CD-ROM drive	These models of CD-ROM drives allow you to write your data to blank disks (recordable media) as well as to read data from standard CD-ROM disks. Recordable CD-ROM disks are excellent media for long-term storage of important computer files. For example, if you were to create an electronic family photo album, you would want to store it on a recordable CD-ROM disk. There are two types of recordable CD-ROM drives. Earlier CD-R drives could only write once to a disk. When the disk got full, or files became obsolete, there was no way to erase data on the disk. Newer CD-RW drives can rewrite data and erase files on more expensive rewriteable disks. A CD-RW drive can also use less expensive write-once disks like CD-R drives.	650MB
DVD drive	A DVD (Digital Video Disk) drive can play the latest generation of DVD disks, and can also read CD-ROM disks. To get the most benefit from a DVD drive, you also need a decoder card to convert the DVD movies into a video format for display on your computer monitor and/or television and to play Dolby Digital™ sound.	Up to 17GB
Removable-disk drive	A removable-disk drive stores data on disk cartridges. By adding more disks, you can create virtually unlimited data storage space. The Iomega Zip™ is one popular example of a removable disk drive. You can store the equivalent of about 75 floppy disks on a single Zip disk. There are other removable disk drives with capacities of up to 1.5GB.	100MB to 250MB

*The abbreviations for capacity are KB for kilobyte, MB for megabyte, and GB for gigabyte. For a description of these, see the glossary.

How Disk Drives Work

Most hard drives use disks covered with a magnetic oxide material, similar to that used for cassette tapes. A read/write head hovers over the disks as they spin at high speed (4800 to 9600 rpm). The read/write head applies positive and negative charges to the surface of the disk to record data. Each positive or negative charge represents one bit of data.

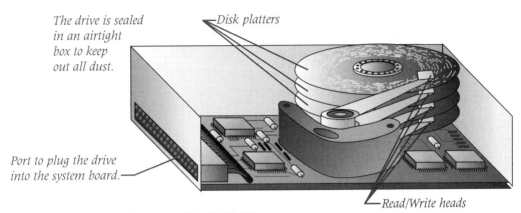

The drive is sealed in an airtight box to keep out all dust.
Disk platters
Port to plug the drive into the system board.
Read/Write heads

Primary components of a standard hard disk drive.

> **TIP!** *Never move a computer while it is running. When the read/write heads are not in the "parked" position, there is a higher risk that they could touch the hard drive platters while the computer is moved.*

Hard drives are extremely reliable, but they can be damaged. Hard drives are sealed in an airtight box to keep out dust particles. If one of the read/write heads touches a disk, it can damage the hard drive and result in the loss of data—perhaps all of the data on the hard drive. When you switch off the computer, the read/write heads are automatically moved to a safe, "park" position, which keeps them away from the data on the hard drive.

RAM Compared to Disk Drives

Although RAM and the capacity of disk drives are both measured in megabytes, they are very different. Many people who are new to computers confuse RAM with storage space on the disk drives. You can avoid this confusion if you think of RAM as the computer's *temporary workbench memory* and disk drives as the computer's *permanent mass-storage* devices.*

There are two important distinctions between RAM and mass storage:

- When you switch off the power to your computer, any data in RAM is erased, whereas data stored on disk drives is saved for future work sessions.
- Most disk drives have capacity for much more data than the RAM on a typical system. A new computer will usually have about 100 MB of disk storage for every 1 MB of RAM.

*The word *permanent* should not be taken literally. Like any electromechanical device, a disk drive might someday fail. It is also possible to inadvertently give a command to erase some or all of the data on the disk drive.

Inside the System Unit, Part 2

Although the microprocessor, RAM, and disk drives are critical to the performance of a computer, they require the support of many other components. Part 2 describes the video system that creates the image on the computer display and the expansion cards that give the computer additional capabilities.

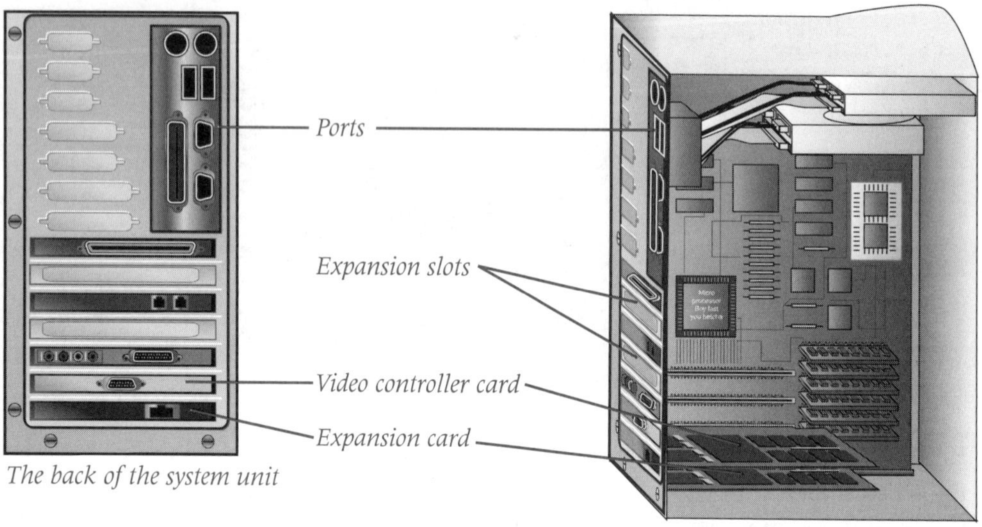
Ports
Expansion slots
Video controller card
Expansion card

The back of the system unit

Cutaway view of the system unit

Computer Video

A computer screen display is made up of hundreds of thousands of individual dots of light called pixels. Each pixel receives commands 60 to 80 times per second that control exactly which color it should display. These commands generate patterns of pixels to create the text, windows, controls, and other images you see on the screen.

My Computer

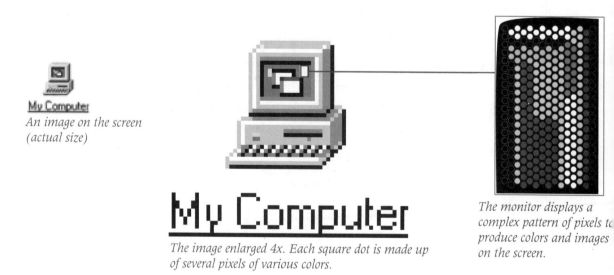

An image on the screen (actual size)

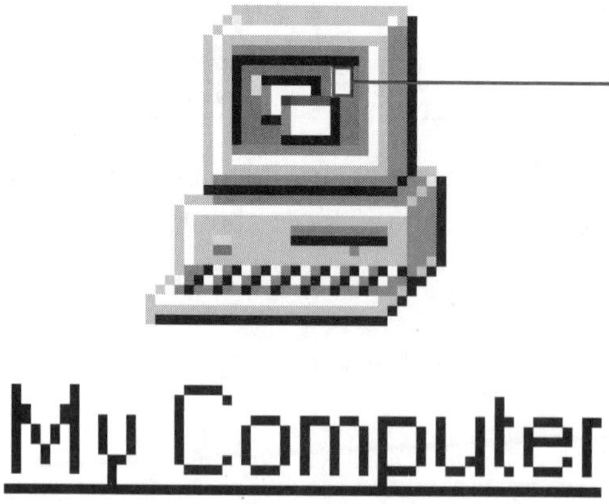
My Computer

The image enlarged 4x. Each square dot is made up of several pixels of various colors.

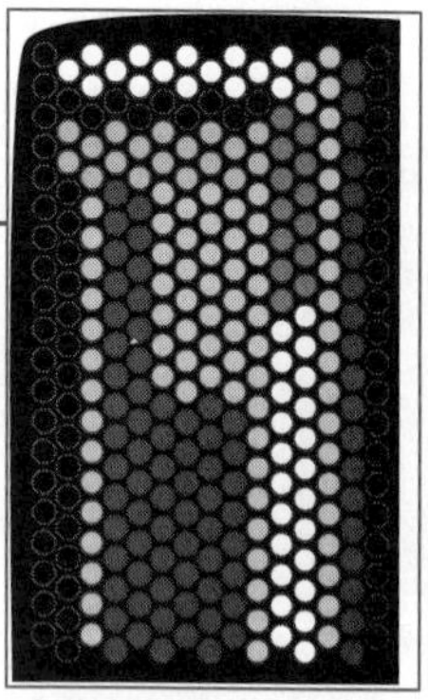

The monitor displays a complex pattern of pixels to produce colors and images on the screen.

Key Components

Three key hardware and software components make up the video subsystem of a computer:

- **Video monitor—**This is similar to a television, but its circuitry is more sophisticated and precise.
- **Video controller—**This is an expansion card inside the computer's system unit, which sends video signals to the monitor. It controls the display of all the images you see on the monitor.
- **Video driver—**This is software that tells Windows how to work effectively with the video controller card and monitor.

Video Performance

There are three important ways to measure the performance of a video controller and monitor:

- **Resolution** is the number of pixels that the monitor can display. Displaying more pixels on your monitor will make the images on your computer screen appear sharper and smaller. The most basic resolution setting is 640 pixels across by 480 pixels down (written 640 × 480). Many computers are capable of almost double this resolution at 1024 × 768.

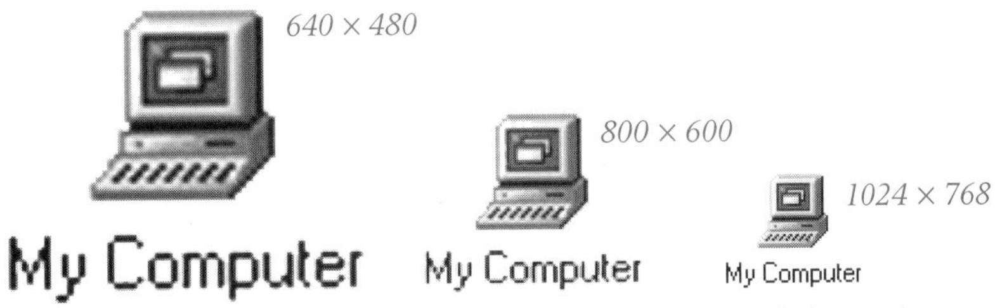
640 × 480
800 × 600
1024 × 768
My Computer
My Computer
My Computer

The higher your monitor's resolution setting, the smaller and sharper images will appear. The examples above show how the My Computer *icon and label would appear at different resolution settings.*

- The **color depth** indicates how many different colors the screen can potentially display. A higher color-depth setting gives the most accurate display of graphics. If you want to display photo-realistic color images, make sure the video controller is capable of 24-bit color, which allows the monitor to display up to 16.7 million colors. Other popular settings are 256 color (8-bit) and 64,000 color (16-bit).

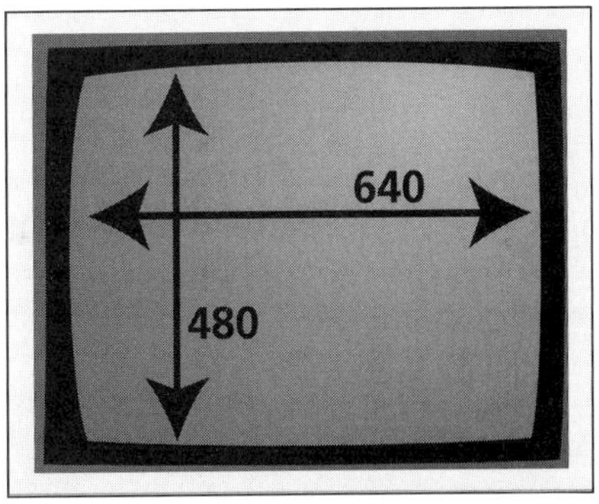
640
480

The screen resolution is measured horizontally and vertically in pixels.

- The **refresh rate** determines how fast the video controller redraws the display on the monitor. This is measured in hertz (cycles per second). A refresh rate of 70 hertz (Hz) or more gives the monitor display a very stable image, without any noticeable flicker. A refresh rate of less than 65Hz can result in noticeable flicker, which may tire your eyes during long work sessions.

Video RAM

The video controller has its own RAM, which is separate from the RAM on the system board. This RAM is devoted to the video display. The table below shows the relationship between video RAM, screen resolution, and the color depth setting. Notice that when a video controller has more RAM, it can display a higher color depth at the higher resolution settings.

MAXIMUM RESOLUTION FOR COLOR DISPLAY		
	Color Depth	
Video Ram	**Millions of Colors**	**Thousands of Colors**
1MB	640 × 480	800 × 600
2MB	800 × 600	1024 × 768
4MB	1024 × 768	1280 × 1024
8MB	1280 × 1024	1600 × 1200

VGA and SVGA

As you shop for a computer and monitor, you will see several popular terms used to describe video performance. Chief among the alphabet soup of acronyms will be *VGA* and *Super-VGA*. Both terms refer to a level of video performance. VGA is short for *Video Graphics Array.*

Term	Level of Performance
VGA	Resolution of 640 × 480 pixels, and the simultaneous display of 16 colors
Super-VGA SVGA	Resolution of 800 × 600 pixels (or more) and the simultaneous display of 256 colors (or more). Nearly all new computers have SVGA displays or better.

3-D Video Controllers

Some video controllers are specially optimized for computer games. Many of the latest computer games have some dazzling 3-D special effects. However, these special effects can appear jagged and jerky on older hardware. The latest generation of 3-D video controllers plug into system boards equipped with an *Accelerated Graphics Port* (AGP) and can display textured 3-D images with great speed and detail.

Purchasing a Monitor

There are several features you should consider when purchasing a monitor. Remember that the screen resolution and refresh-rate settings your monitor is capable of should also be compatible with the capabilities of your computer's video controller.

Feature	Description
Screen size	Like television screens, the size of a computer screen is measured diagonally. Most entry-level computer systems are sold with a 15" monitor. Monitors also have a viewable area rating which measures the largest screen area you can display. For example, many 17" monitors are rated as having a 15.9" viewable area. 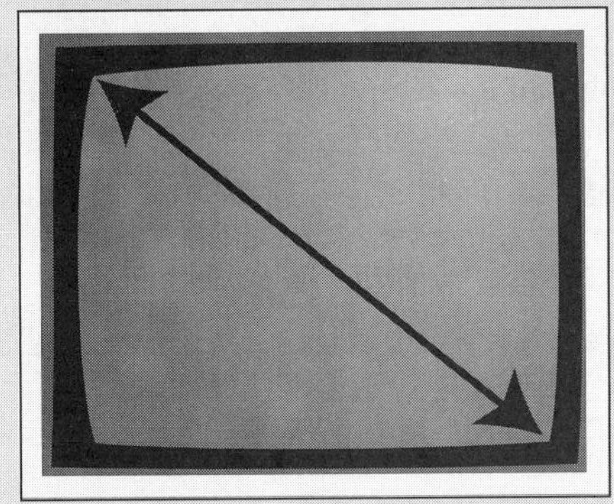 A larger screen allows you to view your work comfortably at a higher resolution setting. This is an advantage for graphics-intensive work such as desktop publishing.
Maximum resolution	Monitors and video controllers are rated for the maximum resolution they can handle. If you set the resolution higher than the monitor is rated, the display may go blank. A high-quality monitor can display a maximum resolution of 1024 × 768 pixels or greater. Some large monitors can handle a display of 1600 × 1200 pixels. This high resolution allows the display of much more information on the screen than the standard 640 × 480 setting.
Dot pitch	Dot pitch refers to the size of the individual points of light (pixels) on the screen. A larger dot pitch causes images on the screen to appear fuzzier and coarser. High-quality monitors will have a dot pitch of around .24 (written ".24 dp"). Cheaper monitors sold with bargain systems may have a dot pitch of .39 or more. *Tip: Purchase a monitor with a dot pitch of .28 or less for the best quality display.*
Vertical frequency	A vertical frequency setting of 70 hertz or better results in a very steady image with no noticeable flicker. Monitors and video controllers are rated for the maximum vertical frequency setting at which they can operate. *Warning: If you set the vertical frequency higher than the monitor can handle, the screen image will be poor. Too high a setting can also damage the monitor.*
Non-interlacing	Cheaper monitors and video controllers may use a technique called interlacing to project an image on the screen. Two passes are made to create the screen image instead of a single pass. Interlacing causes a very noticeable flicker on the screen. *Tip: You should always insist that the monitor you purchase be non-interlacing.*

Expansion Cards

Expansion cards are modular circuit boards that plug into the computer to add new features and capabilities, some of which might not even have existed when the computer was manufactured. For example, you could add an expansion card to connect a scanner or video camera to the computer.

Examples of Expansion Cards

There are numerous expansion cards you can purchase and plug into a computer. Any time you buy an expansion card, it also comes with the software necessary to use its features.

Card type	Description
Modem	A modem lets you dial over a standard phone line to connect to other computers. An internal modem is installed on an expansion card. An external modem is a peripheral. (See pages 24–25 for details on modems).
Sound	A sound card can generate high-quality sound and music on the computer. This is useful for games and for programs such as online encyclopedias. Some sound cards connect to a musical keyboard so you can create your own compositions.
Video capture	This card has a connector for a video camera and software that helps you capture (record) video onto your computer's hard drive. You can edit captured video to add special effects and titles. After editing, you can record the video from the hard drive back to videotape.
Network or LAN	This card lets you connect your computer to a local area network (LAN). If you have network cards on two or more computers in your home, you can set up a small version of a LAN called a peer-to-peer network.
TV	This card can display a television picture in a window on your screen. It can connect to an antenna or cable TV service. The card comes with software to tune in channels.
Scanner	You use a scanner to turn pictures and photographs into computer files. Then you can display the pictures on the screen, send them with an email message to a friend, and print them on a custom card or newsletter.

Expansion Slots

Expansion cards plug into expansion slots on the system board. Most computers sold today come with two types of expansion slots. Before you purchase an expansion card, you should always check to see which types of expansion slots are still open (unused). The open expansion slot and the expansion card must both be the same type.

Slot Type	Description
PCI	This is a very fast connection to your computer's microprocessor. Many new types of expansion cards are designed for this type of slot. For example, video capture and network cards are now typically designed to fit into a PCI slot. PCI is short for Peripheral Component Interconnect.
ISA	This is an older type of slot. It is not as fast as PCI, but there are still many types of expansion cards for which this slot is fast enough for good performance. Most sound cards and modem cards use this older type of slot. ISA is short for Industry Standard Architecture.

The Bus

Expansion slots connect to the microprocessor by a data path called the *bus*. The speed and size of this data path have an important effect on your computer's performance. For example, PCI slots have a wide, 64-bit data path on the system bus (which sends data 64 bits at a time), while the older ISA slot data path is a narrow 16 bits. So a PCI expansion card can exchange data with the rest of the computer system much faster than an ISA card.

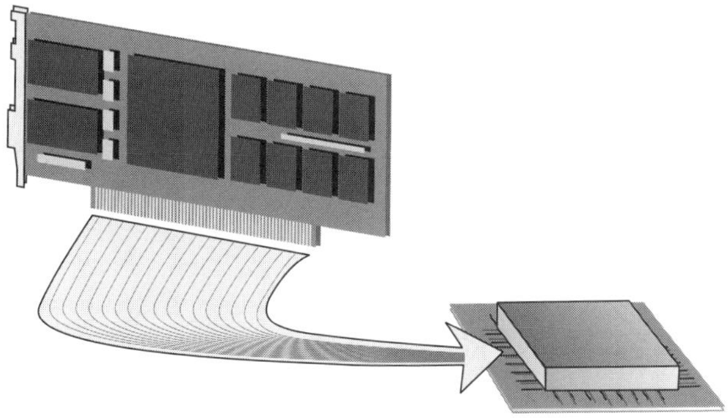

The data bus is like a highway to the system's microprocessor.

Ports

A port is a place to plug a cable or peripheral device into your computer's system unit. The keyboard, mouse, and monitor plug into ports. Many expansion cards provide additional ports for specific devices. For example, a scanner may connect to the computer through a port on an expansion card. All computer systems come with several different ports built into the back of the system unit. Various cables are designed to work with the ports. For example, you would use a parallel cable to connect a printer to the parallel port.

The table below lists the most common types of ports, and they are shown in the figure at the bottom of this page. A computer system may have some or all of these ports.

	This port type . . .	is commonly used to connect . . .
A	PS/2	a mouse and keyboard.
B	USB port	a growing variety of peripheral devices, including scanners, keyboards, cameras, and monitors.
C	Serial (Com1, Com2)	an external modem.
D	Parallel (LPT1)	a printer.
E	SCSI	a scanner or external disk drive.
F	Video	the monitor.
G	Miniplugs	speakers, microphone, and sound sources.
H	Joystick	a joystick for games.
I	Phone jack	a telephone line to an internal modem.
J	RS-14	a network cable.

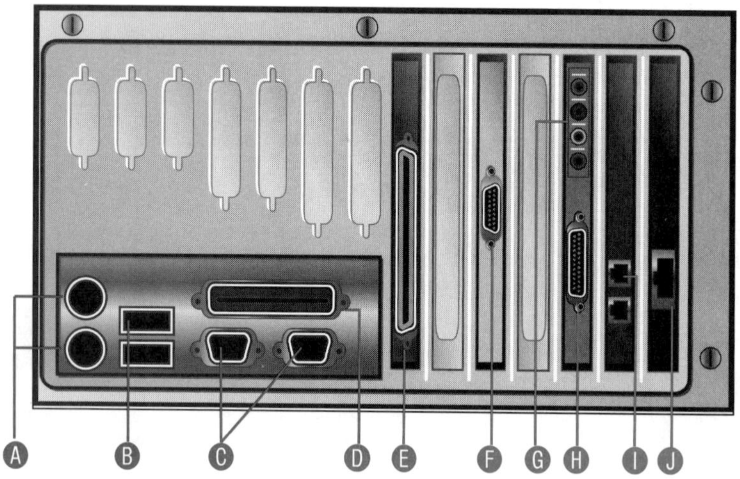
A
B
C
D
E
F
G
H
I
J

Selecting Peripherals

A peripheral is hardware outside the computer's system unit box. Peripherals are usually associated with entering data into the computer (input) or the output of data in the form of screen displays, printouts, and sound. The monitor is one example of a peripheral covered earlier in this lesson.

Keyboard

The keyboard is the main data entry device for a microcomputer. There are numerous makes of keyboards, and they can differ considerably in quality. You may want to consider an ergonomic keyboard. These spread out the keys or even split the keyboard in half to give your hands a more natural typing angle. The style and placement of the computer keyboard is an important factor in healthy computing habits. See page 34 for tips on setting up your computer with the keyboard at the proper height.

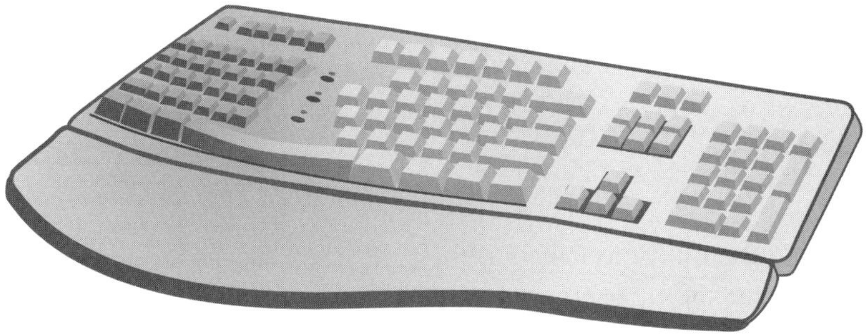

Many ergonomic keyboards have a built-in wrist rest and a curved shape for comfortable hand positioning.

Mouse

The mouse is a pointing device to give commands to the computer by pointing and clicking at specific places on the screen. An ergonomically designed mouse fits very comfortably in your hand; some also have a third button or scroll wheel you can program to issue special commands.

Logitech makes an ergonomic mouse with three buttons.

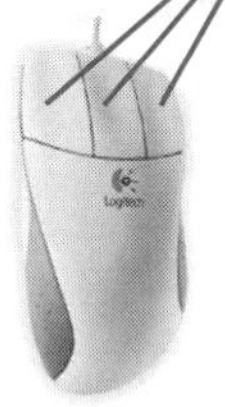

Many new mice feature a thumbwheel for scrolling through information on the screen.

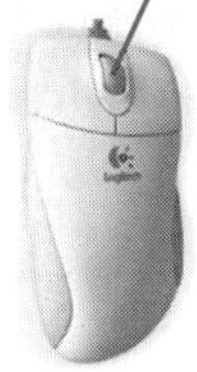

Photos courtesy of Logitech.

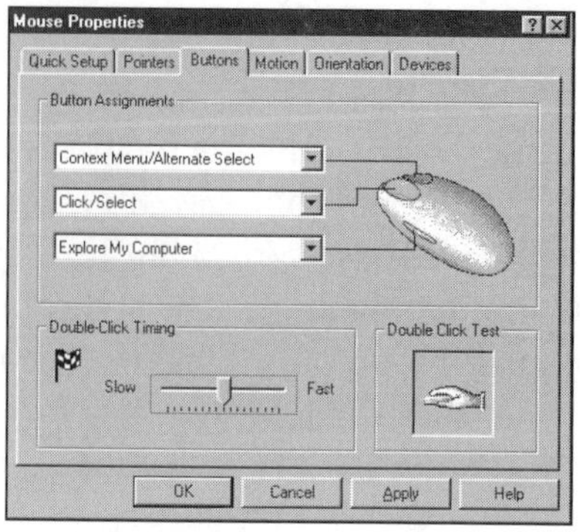
Mouse Properties
Quick Setup
Pointers
Buttons
Motion
Orientation
Devices
Button Assignments
Context Menu/Alternate Select
Click/Select
Explore My Computer
Double-Click Timing
Slow
Fast
Double Click Test
OK
Cancel
Apply
Help

Many mice come with special software programs that allow you to assign commands to the various mouse buttons or thumbwheel.

Trackballs

A popular alternative to the mouse is called a trackball. This uses a rotating ball that you roll with your thumb or fingers. Some users prefer a trackball because it saves desktop space. Others find rolling the trackball more comfortable than moving a mouse. A combined trackball and mouse is also available.

A trackball mouse can save space on your desk.

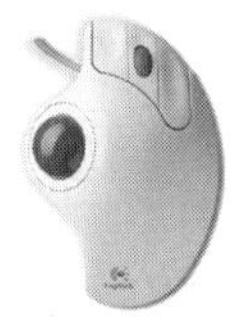

Photo courtesy of Logitech

Modems

A modem (MOdulator/DEModulator) is a device that translates the digital data of computer communication into analog sound waves that can be transmitted over a voice telephone line. At the other end of the line, another modem converts the sound back into digital data. With a modem you can:

- dial up and exchange information with other computers.
- connect to an Internet service provider (ISP) for Web browsing and email.
- use your computer to send and receive faxes.

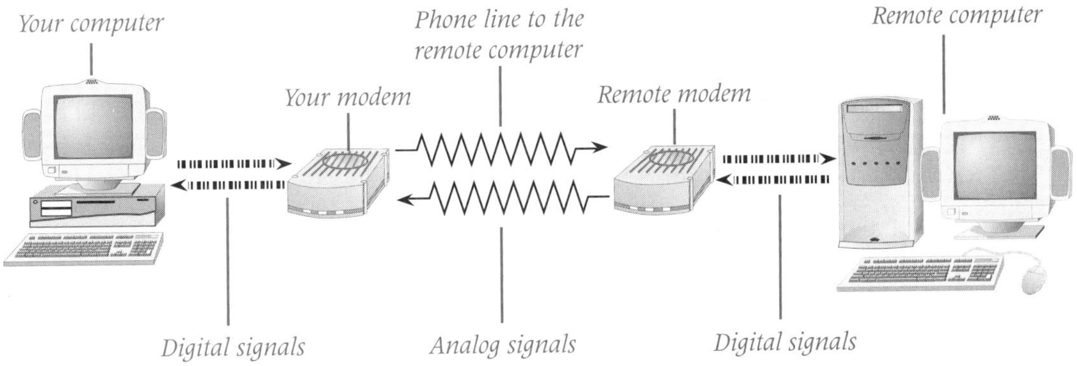
Your computer
Phone line to the remote computer
Remote computer
Your modem
Remote modem
Digital signals
Analog signals
Digital signals

Types of Modems

Photo courtesy of 3Com Corporation.

Modems come in both external and internal models. Internal modems are expansion cards you can plug into an expansion slot inside the system unit. An external modem is a peripheral that sits on your desk and plugs into the back of the computer with a serial cable. Most new computers come with an internal modem as standard equipment. Some modems even offer voice mail capabilities (for example: "To leave a message for Bob, dial 1; to leave a message for Sue, dial 2," and so on).

Modem Speed

A faster modem is useful if you frequently browse the Web. You measure a modem's speed as the bits-per-second of digital data it can transmit over a telephone line under ideal conditions. For example, a 28.8K modem can send and receive data at up to 28,800 bits per second (or about 3,500 bytes per second). Newer modems use a special compression scheme to receive data at nearly 56.6K per second. However, telephone line quality, the facilities of Internet service providers, and other factors may reduce a modem's actual speed to less than its rated speed.

Scanners

Photo courtesy of Hewlett-Packard Corp.

A scanner turns pictures and photographs into computer files that you can place into documents or attach to email messages. Flatbed scanners work similarly to a copy machine. You place the original onto the scanner's glass plate, then run software to select and scan the part of an image you wish to save as a computer file.

Every scanner comes with bundled software to install on the computer. This software allows you to scan and edit pictures and photographs. Additional bundled software may allow you to use the scanner as a copier or fax machine (in conjunction with a modem). Some scanners even come with optical character recognition (OCR) software that converts printed pages from books, magazines, and newspapers into text you can edit in a word processor.

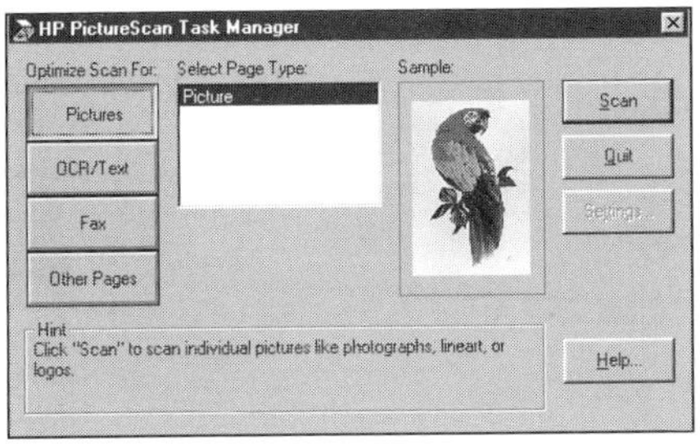
HP PictureScan Task Manager
Optimize Scan For:
Select Page Type:
Sample:
Pictures
OCR/Text
Fax
Other Pages
Picture
Scan
Quit
Settings...
Help...
Hint
Click "Scan" to scan individual pictures like photographs, lineart, or logos.

You use the bundled software to control the scanner. This scanner can also help you send faxes with a fax modem.

Printers

A printer is a very useful peripheral for many types of work. A printer can help you create professional-looking documents, custom business cards, large signs, and other types of printouts. Modern printers produce very sharp output inexpensively and quickly. Two types of printers work best for home and office use:

- **Laser—**Laser printers use a laser to trace a pattern on a drum that picks up toner and fuses it to the paper to print text and graphics. Laser printers are very fast and they print sharp images; however, most laser printers print only in black and white. Color laser printers have become available in recent years, but still cost thousands of dollars more than black-and-white models.
- **Ink-jet—**These printers spray microscopic drops of ink on the page. Compared to laser printers, ink-jets are slower and cannot print as sharply. But most ink-jet printers are capable of color printing. When used with special paper, and set to a low speed, some ink-jet printers can create photo-realistic color pictures.

There are two important measures of printer performance:

- The *resolution* of printing is measured in dots per inch (DPI). The higher the resolution of a printout, the sharper the appearance of graphics and text on the page. Early laser printers and most ink-jet printers can print up to 300 DPI. Most new laser printers now print at 600 DPI.
- The *speed* of a printer is typically measured as the number of pages per minute (PPM) it is able to print.

The table below is a generalized comparison of laser and ink-jet printers.

Printer Type	**Speed**	**Can print color?**	**Printer resolution printing in . . .**	
			Color	**Black and White**
Laser	6–16 PPM	No	n/a	600–1200 DPI
Ink-Jet	1 PPM in color 3–5 PPM in black & white	Yes	300 DPI	600 DPI

Surge Protector

A computer has very sensitive circuitry. A power surge can burn out the most important and expensive components of your computer. To prevent this, your computer and its peripherals should always be connected to a surge protector. Most computer hardware also requires a grounded (three-prong) power outlet. Some surge protectors come with several on-off switches for the outlets. This is very convenient, since it makes it easy to switch off individual components of the computer system when they are not in use.

Photo courtesy of Kensington Technology Group.

Uninterruptible Power Source

If your electrical utility is subject to frequent blackouts and brownouts, you should consider the purchase of an uninterruptible power source (UPS). This device contains a power sensor that instantly switches to a high-capacity battery any time the power to your computer is cut off. The UPS will also sound an audible tone that warns you the computer is running off the battery. The amount of time a UPS can keep the computer running depends on the size of the UPS battery and the computer's power requirements. Typically, the UPS should be able to power the computer for at least five minutes. This provides enough time to save your work and shut down the computer normally.

Photo courtesy of Best Power Technology, Inc.

Computer Software

Computer software is the invisible, logical component of the computer. Most software exists in the form of program instructions that control how the computer functions and performs tasks for you. Software also stores the results of the work you perform on the computer. Without software, a computer is useless.

COMPUTER SOFTWARE

Program Files		User Files
Operating Systems	**Applications**	**User Data**
Windows 98	Word	Letter
Windows 2000 Professional	Excel	Photograph
Macintosh System 8	Myst	Name & address list
Linux	Navigator	Web page

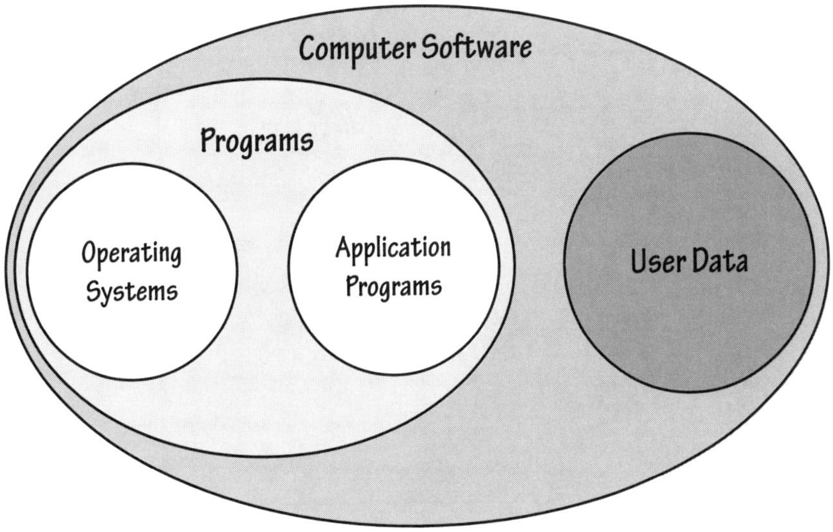
Computer Software
Programs
Operating Systems
Application Programs
User Data

Files

The basic unit of software is the file. A file is a collection of computer data that has some common purpose. Examples of files are application programs, digital images, or a letter you have typed. Depending on the programs you install and use, the computer may have thousands of files stored on its disk drive.

Programs

A program is software code designed to run the computer and help you get work done. A simple program can be a single software file. Complex programs like Word and Excel are made up of dozens of files, each of which helps you use some feature of the program. There are two basic types of programs in a computer system: the operating system and application programs.

Operating System

The operating system (OS) is the basic software your computer needs in order to run. The operating system software takes control of the computer soon after it is turned on and controls all of the basic functions of your computer. The operating system also helps you to browse and organize your user files. This makes it easier to find and open documents and other types of work you have created previously.

Every computer requires an operating system in order to function. Windows 98 is an operating system. Other popular operating systems include System 8 for the Macintosh, Windows NT, and Unix.

32bit ODBC
Add New Hardware
Add/Remove Programs
Date/Time
Display
Find Fast
Fonts
Game Controllers
Internet
Keyboard
Mail and Fax
Modems
Mouse
Multimedia
Network
Passwords
Power Management
Printers
Regional Settings
Sounds
System
Telephony
Users

Most of the settings in the Windows 98 Control Panel are controlled by the operating system.

Here are two examples of how the operating system plays a vital role in every task you perform on the computer:

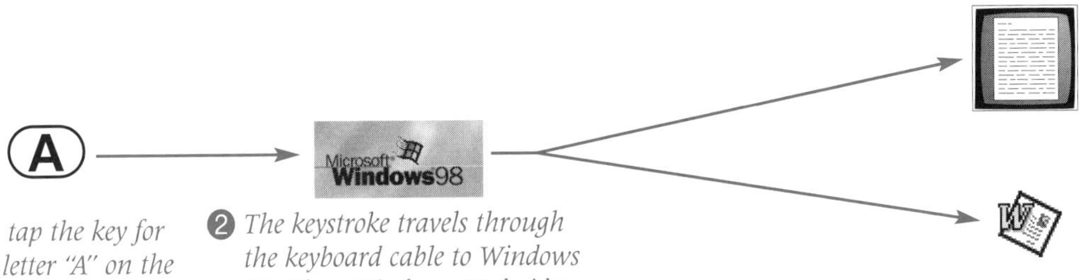
A
Microsoft Windows98

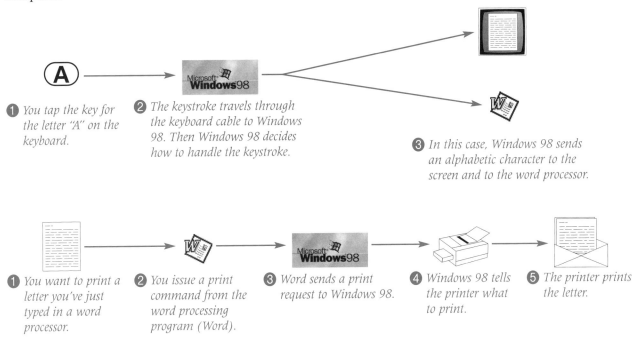

❶ *You tap the key for the letter "A" on the keyboard.*

❷ *The keystroke travels through the keyboard cable to Windows 98. Then Windows 98 decides how to handle the keystroke.*

❸ *In this case, Windows 98 sends an alphabetic character to the screen and to the word processor.*

Microsoft Windows98

❶ *You want to print a letter you've just typed in a word processor.*

❷ *You issue a print command from the word processing program (Word).*

❸ *Word sends a print request to Windows 98.*

❹ *Windows 98 tells the printer what to print.*

❺ *The printer prints the letter.*

Application Programs

Application programs (or simply "applications") help you accomplish tasks. For example, you use a word processing program to type letters and create other documents. You can use financial management programs to balance checkbooks and investment accounts. You use graphics programs to create drawings and other graphic art. Even games for entertainment are a form of application program. Here are some examples of popular application programs:

This application . . .	helps you to . . .
Word	write letters, memos, reports, and other text documents.
Excel	work with numbers on a spreadsheet.
Outlook	keep a schedule, and send and receive electronic mail messages.
Access	keep track of large amounts of data.
PowerPoint	create on-screen presentations.
Internet Explorer	browse sites on the World Wide Web.
Photoshop	edit and add special effects to photographs.
PageMaker	create newsletters, flyers, and books.
Quicken	write checks and keep track of your personal finances.
TurboTax	fill out tax forms and print a tax return, or file the return electronically.
FrontPage	create your own Web sites.

User Files

User files (or simply "files") contain information and work that users have created in application programs. When you finish a piece of work, you will usually save it as a file on a hard drive or floppy disk. Examples of work you might store in user files are:

- letter you typed and saved with a word processor
- drawing or digital photograph
- database of names and addresses
- record of your checking account transactions
- game you have saved to play later

Computer Viruses

A computer virus is a software program designed to cause trouble on a computer system. Viruses can invisibly transmit themselves to "infect" a computer without your knowledge. For example, if you copy a virus-infected program to a floppy disk, then run that program on another computer, the virus may infect other programs on the new "host" computer. There are many types of computer viruses, and new ones are discovered almost every day. Most viruses are harmless, but a very few have been known to do great damage, such as erase your hard drive!

Antivirus Software

A special type of application software designed to detect and erase viruses is called an antivirus program. It is a good idea to purchase and install antivirus software on a new computer. An antivirus program watches all software activities on the computer, and halts the processing of any program it considers to be performing a "suspicious" activity. Antivirus programs can detect the unseen activities of most viruses when they try to invade your system and can usually "clean" (erase) a virus in an infected file.

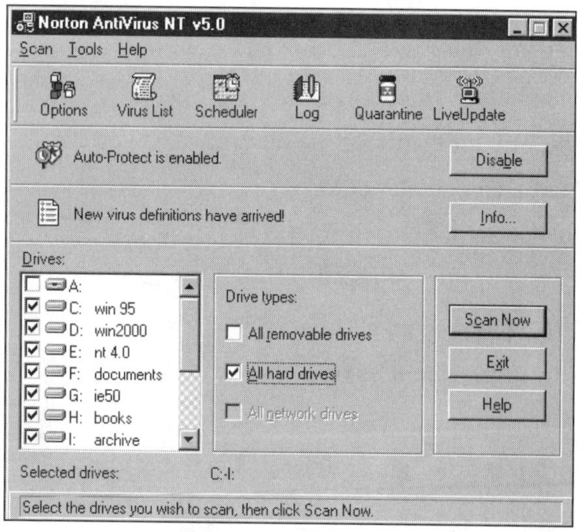

Norton AntiVirus NT v5.0
Scan Tools Help
Options
Virus List
Scheduler
Log
Quarantine
LiveUpdate
Auto-Protect is enabled.
Disable
New virus definitions have arrived!
Info...
Drives:
A:
C: win 95
D: win2000
E: nt 4.0
F: documents
G: ie50
H: books
I: archive
Drive types:
All removable drives
All hard drives
All network drives
Scan Now
Exit
Help
Selected drives: C:-I:
Select the drives you wish to scan, then click Scan Now.

11:30 AM

This antivirus program loads itself automatically when the computer is powered up. It watches for suspicious activity that could indicate a virus attempting to infect the system.

Macro Viruses

A new type of virus has emerged in the past few years. These are small programs embedded in word processor and spreadsheet document files. These so-called macro viruses are the first viruses that are not contained inside program files. (A macro is a saved series of keystrokes and commands that you can "replay" to perform repetitive tasks.) Most modern antivirus software can detect and clean macro viruses.

Virus Definition Updates

New strains (types) of computer virus are discovered almost daily. Since many viruses use similar techniques to invisibly "infect" a computer system, many antivirus programs can detect new strains of virus without having detailed information about them. If the computer has a connection to the Internet or is equipped with a modem, many antivirus programs have an updating feature. This feature dials out and copies (downloads) the most up-to-date virus definitions onto your hard drive. These updates can ensure that your antivirus program has the latest information on new types of viruses.

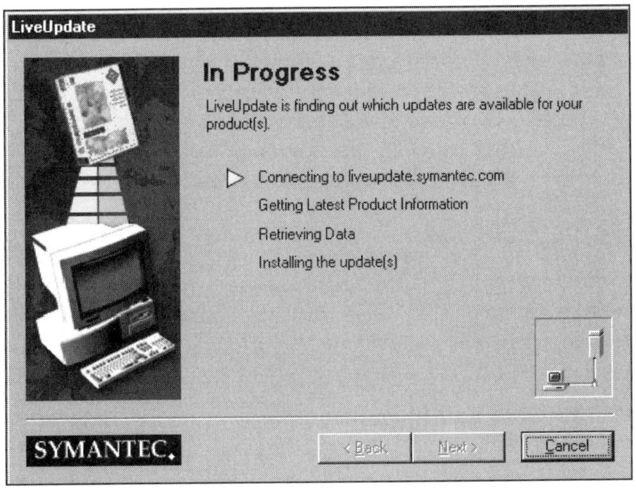
LiveUpdate
In Progress
LiveUpdate is finding out which updates are available for your product(s).
Connecting to liveupdate.symantec.com
Getting Latest Product Information
Retrieving Data
Installing the update(s)
SYMANTEC.
< Back
Next >
Cancel

This screen walks a user through contacting the vendor for the latest virus definitions. Most antivirus software vendors offer a free one-year subscription to this type of update service.

Researching Software

Before you shop for hardware, you should always begin by researching the software you expect to run. Why? Because the usefulness of your new computer depends upon its ability to run the application programs that help you complete tasks, and to store the data files you create as you work. Some application programs require a more powerful computer than others.

Examples

You want to send and receive electronic mail over the Internet (email). Email application programs are generally pretty simple, and even a very inexpensive computer can run them. However, what if you also want to run the latest generation of voice dictation software? These programs allow you to speak into a microphone, with the computer "typing" every word you say. Then you can revise your dictation in a word processor. This type of software makes very high demands on the computer's hardware. If the computer's hardware does not meet the program's requirements, it will not be able to run the voice dictation program at all.

Reading Software Requirements

When you purchase software in a store, the package will indicate the type of hardware and operating system required to run the software. Before you purchase a computer, you should examine the packaging of programs you intend to run. Pay close attention to all of the requirements specified for each program. This research will help you determine exactly which features and equipment are necessary and most valuable. For example, you may discover that the fastest microprocessor on the market will not be as useful to you as more RAM.

Making Your Purchase Decision

After you have completed your software research, you will be ready to make your purchase decision. The table below summarizes the basic specifications to keep in mind when you shop for your computer.

Requirement	Notes	Examples
Microprocessor	This specification tells you the model and speed of the microprocessor required to run the software. A slower or older model microprocessor may not be able to handle the demands of a sophisticated application program. On the other hand, many basic programs will run fine with the slower microprocessor you might find in a used computer.	Pentium-200MHz 486-66MHz
Operating system	Application programs are designed to run with specific versions of Windows or some other operating system. Most programs designed for earlier versions of Windows will also (but not always) work smoothly with a later version of Windows.	Windows 95 or later Windows NT 4.0 or later Macintosh System 8
RAM	More sophisticated programs typically require more RAM to run efficiently. If you intend to run several programs at once, you probably want to have at least twice as much RAM as is required by the most demanding program you will run.	16MB of RAM with Windows 95 32MB of RAM with Windows 2000 Professional
Hard drive storage space	Some programs require a large amount of space on your hard drive to run efficiently. There may be a minimal installation option that takes less hard drive space, and a full installation option that installs all the optional features of the program.	24-60MB of storage space
CD-ROM drive	Many programs now come only on a CD-ROM disk. If your computer does not have a CD-ROM drive, you may need to request floppy disks by mail from the manufacturer. Some programs are so large that they could require 30 or more floppy disks.	32 × CD-ROM drive 64 × CD-ROM drive
Extras	Some software applications may recommend some additional hardware that helps you get more value out of the program.	28.8K modem Sound card

Recommended versus Minimum Configurations

Many software programs list both minimum and recommended hardware configurations. Below is a practical comparison between these two types of requirements, followed by three examples.

- **Minimum**—This configuration is satisfactory only if you intend to run programs on your computer occasionally for brief periods of time. Running the program in the minimum configuration may cause your computer to operate very slowly. This can be very frustrating if you are trying to work efficiently to meet a deadline.
- **Recommended**—This hardware configuration is necessary if you are going to run the application programs frequently. Your computer will be able to deliver its peak performance in this configuration. The recommended RAM is also necessary if you intend to run more than one program at the same time.

The table below compares the minimum and recommended requirements of a very simple application program, a moderately complex program, and a very complex application program.

	Program:	**BORLAND MYST**	**MICROSOFT WORD 97**	**IBM VIA VOICE 98**
	Program Type:	**Game**	**Word Processor**	**Voice Dictation**
	Complexity Level:	**Low**	**Medium**	**High**
Microprocessor	Minimum	386/33	486/66	Pentium/166 MMX*
	Recommended	486/33	Pentium/120	—
RAM	Minimum	4MB	8MB	32–48MB
	Recommended	8MB	16MB	48–64MB
Hard drive storage space	Minimum	4MB	20MB	180MB
	Recommended	—	48-60MB	—
Operating system	Minimum	Windows 3.1	Windows 95 or Windows NT 4.0	Windows 95 or Windows NT 4.0
	Recommended	—	—	—
Other hardware	Minimum	CD-ROM drive	—	Sound board, CD-ROM drive, Microphone
	Recommended	Sound board	Modem, Sound board, CD-ROM drive	—

*MMX stands for MultiMedia eXtensions. These extensions are special software code built right into the microprocessor that helps it process multimedia commands more quickly.

Setting Up a Computer

When you set up a computer, there are measures you can take to make your work and play more productive and comfortable. This section offers advice on setting up a computer and developing healthy work habits that can reduce the risk of discomfort or injury.

Ergonomics

Ergonomics is the science of designing the equipment we work with to maximize productivity and reduce fatigue. When you set up a computer system at home or office, it is important to consider how you can sit and work at the computer as comfortably as possible. A few rules of thumb can help you arrange your computer workstation ergonomically.

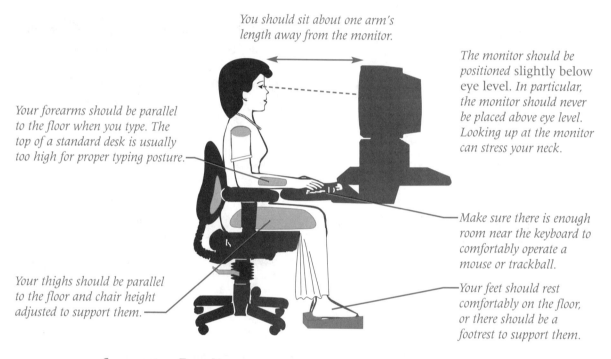

You should sit about one arm's length away from the monitor.
The monitor should be positioned slightly below eye level. In particular, the monitor should never be placed above eye level. Looking up at the monitor can stress your neck.
Your forearms should be parallel to the floor when you type. The top of a standard desk is usually too high for proper typing posture.
Make sure there is enough room near the keyboard to comfortably operate a mouse or trackball.
Your thighs should be parallel to the floor and chair height adjusted to support them.
Your feet should rest comfortably on the floor, or there should be a footrest to support them.

Computer Furniture

Many stores carry furniture designed especially for computers. For example, there are desks equipped with keyboard drawers that place the keyboard at the optimal level for typing. If you expect to spend a great deal of time at the computer, good furniture is a sound investment in your health and comfort.

Photo courtesy of Computer Furniture Direct.

A high-quality chair is another key to working comfortably at the computer. It should have adjustments for the seat back and height. The chair should also give good support to your lower back. If the chair is equipped with arms, they should be adjustable.

An affordable alternative to an expensive computer chair is to purchase an ergonomic backrest instead. Backrests can save you 80% or more over the purchase of a chair.

WEB

See the Lesson 1 *Web page for links to Web sites about computer-related ergonomics.*

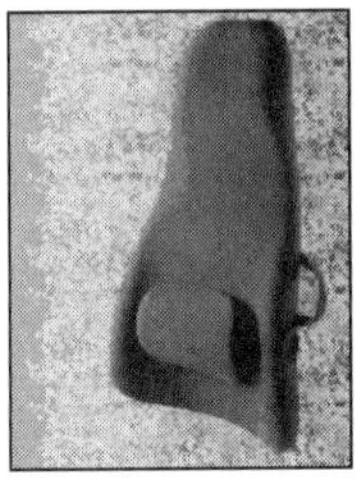

This backrest may give good support at 20% the cost of an equivalent chair.

Photos courtesy of Obusforme.

Healthy Work Habits with Computers

Operating any piece of equipment over a long period of time carries risks. The specific health risks posed by frequent computer operation are still being identified. Some of the risks under study are:

- radiation from computer monitors.
- eye strain from full-time use.
- repetitive stress injuries.

TIP!

Sit at least an arm's length away from the monitor.

Radiation Issues

All computer monitors emit radiation while they are in use. Computer monitors and television sets both use the same cathode ray tube (CRT) technology. However, computer monitors are built with much better shielding to reduce radiation. The amount of radiation emitted by computer monitors is not directly related to the size of the screen. In other words, a small, older monitor may emit more radiation than a new, larger one. Also, monitors put out more radiation from the sides and rear than from the front. Many manufacturers are designing new monitors to emit less radiation.

TIP!

Periodically focus your eyes across the room or out a window (a different distance from the monitor).

Eye Strain

Some computer users have reported blurred vision after long work sessions in front of a monitor. This can be caused by staring at a fixed distance for long periods of time. Our eyes are used to focusing at various distances every few minutes.

TIP!

If you think you are experiencing a repetitive stress injury, seek medical advice as early as possible.

Repetitive Stress Injuries

Repetitive stress injuries (RSIs) can occur when the same motion is repeated over and over again for prolonged periods. If you are typing at a computer keyboard all day long, the muscles in your hands and wrists can be stressed. Some intense projects such as graphic design may require hundreds of motions each hour to maneuver the mouse and give commands from the keyboard.

Awareness Is Key!

Awareness may be the best medicine to prevent the painful and debilitating effects of repetitive stress injuries. One symptom can be numbness and tingling sensations in the wrist, palm, and forearm. In a severe case, every motion of the affected area can become quite painful.

In recent years, there has been an increase in computer-related repetitive stress injuries, including tendonitis and carpal tunnel syndrome. This is a result of the widespread use of computers and the long hours people are working on them. These injuries are difficult to treat, so be careful and take preventive measures.

WEB

See the Lesson 1 *Web page for links to Web sites about computer-related health issues.*

Preventive Measures

With good work habits, your risk of injury is greatly reduced. The following tips can help you avoid a repetitive stress injury, even if you work at a computer many hours each day.

- Take frequent rest breaks.
- Do hand-strengthening exercises (keep a squeeze ball near the computer).
- Maintain proper hand positioning at the keyboard; a wrist rest may help you .
- Invest in ergonomic computer furniture and hardware, including a comfortable chair, keyboard, and mouse.
- Apply an ice pack to your hand and wrist to help reduce inflammation, but see a doctor if any type of discomfort continues.

Concepts Review

True/False Questions

1. The primary chip on a personal computer system board is called a *microprocessor.*	TRUE	FALSE
2. A megabyte is larger than a gigabyte.	TRUE	FALSE
3. Software designed to help you get work done is called *user data files.*	TRUE	FALSE
4. A computer's RAM works just like the storage space on the hard drive.	TRUE	FALSE
5. The sharpness of a printer's output is measured by its *resolution.*	TRUE	FALSE
6. The latest, fastest microprocessor is always the best choice for a new computer.	TRUE	FALSE
7. The image you see on the computer's monitor (screen) is made up of *pixels.*	TRUE	FALSE
8. Floppy disks can hold just as much data as hard drives.	TRUE	FALSE
9. Software that controls the computer's basic functions is called an *operating system.*	TRUE	FALSE
10. Because they are much smaller, notebook computers generally cost less than desktop computers.	TRUE	FALSE

Multiple-Choice Questions

1. Which statement best describes how you should shop for a new computer?
   a. Get the fastest computer available.
   b. Get a computer that meets the requirements of the application program you plan to use.
   c. Get the least expensive computer available.
   d. None of the above

2. Hardware components that are outside the system unit case are called:
   a. accessories
   b. printers and modems
   c. pointing devices
   d. peripherals

3. Among the health risks of working with computers are the following:
   a. Radiation
   b. Gamer's elbow
   c. Repetitive stress injury
   d. Eyestrain
   e. a, c, and d
   f. a, b, c, and d

4. The three primary types of software are:
   a. anti-virus; user data; applications
   b. applications; user data; operating system
   c. operating system; word processor; spreadsheet
   d. applications; utilities; operating system

Concept Matrix

Place a check mark in the correct column for each term:

Item	Hardware	Software
Modem	______	______
Windows 98	______	______
Printer	______	______
Floppy disk	______	______
Word processing application	______	______
Floppy drive	______	______
Letter document file	______	______
Computr system	______	______
Peripherals	______	______
Application program	______	______

Skill Builders

Skill Builder 1.1 Research Software Requirements

- Visit a store that sells computer software.
- Examine at least four software application programs you would like to run on your own computer. They should be programs that help you get useful work done in your job or as a hobby.
- Make notes on the system requirements of each software application program.
- Use these notes to create a basic requirements list for the computer system you will research in the next exercise.

Skill Builder 1.2 Research Your Own Computer System

Look up computer system advertisements in a local periodical or visit a local computer store. Determine the following information for at least two different systems:

- The model of microprocessor and its clock speed
- The system RAM
- The video RAM
- The capacity of the hard drive
- The size of the monitor, its dot pitch, and its resolution

Skill Builder 1.3 Make a Purchase Recommendation

Using the information in this lesson, write a specification for a system you would like to purchase for your use at home or at an office.

- Include any additional peripherals (such as a scanner or video capture card).

LESSON 2—Windows

Working with Windows Programs

As you learned in Lesson 1, the operating system is software that controls the basic functions of the computer. When you work with application programs such as those in the Office 2000 Suite, the Windows operating system controls your interactions with the programs and with peripherals such as the printer. This lesson introduces many basic techniques for working with Windows programs in Windows 95, Windows 98, and Windows 2000. These techniques work with virtually any Windows program, not just the Office 2000 Suite. You will learn how to start programs, adjust the size of program windows, and how to run more than one program at once (multitasking). You will also learn the basics of saving your work and giving commands with menu bars and dialog boxes. By the end of this lesson, you should be able to work with the basic commands of almost any Windows application program.

In This Lesson

Case Study

Michael has just purchased his first computer, a discount model that didn't set him back much but has all the features he needs. It isn't the fastest computer on the market, but Michael made sure it was powerful enough to run the basic types of programs he will use for the next couple of years. The only software that came with the computer was the operating system, Windows 98. But Michael discovers that Windows comes with several basic application programs called *applets.* When a friend asks Michael to help him put together a meeting announcement, he is eager to demonstrate what his computer and printer can do.

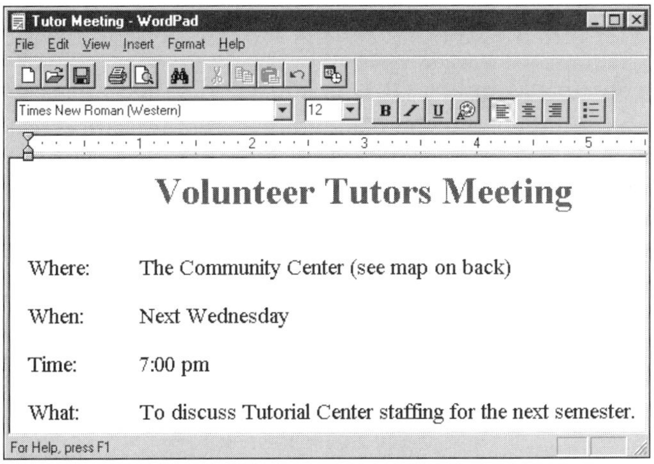
Tutor Meeting - WordPad
File Edit View Insert Format Help
Times New Roman (Western)
12
Volunteer Tutors Meeting
Where: The Community Center (see map on back)
When: Next Wednesday
Time: 7:00 pm
What: To discuss Tutorial Center staffing for the next semester.
For Help, press F1

WordPad is a basic word processing application that you can use to type simple documents, like a one-page letter, with ease.

Michael's friend also wants to print a map with directions to the meeting; so he starts the Paint program and soon has drawn a map showing where the meeting will take place.

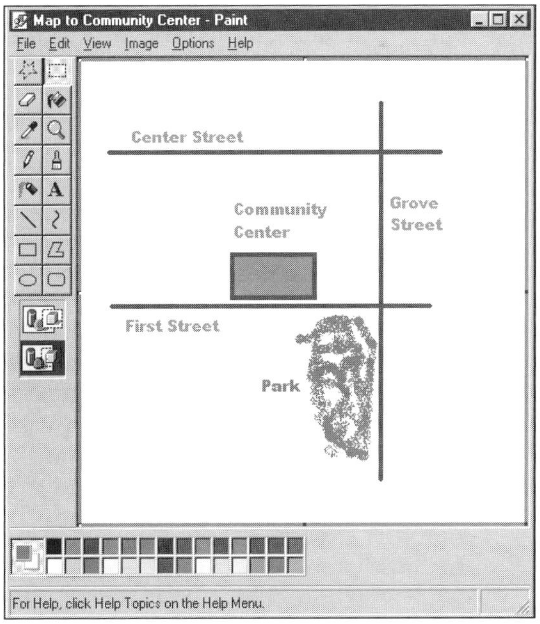
Map to Community Center - Paint
File Edit View Image Options Help
Center Street
Community Center
Grove Street
First Street
Park
For Help, click Help Topics on the Help Menu.

The Paint applet is a simple drawing program. It features tools you use for drawing lines, boxes, circles, and text. It even has a spray paint tool.

Introducing Windows

Windows is an **operating system.** As you may recall from Lesson 1, there are three primary categories of software: the operating system; application programs; and user data files. As the operating system, Windows controls all the basic functions of the computer. Windows serves as the interface between you and the hardware and software that make up the computer system.

Roles of an Operating System

Windows plays several critical roles, such as those described below.

- **Managing file storage—**Windows controls the hard disk drives, floppy drive, and any other storage devices on the computer. For example, if you need to edit a letter you typed recently, Windows tells the computer system where the data for this letter is located and how to retrieve the letter into the word processing program for editing.
- **Managing Random Access Memory (RAM)—**As you learned in Lesson 1, your computer uses RAM as the "workbench" where all of your programs are run. Windows controls RAM and allocates it to the various application programs you run.
- **Managing Programs—**Windows is a multitasking operating system that allows several programs to run at the same time. Windows manages the programs and ensures they have adequate RAM in which to run. Windows controls the interaction of each application program with other software and hardware. It also lets you switch between programs and copy information between them.
- **Managing Hardware and Peripherals—**Windows controls the hardware inside the system unit. For example, when you click with the mouse or tap a key on the keyboard, Windows receives your command and either executes it or passes the command on the application program you are running. Windows also controls the display of everything you see on the computer monitor. When you print a document, Windows sends the commands and data that tell the printer what to print.

Ease of Learning

Imagine if every make of car had its gas and brake pedals in a different location from other makes. Or if you had a turn signal control on the steering wheel in one make of car and on the left side of the dashboard in another. That's the way software was in the early days of personal computers (PCs). Learning one program did not necessarily help you learn the next one. Fortunately, this is no longer the case.

As you make your way through these lessons, you will learn basic commands and techniques that apply to virtually any Windows program you may use in the future. This consistency is an important feature of Windows and of software that uses a Graphic User Interface (GUI). It makes learning how to use computers and various computer programs much easier than it was in the past. Computers were once the realm of programmers and specialists. Now, anyone can learn to use a computer effectively.

Switching On the Computer

You switch on the computer with a power switch on the front or side of the system unit. Most computers also have peripheral devices such as a printer or graphic scanner attached to the system unit. You should switch on these peripherals before you switch on the system unit. This ensures the system unit will recognize the peripherals as it "wakes up."

Hands-On 2.1 Switching On the Computer

In many computer labs, the computers will already be switched on. If yours is not already on, use the steps in this exercise to power up the computer.

1. Remove any floppy disks from the floppy drive.
   The computer will not start properly if a floppy disk is in the drive. There is a small button on the floppy drive you can press to eject floppy disks.
2. If the computer is plugged into a surge protector, make sure the surge protector is switched on.
3. If there is a printer or scanner attached to the computer, switch on any of these devices.
4. Follow these steps to switch on the computer:

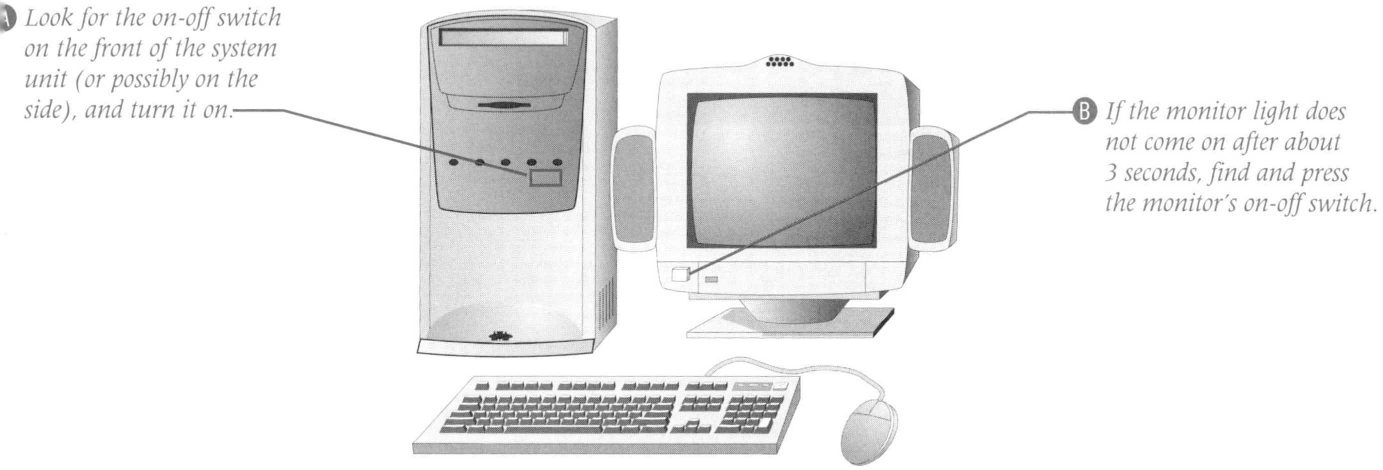

A Look for the on-off switch on the front of the system unit (or possibly on the side), and turn it on.
B If the monitor light does not come on after about 3 seconds, find and press the monitor's on-off switch.

Logging On to Windows

After the computer system completes its power-up routine, you may see a dialog box similar to the two illustrated on the middle of page 44. The *Enter Password* and *Enter Network Password* dialog boxes prompt you to select or type a user name and password. A dialog box is one way to issue commands to Windows. Many home systems are set up to avoid the need to log on, but in most classrooms you will need to follow a log-on procedure.

Entering a User Name

Logging on requires you to select a user name. Your user name is important because it may give you a personal Desktop that can be customized. Also, your user name may restrict your access to devices such as printers. Your instructor will tell you which user name you should select in the Hands-On exercise on the following page.

Hands-On 2.2 Logging On to Windows

NOTE! *You can skip this exercise if your system does not require you to log on.*

1. Get a user name and password from your instructor, and write them in the spaces below.

   User Name: ______________ Password: ______________ ❑ No password required

2. Enter or select your user name in the appropriate box as shown below; then tap the (TAB) key, and enter a password if necessary.
   Notice how asterisks represent the password you type. This prevents someone passing by from reading your password.

Ⓐ *Hold down the (SHIFT) key as you tap the (TAB) key. You will see a highlight in the User Name box. Release the (SHIFT) key.*

Ⓑ *Type your user name here; then tap the (TAB) key to jump to the password box.*

Ⓒ *If necessary, enter your password.*

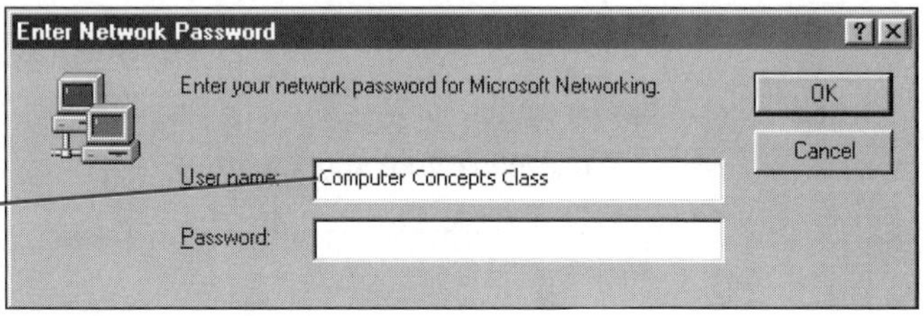
Enter Network Password
Enter your network password for Microsoft Networking.
OK
Cancel
User name:
Computer Concepts Class
Password:

Ⓓ *Tap the ↓ or ↑ arrow keys on the keyboard until the bar highlights your user name. If your user name is not visible, just keep tapping the cursor key until it appears.*

Ⓔ *Tap the (TAB) key; then if necessary enter your password.*

Enter Password
Microsoft Windows98
Select user name:
Excel Class
Internet Class
Student-10
Windows 98 Class
Word Class
Password:
OK
Cancel

3. Tap the (ENTER) key to log on.
   After a brief pause, the Windows Desktop will appear.

The Windows Desktop

After you log on, Windows will display the Desktop. Depending on how the computer is set up, Windows may also automatically run one or more programs. For example you may see an antivirus program start running after the Desktop appears. The Desktop is the workspace where you run programs in Windows. Your Desktop will look similar to the following illustration, but may differ in a few details.

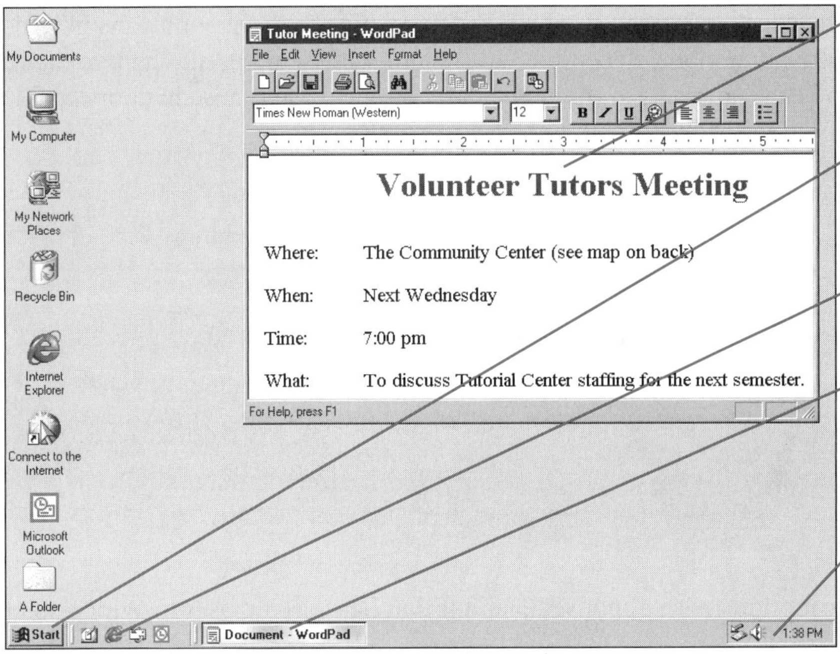
My Documents
My Computer
My Network Places
Recycle Bin
Internet Explorer
Connect to the Internet
Microsoft Outlook
A Folder
Tutor Meeting - WordPad
File Edit View Insert Format Help
Times New Roman (Western)
12
Volunteer Tutors Meeting
Where: The Community Center (see map on back)
When: Next Wednesday
Time: 7:00 pm
What: To discuss Tutorial Center staffing for the next semester.
For Help, press F1
Start
Document - WordPad
1:38 PM

Desktop icons provide access to frequently used Windows features.

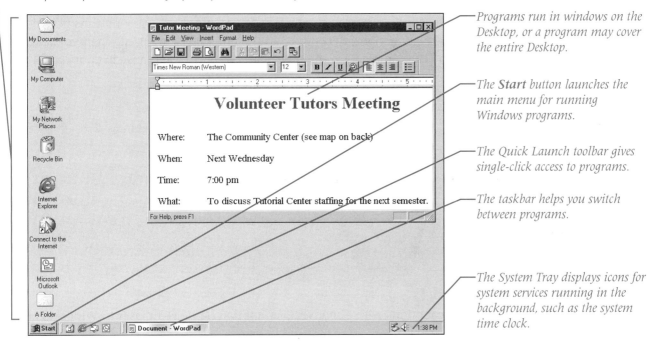

Programs run in windows on the Desktop, or a program may cover the entire Desktop.

*The **Start** button launches the main menu for running Windows programs.*

The Quick Launch toolbar gives single-click access to programs.

The taskbar helps you switch between programs.

The System Tray displays icons for system services running in the background, such as the system time clock.

Displaying the Desktop without Logging On

It is often possible to display the Desktop without actually logging on. A default (generic) Desktop is displayed whenever the **Cancel** button is clicked on the log-on dialog box. However, you may not have access to the normal command menus or printers in the lab if you use this method. Instead, a generic Desktop and Start menu will be displayed. It is best to log on with your assigned user name. Some networked computers in offices won't let you get to the Desktop at all without a user name and password.

Using a Mouse

You will give most of your commands to Windows with a mouse. A mouse is a pointing device. It lets you point to various screen locations and issue commands. The mouse was invented in 1963 by Douglas Englebart, a Stanford University professor. It probably got its name from the tail-like cable that connects it to the computer. If you have never used a mouse before, this lesson—and the ones to follow—will give you plenty of practice.

Mouse Buttons

A typical mouse has two buttons for issuing commands. Some mice have three buttons in which the middle button has various functions, depending on the program being used. The two main mouse buttons are shown below, along with the proper way to grasp the mouse in your hand.

TIP!

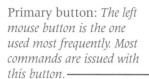

Windows allows you to reverse the right and left mouse buttons. Left-handed users often select this option. Open the Mouse icon in the Windows control panel to see this option. You will do this in the next Hands-On exercise.

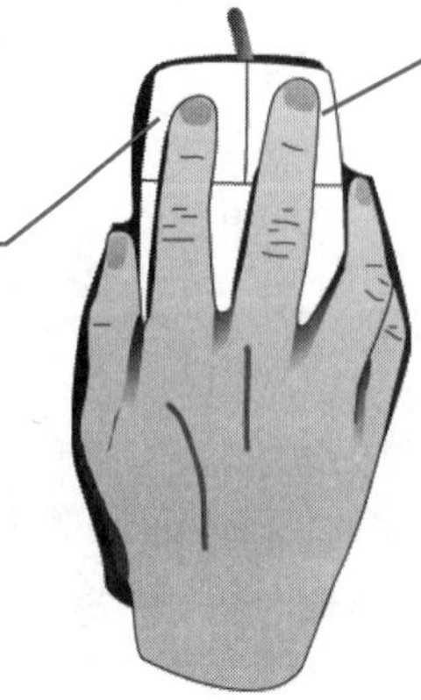
Primary button: *The left mouse button is the one used most frequently. Most commands are issued with this button.*
Secondary button: *The right, or secondary button, often displays a special pop-up menu.*

You can perform five basic motions with a mouse. Each motion has specific uses in Windows and application programs.

Quick Reference

MOUSE MOTIONS

Motion Name	How to Do It
Click	Gently tap and immediately release the primary (left) mouse button. This motion is used to give most commands.
Double-click	Click the primary button twice in rapid succession. This motion is usually a shortcut to open an object on the screen.
Drag	Press and hold down the primary mouse button while you slide the mouse to a new location. Release the mouse button when you reach the destination. This motion is usually used to move objects on the screen.
Right-click	Gently tap and immediately release the secondary (right) mouse button. This is usually used to display special menus.
Point	Slide the mouse without pressing a button until the pointer is in the desired location.

Pointing with the Mouse

When you point with the mouse, you should always remember that the tip of the arrow is the spot you are pointing at. You want to make sure that the tip of the arrow touches any menu or button that you wish to click.

Start

The pointer is too high.

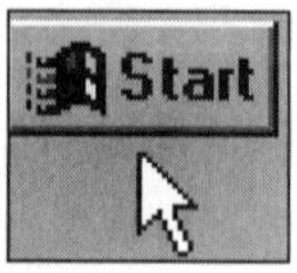
Start

The pointer is too low.

The pointer is just right.

Hands-On 2.3 Use the Mouse

In this exercise, you will practice pointing and clicking. You will see the difference between a normal click and a right-click on the Start button.

1. Follow these steps to practice clicking menu selections:

Ⓐ *Point at the center of the* **Start** *button at the bottom-left corner of the Desktop; then tap and release the* left *mouse button in one smooth motion (click).*

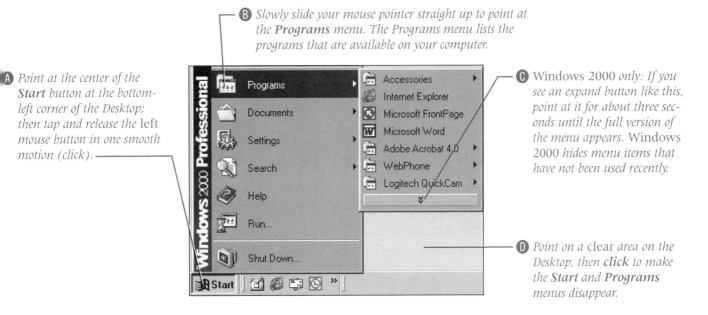

Ⓑ *Slowly slide your mouse pointer straight up to point at the* **Programs** *menu. The Programs menu lists the programs that are available on your computer.*

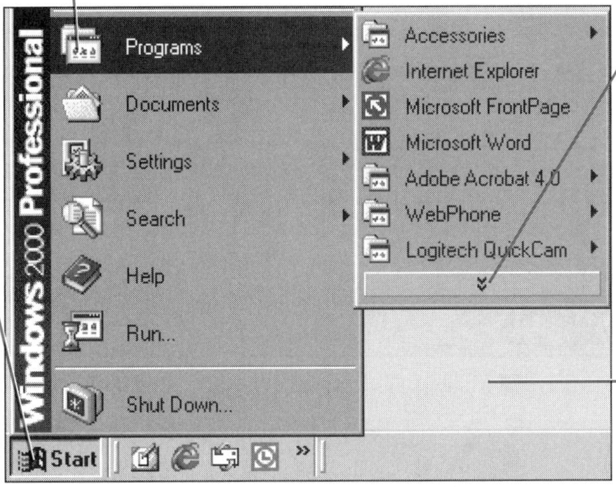

Windows 2000 Professional
Programs
Documents
Settings
Search
Help
Run...
Shut Down...
Start
Accessories
Internet Explorer
Microsoft FrontPage
Microsoft Word
Adobe Acrobat 4.0
WebPhone
Logitech QuickCam

Ⓒ Windows 2000 *only: If you see an expand button like this, point at it for about three seconds until the full version of the menu appears.* Windows 2000 *hides menu items that have not been used recently.*

Ⓓ *Point on a clear area on the Desktop, then* **click** *to make the* **Start** *and* **Programs** *menus disappear.*

2. Follow these steps to practice a right-click:

Ⓐ *Point at the* **Start** *button, but this time tap and release the* **right** *mouse button (a right-click). You will see a pop-up menu appear.*

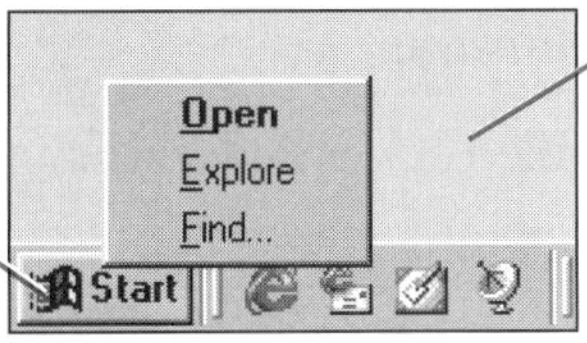

Open
Explore
Find...
Start

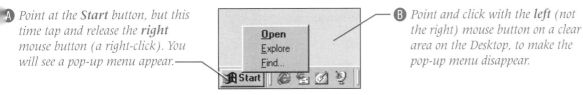

Ⓑ *Point and click with the* **left** *(not the right) mouse button on a clear area on the Desktop, to make the pop-up menu disappear.*

(Continued on the next page)

Practice Double-Clicking and Dragging

Windows lets you adjust the speed of the double-click *mouse motion. In the next steps of this exercise, you will practice adjusting the double-click speed.*

3. Follow these steps to open the Mouse options in Windows control panel:

Ⓐ *Click **Start**.*

Ⓑ *Click **Settings**.*

Ⓒ *Click **Control Panel**.*

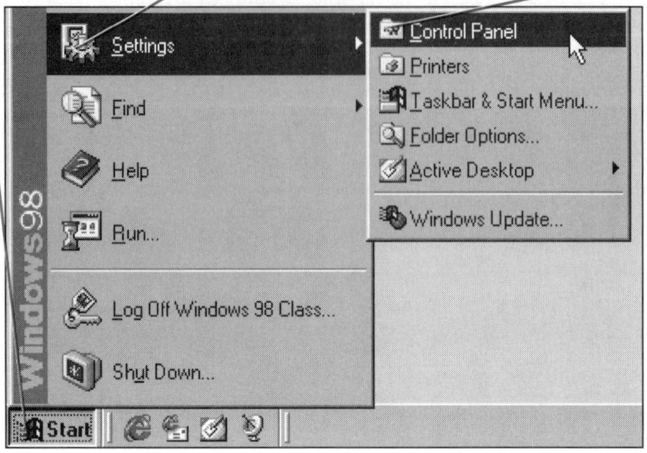

Windows98
Settings
Find
Help
Run...
Log Off Windows 98 Class...
Shut Down...
Start
Control Panel
Printers
Taskbar & Start Menu...
Folder Options...
Active Desktop
Windows Update...

Ⓓ *Look for the Mouse icon. If you do not see it, tap the **M** key on the keyboard two or three times until the mouse icon appears.*

Mou
Open
Create Shortcut

Ⓔ *Click on the Mouse icon with the **right** (not the left) button; then slide the pointer down, and click on the **Open** command in the pop-up menu.*

The Mouse options window will now be displayed.

4. Follow these steps to adjust the double-click speed of the mouse:

Ⓐ *Position the mouse pointer on this slider bar; then press and hold down the* left *mouse button as you drag the bar to the left.*

Ⓑ Release *the mouse button when the slider bar is here. (This will slow down the double-click speed, which makes it easier for beginners to double-click.)*

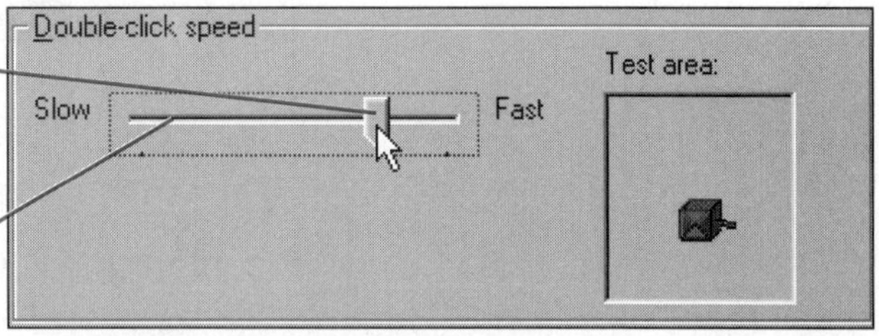

Double-click speed
Slow
Fast
Test area:

Ⓒ Double-click *(quickly tap and release the mouse button twice) in this test area until a jack-in-the-box pops up. It won't pop up until you double-click fast enough. It may take a bit of practice.*

Ⓓ Drag *the slider bar to the right. Try different settings until you can comfortably double-click. Set it toward slow if you're a beginner and toward the middle if you are used to double-clicking.*

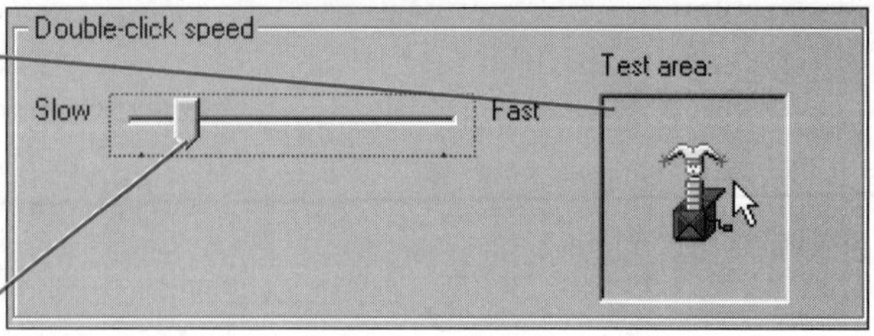

Double-click speed
Slow
Fast
Test area:

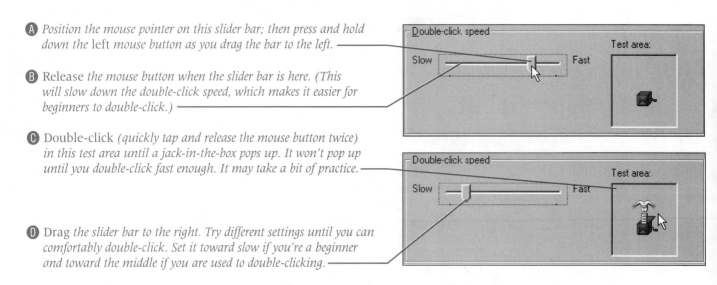

5. Click the **OK** button at the bottom of the Mouse options window to close the window.

6. Click the Close ☒ button at the very top-right corner of the Control Panel window to close that window.

Starting Programs

You can start a program by clicking the Start  button and choosing the desired program from the Programs menu. You can also start a program by double-clicking a Desktop icon for the program (if a Desktop icon exists). For example, the Internet Explorer Web browser program typically has a Desktop icon. Also, some programs can be launched from the Quick Launch toolbar that is next to the Start button.

Internet Explorer

Start

The Quick Launch toolbar lets you start programs with a single click.

Hands-On 2.4 Start WordPad

In this exercise, you will use the Start menu to start the WordPad program. WordPad is an entry-level word processing program you can use to create letters and other simple documents. In a later exercise, you will use WordPad to compose a meeting announcement.

1. Follow these steps to start the WordPad program:

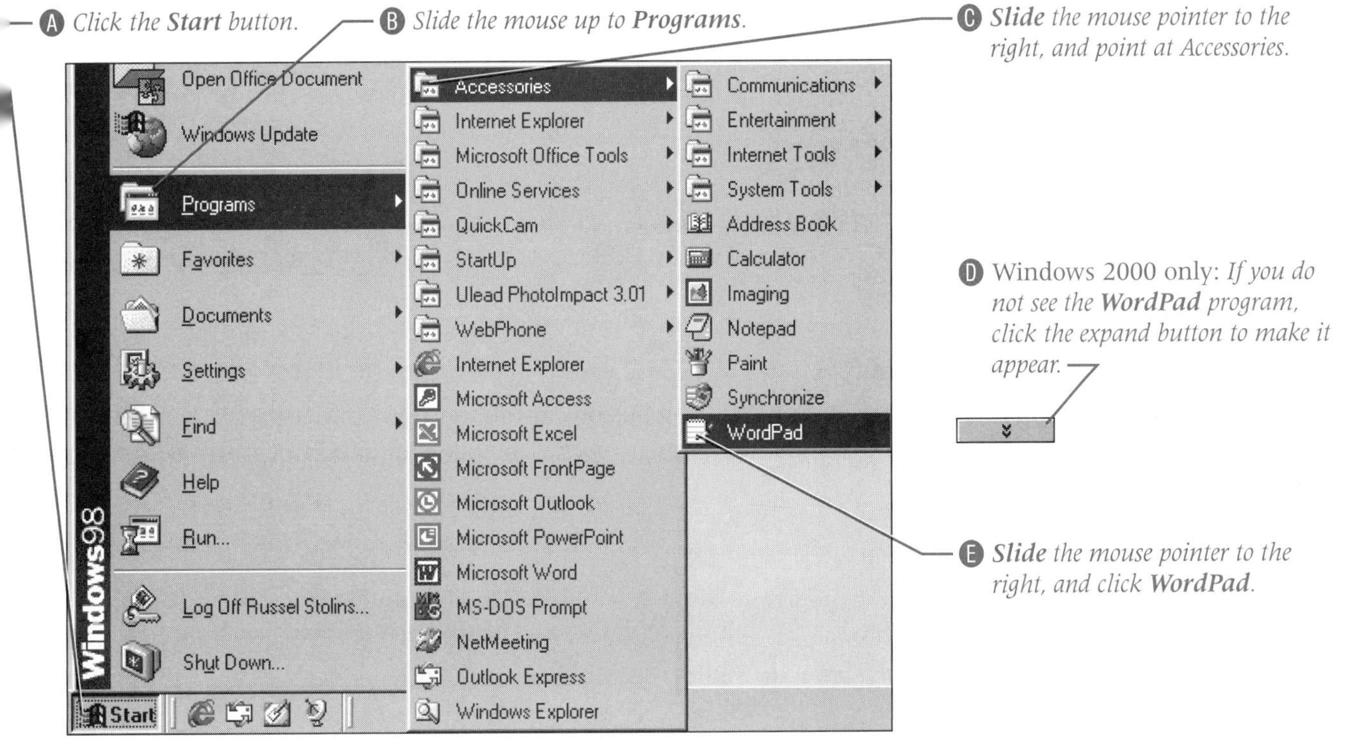
A Click the Start button.
B Slide the mouse up to Programs.
C Slide the mouse pointer to the right, and point at Accessories.
D Windows 2000 only: If you do not see the WordPad program, click the expand button to make it appear.
E Slide the mouse pointer to the right, and click WordPad.
Open Office Document
Windows Update
Programs
Favorites
Documents
Settings
Find
Help
Run...
Log Off Russel Stolins...
Shut Down...
Windows98
Start
Accessories
Internet Explorer
Microsoft Office Tools
Online Services
QuickCam
StartUp
Ulead PhotoImpact 3.01
WebPhone
Internet Explorer
Microsoft Access
Microsoft Excel
Microsoft FrontPage
Microsoft Outlook
Microsoft PowerPoint
Microsoft Word
MS-DOS Prompt
NetMeeting
Outlook Express
Windows Explorer
Communications
Entertainment
Internet Tools
System Tools
Address Book
Calculator
Imaging
Notepad
Paint
Synchronize
WordPad

The WordPad program window will appear on the Desktop.

Elements of a Program Window

Every program runs in its own program window. The WordPad window you have open now is a good example of a typical Windows program. Since the controls in most program windows work similarly, once you have mastered a program such as WordPad, you are well on your way to mastering Windows programs in general. Take a few moments to look over the common features that are shown in the following illustration.

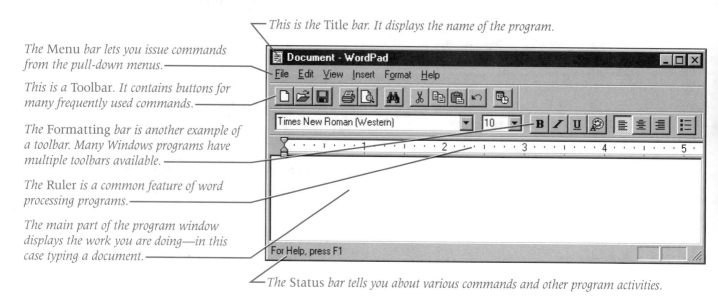

This is the Title bar. *It displays the name of the program.*

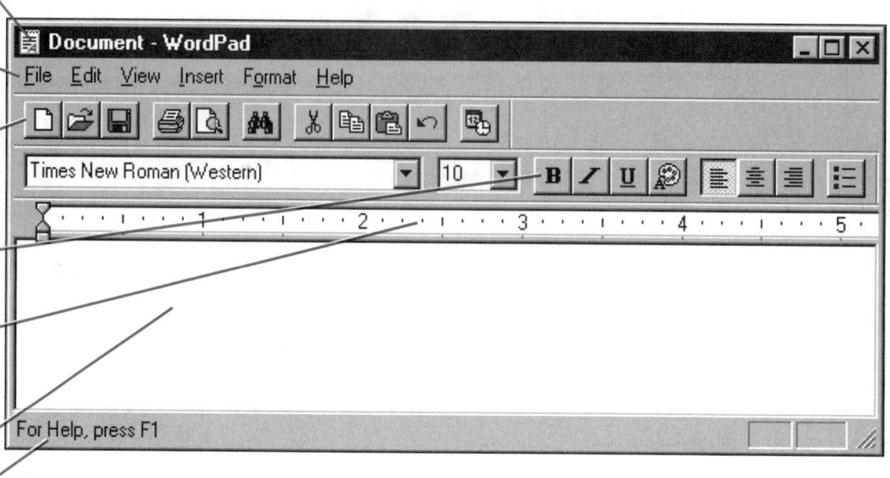
Document - WordPad
File Edit View Insert Format Help
Times New Roman (Western)
10
B I U
For Help, press F1

The Menu *bar lets you issue commands from the pull-down menus.*

This is a Toolbar. *It contains buttons for many frequently used commands.*

The Formatting *bar is another example of a toolbar. Many Windows programs have multiple toolbars available.*

The Ruler *is a common feature of word processing programs.*

The main part of the program window displays the work you are doing—in this case typing a document.

The Status *bar tells you about various commands and other program activities.*

Sizing Program Windows

You can control the position and size of program windows on the Desktop. For example, you may want a program window to occupy the entire Desktop or you may want two or more program windows displayed side-by-side.

Quick Sizing Buttons

Every program window displays quick sizing buttons at the top-right corner that let you give the most common window commands with a single click. The following table describes the function of each quick sizing button.

Button	Description
Minimize	Removes the program window from the Desktop but keeps the program running. Clicking the program button on the Taskbar restores the program window.
Maximize	Expands the program window until it covers the Desktop. Only the maximized program and the Taskbar are visible.
Restore	Restores a program window to the size it was set to before it was maximized. A restored window usually covers only a portion of the Desktop.
Close	Closes a document window or exits a program.

The Switching Restore and Maximize Buttons

The Maximize and Restore buttons never appear together. Instead, when either button is clicked, the window changes and displays the other button, as shown in the example below:

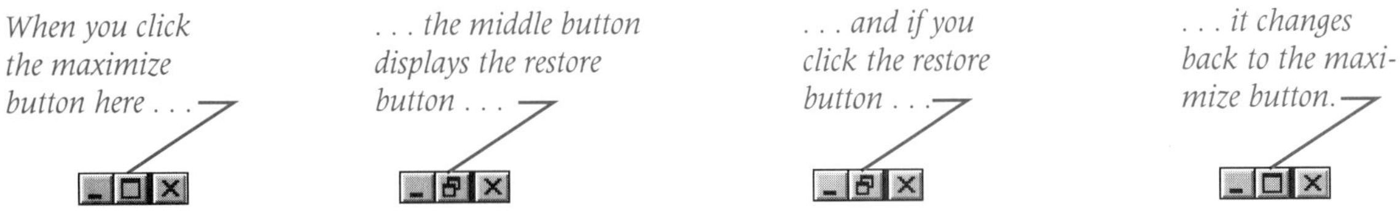

When you click the maximize button here . . .
. . . the middle button displays the restore button . . .
. . . and if you click the restore button . . .
. . . it changes back to the maximize button.

Hands-On 2.5 Use the Quick Sizing Buttons

1. Notice the WordPad Document - WordPad button near the Start button on the Taskbar.
   The button is recessed (pushed in) because WordPad is the active program. A button appears on the Taskbar for each running program.
2. Look at the **top-right** corner of the WordPad window, and you will see three quick sizing buttons.
   If the window is already maximized, then the Restore button will be displayed in the center of the trio. If the last WordPad user had sized the window to cover just part of the Desktop, then the Maximize button will be displayed.
3. If the middle quick sizing button is the Maximize button, then click it.
   At this point, the WordPad window will be maximized. Only the WordPad window, the Taskbar, and the Start button should be visible.
4. Click the Minimize button on the WordPad window.
   The window vanishes, but the WordPad button is still visible on the Taskbar.
5. Click the WordPad Document - WordPad button on the Taskbar and the window will reappear.
   You can always restore a minimized window by clicking that program's button on the Taskbar.
6. Click the Restore button, and the window will occupy only part of the Desktop.
   Leave the WordPad window open.

Moving Program Windows

You can move a window on the Desktop to various screen locations by dragging on its title bar. The only time a window cannot be moved is if it is maximized. You can tell when a window is maximized because it will have a *Restore* quick sizing button.

TIP! *You cannot change the size of a maximized window.*

Changing the Size of a Program Window

You can adjust the size and shape of an open window by dragging the window's borders. When you point to the border of a window that is restored (i.e., not maximized), you will see a double-arrow appear. The arrows will point in the directions you can resize the window.

Hands-On 2.6 Move and Size the WordPad Window

1. Use the following steps to move the WordPad window:

NOTE! *It's OK if your WordPad window has different dimensions than shown below.*

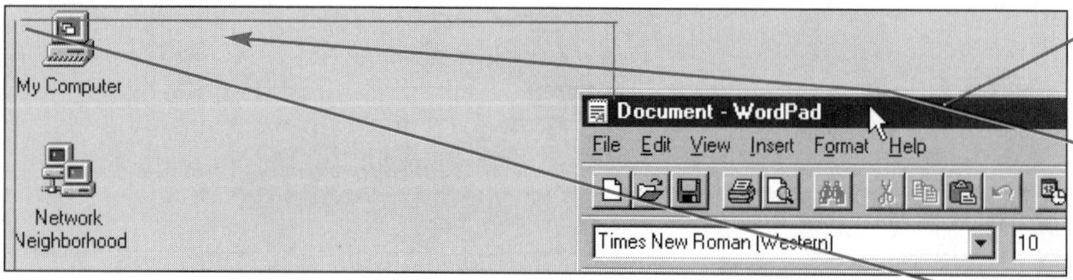

My Computer
Network Neighborhood
Document - WordPad
File Edit View Insert Format Help
Times New Roman (Western)
10

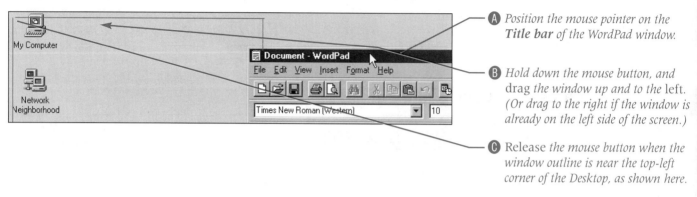

Ⓐ *Position the mouse pointer on the* ***Title bar*** *of the WordPad window.*

Ⓑ *Hold down the mouse button, and* drag *the window up and to the* left. *(Or drag to the right if the window is already on the left side of the screen.)*

Ⓒ Release *the mouse button when the window outline is near the top-left corner of the Desktop, as shown here.*

2. Drag on the title bar of the WordPad window again, but this time drag down toward the **bottom-right** of the Desktop.
3. Drag the title bar once more to place the WordPad window at the **top-center** of the Desktop.

Change the size of the Window

4. Follow these steps to change the size of the WordPad window:

Ⓐ Point *at this border until the double-arrow appears.*

Ⓑ Drag *the border wider until it almost reaches the right side of the Desktop; then release the mouse button.*

Ⓒ Point *at the corner until a diagonal double-arrow appears.*

Ⓓ Drag *up and to the left to make the WordPad window about half as high and wide as it was previously.*

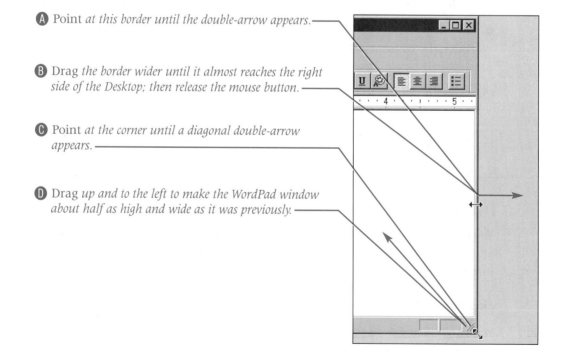

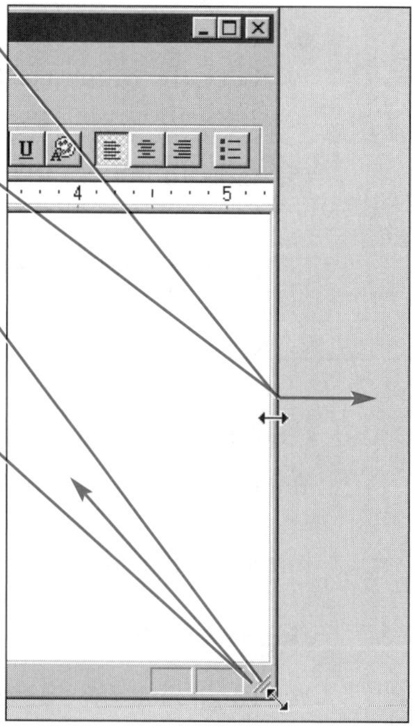

5. Change only the height of the window by dragging the *bottom* border up or down.

6. Practice some more until you can place and size the WordPad window at any desired location on the Desktop.
   This skill will become very useful when you run more than one program at once and need to arrange them on the Desktop so you can see the contents of one window as you work in a different window.

7. When you are finished, maximize the WordPad window.
   It is often easier to work in a maximized window, since it covers any distracting elements that may be on the Desktop.

Working with Programs

Application programs such as WordPad are designed to help you get work done on the computer. There are thousands of application programs available to help you accomplish a wide variety of tasks. Many of the techniques you use to work with the WordPad program in these exercises will apply to using other Windows programs as well. Most programs let you give commands with pull-down menus, toolbars, and keyboard shortcuts. You will use all three types of commands in the Hands-On exercises in this lesson.

Using Toolbars

WordPad's toolbars include buttons for the most frequently used commands. Most of these buttons are either toggles that you switch on and off, or have drop-down lists from which you make a selection.

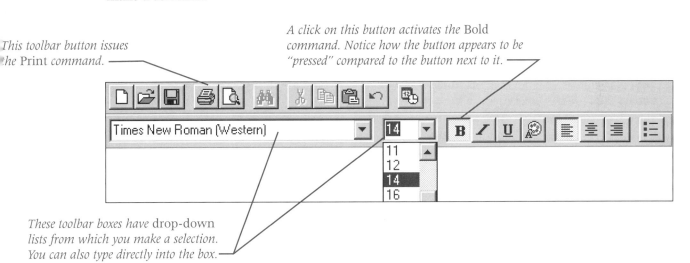

This toolbar button issues the Print *command.*

A click on this button activates the Bold *command. Notice how the button appears to be "pressed" compared to the button next to it.*

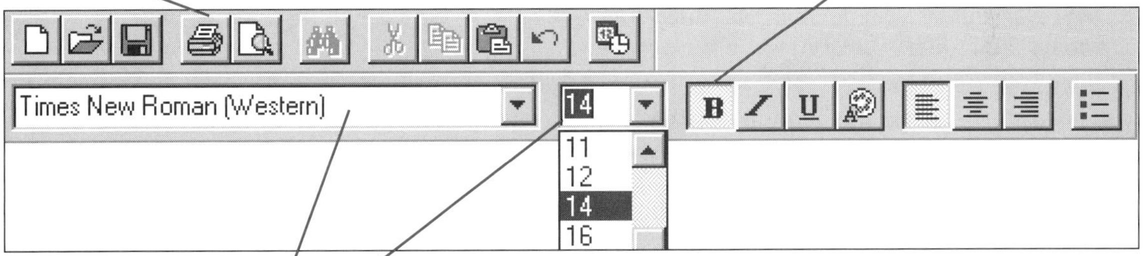

Times New Roman (Western)
14
11
12
14
16

These toolbar boxes have drop-down *lists from which you make a selection. You can also type directly into the box.*

Hands-On 2.7 Type a Meeting Announcement

In this exercise, you will use some of WordPad's toolbar commands as you type a simple meeting announcement. The commands you will use let you change the look of the text in the document.

Format and Type a Heading

1. Tap the (ENTER) key six times to add space to the top margin of the announcement.
   Each time you tap the (ENTER) key in a word processing document, you add a new line to the document. Each new line is usually about one-sixth of an inch high.
2. Follow these steps to set the format for the announcement heading:

Ⓐ Point *(don't click) on the font size drop-down list on the toolbar. Notice the description of the command on the status bar at the bottom-left corner of the WordPad window. If you are running* Windows 95, 98 or 2000, *you will also see a message beneath the font size box indicating the name of the font size list. This is called a* ***ScreenTip****.*

Ⓑ *Click the* drop-down *list button; then click to choose a font size of* ***24****.*

Ⓒ *Click the* ***Bold*** *button to turn on this setting for the text you are about to type. This is an example of a* toggle *that you switch on and off. Notice how the bold button now appears to be "pushed in" on the toolbar.*

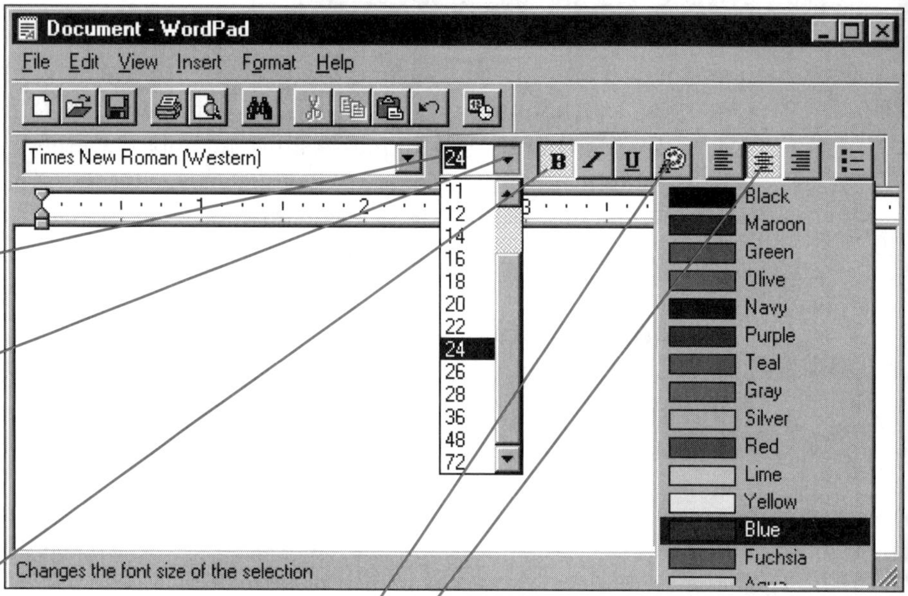

Document - WordPad
File Edit View Insert Format Help
Times New Roman (Western)
24
11
12
14
16
18
20
22
24
26
28
36
48
72
Black
Maroon
Green
Olive
Navy
Purple
Teal
Gray
Silver
Red
Lime
Yellow
Blue
Fuchsia
Changes the font size of the selection

Ⓓ *Click the* ***Color*** *button; then click to choose* ***Blue*** *from the list. If this announcement is printed on a color printer, the heading will be bright blue.*

Ⓔ *Click the* ***Center Align*** *button to center the heading on the page as you type.*

3. Type the heading for the announcement: **`Volunteer Tutors Meeting`**
   The size and color of the letters will match the settings you made in the previous step.
4. Tap the (ENTER) key on the keyboard twice to add space between the heading and the body of the announcement that you are about to type.

Format and Type the Body of the Announcement

5. Follow these steps to format the body text of the announcement:

Ⓐ *Click the* drop-down *list button; then click to choose a font size of* ***14****.*

Ⓑ *Click the* ***Bold*** *button to turn off this setting for the text you are about to type. Since bold was already selected, clicking the button again toggles the setting off. Now the button no longer appears to be "pushed in."*

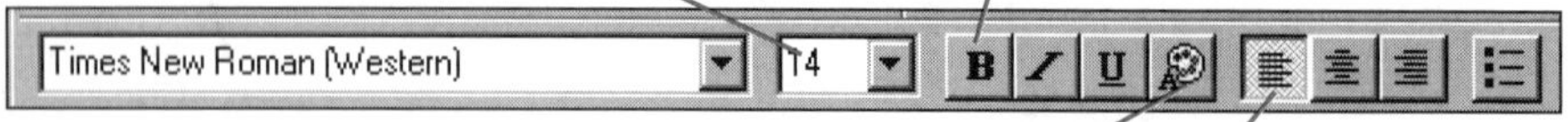

Times New Roman (Western)
14

Ⓒ *Click the* ***Color*** *button; then click to choose* ***Black*** *from the list.*

Ⓓ *Click the* ***Left Align*** *button to align the text with the left margin.*

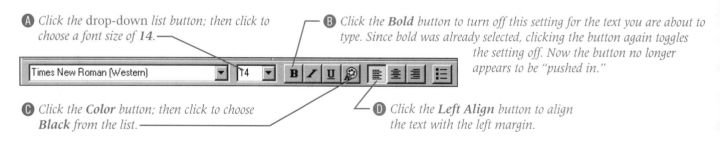

6. Follow these steps to type the body of the announcement:

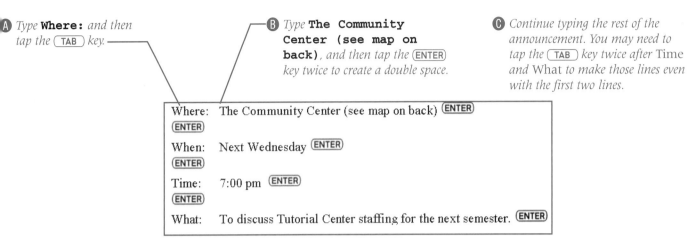

A *Type* **Where:** *and then tap the* TAB *key.*

B *Type* **The Community Center (see map on back)**, *and then tap the* ENTER *key twice to create a double space.*

C *Continue typing the rest of the announcement. You may need to tap the* TAB *key twice after* Time *and* What *to make those lines even with the first two lines.*

Where: The Community Center (see map on back) ENTER
ENTER
When: Next Wednesday ENTER
ENTER
Time: 7:00 pm ENTER
ENTER
What: To discuss Tutorial Center staffing for the next semester. ENTER

Leave the WordPad document open. You will use it again in a moment.

Using Pull-Down Menus

You use pull-down menus frequently in Windows programs to initiate commands. Almost all Windows programs use pull-down menus. There are several symbols that appear on pull-down menus that you should be familiar with. The following illustration displays significant features in WordPad's File menu.

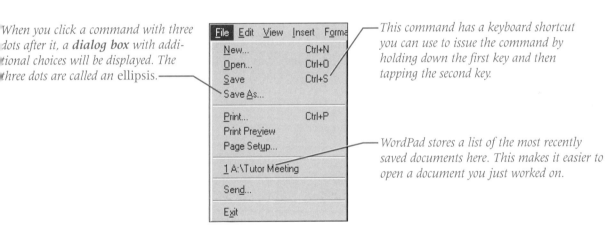

When you click a command with three dots after it, a ***dialog box*** *with additional choices will be displayed. The three dots are called an* ellipsis.

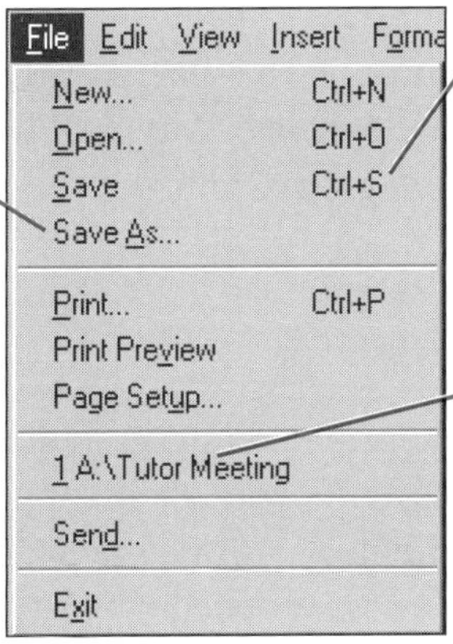
File Edit View Insert Forma
New... Ctrl+N
Open... Ctrl+O
Save Ctrl+S
Save As...
Print... Ctrl+P
Print Preview
Page Setup...
1 A:\Tutor Meeting
Send...
Exit

This command has a keyboard shortcut you can use to issue the command by holding down the first key and then tapping the second key.

WordPad stores a list of the most recently saved documents here. This makes it easier to open a document you just worked on.

Hands-On 2.8 Issue a Command from the Menu Bar

1. Follow these steps to issue a command from the menu bar:

Ⓐ *Click the **File** command on the menu bar.*

Ⓑ *Click the **Print Preview** command in the drop-down menu.*

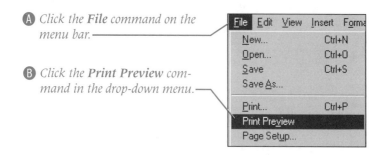

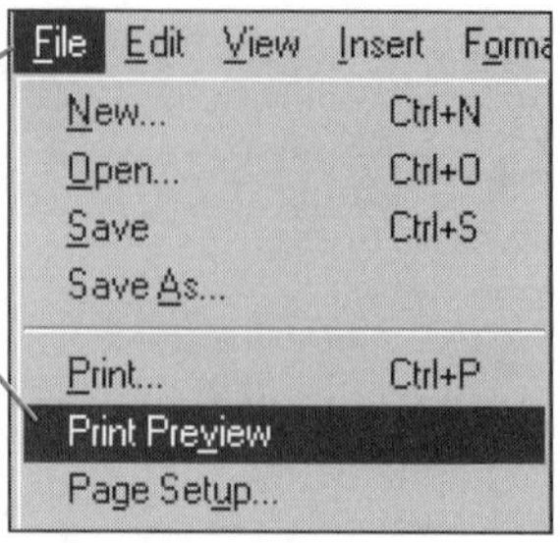
File Edit View Insert Forma
New... Ctrl+N
Open... Ctrl+O
Save Ctrl+S
Save As...
Print... Ctrl+P
Print Preview
Page Setup...

NOTE! *In the rest of this book, a command like this will be written* File→Print Preview.

A preview of the printed page will appear in the WordPad window. This displays exactly how your document will appear when it is printed. The dashed lines are there to show you the margins of the document and will not appear in print.

2. Click the Close button on the top-right side of the WordPad window.
This closes the Print Preview window. Now you are back in the normal document view.

Saving Files

You create documents by using application programs like WordPad. The word **file** refers to any document that has been saved onto a storage device. A typical hard disk drive will have thousands of files stored on it. With most Windows programs, you use the **Save** command to save your work in a file.

Where Your Work Takes Place

Many beginners think that what they see on the computer's monitor is taking place in the hard drive or on a floppy disk. This is not the case. As you use an application program, your work is placed in the computer's random access memory (RAM; see page 11) and is displayed on the monitor. However, RAM is *erased* when the power is switched off or when the system is restarted. This is why you must save your work on a floppy disk, hard disk, or other storage media if you want to save it for later use.

The document you see on the monitor here . . .

. . . is really in RAM in the system unit . . .

. . . until you save the document to a hard drive or floppy disk.

Save and Save As Commands

Most Windows programs provide two commands that let you save documents. The **File→Save** command saves the current document onto a disk. If the document had previously been saved, then the old version is replaced by the new edited version. If the document is new, then a Save As dialog box appears. The *Save As* dialog box lets you name the document and specify the disk drive and folder to which you wish to save the document. You can also use the **File→Save As** command to make a copy of an existing document by saving the document with a new name.

Naming Files

When you save a file for the first time, you must give it a name. Windows has specific rules for how you are allowed to name files. The Quick Reference table below lists the rules for naming files.

Quick Reference

RULES FOR FILE NAMES

Rule	Description
Filename length	A filename can contain up to 255 characters.
Characters that are allowed in filenames	A filename may contain numbers, spaces, periods, commas, semicolons, dashes, and parentheses.
Characters that are not allowed in filenames	A filename cannot contain the following characters: \ / : * ? " < > |.

Hands-On 2.9 Save the Announcement

In this exercise, you will save the WordPad document that is currently in RAM to your floppy disk.

1. Insert your floppy disk into the floppy drive. The disk should be placed with the label side facing up and the metal plate facing in.
   If you are not sure how to insert a floppy disk, ask for assistance.
2. Follow these steps to issue the Save command:

Ⓐ *Click **File** on the WordPad menu bar, and the File menu will drop-down, as shown here.*

Ⓑ *Slide the mouse down, and click **Save** on the drop-down menu.*

Document - WordPad
File Edit View Insert Forma
New... Ctrl+N
Open... Ctrl+O
Save Ctrl+S
Save As...

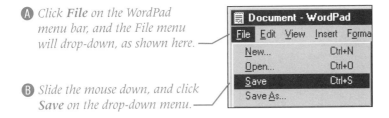

(Continued on the next page)

3. Follow these steps to finish saving the document to your floppy disk:

Ⓐ *Click the **Save in** drop-down list, and choose the 3½* Floppy (A:) *drive.*

Ⓑ *Notice that WordPad proposes the name* Document (or Document.doc) *in the filename field.*

Ⓒ ***Click** in the Filename box to the right of the name* Document. *Use the Backspace key on the keyboard to delete the name* Document, *and then* type *the name* **`Tutor Meeting`**, *as shown here.*

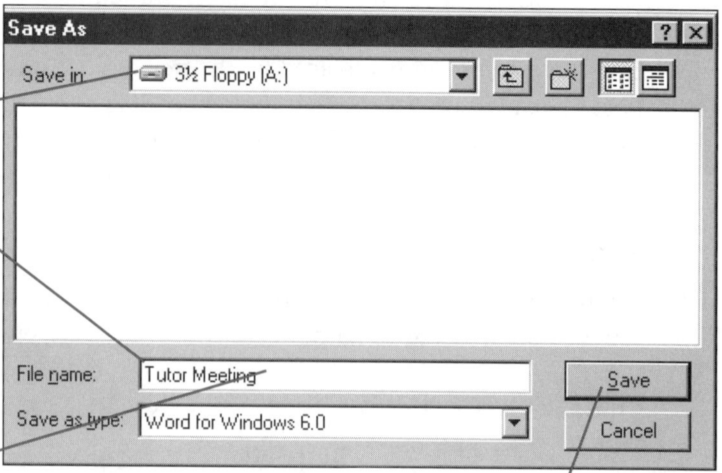
Save As
Save in:
3½ Floppy (A:)
File name:
Tutor Meeting
Save as type:
Word for Windows 6.0
Save
Cancel

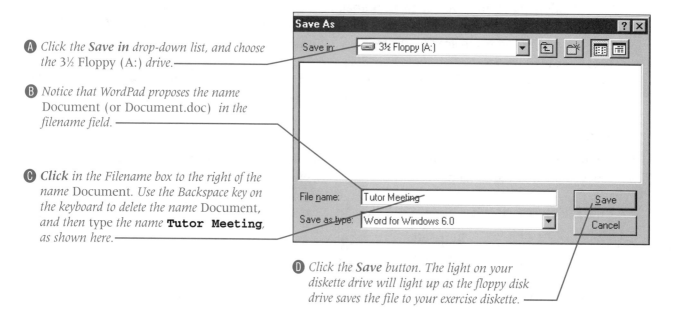

Ⓓ *Click the **Save** button. The light on your diskette drive will light up as the floppy disk drive saves the file to your exercise diskette.*

Notice that the new name of your document is now displayed on the title bar at the top-left corner of the WordPad window.

Tutor Meeting - WordPad
File Edit View Insert Format

Closing Program Windows

From the Keyboard

ALT+F4 to close the active program window.

When you are finished working with a program, you will usually want to close the program window. This not only removes clutter from the Desktop, it also conserves RAM so you can run other programs more efficiently. Virtually all Windows programs have a *File→Exit* command you can use to close the program window. You can also close a program window with the *Close* quick sizing button at the top-right corner of the window.

Hands-On 2.10 Close WordPad

1. Choose **File→Exit** from the menu bar. Click **No** if you are asked if you wish to save your document.
   The program window will close. If you type something in the document after issuing a Save *command, WordPad asks if you wish to save the changes. In this case, there is no need to save the change.*

Editing Files

After you have typed a document, it is easy to make changes. For example, let's say that another volunteer tutor's meeting is to take place next month. Rather than typing the document again from scratch, you can simply change some of the information, then save the document again.

Working on a Previously Saved File

If you want to work on a previously saved file, you must open it in the application program. After you have changed the file, you have two ways to save your changes:

- **Save—**This command will overwrite the old version of the file with the new version you have just edited.
- **Save As—**this command will create a new file with the changes you have made, leaving the old version intact with the old filename.

Hands-On 2.11 Open and Edit a File

In this exercise, you will open the meeting announcement you created earlier, edit it, then save the announcement with a new name.

Open the Meeting Announcement File

1. Click the **Start** button; then slide the mouse pointer up to the **Programs** menu.
2. Slide the mouse pointer to the right, then up to **Accessories**, and then click the **WordPad** program at the bottom of the menu. If you are using Windows 2000 and you do not see the WordPad program in the Accessories menu, click the double-arrow bar to make the entire menu appear.
3. If the WordPad window is not already maximized, click the Maximize quick sizing button to make the WordPad window cover the Desktop.
4. Click the Open button on the WordPad toolbar.
5. Follow these steps to open the announcement file you saved to your floppy disk:

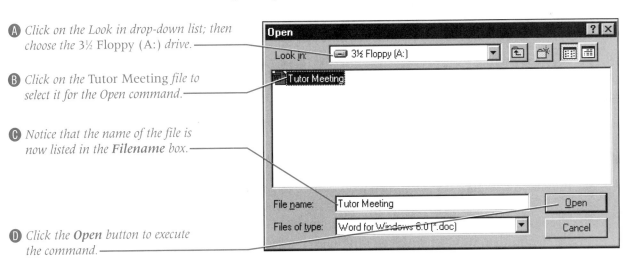

Ⓐ *Click on the Look in drop-down list; then choose the* 3½ Floppy (A:) *drive.*

Ⓑ *Click on the* Tutor Meeting *file to select it for the Open command.*

Ⓒ *Notice that the name of the file is now listed in the* **Filename** *box.*

Ⓓ *Click the* **Open** *button to execute the command.*

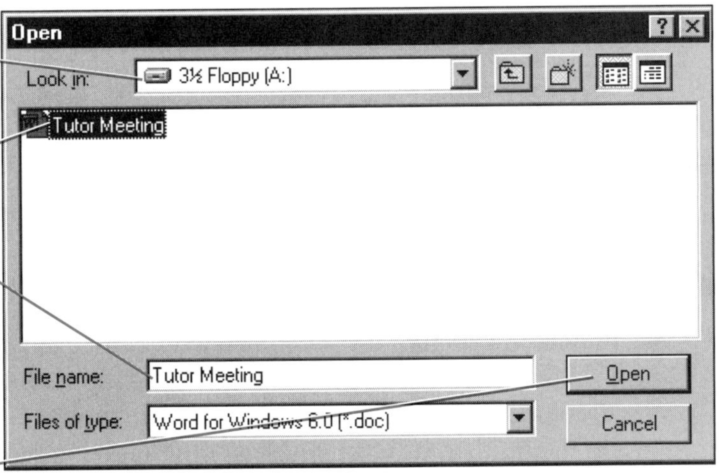

Open
Look in:
3½ Floppy (A:)
Tutor Meeting
File name:
Tutor Meeting
Files of type:
Word for Windows 6.0 (*.doc)
Open
Cancel

You will see the floppy drive light go on as the file is loaded from the floppy drive into the computer's RAM. After it is loaded into RAM, the announcement document will be displayed in the WordPad window.

(Continued on the next page)

Edit the Meeting Announcement Document

6. Follow these steps to change the date for the meeting:

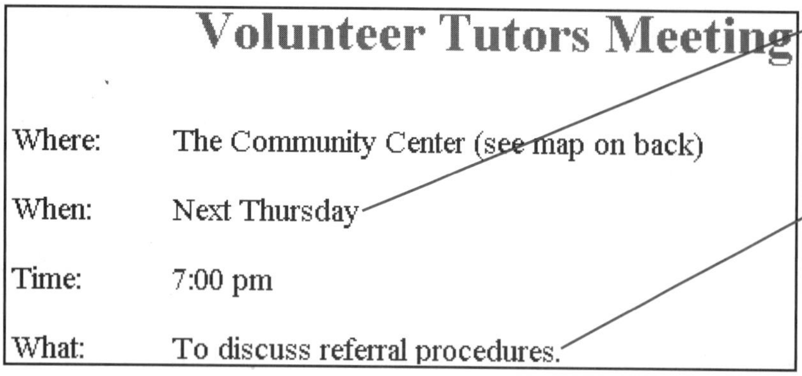

Volunteer Tutors Meeting
Where: The Community Center (see map on back)
When: Next Thursday
Time: 7:00 pm
What: To discuss referral procedures.

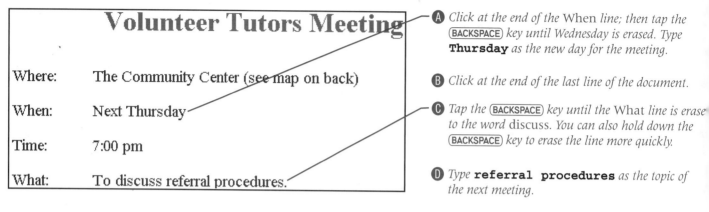

Ⓐ *Click at the end of the* When *line; then tap the* BACKSPACE *key until Wednesday is erased. Type* **`Thursday`** *as the new day for the meeting.*

Ⓑ *Click at the end of the last line of the document.*

Ⓒ *Tap the* BACKSPACE *key until the* What *line is erased to the word* discuss. *You can also hold down the* BACKSPACE *key to erase the line more quickly.*

Ⓓ *Type* **`referral procedures`** *as the topic of the next meeting.*

7. Choose **File→Save As** from the menu bar.

8. Follow these steps to save the file with a new name:

Ⓐ *Click at the end of the filename. If you see .doc at the end of the filename, tap the* BACKSPACE *key until the .doc portion of the filename has been deleted. (WordPad will add the .doc back to the end of the filename when you save the document.)*

File name:
Tutor Meeting

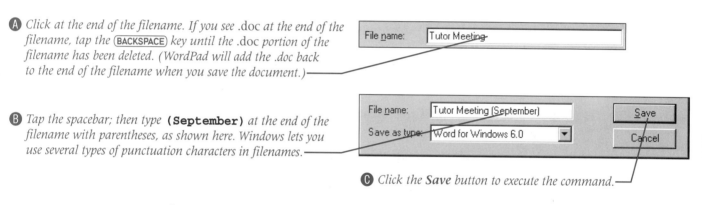

Ⓑ *Tap the spacebar; then type* **`(September)`** *at the end of the filename with parentheses, as shown here. Windows lets you use several types of punctuation characters in filenames.*

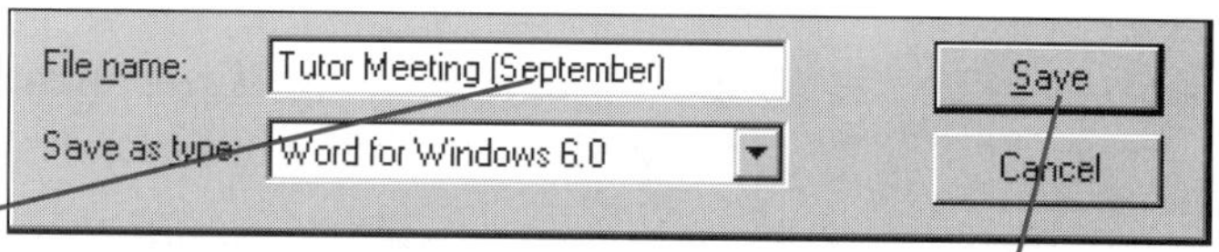

File name:
Tutor Meeting (September)
Save as type:
Word for Windows 6.0
Save
Cancel

Ⓒ *Click the* ***Save*** *button to execute the command.*

Now there are two versions of the announcement saved to your floppy disk. The first version has not been changed.

9. Click the Restore button at the top-right corner of the WordPad window.
Now WordPad occupies just a portion of the Desktop.

Multitasking

One of the most useful features of Windows is the ability to run multiple programs simultaneously. This is known as **multitasking.** For example, you can download files from the Internet, print a long document, and type a letter in a word processor all at the same time. You click program buttons on the Taskbar to switch between multitasked programs.

How Many Programs Can You Multitask?

The number of programs you can run at the same time depends on how much random access memory (RAM) is installed on your computer. The more RAM you have, the more programs you can run efficiently at the same time. Large and complex programs require more RAM than simple programs. If you try to run more than one large program on a computer with a small amount of RAM, Windows will run much more slowly.

Hands-On 2.12 Start Paint

In this exercise, you will start a second program that will run simultaneously with WordPad. Paint is a simple drawing program that comes with Windows.

1. Click the **Start** button; then slide the mouse pointer up to the **Programs** menu.
2. Slide the mouse pointer over to choose the **Accessories** menu; then click the **Paint** program. If you are using Windows 2000 and you do not see the Paint program in the Accessories menu, click the double-arrow bar to make the entire menu appear.
   The Paint program will start.
3. If Paint is not already maximized, click the maximize button.

   Paint's program window now covers the entire Desktop. However, you can see from the two buttons on the Taskbar that WordPad is still running. Since you just started Paint, it is now the active program. Notice how Paint's button on the Taskbar appears "pushed in" compared to the WordPad button.

Switching Between Windows

When you are running multiple programs, only one program at a time can be active. The other program windows are inactive. You use the Taskbar to switch among the programs you are running. As you did in a previous exercise, you also use the Taskbar to restore a minimized program window.

Hands-On 2.13 Switch Between Paint and WordPad

In this exercise, you will practice making WordPad and Paint the active program.

1. Click the Tutor Meeting (September)... button on the Taskbar to make WordPad the active program.
   Now WordPad's Taskbar button appears "pushed in." Notice also that WordPad's title bar has a different color than the title bar for the Paint window.
2. Click the untitled - Paint button on the Taskbar.
   That's all there is to switching from one program to another. The Paint window now appears on top of the WordPad window.
3. Click the Restore button on the **Paint** window.
   Now Paint's window occupies just a portion of the Desktop.
4. If the **WordPad** window is not visible, point at the **title bar** on the Paint window, and drag the Paint window to a new position on the Desktop so that both windows are partially visible. For example, drag the title bar down and to the right.

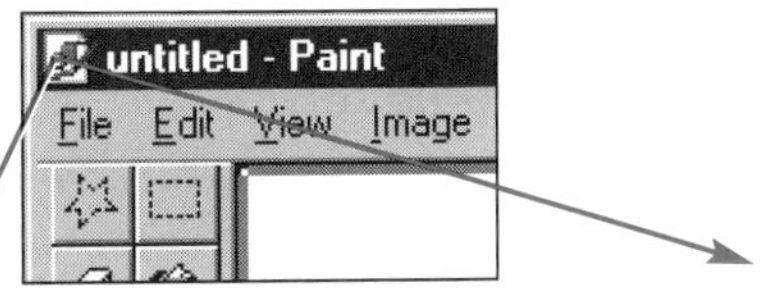
untitled - Paint
File Edit View Image

The Paint window title bar

(Continued on the next page)

5. Click anywhere in the **WordPad** window to make it active.
   Whenever you click in a program window, it becomes the active program.
6. Click the Close button on the WordPad window to exit the program. If WordPad asks you to save changes to the document, click **Yes.**
7. Click the Maximize button on the Paint window.
   Leave the Paint window open, since you will begin drawing in a moment.

Using Dialog Boxes

Dialog boxes let you set options and controls prior to issuing a command. There are a variety of controls that you will encounter in dialog boxes. You used a dialog box earlier in this lesson to adjust the speed of double-clicks with the mouse. The following illustrations describe several types of dialog box controls.

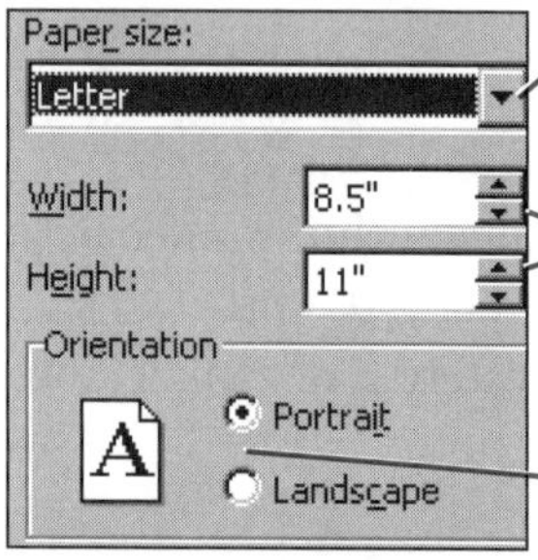

Paper size:
Letter
Width:
8.5"
Height:
11"
Orientation
A
Portrait
Landscape

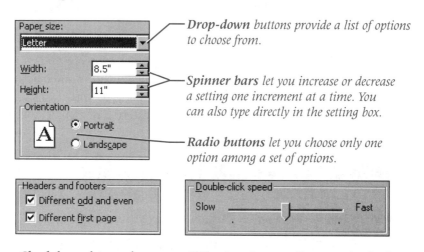

***Drop-down** buttons provide a list of options to choose from.*

***Spinner bars** let you increase or decrease a setting one increment at a time. You can also type directly in the setting box.*

***Radio buttons** let you choose only one option among a set of options.*

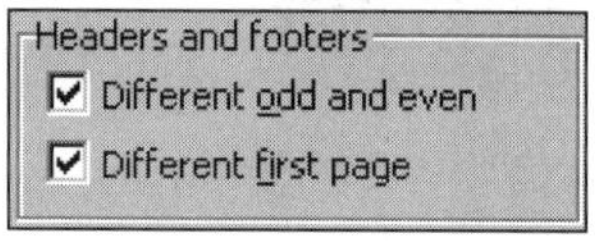

Headers and footers
Different odd and even
Different first page

***Check boxes** let you choose as many boxes as you wish.*

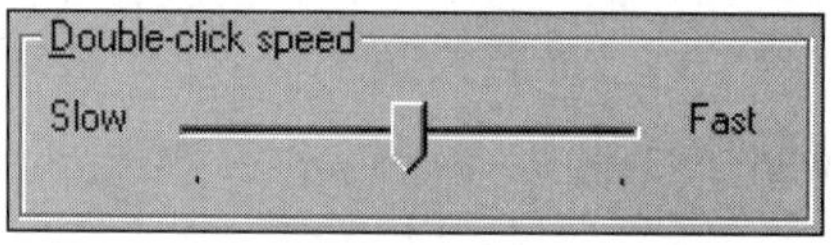

Double-click speed
Slow
Fast

***Slider bars** let you adjust a setting by dragging a bar, as you did in a previous exercise.*

Hands-On 2.14 Set the Drawing Size

In this exercise, you will use a dialog box to specify the size of your drawing. The options you set will reduce the size of the Paint file that you will save to your exercise diskette. This is necessary because the Paint program produces graphic files. Graphic files occupy a large amount of disk space when compared to text files. One Paint file would occupy your entire diskette if you were not to make the settings defined in this exercise.

1. Click **Image** on the Paint menu bar.
   Notice that the Attributes command has three dots (ellipses) after its name. This indicates that this command uses a dialog box.
2. Click the **Attributes** command.
   You will use this dialog box to specify the drawing size. The drawing size also affects the size of the file when you save this drawing.

3. Follow these steps to set the drawing size [make sure you do the steps in order (A, B, C, etc.)]:

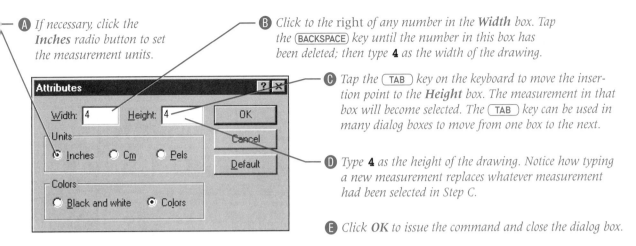

Ⓐ *If necessary, click the* ***Inches*** *radio button to set the measurement units.*

Ⓑ *Click to the right of any number in the* ***Width*** *box. Tap the* (BACKSPACE) *key until the number in this box has been deleted; then type* **4** *as the width of the drawing.*

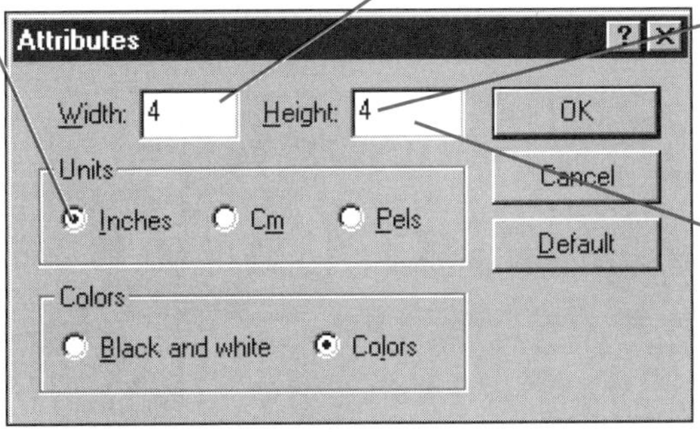

Attributes
Width: 4
Height: 4
OK
Cancel
Default
Units
Inches
Cm
Pels
Colors
Black and white
Colors

Ⓒ *Tap the* (TAB) *key on the keyboard to move the insertion point to the* ***Height*** *box. The measurement in that box will become selected. The* (TAB) *key can be used in many dialog boxes to move from one box to the next.*

Ⓓ *Type* **4** *as the height of the drawing. Notice how typing a new measurement replaces whatever measurement had been selected in Step C.*

Ⓔ *Click* ***OK*** *to issue the command and close the dialog box.*

The image size will be set to 4″ by 4″. In the next few steps, you will save the empty drawing to your exercise diskette. You will use a drop-down button on the Save As *dialog box to set the Save As Type. Most programs have a Save As Type option that lets you specify the type of file you wish to create. In the Paint program, you use the Save As Type option to determine the amount of color information that is stored in the file. You will reduce the amount of color information to conserve space on your diskette.*

4. Choose **File→Save** from the menu bar.

5. Follow these steps to set the image file type for your drawing:

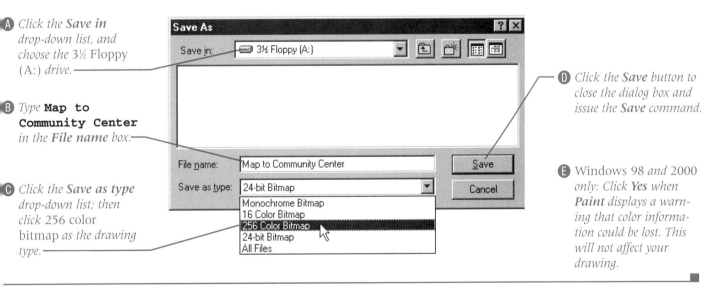

Ⓐ *Click the* ***Save in*** *drop-down list, and choose the* 3½ Floppy (A:) *drive.*

Ⓑ *Type* **`Map to Community Center`** *in the* ***File name*** *box.*

Ⓒ *Click the* ***Save as type*** *drop-down list; then click* 256 color bitmap *as the drawing type.*

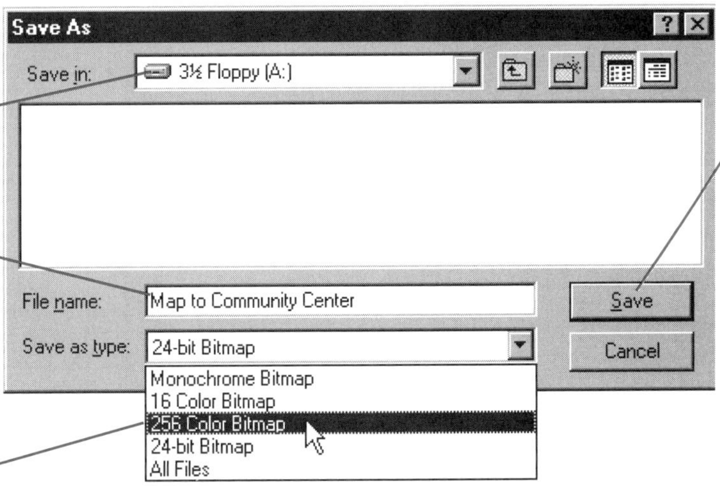

Save As
Save in:
3½ Floppy (A:)
File name:
Map to Community Center
Save as type:
24-bit Bitmap
Save
Cancel
Monochrome Bitmap
16 Color Bitmap
256 Color Bitmap
24-bit Bitmap
All Files

Ⓓ *Click the* ***Save*** *button to close the dialog box and issue the* ***Save*** *command.*

Ⓔ Windows 98 *and* 2000 *only: Click* ***Yes*** *when* ***Paint*** *displays a warning that color information could be lost. This will not affect your drawing.*

Working with the Paint Program

Paint is a small application (called an applet) that is bundled with Windows 98. Paint lets you use a mouse to create drawings and graphic images. Paint is known as a "bit map" program because images are formed by turning dots (called pixels) on and off on the screen. The dots are too tiny to see when printed. However, you can see them if you zoom in on the Paint screen.

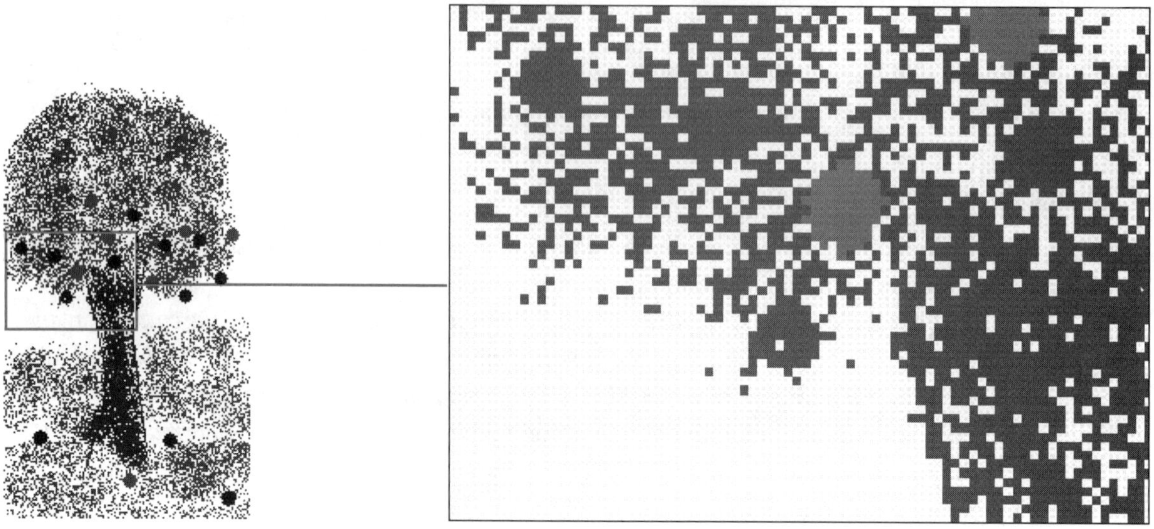

This tree is actually made up of numerous dots (pixels). *A close-up view of the tree drawing.*

Using Tools from a Toolbox

Drawing programs often have a toolbox with buttons representing the various drawing tools. Most toolboxes are designed as floating palettes that can be positioned anywhere on the screen. Paint's toolbox has several tools that are also featured in more sophisticated drawing programs. The illustration to the right shows several of Paint's basic tools.

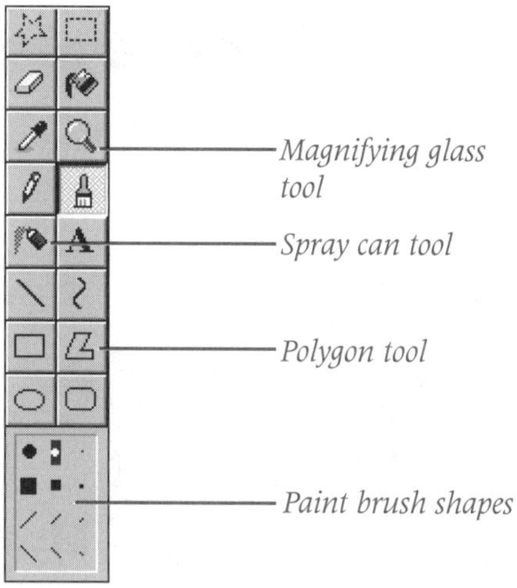
Magnifying glass tool
Spray can tool
Polygon tool
Paint brush shapes

ScreenTips

Like many Windows programs, Paint's toolbox has a feature called **ScreenTips.** When you point at a button in Paint's toolbox for about two seconds, Paint will display a small box with the name of the tool.

Brush

NOTE! *The* Windows NT *version of Paint does not have the ScreenTips feature.*

Hands-On 2.15 Draw a Map

In this exercise, you will use several of Paint's tools to draw a simple map. When you are finished, you will save the drawing. Before you begin, take a look at the map on page 41 to see what the final version of the map will look like.

1. Follow these steps to draw lines for the streets on the map.

TIP! *The (SHIFT) key helps you to draw perfectly straight lines.*

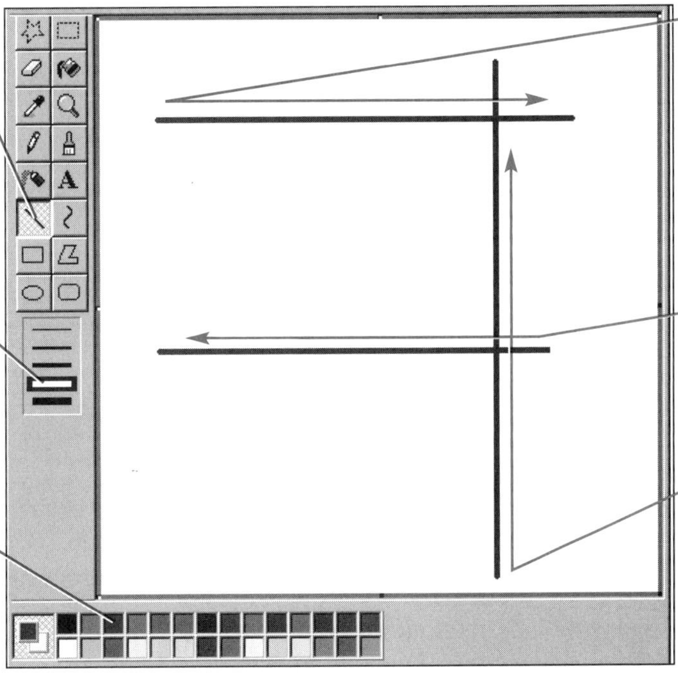

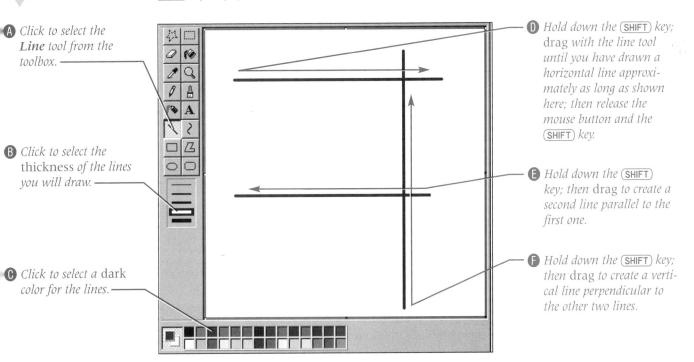

Ⓐ *Click to select the* **Line** *tool from the toolbox.*

Ⓑ *Click to select the* thickness *of the lines you will draw.*

Ⓒ *Click to select a* dark *color for the lines.*

Ⓓ *Hold down the (SHIFT) key;* drag *with the line tool until you have drawn a horizontal line approximately as long as shown here; then release the mouse button and the (SHIFT) key.*

Ⓔ *Hold down the (SHIFT) key; then* drag *to create a second line parallel to the first one.*

Ⓕ *Hold down the (SHIFT) key; then* drag *to create a vertical line perpendicular to the other two lines.*

2. Follow these steps to draw a rectangle for the community center and fill it with color:

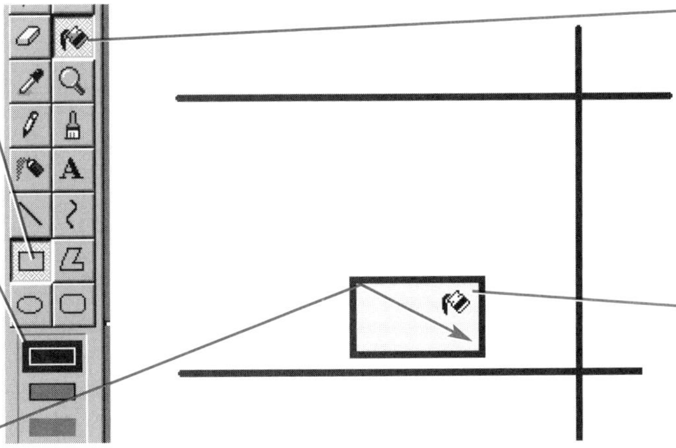

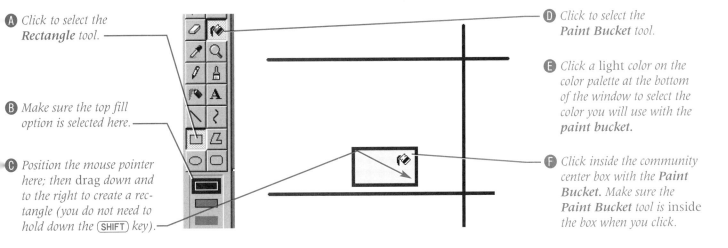

Ⓐ *Click to select the* **Rectangle** *tool.*

Ⓑ *Make sure the top fill option is selected here.*

Ⓒ *Position the mouse pointer here; then drag down and to the right to create a rectangle (you do not need to hold down the (SHIFT) key).*

Ⓓ *Click to select the* **Paint Bucket** *tool.*

Ⓔ *Click a* light color *on the color palette at the bottom of the window to select the color you will use with the* **paint bucket.**

Ⓕ *Click inside the community center box with the* **Paint Bucket.** *Make sure the* **Paint Bucket** *tool is* inside *the box when you click.*

3. Follow these steps to add a park to the drawing:

TIP! *If you do not like the results of a command, choose* Edit→Undo *from the menu bar.*

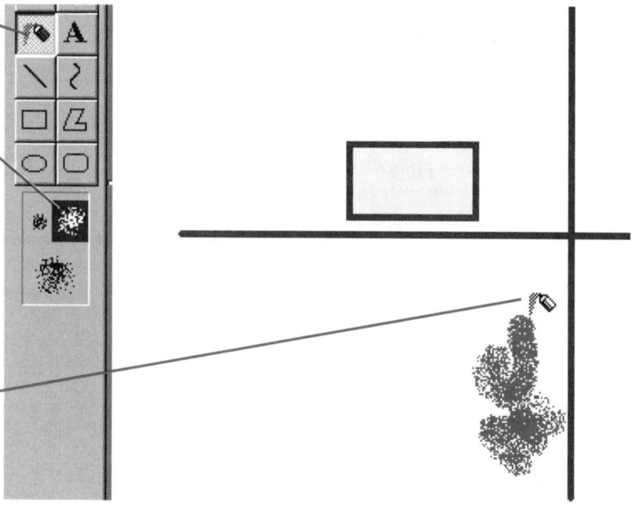

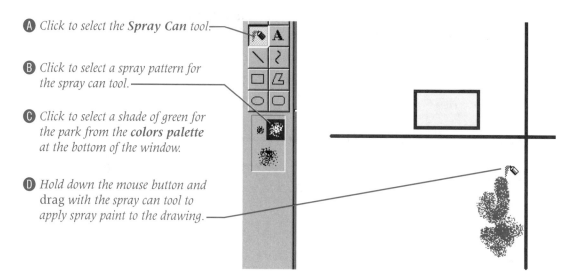

A Click to select the Spray Can tool.
B Click to select a spray pattern for the spray can tool.
C Click to select a shade of green for the park from the colors palette at the bottom of the window.
D Hold down the mouse button and drag with the spray can tool to apply spray paint to the drawing.

Any time you have done a substantial amount of work on a project, it is a good idea to save your work. That way if the computer crashes (stops running) or some other problem occurs, you can still open the most recently saved version of the drawing.

4. Choose **File→Save** from the menu bar to save your drawing.
   You will see the floppy drive light go on as the file is saved. Since you have saved this drawing once already (when you set the drawing type), the ***Save As*** *dialog box does not appear. The blank version of the drawing is replaced by what is on your screen. The drawing is saved with the same settings you made originally.*
5. Follow these steps to add a street name to the drawing:

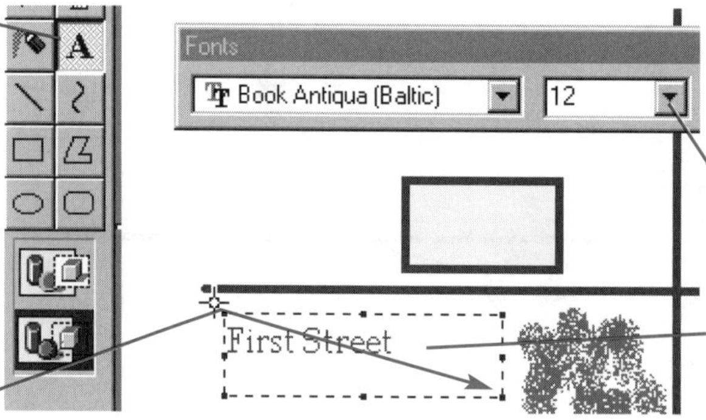

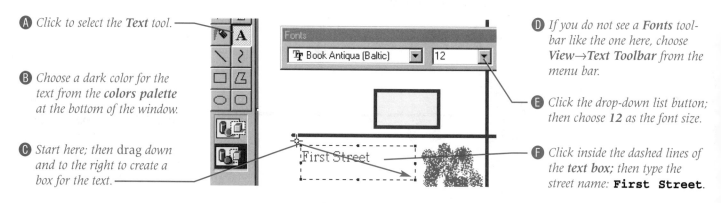

A Click to select the Text tool.
B Choose a dark color for the text from the colors palette at the bottom of the window.
C Start here; then drag down and to the right to create a box for the text.
Fonts
Book Antiqua (Baltic)
12
First Street
D If you do not see a Fonts toolbar like the one here, choose View→Text Toolbar from the menu bar.
E Click the drop-down list button; then choose 12 as the font size.
F Click inside the dashed lines of the text box; then type the street name: First Street.

6. Add additional street names and the community center name to the drawing as shown on page 41. Don't worry if these are not placed perfectly. If you need to move the Fonts toolbar out of the way, drag on the **title bar** (where the word **Fonts** appears).
   Paint has many more features than can be covered in this brief tutorial. Most Windows drawing programs use toolboxes and drawing tools that are similar to the Paint tools you have used in this exercise.

Printing Files

Almost all Windows programs have a *File→Print* command or a Print button on a toolbar that you can use to print your documents. The *File→Print* command usually displays a dialog box that lets you choose the printer, as well as other options. A document with color (such as a Paint drawing) will only print in color if you have a color printer (such as an ink jet printer). Otherwise, the colors will print as shades of gray.

Hands-On 2.16 Print the Map

TIP!

It is always a good idea to save your work before you print.

1. Choose **File→Save** to save your drawing.
2. Choose **File→Print** to view the Print dialog box.
   Look over the Print dialog box options for a moment. There is no need to change any of the options.
3. Click **OK** to print the drawing; then retrieve the drawing from the printer.
4. Feel free to enhance your drawing and experiment with some of the other Paint tools.
5. When you are finished with the drawing, choose **File→Save** from the menu bar to save the finished version of your drawing.
6. Click the Close button to exit the Paint program. If you are asked if you wish to save your drawing, click **Yes.**
   If any changes were made since you last gave the Save command, Paint will ask if you wish to save those changes. If you want to discard the most recent changes, you can click No, *and the changes will not be saved. Usually, however, you will want to save any changes to a file when you exit a program.*

Shutting Down Windows

You must shut down Windows before switching off the computer. The Shut Down command closes all running programs. It also initiates "housekeeping" chores that let Windows start properly the next time the computer is switched on. After the Shut Down command is completed, Windows will display a message that it is safe to switch off power to the computer. On many new computers, the power will be switched off automatically.

Logging Off

If you want to leave the computer on for the next user to log on, you should log off Windows rather than shut the computer down. Logging off prevents unauthorized users from accessing network resources. However, if the computer is running Windows 95 or Windows 98, anyone can get to the Windows Desktop by clicking the *Cancel* button.

Quick Reference

HOW TO SHUT DOWN WINDOWS

Task	Procedure
Log off Windows 98 and Windows 95	■ Click *Start* on the Windows Taskbar. ■ Choose *Log Off [Your User Name]* from the Start menu; then click *Yes* when you are prompted to confirm logging off. Use the log-off procedure for Windows 95 if you do not see *Log Off* in the Start menu.
Log off Windows 95 or Windows NT 4.0	■ Click *Start* on the Windows Taskbar; then choose *Shut down.* ■ Choose the *Close all programs and log on as a different user?* option, and click *Yes.*
Log off Windows 2000 Professional	■ Click *Start* on the Windows Taskbar; then choose *Shut down.* ■ Choose *Log Off [Your User Name]* from drop-down list, and click *OK.*
Shut down Windows (all versions)	■ Click *Start* on the Windows Taskbar; then choose *Shut Down.* ■ Choose the *Shut down* option, and click *Yes* or *OK.*

Hands-On 2.17 Log Off Windows

In this exercise, you will log off and leave the computer running for the next user. Your instructor will tell you whether you should log off or shut down the computer at the end of each class session.

1. Click **Start**; then examine the lower-left side of the Start menu to see which version of Windows you are using.
2. Follow the log-off procedure for the version of windows you are running:
   - **Windows 98 and Windows 95—**Click **Log Off [Your Log on Name]** (just above the Shut Down menu item); then click **Yes** to confirm logging off. Use the procedure for Windows 95 below if you do not see *Log Off* on the Start menu.
   - **Windows 95 and Windows NT—**Click **Shut Down**; then choose the **Close all programs and log on as a different user?** option in the dialog box, and click **Yes.**
   - **Windows 2000—**Click **Shut Down**; then choose the **Log Off [Your Log on Name]** option from the drop-down list, and click **OK.**

You should now be logged off, and a sign-on screen should appear.

Concepts Review

True/False Questions

1. Windows is responsible for file, memory, and program management. TRUE FALSE
2. You double-click by pressing the secondary (right) mouse button twice in rapid succession. TRUE FALSE
3. You can start a program by clicking the Start button and choosing the desired program from the Programs menu. TRUE FALSE
4. The File→Open command is used to save a document to a floppy disk. TRUE FALSE
5. Filenames can have up to 255 characters in Windows. TRUE FALSE
6. Windows is a multitasking operating system. TRUE FALSE
7. You can choose as many radio buttons as desired when setting options in a dialog box. TRUE FALSE
8. You should always shut down Windows prior to switching off the computer system. TRUE FALSE
9. The Windows Taskbar lets you switch between program windows. TRUE FALSE
10. You can change the size of a *maximized* program window by dragging on the window borders. TRUE FALSE

Multiple-Choice Questions

1. Which of the following buttons *restores* a window?
   a. 
   b. 
   c. 
   d. 

2. Which of the following buttons *minimizes* a window?
   a. 
   b. 
   c. 
   d. 

3. Which of the following techniques is used to *move* a program window?
   a. Maximize the window and drag the Title bar.
   b. Restore the window and drag the Title bar.
   c. Minimize the window and drag the Title bar.
   d. Drag a corner-sizing handle.

4. Which of the following commands can be used to *print* in most programs?
   a. File→Save
   b. File→Open
   c. View→Print
   d. None of the above

Skill Builders

Skill Builder 2.1 Type a To Do List

1. Log on to Windows.
2. Choose **Start→Programs→Accessories→WordPad** to start the WordPad program.
3. Maximize the WordPad window.
4. Type `To Do List` as a heading for the document; then tap the ENTER key three times to add lines beneath the heading.
5. Type a list of things you need to do this week. Tap ENTER twice after each line to double-space the list.
6. **Save** your list to your exercise diskette using a descriptive name. Make sure that the **3½ Floppy (A:)** drive is displayed in the **Save in** box. Keep in mind that you can use up to 255 characters in the filename including spaces.
7. Use **File→Print** to print your To Do list.
8. Close WordPad and save any changes (if WordPad gives you that option).

Skill Builder 2.2 Paint a House

1. Start the **Paint** program with **Start→program→accessories→paint.**
2. Choose **File→Save** from the menu bar.
3. Set the **Save as type** (at the bottom of the dialog box) to **16 Color Bitmap.**
   This setting reduces the number of colors you can use in the drawing, but will significantly reduce the size of the file when you save it.
4. Save the empty drawing to your exercise diskette with the name **`My House.`** Make sure that the **3½ Floppy (A:)** drive is displayed in the **Save in** box before you click the **Save** button.
5. Use your investigative skills, your creativity, and some trial and error to draw a house. Try to include objects such as doors, windows, a roof, and perhaps landscaping.

   TIP! *If you make a mistake, immediately select* Edit→Undo *from the menu bar to undo your most recent command. If you are running* Windows 98 *or* Windows 2000, *Paint will let you undo the three most recent commands.*

6. Feel free to print your drawing.
7. Close Paint, and save any changes (if Paint gives you that option).

Skill Builder 2.3 Use the Calculator

This Skill Builder will show you how to use the Windows Calculator applet.

1. Click the Start button, and slide the mouse up to **Programs.**
2. Slide the mouse to **Accessories,** and choose **Calculator.** If you are running *Windows 2000* and you do not see the Calculator in the Accessories menu, click the *menu extension* (double arrow) in the list to display the entire Accessories menu.
3. Follow these steps to add two numbers:

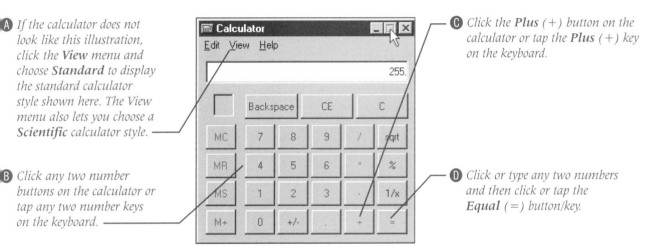

Ⓐ *If the calculator does not look like this illustration, click the **View** menu and choose **Standard** to display the standard calculator style shown here. The View menu also lets you choose a **Scientific** calculator style.*

Ⓑ *Click any two number buttons on the calculator or tap any two number keys on the keyboard.*

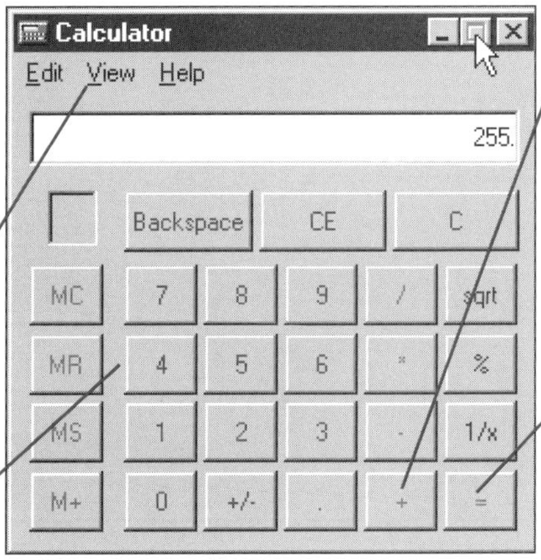
Calculator
Edit View Help
255.
Backspace
CE
C
MC 7 8 9 / sqrt
MR 4 5 6 * %
MS 1 2 3 - 1/x
M+ 0 +/- . + =

Ⓒ *Click the **Plus** (+) button on the calculator or tap the **Plus** (+) key on the keyboard.*

Ⓓ *Click or type any two numbers and then click or tap the **Equal** (=) button/key.*

4. Feel free to experiment with the calculator.
5. Click the Minimize button to minimize the calculator.
6. Click the Calculator button on the Taskbar to restore the calculator. *Notice that you can hide the calculator when you are not using it and display it when you need it. This technique is often used when working with multiple programs.*
7. Feel free to experiment with the calculator.
8. Close the calculator window when you have finished experimenting, and continue with the Assessment exercises.

Assessments

Assessment 2.1 Create and Save a WordPad Document

1. Start the WordPad program.
2. Type the document displayed below.

   Your document does not have to match this document exactly, but it should contain the same information.

   > Parts of a Personal Computer System
   >
   > Hardware
   > System Unit
   > Monitor
   > Mouse
   > Keyboard
   > Printer
   >
   > Software
   > Operating System
   > Application Programs
   > User Files
   >
   > [Your Name]

3. Save the document to your **floppy disk** with the name: **`Assessment Exercise for Lesson 2`**.
4. Have your instructor or a Lab Assistant initial that you have completed this assessment exercise successfully. ______
5. Close ☒ the document.

Assessment 2.2 Open and Print a WordPad Document

1. Start the **WordPad** Program.
2. Open the **Assessment Exercise for Lesson 2** document you created in the previous assessment exercise.
3. Change the title of the document to read: **`Personal Computer Components`**
4. **Save** the change to the document; then **print** the document. Retrieve the printout from the printer.
5. **Close** WordPad.
6. Turn in the printed page for grading.

Assessment 2.3 Configure Two Program Windows

1. Start the **WordPad** Program.
2. If WordPad is maximized, click the **Restore** button to restore the window.
3. Drag on WordPad's program window borders so that the WordPad window covers the **left** half of the Desktop.
4. Start the **Paint** Program. Make sure the Paint window is not maximized.
5. Drag on Paint's program window borders so that the Paint window covers the **right** half of the Desktop.
6. Have your instructor or a Lab Assistant initial that you have completed this assessment exercise successfully. _____
7. Close the program windows.

LESSON 3—Windows

File Management and Online Help

When you begin working with a computer, you will have just a few files to keep track of. But as your use of the computer grows, so will the number of files you must manage. After several months you might have over a hundred of your own files. After a year there might be hundreds more. Fortunately, Windows gives you a very effective tool for managing files: folders. With folders you can group related files together. You can even create folders inside of other folders. As you learn how to use new features such as folders, you should take advantage of the excellent online Help system featured in Windows. Online Help makes it easy to find the answer to many types of questions with three ways to search for the information you need.

In This Lesson

Case Study

Chantal is taking four courses at her community college. As she goes over the syllabi, Chantal notices that three of her courses will require her to submit term papers. She decides to prepare for some of the research she must do. Chantal creates several folders on her computer to help her organize the files she will accumulate as she performs research on each term paper. She creates a folder for each of her classes on the computer. Then she creates folders inside the class folders to further organize her files. For example, she creates *Final* and *Drafts* folders for the word processor documents she will create. Chantal also creates a *Research* folder, to hold the various files, Web pages, and notes she will collect. She creates a folder called *Old Stuff* for everything she thinks she doesn't need, but does not want to delete. She can delete the Old Stuff folder after the term project paper is completed.

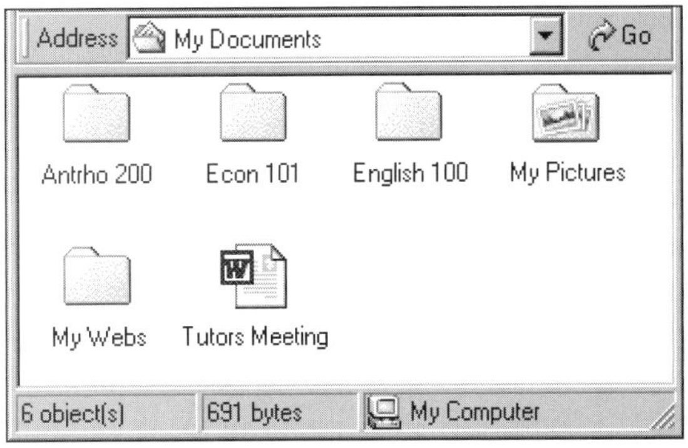

Address
My Documents
Go
Antrho 200
Econ 101
English 100
My Pictures
My Webs
Tutors Meeting
6 object(s)
691 bytes
My Computer

Chantal created these ***folders*** *inside each of her course folders. This makes it easier for her to find the files she needs to work on as the semester progresses.*

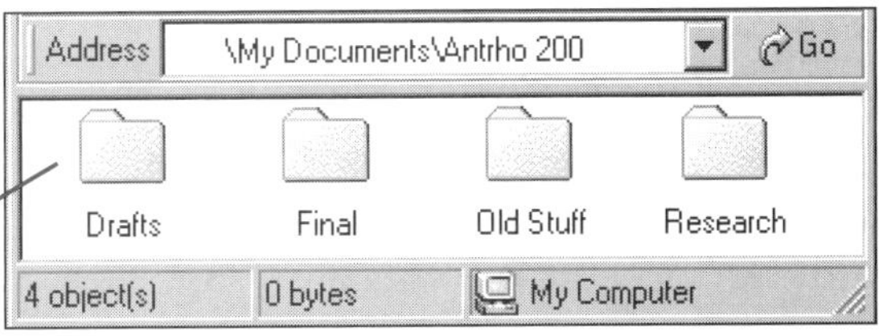

Address
\My Documents\Antrho 200
Go
Drafts
Final
Old Stuff
Research
4 object(s)
0 bytes
My Computer

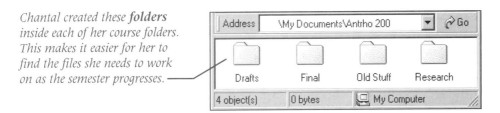

As Chantal learns new ways to organize her work, she also learns how to look up the answers to her questions with online Help. For example, when she could not recall how to create a new folder on her computer, she looked it up in online Help. Chantal likes to be as self-reliant as possible where computers are concerned, and online Help is one of the ways she can do this.

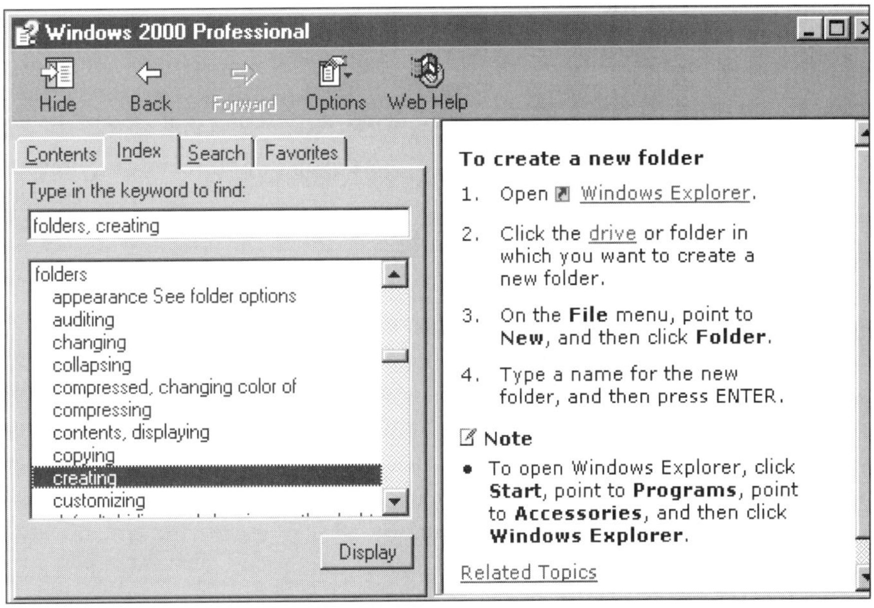

Windows 2000 Professional
Hide
Back
Forward
Options
Web Help
Contents
Index
Search
Favorites
Type in the keyword to find:
folders, creating
folders
appearance See folder options
auditing
changing
collapsing
compressed, changing color of
compressing
contents, displaying
copying
creating
customizing
Display
To create a new folder
1. Open Windows Explorer.
2. Click the drive or folder in which you want to create a new folder.
3. On the File menu, point to New, and then click Folder.
4. Type a name for the new folder, and then press ENTER.
Note
• To open Windows Explorer, click Start, point to Programs, point to Accessories, and then click Windows Explorer.
Related Topics

Using Online Help with Windows

Windows provides an online Help system that can answer questions about running application programs or completing tasks with Windows itself. Online Help has proven so effective that many vendors no longer publish the sort of lengthy manuals that used to come with most programs. For example, the Microsoft Office 2000 Suite does not provide a manual beyond a thin "Getting Started" booklet that helps you install the software.

Finding the Information You Need

Your goal when using online Help is to locate a Help topic. The Help feature provides several methods that you can use to locate topics. All Help topics have keywords that identify them. For example, a Help topic that discusses copying files can probably be located by using the keywords *copying files*. Regardless of which method you use, the goal is to locate a topic. Once you locate the desired topic, you can display it and follow the instructions in the topic.

Search Methods

Depending on the version of Windows you are using, the following methods are available for searching online Help:

Search Method	Description
Contents	The Contents method is useful if you are trying to locate a topic but you aren't really sure how to describe it. The Contents method lets you navigate through a series of categories until the desired topic is located.
Index	The Index method lets you locate a topic by typing keywords. An alphabetically indexed list of topics is displayed from which you can choose the desired topic. This method is most useful if you know the name of the topic or feature that you need assistance with.
Search *(Called* Find *in Windows 95 and NT)*	The Search method searches inside of the Help topics for the keywords you enter. This provides an in-depth search and lets you locate topics that may not be found using the other search methods. However, sometimes this method will find more topics than you really need.
Web Help *(Windows 98 and 2000 only)*	This Help option takes you directly to Microsoft's Web site. Web Help can locate the latest information on the topic for which you are searching.

Quick Reference

STARTING ONLINE HELP

Task	Procedure
Start Windows online Help.	■ Choose *Start→Help* from the Start menu. ■ Choose the desired search method.
Start online Help in an application program.	■ Choose *Help* from the menu bar or tap the F1 function key; then select the type of Help you require.

Hands-On 3.1 Search Online Help

In the first step of this exercise, you will determine which version of Windows you are running. This will determine whether you perform section a, b, or c of the exercise.

1. Click the **Start** button. Read the version of Windows you are running in the vertical title that appears along the left side of the Start menu. Click the **Start** button again to close the menu.

Windows98
Start

2. Select the Hands-On exercise for the version of Windows you are running.
   - **Windows 98—**Complete Hands-On Exercise 3.1a immediately below.
   - **Windows 95 and NT—**Complete Hands-On Exercise 3.1b on page 78.
   - **Windows 2000—**Complete Hands-On Exercise 3.1c on page 79.

Hands-On 3.1a Search Online Help in Windows 98

Windows 98 introduced a new way to search online Help. It is based upon navigation techniques used with Web browsers. In Windows 98, you open Help categories with a single click.

1. Click the **Start** button, and choose  from the menu.
   The Windows Help window will appear. In the next few steps, you will look up a Help topic on copying files or folders.
2. Follow these steps to conduct a search using the Contents method:

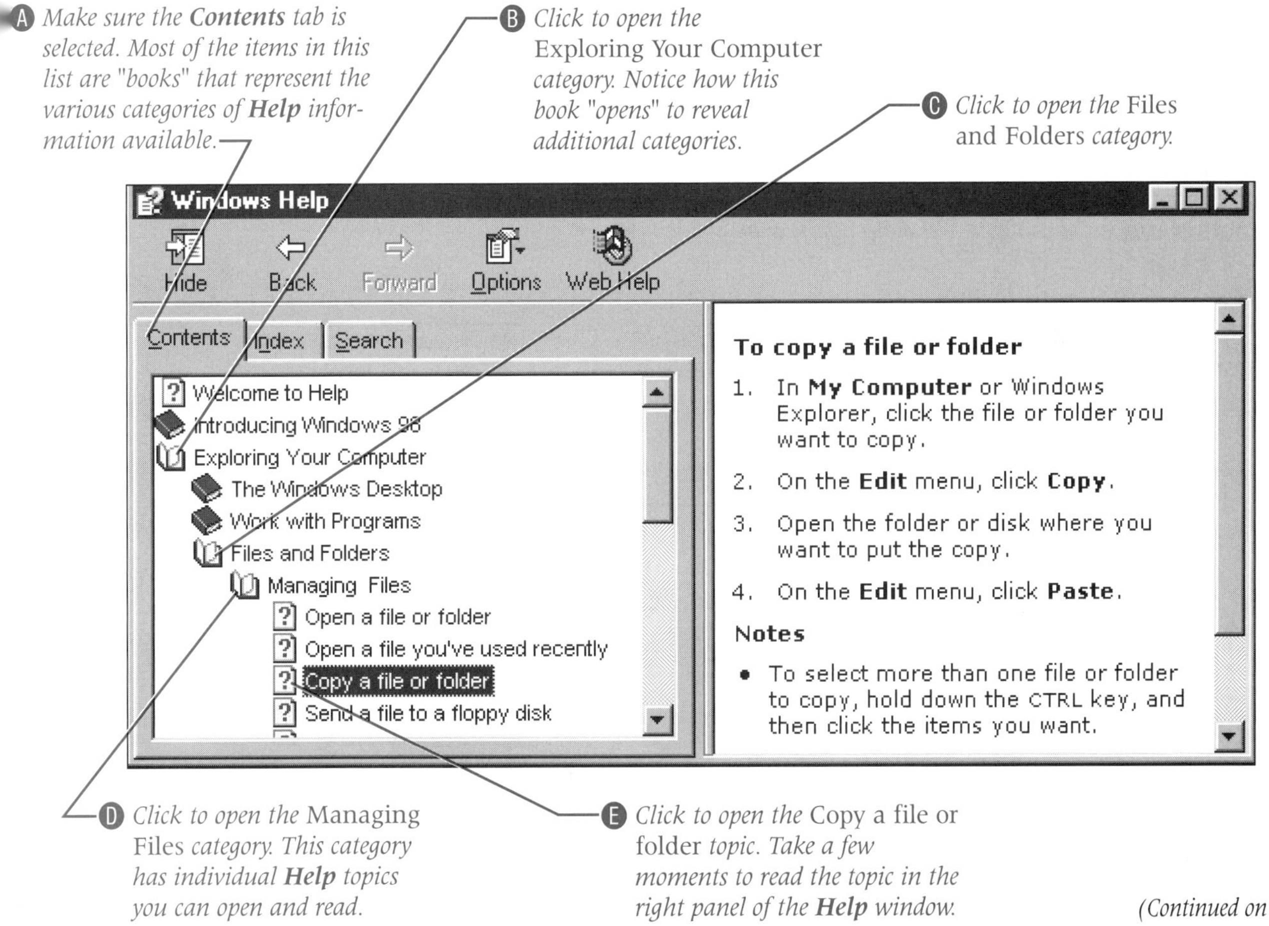
A Make sure the Contents tab is selected. Most of the items in this list are "books" that represent the various categories of Help information available.
B Click to open the Exploring Your Computer category. Notice how this book "opens" to reveal additional categories.
C Click to open the Files and Folders category.
Windows Help
Hide
Back
Forward
Options
Web Help
Contents
Index
Search
Welcome to Help
Introducing Windows 98
Exploring Your Computer
The Windows Desktop
Work with Programs
Files and Folders
Managing Files
Open a file or folder
Open a file you've used recently
Copy a file or folder
Send a file to a floppy disk
To copy a file or folder
1. In My Computer or Windows Explorer, click the file or folder you want to copy.
2. On the Edit menu, click Copy.
3. Open the folder or disk where you want to put the copy.
4. On the Edit menu, click Paste.
Notes
• To select more than one file or folder to copy, hold down the CTRL key, and then click the items you want.
D Click to open the Managing Files category. This category has individual Help topics you can open and read.
E Click to open the Copy a file or folder topic. Take a few moments to read the topic in the right panel of the Help window.

(Continued on the next page)

3. Follow these steps to adjust the size of the panels in the Help window:

Ⓐ *Point at the border between the two panels until you see a double-arrow (↔) appear.*

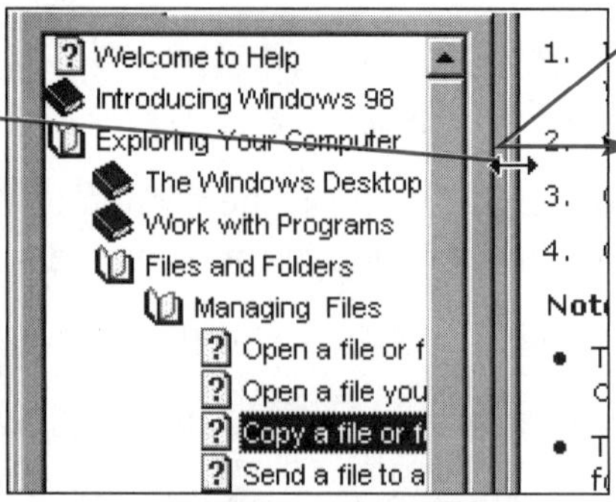
Welcome to Help
Introducing Windows 98
Exploring Your Computer
The Windows Desktop
Work with Programs
Files and Folders
Managing Files
Open a file or f
Open a file you
Copy a file or f
Send a file to a

Ⓑ *Drag the border to the right, until all topics are visible in the left panel.*

4. Click the **Hide** button on the left side of the Help window toolbar.
   This command conserves screen space by hiding the category list. Now only the Help topic you displayed earlier is visible.
5. Click the **Show** button on the left side of the Help window toolbar.
   Now the category list is visible again; thus, this control works as a toggle to switch the display of the category list on and off.

   Leave the Help window open, and continue with the Index Search *topic on page 80.*

Hands-On 3.1b Search Online Help in Windows 95 and Windows NT

1. Click the **Start** button and choose Help from the menu.
   The Windows Help window will appear. In the next few steps, you will look up a Help topic on copying files or folders.
2. Follow these steps to conduct a search using the Contents method:

Ⓐ *Make sure the **Contents** tab is selected. Most of the items in this list are "books" that represent the various categories of **Help** information available.*

Ⓑ *Double-click to open the* How To *category. Notice how this book "opens" to reveal additional categories.*

Ⓒ *Double-click to open the* Work with Files and Folders *category. This category has individual **Help** topics you can open and read.*

Ⓓ *Double-click to open the* Copying a File or Folder *topic. Notice that the **Help Topics** window disappears, and a new **Topic** window appears.*

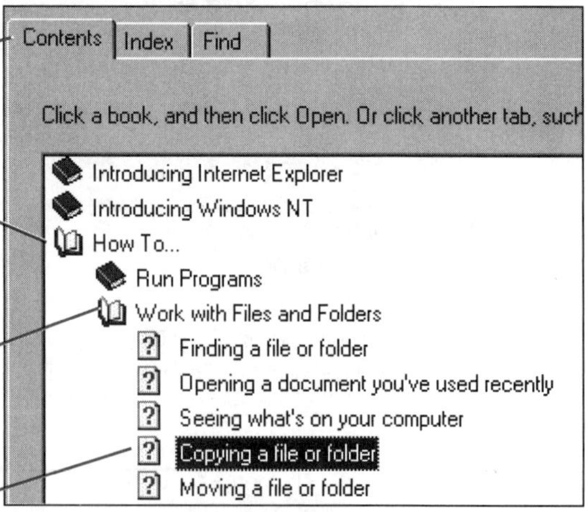
Contents
Index
Find
Click a book, and then click Open. Or click another tab, such
Introducing Internet Explorer
Introducing Windows NT
How To...
Run Programs
Work with Files and Folders
Finding a file or folder
Opening a document you've used recently
Seeing what's on your computer
Copying a file or folder
Moving a file or folder

Ⓔ *Take a few moments to read the **Help** topic. When you are done, click the **Help Topics** button near the top-left corner of the **Topic** window. This will display the **Help Topics** window once again.*

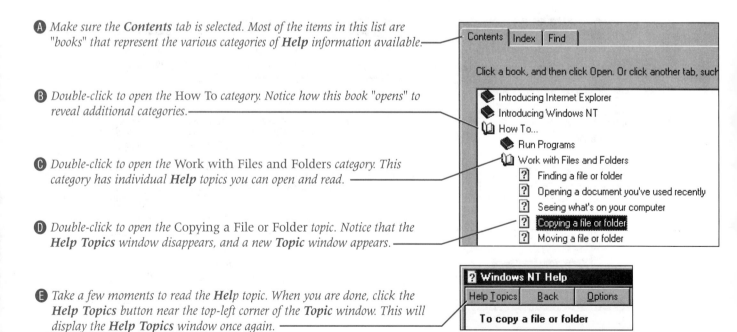

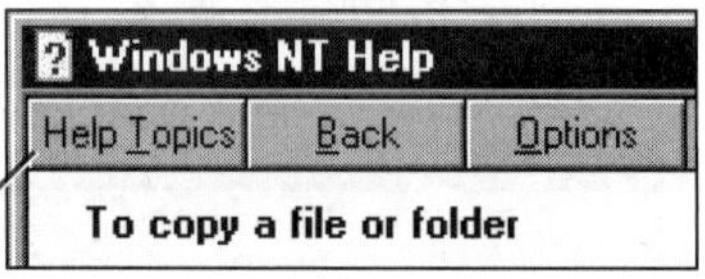
Windows NT Help
Help Topics
Back
Options
To copy a file or folder

Leave the Help window open, and continue with the Index Search topic on page 80.

Hands-On 3.1c Search Online Help in Windows 2000

1. Click the **Start** button, and choose  from the menu.
Help
   The Windows Help window will appear. In the next few steps, you will look up a Help topic on copying files or folders.

2. Follow these steps to conduct a search using the Contents method:

Ⓐ *Make sure the **Contents** tab is selected. Most of the items in this list are "books" that represent the various categories of **Help** information available.*

Ⓑ *Click to open the* Files and Folders *category.*

Ⓒ *Click to open the* Copy or move a file or folder *topic. Take a few moments to read the topic in the right panel of the Help window.*

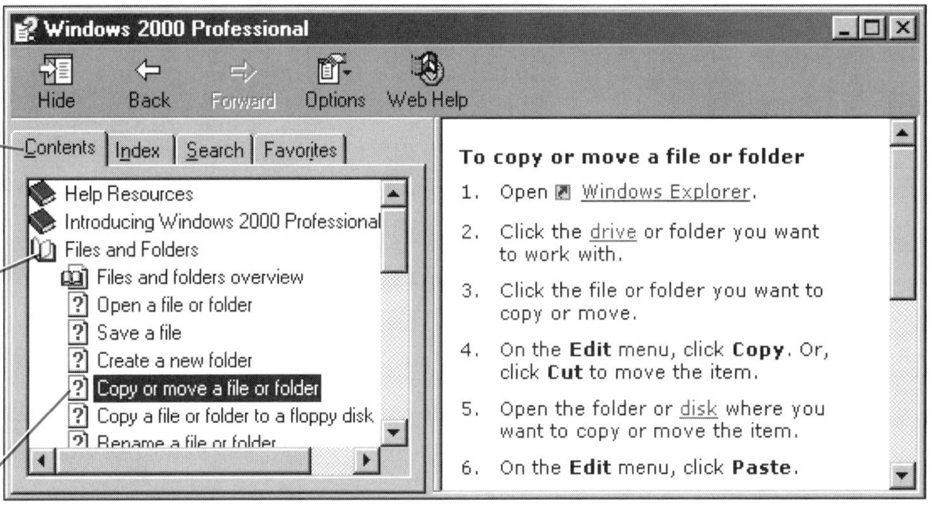
Windows 2000 Professional
Hide
Back
Forward
Options
Web Help
Contents
Index
Search
Favorites
Help Resources
Introducing Windows 2000 Professional
Files and Folders
Files and folders overview
Open a file or folder
Save a file
Create a new folder
Copy or move a file or folder
Copy a file or folder to a floppy disk
Rename a file or folder
To copy or move a file or folder
1. Open Windows Explorer.
2. Click the drive or folder you want to work with.
3. Click the file or folder you want to copy or move.
4. On the Edit menu, click Copy. Or, click Cut to move the item.
5. Open the folder or disk where you want to copy or move the item.
6. On the Edit menu, click Paste.

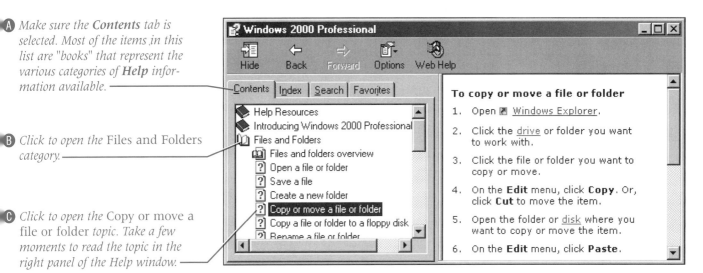

3. Follow these steps to adjust the size of the panels in the Help window:

Ⓐ *Point at the border between the two panels until you see a double-arrow (↔) appear.*

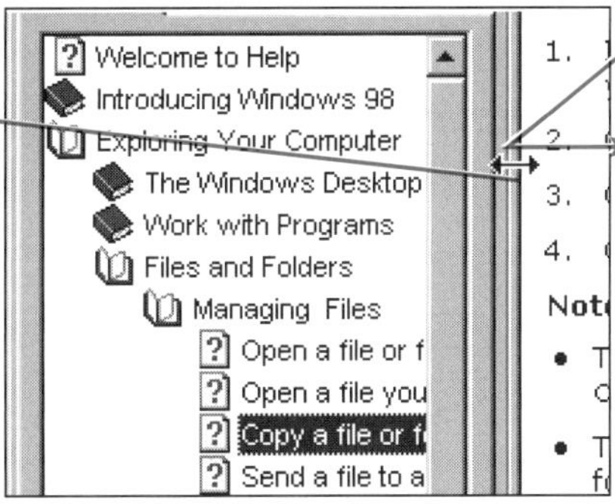
Welcome to Help
Introducing Windows 98
Exploring Your Computer
The Windows Desktop
Work with Programs
Files and Folders
Managing Files
Open a file or f
Open a file you
Copy a file or f
Send a file to a

Ⓑ *Drag the border to the right until all topics are visible in the left panel.*

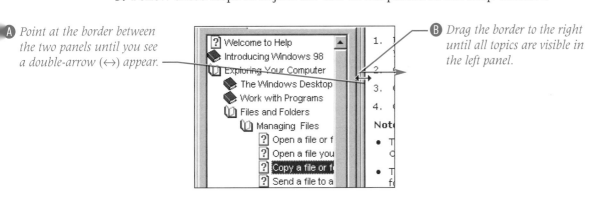

4. Click the **Hide** button on the left side of the Help window toolbar.
   This command conserves screen space by hiding the category list. Now only the Help topic you displayed earlier is visible.

5. Click the **Show** button on the left side of the Help window toolbar.
   Now the category list is visible again; thus, this control works as a toggle to switch the display of the category list on and off.

   Leave the Help window open, and continue with the next topic.

Index Search

The Index search lets you find Help topics by searching for a keyword in the topic titles. Every topic that includes the keyword in its title is displayed in a search results window. In the next exercise, you use the Index search method to find the same topic on copying files and folders.

Hands-On 3.2 Search with the Index Method

1. Follow these steps to perform an Index search:

Ⓐ *Click the* ***Index*** *tab near the top of the* ***Help*** *window.*

Ⓑ *Type the keyword* **`copying`** *in the keyword box.*

Ⓒ *Look over the search results in this list; then use the instructions in the next step to open the appropriate topic.*

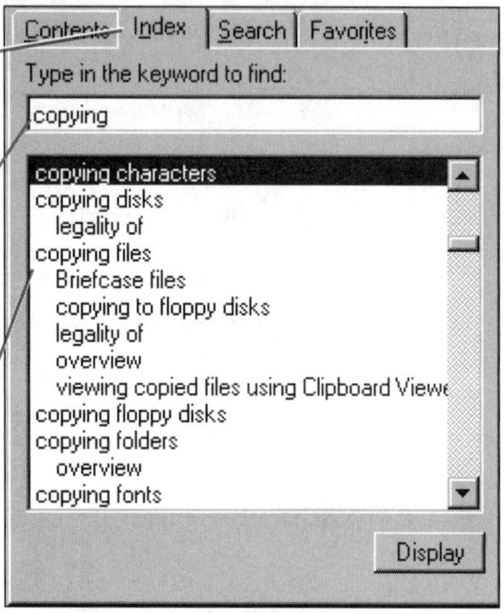

Contents
Index
Search
Favorites
Type in the keyword to find:
copying
copying characters
copying disks
legality of
copying files
Briefcase files
copying to floppy disks
legality of
overview
viewing copied files using Clipboard Viewe
copying floppy disks
copying folders
overview
copying fonts
Display

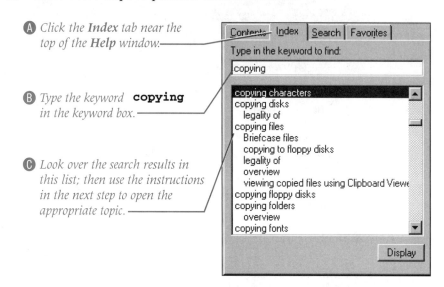

2. Follow the instructions for the version of Windows you are running:

Windows 98

Ⓐ *Double-click the* overview *topic under* copying files or folders*. The topic will be displayed in the right panel of the* **Help** *window.*

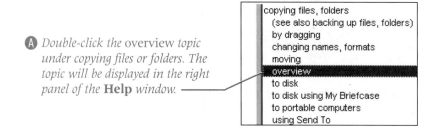

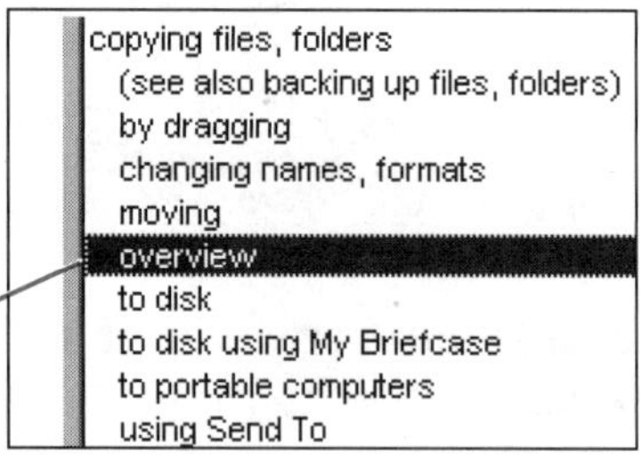

copying files, folders
(see also backing up files, folders)
by dragging
changing names, formats
moving
overview
to disk
to disk using My Briefcase
to portable computers
using Send To

Windows 95 or Windows NT 4.0

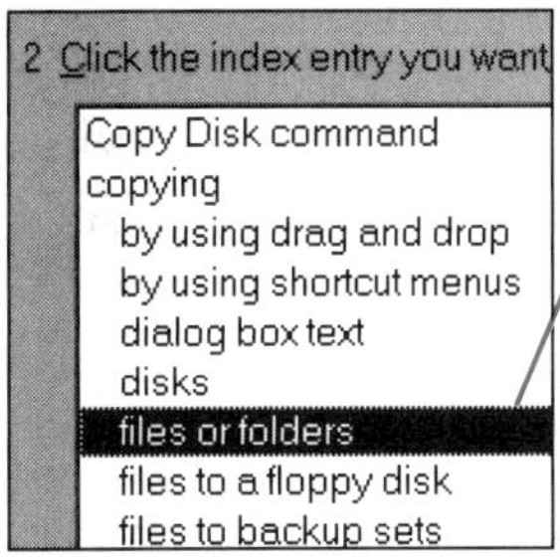
2 Click the index entry you want
Copy Disk command
copying
by using drag and drop
by using shortcut menus
dialog box text
disks
files or folders
files to a floppy disk
files to backup sets

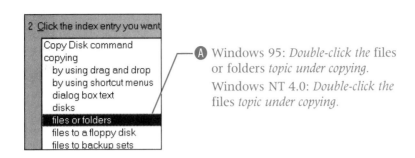

Ⓐ Windows 95: *Double-click the* files or folders *topic under copying.*
Windows NT 4.0: *Double-click the* files *topic under copying.*

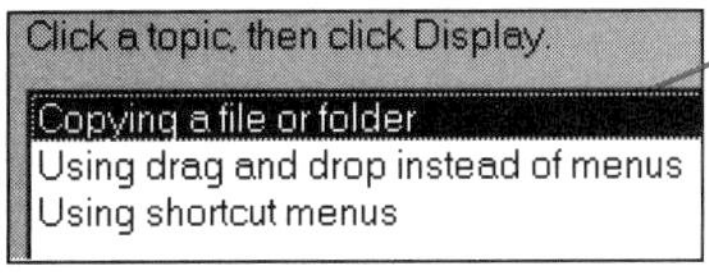
Click a topic, then click Display.
Copying a file or folder
Using drag and drop instead of menus
Using shortcut menus

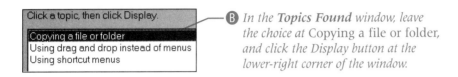

Ⓑ *In the **Topics Found** window, leave the choice at* Copying a file or folder, *and click the Display button at the lower-right corner of the window.*

Windows 2000

Ⓐ *Double-click the* overview *topic under* copying files.

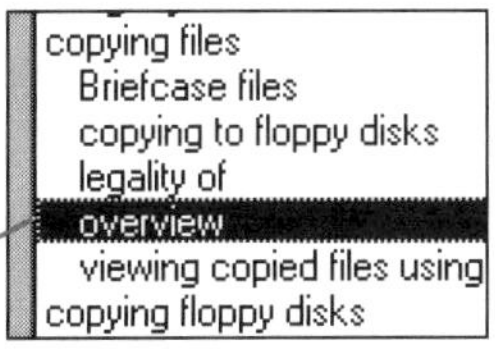
copying files
Briefcase files
copying to floppy disks
legality of
overview
viewing copied files using
copying floppy disks

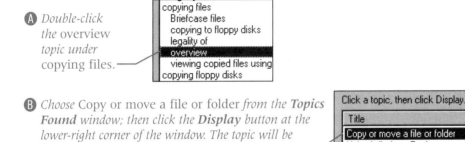

Ⓑ *Choose* Copy or move a file or folder *from the **Topics Found** window; then click the **Display** button at the lower-right corner of the window. The topic will be displayed in the right panel of the **Help** window.*

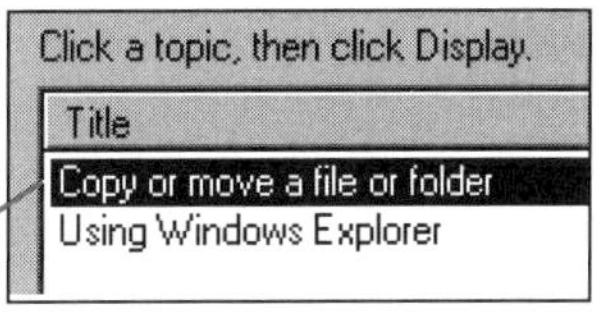
Click a topic, then click Display.
Title
Copy or move a file or folder
Using Windows Explorer

3. Take about 10–15 minutes to try searching for other Help topics. Use the ideas below:
   - Use the *Contents* search method to browse through the new features of the version of Windows you are using. Look for the topic that starts with the words **Introducing Windows.**
   - Use the *Index* search method to find Help on **shutting down** Windows properly.
   - Use the *Index* search method to find Help on **undeleting files.**
4. When you are finished with the additional searches in Step 3, close ☒ any open Help windows before you go on to the next topic.

Accessing Help in an Application Program

From the Keyboard

(F1) to display the Help system.

Most Windows programs have online Help built into them. You access a program's online Help system with the Help command from the program's menu bar. Many Windows application programs use an online Help window that works just like Windows Help. The Microsoft *Office 97* and *Office 2000* Suites feature an **Office Assistant** that lets you search for Help topics by typing a question in plain English.

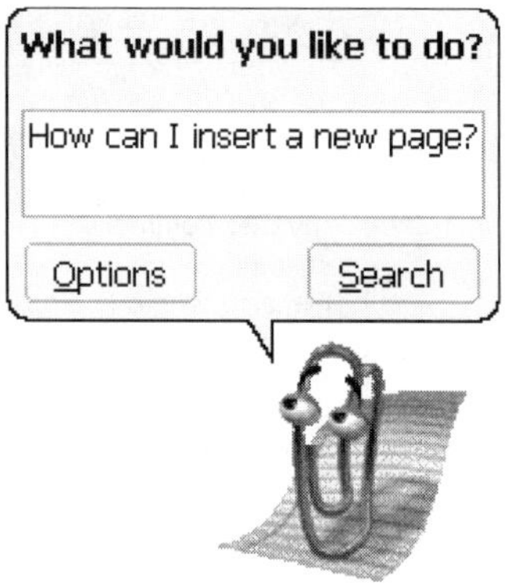
What would you like to do?
How can I insert a new page?
Options
Search

Office Assistants let you search for Help with simple questions.

Hands-On 3.3 Look Up Help for an Application Program

In this exercise, you will start the WordPad program and then look up a Help topic in WordPad's online Help.

1. Choose **Start→Programs→Accessories→WordPad** to start the WordPad program.
2. Choose **Help→Help Topics** from WordPad's menu bar.
   WordPad will display its Help window. This window will look similar to the Help window you used for Windows in the previous exercises.
3. Make sure that the **Index** tab is selected, type **undo** as the search keyword, and then double-click to open the topic in the Topics Found list that begins with the word **undo** or **undoing.**
   WordPad's Help will display the method you can use to undo your most recent action. This can be useful if you accidentally delete some text or make some other mistake as you work.
4. Click the Help Window's Close [X] button.
5. Tap the (F1) function key in the top row of keys on the keyboard.
   Most Windows programs treat (F1) as the Help *key.*
6. Close [X] the Help window again.
7. Close [X] the WordPad window.

Browsing Through Files

In Lesson 2, you stored documents and an image as **files** on your exercise diskette. In this lesson, you will learn how to organize the growing number of files that can accumulate as you work with a computer. Besides your own files, there are hundreds or even thousands of files on the hard drive that run Windows and the application programs you use. Learning how all these files are organized will help you save and find your own files more easily.

How Files Are Organized

Windows uses a flexible hierarchy that is common to most personal computers. The three levels in the hierarchy are listed below:

Level	Definition	Examples
Drive	A physical place where you store files	■ A floppy disk ■ A hard drive
Folder	An electronic location where you store groups of related files. It is also possible to place folders inside of other folders.	■ A folder to store all the files for an application program ■ A folder to store all the letters you type for a project
File	A collection of computer data that has some common purpose	■ A letter you've typed ■ A picture you've drawn

Browsing with the My Computer Window

As you work with Windows programs such as WordPad and Paint, you will want to locate and open files you have created previously. Although you can open files from within an application program, sometimes it is more convenient to search directly through all of the files you have saved to a hard drive or floppy disk. This is the sort of task for which the My Computer window is perfectly suited.

The following illustration describes the major features of the My Computer window. Take a moment to review these features before you start the next Hands-On exercise.

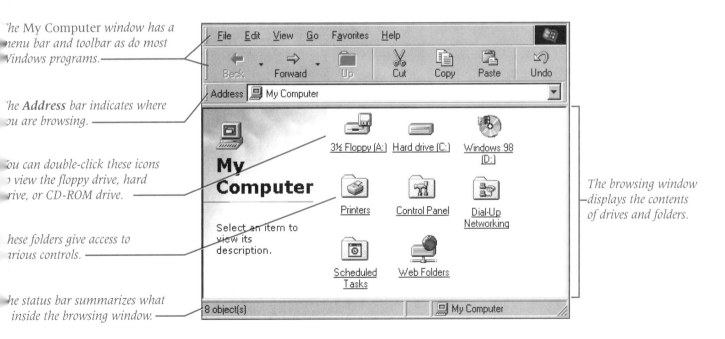

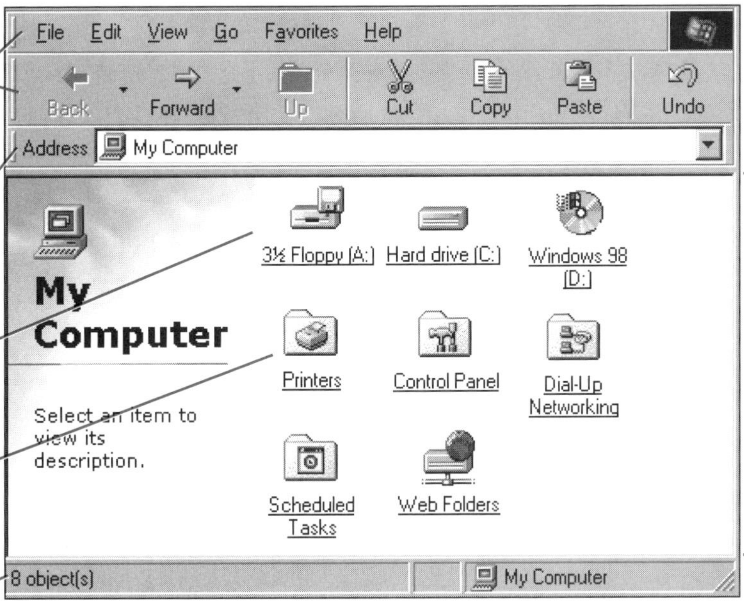
File Edit View Go Favorites Help
Back
Forward
Up
Cut
Copy
Paste
Undo
Address
My Computer
My Computer
Select an item to view its description.
3½ Floppy (A:)
Hard drive (C:)
Windows 98 (D:)
Printers
Control Panel
Dial-Up Networking
Scheduled Tasks
Web Folders
8 object(s)
My Computer

'he My Computer *window has a* ıenu bar and toolbar as do most Vindows programs.*

'he **Address** *bar indicates where* ɔu are browsing.*

ou can double-click these icons ɔ view the floppy drive, hard* rive, or CD-ROM drive.*

hese folders give access to ırious controls.*

he status bar summarizes what inside the browsing window.*

The browsing window displays the contents of drives and folders.

Hands-On 3.4 Open a My Computer Window

In this exercise, you will open a My Computer window and view the contents of your exercise diskette.

1. Close any open windows on the Desktop.
2. *Double-click* the My Computer icon near the top-left corner of the Desktop.
3. If the My Computer window is not already maximized, maximize the window now.
4. Choose **View→Large Icons** from the menu bar.
   This view may have already been selected. It displays easy-to-recognize icons for all of the drives, folders, and files on the computer. Notice that there are icons for the floppy drive, hard drive, and CD-ROM drive.
5. Follow the instructions below for your version of windows.

Windows 98

- Choose **View→Folder Options** from the menu bar.
- Click the **Custom** option.

Custom, based on settings you choose:

- Click the **Settings** button.
- Make sure that the **Browse folders option** is set to **same window** as shown at right.

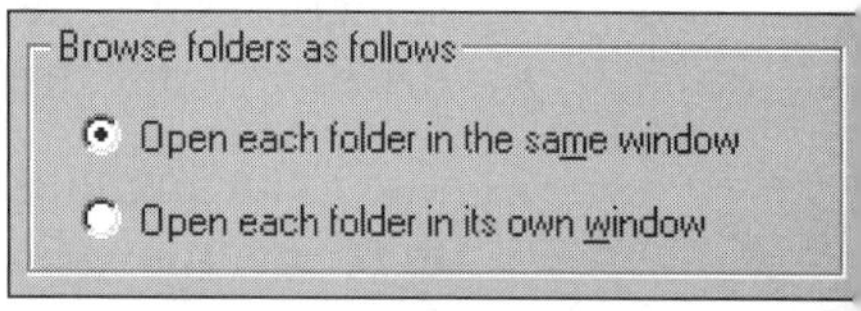
Browse folders as follows
Open each folder in the same window
Open each folder in its own window

- Click **OK;** then click the **Close** button to close the dialog box.

Windows 95 and Windows NT

- Click **View** on the menu bar. Follow the instructions in the **Windows 98** section above if the last item in the view menu reads: **Folder Options.** Otherwise, click **Options** in the View menu.
- Make sure that the **Folders** option is set to **single window** as shown at right.

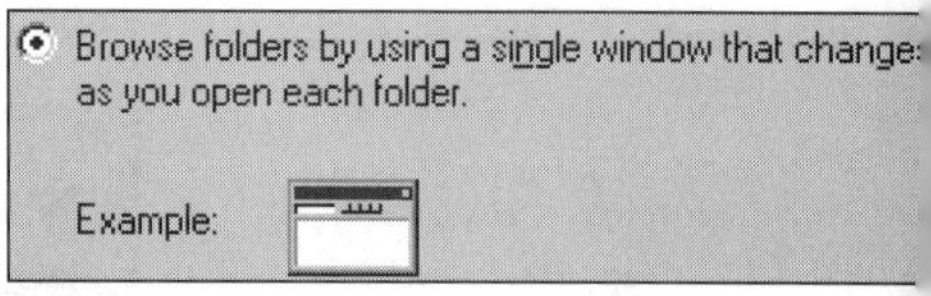
Browse folders by using a single window that change
as you open each folder.
Example:

- Click **OK** to close the dialog box.

Windows 2000

- Choose **Tools→Folder Options** from the menu bar.
- Make sure that the Browse folders option is set to **same window** as shown at right.

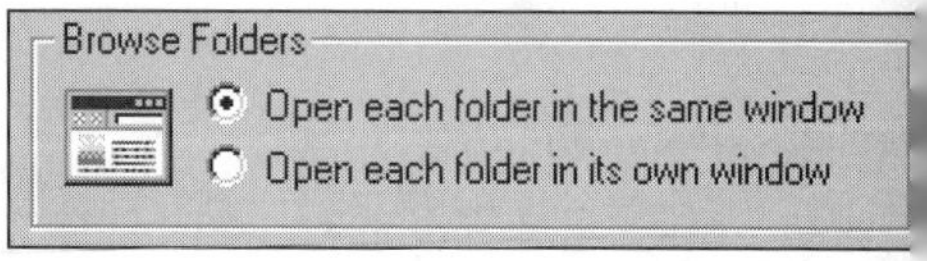
Browse Folders
Open each folder in the same window
Open each folder in its own window

- Click **OK** to close the dialog box.

6. Place your **exercise diskette** in the floppy drive, with the label side up and the metal side in.
7. Double-click the 3½ Floppy (A:) icon to view the exercise diskette.
   You stored some files on this diskette in the previous lesson. But WordPad's Open *and* Save As *dialog boxes only display document files that the program can open. In the My Computer window you can see all of the files on the diskette. Leave the My Computer window open, and continue with the next topic.*

Opening Files

When you double-click on a file in a My Computer window, the program used to create or edit that type of file will be started, and the file will be displayed in the program window. This is a convenient way to start working with a file after you find it.

Hands-On 3.5 Open a Document File

1. *Double-click* on the **Tutor Meeting** document file.
   Windows will start the program that is associated with document files. This will probably be Microsoft Word *or* WordPad. *If Word is installed on the computer, it is programmed to open files that were created with WordPad. However, you can also start WordPad from the Start menu; then use WordPad's Open command to open the file.*
2. Click the **upper** Close button as shown at right. Click **No** if you are asked to save the file.
   Now only the My Computer window should be open.

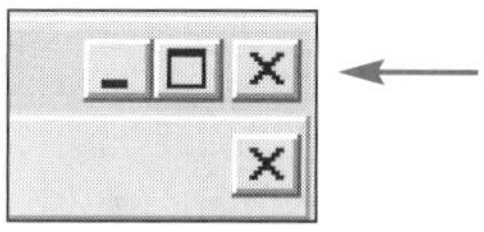

Changing the View

There are four ways to view drives and folders in a My Computer window. You have been using the Large Icons view thus far. This view represents each file and folder with a larger icon than the other views. You can change the view from the My Computer *View* menu or with the *Views* toolbar button. Depending on the version of Windows you are using, the Views button(s) will look like one of the examples below:

Views
Windows 98, 95, *and* NT

Views
Windows 2000

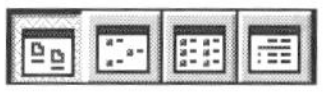
The view buttons on some Windows 95 *and* NT *Toolbars may look like this.*

Hands-On 3.6 Try Out Different Views

1. Choose **View→Small Icons** from the menu bar.
   This view lets you see as many filenames as possible in the window.
2. Choose **View→List** from the menu bar.
   This view doesn't really differ much from the small icons view.
3. Choose **View→Details** from the menu bar.
   This view gives you additional information about the files, such as the date each file was created or modified. Depending on how this view was last used, you may or may not be able to see the entire filename in the leftmost column.
4. Follow these steps to adjust the width of a column in Details view:

(A) Point here until you see the double-arrow; then double-click. The column width will be adjusted to the length of the longest item in the column.

(B) Point here until you see the double-arrow; then press the mouse button and drag to the left to make the column narrower.

(C) Double-click to make the column you just narrowed as wide as its longest item.

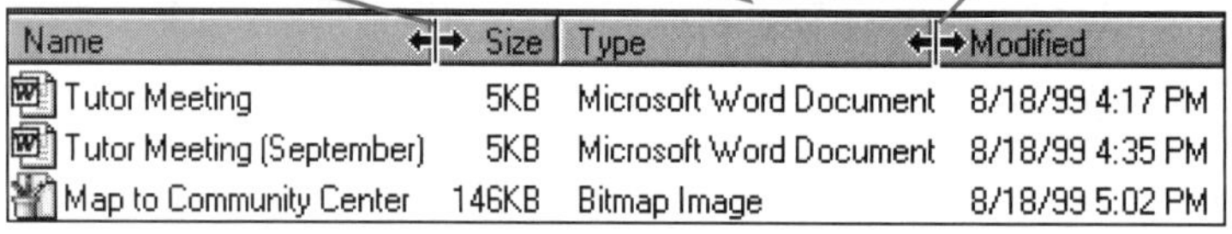
Name
Size
Type
Modified
Tutor Meeting 5KB Microsoft Word Document 8/18/99 4:17 PM
Tutor Meeting (September) 5KB Microsoft Word Document 8/18/99 4:35 PM
Map to Community Center 146KB Bitmap Image 8/18/99 5:02 PM

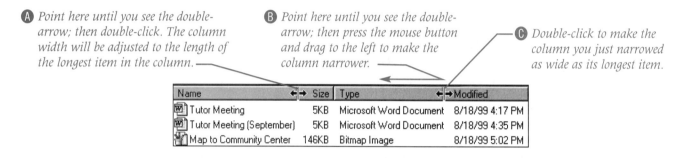

5. If you are running **Windows 2000,** choose **View→Thumbnails** from the menu bar. After you have seen the Thumbnails view, return to the **Details** view.
   The Thumbnails view displays a miniature view of each image file. Notice that the map you created in Lesson 2 is now displayed as a small thumbnail image.

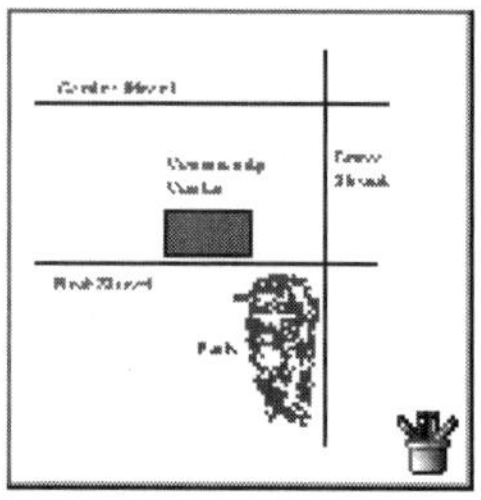

Map to Community Center

Sorting Files

The My Computer window may contain many files and folders. You can sort the files and folders in a variety of ways. This can be useful if you are trying to find a specific file. The files and folders can be sorted by name, size, type, or date. These four parameters are known as **Sort Keys.** You can also sort files in **ascending** order (A to Z) or **descending** order (Z to A). The four sort keys are described in the following table.

Sort Key	How It Sorts the Files and Folders
Name	Alphabetically by filename
Size	By the size of the files
Type	By the function of the file, such as word processing document, spreadsheet, or database
Date	By the date that the file was created or most recently modified

Hands-On 3.7 Sort the Files

In this exercise, you will view the files on your exercise diskette in various sort orders.

1. Follow these steps to sort the files in various ways.

Ⓐ *Click the **Modified** column heading to sort the files by date. The most recently modified file is listed first.*

Ⓑ *Click the **Modified** column heading again. Now files with the most recent date are at the bottom of the list. When you click the same column a second time, the list is sorted in descending rather than ascending order.*

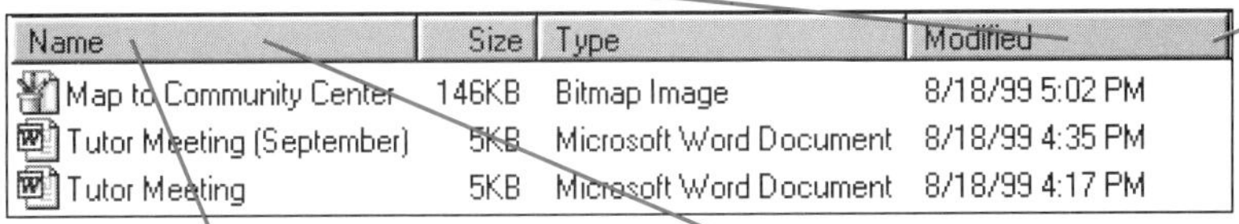

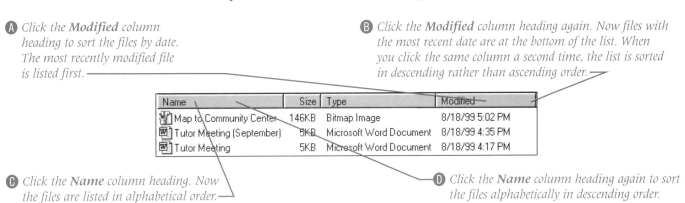

Name
Size
Type
Modified
Map to Community Center
146KB
Bitmap Image
8/18/99 5:02 PM
Tutor Meeting (September)
5KB
Microsoft Word Document
8/18/99 4:35 PM
Tutor Meeting
5KB
Microsoft Word Document
8/18/99 4:17 PM

Ⓒ *Click the **Name** column heading. Now the files are listed in alphabetical order.*

Ⓓ *Click the **Name** column heading again to sort the files alphabetically in descending order.*

2. Try sorting the files by clicking on the other columns.
   Sorting the files can often help you locate a particular file. For example, sorting the files by date can help you find a file you created or modified recently.
3. Set the view to **Large Icons.**
   You can also sort files when you are in one of the other view modes, as you will do in the next step.
4. Choose **View→Arrange Icons→By Size** from the menu bar.
   Your Map to Community Center file should be last in the list. Image files like the map are usually much larger than word processing documents. The Tutor Meeting file appears toward the top of the list, since it is a very small document.
5. Close [X] the My Computer window.

Working with Folders

Folders are important tools for organizing files. You may have just a few files when you begin using a computer, but after a year or two you may have hundreds of files. What if you could only view your files in a single long list? This would be similar to finding a book in a library that had only one long bookshelf. You could find the book eventually, but you would need to scan through many titles before you found the book you were looking for.

Folders Hierarchy

Folders are organized into a hierarchy on each drive of a Windows system. Windows creates many folders when it is installed on the computer. You can create your own folders as well. The following illustration displays a common folders hierarchy on a Windows system. This is an example of the **Exploring** window. You will learn how to open an Exploring window later in this lesson.

Here is the floppy drive. This floppy disk has two folders on it that were created by a user.

The Documents folder is selected for viewing. Notice how it is "open." The contents of the folder are displayed in the right panel of the Exploring window.

This is the computer's hard drive. It contains several folders that were created when Windows was installed and still more folders created as new programs were installed.

The plus signs (+) beside these folders indicate that there are other folders that are not displayed. Clicking the plus sign will expand the list to display folders contained within a folder.

This panel displays the contents of any drive or folder that is selected in the left panel.

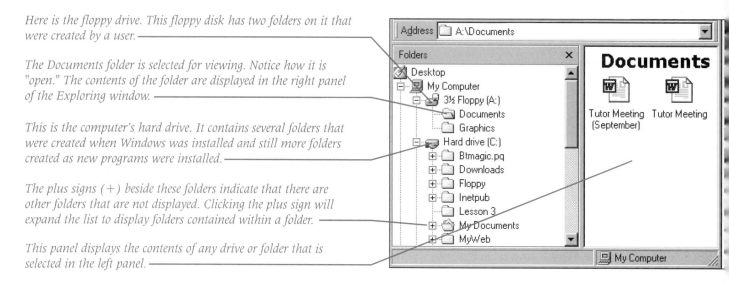

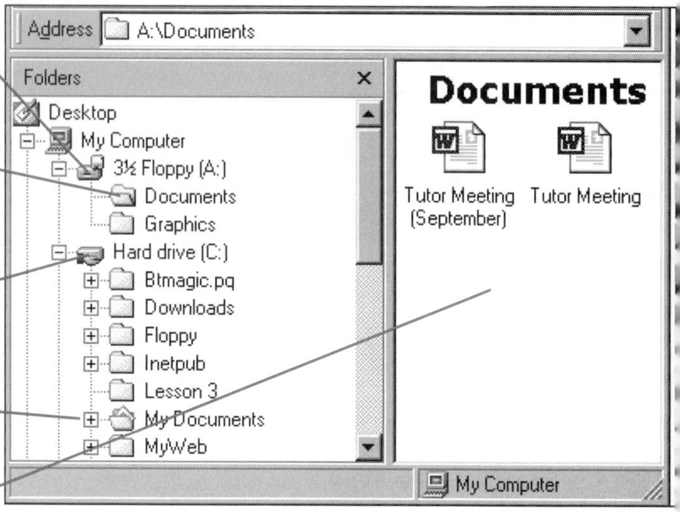
Address
A:\Documents
Folders
Desktop
My Computer
3½ Floppy (A:)
Documents
Graphics
Hard drive (C:)
Btmagic.pq
Downloads
Floppy
Inetpub
Lesson 3
My Documents
MyWeb
Documents
Tutor Meeting (September)
Tutor Meeting
My Computer

My Documents Folder

Windows 98 and Windows 2000 feature a special folder on the Desktop called *My Documents.* This folder stores files on the computer's hard drive. The My Documents folder is associated with your *log-on name.* This means that each user with his or her own log-on name has a unique My Documents folder. If you are running a program in the Office 2000 Suite, you can access the My Documents folder with a single click.

This button in the Word 2000 ***Save As*** *dialog box navigates you to the* ***My Documents*** *folder with a single click.*

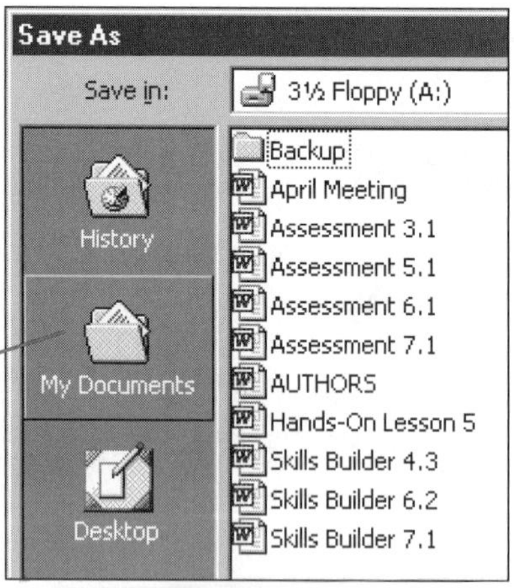
Save As
Save in:
3½ Floppy (A:)
History
My Documents
Desktop
Backup
April Meeting
Assessment 3.1
Assessment 5.1
Assessment 6.1
Assessment 7.1
AUTHORS
Hands-On Lesson 5
Skills Builder 4.3
Skills Builder 6.2
Skills Builder 7.1

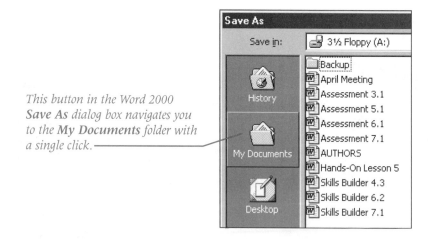

Creating Folders

You can create folders on a floppy disk or the hard drive whenever you need them. Folders can be created while you are viewing a drive in a My Computer or Exploring window. You can also create folders from the *Save As* dialog box of most Windows programs.

Quick Reference

HOW TO CREATE A FOLDER

Task	Procedure
Create a folder from a My Computer window	■ Open a My Computer Window. ■ Navigate to the drive or folder where you wish to create the new folder. ■ Choose *File→New→Folder* from the menu bar. *The new folder will appear in the window. The name of the folder will be selected so you can modify it.* ■ Type a name for the new folder; then tap the (ENTER) key.
Create a folder in the Save As dialog box of an application program	■ Choose *File→Save As* from the program's menu bar. ■ Click the *Create New Folder* button near the top of the Save As window. ■ Type a name for the new folder; then click *OK.*

Hands-On 3.8 Create Folders on Your Floppy Disk

In this exercise, you will create two folders on your floppy disk. Later in this lesson you will move and copy files into these folders.

1. *Double-click* the My Computer icon near the top-left corner of the Desktop. If necessary, Maximize the window.
2. Make sure your **exercise diskette** is in the floppy drive.
3. *Double-click* the 3½ Floppy (A:) icon to view the exercise diskette.
4. Make sure the view is set to **Large Icons.**
5. Follow these steps to create a new folder on your floppy disk:

Ⓐ *Click once on a clear portion of the* ***My Computer*** *window.*

Ⓑ *Choose* ***File→New→Folder*** *from the menu bar.*

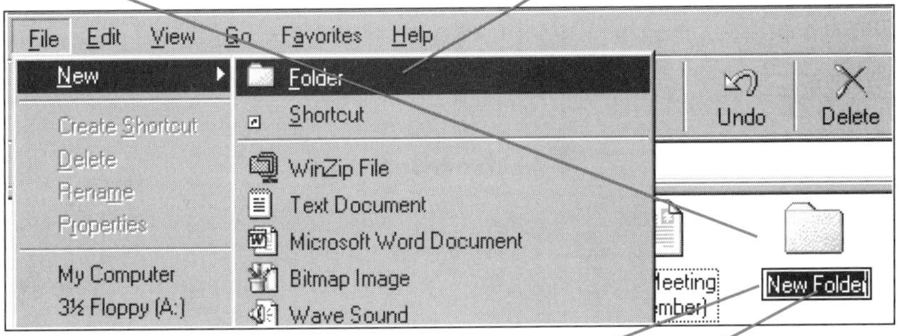
File
Edit
View
Go
Favorites
Help
New
Create Shortcut
Delete
Rename
Properties
My Computer
3½ Floppy (A:)
Folder
Shortcut
WinZip File
Text Document
Microsoft Word Document
Bitmap Image
Wave Sound
Undo
Delete
New Folder

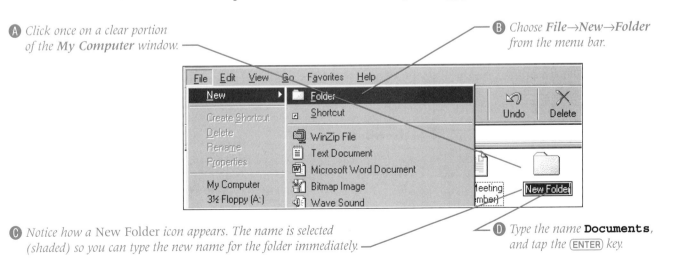

Ⓒ *Notice how a New Folder icon appears. The name is selected (shaded) so you can type the new name for the folder immediately.*

Ⓓ *Type the name* **`Documents`**, *and tap the* (ENTER) *key.*

(Continued on the next page)

6. Double-click the **Documents** folder icon to navigate to your new folder.
   Notice that the name of your folder is displayed in the Address bar near the top of the My Computer window and also in the Title bar. There's nothing in this folder yet. You will place files in it later. If you are running Windows 95 or NT, you may not see the word Address *next to the Address bar.*

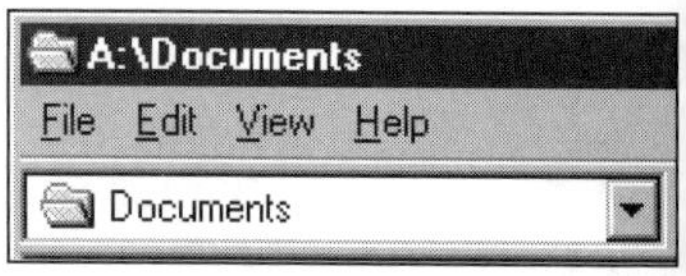

A:\Documents
File Edit View Help
Documents

7. Follow these steps to navigate back to the **3½ Floppy (A:)** level:

Ⓐ *Click the **Address** bar drop-down list button. This button will be on the right side of the **My Computer** window.*

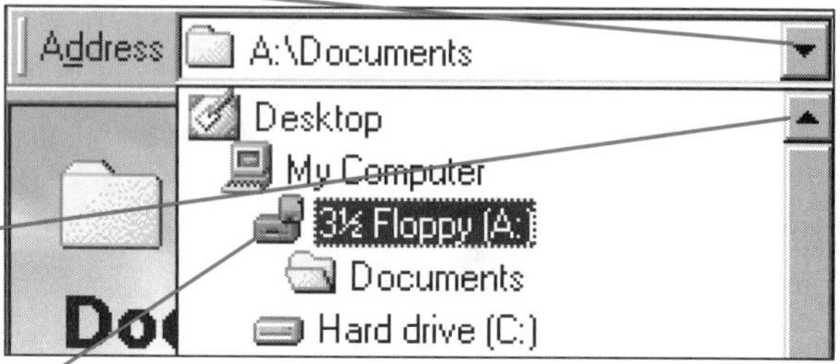

Address
A:\Documents
Desktop
My Computer
3½ Floppy (A:)
Documents
Hard drive (C:)

Ⓑ *Click this scroll button if you do not see the* 3½ Floppy (A:) *drive in the drop down list.*

Ⓒ *Click* 3½ Floppy (A:) *in the list.*

Now the 3½ Floppy (A:) drive is displayed in the Address bar. Looking at the Address bar as you navigate in folders helps you keep track of where you are.

8. Choose **File→New→Folder** from the menu bar. Type **`Graphics`** as the name for the new folder, and tap the ENTER key.
9. *Double-click* on the **graphics** folder.
   Notice that the name of the folder is displayed in the Address bar.
10. Click the Up  button on the toolbar to return to the **3½ Floppy (A:)** drive level.
    The Up button jumps you one level up in the drive/folder hierarchy. This button is often more convenient than the drop-down list you used in Step 7.

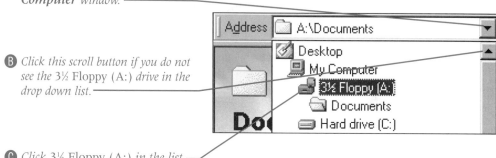

Renaming Files and Folders

In Lesson 2, you learned how to save a file with a new name to create a copy of the file. It is also easy to rename a file without making a copy. To rename a file that is displayed in a My Computer window, *right-click* on the file, and choose **Rename** from the pop-up menu.

Quick Reference

HOW TO RENAME A FILE OR FOLDER

Task	Procedure
Rename a file or folder with the right-click method.	■ *Right-click* on the file or folder icon; then choose *Rename* from the pop-up menu. ■ Type the new name; then tap the ENTER key.
Rename a file or folder with the click-pause method.	■ Click *once* on the filename. ■ Pause about 2 seconds, then *click* on the filename again. ■ Type the new name; then tap the ENTER key.

Filename Extensions

Most Windows filenames have an extension, which consists of three letters following a period at the end of the filename. Filename extensions identify the type of file you are working with. For example the *Tutor Meeting* file is a *word processing* document, so it has a filename extension of *.doc.* Windows application programs add this extension to any filename you type when you save a file. Most windows systems hide the filename extension. But if your system is set to display it, you need to type out the extension whenever you rename a file.

Tutor Meeting.doc

The filename.

The extension. Most Windows systems are set to hide the extension.

Hands-On 3.9 Rename a File

In this exercise, you will use both methods to rename one of the files you created in Lesson 2.

1. Follow these steps to issue the **Rename** command with the right-click method:

Ⓐ *Click with the* right *mouse button (right-click) on the* Tutor Meeting *file* icon *(not the name).*

Ⓑ *Choose* Rename *from the pop-up menu.*

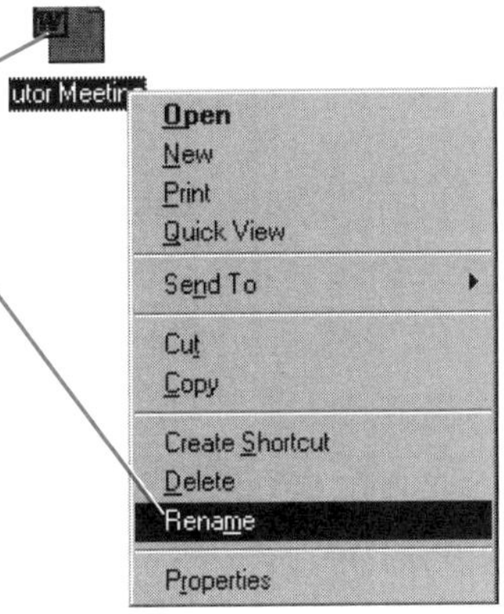
utor Meetin
Open
New
Print
Quick View
Send To
Cut
Copy
Create Shortcut
Delete
Rename
Properties

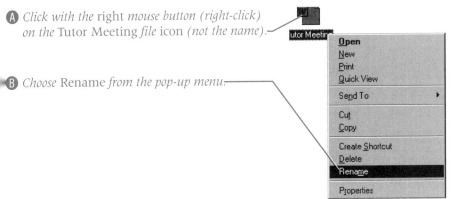

The filename is highlighted for renaming. It may or may not display a three-letter extension of .doc.

2. Examine the filename; then follow the instructions that match the filename:
   - If the filename reads **Tutor Meeting,** type **`April Meeting`** then tap ENTER.
   - If the filename reads **Tutor Meeting.doc,** type **`April Meeting.doc`** then tap ENTER.

   The old name is deleted and replaced by the new name.
3. Click on a **clear area** of the My Computer window to deselect the April Meeting file.
4. Click on the **filename** (not the icon) for the **April Meeting** file. Pause about two seconds, and then click again on the filename.
   The name will be highlighted for editing. You need to pause so that Windows does not mistake your command for a double-click (which is done much faster).
5. Tap the **left arrow** ← key until the insertion point is blinking just to the right of the *l* in April; then tap the BACKSPACE key until the word April is deleted.
   The arrow key allows you to move the insertion point back without deleting the word Meeting.
6. Type **`Tutor`** as the first word in the filename; then tap the ENTER key to complete the rename command.
   Leave the My Computer window open.

Moving and Copying Files

Windows lets you move and copy files from one drive to another, and from one folder to another. There are several techniques you can use to move and copy files. This lesson will teach you three methods:

- **Copy and paste—**copies files into a new location.
- **Cut and paste—**moves files to a new location.
- **Drag and drop—**can either move or copy files to a new location.

Quick Reference

MOVING AND COPYING FILES WITH CUT, COPY, AND PASTE

Task	Procedure
Copy files with Copy and Paste.	■ *Select* the files to be copied. ■ Click the *Copy* button on the toolbar or use the *Edit→Copy* command on the menu bar or use CTRL+*C* from the keyboard. ■ Navigate to the location where the files are to be copied. ■ Click the *Paste* button on the toolbar or use the *Edit→Paste* command on the menu bar or use CTRL+*V* from the keyboard.
Move Files with Cut and Paste.	■ *Select* the files to be moved. ■ Click the *Cut* button on the toolbar, or use the *Edit→Cut* command on the menu bar or use CTRL+*X* from the keyboard. ■ Navigate to the location where the files are to be moved. ■ Click the *Paste* button on the toolbar, or use the *Edit→Paste* command on the menu bar or use CTRL+*V* from the keyboard.

Selecting Multiple Files for Move and Copy Commands

You can move and copy a single file or dozens of files with the same command. Before you give the Cut or Copy command, select the file(s) you wish to be affected by the command. To select a single file, you simply click on it. The two easiest methods to select multiple files are described in the Quick Reference table that follows. You can combine these two techniques as your needs dictate.

Quick Reference

HOW TO SELECT MULTIPLE FILES FOR COMMANDS

Technique	Procedure
CTRL+Click technique to select several files	■ Click the first file you wish to select. ■ Press and hold CTRL while you click on any other files you wish to select. ■ Release the CTRL key when you have made all of your selections.
SHIFT+Click technique to select several files in a row	■ Click the first file you wish to select. ■ Press and hold SHIFT while you click last file in the group that you wish to select; then release SHIFT.
Deselect a selected file	■ Press and hold CTRL while you click on the file you wish to deselect.

Hands-On 3.10 Move and Copy Files

Move a File with Cut and Paste

In this part of the exercise, you will use the Cut and Paste technique to move a single file into one of your new folders.

1. Make sure a My Computer window is displaying the **3½ Floppy (A:)** drive. Look at the top-left corner of the My Computer window's title bar to confirm you are at the right location.

3½ Floppy (A:)
File Edit View

2. Click to select the **Map to Community Center** file in the My Computer window.
3. Choose **Edit→Cut** from the menu bar.
   Notice that the icon for the file you selected is "dimmed." This indicates that the file has been cut and will be moved when you give the Paste command.
4. *Double-click* to open the **Graphics** folder.
   This navigates you to the empty Graphics folder.
5. Choose **Edit→Paste** from the menu bar.
   After the file has been moved, it will be displayed in the window.
6. Click the Up button on the toolbar to return to the **3½ Floppy (A:)** drive level.
   Notice that the Map to Community Center *file is no longer listed with the other files, since it was moved to a different folder.*

NOTE!
This first level of a drive is also called the root.

Copy Multiple Files

In this part of the exercise, you will select more than one file for the Copy and Paste commands.

7. Hold down the CTRL key as you click on the two **Tutor Meeting** Document files; then release the CTRL key.
   Both files should now be selected.
8. Choose **Edit→Copy** from the menu bar.
9. *Double-click* to open the **Documents** folder.
10. Choose **Edit→Paste** from the menu bar.
    The files will appear in the window as they are copied.
11. Click the Up button on the toolbar to return to the **3½ Floppy (A:)** drive level.
    Notice that the document files are still displayed in the window, since they were copied rather than moved.

Moving and Copying Files with Drag and Drop

The Drag-and-Drop technique is an easy way to move or copy files or folders by dragging them to the desired location. The easiest way to use the Drag-and-Drop technique is to hold down the *right* (not the left) mouse button as you drag. This will give you a pop-up menu from which you select the Move or Copy command.

Quick Reference

MOVING AND COPYING WITH DRAG AND DROP

Task	Procedure
Drag and Drop with the right-drag technique.	■ *Select* the files or folders to be moved or copied. ■ Point at one selected file or folder, press and hold the *right* mouse button, and *drag* the files or folders to the desired location. ■ Release the mouse button at the destination; then select *Move Here, Copy Here,* or *Cancel* from the pop-up menu.
Move files on the same disk drive with Drag and Drop.	■ *Select* the files or folders to be moved. ■ Point at one selected file or folder, and *drag* with the *left* mouse button to a new location on the *same* disk drive.
Copy files to a different disk drive with Drag and Drop.	■ *Select* the files or folders to be copied. ■ Point at one selected file or folder, and *drag* with the *left* mouse button to the new location on a *different* disk drive.

Hands-On 3.11 Move Files with Drag and Drop

In this exercise, you will select two files with the CTRL*+Click technique.*

1. Click to select the **Tutor Meeting** file. Press CTRL, click on the **Tutor Meeting (September)** document file; then release CTRL.
2. Follow these steps to move the files with the Drag-and-Drop technique:
   The two files will disappear from the My Computer window as they are moved.

Ⓐ *Point to one of the selected files, press and hold the* right *(not the left) mouse button, and drag the files onto the* Graphics *folder.*

Ⓑ *Release the right mouse button when the* Graphics *folder is selected (shaded), as shown here.*

Ⓒ *Choose* **Move Here** *from the pop-up menu.*

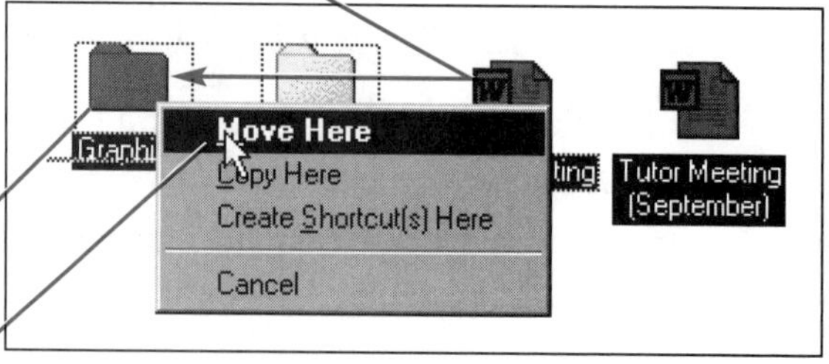
Graphi
Move Here
Copy Here
Create Shortcut(s) Here
Cancel
ting
Tutor Meeting
(September)

3. *Double-click* to open the **Graphics** folder.
   The two files you dragged and dropped should now be in the folder.
4. Click the Up button on the toolbar to return to the **3½ Floppy (A:)** drive level.

Deleting Files and Folders

You can delete files and folders by selecting them then clicking the Delete [X] button on the My Computer or Exploring window toolbar. When you delete a folder, any files inside that folder are deleted as well.

WARNING!

Files and folders deleted from floppy disks *are* not *sent to the Recycle Bin! They are* permanently deleted *when you issue the delete command.*

What Happens to Deleted Files?

Windows does not physically erase a deleted file from the *hard drive.* Instead, the file is placed in the Recycle Bin. The Recycle Bin holds the deleted files until you give a command to empty it, or it runs out of the space allotted to store deleted files. If you delete files from the hard drive, you can recover them by opening the Recycle Bin, selecting the files you wish to recover, then choosing **File→Restore** from the menu bar.

Hands-On 3.12 Delete Files and a Folder

In this exercise, you will delete one of the files in the Documents folder. Then you will delete the Documents folder itself (erasing the other document file).

1. *Double-click* to open the **Documents** folder on your floppy disk.
   You still have a copy of these files in the Graphics folder, so it is safe to delete the ones in this folder.
2. Click to select one of the document files in the folder; then click the Delete [X] button on the toolbar.
   Depending on how Windows is configured, you may see a prompt asking if you really want to delete the file you selected in Step 2. This is a safeguard to help prevent the accidental deletion of files. This confirmation feature can be switched on and off.
3. Click **Yes** if Windows asks you to confirm deleting the file.
   Windows will briefly display an animation of the files being deleted.
4. Click the Up button on the toolbar to return to the **3½ Floppy (A:)** drive level.
5. Click to select the **Documents** folder; then click the Delete [X] button on the toolbar. Click **Yes** if Windows asks you to confirm deleting the folder and any of the files in it.

TIP!

Always make sure you know what's inside a folder before you delete it.

Checking Space on a Drive

As you create and save files to your floppy disk, the disk may eventually run out of space. Thus you may want to check the space available on the floppy disk from time to time. You can use the *Properties* command to display a pie chart of the available space on a drive. Windows 2000 can also display a pie chart as part of a My Computer or Exploring window, as can all other versions of Windows (95, 98, and NT) if they are configured to do so.

Quick Reference

HOW TO CHECK THE AVAILABLE SPACE ON A DISK DRIVE

Task	Procedure
View a pie chart of how much space is available on a disk drive.	■ Open a *My Computer* or *Exploring* window. ■ Right-click on the desired drive; then select *Properties* from the pop-up menu.

Hands-On 3.13 Check the Properties of Your Floppy Disk

1. Click the Up button on the toolbar to return to the **My Computer** level in the computer system.
2. Follow these steps to view the properties of the floppy disk:

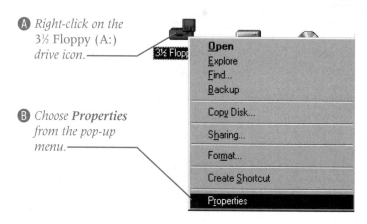

Ⓐ *Right-click on the* 3½ Floppy (A:) *drive icon.*

Ⓑ *Choose* ***Properties*** *from the pop-up menu.*

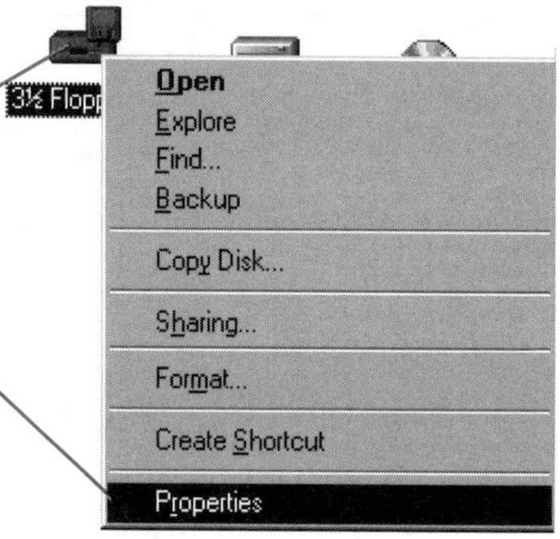

3½ Flopp
Open
Explore
Find...
Backup
Copy Disk...
Sharing...
Format...
Create Shortcut
Properties

A Properties window for the floppy drive will appear. The pie chart and numbers tell you how much space is available on the floppy disk.

3. Close the Properties window.
4. Click (don't double-click) on the **3½ Floppy (A:)** drive.
   Depending on how your version of Windows is configured, you may see a similar pie chart on the left side of the My Computer window.
5. Close the My Computer window.

The Exploring View

Windows gives you two ways to search through files on the computer: the *My Computer* window and the *Exploring* Window. The My Computer window displays these items in a single panel. The Exploring window splits the display into two panels. Below is an example of an Exploring window.

This panel displays the structure of the computer's drives and folders.

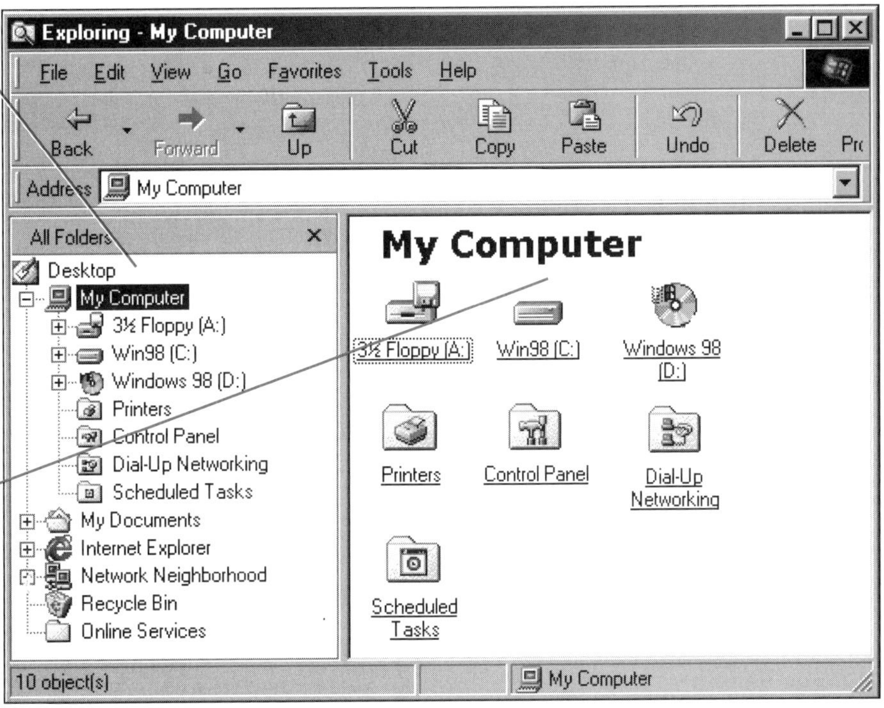

Exploring - My Computer
File Edit View Go Favorites Tools Help
Back
Forward
Up
Cut
Copy
Paste
Undo
Delete
Address
My Computer
All Folders
Desktop
My Computer
3½ Floppy (A:)
Win98 (C:)
Windows 98 (D:)
Printers
Control Panel
Dial-Up Networking
Scheduled Tasks
My Documents
Internet Explorer
Network Neighborhood
Recycle Bin
Online Services
My Computer
3½ Floppy (A:)
Win98 (C:)
Windows 98 (D:)
Printers
Control Panel
Dial-Up Networking
Scheduled Tasks
10 object(s)
My Computer

*This panel displays the contents of any drive or folder that you select for viewing. What you see in this panel is exactly like what you would see in a **My Computer** window.*

Why Two Views?

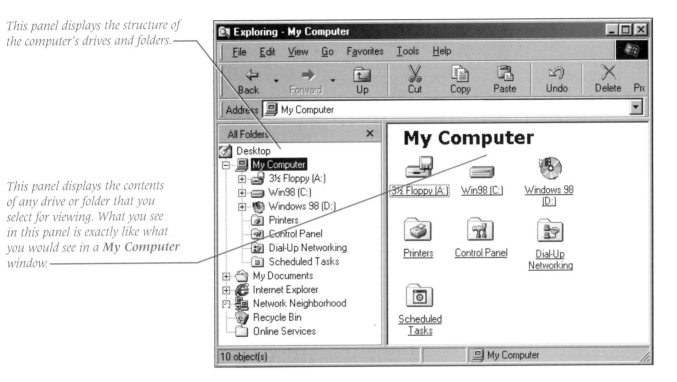

Microsoft researched the way people interact with computers. They found that most beginners are more comfortable with the single-panel view of the My Computer window. It is a simpler, more intuitive view of the computer system. Experienced users tend to prefer the flexibility of the Exploring window. They find it easier to navigate quickly in the computer with the Exploring view. Thus, providing both views satisfies the needs of beginners and experienced users.

You have used the My Computer window for most of the exercises in this lesson. Now you will have an opportunity to try the Exploring window. After you have tried both methods, you can decide which view works best for your file management activities. You may find that you prefer the My Computer view for the first year or two that you work with Windows. That's fine. You can perform the same tasks in either view.

Quick Reference

HOW TO OPEN AN EXPLORING WINDOW

Task	Procedure
Open an Exploring Window.	You can use any of the following methods: ■ *Right-click* on the My Computer icon on the Desktop; then choose *Explore* from the pop-up menu. ■ *Right-click* on the Start button; then choose *Explore* from the pop-up menu. ■ Choose *Start→Programs→Windows Explorer* (or Windows NT Explorer).

Hands-On 3.14 Launch an Exploring Window

In this exercise, you will launch an Exploring window and view your floppy disk. Then you will briefly view folders on the computer's hard drive.

1. Follow these steps to open an Exploring window:

Ⓐ *Right-click on the* **My Computer** *icon near the top-left corner of the Desktop.*

Ⓑ *Choose* Explore *on the pop-up menu.*

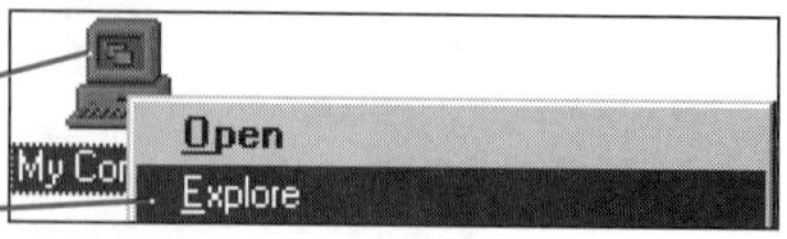

My Cor
Open
Explore

The Exploring window will appear.

2. If the Exploring window is not maximized, click the Maximize button. Set the View to **Large Icons.**
3. Follow these steps to navigate the folders on the **3½ Floppy (A:)** drive in the Exploring window.

Ⓐ *Click the* 3½ Floppy (A:) *icon in the left panel to display the contents of the floppy drive in the right panel of the Exploring window.*

Ⓑ *Click the + to expand the display of the folder inside the* 3½ Floppy (A:) *drive.*

Ⓒ *Click the* Graphics *folder in the left panel.*

Ⓓ *The files inside the* Graphics *folder are displayed in the right panel.*

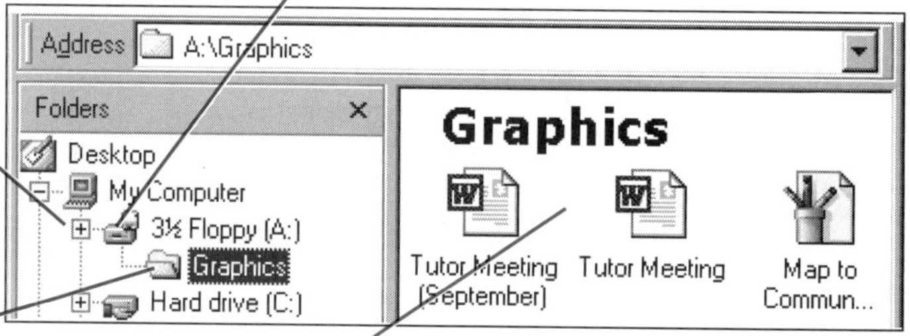

Address
A:\Graphics
Folders
Desktop
My Computer
3½ Floppy (A:)
Graphics
Hard drive (C:)
Graphics
Tutor Meeting (September)
Tutor Meeting
Map to Commun...

The Exploring window makes it easy to navigate directly to folders on a floppy disk or hard drive. However, many beginners do not find it easy to look back and forth from the left panel to the right panel.

Move Files with Drag and Drop

4. Choose **View→List** from the menu bar.
5. Click on the **first** file in the list, and press SHIFT; then click on the **last** file in the list.
   The SHIFT+click *selection technique selects all of the files between your first and last click.*
6. Click on one of the files (do not hold down the SHIFT key).
   Now only the file you clicked is selected. To select more than one file, you must always hold down the SHIFT *or* CTRL *key as you click additional files.*
7. Choose **Edit→Select All** from the menu bar.
   This command selects all of the files displayed in the right panel. This command is faster than the CTRL+Click *or* SHIFT+Click *methods when you want to select all of the files in a folder.*
8. Choose **View→Large Icons** from the menu bar.

9. Follow these steps to move the files back to the top level (root) of the floppy drive with the Drag-and-Drop technique:

Ⓐ *Point to one of the selected files in the right panel, press and hold the right mouse button, and drag the files onto the* 3½ Floppy (A:) *icon in the left panel.*

Ⓑ *Release the right mouse button when the* 3½ Floppy (A:) *icon appears to be selected (shaded) as shown here.*

Ⓒ *Choose **Move Here** from the pop-up menu.*

Folders
Desktop
My Computer
3½ Floppy (A:)
Graphics
Hard drive (C:)
Printers
Control Panel
Web Folders
Graphics
Move Here
Copy Here
Create Shortcut(s) Here
Cancel
Map to Commun...

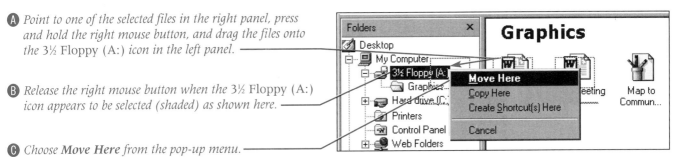

When the Move command is completed, the Graphics folder will be empty.

10. Follow these steps to delete the empty Graphics folder:

Ⓐ *Click to select the* 3½ Floppy (A:) *icon in the left panel.*

Ⓑ *Choose **View→Arrange Icons→By Name** from the menu bar.*

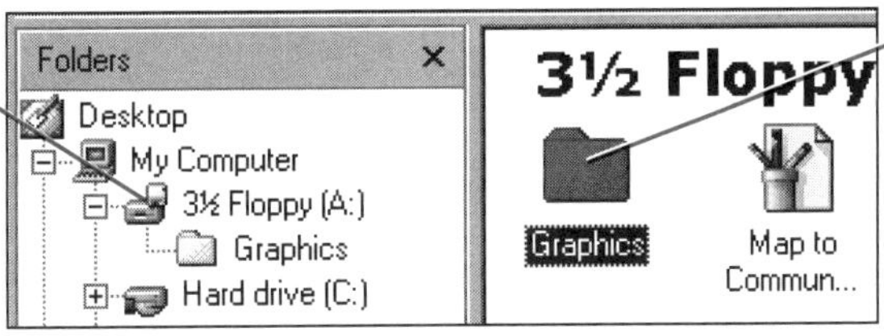

Folders
Desktop
My Computer
3½ Floppy (A:)
Graphics
Hard drive (C:)
3½ Floppy
Graphics
Map to Commun...

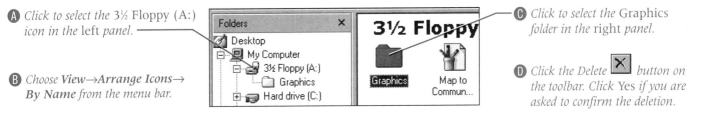

Ⓒ *Click to select the* Graphics *folder in the right panel.*

Ⓓ *Click the Delete* ☒ *button on the toolbar. Click Yes if you are asked to confirm the deletion.*

Explore the Hard Drive

Compared to your floppy disk, a typical hard drive stores many thousands more files in a much more complex folder structure. Now you will browse a few of the folders on a hard drive.

10. Follow these steps to browse folders on the hard drive:

Ⓐ *Click the plus sign (+) next to the* Hard drive (C:) *to expand the view of folders on this drive. The C: drive may not be named the same as the illustration.*

Ⓑ *Click the plus sign (+) next to the* Program Files *folder to expand the view of other folders inside this folder. This folder holds most of the application programs installed on the computer. There may be dozens of folders here.*

Ⓒ *Click to select the* Accessories *folder. Depending on the version of **Windows** you are running and what has been installed, there may only be one or two items in this folder. The contents of the* Accessories *folder is now displayed in the right panel.*

Ⓓ *Click the minus sign (–) beside the* Program Files *folder to collapse the display of folders inside it.*

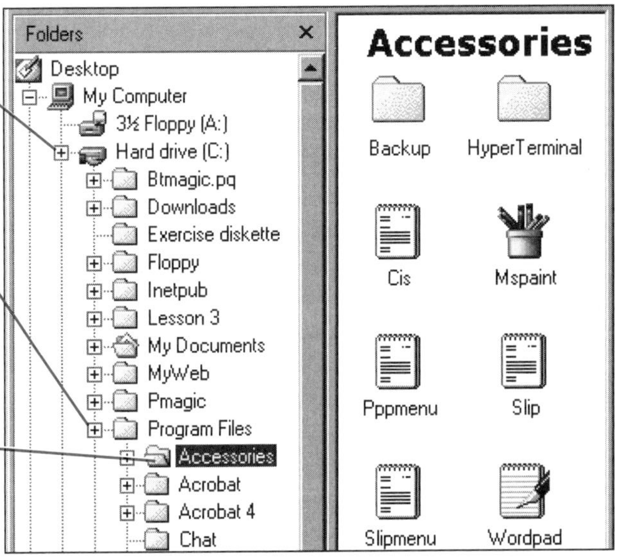

Folders
Desktop
My Computer
3½ Floppy (A:)
Hard drive (C:)
Btmagic.pq
Downloads
Exercise diskette
Floppy
Inetpub
Lesson 3
My Documents
MyWeb
Pmagic
Program Files
Accessories
Acrobat
Acrobat 4
Chat
Accessories
Backup
HyperTerminal
Cis
Mspaint
Pppmenu
Slip
Slipmenu
Wordpad

Program Files
Accessories

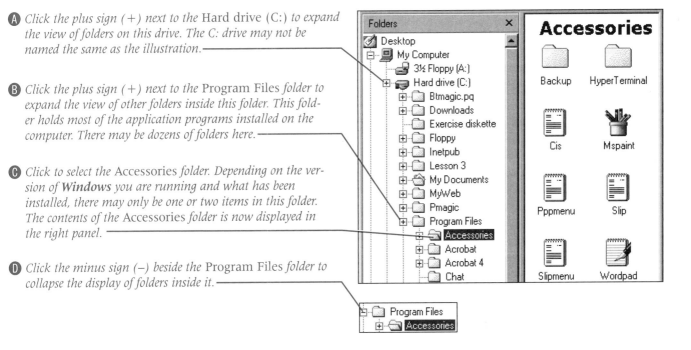

12. Close ☒ the Exploring window.

Concepts Review

True/False Questions

1.	A Contents search of online Help lets you locate Help topics by typing keywords.	TRUE	FALSE
2.	A *My Computer* window lets you view the files and folders on the computer.	TRUE	FALSE
3.	Windows organizes drives and folders in a hierarchy.	TRUE	FALSE
4.	The CTRL key can be used to randomly select a group of files.	TRUE	FALSE
5.	Folders can have subfolders within them.	TRUE	FALSE
6.	You can use the *Cut* and *Paste* commands to move files.	TRUE	FALSE
7.	Files are sent to the Recycle Bin when they are deleted from floppy disks.	TRUE	FALSE
8.	The *Properties* command can display how much space is left on a floppy disk.	TRUE	FALSE
9.	An Exploring window gives you a two-panel view of files and folders.	TRUE	FALSE
10.	A quick way to open a file is to double-click on it in a My Computer windows.	TRUE	FALSE

Multiple-Choice Questions

1. Which of the following methods can be used to view drives and folders on the computer?
   a. Double-click the My Computer icon on the Desktop.
   b. Double-click the My Documents folder on the Desktop (Windows 98 and 2000 only).
   c. Right-click the My Computer icon on the Desktop and choose Explore.
   d. All of the above

2. Which of the following views displays columns with the filename, size, type, and modified date?
   a. Large Icons
   b. Small Icons
   c. List
   d. Details

3. Which command is used to create a new folder?
   a. File→Folder→Create
   b. File→New→Folder
   c. Click the  button.
   d. All of the above

4. If one filename is already selected in a My Computer or Exploring window, which key could be used to select several more files by clicking just once?
   a. SHIFT
   b. ALT
   c. CTRL
   d. None of the above

Skill Builders

Skill Builder 3.1 Work with Online Help

In this exercise, you will practice looking up various topics in Windows' online Help.

1. **Click** the  button, and choose **Help** from the Start menu.
2. Click the **Index** tab in the Help Topics dialog box.
3. Start typing the search keywords **`recycle bin`**. You will notice that the phrase *Recycle Bin* appears after you type the letters **recy**.
   You usually only need to type the first few characters of the desired search phrase.
4. **Double-click** to open the topic according to the operating system you are running:
   - Windows 95: **emptying**
   - Windows 98: **Recycle Bin**
   - Windows NT: **Recycle Bin;** then choose **To empty the Recycle bin.**
   - Windows 2000: **emptying**
5. Read the topic. If you are running **Windows 95** or **NT,** click the **Help Topics** button near the top-left corner of the window to return to the Index search window.
6. Use the **Index** search method to get Help on the following topics.

Windows Version	Search Keyword(s)	Help Topics to Open
Windows 95 or Windows NT	My Computer	opening files or folders
	Windows Explorer	changing the way items are displayed
	Copying	files or folders→copying a file or folder
	drag-and-drop	using drag and drop instead of menus
Windows 98	My Computer	opening files→to open a file or folder
	Windows Explorer	checking disk space
	copying files, folders	overview
	dragging files, folders	to move a file or folder
Windows 2000	My Computer	opening files or folders
	Windows Explorer	copying files or folders
	copying files	overview → copy or move a file or folder
	dragging files	overview → move files by dragging

These Help topics will give you tips and alternatives to the methods you have already learned.

Use the Contents Search Method

7. Click the **Contents** tab.
8. Choose a "book" according to the operating system you are running:
   - **Windows 95 and NT:** How to: Working with files and folders
   - **Windows 98:** Exploring your computer: Files and folders: Managing Files
   - **Windows 2000:** Files and folders
9. Locate five different Help topics in the book listed above for your operating system. Take the time to open the Help topics and read them.
10. Experiment with Help until you are confident that you can find topics when the need arises.
11. Close the Help window ☒.

Skill Builder 3.2 Work with Files and Folders

In this exercise, you will create a new folder and copy files to it.

1. Open a **My Computer** window, and double-click the **3½ Floppy (A:)** drive to display the files on your exercise diskette. If necessary, maximize the window.
2. Double-click the **Map to Community Center** file.
   The Paint program, or another program assigned to open Paint files will start, and your map will be displayed in the program window.
3. Close ☒ the Paint (or other program) window. Click **No** if you are asked to save the file.
4. Choose the **Details** view; then click on the **Modified** heading to sort the files **by date.**
5. Create a **folder** on your exercise diskette named **Backup.** If the folder name is not selected when you create it, **right-click** on the folder icon; then use the **Rename** command to change the name.
6. Follow the remaining instructions for the version of Windows you are running.

Windows 95, 98, and NT 4.0

1. **Sort** the list of files by **size;** then **select** the two smallest files on your diskette.
2. Click the Copy button on the My Computer toolbar.
3. *Double-click* the **Backup** folder.
4. Click the Paste button on the My Computer toolbar.
   After the Copy operation is completed, the two files you had selected should appear in the folder.
5. Click the Up button on the My Computer toolbar.
   The two files that you copied should still be visible at the top level (root) of your exercise diskette. For the moment, these files exist in two locations on the floppy disk.

6. Click to select the **Backup** folder; then **delete** the folder.
7. Close the My Computer window.

Windows 2000

1. **Sort** the list of files by **size;** then **select** the two smallest files on your diskette.
2. Click the Copy to button on the toolbar.
3. Follow these steps to select the destination of the Copy command:

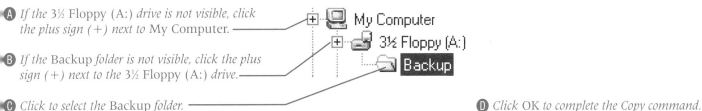

Ⓐ *If the* 3½ Floppy (A:) *drive is not visible, click the plus sign (+) next to* My Computer.

Ⓑ *If the* Backup *folder is not visible, click the plus sign (+) next to the* 3½ Floppy (A:) *drive.*

Ⓒ *Click to select the* Backup *folder.*

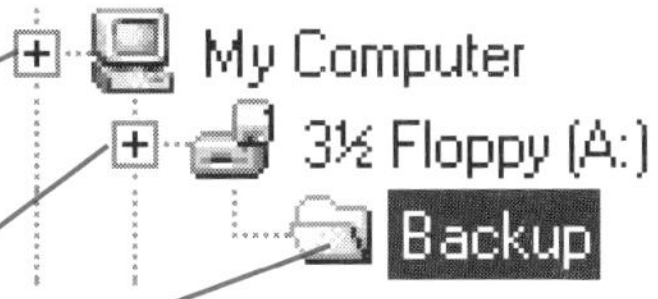
My Computer
3½ Floppy (A:)
Backup

Ⓓ *Click* OK *to complete the Copy command.*

4. Double-click to open the **Backup** folder, and verify that the files were copied.
   The two files you had selected should appear in the folder.
5. Click the Up button on the My Computer toolbar.
6. Click to select the **Backup** folder, and then **delete** the folder.
7. Close the My Computer window.

Skill Builder 3.3 Check the Hard Drive Properties

1. In a **My Computer** window, **right-click** on the **(C:)** drive icon; then choose Properties from the pop-up menu.
2. Write down how much free space there is left on the hard drive: ____________
   There will probably be many megabytes, or even gigabytes, of space available on the hard drive.

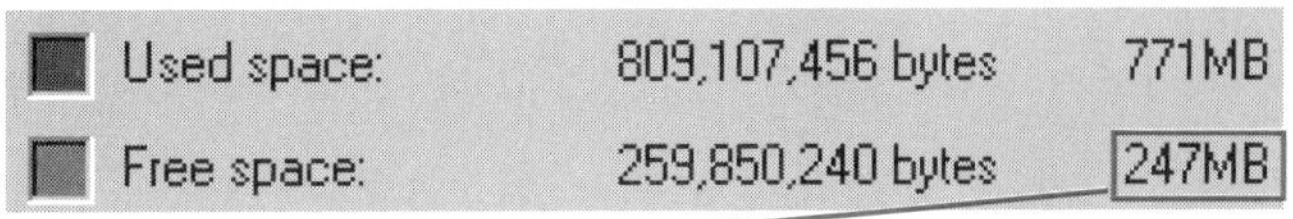
Used space:
809,107,456 bytes
771MB
Free space:
259,850,240 bytes
247MB

Look at the number on the right.

3. Click **Cancel** to close the Properties window.
4. Make sure your exercise diskette is in the floppy drive.
5. Check the **properties** of your exercise diskette.
6. Write down how much free space is left on your exercise diskette: ____________
   The amount of space left your diskette will be quite small compared to the hard drive.
7. Click **Cancel** to close the Properties window.
8. Close the My Computer window.

Assessments

Assessment 3.1 Work with Online Help

1. Start the WordPad program.
2. Type your name at the top of the WordPad document, then tap ENTER twice, type **`Shutting Down the Computer,`** then tap ENTER.
3. Start Windows online Help and look up the following topic: **shutting down the com puter.** (Do not try to look up the topic in WordPad's online Help.)
4. Arrange the **Help** and **WordPad** windows one above the other or side-by-side, so that the Help window is visible as you type in WordPad. Remember that you cannot change the size of a *maximized* window.
5. In WordPad, type the first line of instructions for the Help topic; then tap the ENTER key twice.
6. Type **`Creating a Folder`**; then tap ENTER.
7. Look up the following topic in Windows online Help: **creating a folder**
8. In WordPad, type the first line of instructions for the Help topic; then tap the ENTER key twice.
9. **Save** the WordPad document to your exercise diskette with the name: **`Online Help`**
10. **Print** the document, and turn it in to the instructor for grading.
11. Close ☒ the WordPad and Help windows.

Assessment 3.2 Create a Folder and Copy Files

1. Open a My Computer or Exploring window.
2. **Create** a folder on your exercise diskette named **`Lesson 3`**.
3. Copy the **Tutor Meeting** and the **Tutor Meeting (September)** files to the new folder.
4. Close ☒ the My Computer or Exploring window.

UNIT 2

Internet Explorer 5.0

This unit covers the basics of browsing the World Wide Web with Internet Explorer, including how to navigate the Web with Web addresses (URLs) and hyperlinks. In addition, you will learn how to find Web sites with an Internet search engine and how to print Web pages.

Browsing the Web

The World Wide Web (or "the Web") is one of the most dynamic and exciting service on the Internet. The Web organizes information onto pages connected by objects on those pages called hyperlinks, which you can click to jump to other pages of information. Thousands of new pages are added to the Internet every day. In order to view pages on the Web, you use an application program called a Web browser. Microsoft's Internet Explorer is one of the two most popular Web browsers. In this lesson, you will learn the basics of browsing the Web with Internet Explorer. You will also learn how to use an Internet search engine to find Web pages on almost any topic among the billion or more Web pages now online.

In This Lesson

Case Study

Jasmine has just begun to learn how to work with a Web browser. She has used it a little at the library and the open computer lab at her college. She's enrolled in a computer class this semester. Her instructor tells the class that the next topic will be the history of computers. He hands out a page with some questions about the history of computers. The instructor says there are many Web sites on the Internet with this sort of information, but that he wants the class to begin with the two sites listed on the handout. Jasmine has enjoyed browsing the Web in the past, but this is the first time she's been asked to actually get some work done. The instructor expects her to turn in a page with at least five interesting facts about computers at the next class meeting. Jasmine heads to the computer lab after class and begins looking through the Web pages.

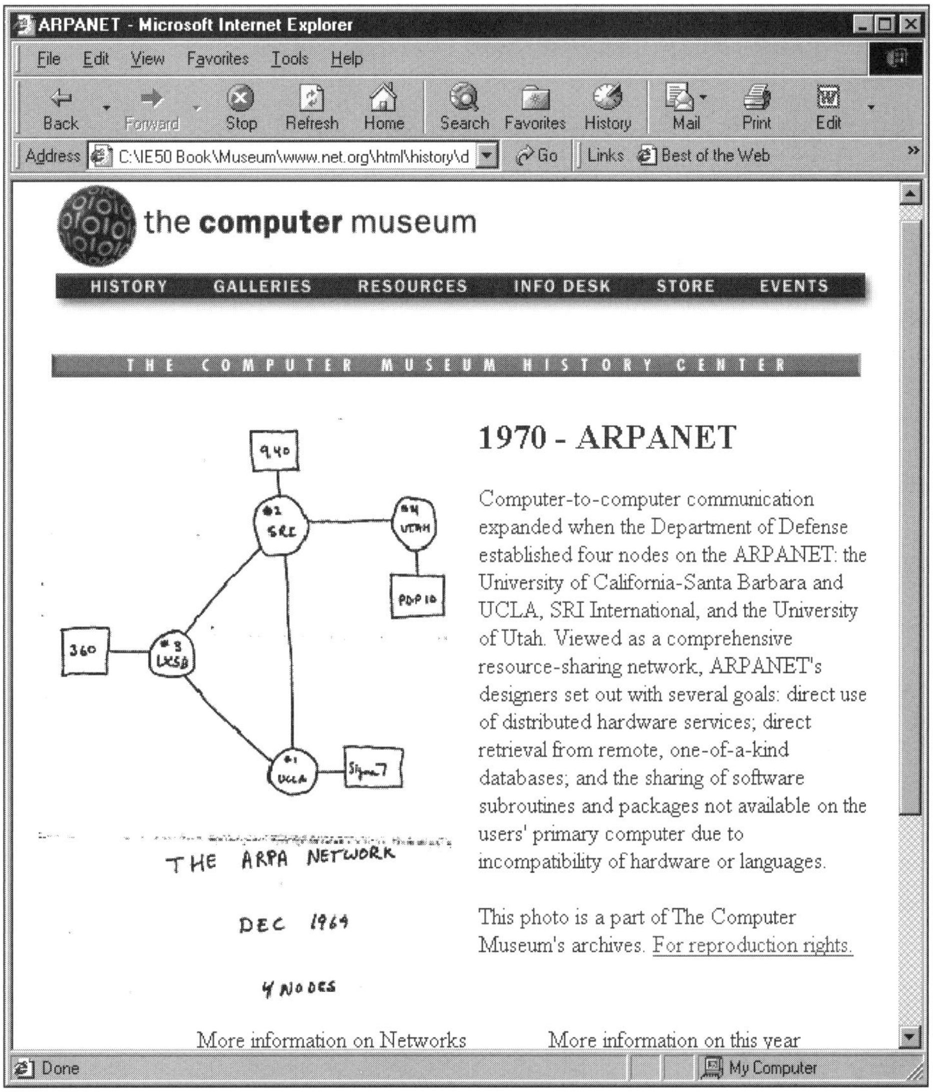

ARPANET - Microsoft Internet Explorer
File Edit View Favorites Tools Help
Back Forward Stop Refresh Home Search Favorites History Mail Print Edit
Address C:\IE50 Book\Museum\www.net.org\html\history\d
Go Links Best of the Web
the computer museum
HISTORY GALLERIES RESOURCES INFO DESK STORE EVENTS
THE COMPUTER MUSEUM HISTORY CENTER
1970 - ARPANET
Computer-to-computer communication expanded when the Department of Defense established four nodes on the ARPANET: the University of California-Santa Barbara and UCLA, SRI International, and the University of Utah. Viewed as a comprehensive resource-sharing network, ARPANET's designers set out with several goals: direct use of distributed hardware services; direct retrieval from remote, one-of-a-kind databases; and the sharing of software subroutines and packages not available on the users' primary computer due to incompatibility of hardware or languages.
This photo is a part of The Computer Museum's archives. For reproduction rights.
THE ARPA NETWORK
DEC 1969
4 NODES
More information on Networks
More information on this year
Done
My Computer

At Web sites such as the Computer Museum, Jasmine can learn about topics like the early predecessor to the Internet, ARPANET.

Launching Internet Explorer

Internet Explorer is an application program similar to a word processor or spreadsheet. It is designed to help you browse Web pages on the Internet. There are several ways to launch Internet Explorer. When you start the browser, it will either begin searching for a page on the Internet, or it may look for a page that is on your hard drive.

Quick Reference

LAUNCHING INTERNET EXPLORER

Task	Procedure
Launch Internet Explorer from the Quick Launch toolbar.	Click the **Internet Explorer** button on the Quick Launch toolbar next to the Start button.
Launch Internet Explorer from the Start menu.	Click **Start→Programs→Internet Explorer**

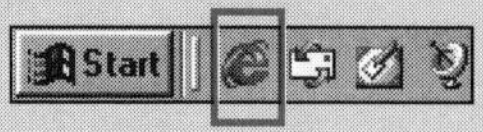
Start

Hands-On 4.1 Launch the Internet Explorer

1. Choose **Start→Programs→Internet Explorer** from the Start menu.
   Internet Explorer will display a Web page. This will probably be the Home page of the institution where you are taking this class.
2. If necessary, Maximize the Internet Explorer window.

The Internet Explorer Window

Like many other application programs, the Internet Explorer has menus and a toolbar that allow you to give commands. The illustration below points out some of the most significant features of the Internet Explorer window. You will use many of these features in this lesson.

You can place buttons for Web addresses on the ***Links*** *bar.*

The Menu bar

The Toolbar contains buttons for frequently used commands.

You use the Address bar to navigate to Web sites.

The browser window displays the content of Web pages.

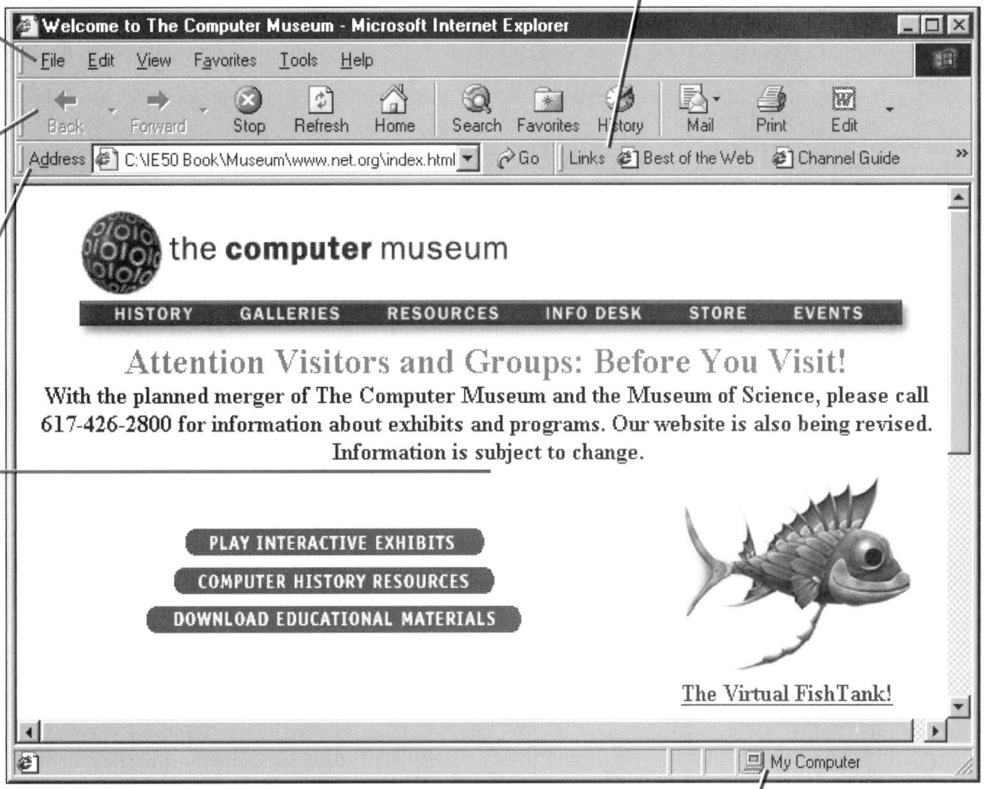

Welcome to The Computer Museum - Microsoft Internet Explorer
File Edit View Favorites Tools Help
Back Forward Stop Refresh Home Search Favorites History Mail Print Edit
Address C:\IE50 Book\Museum\www.net.org\index.html
Go
Links Best of the Web Channel Guide
the computer museum
HISTORY GALLERIES RESOURCES INFO DESK STORE EVENTS
Attention Visitors and Groups: Before You Visit!
With the planned merger of The Computer Museum and the Museum of Science, please call 617-426-2800 for information about exhibits and programs. Our website is also being revised. Information is subject to change.
PLAY INTERACTIVE EXHIBITS
COMPUTER HISTORY RESOURCES
DOWNLOAD EDUCATIONAL MATERIALS
The Virtual FishTank!
My Computer

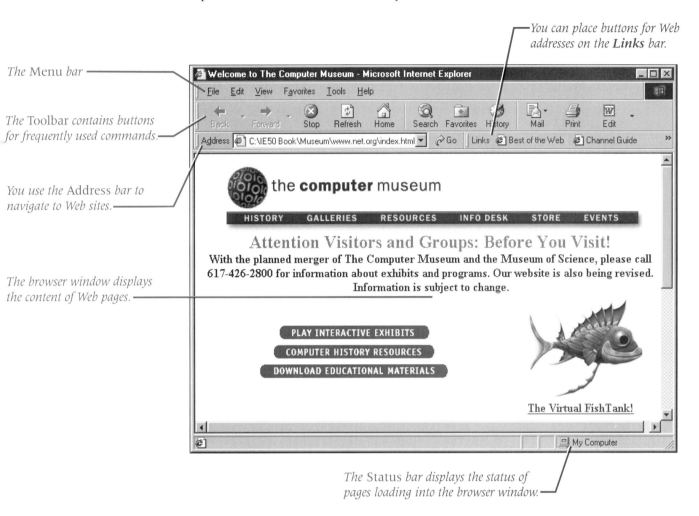

The Status bar displays the status of pages loading into the browser window.

The Home Page

When you launch Internet Explorer, the first page you see displayed is called the *home page.* This page is important, since it is the easiest page to navigate to. Internet Explorer allows you to set any page on the Web as your home page. The home page you are viewing now may be the MSN (Microsoft Network) Web site, or it may be set to a page for the school at which you are studying.

Customizable Home Pages

TIP!

The Lesson 4 Web page contains links to several popular Web portal sites.

There are many Web sites that are designed to serve as your initial point of entry to the Web when you launch Internet Explorer. These sites are often called *portals.* You can even customize the portal's home page to display topics that interest you. For example, you can customize the home page to display breaking news, weather, sports scores, and other information.

Home Page
Make this your home page
Personalize this page

This option on the MSN.com page is typical of many home page sites.

About HTML

Web pages are designed with a programming language called *HTML* (**H**yper**T**ext **M**arkup **L**anguage). Most Web page files end with a filename extension of .htm or .html. These extensions help the computer know what type of data the file contains and thus which program it should use to open the file. The diagram below displays a small example of the HTML code typically behind the Web pages you view.

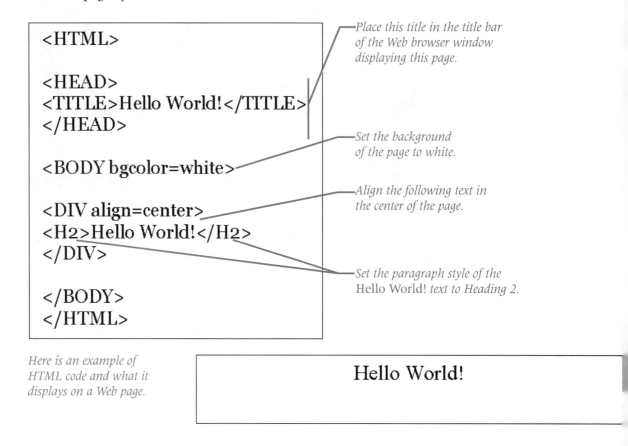

```
<HTML>

<HEAD>
<TITLE>Hello World!</TITLE>
</HEAD>

<BODY bgcolor=white>

<DIV align=center>
<H2>Hello World!</H2>
</DIV>

</BODY>
</HTML>
```

Place this title in the title bar of the Web browser window displaying this page.

Set the background of the page to white.

Align the following text in the center of the page.

Set the paragraph style of the Hello World! *text to Heading 2.*

Here is an example of HTML code and what it displays on a Web page.

Hello World!

Navigating the Web

In order to navigate through the Web, you need to tell your browser which sites you wish to view. Every page on the Web has a unique identifying address, called a *URL* (Universal Resource Locator). When you enter a URL in the Internet Explorer's address bar, the browser loads the Web page contained at that address.

URLs

A URL (pronounced "you are el") is essentially a mailing address for a Web page. Similar to residential addresses, URLs contain several parts that help your browser find the exact page you are looking for. Every URL contains a *domain name.* A URL may also contain file and folder names that point to a specific Web page. If page names and folder names are part of a URL, each is separated by a normal slash (/)—*not* the DOS backslash (\).

The components of a URL are shown below:

TIP!

When you type a domain name, you can leave out the http:// *protocol portion of the URL.*

HTTP://www.labyrinth-pub.com/windows98/home.htm

protocol (HTTP://) — *World Wide Web* (www.) — *domain name* (labyrinth-pub.com) — *folder name* (windows98) — *page name* (home.htm)

Domains

A domain is a particular computer network that is connected to the Internet. A domain can consist of a single computer or hundreds of computers networked together. Every computer connected to the Internet is part of a domain. Most domains have a domain name to make them easier to identify. The most basic identifier for a domain is its top-level domain.

Top-Level Domains

The characters that follow the period at the end of a domain name indicate the top-level domain a Web site belongs to. There are many types of top-level domains. When domain names were first created, several top-level domains were designated. Additional top-level domains have been added to the list over the years. The table below lists several different top-level domains.

Top-level domain	Description	Domain name	Organization
.com	A commercial, for-profit Web site	microsoft.com sears.com	Microsoft, Inc. Sears, Roebuck & Co.
.edu	An educational institution	berkeley.edu stanford.edu	U.C. Berkeley Stanford University
.gov	A government agency	irs.gov state.gov	Internal Revenue Service US Secretary of State
.org	A Web site for a nonprofit organization	npr.org amnesty.org	National Public Radio Amnesty International
.mil	A military organization	navy.mil	The US Navy
.net	An organization dedicated to providing network resources	earthlink.net technet.net	The Earthlink ISP New Mexico Technet
.jp	An organization based in Japan	japantimes.co.jp yahoo.co.jp	Japan Times Publications Yahoo! Japan
.ca	An organization based in Canada	canada.gc.ca aircanada.ca	Government of Canada Air Canada (airline)

Jasmine's teacher has handed out two Web addresses to Web pages in the assignment. Jasmine must navigate to those pages in order to view the information. Jasmine can learn a bit about where the pages are and what they are about just by interpreting the domain names of the URLs. For example, if its URL contains *.edu* in the domain name, Jasmine knows that the Web page is located at an educational institution.

Navigating with the Address Bar

The most basic control for navigating the Web with Internet Explorer is the *Address bar*. This bar allows you to type the URL of the Web page you wish to visit. It also lists the most recent Web sites that have been visited. This can be a handy shortcut when you wish to return to a Web site a day or two later. The Address bar is just one of several shortcuts that help you navigate quickly to favorite sites or sites you have viewed recently.

Labyrinth Publications Home Page - Microsoft Internet Ex
File Edit View Favorites Tools Help
Back
Forward
Stop
Refresh
Home
Search
Address
www.labyrinth-pub.com
Go

You can navigate to any site on the Web by typing its URL in the Address bar*.*

Navigating to Pages

Like a computer's hard drive, the content of sophisticated Web sites is organized into folders. If you know the folder a page is located in and the name of the page, you can navigate directly to that particular page with the Address bar.

Examples: www.offtowork.com/ie/sample.htm

www.labyrinth-pub.com/books/win98/index.htm

AutoComplete

As you type a URL in the Address bar, you may see it display some Web addresses in a drop-down list. This is the *AutoComplete* feature at work. AutoComplete keeps track of all the Web sites you have visited recently. If you start to type the address of one of these sites, AutoComplete displays other URLs similar to what you are entering. If you want to accept a URL in the AutoComplete box, simply click on it with the mouse.

Address
www.lab
Go
http://www.labyrinth-pub.com
http://www.labyrinth-pub.com/books/orders/order.htm
http://www.labyrinth-pub.com/books/os.htm
http://www.labyrinth-pub.com/books/win98/features_bot.htm
http://www.labyrinth-pub.com/books/win98/index.htm

You simply point and click to navigate to a URL displayed in the AutoComplete list.

Quick Reference

NAVIGATING WITH THE ADDRESS BAR

Task	Procedure
Navigate by typing a URL.	■ Click in the Address bar to highlight the current URL. ■ Type the new URL, and tap the ENTER key.
Navigate with AutoComplete.	■ Click in the Address bar to highlight the current URL. ■ Start to type the new URL until you see the AutoComplete list appear with the domain you are navigating to. ■ Tap the Down arrow ↓ key to select the URL you want; then tap the ENTER key, or click on the desired URL with the mouse.

Hands-On 4.2 Navigate to Sites Via the Address Bar

1. Follow these steps to adjust the size of the Address bar.

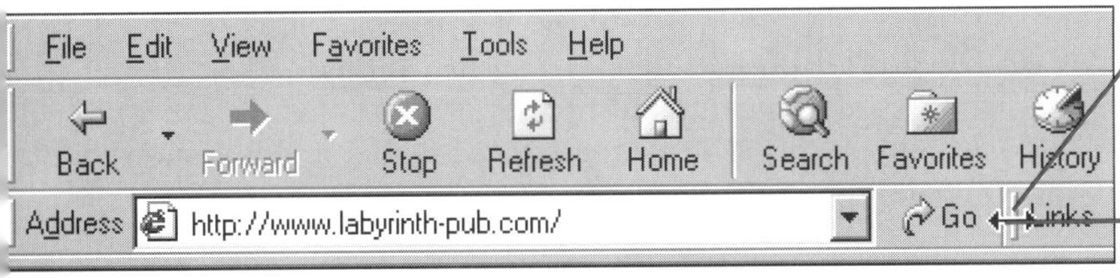

File Edit View Favorites Tools Help
Back
Forward
Stop
Refresh
Home
Search
Favorites
History
Address
http://www.labyrinth-pub.com/
Go
Links

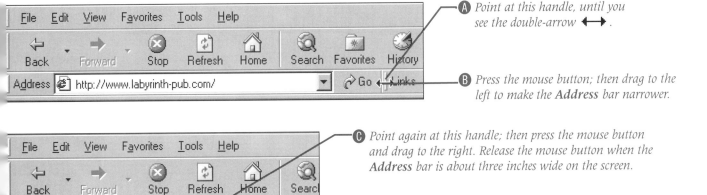

Ⓐ *Point at this handle, until you see the double-arrow ⟷.*

Ⓑ *Press the mouse button; then drag to the left to make the **Address** bar narrower.*

File Edit View Favorites Tools Help
Back
Forward
Stop
Refresh
Home
Address
http://www.la
Go
Links
Best of the

Ⓒ *Point again at this handle; then press the mouse button and drag to the right. Release the mouse button when the **Address** bar is about three inches wide on the screen.*

(Continued on the next page)

2. Follow these steps to navigate to a Web site.

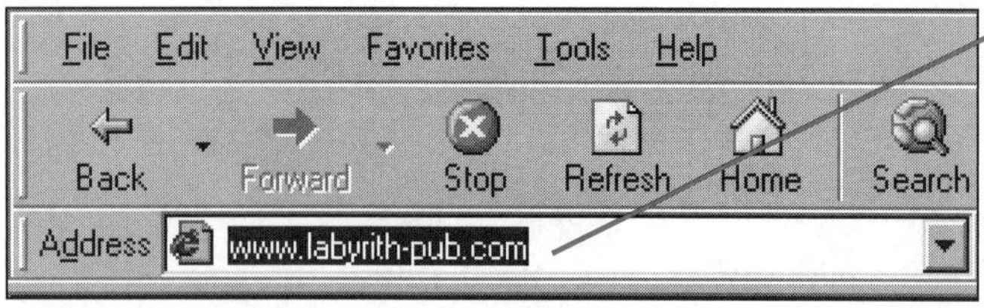

File Edit View Favorites Tools Help
Back
Forward
Stop
Refresh
Home
Search
Address
www.labyrith-pub.com

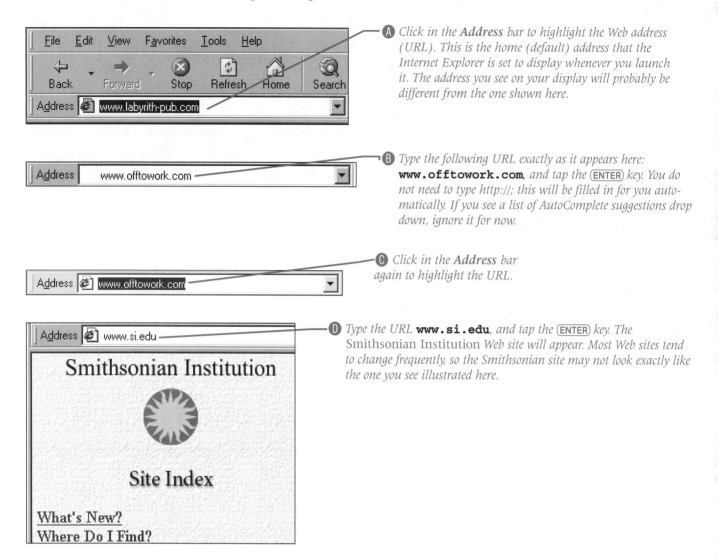

Ⓐ *Click in the **Address** bar to highlight the Web address (URL). This is the home (default) address that the Internet Explorer is set to display whenever you launch it. The address you see on your display will probably be different from the one shown here.*

Address
www.offtowork.com

Ⓑ *Type the following URL exactly as it appears here:* **`www.offtowork.com`**, *and tap the* (ENTER) *key. You do not need to type http://; this will be filled in for you automatically. If you see a list of AutoComplete suggestions drop down, ignore it for now.*

Address
www.offtowork.com

Ⓒ *Click in the **Address** bar again to highlight the URL.*

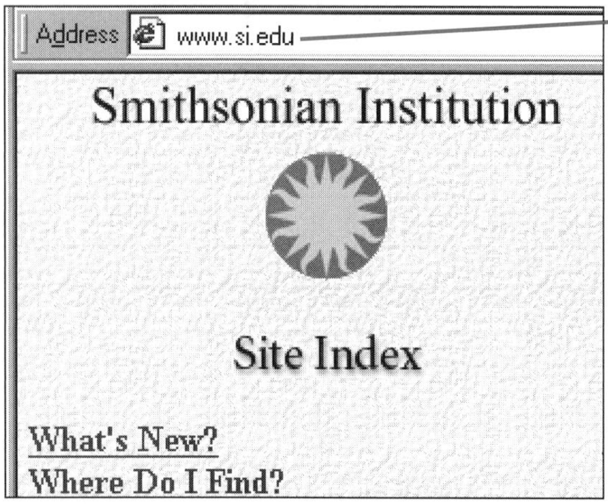

Address
www.si.edu
Smithsonian Institution
Site Index
What's New?
Where Do I Find?

Ⓓ *Type the URL* **`www.si.edu`**, *and tap the* (ENTER) *key. The* Smithsonian Institution *Web site will appear. Most Web sites tend to change frequently, so the Smithsonian site may not look exactly like the one you see illustrated here.*

Try AutoComplete

3. Follow these steps to navigate to a Web site with AutoComplete.

Ⓐ *Click in the **Address** bar to highlight the current URL, and start to type* **`www.offt`**. *AutoComplete will usually display a list of Web addresses that match the first few letters you type.*

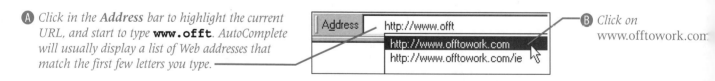

Address
http://www.offt
http://www.offtowork.com
http://www.offtowork.com/ie

Ⓑ *Click on* www.offtowork.com

4. Click in the **Address bar,** and tap the (END) key on the keyboard.
   This removes the selection from the URL. Now you can type at the end of the current URL without the URL being deleted. In the next step, you will navigate to a specific page on the Web site.

5. Type **`modems.htm`** at the end of the URL, and tap the (ENTER) key. Make sure you type the entire word in *lowercase* letters (most URLs are case-sensitive).
   This navigates you to a Web page about modems.

6. Click in the **Address bar** to highlight the current URL; begin to type **`www.si`**, and then pause. Watch for AutoComplete to display a list of URLs, then tap the Down arrow ↓ key on the keyboard to select *http://www.si.edu*. Now navigate to that URL by tapping ENTER.
   You should now be back at the Smithsonian Institution Web site. This technique lets you keep your hands on the keyboard as you select the AutoComplete URL suggestion.
7. Click in the **Address bar** to highlight the current URL, and type **`www.offtowork.com`**. Tap the Forward Slash (/) key; then tap the **`M`** key.
   AutoComplete displays the pages that start with the letter M. *This makes the AutoComplete list much shorter.*
8. Tap the Down arrow ↓ key to choose the *www.offtowork.com/modems.htm* page. Then tap ENTER.
   You are back at the About Modems page. Leave the Internet Explorer window open. You will continue using it in a moment.

Adjusting the Display of Web Pages

You can adjust the size of text displayed in Web pages at any time. For example, you can make the text display larger if it is difficult to read at the normal (medium) setting. It is also possible to make the Internet Explorer window fill the entire monitor, which allows more room to display the content of the Web pages you are browsing.

Quick Reference

ADJUSTING THE VIEW OF WEB PAGES

Task	Procedure
Adjust the size of text.	■ Choose **View→Text Size** from the menu bar. ■ Select the desired size of text from the options menu.
Set Internet Explorer in Full Screen mode.	■ Choose **View→Full Screen** from the menu bar, or tap the F11 function key on the keyboard. ■ Click the Restore button in the top-right corner of the screen to exit full screen mode, or tap the F11 function key again.

Hands-On 4.3 Adjust the Display of Text

1. Follow these steps to adjust the display of text in the Internet Explorer window.

Ⓐ *Choose **View→Text Size→Largest** from the menu bar.*

Ⓑ *If you do not see the illustration, tap the* PGDN *key. Notice that the text in the diagram did not change size. This is because this "text" is a picture of the letters rather than text that can change size.*

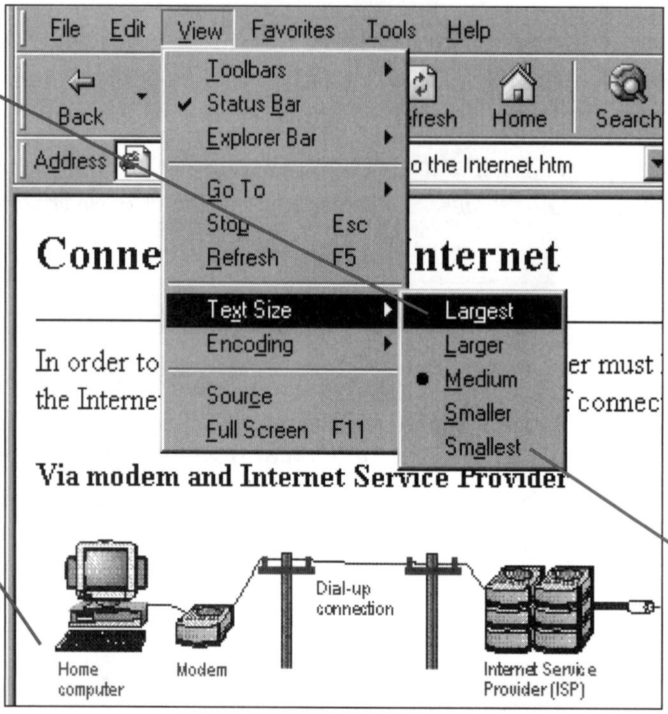

File Edit View Favorites Tools Help
Toolbars
Status Bar
Explorer Bar
Go To
Stop Esc
Refresh F5
Text Size
Encoding
Source
Full Screen F11
Largest
Larger
Medium
Smaller
Smallest
Back
fresh
Home
Search
Address
o the Internet.htm
Conne
nternet
In order to
the Interne
er must
connec
Via modem and Internet Service Provider
Dial-up connection
Home computer
Modem
Internet Service Provider (ISP)

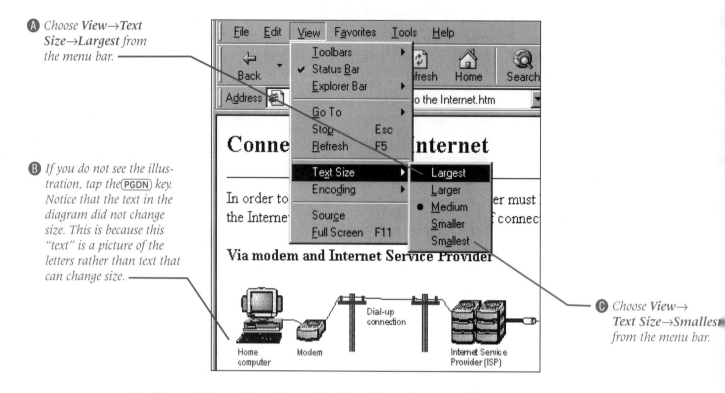

Ⓒ *Choose **View→Text Size→Smallest** from the menu bar.*

2. Choose **View→Text Size→Medium** from the menu bar.
This is the default size for text in Internet Explorer and should work well under most conditions. However, as you browse the Web in this and other lessons, you can change the text size if it makes it easier for you to read the text on Web pages.

3. Choose **View→Full Screen** from the menu bar.
The Internet Explorer window will immediately cover the entire screen. Notice that the Internet Explorer window covers even the Windows Taskbar, which is usually at the bottom of the screen. The navigation buttons at the top-left corner are also smaller. These adjustments provide the maximum amount of space for browsing the content of the Web pages.

4. Click the **restore** button in the *top-right corner* of the screen to restore the Internet Explorer window to the size it had before you gave the Full Screen command.

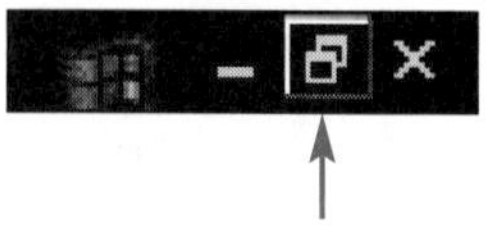

5. Tap the F11 function key at the top of the keyboard.
This function key is a handy shortcut to switch to full-screen mode.

6. Tap the F11 function key again to restore the Internet Explorer window.
This type of command is called a toggle *because tapping the same key toggles you between the full screen and restore commands. Leave the Internet Explorer window open.*

Navigating with Hyperlinks

After URLs, a *hyperlink* is the most basic navigation tool you can use to navigate on the Web. A hyperlink is essentially an object on a Web page that points to some other location on the same page, a different page, or even a different Web site altogether. Web pages with hyperlinks are an example of *hypertext*. Ted Nelson coined this term in 1963, while a sociology student at Harvard. He envisioned a book with hypertext connections to all human knowledge. Hyperlinks usually navigate you to a Web page or a specific location on a Web page. Some hyperlinks may perform other functions, such as generating an email message that is addressed automatically to a particular recipient.

Once Jasmine has navigated to one of the Web sites assigned to her, she also needs to navigate inside the Web site. If Jasmine had to type out the URL for each page she wanted to view, she'd be in for a lot of typing! Fortunately, hyperlinks make it easy to navigate Web pages by simply pointing and clicking.

Examples of Hyperlinks

A hyperlink can take on several forms. It may be some text on a Web page. A hyperlink can also be an image or part of an image. There is one feature that will be consistent for *all* forms of hyperlinks. Whenever you place the mouse pointer over a hyperlink, the mouse pointer will change its shape to a hand. Some examples of hyperlinks are displayed below. You will work with several types of hyperlinks in the following Hands-On exercise.

- Text hyperlinks: *Computer Museum* *David Gutterson* *email the author*
- Buttons:

Web Lessons
About Us
Brewing wisdom

- Navigation bars (navbars)

HOME
BOOKS
SOFTWARE
FOR EDUCATORS
DOWNLOAD
CONTACT US
top
news
tutorials
for students
place an order
about us

HISTORY
GALLERIES
RESOURCES
INFO DESK
STORE
EVENTS

TIP!

If you think an element on a Web page may be a hyperlink, point at it. If the mouse pointer changes to a hand, you know you have found a hyperlink.

Hands-On 4.4 Navigate with Hyperlinks

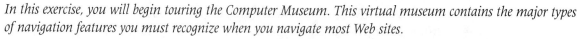

In this exercise, you will begin touring the Computer Museum. This virtual museum contains the major types of navigation features you must recognize when you navigate most Web sites.

Navigate to the Computer Museum

1. Click in the **Address bar,** type the URL **`www.offtowork.com/oe`**, and tap the ENTER key.
2. Click the **Lesson 4** button to display the Web page for this lesson.
3. Click the **Computer Museum** button to display the introduction to this simulation; then click the Continue hyperlink at the bottom of the page.

NOTE! *The Computer Museum is a real Web site. However, for this book, it has been placed into "suspended animation" at the offtowork.com Web site. At the end of the lesson, you can visit the "live site."*

Identify Hyperlinks on the Museum's Home Page

4. Follow these steps to examine some of the hyperlinks on the Computer Museum's home page.

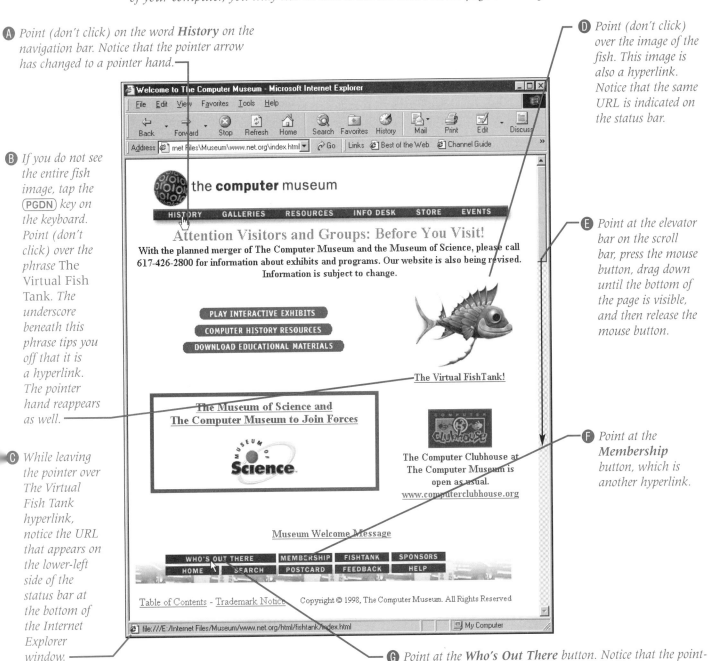

NOTE! *The home page is illustrated in its entirety on the facing page. However, depending on the video setting of your computer, you may not be able to see the entire home page on a single screen.*

Ⓐ *Point (don't click) on the word* ***History*** *on the navigation bar. Notice that the pointer arrow has changed to a pointer hand.*

Ⓑ *If you do not see the entire fish image, tap the* (PGDN) *key on the keyboard. Point (don't click) over the phrase* The Virtual Fish Tank. *The underscore beneath this phrase tips you off that it is a hyperlink. The pointer hand reappears as well.*

Ⓒ *While leaving the pointer over* The Virtual Fish Tank *hyperlink, notice the URL that appears on the lower-left side of the status bar at the bottom of the Internet Explorer window.*

Ⓓ *Point (don't click) over the image of the fish. This image is also a hyperlink. Notice that the same URL is indicated on the status bar.*

Ⓔ *Point at the elevator bar on the scroll bar, press the mouse button, drag down until the bottom of the page is visible, and then release the mouse button.*

Ⓕ *Point at the* ***Membership*** *button, which is another hyperlink.*

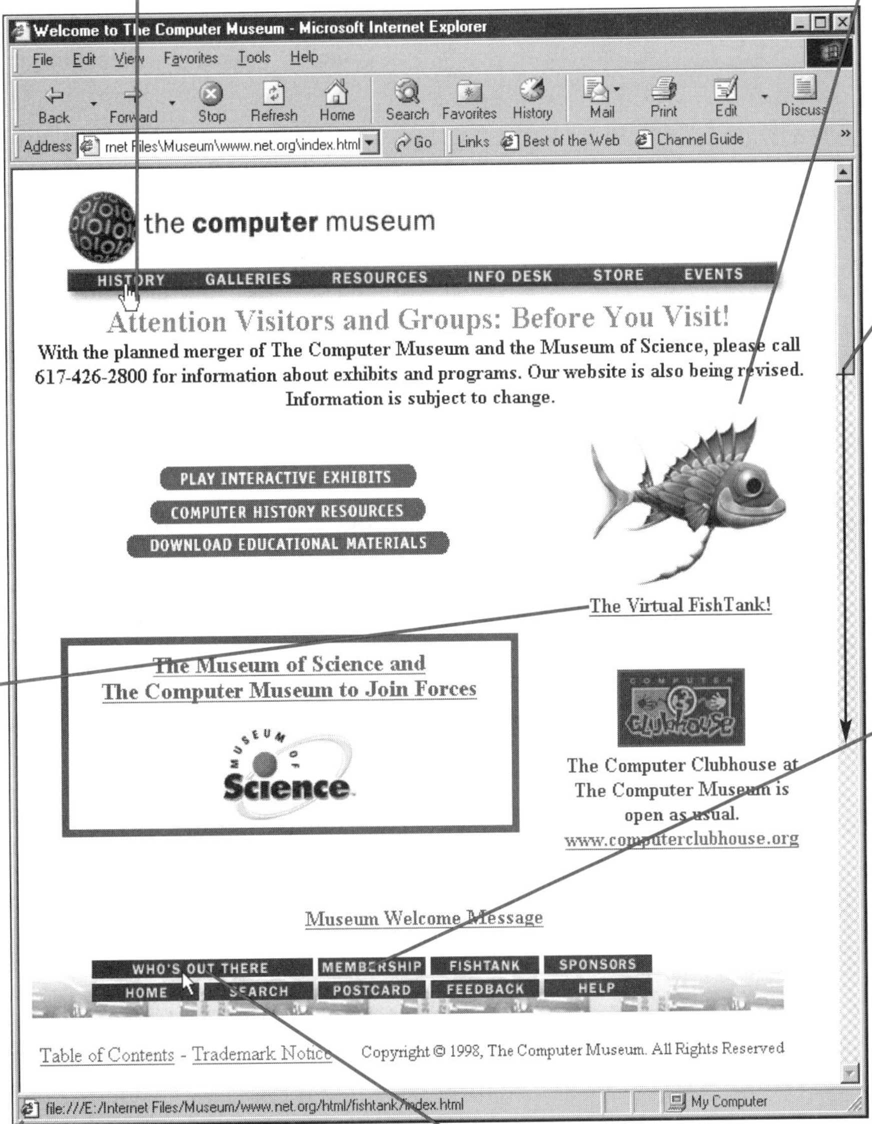

Welcome to The Computer Museum - Microsoft Internet Explorer
File Edit View Favorites Tools Help
Back Forward Stop Refresh Home Search Favorites History Mail Print Edit Discuss
Address rnet Files\Museum\www.net.org\index.html Go Links Best of the Web Channel Guide
the computer museum
HISTORY GALLERIES RESOURCES INFO DESK STORE EVENTS
Attention Visitors and Groups: Before You Visit!
With the planned merger of The Computer Museum and the Museum of Science, please call 617-426-2800 for information about exhibits and programs. Our website is also being revised. Information is subject to change.
PLAY INTERACTIVE EXHIBITS
COMPUTER HISTORY RESOURCES
DOWNLOAD EDUCATIONAL MATERIALS
The Virtual FishTank!
The Museum of Science and The Computer Museum to Join Forces
Museum of Science
The Computer Clubhouse at The Computer Museum is open as usual.
www.computerclubhouse.org
Museum Welcome Message
WHO'S OUT THERE MEMBERSHIP FISHTANK SPONSORS
HOME SEARCH POSTCARD FEEDBACK HELP
Table of Contents - Trademark Notice Copyright © 1998, The Computer Museum. All Rights Reserved
file:///E:/Internet Files/Museum/www.net.org/html/fishtank/index.html
My Computer

Ⓖ *Point at the* ***Who's Out There*** *button. Notice that the pointer arrow does not change to a pointer hand. Apparently, this button on the navigation bar is not yet an active hyperlink.*

5. *Point* (don't click yet) at other spots on the home page. Notice the different URLs of the various hyperlinks on the status bar.

6. When you are finished, tap the (HOME) key on the keyboard to scroll up to the top of the page.

From the Keyboard

(HOME) to jump to the top of the page.

(Continued on the next page)

Navigate with Hyperlinks

7. Click **The Virtual Fish Tank!** hyperlink.
   You've jumped to the Virtual Fish Tank page.

From the Keyboard

END to jump to the bottom of the page.

8. Tap the END key on the keyboard to scroll down to the bottom of the page. If necessary, use the scroll bar to make the hyperlinks visible, as shown in Step 9.
9. Follow these steps to navigate with another hyperlink.

NOTE! *Please read Steps A and B in their entirety before you execute them.*

Ⓐ *Click the* Walk-Through *hyperlink.*

Ⓑ *Immediately focus your attention on the status bar. The status bar will display the progress of loading the next page into your browser. When the blue highlight reaches the border of its section in the status bar, you know the new page has finished loading.*

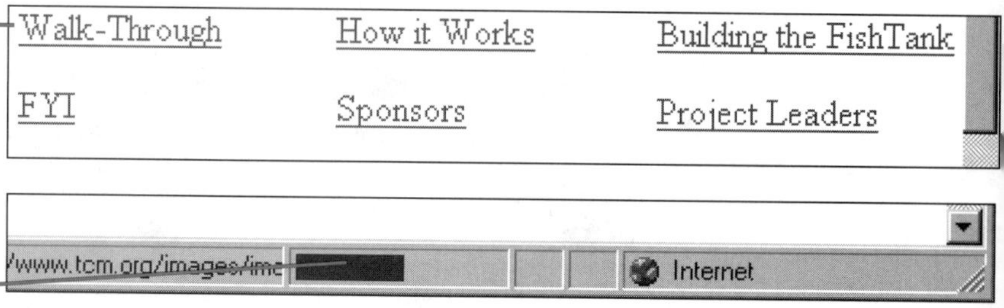

Walk-Through
How it Works
Building the FishTank
FYI
Sponsors
Project Leaders
/www.tcm.org/images/ime
Internet

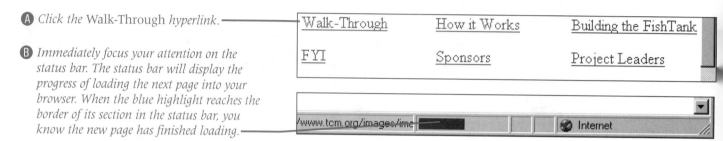

Depending on the speed of your Internet connection and the level of congestion on the Internet in general, the bar may only extend for a few seconds. Over a modem, it might take 30 or more seconds for the entire page to load.

10. Click a few times on the scroll down button on the bottom-right side of the Internet Explorer window to gradually scroll the view down this long page.
11. *Drag* on the **elevator bar** to scroll the rest of the way to the *bottom* of the page. If you see something interesting to read or view as you scroll, feel free to pause and do so. When you have gotten down to the bottom of the page, continue with the next step.
    Notice the hyperlinks at the bottom of the page. Thoughtful Web page designers will often place hyperlinks at the top and bottom of a page so you can navigate without scrolling all the way back to the top.

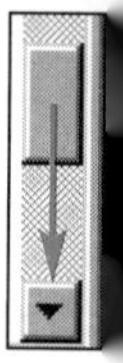

12. Click the **Photo** hyperlink (second link from the right in the second row of hyperlinks). After the photo appears, *scroll down* with the scroll bar until you can view the entire photo.

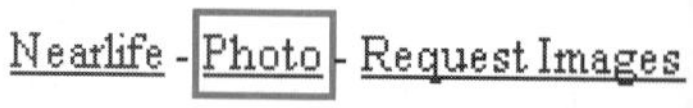

Nearlife - Photo - Request Images

13. Tap the END key to jump to the bottom of the page; then click the **VFT Home** hyperlink (first link to the left on the top row of hyperlinks).
14. *Point* (don't click) at the Computer Museum title at the top of the page. Point at the *ball* as well. Notice the *URL* on the lower-left corner of the status bar.

the computer museum

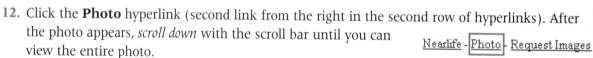

The pointing hand once again tips you off that this is a hyperlink. Many Web sites will navigate you back to the home page if you click on a logo near the top of the page.

15. Click on the spinning ball or the **Computer Museum** logo to navigate back to the home page.

Opening Additional Windows

Sometimes as you browse, you may wish to leave a Web page open on the desktop and browse additional pages. For example, you might want to compare two sites side by side, or browse a hyperlink from one page without losing your place on that page. This is easily done at any time. You can use two methods to open multiple browser windows.

Quick Reference

OPENING ADDITIONAL WINDOWS

Task	Procedure
Open an additional browsing window.	■ Choose **File→New Window** from the Internet Explorer menu bar, or press the CTRL key; then tap the *N* key.
Open an additional browsing window from a hyperlink.	■ *Right-click* on a hyperlink; then choose **Open Link in New Window** from the pop-up menu.

Hands-On 4.5 Open Multiple Browser Windows

Open a Hyperlink in a New Window

1. *Right-Click* on the **History** hyperlink on the navigation bar near the top of the window. Then choose **Open Link in New Window** from the pop-up menu.

HISTORY
GALLERIES
RESOURCES
Open Link
Open Link in New Window

Notice that a new browser window has been opened. Depending on the video display setting of your computer, the entire window may not be visible. For example, you may not be able to see the window-sizing buttons at the top-right corner of the window.

2. Follow these steps to resize this new browser window.
The top-left corner of every window contains a control button. This is handy when you cannot see the window-sizing buttons at the top-right corner.

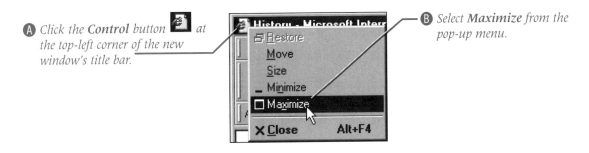

Ⓐ *Click the **Control** button at the top-left corner of the new window's title bar.*

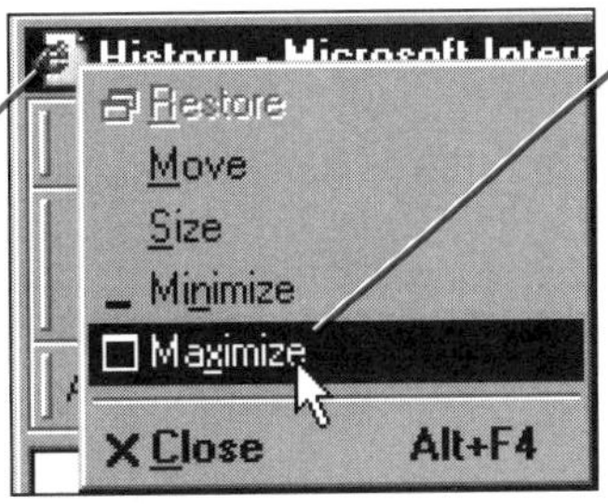
Restore
Move
Size
Minimize
Maximize
Close
Alt+F4

Ⓑ *Select **Maximize** from the pop-up menu.*

3. Tap the Down arrow ↓ key on the keyboard twice to scroll down the page. Then click the BROWSE BY TOPIC hyperlink.
Using the Down arrow ↓ key is another way to slowly scroll down a page.

4. Click the **Computers** hyperlink. Take a moment to scroll down this topic.

(Continued on the next page)

5. Close the ☒ the Internet Explorer window.
Notice that the window for the home page is still open. In fact, it's now the active window. Opening additional windows can be useful when you want to search from a particular point, yet be able to return to that point quickly.

From the Keyboard

CTRL+N to open a new browser window.

Open a New Window

6. Choose **File→New→Window** from the menu bar.

7. Follow these steps to enter a URL in the new window.

Ⓐ *Click in the **Address** bar; then start to type* **www.offto**. *As you type, you will see the AutoComplete feature display one or more URLs that match what you are typing.*

Ⓑ *Point at the corner of the **AutoComplete** list, then drag the AutoComplete list to the right to see any other URLs.*

Address
www.offto
http://www.offtowork.com
http://www.offtowork.com/oe

Ⓒ *Now drag the AutoComplete list to make it narrower, but leave all of the URLs in full view.*

8. Tap the ESC key on the keyboard to cancel the new URL you were typing.
The previous URL is restored and navigation to the new page is cancelled.

Navigating with Browsing Controls

From the Keyboard

ALT+← to navigate back one page
ALT+→ to navigate forward one page
HOME to navigate to the top of the page
END to navigate to the bottom of the page
ESC to stop loading the page

Back

Web pages can have extensive navigation controls built into them or none at all. Fortunately, your Web browser has basic navigation controls that are always available. These basic navigation controls will allow you to navigate reliably in any type of Web site. They also have some features that ordinary hyperlinks lack.

Basic Navigation Buttons

The most basic navigation controls on Internet Explorer are the Forward and Back buttons. There are a few other buttons that you can use to browse Web sites. The diagram below lists and describes the navigation buttons.

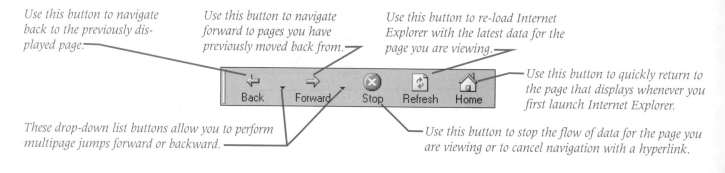

Use this button to navigate back to the previously displayed page.

Use this button to navigate forward to pages you have previously moved back from.

Use this button to re-load Internet Explorer with the latest data for the page you are viewing.

Back
Forward
Stop
Refresh
Home

Use this button to quickly return to the page that displays whenever you first launch Internet Explorer.

These drop-down list buttons allow you to perform multipage jumps forward or backward.

Use this button to stop the flow of data for the page you are viewing or to cancel navigation with a hyperlink.

Hands-On 4.6 Work with the Navigation Buttons

Navigate with Forward and Back

1. Click the HISTORY hyperlink on the navigation bar.
2. Click the EXPLORE THE TIMELINE hyperlink.
3. Click the **'62** hyperlink on the timeline. If you do not see the pictures on this page, tap the (PGDN) key.
   Notice that one of the pictures did not load for this page. Sometimes an image will not load properly when you first navigate to a page.

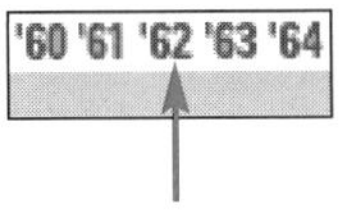
'60 '61 '62 '63 '64

4. Click the Refresh button on the Internet Explorer toolbar.
   There will be a pause as the page is reloaded. If the missing image were indeed on the Web site, this command should have loaded it. Apparently, this image is simply missing from the Web site.
5. If necessary, *scroll down* the page so you can view the pictures and read all of the topics for 1962.
6. Point at the **thumbnail image** above the item *MIT Students Slug . . .* Notice that the pointer changes to a hand, indicating that this thumbnail image is a hyperlink. *Click* on the picture to navigate to this topic, then take a moment to read the topic.
   Space War! was the first interactive computer game. They've certainly come a long way since then. Notice also that the Forward *button is grayed out at this point.*

MIT students Slug Russell, Shag Graetz, and Alan Kotok wrote SpaceWar!

7. Tap the (END) key to jump to the bottom of the page.
   Notice that there is a hyperlink at the bottom of this page that could navigate you back to the 1962 *page. There is also a button leading to the Software category, which would navigate you to the* Categories *area of the museum. A well-designed Web site will frequently feature hyperlinks such as these that can take you to areas of knowledge related to the topic you are currently browsing.*

1962

8. Tap the (HOME) key to jump back to the top of the page.
9. Click the Back button.
   Now you are back to the 1962 page, and the Forward button is no longer grayed out, since you can now navigate forward to a page you visited recently.
10. Click the Forward button.
    You've gone forward to the Space War! page again. Internet Explorer returned to the same view of the page that was displayed when you clicked the Back button to leave the page.

(Continued on the next page)

Navigate with Multipage Jumps

11. Follow these steps to navigate with a drop-down list.
In one jump, you are back to the timeline. It would have taken two clicks of the Back *button to return to this page without the drop-down list.*

Ⓐ *Click the drop-down section of the* **Back** *button to display a list of several pages all the way back to the home page.*

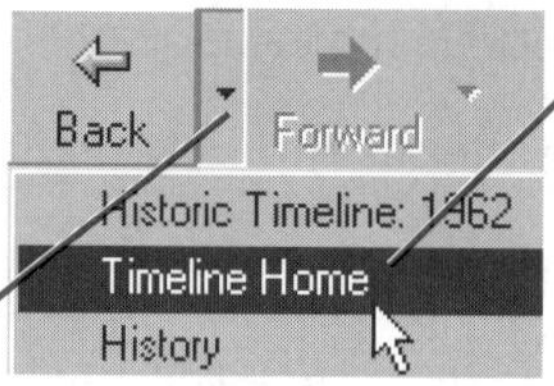
Back
Forward
Historic Timeline: 1962
Timeline Home
History

Ⓑ *Click* Timeline Home *on the drop-down list.*

12. Click the Back button's **drop-down** list section again; then select *Welcome to the Computer Museum.*

13. Click the Forward 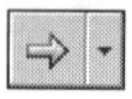 button's drop-down list section; then select *Space War!* from the list.

14. Click the Back 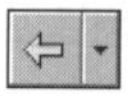 button.
Notice that even though you jumped forward to the Space War! page from the Welcome page in one jump during Step 13, clicking the Back button took you to the 1962 *page this time. That is because Internet Explorer kept track of the entire sequence of pages you jumped through to reach the Space War! page.*

Use the Stop Button

15. Click the Back 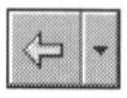 to navigate to the *Timeline Home* page.
Notice that the title of this page appears in the title bar at the top-left corner of the window.

16. Click the **'60** hyperlink on the timeline; then *immediately* click the Stop  button on the Internet Explorer toolbar.
If you clicked Stop before this page had a chance to load completely, you have an example of what can happen if a page stalls while loading.

17. Click the Refresh  button on the Internet Explorer toolbar.
Now the page will reload. If the content of the page did not load completely at Step 15, refreshing the display should allow all of the elements of the page to appear.

18. Click the drop-down list section of the Back 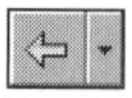 button; then select **Welcome to the Computer Museum.**

19. Click the drop-down list section of the Back button again; then choose **Lesson 4.**

Navigating in Frames

Some Web sites are constructed with a feature called *frames.* A **frame** is a window on a Web page through which other Web pages may be displayed. The advantage of frames is that part of the page can remain static, while other parts of the page change. Since less of the page changes and thus must be loaded into the browser, pages constructed with frames can function faster over a slow Internet connection. Some Web sites use frames as a navigation tool for browsing.

The best way to understand frames is to work with them. You will do just that in the next Hands-On exercise.

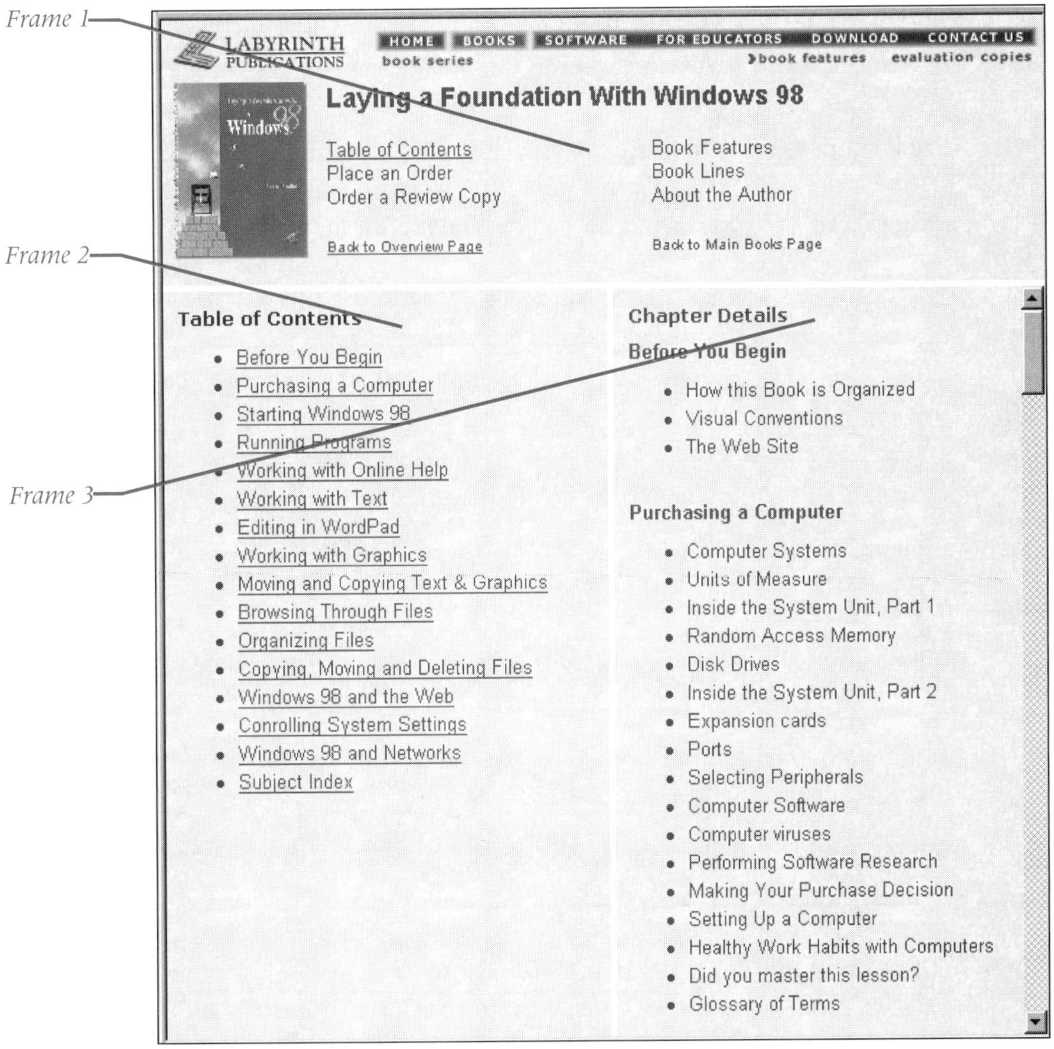
Frame 1
Frame 2
Frame 3
LABYRINTH PUBLICATIONS
HOME BOOKS SOFTWARE FOR EDUCATORS DOWNLOAD CONTACT US
book series
book features evaluation copies
Laying a Foundation With Windows 98
Table of Contents
Place an Order
Order a Review Copy
Back to Overview Page
Book Features
Book Lines
About the Author
Back to Main Books Page
Table of Contents
Before You Begin
Purchasing a Computer
Starting Windows 98
Running Programs
Working with Online Help
Working with Text
Editing in WordPad
Working with Graphics
Moving and Copying Text & Graphics
Browsing Through Files
Organizing Files
Copying, Moving and Deleting Files
Windows 98 and the Web
Conrolling System Settings
Windows 98 and Networks
Subject Index
Chapter Details
Before You Begin
How this Book is Organized
Visual Conventions
The Web Site
Purchasing a Computer
Computer Systems
Units of Measure
Inside the System Unit, Part 1
Random Access Memory
Disk Drives
Inside the System Unit, Part 2
Expansion cards
Ports
Selecting Peripherals
Computer Software
Computer viruses
Performing Software Research
Making Your Purchase Decision
Setting Up a Computer
Healthy Work Habits with Computers
Did you master this lesson?
Glossary of Terms

The white boundaries show the frames on this page. The contents of each frame can change independently, that is, one frame will change while the other frames do not.

Hands-On 4.7 Navigate a Page with Frames

View Frames with Borders

1. Choose **View→Full Screen** on the menu bar to make the Internet Explorer window fill the screen.
2. *Point* for a moment at the very bottom of the screen.
   Notice that when you point to the very bottom of the screen in Full Screen mode, the Windows Taskbar pops up.
3. Click the **Work with Frames** button.
4. Click the **With Borders** button.
   A page will appear describing a Windows textbook. This particular page does not use frames, but the other pages you view next will.

(Continued on the next page)

5. Click the **Table of Contents** hyperlink near the center of the page.
Now you are on a frames page. So you can see exactly how the frames are laid out, they are separated by a white border.

6. Follow these steps to navigate with the Table of Contents frame.
The function of frames in this case is to create a dynamic view of the table of contents. When you encounter frames on a Web page, they will usually serve a purpose to similar what you see here.

Ⓐ *Click the* Purchasing a Computer *hyperlink.*

Ⓑ *Notice that this particular chapter has jumped to the top of the list in this frame.*

Ⓒ *Click the* Working with Online Help *hyperlink. Now this chapter has jumped to the top of the right-hand frame.*

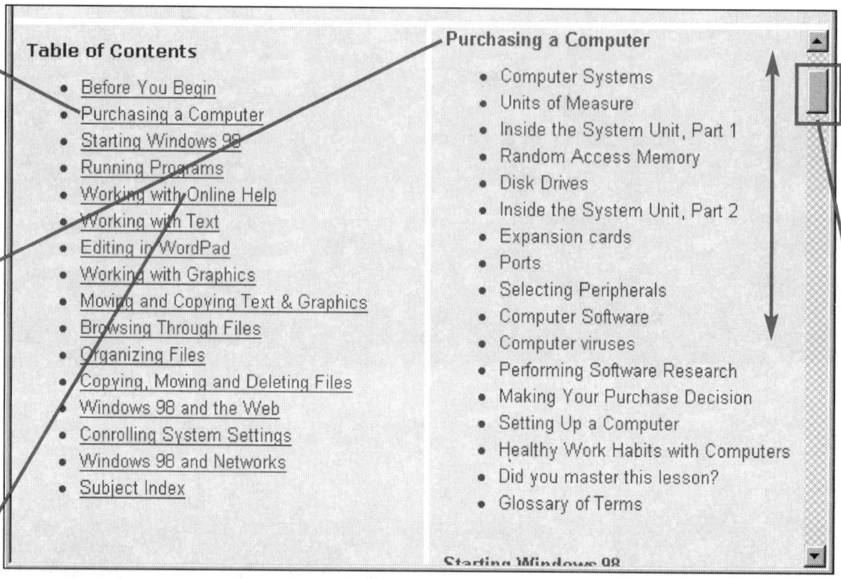

Table of Contents
Before You Begin
Purchasing a Computer
Starting Windows 98
Running Programs
Working with Online Help
Working with Text
Editing in WordPad
Working with Graphics
Moving and Copying Text & Graphics
Browsing Through Files
Organizing Files
Copying, Moving and Deleting Files
Windows 98 and the Web
Conrolling System Settings
Windows 98 and Networks
Subject Index
Purchasing a Computer
Computer Systems
Units of Measure
Inside the System Unit, Part 1
Random Access Memory
Disk Drives
Inside the System Unit, Part 2
Expansion cards
Ports
Selecting Peripherals
Computer Software
Computer viruses
Performing Software Research
Making Your Purchase Decision
Setting Up a Computer
Healthy Work Habits with Computers
Did you master this lesson?
Glossary of Terms

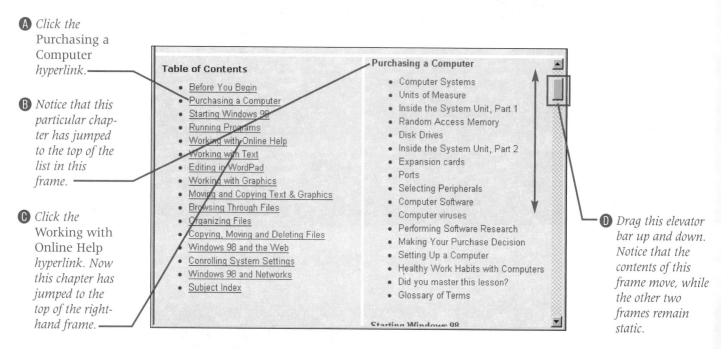

Ⓓ *Drag this elevator bar up and down. Notice that the contents of this frame move, while the other two frames remain static.*

7. Click the **Book Features** hyperlink near the right-center of the page.
This page uses just two frames. Notice that the top frame is identical to the top frame from the Table of Contents page you were viewing a moment ago. When you clicked the Book Features hyperlink, only the contents of the lower frame actually changed.

8. If you see a *scroll bar* next to the item list in the lower frame, *drag* down to view the rest of the items. If you don't see a scroll bar, this means your monitor is able to display all of the contents of this frame without scrolling

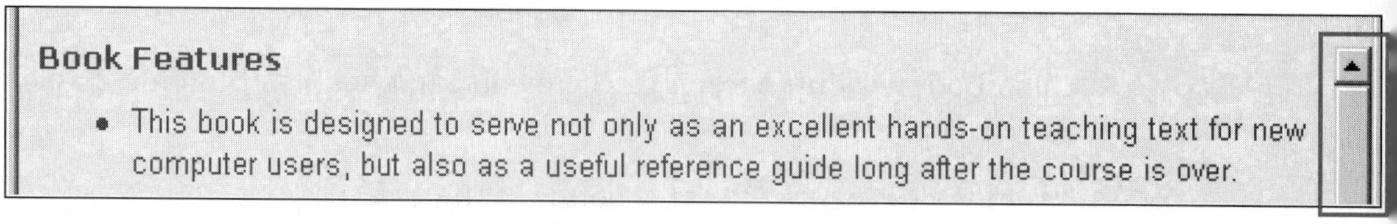

Book Features
This book is designed to serve not only as an excellent hands-on teaching text for new computer users, but also as a useful reference guide long after the course is over.

As you observed in the table of contents in Step 6, the contents of this frame can scroll independently from the other frames.

9. Click the Back button's drop-down list; then select **Work with Frames.**

View Frames without Borders

10. Click the **Without Borders** button.
    There are no borders for the frames in this version of the page. This is actually the way the page was designed to be viewed. Some Web pages that use frames won't be immediately obvious. But once you see parts of the page changing while the rest of the page remains static, you will know you are working with frames.
11. Click the **Table of Contents** hyperlink near the center of the page.
12. Click some of the chapter headings on the *left* side of the Table of Contents frame. Watch the chapter details jump to the top of the list for each chapter you click.
13. Click the **Back to Overview Page** hyperlink.
14. Click the **Restore** button at the top-right corner of the screen to shift out of full screen mode.

15. Minimize this Internet Explorer window.

Printing Web Pages

Introduction

You may often wish to print information from Web pages. For example, if you order a product or travel tickets online and wish to keep a permanent record of the transaction, it is a good idea to print the page when you make a purchase. In general, printing a Web page is like printing a document with a word processor. However, you cannot preview pages before you print them.

Print Options

The Internet Explorer offers several useful print options. Depending on what is on the page you are printing, one or more of these options will be useful.

Option	Description
Print Frames.	If the Web page you are printing uses frames, you have the option to print either the entire page or just the currently selected frame on the page. This option is always grayed out if the page you are about to print does not use frames.
Print linked documents.	This option will print pages for all the hyperlinks on the page you are about to print. *Tip: Use this option with care! If the page has numerous hyperlinks, you may end up with more pages than you want.*
Print a table of links.	This option prints an additional page after the contents of the page itself. A table of hyperlinks is useful if you want to do additional research on the hyperlinks.

Quick Reference

PRINTING A WEB PAGE	
Task	**Procedure**
Print a Web page with the current print options.	■ Click the **Print** button on the Internet Explorer toolbar, or choose **File→Print** from the menu bar.
Print the current Web page and change the print options.	■ Choose **File→Print** from the menu bar. ■ Select the options you desire for the print job.

Hands-On 4.8 Print Web Pages

Print a Topic Page

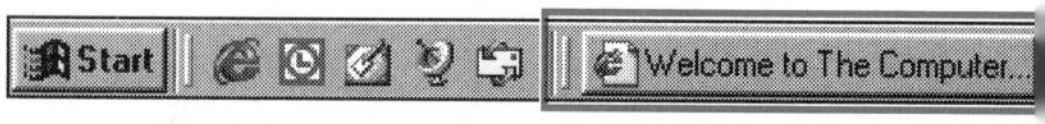
Start
Welcome to The Computer...

1. If it is not already displayed on the screen, click the **Welcome to the Computer** button on the *Windows Taskbar* to activate this window.
2. Click the HISTORY hyperlink on the navigation bar.
3. Click the **Explore the Timeline** hyperlink on the History page.
4. Click **'70** on the timeline; then click the image above the topic that begins *Computer-to-computer communication* . . . If necessary, *scroll down* so you can see the photo.
   The photo on this page depicts the earliest version of the ARPANET, the ancestor of the Internet.

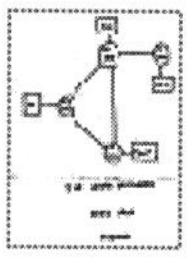
Computer-to-computer communication

5. Choose **File→Print** from the menu bar; then follow these steps to print the Web page.

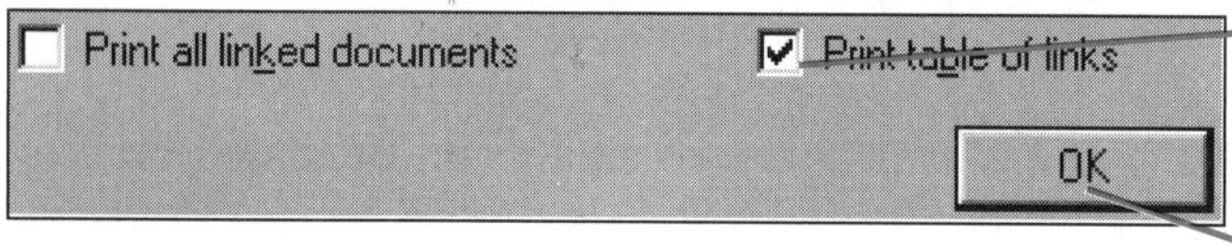
Print all linked documents
Print table of links
OK

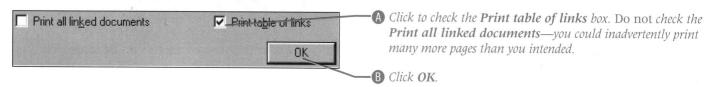

Ⓐ *Click to check the* ***Print table of links*** *box.* Do not *check the* ***Print all linked documents****—you could inadvertently print many more pages than you intended.*

Ⓑ *Click* ***OK****.*

6. Retrieve the printout from the printer.
   The table of links will print a list of all of the hyperlinks available on this page. As you can see, the page contains quite a few hyperlinks.
7. Close ☒ the Computer Museum window.

Print a Frames Page

8. Click the Without Borders - Microso... button on the *Windows Taskbar* to make the *Laying a Foundation with Windows 98* page the active window.
9. Select **File→Print** from the menu bar.
   Notice that the Print Frames *option area is grayed out. This is because this particular page does not use frames.*

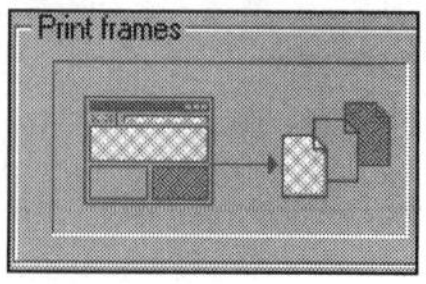
Print frames

10. Click **Cancel** to close the print dialog box without printing.
11. Click the **Table of Contents** hyperlink near the center of the page.

12. Click the **Purchasing a Computer** hyperlink on the lower-left side of the page. [• Purchasing a Computer]
Clicking in this frame has made it the selected frame for printing purposes. This will be important when you select the Print Frames options in the print dialog box.

13. Select **File→Print** from the menu bar; then follow these steps to print the page.

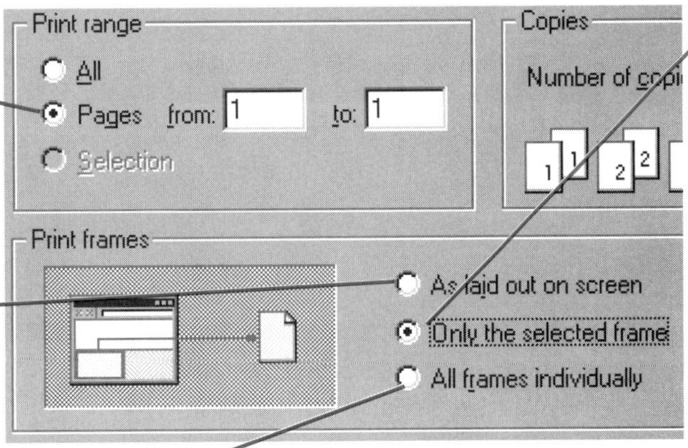

Print range
All
Pages from: 1 to: 1
Selection
Copies
Number of copi
Print frames
As laid out on screen
Only the selected frame
All frames individually

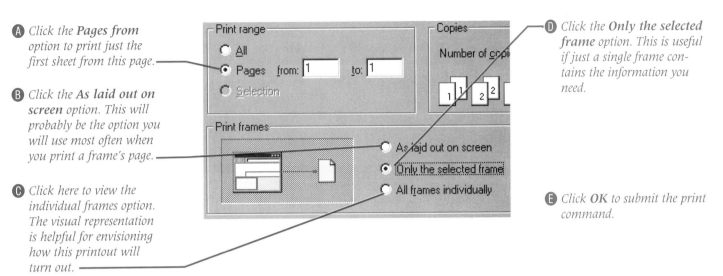

Ⓐ *Click the* ***Pages from*** *option to print just the first sheet from this page.*

Ⓑ *Click the* ***As laid out on screen*** *option. This will probably be the option you will use most often when you print a frame's page.*

Ⓒ *Click here to view the individual frames option. The visual representation is helpful for envisioning how this printout will turn out.*

Ⓓ *Click the* ***Only the selected frame*** *option. This is useful if just a single frame contains the information you need.*

Ⓔ *Click* ***OK*** *to submit the print command.*

14. Retrieve the printout from the printer.
Just the list of chapter titles should have printed.

15. Click on the [Purchasing a Computer] heading in the *right* frame of the page.
Now you have selected this frame to print.

16. Click the Print [printer icon] button on the toolbar; then retrieve the printout from the printer.
This time, the details of the chapters should have printed. Notice that only one page prints out, since you had made this setting in your previous print command.

17. **Close** [X] the Internet Explorer window.

Searching the Web

An *Internet search engine* is a Web site designed to help you locate and navigate to Web pages that contain the information for which you are looking. Search engines typically display a list of links (called *hits*), which you use to navigate to sites that meet your search criteria. As you will see, there are many types of search engines from which to choose, and the search engine you select can make a difference in the success or failure of your searches. This topic will introduce basic techniques for locating Web pages.

NOTE! *Most of the exercises in this lesson will use the* GO.com *search engine because it is an excellent general search engine that is also easy to use. The techniques you use to work with* GO.com *will also work well with other search engines. It will be easier to master your first lesson with search engines by focusing on just one.*

Search Methods

Most search engines offer three different types of search methods to use their Web site database. Most of the time, the standard search method will work best. The advanced search and search directory methods are beyond the scope of this lesson.

Method	Description
Standard search	With this method, you simply enter one or more words or a phrase to conduct a search.
Advanced search	An advanced search allows you to limit the search in specific ways. For example, you could specify that pages that do not have a particular word on them should be included in the list of "hits."
Search Directory	Many search engines also offer a hierarchical directory of the indexed Web pages. Examples of search directory categories include travel, news, education, people, and real estate.

Performing a Standard Search

A *standard search* asks the search engine to find Web pages with a specific word or several words. Standard searches are quick and easy to execute, and will often yield the information you are seeking. The results of a search are typically reported as a results list of Web pages, with a short summary of each page. Each Web page in the search results list is called a "hit." Sometimes, a search may yield no hits at all. Other times, you may get millions of hits—more than you would have time to browse through.

Selecting Search Words

TIP! *Start most of your searches with two to three words.*

A standard search can consist of a singe search word, or several. The more words you include in a search, the more likely it is that the search results will be relevant to your needs. However, you don't want to start out with so many search words that you miss Web sites that did not include some of the search words, but would still be of interest. When you perform a standard search with more than one word, most search engines will show you the pages that contain all the words first, then pages that contain only a few of the words. The illustration on the next page displays the features of a typical search results page.

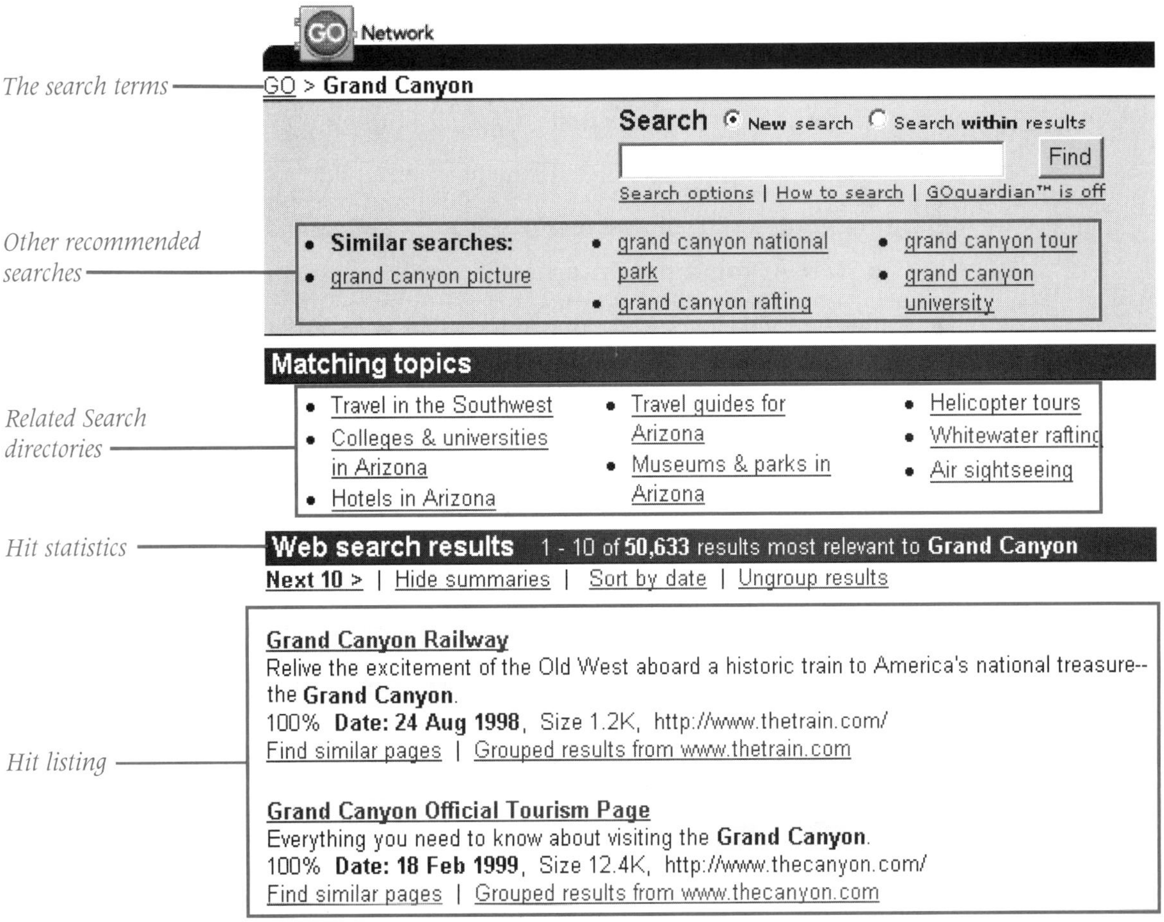

The search terms
Other recommended searches
Related Search directories
Hit statistics
Hit listing
GO Network
GO > Grand Canyon
Search New search Search within results
Find
Search options | How to search | GOguardian™ is off
Similar searches:
grand canyon picture
grand canyon national park
grand canyon rafting
grand canyon tour
grand canyon university
Matching topics
Travel in the Southwest
Colleges & universities in Arizona
Hotels in Arizona
Travel guides for Arizona
Museums & parks in Arizona
Helicopter tours
Whitewater rafting
Air sightseeing
Web search results 1 - 10 of 50,633 results most relevant to Grand Canyon
Next 10 > | Hide summaries | Sort by date | Ungroup results
Grand Canyon Railway
Relive the excitement of the Old West aboard a historic train to America's national treasure--the Grand Canyon.
100% Date: 24 Aug 1998, Size 1.2K, http://www.thetrain.com/
Find similar pages | Grouped results from www.thetrain.com
Grand Canyon Official Tourism Page
Everything you need to know about visiting the Grand Canyon.
100% Date: 18 Feb 1999, Size 12.4K, http://www.thecanyon.com/
Find similar pages | Grouped results from www.thecanyon.com

Every Internet search engine has its own rules and conventions (called *syntax*) for searching. However, the two rules show in the following Quick Reference table will work with most Internet search engines.

TYPING SEARCH WORDS

Rule	Examples
Use capital letters only when typing proper nouns. If you type more than one name in a search, separate each name with a comma.	Robin Williams, Grand Canyon
If you wish to search for an exact phrase, enclose the phrase in quotation marks.	"global warming trends"

Hands-On 4.9 Perform a Standard Search

In this exercise, you will perform a simulated standard search. You will run the simulation from the Off to Work with Internet Explorer Web site.

Launch Internet Explorer and Navigate to the Simulation

1. Use **Start→Programs→Internet Explorer** to start the browser.
2. Enter the following URL in the address bar: **www.offtowork.com/oe**; then tap the (ENTER) key.
3. Click the **Lesson 4** button; then click the **Standard Search** button.
4. Read the instructions on the Standard Search page; then click **Continue** at the bottom of the page.
   You will see a simulation of the GO.com Home page.

Perform a Standard Search

5. Enter the search words **`Grand Canyon`** in the search box; then tap the (ENTER) key. Be sure to capitalize this proper name, since it will help make your search more precise. AutoComplete may display the search words as you type.

GO Network
Search
Grand Canyon
the Web
Find
Search options | How to search | GOguardian™ is off
Powered by Infoseek

   After a pause, the first page of search results will appear. It contains the first ten "hits," as well as other search options you can select.

6. If necessary, scroll down the page until the *Web Search Results* section is visible. Look for the number of hits scored by the search (over 50,000).

Web search results
1 - 10 of 50,633 results most relevant to Grand Canyon
Next 10 > | Hide summaries | Sort by date | Ungroup results

7. *Scroll* the page up and down to briefly glance over the first 10 hits from your search.
   There is a fairly diverse collection of pages here. But notice that the first three hits are quite relevant.

Interpreting Search Results

Most search engines offer several types of information about each hit scored by a search. This helps you select the hits most likely to have the content you are seeking. This is one area where search engines can differ quite a bit. The illustration below displays the hit result list of the *GO.com* search engine.

Page name hyperlink: *This usually comes from a name for the page that is embedded into the page itself by the author. This hyperlink will navigate you to the site.*

Total hits: *The total number of Web pages in the search engine's database that match your search.*

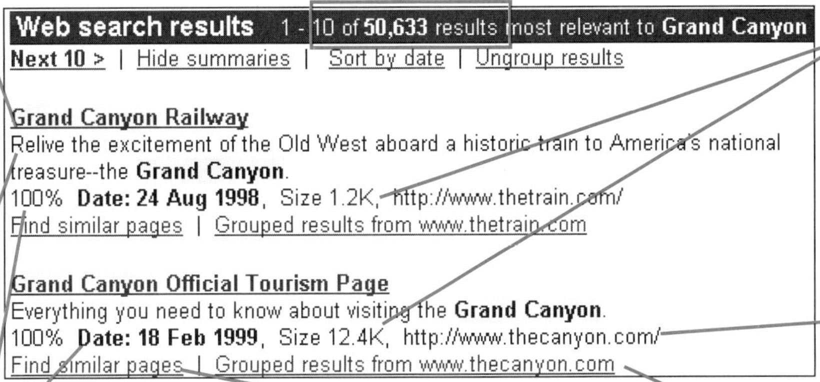
Web search results 1 - 10 of 50,633 results most relevant to Grand Canyon
Next 10 > | Hide summaries | Sort by date | Ungroup results
Grand Canyon Railway
Relive the excitement of the Old West aboard a historic train to America's national treasure--the Grand Canyon.
100% Date: 24 Aug 1998, Size 1.2K, http://www.thetrain.com/
Find similar pages | Grouped results from www.thetrain.com
Grand Canyon Official Tourism Page
Everything you need to know about visiting the Grand Canyon.
100% Date: 18 Feb 1999, Size 12.4K, http://www.thecanyon.com/
Find similar pages | Grouped results from www.thecanyon.com

Summary: *Most search engines display the first few lines of text of the Web site. Or the summary may contain a description of the site that is embedded within the Web page itself.*

Relevance rating: *Gives the search engine's estimate of how likely the hit will contain the information you are looking for.*

Page size: *The size of the Web page and its graphics. Larger pages will take longer to download. Notice the size difference between these two pages.*

URL: *The URL of the page.*

Date: *When the page was first placed on the Web. In some cases, the date may indicate when the page was last updated. Older pages may no longer be online or may contain outdated information.*

Find similar pages: *When you click this hyperlink, the search engine executes a new search for pages similar to this one.*

Grouped results from . . . *Infoseek lists only a single result from each Web site. This keeps the hit list to a more manageable size. Clicking this hyperlink will cause the individual display of additional hits from that site.*

NOTE! *This is just one example of a particular search engine. Other search engines have their own ways of displaying search results.*

Relevance Ratings

When you search with one or more words, search engines look for pages that contain all of the words, and pages that contain any of the words. Pages containing more of your search words are scored higher for *relevance* than pages containing just one or a few of the words. This relevance is usually indicated by a percent rating included with the hit. The higher its relevance rating, the more likely it is that the hit will contain the information you are looking for.

Hands-On 4.10 Browse Search Results

1. *Scroll* the page so that the *Web Search Results* heading is at the top of the page and the first three hits are visible.
   Compare the dates on the first three hits. The date usually (but not always) indicates when the page was last updated. Notice also that every hit on this page has a relevance rating of 100%.
2. Click the **Next 10 >** hyperlink just below the *Web Search Results* heading to view the next 10 search results. Then scroll down the page to look over these hits.
   On the last three hits, notice that the relevance rating is starting to fall below 100%. These pages contain both search words, but they don't contain the words as often as the pages rated 100%.
3. Click the **Next 10 >** hyperlink to view the next 10 search results. Then scroll the page up and down to look over these hits.
   The relevance rating continues to fall but is still in the mid-90s on these pages. The search results are sorted by relevance rating on these pages. Now let's try sorting the pages by date.

Browse by Date

4. Tap the (HOME) key; then click the **Sort by Date** hyperlink. Scroll down the page to view the first hits.

Web search results 11 - 20 of 50,056 results most relevant to grand canyon
< Previous 10 | Next 10 > | Hide summaries | Sort by date | Ungroup results

   Now the most recently updated Web page is listed at the top of results list. If the search engine does not have a date for a page, it uses the date that the search engine last reviewed the page.
5. Click the **Hide Summaries** hyperlink.

Web search results 11 - 20 of 50,056 results most relevant to grand canyon
< Previous 10 | Next 10 > | Hide summaries | Sort by date | Ungroup results

   Notice that now you can view 20 hits on each page rather than just 10. With some types of searches, the summaries won't be as useful as the page titles.
6. Click the **Show Summaries** hyperlink.
7. Click the **Sort by Score** hyperlink.
   Notice that you are still on the 21–30 results page.
8. Click the **< Previous 10** hyperlink *twice* to navigate back to the *first* page of search results.
   When you reach the first page, there will no longer be a **< Previous 10** *hyperlink for you to click.*

Narrowing a Search

When a search yields tens of thousands of hits, it will be very time-consuming to browse through even a fraction of the pages to find the information you are searching for. Fortunately, it is possible to conduct another search only on the hits that were listed for a previous search. This means that you can conduct a broad search, then add more terms to the search to reduce the number of hits. This is called "narrowing" your search, since a narrower cross-section of Web sites will match your multiple search criteria.

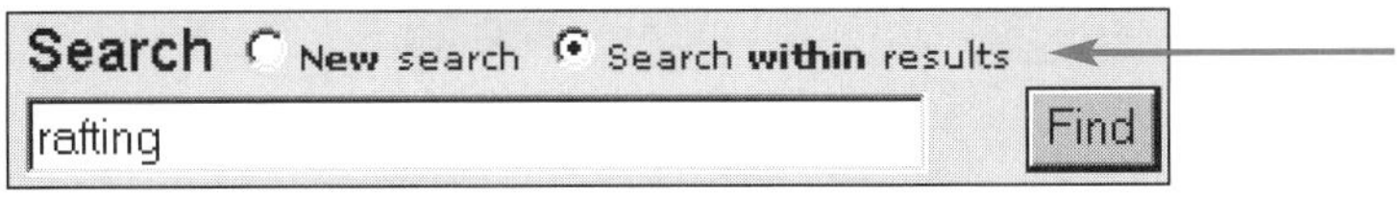
Search
New search
Search within results
rafting
Find

Most search engines allow you to add words to a search and search only within the results from the previous search.

Jasmine likes getting lots of hits on her searches, but soon discovers that there are some disadvantages to a large number of hits. She finds herself looking through screen after screen of hit lists. Since she and her friends decided to take a rafting trip through the Grand Canyon, Jasmine decides to narrow her search to pages that contain references to rafting trips.

Methods

There are two methods you can use to narrow a search. The method that works best depends on the popularity of the topic you are searching.

Method	Example	Notes
Gradual Perform a search for each word, telling the search engine to search only within the previous results.	Perform three searches: ■ *Grand Canyon* Search within results for: ■ *Rafting* ■ *Whitewater*	This method takes more time, but is more likely to end up with relevant sites in your hit list.
Quick Create one search that uses several words you think are relevant to what you are searching for.	Perform one search: ■ *Grand Canyon rafting whitewater*	This method is faster, but you may be more likely to miss a site that does not happen to contain all of the words you entered. There will probably be more irrelevant sites in your search as well.

TIP! *If you are searching on an obscure topic, use the first method.*

Hands-On 4.11 Narrow a Search

1. Tap the (HOME) key to jump to the top of the page.
2. Follow these steps to narrow your search.

Ⓐ *Click to choose the* ***Search within results*** *option*

Search
New search
Search within results
rafting
Find

Ⓑ *Tap the* (TAB) *key to jump the cursor to the search word box; then type the new search word* **`rafting.`**

Ⓒ *Click* ***Find*** *to perform the search (or tap the* (ENTER) *key).*

3. *Scroll down* to the **Web search results** section, and look for the number of *hits* that this narrowed search found. Continue scrolling to briefly review the first ten hits.
The number of hits went down from about 50,000+ to less than 4,000. This is getting to be a more manageable number. Judging by the titles of the pages, these hits are also consistently relevant.
4. Tap the (HOME) key to jump back to the top of the page. Be sure to click the **Search within results** option; then type the search word **`whitewater`**, and tap the (ENTER) key.
5. *Scroll* down the page to the **Web Search Results** section, and review the hit summaries you received.
Now there are less than 2,000 hits. It is also more likely that the hits with a high relevance rating are going to be of interest. Notice that the typical relevance rating of hits on this page is in the 88–85% range
6. Click **Next 10 >** to review the next 10 hits.
The next 10 hits are just a few percentage points lower in their relevance rating. So this narrowed search has resulted in a higher consistency in the relevance rating.

Narrow a Search with Several Search Words (Quick Method)

7. Tap the (HOME) key; then enter the following words for a new search: **`Grand Canyon rafting whitewater`**. Be sure to capitalize *Grand Canyon.*
8. Make sure that the **New search** option is chosen; then tap the (ENTER) key.
9. *Scroll* through the first page of hits, and scan the summaries of the first 10 hits for their relevance to Jasmine's search.
10. Click **Next 10 >**, and scan the 11–20 hits.
Do these first 20 hits appear as consistently relevant as the hits you found with the gradually narrowed search? There appear to be pages without much relevance to rafting in the Grand Canyon. There are also many more hits to review—over 176,000 versus the 1,800 that you found with the gradual method.

Browse Some of the Sites

LIVE LINKS!

In the next few steps, you will navigate to live links on the Internet. Some of them may no longer be online. If you navigate to a site that is not online, just click the Back button and try a different site.

11. Click the **drop-down** button on the Back button then select the second **Search Results for whitewater** from the pop-up menu.
    There were two Search results for whitewater because you looked through two pages of hit results from the search. Since the hits on this list were more consistently relevant, let's browse the results from the gradual method.

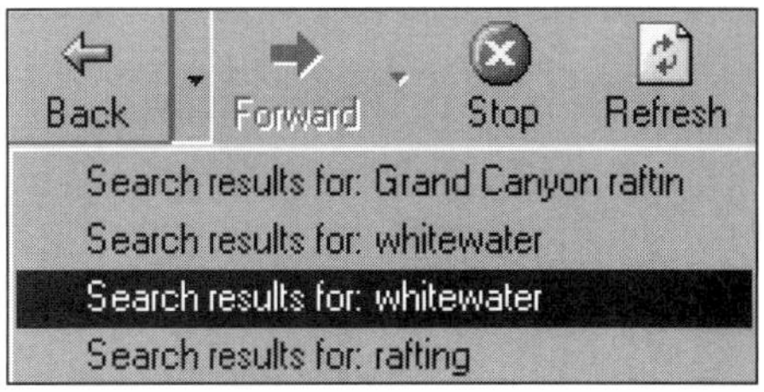
Back
Forward
Stop
Refresh
Search results for: Grand Canyon raftin
Search results for: whitewater
Search results for: whitewater
Search results for: rafting

12. Scroll down the list to the **Grand Canyon Expeditions** link; then *Right-click* on the link, and select **Open in New Window** from the pop-up menu.

Grand Canyon Expeditions-Whitewater rafting
Grand Canyon Expedit
88% Date: 3 Mar 1999,
Open
Open in New Window

13. Take a few minutes to browse this link. Would it help Jasmine and her friends plan a rafting trip? When you are finished browsing the Grand Canyon Expeditions link, close the browser window.
    Your hit list is immediately available for further browsing. By opening the link in a new window, you can return to the hit list without needing to wait for it to reload. This can be a useful timesaver when you are browsing over a modem connection.

14. Close all of the Internet Explorer windows.

Concepts Review

True/False Questions

1.	A URL is essentially the address of a Web page.	TRUE	FALSE
2.	You can only use the Back button to navigate backwards a single page at a time.	TRUE	FALSE
3.	You can always use the Forward button to navigate forward through a Web site.	TRUE	FALSE
4.	The Refresh button reloads text and images into the page you are currently viewing.	TRUE	FALSE
5.	Whenever you print a Web page, it always prints just as you see it on the screen.	TRUE	FALSE
6.	You can have several Internet Explorer browser windows open at the same time, each viewing a different Web site.	TRUE	FALSE
7.	A Web site designed to help you locate Web pages is called an *Internet search engine.*	TRUE	FALSE
8.	The *domain name* of a Web site gives you some clues about the type of organization that is posting that site.	TRUE	FALSE

Multiple-Choice Questions

1. Which save format does not save the images on a Web page?
   a. Web Page, complete
   b. Web page, HTML only
   c. Web Page, archive
   d. None of the above

2. Which of these is *not* a part of a URL?
   a. Domain name
   b. Top-level domain
   c. Page name
   d. Hyperlink name

3. Which of the methods below would you use to navigate the Web using the *Address bar*?
   a. Click its hyperlink.
   b. Enter the URL of the site; then tap the ENTER key.
   c. Enter the domain name of the site; then tap the ENTER key.
   d. All of the above

4. Adding additional search words to reduce the number of hits in a search is called
   a. expanding the search.
   b. a reduced search.
   c. narrowing the search.
   d. All of the above

Skill Builders

Skill Builder 4.1 Browse Another Computer Museum

Compared to the first computer museum you browsed in this lesson, the Obsolete Computer Museum has a much more primitive interface. There is no navbar at the top of the pages. In fact, some pages don't have any hyperlinks at all. However, since you are now familiar with the navigation buttons on the Internet Explorer toolbar, you should find it easy to navigate in this Web site.

Start Internet Explorer and Navigate to the Web Pages

1. Choose **Start→Programs→Internet Explorer.**
2. Click in the Address bar; then enter the URL **`www.offtowork.com/oe`**, and tap the ENTER key.
3. Click the **Lesson 4** button; then click the **Obsolete Computer Museum** button.
4. Read over the introduction to this simulation; then click the **Continue** hyperlink at the bottom of the page.
   The home page of the Obsolete Computer Museum will appear. On the home page is a long list of the computer systems exhibited in the museum. Notice that many of the system names are not underlined as hyperlinks. For space reasons, it was not possible to put the entire museum online here. You can view the full museum later in this exercise.

Browse the Commodore 64 Exhibit

5. *Scroll* the museum's computer list down to the *Commodore* section, and click the **C64** hyperlink
   The Commodore 64 page will appear. This was a popular home microcomputer in the early 1980s. The computer's electronics were all contained within the keyboard unit.
6. Scroll down the page until you see the **C64 Screen Shot** hyperlink, and click the hyperlink.
   Notice that there is no text on this page. There aren't any hyperlinks either. The only way to navigate out of this page is to use the ***Back*** *button on the toolbar.*

   Looks like this computer is booted up. Are you ready to compute?
7. Click the Back  button to navigate back to the Commodore 64 page.
8. Tap the END key to jump to the bottom of the page.

Check the Destination of a Hyperlink

9. Look at the first part of the current address on the *Address bar* at the top of the Internet Explorer window.
   Notice the first part of the URL. The current domain you are browsing is www.offtowork.com.

(Continued on the next page)

10. Follow these steps to analyze one of the hyperlinks.

Ⓐ *Point (don't click) at the* C64 Home Page *hyperlink.*

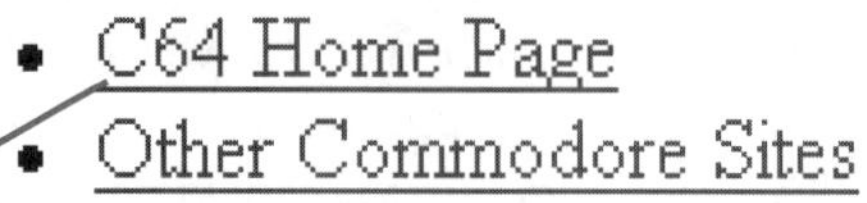
C64 Home Page
Other Commodore Sites

Ⓑ *Look at the hyperlink's destination in the lower-left corner of the status bar. Notice that the URL for this hyperlink is in a* different *domain. This means that the hyperlink will take you to a different Web site.*

http://www.hut.fi/~msmakela/cbm

11. Click the **C64 Home Page** hyperlink.

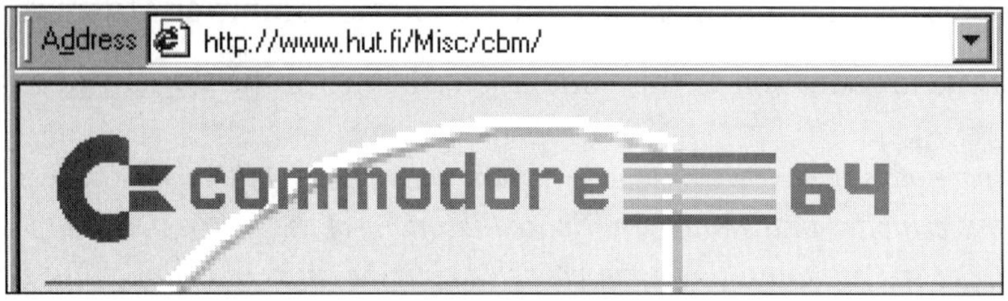
Address
http://www.hut.fi/Misc/cbm/
commodore 64

Depending on the present status of this site, you will navigate to the page or receive an indication that the page is not available because the site has been taken down.

Navigate Back to Your Starting Point

Back
Forward
Stop
Commodore 64
Obsolete Computer Museum

12. Click the drop-down arrow on the **Back** button; then select *Obsolete Computer Museum.*
Now you are back at the Obsolete Computer museum page in a single jump.

13. Click the **Back** button again.
This takes you back to the page which introduced this exercise.

14. If you wish, click the **Obsolete Computer Museum** link to visit the current version of the Web site.

Skill Builder 4.2 Browse with the Address Bar

In this exercise, you will navigate to Web pages with the Address bar.

1. Navigate to the home page of at least two Web sites from the selection of sites listed on page 143. If you see an error message, check for a typo in the Address bar, and try again.
Sometimes a Web site may not be available due to some technical problem on the network. You may need to try the site again in an hour or two, or the next day.

2. If you find a Web site that interests you, feel free to navigate in the site for a few minutes. Look for hyperlinks on the page in the form of navbars, images, and underscored text.

TIP!

Don't forget that many pictures may also be hyperlinks. When you point at a picture, watch for the pointer to change into a hand. Look at the lower-left corner of the status bar to see where the hyperlink is pointing.

http://www.si.edu/activity

Site Name	URL
National Geographic Magazine	www.nationalgeographic.com
National Archives	www.nara.gov/
Yosemite National Park	www.nps.gov/yose/yo_visit.htm
Hertz Rent A Car	www.hertz.com
Amazon	www.amazon.com
Smithsonian Institution	www.si.edu/
Library of Congress	lcweb.loc.gov/ *
Mark Twain	marktwain.miningco.com
eBay Auction site	www.ebay.com/
Project Gutenberg	promo.net/pg/ *
National Aeronautics and Space Administration	www.nasa.gov
Southwest Airlines	www.iflyswa.com

*Note: Not all URL's begin with www. These links are examples.

LIVE HYPERLINKS! *These are live Web links. It is possible for a link to have changed locations or to have shut down since this book was printed. Or, a link may be down temporarily due to technical problems. If you try a link and it does not work, try another link.*

Skill Builder 4.3 Narrow a Search

In this exercise, you will search for Web sites that specialize in the sale of used notebook computers. As you perform your searches, you will record the number of hits at various stages in the table below. Sometimes, fewer hits are far preferable to a large number of hits.

Step	Search word(s)	Number of hits
3	Computer	____________
5	Computer notebook	____________
6	Computer notebook used	____________

1. Use **Start→Programs→Internet Explorer** to start the Web browser.
2. Type the URL **`www.go.com`** in the **Address bar;** then tap the (ENTER) key.

Search with the Narrowing Technique

3. Enter the search word: **`Computer`**; then tap the (ENTER) key.
   Notice the number of hits you received. This search is too general. Let's narrow it by searching within this first hit list.

(Continued on the next page)

4. Check the *Web search results* section and write down the number of hits you obtained in the table at the top of this exercise.

5. Add the search word **`notebook`** to the search field. Make sure that the *Search within results* option is selected; then tap ENTER. When the new hit list appears, write down the number of hits in the table.

Search
New search
Search within results
notebook
Find

The number of hits should be much reduced now.

TIP!
Remember that the search word box and other controls may differ from this illustration. You are searching from a "live" page—not a simulation.

6. Add the search word **`used`** to the search field. Make sure that the *Search within results* option is selected again; then tap ENTER. Check the number of hits, and record it in the table.

7. Look at the number of hits for this search in the Web Results heading, and write it down in the table at the top of this exercise. If the number of hits is not less than the number of hits that you had in the previous search, you probably forgot to select the *Search within results* option. If this happens click the **Back** button, and perform Step 6 again.

8. Scan the descriptions of the first 20 hits. Do most of them appear relevant to searching for a used notebook computer?

9. *Right-click* on a Web site from the hit list; then select **Open in New Window** from the pop-up menu. Take a few minutes to look over the site.

10. When you have finished browsing, close ☒ the new Internet Explorer window for the Web site you were browsing.
Notice that the hit list is still open and ready for you to select another site to browse. The technique of opening hits in new windows is very handy when you want to investigate several Web sites.

11. *Right-click* the hyperlink of another hit result that looks interesting; then select **Open in New Window. Close** the window when you are done.

12. Take a moment to browse one more Web site. *Right-click* on a link from the search results list; then select **Open in New Window** from the pop-up menu. **Browse** the site briefly to determine if it is as relevant as you thought it would be.

13. When you have finished browsing, **close** ☒ all of the Internet Explorer windows.

Assessments

Assessment 4.1 Navigate to Web Pages and Print Them

1. Launch the **Internet Explorer.**
2. Navigate to the Web sites listed below. At each Web site, print the home page.

URL	Description
www.yahoo.com	A popular Internet search engine and portal
www.microsoft.com/ie	Home page for Internet Explorer online support

Assessment 4.2 Navigate with Hyperlinks

1. Navigate to the following Web page: **`www.offtowork.com/oe/test4`**.
   There are no hyperlinks to this page. You must use the Address bar.
2. Navigate with the hyperlinks on this and other pages until you reach the page titled *Stop, you made it!*
   Not all of the hyperlinks will be obvious. You will have to search for them on the pages. Some hyperlinks will be text hyperlinks; others will be images.
3. Print the *Stop, you made it!* page.

Assessment 4.3 Search for Web Pages

1. Start **Internet Explorer** and navigate to *www.go.com*
2. Perform a standard search on one of the topics in the list below. Your search should contain at least three hits that appear to be relevant.
   - A major league sports franchise in or near your city
   - Works by a selected author
   - State government information
   - Travel to your state
   - Travel to a region of your choice
3. After you complete the search, **print** the first search results page.
4. Write your name and the name of your topic at the top of the page.
5. Circle three hits that are relevant to your topic.

UNIT 3

Outlook 2000

This unit has two lessons that introduce the essential features of Outlook 2000. It begins with the basics of sending and receiving email messages. You will learn how to compose email messages, check for incoming email, and how to reply to messages that you receive from others. The unit concludes with topics on other features of Outlook, such as the Contacts list, Calendar, and Task list.

LESSON 5—Outlook

Sending and Receiving Email

Electronic mail (email) is one of the most popular services on the Internet. With an email account, you can exchange messages, documents, images, and virtually any other type of information with other email users anywhere in the world. The use of Internet email is growing so rapidly that it will become as common as the telephone within a few more years. It is not even necessary to have a computer in order to access email. Small, inexpensive devices are being sold that can put email in the palm of your hand. This lesson teaches you the basics of sending, receiving, and replying to email messages.

In This Lesson

Case Study

Daniel has just started a new job at the Acme Trading Company. Acme is an import/export business that works with other vendors in many countries. Daniel will be responsible for tracking Acme's shipments of dishware and glassware. He uses a company email account to correspond with his contacts at other vendor companies. Daniel has never used email before, but he finds it easy to send and receive his first few messages. Soon, he comes to prefer email to sending letters by postal mail. The vendors with whom he exchanges email prefer it too.

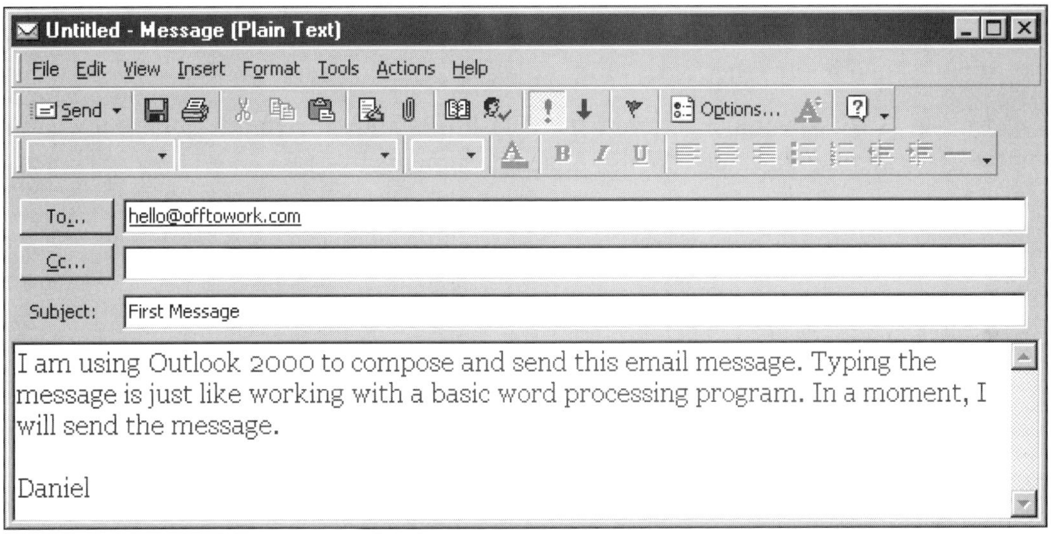
Untitled - Message (Plain Text)
File Edit View Insert Format Tools Actions Help
Send
Options...
To...
hello@offtowork.com
Cc...
Subject:
First Message
I am using Outlook 2000 to compose and send this email message. Typing the message is just like working with a basic word processing program. In a moment, I will send the message.
Daniel

Your first email message will look like this. You will also be replying to email messages you receive and forwarding messages to other email users.

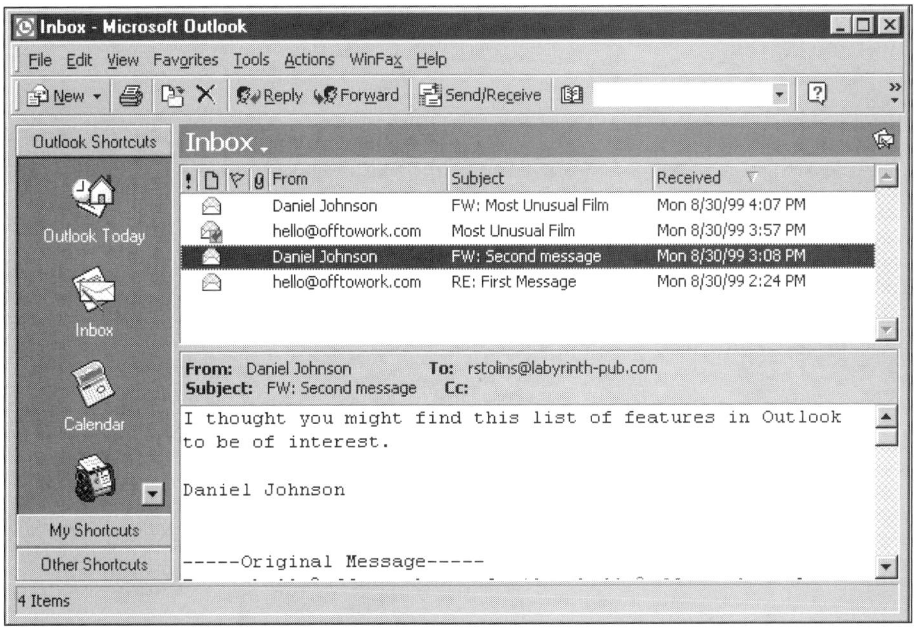
Inbox - Microsoft Outlook
File Edit View Favorites Tools Actions WinFax Help
New
Reply
Forward
Send/Receive
Outlook Shortcuts
Inbox
Outlook Today
Inbox
Calendar
My Shortcuts
Other Shortcuts
From
Subject
Received
Daniel Johnson
FW: Most Unusual Film
Mon 8/30/99 4:07 PM
hello@offtowork.com
Most Unusual Film
Mon 8/30/99 3:57 PM
Daniel Johnson
FW: Second message
Mon 8/30/99 3:08 PM
hello@offtowork.com
RE: First Message
Mon 8/30/99 2:24 PM
From: Daniel Johnson
To: rstolins@labyrinth-pub.com
Subject: FW: Second message
Cc:
I thought you might find this list of features in Outlook to be of interest.
Daniel Johnson
-----Original Message-----
4 Items

Outlook features several views that let you review, respond to, and print email messages. The Inbox *view lists new email messages as they are delivered.*

Starting Outlook

Outlook is a program for managing email, your calendar, names and addresses of contacts, and task lists. The Outlook program has a flexible interface that lets you shift among these various functions. A list of Outlook's basic functions appears below.

- **Electronic Mail (email)—**Outlook lets you send and receive email messages. You can organize messages into folders and create settings that help you manage your email. This lesson concentrates on sending and receiving email with Outlook.
- **Calendar—**Outlook lets you create appointments and display them in daily, weekly, and monthly views. You can set reminders for especially important appointments.
- **Contacts—**Outlook can maintain the names and addresses of all your correspondents. The Contacts list also stores email addresses, web page addresses (URLs), telephone numbers, and many other types of information.
- **Tasks—**Outlook lets you create task lists and set reminders for when various tasks are coming due. You can also attach documents to a task.
- **Notes—**Outlook lets you create the electronic equivalent of yellow sticky notes. You can even display notes directly on the Windows Desktop.

The illustration below describes significant features of the Outlook window.

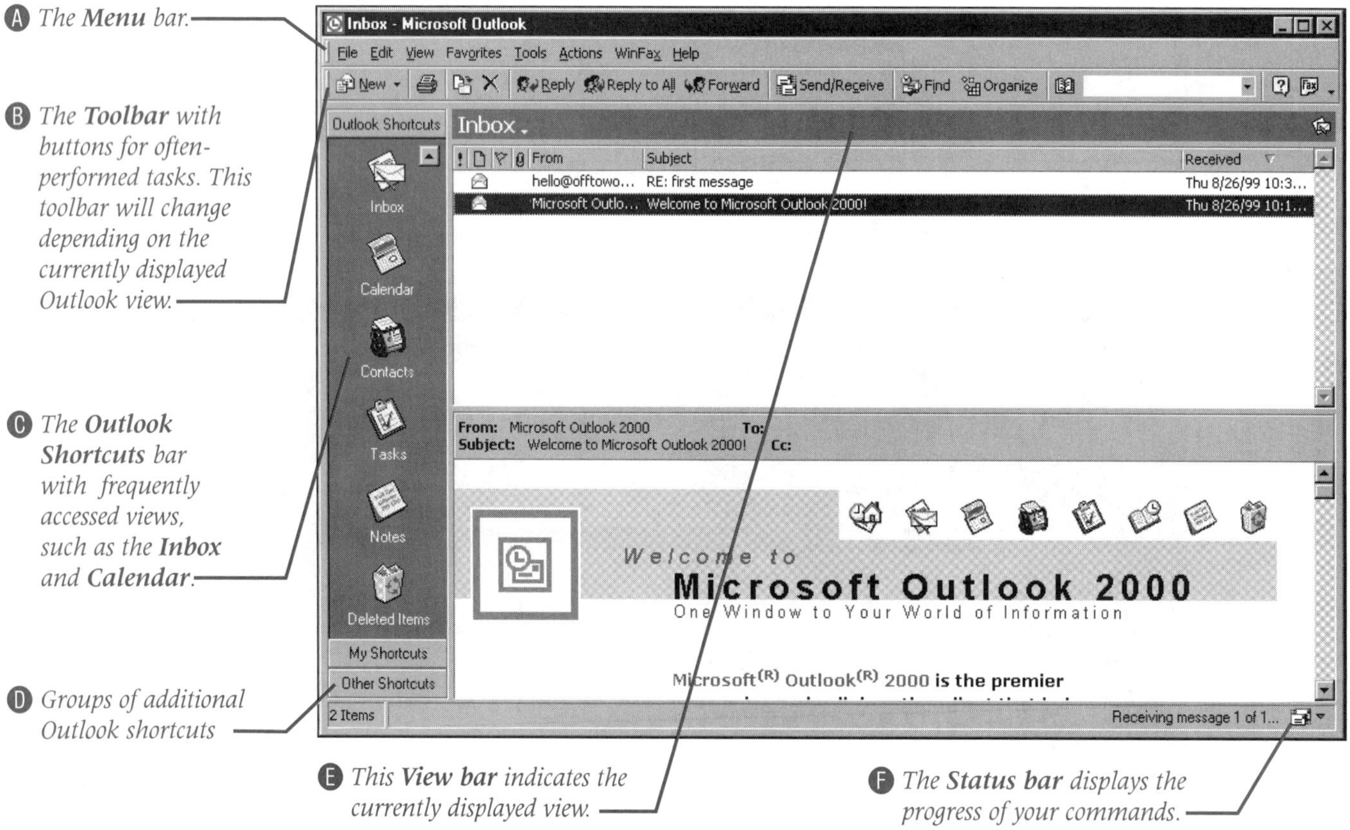

A The *Menu* bar.
B The *Toolbar* with buttons for often-performed tasks. This toolbar will change depending on the currently displayed Outlook view.
C The *Outlook Shortcuts* bar with frequently accessed views, such as the *Inbox* and *Calendar*.
D Groups of additional Outlook shortcuts
E This *View bar* indicates the currently displayed view.
F The *Status bar* displays the progress of your commands.
Inbox - Microsoft Outlook
File Edit View Favorites Tools Actions WinFax Help
New Reply Reply to All Forward Send/Receive Find Organize
Outlook Shortcuts
Inbox
Calendar
Contacts
Tasks
Notes
Deleted Items
My Shortcuts
Other Shortcuts
From Subject Received
hello@offtowo... RE: first message Thu 8/26/99 10:3...
Microsoft Outlo... Welcome to Microsoft Outlook 2000! Thu 8/26/99 10:1...
From: Microsoft Outlook 2000 To:
Subject: Welcome to Microsoft Outlook 2000! Cc:
Welcome to
Microsoft Outlook 2000
One Window to Your World of Information
2 Items
Receiving message 1 of 1...

The Outlook Bar

The Outlook bar is a convenient way to navigate among the various program views. You can customize the Outlook bar to give easy access to the commands and folders that you use frequently. The buttons on the Outlook bar are set up in **groups.** Each group has a button on the Outlook bar that you can click to display the group. The Outlook Shortcuts group contains buttons for all of Outlook's basic functions.

*These shortcut buttons can display the **My Computer** window and the contents of folders in the Outlook window. In this example, the My Computer window is displayed.*

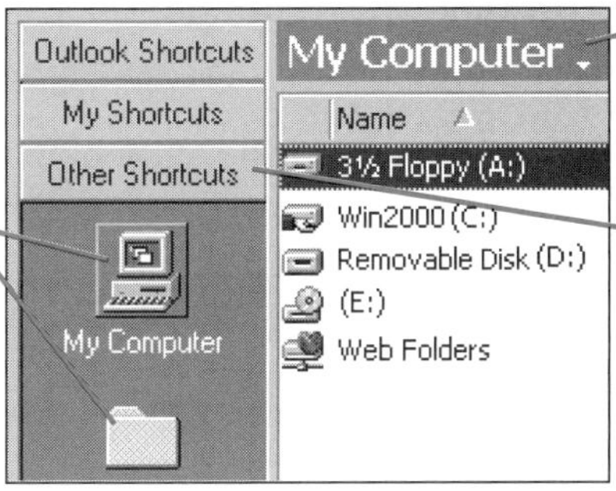

Outlook Shortcuts
My Shortcuts
Other Shortcuts
My Computer
My Computer
Name
3½ Floppy (A:)
Win2000 (C:)
Removable Disk (D:)
(E:)
Web Folders

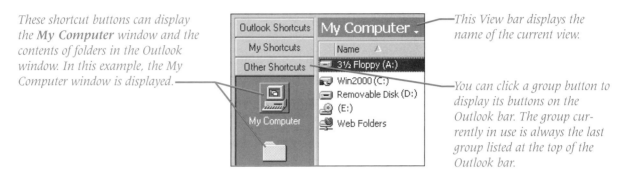

This View bar displays the name of the current view.

You can click a group button to display its buttons on the Outlook bar. The group currently in use is always the last group listed at the top of the Outlook bar.

Hands-On 5.1 Start Outlook

In this exercise, you will start the Outlook program and browse views of some program features.

1. Choose **Start→Programs→Microsoft Outlook** from the Start menu.
   The Outlook program window will appear.
2. Make sure that the Outlook window is Maximized ▣.
3. Follow these steps to view several Outlook features.

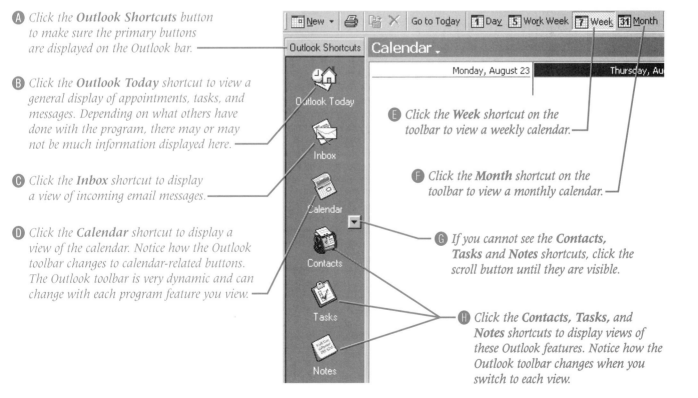

*Ⓐ Click the **Outlook Shortcuts** button to make sure the primary buttons are displayed on the Outlook bar.*

*Ⓑ Click the **Outlook Today** shortcut to view a general display of appointments, tasks, and messages. Depending on what others have done with the program, there may or may not be much information displayed here.*

*Ⓒ Click the **Inbox** shortcut to display a view of incoming email messages.*

*Ⓓ Click the **Calendar** shortcut to display a view of the calendar. Notice how the Outlook toolbar changes to calendar-related buttons. The Outlook toolbar is very dynamic and can change with each program feature you view.*

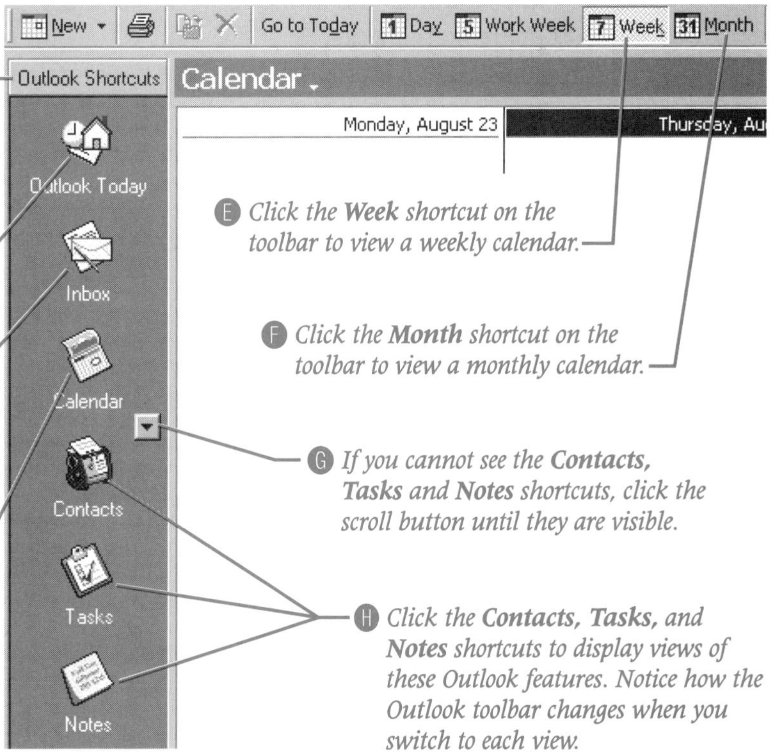

New
Go to Today
Day
Work Week
Week
Month
Outlook Shortcuts
Calendar
Monday, August 23
Outlook Today
Inbox
Calendar
Contacts
Tasks
Notes

*Ⓔ Click the **Week** shortcut on the toolbar to view a weekly calendar.*

*Ⓕ Click the **Month** shortcut on the toolbar to view a monthly calendar.*

*Ⓖ If you cannot see the **Contacts, Tasks and Notes** shortcuts, click the scroll button until they are visible.*

*Ⓗ Click the **Contacts, Tasks,** and **Notes** shortcuts to display views of these Outlook features. Notice how the Outlook toolbar changes when you switch to each view.*

4. Click the **Other Shortcuts** button at the bottom of the Outlook bar.
   The Outlook bar displays a new set of shortcuts to other views. You can add additional shortcuts to any of the button groups.
5. Click the **My Computer** button on the Outlook bar.
   Now the content of My Computer is displayed inside the Outlook window. This is exactly what you would see in an Exploring window.
6. Click the **Outlook Shortcuts** button at the very top of the Outlook bar.
   This restores the basic set of Outlook bar shortcuts.
7. Click the **Inbox** button on the Outlook bar.
   Leave the Outlook window open.

About Electronic Mail

Along with the Web, electronic mail (email) is the most popular of all Internet services. Email is simply the capability to send a message to a specific individual's email address anywhere in the world. An email message can also have one or more computer files (*attachments*) sent along with it. With email you can send and receive messages, send one message to more than one recipient, and exchange documents and images.

Components of Email Service

You need the following services in order to work with email on the Internet:

- **An email account—**Most Internet Service Providers (ISPs) give you an email account when you sign up for service. Your company may also provide you with an email account.
- **An email program (client)—**In order to work with your email account, you must install an email program on the computer. You use this program to create new messages, receive and reply to messages, and organize your messages. Microsoft Outlook 2000 is one example of an email program. Another popular email program is *Eudora Light.* An email program may sometimes be referred to as an email *client.*
- **A mail server—**The company or ISP that provides your email account must run a mail server program on one of its network system computers. The mail server program communicates with other mail servers over the Internet to send and receive email. Of course, in order to function, the mail server program must have a connection to the Internet.

How Email Reaches its Destination

When you send an email message, the following process takes place to move your message to its destination.

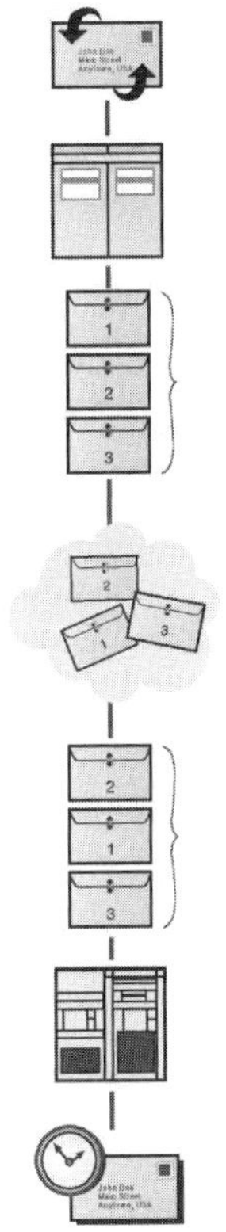

You use Outlook to create and compose the message, then give the send command.

The message is transmitted via your modem or local area network to the outgoing mail server at the office of your ISP or corporate information systems department. The mail server figures out how to find the addressee's mail server at the destination.

The message gets broken up into packets and sent through the Internet to the addressee's incoming *mail server destination.*

The message packets arrive at the incoming mail server and are reassembled into the message.

The addressee gives a send/receive mail *command from his or her email program. The message is transmitted from the incoming mail server to the addressee's email program and is copied to the addressee's hard drive. The addressee can now open, view, and reply to the message.*

Email Settings in Outlook

In order to help you use email, Outlook must have information about your email account. Your email account will probably be set up already. A summary of the email settings Outlook needs is listed in the following table:

Setting	Description	Example
Name	Your name as it will appear on email that you send to others. This name can be changed as needed without affecting the name of your email address.	Bob Smith Betsy Jones
Email address	The address others will use to send you email. Many companies follow a standard convention when they assign email names of first initial, and last name. Some people prefer to use a pseudonym for their email name.	mjones@college.edu clevername@hotmail.com anon@santa-fe.cc.nm.us
Incoming mail server	This is a program on the mail server computer in the network. It controls all *incoming* email.	Pop3.sfsu.edu
Outgoing mail (SMTP) server	This is another program on the mail server computer on the network. It controls all *outgoing* email. *Note: Sometimes the names of the POP server and SMTP server will be identical.*	smtp.sfsu.edu
Account name	This is the name the email system will need to identify you when Outlook logs on to send or receive mail. In most cases, your account name will be identical to your email address, but without the domain name.	mjones clevername
Password	A secret password that allows you to send and receive mail to the mail servers. Some computer facilities have special rules for acceptable passwords. For example, a password may be required to have a certain length or to contain both alphabetic characters and numbers.	Student12 4access What6Ever

Adaptive Menus

Office 2000 programs feature an adaptive menu system that hides menu bar commands that you rarely use. This reduces the number of menu commands that you need to scan when you choose a command from the menu bar. Thus you have two types of menus on the menu bar, as described below.

- **Short menu**—this menu contains only the most frequently used commands. Outlook displays the short menu when you first click on a menu bar command.
- **Expanded menu**—this menu contains all of the available commands. When you choose a command from the expanded menu it is moved to the short menu.

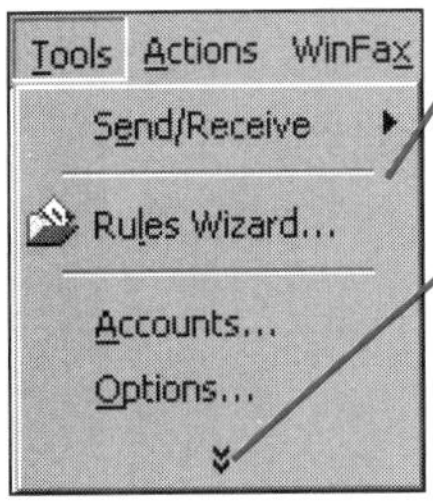
Tools Actions WinFax
Send/Receive
Rules Wizard...
Accounts...
Options...

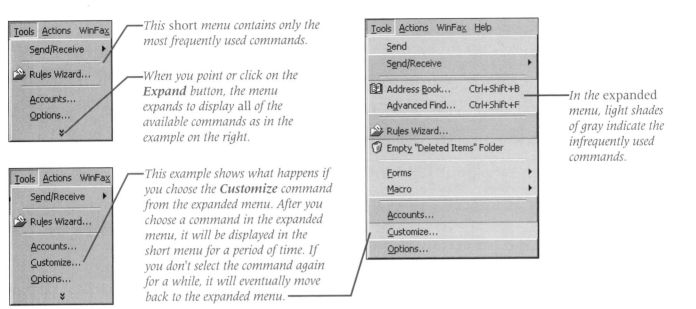

This short menu contains only the most frequently used commands.

*When you point or click on the **Expand** button, the menu expands to display all of the available commands as in the example on the right.*

Tools Actions WinFax
Send/Receive
Rules Wizard...
Accounts...
Customize...
Options...

*This example shows what happens if you choose the **Customize** command from the expanded menu. After you choose a command in the expanded menu, it will be displayed in the short menu for a period of time. If you don't select the command again for a while, it will eventually move back to the expanded menu.*

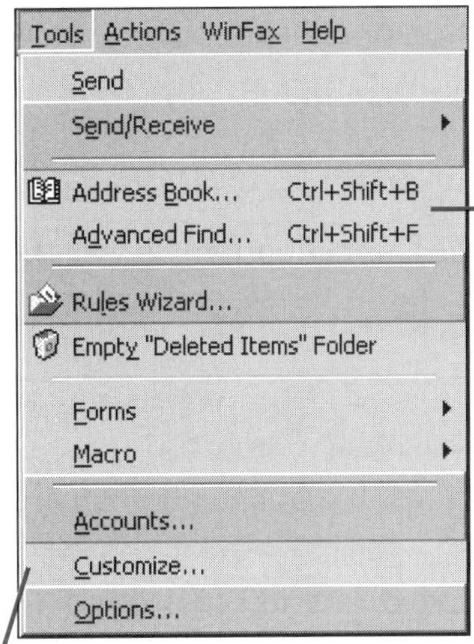
Tools Actions WinFax Help
Send
Send/Receive
Address Book... Ctrl+Shift+B
Advanced Find... Ctrl+Shift+F
Rules Wizard...
Empty "Deleted Items" Folder
Forms
Macro
Accounts...
Customize...
Options...

In the expanded menu, light shades of gray indicate the infrequently used commands.

Hands-On 5.2 View Your Email Settings

In this exercise, you will open a window to display information about your Internet email account. You will enter your own name as the name to display on outgoing email messages.

1. Choose **Tools→Accounts** from the menu bar.
2. Follow these steps to view the properties of your email account.

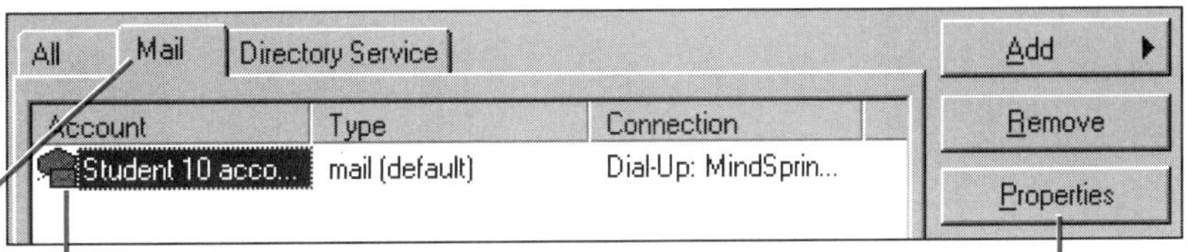
All
Mail
Directory Service
Account
Type
Connection
Student 10 acco...
mail (default)
Dial-Up: MindSprin...
Add
Remove
Properties

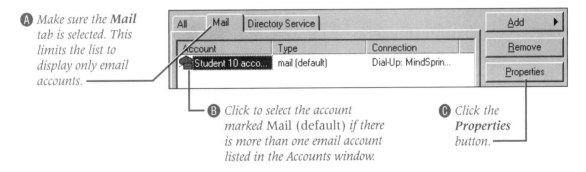

Ⓐ *Make sure the **Mail** tab is selected. This limits the list to display only email accounts.*

Ⓑ *Click to select the account marked* Mail (default) *if there is more than one email account listed in the Accounts window.*

Ⓒ *Click the **Properties** button.*

3. Follow these steps to change the mail user name for your account.

User Information
Name:
Daniel Johnson

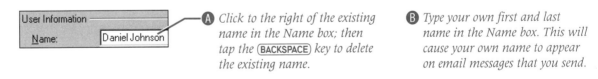

Ⓐ *Click to the right of the existing name in the Name box; then tap the* BACKSPACE *key to delete the existing name.*

Ⓑ *Type your own first and last name in the Name box. This will cause your own name to appear on email messages that you send.*

4. Click the **Apply** button at the bottom-right corner of the Properties dialog box.
   This applies the new name that you typed in the previous step.
5. Click the **Servers** tab near the top of the Properties window.
   This displays the names of the POP (incoming) server and SMTP (outgoing) mail servers for your account. Your account name is also listed. There may or may not be a password in the Password box.

(Continued on the next page)

6. Click the **Connection** tab near the top of the Properties window.
This displays the type of connection you have to the Internet. If you are performing this exercise in a computer classroom, you probably connect to the Internet over a local area network (LAN). If you perform this exercise at home, then your Internet connection is probably over a phone line.
7. Click the **Cancel** button to close the Properties window.
8. Click the **Close** button to close the Accounts window.

Setting Outlook Options

Outlook has many options you can set for its email functions. For example, you can set Outlook to check for new email messages automatically. The settings that are made when Outlook is first installed serve the needs of most users. These initial settings are called **defaults.** However, there may be times when you want to change a default setting. You can do this with the **Tools→Options** command.

Hands-On 5.3 Set Outlook Options

In this exercise, you will set Outlook to hold outgoing email messages until you give the Send/Receive command. You will also set Outlook to automatically check for new email messages every 15 minutes.

1. Choose **Tools→Options** from the menu bar. Click the Expand  button to expand the menu if the Options command is not displayed.
2. Follow these steps to set the Mail Delivery options.

(A) *Click the **Mail Delivery** tab. This displays a new set of options in the dialog box.*

(B) *Make sure that this check box is unchecked. If there is a checkmark in the box, click once to remove the checkmark.*

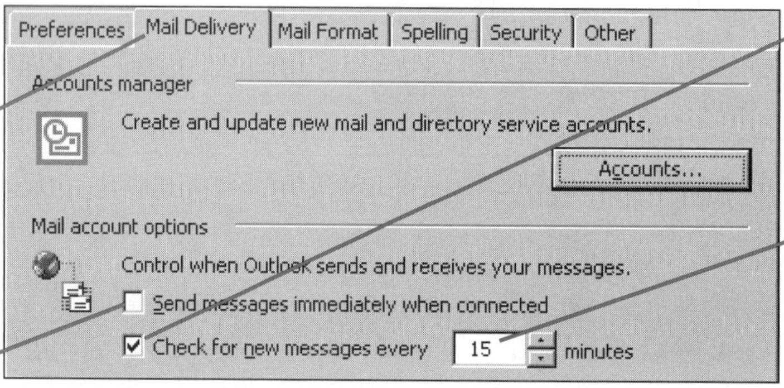
Preferences
Mail Delivery
Mail Format
Spelling
Security
Other
Accounts manager
Create and update new mail and directory service accounts.
Accounts...
Mail account options
Control when Outlook sends and receives your messages.
Send messages immediately when connected
Check for new messages every
15
minutes

(C) *Make sure that this checkbox is checked.*

(D) *Double-click in this checkbox to select the current setting, then type **15** as the new setting.*

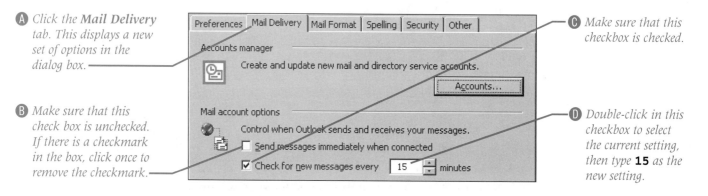

3. Click **OK** to close the Options window.

Sending an Email Message

From the Keyboard

CTRL+SHIFT+M to create a new email message.

Sending an email message is easy. If you know how to use a word processor, you know more than enough to create and send an email message. This topic will take you through the steps of sending your first email message with Outlook. To start an email message, you simply choose **File→New→Mail Message,** or you can click the **New** button on the toolbar and choose Mail Message.

Email Addresses

When you receive an email account, you are also given an email address. The address uniquely identifies your email account and where your mail server can be located. An email address looks similar to, and functions in much the same way as, the URL for a Web page.

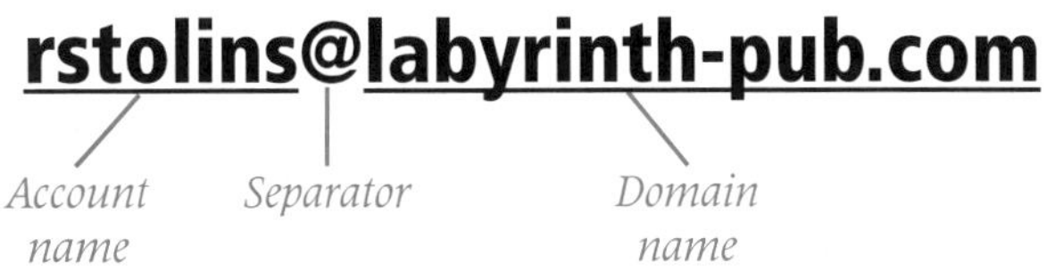

rstolins@labyrinth-pub.com
Account name
Separator
Domain name

Quick Reference

RULES FOR EMAIL ADDRESSES

- Email addresses *always* contain the @ symbol to separate the account name from the domain name.
- An email address *cannot* contain space characters.
- An email address *can* contain certain punctuation characters such as a dash and periods.

Message Importance (Priority)

TIP!

The importance you give a message has nothing to do with how fast it will actually be transmitted. The Internet treats every email message exactly the same, regardless of its importance setting.

When you send a message, you can give it one of three different importance levels, as described below.

- **Normal—**this is the default importance setting for messages. Most messages you send and receive will use this priority.
- **High—**this importance level indicates that the message should be opened and responded to right away.
- **Low—**this importance level is rarely used. If you know your recipient receives a lot of email every day, and your message is not very important, you might consider assigning it a low importance.

When someone receives a high- or low-importance email message, an importance flag will appear on its row in the Inbox.

The message priority column displays symbols for high- and low-priority messages.

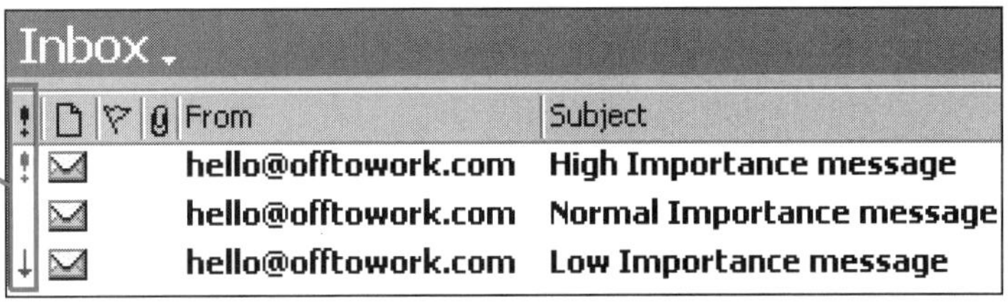

Inbox
From
Subject
hello@offtowork.com
High Importance message
hello@offtowork.com
Normal Importance message
hello@offtowork.com
Low Importance message

SEND AN EMAIL MESSAGE

Task	Procedure
Send an email message.	■ Choose **New→Mail** Message from the menu bar, or click the New button on the Outlook toolbar and choose Mail Message. ■ Address the message, and enter a subject. ■ Fill in the body of the message; then click the Send button.
Assign a priority to an email message.	■ Start the message. ■ Click the appropriate priority button if the message has high or low priority.

Hands-On 5.4 Create and Send an Email Message

In this exercise, you will create a new email message and send it to an email address at offtowork.com. This email address will automatically send a message back to you.

1. Click the New Mail Message button at the left side of the Outlook toolbar.
   A new email message window will appear on the screen. Outlook always gives you a separate window to compose email messages.
2. Follow these steps to start composing the first email message.

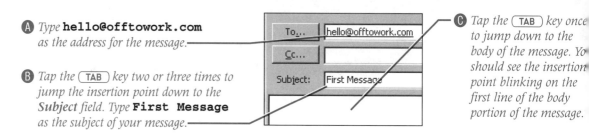

Ⓐ *Type* **hello@offtowork.com** *as the address for the message.*

Ⓑ *Tap the* TAB *key two or three times to jump the insertion point down to the* ***Subject*** *field. Type* **First Message** *as the subject of your message.*

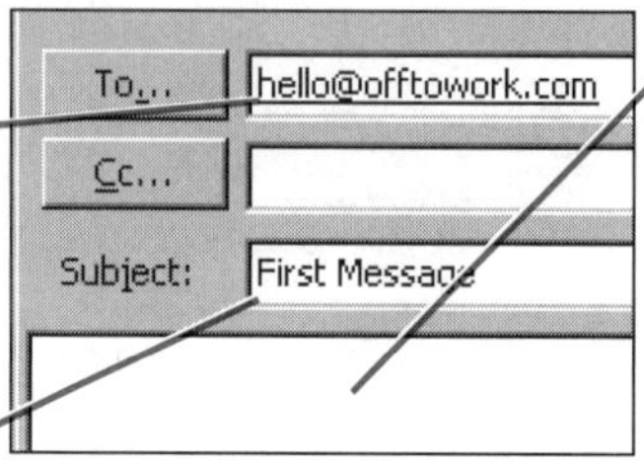

To...
hello@offtowork.com
Cc...
Subject:
First Message

Ⓒ *Tap the* TAB *key once to jump down to the body of the message. Yo should see the insertion point blinking on the first line of the body portion of the message.*

3. Read the comment below; then start typing the message that follows the comment.
   Don't worry about the message lines wrapping around exactly as they appear below. When you type to the end of the message box, a new line will be started for you automatically. You only need to tap ENTER *when you want to start a new line at the end of a paragraph or insert a blank line in the message. If you tap* ENTER *at the end of each line, your message will be difficult for the addressee to read.*

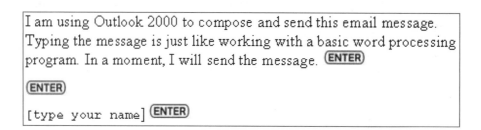

> I am using Outlook 2000 to compose and send this email message. Typing the message is just like working with a basic word processing program. In a moment, I will send the message. ENTER
>
> ENTER
>
> [type your name] ENTER

Set the Message Importance

4. Click the High Importance button on the message toolbar; then move your mouse pointer away from the button.
   The button appears to be "pushed in." This indicates that High Importance is set for this message.
5. Click the High Importance button again; then move the mouse pointer away from the button.
   Now the button no longer appears "pushed in." The High Importance setting has been switched off.
6. Click the High Importance button one last time.

Send the Message

7. Look over the message, and fix any typographic errors you may have made. If you see an error, click just to the right of the error, and tap the BACKSPACE key to delete the error. You can then retype the word, and it will be inserted into the message. After you've made any necessary corrections, go on to the next step.
   Many users make typos in their email messages. It's a good idea to scan your messages for typos before you send them. You should use the same level of care with business correspondence via email as you would use in a standard business letter.

8. Click the 
Send
button on the message toolbar to send your message.
This command does not actually send the message to the mail server system just yet. This is because you configured Outlook in the previous exercise not to send messages immediately upon giving the Send *command.*

9. Click the **My Shortcuts** group button at the bottom of the Outlook bar.
These shortcuts can display additional views that you use less often. Notice the (1) *in parenthesis next to the Outbox shortcut. This indicates that there is one message in the Outbox that is ready for transmission to the outgoing mail server.*

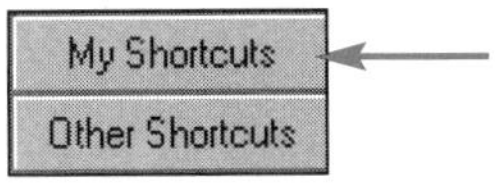
My Shortcuts
Other Shortcuts

10. *Right-click* on the Outlook bar; then choose **Large Icons** from the pop-up menu.
If the Outlook bar had been displaying small icons before, now they should be easier to see.

11. Click the **Outbox** shortcut on the Outlook bar.
Your message should be listed here. The Outbox is a folder that holds all outgoing email messages. When you give the Send/Receive *command, messages in this folder are transmitted to the outgoing mail server on the system that provides your Internet connection.*

12. Click the 
Send/Receive
button on the Outlook toolbar.

13. Use the following steps if you are asked to enter a password

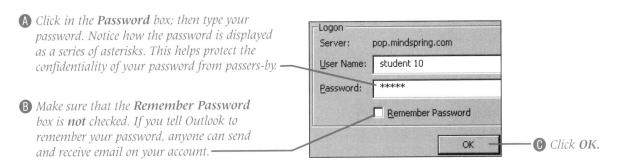

Ⓐ *Click in the **Password** box; then type your password. Notice how the password is displayed as a series of asterisks. This helps protect the confidentiality of your password from passers-by.*

Ⓑ *Make sure that the **Remember Password** box is **not** checked. If you tell Outlook to remember your password, anyone can send and receive email on your account.*

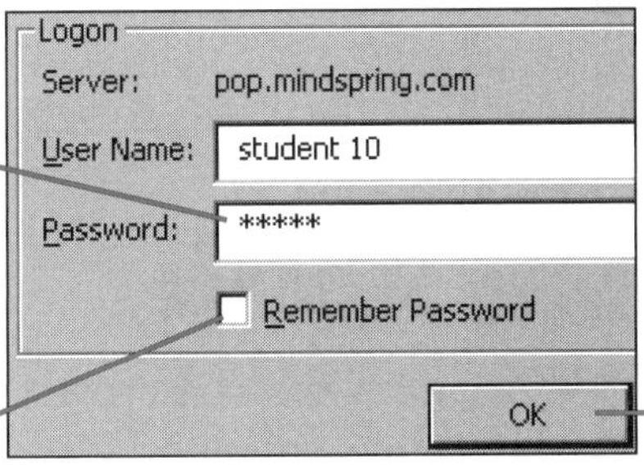
Logon
Server:
pop.mindspring.com
User Name:
student 10
Password:
*****
Remember Password
OK

Ⓒ *Click **OK**.*

Outlook will usually display a window that shows the progress of sending and receiving messages. Since your message is very short, this window may only appear for a few seconds. A portion of the window is displayed here.

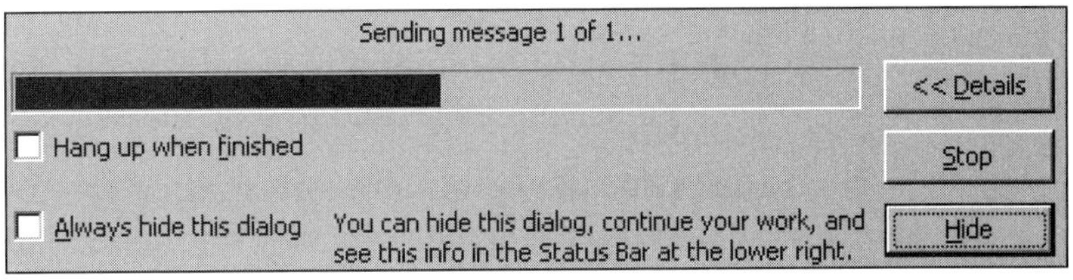
Sending message 1 of 1...
<< Details
Hang up when finished
Stop
Always hide this dialog
You can hide this dialog, continue your work, and see this info in the Status Bar at the lower right.
Hide

If the progress window is not visible, you should see a display at the bottom-right corner of the Outlook window in the Status bar. The Status bar can display information about making a connection to the mail server and the delivery of email messages.

Connecting to server...

Mail Delivery Complete

14. Click the **Sent Items** shortcut on the Outlook bar.
Now your message should appear in this list. Note the time the message was sent in the Sent *column of the list. Outlook keeps a copy of all your sent email messages so you can access them at a later time.*

Congratulations! You've just sent your first email message with Outlook 2000.

(Continued on the next page)

Send a Second Message

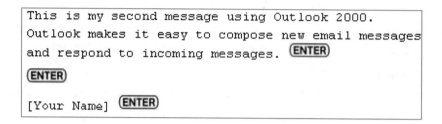

15. Click the New Mail Message [New] button at the left side of the Outlook toolbar.
16. Address the message to: **hello@offtowork.com**.
17. Tap the (TAB) key until the insertion point is blinking in the Subject line, type **Second message**, and tap the (TAB) key to jump to the body of the message.
18. Type the body of the message as shown below:

```
This is my second message using Outlook 2000.
Outlook makes it easy to compose new email messages
and respond to incoming messages. (ENTER)
(ENTER)
[Your Name] (ENTER)
```

19. Click the [Send] button on the message toolbar to send your message.
    The message has been sent to the Outbox, where it will be ready for delivery.
20. Click the [Send/Receive] button on the Outlook toolbar.
    Your message is delivered to the mail server system. It now begins its journey over the Internet to the addressee. Leave the Outlook window open.

Receiving Messages

When a new message arrives, it is stored in the mail server computer at your ISP or business network until you give the Send/Receive command to retrieve it. Outlook gives you two ways to retrieve messages.

- **Give the command manually—**You can click the *Send/Receive* button at any time to check for new messages and to send messages that are currently in your Outbox.
- **Give the command automatically—**You can set Outlook to check for new messages every few minutes or every few hours. You adjusted this setting in a previous Hands-On exercise.

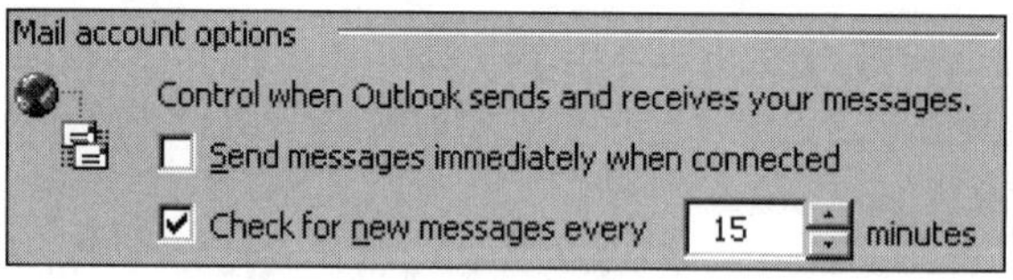
Mail account options
Control when Outlook sends and receives your messages.
Send messages immediately when connected
Check for new messages every
15
minutes

You make a setting in the Outlook options dialog box to check for new messages at a regular time interval.

Quick Reference

SETTING AUTOMATIC CHECKING OF EMAIL

Task	Procedure
Set Outlook to check for new messages automatically.	■ Choose **Tools→Options** from the menu bar. ■ Click the **Mail Delivery** tab. ■ Make sure that the Check for new messages option is checked; then set the time interval for automatic checks.

The Inbox

When messages arrive, they are placed in your *Inbox.* The Inbox normally holds all the messages sent to you until you place them into other folders or delete them. Outlook uses several folders to manage your email. For example, in the previous Hands-On exercise you viewed the *Outgoing* and *Sent Items* folders. You can also create your own email folders in Outlook.

The Send/Receive Command

The *Send/Receive* command in Outlook tells the program to contact your mail server to check for new messages. If there are incoming messages, they will be placed into your *Inbox.* At the same time, Outlook also sends any messages in the *Outbox* to the mail server system for delivery to their destinations.

Outlook has three ways to notify you that one or more new messages have arrived:

- A *new message* sound will play.
- A *number* will appear by the inbox label.
- A *small envelope icon* will appear in the bottom-right side of the Windows taskbar.

5:12 PM

Reading Incoming Messages

You can preview messages in the Outlook window, or you can double-click to open each message in a window of its own. The preview option is handy when you have many messages to review and don't want to open and close a lot of message windows. When you come across a longer message, you may want to open it in a separate message window.

You can sort your email messages alphabetically by sender, by subject, or by the date each message was received. You will practice these techniques in the next Hands-On exercise.

When Things Go Wrong

Sometimes you may receive a message that another message you tried to send did not go through. This may happen for a variety of reasons. For example, you may have typed the wrong address for the message. Or, the recipient's mail server system may have been out of operation. The mail server for your account will make several attempts, if necessary, to deliver each message. When it fails to deliver the message you will receive an error message.

TIP! *If you receive an error message, you should try sending your message again. Select the message in the* Sent Items *view, double-click to open the message, and then choose* Actions→Resend this Message *from the message window menu bar.*

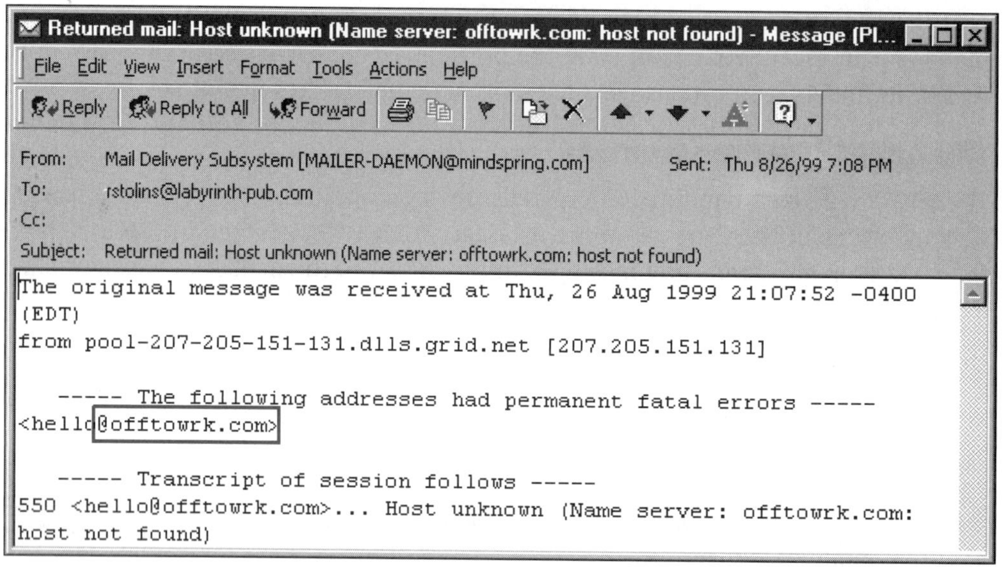

Returned mail: Host unknown (Name server: offtowrk.com: host not found) - Message (Pl...
File Edit View Insert Format Tools Actions Help
Reply
Reply to All
Forward
From: Mail Delivery Subsystem [MAILER-DAEMON@mindspring.com]
Sent: Thu 8/26/99 7:08 PM
To: rstolins@labyrinth-pub.com
Cc:
Subject: Returned mail: Host unknown (Name server: offtowrk.com: host not found)
The original message was received at Thu, 26 Aug 1999 21:07:52 -0400 (EDT)
from pool-207-205-151-131.dlls.grid.net [207.205.151.131]
----- The following addresses had permanent fatal errors -----
<hello@offtowrk.com>
----- Transcript of session follows -----
550 <hello@offtowrk.com>... Host unknown (Name server: offtowrk.com: host not found)

A typographic error in the email address can result in returned email.

Hands-On 5.5 Check for New Messages

1. Follow these steps to view the Inbox.

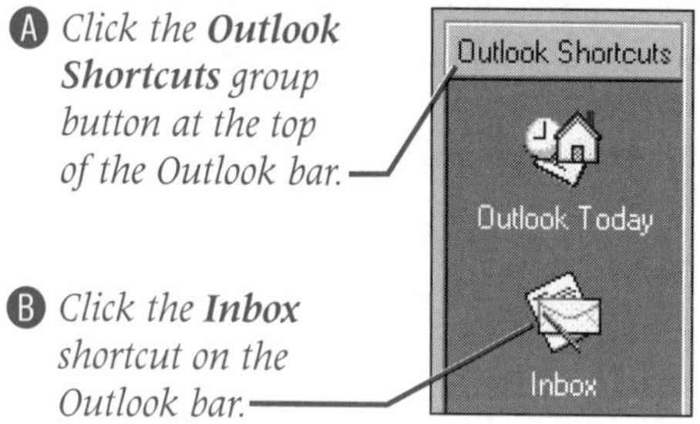

Ⓐ Click the Outlook Shortcuts group button at the top of the Outlook bar.
Ⓑ Click the Inbox shortcut on the Outlook bar.
Outlook Shortcuts
Outlook Today
Inbox

You used the Send/Receive command earlier to transmit your email message to the outgoing mail server. You will use the same command to check the incoming mail server for newly arrived email messages.

2. Click the Send/Receive button on the Outlook toolbar. If you are asked for your password, type your password and click **OK**.
Depending on how Outlook is configured, you may see a dialog box displaying the progress of the Send/Receive command. The status bar will also display the progress of your Send/Receive command.

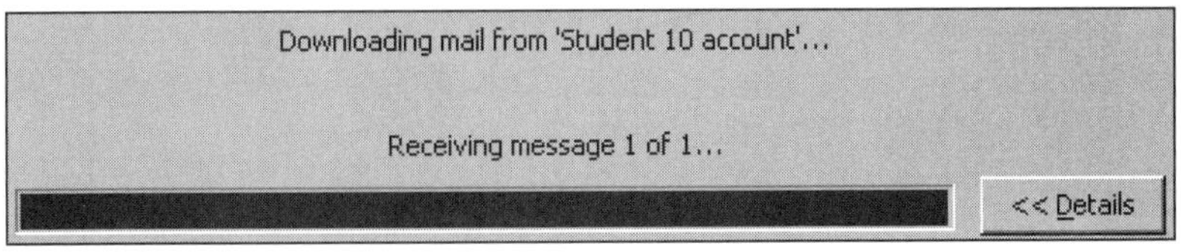
Downloading mail from 'Student 10 account'...
Receiving message 1 of 1...
<< Details

You may be asked to enter your password each time you send and receive email. Without password protection, anyone could send and receive email on your account.

3. If you do not see a message being received, repeat the **Send/Receive** command about every 30 seconds until you receive the message.
Depending on the level of traffic on the Internet, it may take up to two or three minutes for your first message to be received and for the reply to reach the mail server for your email account. Sometimes, the turnaround will take just one minute or less.

4. Notice the **new message** icon next to the system time at the bottom-right corner of the Deskop.

5:12 PM

This icon will remain on the taskbar until you read at least one of the new messages in Outlook.

Read the Newly Arrived Message in the Inbox View

5. Look at the middle of the Inbox view. If you do not see a bar similar to the one shown here, choose **View→Preview Pane** on the menu bar.

From: hello@offtowork.com
To: rstolins@labyrinth-pub.com
Subject: RE: Second message
Cc:

Most Outlook users leave the preview pane switched on.

6. Click on the **RE: Second Message** in the Inbox. Read the response to your second message in the **preview** window in the bottom panel of the Inbox view.

7. Tap the Down arrow ↓ key on your keyboard to view the response to your first message.
The Up and Down arrow keys are a handy way to navigate through your email messages. Also, notice that the icon for your first message has changed from a closed envelope to an opened one.

8. Tap the Up arrow ↑ key on your keyboard to return to the previous message.

(Continued on the next page)

9. Follow these steps to change the height of the Preview Pane.

Ⓐ *Point at the window border until a double-arrow appears; then **drag up** to make the preview window taller. You can always change the height of the preview window in this fashion.*

Ⓑ *Drag the preview window down until it is about half the height of the Outlook window.*

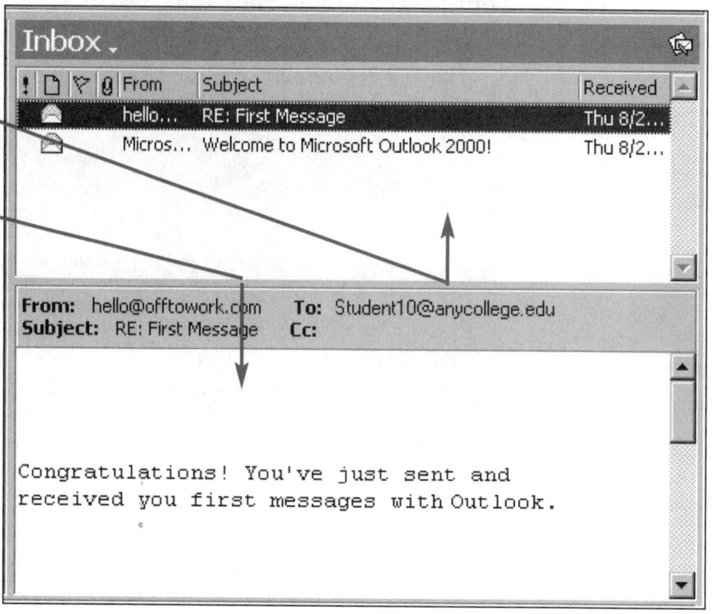

Inbox
From
Subject
Received
hello...
RE: First Message
Thu 8/2...
Micros...
Welcome to Microsoft Outlook 2000!
Thu 8/2...
From: hello@offtowork.com
To: Student10@anycollege.edu
Subject: RE: First Message
Cc:
Congratulations! You've just sent and
received you first messages with Outlook.

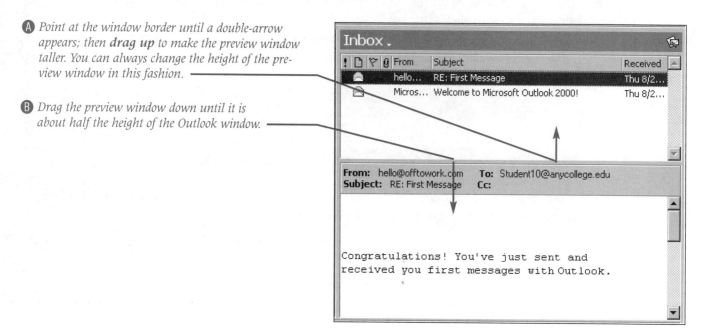

Sort the Inbox Messages

You can sort email messages by clicking on column headings just as you did in the My Computer window in the previous lesson.

10. Follow these steps to practice sorting messages in the Inbox.

Ⓐ *Click the **From** column heading to sort the messages by sender.*

Ⓑ *Notice the small up-pointing triangle. This tells you that the message list is being sorted on this column in **ascending** order. Click the **From** column heading again to sort the messages in descending order. Notice that the small triangle now points down.*

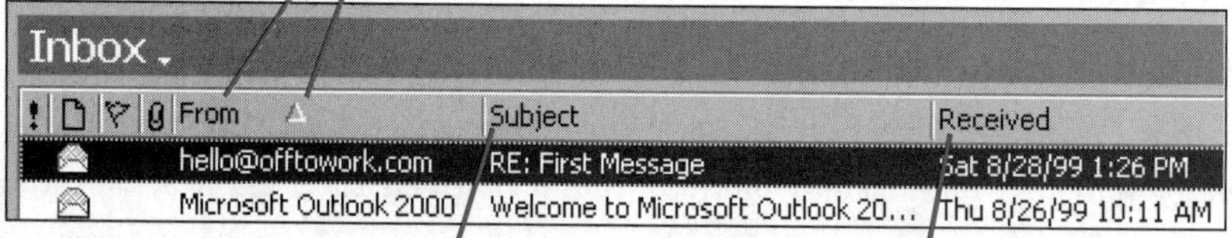

Inbox
From
Subject
Received
hello@offtowork.com
RE: First Message
Sat 8/28/99 1:26 PM
Microsoft Outlook 2000
Welcome to Microsoft Outlook 20...
Thu 8/26/99 10:11 AM

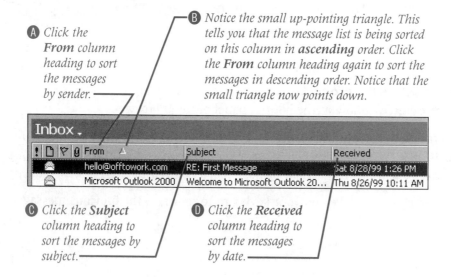

Ⓒ *Click the **Subject** column heading to sort the messages by subject.*

Ⓓ *Click the **Received** column heading to sort the messages by date.*

Read a Message in Its Own Window

11. *Double-click* on the top message in the list. This is the reply to your second message just received from *hello@offtowork.com.*
    The reply is now open in a message window.
12. Minimize the **Outlook** window (not the message window).
13. Point at the bottom border of the message window until you see the double-arrow ↕. Then **drag down** on the bottom margin of the message window to make it larger on the screen for easier reading of the message. You can also drag up on the window's title bar if it is already near the bottom of the Windows Desktop.

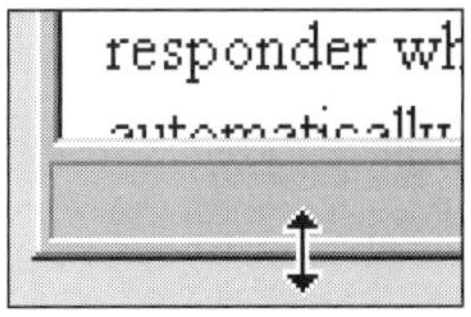

responder wh

14. Click the Next Item button on the message window toolbar to view the next message. This should be the response to your first message.
    You can use the Next and Previous buttons to navigate through all of your messages in the Inbox.
15. Click the Next Item button again.
    The next message in the Inbox will appear, or the message window will close if there are no more messages to display.
16. Close the message window if it is still open.
17. Click the Inbox - Microsoft Outlook button on the Windows Taskbar to restore the program window to the Desktop.

Flagging Messages

You can flag messages in the Inbox as a reminder to follow up. For example, you can flag a message and set a reminder to send a reply or place a phone call to the sender. Flags are especially useful when you need to follow up on specific messages, but don't have the time to do so when you initially read the messages. You can flag the most important messages as you read, then later re-read the flagged messages.

You can type a custom message *for the* ***Flag****.*

You can set a reminder *for the* Flag. *Outlook will display a reminder message at the date and time of the reminder.*

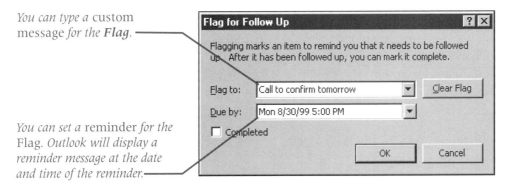

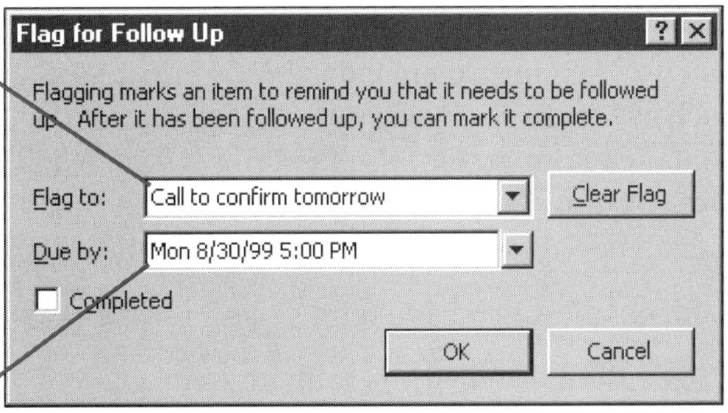

Flag for Follow Up
Flagging marks an item to remind you that it needs to be followed up. After it has been followed up, you can mark it complete.
Flag to:
Call to confirm tomorrow
Clear Flag
Due by:
Mon 8/30/99 5:00 PM
Completed
OK
Cancel

Quick Reference

FLAGGING MESSAGES

Task	Procedure
Flag a message.	■ *Right-click* on the message to be flagged; then choose *Flag* from the pop-up menu.
	■ If you wish, you can change the label for the flag and set a reminder date.
Clear the flag from a message.	■ *Right-click* on the message with the flag; then choose *Clear Flag* from the pop-up menu.

Hands-On 5.6 Flag a Message

1. Make sure that the **Inbox** view is displayed.
2. *Right-click* on the **RE: First Message** you received from *hello@offtowork.com;* then choose **Flag for follow-up** from the pop-up menu.
3. Follow these steps to set the message flag options.

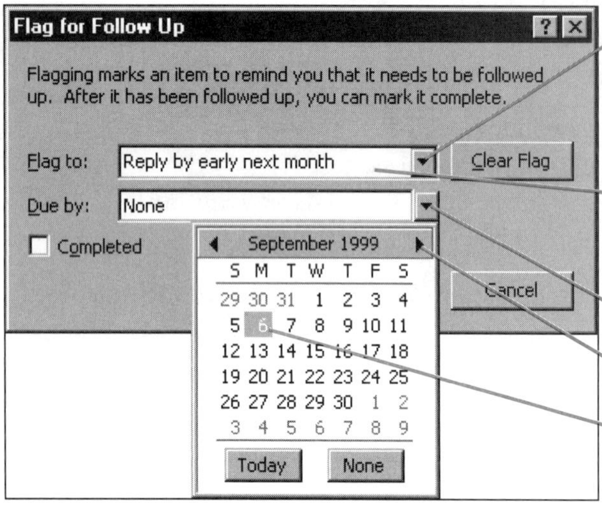

Flag for Follow Up
Flagging marks an item to remind you that it needs to be followed up. After it has been followed up, you can mark it complete.
Flag to:
Reply by early next month
Clear Flag
Due by:
None
Completed
September 1999
S M T W T F S
29 30 31 1 2 3 4
5 6 7 8 9 10 11
12 13 14 15 16 17 18
19 20 21 22 23 24 25
26 27 28 29 30 1 2
3 4 5 6 7 8 9
Today
None
Cancel

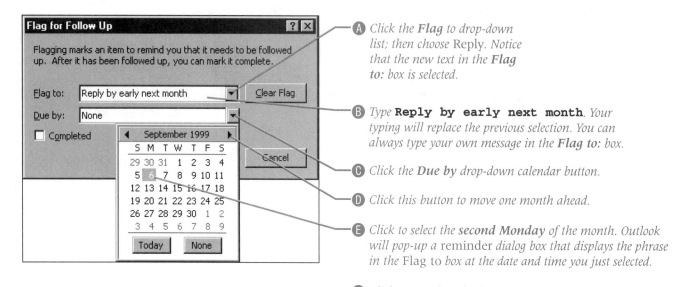

Ⓐ *Click the **Flag** to drop-down list; then choose* Reply. *Notice that the new text in the **Flag to:** box is selected.*

Ⓑ *Type* **Reply by early next month**. *Your typing will replace the previous selection. You can always type your own message in the **Flag to:** box.*

Ⓒ *Click the **Due by** drop-down calendar button.*

Ⓓ *Click this button to move one month ahead.*

Ⓔ *Click to select the **second Monday** of the month. Outlook will pop-up a* reminder *dialog box that displays the phrase in the* Flag to *box at the date and time you just selected.*

Ⓕ *Click **OK** to close the dialog box.*

Notice that a small red flag now appears in the message row. This can be a useful reminder that a message should receive attention in the future.

4. *Right-click* on **RE: First Message;** then choose **Clear Flag** from the pop-up menu.
The flag is cleared from the message. The message is still selected for your next command.

Printing Messages

You use the same commands to print email messages that you use with other Windows programs such as WordPad (File→Print). The toolbar of the Outlook window and each message window contain a Print button. Use the Print button whenever you wish to print the entire message. Outlook also offers a **print preview** option that displays how a message will print. Besides individual messages, you can also print a list of the email messages in the Inbox.

From the Keyboard
CTRL+P to print.

Outlook offers two basic print styles.

- **Items—**When you print an item, Outlook prints whatever type of item is currently selected. For example, Outlook can print an individual email message or an event on the calendar. Items always print with the Memo print style.
- **Views—**Outlook can print the list, calendar, or other type of information displayed in a view. For example, if you are displaying the Inbox view, Outlook can print a list of the email messages displayed in the view.

TIP! *When the print dialog box displays print styles other than* Memo, *these styles print* views *rather than* items.

Quick Reference

PRINTING EMAIL MESSAGES

Task	Procedure
Print an Email message.	■ **Select** the message in the Outlook window. ■ Choose **File→Print** from the menu bar, or click the Print button on the toolbar.
Print a list of messages in the Inbox.	■ Choose **File→Print** from the menu bar. ■ Choose the *Table* print style.

Hands-On 5.7 Print a Message

1. Choose **File→Print** from the menu bar to display the print dialog.
2. Click the **Table Style** option; then click the **Preview** button at the bottom-right corner of the Print dialog box.
   Outlook displays a preview of the message list as it will print. This is an example of printing a view rather than an item, such as an email message.
3. Close the Print Preview window.
4. Click the Print button on the Outlook toolbar. Retrieve the printout from the printer.
   This is an example of printing an item. In the next lesson, you will use the same Print button to print other types of items such as a weekly calendar or an entry in the task list.

Responding to Messages

In a previous exercise, you received a message. There will often be occasions when you want to reply to a message right away. The *Reply* commands make it easy to respond to a message, without the need to retype the email address. In addition, Outlook automatically adds an *RE:* prefix to the subject line so your correspondent knows you are replying to a message.

From: hello@offtowork.com
Date: Tuesday, June 01, 1999 2:38 PM
To: rstolins@labyrinth-pub.com
Subject: RE: check it out

Outlook places an RE: *in front of the original subject line of every reply.*

Reply Compared to *Reply to All*

If you look at the toolbar, you will notice a second reply button. The table below describes the difference between these two commands.

Command	What It Does
Reply	This command creates a message addressed only to the sender of the original message.
Reply to All	This command creates a message addressed to the sender of the original message *and* to every one else who received the original message.

Including the Previous Message

Outlook will automatically place a copy of the message you are responding to in your reply. This helps the person you are replying to know exactly what your reply is about. If you don't want to include the original message in a particular reply, you can always select and delete it as you do in the body of a normal message.

Forwarding Messages

Sometimes you may receive a message that really should be handled by someone else. Or you may want to share it with another correspondent. You could use *copy and paste* to copy the text of the message and paste it into a new message. But it is much easier to use the *forward* command instead. This command makes a copy of the message and lets you address it to a different addressee. The subject line of the message also reflects that the message is being forwarded (i.e., it originated from someone other than you).

Emoticons (Smileys)

One disadvantage of email over making a telephone call is that all you have to communicate with is *words.* Since English is an inflected language, some meaning can be lost when something is expressed in writing alone. One way to overcome the lack of inflection is to use **emoticons** (also called *smileys*) from time to time in your messages. An emoticon can help convey the attitude or emotion behind a phrase. At the right are a few examples of emoticons.

Emoticon	Meaning
:-)	Joking
:-0	Bored
;-)	Winking
:-(	Sad
:-<	Frowning

To create an emoticon, you use some of the punctuation keys on the keyboard. For example, the joking emoticon is composed of a semicolon, followed by a dash, followed by a close parenthesis.

There are literally hundreds of emoticons available. The Web page for this lesson (*www.offtowork.com/oe/lesson5*) contains links to Web pages that list some of the most popular and creative emoticons. In the next exercise, you will use an emoticon.

Hands-On 5.8 Reply to and Forward Messages

In this exercise you will send a reply to the message you received from Hello. You will also forward the message.

1. Follow these steps to create a reply to the message you just received.

Ⓐ *Make sure the reply to your first email message is selected in the* ***Inbox****. If it is not, click once on the message to select it.*

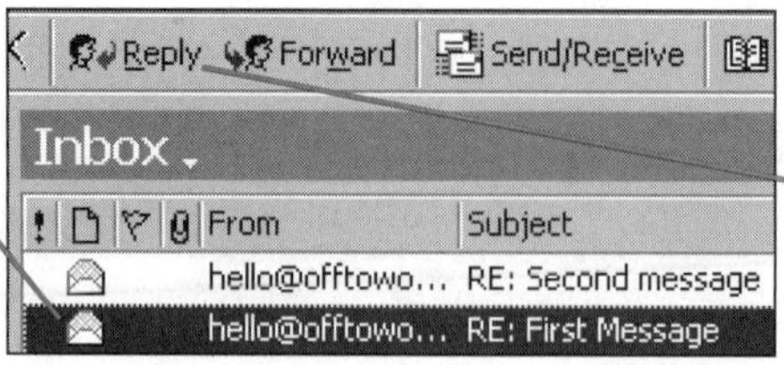

Reply
Forward
Send/Receive
Inbox
From
Subject
hello@offtowo... RE: Second message
hello@offtowo... RE: First Message

Ⓑ *Click the* ***Reply*** *button on the toolbar. A new message window will appear.*

Notice that the address of the sender (hello@offtowork.com) is already typed in the ***To:*** *box. The subject line has been filled in for you as well. There is even a copy of the original message already printed in the message body. The insertion point will be blinking in the first line of the message body, ready for you to type the text of your reply.*

2. Follow these steps to change the subject line of your reply.

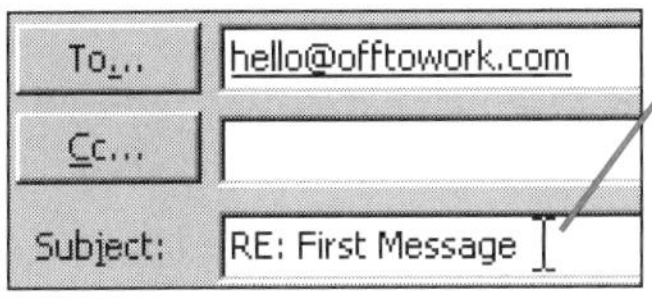
To...
hello@offtowork.com
Cc...
Subject:
RE: First Message

Ⓐ *Point at the end of the subject line until you see the* ***text I-beam*** *; then click.*

Ⓑ *Tap the* BACKSPACE *key to delete the current subject, then type* **Replying** *as the new subject for the message.*

You can change the subject line of a reply at any time.

3. Tap the TAB key to jump the cursor down to the body of the message. Then type the following:

> Thanks for your prompt reply. The way you turned around my message, it seems that you spend all your time watching for new email. Is this a new hobby of yours?

4. Now you will type a smiley *emoticon* that will look like this: **:-)**
   - Tap the SPACE BAR to add a space after the question mark.
   - Type a colon **:**
   - Type a dash **-**
   - While holding down the SHIFT key, type a close parenthesis **)**.
5. Continue typing the rest of the message:

```
(ENTER)

(ENTER)
I will feel free to send other messages your way when I
need the practice. (ENTER)
(ENTER)
[your name] (ENTER)
```

6. Review the message and correct any typos; then click the Send button to send the message to the Outbox.
   Notice that the icon for the message you replied to now displays a small arrow . This indicates that you have replied to the message. The message will be held in the Outbox until you give the Send/Receive command later in this exercise.

(Continued on the next page)

Forward a Message

7. *Double-click* to open the reply to your second message in its own window.
8. Click the [Forward] button on the toolbar of the message window that just popped up.
   A new message window appears with the body of the message you are forwarding already copied. An FW: *prefix has been placed at the beginning of the subject line. The Reply and Forward buttons are always available from the main Outlook window and individual message windows.*
9. In the **To:** box, address the forwarded message to yourself (that is, type your own email address).
10. Tap the (TAB) key *three* times to jump to the body of the message. Then type the following message:

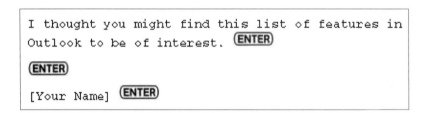

```
I thought you might find this list of features in
Outlook to be of interest. (ENTER)
(ENTER)
[Your Name] (ENTER)
```

11. Click the [Send] button to send the message.
12. Close [X] the message window of the message you just forwarded.
    Notice that the icon for the message you replied to now displays a small arrow. This indicates that you have forwarded the message. Notice also that this arrow points in the opposite direction of the replied to message arrow.

You have forwarded this message.

You have replied to this message.

13. Click [Send/Receive] on the Outlook toolbar to send your outgoing messages and check for new messages. Enter your password, and click **OK** if you are prompted to do so.

Check for New Mail

14. Wait about one minute; then click [Send/Receive] to check for new messages. Keep clicking the Send/Receive button once a minute until you receive the new messages.
15. Read the new messages in the preview window.
    Leave the Outlook window open.

Deleting Messages

As you work with email, there will be times when you want to delete a message that is no longer relevant or a message that is actually junk email (called *spam*). If you delete a message by mistake, it is usually possible to undelete it.

The Deleted Items Folder

Deleted messages always go into the *Deleted Items* folder first. The Deleted Items folder works in a fashion similar to the *Recycle Bin* in Windows. It holds deleted email messages and folders. If you later decide that you wish to keep a message you had deleted previously, you can look for it in the Deleted Items folder and **Retrieve** the message by moving it into a different folder.

When the Deleted Items folder is *emptied,* all the messages in it are permanently erased. To save disk space, you should empty the Deleted Items folder from time to time.

Quick Reference

DELETING AND RETRIEVING MESSAGES

Task	Procedure
Delete a message.	■ Select the message in a view. ■ Drag it to the *Deleted Items* folder, or click the *Delete* button on the toolbar, or tap (DELETE) to delete the selected items.
Retrieve (undelete) a message.	■ Select the *Deleted Items* folder. ■ *Drag* the item to be undeleted to the Outlook bar shortcut, where it should be restored-for example, to the *Inbox* shortcut.
Permanently delete messages.	■ *Right-click* the *Deleted Items* folder. ■ Select *Empty 'Deleted Items' Folder* from the pop-up menu.

Hands-On 5.9 Delete and Retrieve Messages

Delete Messages

1. Make sure that the **Inbox** is displayed in the Outlook window.
2. Follow these steps to delete your email messages.

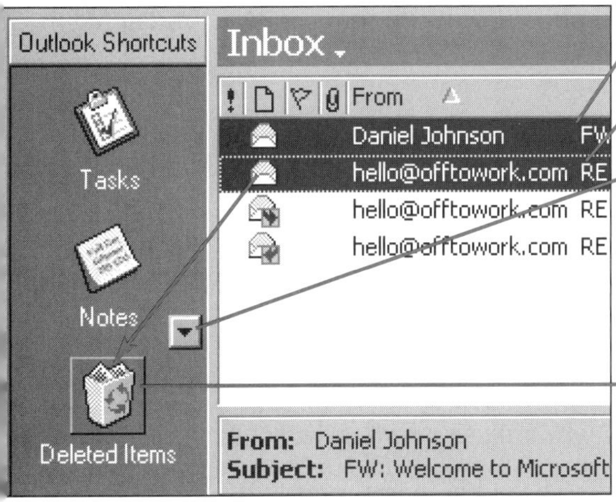

Outlook Shortcuts
Inbox
From
Daniel Johnson
hello@offtowork.com
hello@offtowork.com
hello@offtowork.com
Tasks
Notes
Deleted Items
From: Daniel Johnson
Subject: FW: Welcome to Microsoft

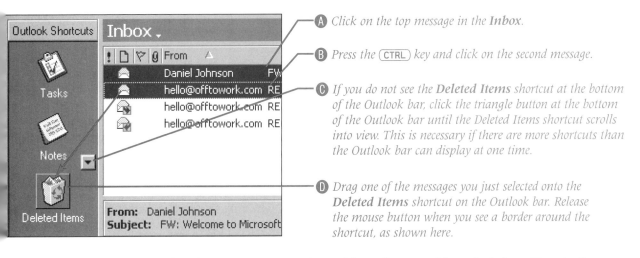

Ⓐ *Click on the top message in the* ***Inbox.***

Ⓑ *Press the* (CTRL) *key and click on the second message.*

Ⓒ *If you do not see the* ***Deleted Items*** *shortcut at the bottom of the Outlook bar, click the triangle button at the bottom of the Outlook bar until the Deleted Items shortcut scrolls into view. This is necessary if there are more shortcuts than the Outlook bar can display at one time.*

Ⓓ *Drag one of the messages you just selected onto the* ***Deleted Items*** *shortcut on the Outlook bar. Release the mouse button when you see a border around the shortcut, as shown here.*

Notice that the two messages you dragged have disappeared from the Inbox. *Now the first message remaining in the Inbox is selected.*

3. Click the Delete [X] button on the Outlook toolbar to delete the selected message.
This message has also been sent to the Deleted Items folder.

(Continued on the next page)

Retrieve One of the Messages

4. Click the **Deleted Items** shortcut on the Outlook bar.
   You will see the messages you just deleted in Steps 2 and 3. The messages will stay in this folder until you empty the Deleted Items folder.
5. Click the Scroll Up button near the top of the Outlook bar if the Inbox shortcut is not visible.
   Notice that the Deleted Items folder and its contents are still displayed.
6. **Drag** one of the messages in the Deleted Items view over the **Inbox** shortcut on the Outlook bar. Release the mouse button when you see a border around the Inbox shortcut, as shown below.

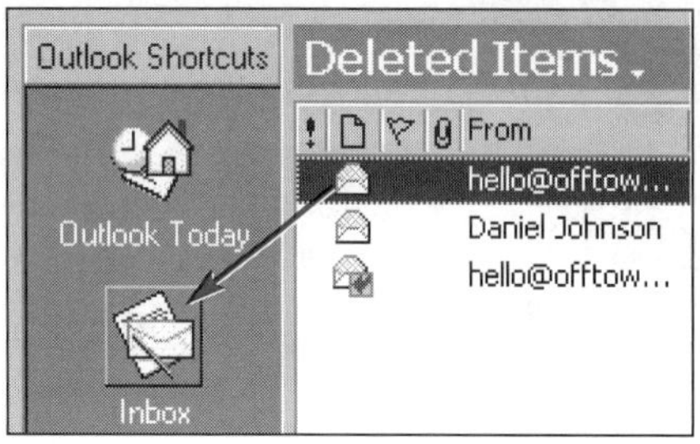

Outlook Shortcuts
Deleted Items
From
hello@offtow...
Daniel Johnson
hello@offtow...
Outlook Today
Inbox

   You have just "undeleted" the message from the Deleted Items folder. Anytime you delete a message by mistake, you can retrieve it from the Deleted Items folder.
7. Click the **Inbox** shortcut on the Outlook bar, and confirm that the message was undeleted.

Empty the Deleted Items Folder

8. If necessary, use the Scroll Down button to scroll the Outlook bar; then click the **Deleted Items** shortcut on the Outlook bar. Notice that two of the messages you deleted earlier are still in this folder.
9. *Right-click* the **Deleted Items** button on the Outlook bar; then choose **Empty→Deleted Items Folder** from the pop-up menu.
   You will see a warning that you are about to permanently delete the contents of this folder. You cannot retrieve items after the Deleted Items folder has been emptied. However, when you permanently delete unneeded messages, they will no longer take up space on the computer's hard drive.
10. Click **Yes** to confirm that the messages in the folder should be permanently deleted.
   The Deleted Items folder should now be empty.
11. Choose **File→Exit** from the menu bar to close the Outlook program window.

TIP! *You must always exit the Outlook window before you shut down or log off Windows. Windows will prompt you to do this if you forget.*

Concepts Review

True/False Questions

1. Outlook's toolbar looks exactly the same, no matter which view you are using (such as the Inbox, Contacts, Calendar, or Tasks).	TRUE	FALSE
2. You can set Outlook to automatically check for new mail.	TRUE	FALSE
3. When an email message arrives at the mail server at your company or ISP, it is immediately transmitted to your Inbox.	TRUE	FALSE
4. When you compose a message and click the *Send* button, the message is always immediately transmitted to the mail server that serves your email account.	TRUE	FALSE
5. To manually check for incoming email messages, you click the Send/Receive button.	TRUE	FALSE
6. When you *reply* to a message, you must manually address it.	TRUE	FALSE
7. You can use Outlook for email even if you do not have an ISP, online service, or business network system with which to connect.	TRUE	FALSE
8. Messages set for a *high* priority get transmitted to their destination faster than messages set for *low* priority.	TRUE	FALSE

Multiple-Choice Questions

1. What must you have in order to use email?
   a. An email program such as Outlook
   b. An email account and an email program
   c. An Internet connection, an email account and an email program
   d. An Internet connection

2. Mail server programs usually run at which locations?
   a. Inside your computer
   b. At the ISP that supports your account
   c. At the company network (if you have a corporate email account)
   d. Both b and c

3. Which of the following is *not* a valid email address?
   a. bsmith@offtowork.com
   b. b smith@offtowork.com
   c. bruce@offtowork.com
   d. www.amazon.com
   e. Both b and d

4. Which of the following views is *not* featured in Outlook?
   a. Email
   b. Calendar
   c. Word Processing
   d. Task List
   e. All of the above views are featured in Outlook.

Skill Builders

Skill Builder 5.1 Send a Message

1. Start Outlook with **Start→Programs→Microsoft Outlook.**
Outlook will check for new messages automatically when you start the program. If you are required to enter a password, you will see a mail delivery error message at the bottom-right corner of the status bar. This message doesn't mean that any email was lost.
2. Make sure that the **Inbox** view is displayed. If you do not see the Inbox shortcut on the Outlook bar, click the **Outlook Shortcuts** button at the top of the Outlook bar.
3. Click the **Send/Receive** button on the Outlook toolbar. Enter your password if prompted to do so. Read any new messages that might have been delivered.

Send a Message

4. Click the New button on the Outlook toolbar to start a new email message.
5. Address the message to **hello@offtowork.com**.
6. Tap the TAB key two or three times until the insertion point is blinking in the Subject box; then type **The best film I've seen lately** in the subject line, and tap the TAB key to jump to the body of the message.

NOTE!
Don't give away the ending! ;-)

7. Compose a brief message about the best film that you've seen recently, with perhaps a line or two about what you liked about it.
8. Click the Send button on the message toolbar to send your message to the Outbox.
9. Click the **Send/Receive** button on the Outlook toolbar. Enter your password if asked to do so.
Your message is transmitted to the outgoing mail server system for delivery over the Internet to the addressee's incoming mail server system.

Print the Message You Just Sent

10. Click the **My Shortcuts** group button at the bottom of the Outlook bar; then choose the Sent Items shortcut.
The message you just sent should be at the top of the list.
11. Make sure that *The best film I've seen lately* message is selected; then click Print on the Outlook toolbar to print the message. Retrieve the message from the printer.
12. Click the **Outlook Shortcuts** group button at the top of the Outlook bar; then click the **Inbox** shortcut.

Skill Builder 5.2 Check for Messages and Respond

In this exercise, you will check for a reply to the message you sent in the previous Skill Builder exercise.

1. Click the **Send/Receive** button on the Outlook toolbar. Continue to check for new messages until you receive a reply from hello to your best film message, with the subject line: Most Unusual Film.
   Depending on the level of traffic on the Internet, the reply might take a little extra time to arrive.
2. Make sure that the **Inbox** view is displayed. Click to **select** the new message and read it in the Preview Pane. If necessary, you may want to change the height of the Preview Pane.

Change the Message Delivery Option

3. Choose **Tools→Options** from the menu bar; then click the **Mail Delivery** tab.
4. Click to check the *Send messages immediately when connected* option. Click **OK** to close the Options window.

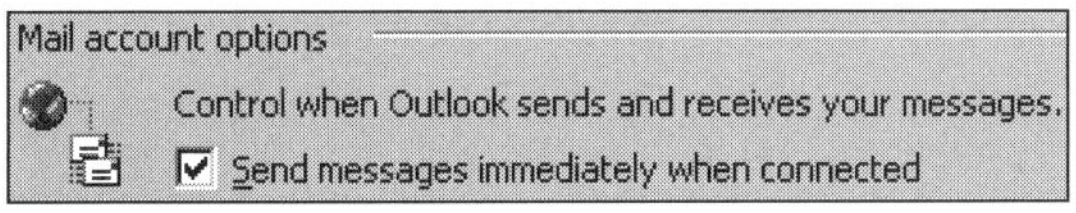
Mail account options
Control when Outlook sends and receives your messages.
Send messages immediately when connected

Now your messages will be transmitted to the outgoing mail server immediately when you click the Send button on the message window.

Forward the Message, and Send a Reply

5. **Forward** the *Most Unusual Film* message to another student in the class or to yourself. In the body of the message, type **`I'm forwarding this interesting comment on a film from someone named "Hello."`** When you have finished typing in the body of the message, click **Send.**
   Outlook will transmit the message immediately. It was unnecessary to type your name at the end of the message since it will appear on the From line when the message is received.
6. Make sure that the Most unusual film message is selected. Click Reply to start a *reply* to this message. Type a line or two about the most unusual film you've ever seen. *Do not* change the subject line. When you are done typing the message, click the **Send** button.
7. After about *one minute,* click the **Send/Receive** button to check for newly arriving messages. If the response from *hello@offtowork.com* does not arrive on your first try, repeat the **Send/Receive** command about every 30 seconds until you receive the response.
8. Read the response from *Hello;* then **print** it.

Skill Builder 5.3 Delete and Retrieve a Message

1. Display the **Inbox** view.
2. Click to select one of the messages you have received from hello@offtowork.com.
3. Click the Delete button on the Outlook toolbar.
   Although the message disappears from the Inbox, it has not yet been permanently deleted. Instead, the message has been moved to the Deleted Items *folder. As long as the message remains in Deleted Items, you can still retrieve it.*
4. Display the **Deleted Items** view. You may need to use the Scroll Down button at the bottom of the Outlook bar to make the Deleted Items shortcut visible.
5. Drag-and-drop the message you just deleted onto the **Inbox** shortcut on the Outlook bar to retrieve (undelete) the message.
6. Click the **Inbox** shortcut on the Outlook bar, and confirm that the message was retrieved.

Assessments

Assessment 5.1 Compose and Send a Message

1. Start Outlook.
2. Start a new email message; then follow these instructions to compose it:

To:	hello@offtowork.com
Subject:	Email Facts
Message body	■ Compose a brief statement on the two most important facts about working with email that you have learned in this lesson. ■ Be sure to type your name at the end of the message.

3. Send the message. Make sure the message goes out to the outgoing mail server.
4. Check for a reply to your message.

Assessment 5.2 Reply to a Message

1. Reply to the *RE: Email Facts* message.
2. In the body of your reply, state one more fact about working with email that you have learned in this lesson, and type your name at the end of the message.
3. **Send** the message; then check for a response to the message.
4. You should now have received a total of two messages from *hello@offtowork.com.*

Assessment 5.3 Print Messages from the Previous Assessment Exercises

1. **Print** both of the messages you received from *hello@offtowork.com* in the previous two assessment exercises.
2. After you have printed the two messages, turn in the printouts to your instructor for grading.

LESSON 6—Outlook

Working with Contacts, Calendars, and Tasks

As your use of email expands, you will have more and more correspondents to keep track of. The Contacts list is tightly integrated with Outlook and gives you a useful tool to manage names, email addresses, and other information about your correspondents. Outlook has several other program features that help you manage your personal information. This lesson also introduces Outlook's Calendar, Tasks, and Notes views. By the end of this lesson, you should be able to use Outlook to manage basic personal, business, and time-management information.

In This Lesson

Case Study

Thus far, Daniel has learned how to send and receive email messages. In the weeks since he started his job, Daniel has received quite a few email messages, and the number of messages he receives each week continues to increase. Daniel realizes that he needs a way to keep information on his growing number of email correspondents. He decides to spend a couple hours learning as much as he can about the Contacts features in Outlook.

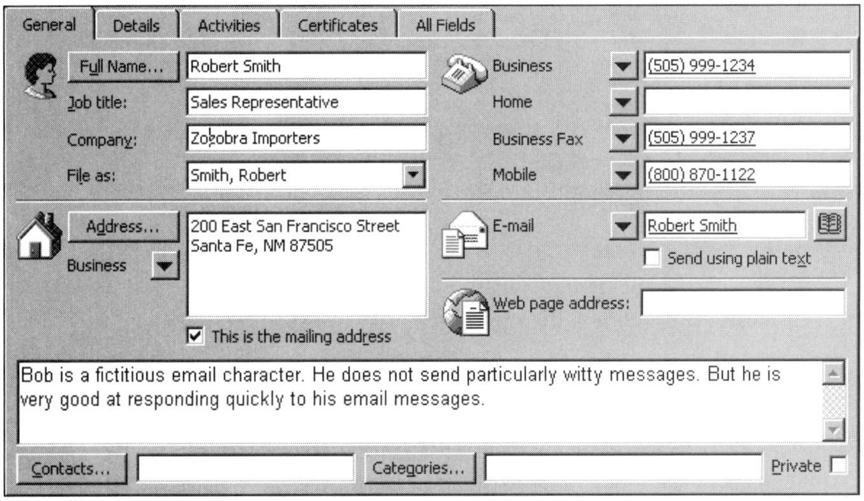
General
Details
Activities
Certificates
All Fields
Full Name...
Robert Smith
Job title:
Sales Representative
Company:
Zobobra Importers
File as:
Smith, Robert
Business
(505) 999-1234
Home
Business Fax
(505) 999-1237
Mobile
(800) 870-1122
Address...
200 East San Francisco Street
Santa Fe, NM 87505
Business
This is the mailing address
E-mail
Robert Smith
Send using plain text
Web page address:
Bob is a fictitious email character. He does not send particularly witty messages. But he is very good at responding quickly to his email messages.
Contacts...
Categories...
Private

Daniel will enter contacts in the Contacts list. This will make it easier for him to send email to his business contacts, and also reduce mistakes due to typographic errors.

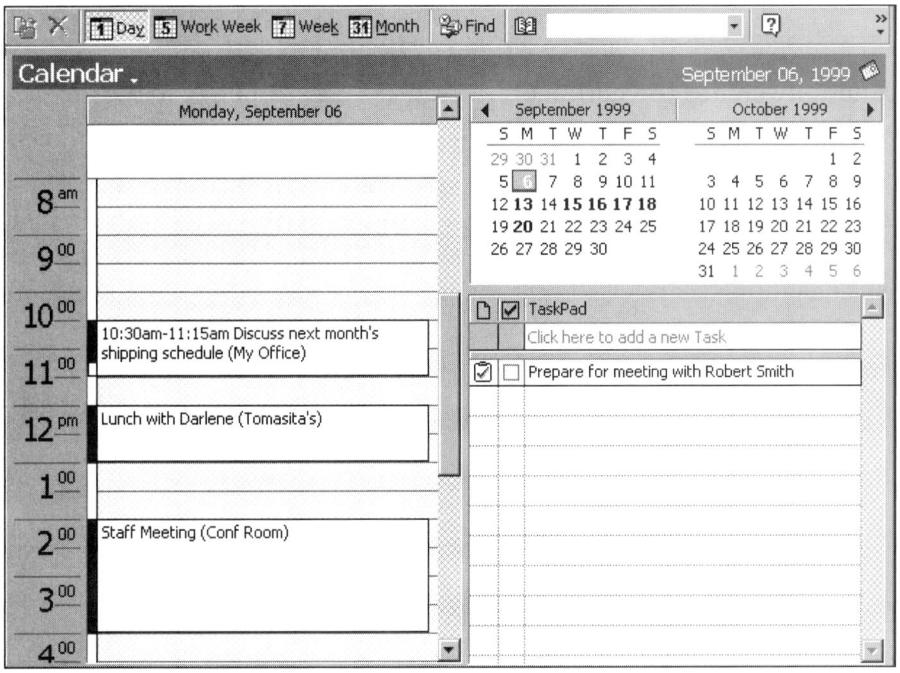
Day
Work Week
Week
Month
Find
Calendar
September 06, 1999
Monday, September 06
September 1999
October 1999
10:30am-11:15am Discuss next month's shipping schedule (My Office)
Lunch with Darlene (Tomasita's)
Staff Meeting (Conf Room)
TaskPad
Click here to add a new Task
Prepare for meeting with Robert Smith

Outlook's Calendar view lets you create appointments and view upcoming events.

Managing Contacts

The Contacts view lets you store email addresses and other information for your correspondents. For example, you can store phone numbers, postal addresses, and notes in the Contacts view. Outlook also lets you initiate email messages and appointments directly from the Contacts view. Other application programs may be able to access information from the Contacts list. For example, you can look up Contacts list contacts while you are working in Microsoft Word. The illustration below displays the primary features of the Contacts view.

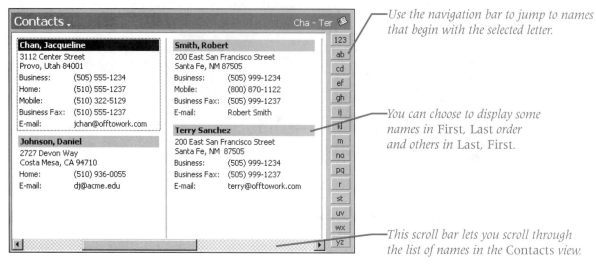

Contacts
Cha - Ter
Chan, Jacqueline
3112 Center Street
Provo, Utah 84001
Business: (505) 555-1234
Home: (510) 555-1237
Mobile: (510) 322-5129
Business Fax: (510) 555-1237
E-mail: jchan@offtowork.com
Johnson, Daniel
2727 Devon Way
Costa Mesa, CA 94710
Home: (510) 936-0055
E-mail: dj@acme.edu
Smith, Robert
200 East San Francisco Street
Santa Fe, NM 87505
Business: (505) 999-1234
Mobile: (800) 870-1122
Business Fax: (505) 999-1237
E-mail: Robert Smith
Terry Sanchez
200 East San Francisco Street
Santa Fe, NM 87505
Business: (505) 999-1234
Business Fax: (505) 999-1237
E-mail: terry@offtowork.com
123
ab
cd
ef
gh
ij
kl
m
no
pq
r
st
uv
wx
yz
Use the navigation bar to jump to names that begin with the selected letter.
You can choose to display some names in First, Last order and others in Last, First.
This scroll bar lets you scroll through the list of names in the Contacts view.

The Contacts view helps you keep track of your correspondents. You can share information about contacts with other Windows applications. The Contacts view can store postal addresses, telephone numbers, fax numbers, and other useful information about each contact.

Inserting Contacts into the Contacts List

There are two ways to insert contacts into the Contacts list:

- **Manually create the contact—**You can add a new contact to the Contacts list at any time. You simply view the Contacts list, give the command to create a new contact, and fill in the contact's information.
- **Automatically create the contact when you reply—**Outlook comes with a default setting to automatically create a new Contacts list contact whenever you send a reply to a *new* email address.

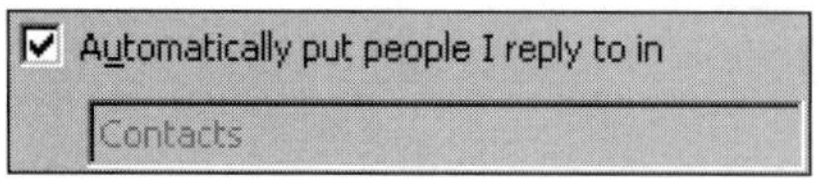
Automatically put people I reply to in
Contacts

This option can add new entries to the Contacts list automatically.

Quick Reference

CREATING NEW CONTACTS

Task	Procedure
Add a new contact to the Contacts list.	■ Choose the Contacts view. ■ Click the New button on the toolbar, or use CTRL+SHIFT+C from the keyboard.
Add new contacts automatically.	■ Choose *Tools→Options* on the Outlook menu bar. ■ Click the *E-mail Options* button. ■ Click to check the *Automatically put people I reply to in* option.

Hands-On 6.1 Add Names to the Contacts List

In this exercise, you will add two new entries to the Contacts list: one for a fictitious character you will correspond with, and one for yourself.

Start Outlook

1. Start Outlook from the Quick Launch toolbar next to the Start button, or click **Start→Programs→Outlook.** Make sure that the Outlook window is *maximized.*

2. Click **Yes** if you are asked to make Outlook your default email client.
   You may be prompted to answer this question if another email program such as Outlook Express is also installed on your computer.

3. Choose the **Inbox** view on the Outlook bar.
   Notice the design of the first button on the Outlook toolbar: 
New

4. Choose the **Contacts** view from the Outlook bar.
   Now notice how the icon on the first toolbar button has changed: 
New
   Outlook's toolbar will change as you shift from one view to another. This toolbar button has transformed from the New Message *button to the* New Contact *button.*

   Depending on contacts added by other students, there may or may not be any contacts in the view. Before you add your first contact, you will make sure that the contact does not exist already.

5. Follow these steps to determine if Robert Smith is already entered as a contact.

Organize
smith

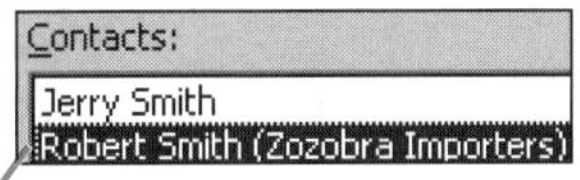
Contacts:
Jerry Smith
Robert Smith (Zozobra Importers)

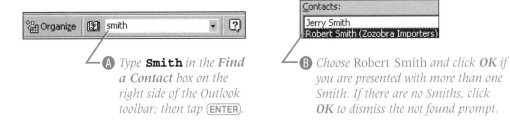

Ⓐ *Type* **Smith** *in the* ***Find a Contact*** *box on the right side of the Outlook toolbar; then tap* ENTER.

Ⓑ *Choose* Robert Smith *and click* ***OK*** *if you are presented with more than one Smith. If there are no Smiths, click* ***OK*** *to dismiss the not found prompt.*

A new window will open for the contact if Robert Smith was found.

6. Choose **File→Delete** from the Contact window menu bar if a contact window for Robert Smith opened in the previous step; otherwise continue to Step 7.
   The contact has been sent to the Deleted Items view. You will learn more about deleting contacts later in the lesson.

(Continued on the next page)

Add a Contact

Robert Smith is a sales representative with whom Daniel often corresponds. You are going to add Robert Smith to the Contacts list.

7. **Click** the New button on the Contacts list toolbar.
   An untitled contact window will appear.

8. Follow these steps to begin adding Robert Smith to the Contacts list.

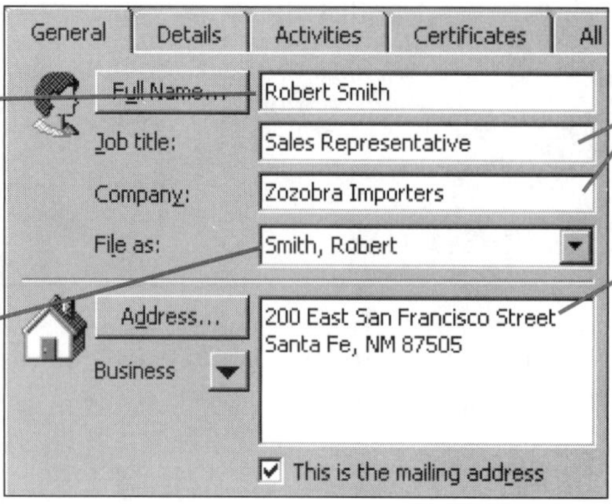

General
Details
Activities
Certificates
All
Full Name...
Robert Smith
Job title:
Sales Representative
Company:
Zozobra Importers
File as:
Smith, Robert
Address...
200 East San Francisco Street
Santa Fe, NM 87505
Business
This is the mailing address

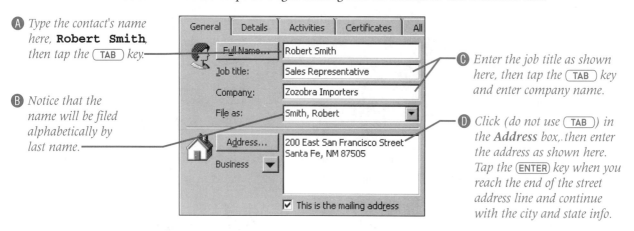

Ⓐ *Type the contact's name here,* **Robert Smith**, *then tap the* TAB *key.*

Ⓑ *Notice that the name will be filed alphabetically by last name.*

Ⓒ *Enter the job title as shown here, then tap the* TAB *key and enter company name.*

Ⓓ *Click (do not use* TAB*) in the* ***Address*** *box,.then enter the address as shown here. Tap the* ENTER *key when you reach the end of the street address line and continue with the city and state info.*

9. Follow these steps to add Robert Smith's telephone numbers and email address.

Business
(505) 999-1234
Home
Business Fax
(505) 999-1237
Pager
(800) 870-1122
E-mail
rsmith@offtowork.com
Send using plain text

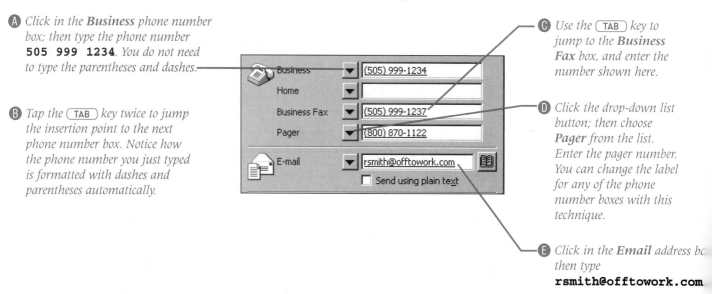

Ⓐ *Click in the* ***Business*** *phone number box; then type the phone number* **505 999 1234**. *You do not need to type the parentheses and dashes.*

Ⓑ *Tap the* TAB *key twice to jump the insertion point to the next phone number box. Notice how the phone number you just typed is formatted with dashes and parentheses automatically.*

Ⓒ *Use the* TAB *key to jump to the* ***Business Fax*** *box, and enter the number shown here.*

Ⓓ *Click the drop-down list button; then choose* ***Pager*** *from the list. Enter the pager number. You can change the label for any of the phone number boxes with this technique.*

Ⓔ *Click in the* ***Email*** *address bo then type* **rsmith@offtowork.com**

10. Follow these steps to continue filling in information on Robert Smith.

Bob is a fictitious email character. He does not send out particularly witty messages. But he is very good at responding quickly to his email messages.
Contacts...
Categories...
Private

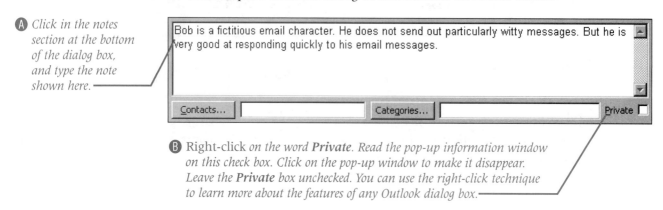

Ⓐ *Click in the notes section at the bottom of the dialog box, and type the note shown here.*

Ⓑ Right-click *on the word* ***Private***. *Read the pop-up information window on this check box. Click on the pop-up window to make it disappear. Leave the* ***Private*** *box unchecked. You can use the right-click technique to learn more about the features of any Outlook dialog box.*

11. Click the **Save and Close** button on the Contact window toolbar.
Now you can see Robert Smith in the Contacts view. His name will be listed as Smith, Robert.

Add Yourself as a Contact

12. Click the New  button on the toolbar.
New

13. Follow these steps to add yourself as a contact.

TIP! *Since others can view this information, you may want to alter some of the personal data that you enter during this exercise.*

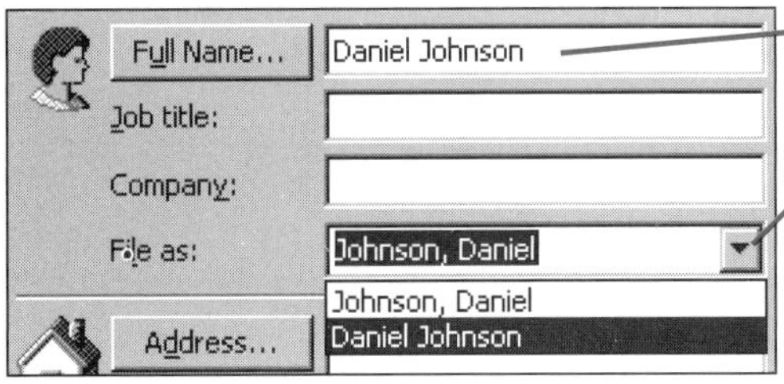

Full Name...
Daniel Johnson
Job title:
Company:
File as:
Johnson, Daniel
Johnson, Daniel
Daniel Johnson
Address...

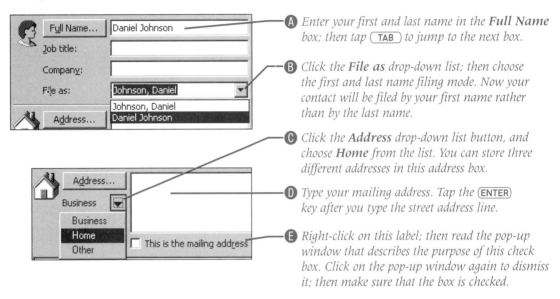

Ⓐ *Enter your first and last name in the* ***Full Name*** *box; then tap* (TAB) *to jump to the next box.*

Ⓑ *Click the* ***File as*** *drop-down list; then choose the first and last name filing mode. Now your contact will be filed by your first name rather than by the last name.*

Ⓒ *Click the* ***Address*** *drop-down list button, and choose* ***Home*** *from the list. You can store three different addresses in this address box.*

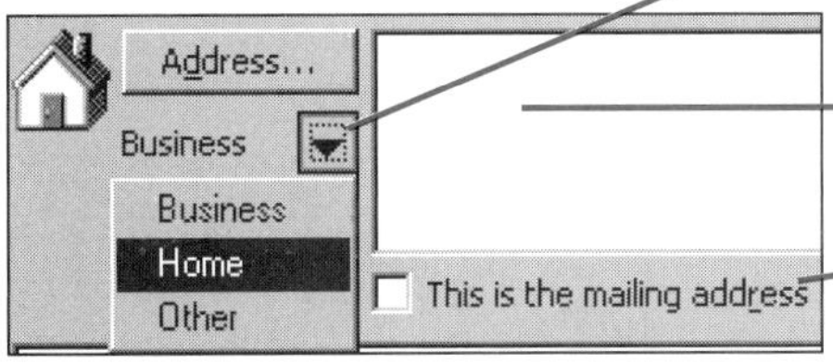

Address...
Business
Business
Home
Other
This is the mailing address

Ⓓ *Type your mailing address. Tap the* (ENTER) *key after you type the street address line.*

Ⓔ *Right-click on this label; then read the pop-up window that describes the purpose of this check box. Click on the pop-up window again to dismiss it; then make sure that the box is checked.*

14. Enter one or more telephone numbers into the appropriate boxes on the right side of the form. Feel free to use the drop-down list buttons beside each telephone number box to change the box label.

15. Be sure to enter your *email address* in the appropriate data box.

16. Choose **File→Save** from the menu bar.
Unlike the Save and Close *button, the* File→Save *command leaves the Contact window open so you can finish adding data for the contact. It is always a good idea to save your work from time to time.*

17. Click the **Details** tab on the dialog box.
A new set of data boxes will appear. Dialog boxes with tabs help to organize the information into logical groups. In this case, the Details data is secondary to the address and phone information you entered under the General *tab.*

18. *Double-click* to select the word **None** in the **Birthday** box, then type a date for your birthday in the Birthday box in the form **`MM/DD/YY`**, and tap (ENTER). Click on the **drop-down list button** beside the Birthday box to display a small calendar. Click anywhere else in the window to dismiss the calendar.
Any data box that stores a date can display a calendar. You can enter a date by navigating to the desired date, then choosing it from the calendar. In this case, it was easier to simply type in a date rather than to navigate month by month to the date with the calendar.

(Continued on the next page)

19. Click the **Save and Close** button on the toolbar when you are done entering contact information for yourself.
Notice that your entry in the contacts list is filed under your first name. This is because you selected the first and last name filing mode as you created your contact entry.

Navigating the Contacts List

The Contacts view has a handy alphabetic navigation bar on the right side of the view. When you click a letter in the navigation bar, Outlook highlights the first name in the contacts list that begins with that letter. Outlook also displays the range of names currently displayed in the Contacts view. If the name you are looking for is not visible after you click the appropriate letter, you should use the *scroll bar* at the bottom of the Contacts view to scroll further down the list.

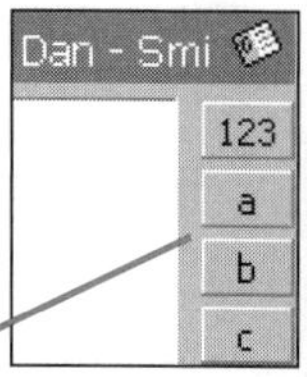

Dan - Smi
123
a
b
c

Navigation bar for the contacts view.

Finding a Contact

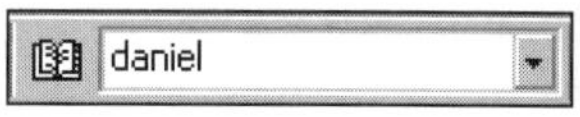

daniel

You can also search the contacts list from the Outlook toolbar. When you type the name of a contact in the *Find a Contact* box on the Toolbar, Outlook displays a list of all contacts with that name. If your contacts list has a lot of names, this method may be somewhat faster than using the navigation bar.

Editing and Deleting Contacts

From the Keyboard

CTRL+O to open a selected item
CTRL+D to delete a selected item

It's easy to open a contact window and edit the data for a contact. Just select the contact in the Contacts view, and double-click to open it. The Delete button on the Outlook toolbar places the deleted items into the Deleted Items view. You can retrieve or empty contacts from Deleted Items just as you did with email messages in the previous lesson.

Quick Reference

EDITING CONTACTS LIST CONTACTS

Task	Procedure
Edit a contact in the Contacts list.	■ Display the *Contacts* view.
	■ *Double-click* to open the dialog box for that contact.
	■ Make the desired changes; then click **OK** to save the changes.
Delete a contact.	■ Display the *Contacts* view.
	■ *Select* the contact(s) to delete. You can use the CTRL+click and SHIFT+click techniques to select more than one contact.
	■ Click the **Delete** button on the Toolbar.

Hands-On 6.2 Find and Edit a Contact Entry

1. *Double-click* on the entry with your name in the Contacts list.
2. Click the **File as** drop-down list button; then choose the **Last, First** depiction of your name from the list.

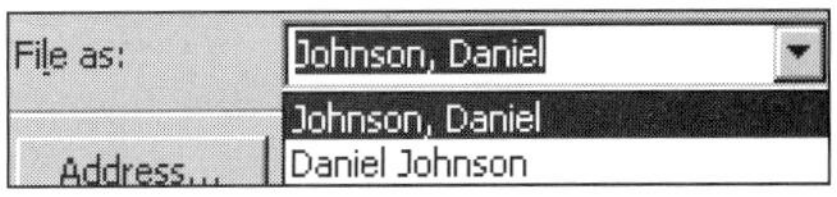
File as:
Johnson, Daniel
Johnson, Daniel
Daniel Johnson
Address...

3. Click the **Save and Close** button on the toolbar to close your entry.
4. Click the **S** or **ST** button on the navigation bar along the right side of the Contacts view.
   The first contact with a name starting with S will be selected. Outlook places a dark blue bar over the name of the selected contact. Depending on the other names in the list, the selection may already be on Robert Smith.

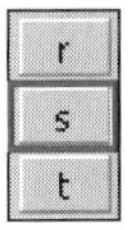
r
s
t

5. *Click* or *drag* the **scroll bar** at the bottom of the Contacts view if you do not see Robert Smith's entry.
6. Click the letter button for your **last name** on the navigation bar. For example, if your last name is Johnson, click the **J** button.
   Now the selection has moved to the first name in the list that begins with the chosen letter.
7. Type your **first name** in the **Find a Contact** box on the Outlook toolbar; then tap the (ENTER) key. *Double-click* on your name if Outlook displays more than one name in a *Choose Contact* window.
   If no other contact has the same first name, Outlook will open your contact entry immediately.

daniel

8. Click the **Save and Close** button on the Contact window toolbar.
   Your entry is filed in the Contacts list by your last name rather than the first name. This is because of the change you made in Step 2 of this exercise. You may prefer to file contacts by first name for friends and family members.

Sending Email to Contacts

It is a good idea to use the Contacts list to address most of your new messages to regular correspondents. For one thing, it relieves you of the need to remember everyone's email address. Another benefit is that you reduce the chance of a typographic error that could cause your message to be undeliverable.

Once contacts are entered in your Contacts list, there are several easy ways you can send them email. Three of the most convenient methods follow:

- **Select a contact, and click the *New Message to Contact* button**—If you have selected a contact in the Contacts list, the *New Message to Contact* button addresses a new email message to the contact automatically.

Find
Contacts
New Message to Contact
Johnson, Daniel
2727 Devon Way
Costa Mesa, CA 94710
Home: (510) 936-0055
E-mail: dj@acme.edu

*The **New Message to Contact** button addresses a new email message to the selected contact automatically.*

(Continued on the next page)

- **Select contacts from a message composition window—**You can use a button such as **To:** next to the address field to display a list of contacts; then select names from the Contacts list.

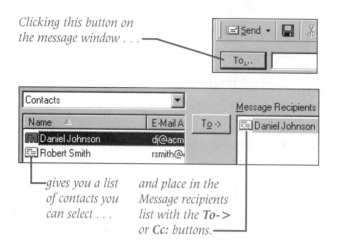

Clicking this button on the message window . . .

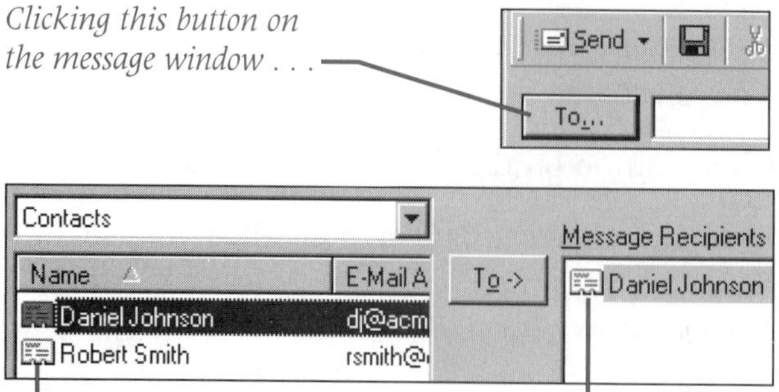
Send
To...
Contacts
Name
E-Mail A
Daniel Johnson
dj@acm
Robert Smith
To ->
Message Recipients
Daniel Johnson

gives you a list of contacts you can select . . . *and place in the Message recipients list with the* ***To->*** *or* ***Cc:*** *buttons.*

- **Type the contact name in the address box—**You can type the *name* of the contact rather than his or her email address directly into an address box. When the message is sent, Outlook will use the contact's email address.

To...
Robert Smith

As Daniel continues to work with Outlook, he exchanges email with a growing list of people. What if he had to memorize each correspondent's email address? Not a happy thought, is it? What's more, think of all the time he would waste typing out each email address in every new message. In the Contacts view Daniel can quickly look up contacts and insert their email addresses into new email messages.

Sending Email to Multiple Addressees

Outlook lets you specify multiple addresses for messages. If a message needs to go to more than one addressee, simply type a *semicolon* (**;**) between each email address in the address box. Outlook also lets you send a Cc (carbon copy) of any message to additional addressees. Just enter email addresses in the Cc box of the message. You should Cc a message when the addressee would find its information useful, but is not responsible for responding to the message. For example, you might Cc a message to your manager so he or she knows about an important piece of information contained in a message to someone else.

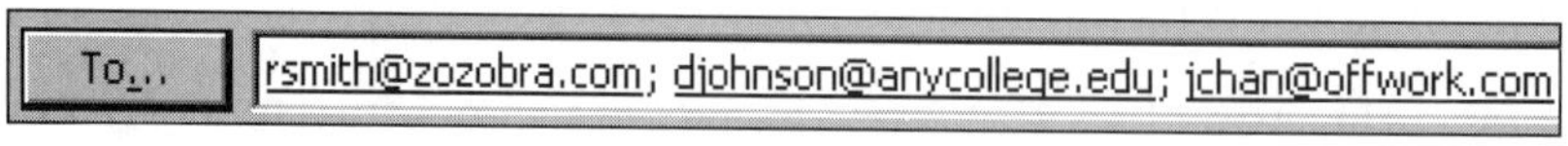
To...
rsmith@zozobra.com; djohnson@anycollege.edu; jchan@offwork.com

A semicolon *separates each individual email address.*

Hands-On 6.3 Send Email to a Contact

Check the Message Delivery Option

In the next two steps, you will make sure that the option to send messages immediately when you give the send command is switched on. This saves you the trouble of giving the *send/receive* command after you click the *Send* button on the message window.

1. Choose **Tools→Options** from the Outlook toolbar; then click the **Mail Delivery** tab near the top of the window.

2. Make sure that the **Send messages immediately when connected** option is checked; then click **OK** to close the Options window.

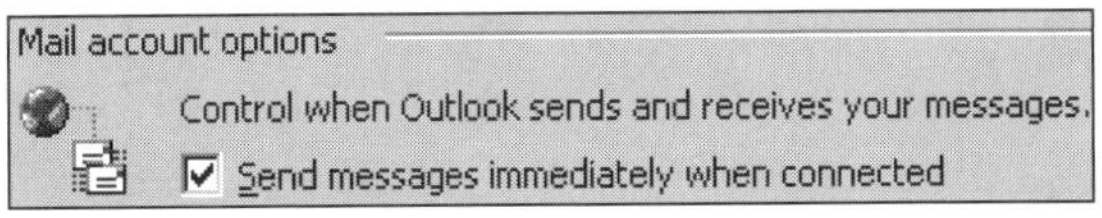
Mail account options
Control when Outlook sends and receives your messages.
Send messages immediately when connected

   Your messages will be transmitted to the outgoing mail server immediately when you click the Send *button on the message window.*

Send a Message to a Contact

3. Make sure *your name* is selected in the Contacts list.

4. Click the New Message to Contact button on the Outlook toolbar.
   A new message window will appear with your email address filled in on the To: *box.*

5. Follow these steps to address the message to another contact.

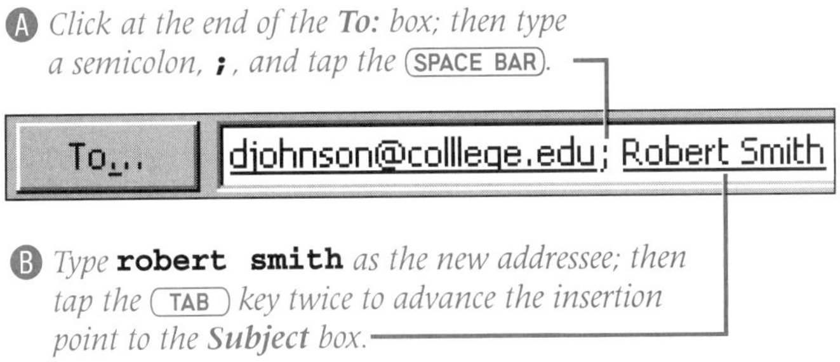
A Click at the end of the To: box; then type a semicolon, ;, and tap the SPACE BAR.
To...
djohnson@colllege.edu; Robert Smith
B Type robert smith as the new addressee; then tap the TAB key twice to advance the insertion point to the Subject box.

   Notice that Robert Smith's name is now underlined and capitalized. You can address email with the name of a person in your contacts list rather than typing out his or her email address.

6. Enter a subject for the message: **`Addressing email`**.

7. Type the following as the body of the message.

```
The same email message can be sent to several people with
a single command. You separate each email address with a
semicolon (;).

If someone should receive a copy of a message but is not
responsible for responding, you can "Cc" the message to
that person. Everyone who receives the message will also
see a list of the people that you Cc'd.
```

8. **Send** the message.

(Continued on the next page)

Find Contacts in the Message Window

9. Display the **Inbox** view.
   The Outlook toolbar transforms to display buttons related to email.
10. Click the New Mail  button on the toolbar.
New
11. Click on the **To:** button next to the email address box.
   The Select Names *window will display a list of your contacts.*
12. Follow these steps to add names from the contacts list.

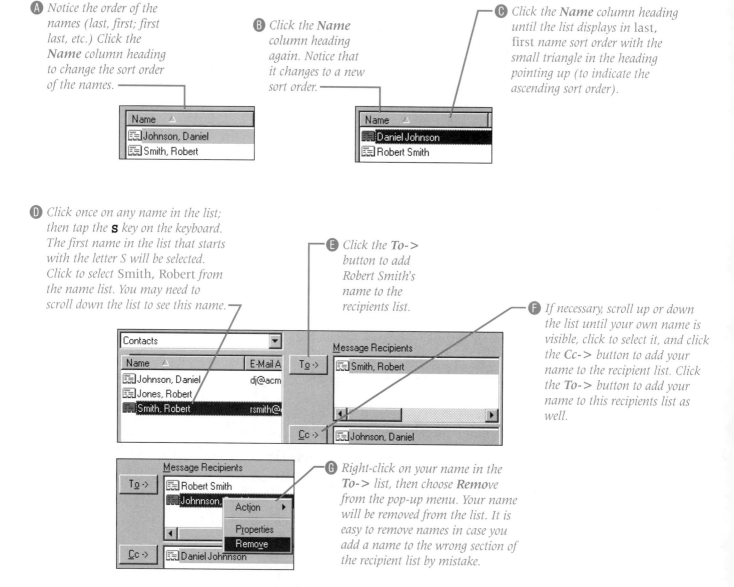

Ⓐ *Notice the order of the names (last, first; first last, etc.) Click the* ***Name*** *column heading to change the sort order of the names.*

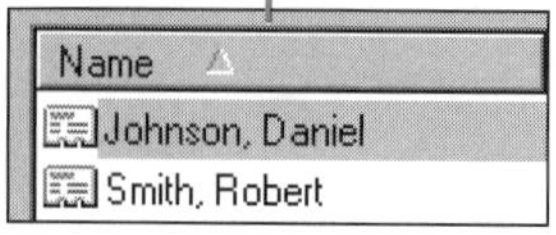
Name
Johnson, Daniel
Smith, Robert

Ⓑ *Click the* ***Name*** *column heading again. Notice that it changes to a new sort order.*

Ⓒ *Click the* ***Name*** *column heading until the list displays in* last, first *name sort order with the small triangle in the heading pointing up (to indicate the ascending sort order).*

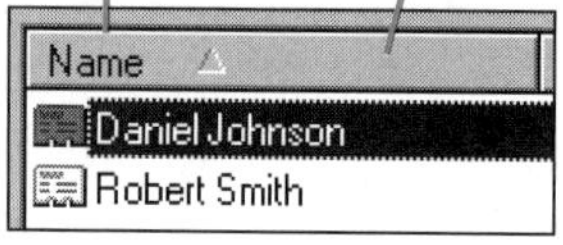
Name
Daniel Johnson
Robert Smith

Ⓓ *Click once on any name in the list; then tap the* **s** *key on the keyboard. The first name in the list that starts with the letter S will be selected. Click to select* Smith, Robert *from the name list. You may need to scroll down the list to see this name.*

Ⓔ *Click the* ***To->*** *button to add Robert Smith's name to the recipients list.*

Ⓕ *If necessary, scroll up or down the list until your own name is visible, click to select it, and click the* ***Cc->*** *button to add your name to the recipient list. Click the* ***To->*** *button to add your name to this recipients list as well.*

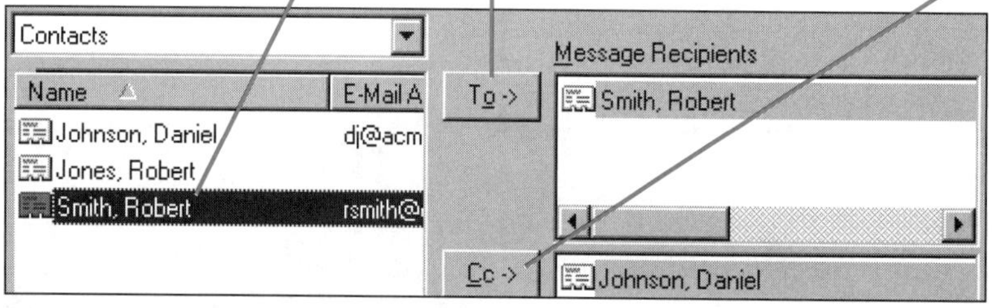
Contacts
Name
E-Mail A
Johnson, Daniel
dj@acm
Jones, Robert
Smith, Robert
rsmith@
Message Recipients
To ->
Smith, Robert
Cc ->
Johnson, Daniel

Ⓖ *Right-click on your name in the* ***To->*** *list, then choose* ***Remove*** *from the pop-up menu. Your name will be removed from the list. It is easy to remove names in case you add a name to the wrong section of the recipient list by mistake.*

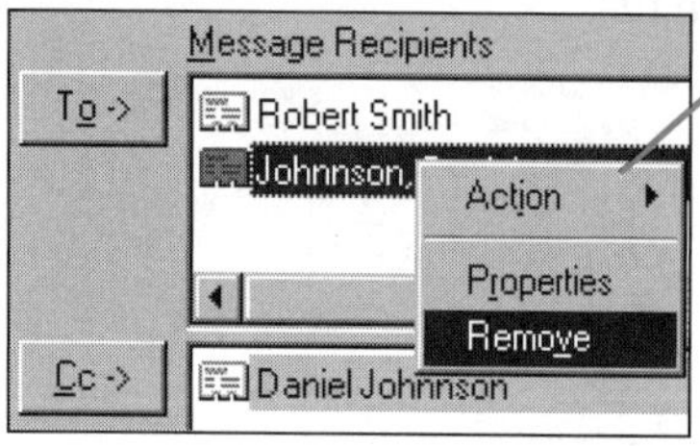
Message Recipients
To ->
Robert Smith
Johnson,
Action
Properties
Remove
Cc ->
Daniel Johnson

13. Click **OK** to close the Select Recipients window.
   The To: *and* Cc: *boxes will display the names of the contacts you selected.*

Compose and Send the Message

14. Enter **`Contacts list`** as the subject of the message. Compose the body of the message as shown below:

```
Hello Bob:
I've just entered you into my Contacts list. This
makes it much easier for me to address messages to
you quickly. It also helps me avoid typos when I
enter your email address. I will look forward to
keeping in touch with you via email.
[Your Name]
```

15. **Send** the message, wait about one minute, and then give the **Send/Receive** command to check for new email messages.

16. Look over replies to your messages in the **Inbox.**

Printing the Contacts list

You can print the entire Contacts list with a single print command, or you can print just a few selected entries. Outlook gives you several styles of printout to choose from. The two most useful styles are *card* and *phone book*. You can preview any printout to determine that it will print the way you want.

Quick Reference

PRINTING THE CONTACTS LIST

Task	Procedure
Print all the contacts.	■ Display the Contacts view. ■ Click the **Print** button on the Contacts list toolbar. ■ Select the print style.
Print one or more contacts.	■ Select one or more entries in the Contacts view. You can use the selected (CTRL)+click and (SHIFT)+click techniques to select multiple entries. ■ Click the **Print** button on the Contacts list toolbar. ■ Set the Print Range option to *Only selected items.*

Hands-On 6.4 Print the Contacts List

1. Display the *Contacts* view.
2. Click the Print button on the toolbar.
   Notice that the Card Style *is already selected in the Print style section of the dialog box.*
3. Click the **Preview** button at the bottom-right corner of the Print dialog box.
   Outlook displays a preview of how a page will print in this style. Notice that your mouse pointer has changed shape to a magnifying glass.
4. Follow these steps to use the Preview window.

*(B) Point (don't click) on the **Page Down** button in the top-left corner of the preview window. Outlook will display a ScreenTip with the name of the button. This can be helpful when you don't know the meaning of a toolbar icon.*

(A) Click on any portion of the preview page to zoom in the view. Now you can see the page in actual size.

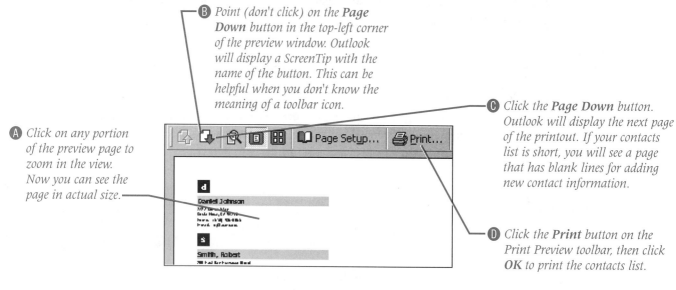

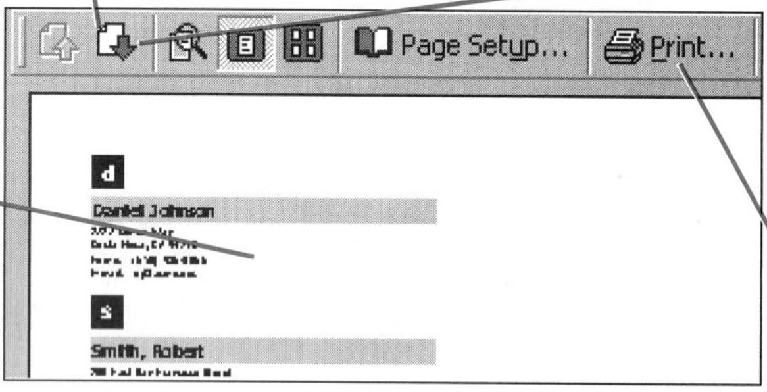
Page Setup...
Print...
d
Daniel Johnson
s
Smith, Robert

*(C) Click the **Page Down** button. Outlook will display the next page of the printout. If your contacts list is short, you will see a page that has blank lines for adding new contact information.*

*(D) Click the **Print** button on the Print Preview toolbar, then click **OK** to print the contacts list.*

5. Retrieve the printout from the printer.

Working with the Calendar

Outlook's Calendar view lets you perform many types of time management activities and display your schedule in a variety of views such as daily, weekly, and monthly. The Calendar view can also display information on items in the *Tasks* list that are active in the time period you are viewing. (You will learn about creating Tasks in Outlook later in this lesson.) The following illustration displays some of the primary features of Outlook's Calendar view.

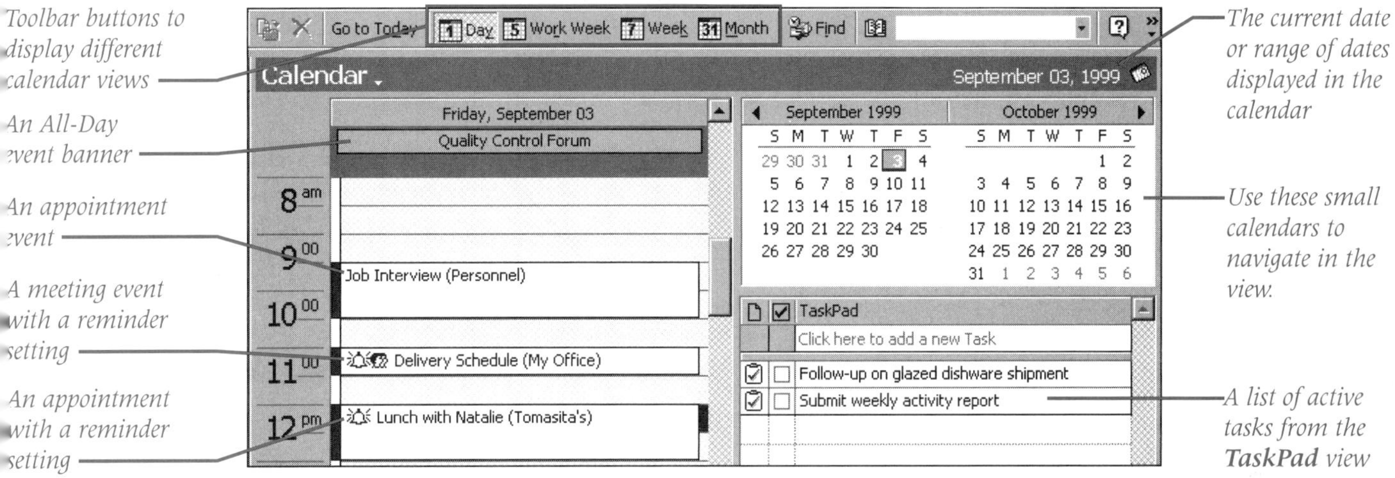

Toolbar buttons to display different calendar views
An All-Day event banner
An appointment event
A meeting event with a reminder setting
An appointment with a reminder setting
The current date or range of dates displayed in the calendar
Use these small calendars to navigate in the view.
A list of active tasks from the TaskPad view
Go to Today
Day
Work Week
Week
Month
Find
Calendar
September 03, 1999
Friday, September 03
Quality Control Forum
8 am
9 00
10 00
11 00
12 pm
Job Interview (Personnel)
Delivery Schedule (My Office)
Lunch with Natalie (Tomasita's)
September 1999
October 1999
TaskPad
Click here to add a new Task
Follow-up on glazed dishware shipment
Submit weekly activity report

Navigating in the Calendar

Outlook offers several methods to display a specific date. You can point and click on a small calendar in the view, use a *scroll bar* (see below) in the weekly and monthly views, or use the *Go to Date* command in any view. You can also navigate to a date in one view and then switch to a different view to add or view events for a specific date or block of time.

Scroll Bars

A scroll bar is a control that lets you control the display of a window or view that is too large to fit on the screen. You have encountered scroll bars in many dialog boxes and program windows. The diagram below displays the primary features of scroll bars.

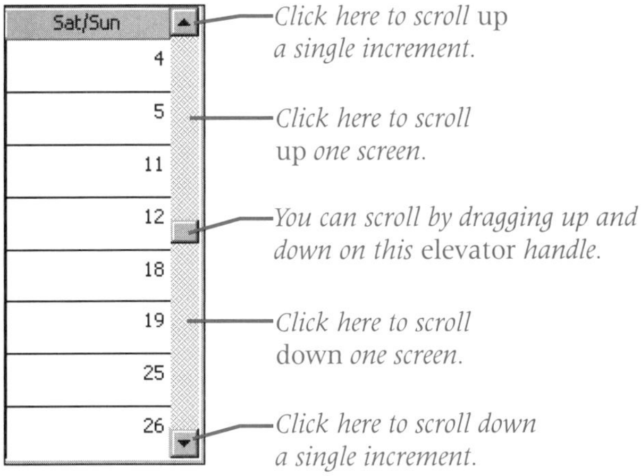

Sat/Sun
4
5
11
12
18
19
25
26
Click here to scroll up a single increment.
Click here to scroll up one screen.
You can scroll by dragging up and down on this elevator handle.
Click here to scroll down one screen.
Click here to scroll down a single increment.

Hands-On 6.5 Navigate in the Calendar

In this exercise, you will practice navigating to various dates and schedule views in the Calendar.

1. Make sure that the Outlook window is *maximized.*
2. Choose **Calendar** on the Outlook bar to display the Calendar view.
3. Click the Day button on the toolbar.
   This gives a detailed view of the selected day's schedule.
4. Follow these steps to navigate in the Day view.

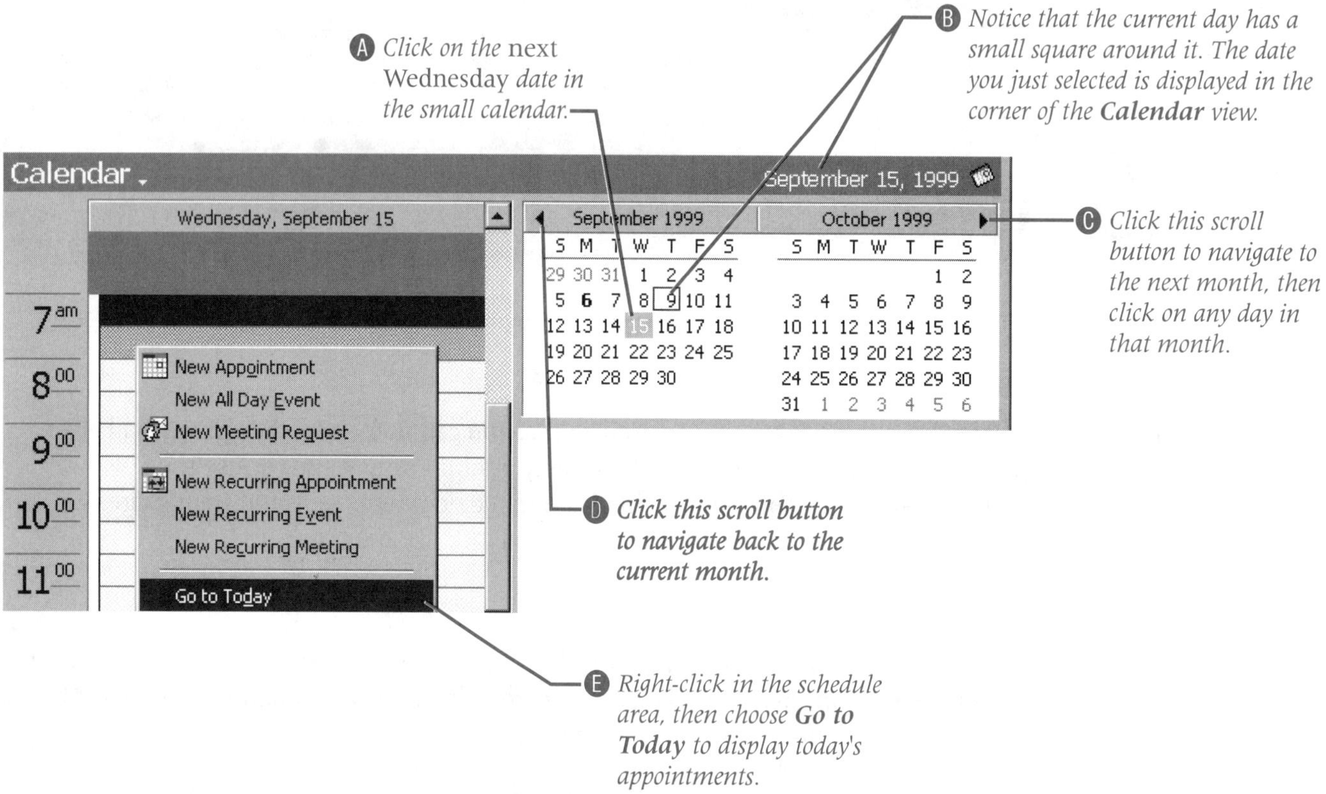
A Click on the next Wednesday date in the small calendar.
B Notice that the current day has a small square around it. The date you just selected is displayed in the corner of the Calendar view.
C Click this scroll button to navigate to the next month, then click on any day in that month.
D Click this scroll button to navigate back to the current month.
E Right-click in the schedule area, then choose Go to Today to display today's appointments.
Calendar
September 15, 1999
Wednesday, September 15
September 1999
October 1999
New Appointment
New All Day Event
New Meeting Request
New Recurring Appointment
New Recurring Event
New Recurring Meeting
Go to Today

5. Click the Work Week button on the toolbar.
   This view lets you see the week in a time schedule format. However, you probably will not be able to see much detail on individual appointments when you use this view.
6. Click the Week button on the toolbar.
   This view has more space to view appointments but lacks the visual display of your scheduled time that is featured in the Work Week *view.*

7. Follow these steps to navigate in the Week view.

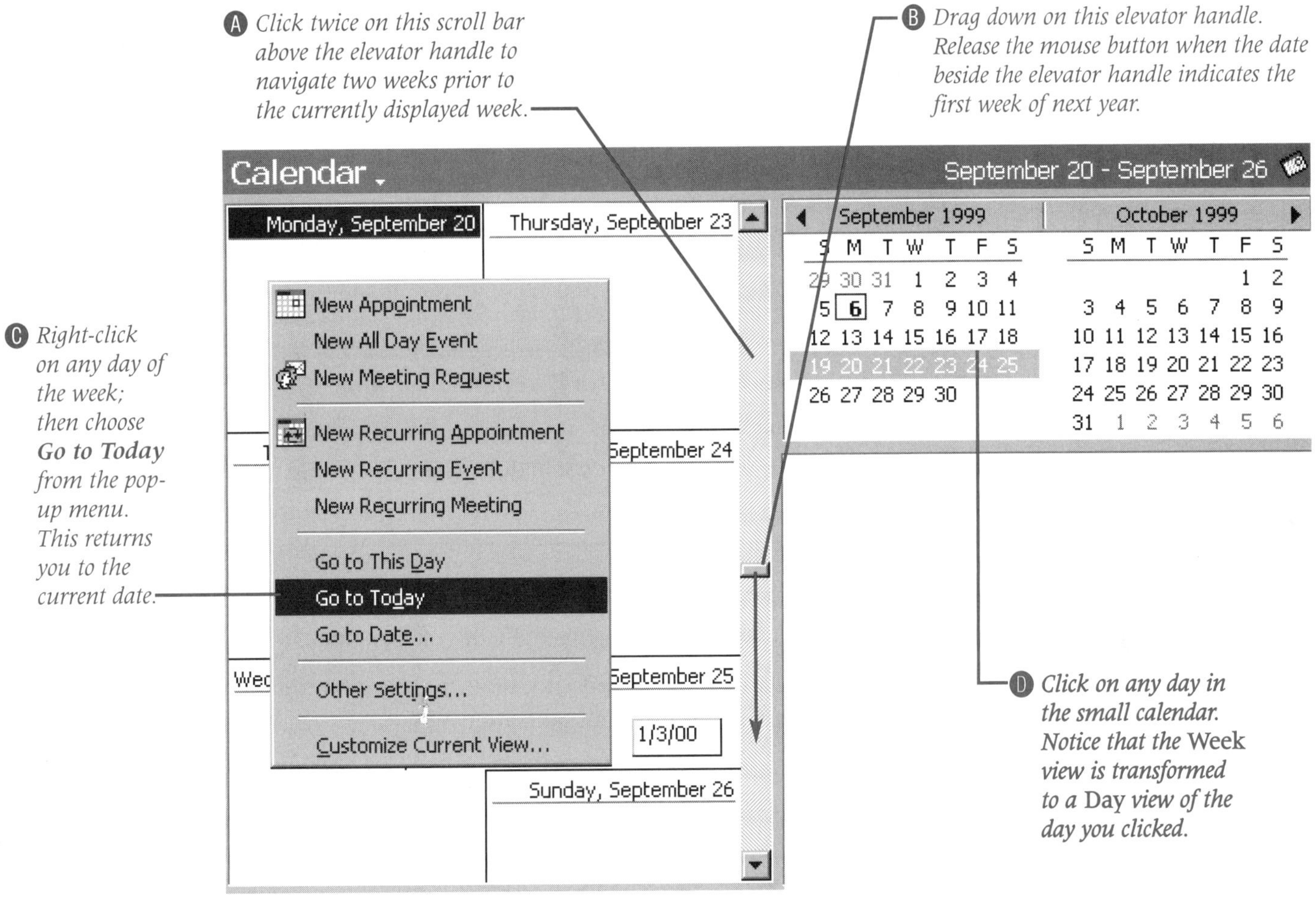
A Click twice on this scroll bar above the elevator handle to navigate two weeks prior to the currently displayed week.
B Drag down on this elevator handle. Release the mouse button when the date beside the elevator handle indicates the first week of next year.
C Right-click on any day of the week; then choose Go to Today from the pop-up menu. This returns you to the current date.
D Click on any day in the small calendar. Notice that the Week view is transformed to a Day view of the day you clicked.
Calendar
September 20 - September 26
Monday, September 20
Thursday, September 23
September 24
September 25
Sunday, September 26
1/3/00
New Appointment
New All Day Event
New Meeting Request
New Recurring Appointment
New Recurring Event
New Recurring Meeting
Go to This Day
Go to Today
Go to Date...
Other Settings...
Customize Current View...
September 1999
October 1999

8. Click the Month [31 Month] button on the toolbar.
This view lets you see which days have activities, but cannot display much detail unless you view it on a large monitor.

9. Follow these steps to navigate forward and back in the Month view.

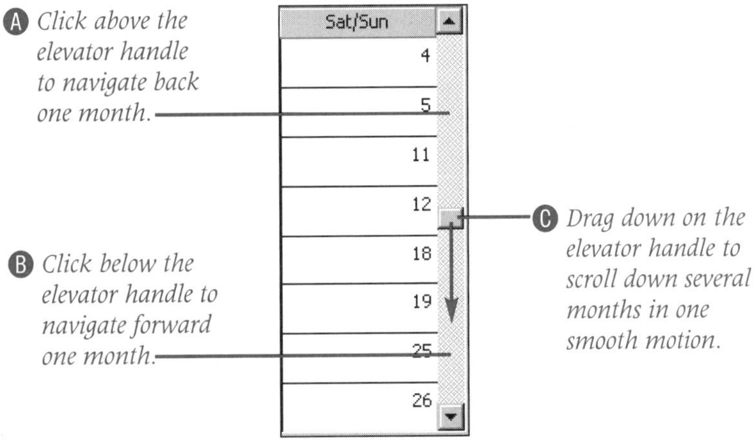
A Click above the elevator handle to navigate back one month.
B Click below the elevator handle to navigate forward one month.
C Drag down on the elevator handle to scroll down several months in one smooth motion.
Sat/Sun

(Continued on the next page)

10. *Right-click* on any day of the month; then choose **Go to This Day** on the pop-up menu. *Outlook displays the* Day *view for that date.*

11. *Right-click* on the label at the top of the day's schedule; then choose **Go to Today** from the pop-up menu. *It's always easy to jump right back to today's date in the calendar.*

Wednesday, August 11

12. *Right-click* again on the label at the top of the day's schedule; then choose **Go to Date** from the pop-up menu.

13. Type your birthday in this format: **`MM/DD`** (do not enter the year); then tap the (ENTER) key.

Date:
9/6

Notice the date in the top-right corner of the Calendar view. Since you did not enter a year, Outlook navigated to the next occurrence *of the date (unless your birthday occurs in the current month). If your birthday has already taken place this year, then you have navigated to next year's date of your birthday.*

September 06, 2000

14. *Right-click* on the label at the top of the day's schedule; then choose **Go to Today** from the pop-up menu.

Creating Events

There are three types of events you can schedule in the Outlook Calendar.

- **Appointments—**These are events that do not require the involvement of any additional people or resources from your company/organization.
- **Meetings—**These are events that require one or more people, or additional resources from your company/organization.
- **All Day Events—**These are activities that last one day or more. All Day events appear as banners in the calendar views rather than as blocks of time.

When you create an event, Outlook sets it for the currently selected date in the calendar. For example, if you click to select the last Friday of the month, and then click the New button, the new event will be set for the date you had just selected. However, you can always change the date and time within the event dialog box when you create the event. If you create an event that conflicts with an already scheduled event (or if the events are in adjacent blocks of time), Outlook will warn you about this.

Reminders

You can set a reminder for any event in the calendar. Reminders display a pop-up window and sound a reminder tone. You can set a reminder to display days, hours, or minutes ahead of the scheduled time. After a reminder goes off, you can either dismiss it or click the **snooze** button to make the reminder appear again later.

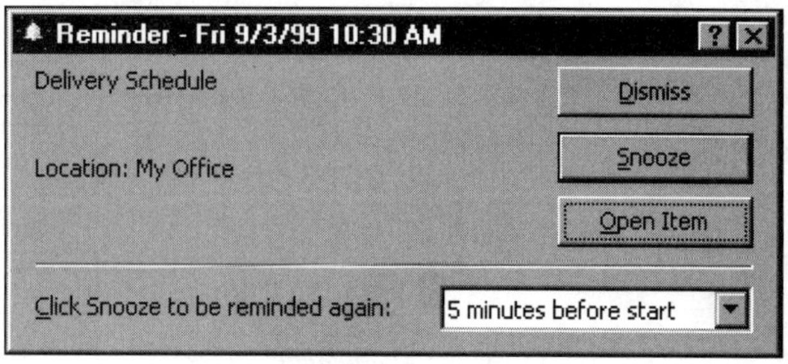
Reminder - Fri 9/3/99 10:30 AM
Delivery Schedule
Location: My Office
Dismiss
Snooze
Open Item
Click Snooze to be reminded again:
5 minutes before start

An example of an appointment reminder.

Although reminders have a drop-down list to display available times, you can also set the time manually to any number of minutes, hours, or days desired. For example, you can select **2 Days** from the drop-down list, then change the reminder to **5 Days,** as shown to the right.

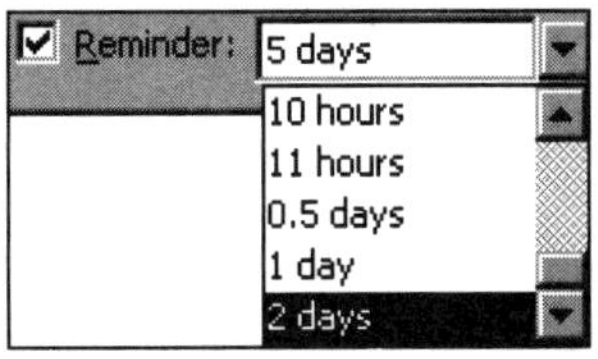
Reminder:
5 days
10 hours
11 hours
0.5 days
1 day
2 days

Quick Reference

HOW TO CREATE EVENTS

Task	Procedure
Create an Appointment event.	■ Select the date for the event in a Calendar view. ■ Click **New** on the Outlook toolbar, or *right-click,* then choose **New Appointment** from the pop-up menu.
Create an All Day event.	■ Select the **start date** for the event in a Calendar view. ■ *Right-click*, then choose **New All Day Event** from the pop-up menu.

Hands-On 6.6 Create an Appointment

In this exercise, you will create an appointment for a visit from Robert Smith.

From the Keyboard

CTRL+N to create a new appointment event.

1. Make sure the view is set to Day. Navigate to *tomorrow* with the small calendar in the upper-right corner of the Calendar view.
2. Follow these steps to select a time block for the new appointment.

10 00
11 00
New Appointment
New All Day Event
New Meeting Request

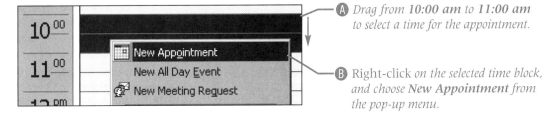

Ⓐ *Drag from* **10:00 am** *to* **11:00 am** *to select a time for the appointment.*

Ⓑ Right-click *on the selected time block, and choose* **New Appointment** *from the pop-up menu.*

An appointment window will appear with the selected date, start, and end times already filled in.

3. Follow these steps to fill in the appointment window.

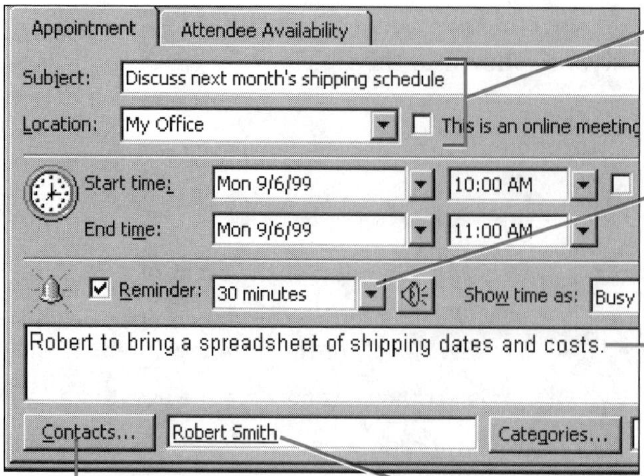
Appointment
Attendee Availability
Subject: Discuss next month's shipping schedule
Location: My Office
This is an online meeting
Start time: Mon 9/6/99 10:00 AM
End time: Mon 9/6/99 11:00 AM
Reminder: 30 minutes
Show time as: Busy
Robert to bring a spreadsheet of shipping dates and costs.
Contacts... Robert Smith
Categories...

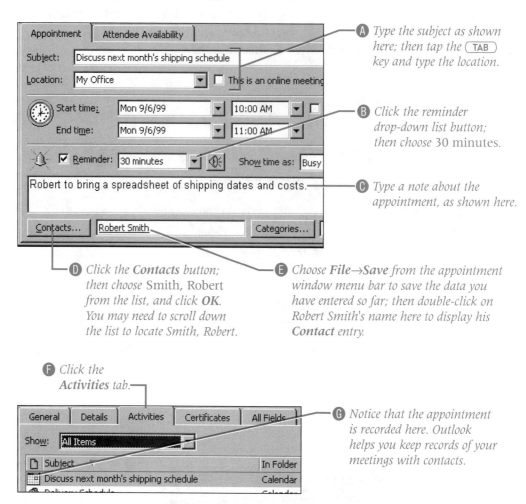

Ⓐ *Type the subject as shown here; then tap the* TAB *key and type the location.*

Ⓑ *Click the reminder drop-down list button; then choose* 30 minutes.

Ⓒ *Type a note about the appointment, as shown here.*

Ⓓ *Click the* ***Contacts*** *button; then choose* Smith, Robert *from the list, and click* ***OK****. You may need to scroll down the list to locate Smith, Robert.*

Ⓔ *Choose* ***File→Save*** *from the appointment window menu bar to save the data you have entered so far; then double-click on Robert Smith's name here to display his* ***Contact*** *entry.*

Ⓕ *Click the* ***Activities*** *tab.*

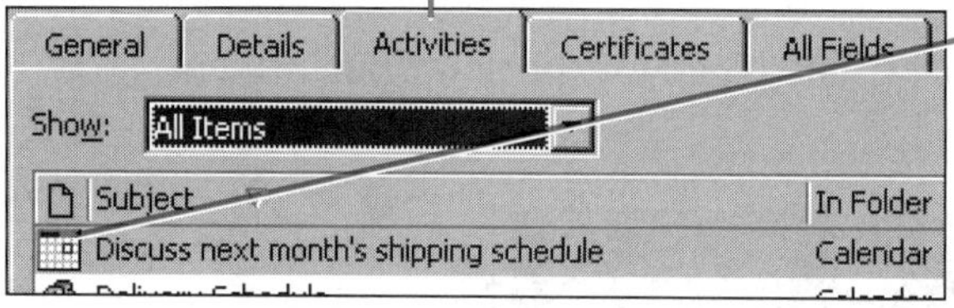
General
Details
Activities
Certificates
All Fields
Show: All Items
Subject
In Folder
Discuss next month's shipping schedule
Calendar

Ⓖ *Notice that the appointment is recorded here. Outlook helps you keep records of your meetings with contacts.*

4. Click the **Save and Close** button on the contact window for Robert Smith.
5. Click the **Save and Close** button for the appointment window.
   Now your appointment should be visible in the calendar window. Notice the small bell icon that indicates a reminder is set for this appointment.

Editing Appointments

From the Keyboard

CTRL+O to open the selected event.

You can *open* any appointment for editing in the calendar view with a double-click. After you make changes to an appointment, click the Save and Close button to save the revisions.

Hands-On 6.7 Edit the Appointment

The day before the appointment, Daniel receives a call from Robert Smith who says he will have to reschedule the meeting for a half-hour later. Daniel indicates that the meeting can be only 45 minutes in that case, since he has another appointment immediately after this one. You will revise the appointment to reschedule the start time and adjust the meeting length.

1. *Double-click* on the appointment in the Day view to display the appointment window.
2. Follow these steps to adjust the appointment time.

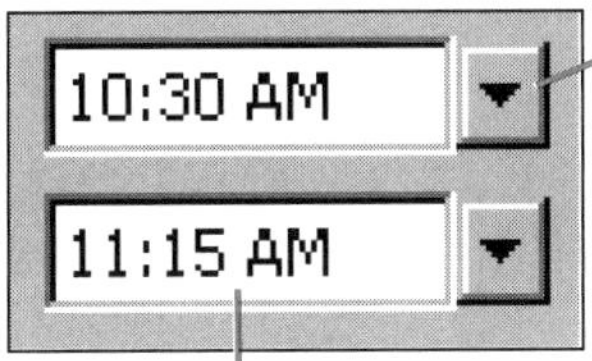
10:30 AM
11:15 AM

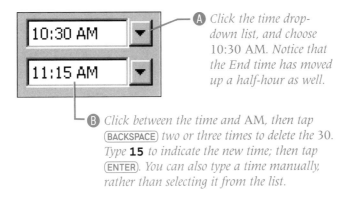

(A) *Click the time drop-down list, and choose* 10:30 AM. *Notice that the End time has moved up a half-hour as well.*

(B) *Click between the time and AM, then tap* (BACKSPACE) *two or three times to delete the 30. Type* **15** *to indicate the new time; then tap* (ENTER). *You can also type a time manually, rather than selecting it from the list.*

3. Click the **Save and Close** button to save the change and close the window.
   The revisions are displayed on the Day view. Notice that the blue bar indicating the meeting duration is now shorter, since you changed the meeting length to 45 minutes.

Creating All Day Events

Unlike appointments or meetings, an All Day event does not occupy a block of time in your schedule. This means you can schedule additional events during All Day events. For example, you might want to schedule an All Day event for the dates of an out-of-town conference and add appointments for specific activities to attend during the conference.

Hands-On 6.8 Create an All Day Event

In this exercise, you will create an All Day event for a conference that will last four days.

1. Click Month on the Outlook toolbar.
2. Click to select **Wednesday** of next week as the event start date.
3. *Right-click* on the selected Wednesday; then choose **New All Day Event** from the pop-up menu.
   A new event window will appear. Notice that the All day event *checkbox is already checked for you. Otherwise, this window looks just like a normal appointment window.*
4. Follow these steps to define the All Day event.

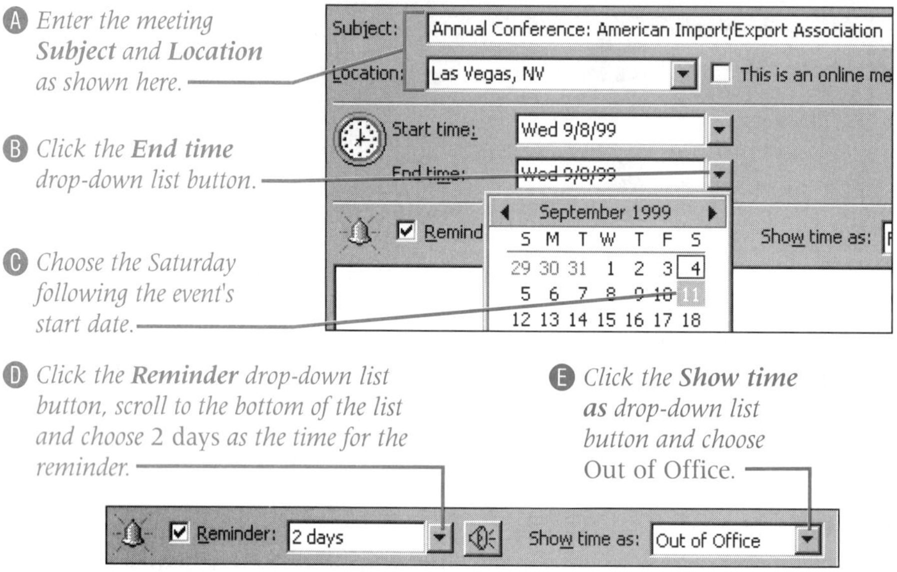

A Enter the meeting Subject and Location as shown here.
B Click the End time drop-down list button.
C Choose the Saturday following the event's start date.
D Click the Reminder drop-down list button, scroll to the bottom of the list and choose 2 days as the time for the reminder.
E Click the Show time as drop-down list button and choose Out of Office.
Subject: Annual Conference: American Import/Export Association
Location: Las Vegas, NV
This is an online me
Start time: Wed 9/8/99
End time: Wed 9/8/99
September 1999
S M T W T F S
29 30 31 1 2 3 4
5 6 7 8 9 10 11
12 13 14 15 16 17 18
Remind
Show time as:
Reminder: 2 days
Show time as: Out of Office

5. Click the **Save and Close** button to close the appointment window.
   Notice the banner that stretches across the four days designated for the event.
6. Click the Week button on the Outlook toolbar.
   Now small banners for the event are displayed on each day of the week.
7. Click the Day button on the Outlook toolbar.
   The All Day event banner appears at the top of the Day schedule. Notice also that numbers for the days of the event are in bold type in the small calendar on the right side of the view. Outlook uses bold type to indicate each date that contains at least one event.

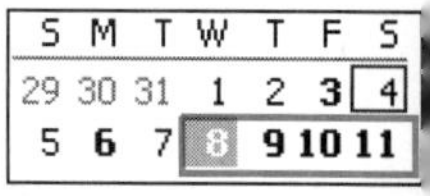

S M T W T F S
29 30 31 1 2 3 4
5 6 7 8 9 10 11

Printing Calendars and Events

Outlook lets you print the Calendar in a wide variety of styles. As was the case with the Contacts list and Inbox messages, you can print either views or individual events. An example of printing a view would be a daily, weekly, or monthly calendar. As with printing from other Outlook views, you can use the Print Preview command to preview what the printed pages will look like. If you wish to print calendars for several days, weeks, or months in a row, simply adjust the print range to reflect the span of time you wish the printout to cover.

Quick Reference

PRINTING THE CALENDAR

Task	Procedure
Print a Calendar view.	■ Display the type of view you would like to print in the Calendar. ■ Click the **Print** button on the toolbar. ■ If desired, choose an alternative print style in the *Print Style* box. ■ If desired, adjust the *Start* and *End* dates in the Print Range for the print command.
Print a Calendar event.	■ Double-click to open the event you would like to print. ■ Click the **Print** button on the toolbar. *Tip: You can also right-click on an event; then choose Print from the pop-up menu.*

Hands-On 6.9 Print from the Calendar

1. *Right-click* on the heading of the Day's schedule; then choose **Go to today** from the pop-up menu.
2. Click to display the **Week** view.
3. Click the Print button on the toolbar.
   Notice that the print range is set to print for the period Monday to Sunday of the coming week.
4. Follow these steps to adjust the print range.

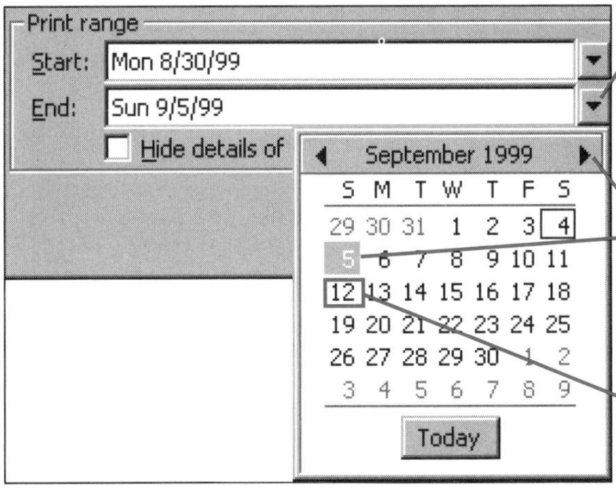

Print range
Start: Mon 8/30/99
End: Sun 9/5/99
Hide details of
September 1999
S M T W T F S
Today

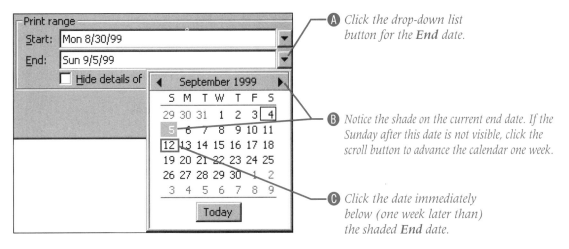

Ⓐ *Click the drop-down list button for the* ***End*** *date.*

Ⓑ *Notice the shade on the current end date. If the Sunday after this date is not visible, click the scroll button to advance the calendar one week.*

Ⓒ *Click the date immediately below (one week later than) the shaded* ***End*** *date.*

5. Click the **Preview** button at the bottom-right corner of the dialog box.
   Outlook will display how the weekly calendar will appear in print.
6. Click on any part of the page to zoom in on the Preview.
7. Click the Page Down button on the Preview toolbar to view the next page.
8. Click the Print button at the top of the preview window.
   This returns you to the Print dialog box. Notice that you could also select the Daily style or any other style listed in the Print style list.

(Continued on the next page)

9. Adjust the *End* date in the *Print range* to print just one week, rather than two weeks. You can select the date from the small calendar or type the new date manually in the End Print Range date box.

10. Click **OK** to print the weekly calendar; then retrieve the printout.

Print an Event

11. Double-click to open the **Discuss next month's shipping schedule** appointment that you created in a previous exercise. Navigate to **today's date** if the appointment is not visible.

12. Click the Print [Print...] button on the event window toolbar.
The event will be sent immediately to the printer.

13. Close [X] the event window.

Working with Tasks

The Tasks view in Outlook lets you maintain a to do list. You can track individual tasks by their due dates, completion status, and priority. The following illustration displays some of the key features of a typical task window.

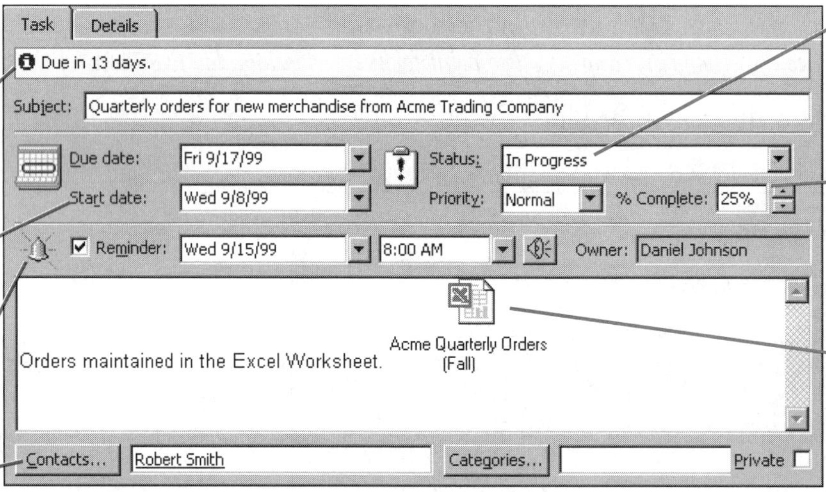

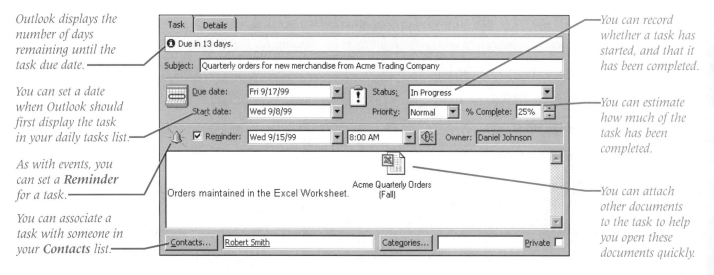

Outlook displays the number of days remaining until the task due date.
You can set a date when Outlook should first display the task in your daily tasks list.
As with events, you can set a **Reminder** for a task.
You can associate a task with someone in your **Contacts** list.
You can record whether a task has started, and that it has been completed.
You can estimate how much of the task has been completed.
You can attach other documents to the task to help you open these documents quickly.
Task
Details
Due in 13 days.
Subject:
Quarterly orders for new merchandise from Acme Trading Company
Due date:
Fri 9/17/99
Start date:
Wed 9/8/99
Status:
In Progress
Priority:
Normal
% Complete:
25%
Reminder:
Wed 9/15/99
8:00 AM
Owner:
Daniel Johnson
Orders maintained in the Excel Worksheet.
Acme Quarterly Orders (Fall)
Contacts...
Robert Smith
Categories...
Private

Creating Tasks

You will usually want to create tasks in the Tasks view. This view displays all of the tasks in your to do list.

Quick Reference

HOW TO CREATE A TASK

Task	Procedure
Add a new task to the Tasks view.	■ Display the *Tasks* view. ■ Type a subject for the new task in the box at the top of the Tasks view; then tap (ENTER). ■ You can also click the New button on the toolbar, or use (CTRL)+N from the keyboard.

Hands-On 6.10 Create a Task

In this exercise, you will create a task to prepare for the meeting with Robert Smith.

1. Click the **Tasks** shortcut on the Outlook bar to display the Tasks view. You may need to scroll down the Outlook bar to make the Tasks shortcut visible.
2. Follow these steps to create the new task.

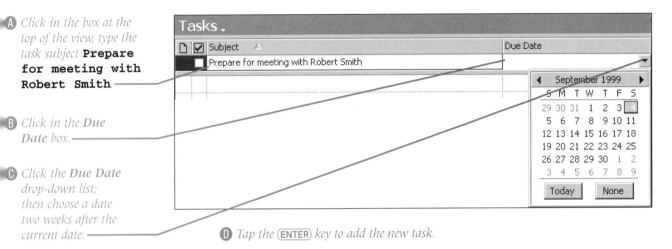

(A) Click in the box at the top of the view, type the task subject **Prepare for meeting with Robert Smith.**

(B) Click in the ***Due Date*** *box.*

(C) Click the ***Due Date*** *drop-down list; then choose a date two weeks after the current date.*

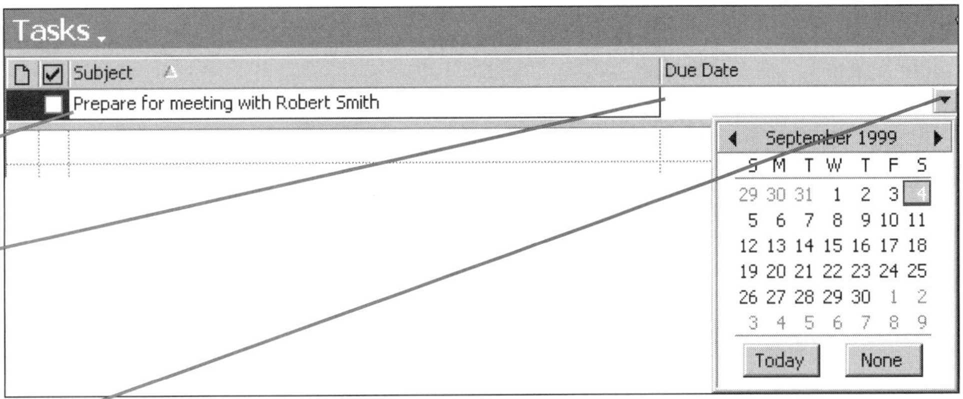

Tasks
Subject
Due Date
Prepare for meeting with Robert Smith
September 1999
S M T W T F S
29 30 31 1 2 3 4
5 6 7 8 9 10 11
12 13 14 15 16 17 18
19 20 21 22 23 24 25
26 27 28 29 30 1 2
3 4 5 6 7 8 9
Today
None

(D) Tap the ENTER *key to add the new task.*

The new task is displayed in the task list.

3. Click the **Outlook Today** shortcut on the Outlook bar. You may need to scroll up the Outlook bar to make the Outlook Today shortcut visible.
Notice that the new task is also displayed in the Tasks section of this view.

Editing and Printing Tasks

When you create a new task in the Tasks view, you can only enter the subject and due date information. If you want to enter additional information, such as a start date or a reminder, you must open the task and edit it. As with email, contacts, and events, you can open any task with a double-click. You can use the same types of commands to print a task list or an individual task that you have used with other Outlook features.

Hands-On 6.11 Edit and Print a Task

1. Display the **Tasks** view.
2. *Double-click* to open the task you just created. Make sure that the Task window is maximized.
3. Follow these steps to edit the new task.

Ⓐ *Click the* ***Start date*** *drop-down list button, then choose a date one week before the due date. If the shaded end date is on the bottom line of the calendar, click the scroll right button to display the next month.*

Ⓑ *Click the* ***% Complete*** *spinner bar button to set the percentage to 50%. You can also manually enter a percentage in this box to reflect how much of the task has been completed.*

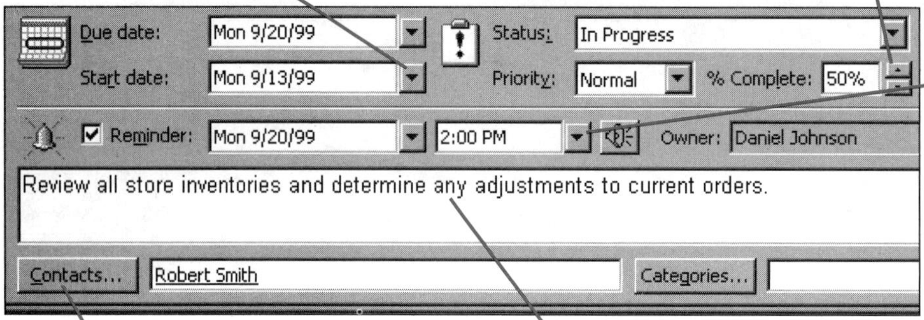
Due date:
Mon 9/20/99
Status:
In Progress
Start date:
Mon 9/13/99
Priority:
Normal
% Complete:
50%
Reminder:
Mon 9/20/99
2:00 PM
Owner:
Daniel Johnson
Review all store inventories and determine any adjustments to current orders.
Contacts...
Robert Smith
Categories...

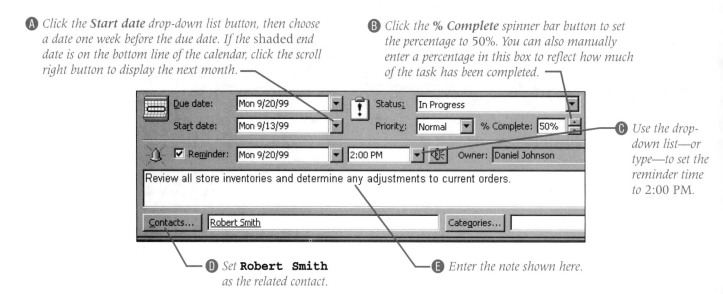

Ⓒ *Use the drop-down list—or type—to set the reminder time to 2:00 PM.*

Ⓓ *Set* **`Robert Smith`** *as the related contact.*

Ⓔ *Enter the note shown here.*

4. Click the **Details** tab near the top of the Task window.
   As with the Details area of a Contact, this area lets you record additional and optional information.
5. Click the **Save and Close** button to save your edits.
6. Make sure that the task is still selected, then click the Print button on the toolbar. Choose the **Memo** print style to print this individual item.
   If you left the print style as Table, *Outlook would print a list of tasks (the view) rather than the details of one or more individual tasks (items).*
7. Click **OK** to execute the print command, and retrieve the printout from the printer.

Working with Notes

Many of us wonder how businesses functioned before the introduction of those ubiquitous yellow sticky notes. Outlook's Notes feature lets you create electronic versions of those notes. Notes are a handy tool to record temporary messages and reminders. You can also place notes on the Windows Desktop. Notes on the Desktop will remain there even if you exit from the Outlook program. You can even change the color of a note. When necessary, it is also possible to print a note.

Quick Reference

WORKING WITH NOTES

Task	Procedure
Create a new note.	■ Choose **File→New→Note** from any view, or use CTRL+SHIFT+N to create a new note.
Place a note on the Desktop.	■ Make sure that the Outlook window is *restored* (not maximized). ■ *Drag-and-drop* the note from the Notes view onto the Windows Desktop. The note can remain on the Desktop until you log off or shut down Windows.
Change the color of a note.	■ *Right-click* on the note; then choose **Colors→[color]** from the pop-up menu.

Hands-On 6.12 Create a Note

1. Display the **Notes** view in the Outlook window.
2. Click the New button at the left side of the Outlook toolbar.
   A new blank note will appear.
3. Type the following text in the note: **`The new rate for shipping is $32.50 per 100 lbs.`**
4. Click the Close button at the top-right corner of the note.
   The note will be reduced to icon size in the Notes view. The first few words of the note serve as its title in this view.
5. Click the List button on the Outlook toolbar.
   This displays the notes in a single column. Outlook displays as much of the Note's contents as will fit in the width of the window.
6. *Right-click* on the note; then choose **Color→Blue** from the pop-up menu.
7. *Double-click* on your new note to open it again. Click at the end of the note, and add **`as of next month`**.
   You do not need to use a Save *command to save your revision—changes to notes are saved automatically as you type.*

(Continued on the next page)

Size the Note, and Place It on the Desktop

8. *Drag* on the bottom-right corner of the note to practice making it larger and smaller. Notice how the text is rearranged as you size the note.
   If you ever add more text to a note than fits in its present size, you can always change its size.
9. Close the note.
10. Restore the Outlook window so that it is no longer maximized. Drag on the borders of the Outlook window, and resize it so that the Desktop is clearly visible.
11. *Drag and drop* the note from the Notes view to any available spot on the Windows Desktop; then minimize the Outlook window.
    The note will remain on the Desktop, even if you close the Outlook window.
12. Double-click to open the note on the Desktop.
13. Click the Close button on the note; then click the **Outlook** button on the Windows taskbar to restore the Outlook window.
14. Click to select the note you created; then click the Delete button on the Outlook toolbar.
    The Note is sent to the Deleted Items *view. It can be retrieved from Deleted Items as with any other Outlook item, such as an email message or an appointment event.*
15. Close the Outlook window.

Concepts Review

True/False Questions

1. When you search for a name in the Contacts list, you must type out the entire name.	TRUE	FALSE
2. When you issue a print command in Outlook, you can print either a view or item(s).	TRUE	FALSE
3. You can only send an email message to one addressee at a time.	TRUE	FALSE
4. You can type a date manually rather than use the drop-down calendar on a data box.	TRUE	FALSE
5. When you schedule a time for an event, you can only select increments that appear in the drop-down list.	TRUE	FALSE
6. Outlook Notes can only be displayed in the Notes view.	TRUE	FALSE
7. The only way to address an email message is to type out the email address as it appears in a contact's data.	TRUE	FALSE
8. You cannot set reminders for Tasks. Reminders can only be set for Calendar Events.	TRUE	FALSE

Multiple Choice Questions

1. Which of the items below *is not* a type of Calendar event?
   a. Appointment
   b. Deadline
   c. Meeting
   d. All Day
   e. All of the above are types of events.

2. Which item in the list below *is not* something you can print in Outlook?
   a. An Item
   b. A View
   c. A Window
   d. None of the above

3. Which item in the list below *is not* a Calendar schedule view?
   a. Daily
   b. Weekly
   c. Monthly
   d. Yearly
   e. All of the above are valid schedule views.

4. When addressing email, which punctuation mark should you use to separate individual email addresses?
   a. Semicolon (;)
   b. Parentheses ()
   c. Colon (:)
   d. Period
   e. Any of the above

Skill Builders

Skill Builder 6.1 Create New Contacts

In this exercise, you will create two new contacts.

1. Start Outlook, and if necessary Maximize the window.
2. Display the **Contacts** view.
3. Click the **New** button on the toolbar; then add the following contact.

TIP! *If you need to change the label for the a phone number box, be sure to do so before you enter the phone number.*

First	**Terry**
Last	**Sanchez**
File as	**Terry Sanchez**
Job Title	**VP, Imports**
Company	**Acme Trading Company**
Business Phone	**[800] 555-1234**
Business Fax	**[800] 555-1237**
Pager	**[800] 345-3737**
Mobile	**[Area*] 322-5129**
Business Address	**3112 Center Street** **[Your City, State & Zip]**
Email Address	**terry@offtowork.com**

4. Click the **Save and Close** button on the contact window when you are done. Leave the Duplicate Contact option on *Update,* and click **OK** if you are prompted that a contact with the same name already exists.
   Outlook warns you so that you do not inadvertently overwrite a contact that already exists. In this case however, you want to overwrite the existing contact.
5. Find and select **Smith, Robert** in the Contacts view.
6. Choose **Actions→New Contact from Same Company** from the menu bar. Click the **Expand Menu** command if you do not see the desired menu item.
   A new contact window will open with basic information copied from Robert Smith's entry. This saves you the time of re-typing the information.

7. Enter the following information for the new contact;

Name	**Jacqueline Chan**
File as	**Chan, Jacqueline**
Job Title	**Manager, Imports**
Company	**Zozobra Importers**
Business Phone	**[505] 555-1220**
Business Fax	**[505] 999-1237**
Pager	**[800] 688-2936**
Mobile	**(None)**
Address	**200 East San Francisco Street** **Santa Fe, NM 87505**
Email Address	**jchan@offtowork.com**

8. *Save and close* the window. Leave the Duplicate Contact option on **Update,** and click **OK** if you are prompted that a contact with the same name already exists.

Skill Builder 6.2 Send Email to Contacts

In this exercise you will send a message to Robert Smith and Cc his manager and Daniel's manager. Daniel is following up on a message he sent last week to which he has not received a reply.

TIP! *Before you begin, if you have not done Skill Builder Exercise 6.1 yet, you should do so before beginning this exercise.*

1. Display the **Contacts** view.
2. Click to select **Smith, Robert** in the Contacts list.
3. Click the New Message to Contact  button on the toolbar.
   A new message addressed to Robert Smith will appear.
4. Click the **Cc:** button on the message window; then add **Jacqueline Chan** and **Terry Sanchez** to the Cc list in the Select Names window. Click **OK** to close the window.

(Continued on the next page)

5. Enter the subject: **Shipment status**. Type the body of the message, as shown below.

```
Hello Bob:

I sent you a message two days ago inquiring about the
shipment of tablecloths to our San Antonio warehouse.
I have not received a reply.

Please notify me right away about the status of the
shipment.

Regards,

Daniel
```

6. **Send** the message.
7. Display the **Inbox,** then check for new messages. Continue checking until you receive a reply from each addressee.

Skill Builder 6.3 Create Appointments

In this exercise, you will create an appointment for the next class meeting. You will also create an All Day event for your next anticipated vacation.

1. Display the **Calendar** view, and set it to display the Day  schedule.
2. Using any method you prefer, navigate to the date of your next class meeting.
3. Click on the *starting time* of your next class meeting in the calendar; then **drag** to the **end time.** If the class does not begin or end on an even hour/half-hour, just come as close as you can—you can adjust the time if necessary in the appointment window.
4. *Right-click* on the time block you selected; then choose **New Appointment** from the pop-up menu.
5. Fill-in the information for this appointment. Enter the title of the class in the *subject* box and the building and room number in the *location* box. If necessary, adjust the start or end times for the appointment to the exact scheduled times for the class. Set the reminder to appear *1 hour* before the appointment.
6. Click **Save and Close** on the toolbar when you are finished.

Create an All Day Event

7. Choose the **Month** schedule for the Calendar view.
8. Using the scroll bar along the right side of the month view, navigate to a month when you would like to take a vacation.
9. Click to select a starting date for the vacation, then *right-click* on the same date and choose **New All Day Event** from the pop-up menu.

10. Enter the name of the destination for your vacation as the Subject and a location, such as the city or country.

11. Enter the ending date for the vacation in the **End time** box, or use the drop-down list button to select the ending date in the calendar.

12. Follow these steps to set a reminder to display *3 days* before the Start time.

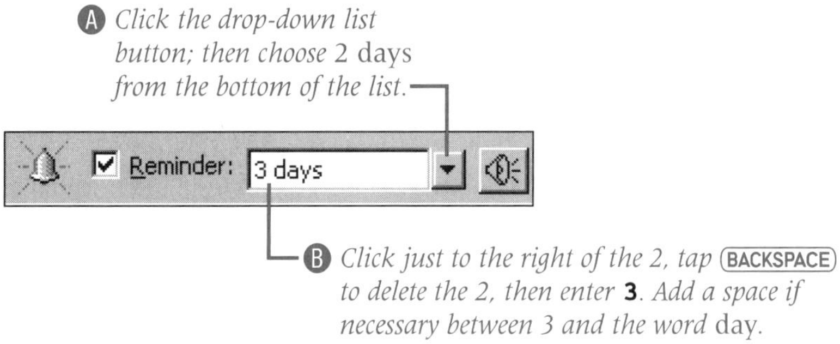

A Click the drop-down list button; then choose 2 days from the bottom of the list.
Reminder: 3 days
B Click just to the right of the 2, tap BACKSPACE to delete the 2, then enter 3. Add a space if necessary between 3 and the word day.

13. **Save and close** the Event.

Skill Builder 6.4 Create a Task

In this exercise, you will create a task and set a reminder.

1. Display the **Tasks** view; then click the **New** button on the toolbar.
   The New button lets you enter all of the information for the new task in one step. In the earlier Hands-On exercise, you had to double-click to open the task after you created it.
2. Follow these steps to enter information on the new task.

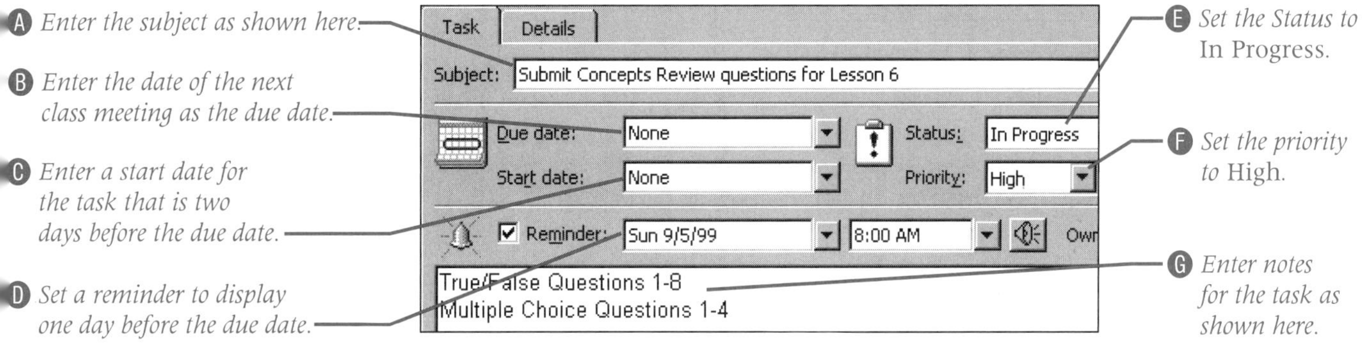

A Enter the subject as shown here.
B Enter the date of the next class meeting as the due date.
C Enter a start date for the task that is two days before the due date.
D Set a reminder to display one day before the due date.
E Set the Status to In Progress.
F Set the priority to High.
G Enter notes for the task as shown here.
Task
Details
Subject: Submit Concepts Review questions for Lesson 6
Due date: None
Start date: None
Status: In Progress
Priority: High
Reminder: Sun 9/5/99
8:00 AM
True/False Questions 1-8
Multiple Choice Questions 1-4

3. **Save and close** the task.
   The task is listed in the Tasks view.
4. Display the **Outlook Today** view.
   This view displays a summary of your appointments, email messages, and to do list. Notice the red exclamation point (!) beside the task you just added—this indicates a high-priority task.

(Continued on the next page)

5. Follow these steps to work with the tasks in the Outlook Today view.

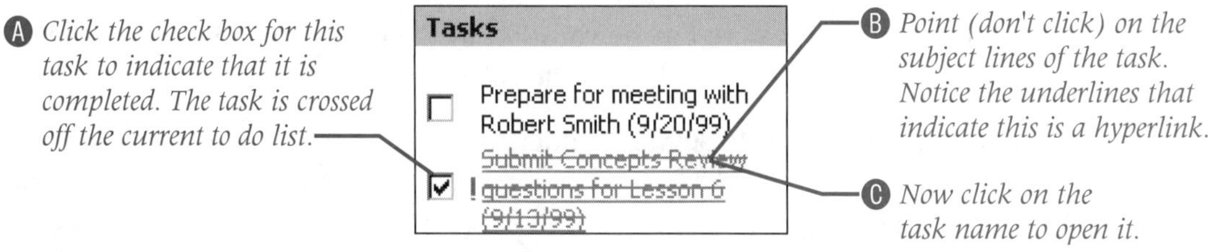

Tasks
Prepare for meeting with Robert Smith (9/20/99)
Submit Concepts Review questions for Lesson 6 (9/13/99)
A Click the check box for this task to indicate that it is completed. The task is crossed off the current to do list.
B Point (don't click) on the subject lines of the task. Notice the underlines that indicate this is a hyperlink.
C Now click on the task name to open it.

Notice that the completion percentage box has been set to 100%. *The Status box has been set to* Completed.

6. Click the spinner bar beside the **% Complete** box to reduce the completion percentage to 75%. *Notice that the Status box has been reset to* In Progress.

7. **Save and Close** the task.
Notice that the task is no longer struck through as completed and the check box is empty.

8. Display the *Tasks* view; then **delete** the task from the Task list.

9. Display the **Deleted Items** view.

10. Scroll down the view until you see your task. Depending on how recently the Deleted Items were emptied, there may be a large number of items in this view.
As you have observed with email messages, the task has not yet been permanently erased. It will stay in the Deleted Items view until you empty the Deleted Items.

11. Use the *drag-and-drop* technique to drag the task from the Deleted Items view to the *Tasks* button on the Outlook bar.
This retrieves the task back to the Tasks view.

12. Display the **Tasks** view to confirm that the task has been retrieved.

Skill Builder 6.5 Create a Note

In this exercise, you will create a note and place it on the Desktop.

1. Display the **Outlook Today** view.

2. Choose **File→New→Note** from the Outlook menu bar.
It was not necessary to display the Notes *view before creating the note. You can create a new note in any of the views.*

3. Type the following in the note: **`Ideas for staff holiday party: Catered luncheon, dinner with dj and dancing, $15 gift exchange.`**

4. Close ☒ the note.

5. Display the **Notes** view, and click the Large Icons [Large Icons] button on the toolbar.
   New notes are always placed in this view. Notice how the first two lines of each note appear in this view.
6. Right-click on the note you just created, choose **Color→Green** from the pop-up menu, and then *double-click* to open the note.
7. If the Outlook window is currently maximized, click the Restore button.
8. If necessary, drag on the borders of the Outlook window to make about half of the Windows Desktop visible.
9. Drag the Note icon to the Desktop; then Close the Outlook window.
   Notice that the note remains on the Desktop even after you have closed the Outlook program. The note will remain on the Desktop until you log off or shut down Windows, or until you close the note.
10. Double-click to open the note on the Desktop.
11. Close the note.
12. Drag any notes on the Desktop to the **Recycle Bin.**
   The notes will still remain in Outlook until you delete them in the Outlook program.

Assessments

Assessment 6.1 Create a New Contact

1. Create a contact with the following information:

First	Graciella
Last	Alvera
Job Title	Store Manager
Company	Imports Warehouse
Email Address	Hello@offtowork.com
Business Address	2020 Tune Road Baltimore, MD 21075
Business Phone	410-999-2222
Business Fax	410-999-2238
Assistant Phone	410-999-2212

2. **Print** the individual entry for this new contact.
3. Print a *list* of all the contacts in your Contacts view.

Assessment 6.2 Send Email to Contacts

1. **Compose** a new message with the following settings:

To:	Jacqueline Chan
Cc:	Robert Smith
Subject:	Contacts List
Body:	This assessment tests my knowledge of the Contacts list and many of its features.

2. **Send** the message.
3. Wait a couple of minutes; then check for new messages.
4. **Print** the message from Jacqueline Chan that you received in response to this message.

Assessment 6.3 Create an Appointment

1. Create an appointment for the final meeting of your class. The appointment should include the following information:
   - **Subject and Location—**fill in the course name and classroom location.
   - **Start and End Times—**day and time of final class meeting.
   - **Reminder—**set for two hours prior to final class meeting.
   - **Notes—**enter a note about any final exam or other activities that will take place on the final class meeting.
2. **Print** the appointment item.

Assessment 6.4 Create a Task

1. Create a task for a class project. The task should include the following information:
   - **Due Date—**date of final class meeting
   - **Start Date—**set for one week prior to final class meeting
   - **Reminder—**set for two days prior to final class meeting
   - **Status—**In Progress
   - **Priority—**High
   - **% Complete—**50%
   - **Note—**enter notes on the lesson in this book that must be completed by the end of the final class meeting.
2. **Print** the task item.
3. **Print** a list of all tasks in the Tasks view.

Assessment 6.5 Create a Note

1. Create a new note with information on this book: Book title, ISBN number, and where it can be purchased. Make sure that all of the information on the note is visible. If necessary resize the note.
2. Place the note on the Desktop.

UNIT 4

Word 2000

Word processing is a fundamental skill that every office worker uses at one time or another. This unit is designed to give you a solid foundation of word processing skills using Word 2000. Word is the most popular word processing program used in businesses. Thus, you will develop marketable skills as you master the techniques in this unit. In addition to word processing skills, you will learn formatting techniques for crafting business letters, memorandums, and reports.

LESSON 7—Word

Creating and Editing Business Letters

In this lesson, you will learn the basics of word processing using Microsoft Word 2000. You will create a variety of business letters while learning proper business document formatting. You will also learn fundamental techniques of entering and editing text, saving documents, and using Word 2000 commands. This lesson is designed to provide you with a solid foundation of word processing skills to prepare you for the advanced features introduced in later lessons.

In This Lesson

Case Study

Susan Adams is the top sales representative for Western Office Supplies. Western Office Supplies distributes office equipment, including copy machines, laser printers, fax machines, and digital scanners to customers throughout the Western United States. Susan and her manager Richard Jones have just delivered a dynamic presentation to Sandra Evans, Vice President of Integrated Office Solutions. Like all top-notch sales representatives, Susan provides excellent follow-through and customer support. As a follow-up to her sales presentation, Susan writes a formal business letter to Sandra Evans thanking her for her time and preparing the next step in the sales process. Susan uses Word 2000 to create and edit her business letter.

June 26, 1999

Ms. Sandra Evans
Vice President
Integrated Office Solutions
2756 Industrial Lane
Los Angeles, CA 90024

Dear Ms. Evans:

It was a pleasure meeting with you and the rest of your staff yesterday. Both Richard Jones and I were quite impressed with your facilities and the quality of your team. You certainly have a group of hard working and creative people.

Our presentation was designed to give you an overview of our high-performance copiers, laser printers, fax machines, and digital scanners. We would like to follow up our presentation with a live demonstration. You must see our products in action to truly appreciate their benefits.

I will contact you early next week to arrange a demonstration. In the meantime, feel free to contact me if I can be of further assistance.

Sincerely,

Susan Adams
Sales Representative

xx

What Is Microsoft Word 2000?

Microsoft Word 2000 is a program that makes word processing a pleasure instead of a chore. Word's powerful suite of tools lets you easily create and modify a variety of documents. Word provides tools to assist you in virtually every aspect of document creation. From desktop publishing to Web publishing, Word has the right tool for the job. For these and many other reasons, Word is the most widely used word processing program in both homes and businesses.

Why Use Word?

Word provides a number of important features and benefits that make it a smart choice to use.

- **IntelliSense Technology—**Word's IntelliSense technology includes automated tools like AutoCorrect to assist you in creating, editing, and formatting documents. This speeds up the process of creating and formatting documents, so that you can focus on content.
- **GUI—**Word's Graphical User Interface is so easy to use that even beginning computer users find it simple. The interface reduces the need to memorize commands, and it will make you more productive.
- **Writing Tools—**Word has powerful writing tools, including automatic grammar checking and spell checking, as you type. These and other tools will help you improve your writing skills.
- **Widely Used—**Word is the most widely used word processing software. Word is the right choice if you are trying to develop marketable skills and find employment.
- **Integration with Other Office Programs—**Word 2000 is part of the Microsoft Office 2000 suite of programs, which also includes Excel, Access, PowerPoint, Outlook, PhotoDraw, and others. The ability to exchange data with these programs is one of the most powerful and attractive features of Word.
- **Web Integration—**Word 2000 lets you easily publish your documents to Web sites on the World Wide Web or to your company Intranet.

It's Time to Master Word!

It's time to put your fears behind and master this wonderful program. You will be amazed at the power and simplicity of Word and how easy it is to learn. The knowledge you are about to gain will give you a marketable skill and make you a master of Word.

Starting Word 2000

The method you use to start Word and other Office programs depends in large part upon whether you intend to create a new document or open an existing document. If you intend to create a new document, then use one of the following methods to start Word. Once the Word program has started, you can begin working in the new document window that appears.

- Click the Start button, and choose Microsoft Word from the Programs menu.
- Click the Microsoft Word  button on the Quick Launch toolbar (located near the Taskbar).
- Click the Start button, choose New Office Document, choose the General tab, and double-click the Blank Document icon.

Use one of the following methods if you intend to open an existing Word document. Once the Word program has started, the desired document will open in a Word window.

- Navigate to the desired document using Windows Explorer or My Computer, and double-click the document.
- Click the Start button and point to Documents. You can choose the desired document from the Documents list. The Documents list displays the most recently used documents.

Hands-On 7.1 Start Word

1. If necessary, start your computer, and the Windows Desktop will be displayed.
2. Click the Start button, and choose **Programs.**
3. Choose **Microsoft Word** from the Programs menu.
The Word program will load, and the document window shown below will appear. Don't be concerned if your document window appears different from this example.

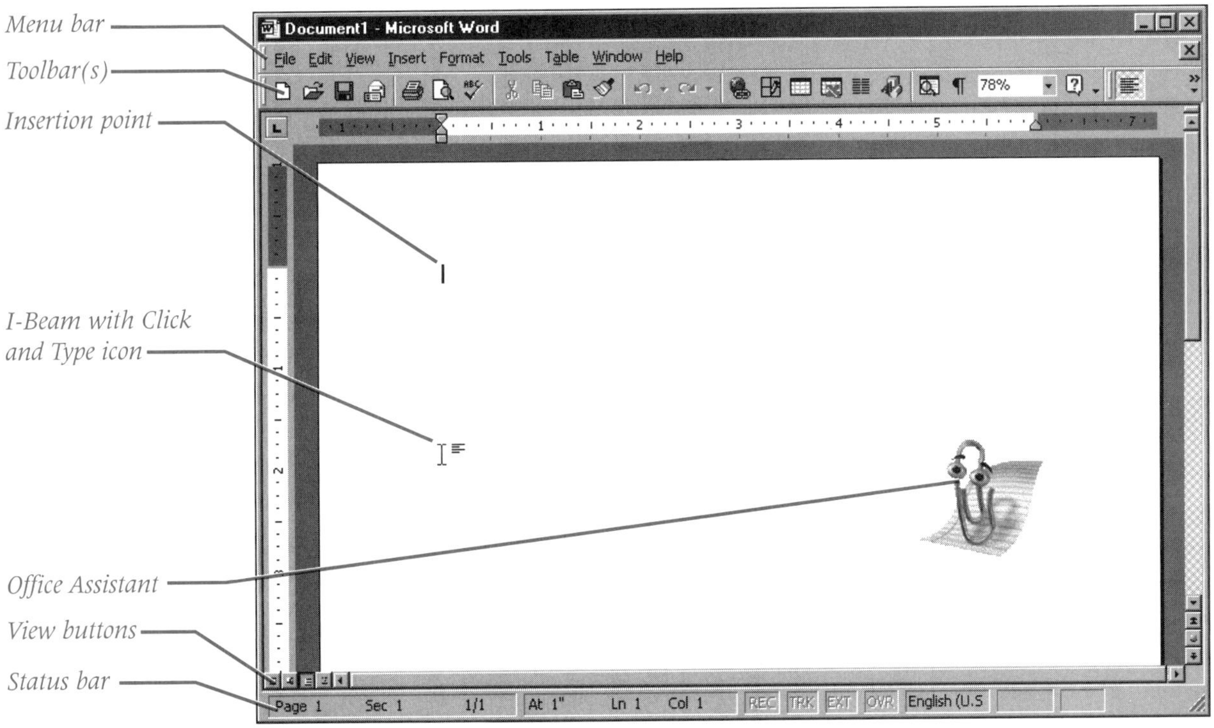

Menu bar
Toolbar(s)
Insertion point
I-Beam with Click and Type icon
Office Assistant
View buttons
Status bar
Document1 - Microsoft Word
File Edit View Insert Format Tools Table Window Help
78%
Page 1 Sec 1 1/1 At 1" Ln 1 Col 1 REC TRK EXT OVR English (U.S

The document window is where you type information into Word. The document window allows you to access Word commands, and it can be customized to suit your particular needs. You will learn how to modify the document window at a later time.

Business Letter Styles

There are several acceptable styles of business letters. The styles discussed in this text include block, modified block, and personal. All business letters contain the same, or similar, elements but with varied formatting.

Block Style Letter

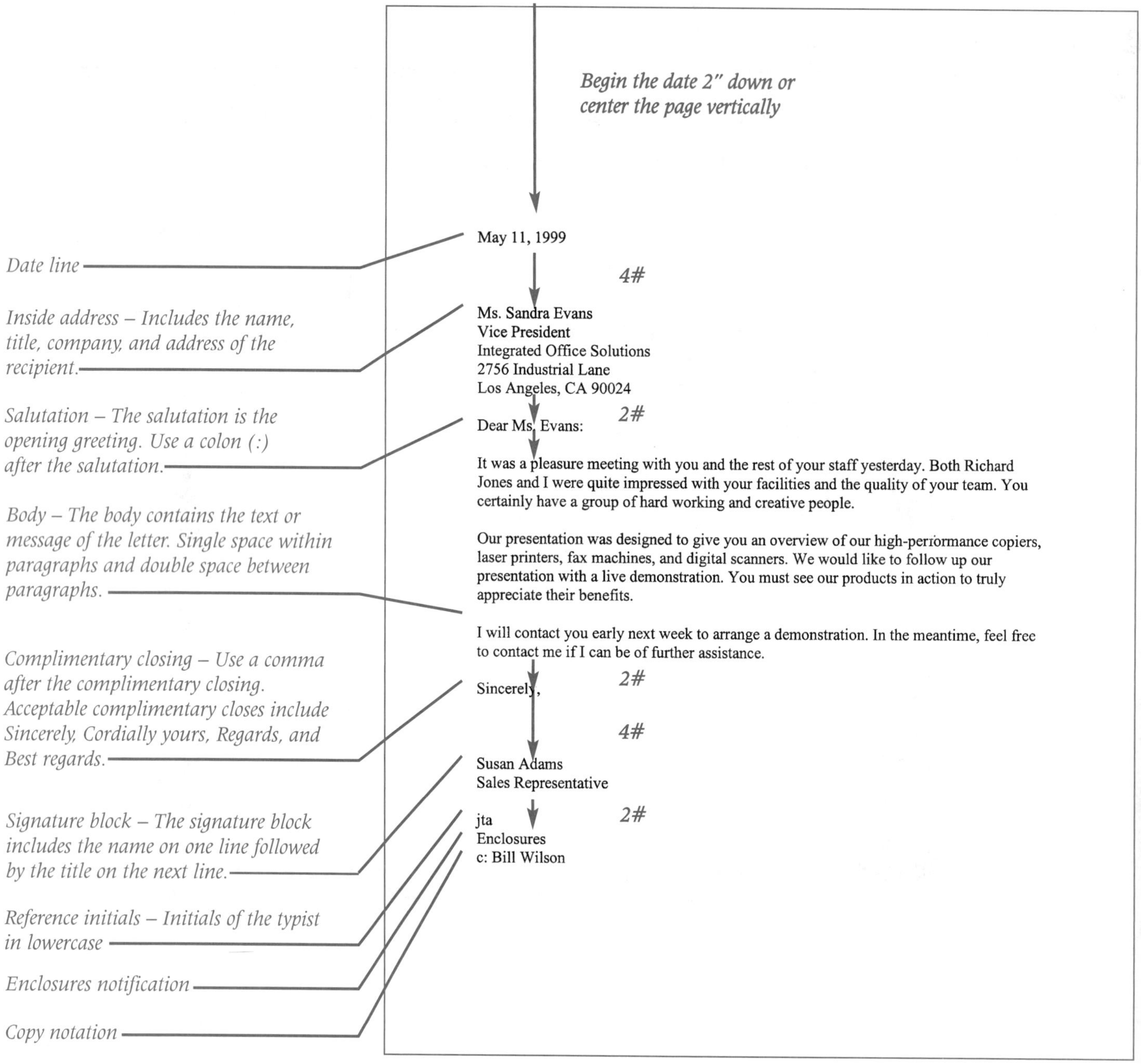

Begin the date 2" down or center the page vertically
4#
2#
2#
4#
2#
Date line
Inside address – Includes the name, title, company, and address of the recipient.
Salutation – The salutation is the opening greeting. Use a colon (:) after the salutation.
Body – The body contains the text or message of the letter. Single space within paragraphs and double space between paragraphs.
Complimentary closing – Use a comma after the complimentary closing. Acceptable complimentary closes include Sincerely, Cordially yours, Regards, and Best regards.
Signature block – The signature block includes the name on one line followed by the title on the next line.
Reference initials – Initials of the typist in lowercase
Enclosures notification
Copy notation

May 11, 1999

Ms. Sandra Evans
Vice President
Integrated Office Solutions
2756 Industrial Lane
Los Angeles, CA 90024

Dear Ms. Evans:

It was a pleasure meeting with you and the rest of your staff yesterday. Both Richard Jones and I were quite impressed with your facilities and the quality of your team. You certainly have a group of hard working and creative people.

Our presentation was designed to give you an overview of our high-performance copiers, laser printers, fax machines, and digital scanners. We would like to follow up our presentation with a live demonstration. You must see our products in action to truly appreciate their benefits.

I will contact you early next week to arrange a demonstration. In the meantime, feel free to contact me if I can be of further assistance.

Sincerely,

Susan Adams
Sales Representative

jta
Enclosures
c: Bill Wilson

Modified Block Style Letter

The modified block style has the same elements and spacing between paragraphs as the block style. However, the date line, complimentary closing, and signature block begin near the center of the lines as shown below.

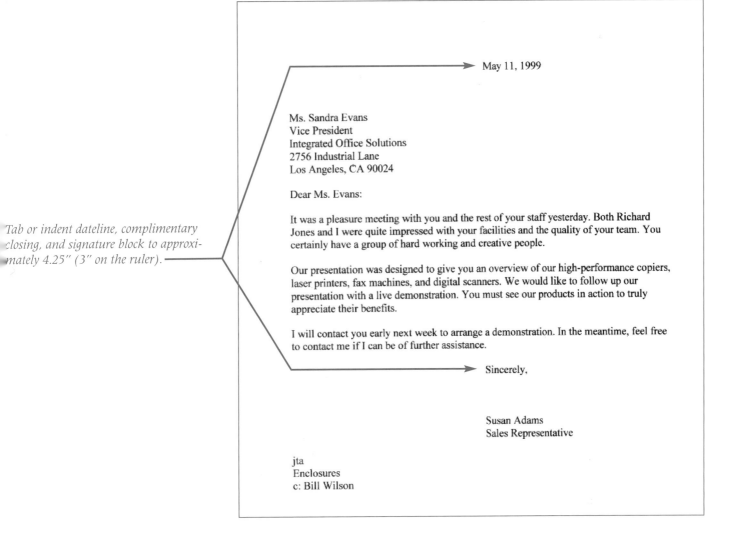

Tab or indent dateline, complimentary closing, and signature block to approximately 4.25″ (3″ on the ruler).

May 11, 1999

Ms. Sandra Evans
Vice President
Integrated Office Solutions
2756 Industrial Lane
Los Angeles, CA 90024

Dear Ms. Evans:

It was a pleasure meeting with you and the rest of your staff yesterday. Both Richard Jones and I were quite impressed with your facilities and the quality of your team. You certainly have a group of hard working and creative people.

Our presentation was designed to give you an overview of our high-performance copiers, laser printers, fax machines, and digital scanners. We would like to follow up our presentation with a live demonstration. You must see our products in action to truly appreciate their benefits.

I will contact you early next week to arrange a demonstration. In the meantime, feel free to contact me if I can be of further assistance.

Sincerely,

Susan Adams
Sales Representative

jta
Enclosures
c: Bill Wilson

Personal Business Letter (Block Style)

Personal business letters are used when an individual representing himself or herself sends a letter to a recipient in a business. Personal business letters can be composed using either the block or modified block style.

Today's Date

Mr. Jake Wilson
Rebate Manager
Sierra Snowboards
4200 University Avenue
Berkeley, CA 94702

Dear Mr. Wilson:

Thank you for your excellent advice on the snowboarding equipment I recently purchased. Sierra Snowboards certainly has the best equipment in the business.

I would like to know when I can expect the rebate on the board I purchased. I mailed in my rebate coupon last month and I have yet to hear from the company. Do rebates normally take this long? Please contact me as soon as possible at (510) 223-3344. Thank you for your assistance.

Sincerely,

Melissa Jackson
1223 Appian Way
El Sobrante, CA 94803

In a personal business letter, the signature block includes the sender's address.

Inserting Text

Text is always inserted into a Word document at the flashing **insertion point.** For this reason, it is important to position the insertion point at the desired location before inserting text. You will learn how to position the insertion point later in this lesson.

Other Ways to Insert Text

Most users insert text using the keyboard. In fact, keyboarding is arguably the most important skill an office user can possess. However, if you have a physical disability or suffer from an ailment such as carpal tunnel syndrome, you may want to invest in voice dictation software such as **IBM's Via Voice.** Via Voice is highly accurate and lets you enter text by dictating into a microphone connected to your computer. You can also insert text with techniques such as Copy and Paste. Later in this course, you will use the Copy and Paste commands to insert text from another document and from a Web page.

Word Wrap

If you continue typing after the insertion point reaches the end of a line, Word automatically wraps the insertion point to the beginning of the next line. This feature is known as **word wrap.** If you are creating a paragraph with two or more lines, then you should let word wrap do its job. Just keep typing until the entire paragraph is complete. Word wrap will format the paragraph by wrapping the lines at the appropriate location. If you let word wrap format the paragraph initially, then the paragraph will also be reformatted as you insert or delete text.

Taking Control With the (ENTER) Key

You use the (ENTER) key to begin a new paragraph or to insert blank lines in a document. (ENTER) inserts a hard carriage return that can only be removed by the user.

AutoComplete and Other Automated Features

Word 2000 has numerous features to assist you in entering text and creating documents. AutoComplete recognizes certain phrases, such as dates and company names, and offers to complete them for you. You accept a phrase that AutoComplete proposes by tapping (ENTER). You can increase the number of phrases that AutoComplete recognizes by adding new AutoText entries to the system. You will learn more about AutoComplete and AutoText later in this course. For now, you will use AutoComplete to enter today's date in a business letter.

Hands-On 7.2 Begin Typing a Business Letter

Use AutoComplete

1. Tap (ENTER) six times.
   Each time you tap (ENTER), the insertion point moves down one line. (ENTER) is used to insert blank lines in documents.

2. Notice the vertical position indicator on the status bar as shown below.

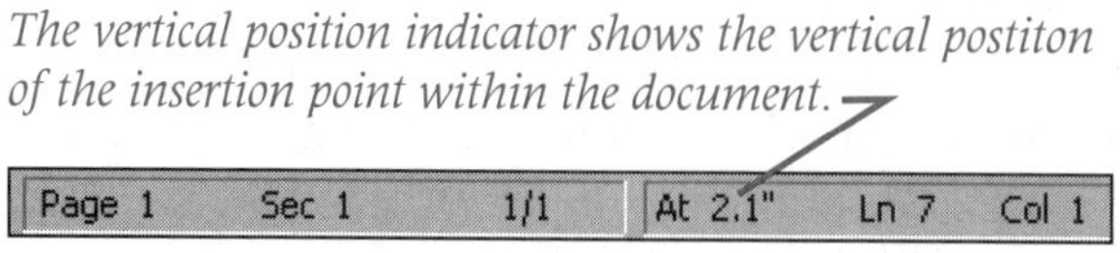
The vertical position indicator shows the vertical postiton of the insertion point within the document.
Page 1
Sec 1
1/1
At 2.1"
Ln 7
Col 1

3. Type today's date, but stop typing when AutoComplete displays a yellow date tip as shown at the right.
   The example at the right uses the date June 26, 1999, but you should type today's date. Also, AutoComplete may not display the date tip. This is because AutoComplete may not be set up to automatically display tips.

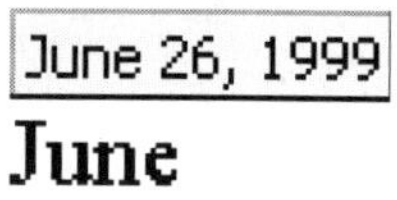
June 26, 1999
June

4. If AutoComplete displays the date tip, then tap (ENTER) to complete the date. Otherwise, complete today's date by typing it.
   You can always accept an item that AutoComplete proposes by tapping (ENTER).

Complete the Inside Address

5. Tap (ENTER) four times.
   Business letters require four returns after the date.

6. Now type the following inside address and salutation.
   Only tap (ENTER) in the locations indicated. The Office Assistant may appear when you tap (ENTER) after typing the salutation. The Office Assistant will be discussed in a moment.

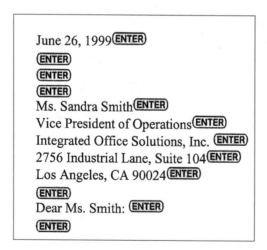

June 26, 1999(ENTER)
(ENTER)
(ENTER)
(ENTER)
Ms. Sandra Smith(ENTER)
Vice President of Operations(ENTER)
Integrated Office Solutions, Inc. (ENTER)
2756 Industrial Lane, Suite 104(ENTER)
Los Angeles, CA 90024(ENTER)
(ENTER)
Dear Ms. Smith: (ENTER)
(ENTER)

The Office Assistant

The Office Assistant is an interactive Help tool that monitors your activities and provides suggestions whenever it assumes you need assistance. The Office Assistant has a balloon window that pops up, allowing you to ask questions and get assistance.

It looks like you're writing a letter.
Would you like help?
Get help with writing the letter
Just type the letter without help
Cancel

TIP!

You can click anywhere in the document window to close the Office Assistant balloon.

7. If the Office Assistant balloon pops up as shown here, then click the **Cancel** button to close it.
   You will work with the Office Assistant and online Help in the next lesson.
8. Now complete the letter as shown in the following illustration. Only tap ENTER in the indicated locations. Use BACKSPACE to correct any typing mistakes. Word 2000 automatically checks spelling and grammar as you type. Word underlines misspelled words with wavy red underlines and grammar errors with wavy green underlines. For now, ignore any red or green underlining that may appear.

Dear Ms. Smith:

It was a pleasure meeting with you yesterday. Both Richard Brown and I were quite impressed with your facilities and the quality of your team. You certainly have a group of hard working people. ENTER
ENTER
Our meeting was designed to give you an overview of our copiers, laser printers, fax machines, and digital scanners. We would like to follow up our presentation with a live demonstration. You must see our products in action to truly appreciate their benefits. I will contact you early next week to arrange a demonstration. ENTER
ENTER
In the meantime, please feel free to contact us if we can be of further assistance. ENTER
ENTER
Sincerely, ENTER
ENTER
ENTER
ENTER
Susan Adams ENTER
Sales Representative

Save Concepts

One important lesson to learn is to save your documents frequently! Power outages and careless accidents can result in lost data. The best protection is to save your documents every 10 or 15 minutes, or after making significant changes. Documents are saved to storage locations such as floppy disks, hard disks, or to Web sites on the World Wide Web.

Save Command

The Save button on the Standard toolbar and the **File→Save** command initiate the Save command. If the document had previously been saved, then Word replaces the previous version with the new edited version. If the document had never been saved, then Word displays the **Save As** dialog box. The Save As dialog box has been significantly enhanced in Word 2000. The Save As dialog box lets you specify the name and storage location of the document. You can also use the Save As dialog box to make a copy of a document by saving it under a new name or to a different location. You can use filenames containing as many as 255 characters. The following illustration describes the Save As dialog box.

From the Keyboard
CTRL+S for save

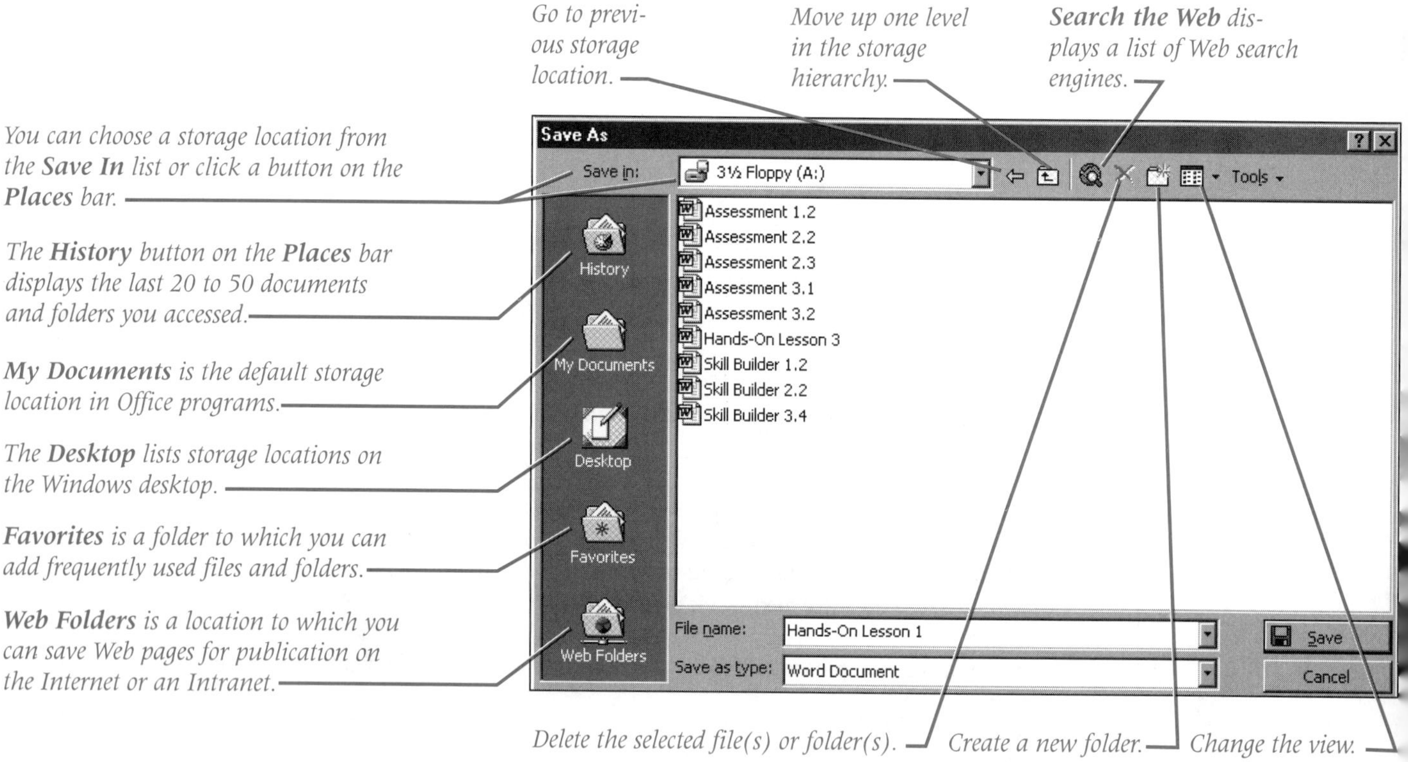

Go to previous storage location.
Move up one level in the storage hierarchy.
Search the Web displays a list of Web search engines.
You can choose a storage location from the *Save In* list or click a button on the *Places* bar.
The *History* button on the *Places* bar displays the last 20 to 50 documents and folders you accessed.
My Documents is the default storage location in Office programs.
The *Desktop* lists storage locations on the Windows desktop.
Favorites is a folder to which you can add frequently used files and folders.
Web Folders is a location to which you can save Web pages for publication on the Internet or an Intranet.
Save As
Save in:
3½ Floppy (A:)
Tools
History
My Documents
Desktop
Favorites
Web Folders
Assessment 1.2
Assessment 2.2
Assessment 2.3
Assessment 3.1
Assessment 3.2
Hands-On Lesson 3
Skill Builder 1.2
Skill Builder 2.2
Skill Builder 3.4
File name:
Hands-On Lesson 1
Save as type:
Word Document
Save
Cancel
Delete the selected file(s) or folder(s).
Create a new folder.
Change the view.

Hands-On 7.3 Save the Letter

In this exercise, you will save the letter that was created in the previous exercise. Your instructor will most likely want you to save your documents onto the exercise diskettes that are provided with this course. You will most likely be saving documents onto the A: disk drive.

1. Click the Save button and the Save As dialog box will appear.
2. Follow these steps to save the letter.
   Keep in mind that your dialog box will contain more files than shown here.

Ⓐ *Click here and choose the disk drive with your exercise diskette. It is most likely 3½ Floppy (A:).*

Ⓑ *Notice that Word proposes the first part of the date as the name. Word always proposes the first line of text as the filename.*

Ⓒ *Type the name* **`Hands-On Lesson 7`** *and it will replace the proposed name. (If you switched disk drives, then you may need to click in the* ***File name*** *box, delete the proposed name with the* DELETE *and/or* BACKSPACE *key, then type the new name.)*

Ⓓ *Click the* ***Save*** *button.*

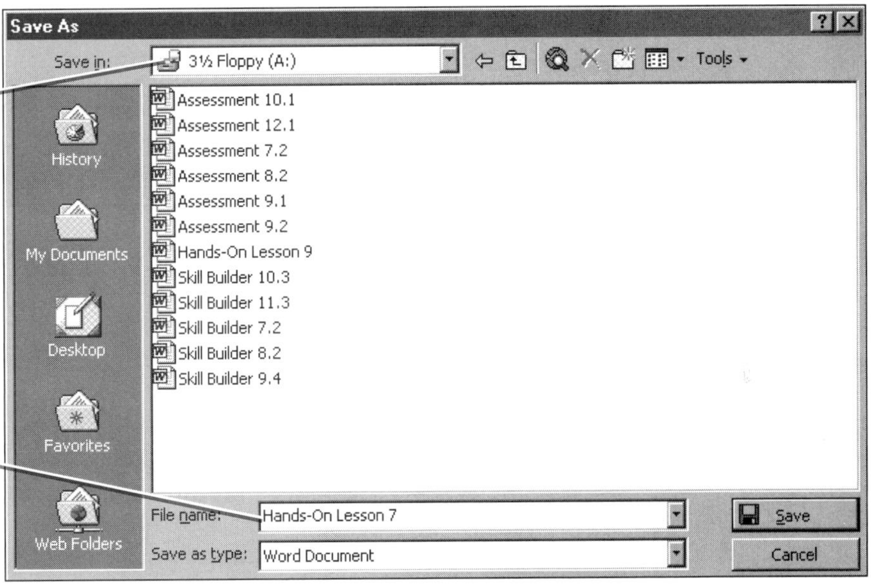
Save As
Save in:
3½ Floppy (A:)
Tools
History
My Documents
Desktop
Favorites
Web Folders
Assessment 10.1
Assessment 12.1
Assessment 7.2
Assessment 8.2
Assessment 9.1
Assessment 9.2
Hands-On Lesson 9
Skill Builder 10.3
Skill Builder 11.3
Skill Builder 7.2
Skill Builder 8.2
Skill Builder 9.4
File name:
Hands-On Lesson 7
Save as type:
Word Document
Save
Cancel

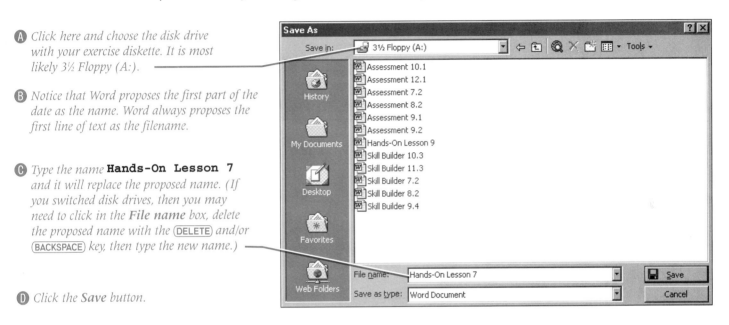

Notice that the letter was saved and remains on the screen. You will continue to use the letter throughout this lesson.

Scrolling Documents and Repositioning the Insertion Point

The vertical and horizontal **scroll bars** let you browse through documents. However, scrolling does not move the insertion point. You must click in the document to reposition the insertion point. The vertical scroll bar is on the right side of the document window and the horizontal scroll bar is at the bottom of the document window. Scroll bars also appear in many dialog boxes. The following illustration shows the scroll bars and their components.

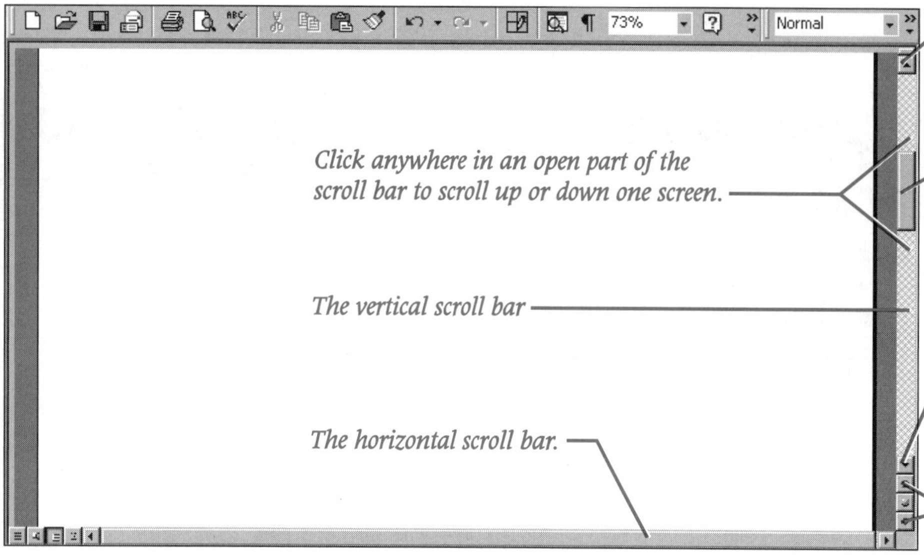

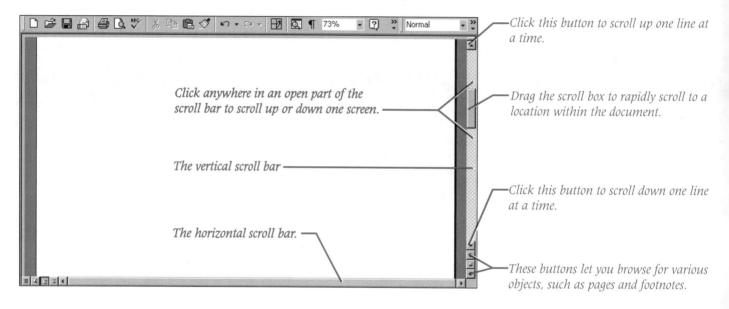

73%
Normal
Click this button to scroll up one line at a time.
Click anywhere in an open part of the scroll bar to scroll up or down one screen.
Drag the scroll box to rapidly scroll to a location within the document.
The vertical scroll bar
Click this button to scroll down one line at a time.
The horizontal scroll bar.
These buttons let you browse for various objects, such as pages and footnotes.

Hands-On 7.4 Practice Scrolling

1. Click the Scroll Down button five times.
   Notice that the document scrolls down, but the insertion point does not move.
2. Click the Scroll Up button until the date is visible at the top of the letter.
3. Slide the mouse; the pointer will have an I-Beam shape when it is in the typing area.
   The pointer must have this I-Beam shape before the insertion point can be repositioned.
4. Click the I-Beam anywhere on the date, and the blinking insertion point will be positioned there.
5. Move the I-Beam into the left margin area, and it will become an arrow.
   This arrow should not *be present if you are trying to reposition the insertion point.*
6. Position the I-Beam on the first line of the inside address just in front of Ms., and click the left mouse button.
   The insertion point should be positioned just in front of Ms. If a black background appears behind the text, then you have accidentally selected it. Selecting is discussed later in this lesson. If you accidentally selected the text, then deselect it by clicking the mouse pointer outside of it.
7. Take a few minutes to practice scrolling and repositioning the insertion point.

Inserting and Overtyping Text

TIP! *You will almost always work in Insert mode.*

Insert mode is the default editing mode in Word. In insert mode, existing text moves to the right as new text is typed. The new text is thus inserted into the document. Thus far, you have been working in insert mode. In **overtype mode,** existing text is replaced as new text is typed. You switch between insert mode and overtype mode by double-clicking the OVR (overtype) indicator on the status bar as shown in the following illustration.

*Double-clicking the **OVR** (overtype) indicator switches between insert mode and overtype mode. The mode is set to overtype when the **OVR** indicator is bold as shown here.*

Page 1
Sec 1
1/1
At 1"
Ln 1
Col 1
REC
TRK
EXT
OVR
English (U.S

Hands-On 7.5 Inserting and Overtyping Text

Insert Text

1. Click just in front of the word **yesterday** in the first body paragraph as shown below.

   Click here

   It was a pleasure meeting with you yesterday.

2. Type the phrase **`and the rest of your staff`**, and tap the (SPACE BAR) once.
3. Use the technique in Steps 1 and 2 to insert the phrase **`and creative`** in front of the word **people** at the end of the paragraph. The completed paragraph is shown below.

   It was a pleasure meeting with you and the rest of your staff yesterday. Both Richard Brown and I were quite impressed with your facilities and the quality of your team. You certainly have a group of hard working and creative people.

Overtype Text

4. Position the insertion point in the inside address in front of the S in Smith.
5. Double-click the **OVR** button on the status bar.
   The OVR button should now appear bold.
6. Type the word **`Evans`**, and Smith should be replaced by Evans.
   If insert mode had been active, the name Smith would have moved to the right, making room for Evans.
7. Now click in front of the name Smith in the salutation line, and type **`Evans`**.
8. Double-click the **OVR** button on the status bar when you have finished.
   The letters OVR will be dimmed on the status bar, indicating that insert mode is active.
9. Click the Save button to save the changes to your exercise diskette.

Selecting Text

You must select text if you wish to perform some action on that text. Suppose you want to delete an entire paragraph. You would select the paragraph first and then tap the DELETE key. Selected text is usually displayed in white on a black background. The illustration to the right shows a selected paragraph in the inside address of your letter.

Ms. Sandra Evans
Vice President of Operations
Integrated Office Solutions, Inc.

Selection Techniques

Word provides many selection techniques using both the mouse and keyboard. The mouse techniques are usually more intuitive; however, beginners may find it difficult to control the mouse. The keyboard techniques tend to provide greater control. You can use the keyboard techniques if you have difficulty controlling the mouse. The following quick reference table illustrates the available selection techniques.

Quick Reference

SELECTION TECHNIQUES

Item to be Selected	Mouse Technique	Keyboard Technique
One word	Double-click the desired word.	Click at beginning of word, press and hold SHIFT and CTRL while tapping →.
A phrase or continuous section of text	Drag the I-beam in any direction over the desired text.	Click at beginning of phrase, press and hold SHIFT while tapping any arrow keys. You can also click at beginning of phrase, press and hold SHIFT, and then click at end of phrase.
A line	Position the mouse pointer to the left of the line, and click when the pointer has an arrow shape.	Press SHIFT + END to select from insertion point to end of line. Press SHIFT + HOME to select from insertion point to beginning of line.
One paragraph	Triple-click anywhere on the paragraph. You can also position the mouse pointer to the left of the paragraph in the margin and double-click when the pointer has an arrow shape.	
Multiple paragraphs	Drag the I-beam over the desired paragraphs. You can also position the mouse pointer to the left of the paragraphs and drag up or down when the pointer has an arrow shape.	
Entire document	Triple-click to the left of any paragraph, or press and hold CTRL and click to the left of any paragraph.	Press CTRL + A to execute Select All command, or press CTRL and click in left margin.

Hands-On 7.6 Practice Selecting Text

Select Using the Left Margin

1. Follow these steps to select text using the left margin.

Ⓐ *Place the mouse pointer to the left of this line and it will have this shape. Click the mouse button to select the entire line.*

Ⓑ *Click here to select this line. Notice that the previously selected paragraph is no longer selected.*

Ⓒ *Select this paragraph by double-clicking in front of it.*

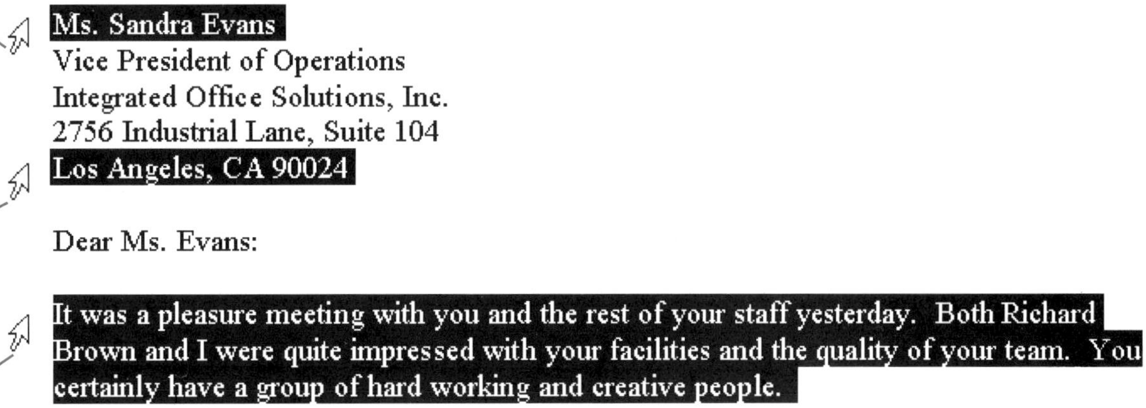

Ms. Sandra Evans
Vice President of Operations
Integrated Office Solutions, Inc.
2756 Industrial Lane, Suite 104
Los Angeles, CA 90024

Dear Ms. Evans:

It was a pleasure meeting with you and the rest of your staff yesterday. Both Richard Brown and I were quite impressed with your facilities and the quality of your team. You certainly have a group of hard working and creative people.

2. Try dragging the mouse pointer down in the left margin.
   Be sure to press and hold the left mouse button as you drag, and multiple lines will be selected.
3. Try triple-clicking the mouse pointer anywhere in the left margin.
   The entire document will become selected. Triple clicking can be tricky, so you may need to try it several times. Also, you can select the entire document by pressing CTRL *and clicking in the left margin.*
4. Deselect the document by clicking anywhere on the selected text.

Select Words

5. Double-click the I-beam on any word.
   The word should become selected.
6. Double-click a different word, and notice that the previous word has been deselected.
7. Select five different words one after another by double-clicking them.
8. Deselect the last word you selected by clicking the I-Beam anywhere outside of it.

(Continued on the next page)

Drag Select

9. Follow these steps to drag select a phrase.

Ⓐ *Position the I-beam here just in front of* It was a pleasure . . .

Ⓑ *Press and hold the left mouse button, then drag to the right until the phrase* It was a pleasure meeting with you *is selected.*

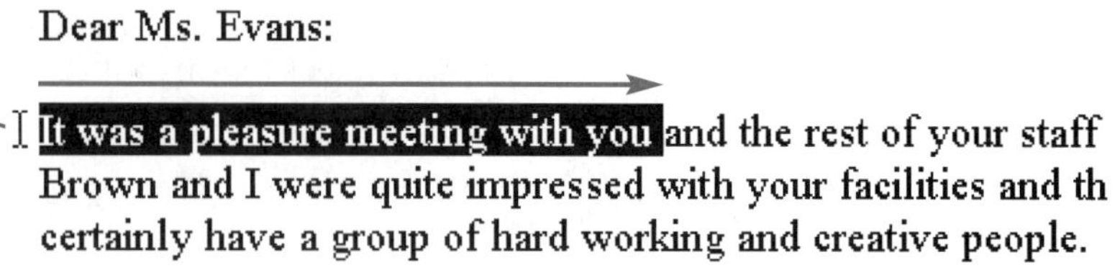
Dear Ms. Evans:

It was a pleasure meeting with you and the rest of your staff
Brown and I were quite impressed with your facilities and th
certainly have a group of hard working and creative people.

Ⓒ *Release the mouse button and the text will remain selected.*

TIP!
Use Undo if you accidentally move text.

10. Practice drag selecting text in the second large paragraph. Try dragging the mouse in all directions.
Notice how the selection block expands and contracts as you move the mouse.
11. Deselect by clicking anywhere on the selected text.
12. Take two minutes to practice selecting text using the drag technique.
13. Take five minutes to practice selecting text using all of the techniques discussed in the table at the beginning of this topic. In particular, try using the keystroke techniques discussed in the Quick Reference Selection Techniques table.

Editing Text

From the Keyboard
CTRL+BACKSPACE to delete from insertion point to beginning of word.
CTRL+DELETE to delete from insertion point to end of word.

The DELETE and BACKSPACE keys are used to remove text from a document. DELETE removes the character to the right of the insertion point and BACKSPACE removes the character to the left of the insertion point. You can also remove an entire selection by tapping DELETE or BACKSPACE. If you are removing just a few characters, it is usually more efficient to click in front of the characters and tap DELETE one or more times. If you are removing a word, phrase, or paragraph, it is more efficient to select the desired text and then tap DELETE to remove the selection.

You can replace text by selecting the desired text and then typing the replacement text. Selected text is removed as you begin typing replacement text. The replacement text is then inserted in the document as you continue to type.

Undo and Redo

From the Keyboard
CTRL+Z to undo
CTRL+Y to redo

Word's Undo button lets you reverse your last editing action(s). You can reverse simple actions such as accidental text deletions, or you can reverse more complex actions such as margin changes. Most actions can be undone. Actions that cannot be undone include commands such as printing documents and saving documents.

The Redo button reverses Undo. Use Redo when you Undo an action but decide to go through with that action after all.

Undoing and Redoing Multiple Actions

The arrows ▾ on the Undo and Redo buttons display lists of actions that can be undone or redone. You can undo or redo multiple actions by dragging the mouse over the desired actions. You can undo or redo an almost unlimited number of actions using this method. However, you must undo or redo actions in the order in which they appear on the drop-down list.

Repeat

The **Edit→Repeat** command lets you repeat your last action. For example, imagine you want to change the font size at several locations in a document. To accomplish this, you could change the font size at one location, reposition the insertion point, and then issue the Repeat command. The Repeat command would set the font size at the new location to the same size you set at the previous location. You can repeat an action as many times as desired. However, the Repeat command is only available when the Redo button is unavailable. The **Edit→Repeat** command changes to **Edit→Redo** as soon as you undo an action.

From the Keyboard

CTRL+Y to repeat.

Hands-On 7.7 Edit the Letter and Use Undo

Delete Several Words

1. Follow these steps to delete text from the inside address block.

Ms. Sandra Evans
Vice President of Operations
Integrated Office Solutions, Inc.
2756 Industrial Lane, Suite 104

A *Drag the mouse pointer over the phrase* of Operations *as shown here.*

B *Tap* DELETE *to remove the phrase, then tap* BACKSPACE *to remove the space after the word* President.

C *Select the word* Inc *by double-clicking it, then tap* DELETE *to delete the word.*

D *Tap* DELETE *once to remove the period, then tap* BACKSPACE *once to remove the comma.*

E *Click in front of this comma, then tap* DELETE *repeatedly to remove the phrase,* Suite 104.

Select and Replace Words

2. Follow these steps to select and replace several words and to insert a phrase.

It was a pleasure meeting with you and the rest of your staff yesterday. Brown and I were quite impressed with your facilities and the quality of certainly have a group of hard working and creative people.

Our meeting was designed to give you an overview of our copiers, laser machines, and digital scanners. We would like to follow up our present demonstration. You must see our products in action to truly appreciate will contact you early next week to arrange a demonstration.

In the meantime, please feel free to contact us if we can be of further as

A *Double-click the last name* Brown *and type the replacement name* **Jones**.

B *Double-click the word* meeting *and type the replacement word* **presentation**.

C *Click in front of the word* copiers, *type the phrase* **high-performance**, *and tap* SPACE BAR. *The new phrase should be inserted in front of the word* copiers.

D *Select the word* us *and type the replacement word* **me**.

E *Replace* we *with* **I**.

(Continued on the next page)

TIP!

To turn off Auto capitalization, choose Tools→AutoCorrect and uncheck the Capitalize first letter of sentences box.

Use Undo to Override AutoCorrect

AutoCorrect is a Word 2000 tool that automatically corrects many common spelling errors and looks for other potential problems. One of these potential problems is the lack of capitalization at the start of a sentence. AutoCorrect will automatically capitalize the first letter of a sentence if you fail to capitalize it yourself. This is acceptable most of the time, but there are occasions when you may want to override AutoCorrect.

3. Scroll to the bottom of the document, and click to the right of the title Sales Representative in the signature block.
4. Tap (ENTER) twice.
5. Type your initials in lowercase, and then type a colon (**:**).
   AutoCorrect should spring into action, capitalizing your first initial. Unfortunately, typists initials should appear in lowercase in business correspondence.
6. Click Undo, and the capital letter should return to lowercase.
   You can always use Undo to override AutoCorrect.
7. Tap (SPACE BAR), and type the document name **Hands-On Lesson 7**.
   The completed signature block should be xx: Hands-On Lesson 7, where xx are your initials.
8. Click Save to save the changes to your document.

IMPORTANT!

It is important to save now because you will experiment with Undo and Redo in the remainder of this exercise.

Practice Using Undo and Redo

9. Delete any word in the letter.
10. Click Undo and the word will be restored.
11. Select any paragraph, then tap (DELETE) to remove the paragraph.
12. Click Undo to restore the paragraph.
13. Click Redo and the paragraph will vanish again.
    Redo always reverses the most recent Undo.
14. Click Undo again to restore the paragraph.

Undo and Redo Multiple Actions

15. Follow these steps to explore the Undo actions list, and to delete three items.

Ⓐ *Click the drop-down button next to* ***Undo****, and a list of all preceding actions will be displayed. Don't worry if your list does not match the list in this illustration.*

Ⓑ *Use the scroll bar to browse through the list of actions. Scroll to the top of the list when you are finished browsing and make a mental note of the first three or four actions on the list.*

Ⓒ *Tap the* ESC *key to close the list.*

Ⓓ *Select the month, and delete it.*

Ⓔ *Delete the word* Vice *from the title* Vice President.

Ⓕ *Select the street number 2756, and type the replacement number* **2989**.

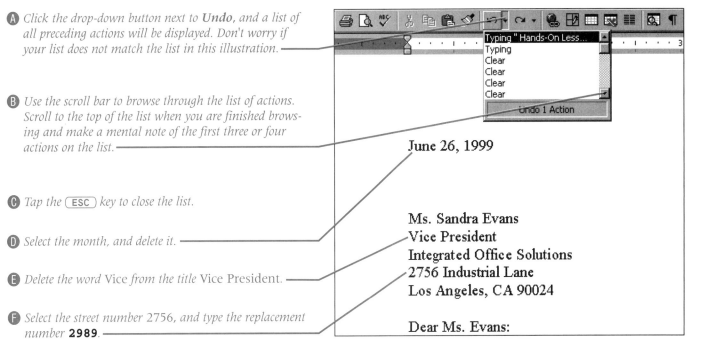

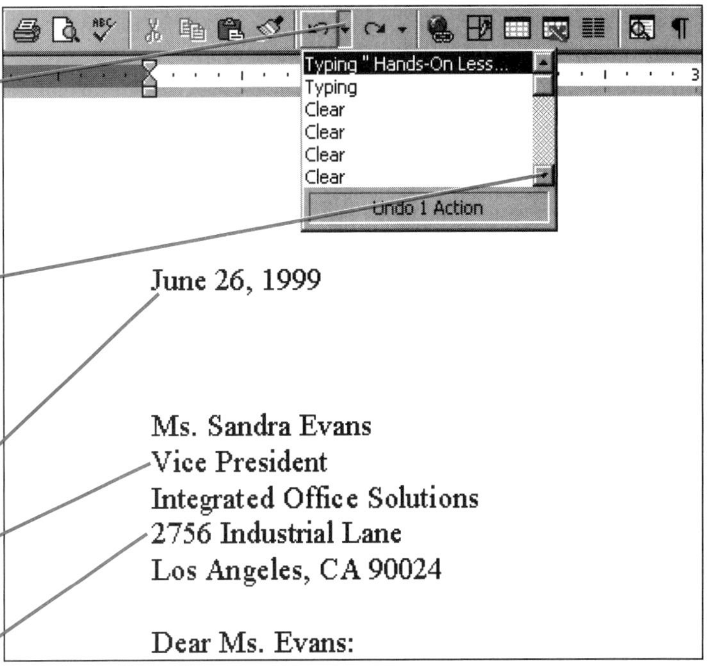
Typing " Hands-On Less...
Typing
Clear
Clear
Clear
Clear
Undo 1 Action
June 26, 1999
Ms. Sandra Evans
Vice President
Integrated Office Solutions
2756 Industrial Lane
Los Angeles, CA 90024
Dear Ms. Evans:

16. Follow these steps to undo the last three actions:

Ⓐ *Click the* ***Undo*** *drop-down button, and notice that there are three new actions at the top of the list. Your most recent action was typing the number 2989, so it appears on top of the list. Each action is given a descriptive name to help identify it.*

Ⓑ *Position the mouse pointer on the first action,* Typing "2989," *then slide the mouse down (there is no need to press the mouse button) highlighting the first three actions as shown here.*

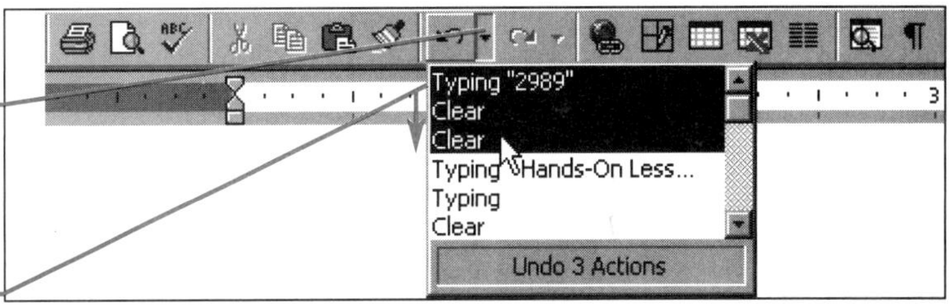
Typing "2989"
Clear
Clear
Typing "Hands-On Less...
Typing
Clear
Undo 3 Actions

Ⓒ *Click when the actions are selected, and all three actions will be undone. Your document should be exactly as it was prior to making the changes.*

17. Feel free to experiment with Undo and Redo.

Closing Documents

The **File→Close** command is used to close an open document. When you close a document, Word prompts you to save the changes. If you choose Yes at the prompt and the document had previously been saved, then Word saves the changes. If the document is new, Word displays the Save As dialog box, allowing you to assign a name and storage location to the document.

Hands-On 7.8 Close the Document

1. Choose **File→Close** from the menu bar.
2. Click the **No** button if Word asks you to save the changes.
   You can always close without saving to eliminate changes that have occurred since the last save. The next exercise will instruct you to open the letter. You will notice that the most recent changes have not been saved.
3. Finally, notice that there is no document in the document window.
   The document window always has this appearance when all documents have been closed.

Opening Documents

From the Keyboard

CTRL+O to display open dialog box.

The Open button on the Standard toolbar and the **File→Open** command display the Open dialog box. The Open dialog box lets you navigate to any storage location and open previously saved documents. Once a document is open, you can browse it, print it, or even make editing changes. The organization and layout of the Open dialog box is similar to the Save dialog box discussed earlier in this lesson.

Hands-On 7.9 Open the Letter

1. Click Open on the Standard toolbar.
2. Follow these steps to open the Hands-On Lesson 7 document.
   Keep in mind that your dialog box will contain more files than shown here.

Ⓐ *Choose the disk drive containing your exercise diskette. It is most likely in 3½ Floppy (A:).*

Ⓑ *Choose* Hands-On Lesson 7.

Ⓒ *Click the* ***Open*** *button.*

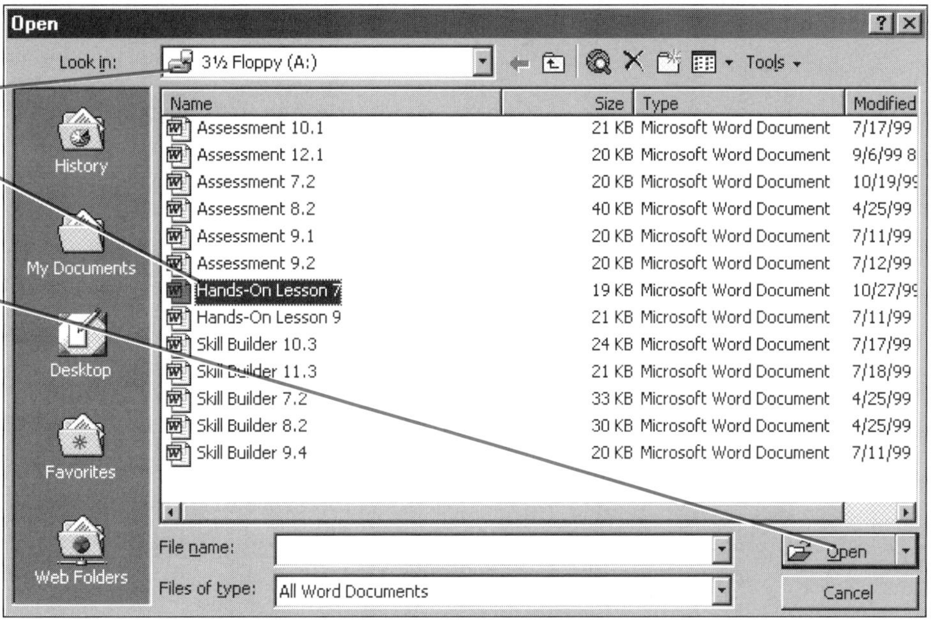
Open
Look in:
3½ Floppy (A:)
Tools
History
My Documents
Desktop
Favorites
Web Folders
Name
Size
Type
Modified
Assessment 10.1 21 KB Microsoft Word Document 7/17/99
Assessment 12.1 20 KB Microsoft Word Document
Assessment 7.2 20 KB Microsoft Word Document
Assessment 8.2 40 KB Microsoft Word Document 4/25/99
Assessment 9.1 20 KB Microsoft Word Document 7/11/99
Assessment 9.2 20 KB Microsoft Word Document 7/12/99
Hands-On Lesson 7 19 KB Microsoft Word Document
Hands-On Lesson 9 21 KB Microsoft Word Document 7/11/99
Skill Builder 10.3 24 KB Microsoft Word Document 7/17/99
Skill Builder 11.3 21 KB Microsoft Word Document 7/18/99
Skill Builder 7.2 33 KB Microsoft Word Document 4/25/99
Skill Builder 8.2 30 KB Microsoft Word Document 4/25/99
Skill Builder 9.4 20 KB Microsoft Word Document 7/11/99
File name:
Files of type:
All Word Documents
Open
Cancel

TIP! *You can also double-click a document on the list.*

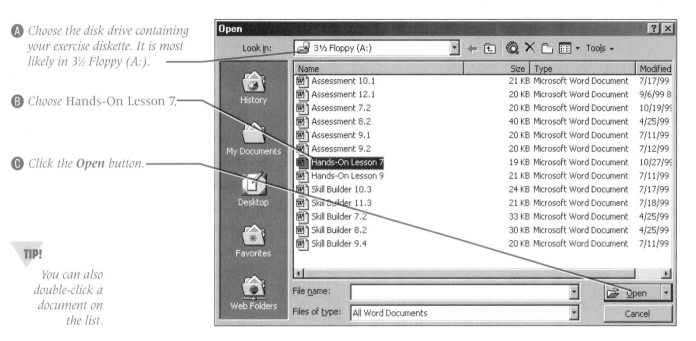

3. Take a few moments to scroll through the letter. Notice that the most recent changes were not saved (because you closed without saving).

Showing Nonprinting Characters

The Show All ¶ button on the Standard toolbar shows or hides all nonprinting characters in a document. Nonprinting characters include spaces, tab characters, and carriage returns that do not appear on the printed page. Showing these characters can be important, especially when editing a document. For example, you may need to display the nonprinting characters to determine whether the space between two words was created with SPACE BAR or TAB. The following illustration shows the location of the Show All button and the characters that are inserted whenever SPACE BAR and ENTER are tapped.

From the Keyboard

CTRL+SHIFT+8 to show or hide characters

*The **Show All** button has been pushed in.*

These symbols are called paragraph marks. They are inserted whenever ENTER is tapped.

The dots between words are inserted whenever SPACE BAR is tapped.

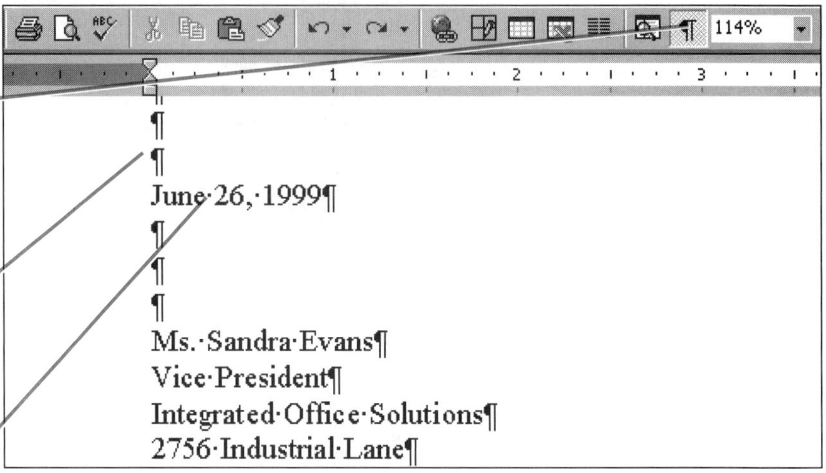
114%
June·26,·1999¶
Ms.·Sandra·Evans¶
Vice·President¶
Integrated·Office·Solutions¶
2756·Industrial·Lane¶

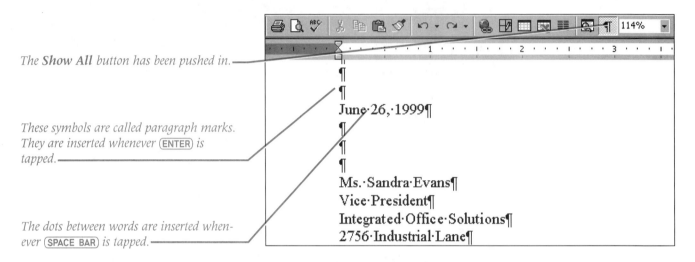

Inserting and Deleting Paragraph Marks

Paragraph marks ¶ (or carriage returns) play an important role in Word documents. Every paragraph ends with a paragraph mark. A paragraph mark is inserted whenever ENTER is tapped. Paragraph marks affect the appearance and format of documents. You may need to delete paragraph marks as you edit and format documents. For example, suppose you want to combine two paragraphs into one large paragraph. To accomplish this, you would delete the paragraph mark separating the paragraphs. It is usually best to display the nonprinting characters with the Show All button before deleting paragraph marks and other nonprinting characters. You can delete the paragraph mark to the right of the insertion point using DELETE. Likewise, the paragraph mark to the left of the insertion can be removed with BACKSPACE.

Hands-On 7.10 Insert and Delete Paragraph Marks

In this exercise, you will restructure several paragraphs in the letter. Remember to use Undo if you make a mistake.

Combine Two Paragraphs

1. Click Show All ¶ to display the symbols.
2. Position the insertion point in front of the paragraph mark at the end of the second main paragraph as shown here.

presentation·with·a·live·demonstration.·You·must·see·our·products·in·action·to·truly·
appreciate·their·benefits.·I·will·contact·you·early·next·week·to·arrange·a·demonstration.¶
¶
In·the·meantime,·please·feel·free·to·contact·me·if·I·can·be·of·further·assistance.¶

*Position **insertion point** here.*

3. Tap (DELETE) once.
   The paragraph mark to the right of the insertion point will be deleted. The mark below the paragraph will immediately move up to take its place. Notice that the gap between the paragraphs is no longer a double space.
4. Tap (DELETE) again, and the paragraphs will be joined together.
5. Tap (SPACE BAR) once to create space between the two sentences in the combined paragraph.

Split the Combined Paragraph

6. Follow these steps to split the paragraph into two smaller paragraphs.

Our·presentation·was·designed·to·give·you·an·overview·of·our·high-performance·copiers,·
laser·printers,·fax·machines,·and·digital·scanners.·We·would·like·to·follow·up·our·
presentation·with·a·live·demonstration.·You·must·see·our·products·in·action·to·truly·
appreciate·their·benefits.·I·will·contact·you·early·next·week·to·arrange·a·demonstration.·In·
the·meantime,·please·feel·free·to·contact·me·if·I·can·be·of·further·assistance.¶

Ⓐ *Click here just in front of the word I.*

Ⓑ *Tap (ENTER) twice to push the last two sentences down and to form a new paragraph.*

7. Click Show All ¶ to turn off the symbols.
   At this point, your letter should match the example shown in the case study at the start of this lesson (except for the date).

Print Preview

The Print Preview button and the **File→Print Preview** command display the Print Preview window, which shows how a document will look when it is printed. Print Preview can save time, paper, and wear-and-tear on your printer. Print Preview is especially useful when printing long documents, or with documents containing intricate graphics and formatting. It is always wise to preview a long or complex document before sending it to the printer.

When you display the Print Preview window, the standard toolbars are replaced by the Print Preview toolbar. The following illustration explains the important buttons on the Print Preview toolbar.

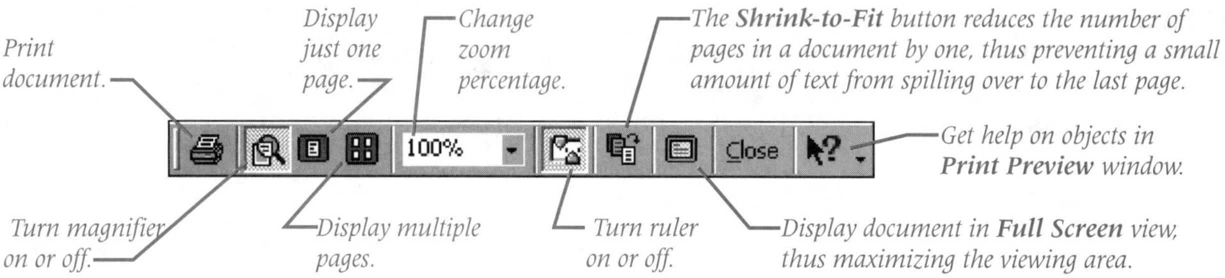
Print document.
Display just one page.
Change zoom percentage.
The Shrink-to-Fit button reduces the number of pages in a document by one, thus preventing a small amount of text from spilling over to the last page.
100%
Close
Get help on objects in Print Preview window.
Turn magnifier on or off.
Display multiple pages.
Turn ruler on or off.
Display document in Full Screen view, thus maximizing the viewing area.

Hands-On 7.11 Use Print Preview

1. Click Print Preview on the Standard toolbar.
2. Make sure the Magnifier button is pushed in on the toolbar.
3. Position the mouse pointer over the document, and the pointer will look like a magnifying glass.
4. Zoom in by clicking anywhere on the document.
5. Zoom out by clicking anywhere on the document.
   You can zoom in and out whenever the magnifier is on. When the magnifier is off, the mouse pointer functions normally, allowing you to edit the document in Print Preview mode.
6. Feel free to experiment with the other buttons on the Print Preview toolbar.
7. When you have finished, click the **Close** button on the Print Preview toolbar to exit from Print Preview.

Printing

The Print button on the Standard toolbar sends the entire document to the current printer. You must display the Print dialog box if you want to change printers, specify the number of copies to be printed, print selected pages, and to set other printing options. The Print dialog box is displayed with the **File→Print** command. When you print a document, a printer icon appears on the status bar. The Printer icon indicates that Word is processing the print job and is preparing to send the job to the printer. The following illustration explains the most important options available in the Print dialog box.

From the Keyboard

CTRL+P to display Print dialog box

You choose printers from this drop-down list.

You can specify the number of copies here. The ***Collate*** *option is useful when you are printing more than one copy of a multiple page document. If the* ***Collate*** *box is checked, the first copy is printed before the second copy begins printing, etc.*

You can choose to print all pages, the current page, or a range of pages. You specify a range of pages by typing the desired range in the ***Pages*** *box. The example text below the* ***Pages*** *box shows the entry required to print pages 1, 3, and 5 through 12.*

You can choose to print odd or even pages only with the ***Print*** *option.*

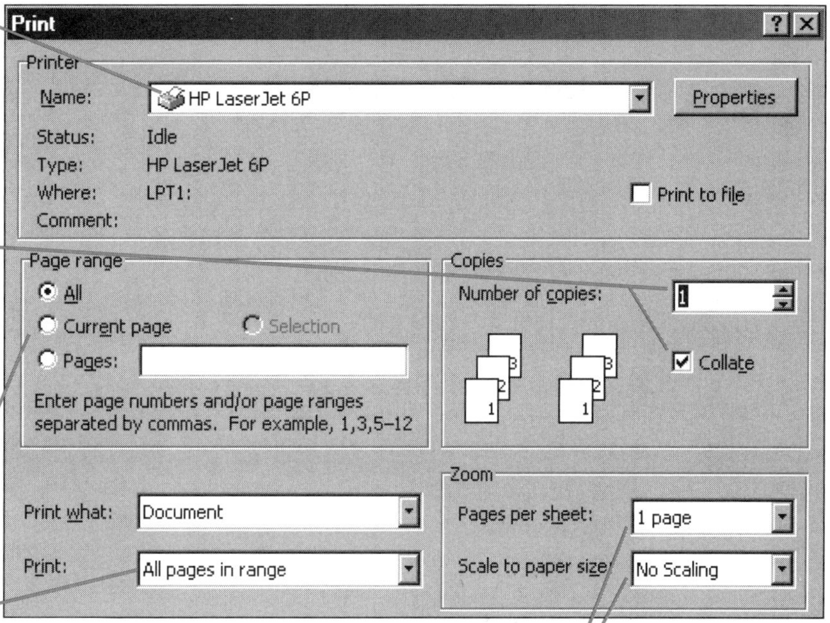

Print
Printer
Name:
HP LaserJet 6P
Properties
Status:
Idle
Type:
HP LaserJet 6P
Where:
LPT1:
Comment:
Print to file
Page range
All
Current page
Selection
Pages:
Enter page numbers and/or page ranges separated by commas. For example, 1,3,5–12
Copies
Number of copies:
1
Collate
Print what:
Document
Print:
All pages in range
Zoom
Pages per sheet:
1 page
Scale to paper size:
No Scaling

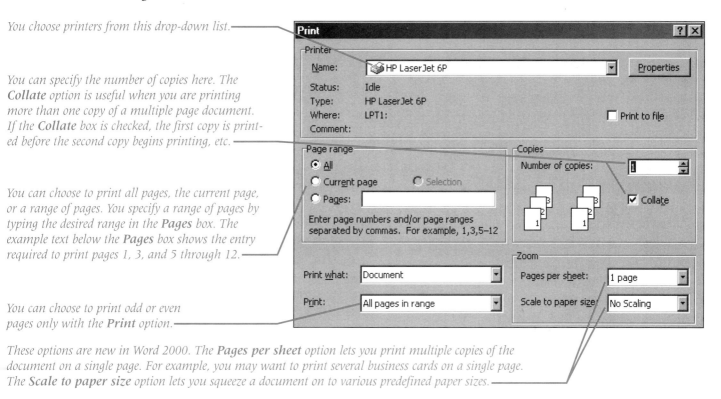

These options are new in Word 2000. The ***Pages per sheet*** *option lets you print multiple copies of the document on a single page. For example, you may want to print several business cards on a single page. The* ***Scale to paper size*** *option lets you squeeze a document on to various predefined paper sizes.*

Hands-On 7.12 Print the Document

1. Choose **File→Print** to display the Print dialog box.
2. Take a few moments to check out the dialog box options.
3. When you are ready to print, make sure the options are set as shown in the preceding illustration, and click the **OK** button.
   Keep in mind that your printer will probably be different than the printer shown in the Name box in the illustration.
4. Retrieve your document from the printer.

Canceling Print Jobs

Sometimes you will want to cancel a print job after issuing the Print command. When you print a document, Word processes the print job and sends it to the printer. Most modern printers contain memory where the Print job is stored while it is being printed. For this reason, it is not always possible to terminate a print job from Word or other Office programs. The difficult work of canceling the print job must often be done at the printer. This is especially true with newer computers. Newer computers are so fast that the print job is often sent to the printer before you have time to cancel it from within the application. The following quick reference steps can be used to effectively cancel print jobs. This sequence of steps is designed to save paper, prevent jamming of the printer, and effectively terminate the print job.

Quick Reference

CANCELLING PRINT JOBS

- Remove the paper stack from the printer, or remove the paper tray. You should be able to do this even if the printer is in the middle of printing a page.
- Double-click the Printer icon on the status bar. This will terminate further processing of the job by Word. The Printer icon won't be visible if Word has finished processing the job.
- If a page was being printed when you pulled out the paper tray, make sure it has finished printing.
- Switch off the power on the printer. This will clear the job out of the printer's memory.
- Pause 30 seconds and turn the printer back on.
- Reinsert the paper stack or the paper tray.

WARNING!

Turning off the printer may disrupt other users in a networked computer lab or office environment.

Exiting From Word

The **File→Exit** command is used to close the Word program. You should close Word and other programs if you are certain you won't be using them for some time. This will free up memory for other programs. When you close Word, you will be prompted to save any documents that have unsaved edits.

Hands-On 7.13 Exit from Word

1. Choose **File→Exit** from the menu bar.
2. Choose **Yes** when Word asks if you would like to save the changes.
   Word will close, and the Windows desktop will appear. Continue with the questions and exercises on the following pages.

Concepts Review

True/False Questions

1. The insertion point is automatically repositioned when you scroll through a document. TRUE FALSE
2. (ENTER) can be used to end one paragraph and begin another. TRUE FALSE
3. The Show All button is used to display nonprinting characters, such as paragraph marks. TRUE FALSE
4. The OVR button toggles Word between insert mode and overtype mode. TRUE FALSE
5. A single word can be selected by clicking once on the word. TRUE FALSE
6. Paragraph marks cannot be deleted once they have been inserted in a document. TRUE FALSE
7. (BACKSPACE) deletes the character to the right of the insertion point. TRUE FALSE
8. Overtype mode is the default editing mode in Word. TRUE FALSE

Multiple-Choice Questions

1. Which shape does the mouse pointer have when it is in the text area?
   a. Right-pointing arrow
   b. I-beam
   c. Left-pointing arrow
   d. None of the above

2. Which of the following methods can be used to select a paragraph?
   a. Double-click anywhere in the paragraph.
   b. Triple-click anywhere in the paragraph.
   c. Triple-click anywhere in the left margin.
   d. None of the above

3. What is happening if your existing text is disappearing as you type new text?
   a. You are in overtype mode.
   b. You are in insert mode.
   c. You are tapping (DELETE) by accident.
   d. None of the above

4. Which of the following statements is true?
   a. Undo is only available if Redo has been used.
   b. Redo is only available if Undo has been used.
   c. Both a and b
   d. Neither a nor b

Skill Builders

Skill Builder 7.1 Create a Block Style Letter

1. Start Word, and a new document window will appear. If you did not exit Word at the end of the last exercise, then click the New button on the Standard toolbar (first button on the toolbar). The New button is used to open a new document.
2. Type the following letter, tapping (ENTER) only as indicated. Notice the six hard returns shown at the top of the document. These hard returns position the date at approximately the 2″ position.

(ENTER)
(ENTER)
(ENTER)
(ENTER)
(ENTER)
(ENTER)
June 26, 1999(ENTER)
(ENTER)
(ENTER)
(ENTER)
Ms. Melissa Thompson(ENTER)
Customer Service Representative(ENTER)
Urbana Software Services(ENTER)
810 Ivanhoe Way(ENTER)
Urbana, IL 61801(ENTER)
(ENTER)
Dear Ms. Thompson:(ENTER)
(ENTER)
I would like to take this opportunity to thank you for your excellent customer service. You were patient, courteous, and very helpful. The installation assistance you provided was invaluable.(ENTER)
(ENTER)
I have already put your program to good use. As you know, application programs can boost personal productivity. Your program has allowed me to manage my business much more effectively. I have enclosed the $45 fee you requested.(ENTER)
(ENTER)
Please send me a receipt and a catalog.(ENTER)
(ENTER)
Sincerely,(ENTER)
(ENTER)
(ENTER)
(ENTER)
Denise Smith(ENTER)
Administrative Assistant(ENTER)

3. Use Show All [¶] to display the hidden characters.
4. Position the insertion point just in front of the sentence **I have enclosed the $45 . . .** in the second paragraph, and tap (ENTER) twice to create a new paragraph.
5. Position the insertion point at the end of the new paragraph just in front of the paragraph mark.
6. Tap (DELETE) twice to remove the two paragraph marks separating the new paragraph from the following paragraph.
7. Tap (SPACE BAR) once to insert a space between the two sentences in the combined paragraph.
8. Position the insertion point just to the right of the sentence **The installation assistance . . .** at the end of the first paragraph. The insertion point should be just to the right of the period ending the sentence.
9. Tap (SPACE BAR), and then type the sentence **`I also appreciate the overnight delivery.`**
10. Type **`The program is also a lot of fun.`** at the end of the second paragraph.
11. Insert your initials, below the signature block.
12. Save the document to your exercise diskette with the name **Skill Builder 7.1;** then close the document.

Skill Builder 7.2 Edit a Document

1. Click Open on the Standard toolbar.
2. Navigate to your exercise diskette, and double-click the file named Skill Builder 7.2.
   You will edit this document during this exercise. Notice that this document contains formatting that you have not yet learned about. For example, the title is centered and bold, and the paragraphs are formatted with double line spacing. This document is formatted like this because it is a report. You will learn about reports and formatting documents as you progress through this course.

(Continued on the next page)

3. Use these guidelines to make the editing changes shown in the following document.
   - If only one or two characters require deletion, then position the insertion point in front of the character(s) and use (DELETE) to remove them.
   - If one or more words require deletion, then select the text and use (DELETE) to remove the selected text.
   - If a word or phrase needs to be replaced with another word or phrase, then select the desired text and type the replacement text.
   - Use Undo [Undo button] if you make mistakes.
4. When you have finished, **Save** the changes, and **Close** the document.

MAINE – THE PINE TREE STATE

healthful

Maine is recognized as one of the most ~~healthy~~ states in the nation with ^ temperatures

5 summer

averaging 70°F and winter temperatures averaging 20°F. It has 3,~~7~~00 miles of coastline, is about 320 miles long and 210 miles wide, with a total area of 33,215 square miles or about as big as all of the other five New England States combined. It comprises 16 counties with 22 cities, 424 towns, 51 plantations, and 416 unorganized townships. Aroostook county is so large (6,453 square miles) that it covers an area greater than the combined size of Connecticut ^.

and Rhode Island

Maine abounds in natural assets—542,629 acres of state and national parks, including the 92-mile Allagash Wilderness Waterway, Acadia National Park (second most visited national park in the United States), and Baxter State Park (location of Mt. Katahdin and the northern end

that

of the Appalachian Trail). Maine has one mountain ~~which~~ is approximately one mile high—Mt. Katahdin (5,268 ft. above sea level) and also claims America's first chartered city: York, 1641.

Maine's blueberry crop is the largest ~~blueberry crop~~ in the nation—98% of the low-bush blueberries ^. Potatoes rank third in acreage and third in production nationally. Maine is nationally

in the United States lobster

famed for its shellfish; over 46 million pounds of ~~shellfish~~ were harvested in 1997. The total of all shellfish and fin fish harvested was approximately 237 million pounds with a total value of

in 1997

$ ^ 273 million ~~during the 1997 fishing season.~~

Skill Builder 7.3 Create a Modified Block Style Letter

A modified block style letter has the same elements and similar formatting as a block style letter. However, the modified block style positions the date, complimentary close, and signature block near the center of the lines.

1. Click New [New button] to open a new document window.
2. Type the following modified block style letter. Start the letter approximately 2" down from the top of the page. Tap TAB seven times to begin the date, complimentary close, and signature block just past the center of the lines. Finally, use the correct number of hard returns between the various paragraphs so that you have a properly formatted business letter.
3. When you have finished, save the document with the name **Skill Builder 7.3,** and then close the document.

Today's Date

Ms. Jessica Simms
811 Fairview Drive
Kansas City, MO 64106

Dear Ms. Simms:

I am pleased to inform you that you had excellent scores on all of your placement tests. You scored 98% on the word processing test, 97% on the spreadsheet test, and 99% on the office procedures test. These scores were far above average and are a testament to the quality of the vocational training program you recently completed.

I am pleased to offer you employment with Wilkinson Legal Services. Sarah Adams is looking forward to working with you should you decide to accept our offer.

I know you have several other job offers, and I hope you will give Wilkinson serious consideration. Sarah has already expressed an interest in having you train our staff members due to your excellent knowledge in Word and Excel. You will certainly have a bright future at Wilkinson.

Ms. Simms, please contact me soon. We look forward to having you as part of the Wilkinson team.

Sincerely,

Cynthia Lentz
Director, Human Resources

xx

Assessments

Assessment 7.1 Block Style Letter

1. Create the block style business letter shown below. Space down the proper distance from the top of the page, and use proper spacing between paragraphs.
2. Save the letter to your exercise diskette with the name **Assessment 7.1.**
3. Print the letter, and then close the document.

Today's Date

Mrs. Suzanne Lee
8445 South Princeton Street
Chicago, IL 60628

Dear Mrs. Lee:

Thank you for your interest in the Back Bay Users Group. We will be holding an orientation for new members on the first Thursday in April at our headquarters.

Please let us know if you can attend by calling the phone number on this letterhead. Or, if you prefer, you may respond in writing or via email.

Sincerely,

Jack Bell
Membership Chair

xx

Assessment 7.2 Editing Skills

1. Open the document on your exercise diskette named Assessment 7.2.
2. Make the editing changes shown in the following document.
3. Use (ENTER) to push the entire document down so that the date is positioned at approximately the 2″ position.
4. Use (TAB) to move the date, complimentary close, and signature block to approximately the 3″ position. This will convert the letter from block style to modified block style.
5. When you have finished, save the changes, print the letter, and close the document.

Today's Date

~~Ms. Cynthia Wilson~~ Mr. Roosevelt Jackson
~~118 Upper Terrace~~ 8 Spring Street
~~Freehold, NJ 08845~~ Martinville, NJ 08836

Dear ~~Ms. Wilson~~: Mr. Jackson

Thank you for your recent letter concerning back injuries in your office. Yes, back injuries are a common problem for office workers today. It was estimated by the U. S. Bureau of Labor Statistics that in one year over ~~490~~ 580,000 employees took time from work due to back injuries.

Encourage your office employees to make certain their work surface is at a ~~suitable~~ comfortable height. They should also be encouraged to take frequent breaks from their desks.

~~Feel free to~~ Please contact my office if you would like more information.

Sincerely,

Elaine Boudreau
Ergonomics Specialist

LESSON 8—Word

Creating a Memorandum and Press Release

In this lesson, you will expand upon the basic skills you developed in the previous lesson. You will create a two-page document that uses a page break to separate the pages. Paragraph formatting is an important technique in Word. This lesson introduces paragraph formatting and paragraph alignment techniques. You will learn how to apply various text formats, and you will use Cut, Copy, and Paste to rearrange text and paragraphs. Word has powerful editing tools that go beyond the traditional Cut, Copy, and Paste tools. This lesson introduces three of those tools: the new Office Clipboard, the Spike, and document scraps. Finally, you will unleash the power of Word's Format Painter—a powerful tool that is used to rapidly format text and ensure formatting consistency throughout a document.

In This Lesson

Case Study

Lashanda Robertson is the Public Affairs Representative for Flexico, Inc., a fabrics manufacturer specializing in materials for active wear. Image and public perception are important determinants of success in the high-profile world of fashion design. Flexico is a progressive company that understands the importance of image. As the Public Affairs Representative for Flexico, Lashanda's responsibilities include issuing press releases to inform clothing manufacturers and other potential customers of forthcoming fabrics and materials. Lashanda creates a memorandum to which she attaches her latest press release announcing the new FlexMax line of fabrics for active wear. Memorandums are used for internal communication within a company or organization, whereas business letters are used for external communication. A sample of the memorandum and press release are shown below.

MEMO TO: Bill Watson

FROM: Lashanda Robertson

DATE: April 25, 1999

SUBJECT: Flexico® Press Release

I have attached a press release to announce the launch of our new FlexMax™ line of fabrics. Please review the press release and let me know if you have comments or suggestions. I will submit this press release to the media organizations next week.

xx
Attachment

Flexico,® Inc.

Press Release

Flexico Announces FlexMax™ Fabric

Announcement
San Francisco, Ca.—July 10, 1999—Flexico, Inc. today announced the FlexMax fabric for active wear. This revolutionary fabric is designed by Flexico and allows for maximum range of motion while providing support, comfort, and moisture protection. Flexmax fabric is ideally suited for active wear such as biking, hiking, and aerobics attire.

Delivery and Availability
FlexMax products are expected to reach retailers shelves by the third quarter of this year. Look for the distinctive Flexico logo and the FlexMax trademark. FlexMax products will be available at most quality sporting goods stores.

FlexMax Styles
Initially, FlexMax fabric will be available in two weights and a variety of colors. Contact Flexico or your distributor for information and samples.

About Flexico
Founded in 1988, Flexico is a leading manufacturer of fabrics for active wear and outdoor activities. Flexico fabrics are used in fine active wear products worldwide.

Memorandum Styles

There are a variety of acceptable memorandum styles in use today. All memorandum styles contain the same elements but with varied formatting. Many new formats have emerged since the widespread use of computer and word processing technology. The style illustrated below is a traditional memorandum style with minimal formatting.

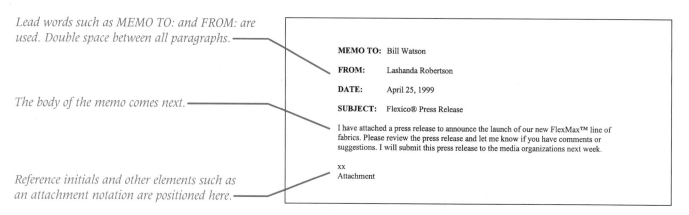

Lead words such as MEMO TO: and FROM: are used. Double space between all paragraphs.

The body of the memo comes next.

Reference initials and other elements such as an attachment notation are positioned here.

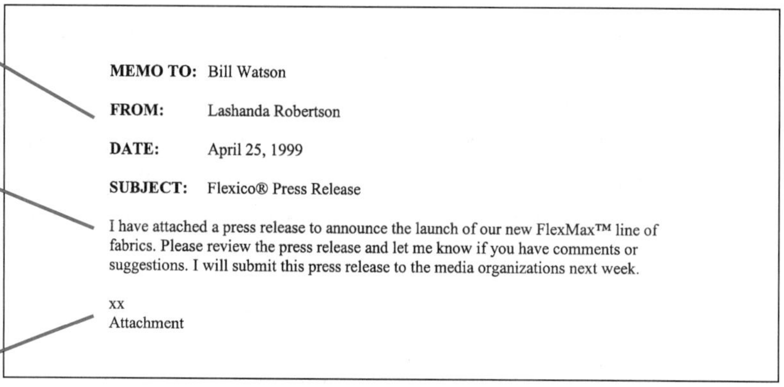
MEMO TO: Bill Watson

FROM: Lashanda Robertson

DATE: April 25, 1999

SUBJECT: Flexico® Press Release

I have attached a press release to announce the launch of our new FlexMax™ line of fabrics. Please review the press release and let me know if you have comments or suggestions. I will submit this press release to the media organizations next week.

xx
Attachment

Adaptive Menus

Word's menus now consist of a short section containing the commands you use most frequently and an expanded section containing commands that are rarely used. These adaptive menus reduce the number of commands on the main (short) menu, thereby reducing screen clutter. The following illustrations outline the adaptive menus in Word 2000.

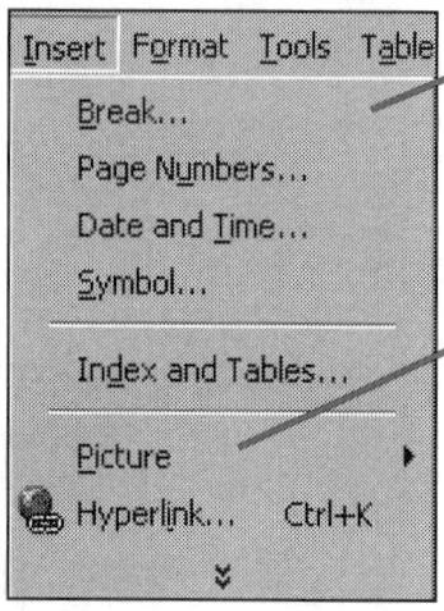
Insert
Format
Tools
Table
Break...
Page Numbers...
Date and Time...
Symbol...
Index and Tables...
Picture
Hyperlink... Ctrl+K

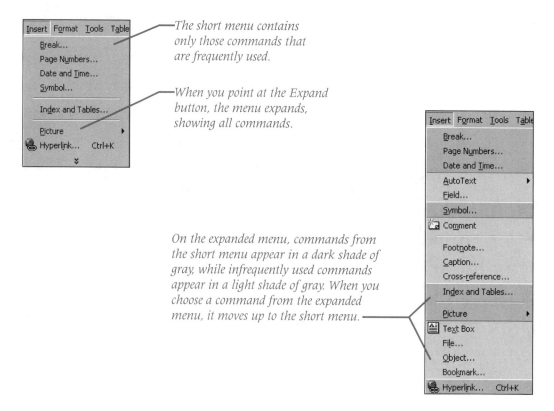

The short menu contains only those commands that are frequently used.

When you point at the Expand button, the menu expands, showing all commands.

On the expanded menu, commands from the short menu appear in a dark shade of gray, while infrequently used commands appear in a light shade of gray. When you choose a command from the expanded menu, it moves up to the short menu.

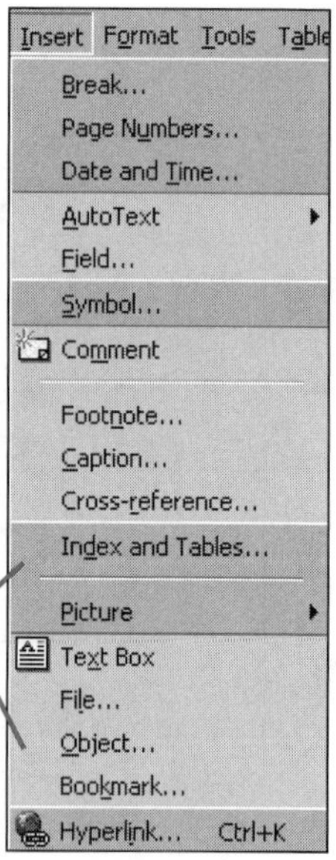
Insert
Format
Tools
Break...
Page Numbers...
Date and Time...
AutoText
Field...
Symbol...
Comment
Footnote...
Caption...
Cross-reference...
Index and Tables...
Picture
Text Box
File...
Object...
Bookmark...
Hyperlink... Ctrl+K

Working with Toolbars

In Word 2000, the Standard toolbar and Formatting toolbar are placed side by side on a single row just below the menu bar. This is a change from earlier versions of Word, where the Formatting toolbar was positioned below the Standard toolbar. In addition to the Standard toolbar and Formatting toolbar, Word has approximately 20 additional toolbars that are used with various program features.

Adaptive Toolbars

Like adaptive menus, adaptive toolbars may change depending upon how you use Word. Buttons may automatically be added to or removed from these toolbars. The right end of each Word toolbar now contains a button named More Buttons. You use this button to display buttons not currently visible on the toolbar and to add or remove buttons from a toolbar. The following illustration uses the Formatting toolbar to discuss adaptive toolbars in Word 2000.

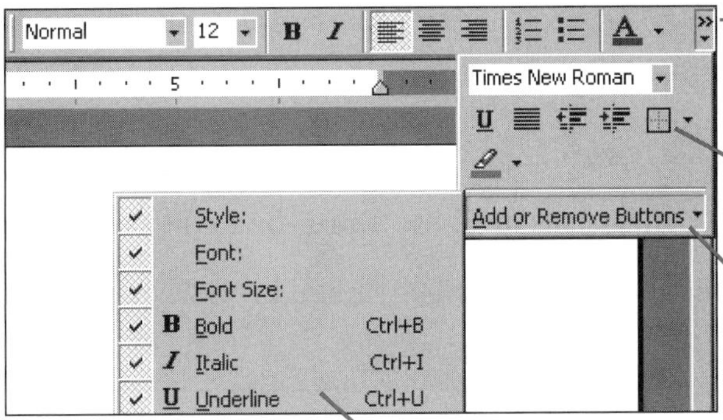

Normal
12
Times New Roman
Add or Remove Buttons
Style:
Font:
Font Size:
Bold
Ctrl+B
Italic
Ctrl+I
Underline
Ctrl+U

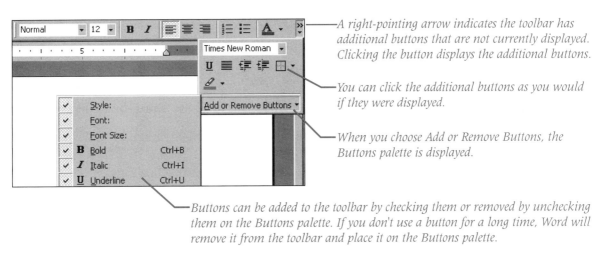

A right-pointing arrow indicates the toolbar has additional buttons that are not currently displayed. Clicking the button displays the additional buttons.

You can click the additional buttons as you would if they were displayed.

When you choose Add or Remove Buttons, the Buttons palette is displayed.

Buttons can be added to the toolbar by checking them or removed by unchecking them on the Buttons palette. If you don't use a button for a long time, Word will remove it from the toolbar and place it on the Buttons palette.

Displaying and Hiding Toolbars

You can display and hide toolbars by choosing **View→Toolbars** from the menu bar and checking or unchecking the desired toolbars. You can also display or hide toolbars by right-clicking any toolbar on the screen and checking or unchecking the desired toolbar.

Moving Toolbars

You can move a toolbar to any screen location. For example, many users prefer to move the Formatting toolbar below the Standard toolbar as in previous versions of Word. You move toolbars by dragging the Move handle located on the left end of the toolbar.

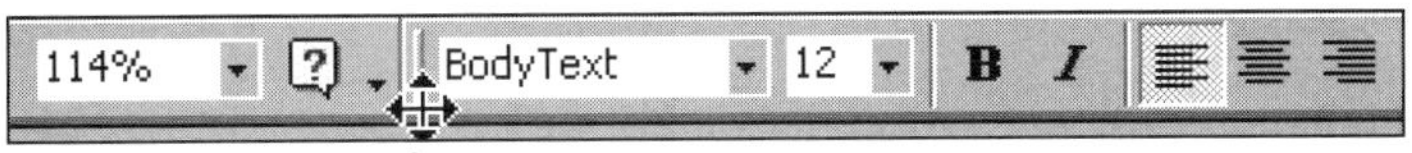

114%
BodyText
12

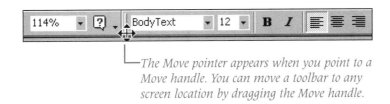

The Move pointer appears when you point to a Move handle. You can move a toolbar to any screen location by dragging the Move handle.

Displaying the Formatting Toolbar on a Separate Row

Dragging the Formatting toolbar below the Standard toolbar can be tricky. Fortunately, Word provides an easier way to display the Standard and Formatting toolbars on separate rows.

Quick Reference

DISPLAYING THE STANDARD AND FORMATTING TOOLBARS ON SEPARATE ROWS

- Choose View→Toolbars→Customize from the menu bar.
- Click the Options tab in the Customize dialog box.
- Uncheck the *Standard and Formatting toolbars share one row* checkbox.

Hands-On 8.1 Display the Formatting Toolbar on a Separate Row

IMPORTANT!

From this point forward, the instructions in this text will assume the Standard and Formatting toolbars are displayed on separate rows. This will make it easier for you to locate buttons when instructed to do so.

1. Start Word, and choose **View→Toolbars→Customize** from the menu bar.
2. Click the Options tab in the Customize dialog box.
3. Uncheck the **Standard and Formatting toolbars share one row** checkbox.
4. Click the **Close** button, and the Formatting toolbar should be positioned below the Standard toolbar.

Inserting the Date and Time

From the Keyboard

ALT+SHIFT+D to insert date

ALT+SHIFT+T to insert time

Word lets you insert the current date and time using a variety of formats. For example, the date could be inserted as 4/25/99, April 25, 1999 or 25 April 1999. You insert the date and time with the **Insert→Date and Time** command.

Update Automatically Option

You can insert the date and time as **text** or as a **field.** Inserting the date as text has the same effect as typing the date into a document. Fields, however, are updated whenever a document is opened or printed. For example, imagine you created a document on April 25, 1999, and you inserted the date as a field. If you had opened the document the next day, then the date would have automatically been updated to April 26, 1999. The date and time are inserted as fields whenever the Update Automatically box is checked, as shown to the right.

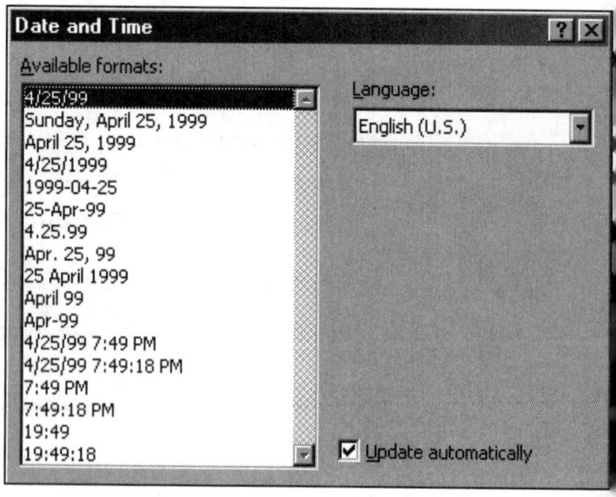
Date and Time
Available formats:
4/25/99
Sunday, April 25, 1999
April 25, 1999
4/25/1999
1999-04-25
25-Apr-99
4.25.99
Apr. 25, 99
25 April 1999
April 99
Apr-99
4/25/99 7:49 PM
4/25/99 7:49:18 PM
7:49 PM
7:49:18 PM
19:49
19:49:18
Language:
English (U.S.)
Update automatically

When to Use the Update Automatically Option

Maintaining the original date in a document may be important. For example, the date is important in documents such as business letters and legal agreements. If you insert the date in such documents using the Update Automatically option, then you will lose the original date the next time you open the document.

TIP!

To find the original date that a document was created, right-click the document in My Computer or Windows Explorer, choose Properties, and click the General tab.

Hands-On 8.2 Set Up the Memo and Insert the Date

Set Up the Memo

1. Use (ENTER) to space down to approximately the 2" position.
   Memorandums generally begin 2" down from the top of the page.
2. Type **MEMO TO:** and tap the (TAB) key.
3. Type **Bill Watson,** and tap (ENTER) twice.
4. Type **FROM:** and tap the (TAB) key.
5. Type **Lashanda Robertson,** and tap (ENTER) twice.
6. Type **DATE:** and tap the (TAB) key **twice.**
   It was necessary to tap (TAB) twice to align the date with the names. The first tab aligned the insertion point with the ½" mark on the ruler (located just above the document). The second tab aligned the insertion point with the 1" position on the ruler.

Insert the Date

7. Choose **Insert→Date and Time** from the menu bar.

TIP!

If the date and time are not accurate on your computer, double-click the clock on the right end of the Taskbar, set the correct date and time, and click OK.

8. Make sure the Update Automatically box is checked at the bottom of the dialog box.
   This option instructs Word to insert the date as a field. Once again, be careful when using this option. It is being used in this memorandum for instructional purposes only. You may want to avoid using this feature in business correspondence.
9. Choose the third date format on the list, and click OK.
   Notice that the date appears to be in a shaded box. The shaded box indicates that the date has been inserted as a field.

(Continued on the next page)

10. Complete the remainder of the memorandum as shown in the following illustration.
Make sure you double-space after the date line, the subject line, and after the main paragraph. Also, use (TAB) *to line up the phrase Flexico Press Release after the SUBJECT: lead word.*

MEMO TO:	Bill Watson
FROM:	Lashanda Robertson
DATE:	April 25, 1999
SUBJECT:	Flexico Press Release

I have attached a press release to announce the launch of our new FlexMax line of fabrics. Please review the press release and let me know if you have comments or suggestions. I will submit this press release to the media organizations next week.

xx
Attachment

11. Click the Save button, and save the memorandum as **`Hands-On Lesson 8`**.
You will continue to enhance the memorandum throughout this lesson.

Inserting Symbols

Word lets you insert a variety of symbols, typographic characters, and international characters not found on the keyboard. Most symbols are inserted by using the **Insert→Symbol** command and choosing the desired symbols from the Symbol dialog box. You can also use keystrokes to insert common typographic symbols such as the Registered ® symbol and some international characters. The following illustration shows the organization of the Symbol dialog box.

The special characters tab contains commonly used characters such as the Registered ® symbol, and various English language symbols.

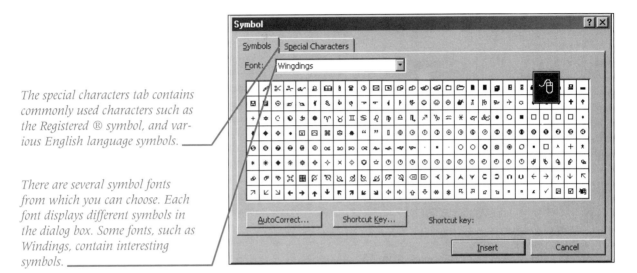

There are several symbol fonts from which you can choose. Each font displays different symbols in the dialog box. Some fonts, such as Windings, contain interesting symbols.

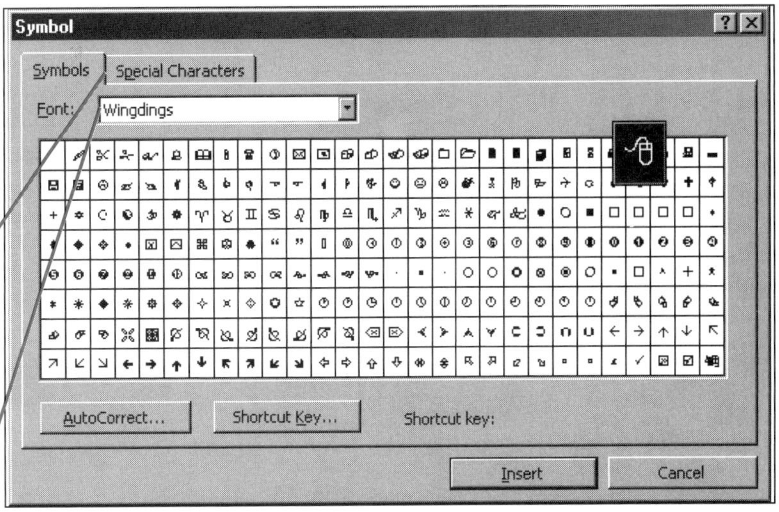
Symbol
Symbols
Special Characters
Font:
Wingdings
AutoCorrect...
Shortcut Key...
Shortcut key:
Insert
Cancel

Hands-On 8.3 Insert Symbols

1. Position the insertion point to the right of the word Flexico on the SUBJECT: line.
   You will insert a Registered Trademark ® symbol in the next few steps. A registered trademark gives a company the exclusive right to use a trademark (Flexico in this case) nationwide.
2. Choose **Insert→Symbol** from the menu bar.
3. Click the Special Characters tab.
4. Choose the Registered symbol, and click the Insert button.
   Notice that the Registered ® symbol appears in your document, and the Symbol dialog box remains open. Word leaves the dialog box open in case you wish to insert additional symbols.
5. Click the insertion point to the right of the word FlexMax in the main paragraph (you may need to drag the dialog box out of the way in order to see the word).
6. Insert the Trademark ™ symbol.
   The Trademark symbol indicates that a company claims a phrase or icon as their trademark, but they have not received federal protection (indicated by the Registered ® symbol).

(Continued on the next page)

7. Click the Symbols tab on the Symbol dialog box.
8. Click any symbol, and it will be magnified.
9. Try choosing a different font from the Font list, and you will see a new set of symbols.
10. When you have finished experimenting, click the Close button to close the dialog box.
11. Click the Save button to save the changes.

Views

Normal
Print Layout
Web Layout
Outline

Word lets you view documents in several ways. Each view is optimized for specific types of work, thus allowing you to work efficiently. The views change the way documents appear onscreen but have no impact on the appearance of printed documents. You can choose the desired view from the View menu or from the View bar at the left end of the horizontal scroll bar as shown to the right. The following table outlines the views available in Word 2000.

Quick Reference

VIEWS

View	Description
Print Layout	Print Layout is the default view in Word 2000. In Print Layout, documents look almost exactly as they will when printed. Print Layout is the most versatile view, allowing you to see text, graphics, headers and footers, and other types of objects. You will probably use Print Layout view most of the time.
Normal	Normal view simplifies page layout by eliminating page numbers, page breaks, and a few other elements from the view. Normal view can be useful if you want to concentrate on the text in your document. Normal view may also speed up scrolling and other tasks, especially if you have an older computer or large documents with many graphics.
Web Layout	Web Layout displays your document as it would look on a Web page. Text, graphics, and background patterns are visible. The document is displayed on one long page without page breaks.
Outline	Outline view is useful for organizing documents.

Hands-On 8.4 Experiment with Views

1. Locate the Views bar on the left end of the horizontal scroll bar.
2. Position the insertion point over each button, and a descriptive ScreenTip will pop up.
3. Click each button to see how the appearance of the document changes.
   You may not notice much of a difference because your document lacks graphics and other more advanced elements.
4. Switch to Print Layout view when you have finished experimenting.

Zooming

The Zoom Control lets you "zoom in" to get a close-up view of a document or "zoom out" to see the "big picture." Zooming changes the size of onscreen text and graphics but has no affect on printed text and graphics. You can zoom from 10% to 500%.

You can type a zoom percentage in the Zoom box and tap Enter, or . . .

. . . you can click the drop-down button . . . and choose an option from the list.

Notice how large the onscreen text appears; however, it will print in the normal size.

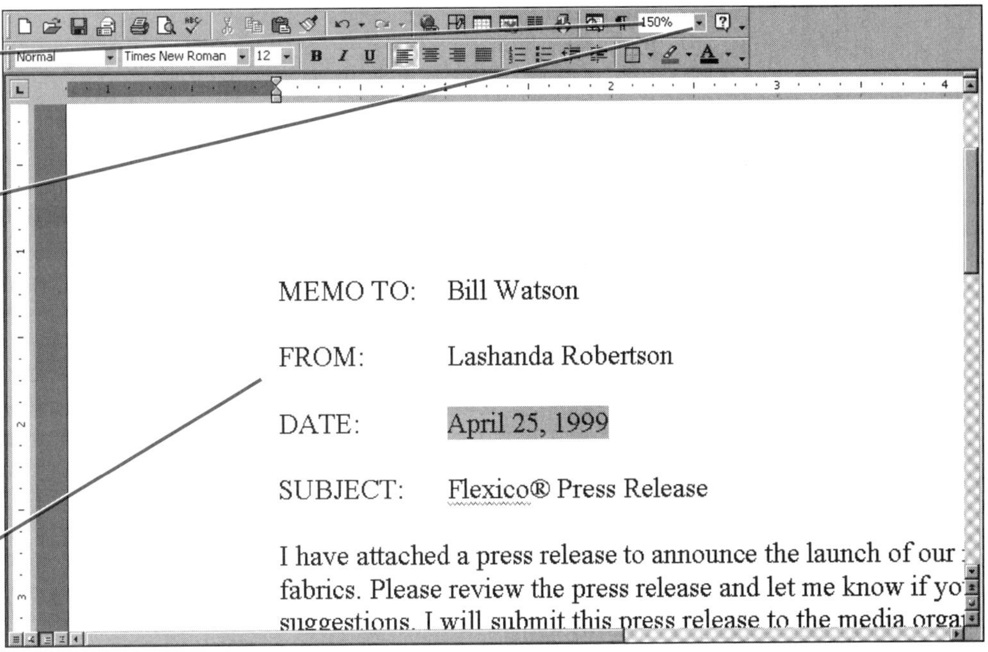

150%
Normal
Times New Roman
12
MEMO TO: Bill Watson
FROM: Lashanda Robertson
DATE: April 25, 1999
SUBJECT: Flexico® Press Release
I have attached a press release to announce the launch of our
fabrics. Please review the press release and let me know if yo

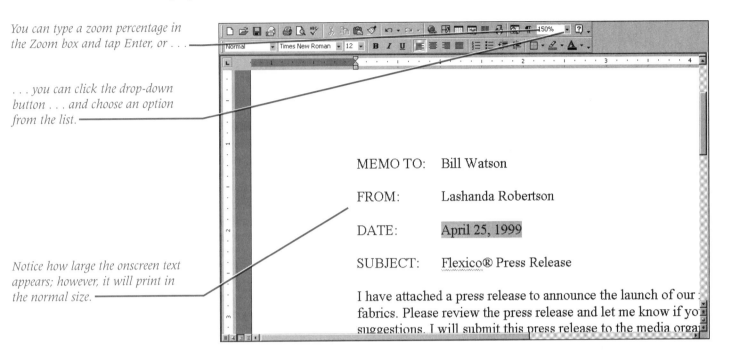

Hands-On 8.5 Use the Zoom Control

1. Follow these steps to experiment with the zoom control.

A *Click in this box, type* **123**, *and then tap* ENTER. *You can zoom to any percentage between 10 and 500.*

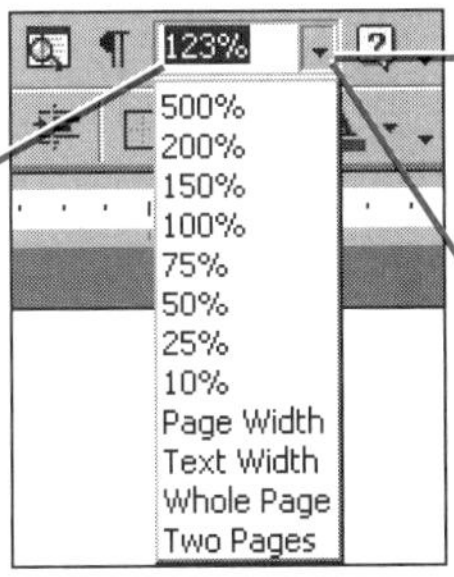

123%
500%
200%
150%
100%
75%
50%
25%
10%
Page Width
Text Width
Whole Page
Two Pages

B *Click the drop-down button, and choose 150%.*

C *Click this button again, and choose Page Width. Page Width adjusts the zoom to the width of the page. Some zoom options, like Page Width, are not available in Normal or Web Layout views.*

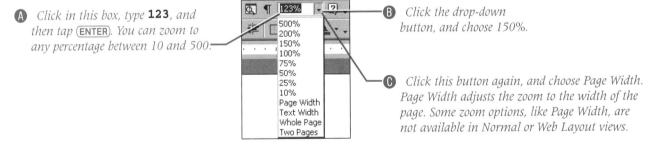

2. Use the zoom control to select the following three zoom settings: Whole Page, 75%, and Page Width. Feel free to experiment with the zoom control.

Page Breaks

If you are typing text and the insertion point reaches the bottom of a page, Word automatically breaks the page and begins a new page. This is known as an **automatic page break.** The location of automatic page breaks may change as text is added to or deleted from a document. Automatic page breaks are convenient when working with long documents that have continuously flowing text. For example, imagine you were writing a novel, and you decided to insert a new paragraph in the middle of a chapter. With automatic page breaks, you could insert the paragraph, and Word would automatically repaginate the entire chapter.

From the Keyboard

CTRL+ENTER to insert page break

You can force a page break to occur at any location in a document by inserting a **manual page break.** A manual page break remains in place unless you remove the break. You insert manual page breaks whenever you want to control the starting point of a new page. You can insert a manual page break with the **Insert→Break** command.

Removing Manual Page Breaks

In Normal view, manual page breaks appear as a horizontal line with the phrase Page Break appearing on the line. The page break line also appears in Print Layout view if you click the Show All button. You can remove a manual page break by positioning the insertion point on the page break line and tapping DELETE, as shown in the following illustration.

You can remove a manual page break by showing the nonprinting characters, clicking on the Page Break line, and tapping DELETE.

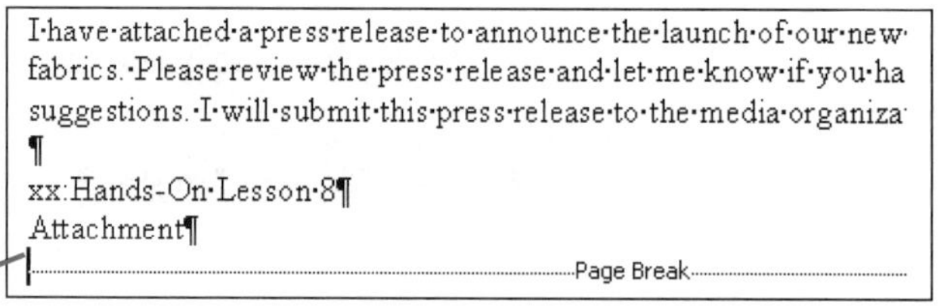
I·have·attached·a·press·release·to·announce·the·launch·of·our·new·
fabrics.·Please·review·the·press·release·and·let·me·know·if·you·ha
suggestions.·I·will·submit·this·press·release·to·the·media·organiza·
¶
xx:Hands-On·Lesson·8¶
Attachment¶
Page Break

Hands-On 8.6 Page Breaks

Insert a Page Break

1. Make sure you are in Print Layout view.
2. Position the insertion point to the right of the word *Attachment* on the attachment line.
3. Choose **Insert→Break** from the menu bar. If the Break option is not on the menu, you will need to click the Expand button at the bottom of the Insert menu, and then choose Break.
   Notice that several types of breaks are listed on the Breaks menu. This lesson only introduces page breaks.
4. Make sure **Page break** is chosen, and click **OK.**
   You should be able to see the bottom portion of page 1 and the top of page 2.
5. Look at the Status bar at the bottom of the screen; it will show the insertion point is on Page 2.

Page 2
Sec 1
2/2

TIP! *You can remove a break without showing the nonprinting characters. However, this takes a little practice.*

Remove the Page Break

6. Scroll up until the attachment line is visible.
7. Click the Show All button, and a Page Break line will appear.
8. Click on the Page Break line, and tap DELETE.
9. Try scrolling down to the second page, and you will see that it has been removed.

Reinsert the Break

10. Scroll up, and the insertion point should be just below the attachment line.
11. Press CTRL+ENTER to reinsert the page break.
    This shortcut keystroke is useful to remember because page breaks are inserted often.
12. Click Show All to hide the nonprinting characters.
    The insertion point should be positioned at the top of the second page.

Paragraph Concepts

The word paragraph has a special meaning in Word. A paragraph includes any text, graphics, or objects followed by a paragraph mark. Word lets you format paragraphs in a variety of ways. For example, you can change paragraph alignment, add bullets and numbering to paragraphs, and indent paragraphs.

¶

A paragraph mark

You can click anywhere in a paragraph and apply the desired formats. When you tap ENTER, the formats from the current paragraph are applied to the new paragraph. For example, if a heading is centered and you tap ENTER, then the new paragraph will also be centered. You can format several paragraphs by first selecting the desired paragraphs and then applying the formats.

Aligning Text

From the Keyboard
CTRL+L Align Left
CTRL+E for Center
CTRL+R for Align Right
CTRL+J for Justify

The alignment buttons on the Formatting toolbar allow you to align paragraphs horizontally. Text can be left or right-aligned, centered, or justified. The alignment commands affect all text in a paragraph. To mix alignments within a line, you must use customized tab stops or tables.

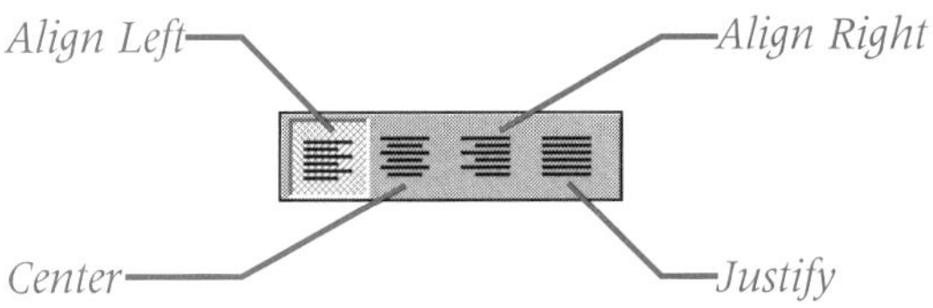
Align Left
Align Right
Center
Justify

Hands-On 8.7 Set Up a Press Release

In this exercise, you will set up a press release. A press release is a type of announcement, so you will begin the first line 2″ down from the top of the page.

Set Up the Title Lines

1. Make sure the insertion point is at the top of the new page, and tap (ENTER) several times to space down to approximately the 2″ position.
2. Locate the alignment buttons on the Formatting toolbar, and notice that the Align Left button is pushed in.
   Left alignment is the default setting in Word.
3. Click the Center button.
   The insertion point moves to the center of the line.
4. Type the title **Flexico Announces FlexMax™Fabric**, inserting the Trademark symbol as shown.
5. Tap (ENTER) twice, and notice that the center alignment is still in effect.
   Paragraph formats (including alignments) are copied to the next paragraph when (ENTER) is tapped.
6. Type **Press Release**, and tap (ENTER) twice.
7. Type **Flexico,® Inc.** inserting the Registered symbol as shown.
8. Tap (ENTER) twice; then click Align Left to restore left alignment.
   You are now ready to set up the body of the press release.

Set Up the Body

9. Type the heading **Announcement**, and tap (ENTER).
10. Type the phrase **San Francisco, Ca**.
    In the next step, you will insert an em dash. Em dashes are used as connectors within sentences and are available on the Symbols dialog box.
11. Display the Symbols dialog box, choose Em Dash from the Special Characters tab, and click Insert.
12. If necessary, move the Symbol dialog box out of the way, and click in the document to the right of the em dash.
13. Type **Today's Date**, and insert another em dash.

From the Keyboard

Type two hyphens with no spaces before or after hyphens. Word will convert hyphens to em dash when (SPACE BAR) is tapped after typing second connector word.

14. Close the Symbol dialog box, and complete the press release as shown below.

Flexico Announces FlexMax™ Fabric

Press Release

Flexico,® Inc.

Announcement
San Francisco, Ca.—April 25, 1999—Flexico, Inc. today announced the FlexMax fabric for active wear. Flexmax fabric is ideally suited for active wear such as biking, hiking, and aerobics attire. This revolutionary fabric is designed by Flexico and allows for maximum range of motion while providing support, comfort, and moisture protection.

About Flexico
Founded in 1988, Flexico is a leading manufacturer of fabrics for active wear and outdoor activities. Flexico fabrics are used in fine active wear products worldwide.

FlexMax Styles
Initially, FlexMax fabric will be available in two weights and a variety of colors. Contact Flexico or your distributor for information and samples.

Delivery and Availability
FlexMax products are expected to reach retailers shelves by the third quarter of this year. Look for the distinctive Flexico logo and the FlexMax trademark. FlexMax products will be available at most quality sporting goods stores.

15. Save the changes, and continue with the next topic.

Formatting Text

From the Keyboard

CTRL+B for Bold
CTRL+U for Underline
CTRL+I for Italics
CTRL+] to increase size one point
CTRL+[to decrease size one point

In Word and other Office programs, you can format text by changing the font, font size, and color. You can also apply various font formats including bold, italics, and underline. If no text is selected, the format settings take effect from that point forward or until you change them again. If you wish to format existing text, you must select the text and then apply the desired formats. You can format text with buttons on the Formatting toolbar, as shown in the following illustration.

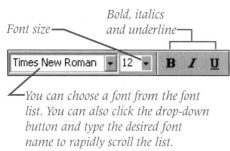

Font size

Bold, italics and underline

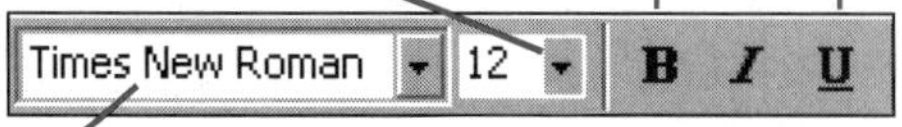

Times New Roman
12
B
I
U

You can choose a font from the font list. You can also click the drop-down button and type the desired font name to rapidly scroll the list.

The Font Color button is on the right end of the Formatting toolbar. The color palette appears when you click the drop-down button. Once you choose a color, the color is displayed on the button. From that point forward, you can rapidly apply the color by clicking the button.

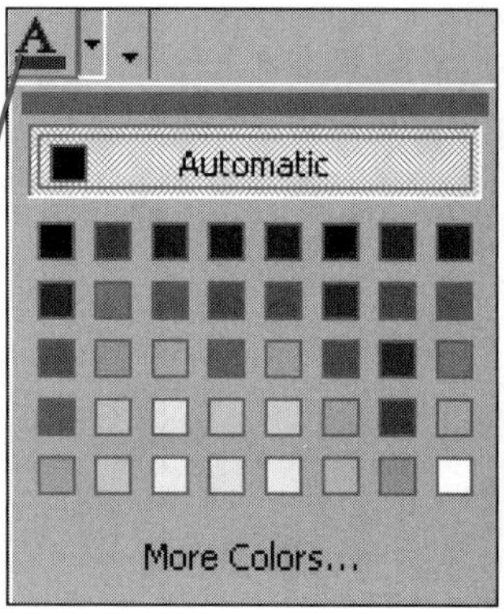

Automatic
More Colors...

Character Effects and Animation

The **Format→Font** command displays the Font dialog box. Any text formats that can be applied with the Formatting toolbar can also be applied using the Font dialog box. In addition, the font dialog box lets you apply underlining options, character effects (such as superscript and strikethrough), and animation. The Font dialog box also provides a Preview window that lets you preview the formatted text before it is applied. The Preview window is helpful if you want to experiment with various font and effect combinations.

Hands-On 8.8 Format Text

Format the Press Release Title Lines

1. Follow this step to select the press release title lines.

Ⓐ *Position the mouse pointer in the left margin, and drag down.*

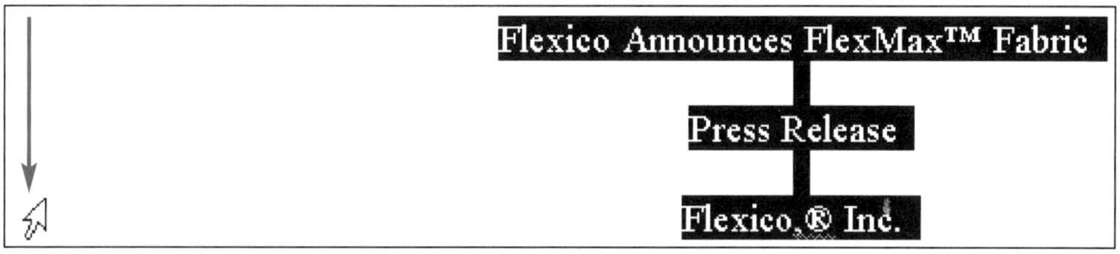

Flexico Announces FlexMax™ Fabric
Press Release
Flexico,® Inc.

2. Follow these steps to format the title lines.

Ⓐ *Click this button to drop down the font list.*

Ⓑ *Notice this dividing line. The names of recently used fonts are placed above the dividing line at the top of the menu. This makes it easy to choose the fonts you use most often.*

Ⓒ *If necessary, scroll down the list, and choose Arial.*

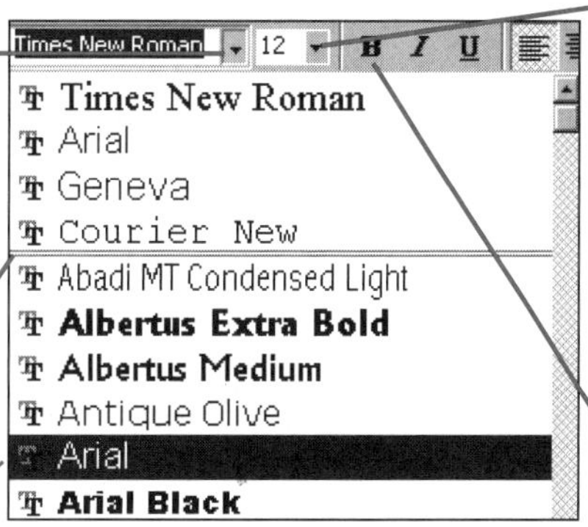

Times New Roman
12
Times New Roman
Arial
Geneva
Courier New
Abadi MT Condensed Light
Albertus Extra Bold
Albertus Medium
Antique Olive
Arial
Arial Black

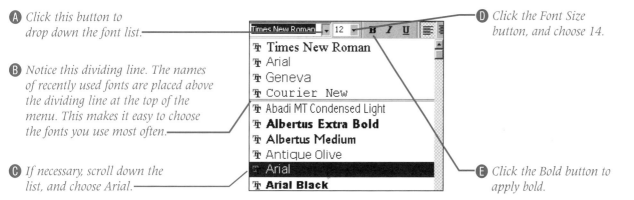

Ⓓ *Click the Font Size button, and choose 14.*

Ⓔ *Click the Bold button to apply bold.*

3. Click the drop-down button on the Font Color button (on the right end of the Formatting toolbar), and choose your favorite color.

Use Keystrokes to Select and Format

The following steps show you how to select using the keyboard. In some situations, keyboard selecting can give you greater precision and control.

4. Scroll up to the first page of the document to view the memorandum.
5. Follow these steps to select the phrase MEMO TO:

Ⓐ *Click just in front of the word MEMO when the mouse pointer has an I-beam shape as shown here.*

Ⓑ *Press and hold the* SHIFT *key, and tap the → key until the phrase MEMO TO: is selected as shown here.*

MEMO TO:
Bill Watson

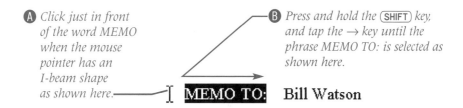

6. Press CTRL+B to apply bold to the phrase.
7. Use the techniques in the previous two steps to apply bold to the next lead word, **FROM:**.

(Continued on the next page)

8. Now apply bold to the lead word **DATE:**. You should see the date move one tab stop to the right, thus throwing off the alignment.
   This occurred because the bold format increased the size of the lead word DATE:. The increased size pushed the lead word past the tab stop at the ½" position on the ruler. This in turn pushed the date past the tab stop at the 1" position. In the next few steps, you will solve this dilemma by removing a tab stop.

Remove a Tab Stop

9. Click the Show All ¶ button to display the nonprinting characters.
10. Notice the tab → symbols between DATE: and the date.
    The tab symbols show each location where the (TAB) *key was tapped.*
11. Click between the tab → symbols, and tap (DELETE) to remove the second symbol.
    The date will move to the left, restoring proper alignment.
12. Click Show All ¶ to hide the nonprinting characters.
13. Now apply bold to the **SUBJECT:** heading.
14. Save the changes, and continue with the next topic.

Cut, Copy, and Paste

Cut, Copy, and Paste are available in all Office 2000 applications. With Cut, Copy, and Paste you can move or copy text within a document, between documents, or between different Office applications. For example, you could use the Copy command to copy an important paragraph from one document, and the Paste command to paste the paragraph to another document. Cut, Copy, and Paste are most efficient for moving or copying text a long distance within a document or between documents. Cut, Copy, and Paste are easy to use if you remember the following concepts:

- You must **select text** before issuing a Cut or Copy command.
- You must **position the insertion point** at the desired location before issuing the Paste command. Otherwise, you will paste at the wrong location.

Quick Reference

USING CUT, COPY, AND PASTE

Command	Description	How to Issue the Command
Cut	The Cut command removes selected text from its original location and places it on the Office Clipboard.	Click the Cut button, or press (CTRL)+X.
Copy	The Copy command also places selected text on the Office Clipboard, but it leaves a copy of the text in the original location.	Click the Copy button, or press (CTRL)+C.
Paste	The Paste command pastes the most recently cut or copied text into the document at the insertion point location.	Click the Paste button, or press (CTRL)+V.

The Office 2000 Clipboard

Office 2000 introduces a new clipboard that can hold up to 12 cut or copied items. The Clipboard toolbar appears once you have cut or copied two or more items. The Clipboard toolbar displays an icon representing each cut or copied item. You can paste any item by choosing it from the Clipboard toolbar. You can paste all items from the toolbar by clicking the Paste All button. The items are pasted in the order in which they were cut or copied to the toolbar.

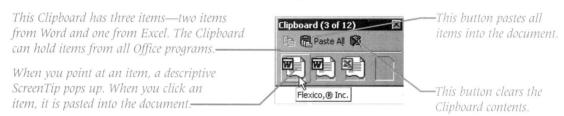

Clipboard (3 of 12)
Paste All
Flexico,® Inc.
This Clipboard has three items—two items from Word and one from Excel. The Clipboard can hold items from all Office programs.
When you point at an item, a descriptive ScreenTip pops up. When you click an item, it is pasted into the document.
This button pastes all items into the document.
This button clears the Clipboard contents.

Hands-On 8.9 Use Cut and Paste

In this exercise, you will use Cut and Paste to rearrange the title lines in the press release.

1. Scroll down to the press release page.
2. Follow these steps to Cut and Paste a title line.

Flexico Announces FlexMax™ Fabric
Press Release
Flexico,® Inc.
A Select this title line and the empty paragraph below it by dragging in the left margin.
B Click the Cut button on the Standard toolbar. The text will be removed and placed on the Office Clipboard.
C Click the I-beam just in front of the first title line as shown here.
D Click the Paste button.

The Press Release *title and the paragraph mark below it should have pushed the* Flexico Announces *heading down, maintaining the double-spacing of the title lines. This occurred because of the way you selected the text prior to issuing the Cut command. By dragging in the margin to the left of the text, you selected both the text and the paragraph marks. The paragraph marks were pasted along with the text. The paragraph marks pushed the* Flexico Announces *paragraph down, maintaining the double-spacing. This was, by the way, the intended result.*

3. Now select the third title line, **Flexico,® Inc.,** and the empty paragraph below it by dragging in the left margin.
4. Click the Cut button, and the Clipboard toolbar should appear. If the Clipboard toolbar did not appear, then choose **View→Toolbars→Clipboard** from the menu bar.
   You will use the Clipboard toolbar in a moment.

(Continued on the next page)

5. Position the insertion point just in front of the first heading, **Press Release**.
6. Click the Paste button on the Standard toolbar (not the Clipboard toolbar).
   Your headings should now have the arrangement shown to the right.

Flexico,® Inc.
Press Release
Flexico Announces FlexMax™ Fabric

Use the Clipboard Toolbar

7. Click the drop-down button on the Undo button.
   If you performed the preceding steps correctly, the first four items on the Undo list should be Paste, Cut, Paste, Cut.
8. Slide the mouse pointer over the first four items to select them, and click the mouse button.
   The press release headings should be in the same order they were in prior to cutting and pasting.
9. Click the Clear Clipboard button on the Clipboard toolbar.
   The two icons should be cleared from the Clipboard.
10. Select the **Press Release** heading and the empty paragraph below it.
11. Click the Cut button.
12. Select the **Flexico,® Inc.** heading and the empty paragraph below it.
13. Click the Cut button.
    The Clipboard toolbar should display two icons.
14. Position the insertion point just in front of the **Flexico Announces** title line.
15. Point at the first icon on the Clipboard toolbar, and the ScreenTip shown to the right should pop up.
    This heading was the first heading you cut to the Clipboard so it is in the first position on the Clipboard.

Clipboard (2 of 12)
Paste All
Press Release

16. Click the icon; the **Press Release** heading and empty paragraph should be pasted above the **Flexico Announces** title line.
    If you selected the title line and the paragraph mark following it prior to cutting, then the Flexico Announces *heading should be pushed down to the second line.*
17. Position the insertion point just in front of the **Press Release** title line.
18. Click the second icon on the Clipboard to paste the **Flexico,® Inc.** heading.
    As you can see, the Clipboard toolbar can be useful if you are collecting items from several places in a document. Keep in mind, however, that Cut, Copy, and Paste can be used in the traditional manner without change, and without using the Clipboard toolbar.
19. Click the Clear Clipboard button to clear the Clipboard contents.
20. Close the Clipboard toolbar by clicking its Close button.

Drag and Drop

Drag and drop produces the same result as Cut, Copy, and Paste. However, Drag and Drop is usually more efficient if you are moving or copying text a short distance within the same document. If the original location and destination are both visible in the current window, then it is usually easier to use Drag and Drop. With Drag and Drop, you select the text you wish to move or copy and release the mouse button. Then you drag the text to the desired destination. If you press the (CTRL) key while releasing the mouse button, the text is copied to the destination.

Right Dragging

Right dragging is a variation of the drag-and-drop technique. Many beginners find Drag and Drop difficult to use because they have difficulty controlling the mouse. This difficulty is compounded if they are trying to copy text using Drag and Drop. This is because copying requires the (CTRL) key to be held while dragging the text. With the Right-Drag method, the right mouse button is used when dragging. When the right mouse button is released at the destination, a pop-up menu appears. The pop-up menu lets you choose Move, Copy, or Cancel. This provides more control because there is no need to use the (CTRL) key when copying, and you have the option of canceling the move or copy. The Right-Drag pop-up menu is shown in the illustration to the right.

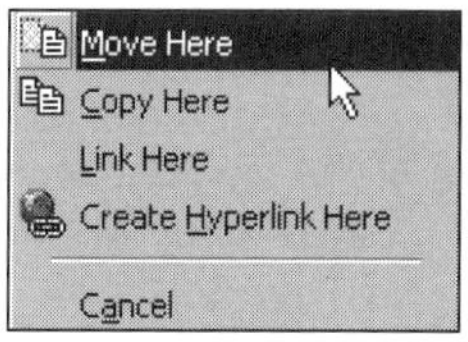

Move Here
Copy Here
Link Here
Create Hyperlink Here
Cancel

Right-Drag Pop-Up Menu

Hands-On 8.10 Use Drag and Drop and Right Drag

In this exercise, you will use Drag and Drop and the Right-Drag method to rearrange paragraphs.

Use Drag and Drop

1. If necessary, scroll down until the paragraphs with the headings About Flexico, FlexMax Styles, and Delivery and Availability are all visible on the screen.
   Drag and Drop is most effective for moving or copying a short distance on the screen.
2. Follow these steps to move the **Delivery and Availability** paragraph and heading.

Ⓐ *Select from the empty paragraph above the* Delivery and Availability *heading to the end of the paragraph as shown in the illustration.*

Ⓑ *Release the mouse button.*

Ⓒ *Position the mouse pointer on the selected text, and drag the text up until the move pointer is just above the* About Flexico *heading, as shown here.*

Ⓓ *Release the mouse button to drop the text above the* About Flexico *heading.*

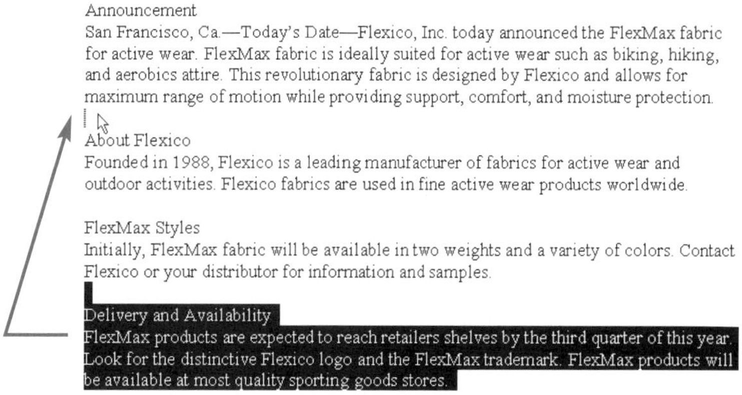

Announcement
San Francisco, Ca.—Today's Date—Flexico, Inc. today announced the FlexMax fabric for active wear. FlexMax fabric is ideally suited for active wear such as biking, hiking, and aerobics attire. This revolutionary fabric is designed by Flexico and allows for maximum range of motion while providing support, comfort, and moisture protection.
About Flexico
Founded in 1988, Flexico is a leading manufacturer of fabrics for active wear and outdoor activities. Flexico fabrics are used in fine active wear products worldwide.
FlexMax Styles
Initially, FlexMax fabric will be available in two weights and a variety of colors. Contact Flexico or your distributor for information and samples.
Delivery and Availability
FlexMax products are expected to reach retailers shelves by the third quarter of this year. Look for the distinctive Flexico logo and the FlexMax trademark. FlexMax products will be available at most quality sporting goods stores.

If you selected the empty paragraph above the text as shown and dropped the text in the empty space above the About Flexico *heading, then your paragraphs should be properly spaced.*

Use Right Drag

3. Follow these steps to move the FlexMax Styles paragraph and heading.

Ⓐ *Select from the empty paragraph above the* FlexMax Styles *heading to the end of the paragraph as shown here; then release the mouse button.*

Ⓑ *Position the mouse pointer on the selected text, and press and hold the right mouse button.*

Ⓒ *Drag the mouse up while holding the right button until the move pointer is positioned just above the* About Flexico *heading, as shown here.*

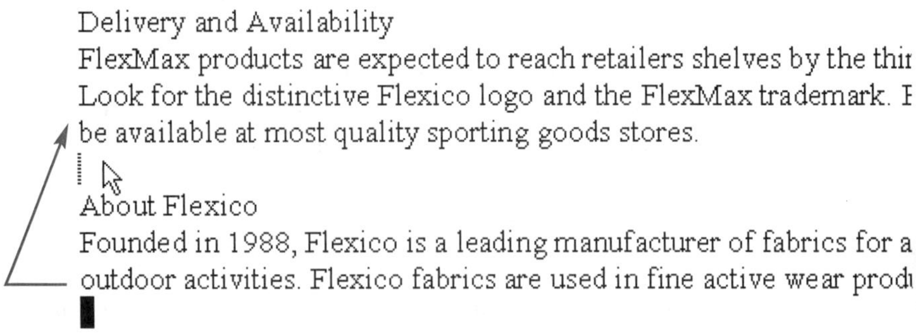

Delivery and Availability
FlexMax products are expected to reach retailers shelves by the thi
Look for the distinctive Flexico logo and the FlexMax trademark. F
be available at most quality sporting goods stores.
About Flexico
Founded in 1988, Flexico is a leading manufacturer of fabrics for a
outdoor activities. Flexico fabrics are used in fine active wear prod

Ⓓ *Release the mouse button, and choose* **Move Here** *from the pop-up menu that appears. Notice that the pop-up menu would have allowed you to cancel the move if desired.*

Move a Sentence

4. Use any of the move techniques you have learned thus far to move the last sentence in the Announcement paragraph as shown in the following illustration. You can use Cut and Paste, Drag and Drop, or Right Drag.

Move the selected sentence to this location in front of the previous sentence. You will probably need to insert a space after moving the sentence.

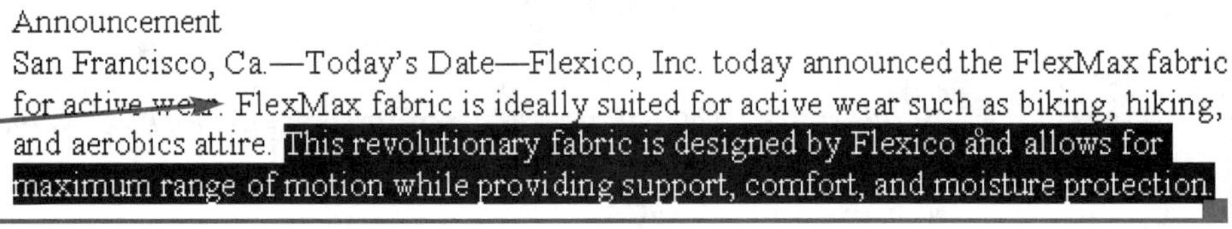

Announcement
San Francisco, Ca.—Today's Date—Flexico, Inc. today announced the FlexMax fabric
for active wear. FlexMax fabric is ideally suited for active wear such as biking, hiking,
and aerobics attire. This revolutionary fabric is designed by Flexico and allows for
maximum range of motion while providing support, comfort, and moisture protection.

The Spike

The Spike is another tool that allows you to gather text from various parts of Word documents. The primary benefit of the Spike is that there is no limit to the number of text items you can place on it. However, you can only place text on the Spike, not graphics, tables, or other Word objects. Also, text formatting is not saved when text is cut to the Spike. When you have finished gathering text with the Spike, you paste all text items at one location. The Spike's contents are pasted in the order in which they were placed on the Spike. The following Quick Reference table shows you how to use the Spike. You will use the Spike in a Skill Builder exercise later in this lesson.

Quick Reference

USING THE SPIKE

- Select text you would like to place on the Spike.
- Press CTRL+F3 to cut the text to the Spike.
- Continue to cut as many text items as desired.
- Position the insertion point at the location where you want to paste the Spike's contents.
- Press CTRL+SHIFT+F3 to paste the Spike's contents and clear the Spike.

Document Scraps

Document Scraps are a useful way to copy text to or from a Word document. To create a document scrap, you drag text from a Word document onto the Windows Desktop. Likewise, you can drag a document scrap from the Desktop and drop it in any Word document. A document scrap is a self-contained document residing on the Windows Desktop. Document scraps are useful if you have a frequently used block of text that you would easily like to add to documents.

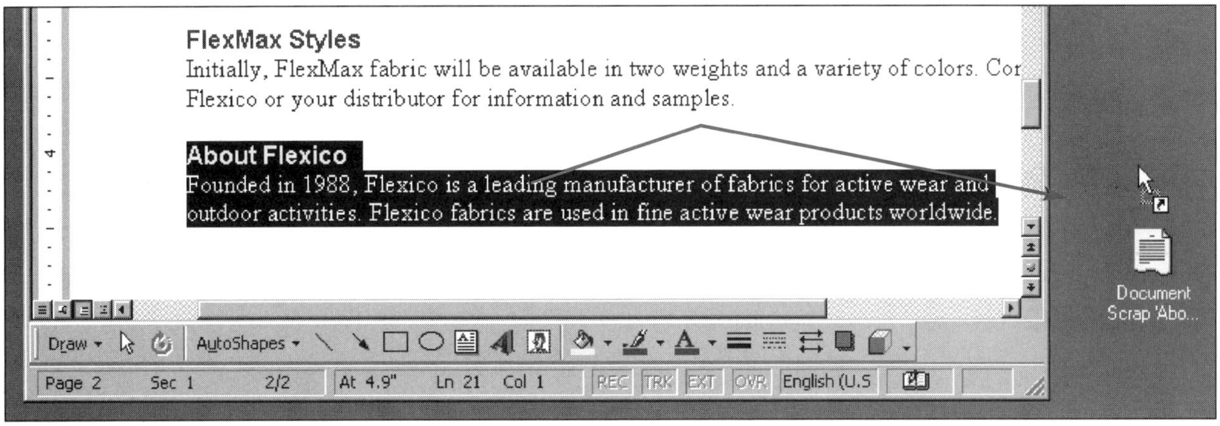

FlexMax Styles
Initially, FlexMax fabric will be available in two weights and a variety of colors. Cor
Flexico or your distributor for information and samples.
About Flexico
Founded in 1988, Flexico is a leading manufacturer of fabrics for active wear and outdoor activities. Flexico fabrics are used in fine active wear products worldwide.
Document Scrap 'Abo...
Draw
AutoShapes
Page 2 Sec 1 2/2 At 4.9" Ln 21 Col 1 REC TRK EXT OVR English (U.S

Creating a Document Scrap

The Format Painter

The Format Painter lets you copy text formats from one location to another. This is convenient if you want the same format(s) applied to text in different locations. The Format Painter copies all text formats, including the font, font size, color, and character effects. The Format Painter saves time and helps create consistent formatting throughout a document. The Format Painter can also be used to copy paragraph formats, such as alignment settings.

Quick Reference

COPYING TEXT FORMATS WITH THE FORMAT PAINTER

- Click on the text with the format(s) you wish to copy.
- Click the Format Painter once if you want to copy formats to one other location, or double-click if you want to copy to multiple locations.
- Select the text at the new location(s) that you want to format. If you double-clicked in the previous step, the Format Painter will remain active, allowing you to select text at multiple locations. You can even scroll through the document to reach the desired location(s).
- If you double-clicked in the first step, then click the Format Painter button when you have finished. This will turn off the Format Painter.

Hands-On 8.11 Use the Format Painter

Format Text

1. Click on the **Announcement** heading (just above the first large paragraph of text).
2. Choose **Format→Font** to display the Font dialog box.

Ⓐ *Scroll through the list of fonts, and choose Arial.*

Ⓑ *Set the font size to 14.*

Ⓒ *Click the Font color button, and choose the same color you choose for the title lines.*

Ⓓ *Notice the Effects section. You can apply one or more character effects to text (but don't do it now).*

Ⓔ *Click OK to apply the formatting to the Announcement heading.*

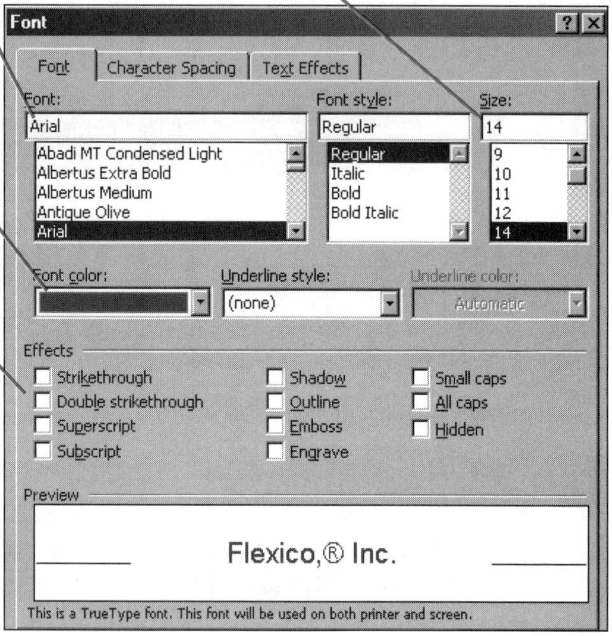
Font
Font
Character Spacing
Text Effects
Font:
Arial
Abadi MT Condensed Light
Albertus Extra Bold
Albertus Medium
Antique Olive
Arial
Font style:
Regular
Regular
Italic
Bold
Bold Italic
Size:
14
9
10
11
12
14
Font color:
Underline style:
(none)
Underline color:
Automatic
Effects
Strikethrough
Double strikethrough
Superscript
Subscript
Shadow
Outline
Emboss
Engrave
Small caps
All caps
Hidden
Preview
Flexico,® Inc.
This is a TrueType font. This font will be used on both printer and screen.

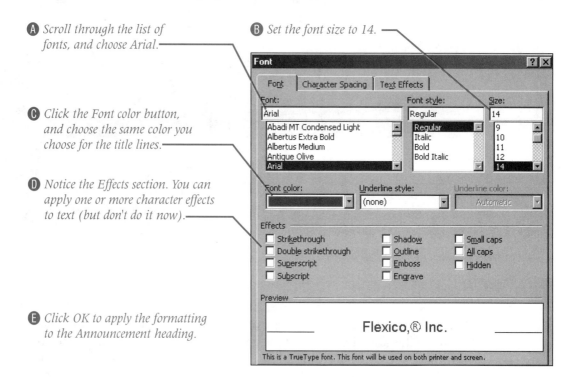

Notice that you were able to format the word Announcement without actually selecting it. You can format a single word by clicking on the word and applying the desired formats.

Copy Formats to One Location

3. Make sure the insertion point is on the Announcement heading.
4. Click the Format Painter button on the Standard toolbar.
   An animated paintbrush icon will be added to the I-beam pointer.
5. Drag the mouse pointer across the Delivery and Availability heading.
   The Arial, 14pt, bold, colored formats should be copied to the heading. The animated paintbrush icon also vanished because you clicked the Format Painter button just once in the previous step. If you want to copy formats to multiple locations, you must double-click the Format Painter. Actually, the 14pt heading is too large for these paragraphs. In the next few steps, you will change the size to 12pt for the Announcement heading and then copy the formats to the other headings in the press release.

Copy Formats to Several Locations

6. Click anywhere on the Announcement heading.
7. Click the Font Size 14 drop-down button on the Formatting toolbar, and choose 12.
   Once again, you can format an individual word by just clicking on the word and applying the desired formats.

8. Double-click the Format Painter .
9. Select the heading **Delivery and Availability** by either dragging the mouse over the heading or by clicking in front of the heading in the margin.
10. Select the **FlexMax Styles** heading to copy the formats to that heading.
11. If necessary, scroll down, and then select the **About Flexico** heading.
12. Click the Format Painter to turn it off.
13. Scroll through your document, and take a moment to appreciate your work.
14. Feel free to experiment with any of the techniques you have learned in this lesson.
15. When you have finished, save the changes to your document; then close the document.
    Continue with the end-of-lesson questions and exercises.

Concepts Review

True/False Questions

1. The zoom control changes the size of printed text. TRUE FALSE
2. The Formatting toolbar can be used to set all text formats and character effects. TRUE FALSE
3. Normal view is the default view in Word 2000. TRUE FALSE
4. The Format Painter is used to copy and paste text. TRUE FALSE
5. Manual page breaks remain in place until the user removes them. TRUE FALSE
6. The Right-Drag method displays a pop-up menu when the mouse button is released. TRUE FALSE
7. The Office Clipboard can hold up to 12 cut or copied items. TRUE FALSE
8. Items must be pasted from the Office Clipboard in the same order that they were placed on the Clipboard. TRUE FALSE

Multiple-Choice Questions

1. In order to copy text formats to several locations in a document, you must
   a. click the Format Painter button and then select the desired text.
   b. double-click the Format Painter button and then select the desired text.
   c. use the Copy button.
   d. This cannot be done in Word.

2. Which of the following statements can be used to describe manual page breaks?
   a. Manual page breaks remain in place until they are deleted.
   b. Manual page breaks are inserted by the user.
   c. Manual page breaks can be inserted by pressing CTRL+ENTER.
   d. All of the above

3. What is the percentage range of the zoom control?
   a. 25%–200%
   b. 10%–500%
   c. 25%–500%
   d. None of the above

4. Which key should you press if you want to copy while using drag-and-drop?
   a. SHIFT
   b. CTRL
   c. ALT
   d. HOME

Skill Builders

Skill Builder 8.1 Alignment and Formatting Practice

1. Click New to start a new document.
2. Click the Center button.
3. Tap (ENTER) several times to space down to 2″.
4. Set the font to Arial, the point size to 18, and turn on bold.
5. Click the drop-down button on the Font Color button (on the right end of the Formatting toolbar), and choose your favorite color.
6. Type **The Wilson Family**, and tap (ENTER) *twice.*
   Notice you can apply text formats prior to typing text. The formats remain in effect until you change them or move the insertion point to a location with different formats.
7. Set the font size to 14.
8. Type **Is Having a**, and tap (ENTER) *twice.*
9. Set the font size to 18.
10. Type **Big Yard Sale**, tap (ENTER) twice, and set the alignment to Left.
11. Set the font to Times New Roman, the size to 14, turn off bold, and set the color to black.
12. Complete the document as shown below. You will need to apply bold formatting to the date and time as shown.
13. Save the document as **Skill Builder 8.1**, then close the document.

The Wilson Family

Is Having a

Big Yard Sale

Stop by our home at 22 Maple Street in Walnut Grove on July 21 for the yard sale of the summer! We'll have furniture, toys, electronics, antiques, and much more. We start at 8:00, so arrive early and be prepared to find bargains, one-of-a-kind items, and rare antiques!

Skill Builder 8.2 The Spike, Format Painter, Drag and Drop

In this exercise, you will open a document on your exercise diskette. You will use the Spike to rearrange paragraphs, the Format Painter to paint formats, and Drag and Drop to move blocks of paragraphs.

Use the Spike

1. Open the document named Skill Builder 8.2 on your exercise diskette.
   Notice that the document contains a list of professional contacts. In the next few steps, you will use the Spike to reorganize the contacts by contact type. In other words, all of the attorneys will be grouped together, followed by the designers, then the bookkeepers.
2. Select the first attorney contact, **David Roberts, Attorney,** by clicking in front of the contact in the left margin.
3. Press CTRL+F3 to cut the text and place it on the Spike.
4. Select the next attorney, **Lisa Wilson, Attorney**, and press CTRL+F3 to cut the text to the Spike.
5. Cut the remaining attorney contacts to the Spike. Use Undo if you make a mistake. However, try to be extra careful because even if you use Undo, the item you cut will remain on the Spike.
6. Cut the designer contacts to the Spike.
   The bookkeeper contacts should now be grouped together in the document. The insertion point should also be at the end of the document.
7. Press CTRL+SHIFT+F3 to paste the Spike's contents.
   The Spike pastes the contents and inserts an empty paragraph between each contact. Notice that the attorneys are now grouped together, and the designers are grouped together.

Create Headings

8. Click in the empty space between any two contacts, and tap DELETE to remove the empty space.
   You are actually deleting a paragraph mark when you do this.
9. Remove the remaining empty paragraphs between the contacts.
10. Click in front of the first bookkeeper contact, and tap ENTER to create a blank line.
11. Click on the blank line, and type **`Bookkeepers`**.
12. Use this technique to create an **`Attorneys`** heading above the first attorney contact, and a **`Designers`** heading above the first designer contact.

Use the Format Painter

13. Click on the **Professional Contacts** heading at the top of the document.
14. Double-click the Format Painter .
15. Click the **Bookkeepers** heading to copy the formats to that heading.
16. Click the **Attorneys** and **Designers** headings.
17. Turn off the Format Painter .
18. Select the **Professional Contacts** heading, and increase the size to 14.

Use Drag and Drop

19. Select the **Attorneys** heading and the four attorney contacts by dragging in the left margin.
20. Release the mouse button.
21. Position the mouse pointer on the selection, and drag up until the pointer is just in front of the **Bookkeepers** heading.
22. Release the mouse button to move the **Attorneys** block above the **Bookkeepers**.
23. Now move the **Designers** heading and the designer contacts above the **Bookkeepers**.

Create Space and Center the Title

24. Position the insertion point just in front of the **Attorneys** heading, and tap (ENTER) to create a blank line between the **Professional Contacts** heading and the **Attorneys** heading.
25. Insert blank lines above the **Designers** and **Bookkeepers** headings.
26. Click on the **Professional Contacts** heading, and click the Center Align button.
27. Use (ENTER) to push the entire document down to the 2″ position.
28. Save the changes, and close the document when you have finished.

Skill Builder 8.3 Create a Memorandum

1. Follow these guidelines to create the memorandum shown below.
   - Position the MEMO TO: line approximately 2″ down from the top of the page.
   - Double space between all paragraphs, and apply bold to the lead words MEMO TO:, FROM:, DATE:, and SUBJECT:.
   - Apply bold formatting as shown in the body paragraph.
2. Save the memo with the name **Skill Builder 8.3,** and then close the document.

MEMO TO: Jason Alexander

FROM: Tamika Jackson

DATE: Today's Date

SUBJECT: Monthly Sales Meeting

Our monthly sales meeting will be held in the conference room at **10:00 a.m.** on **Thursday, July 24**. Please bring your sales forecast for August and any important accounts that you wish to discuss. I will give you a presentation on our new products that are scheduled for release in September. I look forward to seeing you then.

xx

Assessments

Assessment 8.1 Create a Memorandum

1. Follow these guidelines to create the memorandum shown below.
   - Begin the document 2″ down from the top of the page.
   - Boldface the lead words MEMO TO, FROM, DATE, and SUBJECT as shown.
   - Use the em dash after the department names.
   - Type your initials at the bottom of the memo.
2. Save the document to your exercise diskette with the name **Assessment 8.1.**
3. Print the document, and then close it.

MEMO TO: Mark Paxton

FROM: Tamara Niu

DATE: Today's Date

SUBJECT: Purchase Orders

The following departments have requested that purchase orders be issued for the specified products. Please conduct the necessary research and issue purchase orders as soon as possible.

Marketing—A cordless mouse that can be used at least six feet away from the base unit.

Systems—A flatbed scanner with high resolution. It should have software that allows enhancing of images even as scanning is taking place.

Research—A video camera that is supported by the Universal Serial Bus (USB) standard. The price should be lower than what we paid for the analog camera.

xx

Assessment 8.2

1. Open the document named Assessment 8.2 on your exercise diskette.
2. Follow these guidelines to modify the memorandum.
   - Apply bold formatting as shown below.
   - Insert the *Do Not Try to Please Everyone* line and the paragraphs following it as shown below, including the initials line and the attachment line.

MEMO TO: Office Staff

FROM: Ariel Ramirez

DATE: Today's Date

SUBJECT: Multiple Supervisors

Most executive assistants at our firm have multiple supervisors. Therefore, we are offering the following suggestions to make your work easier.

Prioritize—What is important may take preference over what is urgent. Which project can be delayed? Overall, which has the greatest importance to our firm? Evaluate and schedule your time accordingly.

Refuse Assignments—If you do not have the time, ask your supervisor if someone else can do the assignment. It's better to say no than to not meet the deadline.

Enjoy Multiple Projects—Learn to enjoy the challenge of switching from one project to another. You may not be able to finish them all, but realize the contribution you have made to each one.

Do Not Try to Please Everyone—There is no way you will please all of your supervisors all of the time. Set your own approval rating and go with it.

Listed on the attached sheet are some related workshops you may want to attend. Contact Human Resources for registration forms.

xx
Attachment

(Continued on the next page)

3. Tap (ENTER) once after the Attachment line; then insert a page break.

4. Follow these guidelines to create the following page.
   - Start the title line 2″ down.
   - Center and bold the title as shown.
   - Apply the color of your choice to the title.
   - Double-space between all paragraphs.

RECOMMENDED WORKSHOPS

How to Manage Your Boss, April 23, Holiday Inn, Fremont, Phoenix Extension

The Perfect Support Person, April 30, Hyatt at the Airport, ProPeople Associates

Prioritizing Made Easy, May 5, Sheraton at the Wharf, CareerTech

Office Procedures for the Executive Assistant, May 7, SF Marriott, Phoenix Extension

5. Save the changes, print the document, and then close it.

LESSON 9—Word

Professional Writing and Editing Tools

In this lesson, you will use the Office Assistant, online Help, and professional writing and editing tools. The Office Assistant and online Help allow you to get assistance at any time. Word 2000 provides spell checking, grammar checking, and a powerful thesaurus. Word 2000 even has automatic spell checking and grammar checking that check your work as you write. Another powerful tool in Word 2000 is Find and Replace. Find and Replace is especially useful for finding and replacing text in large documents. Once you master the writing tools in Word 2000, you'll be able to write business documents, research papers, and reports with confidence.

In This Lesson

Case Study

Sarah Thomas is a Health Science major at Upper State University. In order to fulfill the requirements of her Nutritional Studies class, Sarah has chosen to write a research paper on diabetes. Sarah is enthusiastic about this topic since one of her family members was recently afflicted with diabetes. Sarah takes full advantage of the powerful writing and editing tools in Word 2000. She uses the spelling and grammar checkers to proof her paper prior to submission. She uses the thesaurus to find the best words to express her ideas. Finally, Sarah uses the find and replace feature to make changes and ensure consistency throughout her paper.

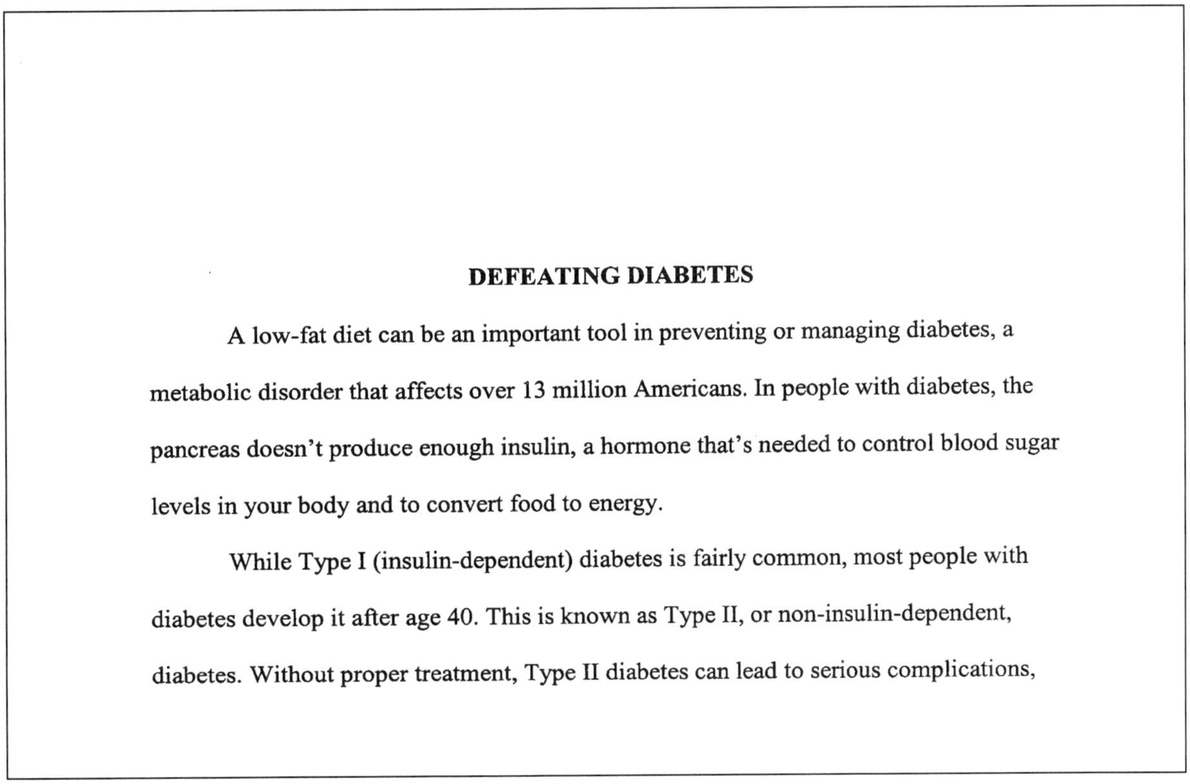

DEFEATING DIABETES

A low-fat diet can be an important tool in preventing or managing diabetes, a metabolic disorder that affects over 13 million Americans. In people with diabetes, the pancreas doesn't produce enough insulin, a hormone that's needed to control blood sugar levels in your body and to convert food to energy.

While Type I (insulin-dependent) diabetes is fairly common, most people with diabetes develop it after age 40. This is known as Type II, or non-insulin-dependent, diabetes. Without proper treatment, Type II diabetes can lead to serious complications,

A polished paper, thanks to Word 2000's writing tools.

The Office Assistant

It looks like you're writing a letter.
Would you like help?
Get help with writing the letter
Just type the letter without help
Cancel

Assistant offering assistance

The Office Assistant is an interactive Help tool available in all Office 2000 applications. The Assistant monitors your activities and provides tips, suggestions, and alert messages whenever it assumes you need assistance. For example, the Assistant recognizes certain phrases such as salutations beginning with the word *Dear.* The Assistant displays a **speech balloon** when it recognizes such a phrase. The speech balloon contains the suggestion or alert message. The Assistant can also be configured to display a tip of the day when Word is started.

Using the Assistant to Get Help

The Assistant's speech balloon contains a search box where you can enter phrases and questions. When you click the Search button, the Assistant interprets the phrase or question in the search box and displays a list of topics relating to the search box text. When you click a topic, Word displays a Help window providing you with detailed help information.

Controlling the Assistant

You can control all aspects of the Assistant. For example, you may not want the Assistant to display a tip of the day, or you may want to turn the Assistant off. You can set options for the Assistant in the Office Assistant dialog box. The following Quick Reference table outlines various methods of controlling the Assistant.

Quick Reference

CONTROLLING THE OFFICE ASSISTANT

Task	Procedure
Display the Assistant's speech balloon (four different methods).	■ Click anywhere on the Assistant. ■ Press (F1). ■ Click the Help button on the Standard toolbar. ■ Choose Microsoft Word Help from the Help menu.
Close the speech balloon.	Click anywhere in the document, or tap (ESC).
Display Office Assistant dialog box.	Display the speech balloon, and click the Options button.
Change animated character.	Display the Office Assistant dialog box, click the Gallery tab, use the Next button to browse the available characters, choose a character, and click OK.
Temporarily hide the Assistant.	Choose Help→Hide the Office Assistant, or right-click the Assistant, and choose Hide from the pop-up menu.
Turn Assistant off completely.	Display the Office Assistant dialog box, and uncheck the Use the Office Assistant box.
Unhide the Assistant or turn on the Assistant.	Choose Help→Show the Office Assistant.

Hands-On 9.1 Use the Office Assistant

In this and the following exercise, you will use the Assistant to learn more about inserting dates. You learned about inserting dates in the previous lesson.

Display the Speech Balloon

1. Start Word, and the Assistant should appear.
2. If the Assistant is not visible on your screen, choose Help→Show the Office Assistant.
   This text shows the default Assistant character known as "Clippit." The Assistant on your machine may be different.
3. Click the Assistant and the speech balloon will pop up.
4. Click anywhere in the document window to close the speech balloon.
5. Position the mouse pointer on the Assistant, and drag the Assistant to a new screen location.
   You can always reposition the Assistant even if the speech balloon is displayed.

Get Help

6. Click the Assistant to display the speech balloon.
7. Follow these steps to get help on inserting the date in documents.

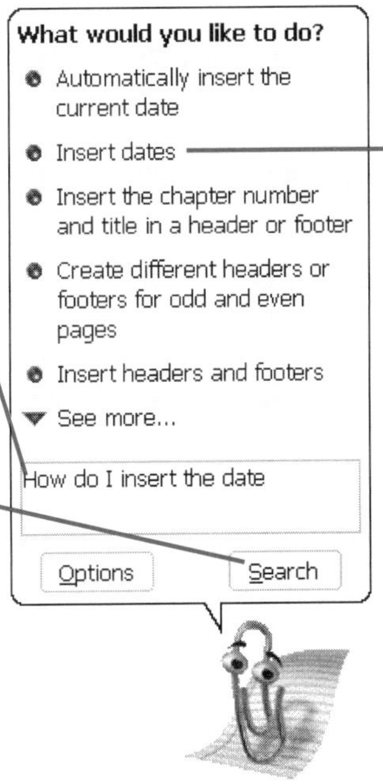

What would you like to do?
Automatically insert the current date
Insert dates
Insert the chapter number and title in a header or footer
Create different headers or footers for odd and even pages
Insert headers and footers
See more...
How do I insert the date
Options
Search

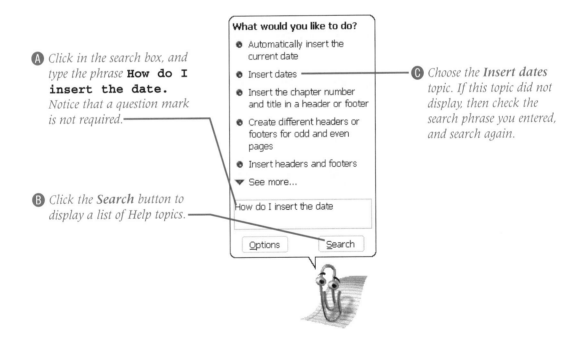

A *Click in the search box, and type the phrase* **`How do I insert the date.`** *Notice that a question mark is not required.*

B *Click the* ***Search*** *button to display a list of Help topics.*

C *Choose the* ***Insert dates*** *topic. If this topic did not display, then check the search phrase you entered, and search again.*

Word will display a Help window relating to Inserting the date and time. The Help window will most likely appear beside the Word document window. As you can see, the Assistant can be used to display Help windows. You will learn more about inserting the date and time and online Help in a moment.

(Continued on the next page)

8. For now, click the Close [X] button at the top–right corner of the Help window.
The Help window should close, and the Word window will return to its original size.

9. Type the word **`date`** in the Assistant's search box.

10. Click the Search button, and a list of topics will appear.
Notice that Insert dates is one of the topics. This is the same topic you searched for previously when you entered the search phrase "How do I insert the date." This example shows that it isn't always necessary to type long phrases in the search box. Often, a single word is enough to locate a desired topic.

Check Out the Options

11. Click the Options button on the speech balloon.

12. If necessary, click the Options tab in the dialog box that appears.

13. Click the Question Mark [?] button at the top-right corner of the dialog box, and then click on any option check box.
Word will provide a ScreenTip describing the purpose of the option.

14. Tap the (ESC) key to close the ScreenTip.

15. Feel free to get help on the various Office Assistant options. You may also want to click the Gallery tab in the dialog box to check out the other Assistant characters. If you are studying in a computer lab, it is recommended that you not change any options.

16. Close the Office Assistant dialog box when you have finished.

Online Help

Word's online Help puts a complete reference book at your fingertips. Help is available for just about any topic you can imagine. Online Help is important because Microsoft does not provide reference manuals with Office 2000. The reference manuals are now integrated into online Help.

Locating Help Topics

Your goal when using online Help is to locate Help topics. There are several different search methods you can use to locate topics. All Help topics have key words that identify them. For example, a Help topic that discusses printing documents can probably be located by including the key word *printing* in your search method. Regardless of which search method you use, the goal is to locate a topic. Once you locate the desired topic, you can display it and follow the instructions in the topic.

When Help Is Available

In Word 2000, you can display the Help window directly only when the Office Assistant is turned off. You learned how to turn off the Office Assistant in the previous topic. When the Office Assistant is turned off, the Help window can be displayed using any of the following methods:

- Click the Help [?] button on the Standard toolbar.
- Press (F1).
- Choose Help→Microsoft Word Help from the menu bar.

The following Quick Reference table explains the various methods for locating Help topics.

Quick Reference

LOCATING HELP TOPICS

Search Method	Procedure
Contents	The Contents method is useful if you are trying to locate a topic but you aren't really sure how to describe it. The Contents method lets you navigate through a series of categories until the desired topic is located.
Answer Wizard	The Answer Wizard lets you find topics the same way that you find them with the Office Assistant. You type a phrase into a search box and execute a search.
Index	The Index method lets you locate a topic by typing key words. An alphabetically indexed list of topics is displayed from which you can choose the desired topic. This method is most useful if you know the name of the topic or feature for which you need assistance.

The Help Window Toolbar

The Help window contains a toolbar to assist you with online Help. The following illustration defines the buttons on the Help toolbar.

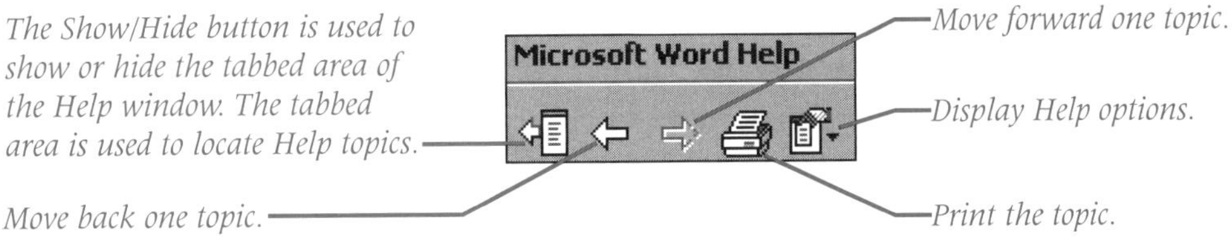
The Show/Hide button is used to show or hide the tabbed area of the Help window. The tabbed area is used to locate Help topics.
Move back one topic.
Microsoft Word Help
Move forward one topic.
Display Help options.
Print the topic.

Hands-On 9.2 Use Online Help

Turn Off the Office Assistant

1. Click the Office Assistant, and then click the Options button.
2. Make sure the Options tab is active, and remove the check from the Use the Office Assistant box.
3. Click **OK,** and the Office Assistant will vanish.
   Once the Office Assistant is turned off, commands that would normally display the Office Assistant display the Help window instead.

Use an Index Search

4. Choose **Help→Microsoft Word Help** from the menu bar.
   The Help window will be displayed beside the Word window. If the Office Assistant had been active, this command would have popped up the Assistant's speech balloon.
5. If the tabbed area of the Help window is not displayed, then click the Show button on the Help toolbar.

(Continued on the next page)

6. Click the Index tab.
7. Type the word **`date`** in the Type keywords box, and click the **Search** button.
   The topic Insert the current date and time *should appear in the right side of the Help window.*
8. Click the **Insert the current date and time** topic.
   The Help information for that topic will appear in the right side of the Help window.
9. Take a moment to read the help information; then click the **Show Me** hyperlink that appears in Step 2.
   The Show Me *hyperlink displays the actual dialog box that is used for setting the date and time.*
10. Click the Cancel button on the Date and Time dialog box.

Experiment with Help

11. Click in the Help window to redisplay the entire window.
12. Feel free to experiment with Help. Try using the Contents method to locate Help topics, and try using the Index method to locate additional topics.
13. When you have finished, click the Close ☒ button on the Help window.
14. Finally, turn the Office Assistant back on with the **Help→Show the Office Assistant** command. If necessary, close the Assistant's speech balloon.

Spell Checking

Word checks a document for spelling errors by comparing each word to the contents of a main dictionary. The main dictionary is a standard, college-level dictionary. The spell checker also looks for double words such as *the the,* words with numbers such as *99budget,* and a variety of capitalization errors.

Custom Dictionaries

Word actually compares your document with two (or more) dictionaries: the main dictionary and one or more custom dictionaries. Custom dictionaries contain words such as last names or company names that may not be in the main dictionary. You can add words to a custom dictionary during a spell check. For example, you may want to add last names or company names you frequently use in your work. The spell checker will ignore those words during future spell checks. Word also lets you use dictionaries for languages other than English. You can even purchase dictionaries with specific terminology, such as medical or legal terminology.

Automatic Spell Checking

Word can automatically check your spelling as you type. Word flags spelling errors by underlining them with wavy red lines. You can correct a flagged error by right-clicking the error and choosing a suggested replacement word or other option from the pop-up menu that appears.

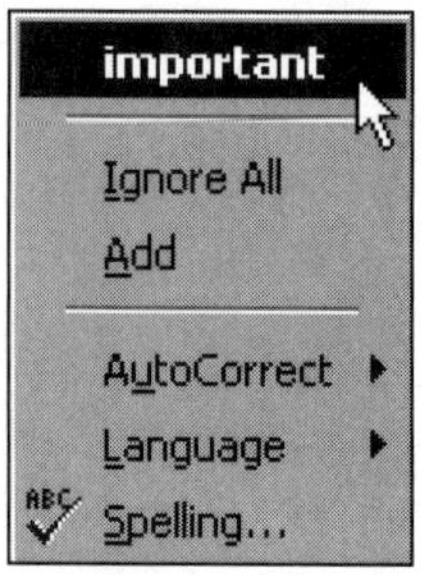
important
Ignore All
Add
AutoCorrect
Language
Spelling...

Spell Check Pop-Up Menu

Hands-On 9.3 Use Automatic Spell Checking

Correct Spelling Errors

1. Open the document named **Hands-On Lesson 9** on your exercise diskette.
   This document has plenty of spelling errors for you to correct.
2. Notice that the mispelled word *iportant* in the first sentence has a wavy red underline.
   Misspelled words are identified by wavy red underlines.
3. *Right-click* the word *iportant,* and the following pop-up menu will appear.
   Take a few moments to study the following illustration.

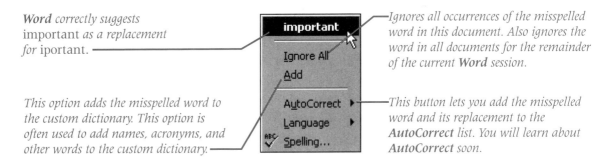

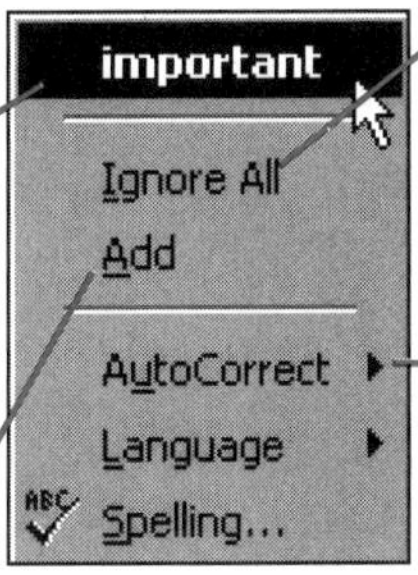
important
Ignore All
Add
AutoCorrect
Language
Spelling...
Word correctly suggests important as a replacement for iportant.
This option adds the misspelled word to the custom dictionary. This option is often used to add names, acronyms, and other words to the custom dictionary.
Ignores all occurrences of the misspelled word in this document. Also ignores the word in all documents for the remainder of the current Word session.
This button lets you add the misspelled word and its replacement to the AutoCorrect list. You will learn about AutoCorrect soon.

4. Choose **important** from the top of the list as shown in the preceding illustration.
   Important will replace iportant.
5. *Right-click* the word *millionAmericans* on the second line of the first paragraph, and choose **million Americans** from the pop-up menu.

Double Word and Capitalization Errors

6. Notice the double word *with with* on the second line.
   Word reports these types of errors as well.
7. *Right-click* the second occurrence of *with,* and choose **Delete Repeated Word** from the pop-up menu.
8. *Right-click* the word *WHile* at the start of the second paragraph.
9. Choose **While** from the pop-up menu.
   As you can see, the spell checker looks for spelling, double words, and capitalization errors. You can always correct spelling as you type by right-clicking words with a wavy red underline and choosing an option from the pop-up menu.

Grammar Checking

Word has a sophisticated grammar checker that can help improve your writing skills. Like the spell checker, the grammar checker can check grammar as you type. The grammar checker "flags" grammar errors by underlining them with wavy green lines. You can correct a flagged error by right-clicking the error and choosing a replacement phrase or other option from the pop up menu. Be careful when using the grammar checker, however, because it isn't perfect. There is no substitute for careful proofreading.

The Spelling and Grammar Dialog Box

From the Keyboard

Press F7 to start Spelling and Grammar checker

The Spelling and Grammar dialog box is useful when you are spell checking and/or grammar checking a large document. It also provides access to customization options. For example, you use the Spelling and Grammar dialog box to choose a customized dictionary for the spell checker and to choose the writing style for the grammar checker. The available writing styles are casual, standard, formal, technical, and custom. The Spelling and Grammar dialog box is displayed with the **Tools→Spelling and Grammar** command or by clicking the Spelling and Grammar button on the Standard toolbar.

Hands-On 9.4 Use the Spelling and Grammar Dialog Box

1. Click the Spelling and Grammar button on the Standard toolbar.
   The spell check will begin, and the speller should stop on the misspelled word famil in the third paragraph.
2. Take a few moments to study the following illustration.

*You can choose a suggestion from this list and click the **Change** button.*

You can change the custom dictionary, writing style, turn on grammar checking as you type, and set other options.

This box turns on grammar checking when using this dialog box; however, it does not activate grammar checking as you type.

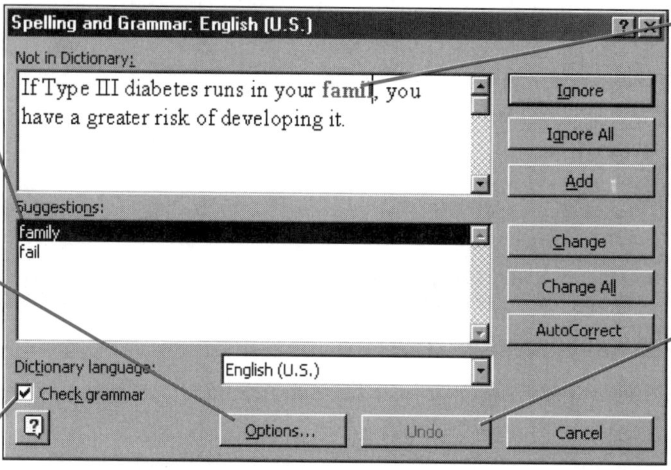
Spelling and Grammar: English (U.S.)
Not in Dictionary:
If Type III diabetes runs in your famil, you have a greater risk of developing it.
Ignore
Ignore All
Add
Suggestions:
family
fail
Change
Change All
AutoCorrect
Dictionary language:
English (U.S.)
Check grammar
Options...
Undo
Cancel

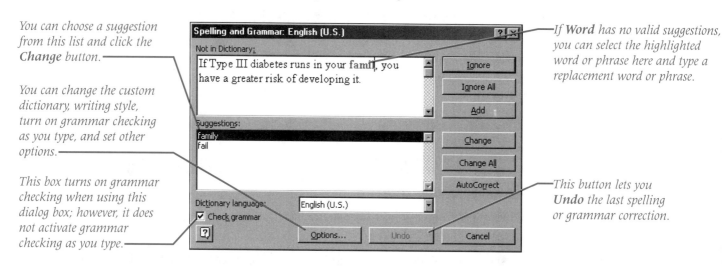

*If **Word** has no valid suggestions, you can select the highlighted word or phrase here and type a replacement word or phrase.*

*This button lets you **Undo** the last spelling or grammar correction.*

3. Choose **family** from the suggestions list, and click the **Change** button.
4. Use the following guidelines to spell check and grammar check the remainder of this document.
   - Use your best judgment to determine the correct spelling of all misspelled words.
   - Use your best judgment to determine the correct grammar if Word reports grammar errors.
   - From time-to-time, messages may pop up helping you with reported spelling and grammar errors. The messages will vanish as soon as you take any kind of action.
5. When the spell check is complete, the Office Assistant will display a message. Click anywhere in the document to close the message.
6. Click the Save button to update the changes.
   Leave the document open; you will continue to use it.

Thesaurus

The thesaurus can help improve your vocabulary and writing skills by providing synonyms (words with the same meaning) for words or phrases. The thesaurus can help you choose just the right words or phrases to accurately express your ideas. You can easily display of list of synonyms by right-clicking a selected word or phrase and choosing Synonyms from the pop up menu that appears. The thesaurus dialog box can also be used to display synonyms and antonyms (words or phrases with the opposite meaning). You display the Thesaurus dialog box with the **Tools→Language→Thesaurus** command.

From the Keyboard

SHIFT+F7 to display the Thesaurus dialog box

Hands-On 9.5 Use the Thesaurus

1. Scroll up and **right-click** the word *manufacture* in the third line of the first paragraph.
2. Choose **Synonyms** from the bottom of the pop-up menu.
3. Choose **produce** from the synonym list.
4. Use the preceding steps to replace the word **manage** with **control** also on the third line of the first paragraph.
5. Click anywhere on the word **control**, and choose **Tools→Language→Thesaurus** from the menu bar.
6. Follow these steps to explore the thesaurus dialog box.

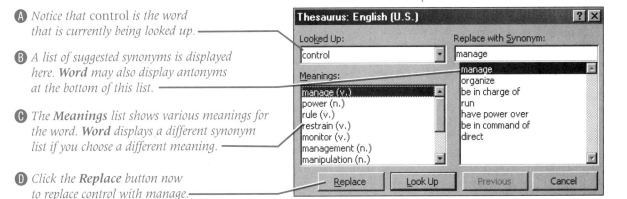

Ⓐ *Notice that* control *is the word that is currently being looked up.*

Ⓑ *A list of suggested synonyms is displayed here.* **Word** *may also display antonyms at the bottom of this list.*

Ⓒ *The* **Meanings** *list shows various meanings for the word.* **Word** *displays a different synonym list if you choose a different meaning.*

Ⓓ *Click the* **Replace** *button now to replace control with manage.*

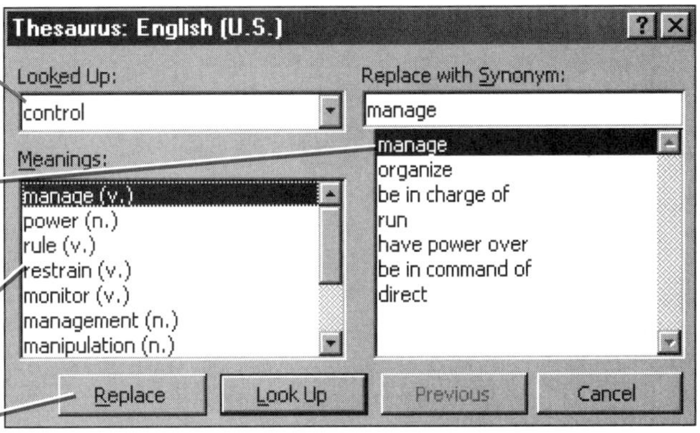

Thesaurus: English (U.S.)
Looked Up:
control
Replace with Synonym:
manage
Meanings:
manage (v.)
power (n.)
rule (v.)
restrain (v.)
monitor (v.)
management (n.)
manipulation (n.)
manage
organize
be in charge of
run
have power over
be in command of
direct
Replace
Look Up
Previous
Cancel

7. **Right-click** the word *manage,* and choose **control** from the Synonyms list on the pop-up menu.
8. Feel free to experiment with the thesaurus.
9. Save your document when you have finished experimenting.

Find and Replace

From the Keyboard

Press (CTRL)+F for Find
Press (CTRL)+H for Replace

Word's Find command lets you search a document for a particular word or phrase. You can also search for text formats, page breaks, and a variety of other items. Find is often the quickest way to locate a phrase, format, or item in a document. The Replace option lets you replace the found phrase, format, or item with a replacement phrase, format, or item. The Find and Replace dialog box is displayed with either the **Edit→Find** command or the **Edit→Replace** command.

Hands-On 9.6 Use Find

Find a Word

1. Position the insertion point at the top of the document, and make sure that no text is selected.
2. Choose **Edit→Find** from the menu bar.
3. Follow these steps to search for the word *pancreas*.

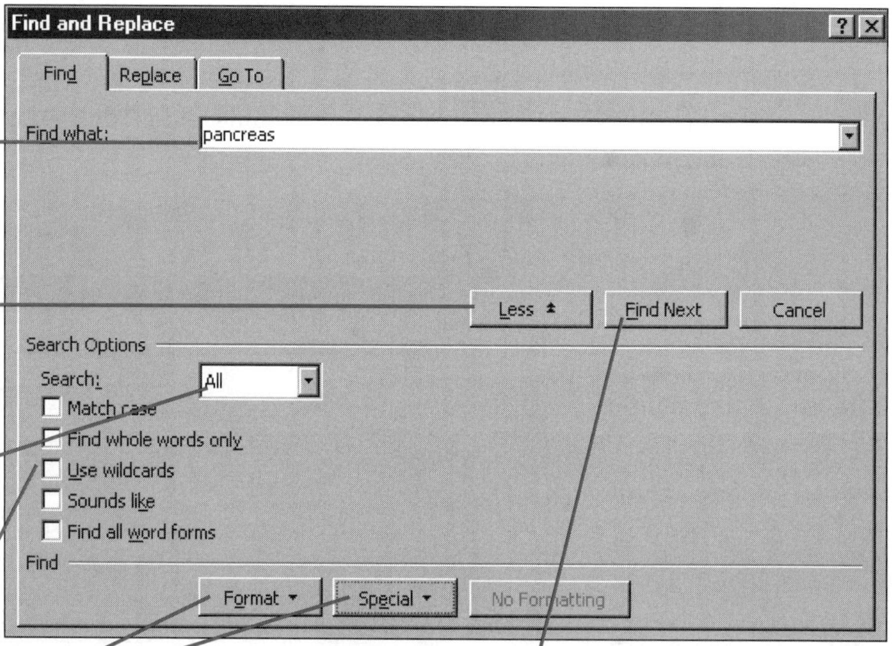

Find and Replace
Find
Replace
Go To
Find what:
pancreas
Less
Find Next
Cancel
Search Options
Search:
All
Match case
Find whole words only
Use wildcards
Sounds like
Find all word forms
Find
Format
Special
No Formatting

Ⓐ *Type* **pancreas** *in the* ***Find what*** *box. Notice the drop-down button. The drop-down button displays a list of previous words for which you have searched.*

Ⓑ *Click this button if it is labeled* ***More.*** *The* ***Search*** *and* ***Find*** *options will appear as shown here.*

Ⓒ *Make sure this option is set to* ***All.*** *You can search up or down from the insertion point or through the entire document.*

Ⓓ *Notice these check boxes. You will use these boxes later in this exercise.*

Ⓔ *These options let you search for formats and other types of elements.*

Ⓕ *Click the* ***Find Next*** *button to initiate the search.*

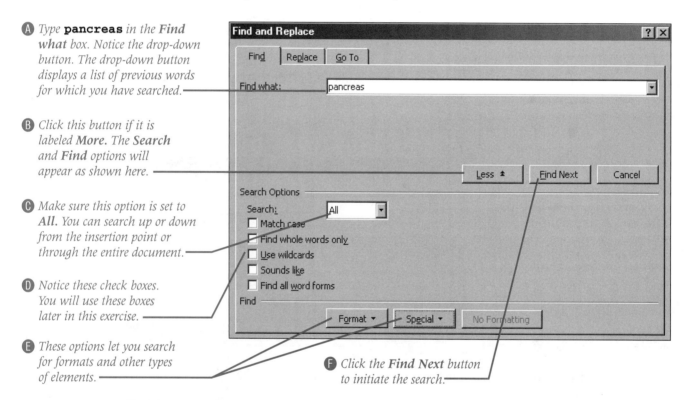

Find Another Word

4. Click in the **Find what** box, delete *pancreas* and type **With** (with a capital *W*) in its place.
5. Click the **Find Next** button, and *With* should be located in the second paragraph.
6. Click **Find Next** again, and the word *Without* should be located in the second paragraph. *Notice that* With *was found even though it is part of the word* Without. *By default,* ***Find*** *is not case-sensitive, and it doesn't recognize the difference between a whole word or part of the word. You will change this, however, in the next few steps.*

Use Match Case

7. Click the **Match case** check box under the search options.
This box instructs Word to find only occurrences of the search string with the same matching case.
8. Click the **Find Next** button, and Word will locate the capitalized word *With* further down in the document.
9. Click **Find Next** again, and the Office Assistant will indicate the entire document has been searched.
Word skipped over several occurrences of with in lowercase.
10. Uncheck the **Match case** check box.

Search for a Whole Word

11. Scroll to the top of the document, and click the insertion point anywhere on the document title. Notice you can scroll while the Find and Replace box is open, although you may need to move the box out of your way.
12. Check the **Find whole words only** check box.
13. Click **Find Next** several times until the Office Assistant indicates that the entire document has been searched.
Notice that the word without was not located this time.
14. Uncheck the **Find whole words only** check box.

Search for Text Formats and Tab Characters

Notice the Format and Special buttons at the bottom of the dialog box.

15. Click the **Special** button, and a list of items will appear.
You can search a document for the presence of any item.
16. Choose **Tab Character** (the second item on the list).
Word will place a ^t character in the Find what box. This character tells Word to search for a tab.
17. Click **Find Next.**
Word will select the space at the front of the credit line at the end of the document. A tab created this space.
18. Click the **Format** button at the bottom of the dialog box.
The Format button lets you search for specific fonts, paragraph formats, and other formats.
19. Choose **Font** from the list.
20. Choose **Bold** from the Font Style list, and click **OK.**
The words Format: Font: Bold *should appear below the Find what box.*
21. Remove the **^t** character from the Find what box; then **click** the **Find Next** button.
Word should select the title because it is in bold.
22. **Click** the **Cancel** button to close the Find and Replace dialog box.
23. Click anywhere on the title to remove the selection.

(Continued on the next page)

Use Replace

24. Press (CTRL)+H to display the Find and Replace dialog box.
    Notice that the Replace tab is active in the dialog box. The shortcut keystroke you use determines which tab displays when the dialog box appears. Notice that there are tabs for Find, Replace, and Go To. Go To is covered later in this lesson.

25. Click the **No Formatting** button at the bottom of the dialog box.
    This turns off the bold setting that you searched for in the previous exercise. In the next step, you will begin replacing the Roman numeral III with II.

26. Type the Roman numeral **III** (3 capital I's) in the **Find wha**t box and **II** in the **Replace** box.

27. Click the **Find Next** button.
    Word will locate and select the first occurrence of III.

28. Click the **Replace** button.
    Word replaces III with II and selects the next occurrence of III in the document.

29. Now click **Replace All**, and Word will replace all occurrences of III with II.
    The Office Assistant will display a pop-up message indicating the number of replacements that were made.

30. Click anywhere in the dialog box to close the pop-up message.
    Be careful with Replace All because you may make accidental replacements. For example, if you replace cat *with* dog, *then words like* catapult *may become* dogapult. *You should use the Find Whole Words Only option if the word you are replacing might be part of a larger word (like* cat *and* catapult*).*

31. Use Replace to replace all occurrences of the word *Boulder* with *Denver.* Make sure you type the word *Denver* with an uppercase D in the replace box. This way, it will be capitalized in the document.

32. Feel free to experiment with find and replace.

33. Close the Find and Replace dialog box when you have finished, but leave the document open.

Word Count

The word count feature counts the number of words, sentences, paragraphs, and pages in a document. Word count can be useful if you need to adjust your document to a specific length. For example, students who are creating reports or research papers often have length limitations. Word count is particularly useful to word processing professionals who bill clients by the word or page. You initiate word count with the **Tools→Word Count** command.

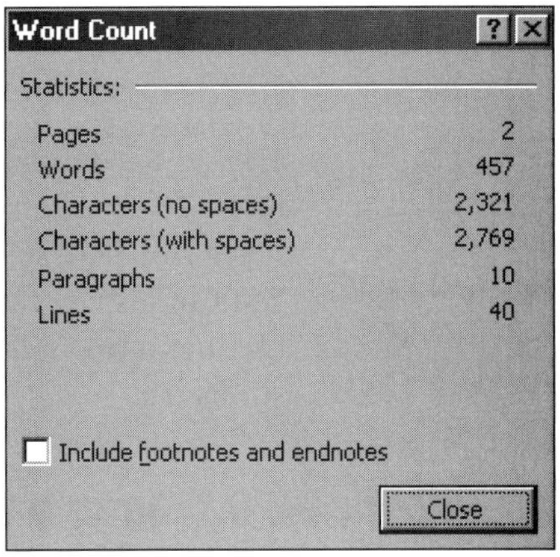

Word Count
Statistics:
Pages 2
Words 457
Characters (no spaces) 2,321
Characters (with spaces) 2,769
Paragraphs 10
Lines 40
Include footnotes and endnotes
Close

Word Count Statistics

Hands-On 9.7 Use Word Count

1. Click anywhere in the document to make sure no words are selected.
2. Choose **Tools→Word Count** from the menu bar.
   Word will analyze the document and display the statistics.
3. Take a few moments to study the results; then click the **Close** button.
4. Save the changes to the document; then close the document.

Recently Used File List

Word and other Office applications list up to nine of the most recently used files at the bottom of the File menu. You can open any of these documents by choosing them from the list. This is often the most efficient way to open a recently used document. The following Quick Reference steps explain how to adjust the number of files displayed on the recently used file list.

MODIFYING THE RECENTLY USED FILE LIST

- Choose Tools→Options from the menu bar.
- Click the General tab.
- Adjust the number of entries in the *Recently used file list* box.

Hands-On 9.8 Use the Recently Used Files List

1. Choose **File** from the menu bar.
   You will notice up to nine recently used documents are listed at the bottom of the menu. The Hands-On Lesson 3 document should be at the top of the list because you used it in the previous exercise.
2. Choose **Hands-On Lesson 9** from the list, and the document will open.
   Leave the document open; you will continue to use it in the next exercise.

The Go To Command

From the Keyboard

CTRL+G to display Go To dialog box

The Go To command lets you rapidly locate a specific page in a document. Go To can also be used to locate objects (which you have not learned about) such as bookmarks, tables, footnotes, and endnotes. You choose the object you wish to go to in the Go To tab of the Find and Replace dialog box. You can display the Go To tab of the Find and Replace dialog box by choosing **Edit→Go To** from the menu bar. You can also display the Go To tab by double-clicking the page number section of the status bar.

Hands-On 9.9 Go to a Page

Use the Keyboard

1. Press CTRL+G, and the Go To tab of the Find and Replace dialog box will appear.
2. Type **2** into the Enter page number box, and click the **Go To** button.
   The insertion point should move to the top of page 2.
3. Click the **Close** button on the dialog box.

Use the Status Bar

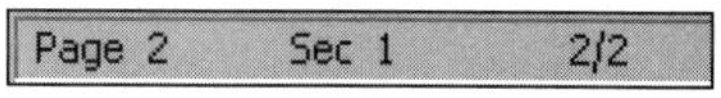

Page 2
Sec 1
2/2

4. Double-click anywhere on the page number section of the status bar to display the Go To tab of the Find and Replace dialog box.
   Notice that you can go to other locations, such as Sections, Lines, etc.
5. Type **1** into the Enter Page Number box, and then click the **Go To** button.
6. Close the Find and Replace dialog box.

Hyphenation

Word lets you hyphenate text automatically or manually. With **automatic** hyphenation, Word hyphenates words whenever it determines that hyphenation is necessary. With **manual** hyphenation, Word searches the document for words to hyphenate. When a word requiring hyphenation is located, Word prompts you to confirm the hyphen location within the word. Hyphenation is most useful in documents with short line lengths, such as documents containing newspaper style columns.

Quick Reference

HYPHENATING TEXT

To Hyphenate a Document Automatically:

- Choose Tools→Language→Hyphenation from the menu bar.
- Check the *Automatically hyphenate document box,* and click OK.

To Hyphenate a Document Manually:

- Choose Tools→Language→Hyphenation from the menu bar.
- Click the Manual button.
- If Word identifies a word to hyphenate and you want the hyphen positioned at the location Word proposes, click Yes. If you want the hyphen positioned at a different location in the word, then use the arrow keys on the keyboard to adjust the position, and then click Yes.

The Hyphenation Zone

The Hyphenation dialog box contains a Hyphenation Zone setting. The hyphenation zone lets you adjust the sensitivity of the hyphenation. You can widen the hyphenation zone by entering a larger number in the Hyphenation Zone box. This will reduce the number of words that are hyphenated. Likewise, you can increase the number of words that are hyphenated by entering a smaller number for the hyphenation zone.

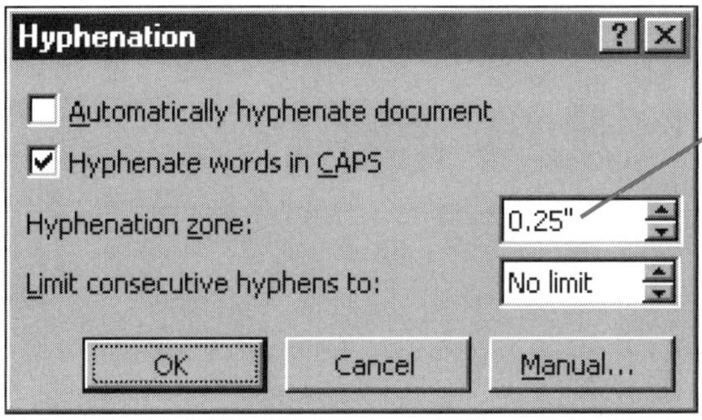
Hyphenation
Automatically hyphenate document
Hyphenate words in CAPS
Hyphenation zone:
0.25"
Limit consecutive hyphens to:
No limit
OK
Cancel
Manual...

*Increasing the **Hyphenation zone** decreases the number of hyphenated words and vice-versa.*

Nonbreaking Hyphens Nonbreaking Spaces

Some phrases (such as *easy-to-use*) require hyphens between the words in the phrase. You can use nonbreaking hyphens to ensure that all words in the phrase stay together on the same line. If you use nonbreaking hyphens and there is not enough space on a line for the entire phrase, then Word will move the entire phrase to the beginning of the next line. You insert nonbreaking hyphens with the (CTRL)+(SHIFT)+Hyphen keystroke combination. Likewise, you can insert nonbreaking spaces with the (CTRL)+(SHIFT)+(SPACE BAR) keystroke combination.

Hands-On 9.10 Use Hyphenation

1. Browse through the document and notice that there is only one hyphenated word at the end of the lines.
   This is because automatic hyphenation is turned off. Any words currently hyphenated in the document had the hyphens inserted when the document was created.
2. Scroll to the top of the document, and click on the title.
3. Choose **Tools→Language→Hyphenation** from the menu bar.
4. Make sure the hyphenation zone setting is set to .25″, and click the **Automatically hyphenate document** check box.
5. Click **OK**, and browse through the document counting the number of end-of-line hyphens.
   You will increase the hyphenation zone setting in the next few steps and notice how this affects the number of hyphens.
6. Choose **Tools→Language→Hyphenation** from the menu bar.
7. Set the hyphenation zone to .5″ and click **OK.**
8. Browse through the document, count the number of hyphens.
   The number of hyphens should have been reduced.

(Continued on the next page)

9. Choose **Tools→Language→Hyphenation** from the menu bar.
10. Uncheck the **Automatically hyphenate document** box, and click **OK.**
11. Browse through the document and notice that all automatic hyphens have been removed. *The only hyphens that remain are for words that were manually hyphenated when the document was created.*
12. Save the document, close it, and continue with the end-of-lesson questions and exercises.

CONCEPTS REVIEW

True/False Questions

1. The Office Assistant cannot be turned off in Word 2000.	TRUE	FALSE
2. Word marks misspelled words with wavy red underlines.	TRUE	FALSE
3. You can correct a misspelled word by clicking it with the left mouse button and choosing a suggested replacement from the pop-up menu.	TRUE	FALSE
4. The Ignore All command on the Spelling and Grammar dialog boxignores a misspelled word for the current spell check only.	TRUE	FALSE
5. The spell checker can identify certain types of capitalization errors.	TRUE	FALSE
6. The Go To command can be initiated by pressing ALT+G.	TRUE	FALSE
7. The thesaurus lets you find and replace misspelled words.	TRUE	FALSE
8. Increasing the hyphenation zone measurement increases the number of hyphenated words.	TRUE	FALSE

Multiple-Choice Questions

1. Which of the following statements is true?
   a. The spell checker uses only a main dictionary.
   b. The only time a custom dictionary is used is with legal documents.
   c. The spell checker uses a main and custom dictionary for all spell checks.
   d. None of the above

2. Which command initiates Word Count?
   a. Tools→Word Count
   b. Edit→Word Count
   c. Format→Word Count
   d. None of the above

3. What will happen if the Office Assistant is turned off and you click the Help button on the Standard toolbar?
   a. The Office Assistant will appear.
   b. You will receive an error message.
   c. The online Help window will appear.
   d. The Save dialog box will appear.

4. On which menu is a list of the most recently used documents displayed?
   a. File
   b. Edit
   c. Insert
   d. Format

Skill Builders

Skill Builder 9.1 Use the Office Assistant and Online Help

1. Make sure the Office Assistant is displayed. If it isn't displayed, use the **Help→Show the Office Assistant** command.
2. Click the Assistant to display the speech balloon.
3. Type the phrase `Office Clipboard` in the search box, and click the Search button.
4. Click the **View the contents of the Office Clipboard** topic that appears.
5. Take a moment to read the topic, and notice the word *docked* is displayed in color.
6. Clicked the word *docked* and take a moment to read the definition that pops up.
7. Close the definition by clicking in the Help window.
8. If necessary, click the Office Assistant to display the speech balloon.
9. Use the Assistant to locate the Help topic **Create and use custom dictionaries.**
10. Click the **Create and use custom dictionaries** topic, then click the **Creating and using custom dictionaries** hyperlink in the Help window.
11. Take a moment to read the topic, then click the Back button on the Help toolbar to return to the previous topic screen.
    You can always use the Back and Forward buttons to revisit topics.
12. Click the Show button to display the tabs in the Help window.
13. Click the Contents tab.
    The Contents tab contains a list of books that you can expand or collapse to locate a Help topic. This method is most useful if you have a general idea of the topic you are trying to locate but don't know the name of the topic.
14. Click the plus + sign to the left of the **What's New?** book at the top of the window.
    The book will open, displaying a single topic.
15. Click the **What's new in Microsoft Word 2000?** topic to display a list of topics in the right pane of the Help window.
16. Feel free to click any topic to find out about the new features in Word 2000. When you have finished reading a topic, use the Back button to return to the list of new features in Word 2000.
17. Feel free to experiment with Online Help and the Office Assistant.
18. When you have finished, close the Help window, and continue with the next exercise.

Skill Builder 9.2 Spell Checking/Find and Replace

1. Start a new document, and type the business letter shown below. Use Word's automatic spell checking and grammar checking as you type the letter. Format the text with bold and italics as shown.

> Today's date
>
> Mr. Juan Lopez
> Editor-in-Chief
> Western Wildlife Publications
> 1450 Parker Lane
> Ventura, CA 93003
>
> Dear Mr. Lopez:
>
> A short time ago, I subscribed to *Birds of Prey* magazine and I am enjoying it immensely. Your monthly tips have been especially useful. I have spotted more than twenty new species in my local area since I first subscribed to *Birds of Prey*. **Keep up the good work!**
>
> One thing that I would like to see more of in *Birds of Prey* is recommendations on bird watching sites in the Western United States. I am especially interested in bald eagles and golden eagles. I would appreciate any suggestions you may have.
>
> Sincerely,
>
> Jason Torval
> 450 Lighthouse Lane
> Manhattan Beach, CA 90266

2. Press CTRL+H to open the Find and Replace dialog box.
3. Replace all occurrences of *Birds of Prey* with *Bird Watcher.*
   Word should automatically italicize the phrase Bird Watcher *because* Birds of Prey *was italicized.*
4. Make sure there are no spelling errors in the document.
5. Save the document with the name **Skill Builder 9.2,** then close the document.

Skill Builder 9.3 Using the Thesaurus

In this exercise, you will modify the letter you created in the previous exercise.

1. Choose **File** from the menu bar, and then choose Skill Builder 9.2 from the list of recently used files.
   Suppose you want to use a word other than especially *in the second paragraph.*
2. **Right-click** anywhere on the word *especially* in the second paragraph.
3. Choose **Synonyms** from the pop-up menu, and then choose **particularly**.
4. Use the thesaurus to find replacements for the word **useful** in the first paragraph and **appreciate** in the second paragraph.
5. Select the phrase **A short time ago** at the beginning of the first paragraph.
6. **Right-click** the selected phrase.
7. Choose the replacement phrase *not long ago,* from the Synonym list.
   Notice that Word replaces the phrase but does not capitalize the first word of the sentence.
8. Click Undo to restore the original phrase.
9. Choose **Tools→Language→Thesaurus** from the menu bar.
10. Choose the replacement phrase *not long ago,* and click **Replace.**
    In this case, Word should have replaced the phrase and capitalized the first word of the sentence. This is one minor advantage to using the dialog box over the right-click method.
11. Choose **File→Save As** from the menu bar.
    This command can be used to save a document under a new name.
12. Change the name Skill Builder 9.2 in the filename box to **Skill Builder 9.3,** and click the Save button.
    The Skill Builder 9.2 file remains unchanged, and Skill Builder 9.3 now also resides on your diskette.
13. Close the document, and continue with the next exercise.

Skill Builder 9.4 Editing a Business Letter

1. Open the document on your exercise diskette named Skill Builder 9.4.
2. Use Find and Replace to replace all occurrences of the word *bill* with *account.*
3. Use Find and Replace to replace all occurrences of the word *payment* with *check.*
4. Spell check the entire document.
5. Select the entire document, and change the font size to 12.
6. Use ENTER to start the date line at approximately the 2″ position.
7. Replace the phrase Today's Date with the current date.
8. Move the address block from the bottom of the letter to the space between the last body paragraph and the complimentary close (Sincerely). If necessary, insert or remove hard returns until there is a double space between the address block and the last body paragraph, and between the address block and the complimentary close (sincerely).
9. Center the three address block lines horizontally on the page.
10. Insert your typist's initials and the document name below the signature block.
11. Save the changes; then close the document.

Assessments

Assessment 9.1

1. Open the document on your exercise diskette named Assessment 9.1.
2. Spell check the document. Use your best judgment to determine which replacement words to use for incorrectly spelled words. Assume all proper names are spelled correctly.
3. Use Find and Replace to make the following replacements. Also, write the number of replacements in the third column of the table.

Word	Replace With	Number of Replacements
Mary	Chitra	______________
arthritis	cancer	______________

4. Print the document when you have finished.
5. Save the changes; then close the document.

Assessment 9.2

1. Open the document on your exercise diskette named Assessment 9.2.
2. Replace the phrase Today's Date with the current date, using the Date and Time feature. Insert the date as a field so that it updates automatically.
3. Spell check the document. Use your best judgment to determine which replacement words to use for incorrectly spelled words. Assume all proper names are spelled correctly.
4. Use Find and Replace to make the following replacements. Make sure the case (lowercase or uppercase) remains the same for all replacements. Also, write the number of replacements in the third column of the table.

Word or phrase	**Replace With**	**Number of Replacements**
Dan	Mr. Heywood	____________
Do not replace Dan in the inside address		
families	people	____________
special consideration	something special	____________

5. Print the document when you have finished.
6. Save the changes; then close the document.

LESSON 10—Word

Creating a Simple Report

In this lesson, you will create a simple report. Reports are important documents often used in business and education. You will format your report using various paragraph formatting techniques. Paragraphs are a fundamental part of any Word document. You will learn how to use Word 2000's new Click and Type feature and change line spacing. In addition, you will master indenting techniques using the ruler and the indent buttons on the Formatting toolbar. This lesson will prepare you for more advanced report techniques discussed in the next lesson.

In This Lesson

Case Study

Bill Nelson is a freshman at West Side Junior College. Bill has enrolled in an information systems course in which Office 2000 is an important component. Bill has been assigned the task of preparing a report on the importance of computer technology in the twenty-first century. Professor Williams has instructed Bill to use Word 2000. After conducting the necessary research, Bill uses the paragraph formatting techniques in Word 2000 to prepare a report that is easy to read, properly formatted, and has a professional appearance.

COMPUTER TECHNOLOGY IN THE TWENTY-FIRST CENTURY

Our society has changed from a manufacturing-oriented society to an information society. Those with access to capital had power in the early 1900s. In the twenty-first century, however, power will come from access to information. The amount of worldwide information is growing at a rapid pace. Computer technology is responsible for much of this growth, but it can also help us manage the information.

Information management is an important use of computer technology. Daryl Richardson of Harmond Technology describes four other reasons why the average person may want to acquire thorough knowledge of computers.

> Computer skills are becoming more important in the business world. Many companies need employees with excellent computer skills.
>
> The Internet and other information resources provide access to a global database of information.
>
> Computer skills can often simplify ones personal life. Computers can be used to entertain, to manage finances, and to provide stimulating learning exercises for children.
>
> Using computers can provide a sense of accomplishment. Many people suffer from "computerphobia." Learning to use computers often creates a feeling of connection with the information age.

Report Formats

Overview

There are a variety of acceptable report formats. The example below shows a traditional business report in unbound format. Other report formats can be used for research papers and other types of documents.

Traditional Unbound Business Report Format

Double-spacing is typically set before beginning the report. Three double-spaced returns are used to space the title down to approximately the 2" position.

The title is typed in uppercase, centered, and bold face. You can also apply a distinctive font to the title.

The body of the report is double-spaced. The first line of each body paragraph is indented to 0.5".

Quotations and other text you wish to emphasize are single-spaced and indented 0.5" to 1" on the left and right. You should double-space (by tapping ENTER twice) between quotes.

COMPUTER TECHNOLOGY IN THE TWENTY-FIRST CENTURY

Our society has changed from a manufacturing-oriented society to an information society. Those with access to capital had power in the early 1900s. In the twenty-first century, however, power will come from access to information. The amount of worldwide information is growing at a rapid pace. Computer technology is responsible for much of this growth, but it can also help us manage the information.

Information management is an important use of computer technology. Daryl Richardson of Harmond Technology describes four other reasons why the average person may want to acquire thorough knowledge of computers.

> Computer skills are becoming more important in the business world. Many companies need employees with excellent computer skills.
>
> The Internet and other information resources provide access to a global database of information.
>
> Computer skills can often simplify ones personal life. Computers can be used to entertain, to manage finances, and to provide stimulating learning exercises for children.
>
> Using computers can provide a sense of accomplishment. Many people suffer from "computerphobia." Learning to use computers often creates a feeling of connection with the information age.

Click and Type

Click and Type is a new feature in Word 2000 that lets you automatically apply formatting in blank areas of a document. Click and Type lets you set paragraph alignments (Align Left, Center, and Align Right), customize tab stops, insert tables, and apply other formats. To use Click and Type, position the mouse pointer in a blank area of a document and double-click. Click and Type inserts hard returns and adjusts the paragraph alignment as necessary to achieve the formatting you desire. Click and Type is only available in Print Layout and Web Layout views. The following illustrations demonstrate the use of Click and Type.

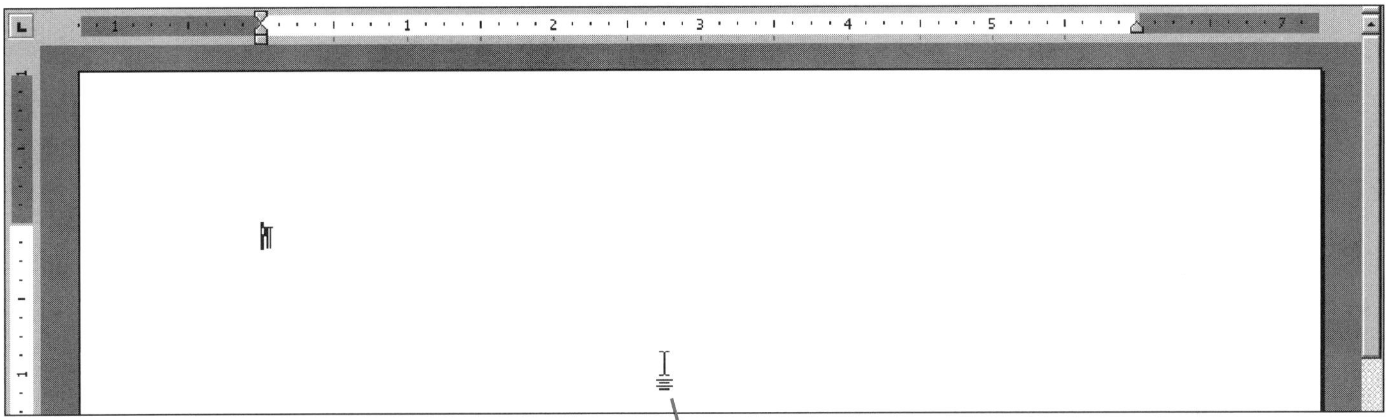

With Click and Type, the mouse pointer changes shape to reflect the formatting that will be applied when you double-click. In this example, the mouse pointer shows that center alignment will be applied.

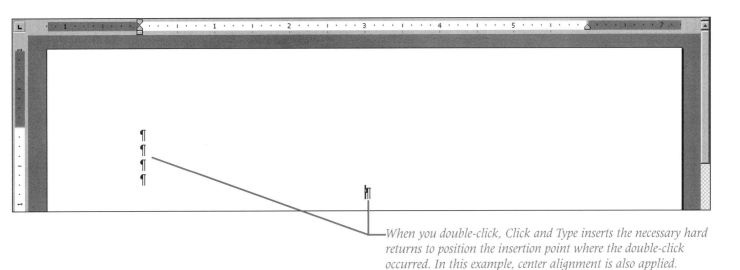

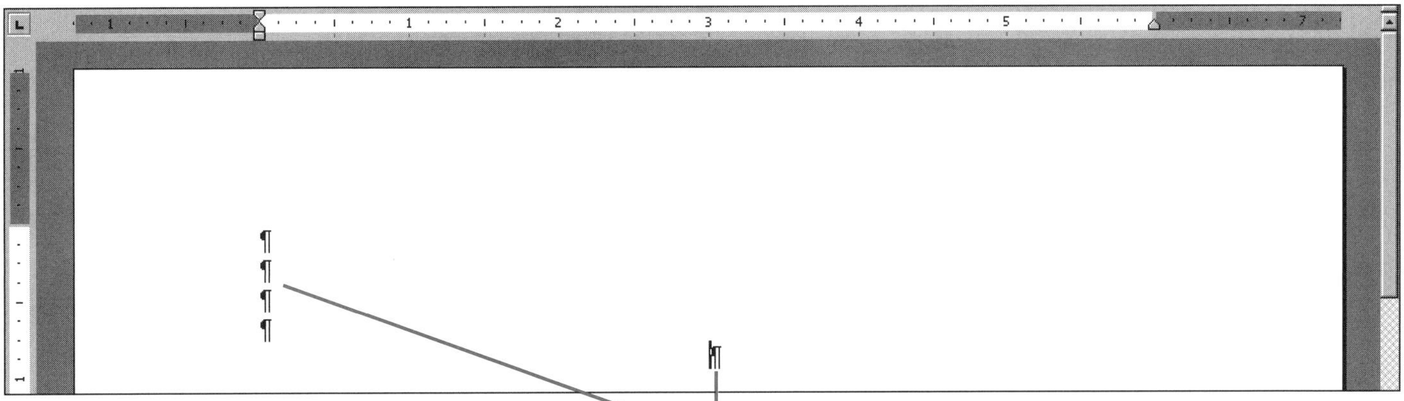

When you double-click, Click and Type inserts the necessary hard returns to position the insertion point where the double-click occurred. In this example, center alignment is also applied.

Hands-On 10.1 Use Click and Type

1. Start Word, and a blank document window will appear.
2. Make sure you are in Print Layout view. If necessary, use the View→Print Layout command to switch to Print Layout view.
3. Slide the mouse pointer to various locations in the blank document, and notice how the mouse pointer changes shape.
   The align left or align right shapes reflect the formatting that would be applied if you were to double-click.
4. Click the Show All ¶ button to display the symbols.
5. Make sure the ruler is displayed at the top of the document window. If necessary, use the View→Ruler command to display the ruler.
6. Follow these steps to use Click and Type to format the title line of the report.

(A) Position the mouse pointer approximately 2" down and centered on the line. You can tell you are two inches down by looking at the vertical ruler. The 1" position on the white section of the vertical ruler means you are 2" down on the page. This is because the ruler's white section begins at the top margin, which is already 1" down from the top of the page.

(B) Double-click when the mouse pointer has the center alignment shape, as shown here.

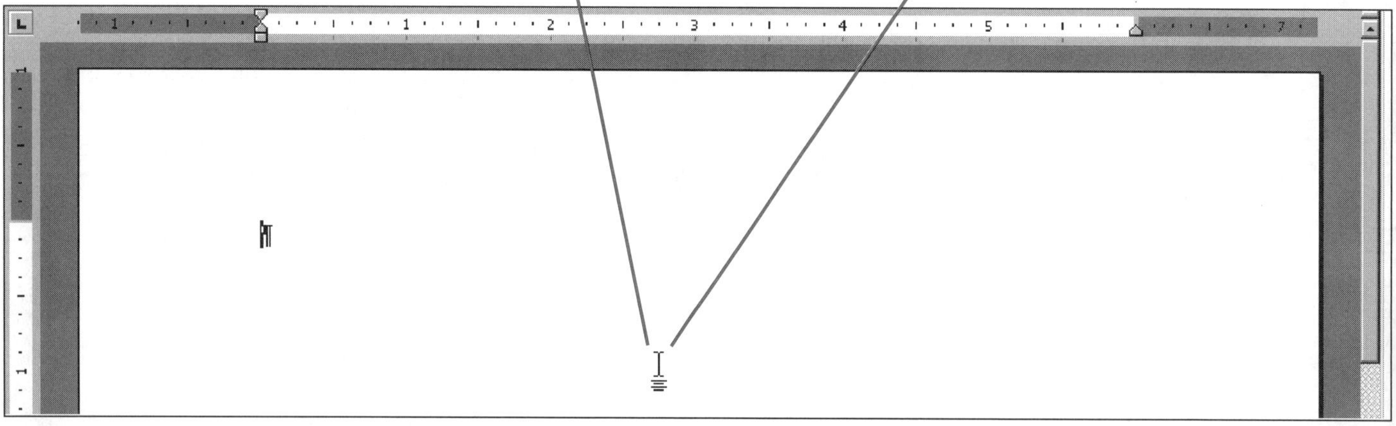

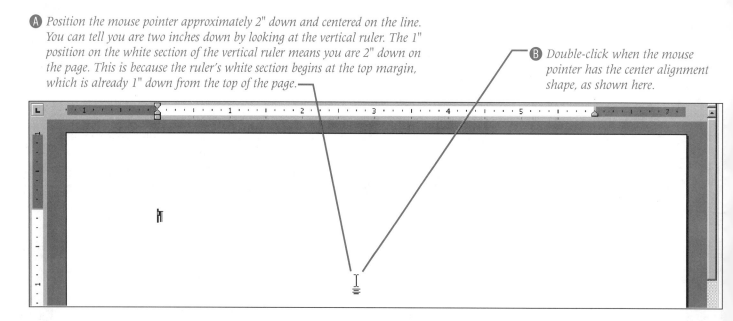

Word inserts paragraph marks as necessary and applies center alignment. Check the Status bar at the bottom of the window to ensure the insertion point is at approximately the 2″ position. As you can see, Click and Type can be useful for rapidly applying formats. However, it does lack the precision that may be required for formatting some types of documents.

7. If the insertion point is not at the 2″ position, use ENTER to insert hard returns as necessary to force it to the 2″ position.
8. Turn on CAPS LOCK, and click the Bold **B** button.
9. Type the report title **`COMPUTER TECHNOLOGY IN THE TWENTY-FIRST CENTURY`**.
10. Turn off Bold, and tap ENTER twice.

11. Slide the mouse pointer to the left end of the current line.

12. Double-click when the mouse pointer has this shape.
The alignment should change to left, and the insertion point should be positioned two lines below the title. Use Undo and try again if the alignment is not set to left.

13. Save the document to your exercise diskette with the name **Hands-On Lesson 10.**

Line Spacing

From the Keyboard

CTRL+1 for single spacing
CTRL+5 for 1.5 spacing
CTRL+2 for double spacing

Line spacing determines the amount of vertical space between lines in a paragraph. The default line spacing is single. Word makes a single-spaced line slightly higher than the largest character in the line. For example, if you are using a 12-point font, then single line spacing is slightly larger than 12 points. You apply line spacing by selecting the desired paragraph(s) and choosing the desired line spacing from the Paragraph dialog box. The following table describes Word's line spacing options.

Line Spacing	Description
Single	Default spacing in Word
1.5 Lines	1.5 times single-spacing
Double	Twice single-spacing
At Least	Specifies the minimum line spacing. The spacing may increase if the font size increases. However, the line spacing will never be smaller than the number of points specified in the At Least setting.
Exactly	Fixes the line spacing at the number of points specified. The line spacing remains fixed even if the font size of characters within the line changes.
Multiple	Lets you precisely control the line spacing by setting multiples such as 1.3 or 2.4.

Hands-On 10.2 Set Line Spacing

1. Make sure the insertion point is on the second blank line below the title.

2. Choose **Format→Paragraph** from the menu bar.

3. Click the Line spacing drop-down button, and notice the various options.

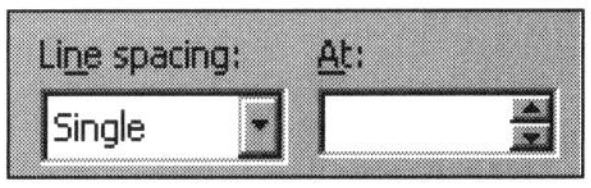
Line spacing:
At:
Single

4. Choose **Double** from the list, and click **OK.**

5. Tap the TAB key once to create a 0.5″ indent at the start of the paragraph.

(Continued on the next page)

6. Now type the following paragraph, but only tap ENTER after the last line in the paragraph.
   The lines will be double-spaced as you type them.

> Our society has changed from a manufacturing-oriented society to an information society. Those with access to capital had power in the early 1900s. In the twenty-first century, however, power will come from access to information. The amount of worldwide information is growing at a rapid pace. Computer technology is responsible for much of this growth, but it can also help us manage the information.

7. Make sure you tap ENTER after the last line. Then TAB once, and type the following paragraph.
   Notice the double-spacing has been carried to the new paragraph.

> Information management is an important use of computer technology. Daryl Richardson of Harmond Technology describes four other reasons why the average person may want to acquire thorough knowledge of computers.

8. Tap ENTER to complete the paragraph, then press CTRL+1 to set single-spacing.
   The shortcut keystrokes can be quite useful for setting line spacing.
9. Now type the following paragraphs, tapping ENTER twice between paragraphs. There is no need to tab at the beginning of these paragraphs.

> Computer skills are becoming more important in the business world. Many companies need employees with excellent computer skills.
>
> The Internet and other information resources provide access to a global database of information.
>
> Computer skills can often simplify one's personal life. Computers can be used to entertain, to manage finances, and to provide stimulating learning exercises for children.
>
> Using computers can provide a sense of accomplishment. Many people suffer from "computerphobia." Learning to use computers often creates a feeling of connection with the information age.

10. Save the changes, and continue with the next topic.

Indenting Text

Indenting offsets text from the margins. The **left indent** is the most widely used indent. The left indent sets off all lines in a paragraph from the left margin. Likewise, the **right indent** sets off all lines from the right margin. The **first line indent** sets off just the first line of paragraphs. This is similar to using TAB at the start of a paragraph. The **hanging indent** sets off all lines except for the first line.

From the Keyboard

CTRL+M for left indent
CTRL+SHIFT+M to remove left indent
CTRL+T for hanging indent
CTRL+SHIFT+T to remove hanging indent

The Increase Indent button and Decrease Indent button on the Formatting toolbar let you adjust the **left** indent. These buttons increase or decrease the left indent to the nearest tab stop. The default tab stops are set every 0.5″, so the left indent changes 0.5″ each time you click the buttons. You can also set indents using keystrokes, the Paragraph dialog box, and by dragging indent markers on the horizontal ruler.

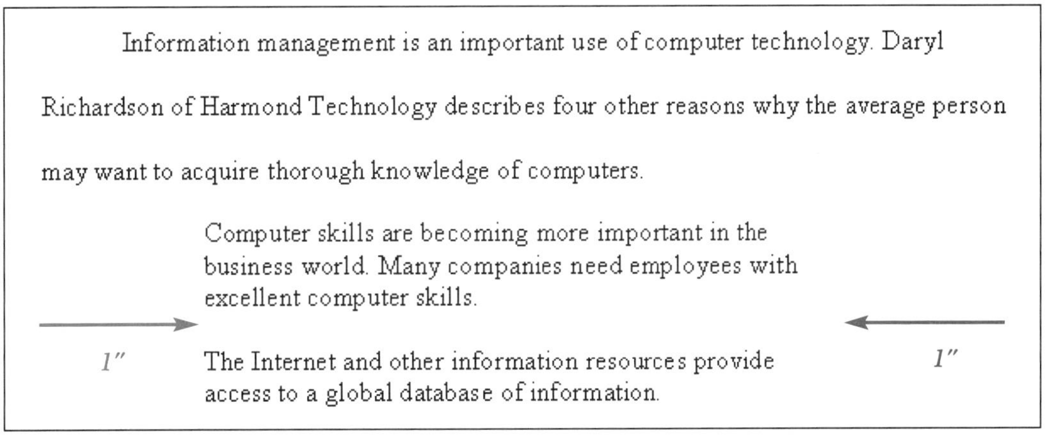
Information management is an important use of computer technology. Daryl Richardson of Harmond Technology describes four other reasons why the average person may want to acquire thorough knowledge of computers.

Computer skills are becoming more important in the business world. Many companies need employees with excellent computer skills.

1″ The Internet and other information resources provide access to a global database of information. 1″

These paragraphs are indented 1″ from the left and right margins.

Hands-On 10.3 Experiment with Left Indents

Indent One Paragraph

1. Click on one of the single-spaced paragraphs you just typed.
2. Click the Increase Indent button near the right end of the Formatting toolbar.
   The paragraph should be indented 0.5″ on the left.
3. Click the Decrease Indent button to remove the indent.

Indent Several Paragraphs

4. Use the mouse to select any part of two or more paragraphs.
   You only need to select part of a paragraph when indenting or applying other paragraph formats.
5. Click Increase Indent **twice** to create a 1″ left indent on each of the selected paragraphs.
6. Now click Decrease Indent **twice** to remove the indents.
   You will continue to work with indents in the next Hands-On exercise.

The Horizontal Ruler

You can set indents, margins, and tab stops by dragging markers on the horizontal ruler. When you use the ruler, you can see formatting changes as they are applied. The horizontal ruler is positioned just above the document in the document window. You can display or hide the ruler with the **View→Ruler** command. The following illustration shows the ruler, the margin boundaries, and the various indent markers.

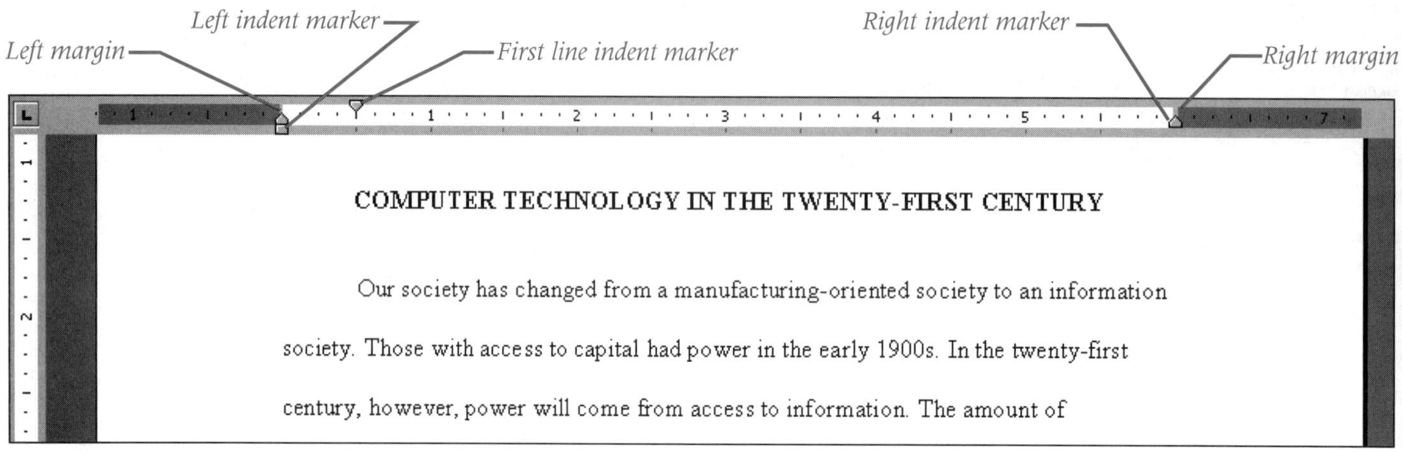

Left indent marker
Left margin
First line indent marker
Right indent marker
Right margin
COMPUTER TECHNOLOGY IN THE TWENTY-FIRST CENTURY
Our society has changed from a manufacturing-oriented society to an information
society. Those with access to capital had power in the early 1900s. In the twenty-first
century, however, power will come from access to information. The amount of

Quick Reference

INDENT MARKERS

Indent Type	How to Set It
First line	Drag this marker.
Hanging	Drag the top triangle.
Left	Drag the bottom square.
Right	Drag this marker on the right end of the ruler.

Hands-On 10.4 Use the Ruler to Indent Paragraphs

Set Left and Right Indents

1. If necessary, scroll down until the four single-spaced paragraphs at the bottom of your document are visible.
2. Select all four paragraphs by dragging the mouse pointer in the left margin.

3. Use the following steps to adjust the left and right indents.

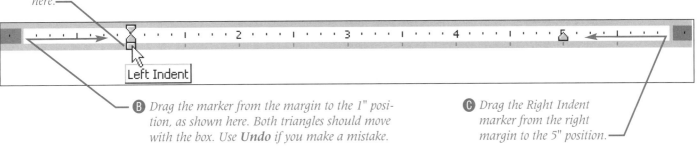

Ⓐ *Position the pointer on the Left Indent marker (the bottom box). A yellow* Left Indent *ScreenTip will appear, as shown here.*

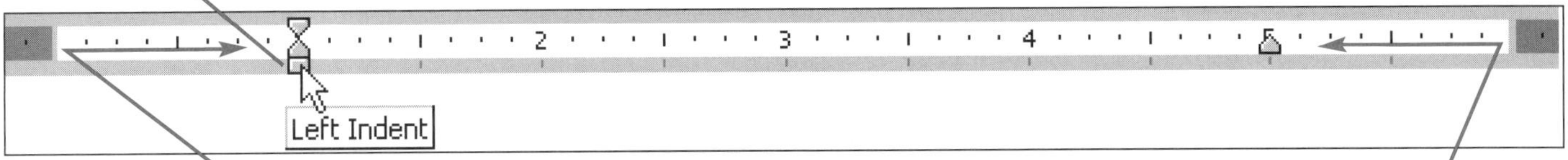
2
3
4
Left Indent

Ⓑ *Drag the marker from the margin to the 1" position, as shown here. Both triangles should move with the box. Use* **Undo** *if you make a mistake.*

Ⓒ *Drag the Right Indent marker from the right margin to the 5" position.*

Convert Tab Stops to First Line Indents

4. Scroll to the top of the document.
5. Make sure the nonprinting characters are displayed in your document. If necessary, use the Show All button to display the nonprinting characters.
   In the next step, you are instructed to remove the tab → symbol from the start of the first paragraph. You should have inserted the tab when you created the paragraph. It is possible that your paragraph will not have a tab symbol (even if it is indented). Skip the following step if there is no tab symbol.
6. Follow these steps to remove the tab symbol at the start of the first body paragraph.

   Ⓐ *Click to the left of the tab symbol.*

   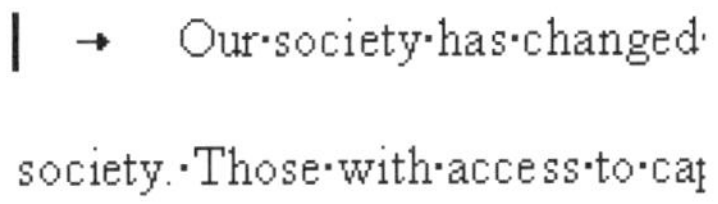
   Our·society·has·changed·
society.·Those·with·access·to·ca

   Ⓑ *Tap the* DELETE *key.*

   The space created by the tab should be removed from the first line.
7. Make sure the insertion point is at the start of the paragraph and tap the TAB key.
   The first line will be indented 0.5" although you won't see a tab → symbol in the document. The First Line Indent marker should have moved to the 0.5" position on the ruler. Word 2000 automatically creates a first line indent when you tap the TAB *key at the start of an existing paragraph. This has the same effect as inserting a tab symbol. This feature is known as AutoIndent.*
8. Use the technique in Step 6 to remove the tab → symbol from the beginning of the second double-spaced paragraph.
9. Now drag the First Line Indent marker to the 0.5" position on the ruler.
   The paragraph should have the same 0.5" indent as the first paragraph. As you can see, there are several ways to indent the first line of a paragraph.

(Continued on the next page)

Experiment with the Indent Markers

10. Select both of the double-spaced paragraphs.
11. Drag the First Line Indent marker to the left or right.
The first line indent of both paragraphs will be adjusted.
12. Make sure the paragraphs are still selected, and drag the Left Indent marker (bottom square).
The left indent affects all lines in the paragraph because it moves both the First Line Indent marker and the Hanging Indent marker.
13. Feel free to experiment with indents, but restore the 0.5" first line indents when you have finished.
14. Save the changes to your document, and then close the document.

Concepts Review

True/False Questions

1. The Increase Indent button changes the right indent. TRUE FALSE
2. The Decrease Indent button changes the right indent. TRUE FALSE
3. The ruler can be used to indent paragraphs. TRUE FALSE
4. The CTRL+D keystroke combination is used to set double-spacing. TRUE FALSE
5. The CTRL+1 keystroke combination is used to set single-spacing. TRUE FALSE
6. The Ruler is displayed with the Edit→Ruler command. TRUE FALSE
7. First Line indents only affect the first line of each selected paragraph. TRUE FALSE
8. The title begins 2″ from the top of the page in a traditional business report. TRUE FALSE

Multiple-Choice Questions

1. In which of the following view modes is Click and Type available?
   a. Print Layout
   b. Web Layout
   c. Outline
   d. Both a and b

2. What will happen if you tap the TAB key at the beginning of an existing paragraph?
   a. The Left indent will increase.
   b. The First Line indent will increase.
   c. A tab symbol will be inserted.
   d. None of the above

3. Which of the following actions should you take to adjust the right indent of three paragraphs?
   a. Drag the Right Indent marker.
   b. Select the paragraphs, and then drag the Right Indent marker.
   c. Select the paragraphs, and tap the Tab key.
   d. All of the above

4. Which command is used to display the horizontal ruler?
   a. View→Ruler
   b. Edit→Display Ruler
   c. Insert→Ruler
   d. File→Ruler

Skill Builders

Skill Builder 10.1 Indents and Line Spacing

1. Start a new document, and choose **Format→Paragraph** from the menu bar.
2. Set the line spacing to double, and click **OK.**
3. Click the Center button, and tap (ENTER) three times to double-space down to the 2″ position.
4. Set the font to Arial, bold, 12pt, and type the title shown below.
5. Tap (ENTER), and set the alignment to left.
6. Turn off bold and set the font size to 11.
7. Type the first paragraph shown below, tapping (ENTER) once at the end of the paragraph.
8. Choose **Format→Paragraph** from the menu bar, and set the line spacing to single and the left and right indents to 1″.
   The Paragraph dialog box is useful when setting several options, or when you want to precisely set line spacing, indents, or other options.
9. Click Italics and type the quotations shown below. Use the Em Dash symbol from the Symbols dialog box between the end of paragraph periods and the author's names. Do not use italics on the author's names.

FAMOUS AMERICAN QUOTATIONS

Quotations have the power to inspire and define moments in our history. They are windows into the minds and lives of great people. Famous Americans certainly have contributed their share of famous quotations.

> *There was never yet an uninteresting life. Such a thing is an impossibility. Inside of the dullest exterior, there is a drama, a comedy, and a tragedy.*—Mark Twain
>
> *We hold these truths to be sacred and undeniable; that all men are created equal and independent, that from that equal creation they derive rights inherent and inalienable, among which are the preservation of life, and liberty, and the pursuit of happiness.*—Thomas Jefferson
>
> *I think, at a child's birth, if a mother could ask a fairy godmother to endow it with the most useful gift, that gift would be curiosity.*—Eleanor Roosevelt

10. Save the document with the name **Skill Builder 10.1.**
    You will continue to use the document in the next exercise.

Skill Builder 10.2 Add Another Quotation

In this exercise, you will add a new quotation, and a paragraph to the Skill Builder 10.1 document. The document should be open from the previous exercise.

1. Position the insertion point in front of the word *We* at the beginning of the second quote.
2. Tap (ENTER) twice to push the last two quotations down.
3. Tap ↑ twice to move the insertion point into the blank space between the paragraphs.
4. Now type the following quotation.

> *No one has been barred on account of his race from fighting or dying for America—There are no "white" or "colored" signs on the foxholes or graveyards of battle.—John F. Kennedy*

5. Now add the paragraph shown below to the bottom of the document. Make sure you double-space with (ENTER) between the last quote and the new paragraph. For the new paragraph, set the left and right indents to zero, the first line indent to 0.5″, and the line spacing to double. You will also need to turn off italics.

> Famous quotations help us express those hard-to-find words and feelings that are in all of our hearts. They become a part of our national conscience and memory.

6. Choose **File→Save As** from the menu bar.
7. Change the name of the document to **Skill Builder 10.2,** save it, and close it.

Skill Builder 10.3 Format an Existing Document

In this exercise, you will open a report on your exercise diskette. You will adjust the line spacing and indents and spell check the document.

Adjust the First Line Indent and Line Spacing

1. Open the document named Skill Builder 10.3.
2. Use the Zoom Control to switch to a Whole Page zoom.
3. Select the entire document by triple-clicking in the left margin, or choose **Edit→Select All** from the menu bar.
4. Drag the First Line Indent marker to the 0.5″ position on the ruler.
   This will indent the first line of all paragraphs by 0.5″ (including the title).
5. Set the line spacing to double.
6. Use the Zoom Control to switch to a Page Width zoom.

Format the Title and Credit Line

7. Use (ENTER) to push the title down to approximately the 2″ position.
8. Center the title.
   Look at the ruler, and notice that the First Line Indent marker is at the 0.5″ position. This will cause the title to be slightly off center.
9. Set the First Line Indent for the title paragraph to zero.
10. Format the title as Arial Bold, 14pt.
11. Click on the credit line at the bottom of the report.
12. Set the First Line Indent to zero, and right-align the paragraph.
    The paragraph should be flush with the right margin.
13. Format the title *The Forest People* in the credit line with italics.
14. Spell check the entire document. Assume that the names of all people and places are correct.
15. Save the changes, and close the document.

Assessments

Assessment 10.1 Format an Existing Document

1. Open the document named Assessment 10.1 on your exercise diskette.
2. Apply double-spacing to the entire document.
3. Center the title, and apply bold formatting to the title.
4. Apply bold formatting to the two capitalized headings.
5. Apply a 0.5″ First Line indent to all body paragraphs except for the headings.
6. Print the document, save the changes, and close the document.

Assessment 10.2 Create a Report Using Indents

1. Use the skills and report formatting knowledge you have acquired to create the report shown below. The single-spaced paragraphs are indented 1″ on both the left and right.
2. Print the report, save it as **Assessment 10.2,** but leave it open, as you will continue to use it.

CLASSIFICATIONS OF EMPLOYMENT

CFEB Associates—Company Handbook

It is important that you understand how CFEB Associates classifies its employees. We have established the following classifications for purposes of salary administration and eligibility for overtime payment and benefits.

Full-Time Regular Employees. These are staff members hired to work CFEB's normal, full-time workweek on a regular basis.

Part-Time Regular Employees. These are staff members hired to work at CFEB fewer than thirty-five hours per week on a regular basis.

Exempt Employees. These are staff members of CFEB Associates who are not required to be paid overtime, in accordance with applicable federal wage and hour laws, for work performed beyond forty hours in a workweek.

Nonexempt Employees. These are staff members of CFEB Associates who are required to be paid overtime at the rate of time and one-half their regular rate of pay for all hours worked beyond forty hours in a workweek.

LESSON 11—Word

Margins and Lists

In this lesson, you will expand upon the formatting techniques you learned in the previous lesson, and you will use margins, bulleted lists, and hanging indents to create a more sophisticated document. You will also learn how to customize bulleted and numbered lists, and you will work with outline-style numbered lists.

In This Lesson

Case Study

Lisa Madison has found the summer job that most students dream about: she is a whitewater-rafting guide for Outdoor Adventures. Outdoor Adventures has been wooing thrill seekers for 25 years with rafting trips, helicopter skiing, wilderness trekking, and other high-octane adventures. Recently, Lisa realized that many guests have been forgetting to bring items, while others have been getting lost on the way to the starting points. Lisa decides to take charge of this situation using the power of Word 2000 to design a pre-trip checklist that includes a list of recommendations, a bulleted list of items to bring, and directions to the starting points. With her take-charge attitude and her Office 2000 skills, Lisa should have no problem navigating the turbulent waters awaiting her in today's rough-and-tumble business world.

OUTDOOR ADVENTURES

Pre-Trip Checklist

The following checklist and directions will help you prepare for your trip. Also, remember to keep three important things in mind:

1. Pack light—We have limited space on our rafts, and you must carry all of your belongings with you. You will make more friends if you pack light.

2. Bring waterproof bags—One thing you can count on is that you bag(s) will get wet. Make sure they are waterproof and they float.

3. No valuables please—Leave valuables such as camcorders and cameras at home. Inexpensive 35mm cameras are the safest bet.

Checklist:

- ❑ Sunglasses
- ❑ Sunscreen
- ❑ Insect repellant
- ❑ Three sets of dry clothing
- ❑ Tennis shoes
- ❑ A warm, waterproof jacket

Directions:

Upper Granite Canyon—Take Highway 240 to the Forest Lake exit. Take Forest Lake Drive to Creekside Lane, and look for the starting point.

Middle Granite Canyon—Take Highway 240 to the Pine Meadows turnoff. Go right for two miles until you see a fork in the road. Go right for one mile to the starting point.

Margins

Margins determine the overall size of the text area on a page. In Word, the default top and bottom margins are 1″, and the left and right margins are 1.25″. You can set margins by dragging the margin boundaries on the rulers. You can also use the **File→Page Setup** command and set the margins in the Margins tab of the Page Setup dialog box. Margin settings are applied to the entire document or to an entire section (if the document has multiple sections). Sections are not discussed in this lesson.

Differences Between Margins and Indents

The margins determine the space between the text and the edge of the page. Indents are used to offset text from the margins. For example, imagine a document has a 1″ left margin, and one of the paragraphs in that document has a 0.5″ indent. The margin plus the indent will position the paragraph 1.5″ from the edge of the page. If the margin were changed to 2″, then the indented paragraph would be positioned 2.5 ″ from the edge of the page (the 2″ margin plus the 0.5″ indent).

Hands-On 11.1 Set Margins

1. Start Word, and choose **File→Page Setup** from the menu bar.
   The Page Setup dialog box lets you adjust a number of important settings that affect pages; for example, margins, paper size, page orientation, and headers and footers.
2. Make sure the Margins tab is selected, and notice the default settings for the margins.
3. Change the top margin to 1.5″ and the left and right margins to 1″.
4. Click **OK** to apply the changes.
   The top of the vertical ruler will have a 1.5″ dark gray area representing the top margin. Also, the Status bar will indicate that the insertion point is at the 1.5″ position.
5. Set the font size to 14, and type the following text. Use (ENTER) to double-space between the title and subtitle and to triple-space between the subtitle and body paragraph. Also, use (ENTER) to double-space after the body paragraph.

OUTDOORS ADVENTURES Pre-Trip Checklist   The following checklist and directions will help you prepare for your trip. Also, remember to keep three important things in mind:

6. Format the title with an Arial 18 pt bold font, and the subtitle with an Arial 16 pt bold font.
7. Save the document with the name **Hands-On Lesson 11.**
   You will continue to enhance this document throughout the lesson.

Setting Margins with the Rulers

You can set all four margins by dragging the margin boundaries on the rulers. The benefit of this technique is that you can see the effect immediately in the document. If you press the (ALT) key when dragging a margin boundary, Word displays the precise margin measurement; on the rulers however, you must press (ALT) after you have begun dragging the margin boundary.

Hands-On 11.2 Change Margins with the Ruler

1. Follow these steps to adjust the margins.

(A) *Position the mouse pointer here on the top margin boundary so that a double-headed arrow will appear.*

(B) *Drag the margin boundary down until the numeral 2 appears at the top of the ruler. This indicates that the margin is set to 2".*

(C) *Try adjusting the top margin again but press and hold the (ALT) key after you begin dragging. Word will display the margin measurements on the ruler.*

(D) *Set the top margin to 2".*

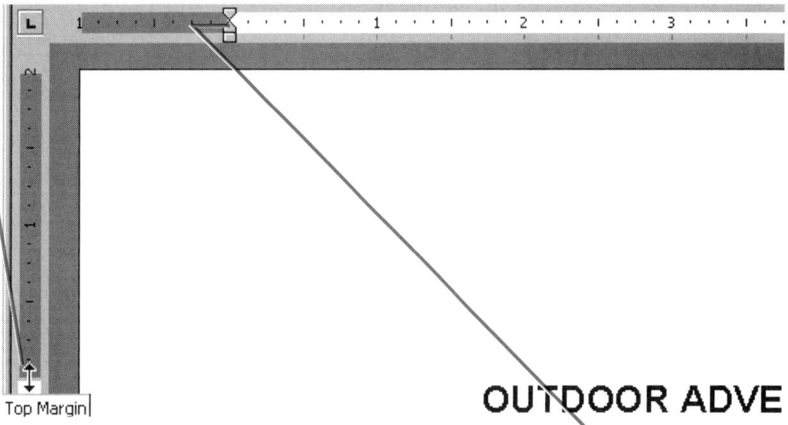
Top Margin
OUTDOOR ADVE

(E) *Try changing the left margin by dragging this margin boundary. However, be patient because the indent markers may prevent the double-headed arrow from appearing. When you have finished, make sure the left margin is set to 1".*

Bulleted and Numbered Lists

You can create bulleted and numbered lists with the Bullets and Numbering buttons on the Formatting toolbar. In Word, a list is a series of two or more paragraphs. You can apply bullets and numbers to paragraphs by selecting the paragraphs and clicking the desired button. For a new list, you can turn on bullets or numbers when you begin typing the list. Word will format the first paragraph with a bullet or number. When you complete the paragraph and tap (ENTER), Word formats the next paragraph with a bullet or number. In a numbered list, Word numbers the paragraphs sequentially. Paragraphs in a numbered list are automatically renumbered if paragraphs are inserted or deleted.

AutoFormat as You Type

You can also start a bulleted list by typing an asterisk * followed by a space or a tab at the beginning of a new paragraph. When you complete the paragraph and tap (ENTER), Word converts the asterisk to a bullet character. Likewise, you can begin a numbered list by typing 1 followed by a space or tab and tapping (ENTER). This feature is known as **AutoFormat as You Type.**

Turning Bullets and Numbering Off

You can remove bullets or numbers from paragraphs by selecting the paragraphs(s) and clicking the Bullets button or the Numbering button. If you are typing a list, you should complete the list by tapping (ENTER) after the last paragraph in the list. You can then turn off bullets or numbering for the first paragraph following the list by clicking the Bullets button or the Numbering button.

Hands-On 11.3 Bullets and Numbers

Create a Numbered List

1. Position the insertion point at the bottom of the document.
   The insertion point should be on the second blank line below the body paragraph.
2. Click the Numbering button on the Formatting toolbar.
   The indented numeral 1 appears followed by a period.
3. Type the following text, inserting the Em Dash symbol as shown.

   > 1. **Pack light—We have limited space on our rafts, and you must carry all of your belongings with you. You will make more friends if you pack light.**

4. Tap (ENTER) once after typing the text.
   Notice that Word begins the next paragraph with the numeral 2. Paragraphs are numbered sequentially unless you tell Word otherwise. You will learn how to change the starting number later in this lesson.
5. Tap (ENTER) again, and numbering will be turned off for the new paragraph.
   Word assumes you want to turn off numbering when you tap (ENTER) without typing any text.
6. Click the Numbering button again.
   Word will number the new blank paragraph with the numeral 2. Word continues the numbering from the previous list.
7. Type the following text.

   > 2. **Bring waterproof bags—One thing you can count on is that your bag(s) will get wet. Make sure they are waterproof and they float.**

8. Tap (ENTER) and notice that Word creates a double-space and starts the numbering at 3.
   Word now understands that you want a double-space between each paragraph in the list.
9. Type the following text.

   > 3. **No valuables please—Leave valuables such as camcorders and cameras at home. Inexpensive 35mm cameras are the safest bet.**

10. Tap (ENTER) and another double-space will be inserted.
11. Click the Numbering button to turn off numbering for the new paragraph.

Create a Bulleted List

12. Type **`Checklist`**: and tap (ENTER) once.
13. Click the Bullets button on the Formatting toolbar.
    Word will most likely insert a round • bullet (although another bullet style may appear). Also, the bullet may be indented farther than the numbers in the numbered list.
14. Type **`Sunglasses`**, and tap (ENTER).
    Word formats the new paragraph with the bullet style.
15. Complete the following checklist.

> Checklist:
> - Sunglasses
> - Sunscreen
> - Insect repellant
> - Three sets of dry clothing
> - Tennis shoes
> - A warm, waterproof jacket

16. Tap (ENTER) twice after the last list item to turn off bullets.

The Bullets and Numbering Dialog Box

The **Format→Bullets and Numbering** command displays the Bullets and Numbering dialog box. The Bullets and Numbering dialog box lets you choose a style for your bulleted or numbered list, customize lists, and create outline numbered lists.

Built-in Bullet and Numbering Styles

Word provides seven built-in styles for bulleted and numbered lists. The styles are displayed in **style galleries** in the Bullets and Numbering dialog box. You can easily change the appearance of a bulleted or numbered list by choosing a style from the style galleries. The following illustration shows the built-in bullet and number styles available.

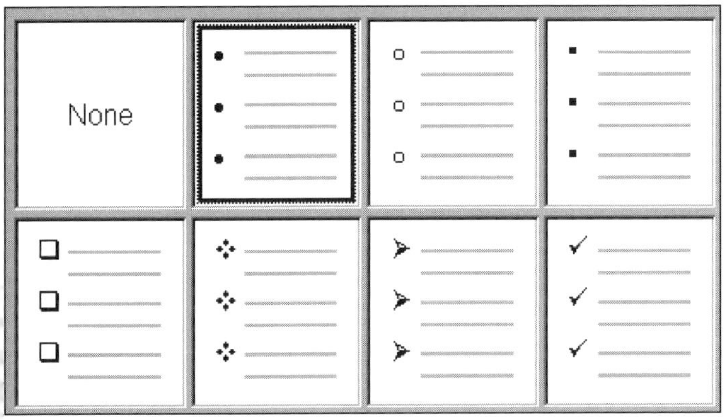
None

Bullet style gallery

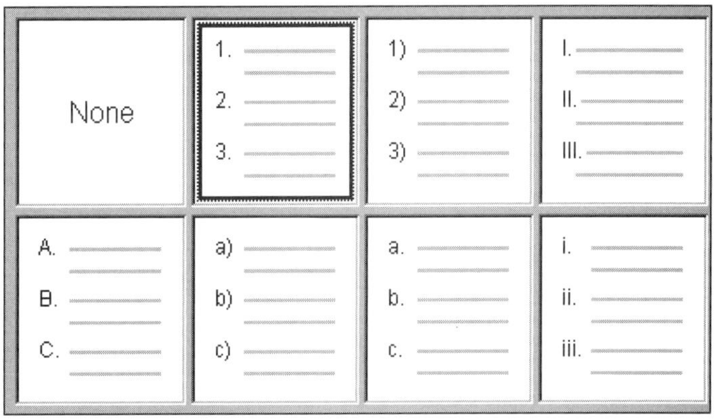
None
1.
2.
3.
1)
2)
3)
I.
II.
III.
A.
B.
C.
a)
b)
c)
a.
b.
c.
i.
ii.
iii.

Number style gallery

Hands-On 11.4 Change the Bullet Style

1. Select the bulleted list as shown below.

Checklist:

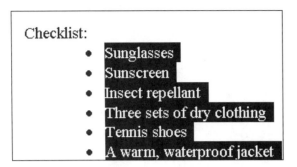

- Sunglasses
- Sunscreen
- Insect repellant
- Three sets of dry clothing
- Tennis shoes
- A warm, waterproof jacket

2. Choose **Format→Bullets and Numbering** from the menu bar.
3. Choose the Checkbox style from the bullets gallery, and click **OK.**

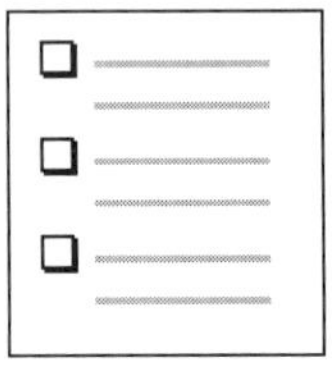

Customizing Bullet and Number Styles

You can customize the built-in bullet and number styles in several ways. For example, you may want to use a bullet character other than the built-in bullet characters, or you may want to change the default indentation of a particular built-in bullet or number style. These and other customization options are available in the Customization dialog box. To display the Customization dialog box first display the Bullets and Numbering dialog box, and then choose a bullet or number style from the style galleries, and click the Customize button.

Resetting Customized Bullet and Number Styles

Once you customize a built-in bullet or number style, the new customized style replaces the built-in style in the style gallery from that point onward. Fortunately, the Bullets and Numbering dialog box contains a Reset button that restores a style in the gallery to its original built-in format. To reset a style, you choose the style from the style galleries and click the Reset button.

Modifying List Numbering

Many documents have more than one numbered list. In some documents, you may want the numbering to continue sequentially from one list to the next. For example, if one list ends with the numeral 4 you may want the next list to begin with the numeral 5. Then again, you may want the numbering in each new list to begin with 1. Fortunately, Word has two options on the Numbered tab of the Bullets and Numbering dialog box that let you control the list numbering:

- **Restart numbering option—**This option forces a list to begin with the numeral 1.
- **Continue previous list option—**This option forces the numbering to continue from the previous list.

Hands-On 11.5 Experiment with Customization

1. Scroll up, and click anywhere on the first numbered paragraph.
2. Choose **Format→Bullets and Numbering** from the menu bar.
   Notice the seven different number styles in the gallery. As with bullets, you can apply a style by choosing it from the gallery and clicking OK. When you use the Numbering button on the Formatting toolbar, it always applies the most recently used number style.
3. Notice the **Restart numbering** and **Continue previous list** options below the number styles.
   These options are used to adjust the starting number of a numbered list. These options will not be available for the paragraph numbered 1 because it is the first numbered paragraph in the document.
4. Click the **Customize** button.
5. Follow these steps to explore the Custom Numbered List dialog box.

Ⓐ *Notice that you can change the font for the numbers and the number format. The* ***Number format*** *can be customized by adding text in front of the shaded number. For example, you could type the word Step in front of the shaded number to begin each item in a numbered list with the word Step (e.g. Step 1, Step 2).*

Ⓑ *This option lets you start a list with any number.*

Ⓒ *You can adjust the number position and the indent of the text from the number with these options.*

Ⓓ *Now, change the* ***Indent at*** *setting to 0.75" and click OK.*

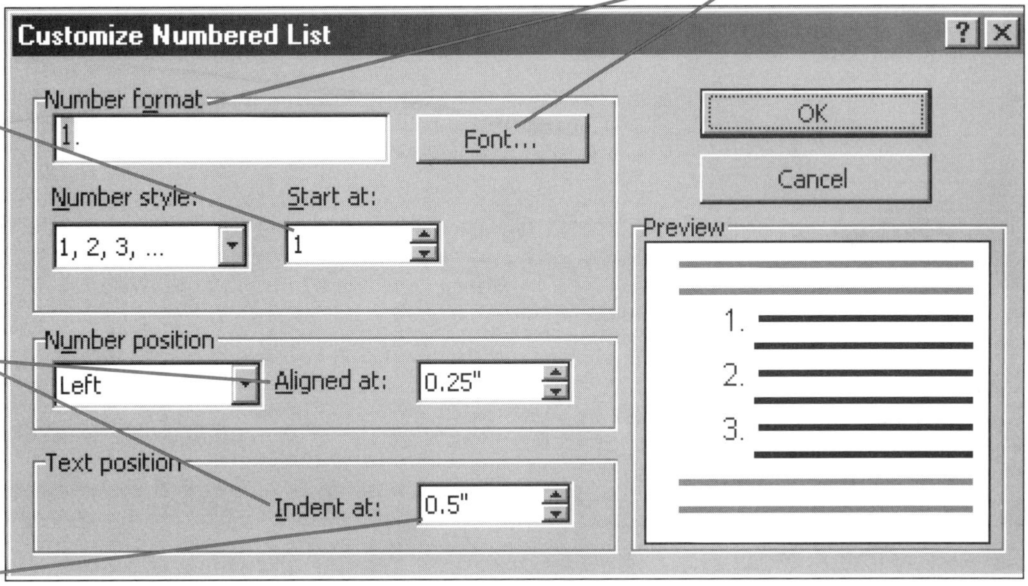

Customize Numbered List
Number format
1.
Font...
Number style:
1, 2, 3, ...
Start at:
1
OK
Cancel
Preview
1.
2.
3.
Number position
Left
Aligned at:
0.25"
Text position
Indent at:
0.5"

The new number style should be applied to all numbered paragraphs. This will move the text following the number to the 0.75" position.

6. Make sure the insertion point is somewhere on the first paragraph in the numbered list.
7. Choose **Format→Bullets and Numbering** from the menu bar.
   The current number style should be highlighted in the gallery.
8. Locate the **Reset** button at the bottom of the dialog box.
   The Reset button will be available because the current number style has been customized.
9. Click the **Reset** button.

(Continued on the next page)

10. Click **Yes** on the message box that appears.
Word asks if you want to restore the gallery position to the default style. Each style has a position in the gallery. When you reset a style, you are resetting a particular gallery position to the default formats for that position. Notice that the Reset button is no longer available. The Reset button is only available if the highlighted gallery style has been customized.

11. Click **OK,** and the numbered paragraphs will be restored to their original format.
Keep in mind that you can customize bullet styles in a similar manner to number styles.

Adjusting Bullet and Number Alignment with the Ruler

You can easily adjust the indents of bulleted and numbered lists and the text following the bullets and numbers by dragging markers on the ruler. This technique is useful because it can be applied to specific paragraphs without changing the built-in styles in the style galleries. Drag the First Line Indent marker to adjust the bullet position and a Left Tab marker to adjust the text position.

Hands-On 11.6 Adjust Bullet Position and the Text Indent

1. Scroll to the bottom of the document, and select all of the bulleted paragraphs.
2. Follow this step to adjust the **First Line Indent** marker.

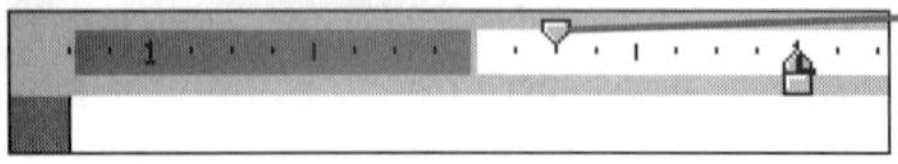

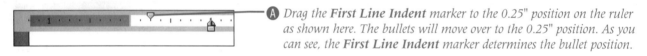

Ⓐ *Drag the **First Line Indent** marker to the 0.25" position on the ruler as shown here. The bullets will move over to the 0.25" position. As you can see, the **First Line Indent** marker determines the bullet position.*

3. Follow these steps to adjust the **Left Tab** marker.

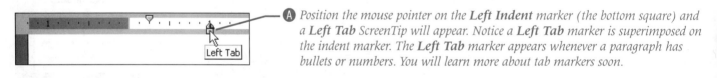

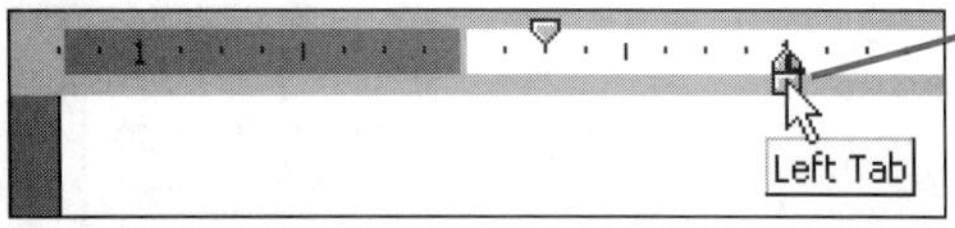
Left Tab

Ⓐ *Position the mouse pointer on the **Left Indent** marker (the bottom square) and a **Left Tab** ScreenTip will appear. Notice a **Left Tab** marker is superimposed on the indent marker. The **Left Tab** marker appears whenever a paragraph has bullets or numbers. You will learn more about tab markers soon.*

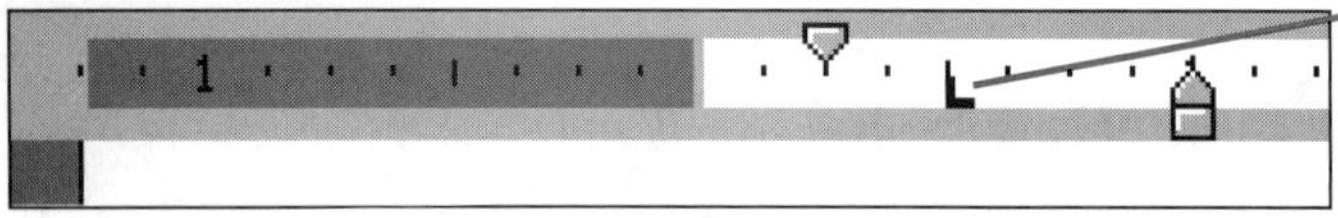

Ⓑ *Drag the **Left Tab** marker until it is positioned at the 0.5" position as shown here. The bullet text should now be aligned at the 0.5" position.*

4. Follow these steps to adjust the **Hanging Indent** marker.

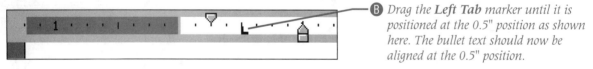

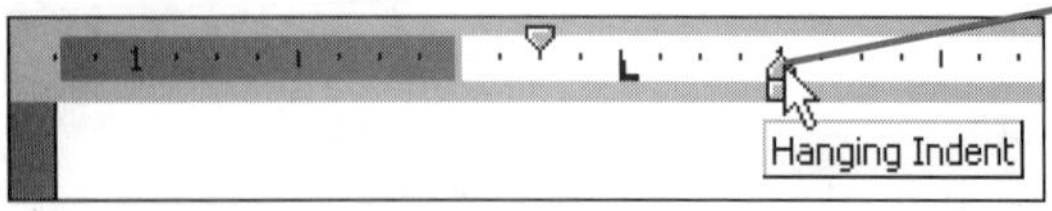
Hanging Indent

Ⓐ *Position the mouse pointer on the **Hanging Indent** marker (the upward pointing triangle) and a **Hanging Indent** ScreenTip will appear.*

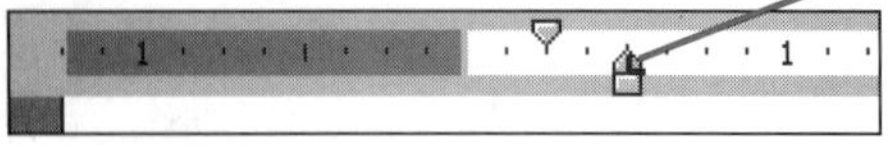

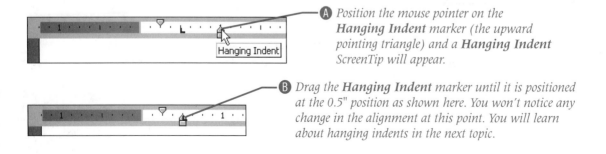

Ⓑ *Drag the **Hanging Indent** marker until it is positioned at the 0.5" position as shown here. You won't notice any change in the alignment at this point. You will learn about hanging indents in the next topic.*

The bulleted checklist should have the appearance and alignment shown below.

> 3. No valuables please—Leave valuables such as camcorders and cameras at home. Inexpensive 35mm cameras are the safest bet.
>
> Checklist:
> - ❑ Sunglasses
> - ❑ Sunscreen
> - ❑ Insect repellant
> - ❑ Three sets of dry clothing
> - ❑ Tennis shoes
> - ❑ A warm, waterproof jacket

5. Save the changes, and continue with the next topic.

Hanging Indents

The Hanging Indent marker (upward-pointing triangle) offsets all lines of a paragraph except for the first line. Hanging indents are often used in bibliographic entries, glossary terms, and bulleted and numbered lists. You create hanging indents by dragging the Hanging Indent marker on the ruler or with the Paragraph dialog box.

> Middle Granite Canyon—Take Highway 240 to the Pine Meadows turnoff. Go right for two miles until you see a fork in the road. Go right for one mile to the starting point.

Hands-On 11.7 Create Hanging Indents

1. Position the insertion point on the second blank line below the checklist.
2. Type **Directions:** and tap ENTER.
3. Type the following text:

> Upper Granite Canyon—Take Highway 240 to the Forest Lake exit. Take Forest Lake Drive to Creekside Lane and look for the starting point.

(Continued on the next page)

4. Click anywhere on the paragraph you just typed.
5. Follow these steps to create a hanging indent.

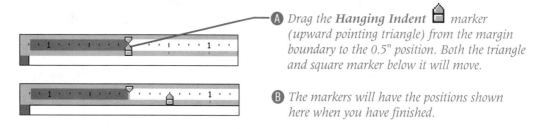

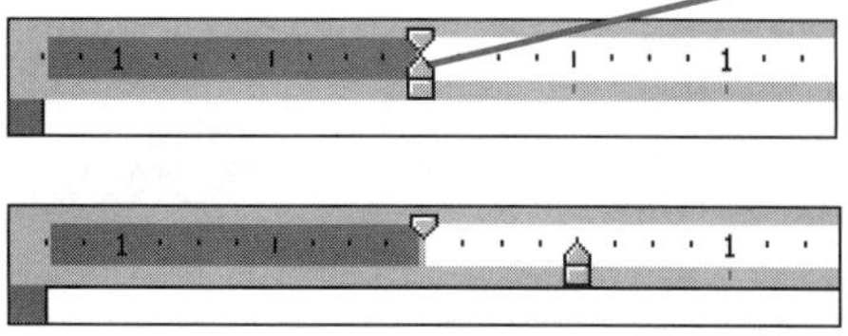
1
1
1
1

Ⓐ *Drag the **Hanging Indent** marker (upward pointing triangle) from the margin boundary to the 0.5" position. Both the triangle and square marker below it will move.*

Ⓑ *The markers will have the positions shown here when you have finished.*

The formatted paragraph should match the following example. Notice how the second line is indented, but the first line remains at the margin.

> Upper Granite Canyon—Take Highway 240 to the Forest Lake exit. Take Forest
> Lake Drive to Creekside Lane and look for the starting point.

6. Now click the Increase Indent button to increase both the First Line indent and the Hanging indent.
7. Position the insertion point at the end of the paragraph (to the right of the period).
8. Tap (ENTER) twice, then type the following text.

> Middle Granite Canyon—Take Highway 240 to the Pine Meadows turnoff.
> Go right for two miles until you see a fork in the road. Go right for
> one mile to the starting point.

9. Tap (ENTER) twice, and drag the First Line Indent marker and the Hanging Indent marker to the 0″ position on the ruler.
10. Save the changes, and continue with the next topic.

Outline-Style Numbered Lists

An outline-style numbered list can have up to nine levels of numbers or bullet characters. Outline-style lists are often used in the legal profession where multiple numbering levels are required. You format paragraphs as an outline-style numbered list by displaying the Bullets and Numbering dialog box and choosing the desired style from the style gallery on the Outline Numbered tab.

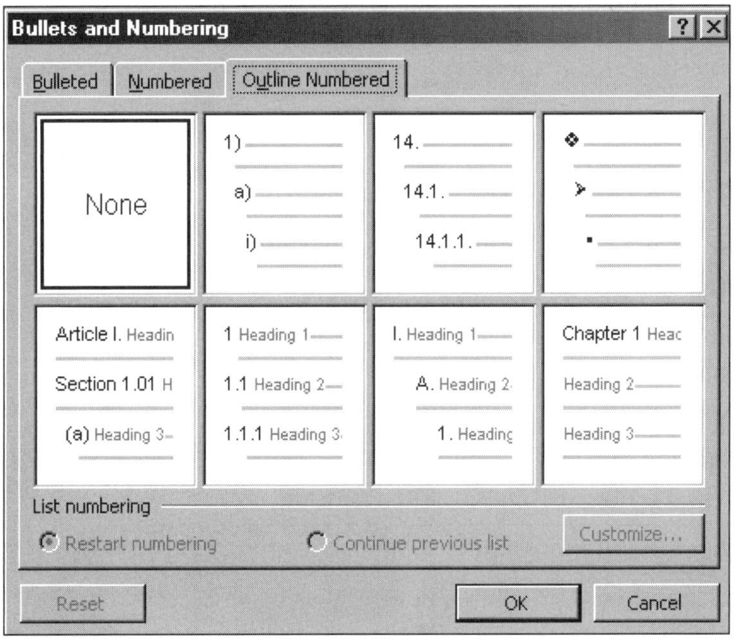
Bullets and Numbering
Bulleted
Numbered
Outline Numbered
None
1)
a)
i)
14.
14.1.
14.1.1.
Article I. Headin
Section 1.01 H
(a) Heading 3
1 Heading 1
1.1 Heading 2
1.1.1 Heading 3
I. Heading 1
A. Heading 2
1. Heading
Chapter 1 Heac
Heading 2
Heading 3
List numbering
Restart numbering
Continue previous list
Customize...
Reset
OK
Cancel

Outline numbered list styles

Promoting and Demoting List Items

From the Keyboard

TAB to demote
SHIFT+TAB to promote

The Increase Indent button and the Decrease Indent button are used to promote or demote paragraphs in an outline-style numbered list. The Increase Indent button indents selected paragraphs one level, thus demoting them one level. The Decrease Indent button reduces the indentation level and thus promotes the paragraph one level.

Hands-On 11.8 Create a Policies and Procedures Page

In this exercise, you will use outline-style numbered lists to create a policies and procedures page at the end of the document.

Set Up the New Page

1. Make sure the insertion point is at the end of the document and that the paragraph has no preset indents.
2. Press CTRL+ENTER to insert a page break.
   Notice that the top margin is still set to 2″.
3. Click the Center button.
4. Type **OUTDOOR ADVENTURES**, and tap ENTER twice.
5. Type **Policies and Procedures**, and tap ENTER three times.
6. Click the Align Left button.

(Continued on the next page)

Create an Outline-Style Numbered List

7. Choose **Format→Bullets and Numbering** from the menu.
8. Click the Outline Numbered tab.
9. Click the first style in the gallery. If the Reset button is available at the bottom of the dialog box, click it to restore the style to the default setting. The style should match the example shown to the right.

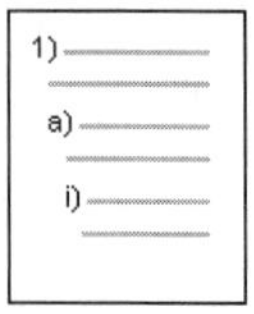

1)
a)
i)

10. Click **OK** to apply the style.
11. Type **Medical and Injury**, and tap (ENTER).
    The heading Medical and Injury should be preceded by the number 1 followed by a closing parenthesis, and the number 2) should be applied to the new paragraph.
12. Click the Increase Indent  button to demote the new paragraph.
    The number 2) should now become the letter a).
13. Type **All guests must have medical insurance**, and tap (ENTER).
    The new paragraph will be preceded by the letter b).
14. Complete items b) and c) as shown below, tapping (ENTER) once after each paragraph. The insertion point should be on the new paragraph d) when you have finished.

> 1) Medical and Injury
>   a) All guests must have medical insurance
>   b) All guests must sign an injury waiver
>   c) All guests agree to pay out-of-pocket medical expenses including:
>   d)

15. Click the Increase Indent  indent to demote the new paragraph.
    The new paragraph will be preceded by the letter i).
16. Type **Injuries resulting from on-trip accidents**, and tap (ENTER).
17. Complete the document as shown on the following page. You should double-space between the three list headings as shown. When you do this, the outline numbering will be turned off for the new heading paragraph. Turn the numbering on again using the Numbering button on the Formatting toolbar. Finally, format the title with an Arial 18 pt bold font and the subtitle with an Arial 16 pt bold font.
18. Save the changes, and close the document.

OUTDOOR ADVENTURES

Policies and Procedures

1) Medical and Injury
   a) All guests must have medical insurance
   b) All guests must sign an injury waiver
   c) All guests agree to pay out-of-pocket medical expenses including:
      i) Injuries resulting from on-trip accidents
      ii) Aero medical evacuation
      iii) Rehabilitation costs

2) Cancellations and Refunds
   a) A full refund will be given for cancellations with 60 days notice
   b) A 50% refund will be given for cancellations with 30 days notice
   c) No refund for cancellations with less than 30 days notice

3) Alternate Trip Destinations and Cancellations
   a) Your trip may be cancelled for any of the following reasons:
      i) Inclement weather
      ii) Poor water flow
      iii) Insufficient number of guests
      iv) Unavailability of a guide
   b) Your trip destination may be changed for any of the following reasons:
      i) Inclement weather
      ii) Poor water flow
      iii) Insufficient guest turnout requiring reorganization of trips

Concepts Review

True/False Questions

1. Margins can be set with the ruler. TRUE FALSE
2. The **File→Page Setup** command displays a dialog box that can be used to adjust margins. TRUE FALSE
3. Bullets can be offset from the margins. TRUE FALSE
4. Numbering always continues sequentially from one list to the next in documents with multiple lists. TRUE FALSE
5. Bullet formats are carried to the next paragraph when (ENTER) is tapped. TRUE FALSE
6. Bullet formats cannot be changed once (ENTER) is tapped. TRUE FALSE
7. Only the first line of a paragraph is indented when a hanging indent is applied. TRUE FALSE
8. Outline-style numbered lists can have up to seven numbering levels. TRUE FALSE

Multiple-Choice Questions

1. Which of the following keys is used to display measurements on the ruler while the margin boundary is dragged?
   a. (ALT)
   b. (SHIFT)
   c. (CTRL)
   d. None of the above

2. Which command displays the Bullets and Numbering dialog box?
   a. Format→Bullets and Numbering
   b. Edit→Bullets and Numbering
   c. Format→Paragraph
   d. None of the above

3. Which technique indents the *bullets* in a bulleted list?
   a. Select the desired paragraphs, and drag the First Line Indent marker.
   b. Select the desired paragraphs, and drag the Left Tab symbol on the indent marker.
   c. Use the (TAB) key.
   d. None of the above

4. Which technique should you use to indent the **text** in a bulleted list?
   a. Select the desired paragraphs, and drag the First Line Indent marker.
   b. Select the desired paragraphs, and drag the Left Tab symbol on the indent marker.
   c. Use the (TAB) key.
   d. None of the above

Skill Builders

Skill Builder 11.1 Create a Personal Business Letter

In this exercise, you will create the document shown on the following page.

Set-Up the Letter

1. Start a new document, and Choose **File→Page Setup** from the menu bar.
2. Set the left and right margins to 1" and click **OK.**
3. Type the date, address, salutation, and first paragraph as shown on the following page.

Create the Numbered List

4. Tap (ENTER) twice after the first main paragraph, and then click the Numbering button.
   It's OK if the number style and indentation are different than shown on the following page. You will adjust the style and indentation soon.
5. Type the three numbered paragraphs, tapping (ENTER) once after each paragraph.
6. Tap (ENTER) twice after the third numbered paragraph.
   This will turn off numbering.
7. Now complete the document as shown on the following page. Turn bullets on and off as necessary, and tap (ENTER) either once or twice between paragraphs as shown. Don't be concerned with text formats or bullet alignments at this point. You will be instructed to make those changes in the following steps.

(Continued on page 339)

Today's Date

Mr. Dave Olson, President
Financial Freedom Network
300 South Meyers Fork Road
San Jose, CA 95136

Dear Mr. Olson:

I recently attended your quick start seminar on tax planning for retirement, and I was impressed with both the speaker and content of the presentation. I spoke with Mr. Barry after the presentation, and he asked me to provide you with three types of feedback:

1. Topics that I feel should be included in next year's presentation
2. Ways to improve the presentation
3. Comments on the facilities

I have organized my comments into the three lists that follow.

Topics to Include Next Year
- ✓ Information on 401K plans
- ✓ Method for calculating projected net worth
- ✓ Planning for children's college expenses

How to Improve the Presentation
- ✓ Make it longer (8 hours).
- ✓ Include more visuals.
- ✓ Have multiple speakers.

About the Facilities
- ✓ The food was excellent.
- ✓ The chairs were a little uncomfortable.
- ✓ The employees were very friendly and helpful.

Mr. Olson, I hope my feedback helps you plan for and improve next year's presentation. Please feel free to contact me if you need additional information.

Sincerely,

Richard Ellison, Seminar Participant
2400 Fairview Lane
Richmond, CA 94803

Format the Lists and Headings

8. Select the three paragraphs in the numbered list.
9. Drag the First Line Indent marker to the 0″ position on the ruler to align the numbers with the left margin.
10. Drag the Left Tab marker and the Hanging Indent marker to the 0.5″ position on the ruler. This will indent the text 0.5″ from the numbers.
11. Now align the bulleted paragraphs the same way.
12. Format the headings with bold as shown on the preceding page.
13. If necessary, use the **Format→Bullets and Numbering** command to choose the numbering style and bullet style shown on the preceding page.
14. Save the document with the name **Skill Builder 11.1,** then close the document.

Skill Builder 11.2

1. Start a new document.
2. Set the top margin to 2″ and the left and right margins to 1.5″.
3. Follow these guidelines to create the document shown below.
   - Use a Times New Roman 16 pt font for all text except for the title and subtitle. Use an Arial Bold 18 pt font for the title and an Arial Bold 16 pt font for the subtitle.
   - Use (ENTER) to create the single-, double-, and triple-spacing shown below.
   - Use the bullet style shown below.
4. Save the document as **Skill Builder 11.2,** and close the document.

Baron's Model Train Supply

Going Out of Business Sale

Baron's Model Train Supply has provided the widest selection of model train accessories for over 43 years, but our lease has run out. We have decided to close up shop and liquidate our inventory. Please stop by before the end of June to take advantage of rock-bottom prices and a wide selection of accessories and collectibles. Here is just a sample of what you will find.

Accessories
- ❖ Scenery
- ❖ Tracks and switches
- ❖ Buildings

Collectibles
- ❖ Antique locomotives
- ❖ Antique cabooses
- ❖ Figures: Switchmen, engineers, animals, and more

Skill Builder 11.3

In this exercise, you will open a document on your exercise diskette. You will format the document until it matches the document on the following page.

1. Open the document named Skill Builder 11.3.
2. Set the left and right margins to 1″.
3. Look at the document on the following page, and notice the title shown at the top of the document. Insert the title, separating it from the first body paragraph with three hard returns (tap (ENTER) three times). Format the title with an Arial 14 pt bold font.
4. Select the first four body paragraphs, and apply double-spacing to them. Adjust the first line indent of the first four body paragraphs to 0.5″.
5. Apply the bullet style shown on the following page to the next three paragraphs. Use (ENTER) to double-space between the paragraphs.
6. Indent the last paragraph 1″ on both the left and right as shown. You will also need to insert hard returns above and below the paragraph with the phrase "Levy concludes that".
7. Your completed document should match the document on the following page.
8. Save the changes to the document, and close it.

(Continued on the next page)

LEFT BRAIN/RIGHT BRAIN

In recent years it has become popular to speak of people as being either "left-brained" or "right-brained." The notion is that the hemispheres of the brain are involved in very different kinds of intellectual and emotional functions and responses.

Like other popular ideas, the "left brain / right brain" notion is exaggerated. Research does suggest that the dominant hemisphere is somewhat more involved in intellectual undertakings that require logic and problem solving, whereas the non-dominant hemisphere is more concerned with decoding visual information, aesthetic and emotional responses, imagination, understanding metaphors, and creative mathematical reasoning.

Despite these differences, it would be erroneous to think that the hemispheres of the brain act independently, or that some people are "left-brained" and others are "right-brained." The functions of the left and right hemispheres tend to respond simultaneously as we focus our attention on one thing or another.

Biological psychologist Jerre Levy summarized left-brain and right-brain similarities and differences as follows:

- The hemispheres are similar enough so that each can function quite well independently, but not as well as they function in normal combined usage.
- The left hemisphere seems to play a special role in understanding and producing language, while the right hemisphere seems to play a special role in emotional response.
- Creativity is not confined to the right hemisphere.

Levy concludes that:

> There are significant differences between the right and left brains; however, these differences may not be as significant as we have been led to believe.

Assessments

Assessment 11.1

1. Follow these guidelines to create the document shown below.
   - Set the top margin to 2″.
   - Insert the date as a field using the Insert→Date and Time command.
   - Use the bullet style shown for the bulleted list.
2. Print the document, save it with the name **Assessment 11.1,** and close the document.

Current Date

Mr. John Upshaw
1204 Wilkins Drive
Sacramento, CA 90518

Dear Mr. Upshaw:

I am pleased to inform you that you have won the grand prize in our sweepstakes contest. Please contact me as soon as possible to verify receipt of this letter. You may contact me in any of the following ways.

- ➢ Stop by our office at 2400 Gerber Road.
- ➢ Call 1-916-682-9090 between the hours of 9:00 a.m. and 5:00 p.m.
- ➢ Write to me at the address listed on this letterhead.

I look forward to hearing from you soon. Please be prepared to present us with your verification number. Your verification number is JB101.

Sincerely,

Jerry Williams
Prize Notification Manager

Assessment 11.2

1. Follow these guidelines to create the document shown below.
   - Set the top margin to 2″ and the left and right margins to 1″.
   - Use an Arial Bold 16 pt font for the title and a Times New Roman 14 pt font for all other text.
   - Center the title, and use three hard returns after the title.
   - Use single-spacing and double-spacing as necessary to format the document as shown.
   - Set the First Line indent of the two body paragraphs to 0.5″ as shown. Adjust the indents of the numbered paragraphs and the quotation as shown.
2. Print the document, save it with the name **Assessment 11.2,** and close the document.

SUCCESS

The quest for success is a driving force in the lives of many Americans. This force drives the business world and often results in huge personal fortunes. However, success can come in many forms, some of which are listed below.

1. Many people in America view success monetarily.
2. Our society also views public figures such as movie stars, athletes, and other celebrities as being successful.
3. Educational achievement such as earning an advanced degree is often perceived as successful.

It is easy to see that success means many things to many people. The poet Ralph Waldo Emerson provides this elegant definition of success:

> To laugh often and much; to win the respect of intelligent people and the affection of children; to earn the appreciation of honest critics and endure the betrayal of false friends; to appreciate beauty, to find the best in others; to leave the world a bit better, whether by a healthy child, a garden patch or a redeemed social condition; to know even one life has breathed easier because you have lived. This is to have succeeded.

Assessment 11.3

1. Follow these guidelines to create the document shown below.
   - Set the top margin to 2″.
   - Center the title, and use three hard returns after the title.
   - Use an Arial Bold 16 pt font for the title and a Times New Roman 14 pt font for all other text. Apply bold to the list headings as shown.
   - Apply line spacing, indents, and bullets as shown.
2. Print the document, save it with the name **Assessment 11.3,** and close the document.

THE GOLDEN STATE

With more than thirty million people, California has become the most populous state in America. From the beaches of Southern California to the great redwood forests of Northern California, the Golden State is home to a diverse population and a vibrant economy.

A recent poll asked Californians to list the five things they liked best about life in California. The same poll also asked them to list the five biggest drawbacks to life in the Golden State. The poll results appear below.

Five Best Things
- Climate
- Cultural attractions
- Economic opportunities
- Educational opportunities
- Recreational activities

Five Biggest Drawbacks
- Air pollution
- Cost of living
- Crime
- Taxes
- Traffic and congestion

LESSON 12—Word

Desktop Publishing

In this lesson, you will use desktop publishing techniques in Word 2000. Word 2000 makes desktop publishing fun and easy. Everyone from beginners to advanced users will find something exciting in Word 2000. As you progress through this lesson, you will work with a variety of graphic objects, including WordArt, clip art, and drawing objects. You will also visit Microsoft's ClipGallery Live Web page, where thousands of high-quality clip art images are available for download. In addition, you will enhance the appearance of paragraphs with drop caps.

In This Lesson

Case Study

Jane Thompson is the owner of West Side Bakery. West Side Bakery is located on the fringes of a major university and caters to the large student population on campus. Jane has decided to produce an inexpensive flyer to be handed out around campus. The flyer is designed to entice students to visit the store for the first time. Jane uses the desktop publishing features of Word 2000 to produce the flyer on her office computer. Once the flyer is produced, Jane will take it to the nearest copy shop to have it duplicated.

The Best Bakery in Ocean City!
Stop by the West Side Bakery before June 30, and get a free loaf of sourdough bread when you buy a dozen muffins. Our award-winning muffins will please your palette and satisfy your hunger. All of our breads and muffins are made with the finest ingredients. We are located at 1450 Market Street in Ocean City.
Huge Muffins
We're fresh from the oven.

Drawing Object Concepts

Office 2000 has an excellent set of drawing tools that let you draw lines, arrows, rectangles, callouts, WordArt, and many other objects. Drawing objects are easy to work with and a lot of fun! Drawing objects are particularly useful for creating flyers and other types of graphically-rich documents. You insert a drawing object by choosing the desired object from the Drawing toolbar and then dragging the mouse in the document.

The Drawing button on the Standard toolbar is used to display and hide the Drawing toolbar. The Drawing toolbar is usually located at the bottom of the document window just above the status bar. You can also display or hide the drawing toolbar with the **View→Toolbars→Drawing** command. The following illustration explains the buttons on the Drawing toolbar.

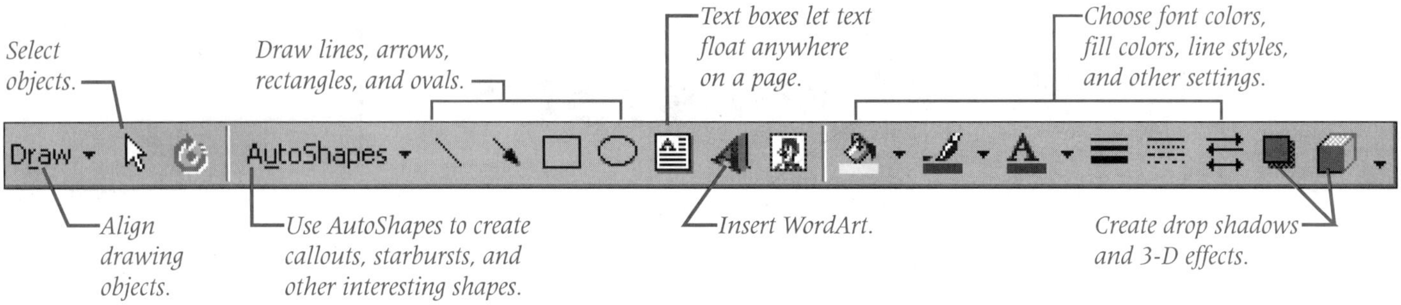

Select objects.
Draw lines, arrows, rectangles, and ovals.
Text boxes let text float anywhere on a page.
Choose font colors, fill colors, line styles, and other settings.
Draw
AutoShapes
Align drawing objects.
Use AutoShapes to create callouts, starbursts, and other interesting shapes.
Insert WordArt.
Create drop shadows and 3-D effects.

Object Layers

Drawing objects reside on invisible layers in the document that are independent of the text layer. For this reason, drawing objects can be placed behind the text layer or in front of the text layer. This allows you to superimpose drawing objects over text or hide objects behind text. You can also place drawing objects in front of or behind other drawing objects.

The Grid

In Word, a hidden grid is used to align drawing objects. When you move or size an object, it will snap to a grid point. The grid makes it easy to align objects along horizontal or vertical lines. You can display the grid by choosing the *Display gridlines on screen* option in the Grid dialog box. You display the Grid dialog box by clicking the Draw button on the Drawing toolbar and choosing Grid.

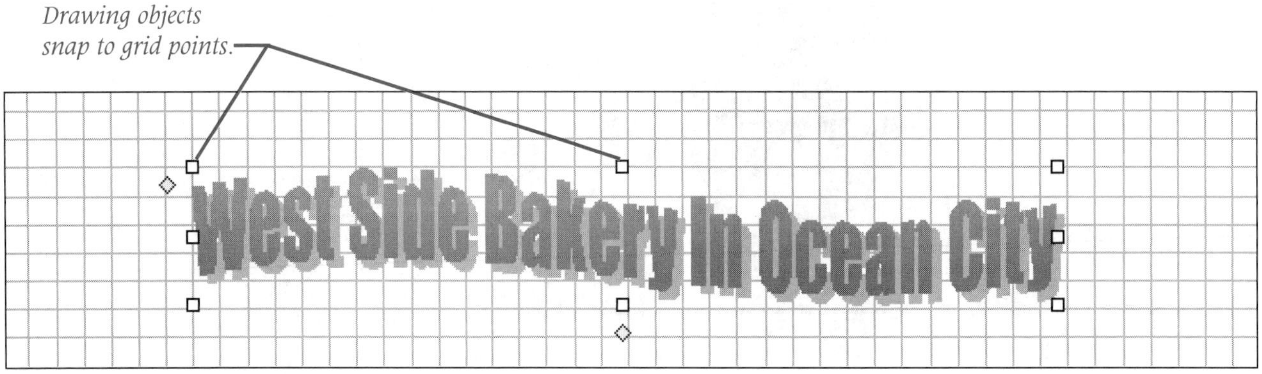

Drawing objects snap to grid points.
West Side Bakery In Ocean City

Hands-On 12.1 Display and Hide Gridlines

1. Start Word, and locate the Drawing toolbar at the bottom of the Word window. If the Drawing toolbar isn't displayed, use the **View→Toolbars→Drawing** command to display the toolbar.
2. Click the **Draw** button on the left end of the Drawing toolbar, and choose Grid from the menu.
   Notice the Snap objects to grid *option is checked at the top of the dialog box. This option is set by default.*
3. Check the **Display gridlines on screen** box, and click **OK.**
   The grid will be displayed. As you work with objects in the following exercises, they will snap to points on the grid.
4. Display the Grid dialog box, and turn off the gridline display.
   Objects will still snap to the gridlines even though the grid is not displayed.

WordArt

The **WordArt**  button on the Drawing toolbar displays the WordArt Gallery. You can add special effects to text by choosing a style from the gallery. Once you choose a style, Word displays a dialog box where you enter the text and choose the font and font size for your stylized WordArt text. The WordArt gallery is shown below.

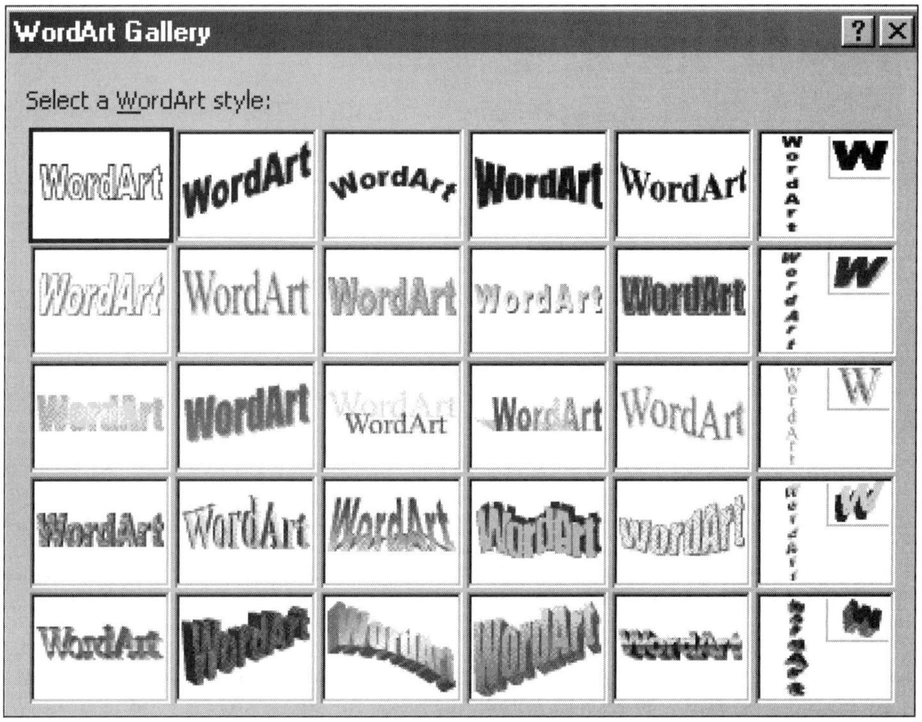
WordArt Gallery
Select a WordArt style:

Hands-On 12.2 Insert and Edit WordArt Text

1. Click the **WordArt** button on the Drawing toolbar.
   The WordArt Gallery appears.
2. Choose the style in the third row and fifth column, and click **OK.**
   The Edit WordArt Text box appears. This is where you enter your WordArt text.
3. Type the phrase **`West Side Bakery in Ocean City`**.
4. Choose Impact from the font list, and set the font size to 28. Choose Arial as the font if Impact is not available.
5. Click **OK** to insert the *WordArt* object in your new document.
   The WordArt toolbar should have appeared. The WordArt toolbar lets you edit the text in the WordArt object and format the object.
6. Click the **Edit Text** button on the WordArt toolbar.
7. Select the first two words (West Side), and replace them with the words **`The Best`**.
8. Click at the end of the phrase, and type an exclamation point.
   The phrase in the Edit WordArt Text box should now be The Best Bakery in Ocean City!
9. Change the font size to 32, and click **OK.**

Selecting, Moving, and Sizing Objects

You must select objects before you can move or size them. The easiest way to select an object is to click anywhere on the object. Small squares called sizing handles appear on the corners and four sides of a selected object. The following Quick Reference table explains the techniques you can use to select, move, and size objects. The methods apply to both drawing objects and pictures. You will work with pictures later in this lesson.

Quick Reference

SELECTING, MOVING, AND SIZING OBJECTS

Task	Method
Select a single object.	Click the object
Select multiple objects.	Click the Select Objects button on the Drawing toolbar, and drag to enclose the desired objects in the selection box. You can also press SHIFT while you click the desired objects.
Move an object with the mouse.	Drag the object (not the sizing handles) to a new location. You can also press and hold ALT while dragging an object to prevent the object from snapping to the grid.
Move an object with the keyboard.	Tap ← → ↑ or ↓ to nudge the object to the next grid point. You can also press CTRL while tapping the arrow keys to nudge the object a tiny amount.
Size an object.	Drag any sizing handle. Dragging a corner sizing handle lets you change both the width and height at the same time.
Size an object while maintaining the original shape and proportions.	Press SHIFT while dragging a corner sizing handle to maintain the original shape and proportions of the object.

Hands-On 12.3 Move and Size the WordArt Object

1. Follow these steps to move and size the WordArt object.

The Best Bakery in Ocean City!

Ⓐ *Drag any sizing handle to increase the size.*

Ⓑ *Click* ***Undo*** *to restore the original size.*

Ⓒ *Position the mouse pointer on the object and drag it towards the top of the document. You will notice the object snaps to grid points as it moves. Position the object about 1" from the top, and center it horizontally. Use the horizontal ruler to help you align the object horizontally.*

2. Click anywhere outside of the object, and it will become deselected.
3. Now click the object, and it will become selected (sizing handles will appear).
4. Feel free to experiment with the buttons on the WordArt toolbar.
   The object must be selected (with sizing handles) in order to edit it. Use Undo if you make a mistake or wish to reverse an action.
5. Save the document as **Hands-On Lesson 12.**

Object Anchors

All objects are anchored to paragraphs when they are inserted into a document. As a document changes, an object moves with the paragraph to which it is anchored, thus maintaining the same position relative to the paragraph. When you move an object, its anchor will change to a paragraph in close proximity to the object's new location. You can determine the paragraph to which an object is anchored by selecting the object and using the Show All button to display the nonprinting characters.

An anchor symbol appears next to the paragraph to which an object is anchored.

The Best Bakery in Ocean City!

Hands-On 12.4 Move the Anchor

1. Click anywhere outside of the WordArt object to deselect the object.
   The insertion point will be positioned at the top of the document.
2. Tap ENTER *four* times.
   The object should move down each time you tap ENTER because it was anchored to the first paragraph mark, which has now been pushed down four lines.
3. Click the Show All ¶ button on the Standard toolbar.
4. Click the object to select it, and an anchor ⚓ symbol will appear to the left of the last paragraph mark.
   The object is anchored to that paragraph.
5. Drag the WordArt object up until the anchor is positioned to the left of the first paragraph mark.
   Now the object will move only when the first paragraph mark moves. In a moment, you will add additional paragraphs to the bottom of the document, and the WordArt object will remain stationary. The purpose of this exercise is to help you understand what is going on "behind the scenes." Normally, you can move an object without being concerned about the anchor position.
6. Now click the insertion point in front of the last paragraph mark.
7. Tap ENTER *twice,* then click Show All ¶ to hide the nonprinting characters.

Drop Caps

TYPE TEXT FIRST

Word's Drop Caps feature lets you easily create large drop-down capitals at the beginning of paragraphs. To create a drop cap, click anywhere in the desired paragraph and issue the **Format→Drop Cap** command. The dialog box options are quite simple, as described below.

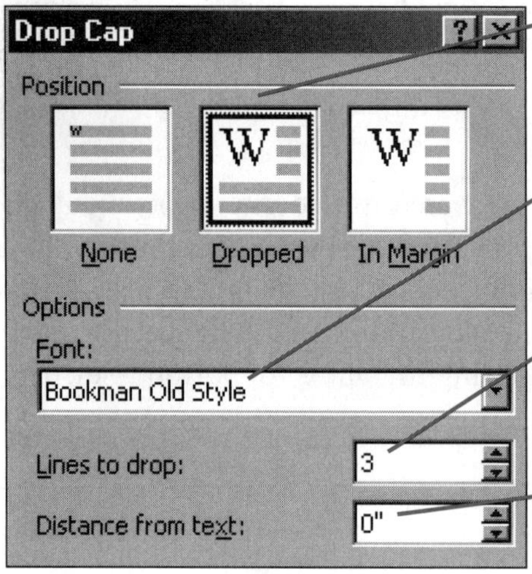
Drop Cap
Position
None
Dropped
In Margin
Options
Font:
Bookman Old Style
Lines to drop:
3
Distance from text:
0"

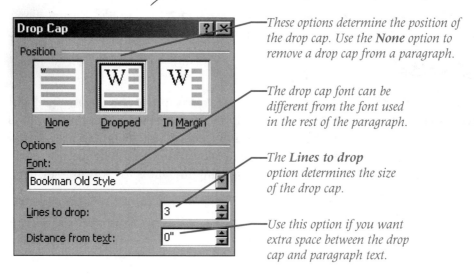

*These options determine the position of the drop cap. Use the **None** option to remove a drop cap from a paragraph.*

The drop cap font can be different from the font used in the rest of the paragraph.

*The **Lines to drop** option determines the size of the drop cap.*

Use this option if you want extra space between the drop cap and paragraph text.

Hands-On 12.5 Drop Caps

Create the Drop Cap

1. Change the font size to 18, and type the following paragraph.

> Stop by the West Side Bakery before June 30, and get a free loaf of sourdough bread when you buy a dozen muffins. Our award-winning muffins will please your palette and satisfy your hunger. All of our breads and muffins are made with the finest ingredients. We are located at 1450 Market Street in Ocean City.

2. Make sure the insertion point is positioned somewhere in the paragraph you just typed.
   The insertion point can be positioned anywhere in the paragraph when creating a drop cap.
3. Choose **Format→Drop Cap** from the menu bar.
4. Choose the Dropped position (the middle position), and click **OK.**
   Notice that the drop cap is surrounded by a border and sizing handles. The drop cap is also a type of object.
5. Click anywhere in the paragraph, and the drop cap border will disappear.

Remove and Restore the Drop Cap

6. Choose **Format→Drop Cap** from the menu bar.
7. Choose the None option, and click **OK.**
   As you can see, removing a drop cap is just as easy as creating one.
8. Click Undo  to restore the drop cap, and continue with the next topic.

Clip Art and Pictures

You can dress up your documents using the professionally designed clip art provided with Office 2000. The clip art that is built into Office 2000 is in a Windows metafile format. The metafile format lets you size and scale the clip art while preserving the image quality. You can also use your own clip art or digitized pictures. Digitized pictures are usually created using a scanner or a digital camera. Digitized pictures have a bit-mapped format, which may cause images to look grainy or decrease in quality as they are enlarged and scaled.

The Office 2000 Clip Gallery

The Insert Clip Art button on the Drawing toolbar displays the Clip Gallery. The Clip Gallery has been redesigned in Office 2000 to make it easier to locate and manage clip art and pictures. The Clip Gallery organizes clip art into categories such as Business, Animals, and Academic. The Clip Gallery can also be displayed with the **Insert→Picture→Clip Art** command.

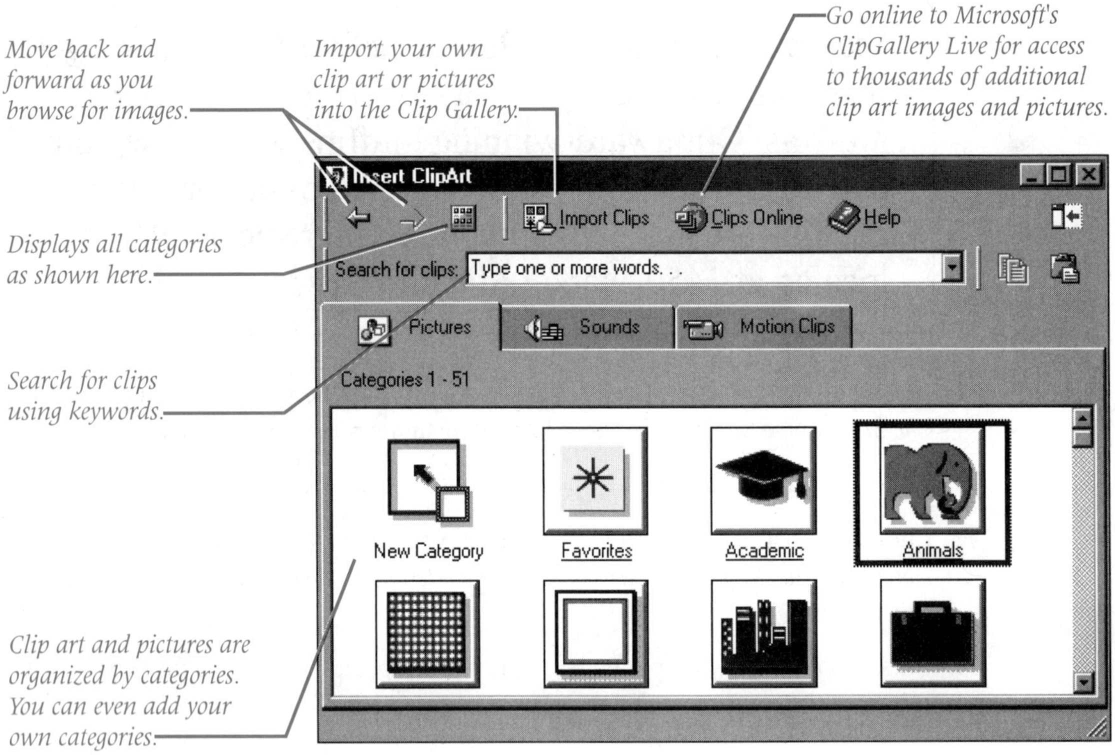
Move back and forward as you browse for images.
Import your own clip art or pictures into the Clip Gallery.
Go online to Microsoft's ClipGallery Live for access to thousands of additional clip art images and pictures.
Displays all categories as shown here.
Search for clips using keywords.
Clip art and pictures are organized by categories. You can even add your own categories.
Insert ClipArt
Import Clips
Clips Online
Help
Search for clips:
Type one or more words. . .
Pictures
Sounds
Motion Clips
Categories 1 - 51
New Category
Favorites
Academic
Animals

Hands-On 12.6 Use the Clip Gallery

In this exercise, you will explore the Clip Gallery and insert a picture. You will also explore Microsoft's ClipGallery Live Web page.

Explore the Clip Gallery and Insert a Clip

1. Click in the middle of the large paragraph with the drop cap.
2. Click the Insert Clip Art button on the Drawing toolbar.
3. Click the Academic category to display clips related to academia.

4. Follow these steps to preview a clip.

Pictures
Sounds
Motion Clips
Clips 1 - 8 in Academic
Preview clip

Ⓐ *Click the books clip.*

Ⓑ *Point (but don't click) at each button on the pop-up menu, and the button's function will appear in a ScreenTip.*

Ⓒ *Click the **Preview clip** option to display an enlarged preview of the clip.*

Ⓓ *Click the Close* ☒ *button on the Preview window.*

5. Follow these steps to navigate in the Clip Gallery and to search for a clip.

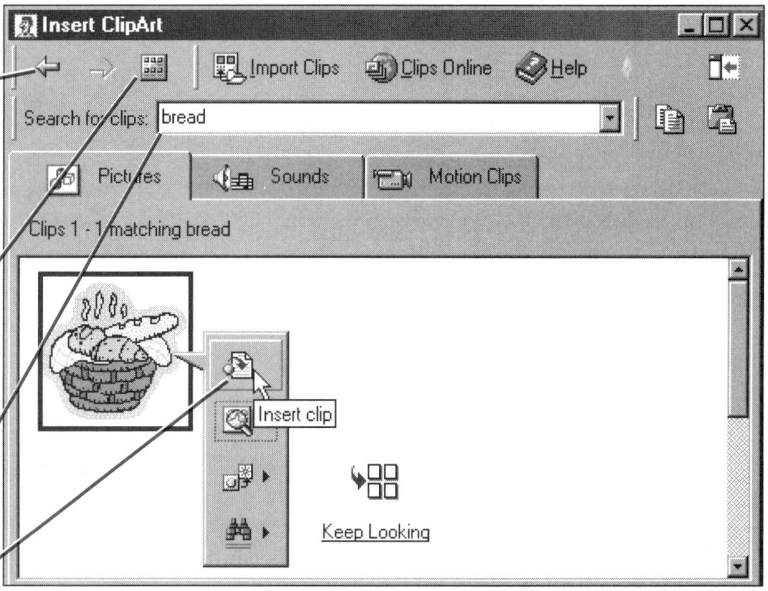

Insert ClipArt
Import Clips
Clips Online
Help
Search for clips:
bread
Pictures
Sounds
Motion Clips
Clips 1 - 1 matching bread
Insert clip
Keep Looking

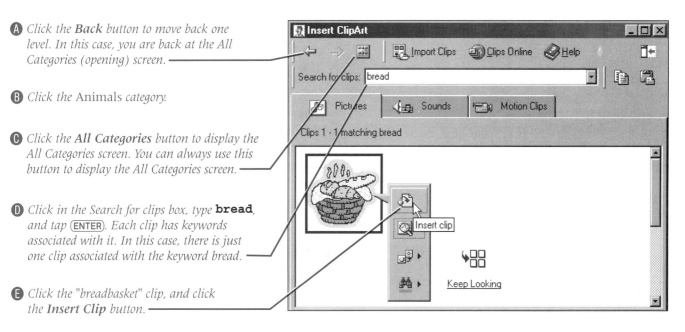

Ⓐ *Click the **Back** button to move back one level. In this case, you are back at the All Categories (opening) screen.*

Ⓑ *Click the* Animals *category.*

Ⓒ *Click the **All Categories** button to display the All Categories screen. You can always use this button to display the All Categories screen.*

Ⓓ *Click in the Search for clips box, type* **bread***, and tap* (ENTER)*. Each clip has keywords associated with it. In this case, there is just one clip associated with the keyword bread.*

Ⓔ *Click the "breadbasket" clip, and click the **Insert Clip** button.*

6. Click the Close ☒ button on the Clip Gallery.
As you can see, the bread basket picture is quite large, and it has been inserted in the middle of the paragraph. By default, pictures are inserted in line *with the text. They do not "float" on the page as do drawing objects and WordArt. In the next exercise, you will size the picture and change it's text wrapping settings to allow it to float on the page.*

7. Use the Zoom Control to switch the zoom to Whole Page.
This will allow you to see the layout of the entire page.

(Continued on the next page)

Explore Microsoft's ClipGallery Live Web Page

In order to complete the remainder of this exercise, you will need an Internet connection and a Web browser. This exercise will assume you are using Microsoft's Internet Explorer 5.0 Web browser.

8. Click the Insert Clip Art button on the Drawing toolbar.
9. Click the Clips Online button on the Clip Gallery toolbar.
   The Internet Explorer Web browser will start, and a Connect to Web dialog box may appear.
10. If the Connect to Web dialog box appears, click **OK** to continue to Microsoft's Web page.
11. Read the licensing terms page, then click **OK.**
12. Follow these steps to explore the ClipGallery Live page.

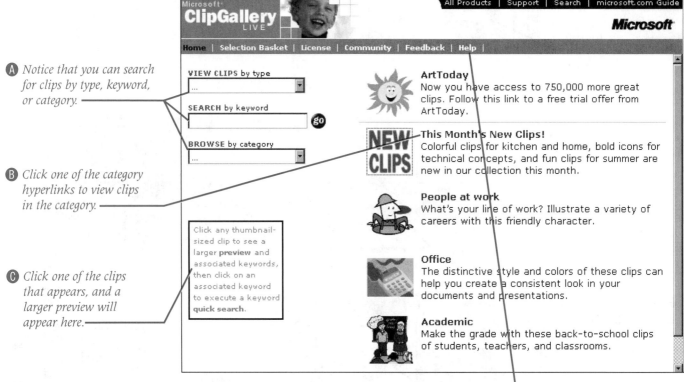

(A) *Notice that you can search for clips by type, keyword, or category.*

(B) *Click one of the category hyperlinks to view clips in the category.*

(C) *Click one of the clips that appears, and a larger preview will appear here.*

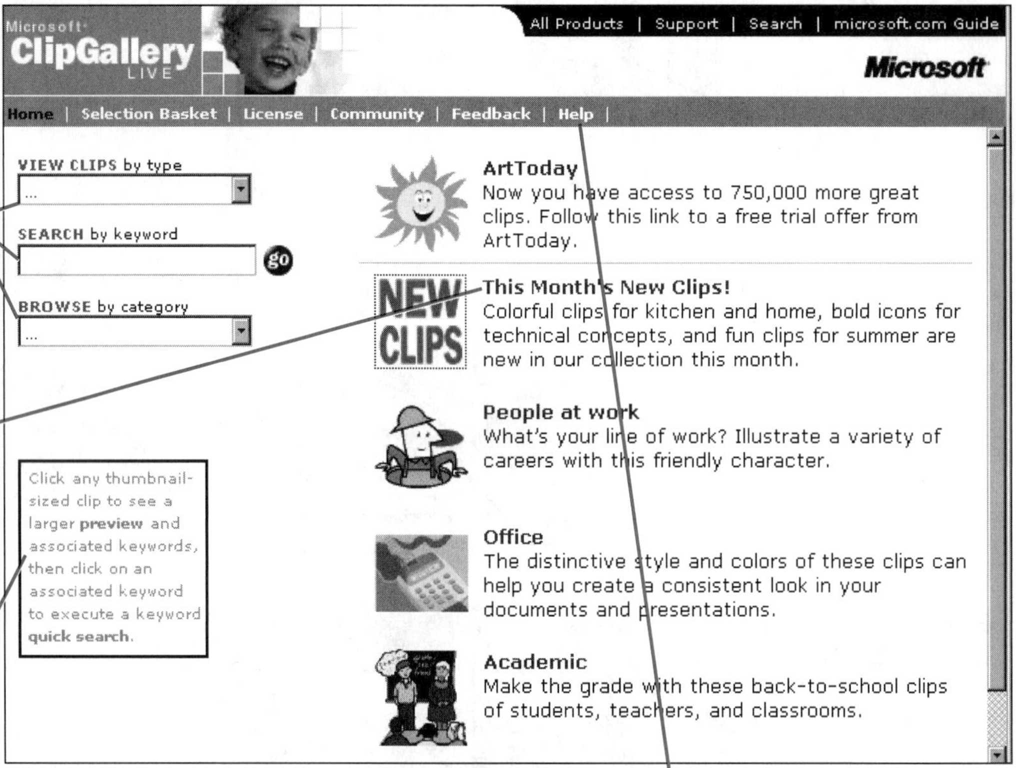
Microsoft
ClipGallery
LIVE
All Products | Support | Search | microsoft.com Guide
Microsoft
Home | Selection Basket | License | Community | Feedback | Help |
VIEW CLIPS by type
SEARCH by keyword
go
BROWSE by category
Click any thumbnail-sized clip to see a larger preview and associated keywords, then click on an associated keyword to execute a keyword quick search.
ArtToday
Now you have access to 750,000 more great clips. Follow this link to a free trial offer from ArtToday.
NEW CLIPS
This Month's New Clips!
Colorful clips for kitchen and home, bold icons for technical concepts, and fun clips for summer are new in our collection this month.
People at work
What's your line of work? Illustrate a variety of careers with this friendly character.
Office
The distinctive style and colors of these clips can help you create a consistent look in your documents and presentations.
Academic
Make the grade with these back-to-school clips of students, teachers, and classrooms.

(D) *Click the **Help** option, and take a few minutes to browse through the Help topics. Help is quite thorough, and you should be able to learn everything you need to about choosing and downloading clips. However, don't download any clips if you are working in a computer lab, because the clips are automatically added to the ClipGallery. When you have finished using Help, you can click the **Home** link on the left end of the ClipGallery Live menu bar to return to the opening screen.*

13. When you have finished browsing the ClipGallery Live site, click the Close button on the Internet Explorer window.
14. Continue with the next topic, where you will learn how to position the breadbasket clip.

Formatting Objects

You can format drawing objects, clip art, and pictures using the Format dialog box that is associated with each object type. The easiest way to display the dialog box is to right-click the object and choose Format (Object Type) from the pop-up menu. You can also click the object, choose Format from the menu bar, then choose the object type from the drop-down menu. The following illustration explains the Format Picture dialog box.

*The **Colors and Lines, Size, Layout,** and **Web** tabs are available for all object types.*

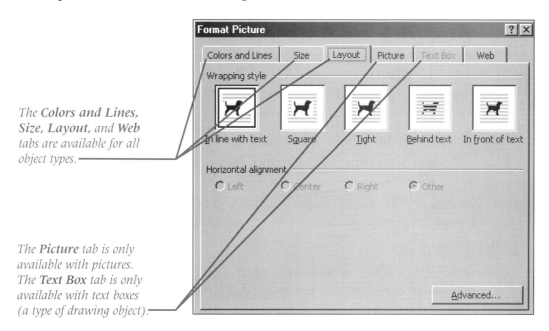

*The **Picture** tab is only available with pictures. The **Text Box** tab is only available with text boxes (a type of drawing object).*

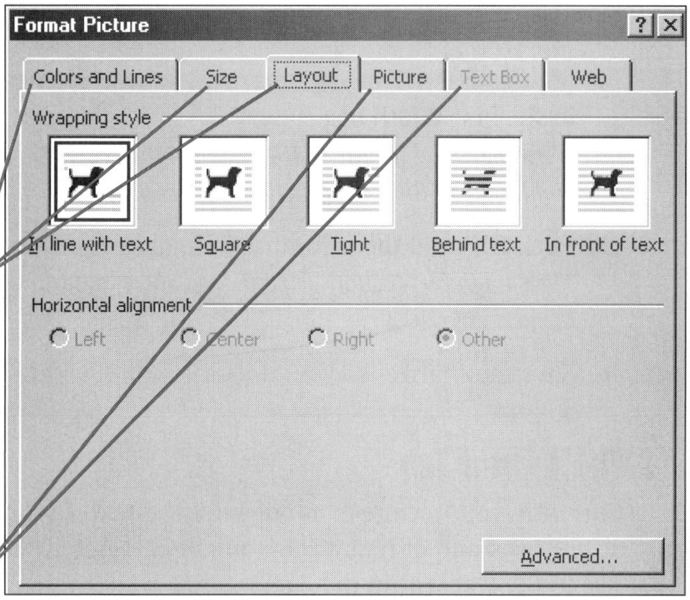

Format Picture
Colors and Lines
Size
Layout
Picture
Text Box
Web
Wrapping style
In line with text
Square
Tight
Behind text
In front of text
Horizontal alignment
Left
Center
Right
Other
Advanced...

The Size Tab

Earlier in this lesson, you learned how to change the size of objects by dragging sizing handles. You can use the Size tab on the Format Object dialog box to size an object with precision. You can specify the width and height in inches or you can scale the original width and height by a percentage. The Size tab also has a Lock aspect ratio check box. If this box is checked, you can adjust either the width or height, and Word will determine the other measurement (width or height) to ensure that the object has the original proportions. For example, in the following exercise, you will specify the height for the picture in your document. Word will adjust the width as necessary to maintain the current proportions.

Hands-On 12.7 Size the Picture

1. Make sure that the picture is selected in your document and that the zoom control is set to *Whole Page.*
2. Right-click the picture (click the right mouse button), and choose **Format→Picture** from the pop up menu.
3. Click the Size tab in the Format Picture dialog box.
4. Set the first height measurement to 1, make sure the *Lock aspect ratio* box is checked, and click in the first Width box.
   Word should adjust the width to 1.06", thus maintaining the original proportions. Notice that the width and height in the scaling section have been set to 27%. The height you chose is 27% of the original height.
5. Click **OK,** and the picture size should be reduced in your document.
   The paragraph text may be positioned above and below the picture. You will adjust the layout options in the next exercise.
6. Save the changes to your document, and continue with the next topic.

The Layout Tab

Currently, your picture is in line with the text. In other words, the picture behaves like a text character. If you add or remove text in the paragraph, the picture will remain in the same position relative to the text within the paragraph. Earlier in this lesson, you moved the WordArt object by dragging it with the mouse. You were able to position the WordArt object anywhere on the page because it uses a different Wrapping style than your picture. The Wrapping style is chosen in the Layout tab of the Format Object dialog box. You can change the Wrapping style of a picture so that it behaves like a drawing object. In the following exercise, you will do this, so that the picture floats near the bottom of the page.

Hands-On 12.8 Work with Layout Options

1. Try dragging the picture down to the bottom edge of the page.
   Notice that the furthest you can drag the picture is into the last line of text within the paragraph. At this point, the picture is like any other character in the paragraph. You can't drag it beyond the paragraph unless you use the (ENTER) *key to create space below the paragraph.*
2. Drag the picture up, and place it in the middle of the paragraph.
3. Right-click the picture, and choose **Format→Picture** from the pop-up menu.

4. Click the Layout tab, and notice that the Wrapping style is currently set to *In line with text.* *This Wrapping style is always used when a picture is first inserted. Notice the other available wrapping styles. In particular, notice the way the text flows around the sample picture in the various Wrapping styles.*
5. Choose the Tight wrapping style, and notice that the horizontal alignment options are now available.
   The horizontal alignment options are not available if the Wrapping style is set to In line with text. The alignment options are used to align a floating object horizontally on the page.
6. Click **OK,** and the picture should now have text wrapping around it within the paragraph.
7. Drag the picture to another location within the paragraph.
   The text will adjust to wrap around the picture.
8. Drag the picture down until it is around 2″ from the bottom of the page.
   Now the picture is floating on the page, so it behaves like a drawing object. You can position it anywhere on the page.
9. Right-click the picture, and choose Format Picture from the pop-up menu.
10. Click the Layout tab and notice the *Behind text* and *In front of text* Wrapping styles.
    These styles let you place the picture on a layer behind or in front of the text layer. Currently, the picture is on the same layer as the text. This is why the text wrapped around the picture when it was in the large body text paragraph.
11. Click the Size tab.
12. Set the Height to 3″, and make sure the *Lock aspect ratio* box is checked.
13. Click the Layout tab and continue with the next topic.

Advanced Text-Wrapping Options

The Advanced button on the Layout tab of the Format Object dialog box displays the Advanced Layout options. The Advanced Layout options give you two additional text-wrapping options and more control over the positioning of objects on the page.

Hands-On 12.9 Set Advanced Text Wrapping and Position Options

In this exercise, you will use advanced options to precisely position the picture on the page.

1. Click the Advanced button on the dialog box.
2. If necessary, click the Text Wrapping tab.
   Notice that the Advanced Layout box gives you access to two additional wrapping options: Through, and Top and Bottom. Also, you can specify the sides you want text to wrap on and the distance of the object from the text.
3. Click the Picture Position tab, and follow these steps to position the picture on the page.

Ⓐ *Set the* ***Horizontal Alignment*** *to* Centered *relative to* Page. *This will center the picture horizontally.*

Ⓑ *Set the* ***Vertical Alignment*** *to* Bottom *relative to* Margin. *This will place the bottom edge of the picture at the bottom margin. The bottom margin is 1", so the picture will be placed 1" from the bottom edge of the page.*

Ⓒ *Uncheck the* Move object with text *box. When this box is checked, it causes the picture to move with the paragraph to which it is anchored. You unchecked the box to force the picture to remain stationary. This box is checked when objects are first inserted.*

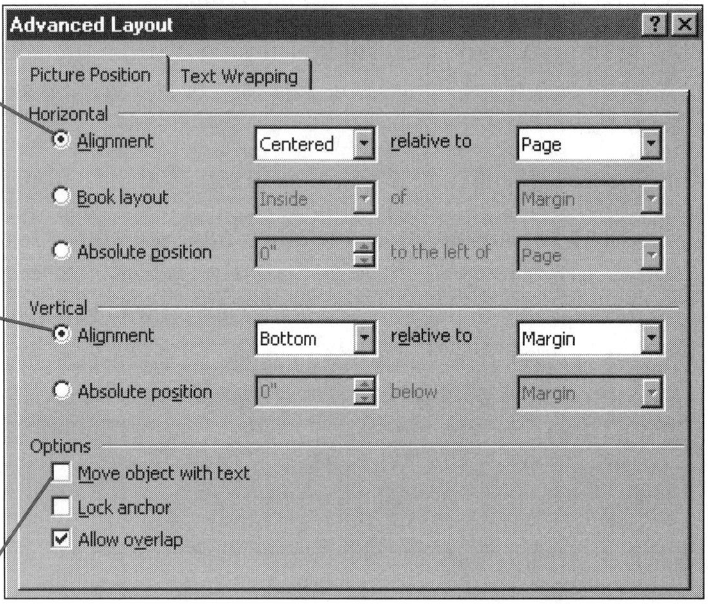
Advanced Layout
Picture Position
Text Wrapping
Horizontal
Alignment
Centered
relative to
Page
Book layout
Inside
of
Margin
Absolute position
0"
to the left of
Page
Vertical
Alignment
Bottom
relative to
Margin
Absolute position
0"
below
Margin
Options
Move object with text
Lock anchor
Allow overlap

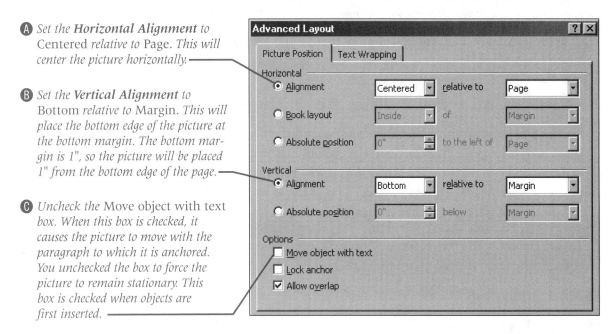

4. Click **OK** to close the Advanced Layout box, and click **OK** again to apply the settings.
   Your picture should now be centered horizontally and positioned 1" from the bottom edge of the page.
5. Right-click the WordArt object at the top of the page, and choose Format WordArt from the pop-up menu.
6. If necessary, click the Layout tab.
7. Set the horizontal alignment to Center, and click **OK.**
   Notice that there is no need to use the advanced alignment options when setting the horizontal alignment.

Remaining Tabs

The four remaining tabs in the Format Object box are defined in the following table. You will receive hands-on experience with some of these options later in this lesson.

Tab	Purpose
Colors and Lines	This tab lets you apply fill colors and borders to objects. The Arrows options are used to change the arrowhead styles on lines.
Pictures	The Pictures tab has several options that are only used with pictures. For example, you can crop the picture (chop off a portion of the picture) and change the image brightness and contrast.
Text Box	The Text Box tab lets you set internal margins for text boxes. Text boxes let you float text anywhere on a page.
Web	The Web tab is useful if you intend to post your document on the Web. You can type alternative text in the box on the Web tab. The alternative text is displayed on a Web page as the picture is loading or if the picture is missing.

AutoShapes and Other Shapes

You can use AutoShapes to add a variety of fun shapes to your documents. AutoShapes are predefined shapes organized by categories, such as stars and banners, callouts, and flowchart symbols. You choose AutoShapes with the AutoShapes button on the Drawing toolbar. You can also draw lines, arrows, rectangles, and ovals in your documents. To draw a shape, click the desired button on the Drawing toolbar, then either click or drag in the document.

AutoShapes are organized by categories. You choose a shape from a category and drag in the document to draw the shape.

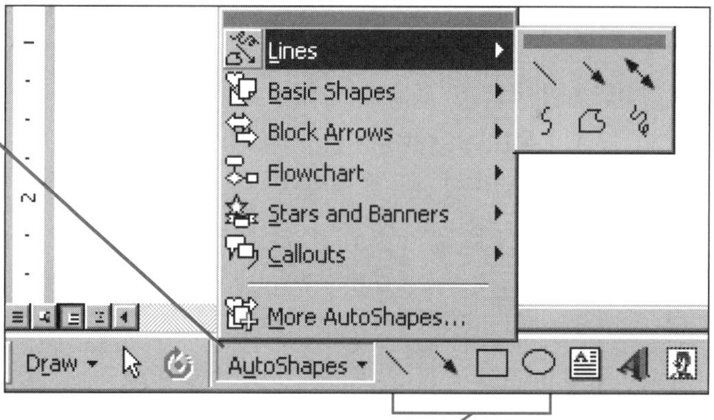

Lines
Basic Shapes
Block Arrows
Flowchart
Stars and Banners
Callouts
More AutoShapes...
Draw
AutoShapes

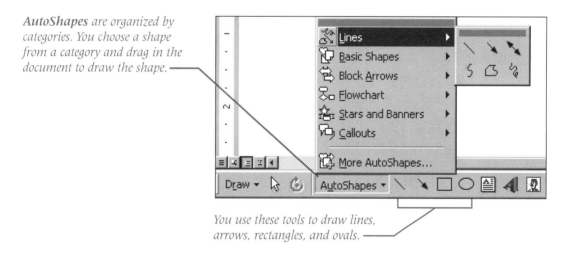

You use these tools to draw lines, arrows, rectangles, and ovals.

Constraining Objects

You can constrain objects to specific shapes or angles as you draw. These techniques are explained in the following Quick Reference table.

Quick Reference

CONSTRAINING OBJECTS

Task	Procedure
Draw or insert squares.	Choose the Rectangle tool, and click in the document. You can also press the SHIFT key while drawing a new rectangle. If you press SHIFT while sizing an existing rectangle, then the original shape of the rectangle is maintained.
Draw or insert circles.	Choose the Oval tool, and click in the document. You can also press the SHIFT key while drawing a new oval. If you press SHIFT while sizing an existing oval, then the original shape of the oval is maintained.
Draw lines at 15-degree increments.	Press the SHIFT key while drawing a line or arrow.

Deleting Objects

You can delete pictures and drawing objects by selecting the objects and tapping the DELETE key. If you accidentally delete an object, you can always use Undo to restore it.

Hands-On 12.10 Draw AutoShapes

In this exercise, you will draw a starburst and cloud AutoShape. The Zoom Control should still be set to Whole Page.

Draw a Starburst

1. Click the insertion point at the end of the large paragraph. The insertion point should be just to the right of the period in the last sentence.
2. Tap ENTER to insert a blank line below the paragraph.
   Notice that the picture remains at the same location on the page. The picture remains stationary because you unchecked the Move object with text box in the previous exercise.
3. Click the AutoShapes button on the Drawing toolbar.
4. Follow these steps to choose a starburst shape.

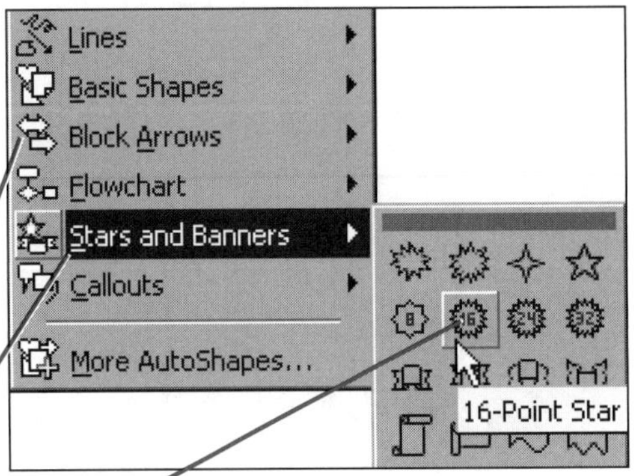

Lines
Basic Shapes
Block Arrows
Flowchart
Stars and Banners
Callouts
More AutoShapes...
16-Point Star

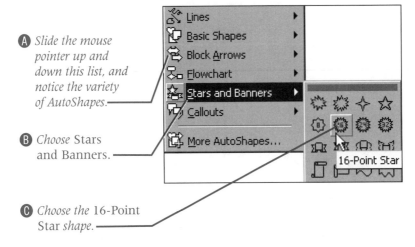

Ⓐ *Slide the mouse pointer up and down this list, and notice the variety of AutoShapes.*

Ⓑ *Choose* Stars and Banners.

Ⓒ *Choose the* 16-Point Star *shape.*

5. Follow these steps to draw the starburst.

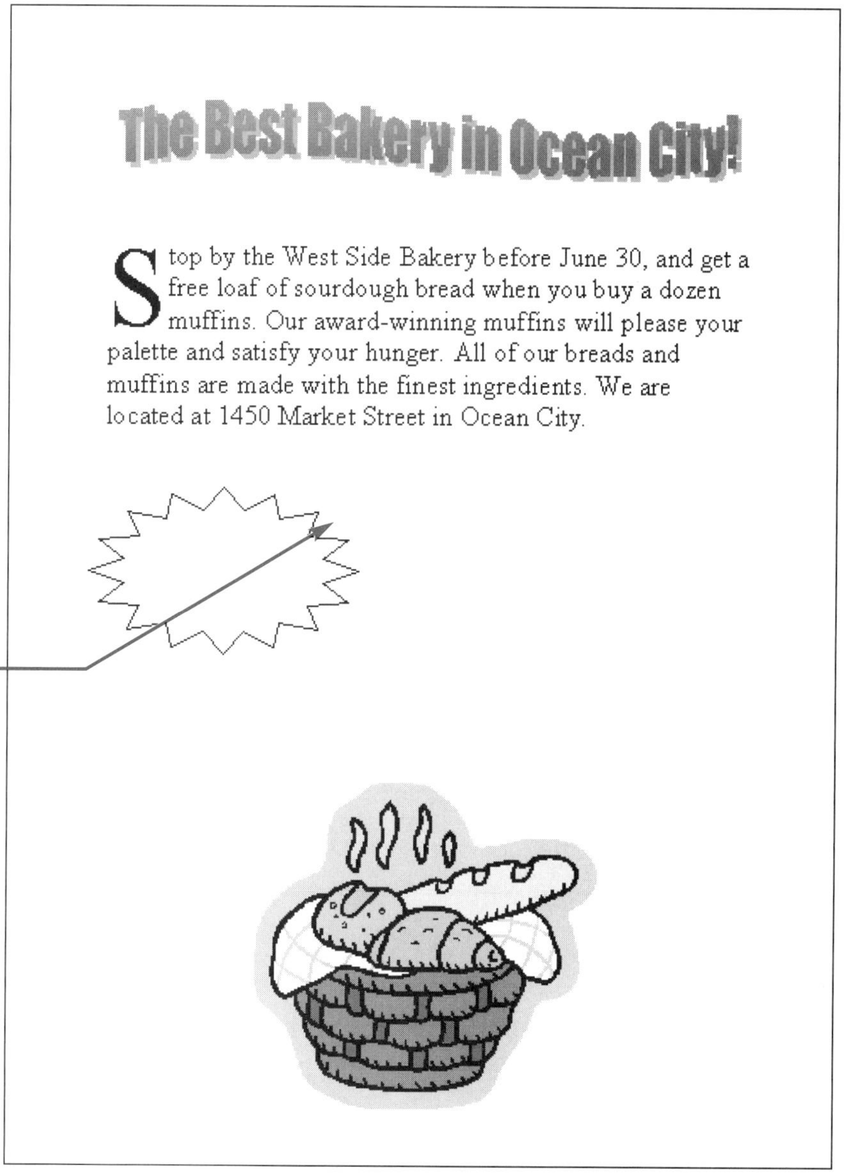
The Best Bakery in Ocean City!
Stop by the West Side Bakery before June 30, and get a free loaf of sourdough bread when you buy a dozen muffins. Our award-winning muffins will please your palette and satisfy your hunger. All of our breads and muffins are made with the finest ingredients. We are located at 1450 Market Street in Ocean City.

Ⓐ *Position the mouse pointer here, and drag up to the right until the starburst has approximately this shape and size.*

Ⓑ *Release the mouse button to complete the starburst. You will add text to the starburst later.*

6. Tap the DELETE key to delete the selected starburst.
   You can always delete an object by selecting it and tapping DELETE.
7. Click Undo to restore the starburst.

(Continued on the next page)

Draw a Callout

8. Click the AutoShapes button, and choose Callouts.
9. Choose the Cloud Callout shape (fourth button on the top row).
10. Follow this step to draw the callout.
    If you make a mistake, delete the callout and start over.

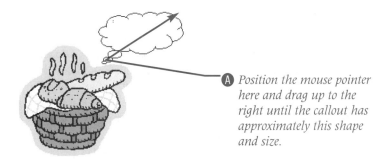

A
Position the mouse pointer here and drag up to the right until the callout has approximately this shape and size.

Formatting Buttons on the Drawing Toolbar

TIP!
Use the Format Object dialog box for size, layout, and position formatting.

The Drawing toolbar has several buttons that let you format drawing objects. You can use the Drawing toolbar to format AutoShapes, rectangles, ovals, lines, text boxes, and other drawing objects. To format an object, you must select the object first and then apply the desired format(s). You can also select several objects and format them as a group. The following Quick Reference table discusses the formatting buttons on the Drawing toolbar.

Quick Reference

FORMATTING BUTTONS ON THE DRAWING TOOLBAR

Button	Function
Fill Color	Fills an object with a solid color, pattern, or gradient
Line Color	Changes the color of lines, or applies a line pattern
Font Color	Changes the font color of text in a text box or other object
Line Style	Changes thickness and style of lines and object borders
Dash Style	Formats lines and borders with various dash styles
Arrow Style	Applies arrowheads to lines, or changes the arrowhead style of lines
Shadow	Applies a shadow effect to objects
3-D	Applies a 3-D effect to objects

Hands-On 12.11 Format Objects

Add Text to the Callout, and Format the Text

One of the benefits of a callout is that you can type text directly into it. Other AutoShapes, such as the star-burst you drew earlier, lack this capability.

1. Set the Zoom Control to Page Width.
2. If necessary, scroll up or down until the callout is visible.
3. Click inside the callout cloud and type the phrase `We're fresh from the oven`.
   The phrase will wrap within the callout.
4. Select the entire phrase within the callout. If a portion of the text is not visible within the call-out, then click on the callout and drag a sizing handle to enlarge the callout.
5. Set the font size to 18.
6. Add color to the text with the Font Color 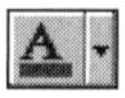 button on the Drawing toolbar or the Standard toolbar.
7. Click the Center Align  button to center the text.
8. Click anywhere outside the callout. It should closely match the following example.

We're fresh
from the oven.

Format the Callout

9. Follow these steps to format the callout using buttons on the Drawing toolbar.

We're fresh
from the oven.

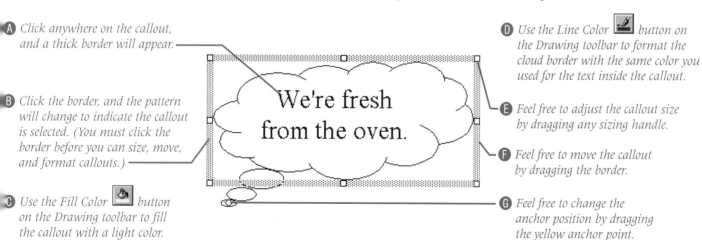

A *Click anywhere on the callout, and a thick border will appear.*

B *Click the border, and the pattern will change to indicate the callout is selected. (You must click the border before you can size, move, and format callouts.)*

C *Use the Fill Color*  *button on the Drawing toolbar to fill the callout with a light color.*

D *Use the Line Color*  *button on the Drawing toolbar to format the cloud border with the same color you used for the text inside the callout.*

E *Feel free to adjust the callout size by dragging any sizing handle.*

F *Feel free to move the callout by dragging the border.*

G *Feel free to change the anchor position by dragging the yellow anchor point.*

10. Save the changes, and continue with the next topic.

Text Boxes

You use the Text Box tool to draw text boxes. Text boxes are one of the most useful drawing objects. They look like rectangles when they are inserted; however, unlike rectangles, you can type text inside a text box. Text boxes let you position text anywhere on a page. You can use text boxes to superimpose text on other text, pictures, and other graphics. For example, in the following exercise, you will use a text box to superimpose text on the starburst you inserted in the previous exercise.

Layering Objects

Drawing objects reside on different layers than the text in your document. Drawing objects can be placed in front of or in back of the text layer. You can also layer drawing objects on top of one another. For example, the text box that you will draw in the following exercise will be on a layer in front of the starburst. Thus, the text box text will appear to float on top of the starburst. You can change the layering of drawing objects by clicking the Draw button on the Drawing toolbar and choosing layering options from the Order menu.

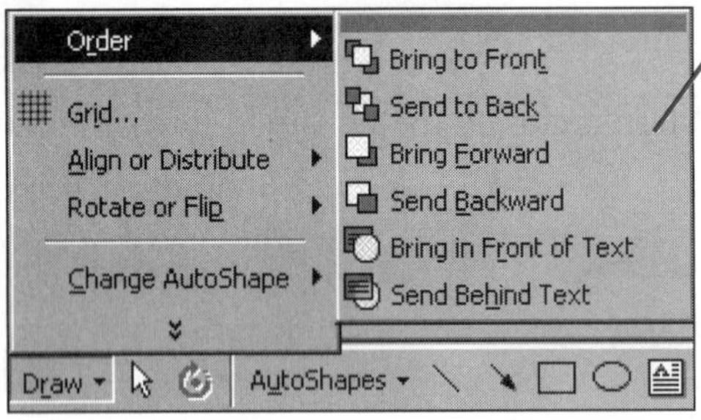
Order
Grid...
Align or Distribute
Rotate or Flip
Change AutoShape
Bring to Front
Send to Back
Bring Forward
Send Backward
Bring in Front of Text
Send Behind Text
Draw
AutoShapes

The layering options appear on the Order menu.

Hands-On 12.12 Draw a Text Box, and Layer Objects

Draw the Text Box

1. If necessary, scroll up or down until the starburst is visible.
2. Click the Text Box button on the Drawing toolbar.
3. Follow this step to draw the text box.

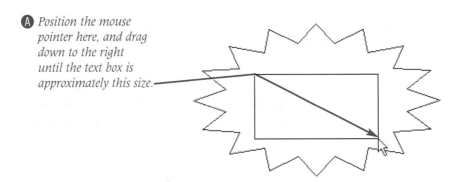

Ⓐ *Position the mouse pointer here, and drag down to the right until the text box is approximately this size.*

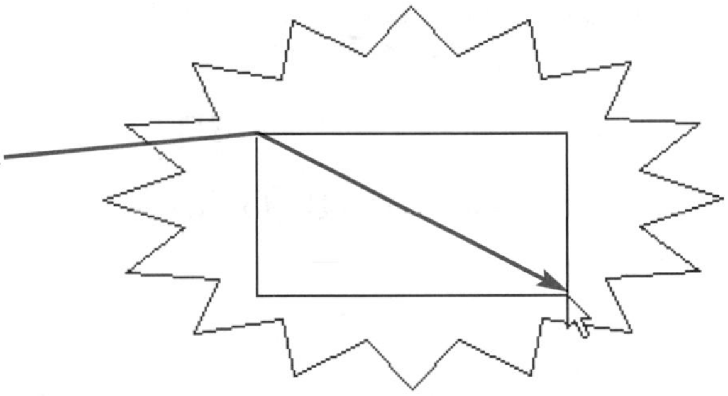

4. Type the word **Huge** in the text box, and then tap ENTER.
5. Type the word **Muffins**.

Format Text Within the Text Box

6. Select both of the paragraphs you just typed, and set the font size to 18.
7. If necessary, adjust the width and/or height of the text box and starburst.
   The text should fit in the box without wrapping, and the text box should fit inside of the starburst.
8. Select the text in the text box, and use the Font Color button on the Drawing toolbar to apply the same font color that was used in the callout.
9. Now Center Align the paragraphs within the text box.
10. Click anywhere outside the textbox.
    The text box and starburst should closely match the example shown to the right.

Huge
Muffins

Experiment with Layering

11. Follow this step to select the text box.

Huge
Muffins
A Click any edge of the text box, and a border with sizing handles will appear.

12. Click the Draw button on the Drawing toolbar.
13. Choose Order from the Draw menu, and then choose Send to Back.
    The text box text should vanish as it is sent behind the starburst.
14. Click the Draw button, choose Order, and then choose Bring to Front.
    The text should reappear, since it is now in front of the starburst. You can also use the Send Backward and Bring Forward commands to move objects backward and forward one layer at a time. This is useful with complex graphics where you have several drawing layers. The Bring in front of text and Send behind text options are useful for placing drawing objects in front of and behind the text layer.

Remove the Text Box Border, and Nudge the Text Box

15. Make sure the text box is still selected.
16. Click the Line Color drop-down button on the Drawing toolbar.
    A color palette will be displayed.
17. Choose No Line from the top of the color palette.
18. Now fine tune the position of the text box within the starburst by pressing the CTRL key while you tap any of these ← → ↑ ↓ keys. Adjust the position until you are satisfied with its placement.
    You can always nudge a selected object by using this keystroke technique.

(Continued on the next page)

Format the Starburst

19. Click anywhere on the starburst, and sizing handles will appear.
20. Click the Line Style button on the Drawing toolbar.
21. Choose a 1½ pt line style.
    The starburst should now have a much thicker line.
22. Use the Line Color drop-down button to apply the same line color to the starburst as you used for the border of the cloud callout.
23. Select the cloud callout by clicking it once.
24. Use the Line Style button to apply a 1½ pt line style to the cloud callout.
25. Save the changes, and continue with the next topic.

Paragraph Spacing

The amount of space inserted between paragraphs by the ENTER key is dependent upon the font size in effect when ENTER is tapped. Up until now, you have been limited to single spacing or double-spacing between paragraphs. You can add additional space before and after paragraphs with the Spacing Before and Spacing After options on the Paragraph dialog box. These options are quite useful in desktop publishing where spatial arrangements are important.

Paragraph Spacing vs. Line Spacing

Line spacing affects the spacing within and after a paragraph. Paragraph spacing has no impact on spacing within a paragraph. Paragraph spacing only changes the spacing before or after a paragraph. For example, in the following exercise, you will change the spacing before the paragraph in the cloud callout. This will allow you to precisely control the vertical position of the text within the callout without changing the spacing between the two lines of text. The following illustration shows the text in the cloud callout before and after Spacing Before has been applied. Notice that the text has been pushed down slightly in the second cloud.

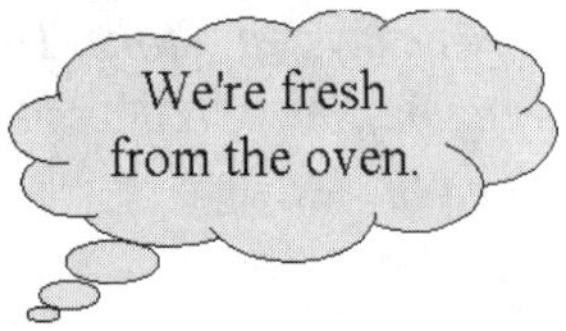
We're fresh
from the oven.

Spacing Before 0

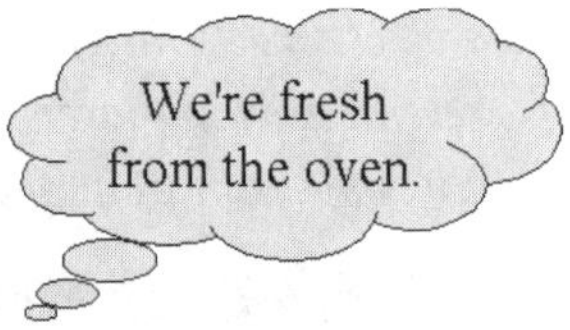
We're fresh
from the oven.

Spacing Before 4 pt

Hands-On 12.13 Increase Paragraph Spacing

1. Click anywhere on the text inside the cloud.
2. Choose **Format→Paragraph** from the menu bar.
3. Set the paragraph Spacing Before to 4 pt, as shown on the right.
4. Click **OK** to push the callout text down slightly.

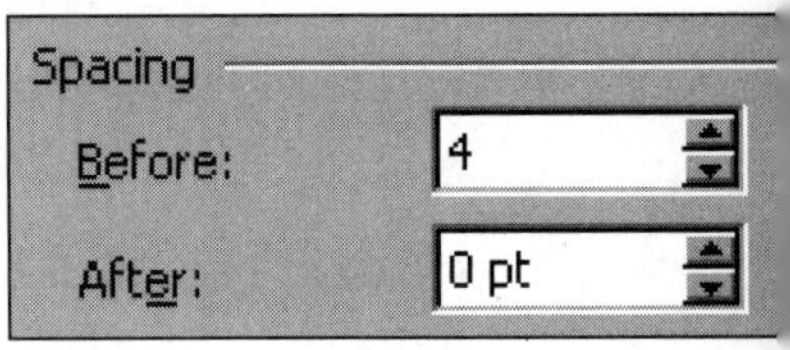
Spacing
Before:
4
After:
0 pt

5. If necessary, continue to adjust the paragraph Spacing Before until you are satisfied with the text position within the callout.
Now continue with the last topic in this lesson.

Page Borders

Word 2000 lets you apply borders to pages. Page borders are applied to all pages in a document unless the document is organized into sections. If a document is organized in sections, you can apply page borders to individual sections. You use the **Format→Borders and Shading** command to display the Borders and Shading dialog box. You use the options on the Page Border tab to apply page borders.

Hands-On 12.14 Apply a Page Border

1. Click anywhere on the main paragraph in your flyer.
You must make sure no objects are selected before issuing the Borders and Shading command. Otherwise, a different dialog box will be displayed.
2. Choose **Format→Borders and Shading** from the menu bar.
3. Follow these steps to apply a page border.

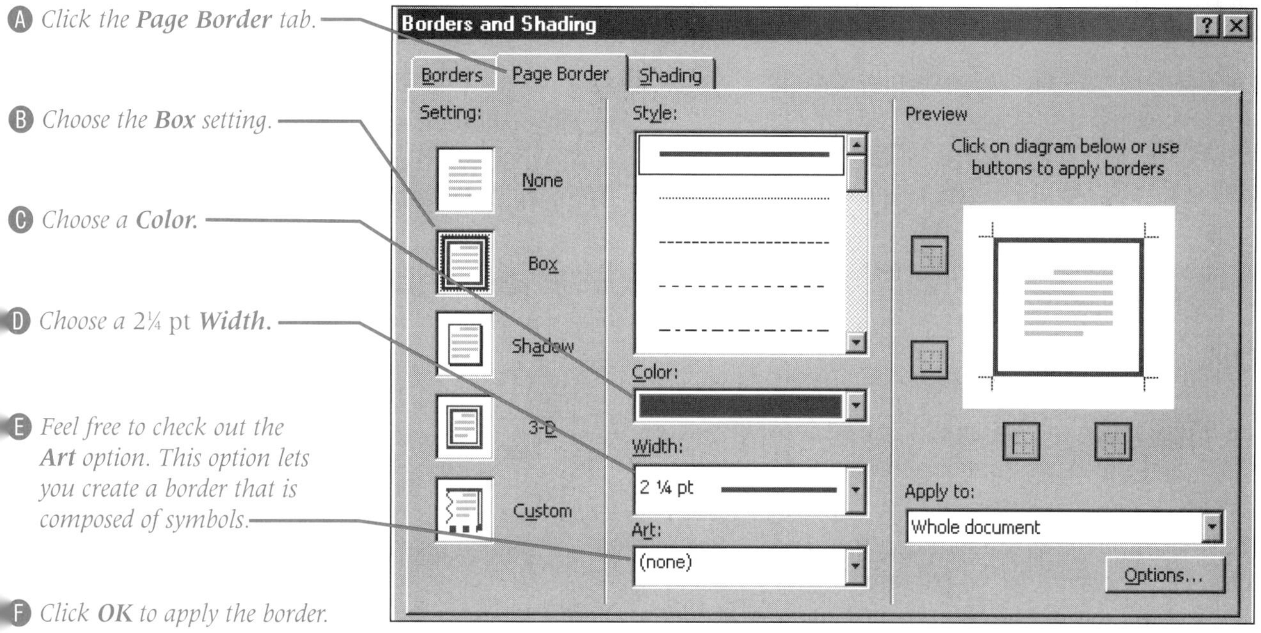
A Click the Page Border tab.
B Choose the Box setting.
C Choose a Color.
D Choose a 2¼ pt Width.
E Feel free to check out the Art option. This option lets you create a border that is composed of symbols.
F Click OK to apply the border.
Borders and Shading
Borders
Page Border
Shading
Setting:
None
Box
Shadow
3-D
Custom
Style:
Color:
Width:
2 ¼ pt
Art:
(none)
Preview
Click on diagram below or use buttons to apply borders
Apply to:
Whole document
Options...

4. Click the Print Preview button to view your completed flyer.
You should now have a border around the entire page. Word places the border approximately 0.5″ from the edges of the page. Keep in mind that you can always remove a border by issuing the Format→Borders and Shading command, and choosing the None option. Your flyer should closely match the flyer shown in the case study at the start of this lesson.
5. Click the Close button to exit from Print Preview.
6. Save the changes, close the document, and continue with the questions and exercises.

Concepts Review

True/False Questions

1. You can change the size of pictures after they have been inserted. TRUE FALSE
2. The Drawing button displays and hides the Drawing toolbar. TRUE FALSE
3. Clicking the Select Objects tool displays the Format Object dialog box. TRUE FALSE
4. The paragraph Spacing Before and After settings are used to create additional space between the lines within a paragraph. TRUE FALSE
5. Text boxes can be used to superimpose text on other text or objects. TRUE FALSE
6. Drop Caps are inserted with the **Insert→Drop Cap** command. TRUE FALSE
7. WordArt objects cannot be moved once they have been inserted. TRUE FALSE
8. Pictures are always positioned in line with text. TRUE FALSE

Multiple-Choice Questions

1. Which technique can be used to display an object's anchor?
   a. Use the Show All button to display the nonprinting characters, then select the desired object.
   b. Select the desired object. There is no need to display the nonprinting characters.
   c. Display the nonprinting characters. There is no need to select the object.
   d. None of the above

2. Which of the following statements most accurately describes the paragraph Spacing Before command?
   a. The Spacing Before command only adds space before each selected paragraph.
   b. The Spacing Before command adds space before each selected paragraph and to each line within the selected paragraphs.
   c. The Spacing Before command adds space before and after each selected paragraph.
   d. None of the above

3. Which command displays the Borders and Shading dialog box?
   a. Format→Paragraph
   b. Edit→Borders and Shading
   c. Format→Borders and Shading
   d. None of the above

4. Which keyboard key is used to select multiple drawing objects?
   a. SHIFT
   b. ALT
   c. CTRL
   d. None of the above

Skill Builders

Skill Builder 12.1 Create a Flyer on Your Own

1. Create the flyer shown below. Use WordArt to insert the "Protected Wetlands" title. The clip art can be found in the Animals category of the Clip Gallery. You can leave the layout of the clip art set to **In line with text** and use the Center Align button on the Formatting toolbar to center align the clip. Use any page border thickness and style that you desire. Insert the drop cap as shown. Use a Times New Roman font for the body paragraph and an Arial font for all other text. Use bold and italics as necessary, and choose font sizes to give the document the appearance shown below.
2. Save the document as **Skill Builder 12.1,** then close the document.

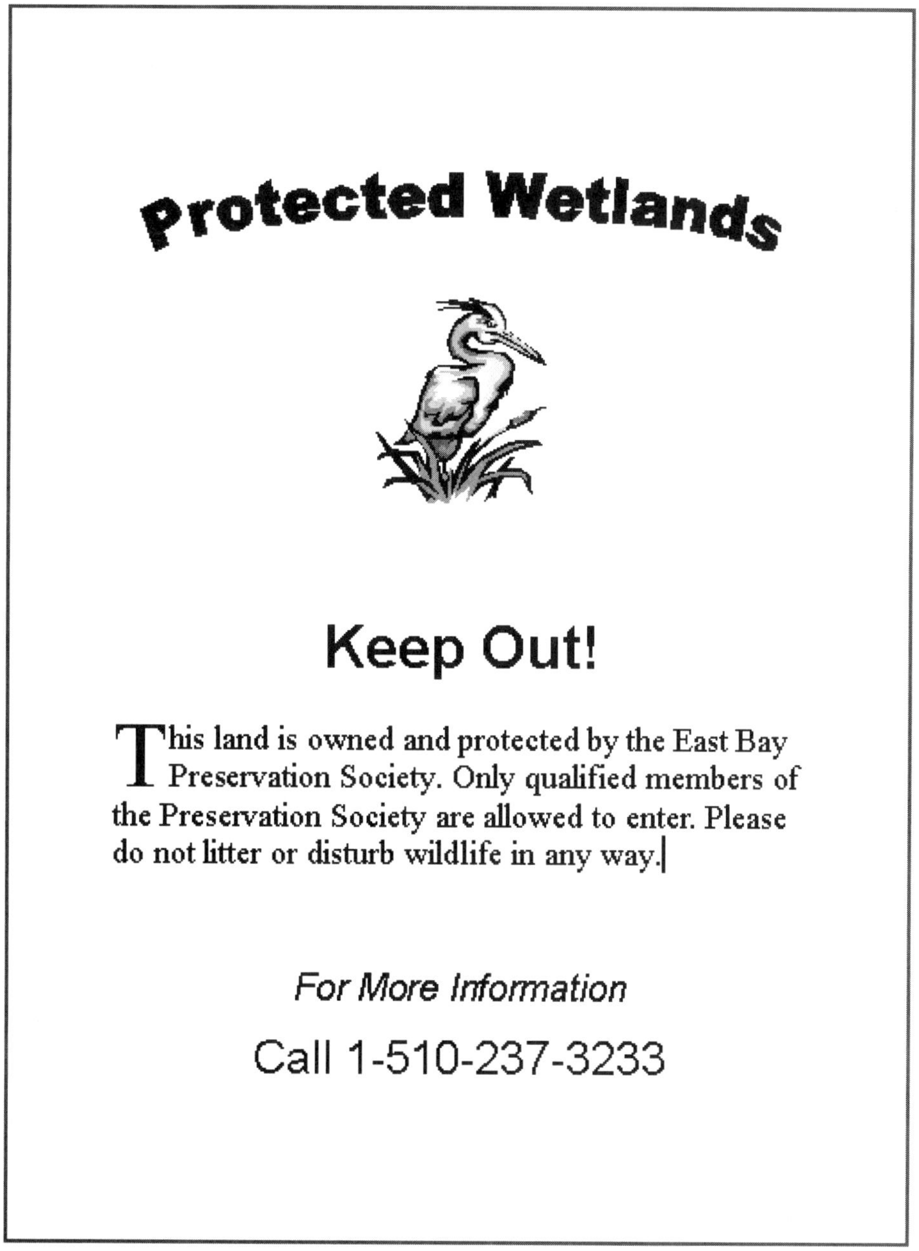
Protected Wetlands

Keep Out!

This land is owned and protected by the East Bay Preservation Society. Only qualified members of the Preservation Society are allowed to enter. Please do not litter or disturb wildlife in any way.

For More Information

Call 1-510-237-3233

Skill Builder 12.2 Practice with Drawing Objects

In this exercise, you will use WordArt, text boxes, and lines to create the family tree shown at the end of this Skill Builder, 12.2.

Insert WordArt, and Draw and Format the First Text Box

1. Start a new document, and insert the WordArt object shown in the completed document at the end of this exercise. Position the object approximately 2″ down from the top of the page and centered horizontally.
2. Click the Text Box button on the Drawing toolbar.
3. Draw a box approximately 0.5″ high by 1.5″ wide that is centered horizontally about 1″ below the WordArt object. Don't be too concerned about the size and position of the box. You can always adjust the size and position later.
4. Type the name **`Wayne Westover`** in the box.
5. Select the text within the box and format it as Arial 11 Bold.
6. Center align the text within the box.
7. If necessary, adjust the size of the box until it has the approximate dimensions shown in *Diedre's Family Tree.*
8. Use the **Format→Paragraph** command and the Spacing Before option to insert a small amount of space above the text. Your objective is to center the text vertically within the box. You will need to insert between 1 and 10 points.

Draw the First Connector Line

Take a moment to study the Diedre's Family Tree. *Notice the position of the vertical line under the first text box. The line is centered horizontally on the box and intersects the bottom edge of the box. When you draw the line, it will connect to the bottom of the box because it will snap to a grid point on the box. The Snap to Grid feature makes it easy to connect objects.*

9. Click the Line button on the Drawing toolbar.
10. Position the mouse pointer on the bottom center edge of the text box, and drag down about 0.5″.
11. Release the mouse button to complete the line. If you aren't satisfied with your line, you can click Undo and start over.

Make Copies of the Box and Line

12. Follow this step to copy the box and line using right drag.

TIP!
You can also press the (CTRL) key and drag with the left mouse button.

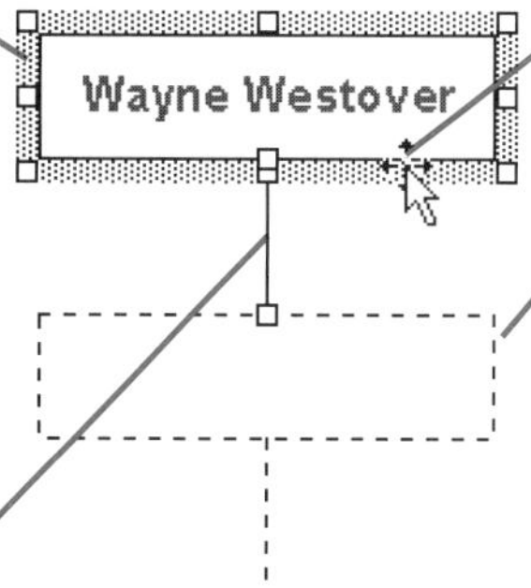

Wayne Westover

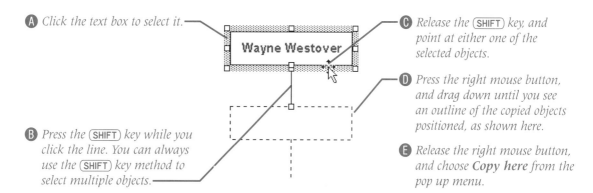

A Click the text box to select it.

B Press the (SHIFT) key while you click the line. You can always use the (SHIFT) key method to select multiple objects.

C Release the (SHIFT) key, and point at either one of the selected objects.

D Press the right mouse button, and drag down until you see an outline of the copied objects positioned, as shown here.

*E Release the right mouse button, and choose **Copy here** from the pop up menu.*

13. If you made a mistake, click Undo, and try again.
14. Change the text in the copied box to Miah Healy.
15. Repeat the procedure once more to create the Jean Healy box and the line below it.
16. Now copy just the Jean Healy box (not the line) three times to create the Yvonne Healy, Deidre Westover, and Joan Westover boxes. You will need to position the copied boxes in the approximate locations shown on the following page. Also, type the correct names in the boxes.
17. Add a light fill color to the Deidre Westover and Joan Westover boxes.

Draw, Copy, and Flip Arrows

18. Use the Arrow tool to draw an arrow from the Yvonne Healy box to the Deidre Westover box.
19. Use the Copy and Paste buttons to make a copy of the arrow.
20. Make sure the copied arrow is selected, and click the Draw button on the Drawing toolbar.
21. Choose Rotate or Flip from the Draw menu, and then choose Flip Horizontal.
    The arrow will now point in the opposite direction.
22. Now drag the flipped arrow to the proper position as shown on the following page.
23. Set the zoom control to Whole Page.
24. Click the Select Objects button on the Drawing toolbar.
25. Drag the mouse in the document to enclose all of the objects (except the WordArt object) in a box. This will select all of the objects.

(Continued on the next page)

26. Use the Line Color button and the Line Style button on the Drawing toolbar to apply a blue 1pt line to the selected objects. If necessary, use the arrow keys or the mouse to move the selected objects to the desired location below the WordArt object. Your completed document should closely match the document shown below.

27. Save the document as **Skill Builder 12.2,** then close the document.

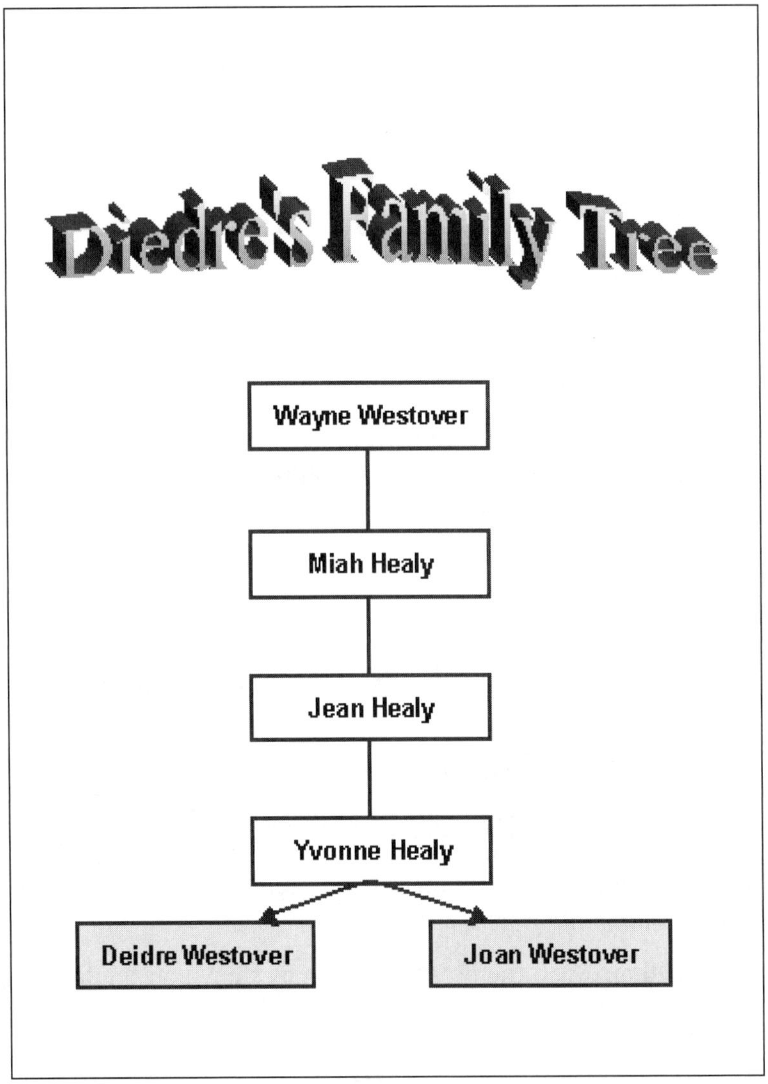
Diedre's Family Tree
Wayne Westover
Miah Healy
Jean Healy
Yvonne Healy
Deidre Westover
Joan Westover

Skill Builder 12.3 Draw an Organizational Chart

1. Use the techniques you used in Skill Builder 12.3 to create the organizational chart shown below. This project is actually quite easy if you use right drag to copy objects. The names shown below the boxes are created with text boxes that have had the lines removed. Make sure you set up the first few objects correctly, then use the right-drag method to duplicate the objects. Once you create the Dale Jones branch of the chart, you can copy the entire branch to the Paula Williams and Allen Smith branches. Then change the text in the new branches.
2. Save the document as **Skill Builder 12.3,** then close the document.

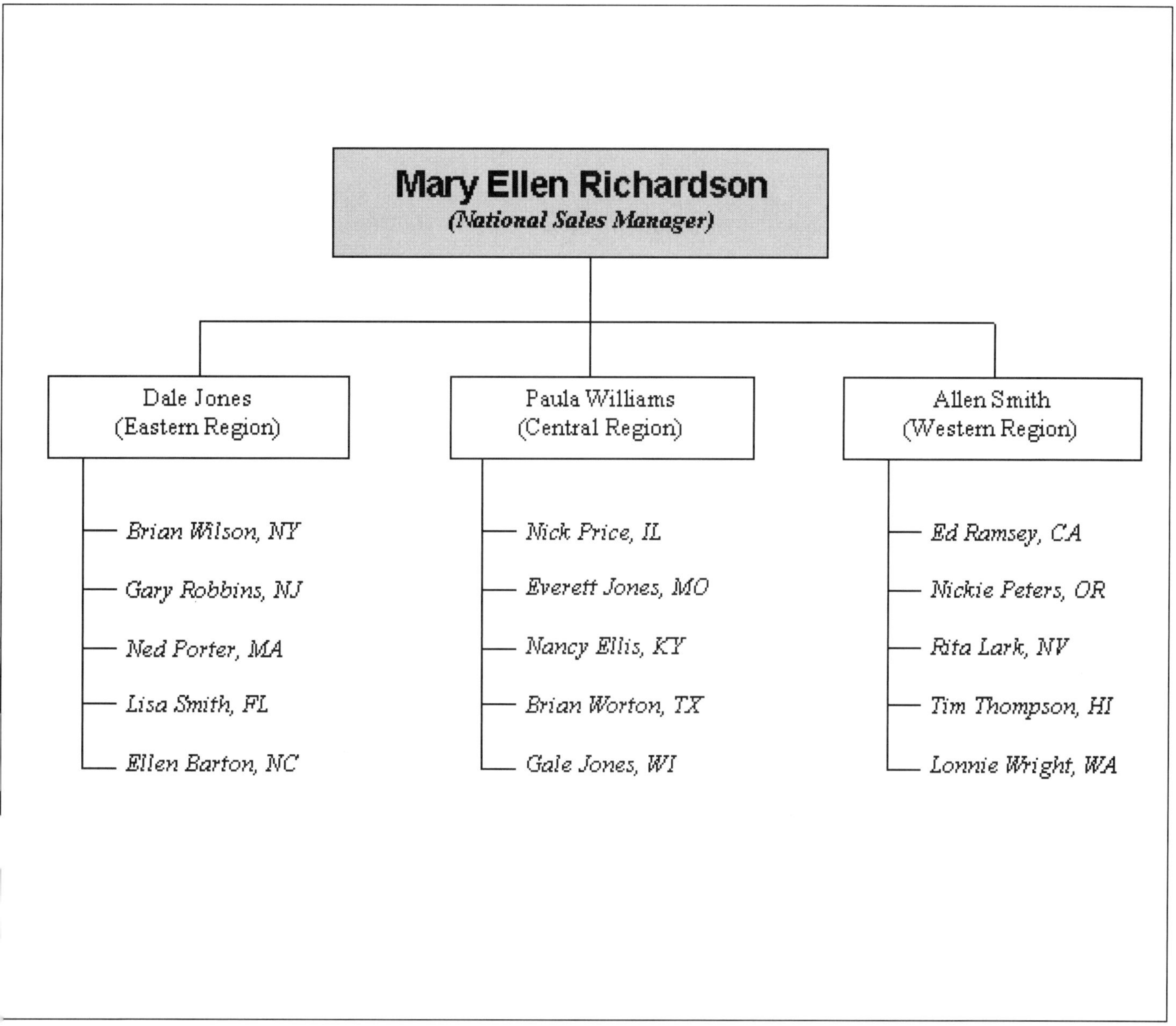

Mary Ellen Richardson
(National Sales Manager)
Dale Jones
(Eastern Region)
Paula Williams
(Central Region)
Allen Smith
(Western Region)
Brian Wilson, NY
Gary Robbins, NJ
Ned Porter, MA
Lisa Smith, FL
Ellen Barton, NC
Nick Price, IL
Everett Jones, MO
Nancy Ellis, KY
Brian Worton, TX
Gale Jones, WI
Ed Ramsey, CA
Nickie Peters, OR
Rita Lark, NV
Tim Thompson, HI
Lonnie Wright, WA

Assessments

Assessment 12.1 Format a Document

In this assessment, you will modify a document until it matches the document below.

1. Open the document named Assessment 12.1.
2. Follow these instructions to modify the document.
   - Insert the title 2″ down from the top of the page. Format the title with an Arial 20 Bold font, and center it on the line.
   - Begin the first body paragraph two lines below the title, as shown below.
   - Add drop caps to the two body paragraphs as shown. Notice the drop caps only drop down two lines.
   - Insert a picture in the second paragraph. The picture shown below is available in the Special Occasions category in the Clip Gallery. Set the height of your picture to 1.25″, and align it in the paragraph as shown.
3. Print the document when you have finished.
4. Save the document as **Assessment 12.1,** then close the document.

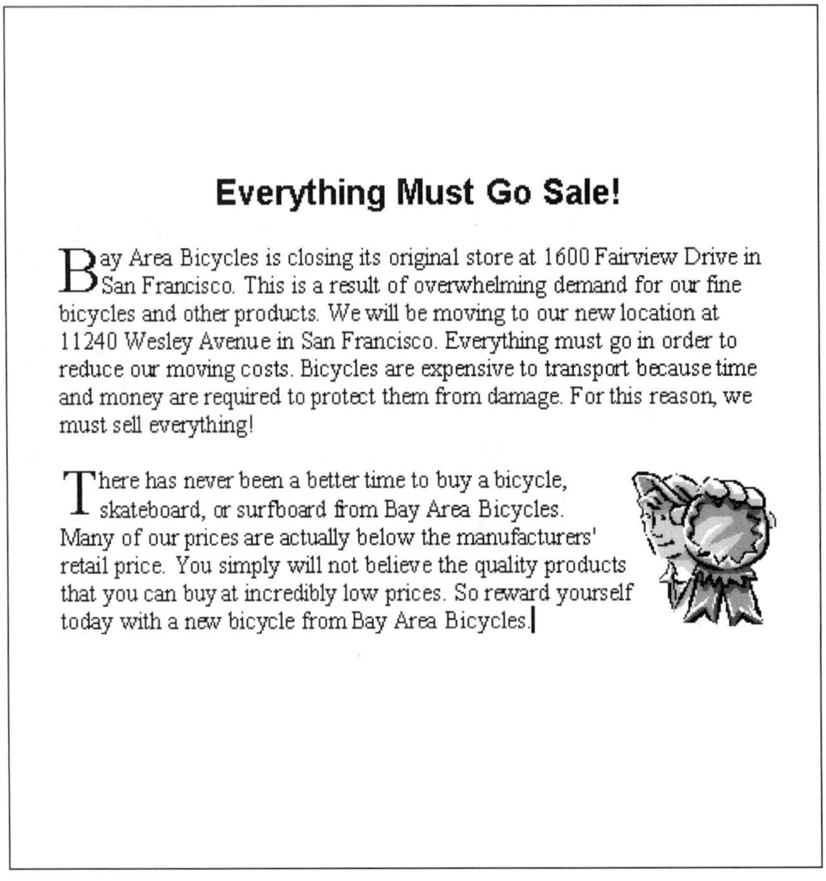

Everything Must Go Sale!

Bay Area Bicycles is closing its original store at 1600 Fairview Drive in San Francisco. This is a result of overwhelming demand for our fine bicycles and other products. We will be moving to our new location at 11240 Wesley Avenue in San Francisco. Everything must go in order to reduce our moving costs. Bicycles are expensive to transport because time and money are required to protect them from damage. For this reason, we must sell everything!

There has never been a better time to buy a bicycle, skateboard, or surfboard from Bay Area Bicycles. Many of our prices are actually below the manufacturers' retail price. You simply will not believe the quality products that you can buy at incredibly low prices. So reward yourself today with a new bicycle from Bay Area Bicycles.

Assessment 12.2 Create a Flyer

In this assessment, you will create the flyer shown below.

1. Follow these instructions to create the flyer.
   - Set all four margins to 1.5″.
   - Set the font to Times New Roman 24.
   - Position the first body paragraph approximately 3.5″ down from the top of the page.
   - Add drop caps to the two main paragraphs as shown.
   - Add the WordArt object to the top of the document as shown. Use the fourth WordArt style in the top row of the WordArt Gallery. Position the WordArt object in the blank space at the top of the document.
   - Insert the clip art shown at the bottom of the document. The clip is available in the Places category. Adjust the size and position of the clip art as shown.
   - Add a 3 pt, blue, page border with a Box style.
2. Print the document when you have finished.

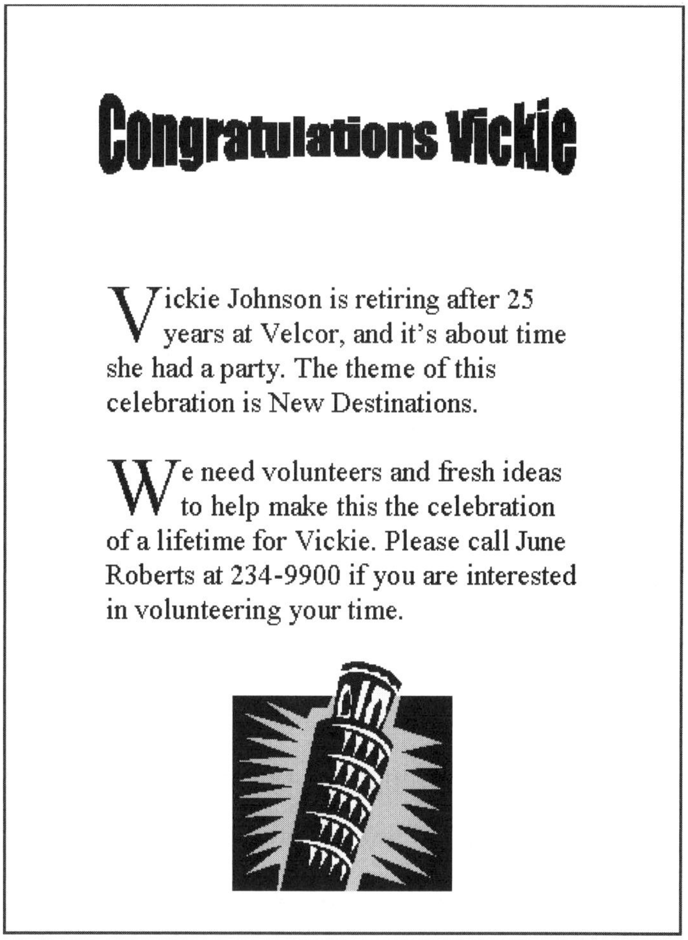
Congratulations Vickie

Vickie Johnson is retiring after 25 years at Velcor, and it's about time she had a party. The theme of this celebration is New Destinations.

We need volunteers and fresh ideas to help make this the celebration of a lifetime for Vickie. Please call June Roberts at 234-9900 if you are interested in volunteering your time.

3. Save the document as **Assessment 12.2,** then close the document.

Online Collaboration

Team projects are a key business activity. As email becomes a routine tool in business, project teams can now be composed of people from various parts of the country. By attaching documents and other types of files to email messages, team members located across the country can exchange feedback and revisions as if they were working in the same building. In this lesson, you will learn how to participate in an online collaboration. You will set up folders for project files, receive an attachment from email, and place comments into a working document.

In This Lesson

Case Study

Grace works at a property tax accounting firm. She's played a key role supporting one of their most important clients for the past year. When she was called into a meeting with her manager, Grace figured that it had to do with this client, but she was wrong. Instead, they talked about a potential client whose business the company wants to secure. Grace was asked to help develop a sales proposal to the prospective client. The "meeting" turned out to be a conference call over the phone with people in other states. Grace's manager introduced her to Terry Sanchez, a sales representative in San Antonio and Robert Smith, a writer in their New York Headquarters. Grace, Robert, and Terry will work to develop the sales proposal and presentation. Grace was asked to participate because of her in-depth knowledge of her company's day-to-day services to a key client. To start the project, Terry will send a draft proposal document for Grace and Robert Smith to review. They must have a final version of the proposal ready by the end of the week.

Terry attached a Word document to his message. Grace can open the document with a double-click and read it like any other Word document. Later, Grace can attach the document to an email message to send it back to Terry.

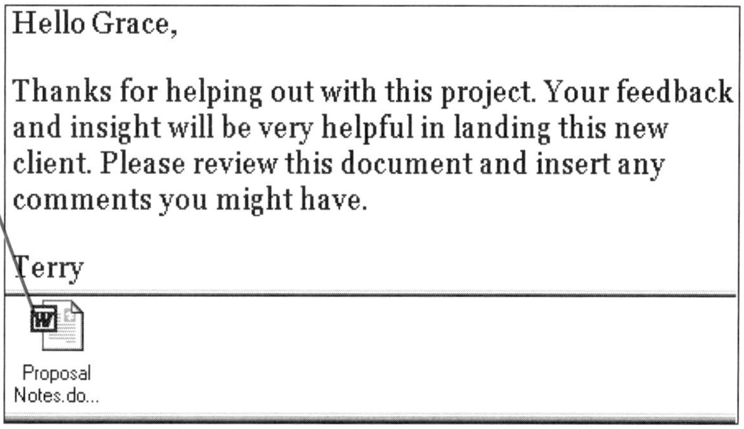
Hello Grace,
Thanks for helping out with this project. Your feedback and insight will be very helpful in landing this new client. Please review this document and insert any comments you might have.
Terry
Proposal Notes.do...

The shaded area of this message indicates there is a comment embedded in the document.

When Grace points at the shaded highlight, she sees a question from Terry about a statement in the draft document.

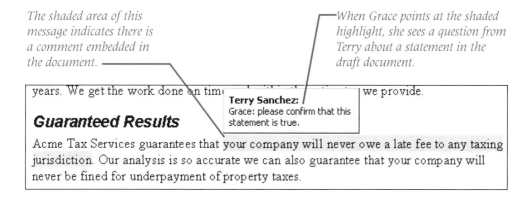

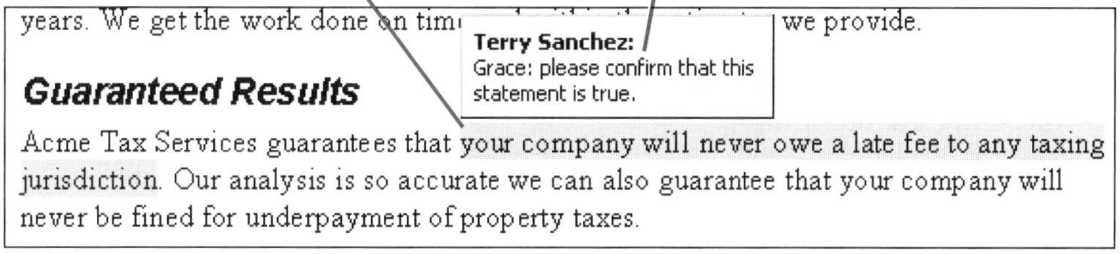
Terry Sanchez:
Grace: please confirm that this statement is true.
Guaranteed Results
Acme Tax Services guarantees that your company will never owe a late fee to any taxing jurisdiction. Our analysis is so accurate we can also guarantee that your company will never be fined for underpayment of property taxes.

Organizing a Project

When you work on a project, it is usually a good idea to create one or more folders on the computer to store the documents and other types of files with which you will work. You learned how to create folders in an earlier lesson. This topic will give you some additional practice in creating folders and teach you techniques to access these new folders quickly.

Project Folders

Depending on the size of the project and the number of files you must organize, you may need to create more than one folder. Windows lets you create folders inside of other folders. Thus you can have one main folder for the project, and create subfolders inside it for major types of documents or major sections of the project. The following diagram displays an example of project folders.

*This My Computer window is displaying the **Sales Proposal** folder that Grace created for this online team project.*

*Grace will use these folders to store additional files, leaving the **Sales Proposal** folder clear to store just the proposal files.*

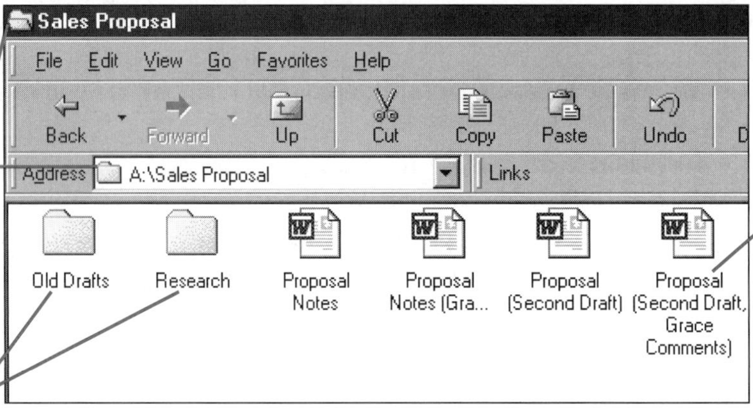

Sales Proposal
File Edit View Go Favorites Help
Back
Forward
Up
Cut
Copy
Paste
Undo
Address A:\Sales Proposal
Links
Old Drafts
Research
Proposal Notes
Proposal Notes (Gra...
Proposal (Second Draft)
Proposal (Second Draft, Grace Comments)

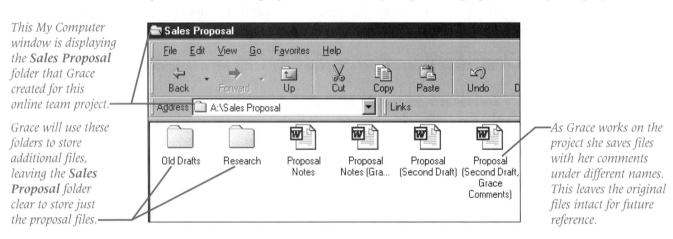

As Grace works on the project she saves files with her comments under different names. This leaves the original files intact for future reference.

Grace sets up a special project folder in the *My Documents* folder on her hard drive. She also creates a subfolder for old drafts (in case something that was deleted earlier might be useful) and for research documents. This will keep the list of files in any given folder from becoming long and confusing.

Hands-On 13.1 Create Project Folders

In this exercise, you will create Grace's three folders for the project on your floppy disk. Two of these folders will be subfolders.

1. *Double-click* the My Computer icon near the top-left corner of the Desktop. If necessary, Maximize the window.
2. Follow the instructions on the next page for your version of windows.
   Some computers may be set to display a new window for each new drive or folder that you browse. You will set the My Computer window to display just a single window as you browse—to avoid cluttering the Desktop with too many windows.

Windows 98

- Choose **View→Folder Options** from the menu bar.
- Click the **Settings** button.
- Make sure that the Browse folders option is set to *same window* as shown at right.

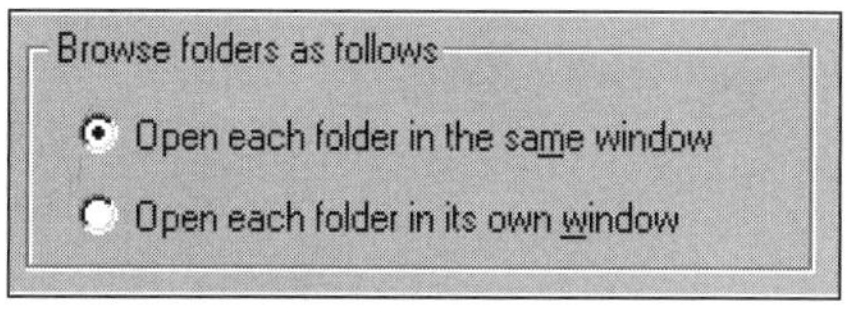
Browse folders as follows
Open each folder in the same window
Open each folder in its own window

- Click **OK;** then click the **Close** button to close the dialog box.

Windows 95 and Windows NT

- Click **View** on the menu bar. Follow the instructions in the *Windows 98* section above if the last item in the view menu reads: *Folder Options.* Otherwise, click **Options** in the View menu.
- Make sure that the Folders option is set to *single window* as shown at right.

Browse folders by using a single window that changes as you open each folder.
Example:

- Click **OK** to close the dialog box.

Windows 2000

- Choose **Tools→Folder Options** from the menu bar.
- Make sure that the Browse folders option is set to *same window* as shown at right.

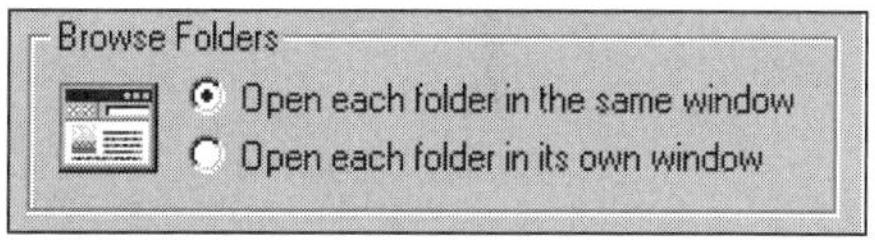
Browse Folders
Open each folder in the same window
Open each folder in its own window

- Click **OK** to close the dialog box.

3. Make sure your *exercise diskette* is in the floppy drive.
4. *Double-click* the 3½ Floppy (A:)  icon to view the exercise diskette.
5. Make sure the view is set to *Large Icons.*
6. Follow these steps to create a new folder on your floppy disk.

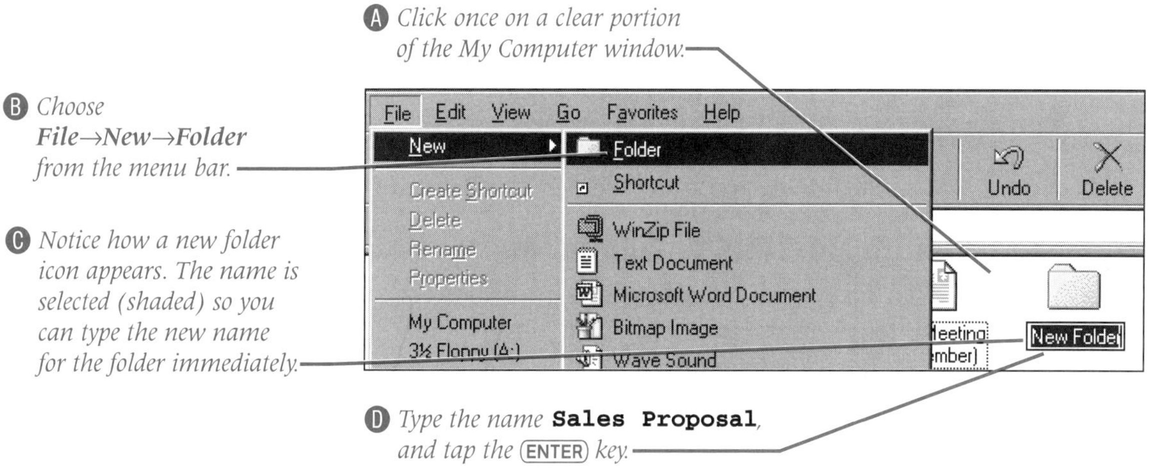
A Click once on a clear portion of the My Computer window.
B Choose File→New→Folder from the menu bar.
C Notice how a new folder icon appears. The name is selected (shaded) so you can type the new name for the folder immediately.
D Type the name Sales Proposal, and tap the ENTER key.
File
Edit
View
Go
Favorites
Help
New
Create Shortcut
Delete
Rename
Properties
My Computer
Folder
Shortcut
WinZip File
Text Document
Microsoft Word Document
Bitmap Image
Wave Sound
Undo
Delete
New Folder

7. Double-click the **Sales Proposal** folder icon to navigate to your new folder.
Notice that the name of the folder is displayed in the Address bar near the top of the My Computer window and also in the Title bar.

(Continued on the next page)

Create SubFolders

Now that you have created a new project folder, you can add the two subfolders to it. Any new folders you create will be added inside *the Sales Proposal folder, since this is the currently displayed folder.*

8. Choose **File→New→Folder** from the menu bar. Type **`Old Drafts`** as the name for the new folder, and tap the ENTER key.
9. Choose **File→New→Folder** from the menu bar. The **New** command may appear further down the menu than it did previously. Type **`Research`** as the name for the new folder, and tap the ENTER key.
   There should now be two folders displayed in the Sales Proposal folder.
10. Minimize the *My Computer* window.

Placing a Shortcut on the Desktop

Shortcut to
Sales Proposal

A shortcut is a type of file that points to some other file, folder, drive, or device on your system. You can recognize a shortcut by the small arrow in the lower left corner of its icon.

When to Use a Shortcut

You should use a shortcut if you want to access a file, folder, or drive from more than one location. For example, you might keep a file named *Sales Proposal First Draft* in a folder named *Sales Proposal,* but you also want to access the file from another folder named *Current Work.* You could place a shortcut to Staff Assignments inside *Current Work,* and leave the actual file in the *Sales Proposal* folder.

The Benefits of Shortcuts

A shortcut occupies less storage space (about one kilobyte) than another complete copy of the same file. You could make copies of a file or folder and place them at different locations on your system. However, this would have two disadvantages:

- Each copy of the file would occupy additional storage space on a drive. Since shortcuts are just one kilobyte in size, they take up very little space compared to the file they point to.
- If you wanted to change the file, you would have to change *each* copy of the file individually. This could become very confusing and time-consuming. When you use shortcuts to the file or folder, only one file needs to be modified.

TIP!

Avoid placing folders on the Desktop. Place shortcuts to folders on the Desktop instead.

Placing Shortcuts to Folders on the Desktop

You can easily open a folder by placing a shortcut to it on the Desktop. It is a bad idea to place the actual folder on the Desktop. If you move a folder to the Desktop, it loses its place in the hierarchy on your floppy or hard drive. Shortcuts help you work around this problem. The actual folder can be in its proper spot in the disk drive/folder hierarchy while the shortcut sits on the Desktop ready for quick access.

Quick Reference

HOW TO CREATE A FOLDER SHORTCUT ON THE DESKTOP

Task	Procedure
Create a shortcut to a folder on the Desktop.	■ Open a *My Computer* or *Exploring* window, and *restore* the window so part of the Desktop is visible. ■ Navigate to the item for which you are creating a shortcut. ■ Drag the folder with the *right* mouse button (right-drag) from the My Computer window to a spot over the Desktop; then release the mouse button. ■ Choose *Create Shortcut(s) here* from the pop-up menu.

Since she will be working with files on this project a great deal during the coming week, Grace places a shortcut to the folder on the Desktop. This makes it easy to open the folder quickly, while keeping it in its proper location on her hard drive (or on your floppy disk).

Using Favorites for Folders

A Favorite works like a command that points to a specific folder or file on a disk drive. There may be some folders on your system that you will want to jump to frequently. Although you could create shortcuts to these folders, a Favorite may be a better choice. You can access Favorites from the Favorites menu in a My Computer or Exploring window or in the Open and Save dialog boxes in Office 2000 application programs, such as Word. Because you access Favorites from a menu, they are often more convenient than shortcuts, which must always reside on the Desktop or in a specific location on a hard drive or floppy disk.

Uses for Favorites

You can use Favorites to quickly navigate to three different types of locations:

- Folders on the computer system or on a network
- Disk drives on your computer or on a network
- Web pages

Creating Favorites

You can create a new favorite whenever you need one. You create favorites in My Computer and Exploring windows, in Internet Explorer, or in the *Open* and *Save* dialog boxes of Office 2000 applications, such as Word, Excel, and Outlook.

Quick Reference

WORKING WITH FAVORITES TO FOLDERS AND FILES

Task	**Procedure**
Create a Favorite to a folder from a My Computer or Exploring window.	■ Navigate to display the folder for the Favorite. ■ Choose **Favorites→Add to Favorites** from the menu bar. ■ Revise the name for the Favorite if necessary; then click **OK.** *Note: Some versions of Windows 95 and NT 4.0 do not support this method.*
Create a Favorite to a folder from an Open or Save dialog box.	■ Use **File→Save As** or **File→Open** to view a dialog box. ■ Click to select the disk drive, folder, or file for which to create a Favorite. ■ Click the Tools button in the dialog box; then choose **Add to Favorites** from the drop-down menu.
Access a Favorite from an Office 2000 Open or Save dialog box.	■ Use **File→Save As** or **File→Open** to view a dialog box. ■ Click the **Favorites** button to view all of your Favorites.
Access a Favorite from a My Computer or Exploring Window.	■ Open a *My Computer, Exploring,* or *Internet Explorer* window. ■ Click **Favorites** on the menu bar, and choose the Favorite to which you wish to navigate. *Note: Some versions of Windows 95 and NT 4.0 do not support this method.*

Hands-On 13.2 Create a Shortcut and a Favorite

In this exercise, you will create a Favorite that opens the Sales Proposal folder on your floppy disk. You will also create a shortcut the on the Desktop to the Sales Proposal folder.

Create a Favorite

1. Start Microsoft Word; then click the Open button on the toolbar.
2. Follow these steps to create the Favorite.

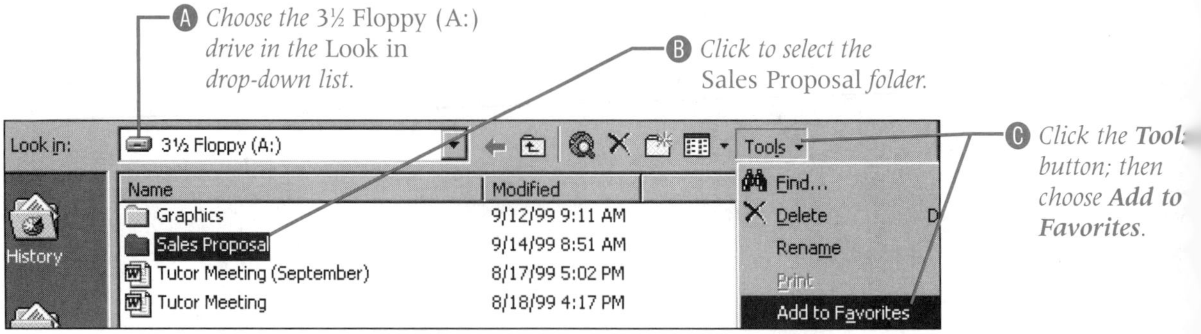
A Choose the 3½ Floppy (A:) drive in the Look in drop-down list.
B Click to select the Sales Proposal folder.
C Click the Tools button; then choose Add to Favorites.
Look in:
3½ Floppy (A:)
Tools
Name
Modified
Graphics
9/12/99 9:11 AM
Sales Proposal
9/14/99 8:51 AM
Tutor Meeting (September)
8/17/99 5:02 PM
Tutor Meeting
8/18/99 4:17 PM
History
Find...
Delete
Rename
Print
Add to Favorites

3. Click the **Favorites** button on the left side of the dialog box.
The dialog box will display a list of all of the Favorites defined for your log-on name. Each log-on name can maintain a custom list of Favorites.

4. Tap the letter **s** on the keyboard until you see a Favorite named *Sales Proposal* or *Sales Proposal folder.*

5. If you see a Favorite named **Sales Proposal folder,** click the **icon** (not the name) to select the Favorite; then tap the DELETE key. Click **Yes** if you are asked to confirm the deletion.
Another student may have created this Favorite previously. There is no need to have more than one Favorite to this folder.

6. Follow these steps to rename the Favorite.

Wende
MyIP -
Sales P
Rename
Properties

Ⓐ *Right-click on the* Sales Proposal *Favorite; then choose* ***Rename*** *from the pop-up window.*

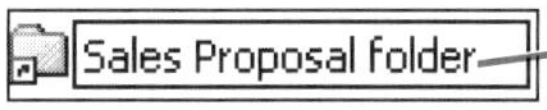
Sales Proposal folder

Ⓑ *Tap the* END *key, tap the* SPACE BAR *and type* **folder** *at the end of the Favorite name; then tap the* ENTER *key.*

You can use this technique to rename any file or folder that you view in an Open *or* Save As *dialog box.*

7. Click the **Cancel** button to close the dialog box, and then minimize the Word window.
The Cancel *button cancels the* Open File *command, not the creation of the Favorite. The Favorite you created in this dialog box will remain after you give the Cancel command.*

Create a Shortcut to the Folder

8. If you see a shortcut on the Desktop named **Shortcut to Sales Proposal,** drag it to the **Recycle Bin.** Click **Yes** if you are asked to confirm the deletion.

9. Click the **Sales Proposal** button on the Windows Taskbar to make the window active.

10. Click the Restore button at the top-right corner of the My Computer window. If necessary, *drag* on the borders of the window to make a portion of the Desktop visible.

11. Click the Up button to return to the first (root) level of the floppy drive.
Now the 3½ Floppy (A:) *drive is displayed in the Address bar. Looking at the Address bar as you navigate in folders helps you keep track of where you are.*

(Continued on the next page)

12. Follow these steps to create the shortcut.

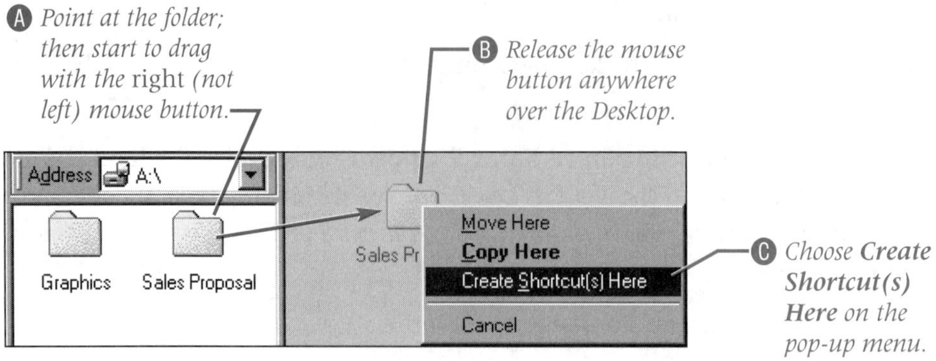

A Point at the folder; then start to drag with the right (not left) mouse button.
B Release the mouse button anywhere over the Desktop.
C Choose **Create Shortcut(s) Here** on the pop-up menu.
Address A:\
Graphics
Sales Proposal
Sales Pr
Move Here
Copy Here
Create Shortcut(s) Here
Cancel

Now a shortcut to the folder will appear on the Desktop. Notice the small arrow on the icon that identifies it as a shortcut.

Shortcut to Sales Proposal

13. Close the *My Computer* window.

Navigate with the Shortcut and Favorite

14. Double-click on the **Sales Proposal** folder shortcut.
A new My Computer window will open to display the folder.

15. Close the *My Computer* window.

16. *Double-click* the **My Computer** icon to open a new *My Computer* window.

17. Choose **Favorites→Sales Proposal folder** from the menu bar. If you do not see **Favorites** on the menu bar, skip to Step 18—your version of Windows does not support this menu command in the My Computer window.
The contents of the Sales Proposal folder are displayed immediately. You can access this folder from any window that features the Favorites command. You will see a Favorites command in Word's Open *dialog box later in this lesson; which even works with versions of Windows that do not have a Favorites command on the My Computer window menu bar.*

18. Close the My Computer window.

Email Attachments

An *attachment* is a file you include with an email message. Some types of information are not as easy to work with in the form of an email message. For example, if you needed to submit a multi-page report for review by others, you could lose some of the document formatting (such as pagination) if you converted the report from a word processor file to an email message. It would be much simpler to send the report document as an attachment. An attachment can be any type of file.

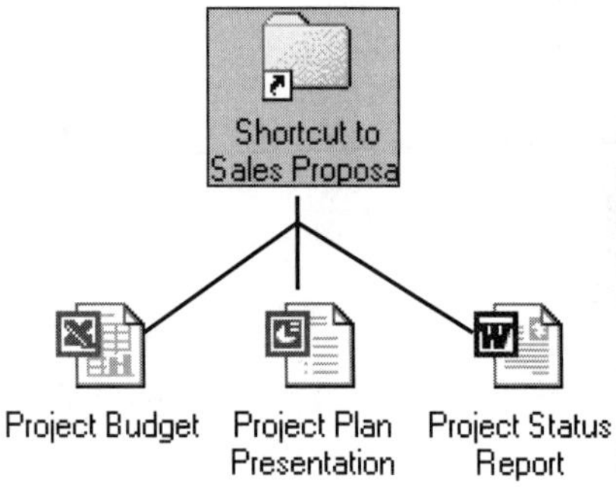

Shortcut to Sales Proposa
Project Budget
Project Plan Presentation
Project Status Report

Here are some examples of attachments:

- A Word document, Excel worksheet, or PowerPoint presentation.
- A photograph (converted to an image file).

Receiving and Opening Attachments

When you receive a file that has an attachment, Outlook will indicate that the file has an attachment by displaying a small paper clip next to the message name. As you view the message in the Outlook window, you will also see a paper clip at the top-right corner of the Preview pane. Clicking on the paper clip will display the names of all the attachments. If you double-click to open an email message, any attachments are displayed as icons at the bottom of the message window.

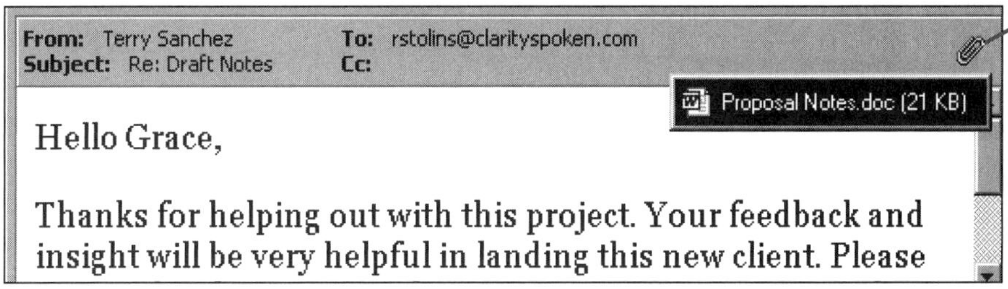
From: Terry Sanchez
To: rstolins@clarityspoken.com
Subject: Re: Draft Notes
Cc:
Proposal Notes.doc (21 KB)
Hello Grace,
Thanks for helping out with this project. Your feedback and insight will be very helpful in landing this new client. Please

*When you click the **paper clip** icon in Outlook's message preview pane; a menu displays the available attachments.*

File Compatibility

In order to open an attachment, you must have installed an application program that is capable of opening the attachment file. For example, if the file is an Access database file, you must have Access (or another program capable of opening Access database files) installed on your computer. If Windows cannot find a program that can open the file, it will ask you to select an application program. Fortunately, most attachments you receive will probably be word processing and workbook files, so file compatibility will rarely be an issue.

Quick Reference

OPENING ATTACHMENTS

Task	Procedure
Open an attachment from the *Inbox* view.	■ Click to select the message with the attachment. ■ Click the **paper clip icon** on the right corner of the Preview pane; then select the attachment you wish to open.
Open an attachment from a *message* window.	■ Double-click to **open** the message in a message window. ■ *Double-click* the *icon* for the attachment, or *right-click* on the icon; then choose **Open** from the pop-up menu.

Saving Attachments

After you receive an attachment, you may wish to store it somewhere else on the hard drive or a floppy disk. Outlook stores attachments as a part of the email message. In order to work with the attachment apart from the email message it was attached to, you must save the attachment file(s). One way to save an attachment is to open it in an application program, then use the programs' *Save As* command. You can also right-click on an attachment in a message window, and then give the *Save As* command.

TIP! *When you delete a message that has attachments, the attachment files are deleted as well—unless you have already saved the attachments.*

When Grace gets the email message from Terry with the draft proposal, she saves it into the project folder she set up earlier. Otherwise, it would be difficult to locate the document later unless she looked up the email message it was attached to.

Attachments and Computer Viruses

Remember that an attachment may contain a computer virus. This will probably be rare, but you should always be cautious when handling attachments from users you do not know well. Even co-workers can unknowingly transmit a virus through a *macro virus* in a document file.

Quick Reference

SAVING ATTACHMENTS

Task	Procedure
Save an attachment in a message window.	■ Double-click to open the message with the attachment. ■ Right-click on the attachment file icon at he bottom of the message window; then choose File→Save As from the pop-up menu.

Hands-On 13.3 Save an Attachment

In this exercise, you will save an attachment to an email message in one of the project folders.

Before you begin, *if you do not have access to email in the computer lab, you should skip directly to the* Save Files Off the Web Page *section (Step 7) near the end of this exercise.*

1. Start **Outlook**, and display the *Inbox* view.
2. Create a new email message with the settings below.

Addressee	**Terry@offtowork.com**
Subject	**Draft Notes**
Body	**Hello Terry:** **Please send me your current notes on the proposal draft as we discussed in this morning's phone call. I will look them over and give you my input.** **Regards,** **Grace**

3. Send the message, then click the Send/Receive button. Wait about a minute, and then check for a reply. The reply will have an attachment.
   Notice the small paper clip for the message in the message list. This indicates that the message contains an attachment.

Terry Sanchez
Re: Draft Notes

4. *Double-click* to open the Re: Draft Notes message in its own message window.
   The attachment will appear at the bottom of the message.

5. Follow these steps to save the attachment to your floppy disk.

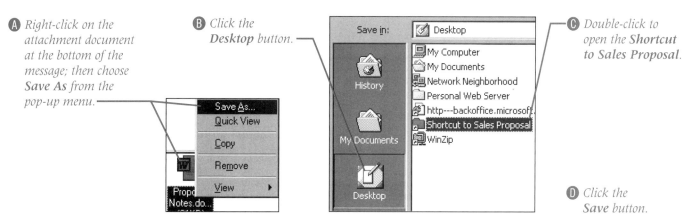

(A) *Right-click on the attachment document at the bottom of the message; then choose* ***Save As*** *from the pop-up menu.*

(B) *Click the* ***Desktop*** *button.*

Save As...
Quick View
Copy
Remove
View
Notes.do...

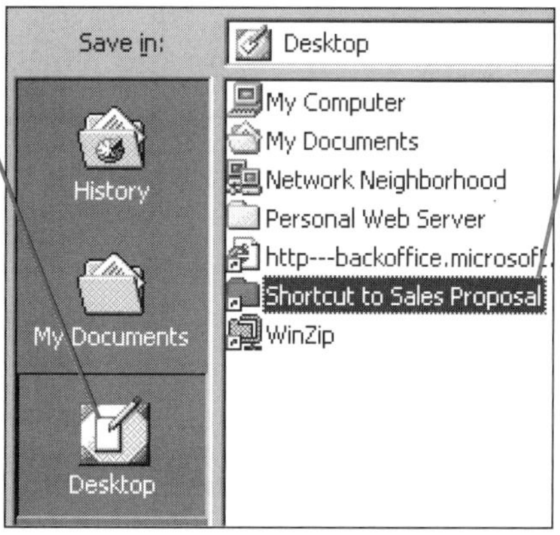

Save in:
Desktop
History
My Documents
Desktop
My Computer
My Documents
Network Neighborhood
Personal Web Server
http---backoffice.microsof
Shortcut to Sales Proposal
WinZip

(C) *Double-click to open the* ***Shortcut to Sales Proposal****.*

(D) *Click the* ***Save*** *button.*

6. Close ☒ the **message** window; then minimize ▭ the **Outlook** window.
You should skip the next section of this exercise, and continue with Step 13 *near the end of this exercise.*

Save the Files Off the Web Page

If you do not have access to email in the computer lab, you should use this alternative process to save the files Terry Sanchez was to send as attachments off of a Web page.

7. Start **Internet Explorer** and navigate to the Lesson 13 Web page at:
www.offtowork.com/oe/lesson13

8. Follow these steps to save the first document file:

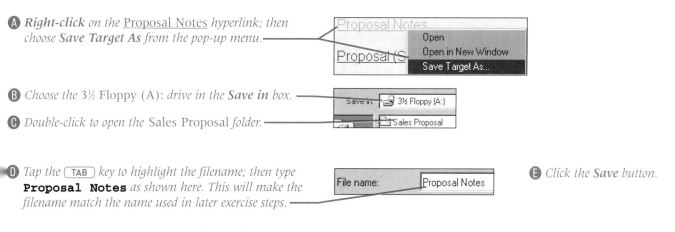

(A) ***Right-click*** *on the* Proposal Notes *hyperlink; then choose* ***Save Target As*** *from the pop-up menu.*

Proposal Notes
Proposal (S
Open
Open in New Window
Save Target As...

(B) *Choose the* 3½ Floppy (A): *drive in the* ***Save in*** *box.*

(C) *Double-click to open the* Sales Proposal *folder.*

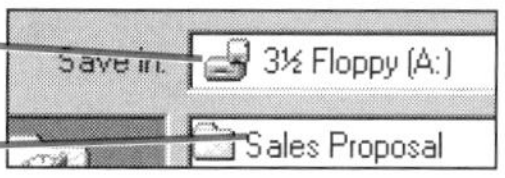

3½ Floppy (A:)
Sales Proposal

(D) *Tap the* TAB *key to highlight the filename; then type* **`Proposal Notes`** *as shown here. This will make the filename match the name used in later exercise steps.*

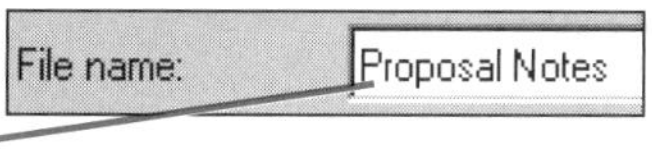

File name:
Proposal Notes

(E) *Click the* ***Save*** *button.*

Internet Explorer will display a dialog box showing the progress of copying the file from the Web page to your floppy disk.

9. Click the **Close** button on the *Download Complete* dialog box.

10. *Right-click* on the **Proposal (Second Draft)** hyperlink on the Web page; then choose *Save Target As* from the pop-up menu. Save the file to the Sales Proposal folder with the name **`Proposal (Second Draft)`**. Close the **Download Complete** window.

11. Close ☒ the Internet Explorer window.

12. Start **Outlook;** then minimize ▭ the Outlook window.
This step ensures that your Windows Taskbar matches the instructions later in this exercise.

(Continued on the next page)

Open the Document

13. Double-click the **Shortcut to Sales Proposal** shortcut on the Desktop.
14. Double-click to open the **Proposal Notes** document in Word.

Sending Attachments

Sending one or more attachments with an email message is easy to do. You simply create an email message in Outlook and then give the command to attach one or more files to the message. The files you select to attach can be anywhere on the computer's hard drive or on your floppy disk. You can use either of two methods to send one or more files as attachments:

- **From My Computer and Exploring windows—**You can attach any file by dragging and dropping it from a My Computer or Exploring window into the desired email message.
- **From the Message window—**While you are composing a message, you always have the option to attach one or more files to the message with the **Insert→File Attachment** command, or the *Insert File* button.

Quick Reference

SENDING ATTACHMENTS

Task	Procedure
Attach one or more files to a message you are composing.	■ Start composing the new message. ■ Click the Insert File button on the message toolbar. ■ Navigate to the file you wish to attach; then double-click to select it, or click the **Insert** button. ■ To select more than one file in a folder, press the CTRL key as you click to select each file. ■ If you need to attach additional file(s) from another folder or drive on your computer, click the **Insert File** button again, and repeat the previous two steps.

TIP!

You will send an attachment later in this lesson.

Working with Comments

Word's Comment feature is a great tool for online collaboration. A *comment* is a text note that you can embed inside a Word document without cluttering the actual text of the document page. When someone inserts a comment, Word places a yellow highlight over the text associated with the comment. When you point over the highlight, Word will display the name of the author and the text of the comment. You can also display a list of comments in a document and print it. The illustration on the next page shows highlighted text and an associated comment.

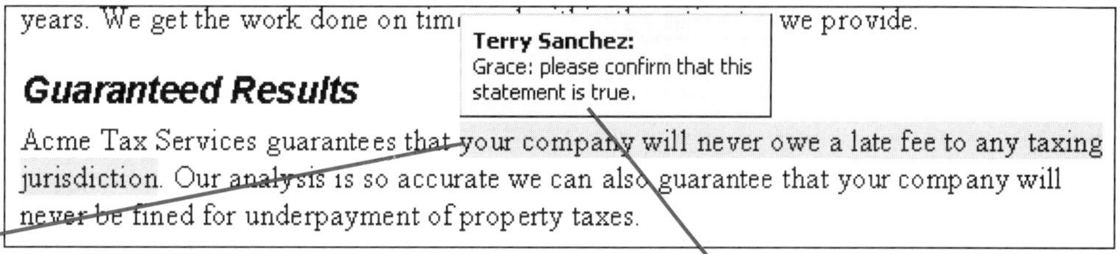
years. We get the work done on tim
we provide.
Terry Sanchez:
Grace: please confirm that this statement is true.
Guaranteed Results
Acme Tax Services guarantees that your company will never owe a late fee to any taxing jurisdiction. Our analysis is so accurate we can also guarantee that your company will never be fined for underpayment of property taxes.

The shaded area of this message indicates there is a comment embedded in the document.

When Grace points at the shaded highlight, she sees a question from Terry about a statement in the draft document.

When to Use a Comment

Comments are an excellent way to handle situations such as the following:

- When you want to document a piece of writing or record what you had in mind as you wrote the text.
- To record a question about the writing, such as a fact you are not quite sure of.
- To ask a question of an online collaborator without placing it into the normally printed page of the document.

Viewing Comments

To read comments, simply point over the yellow comment highlight. You can also view comments with the **View→Comments** command to open the Comments panel. The Comments panel lets you view comments by a specific author, or by all authors. It is also possible to print out comments by setting an option in Word's *Print Options* dialog box.

Navigating Comments

You can jump from one comment to the next in the Comments panel. When you click on a comment in the panel while in *Normal* or *Print Layout* view, Word displays the highlighted text associated with the comment on the top line of the document window. This makes it easy to move from comment to comment without the need for a page-by-page search through the document.

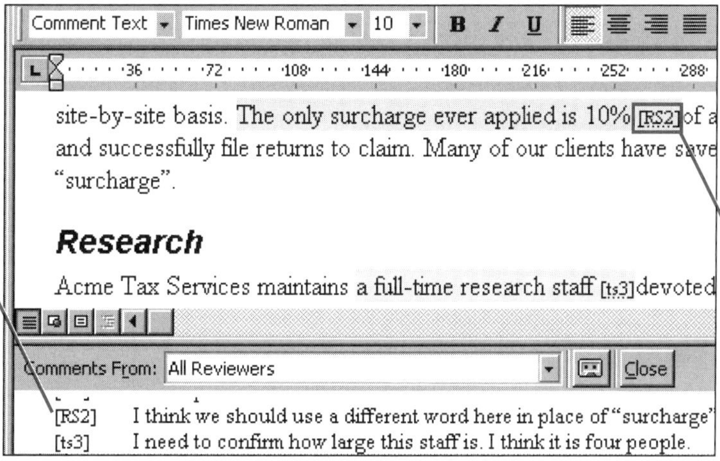
Comment Text
Times New Roman
10
B I U
site-by-site basis. The only surcharge ever applied is 10%[RS2]of a
and successfully file returns to claim. Many of our clients have save
"surcharge".
Research
Acme Tax Services maintains a full-time research staff [ts3]devoted
Comments From: All Reviewers
Close
[RS2] I think we should use a different word here in place of "surcharge"
[ts3] I need to confirm how large this staff is. I think it is four people.

A click on a comment in the ***Comments*** *panel lets you view the associated text in the document window. In this example, Comment [RS2]has just been clicked in the comments panel.*

The author's initials and comment number are visible when the Comments panel is open. When the Comments panel is closed, only the yellow highlight remains visible.

Hands-On 13.4 Review Comments

In this exercise, you will review comments inserted into the document previously by Robert Smith and Terry Sanchez.

1. Point at the yellow highlighted text in the *Guaranteed Results* paragraph. Leave the pointer on the highlighted text until you see a small pop-up window.
   This window contains the text of a comment from Terry Sanchez. Later, you will edit this comment to insert Grace's answer to the question.
2. Point at the yellow highlighted text in the *Fee Structure* paragraph.
   This comment is from Robert Smith. Word makes it easy to identify the author of any comment.
3. Scroll down the page, and point to read the remaining two comments.
4. Choose **View→Comments** from the menu bar.
   The Comments panel will appear at the bottom of the Word window to display all of the comments for this document.
5. Follow these steps to begin working with the Comments panel.

(A) Point at the panel border until you see a double-arrow; then drag up or down until the four comments are in view.

(B) Click on the last comment in the panel.

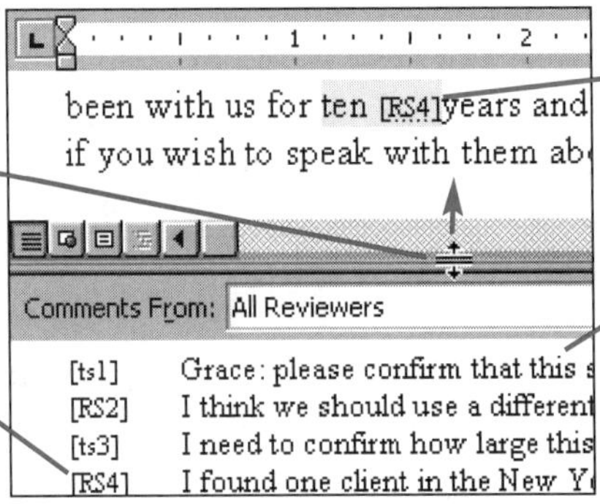
been with us for ten [RS4]years and
if you wish to speak with them ab
Comments From: All Reviewers
[ts1] Grace: please confirm that this
[RS2] I think we should use a different
[ts3] I need to confirm how large this
[RS4] I found one client in the New Y

(C) Notice that the line with this comment appears on the top line of the document window. You can also see the comment number next to the highlighted text.

(D) Click the first comment in the Comments panel. Now the line with the first comment appears at the top of the document window. It's easy to navigate to specific comments in the document with this method.

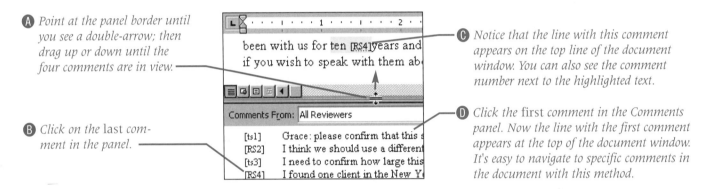

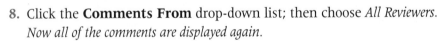

6. Click the *second* and *third* comments in the Comments panel.
7. Click the **Comments From** drop-down list; then choose *Terry Sanchez*.

   Comments From: Terry Sanchez
   Now only comments from this author are displayed.
8. Click the **Comments From** drop-down list; then choose *All Reviewers*.
   Now all of the comments are displayed again.
9. Click the  Close button on the comments panel.
   The comments panel is closed. You can reopen it at any time with the ***View→Comments*** *command.*

Inserting Comments

You can insert comments into any part of a Word document or Excel worksheet. You can select the text that the comment applies to before you give the **Insert→Comment** command. After you insert the comment, any text you had selected is automatically highlighted in a light yellow. This yellow is dimmer than the color created by the yellow *highlighter* tool that you will learn about later in this lesson. The author's initials and a comment number identify each comment.

Setting the Author's Initials

Name:
Grace Singleton
Initials:
GS

Before you insert comments, you should make sure that Word has your name and initials. You make this setting in Word's **Tools→Options** window, under the *User Information* tab. Once you set the author name and initials, Word will keep this setting until someone else changes it again.

Grace shares her computer with a co-worker who comes into the office part-time. Before she starts working on the draft proposal, Grace checks to make sure her own name and initials are set in Word's User Information tab.

Editing Comments

You can edit a comment at any time. You can even edit or add to comments made by other authors. When you edit a comment made by another author, that author's initials remain with the comment ID number. You edit comments in the Comments window.

As she reads comments inserted by one of the team members, Grace notices one that requests her opinion. Rather than insert a new comment, Grace decides to add her answer by editing the existing comment. Grace also applies a different text color to this edit, so that the other readers can readily distinguish her addition from the original comment.

Quick Reference

WORKING WITH COMMENTS IN WORD

Task	Procedure
Insert a comment.	■ Select the text to which your comment applies; then choose **Insert→Comment** from the menu bar. ■ Type the text of your comment. ■ Click the **Close** button to close the Comments panel, or continue your work with the Comments panel left open.
Associate your initials with comments.	■ Choose **Tools→Options** from the menu bar. ■ Click the **User Information** tab. ■ Enter your name and initials; then click **OK.**
View a comment in a document window.	■ *Point* on the comment highlight for about 2 seconds.
View all of the comments for a document.	■ Choose **View→Comments** from the menu bar. ■ Click on a comment in the Comments panel to view its associated text at the top of the document window.
Edit a comment.	■ *Point* on the comment highlight; then *right-click* on the comment highlight, and choose **Edit Comment** from the pop-up menu. ■ Edit the comment text normally. ■ Click **Close** to close the Comments panel.
Delete a comment.	■ *Point* on the comment highlight. ■ *Right-click* on the comment highlight; then choose **Delete Comment** from the pop-up menu.

Hands-On 13.5 Insert and Edit Comments

In this exercise, you will insert one of Grace's comments into the document and edit an existing comment with her answer to a question.

Set the Author's Initials

1. Choose **Tools→Options** from the menu bar; then click the **User Information** Tab.

Name:
Grace Singleton
Initials:
GS

2. Enter your first and last name in the *Name* box; then tap the TAB key, and enter two or three initials. The initials can be in upper- or lowercase letters.
3. Click **OK** to save the change.

Insert a Comment

4. Use CTRL+END to jump to the bottom of the document. Tap ENTER to add another line; then type the following text.

   > Computer Automation
   > Acme analysts use a state-of-the-art information system to track property tax data.

5. *Drag* to select the *Computer Automation* line that you just typed; then choose **Insert→Comment** from the menu bar.
   The Comments panel will open with the insertion point on a new line for your comment. Notice that your initials are placed as a prefix to the new comment number.
6. Type the following comment: TAB **`You should include information on the computer system I use to serve clients.`**
7. Click the Close button on the **Comments** panel.
8. *Point* (don't click) on the yellow highlighted text in the *Computer Automation* line to display your comment.
   Notice that your name is spelled out as you entered it under the User Information *tab.*

Edit a Comment

9. Use CTRL+HOME to jump to the top of the document.
10. *Point* to display the first comment in the document under *Guaranteed Results.*
11. *Right-click* on the comment; then choose **Edit Comment** from the pop-up menu.
    The comments panel will open to display the text of the comment you selected to edit.

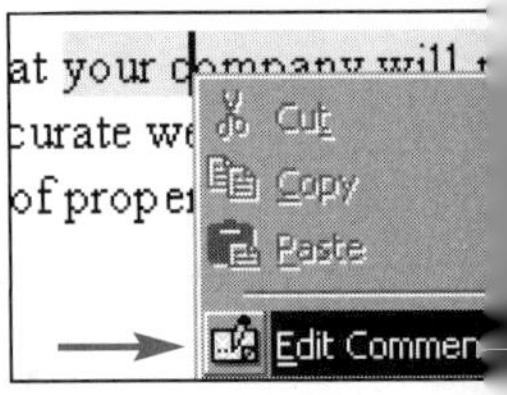
Cut
Copy
Paste
Edit Comment

12. Follow these steps to edit the comment.

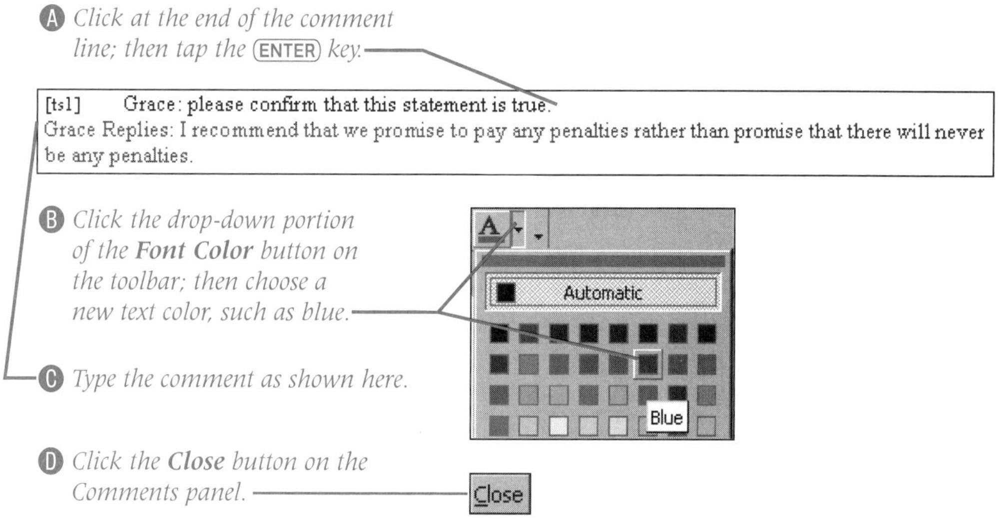
A Click at the end of the comment line; then tap the ENTER key.
[ts1] Grace: please confirm that this statement is true.
Grace Replies: I recommend that we promise to pay any penalties rather than promise that there will never be any penalties.
B Click the drop-down portion of the Font Color button on the toolbar; then choose a new text color, such as blue.
Automatic
Blue
C Type the comment as shown here.
D Click the Close button on the Comments panel.
Close

13. Point at the yellow highlight for the comment to view your editing.
Notice that none of the formatting you used in the comment is visible in the pop-up comment. You may want to remind readers that they may need to read your comments in the Comments view rather than just the pop-up window.

14. Choose **File→Save As** from the menu bar. Save the document with a new name: **`Proposal Notes (Grace Comments)`**.
By saving the file with a new name, you preserve the original version for future reference. The new name will also let you and the other team members know that it contains your comments.

Printing Comments

Word does not normally print comments. To print the comments in a document, you must select this option in Word's *Print Options* dialog box. When you choose to print comments, Word will automatically print the author's initials and the comment number beside each comment in the document. Word also prints one or more sheets with the text of all comments.

Quick Reference

PRINTING COMMENTS IN WORD

Task	Procedure
Print comments.	■ Choose **File→Print** from the menu bar. ■ Click the **Options** button. ■ Click the check box by **Comments;** then click **OK.**

TIP!

To stop printing comments reverse the above procedure.

Hands-On 13.6 Print Comments

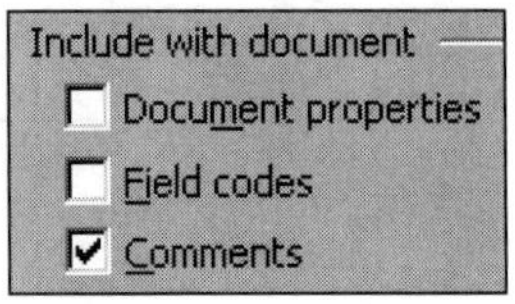
Include with document
Document properties
Field codes
Comments

1. Choose **File→Print** from the menu bar.
2. Click the **Options** button.
3. Make sure the **Comments** check box is checked.
4. Click **OK;** then click **OK** again to print the document with comments, and retrieve the printout from the printer.
   Notice that the printout includes the initials and comment number of each comment. A separate sheet was printed that contains the text of the comments themselves.

Emailing the Document

When you send someone a Word document, you have two choices. You can send the document as an attachment similar to the one you received earlier in this lesson, or you can send the document itself as the message. Each method has its uses. Sending the document as a message may cause some formatting to be lost. However, if it is a short document, sending it as an email message may be more convenient for the recipient to open and print.

TIP! *Documents of several pages or more are best sent as attachments rather than as messages.*

The Send To Command

Word's **Send To** command lets you choose whether the document should be sent as an email message or as an attachment. You simply choose **File→Send To** from the menu bar; then choose the method of transmission. If you want to send the document as an email message, Word offers an even faster way to give this command.

The E-mail Button

The Word 2000 toolbar contains a button that makes it easy to send any document as an email message. When you click the **E-mail** button on the toolbar, Word immediately displays boxes for you to fill in, the To: and Cc: addresses, the subject, and a **Send** button to send the message.

TIP! *If you click the E-mail button by mistake, just click it again to dismiss the command.*

Quick Reference

SENDING A DOCUMENT VIA EMAIL

Task	Procedure
Send a document as an email message.	■ Open or create the document to be sent. ■ Click the **E-mail** button on the Word toolbar. ■ *Address* the message, and accept or revise the default *subject* for the message (the document name). ■ Click the **Send a Copy** button on the Word toolbar.
Send a document as an attachment to an email message.	■ Open or create the document to be sent. ■ Choose **File→Send To→Mail Recipient as Attachment** from the menu bar. A new message will be created in a normal Outlook (Or Outlook Express) message window. ■ *Address* the message, and accept or revise the default *subject* for the message (the document name). ■ Click the **Send** button on the message toolbar.

Hands-On 13.7 Send a Document

In this exercise, you will send the Proposal Notes document twice: once with the E-mail button and once as an attachment.

Use the Email Message Command

1. Click the E-mail button on the Word toolbar.
   A new toolbar will appear at the top of the Word window. It has boxes that let you address the message and enter a subject, just like the Outlook message window. Your Word document has become the "body" of the message.
2. Click once on any email address that may already be in the To: box and tap (DELETE). Take care to place a semicolon between the two addresses, and address the message as shown here: **terry@offtowork.com; rsmith@offtowork.com**.
3. Change the subject line to read: **Grace's feedback**.
   Although you could type the body of the message, in this case it is unnecessary. Both correspondents will recognize the document immediately and see the highlighting for your comments.
4. Click the Send a Copy button on the Word toolbar.
   The message is placed into Outlook's Outbox view for delivery. It will be sent the next time Outlook checks your email account.

Send the Document as an Attachment

5. Choose **File→Send To→Mail Recipient as Attachment** from the Word menu bar.
   A new message will be created in a normal Outlook message window.
6. Address the message to **terry@offtowork.com**.
7. Change the message subject to: **Comments Attached**

(Continued on the next page)

8. Type the body of the message as shown below:

```
Hello Terry:

Here are my comments on the Proposal Notes document.
Please let me know how else I may assist you.

Regards,

Grace
```

9. Click the **Send** button on the message window toolbar.
   The message is sent to the Outlook outbox for delivery.
10. Follow these steps to close the document.

Notice that there are two close window *quick-sizing buttons at the top-right corner of the Word window.*

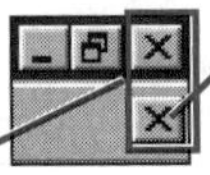

Click the lower *close button to close the document without closing the Word window. Click* **Yes** *if you are asked to save the document.*

Open an Attachment from the Preview Pane

11. Click the **Outlook** button on the Windows Taskbar to activate the window.
12. Click the **Send/Receive** button to send the outgoing messages and receive incoming messages. Continue to check for new messages until you have received *two* replies from Terry Sanchez and *one* from Robert Smith.
13. Click to select the **Latest Draft** message from Terry Sanchez in the **Inbox** view.
14. Click on the paper clip at the right side of the Preview pane; then choose the **Proposal (Second Draft)** attachment.
    The attachment will open in the Word window.
15. Choose **File→Save As** from the menu bar.
    Notice that Temp *is listed as the* Save in *folder at the top of the dialog box. This means that the document is currently stored in that folder. You will now save the document to the* Sales Proposal folder *instead.*
16. Click the **Favorites** button in the Open dialog box; then *double-click* to open the *Sales Proposal folder* favorite. You may need to scroll through the list to find this Favorite.
    The contents of the folder will be displayed. This Favorite saves you time navigating through the system to the folder.

Sales Proposal folder
Favorites

17. Click the **Save** button to save the document in the Sales Proposal folder.

Other Composition Tools

Word includes additional composition tools that may be useful in a collaborative project. This topic covers three of these tools: the highlighter, hyperlinks, and cross-references.

Adding Cross-References

A *cross-reference* is special item you can insert into a Word document that points to another element somewhere else in the document. For example, you can add a cross-reference that points to a heading on another page. When you place a cross-reference in a document, you must also choose the type of information it displays. For example, a cross-reference might contain the text of a heading in the document or the page number where the heading appears.

Example

In the example below, both cross-references refer to the same heading, but the first appears as the text of the heading, and the second appears as the page number.

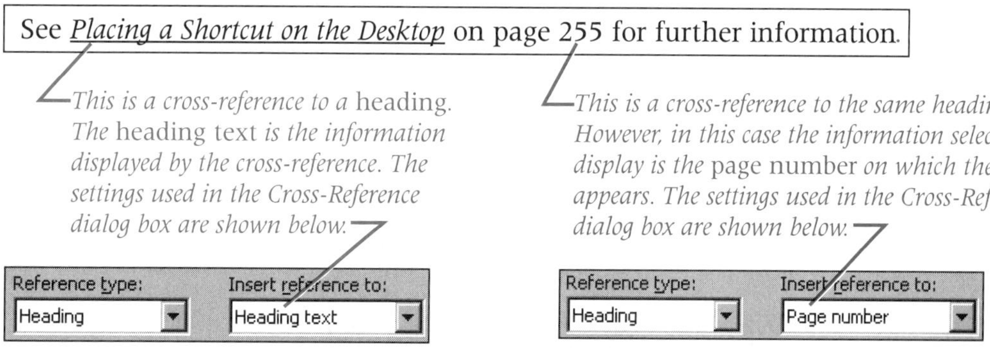

See Placing a Shortcut on the Desktop on page 255 for further information.
This is a cross-reference to a heading. The heading text is the information displayed by the cross-reference. The settings used in the Cross-Reference dialog box are shown below.
This is a cross-reference to the same heading. However, in this case the information selected to display is the page number on which the heading appears. The settings used in the Cross-Reference dialog box are shown below.
Reference type:
Heading
Insert reference to:
Heading text
Reference type:
Heading
Insert reference to:
Page number

Cross-References as Hyperlinks

Any cross-reference you insert can also act as a hyperlink. When you click on the cross-reference, Word will immediately jump the view to the location of the cross-reference item. For example, if you place a cross-reference to a heading in the document, clicking that cross-reference will immediately jump the view to the page containing the cross-referenced heading.

As Grace writes, she sees where two different topics are closely related. Grace places a cross-reference to the other topic so it will be easy to jump between the topics to make comparisons.

Using the Highlighter

Word's *highlighter* tool works just like its real-life counterpart (except that you can easily erase this highlighter). The highlighter tool applies a transparent color to the background of text. You can apply the highlighter by selecting a highlight color and then dragging, or you can select the text first and then click to apply the highlight color.

As Grace makes additions to the draft document, she highlights each change in blue. This will make it easy for the other team members to quickly identify and review her additions.

Hands-On 13.8 Create a Cross-Reference and Highlights

In this exercise, you will insert a cross-reference to a heading in the document. You will also highlight new text that you will type and remove a highlight applied by another user.

1. The **Proposal (Second Draft)** document should now be open in the Word window. If you did not receive the attachment in the previous exercise because you do not have an email account, make *Word* the active window and use the **File→Open** command to open the document from the **Sales Proposal folder.**
   Now you will type an addition to one of the points in the proposal. You will stop mid-sentence in the addition to add a cross-reference.
2. Click to the right of the period after the word *provide* at the very end of the paragraph beneath the *Reliability* heading.
3. Type the following text at the end of the paragraph.

```
One reason we are able to provide such a high level of
reliability is due to Acme's proprietary ATTACK system. See
```

4. Choose **Insert→Cross-reference** from the menu bar.
5. Follow these steps to insert the cross-reference.

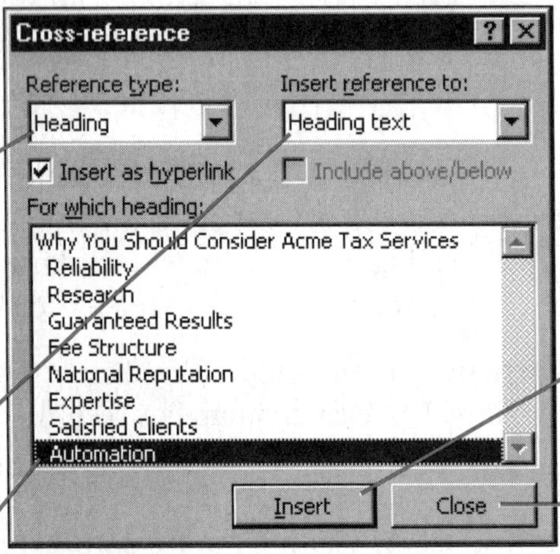

Cross-reference
Reference type:
Heading
Insert reference to:
Heading text
Insert as hyperlink
Include above/below
For which heading:
Why You Should Consider Acme Tax Services
Reliability
Research
Guaranteed Results
Fee Structure
National Reputation
Expertise
Satisfied Clients
Automation
Insert
Close

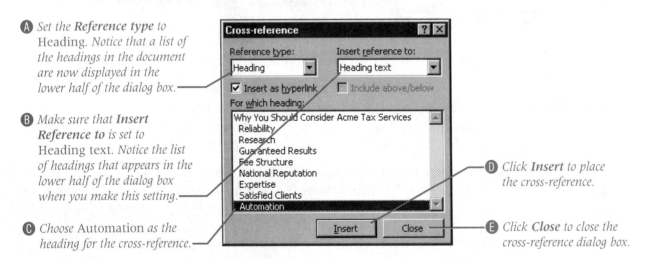

Ⓐ *Set the* ***Reference type*** *to* Heading. *Notice that a list of the headings in the document are now displayed in the lower half of the dialog box.*

Ⓑ *Make sure that* ***Insert Reference to*** *is set to* Heading text. *Notice the list of headings that appears in the lower half of the dialog box when you make this setting.*

Ⓒ *Choose* Automation *as the heading for the cross-reference.*

Ⓓ *Click* ***Insert*** *to place the cross-reference.*

Ⓔ *Click* ***Close*** *to close the cross-reference dialog box.*

6. Hold down the (SHIFT) key; then tap the right arrow → key to select the new hyperlink.
7. Click the Underline [U] button on the toolbar.
   As you learned in a previous lesson, most hyperlinks on Web pages are underlined. An underline makes it easier for readers of this document to identify the hyperlink.

8. *Point* (don't click) on the Automation cross-reference. Notice that the pointer changes to a hand, which indicates that this text is a hyperlink.

9. Click on the *Automation* cross-reference.
   Your pointer jumps to the Automation heading on page 2. Notice that the Style box at the top-left corner of the Word toolbar reads Heading 2. *Automation was listed as a heading earlier because this heading style had been applied to the paragraph.*

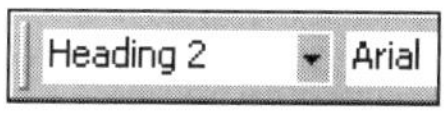

Heading 2
Arial

   Notice also that a new toolbar has appeared in the Word window. This is the Web *toolbar. Its controls are similar to those you used in Internet Explorer.*

10. Click the Back  button on Word's Web toolbar.
    This navigates you back to the hyperlink you clicked in Step 9.

Highlight and Unhighlight Text

11. Tap the (END) key to jump to the end of the current line. If the Underline  button appears to be "pressed," click the button to *switch off* the text underline.

12. Type the following text to complete the addition to this paragraph: **`on the following page.`**

13. Follow these steps to highlight the new text you typed in this exercise.

Ⓐ *Drag down to select the additions you just made to the* Reliability *paragraph.*

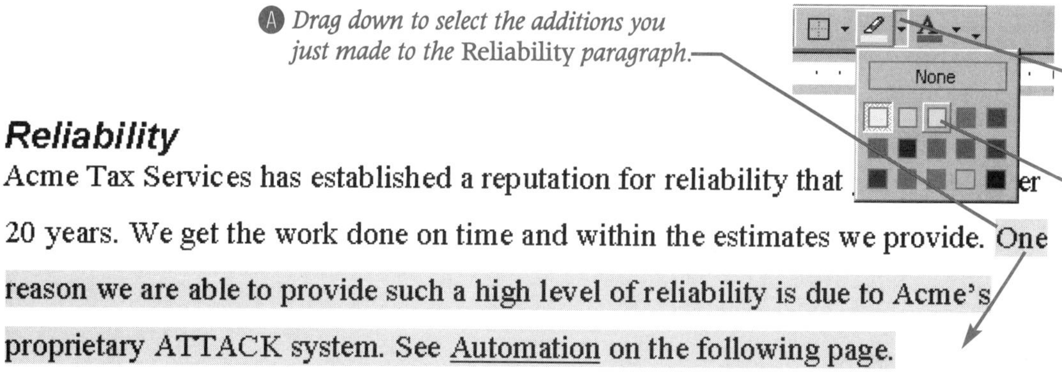

None
Reliability
Acme Tax Services has established a reputation for reliability that
er
20 years. We get the work done on time and within the estimates we provide. One
reason we are able to provide such a high level of reliability is due to Acme's
proprietary ATTACK system. See Automation on the following page.

Ⓑ *Click the* **Highlight** *drop-down list button.*

Ⓒ *Choose the color* turquoise *from the drop-down palette.*

   The highlight color is applied immediately to the selected text.

14. Scroll down the page to the **Guaranteed Results** topic. Read the comment on this heading.

15. *Right-click* on the comment; then choose **Delete Comment** from the pop-up menu.
    The comment and its highlight are removed. You cannot delete a comment by deleting the text in the comment inside the Comments panel. You must delete the comment in the Document window.

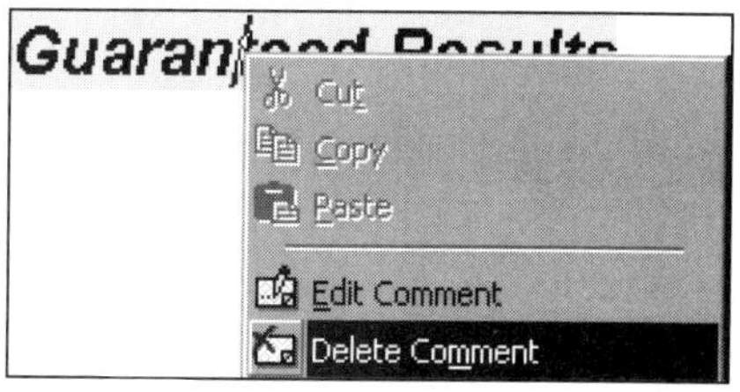

Cut
Copy
Paste
Edit Comment
Delete Comment

16. Drag to select the text with the green highlight; then click the **drop-down** portion of the **Highlight** button on the toolbar and choose **None.**
    The highlight is removed from the selected text.

17. Use (CTRL)+(END) to jump to the top of the page; then click the Automation hyperlink to navigate to that section of the following page.

(Continued on the next page)

18. Type the following text at the *end* of the last paragraph: **`This allows us to serve our clients with unexcelled reliability.`**

19. Follow these steps to highlight the sentence you just typed.

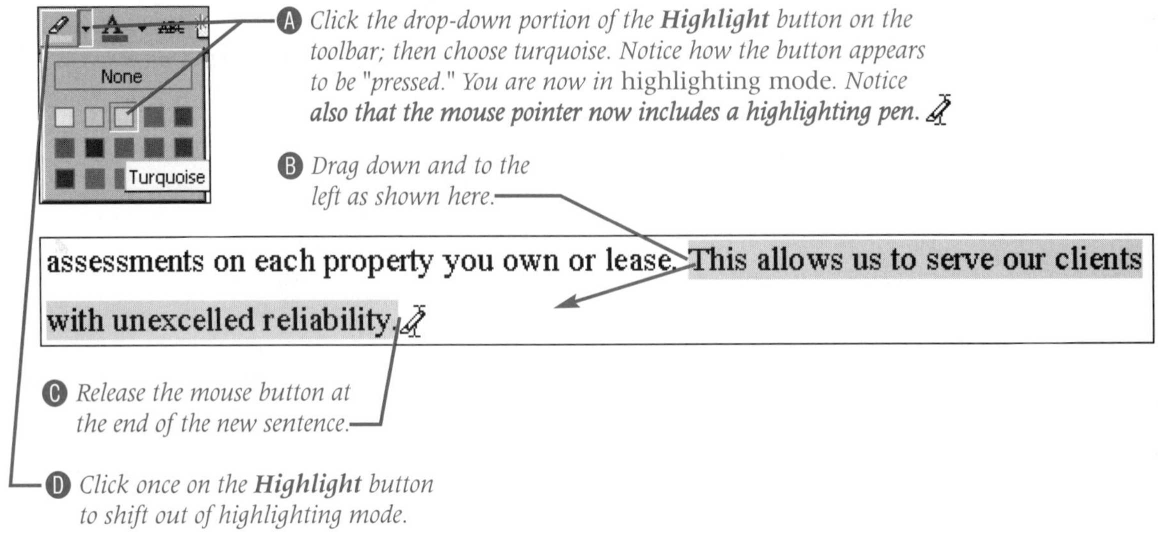

None
Turquoise
A Click the drop-down portion of the **Highlight** button on the toolbar; then choose turquoise. Notice how the button appears to be "pressed." You are now in highlighting mode. Notice also that the mouse pointer now includes a highlighting pen.
B Drag down and to the left as shown here.
assessments on each property you own or lease. This allows us to serve our clients
with unexcelled reliability.
C Release the mouse button at the end of the new sentence.
D Click once on the **Highlight** button to shift out of highlighting mode.

20. Save the document.

Adding Hyperlinks

Word makes it easy to insert hyperlinks to Web pages and other types of documents. For example, if a Web site contains information that would be useful in writing a document, you can embed a hyperlink to that Web site directly into your text. When another user clicks on the hyperlink, Word will transform its window into an Internet Explorer window and open up the linked Web site.

Quick Reference

HOW TO INSERT A HYPERLINK

Task	Procedure
Insert a hyperlink to a Web page.	■ Click where you wish to insert the hyperlink. ■ Choose **Insert→Hyperlink** from the menu bar, or click the **Insert Hyperlink** button on the toolbar, or use CTRL+K from the keyboard. ■ Click the **Web Page** button; then navigate in Internet Explorer to the desired page, or type the URL into the dialog box. ■ Make Word the active program window; then click **OK** to insert the hyperlink.

During her research, Grace looks at a competitor's Web site. She notices a few services and benefits on one page that her company might address in its own proposal. Grace decides to place a hyperlink directly into her input on the draft proposal document.

Hands-On 13.9 Insert Hyperlinks to Web Pages

In this exercise, you will add a hyperlink to a Web page. When Terry and Robert click on this hyperlink, it will navigate them directly to that Web page.

1. Tap (ENTER) twice to add blank lines to the bottom of the document.
2. Type the following text: **`Terry: Check this competitor's Web site for some interesting information about their tax data system.`**
3. Tap the (SPACE BAR) twice to add space after the period.
4. Click the Insert Hyperlink button on the toolbar.
   Word will display the Insert Hyperlink dialog box. This dialog box offers several different methods to insert hyperlinks. In this exercise, you will use the method that lets you navigate to the Web page with Internet Explorer.
5. Click the **Web Page** button on the right side of the dialog box.
   Word will launch the Internet Explorer browser and display the Home page.
6. Navigate to the *Office Essentials* Web page (www.offtowork.com/oe).
7. Click the **Lesson 13** button; then click the **Competition** button.
   A simulated competitor's Web page will appear. Now that you are displaying the Web page to be linked, you will return to Word and insert the hyperlink.
8. Click the **Proposal (Second Draft)** button on the Windows Taskbar to make Word the active program.
9. Follow these steps to complete the Insert Hyperlink command.

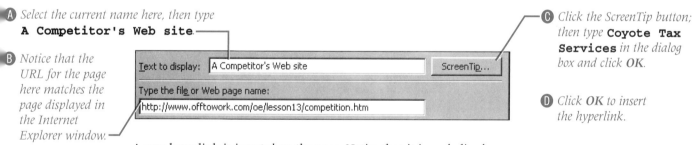

Ⓐ *Select the current name here, then type* **`A Competitor's Web site`**

Ⓑ *Notice that the URL for the page here matches the page displayed in the Internet Explorer window.*

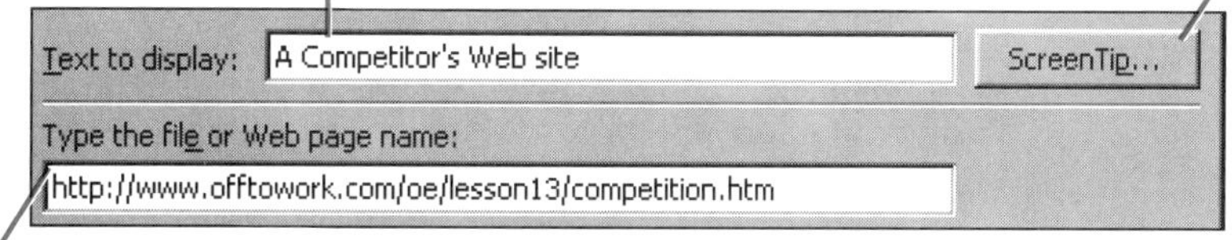
Text to display:
A Competitor's Web site
ScreenTip...
Type the file or Web page name:
http://www.offtowork.com/oe/lesson13/competition.htm

Ⓒ *Click the ScreenTip button; then type* **`Coyote Tax Services`** *in the dialog box and click* ***OK***.

Ⓓ *Click* ***OK*** *to insert the hyperlink.*

A new hyperlink is inserted on the page. Notice that it is underlined.

10. *Point* (don't click) over the new hyperlink.
    A pointer hand appears on the hyperlink. Notice that your ScreenTip appears as well.

(Continued on the next page)

NOTE!

Some computers may display a new Internet Explorer window instead of transforming the Word window.

11. **Click** once on the hyperlink to test it.
The Word window will temporarily transform into an Internet Explorer window to display the Web page. Notice that all of the toolbar buttons have changed. You can navigate in the Web site from this window just as you would with Internet Explorer.

12. Click the Back button on the Internet Explorer toolbar to return to the Word document.
The normal Word toolbars will return to the window.

Pasting Data from Other Sources

In previous lessons, you have used the copy and paste command to paste information from one place to another within the same document. However, it is also possible to copy and paste information from *one application program* to another. For example, you can copy and paste text from a Web page displayed in *Internet Explorer* into a *Word* document.

Pasting Various Formats

The information you work with in various applications can be pasted in a variety of formats. Each format has features that may make it well- or ill-suited for pasting into a document. For example, some formats may include additional codes that you would not want to appear in the Word document. The following table lists three examples of commonly used formats.

Format Name	Description
Formatted Text (RTF)	This format transfers any font or paragraph-level formatting such as bold, italics, and indents, and table formatting.
Unformatted Text	This format will lose any font or paragraph-level formatting in the original text. The pasted text will be formatted according to the current settings in the paragraph where you give the Paste command.
HTML format	This format will retain any types of formatting of text that you copy from a Web page. For example, if the text appears in a table on the Web page, the Paste command will paste the table into your document as well.

Paste Special Command

Word's *Paste Special* command lets you select the format for the content you paste into a document. When you give the Paste Special command, Word will list all of the available formats you can choose. Depending on the type of content you are pasting, there may be several formats in the list, or just one.

As she searches Acme's Web site, Grace notices some details that will be useful in preparing the sales proposal. Since the Web page contains other information that is not of interest, Grace decides to copy and paste the useful content on the Web page directly into the Word document. To ensure that the content is formatted clearly, and to save the time of manually formatting it herself, Grace uses the *Paste Special* command to paste the content into the Word document.

Hands-On 13.10 Navigate to a Web Page and Copy Text From It

1. Click Competition - Microsoft I... on the Windows Taskbar to activate the *Internet Explorer* window.
2. Click the Back button on the Internet Explorer toolbar to return to the *Lesson 13* Web page.
3. Click the **Acme Tax Services** button.
4. Make sure that the Internet Explorer window is *maximized.*
5. Follow these steps to copy the table from this Web page.

Ⓐ *Point here; then drag down and to the right.*

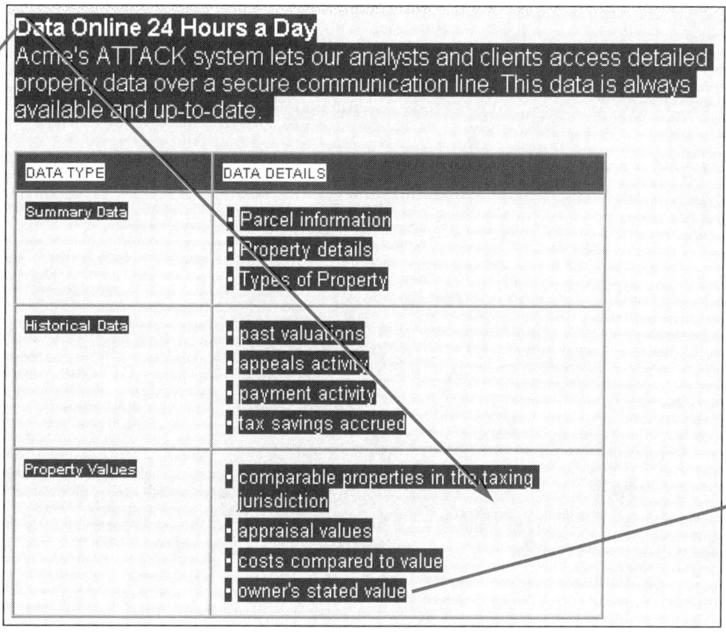

Data Online 24 Hours a Day
Acme's ATTACK system lets our analysts and clients access detailed property data over a secure communication line. This data is always available and up-to-date.
DATA TYPE
DATA DETAILS
Summary Data
Parcel information
Property details
Types of Property
Historical Data
past valuations
appeals activity
payment activity
tax savings accrued
Property Values
comparable properties in the taxing jurisdiction
appraisal values
costs compared to value
owner's stated value

Ⓑ *Release the mouse button here. You should see a shaded selection over the table.*

6. Choose **Edit→Copy** from the menu bar.
7. Minimize the Internet Explorer window.
   The Word window should now be displayed as the active program.

Paste the Web Page Information

8. Use the *Zoom* box on the Word toolbar to set the magnification to 75%.
   This will let you see more of the pasted text when you use the paste command later.
9. Use CTRL+END to jump to the bottom of the document. Tap ENTER twice to add space below the last line of the document.
10. Use CTRL+ENTER to create a page break in the document; then type the following note:
    `Terry: let's also include this information about our data system.`
11. Tap ENTER to add a new line after the text you just typed.
12. Choose **Edit→Paste Special** from the menu bar.

(Continued on the next page)

13. Choose **Unformatted Text** from the paste special dialog box; then click **OK.**

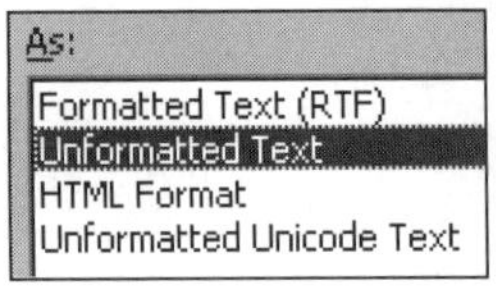
As:
Formatted Text (RTF)
Unformatted Text
HTML Format
Unformatted Unicode Text

14. Scroll back up the page to review the text that you just pasted.
    Notice that the pasted text does not appear as it did on the Web page. All of the formatting (including the table) has been stripped away from the text. Only the words were pasted.
15. Click the Undo button on the toolbar.
16. Choose **Edit→Paste Special** from the menu bar; then choose **Formatted Text (RTF)** from the option list, and click **OK.** Scroll if necessary to review the pasted text.
    Now the table looks pretty good, and the text is still formatted as well. The Paste Special command lets you choose a paste format that gives the most useful results.

Send the Message

17. Choose **File→Save As** from the menu bar. Save the message to the Sales Proposal folder as: `Proposal (Second Draft, Grace Comments)`.
18. Choose **File→Send To→Mail Recipient As Attachment** from the menu bar.
    This will transmit the document as a normal Word file rather than inside an email message. Working with a normal document should make it easier for Terry to complete the final version of the proposal.
19. Compose the following message.

To:	**[yourself]**
Subject:	**Additions**
Body:	**Hello Terry and Robert:** **Attached are my additions to the second proposal draft. All additions are highlighted in blue. Let me know if there is anything else you need for me to contribute. Good luck with the proposal.** **Regards,** **Grace**

20. **Send** the message.
21. Close any open Word, Internet Explorer, and My Computer windows.
22. Activate the *Outlook* window; then use *Send/Receive* to check for new messages.
23. Click the message you just sent yourself in the **Inbox** view. Click on the **paper clip** icon in the Preview pane, and choose the attachment document.
    This is how Terry and Robert would receive the attachment Grace sent to them.
24. Close the Word and Outlook windows.

Concepts Review

True/False Questions

1. Windows lets you create folders inside of other folders.	TRUE	FALSE
2. A shortcut lets you access a folder from the Desktop.	TRUE	FALSE
3. An attachment is a file that is sent along with an email message.	TRUE	FALSE
4. Word always automatically prints the comments in any document.	TRUE	FALSE
5. A cross-reference can also work like a hyperlink.	TRUE	FALSE
6. A hyperlink in a Word document to a Web page works just like a hyperlink on a typical Web page.	TRUE	FALSE
7. It doesn't matter which format you select when you use the Paste Special command.	TRUE	FALSE
8. Word's E-mail button on the toolbar sends the document as an attachment.	TRUE	FALSE
9. Word's highlighter tool lets you insert comments into a document.	TRUE	FALSE
10. A Favorite can help you navigate quickly to a folder or disk drive.	TRUE	FALSE

Multiple-Choice Questions

1. Which statement about email message attachments is true?
   a. An attachment can be any type of file.
   b. An attachment must be a Word document file.
   c. An attachment is a second email message attached to the first one.
   d. None of the above

2. What controls the initials and name that identify a comment?
   a. The initials are set up in the Comments window.
   b. You must reinstall Word in order to change the initials.
   c. The initials are set in the Options window.
   d. Word sets the initials according to your log-on name.

3. Which description of a cross-reference in Word is true?
   a. A cross-reference can also act as a hyperlink.
   b. A cross-reference can be the text of a heading or a page number.
   c. A cross-reference is created with the Insert→Cross-Reference command.
   d. All of the above

4. Which statement best describes how the Paste Special command differs from an ordinary Paste command?
   a. Paste Special can only be used to paste particular types of data.
   b. Paste Special lets you select the format of the data you paste.
   c. Paste Special works exactly like the Paste command.
   d. Paste Special never pastes text formatting.

UNIT 5

Excel 2000

Excel 2000 is a powerful tool for organizing and analyzing financial data. Few businesses can thrive in today's competitive business environment without programs such as Excel. Two of its most important features are its flexibility and its array of tools. In addition, Excel is very easy to use. These features have made Excel popular at all organizational levels. Whether you are a receptionist or the CEO of a Fortune 500 company, chances are you will use Excel. The techniques covered in this unit will guide you from the basics of data entry to the creation of complex charts. You will develop marketable skills using a remarkable program.

LESSON 14—Excel

Creating and Editing a Simple Worksheet

In this lesson, you will develop fundamental Excel 2000 skills. This lesson will provide you with a solid foundation of skills so that you are prepared to master the advanced features introduced in later lessons. For example, you will learn basic skills, including selecting cells, entering and editing text and numbers, and aligning cell entries. In addition, you will use Excel's powerful yet easy-to-use AutoSum tool to sum rows and columns of numbers.

In This Lesson

Case Study

Susan Lee is a student intern at Computer Depot, a discount retailer of computers and computer accessories. Joel Williams, the buyer for Computer Depot, has asked Susan to report the number of PCs, laptop computers, printers, and monitors sold during a five-day period. Joel has instructed Susan to report the data on a daily basis and to include the number of units sold by each manufacturer. After analyzing Joel's request, Susan decides that Excel 2000 is the right tool for the job. She organizes the data in an Excel worksheet and uses Excel's AutoSum feature to compute the necessary totals.

	A	B	C	D	E	F	G	H
1	Computer Depot Weekly Sales Data							
2								
3			Wednesday	Thursday	Friday	Saturday	Sunday	
4	PCs							Totals
5		Compaq	3	10	12	15	16	56
6		IBM	4	8	10	13	14	49
7		Acer	6	13	15	18	19	71
8		Total	13	31	37	46	49	176
9								
10	Laptops							
11		IBM	2	5	4	10	8	29
12		Apple PowerBook	3	7	5	12	10	37
13		Compaq	4	8	11	14	14	51
14		Toshiba	2	3	5	5	3	18
15		Total	11	23	25	41	35	135
16								
17	Printers							
18		IBM	3	5	5	6	8	27
19		HP	6	1	2	3	7	19
20		Canon	8	2	3	4	5	22
21		Total	17	8	10	13	20	68
22								
23	Monitors							
24		NEC	3	6	8	7	2	26
25		Sony	5	3	2	2	1	13
26		Compaq	2	2	6	8	3	21
27		Total	10	11	16	17	6	60

What Is Microsoft Excel?

Microsoft Excel is an electronic spreadsheet (also known as a worksheet) program that makes working with numbers a pleasure instead of a chore. Excel provides tools to assist you in virtually every aspect of worksheet creation and analysis. Whether you are creating dynamic charts for a presentation or interactive worksheets for group collaboration, Excel has the right tool for the job. For these and many other reasons, Excel is the most widely used worksheet program in both homes and businesses.

Why Use Excel?

Excel provides a number of important features and benefits that make it a smart choice.

1. **IntelliSense technology—**Excel's IntelliSense technology includes automated tools to assist you in entering, editing, and analyzing data. This speeds up the process of creating worksheets so that you can focus on analysis and other tasks.
2. **GUI—**Excel's Graphical User Interface is so easy to use that even beginning computer users find it simple. The interface reduces the need to memorize commands, and it will make you more productive.
3. **Charting—**Have you heard the expression, "One picture is worth a thousand words?" This is especially true with financial or numeric data. Excel's powerful charting and formatting features let you display your data in a powerful and convincing graphic format.
4. **Widely used—**Excel is the most widely used worksheet software. Excel is the right choice if you are trying to develop marketable skills and find employment.
5. **Integration with other Office programs—**Excel 2000 is part of the Microsoft Office 2000 suite of programs, which also includes Word, Access, PowerPoint, Outlook, PhotoDraw, and others. The ability to exchange data with these programs is one of the most powerful and attractive features of Excel.
6. **Web integration—**Excel 2000 lets you easily publish your worksheets to Web sites on the World Wide Web or to your company Intranet.

It's Time to Learn Excel!

It's time to put your fears behind and learn this wonderful program. You will be amazed at the power and simplicity of Excel and how easy it is to learn. The knowledge you are about to gain will give you a marketable skill and make you an Excel master.

Starting Excel

The method you use to start Excel and other Office programs depends in large part upon whether you intend to create a new workbook or open an existing workbook. A workbook is a file containing one or more worksheets. If you intend to create a new workbook, then use one of the following methods to start Excel. Once the Excel program has started, you can begin working in the new workbook that appears.

- Click the 
Start
button, and choose Microsoft Excel from the Programs menu.
- Click the Microsoft Excel  button on the Quick Launch toolbar (located near the Taskbar).
- Click the Start button, choose New Office Document, choose the General tab, and double-click the Blank Workbook icon.

Use one of the following methods if you intend to open an existing Excel workbook. Once the Excel program has started, the desired workbook will open in an Excel window.

- Navigate to the desired document using Windows Explorer or My Computer, and double-click the workbook.
- Click the Start button and point to Documents. You can choose the desired workbook from the Documents list. The Documents list displays the most recently used Office documents.

Hands-On 14.1 Start Excel

In this exercise, you will start the Excel program.

1. Start your computer, and the Windows desktop will be displayed.
2. Click the Start button and choose **Programs.**
3. Choose Microsoft Excel from the Programs menu.
   The Excel program will load, and the Excel window will appear. Don't be concerned if your window appears different from the example shown in the following illustration.

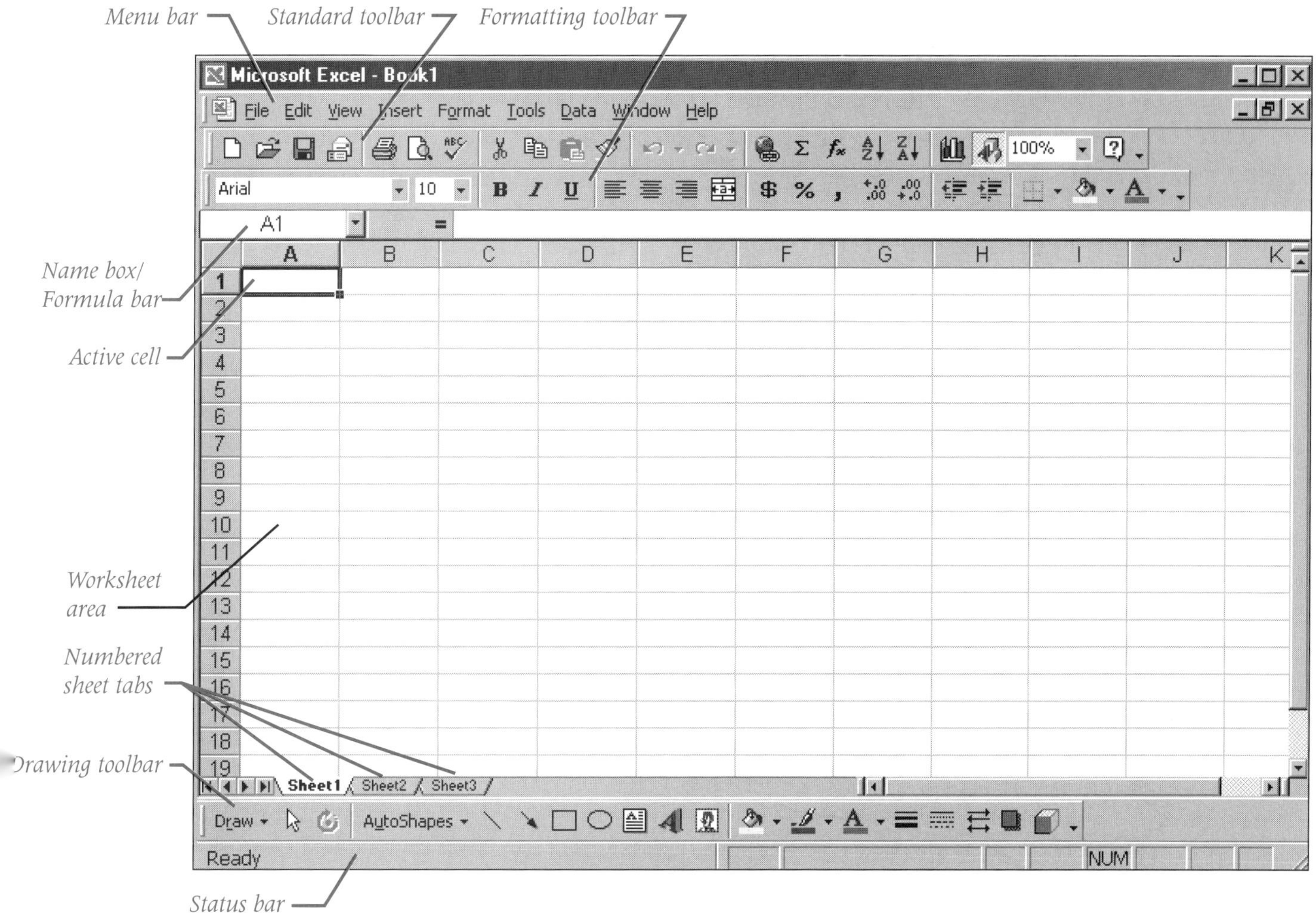

Menu bar
Standard toolbar
Formatting toolbar
Microsoft Excel - Book1
File Edit View Insert Format Tools Data Window Help
Name box/
Formula bar
Active cell
Worksheet
area
Numbered
sheet tabs
Drawing toolbar
Sheet1 Sheet2 Sheet3
Draw AutoShapes
Ready
NUM
Status bar

Worksheets and Workbooks

Excel displays a blank **workbook** the moment you start the program. A workbook is composed of **worksheets.** This is similar to a paper notebook with many sheets of paper. You enter text, numbers, formulas, charts, and other objects in worksheets. Excel displays three worksheets in a new workbook. You can insert new worksheets, up to a maximum of 255 worksheets per workbook.

A worksheet has a grid structure with horizontal rows and vertical columns. A new worksheet has 256 columns and 65,536 rows. However, at any given time, only a small number of the rows and columns are visible in the worksheet window. The intersection of each row and column is a **cell.** Each cell is identified by a **reference.** The reference is the column letter followed by the row number. For example, A1 is the reference of the cell in the top–left corner of the worksheet. So, we refer to this cell as Cell A1.

The Highlight

The **highlight** is a thick line surrounding the active cell. You can move the highlight by clicking in a cell or by using the keyboard. Moving the highlight is important because data is entered into the active cell. The vertical and horizontal scroll bars let you scroll through a worksheet. However, scrolling does not move the highlight. You must position the highlight in the desired cell after scrolling. The following table lists important keystrokes that move the highlight.

Quick Reference

NAVIGATING A WORKSHEET

Keystroke(s)	How the Highlight Is Moved
→ ← ↑ ↓	One cell to the right, left, up, or down
HOME	To the beginning of current row
CTRL+→	End of current row
CTRL+HOME	Home cell, usually Cell A1
CTRL+END	Last cell in active part of worksheet
PGDN	Down one screen
PGUP	Up one screen
ALT+PGDN	One screen to the right
ALT+PGUP	One screen to the left
CTRL+G	Displays Go To dialog box. Enter cell reference and click OK to go to that cell.

Hands-On 14.2 Move the Highlight and Explore the Excel Window

1. Slide the mouse, and the pointer will have a thick cross ✜ shape when it is in the worksheet area.
2. Click the pointer on any cell, and the highlight will move to that cell.
3. Move the highlight five times by clicking in various cells.

Use the Keyboard to Move the Highlight

In the next few steps, you will move the highlight with the keyboard. You can use the keys on the main part of your keyboard or on the Numeric keypad at the bottom right corner of your keyboard. Keep in mind, however, that you must have the (NUM LOCK) *key turned off if you want to move the highlight with the Numeric keypad. The word NUM will disappear from the Status bar when Num Lock is turned off.*

4. Use the arrow → ← ↑ ↓ keys to position the highlight in Cell F10.
5. Tap the (HOME) key, and the highlight will move to Cell A10.
   The (HOME) *key always moves the highlight to Column A in the active row.*
6. Press (CTRL)+(HOME) to move the highlight to Cell A1.
7. Tap the (PGDN) key two or three times.
   Notice that Excel displays the next twenty or so rows each time you tap (PGDN).
8. Press and hold the ↑ key until the highlight is in Cell A1.

Use the Scroll Bars

9. Click the Scroll Right ▶ button on the horizontal scroll bar until Columns AA and AB are visible.
   Excel labels the first 26 columns A–Z and the next 26 columns AA–AZ. A similar labeling scheme is used for the remaining columns.
10. Take a few minutes to practice scrolling and moving the highlight.

(Continued on the next page)

Explore the Excel Window

11. Follow these steps to explore the Excel window.

Ⓐ *Notice the Name box on the Formula bar. Don't worry if your Formula bar is not displayed. You will learn to display and hide the Formula bar soon. The Name box displays the name or reference of the active cell.*

Ⓑ *Click the Sheet2 tab, and another blank worksheet will be displayed. A workbook can have up to 255 worksheets.*

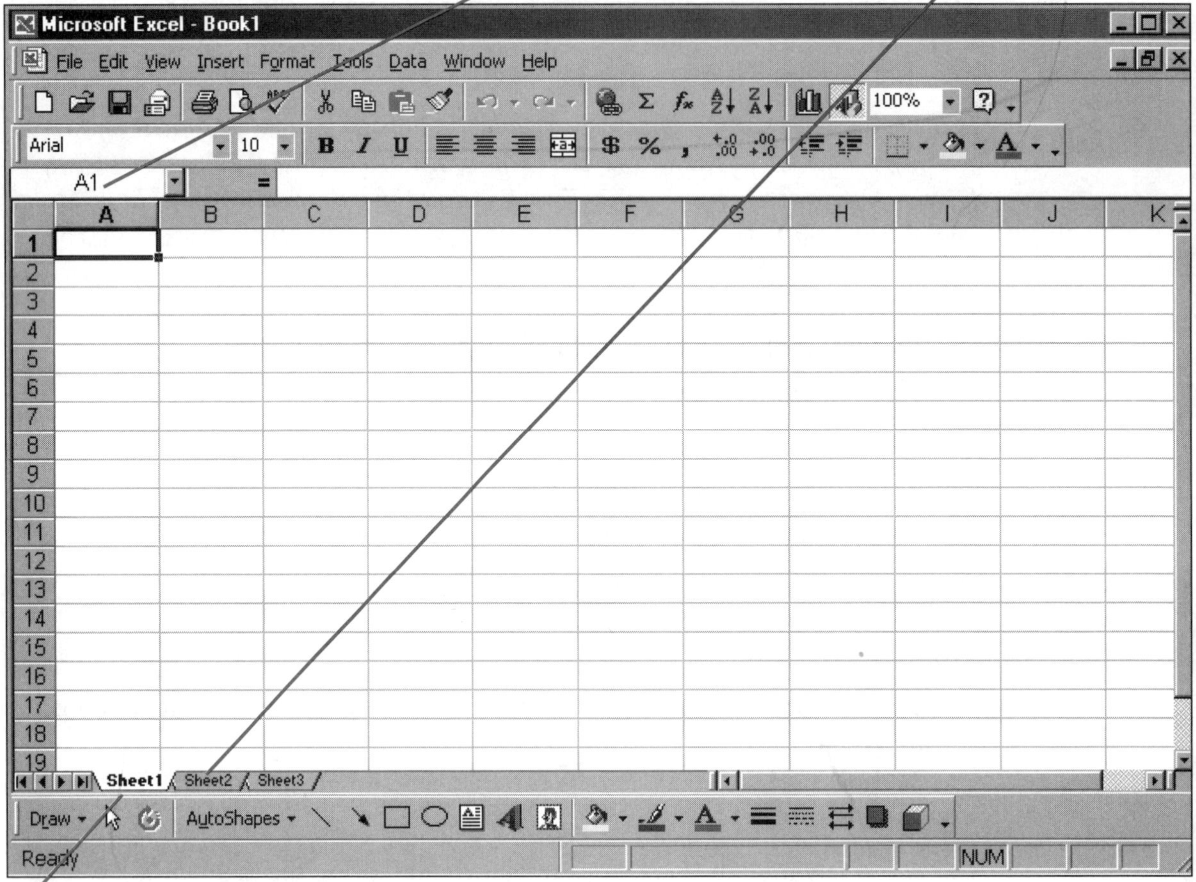
Microsoft Excel - Book1
File Edit View Insert Format Tools Data Window Help
100%
Arial
10
A1
A B C D E F G H I J K
Sheet1 Sheet2 Sheet3
Draw AutoShapes
Ready
NUM

Ⓒ *Click the Sheet1 tab.*

12. Press (CTRL)+(HOME) to move the highlight to Cell A1.

Entering Data

You can begin entering data the moment Excel is started. Data is entered into the active cell (the cell with the highlight). You can enter text, numbers, or formulas into cells. Text and numbers are used for different purposes in a worksheet. Text is used for descriptive headings and entries that require alphabetic characters or a combination of alphabetic and numeric characters. Numbers can be calculated using formulas. Excel recognizes the data you enter and decides whether the entry is text, a number, or a formula.

Long Text Entries

Text entries are often too long to fit in a cell. These entries are known as **long entries.** Excel uses the following rules when deciding how to display long entries.

- If the cell to the right of the long entry is empty, then the long entry displays over the adjacent cell.
- If the cell to the right of the long entry contains an entry, then Excel shortens, or **truncates,** the display of the long entry.

Keep in mind that Excel does not actually change the long entry, it simply truncates the display of the entry. You can always widen a column to accommodate a long entry.

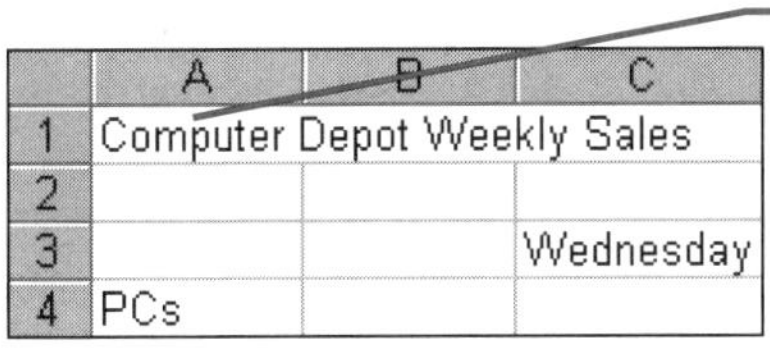
A
B
C
1
Computer Depot Weekly Sales
2
3
Wednesday
4
PCs

The entry, Computer Depot Weekly Sales *is a long entry. The entire phrase is entered in Cell A1 although it displays over Cells B1 and C1.*

Completing Cell Entries

Enter text or numbers by positioning the highlight in the desired cell, typing the desired text or number, and completing the entry. You can use (ENTER) and any of the arrow → ← ↑ ↓ keys to complete an entry. When you complete an entry with (ENTER), the text or number is entered in the cell, and the highlight moves down to the next cell. When you complete an entry with an arrow key, the text or number is entered in the cell, and the highlight moves to the next cell in the direction of the arrow key. If you are entering text or numbers and change your mind prior to completing the entry, you can press (ESC) to cancel the entry.

The Enter and Cancel Buttons

The Enter button and Cancel button appear on the Formula bar whenever you are entering or editing an entry. The Enter button completes the entry, and the highlight remains in the current cell. The Cancel button cancels the entry, as does the (ESC) key.

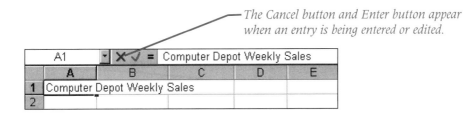

The Cancel button and Enter button appear when an entry is being entered or edited.

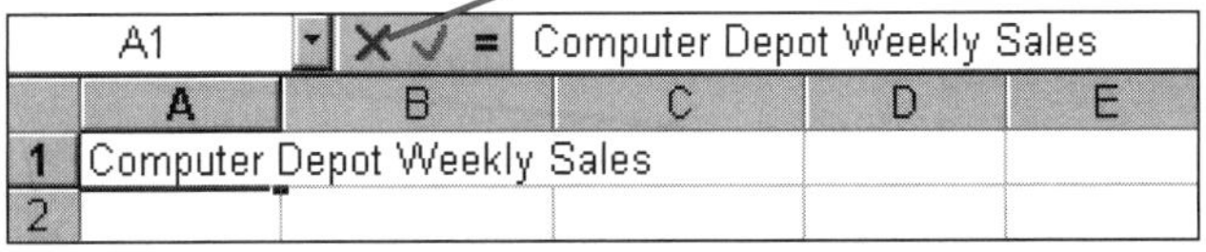
A1
=
Computer Depot Weekly Sales
A
B
C
D
E
1
Computer Depot Weekly Sales
2

Deleting and Replacing Entries

You can delete an entry after it has been completed by clicking in the cell and tapping (DELETE). Likewise, you can replace an entry by clicking in the cell and typing a new entry. The new entry will replace the original entry.

Undo and Redo

Excel's Undo button lets you reverse your last 16 action(s). You can reverse simple actions such as accidentally deleting a cell's content, or you can reverse more complex actions such as deleting an entire row. Most actions can be undone. Actions that can't be undone include commands such as printing workbooks and saving workbooks.

From the Keyboard

CTRL+Z for undo

CTRL+Y for redo

The Redo button reverses Undo. Use Redo when you Undo an action but decide to go through with that action after all.

Undoing and Redoing Multiple Actions

The arrows on the Undo and Redo buttons display lists of actions that can be undone or redone. You can undo or redo multiple actions by dragging the mouse over the desired actions. You can undo or redo up to 16 actions using this method. However, you must undo or redo actions in the order in which they appear on the drop-down list.

Repeat

The **Edit→Repeat** command lets you repeat your last action. For example, imagine you want to change the font size for several cells in a worksheet. To accomplish this, you could change the font size in one cell, reposition the highlight, and then issue the Repeat command. The Repeat command will set the font size for the new cell to the same size you set in the previous cell. You can repeat an action as many times as desired. However, the Repeat command is only available when the Redo button is unavailable. The **Edit→Repeat** command changes to **Edit→Redo** as soon as you undo an action.

From the Keyboard

CTRL+Y for repeat

Hands-On 14.3 Entering Text

Type a Long Entry

1. Make Cell A1 active by clicking the mouse pointer in it.
2. Type **`Computer Depot Weekly Sales`**, and tap ENTER.
   The text should be entered in the cell, and the highlight should move down to Cell A2. Excel moves the highlight down when you tap ENTER because most people enter data column by column. Notice that the entry displays over Cells B1 and C1. The long entry would not display over these cells if they contained data.
3. Click in Cell A1, and note the appearance of the Formula bar.

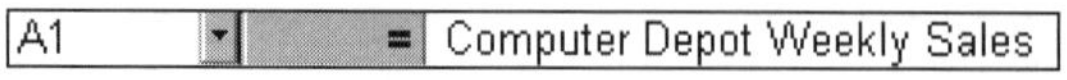
A1
=
Computer Depot Weekly Sales

Notice that the Formula bar displays the name of the active Cell (A1) and the cell's content. In this example, the cell's content is the title Computer Depot Weekly Sales. The title is a long entry because it is wider than Cell A1. Cells B1 and C1 are empty, so the long entry is displayed over them. Keep in mind; however, that the entire entry belongs to Cell A1. This concept will be demonstrated in the next few steps.

Delete the Entry and Use Undo and Redo

4. Tap (DELETE) and the entire entry is deleted.
   Notice that the entire entry was deleted because it belonged to Cell A1.
5. Click Undo to restore the entry.
6. Click Redo, and the entry will be deleted again.
   Redo always reverses Undo.
7. Click Undo again to restore the entry.

Verify That the Entry Belongs to Cell A1

8. Tap the → key to make Cell B1 active.
9. Look at the Formula bar, and notice that Cell B1 is empty.
   Once again, the long entry belongs to Cell A1 even though it is displayed over Cells B1 and C1.

Type Additional Text Entries

10. Use the → and ↓ keys to position the highlight in Cell C3.
11. Type **Wednesday**, and tap → once.
    Notice that the entry is completed and the highlight moves to Cell D3. You can always use the arrow keys to complete an entry and move the highlight in the desired direction.
12. Type **Thursday** in Cell D3, and tap →.
    Notice that the display of Wednesday is shortened or truncated. A long entry is always truncated when the cell to the right contains text or a number.
13. Enter the remaining text entries as shown in the illustration on the following page.
    Use Undo if you make a mistake. Also, you can change any entry by clicking in the desired cell and retyping the entry.

(Continued on the next page)

	A	B	C	D	E	F	G
1	Computer Depot Weekly Sales						
2							
3			Wednesda	Thursday	Friday	Saturday	Sunday
4	PCs						
5		Compaq					
6		IBM					
7		Acer					
8		Total					
9							
10	Laptops						
11		IBM					
12		Apple					
13		Empower					
14		Toshiba					
15		Total					
16							
17	Printers						
18		IBM					
19		HP					
20		Canon					
21		Total					
22							
23	Monitors						
24		NEC					
25		Sony					
26		Compaq					
27		Total					

You will continue to enhance your worksheet in the next exercise.

Number Entries

Numbers can only contain the digits 0–9 and a few other characters. Excel initially right-aligns numbers in cells, although you can change the alignment. The following table lists characters Excel will accept as part of a number entry.

Valid Characters in Number Entries
Digits 0–9
The following characters: + – ( ) , / $ % .

Number Formats

It isn't necessary to type commas, dollar signs, or other number formats when entering numbers. It is easier to just enter the numbers and then use Excel's formatting commands to add the desired number format(s). You will learn how to format numbers soon.

Decimals and Negative Numbers

You should always type a decimal point if the number you are entering requires one. Likewise, you should precede a negative number entry with a minus sign or enclose it in parenthesis ( ).

Hands-On 14.4 Enter Numbers

Use the Enter Button

1. Position the highlight in Cell C5.
2. Type **3**, but don't complete the entry.
3. Look at the Formula bar, and notice the Cancel ☒ and Enter ☑ buttons.
   These buttons appear whenever you begin entering or editing data in a cell.
4. Click the Enter ☑ button to complete the entry.
   Notice that the highlight remains in Cell C5. You can use the Enter button to complete entries; however, it is more efficient to complete entries with the keyboard when building a worksheet. This is because the highlight automatically moves to the next cell. The Enter button is most useful when editing entries.

Use the Cancel Button and the ESC Key

5. Position the highlight in Cell C6 and type **4**, but don't complete the entry.
6. Click the Cancel ☒ button on the Formula bar to cancel the entry.
7. Type **4** again, but this time tap ESC on the keyboard.
   ESC *has the same effect as the Cancel button.*
8. Type **4** once again, and tap ↓.
   Notice that Excel right-aligns the number in the cell.
9. Enter the remaining numbers as shown in the illustration on the following page.
   Keep in mind that some of the numbers you enter will cause entries in Column B to be truncated. You will solve this problem by widening Column B later in this exercise.

(Continued on the next page)

	A	B	C	D	E	F	G
1	Computer Depot Weekly Sales						
2							
3			Wednesda	Thursday	Friday	Saturday	Sunday
4	PCs						
5		Compaq	3	10	12	15	16
6		IBM	4	8	10	13	14
7		Acer	6	13	15	18	19
8		Total					
9							
10	Laptops						
11		IBM	2	5	4	10	8
12		Apple	3	7	5	12	10
13		Empower	4	8	11	14	14
14		Toshiba	2	3	5	5	3
15		Total					
16							
17	Printers						
18		IBM	3	5	5	6	8
19		HP	6	1	2	3	7
20		Canon	8	2	3	4	5
21		Total					
22							
23	Monitors						
24		NEC	3	6	8	7	2
25		Sony	5	3	2	2	1
26		Compaq	2	2	6	8	3
27		Total					

10. Take a moment to check the accuracy of your text and numbers.
It is very important to be accurate when entering data in worksheets. Excel's formulas, charts, and other features are of little use unless your data is accurate. You will learn how to save the workbook in the next topic.

Save Concepts

One important lesson to learn is to save your workbooks frequently! Power outages and careless accidents can result in lost data. The best protection is to save your workbooks every 10 or 15 minutes, or after making significant changes. Workbooks are saved to storage locations such as floppy disks, hard disks, or to Web sites on the World Wide Web.

Save Command

The Save button on the Standard toolbar and **File→Save** initiate the Save command. If a document has previously been saved, Excel then replaces the original version with the new edited version. If a document has never been saved, Excel then displays the **Save As** dialog box. The Save As dialog box has been significantly enhanced in Excel 2000. The Save As dialog box lets you specify the name and storage location of the document. You can also use the Save As dialog box to make a copy of a document by saving it under a new name or to a different location. You can use filenames containing as many as 255 characters. The following illustration outlines the Save As dialog box functions.

From the Keyboard

CTRL+S for Save

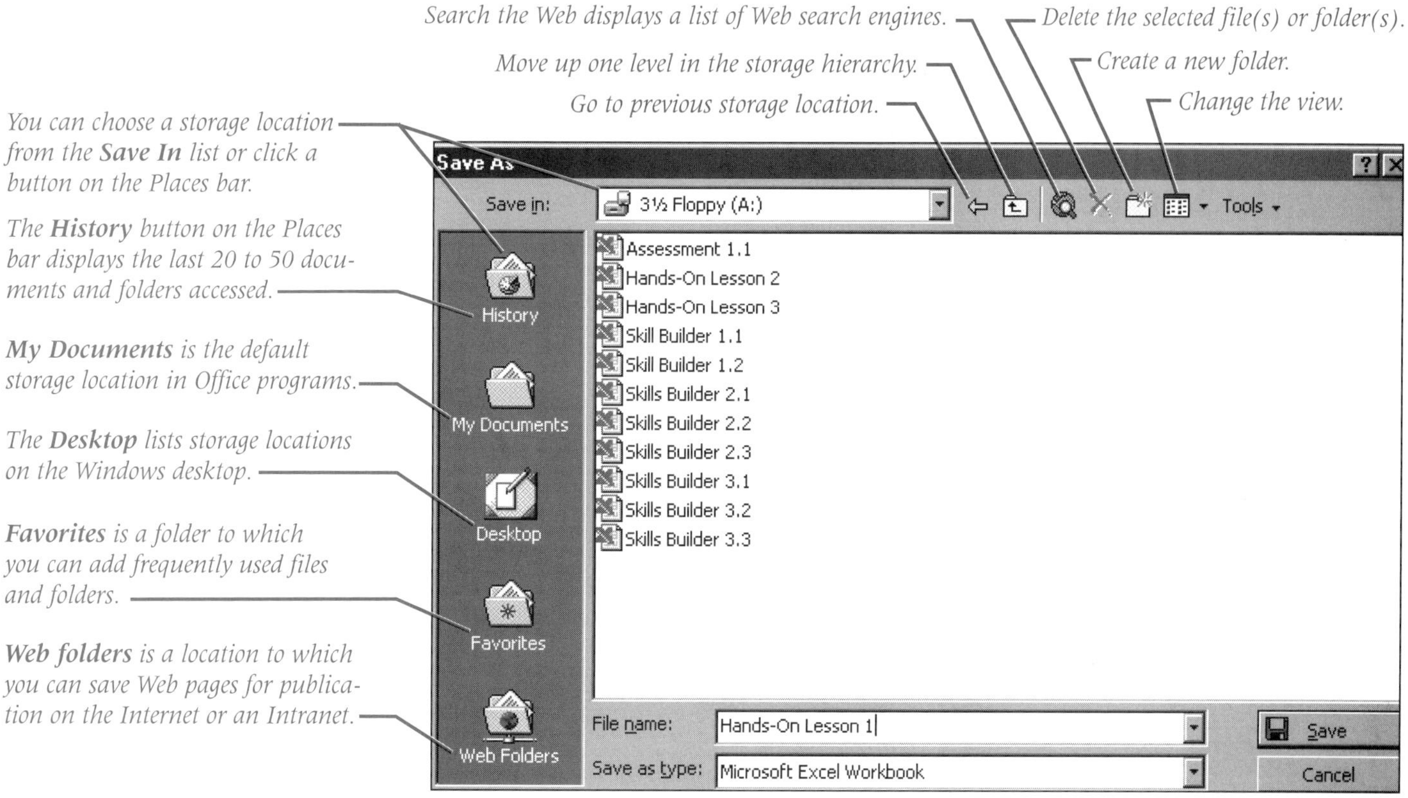

Search the Web displays a list of Web search engines.
Delete the selected file(s) or folder(s).
Move up one level in the storage hierarchy.
Create a new folder.
Go to previous storage location.
Change the view.
You can choose a storage location from the Save In list or click a button on the Places bar.
The History button on the Places bar displays the last 20 to 50 documents and folders accessed.
My Documents is the default storage location in Office programs.
The Desktop lists storage locations on the Windows desktop.
Favorites is a folder to which you can add frequently used files and folders.
Web folders is a location to which you can save Web pages for publication on the Internet or an Intranet.
Save As
Save in:
3½ Floppy (A:)
Tools
History
My Documents
Desktop
Favorites
Web Folders
Assessment 1.1
Hands-On Lesson 2
Hands-On Lesson 3
Skill Builder 1.1
Skill Builder 1.2
Skills Builder 2.1
Skills Builder 2.2
Skills Builder 2.3
Skills Builder 3.1
Skills Builder 3.2
Skills Builder 3.3
File name:
Hands-On Lesson 1
Save as type:
Microsoft Excel Workbook
Save
Cancel

Hands-On 14.5 Save the Workbook

In this exercise, you will save the workbook created in the previous exercises. Your instructor will most likely want you to save your workbooks onto the exercise diskette that is provided with this book. You will most likely be saving workbooks onto the A: disk drive.

1. Click the Save button, and the Save As dialog box will appear.
2. Follow these steps to save the workbook.
   Keep in mind that your dialog box will contain more files than shown here.

Ⓐ *Click here, and choose the disk drive with your exercise diskette. It is most likely* 3½ Floppy (A:).

Ⓑ *Notice that Excel proposes the filename* Book1 *in the File name box.*

Ⓒ *Type the name* **Hands-On Lesson 14**, *and it will replace the proposed name. (If you switched disk drives, then you may need to click in the* File name *box, delete the proposed name with the* DELETE *and/or* BACKSPACE *keys, and then type the new name.)*

Ⓓ *Click the* **Save** *button.*

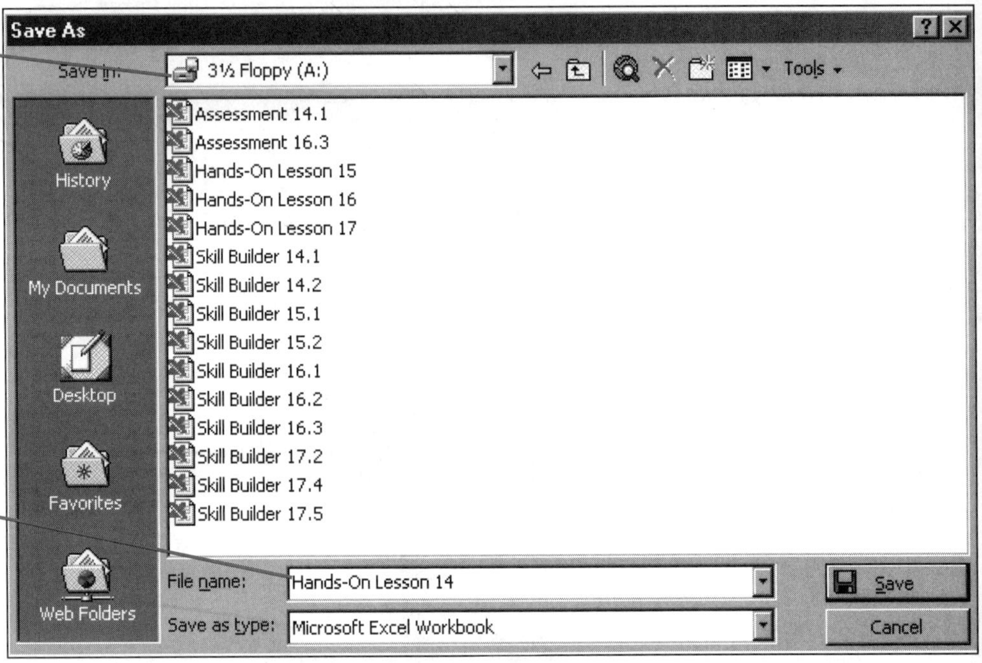

Save As
Save in:
3½ Floppy (A:)
Tools
History
My Documents
Desktop
Favorites
Web Folders
Assessment 14.1
Assessment 16.3
Hands-On Lesson 15
Hands-On Lesson 16
Hands-On Lesson 17
Skill Builder 14.1
Skill Builder 14.2
Skill Builder 15.1
Skill Builder 15.2
Skill Builder 16.1
Skill Builder 16.2
Skill Builder 16.3
Skill Builder 17.2
Skill Builder 17.4
Skill Builder 17.5
File name:
Hands-On Lesson 14
Save as type:
Microsoft Excel Workbook
Save
Cancel

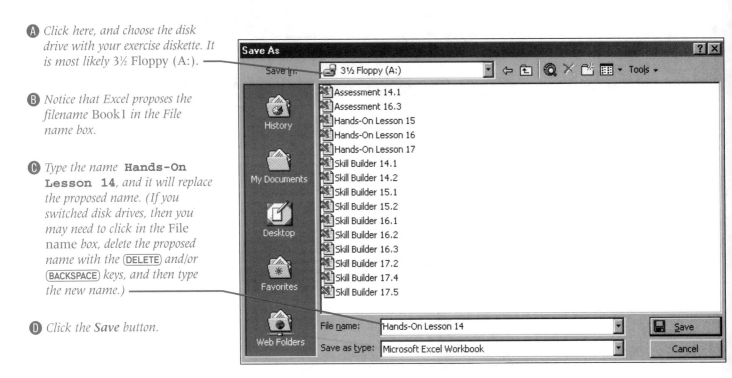

Notice that the workbook was saved and remains on the screen. You will continue to use this workbook throughout the lesson.

Editing Entries

You can edit the active cell by clicking in the Formula bar and making the desired changes. You can also double-click a cell and then edit the contents directly in the cell. This technique is known as **in-cell editing.**

Replacing Entries

Editing an entry is efficient if the entry is long enough that retyping it would be time-consuming. Editing can also be efficient with complex formulas and other functions that are difficult to recreate. If the entry requires little typing, however, it is usually easier to just replace it.

Deleting Characters

From the Keyboard

CTRL+DELETE to delete text to end of line

Use the DELETE and BACKSPACE keys to edit entries in the Formula bar or within a cell. The DELETE key removes the character to the right of the insertion point, while the BACKSPACE key removes the character to the left of the insertion point.

Hands-On 14.6 Edit Entries

The Hands-On Lesson 14 workbook should be open from the previous exercise.

Edit in the Formula Bar

1. Click Cell A1.
2. Follow these steps to edit Cell A1 using the Formula bar.

A Click in the Formula bar just to the right of the word Sales.
B Tap the SPACE BAR, and type the word Data.
A1
Computer Depot Weekly Sales Data
C Click the ENTER button.

Replace an Entry

3. Click Cell B13.
4. Type **Compaq**, and tap ENTER.
   The entry Compaq will replace Empower.

Use In-Cell Editing

5. *Double-click* Cell B12 (the cell with the word *Apple*).
6. Use the mouse or the → key to position the flashing insertion point to the right of the word *Apple*.
7. Tap the SPACE BAR once, and type **PowerBook**.
8. Tap ENTER or click Enter to complete the change.
   The entry should now read Apple PowerBook (although the entry will be slightly truncated). You will fix the truncation by widening the column later in this lesson.
9. Click the Save button to update the changes.
   The Save button automatically saves changes to a workbook that has previously been saved.

Selecting Cells

In Excel, you can select cells using both the mouse and the keyboard. You can perform a variety of actions on selected cells, including moving, copying, deleting, and formatting.

A **range** is a rectangular group of cells. Earlier in this lesson, you learned that each cell has a reference. For example, A1 refers to the first cell in a worksheet. Likewise, a range reference specifies the cells that are included within a range. The range reference includes the first and last cells in the range separated by a colon (:). For example, the Range C3:G3 includes all cells between C3 and G3. The following illustration highlights several ranges and their corresponding range references.

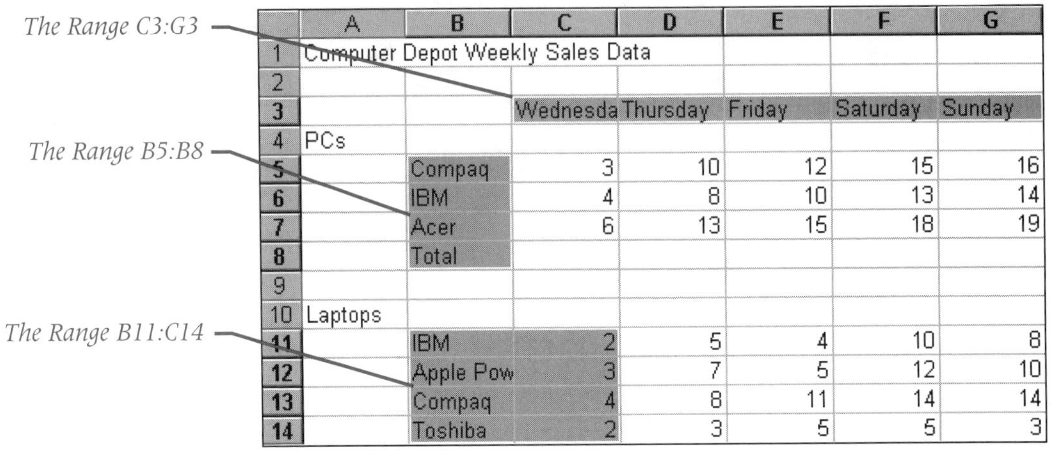

The Range C3:G3
The Range B5:B8
The Range B11:C14

	A	B	C	D	E	F	G
1	Computer Depot Weekly Sales Data						
2							
3			Wednesda	Thursday	Friday	Saturday	Sunday
4	PCs						
5		Compaq	3	10	12	15	16
6		IBM	4	8	10	13	14
7		Acer	6	13	15	18	19
8		Total					
9							
10	Laptops						
11		IBM	2	5	4	10	8
12		Apple Pow	3	7	5	12	10
13		Compaq	4	8	11	14	14
14		Toshiba	2	3	5	5	3

The following Quick Reference table describes selection techniques in Excel.

Quick Reference

SELECTION TECHNIQUES

Technique	**How to Do It**
Select a range.	Drag the mouse pointer over the desired cells.
Select several ranges.	Select a range; then press CTRL while selecting additional range(s).
Select an entire column.	Click a column heading, or press CTRL+SPACE BAR.
Select an entire row.	Click a row heading, or press SHIFT+SPACE BAR.
Select multiple columns or rows.	Drag the mouse pointer over the desired column or row headings.
Select an entire worksheet.	Click the Select All button at the top–left corner of the worksheet, or press CTRL+A.
Select a range using the SHIFT key.	Position the highlight in the first cell you wish to select, press SHIFT, and click the last cell in the range.
Extend a selection with the SHIFT key.	Press SHIFT while tapping any arrow key.

Hands-On 14.7 Practice Selecting

1. Position the mouse pointer ✣ over Cell C3.
2. Press and hold the left mouse button while dragging the mouse to the right until the range C3:G3 is selected.
3. Deselect the cells by clicking anywhere in the worksheet.

Select Multiple Ranges

4. Select the range C3:G3 as you did in steps 1 and 2.
5. Press and hold CTRL while you select the range B5:B8, as shown to the right.
   Both the C3:G3 and B5:B8 ranges should be selected. The CTRL *key lets you select more than one range at the same time.*

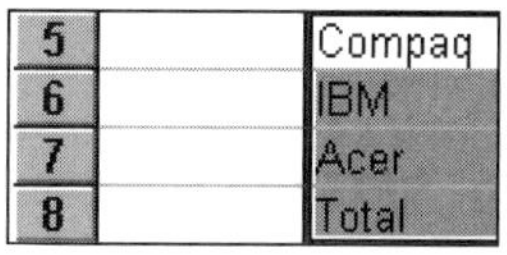
5
6
7
8
Compaq
IBM
Acer
Total

6. Press and hold CTRL while you select another range.
   There should now be three ranges selected.
7. Deselect the ranges by releasing CTRL and clicking anywhere in the worksheet.

Select Entire Rows and Columns

8. Follow these steps to select various rows and columns.

Ⓐ *Click on the* ***Column A*** *heading to select the entire column.*

Ⓑ *Position the mouse pointer on the* ***Column C*** *heading, then drag to the right until* ***Columns C, D,*** *and* ***E*** *are selected.* ***Column A*** *will be deselected.*

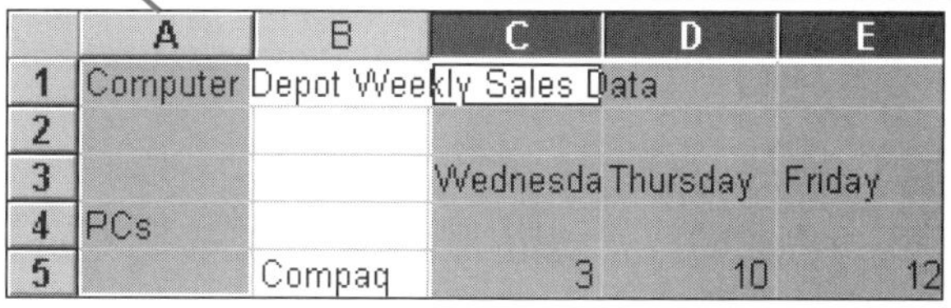
A B C D E
1 Computer Depot Weekly Sales Data
2
3 Wednesda Thursday Friday
4 PCs
5 Compaq 3 10 12

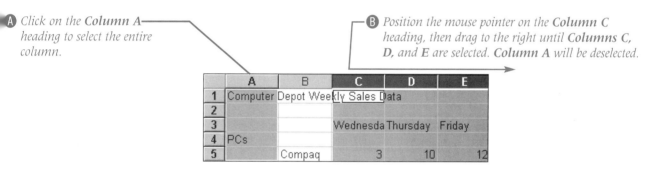

Ⓐ *Click the Select All button to select the entire worksheet.*

Ⓑ *Click the Row 1 heading to select Row 1.*

Ⓒ *Drag the mouse pointer down over the headings to Rows 5–8 to select them.*

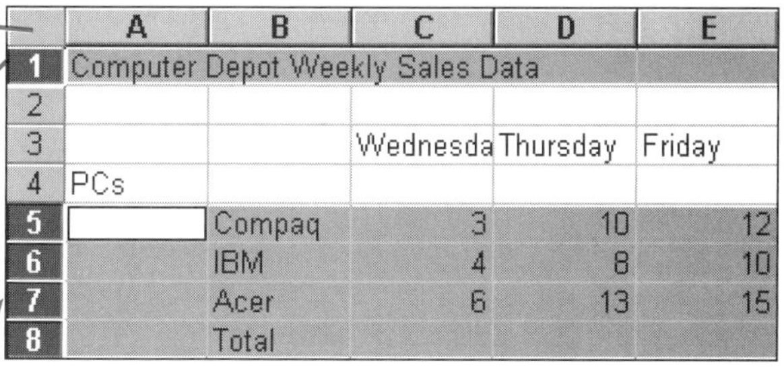
A B C D E
1 Computer Depot Weekly Sales Data
2
3 Wednesda Thursday Friday
4 PCs
5 Compaq 3 10 12
6 IBM 4 8 10
7 Acer 6 13 15
8 Total

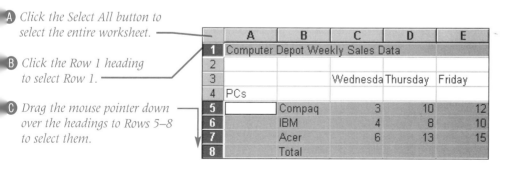

(Continued on the next page)

Use Keyboard Techniques

9. Click Cell B5.
10. Press and hold SHIFT; then click Cell G8 to select the range B5:G8.
11. Click Cell B11.
12. Press and hold SHIFT then tap → five times, and ↓ four times.
    The range B11:G15 should be selected. Notice that the SHIFT key techniques give you precise control when selecting. You should use the SHIFT key techniques if you find it difficult to select with the mouse.
13. Take a moment to practice selection techniques.

Aligning Cell Entries

The Align Left, Center, and Align Right buttons on the Formatting toolbar let you align entries within cells. By default, text entries are left-aligned and numbers are right-aligned. To change alignment, select the cell(s) and click the desired alignment button.

Hands-On 14.8 Align Text Entries and Widen Columns

In this exercise, you will align the entries in Row 3. You will also widen Columns B and C.

1. Select the range C3:G3.

Wednesda Thursday Friday Saturday Sunday

2. Click the Align Right button on the Formatting toolbar.
   Each entry in the range (except Wednesday) should appear right-aligned. Wednesday does not appear right aligned because it is too wide for the cell. You will change the width of Column C in a moment.

Adjust Column Widths

In the next few steps, you will adjust the width of Columns B and C. This exercise provides a brief introduction to adjusting column widths. A complete discussion of adjusting column widths is given in a later lesson.

3. Follow these steps to adjust the width of Column B.

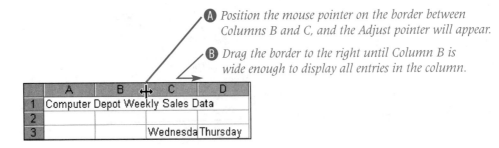

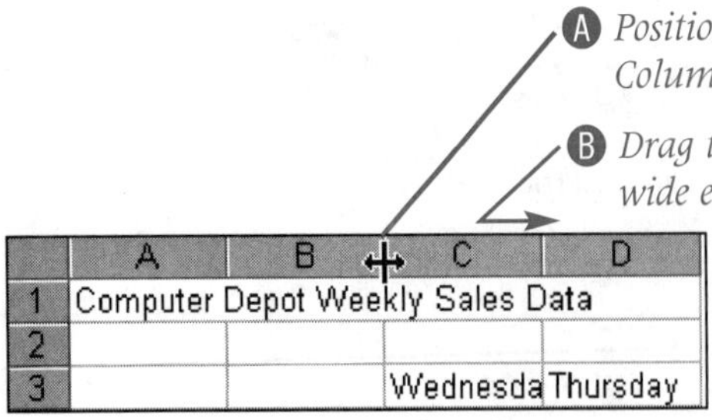
A Position the mouse pointer on the border between Columns B and C, and the Adjust pointer will appear.
B Drag the border to the right until Column B is wide enough to display all entries in the column.
A B C D
1 Computer Depot Weekly Sales Data
2
3 Wednesda Thursday

4. Widen Column C until the word *Wednesday* is completely visible in Cell C3.
   You will need to drag the border between the column headings C and D.
5. Click the Save button to save the changes.

AutoSum

The power of Excel becomes apparent when you begin using formulas and functions. The most common type of calculation is when a column or row of numbers is summed. In fact, this type of calculation is so common that Excel provides the AutoSum function specifically for this purpose.

The AutoSum button on the Standard toolbar automatically sums a column or row of numbers. When you click AutoSum, Excel proposes a range of numbers. You can accept the proposed range or drag in the worksheet to select a different range. When you complete the entry, Excel inserts a SUM function in the worksheet, which adds the numbers in the range.

From the Keyboard
ALT+= for AutoSum

Hands-On 14.9 Use AutoSum

In this exercise, you will use AutoSum to compute several totals. Keep in mind that this section provides an introduction to formulas. You will learn more about formulas as you progress through this course.

Compute One Column Total

1. Click Cell C8.
2. Click the AutoSum button.
3. Follow these steps to review the formula and complete the entry.

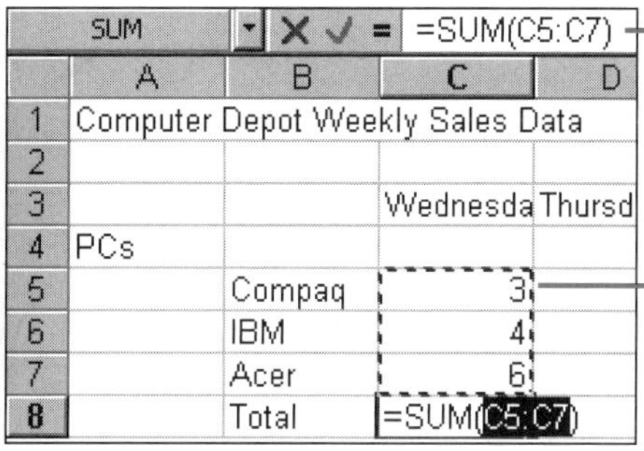
SUM
=SUM(C5:C7)
A
B
C
D
1 Computer Depot Weekly Sales Data
2
3 Wednesda Thursd
4 PCs
5 Compaq 3
6 IBM 4
7 Acer 6
8 Total =SUM(C5:C7)

A *Notice that Excel proposes the formula =SUM(C5:C7) in Cell 8 and in the Formula bar. All formulas begin with an equal (=) sign. SUM is a built-in function that adds the numbers in a range (in this example the range is C5:C7).*

B *Notice the flashing marquee surrounding the range C5:C7. AutoSum assumes you want to add together all cells above C8 until the first empty cell is reached. The marquee identifies this range of cells.*

C *Click the Enter button on the Formula bar to complete the entry. The total should be 13.*

4. Click Cell D8.
5. Click AutoSum and complete the entry.
6. Use the preceding technique to compute the column totals in Cells E8, F8, and G8.

(Continued on the next page)

Compute Several Totals With One Command

7. Select the Range C15:G15. 
15
Total

8. Click the AutoSum button.
The column totals for Cells C15, D15, E15, F15, and G15 should automatically be computed. AutoSum displays the marquee and requires confirmation only when you are computing a single total.

9. Use the preceding steps to compute the column totals in Rows 21 and 27.

Make Column H a Totals Column

10. Click Cell H4, type the word **`Totals`**, and complete the entry.

11. Use the Align Right button to right-align the entry in Cell H4.

12. Click Cell H5.

13. Click AutoSum and Excel will propose the Range C5:G5, which includes all numbers in Row 5.

14. Complete the entry and the row sum should total 56.

15. Use the preceding steps to compute the row total in Cell H6.

Override the Range AutoSum Proposes

16. Click Cell H7, and then click AutoSum .
Notice that Excel assumes you want to sum the Cells H5 and H6, above H7. This assumption is incorrect. Excel made this assumption because there were two cells above H7, which is enough to make a range. Excel will always propose a column summation if it has a choice between a column and row summation.

17. Follow these steps to override the proposed range.

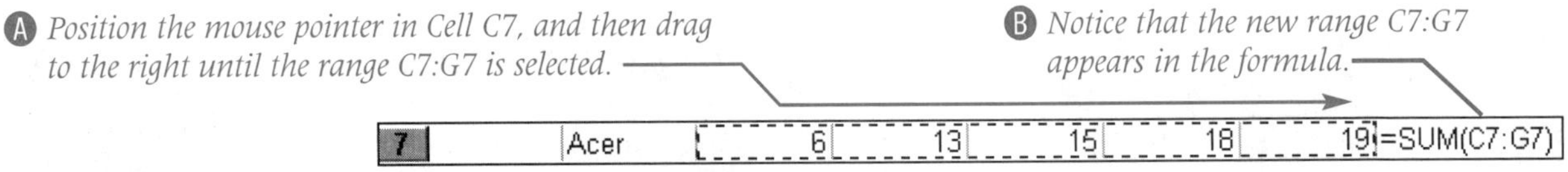
A Position the mouse pointer in Cell C7, and then drag to the right until the range C7:G7 is selected.
B Notice that the new range C7:G7 appears in the formula.
7
Acer
6
13
15
18
19
=SUM(C7:G7)

18. Complete the entry, and the row sum should total 71.

19. Use the preceding technique to compute the row total in Cell H8 (the total should equal 176).
Actually, you could have accepted the formula that AutoSum proposed for Cell H8. In this case, the column and row summations would have been the same.

Compute Several Totals with One Command

You can eliminate the problem of AutoSum proposing the wrong formula by summing a range of row totals with one command. This is the same technique you used to sum the column totals.

20. Select the range H11:H15 as shown in the following illustration.

	A	B	C	D	E	F	G	H
9								
10	Laptops							
11		IBM	2	5	4	10	8	
12		Apple PowerBook	3	7	5	12	10	
13		Compaq	4	8	11	14	14	
14		Toshiba	2	3	5	5	3	
15		Total	11	23	25	41	35	

21. Click the AutoSum [Σ] button.
The five row totals should be computed.

22. Use the preceding steps to compute the row totals for the ranges H18:H21 and H24:H27.
Your completed worksheet should match the worksheet shown in the Case Study at the start of this lesson.

AutoCalculate

The AutoCalculate box on the Status bar lets you view the sum of a range of numbers without actually inserting a SUM function in the worksheet. You can also right-click on the AutoCalculate box to see the average, minimum, or maximum of the selected range. The following illustration highlights these concepts.

To use AutoCalculate, first select a range. Excel displays the sum in the AutoCalculate box on the Status bar.

If desired, you can right-click the AutoCalculate box and choose another function from the pop-up menu.

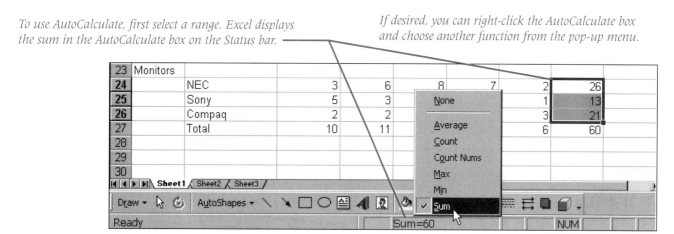

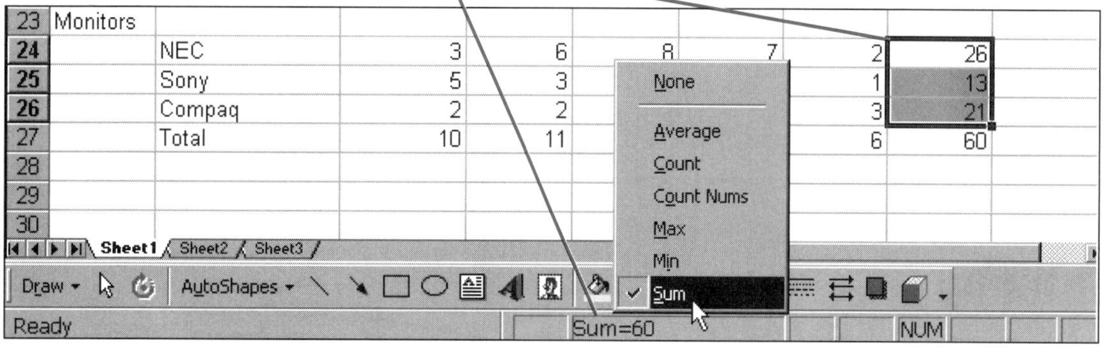
23 Monitors
24 NEC 3 6 8 7 2 26
25 Sony 5 3 1 13
26 Compaq 2 2 3 21
27 Total 10 11 6 60
28
29
30
Sheet1 Sheet2 Sheet3
None
Average
Count
Count Nums
Max
Min
Sum
Draw AutoShapes
Ready
Sum=60
NUM

Hands-On 14.10 Use AutoCalculate

1. Select any range of numbers in your worksheet.
2. Locate the AutoCalculate box on the Status bar. The sum of the selected numbers should be displayed.
3. *Right-click* the AutoCalculate box, and the pop-up menu will appear.
4. Choose **Average** from the pop-up menu to display the average of the numbers in the AutoCalculate box.
5. Select another range to display the average in the AutoCalculate box.
6. *Right-click* the AutoCalculate box, and choose **Sum** from the pop-up menu.

Print Preview

The Print Preview button on the Standard toolbar displays the Print Preview window. Print Preview lets you see exactly how a worksheet will look when it is printed. Print Preview can save time, paper, and wear-and-tear on your printer. Print Preview is especially useful when printing large worksheets, or with worksheets containing charts and intricate formatting. It is always wise to preview a large or complex worksheet before sending it to the printer. When you display the Print Preview window, the standard toolbars are replaced by the Print Preview toolbar.

Hands-On 14.11 Use Print Preview

1. Click the Print Preview button on the Standard toolbar.
2. Zoom in by clicking anywhere on the worksheet.
3. Zoom out by clicking anywhere on the worksheet.
4. Click the **Close** button on the Print Preview toolbar to exit without printing.

Printing

From the Keyboard

CTRL+P to display Print dialog box

The Print button on the Standard toolbar sends the entire worksheet to the current printer. You must display the Print dialog box if you want to change printers, adjust the number of copies to be printed, or set other printing options. Display the Print dialog box with the **File→Print** command. The illustration on the following page explains the most important options available in the Print dialog box.

Choose a printer from this drop-down list.

Specify the number of copies here. The Collate option is useful when you are printing more than one copy of a multiple page worksheet. If the Collate box is checked, the first copy is printed before the second copy begins printing, etc.

Choose to print all pages or a range of pages.

Choose to print only selected cells, the active sheet(s), or the entire workbook here.

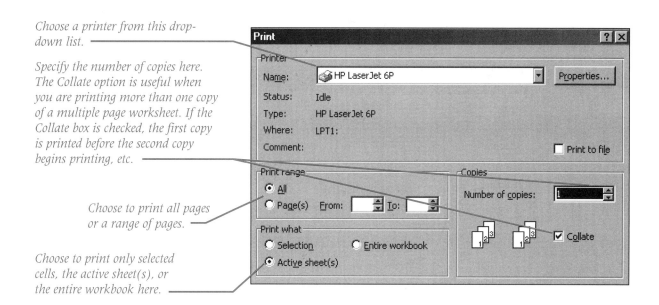

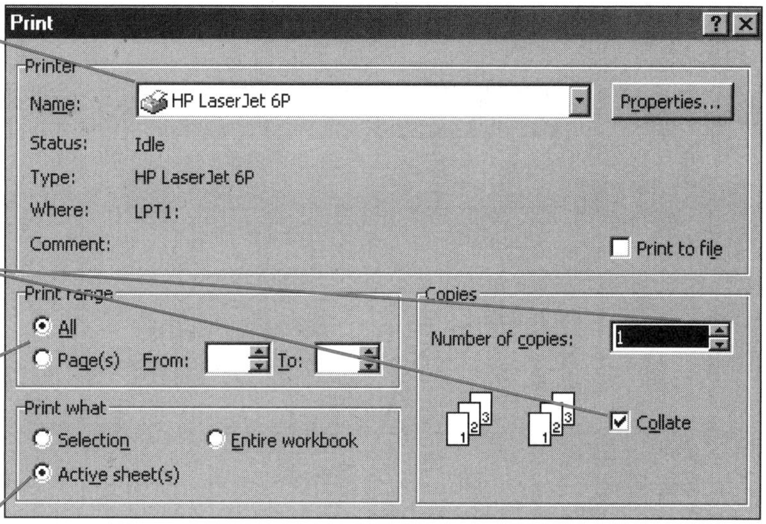

Print
Printer
Name: HP LaserJet 6P
Properties...
Status: Idle
Type: HP LaserJet 6P
Where: LPT1:
Comment:
Print to file
Print range
All
Page(s) From: To:
Copies
Number of copies: 1
Collate
Print what
Selection
Entire workbook
Active sheet(s)

Hands-On 14.12 Print the Worksheet

1. Choose **File→Print** to display the Print dialog box.
2. Take a few moments to review the dialog box options.
3. When you are ready to print, make sure the options are set as shown in the preceding illustration, then click the **OK** button.
   Keep in mind that your printer will probably be different than the printer shown in the illustration.
4. Retrieve your worksheet from the printer.

Closing Workbooks

The **File→Close** command is used to close an open workbook. When you close a workbook, Excel prompts you to save the changes. If you choose *Yes* at the prompt and the workbook has previously been saved, then Excel saves the changes. If the workbook is new, Excel displays the Save As dialog box, allowing you to assign a name and storage location to the workbook.

Hands-On 14.13 Close the Workbook

1. Choose **File→Close** from the menu bar.
2. Click the **Yes** button if Excel asks you to save the changes.
   Notice that there is no workbook in the Excel window. The Excel window always has this appearance when all workbooks have been closed.

Opening Workbooks

The Open button on the Standard toolbar and the **File→Open** command display the Open dialog box. The Open dialog box lets you navigate to any storage location and open previously saved workbooks. Once a workbook is open, you can browse it, print it, or even make editing changes. The organization and layout of the Open dialog box are similar to the Save dialog box discussed earlier in this lesson.

From the Keyboard

CTRL+O to Open

Hands-On 14.14 Open the Workbook

1. Click Open on the Standard toolbar.
2. Follow these steps to open the Hands-On Lesson 14 workbook.
   Keep in mind that your dialog box will contain more files than shown here.

A Choose the disk drive containing your exercise diskette. It is most likely in 3½ Floppy (A:).

B Choose Hands-On Lesson 14.

C Click the Open button.

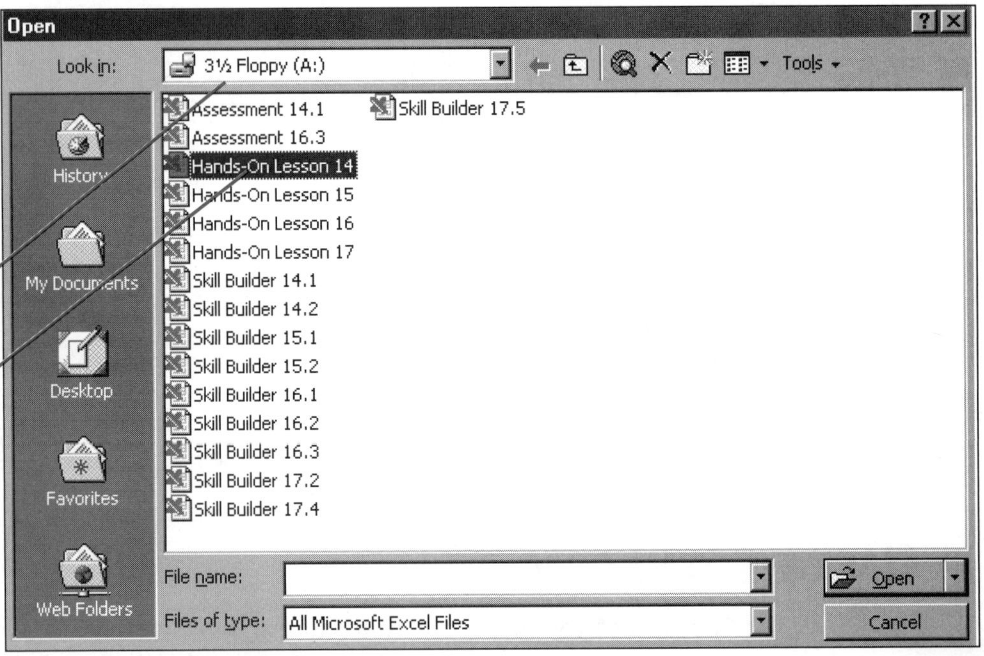
Open
Look in:
3½ Floppy (A:)
Tools
History
My Documents
Desktop
Favorites
Web Folders
Assessment 14.1
Assessment 16.3
Hands-On Lesson 14
Hands-On Lesson 15
Hands-On Lesson 16
Hands-On Lesson 17
Skill Builder 14.1
Skill Builder 14.2
Skill Builder 15.1
Skill Builder 15.2
Skill Builder 16.1
Skill Builder 16.2
Skill Builder 16.3
Skill Builder 17.2
Skill Builder 17.4
Skill Builder 17.5
File name:
Files of type:
All Microsoft Excel Files
Open
Cancel

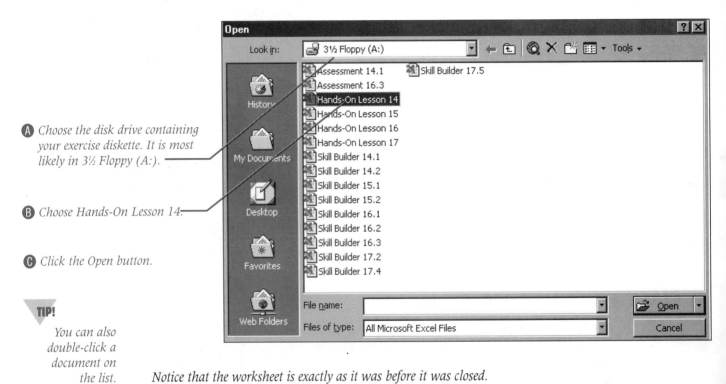

TIP! *You can also double-click a document on the list.*

Notice that the worksheet is exactly as it was before it was closed.

Exiting from Excel

The **File→Exit** command is used to close the Excel program. You should close Excel and other programs if you are certain you won't be using them for some time. This will free up memory for other programs. When you close Excel, you will be prompted to save any workbooks that have unsaved edits.

Hands-On 14.15 Exit from Excel

1. Choose **File→Exit** from the menu bar.
   Excel will close without prompting you to save the workbook because you have not changed the workbook since it was opened last.

Concepts Review

True/False Questions

1. Each workbook can have a maximum of one worksheet.	TRUE	FALSE
2. A worksheet is composed of horizontal rows and vertical columns.	TRUE	FALSE
3. Text entries can contain spaces.	TRUE	FALSE
4. Numbers can only contain the digits 0–9. No other characters are permitted.	TRUE	FALSE
5. The Undo button lets you reverse up to the last 16 actions.	TRUE	FALSE
6. A colon (:) is used to separate the beginning and ending cells in a range reference.	TRUE	FALSE
7. You can select an entire row by clicking the row header.	TRUE	FALSE
8. When given a choice, AutoSum will always sum the numbers to the left of the active cell instead of summing the numbers above the active cell.	TRUE	FALSE

Multiple-Choice Questions

1. Which of the following keystrokes moves the highlight to Cell A1?
   a. HOME
   b. CTRL+PGUP
   c. CTRL+HOME
   d. CTRL+INS

2. What happens when you enter text in a cell that already contains an entry?
   a. The text replaces the original entry.
   b. Excel rejects the new entry, keeping the original entry intact.
   c. The cell contains both the original entry and the new entry.
   d. None of the above

3. What happens when you insert an entry in the cell to the **right** of a long text entry?
   a. The display of the long entry is truncated.
   b. The long entry is replaced by the entry in the cell to the right.
   c. It has no effect on the long entry.
   d. None of the above

4. What happens when you insert an entry in the cell to the **left** of a long text entry?
   a. The display of the long entry is truncated.
   b. The long entry is permanently truncated.
   c. It has no effect on the long entry.
   d. None of the above

Skill Builders

Skill Builder 14.1 Edit a Worksheet

In this exercise, you will edit a worksheet. This exercise demonstrates that sometimes it is easier to replace entries, and at other times it is easier to edit them.

Replace Several Entries

1. Start Excel and click the Open button on the Standard toolbar.
2. Navigate to your exercise diskette, and double-click the workbook named Skill Builder 14.1.
3. Click Cell A4.
4. Type **Ralph**, and tap ENTER.
   Notice that it was easy to replace the entry because the name Ralph is easy to retype.
5. Replace the name Calvin in Cell A6 with the name **Steven**.

Edit Using the Formula Bar

6. Click Cell C4.
7. Click in the Formula bar just in front of the telephone prefix 222.
8. Tap DELETE three times to remove the prefix.
9. Type **333** and complete the entry.
10. Change the area code in Cell C8 from 714 to **814**.

Use In-Cell Editing

11. Double-click Cell D4.
    The flashing insertion point should appear in the cell.
12. Use → or ← to position the insertion point in front of the word *Lane*.
13. Use DELETE to remove the word *Lane*.
14. Type **Reservoir**, and complete the entry.

(Continued on the next page)

15. Edit the next five addresses using either the Formula bar or in-cell editing. The required changes appear bold in the following table.

Cell	Make These Changes
D5	2900 **Carlton** Drive, San Mateo, CA 94401
D6	**2300** Palm Drive, Miami, FL 33147
D7	888 Wilson Street, **Concord**, CA **94518**
D8	320 Main Street, **Pittsburgh**, PA 17951
D9	132nd Street, Los Angeles, CA **90045**

16. When you have finished, choose **File→Close** from the menu bar, and click the **Yes** button when Excel asks if you wish to save the changes.

Skill Builder 14.2 Use AutoSum and Align Entries

In this exercise, you will edit a worksheet. You will use AutoSum to compute totals, and the alignment buttons to align entries.

Compute Totals

1. Click the Open button on the Standard toolbar.
2. Navigate to your exercise diskette, and double-click the workbook named Skill Builder 14.2.
3. Click Cell C10, and then click AutoSum.
   Notice that Excel proposes the formula =SUM(C8:C9). Excel proposes this incorrect formula because there are empty cells in the range you are to sum.
4. Drag the mouse pointer over the range C5:C9. The flashing marquee will surround the range C5:C9, as shown to the right.

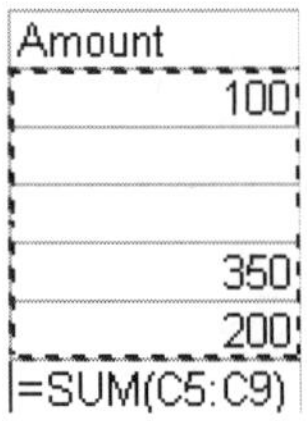
Amount
100
350
200
=SUM(C5:C9)

5. Complete the entry; the total should equal 650.
6. Use the preceding steps to compute the totals in Cells E10, G10, and I10.
   You may need to scroll to the right to see Column I.

Align the Entries

7. Follow these steps to align the cell entries for Q1.

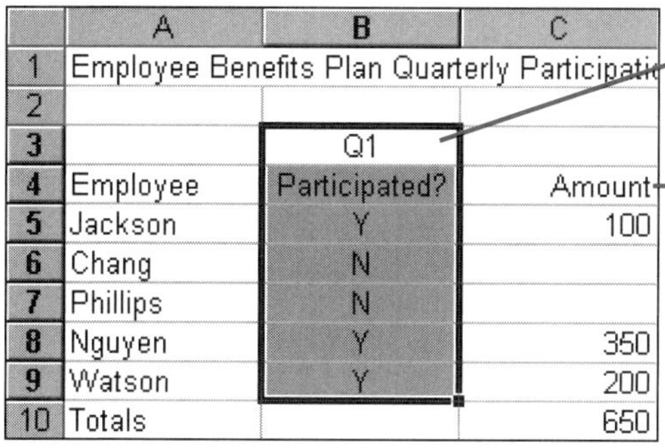

A
B
C
1 Employee Benefits Plan Quarterly Participati
2
3 Q1
4 Employee Participated? Amount
5 Jackson Y 100
6 Chang N
7 Phillips N
8 Nguyen Y 350
9 Watson Y 200
10 Totals 650

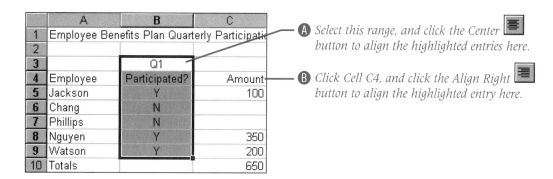

Ⓐ *Select this range, and click the Center button to align the highlighted entries here.*

Ⓑ *Click Cell C4, and click the Align Right button to align the highlighted entry here.*

8. Align the entries for Q2, Q3, and Q4 as you just did for Q1. You can do this quickly by using the CTRL key to select all three ranges and aligning them with a single click of the Center button.

9. Right-align the word *Amount* in Cells E4, G4, and I4. Once again, you can use CTRL to select all three cells and then issue the command.

10. Save the changes to your workbook, and then close the workbook.

Skill Builder 14.3 Create a Worksheet with Decimal Numbers

In this exercise, you will create the worksheet shown on the following page. You will enter numbers containing two decimal places. You will also use the alignment buttons to align the text and numbers.

Enter Text and Widen Columns

1. Click the New button on the Standard toolbar.
   You can always use the New button to display a new workbook.

2. Enter text in Rows 1–3 as shown in the following illustration.
   Make sure you enter the entire phrase ***Order Tracking Sheet*** *into Cell D1. Also, the entries in Cells A3, B3, and E3 will be truncated. You will correct this by widening the columns in the following steps.*

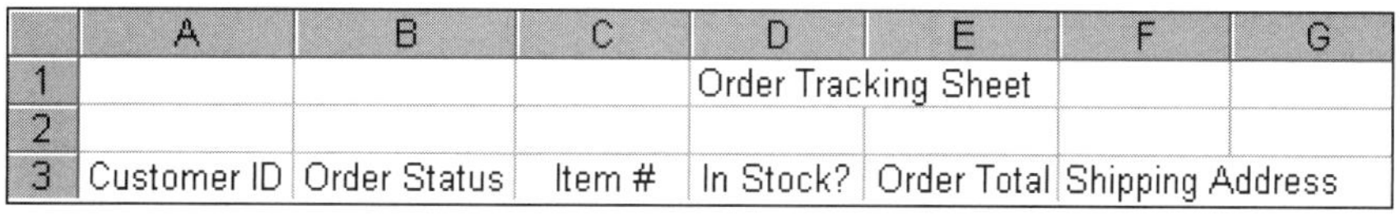

A B C D E F G
1 Order Tracking Sheet
2
3 Customer ID Order Status Item # In Stock? Order Total Shipping Address

(Continued on the next page)

3. Position the mouse pointer on the border between the column headings A and B, and the Adjust pointer will appear.

4. Drag the border to the right until Column A is wide enough for the Customer ID entry.

5. Widen Columns B and E until the entries in those columns are completely visible.

Enter Numbers with Decimals

6. Click Cell E4.

7. Type **`100.91`**, and tap (ENTER).
   You should always type a decimal point if the number requires one.

8. Type **`45.87`**, and tap (ENTER).

9. Enter the numbers shown below in Cells E6, E7, and E8 (don't type the total 292.38 in Cell E9).

Use AutoSum

10. Click Cell E9.

11. Click AutoSum [Σ], and then complete the entry.
    The total should be 292.38 as shown below.

12. Complete the worksheet as shown below. You will need to enter the numbers and text shown. Make sure you enter each shipping address into a single cell. For example, the address **`1603 Catalina`** . . . should be entered in Cell F4. Also, you will need to select the range A3:D8 and use the Center button to center the entries. Align all other entries as shown below.

13. When you have finished, click the Save button, and save the workbook as **Skill Builder 14.3.** Close the workbook after it has been saved.

	A	B	C	D	E	F	G	H	I	J
1				Order Tracking Sheet						
2										
3	Customer ID	Order Status	Item #	In Stock?	Order Total	Shipping Address				
4	341	S	A423	Y	100.91	1603 Catalina Avenue, Redondo Beach, CA 90277				
5	234	S	A321	Y	45.87	Will Pickup				
6	567	I	S345	N	43.23	450 Terrace Drive, Santa Clara, CA 95050				
7	879	H	D567	N	78.92	No address at this point				
8	233	I	S230	Y	23.45	23 Maple Lane, Crawfordsville, IN 47933				
9	Total Orders				292.38					

Assessments

Assessment 14.1

1. Open the workbook named Assessment 14.1 on your exercise diskette.
2. Edit the title in Cell A1 to read **`Computer Depot Sales Bonuses`**.
3. Widen Column A until all names in the column are visible.
4. Right-align the headings in Row 3.
5. Use AutoSum to compute the totals in Row 9.
6. Change the name Mary Johnson in Cell A5 to **`Sally Adams`**.
   Your completed worksheet should match the worksheet below.
7. Print the completed worksheet, save the changes, and then close the workbook.

	A	B	C	D	E	F	G
1	Computer Depot Sales Bonuses						
2							
3		January	February	March	April	May	June
4	Employee						
5	Sally Adams	100	125	300	235	125	300
6	Cliff Packard	200	200	200	210	210	250
7	Helen Martinez	200	350	250	120	230	225
8	Sarah Stonestown	150	125	235	250	135	175
9	Total	650	800	985	815	700	950

Assessment 14.2

1. Click the New button to open a new workbook.
2. Use the following guidelines to create the following worksheet.
   - Widen the columns as necessary to prevent long entries from being truncated.
   - Use AutoSum to compute the totals. Be careful, as certain rows and columns contain blank cells. You will need to manually override the ranges proposed by AutoSum.
   - Align the text entries in Row 3 as shown.
3. When you have finished, click the Print button on the Standard toolbar to print the worksheet.
4. Save the workbook as **Assessment 14.2,** and then close the workbook.

	A	B	C	D	E	F	G
1	Computer Depot Employee Time Log						
2							
3	Employee	Wednesday	Thursday	Friday	Saturday	Sunday	Totals
4	Mary Johnson	6.5		5	6.5	4	22
5	Cliff Packard	4	6	6.5	6.5	4	27
6	Helen Martinez	4	6	6.5	6.5		23
7	Sarah Stonestown		4	4	4		12
8	Totals	14.5	16	22	23.5	8	84

Assessment 14.3

1. Open a New workbook.
2. Create the worksheet shown in the following illustration. Make sure the numbers and totals match the worksheet. Widen columns and align entries as shown.
3. Print the workbook when you have finished.
4. Save the workbook as **Assessment 14.3,** and then close the workbook.

	A	B	C	D	E	F
1	Big City Diner Q1 Expenses					
2						
3	Item		January	February	March	Q1 Totals
4	Rent and Utilities	Rent	800	800	800	2400
5		Utilities	340	400	250	990
6		Phone	250	200	300	750
7		Insurance	350			350
8		Total	1740	1400	1350	4490
9						
10	Cost of goods sold	Produce	2500	2320	1700	6520
11		Meat	4000	3400	3700	11100
12		Grains	1000	1200	890	3090
13		Total	7500	6920	6290	20710
14						
15	Salaries	Simmons	800	780	800	2380
16		Swanson	750	650	870	2270
17		Martinez	900	780	680	2360
18		Richardson	1200	1000	990	3190
19		Total	3650	3210	3340	10200
20						
21	Other	Advertising	500	300		800
22		Uniforms		340		340
23		Janitorial	200	200	200	600
24		Miscellaneous	100	2000		2100
25		Total	800	2840	200	3840

LESSON 15—Excel

Expanding on the Basics

In this lesson, you will expand upon the basic skills you learned in the previous lesson. You will use several types of formulas to create totals, calculate profits, and determine financial ratios. You will also learn powerful tools and techniques such as the fill handle and the Format Painter. When you have finished this lesson, you will have developed the skills necessary to produce more sophisticated worksheets.

In This Lesson

Case Study

Donna Prusko is an entrepreneur and the founder of Donna's Deli. Donna recently resigned from her corporate position to pursue her dream and passion—a deli that serves delicious, healthy food at reasonable prices. Donna also realizes that the health of her business is just as important as the health of her customers. For this reason, she wants to develop a worksheet to track her income and expenses. The worksheet will use formulas to determine gross profits, net profits, and important financial ratios. Microsoft Excel is an important tool for any entrepreneur in today's highly competitive business world.

	A	B	C	D	E
1	**Donna's Deli - Income and Expense Worksheet**				
2					
3			Quarterly Income		
4	Food Sales	**Q1**	**Q2**	**Q3**	**Q4**
5	Dine-in Sales	21,000	23,000	28,000	42,000
6	Takeout Sales	12,000	16,000	25,000	56,000
7	Subtotal	**$33,000**	**$39,000**	**$53,000**	**$98,000**
8	Other Income				
9	Tips	2,500	2,700	3,000	4,500
10	Sublease	500	500	500	500
11	Subtotal	**$3,000**	**$3,200**	**$3,500**	**$5,000**
12	Total Income	**$36,000**	**$42,200**	**$56,500**	**$103,000**
13					
14			Quarterly Expenses		
15	Expenses	**Q1**	**Q2**	**Q3**	**Q4**
16	Rent	3,000	3,000	3,000	3,000
17	Utilities	400	310	290	380
18	Marketing	800	800	800	800
19	Salaries	12,000	12,000	14,000	14,000
20	Supplies	15,000	15,500	18,000	24,000
21	Equipment	6,000	2,000	1,000	-
22	Total Expenses	**$37,200**	**$33,610**	**$37,090**	**$42,180**
23					
24	Gross Profit	**($1,200)**	**$8,590**	**$19,410**	**$60,820**
25	Net Profit	**($1,200)**	**$8,590**	**$16,499**	**$45,615**
26	Gross Profit vs. Income	**-3%**	**20%**	**34%**	**59%**

Adaptive Menus

Excel's menus now consist of a short section containing the commands you use most frequently and an expanded section containing commands that are rarely used. These adaptive menus reduce the number of commands on the main (short) menu, thereby reducing screen clutter. The following illustrations define the adaptive menus in Excel 2000.

Insert Format Tools Data
Rows
Columns
Worksheet
Chart...
Function...
Name
Comment
Picture
Hyperlink... Ctrl+K

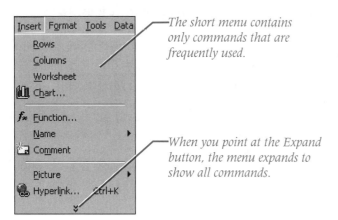

The short menu contains only commands that are frequently used.

When you point at the Expand button, the menu expands to show all commands.

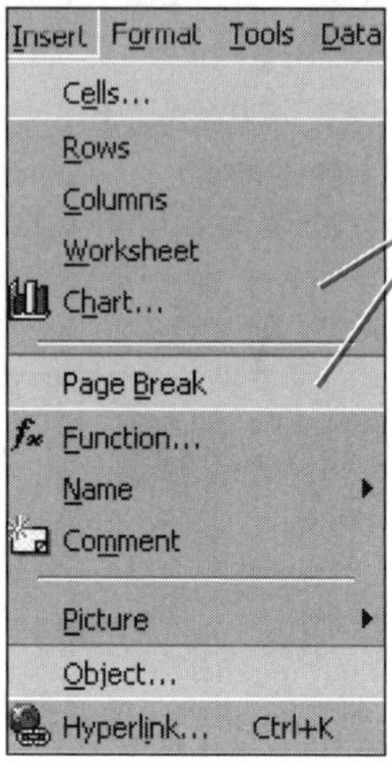
Insert Format Tools Data
Cells...
Rows
Columns
Worksheet
Chart...
Page Break
Function...
Name
Comment
Picture
Object...
Hyperlink... Ctrl+K

On the expanded menu, commands from the short menu appear in a dark shade of gray, while infrequently used commands appear in a light shade of gray. When you choose a command from the expanded menu, it moves up to the short menu.

Working with Toolbars

In Excel 2000, the Standard toolbar and Formatting toolbar are placed side by side on a single row just below the menu bar. This is a change from earlier versions of Excel where the Formatting toolbar was positioned below the Standard toolbar. In addition to the Standard toolbar and Formatting toolbar, Excel has approximately 15 additional toolbars that are used with various program features.

Adaptive Toolbars

Like adaptive menus, adaptive toolbars may change depending upon how you use Excel. Buttons may automatically be added to or removed from these toolbars. The right end of each Excel toolbar now contains a button named More Buttons. Use this button to display buttons not currently visible on the toolbar, and to add or remove buttons from a toolbar. The following illustration uses the Formatting toolbar to outline adaptive toolbars in Excel 2000.

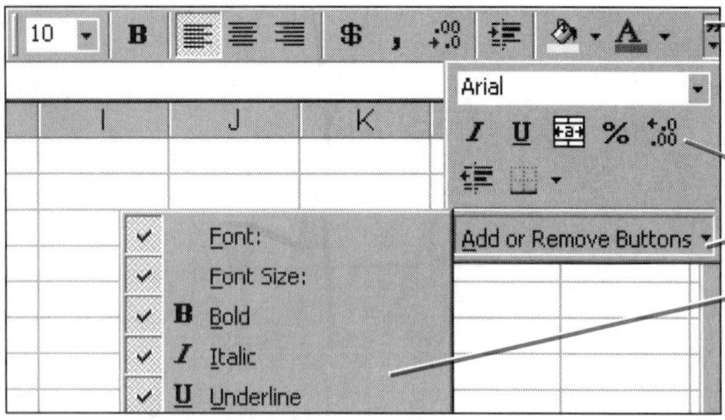
10
Arial
I
J
K
Add or Remove Buttons
Font:
Font Size:
Bold
Italic
Underline

A right-pointing arrow indicates the toolbar has additional buttons that are not currently displayed. Clicking the button displays the additional buttons.

You can click the additional buttons as you would if they were displayed.

When you choose Add or Remove Buttons, the Buttons palette is displayed.

Buttons can be added to the toolbar by checking them, or removed by unchecking them on the Buttons palette. If you don't use a button for a long time, Excel will remove it from the toolbar and place it on the Buttons palette.

Displaying and Hiding Toolbars

You can display and hide toolbars by choosing **View→Toolbars** from the menu bar and checking or unchecking the desired toolbars. You can also display or hide toolbars by right-clicking any toolbar on the screen and checking or unchecking the desired toolbar.

Moving Toolbars

You can move a toolbar to any screen location. For example, many users prefer to move the Formatting toolbar below the Standard toolbar, as in previous versions of Excel. Move toolbars by dragging the Move handle located on the left end of the toolbar.

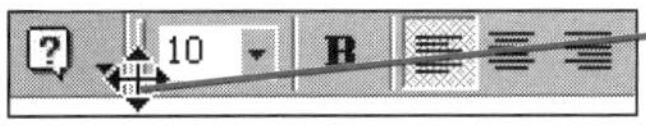

The Move pointer appears when you point to a Move handle. You can move a toolbar to any screen location by dragging the Move handle.

Displaying the Formatting Toolbar On a Separate Row

Dragging the Formatting toolbar below the Standard toolbar can be tricky. Fortunately, Excel provides an easier way to display the Standard and Formatting toolbars on separate rows. This technique is explained in the following Quick Reference table.

Quick Reference

DISPLAYING THE STANDARD AND FORMATTING TOOLBARS ON SEPARATE ROWS

- Choose View→Toolbars→Customize from the menu bar.
- Click the Options tab in the Customize dialog box.
- Uncheck the *Standard and Formatting toolbars share one row* checkbox.

Hands-On 15.1 Display the Formatting Toolbar on a Separate Row

1. Start Excel and choose **View→Toolbars→Customize** from the menu bar.
2. Click the Options tab in the Customize dialog box.
3. Uncheck the **Standard and Formatting toolbars share one row** checkbox.
4. Click the **Close** button. The Formatting toolbar should be positioned below the Standard toolbar.

IMPORTANT! *From this point forward, the instructions in this text will assume the Standard and Formatting toolbars are displayed on separate rows. This will make it easier for you to locate buttons when instructed to do so.*

The Fill Handle

The fill handle is a small black square visible at the bottom right corner of the active cell. A black cross appears when you position the mouse pointer on the fill handle. You can drag the fill handle to fill adjacent cells as described below:

- **Copying an entry—**If the entry in the active cell is a number, a formula, or a typical text entry, the fill handle copies the entry to adjacent cells.
- **Expanding a repeating series of numbers—**If you select two or more cells containing numbers, Excel assumes you want to expand a repeating series. For example, if you select two cells containing the numbers 5 and 10 and drag the fill handle, Excel will fill the adjacent cells with the numbers 15, 20, 25, etc.
- **AutoFill of date entries—**If the active cell contains a date entry, then Excel will increment the date value filling in the adjacent cells. For example, if the current cell contains the entry Q1 and you drag the fill handle, AutoFill will insert the entries Q2, Q3, and Q4 in the adjacent cells.

Q1

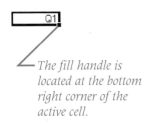

The fill handle is located at the bottom right corner of the active cell.

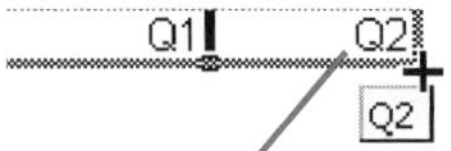

Q1
Q2
Q2

If the active cell contains a date entry such as Q1, AutoFill automatically fills the adjacent cell with the next item in the series (Q2).

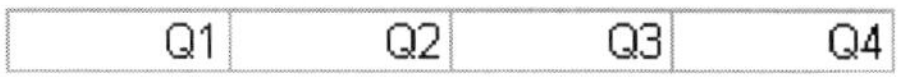

Q1
Q2
Q3
Q4

The completed series.

Hands-On 15.2 Use the Fill Handle

1. Open the workbook named **Hands-On Lesson 15** from your exercise diskette.

Use AutoFill to Expand the Q1 Series

2. Click Cell B4.
   Notice that Cell B4 contains the heading Q1. Excel recognizes Q1 as the beginning of the series Q1, Q2, Q3, and Q4.
3. Follow these steps to fill the adjacent cells.

(A) Position the mouse pointer on the bottom right corner of the active cell, and a black cross will appear.

(B) Drag to the right over the next three cells, and a shaded rectangle will appear.

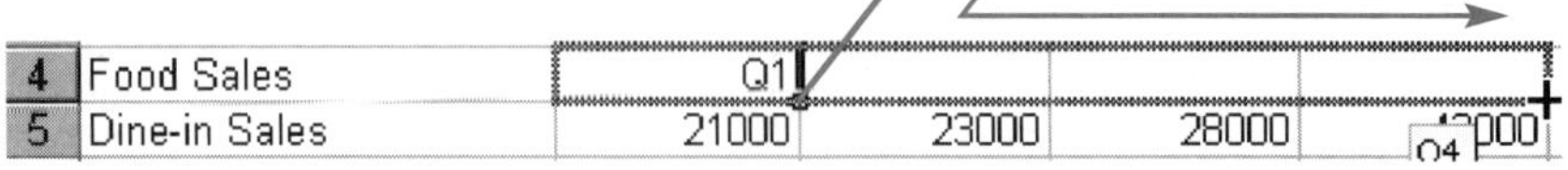

4
Food Sales
Q1
5
Dine-in Sales
21000
23000
28000
Q4

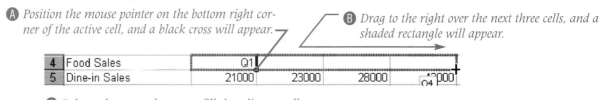

(C) Release the mouse button to fill the adjacent cells.

Excel recognizes Q1, days of the week (Sunday), months (January), and other date values as the beginning of a series. You can expand any of these series with the fill handle.

4. Click Cell B15, and use the fill handle to expand Q1 to Q1–Q4, as you did in the previous step.

Use the Fill Handle to Copy Cells

5. Click Cell B7.
6. Click AutoSum Σ, and complete the entry.
   The subtotal should equal 33000.
7. Make sure Cell B7 is active; then drag the fill handle + to the right until the shaded rectangle is over Cells C7, D7, and E7.
8. Release the mouse button. The formula should be copied to those cells.
   Excel determines whether it should copy the cell or expand a series.
9. Click Cell B11, and use AutoSum to compute the subtotal.
10. Use the fill handle to copy the formula in Cell B11 to Cells C11, D11, and E11.
11. Use these techniques to compute the total expenses in Row 22 (not total income in Row 12).
    It actually would have been easier to select the four cells in these examples and use AutoSum to compute the totals. However, there are times when it is easier to copy cells with the fill handle, as you will see in the next topic.

Formulas

You have already learned how to compute totals with AutoSum. AutoSum provides a convenient method for summing a range of numbers. However, you will need to use many other types of formulas in Excel. In fact, many worksheets, such as financial models, require hundreds or even thousands of complex formulas.

Beginning Character in Formulas

If you are typing a formula in a cell, it is recommended that you always begin the formula with an equal (=) sign. You can also begin formulas with a plus (+) or minus (–) sign; however; it is better to adopt one method in order to create consistency.

Cell and Range References

Formulas derive their power from the use of cell and range references. For example, in the previous exercise, you used AutoSum to insert the formula =SUM(B16:B21) in Cell B22. Because the range reference (B16:B21) was used in the formula, you were able to copy the formula across the row using the fill handle. There are two important benefits to using references in formulas.

- When references are used, formulas can be copied to other cells.
- Since a reference refers to a cell or a range of cells, the formula results are automatically recalculated when the data is changed in the referenced cell(s).

Arithmetic Operators and Spaces

Formulas can include the standard arithmetic operators shown in the following table. You can also use spaces within formulas to improve their appearance and readability. Notice that each formula in the table begins with an equal (=) sign. Also, keep in mind that each formula is entered into the same cell that displays the resulting calculation.

Quick Reference

ARITHMETIC OPERATORS IN FORMULAS

Operator	Example	Comments
+ (addition)	=B7+B11	Adds the values in B7 and B11.
– (subtraction)	=B7–B11	Subtracts the value in B11 from B7.
* (multiplication)	=B7*B11	Multiplies the values in B7 and B11.
/ (division)	=B7/B11	Divides the value in B7 by the value in B11.
^ (exponentiation)	=B7^3	Raises the value in B7 to the third power (B7*B7*B7).
% (percent)	=B7*10%	Multiplies the value in B7 by 10% (.10).
( ) (calculations)	=B7/(C4–C2)	Parentheses change the order of calculations. In this example, C2 would be subtracted from C4, and then B7 would be divided by the result. Order of calculations is discussed in detail in a later lesson.

Hands-On 15.3 Use the Keyboard to Enter Formulas

1. Click Cell B12.
2. Type **=B7+B11**, and complete the entry.
   The result should be 36000. This is the summation of the two subtotals in Cells B7 and B11.
3. Click Cell C12.
4. Type **=C7+C11**, and complete the entry.
   The result should be 42200.

Relative Cell References

All formulas use relative cell references unless you specifically instruct Excel to use an absolute reference. Relative references make it easy to copy formulas to other cells. For example, in the Hands-On Lesson 15 worksheet, Cell C12 contains the formula =C7+C11. If this formula is copied to Cell D12, then the formula in D12 will become =D7+D11. The references to Cells C7 and C11 are updated to reflect the new location of the formula.

Point Mode

One potential danger that can occur when typing formulas is that you will accidentally type the wrong cell reference. This is easy to do, especially if the worksheet is complex and contains large numbers of cells. Point mode can help you avoid this problem. With point mode, you can insert a cell reference in a formula by clicking the desired cell as you are typing the formula. Likewise, you can insert a range reference in a formula by dragging over the desired cells. You will use point mode in the following exercise.

Hands-On 15.4 Use Point Mode

1. Click Cell D12.
2. Type an equal (=) sign.
   Notice that Excel begins building the formula by entering the equal = sign in the Formula bar.
3. Click Cell D7.
   Notice that Excel adds the reference D7 to the formula in the Formula bar.
4. Type a plus (+) sign (try tapping the plus (+) key on the numeric keypad).
5. Click Cell D11.
   The Formula bar should contain the formula =D7+D11.
6. Complete the entry. The total should be 56500.
7. Make sure the highlight is in Cell D12, and then drag the fill handle one cell to the right.
   The formula should be copied to Cell E12, and the result should be 103000.
8. Click Cell E12, and notice the formula in the Formula bar.
   The formula should be =E7+E11. The references were updated to reflect the new formula location.

Using the Formula Bar to Enter Formulas

You can enter a formula by first clicking the Edit Formula button on the Formula bar. When you click this button, the Formula bar expands to include a function box containing a list of recently used functions, an area that displays the formula results as the formula is constructed, an OK button, and a Cancel button. You may want to use this technique because it is often helpful to view the formula results as the formula is constructed.

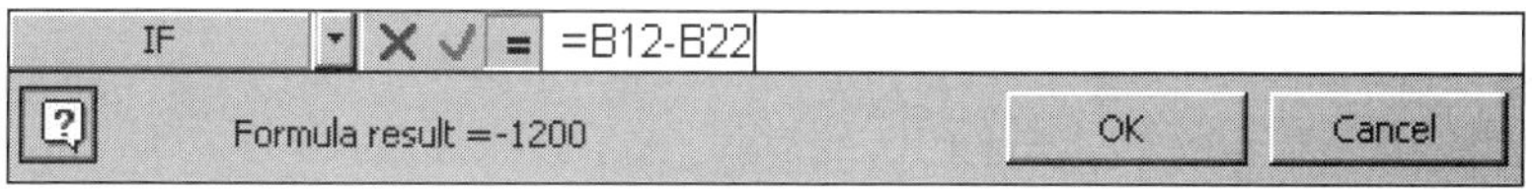
IF
=B12-B22
Formula result =-1200
OK
Cancel

Hands-On 15.5 Enter Formulas with the Formula Bar

Calculate the Gross Profit

1. If necessary, scroll down until Rows 12–26 are visible.
2. Click Cell B24.
   Cell B24 will contain the gross profit. The gross profit is calculated as the total income in Cell B12 minus the total expenses in Cell B22.
3. Click the Edit Formula button on the Formula bar.
   Excel will enter an equal (=) sign in the Formula bar, and the Formula bar will expand. Also, the Office Assistant may pop up. The Office Assistant is an interactive Help tool that monitors your activities and provides suggestions whenever it assumes you need assistance. For now, ignore the Office Assistant and continue with the next step.

(Continued on the next page)

4. Click Cell B12, and the Formula bar will indicate a result of 36000.
5. Type a minus (**–**) sign, then click Cell B22.
6. Complete the formula by clicking the OK button on the Formula bar.
   The gross profit should equal –1200. As you can see, Donna's Deli is not profitable in the first quarter.
7. Copy the formula to the next three cells by dragging the fill handle to the right.

Calculate the Net Profit

*You will calculate the net profit in the next few steps. You will use a simplified net profit calculation: that is, the gross profit minus income taxes. We will make the assumption that Donna will pay no taxes in Q1 and Q2. This is because she lost money in Q1, and her gross profit was only $8,590 in Q2. Furthermore, we will assume that Donna's tax rate will be 15% for Q3 and 25% for Q4. The formula is, Net Profit = Gross Profit * (1–Taxrate). For example, if the tax rate is 15%, then Donna will keep 85% of her gross profit. So the Net Profit = Gross Profit * 0.85.*

8. Click Cell B24.
   Look at the Formula bar and notice the gross profit is calculated as B12–B22. In the next few steps, you will attempt to copy the gross profit formula from Cell B24 to Cell B25.
9. Follow this step to copy the formula from Cell B24 to B25.

24 Gross Profit -1200
25 Net Profit

Ⓐ *Drag the fill handle down to cell B25.*

10. Click Cell B24, and notice that the gross profit formula in the Formula bar is =B12–B22.
11. Click Cell B25, and notice that the net profit formula is =B13–B23.
12. Look at Cells B13 and B23 in the worksheet, and you will see they are empty.
   The formula result is 0 because Cells B13 and B23 are empty. This example demonstrates that you must be careful when copying formulas. Excel updated the cell references when you copied the formula. This produced an incorrect result because the formula is referencing incorrect cells.
13. Click Undo to reverse the copy procedure.
14. Click Cell B25, type the formula **=B24**, and complete the entry.
   This simple formula makes Cell B25 equal to Cell B24.
15. Click Cell C25, type the formula **=C24**, and complete the entry.
   Once again, the net profit and gross profit should be equal in Q2 because Donna has no tax liability in the second quarter.
16. Click Cell D25, and enter the formula **=D24*85%**.
   The result should be 16498.5. We are assuming a tax rate of 15% in Q3, so Donna gets to keep 85% of her gross profit.
17. Click Cell E25, and enter the formula **=E24*75%**.
   The result should be 45615. Keep in mind that you can either type the formulas or use point mode and the Formula bar. From this point forward, you will simply be instructed to enter a formula. You should use whichever method works best for you.

Calculate the Ratios

Donna wants to determine the ratio of gross profit to total income, or GP/TI. This ratio is important in determining the health of a business. This ratio is one indicator that will show Donna how fast she can grow her business by reinvesting the money she earns. This ratio will show Donna the amount of profit she will earn from each dollar of product she sells.

18. Click Cell B26, and enter the formula **=B24/B12**.
    The result should be –0.03333. You will convert this number to a percentage later in this lesson.

19. Use the fill handle to copy the formula to Cells C26, D26, and E26.
    The results should match the following example.

26	Gross Profit vs. Income	-0.03333	0.203555	0.34354	0.590485

20. Click Cell C26, and notice the formula =C24/C12.
    Once again, Excel updated the cell references when the formula was copied. In this case, it is good that the references were updated because the formula now refers to the correct gross profit and total income in cells C24 and C12.

21. Click the Save button to save the changes.

Number Formats

Excel lets you format numbers in a variety of ways. Number formats change the way numbers are displayed; however, they do not change the actual numbers. The following Quick Reference table describes the most common number formats.

Quick Reference

NUMBER FORMATS

Number Format	Description
General	Numbers have a General format when they are first entered. The General format does not apply any special formats to the numbers.
Comma	The Comma format inserts a comma between every third digit in the number. An optional decimal point with decimal places can also be displayed.
Currency	The Currency format is the same as the Comma format, except a dollar $ sign is placed in front of the number.
Percent	A percent % sign is inserted to the right of the number. The number is multiplied by 100, and the resulting percentage is displayed in the cell.

The following table provides several examples of formatted numbers.

Number Entered	Format	How the Number Is Displayed
1000.984	General	1000.984
1000.984	Comma with 0 decimal places Comma with 2 decimal places	1,000 1,000.98
1000.984	Currency with 0 decimal places Currency with 2 decimal places	$1,000 $1,000.98
.5366	Percent with 0 decimal places Percent with 2 decimal places	54% 53.66%

Applying Number Styles with the Formatting Toolbar

From the Keyboard

CTRL+SHIFT+$ for Currency style
CTRL+SHIFT+% for Percent style
CTRL+SHIFT+! for Comma style
CTRL+SHIFT+~ for General style

The Formatting toolbar contains buttons that allow you to apply the Currency, Comma, and Percent number styles. These are the most common types of number styles. The Formatting toolbar also includes buttons that allow you to increase or decrease the number of displayed decimals. The following illustration displays the number formatting buttons on the Formatting toolbar.

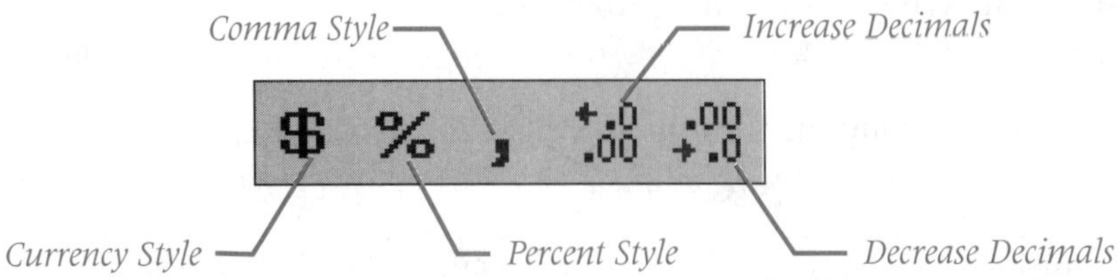
Comma Style
Increase Decimals
Currency Style
Percent Style
Decrease Decimals

Changing the Number of Displayed Decimals

The Increase Decimals and Decrease Decimals buttons change the number of displayed decimal places. For example, you could enter the number 100.37 and then decrease the decimals to 0. The number would then be displayed as 100. However, the actual number would remain 100.37. The number 100.37 would be used in any calculations referencing the cell.

Hands-On 15.6 Format Numbers

In this exercise, you will format numbers using buttons on the Formatting toolbar.

Apply the Currency Style

1. Scroll up until the top row of the worksheet is visible.
2. Select the four subtotals in Row 7 (be careful not to drag the fill handle).
   The fill handle is not used to select cells. It is only used to copy cells or to expand a series. Make sure your pointer has the thick white cross shape whenever you wish to select cells.
3. Click the Currency Style button, and the cells should be formatted as shown below.

7	Subtotal	$33,000.00	$39,000.00	$53,000.00	$98,000.00

Notice that the Currency style adds a dollar sign in front of the number and a comma between every third digit. It also adds a decimal point with two decimal places. Excel should also have widened the columns to accommodate the additional characters and numbers.

Decrease the Decimals

4. Make sure the four cells you just formatted are selected.
5. Click the Decrease Decimal button twice to remove the displayed decimals.
   Notice that the dollar signs $ are positioned on the left side of the cells. You will adjust this alignment later in the lesson.

6. Select the subtotal and total income cells in Rows 11 and 12, as shown below.

11	Subtotal	3000	3200	3500	5000
12	Total Income	36000	42200	56500	103000

7. Click the Currency Style button; then decrease the decimals to 0.
8. Format the numbers in Rows 22, 24, and 25 as currency with 0 decimals.

Apply the Comma Style

9. Select the numbers in Rows 5 and 6.
10. Click the Comma Style button, and then decrease the decimals to 0.
    Notice that the Comma style is similar to the Currency style, except a dollar sign is not displayed. Also notice that the numbers now line up with the currency formatted numbers in the subtotal row.
11. Format the numbers in the ranges B9:E10 and B16:E21 as Comma style with 0 decimals.

Apply the Percent Style

12. Select the numbers in the last row of the worksheet.
13. Click the Percent Style button.
    The numbers should be formatted as percent with 0 decimal places. The Percent style does not display decimals; however, you can always use the Increase Decimal button to display decimals.

Setting Number Styles with the Format Cells Dialog Box

From the Keyboard

CTRL+1 to display Format Cells dialog box

The **Format→Cells** command displays the Format Cells dialog box. This dialog box provides additional built-in number styles that are not available on the Formatting toolbar. You can format numbers with one of the built-in styles by displaying the dialog box and choosing the desired style. You can even create your own customized number styles to suit your needs.

Accounting and Currency Styles

The dollar signs $ in the Hands-On Lesson 15 worksheet currently have a fixed format. In other words, they are fixed on the left side of the cells. You can use the Format Cells dialog box to choose a number style that floats the dollar signs next to the numbers. There are two number styles that apply currency symbols (such as dollar signs) to numbers, as discussed below.

- **Accounting style—**The Currency Style button on the Formatting toolbar actually applies an Accounting style to numbers. The Accounting style lines up dollar signs and decimal points in columns. The dollar signs appear fixed at the left edges of the cells.
- **Currency style—**The Currency style floats dollar signs next to the numbers. Like the Accounting style, the Currency style displays a comma between every third digit, and it displays decimals and a decimal point.

Displaying Negative Numbers

Negative numbers can be displayed either preceded by a minus sign or surrounded by parentheses. You can also display negative numbers in red. The Currency option and Number option in the Format Cells dialog box let you choose the format for negative numbers.

The negative numbers format you choose affects the alignment of numbers in cells. If the format displays negative numbers in parentheses, then a small space equal to the width of a closing parenthesis appears on the right edge of cells containing positive numbers. Excel does this so that decimal points are aligned in columns containing both positive and negative numbers. These concepts are described in the following illustration.

15	Expenses	Q1
16	Rent	3,000
17	Utilities	400
18	Marketing	800
19	Salaries	12,000
20	Supplies	15,000
21	Equipment	6,000
22	Total Expenses	$ 37,200
23		
24	Gross Profit	$ (1,200)
25	Net Profit	$ (1,200)

Notice the slight space between positive numbers and the right edge of the cells.

Notice that the closing parenthesis of negative numbers is flush with the right edge of the cell.

15	Expenses	Q1
16	Rent	3,000.00
17	Utilities	400.00
18	Marketing	800.00
19	Salaries	12,000.00
20	Supplies	15,000.00
21	Equipment	6,000.00
22	Total Expenses	37,200.00
23		
24	Gross Profit	(1,200.00)
25	Net Profit	(1,200.00)

When the numbers are displayed with decimals, this slight shift of the positive numbers lines up the decimal points of both the positive and negative numbers.

Hands-On 15.7 Use the Format Cells Dialog Box

1. Select the numbers with the Currency style in Row 7.
2. Choose **Format→Cells** from the menu bar.
3. Make sure the Number tab is active at the top of the dialog box.
4. Notice that the Custom option is chosen at the bottom of the Category list.
   The Custom option is chosen because you modified the number style when you decreased the decimal places in the previous exercises, creating a custom number format.

5. Follow these steps to format the numbers with floating dollar ($) signs.

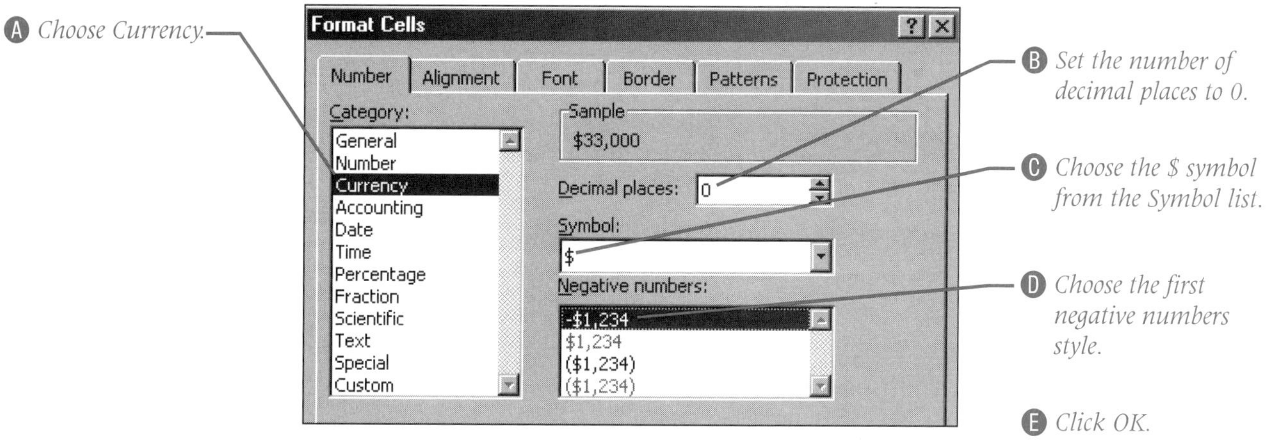
A Choose Currency.
Format Cells
Number
Alignment
Font
Border
Patterns
Protection
Category:
General
Number
Currency
Accounting
Date
Time
Percentage
Fraction
Scientific
Text
Special
Custom
Sample
$33,000
Decimal places:
0
Symbol:
$
Negative numbers:
-$1,234
$1,234
($1,234)
($1,234)
B Set the number of decimal places to 0.
C Choose the $ symbol from the Symbol list.
D Choose the first negative numbers style.
E Click OK.

Notice that the dollar signs are now floating just in front of the numbers. Also, notice that the numbers are now shifted slightly to the right, and that they no longer line up with the numbers above them. This is because of the Negative Numbers option you set. You will adjust the Negative Numbers option in the next step.

Adjust the Negative Numbers Option

6. Make sure Cells B7:E7 are still selected, and choose **Format→Cells** from the menu bar.
7. Notice the various negative numbers formats.
   Formats that are red display negative numbers in red. Also notice that some of the formats are surrounded with parentheses. Formats with parentheses cause positive numbers to shift slightly to the left. as discussed earlier.
8. Choose the third Negative Numbers format ($1,234), and click **OK.**
   The numbers should now be right-aligned with the numbers in Rows 5 and 6. The numbers in Rows 5 and 6 are formatted with the Comma style. The Comma style displays negative numbers in parentheses. This is why the positive numbers in Rows 5 and 6 are shifted slightly to the left.

Check Out the Accounting Style

9. Make sure Cells B7:E7 are still selected, and choose **Format→Cells** from the menu bar.
10. Choose the Accounting category.
11. Make sure the symbol type is set to $ and the decimal places are set to 0.
12. Click **OK,** and the dollar ($) signs will once again have a fixed placement on the left side of the cells.
    Notice that this was how the numbers were formatted when you first clicked the Currency Style button in an earlier exercise. The Currency Style button actually applies the Accounting style to numbers.
13. Click Undo to restore the Currency style.

(Continued on the next page)

Explore Other Number Styles

14. Choose **Format→Cells** from the menu bar.
15. Take a few minutes to browse through the various number styles in the Category list.
    Feel free to choose a style, and then read the description that appears at the bottom of the dialog box.
16. Click the **Cancel** button when you have finished exploring.
    You will continue to format numbers in a later exercise.
17. Save the changes, and continue with the next topic.

Merging Cells

Excel's merge cells option lets you merge cells together. Merged cells behave as one large cell. You can merge cells vertically or horizontally. The merge cells option is useful if you want to place a large block of text (such as a paragraph) in the worksheet. You merge cells by selecting the desired cells, issuing the **Format→Cells** command, and checking the Merge Cells box on the Alignment tab. Likewise, you can split a merged cell into the original cell configuration by removing the check from the Merge Cells box.

The Merge and Center Button

The Merge and Center button merges selected cells and changes the alignment of the merged cell to center. This technique is often used to center a heading across columns. Keep in mind that the Merge and Center button has the same effect as merging cells, and then changing the alignment of the merged cell to center. You can split a merged and centered cell the same way you would split any other merged cell. The following example shows a heading centered across Columns B through E.

The Quarterly Income heading is centered above Columns B–E.

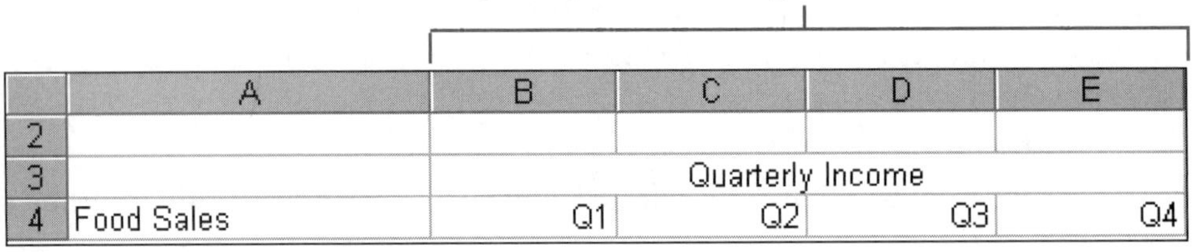
A
B
C
D
E
2
3
Quarterly Income
4
Food Sales
Q1
Q2
Q3
Q4

Hands-On 15.8 Use Merge and Center

1. Select the range B3:E3, as shown to the right.
   Notice that this range includes the heading you wish to center (Quarterly Income) and the range of cells you wish to center this heading across (B3:E3).

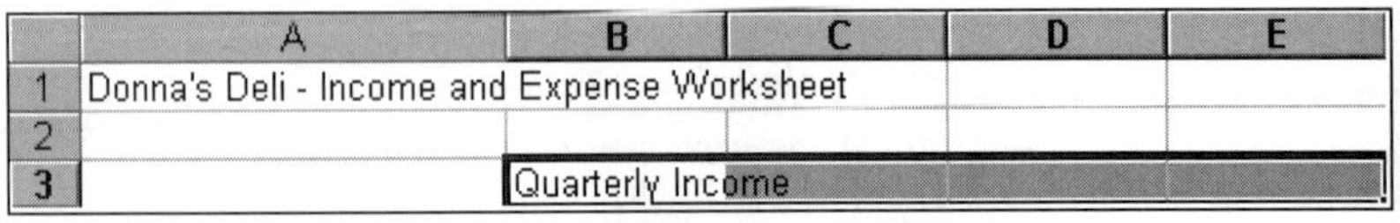
A
B
C
D
E
1
Donna's Deli - Income and Expense Worksheet
2
3
Quarterly Income

2. Click the Merge and Center button (near the middle of the Formatting toolbar).
   Notice that the cells have been merged together and the Center button on the Formatting toolbar is pushed in.
3. Click the Align Left button and the entry will move to the left side of the merged cell.
4. Click the Center button to center the entry in the merged cell.
5. Choose **Format→Cells** from the menu bar.
6. Click the Alignment tab on the Format Cells dialog box.
   Notice that the Merge Cells box is checked. This box is checked whenever cells are merged.
7. Remove the check from the Merge Cells box and click **OK.**
8. Click anywhere to deselect the cells, and notice that they are no longer merged.
   You use this technique to split merged cells.
9. Click Undo to restore the merged cell.
10. Select the range B14:E14.
11. Click the Merge and Center button to center the Quarterly Expenses heading.

Indenting Entries

The Increase Indent button and Decrease Indent button on the Formatting toolbar let you offset entries from the left edges of cells. Indenting is useful in conveying the hierarchy of entries. The following illustration shows indented cells.

These cells are indented to show their subordination to the Food Sales heading.

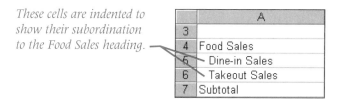

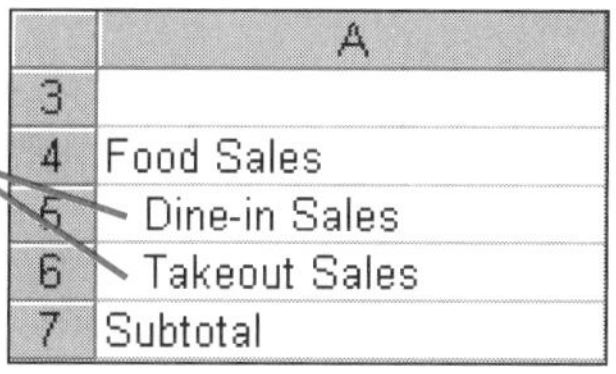
A
3
4 Food Sales
5 Dine-in Sales
6 Takeout Sales
7 Subtotal

Hands-On 15.9 Indent Entries

1. Click Cell A5.
2. Click the Increase Indent button twice.
   Notice that the entry is indented slightly each time you click the button.
3. Click the Decrease Indent button once.
4. Click Cell A6, and increase the indent once.
5. Select Cells A9 and A10.
6. Press and hold the CTRL key while you select the range A16:A21.
   The range A16:A21 contains the Rent, Utilities, etc. subheadings below the Expenses heading in Column A.
7. Increase the indent once.

Formatting Entries

From the Keyboard

CTRL+B for Bold
CTRL+U for Underline
CTRL+I for Italics

In Excel and other Office programs, you can format text by changing the font, font size, and color. You can also apply various font formats, including bold, italics, and underline. To format cells, select the desired cells and apply formats using buttons on the Formatting toolbar. You can also choose formats from the Font tab of the Format Cells dialog box.

You can choose a font from the font list. You can also click the drop-down button and type the desired font name to rapidly scroll the list.

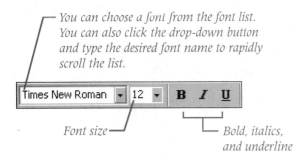

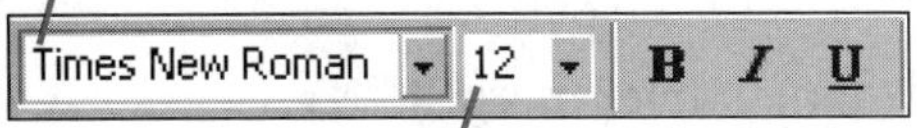
Times New Roman
12
B
I
U

Font size

Bold, italics, and underline

The Font Color button is on the right end of the Formatting toolbar. The color palette appears when you click the drop-down button. Once you choose a color, the color is displayed on the button. From that point forward, you can rapidly apply the color by clicking the button.

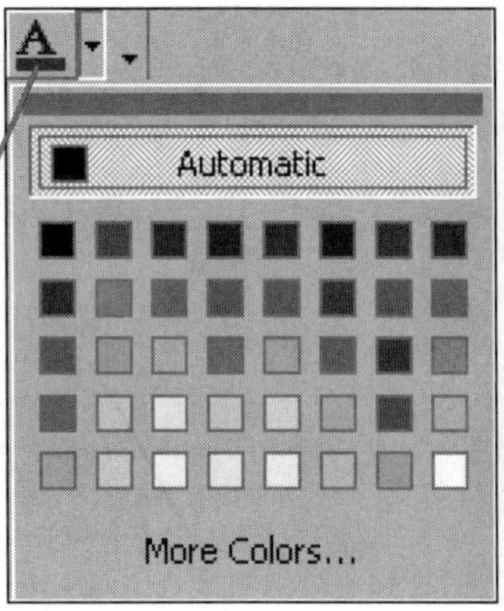
A
Automatic
More Colors...

Hands-On 15.10 Format Entries

1. Click Cell A1.
2. Click the Font Size button on the Formatting toolbar, and choose **14.**
3. Click the Bold button on the Formatting toolbar.
   Notice that the entire title is formatted. Once again, the entire title belongs to Cell A1, even though it is displayed over the adjacent cells.
4. Click the drop-down button on the Font Color button located at the right end of the Formatting toolbar.
5. Choose one of the dark blue shades from the color palette.
   Notice that the color you chose is now displayed on the Font Color button. You can now apply the same color to other cells by selecting the cells and then clicking the button.
6. Click Cell B3.
   Cell B3 is now part of the large merged cell in the range B3:E3.
7. Click the Font Color button, and the same color will be applied to the Quarterly Income cell.
8. Increase the size of the Quarterly Income cell to **12,** and apply **bold** formatting.
9. Select the Q1–Q4 headings in Row 4.
10. Apply bold formatting, and then choose a different color from the Font Color button's color palette.
    In the next exercise, you will use the Format Painter to copy font and number formats to other cells.

The Format Painter

The Format Painter lets you copy text and number formats from one cell to another. The Format Painter copies all text and number formats from the source cell to the target cell(s). The Format Painter saves time and helps create consistent formatting throughout a workbook.

Quick Reference

USING THE FORMAT PAINTER

- Click on the cell with the format(s) you wish to copy.
- Click the Format Painter once if you want to copy formats to one other cell or range. Double-click if you want to copy to multiple cell(s) or range(s).
- Select the cells to which you want to copy the format(s). If you double-clicked in the previous step, the Format Painter will remain active, allowing you to select cells at multiple locations. You can even scroll through the workbook to reach the desired location(s).
- If you double-clicked in the first step, then click the Format Painter when you have finished. This will turn off the Format Painter.

Hands-On 15.11 Use the Format Painter

Copy Text Formats

1. Click Cell B3 (the merged cell with the Quarterly Income heading).
2. Click the Format Painter on the Standard toolbar, and an animated paintbrush icon will be attached to the mouse pointer.
3. Click Cell B14 (the merged cell with the Quarterly Expenses heading).
   The text formats should be copied to that heading. The animated paintbrush icon also vanished because you clicked the Format Painter button just once in the previous step. If you want to copy formats to multiple locations, you must double-click the Format Painter.
4. Click Cell B4.
   This cell should contain the heading Q1.
5. Click the Format Painter .
6. Select the range B15:E15 to copy the formats to those cells, as shown below.

15	Expenses	Q1	Q2	Q3	Q4

Copy Number Formats

7. Select the cells containing numbers in Row 7, and apply bold formatting to the numbers.
   Notice that the numbers in Row 7 have a Currency style with a floating dollar sign. In the next few steps, you will use the Format Painter to copy both the number and text formats to the numbers in Rows 11, 12, and 22–25. Notice that these rows currently have fixed dollar signs on the left edges of the cells.

(Continued on the next page)

8. Click Cell B7.

9. *Double-click* the Format Painter.

10. Select the range B11:E12 to copy the formats to those cells, as shown below.

11	Subtotal	$3,000	$3,200	$3,500	$5,000
12	Total Income	$36,000	$42,200	$56,500	$103,000

11. Select the range B22:E26 to copy the formats to those cells, as shown below.

22	Total Expenses	$37,200	$33,610	$37,090	$42,180
23					
24	Gross Profit	($1,200)	$8,590	$19,410	$60,820
25	Net Profit	($1,200)	$8,590	$16,499	$45,615
26	Gross Profit vs. Income	($0)	$0	$0	$1

12. Click the Format Painter to turn it off.
Notice that you had to turn the Format Painter off this time because you double-clicked it initially. Also, notice the Percent number style in Row 26 has been removed. Be careful when you are trying to copy text formats but not number formats. In this example, you wanted to copy the bold text style to Row 26 but not the Currency style. Keep in mind that the Format Painter copies both text formats and number formats.

13. Select the numbers in Row 26 and use the Percent Style % button to reapply the Percent style.

14. Save the changes, and continue with the next topic.

Clearing Cell Contents and Formats

The **Edit→Clear** command displays a submenu that lets you clear the content, formats, or comments from cells. The submenu also contains an All option that clears all of these items from the selected cells. Each of these items is defined below.

- **Content—**Clearing the content has the same effect as tapping the DELETE key. This deletes a cell's contents, but any format applied to the cell will still be in effect if new data is entered in the cell.
- **Formats—**The Formats option removes all text and number formats, leaving unformatted entries in the cell(s).
- **Comments—**You can insert comments in cells to document your worksheet. The Comments option removes comments from the selected cells.

Hands-On 15.12 Clear Formats

1. Notice the formatting applied to the Q1–Q4 headings in Rows 4 and 15.
   These headings will probably look better if they have simple bold formatting like the numbers in the subtotal and total rows.
2. Select the Q1–Q4 headings in Row 4 and choose **Edit→Clear→Formats.**
   Excel will remove all formats, including the right alignment.
3. Click the Align Right  button, and then apply bold formatting to the cells.
4. Clear the formats from the Q1–Q4 headings in Row 15.
5. Right-align the Q1–Q4 headings in Row 15, and apply bold formatting to the headings.
   Your completed worksheet should match the worksheet shown in the case study at the start of this lesson.
6. Save the changes to your workbook.
7. Feel free to experiment with the **Edit→Clear** command.
8. When you have finished experimenting, close the workbook without saving the changes.
   Continue with the end-of-lesson questions and exercises.

Concepts Review

True/False Questions

1. The fill handle cannot be used to copy formulas. TRUE FALSE
2. The Merge and Center button can only be used with numbers. TRUE FALSE
3. Formulas must always begin with an open parenthesis (. TRUE FALSE
4. Formulas can include both cell and range references. TRUE FALSE
5. The asterisk * is used to represent multiplication in formulas. TRUE FALSE
6. Point mode can be used to insert cell references in formulas. TRUE FALSE
7. The Comma number style inserts a dollar sign in front of the number. TRUE FALSE
8. The Format Painter copies text formats, but not number formats. TRUE FALSE

Multiple-Choice Questions

1. What should you do before clicking the Merge and Center button?
   a. Click the cell that contains the entry you wish to center.
   b. Select the cells you wish to center the entry across, while making sure the entry is included in the selection.
   c. Select the entire row that contains the entry you wish to center.
   d. None of the above

2. Which of the following symbols can be used to begin a formula?
   a. +
   b. –
   c. =
   d. All of the above

3. How would the number 10000.367 be displayed if you format it as comma with 2 decimals?
   a. 10,000.38
   b. $10,000.38
   c. 10,000
   d. None of the above

4. How is the dollar sign positioned with the Accounting number style?
   a. Floats to the immediate left of the number
   b. Fixed on the left edge of the cell
   c. The Accounting style does not place a dollar sign in front of the number.
   d. The answer depends on whether the number has a decimal point.

Skill Builders

Skill Builder 15.1 Formatting and Formulas

In this exercise, you will open a home budget worksheet on your exercise diskette. You will format the worksheet using the skills you have learned in this lesson.

1. Open the workbook named Skill Builder 15.1 on your exercise diskette.
2. Widen Column A until the text entries in that column are visible.
3. Select the range A1:G1, as shown below.

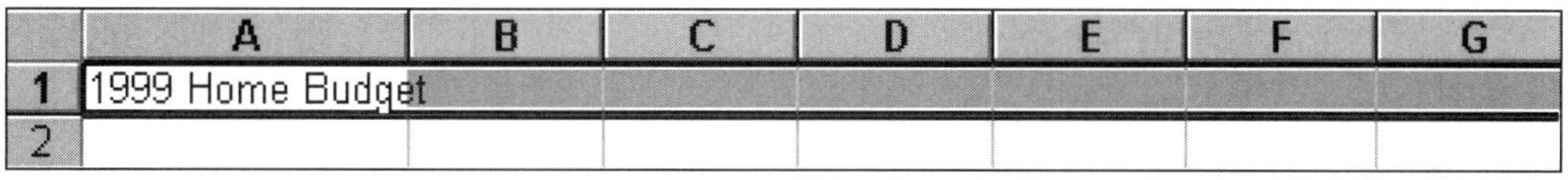
A
B
C
D
E
F
G
1
1999 Home Budget
2

4. Click the Merge and Center button to center 1999 Home Budget above the worksheet.

Use AutoFill

5. Follow these steps to AutoFill the headings in Row 3.

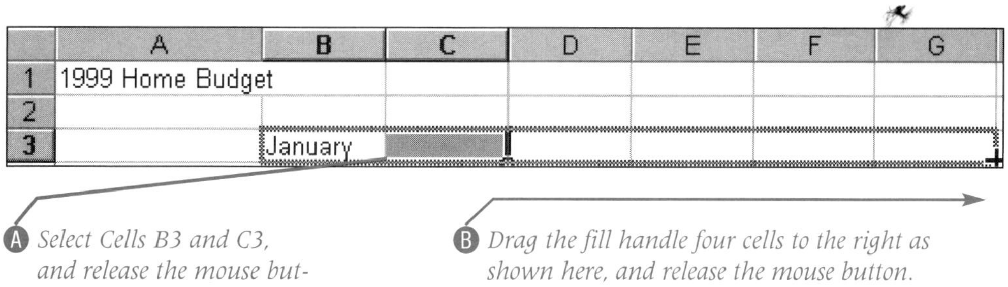
A
B
C
D
E
F
G
1
1999 Home Budget
2
3
January
A Select Cells B3 and C3, and release the mouse but-
B Drag the fill handle four cells to the right as shown here, and release the mouse button.

Excel assumes you want the series January–March with an empty cell between each month. This is a correct assumption, and the resulting cells are shown below.

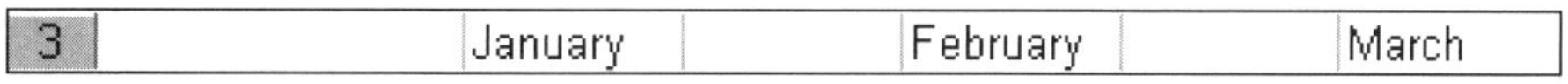
3
January
February
March

6. Select Cells B4 and C4 (the Budget and Spent cells).
7. Drag the fill handle over the next four cells to the right, and Excel will copy Cells B4 and C4 to those cells.
   You should now have three sets of Budget and Spent cells. As you can see, the fill handle is used for a variety of purposes.

(Continued on the next page)

Use Merge and Center

8. Select Cells B3 and C3 (the January cell and the blank cell to the right of it).
9. Click Merge and Center to center the January heading over the Budget and Spent columns.
10. Merge and center the February and March headings over their Budget and Spent columns.
11. Select Row 4, and right-align the Budget and Spent headings.

Calculate the Subtotals

12. Select the range B9:G9 (the subtotal cells in Row 9).
13. Press and hold the CTRL key while you select the subtotal ranges B14:G14 and B19:G19.
    All three of the subtotal ranges should be selected.
14. Click AutoSum to calculate all subtotals with a single command.

Calculate the Totals and Differences

15. Click Cell B21.
16. Enter the formula **=B9+B14+B19.**
17. Use the fill handle to copy the formula across the row.
18. Click Cell B22.
    This cell will contain the difference between the January budget and January spent in Row 21.
19. Enter the formula **=B21-C21**.
    The result should equal 158.
20. Calculate the differences in Cells D22 and F22. You may want to use some shortcut to enter these formulas. For example, you could use the fill handle to copy the formula in Cell B22 across and then delete the formulas in Cells C22, E22 and G22.
    The results should equal 118 and –739.

Copy Number Formats

21. Select the subtotal numbers in Row 9.
22. Click the Currency Style button.
23. Click the Decrease Decimal button twice to reduce the decimals to 0.
    If you want the dollar ($) signs to float next to the numbers, make sure the cells are selected, and use the Format→Cells command. Choose the Currency style and set the number of decimal places and other options as desired.

24. Click Cell B9.

25. *Double-click* the Format Painter .

26. Drag the animated paintbrush over the subtotal numbers in Rows 14 and 19, and then drag over the totals and differences in Rows 21 and 22.
The Currency format will be copied to the numbers in those rows.

27. Click the Format Painter to turn it off.

Format Text Entries

28. Click Cell A1 (the large merged cell).

29. Set the font size to 16, apply bold formatting, and choose a color .

30. Apply bold formatting to the headings in Row 3, and apply the same color you used for the title in Cell A1.

31. Format the headings in Row 4 with the same color you used in Row 3.

32. Apply bold formatting to the subtotals in Rows 9, 14, and 19.

33. Format the totals and differences rows with the same color you used in Rows 3 and 4.

Recalculate Formulas

34. Click Cell G5.
Imagine you have an adjustable rate mortgage, and the monthly payment just went up. In the next step, you will change the number in Cell G5. Keep an eye on the totals and differences formulas at the bottom of the worksheet when you change the number. The formulas will automatically recalculate the numbers.

35. Type **1075**, and complete the entry.
The new total in Cell G21 should equal 2879, and the new difference in Cell F22 should equal –814.

36. Save the changes to the workbook, and then close the workbook.

Skill Builder 15.2 Formatting Practice

In this exercise, you will open a workbook on your exercise diskette. You will format the worksheet until it closely matches the completed worksheet shown below.

1. Open the workbook named Skill Builder 15.2.
2. Merge and Center the title, Corporate Budget, across Columns A–E.
3. Use the fill handle to expand the series Q1 to Q1–Q4.
4. Right-align the headings Q1–Q4.
5. Calculate the subtotals and totals.
6. Widen Column A until the entries in the column are visible.
7. Format the numbers as shown below.
8. Format the title and headings with text formats of your choice.
9. Format the subtotal rows with italics as shown.
10. Format the total row with bold and italics as shown.
11. When you have finished, save the changes, and then close the workbook.

	A	B	C	D	E
1	**Corporate Budget**				
2					
3		**Q1**	**Q2**	**Q3**	**Q4**
4	Marketing	1,234,890	2,346,890	2,156,580	1,900,890
5	Sales	2,316,780	2,145,670	2,134,670	2,145,760
6	*Subtotal*	*$ 3,551,670*	*$ 4,492,560*	*$ 4,291,250*	*$ 4,046,650*
7					
8	Manufacturing	8,909,800	8,769,870	7,869,870	9,878,760
9	Distribution	3,456,570	3,245,670	2,314,560	3,897,860
10	*Subtotal*	*$ 12,366,370*	*$ 12,015,540*	*$ 10,184,430*	*$ 13,776,620*
11					
12	Customer Support	93,450	72,150	63,670	93,670
13	Human Resources	65,640	87,890	65,670	86,780
14	*Subtotal*	*$ 159,090*	*$ 160,040*	*$ 129,340*	*$ 180,450*
15					
16	***Total***	***$ 16,077,130***	***$ 16,668,140***	***$ 14,605,020***	***$ 18,003,720***

Assessments

Assessment 15.1

In this assessment, you will develop the completed worksheet shown below.

1. Click the New button to start a new workbook.
2. Create the completed worksheet shown at the below. You must use formulas in Columns D and F and Row 11. Make sure the formula results match the completed worksheet. Format the numbers and text as shown.
3. Use print preview when you have finished, and then print the worksheet.
4. Save your workbook as **Assessment 15.1,** and then close the workbook.

	A	B	C	D	E	F
1	Donna's Deli - Customer Credit Lines					
2						
3	Customer	Previous Balance	New Charges	Subtotal	Payment Amount	New Balance
4	George Lopke	100	50	150	150	0
5	Wanda Watson	230	85	315	315	0
6	Alicia Thomas	58	100	158	100	58
7	Bill Barton	60	35	95	0	95
8	Latisha Robertson	140	80	220	0	220
9	Amy Chang	200	150	350	350	0
10	Dan Long	90	65	155	100	55
11	**Total Credit**	**$878**	**$565**	**$1,443**	**$1,015**	**$428**

Assessment 15.2

1. Create the following worksheet, formatting the cells as shown.
2. Print the worksheet, save the workbook as **Assessment 15.2,** and then close the workbook.

	A	B	C	D
1	Donna's Deli - Customer Survey Results			
2				
3	Category	January	February	March
4	Flavor	4.80	4.75	4.80
5	Service	4.60	4.50	4.70
6	Nutritional Value	4.95	4.95	4.83
7	Presentation	4.20	4.35	4.30
8	Price	4.20	4.20	4.45
9	Convenience	4.30	4.40	4.20
10	**Total**	**27.05**	**27.15**	**27.28**

LESSON 16—Excel

Powerful Features and Automated Tools

In this lesson, you will be introduced to Excel functions. Excel has hundreds of built-in functions including the AVERAGE, MIN, MAX, and COUNT functions which are introduced in this lesson. This lesson will also give you the skills necessary to move and copy cells. You will learn the Cut, Copy, and Paste techniques as well as Drag and Drop. Finally, you will learn how to apply borders and fill colors to cells and use Excel's powerful AutoFormat command.

In This Lesson

Case Study

Lisa Wilkins is the National Sales Manager for Centron Cellular—a nationwide distributor of cellular telephone equipment. Lisa has instructed her assistant, Carl Jenkins, to provide her with a commission report for her sales force. Lisa wants the report separated into two regions. She wants to know the monthly sales and commissions for each sales rep. She also wants the total, average, minimum, and maximum sales of the reps in each region on a monthly basis. This would be a formidable task for most people, but Carl Jenkins is not concerned. Carl has expert knowledge of Excel 2000. With a little planning and the power of Excel 2000, Carl will produce this worksheet with ease.

	A	B	C	D	E	F	G
1				Centron Cellular			
2							
3				Region 1			
4	**Sales Rep**	*Jan Sales*	*Jan Comm*	*Feb Sales*	*Feb Comm*	*Mar Sales*	*Mar Comm*
5	**Branston**	32000	4800	32000	4800	23000	3450
6	**Barton**	15000	2250	32000	4800	23890	3583.5
7	**Alexander**	45000	6750	8900	1335	43000	6450
8	**Alioto**	23000	3450	19000	2850	10900	1635
9	**Chin**	34000	5100	34000	5100	32000	4800
10	**Total**		22350		18885		19918.5
11	**Average**		4470		3777		3983.7
12	**Maximum**		6750		5100		6450
13	**Minimum**		2250		1335		1635
14							
15							
16				Region 2			
17	**Sales Rep**	*Jan Sales*	*Jan Comm*	*Feb Sales*	*Feb Comm*	*Mar Sales*	*Mar Comm*
18	**Richardson**	18000	2700	54000	8100	36790	5518.5
19	**Thomas**	12000	1800	35900	5385	45678	6851.7
20	**Carter**	56000	8400	34900	5235	72490	10873.5
21	**Williams**	39000	5850	54000	8100	21000	3150
22	**Jones**	23000	3450	89000	13350	38900	5835
23	**Total**		22200		40170		32228.7
24	**Average**		4440		8034		6445.74
25	**Maximum**		8400		13350		10873.5
26	**Minimum**		1800		5235		3150

The Office Assistant

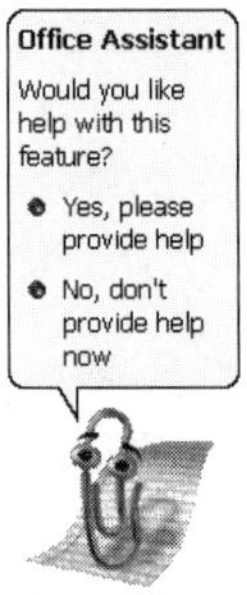
Office Assistant
Would you like help with this feature?
Yes, please provide help
No, don't provide help now
The Office Assistant

The Office Assistant is an interactive Help tool available in all Office 2000 applications. The Assistant monitors your activities and provides tips, suggestions, and alert messages whenever it assumes you need assistance. For example, the Assistant displays a **speech balloon** when it recognizes certain actions such as clicking the Edit Formula button on the Formula bar. You can use the speech balloon to get help with the action.

Using the Assistant to Get Help

The Assistant's speech balloon contains a search box where you can enter phrases and questions. When you click the Search button, the Assistant interprets the phrase or question in the search box and displays a list of topics relating to the search box text. When you click a topic, Excel displays a Help window providing you with detailed help information.

Controlling the Assistant

You can control all aspects of the Assistant. For example, you may not want the Assistant to display a tip of the day, or you may want to turn the Assistant off. You set options for the Assistant in the Office Assistant dialog box. The following Quick Reference table describes various methods of controlling the Assistant.

Quick Reference

CONTROLLING THE OFFICE ASSISTANT

Task	Procedure
Display the Assistant's speech balloon. (four different methods)	■ Click anywhere on the Assistant. ■ Press (F1). ■ Click the Help button on the Standard toolbar. ■ Choose Microsoft Excel Help from the Help menu.
Close the speech balloon.	Click anywhere in the worksheet, or tap (ESC).
Display Office Assistant dialog box.	Display the speech balloon, and click the Options button.
Change animated character.	Display the Office Assistant dialog box, click the Gallery tab, use the Next button to browse the available characters, choose a character, and click OK.
Temporarily hide the Assistant.	Choose Help→Hide the Office Assistant, or right-click the Assistant, and choose Hide from the pop-up menu.
Turn Assistant off completely.	Display the Office Assistant dialog box, and uncheck the Use the Office Assistant box.
Unhide the Assistant or turn the Assistant back on.	Choose Help→Show the Office Assistant

Hands-On 16.1 Use the Office Assistant

In this exercise, you will use the Assistant to learn about functions.

Display the Speech Balloon

1. Start Excel, and the Assistant should appear.
2. If the Assistant is not visible on your screen, choose Help→Show the Office Assistant.
   This text shows the default Assistant character known as "Clippit." The Assistant on your machine may be different.
3. Click the Assistant, and the speech balloon will pop up.
4. Click anywhere in the worksheet to close the speech balloon.
   You can always close the speech balloon by clicking in the worksheet or by tapping ESC.
5. Position the mouse pointer on the Assistant and drag it to a new screen location.
   You can always reposition the Assistant, even if the speech balloon is displayed.

Get Help

6. Click the Assistant to display the speech balloon.
7. Follow these steps to get help with functions.

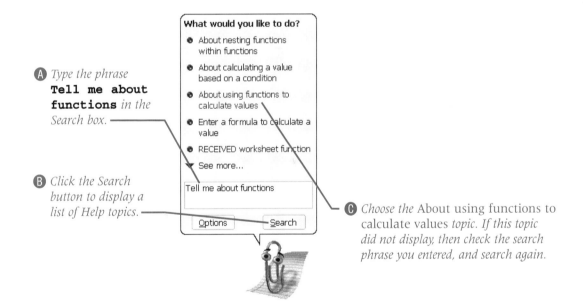

Ⓐ *Type the phrase* **Tell me about functions** *in the Search box.*

Ⓑ *Click the Search button to display a list of Help topics.*

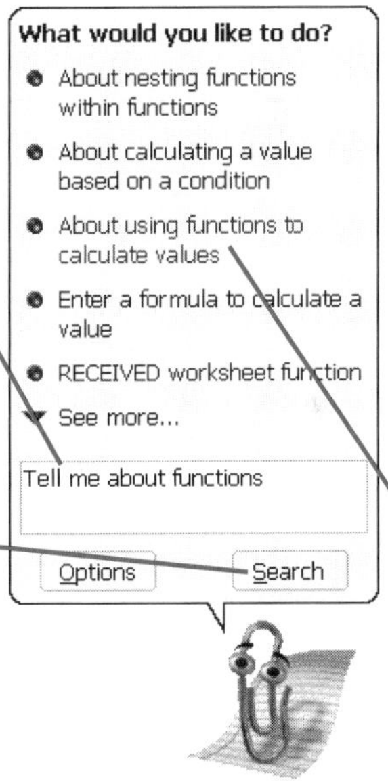
What would you like to do?
About nesting functions within functions
About calculating a value based on a condition
About using functions to calculate values
Enter a formula to calculate a value
RECEIVED worksheet function
See more...
Tell me about functions
Options
Search

Ⓒ *Choose the* About using functions to calculate values *topic. If this topic did not display, then check the search phrase you entered, and search again.*

Excel will display a Help window relating to functions. The Help window will most likely appear beside the Excel document window. As you can see, the Assistant can be used to display Help windows. You will learn more about functions and online Help in a moment.

(Continued on the next page)

8. For now, click the Close ☒ button at the top-right corner of the Help window.
   The Help window should close, and the Excel window will return to its original size.
9. Type the word **`functions`** in the Assistant's search box.
10. Click the **Search** button, and a list of topics will appear.
    Notice that About using functions to calculate values *is one of the topics. This is the same topic you searched for previously when you entered the search phrase "Tell me about functions." This example shows that it isn't always necessary to type long phrases in the search box. Often, a single word is enough to locate a desired topic.*

Check Out the Options

11. Click the Options button on the speech balloon.
12. If necessary, click the Options tab in the dialog box that appears.
13. Click the Question Mark [?] button at the top-right corner of the dialog box, and then click on any option check box.
    Excel will provide a ScreenTip describing the purpose of the option.
14. Tap the (ESC) key to close the ScreenTip.
15. Feel free to get help on the various Office Assistant options. You may also want to click the Gallery tab in the dialog box to check out the other Assistant characters. If you are studying in a computer lab, it is recommended that you not change any options.
16. Close the Office Assistant dialog box when you have finished.

Online Help

Excel's online Help puts a complete reference book at your fingertips. Help is available for just about any topic you can imagine. Online Help is important because Microsoft does not provide reference manuals with Office 2000. The reference manuals are now integrated into online Help.

Locating Help Topics

Your goal when using online Help is to locate Help topics. There are several different search methods you can use to locate topics. All Help topics have key words that identify them. For example, a Help topic that discusses printing workbooks can probably be located by including the key word *printing* in your search method. Regardless of which search method you use, the goal is to locate a topic. Once you locate the desired topic, you can display it and follow the instructions in the topic.

When Help Is Available

In Excel 2000, you can display the Help window directly only when the Office Assistant is turned off. You learned how to turn off the Office Assistant in the previous topic. When the Office Assistant is turned off, the Help window can be displayed using any of the following methods:

- Click the Help button on the Standard toolbar.
- Press (F1).
- Choose Help→Microsoft Word Help from the menu bar.

The following Quick Reference table describes the various methods for locating Help topics.

Quick Reference

LOCATING HELP TOPICS

Search Method	Procedure
Contents	The Contents method is useful if you are trying to locate a topic but you aren't really sure how to describe it. The Contents method lets you navigate through a series of categories until the desired topic is located.
Answer Wizard	The Answer Wizard lets you find topics the same way that you find them with the Office Assistant. You type a phrase into a search box and execute a search.
Index	The Index method lets you locate a topic by typing key words. An alphabetically indexed list of topics is displayed from which you can choose the desired topic. This method is most useful if you know the name of the topic or feature for which you need assistance.

The Help Window Toolbar

The Help window contains a toolbar to assist you with online Help. The following illustration describes the buttons on the Help toolbar.

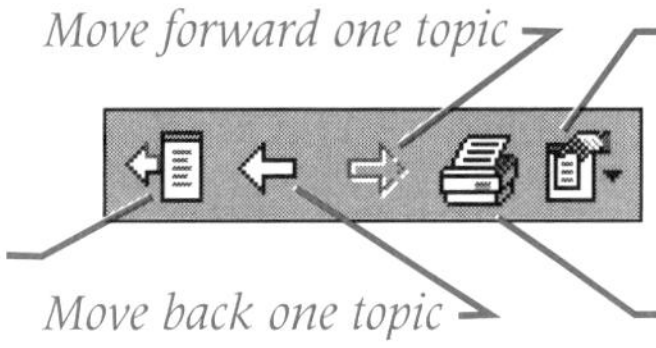

The Show/Hide button is used to show or hide the tabbed area of the Help window. The tabbed area is used to locate Help topics.
Move forward one topic
Display Help options
Move back one topic
Print the topic

Hands-On 16.2 Use Online Help

Turn Off the Office Assistant

1. Click the Office Assistant, and then click the Options button.
2. Make sure the Options tab is active, and remove the check from the **Use the Office Assistant** box.
3. Click **OK,** and the Office Assistant will vanish.
   Once the Office Assistant is turned off, commands that would normally display the Office Assistant display the Help window instead.

(Continued on the next page)

Use an Index Search

4. Choose **Help→Microsoft Excel Help** from the menu bar.
   The Help window will be displayed beside the Excel window. If the Office Assistant had been active, this command would have popped up the Assistant's speech balloon.
5. If the tabbed area of the Help window is not displayed, then click the Show button on the Help toolbar.
6. Click the **Index** tab.
7. Type the word **`function`** in the Type keywords box, and click the **Search** button.
   A list of Help topics is displayed in the bottom section of the Help window. The About using functions to calculate values *topic should be the third one on the list.*
8. Click the **About Using Functions to Calculate Values** topic to display the topic in the right side of the Help window.
   This is the same Help topic you located earlier with the Office Assistant.
9. Take a moment to read the help information. Notice the blue phrases such as **cell references** that are scattered throughout the topic.
10. Click the **cell references** phrase, and a definition will pop up.
11. Tap (ESC) to close the definition.

Experiment with Help

12. Try using the Index method to locate additional Help topics. You can type keywords in the Keyword box, click the Search button, and click the desired topic. Try locating Help topics for Excel features you have already learned or for new features to be covered in this lesson.
13. Try using the Contents tab to locate topics. You must double-click closed books in the Contents tab to locate topics.
14. When you have finished, click the Close button on the Help window.
15. Finally, turn the Office Assistant back on with the **Help→Show the Office Assistant** command. If necessary, close the Assistant's speech balloon.

AutoCorrect

Excel's AutoCorrect feature can improve the speed and accuracy of entering text. AutoCorrect is most useful for replacing abbreviations with a full phrase. For example, you could set up AutoCorrect to substitute ***as soon as possible*** whenever you type ***asap.*** AutoCorrect also automatically corrects common spelling errors. For example, the word ***the*** is often misspelled as ***teh*** and the word ***and*** is often misspelled as ***adn.*** These and other common spelling mistakes are built into AutoCorrect, so they are fixed automatically. AutoCorrect also automatically capitalizes the first letter of a day if you type the day in lowercase. For example, if you type ***sunday*** and complete the entry, AutoCorrect will enter ***Sunday*** in the cell. Finally, AutoCorrect fixes words that have two initial capital letters by switching the second letter to lowercase.

Expanding AutoCorrect Entries

AutoCorrect goes into action when you type a word in a text entry and tap SPACE BAR or when you complete a text entry. The word or entry is compared to all entries in the AutoCorrect table. The AutoCorrect table contains a list of words and their replacement phrases. If the word you type matches an entry in the AutoCorrect table, then a phrase from the table is substituted for the word. This is known as expanding the AutoCorrect entry.

Creating and Editing AutoCorrect Entries

The **Tools→AutoCorrect** command displays the AutoCorrect dialog box. You use the AutoCorrect dialog box to add entries to the AutoCorrect table, to delete entries from the table, and to set other AutoCorrect options. To add an entry, you type the desired abbreviation in the Replace box and the desired expansion for the abbreviation in the With box.

AutoComplete

The AutoComplete feature is useful if you want the same entry repeated more than once in a column. If the first few characters you type match another entry in the column, then AutoComplete will offer to complete the entry for you. You can accept the offer by completing the entry or you can reject the offer by typing the remainder of the entry yourself.

Hands-On 16.3 Use AutoCorrect and AutoComplete

In this exercise, you will open a workbook from your exercise diskette. You will experiment with AutoCorrect and AutoComplete, and create a new AutoCorrect entry.

Use AutoCorrect

1. Open the workbook named **Hands-On Lesson 16.**
2. Type **adn** (that's adn, not and) in Cell A1, and tap ENTER.
   Excel should correct the misspelling and enter the word and *in the cell.*
3. Click Cell A1, and type **This adn that**, but don't complete the entry.
   Notice that AutoCorrect fixes the typo immediately after you tap SPACE BAR.
4. Tap ESC to cancel the entry.

(Continued on the next page)

Create a New AutoCorrect Entry

5. Choose **Tools→AutoCorrect** from the menu bar.

6. Follow these steps to create a new AutoCorrect entry.

Ⓐ *Notice these check boxes. They instruct AutoCorrect to automatically make the specified corrections in your worksheets.*

Ⓑ *Type* **cc** *in the Replace box.*

Ⓒ *Type* **Centron Cellular** *in the With box.*

Ⓓ *Click the* ***Add*** *button to add the entry to the list.*

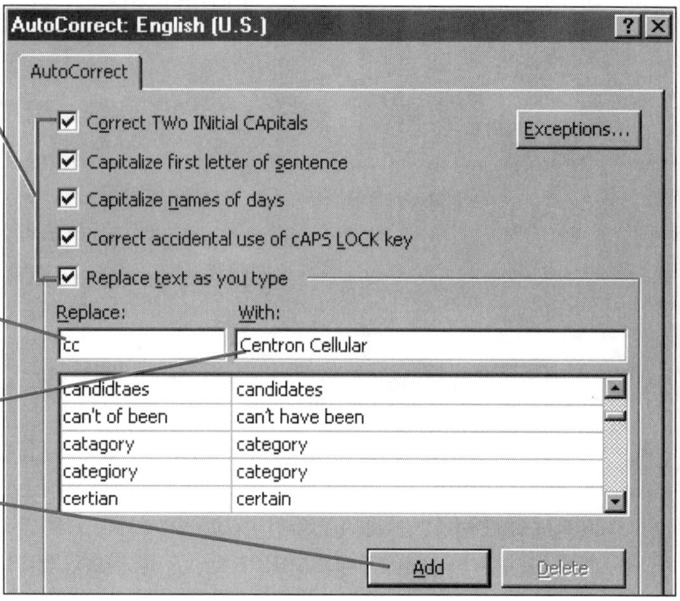
AutoCorrect: English (U.S.)
AutoCorrect
Correct TWo INitial CApitals
Exceptions...
Capitalize first letter of sentence
Capitalize names of days
Correct accidental use of cAPS LOCK key
Replace text as you type
Replace:
With:
cc
Centron Cellular
candidtaes
candidates
can't of been
can't have been
catagory
category
categiory
category
certian
certain
Add
Delete

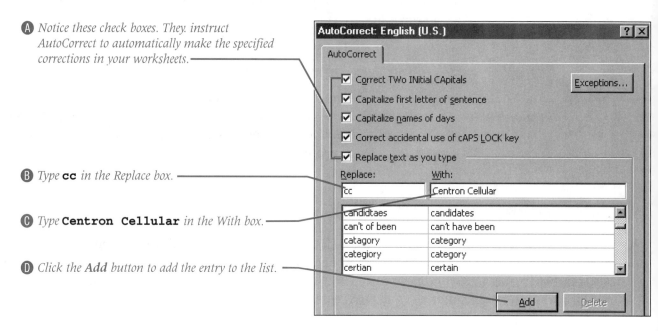

Ⓔ *Feel free to scroll through the list. You will see hundreds of AutoCorrect entries. All Office 2000 programs share the same AutoCorrect entries.*

Ⓕ *Click OK.*

7. Click Cell A1, type **cc**, and tap (ENTER).
   AutoCorrect should replace cc with Centron Cellular. Notice that you can use AutoCorrect as a type of shorthand. AutoCorrect can replace abbreviations with phrases you use often such as your company name or address.

Delete the AutoCorrect Entry

8. Choose **Tools→AutoCorrect** from the menu bar.

9. Scroll through the list of AutoCorrect entries and choose the **cc, Centron Cellular** entry.

10. Click the **Delete** button below the AutoCorrect table, and then click **OK.**
    The entry is deleted from the AutoCorrect table, but the phrase Centron Cellular will remain in Cell A1.

Use AutoComplete

11. Click Cell A5, type **Branston**, and then tap (ENTER).

12. Type the letter **B** in Cell A6 and AutoComplete will display the word Branston in the cell.
    You could accept this proposal by completing the entry; however, you will continue to type in the next step thus typing over the proposed entry.

13. Type **arton** (to make the entry Barton), and tap (ENTER).
    AutoComplete will constantly try to assist you in completing entries. You can either ignore AutoComplete and continue typing your entries or complete the entries that AutoComplete proposes.

14. Enter the following sales rep names into the next three cells.

7	Alexander
8	Alioto
9	Chin

You will continue to enhance the worksheet throughout this lesson.

Functions

Excel has over 400 built-in functions. Functions are predefined formulas that perform calculations. Functions must be constructed using a set of basic rules known as **syntax.** Fortunately, most functions use the same or similar syntax. The following illustration defines the syntax of the SUM function. This syntax also applies to the MIN, MAX, AVERAGE, and COUNT functions, which are discussed in the Quick Reference table following the illustration.

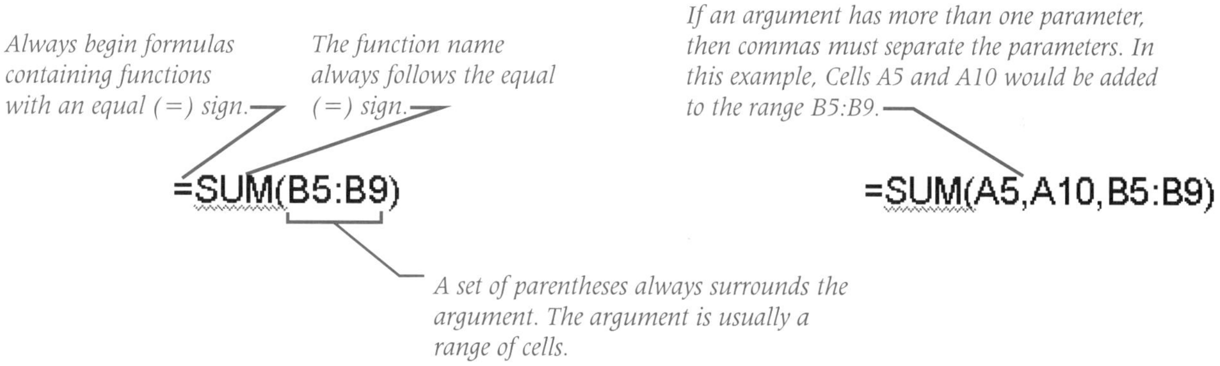
Always begin formulas containing functions with an equal (=) sign.
The function name always follows the equal (=) sign.
If an argument has more than one parameter, then commas must separate the parameters. In this example, Cells A5 and A10 would be added to the range B5:B9.
=SUM(B5:B9)
=SUM(A5,A10,B5:B9)
A set of parentheses always surrounds the argument. The argument is usually a range of cells.

COMMON FUNCTIONS

Function	What It Does	Syntax Example
MIN	Returns the minimum value of a range	=MIN(B5:B9)
MAX	Returns the maximum value of a range	=MAX(B5:B9)
AVERAGE	Returns the average of values in a range	=AVERAGE(B5:B9)
COUNT	Determines how many cells in a range contain numbers, dates, or formulas	=COUNT(B5:B9)

Entering Functions with the Keyboard

You can type a function and its argument(s) directly in the desired cell. You can also click in the desired cell and type the function in the Formula bar. If you choose to type a function, you can use point mode to assist you in entering the function arguments.

Hands-On 16.4 Enter Functions with the Keyboard

Do a Little Detective Work and Use AutoSum

1. Notice that the Hands-On Lesson 16 worksheet has a January Commissions column (Jan Comm).
   The commissions in Column C are calculated with a simple formula.
2. What commission rate is being used to calculate the sales rep's commissions?
   You can find this out by clicking a commission cell in Column C and reviewing the formula in the Formula bar.
3. Click Cell C10, click AutoSum, and complete the entry.
   The total commissions for January should equal 20550.
4. Look at the Formula bar and notice the function =SUM(C5:C9) that AutoSum has placed in the cell.
   The SUM function uses the standard function syntax discussed at the beginning of this topic.

Type the AVERAGE Function

5. Click Cell C11, type the function **=AVERAGE(C5:C9)**, and complete the entry.
   The result should equal 4110. This is the average of the values in the range C5:C9. Notice that the syntax is the same as the SUM function syntax, except you used the function name AVERAGE instead of SUM.

Pasting Functions

The Paste Function button on the Standard toolbar displays the Paste Function box. The Paste Function box provides access to all built-in functions in Excel. The Paste Function box organizes functions into various categories to help you easily locate the desired function. When you choose a function and click OK, Excel displays the Formula Palette below the Formula bar. The Formula Palette can assist you in constructing the function by helping you enter the arguments. The Paste Function box and the Formula Palette are shown in the following illustrations.

*The **Paste Function** box organizes functions into categories. This example shows some of the functions in the* Statistical *category.*

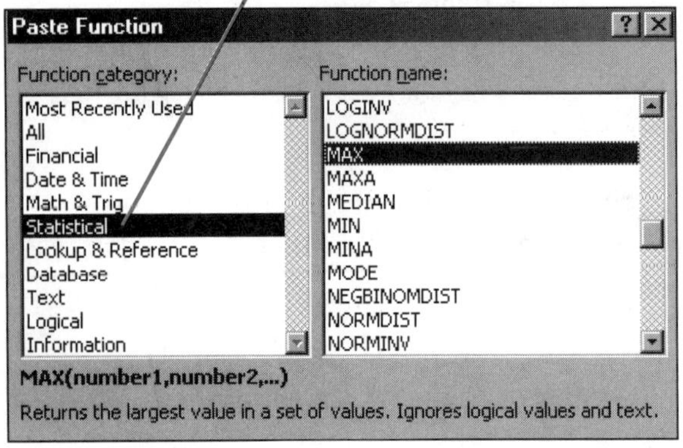
Paste Function
Function category:
Most Recently Used
All
Financial
Date & Time
Math & Trig
Statistical
Lookup & Reference
Database
Text
Logical
Information
Function name:
LOGINV
LOGNORMDIST
MAX
MAXA
MEDIAN
MIN
MINA
MODE
NEGBINOMDIST
NORMDIST
NORMINV
MAX(number1,number2,...)
Returns the largest value in a set of values. Ignores logical values and text.

The Formula Palette appears below the Formula bar when you choose a function and click OK.

As you build the formula, Excel displays it in the Formula bar.

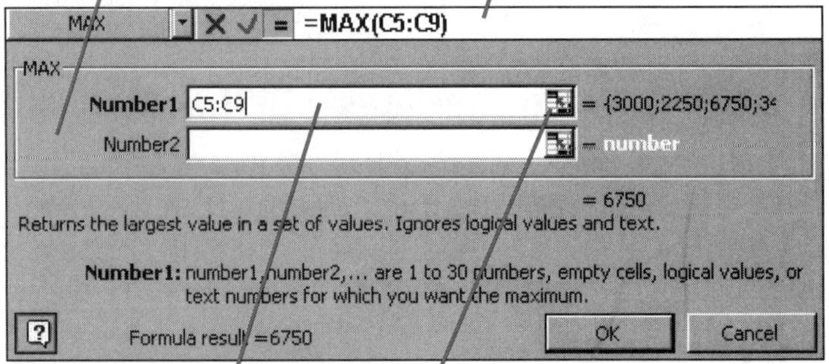
MAX
=MAX(C5:C9)
MAX
Number1 C5:C9
= {3000;2250;6750;3
Number2
= number
= 6750
Returns the largest value in a set of values. Ignores logical values and text.
Number1: number1,number2,... are 1 to 30 numbers, empty cells, logical values, or text numbers for which you want the maximum.
Formula result =6750
OK
Cancel

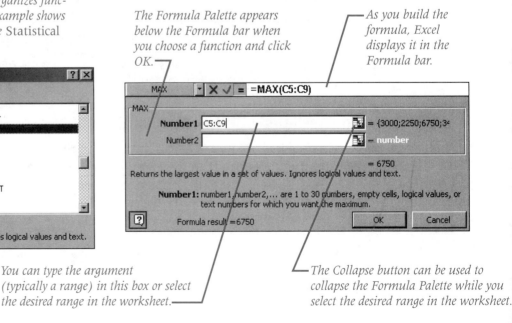

You can type the argument (typically a range) in this box or select the desired range in the worksheet.

The Collapse button can be used to collapse the Formula Palette while you select the desired range in the worksheet.

The Function Box

When you click the Edit Formula button, the Function box appears on the left end of the Formula bar. The Function box has a drop-down button containing a list of the 10 most recently used functions. When you choose a function from the list, the Formula Palette appears below the Formula bar. This technique has the same result as displaying the Paste Function box; however, it is more efficient if you are pasting a function that has recently been used.

The Function box also has a More Functions choice at the bottom of the drop-down menu that displays the Paste Function dialog box. This is convenient if the function you desire is not on the 10 most recently used functions list.

Clicking the Function box drop-down button displays the 10 most recently used functions.

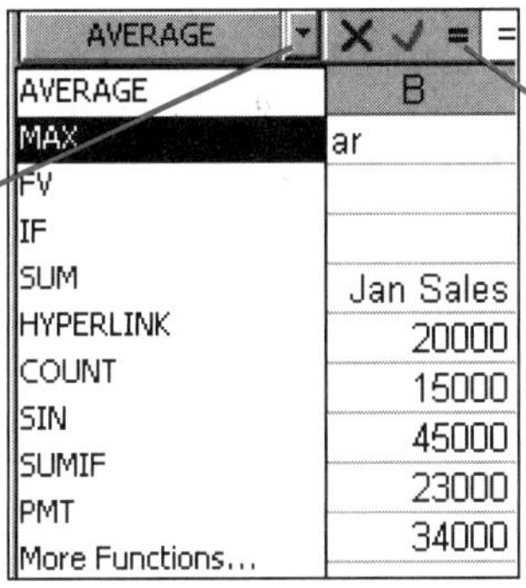

AVERAGE
AVERAGE
MAX
FV
IF
SUM
HYPERLINK
COUNT
SIN
SUMIF
PMT
More Functions...
B
ar
Jan Sales
20000
15000
45000
23000
34000

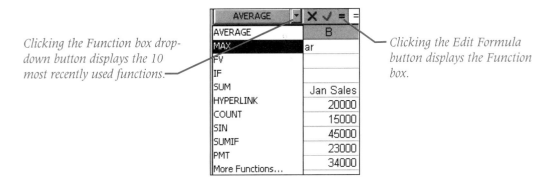

Clicking the Edit Formula button displays the Function box.

Hands-On 16.5 Paste a Function and Use Point Mode

In this exercise, you will insert the MAX and MIN functions in your worksheet.

Paste the MAX Function

1. Click Cell C12, and then click the Edit Formula button on the Formula bar.
2. Follow these steps to explore the Function box.

(A) Click the Function box drop-down button. The list shows the 10 most recently used functions on your computer.

(B) Notice that the most recently used function (in this case, AVERAGE) appears on the button and at the top of the list.

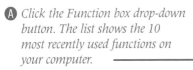

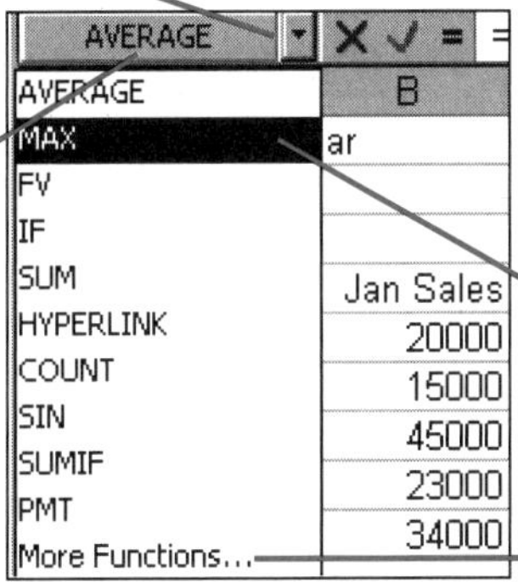

AVERAGE
AVERAGE
MAX
FV
IF
SUM
HYPERLINK
COUNT
SIN
SUMIF
PMT
More Functions...
B
ar
Jan Sales
20000
15000
45000
23000
34000

(C) The MAX function will probably appear on your list. You could choose MAX at this point; however, you will choose the MAX function in the next step using the Paste Function box.

(D) Choose More Functions to display the Paste Function box.

(Continued on the next page)

3. Follow these steps to choose the MAX function.

Ⓐ *Notice that the functions are organized by categories. The functions for the highlighted category are displayed to the right.*

Ⓑ *Choose the Statistical category.*

Ⓒ *Scroll down through the list of functions and choose MAX.*

Ⓓ *Click **OK**.*

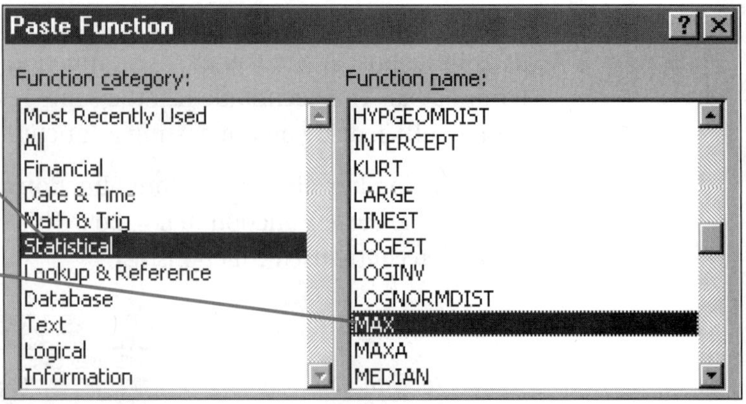
Paste Function
Function category:
Function name:
Most Recently Used
All
Financial
Date & Time
Math & Trig
Statistical
Lookup & Reference
Database
Text
Logical
Information
HYPGEOMDIST
INTERCEPT
KURT
LARGE
LINEST
LOGEST
LOGINV
LOGNORMDIST
MAX
MAXA
MEDIAN

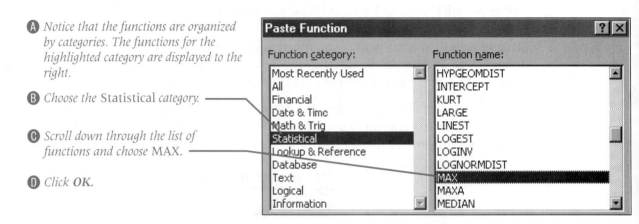

Notice the MAX(C11) function appears in the Formula bar. This is the correct function; however, the range C11 is incorrect. You could type the correct range, C5:C9, in the Formula Palette or the Formula bar; however, you will insert the range by dragging in the worksheet in the following steps.

4. Follow this step to collapse the Formula Palette.

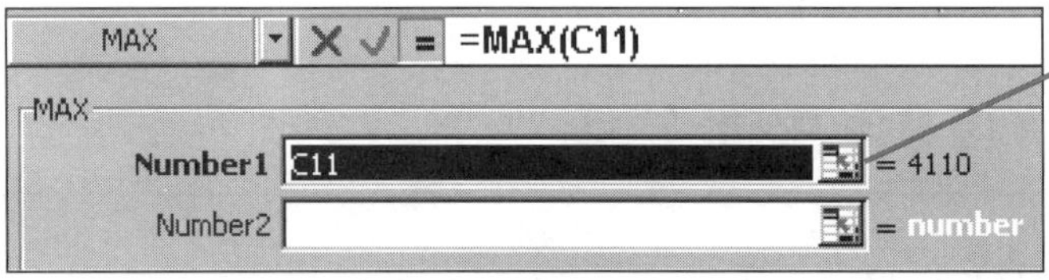
MAX
=MAX(C11)
MAX
Number1
C11
= 4110
Number2
= number

Ⓐ *Click the Collapse button on the Formula Palette.*

5. Follow these steps to select the appropriate range of cells and restore the Formula Palette.

Ⓐ *Drag the mouse over the range C5:C9, as shown here.*

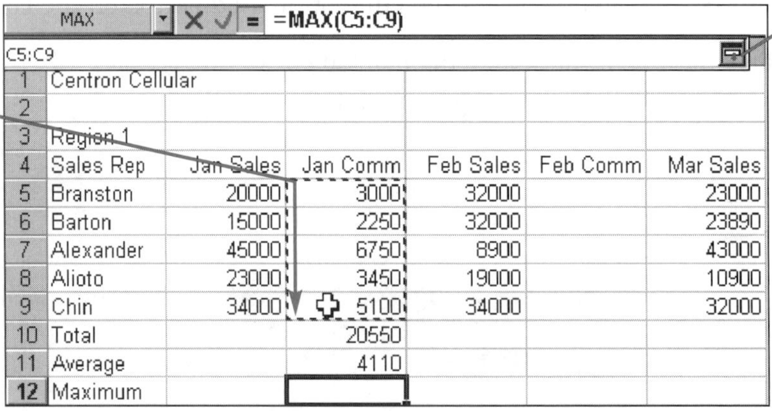
MAX
=MAX(C5:C9)
C5:C9
Centron Cellular
Region 1
Sales Rep
Jan Sales
Jan Comm
Feb Sales
Feb Comm
Mar Sales
Branston 20000 3000 32000 23000
Barton 15000 2250 32000 23890
Alexander 45000 6750 8900 43000
Alioto 23000 3450 19000 10900
Chin 34000 5100 34000 32000
Total 20550
Average 4110
Maximum

Ⓑ *Click the Collapse button to restore the Formula Palette.*

Take a moment to equal the formula in the Formula bar. It should be =MAX(C5:C9).

6. Complete the function by clicking **OK** on the Formula palette (the result should equal 6750).

Use Point Mode to Enter the MIN Function

7. Click Cell C13 and type **`=min(`**.
   If you type a function in lowercase, Excel will convert it to uppercase when you complete the entry. Remember, you must always type the opening parenthesis when entering a function in point mode.
8. Drag the mouse down the range **C5:C9.**
9. Type a closing parenthesis **`)`**, and your formula should be =min(C5:C9).
10. Complete the entry. The result should equal 2250.
    In this exercise, you used two different methods to create functions. You can also insert functions by typing them directly into the cell or Formula bar. In the future, use whichever method you prefer.

Change the Values

You may be wondering why you used the MIN and MAX functions in this worksheet when it is relatively easy to see which sales reps had the minimum and maximum commissions. The benefit of using the functions becomes apparent when the values change or when there are a large number of rows. The functions automatically recalculate the SUM, AVERAGE, MAX, and MIN values when other values in the worksheet change.

11. Click Cell B5, change the sales number from 20000 to 32000, and complete the entry.
    Notice how the functions in Cells C10 and C11 recalculate the sum and average.
12. Click Undo  to change the number back to 20000.

Cut, Copy, and Paste

Cut, Copy, and Paste are available in all Office 2000 applications. With Cut, Copy, and Paste you can move or copy cells within a worksheet, between worksheets, or between different Office applications. For example, you could use the Copy command to copy a range from one worksheet and the Paste command to paste the range into another worksheet. Cut, Copy, and Paste are most efficient for moving or copying cells a long distance within a worksheet or between worksheets. Cut, Copy, and Paste are easy to use if you remember the following concepts.

- You must select cells before issuing a Cut or Copy command.
- You must position the highlight at the desired location before issuing the Paste command. This is important because the range you paste will overwrite any cells in the paste area.

Command	Discussion	Procedure
Cut	The Cut command removes entries from selected cells and places them on the Windows clipboard.	Click the Cut  button, or press CTRL+X.
Copy	The Copy command also places entries on the Windows clipboard, but it leaves a copy of the entries in the original cells.	Click the Copy  button, or press CTRL+C.
Paste	The Paste command pastes entries from the Windows clipboard to worksheet cells beginning at the highlight location.	Click the Paste  button, or press CTRL+V.

The Office 2000 Clipboard

Office 2000 introduces a new clipboard that can hold up to 12 cut or copied items. The Clipboard toolbar appears once you have cut or copied two or more items. The Clipboard toolbar displays an icon representing each cut or copied item. You can paste any item by choosing it from the Clipboard toolbar. You can paste all items from the toolbar by clicking the Paste All button. The items are pasted in the order in which they were cut or copied to the toolbar.

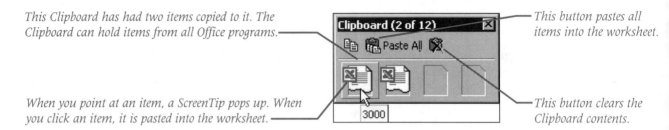

This Clipboard has had two items copied to it. The Clipboard can hold items from all Office programs.

When you point at an item, a ScreenTip pops up. When you click an item, it is pasted into the worksheet.

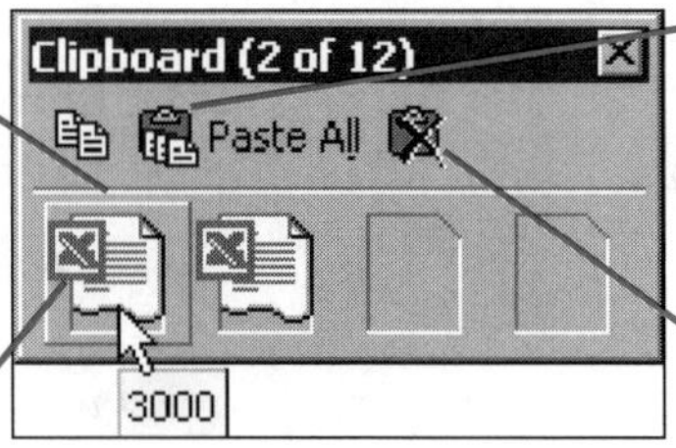
Clipboard (2 of 12)
Paste All
3000

This button pastes all items into the worksheet.

This button clears the Clipboard contents.

Hands-On 16.6 Use Copy and Paste

Copy the Commission Formula to Cell E5

1. Click Cell C5, and take a moment to review the formula in the Formula bar.
   Your objective is to copy this formula to the February and March commission columns. This cannot be done with the fill handle because those cells are not adjacent to Cell C5.
2. Click the Copy button on the Standard toolbar.
   Notice the flashing marquee in Cell C5. This indicates that the sales commission formula is on the clipboard and ready to be pasted.
3. Click Cell E5, and then click the Paste button.
   The formula will be pasted, and it will calculate the commission as 4800. The flashing marquee in Cell C5 indicates the formula is still available for pasting into other cells.

Paste to a Range

4. Select the range E6:E9.
5. Click the Paste button to paste the formula.
   You can always copy a single cell and paste it into a range of cells.
6. Select the range G5:G9 and paste the formula into those cells.
   You can continue to paste as long as the marquee is flashing.
7. Tap ESC on the keyboard, and the marquee will stop flashing.
   You can always turn off the flashing marquee with the ESC key.
8. Click any cell that you just pasted into, and review the formula in the Formula bar.
   Excel updates the references in the formulas to reflect the new formula locations.

Paste to Multiple Ranges

9. Click Cell C10, and click the Copy button.
10. Click Cell E10.
11. Press and hold the CTRL key, and click Cell G10.
    Both Cells E10 and G10 should be selected.
12. Click the Paste button to paste the formula into both cells.
13. Use the preceding techniques to copy the AVERAGE, MAX, and MIN functions from Column C to Columns E and G. You can copy the functions one at a time, or you can select all three functions, and copy and paste them simultaneously.

Copy the Heading Rows

14. Select all entries in Rows 3 and 4 by dragging over the cells.
15. Click the Copy button, and then click Cell A16.
    In the next step, you will paste the range to Cell A16. You should always paste a large range like this to one cell (A16 in this case). Excel will use Cell A16 as the starting location of the pasted range. However, you must be careful when using this technique because Excel will overwrite any cells in the pasted range.
16. Click the Paste button.
    In the next exercise, you will continue to copy cells with the drag-and-drop technique. For now, continue with the data entry task in the next step.
17. Enter the following names into the range A18:A22.

18	Richardson
19	Thomas
20	Carter
21	Williams
22	Jones

18. Change the heading in Cell A16 from Region 1 to Region 2.

Drag and Drop

Drag and Drop produces the same results as Cut, Copy, and Paste. However, Drag and Drop is usually more efficient if you are moving or copying entries a short distance within the same worksheet. If the original location and destination are both visible in the current window, then it is usually easier to use Drag and Drop. With Drag and Drop, you select the cells you wish to move or copy and release the mouse button. Then you point to the edge of the selected range and drag the range to the desired destination. If you press the CTRL key while releasing the mouse button, the cells are copied to the destination.

Right Dragging

Right dragging is a variation of the drag and drop technique. Many beginners find Drag and Drop difficult to use because they have difficulty controlling the mouse. This difficulty is compounded if they are trying to copy entries using drag and drop. This is because copying requires the (CTRL) key to be held while the selected range is dragged. With the Right-Drag method, the right mouse button is used when dragging. When the right mouse button is released at the destination, a pop-up menu appears. The pop-up menu allows you to choose Move, Copy, or Cancel. This provides more control because there is no need to use the (CTRL) key when copying, and you have the option of canceling the move or copy.

Hands-On 16.7 Use Drag and Drop

In this exercise, you will use Drag and Drop to move and copy text and formulas in the worksheet.

Move Entries

1. Follow these steps to drag-and-drop text entries.

10 Total
11 Average
12 Maximum
13 Minimum
14
15
16 Region 2
17 Sales Rep
18 Richardson
19 Thomas
20 Carter
21 Williams
22 Jones
23
24
25
26

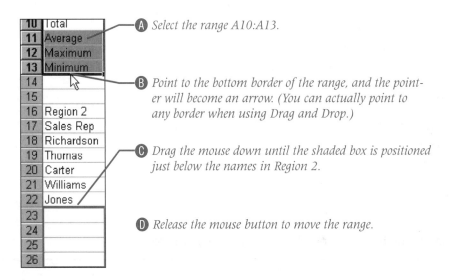

Ⓐ *Select the range A10:A13.*

Ⓑ *Point to the bottom border of the range, and the pointer will become an arrow. (You can actually point to any border when using Drag and Drop.)*

Ⓒ *Drag the mouse down until the shaded box is positioned just below the names in Region 2.*

Ⓓ *Release the mouse button to move the range.*

Notice how easy it was to move the cells using Drag and Drop. You should focus on using Drag and Drop if the move is a short distance within the same worksheet. Unfortunately, you should have copied the cells instead of moving them. You will correct this in the next few steps.

2. Click Undo [Undo button] to reverse the move.

Use Right Drag

3. Make sure the range A10:A13 is still selected.
4. Position the mouse pointer on the bottom edge of the selected range and press and hold the **right** mouse button.

5. Drag the mouse down until the range A23:A26 is highlighted as in the previous steps, and release the right mouse button.
A pop-up menu will appear with several choices.
6. Choose **Copy Here** from the pop-up menu.
The selected range will be copied.

Use Right Drag to Copy Formulas

7. Follow these steps to copy the January commission formulas to Region 2.

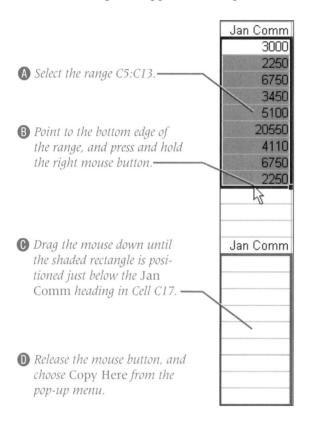

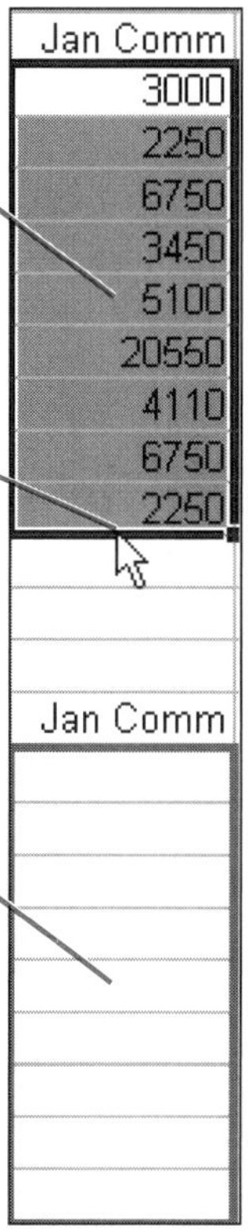

Jan Comm
3000
2250
6750
3450
5100
20550
4110
6750
2250
Jan Comm

Ⓐ *Select the range C5:C13.*

Ⓑ *Point to the bottom edge of the range, and press and hold the right mouse button.*

Ⓒ *Drag the mouse down until the shaded rectangle is positioned just below the* Jan Comm *heading in Cell C17.*

Ⓓ *Release the mouse button, and choose* Copy Here *from the pop-up menu.*

(Continued on the next page)

8. Use the right-drag method to copy the February and March commission formulas to Region 2.

9. Save the changes to your workbook.
At this point, your worksheet should match the following worksheet.

	A	B	C	D	E	F	G
1	Centron Cellular						
2							
3	Region 1						
4	Sales Rep	Jan Sales	Jan Comm	Feb Sales	Feb Comm	Mar Sales	Mar Comm
5	Branston	20000	3000	32000	4800	23000	3450
6	Barton	15000	2250	32000	4800	23890	3583.5
7	Alexander	45000	6750	8900	1335	43000	6450
8	Alioto	23000	3450	19000	2850	10900	1635
9	Chin	34000	5100	34000	5100	32000	4800
10	Total		20550		18885		19918.5
11	Average		4110		3777		3983.7
12	Maximum		6750		5100		6450
13	Minimum		2250		1335		1635
14							
15							
16	Region 2						
17	Sales Rep	Jan Sales	Jan Comm	Feb Sales	Feb Comm	Mar Sales	Mar Comm
18	Richardson	18000	2700	54000	8100	36790	5518.5
19	Thomas	12000	1800	35900	5385	45678	6851.7
20	Carter	56000	8400	34900	5235	72490	10873.5
21	Williams	39000	5850	54000	8100	21000	3150
22	Jones	23000	3450	89000	13350	38900	5835
23	Total		22200		40170		32228.7
24	Average		4440		8034		6445.74
25	Maximum		8400		13350		10873.5
26	Minimum		1800		5235		3150

Cell Borders

The Borders 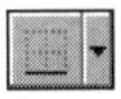 button on the Formatting toolbar lets you add borders to cell edges. When you click the Borders drop-down button, a tear-off palette of popular border styles appears. You can apply a style to all selected cells by choosing it from the palette. You can also use the **Format→Cells** command to display the Format Cells dialog box. The Borders tab on the dialog box lets you apply additional border combinations. You can also choose a color from the dialog box to apply colored borders.

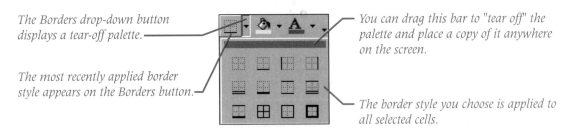

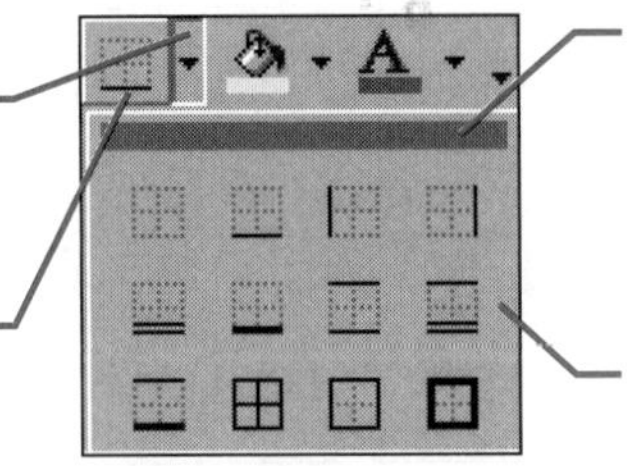
The Borders drop-down button displays a tear-off palette.
The most recently applied border style appears on the Borders button.
You can drag this bar to "tear off" the palette and place a copy of it anywhere on the screen.
The border style you choose is applied to all selected cells.

Fill Colors and Patterns

The Fill Color button on the Formatting toolbar lets you fill selected cells with color. When you click the Fill Color drop-down button, a tear-off palette of colors appears. You can apply a color to all selected cells by choosing it from the palette. The fill color is independent of the font color used to format text and numbers. You can also use the Format→Cells command to display the Format Cells dialog box. The Patterns tab on the dialog box lets you apply fill colors and a variety of patterns.

Hands-On 16.8 Add Borders and Fill Colors

Format the Title Cells

1. Select the range A1:G1 in Row 1, and click the Merge and Center button.
2. Make sure the range is selected, and click the Borders drop-down button.
3. Follow these steps to put a thick border around the range.

(A) Take a moment to review the various border styles. The first style removes all borders from the selected cells. Notice the other styles place thin, thick, or double lines on various borders.

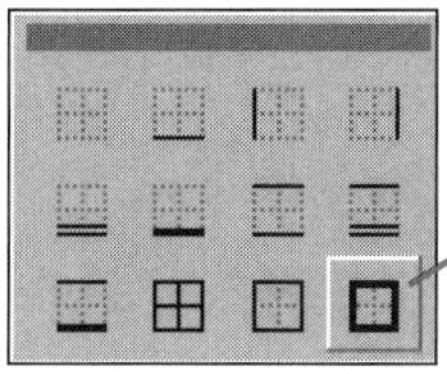

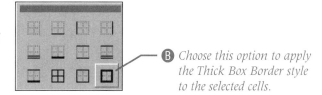

(B) Choose this option to apply the Thick Box Border style to the selected cells.

4. Make sure the range is selected, click the Fill Color drop-down button, and choose any color.
5. Make sure the range is selected, and click the Font Color drop-down button.
6. Choose a color that will provide adequate contrast to the fill color you chose.
7. Click outside the range, and you will be able to see the formats.
   The lines on the top and left sides of the range may not be visible because the column and row headings are blocking them. Notice the fill color fills the range, while the font color only affects the text. Also notice that the colors and line style you chose now appear on the buttons. If desired, you could apply these same colors and line style to other selected cells by clicking the buttons.
8. Click the Print Preview button.
9. Click anywhere on the worksheet to zoom in.
   The lines on the top and left sides of the range should now be visible. However, the colors will not be visible if you have a black-and-white printer. Print Preview displays colors in gray shades, as they will appear on the printed page.

(Continued on the next page)

Add Additional Borders

10. Click the **Close** button to exit from Print Preview.
11. Select the range A2:G26.
    This range includes all cells in the active worksheet area except for the title row.
12. Click the Borders drop-down button.
13. Choose the All Borders style (second style on the bottom row).
14. Click the Print Preview button.
    Notice that the lines on every border of every cell appear too busy. You will change the borders in the next few steps.

Remove Borders and Reapply Borders

15. Close the Print Preview window.
16. Make sure the range A2:G26 is still selected.
17. Click the Borders drop-down button, and choose Thick Box Border style.
18. Click Print Preview and notice that a thick border has been applied to the outside of the range but the inside borders have not been removed.
19. Close the Print Preview window.
20. Click the Borders drop-down button, and choose No Borders style (first button).
    This will remove the borders from the selected range.
21. Click the Borders drop-down button, and choose Thick Box Border style.
22. Click Print Preview, review the results, and then close Print Preview.

Apply Fill Color and Font Color

23. Select the range A10:G13.
    This range includes all cells containing entries in Rows 10, 11, 12, and 13.
24. Click the Fill Color button (not the drop-down button) to apply the same fill color that was applied to the large merged cell at the top of the worksheet.
25. Click the Font Color button (not the drop-down button) to apply the same font color that was applied to the merged cell.
26. Apply the same fill color and font color to the range A23:G26.
27. Save the changes to your workbook.
28. Take a few moments to experiment with borders and fill colors. Use Undo to reverse any changes you make.

AutoFormat

NOTE!
You must select a range before applying an AutoFormat.

The **Format→AutoFormat** command lets you choose from a variety of predefined formats. The predefined formats automatically apply number formats, borders, fill colors, font colors, font sizes, and other formats to a selected range. You may be pleasantly surprised when you see the professional formatting that AutoFormat can apply.

The AutoFormat box shows previews of the available formats.

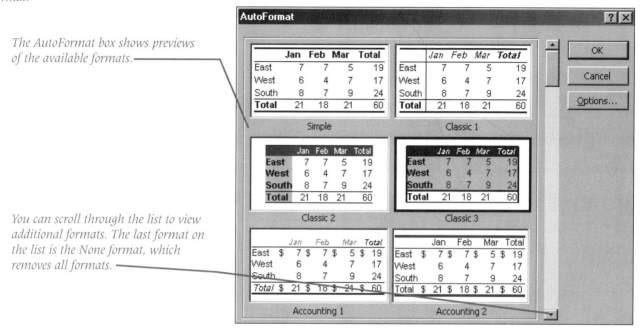

You can scroll through the list to view additional formats. The last format on the list is the None format, which removes all formats.

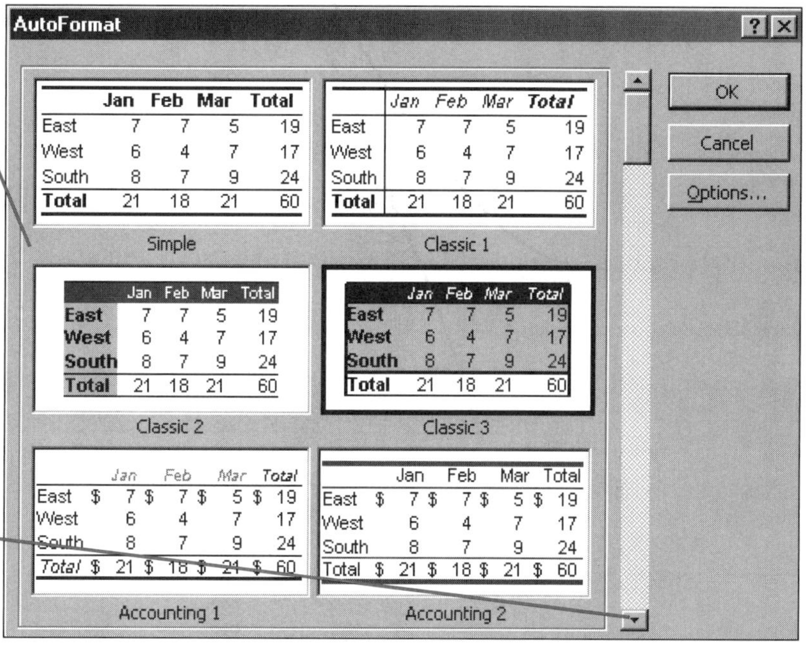

AutoFormat
OK
Cancel
Options...
Simple
Classic 1
Classic 2
Classic 3
Accounting 1
Accounting 2

Hands-On 16.9 Use AutoFormat

Use AutoFormat on Region 1

1. Select the range A3:G13, which includes all cells for Region 1.
2. Choose **Format→AutoFormat** from the menu bar.
3. Click the Options button just below the Cancel button on the right side of the box.
   Check boxes will appear at the bottom of the dialog box. These boxes determine the formats that AutoFormat will apply. Make sure all of the boxes are checked.
4. Scroll through the list and notice the various formats.
5. Scroll to the top of the list and choose **Classic 3** style.
6. Click **OK,** and then click anywhere in the worksheet to view the formats.
   Notice that AutoFormat detected rows containing formulas and formatted those rows in a different manner than the body and header rows. AutoFormat makes its formatting decisions by determining which rows and columns have text, numbers, and formulas.

(Continued on the next page)

Remove the AutoFormats

7. Select the range A3:G13 (the range you just formatted).
8. Choose **Format→AutoFormat** from the menu bar.
9. Scroll to the bottom of the list and choose the **None** format.
10. Click **OK,** and the formats will be removed.
    You can use this technique to remove all formats, whether or not they were applied with AutoFormat.

Format Other Ranges

11. Click Undo to restore the AutoFormats to Region 1.
12. Select the range A16:G26, which includes all cells for Region 2.
13. Choose **Format→AutoFormat,** and apply the **Classic 3** style.
14. Click in the large merged cell at the top of the worksheet.
15. Apply the Classic 3 AutoFormat to the merged cell.
16. Increase the font size of the merged cell to 12, and remove italics.
17. Save the changes to your workbook.
18. Feel free to experiment with AutoFormat, and then continue with the next topic.

Zooming

The Zoom Control lets you "zoom in" to get a close-up view of a worksheet or "zoom out" to see the full view. Zooming changes the size of the onscreen worksheet but has no effect on the printed worksheet. You can zoom from 10% to 400%.

Notice how large the onscreen worksheet appears. However, it will print in the normal size.

You can type a zoom percentage in the Zoom box and tap ENTER *or . . .*

. . . you can click the drop-down button and choose an option from the list.

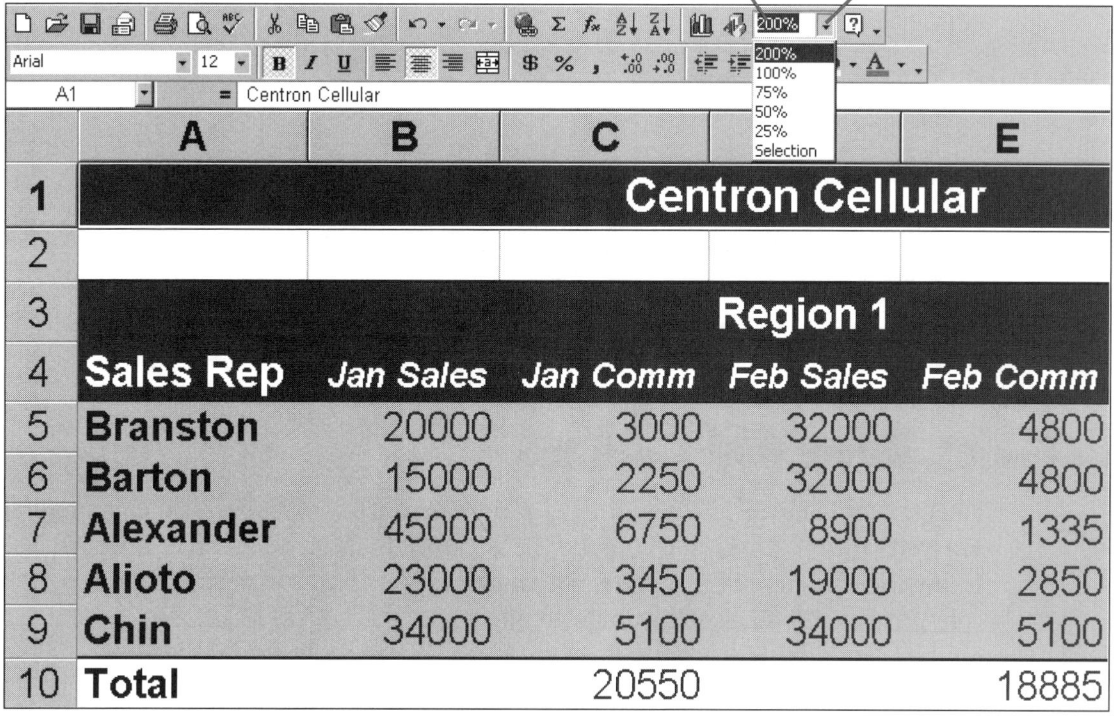
200%
Arial
12
200%
100%
75%
50%
25%
Selection
A1
= Centron Cellular
A
B
C
E
Centron Cellular
Region 1
Sales Rep
Jan Sales
Jan Comm
Feb Sales
Feb Comm
Branston 20000 3000 32000 4800
Barton 15000 2250 32000 4800
Alexander 45000 6750 8900 1335
Alioto 23000 3450 19000 2850
Chin 34000 5100 34000 5100
Total 20550 18885

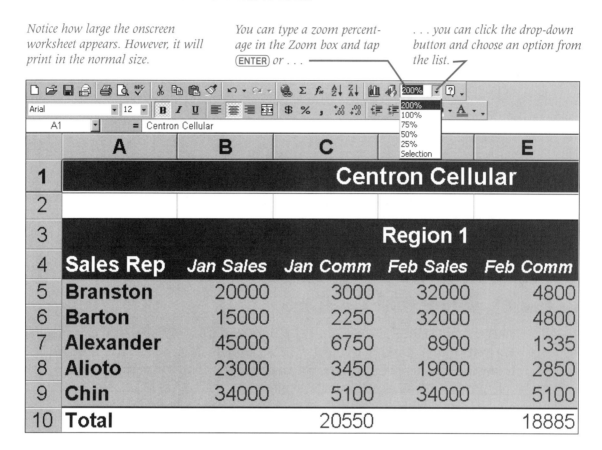

Hands-On 16.10 Use the Zoom Control

1. Follow these steps to adjust the zoom percentage.

Ⓐ *Click in the Zoom box, type* **150**, *and tap* ENTER.

Ⓑ *Click the Zoom drop-down button, and choose 200%.*

Ⓒ *Zoom to 100%.*

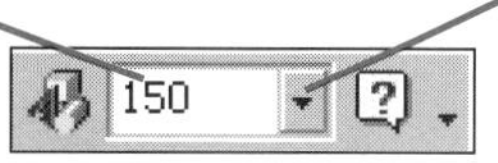
150

2. Select the range A4:C13.
   Imagine that you want to analyze just the January sales numbers. You can zoom in to get a close-up view of just this range.
3. Click the Zoom drop-down button, and choose **Selection.**
   Excel will zoom to the maximum percentage possible for that selection.
4. Zoom to 100%, and continue with the next topic.

Hiding Rows and Columns

You can hide selected rows and columns with the **Format→Row→Hide** command and the **Format→Column→Hide** command. Hidden rows and columns are not visible in the worksheet, and they are not printed when the worksheet is printed. However, hidden rows and columns are still part of the worksheet. Their values and formulas can be referenced by other formulas in the visible rows and columns. Hiding rows and columns can be useful if you are trying to focus attention on other parts of the worksheet.

Notice that Columns B, D, and F have been hidden. These columns are hidden to draw attention to the commission columns.

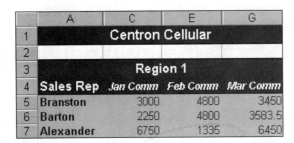

	A	C	E	G
1		Centron Cellular		
2				
3		Region 1		
4	Sales Rep	Jan Comm	Feb Comm	Mar Comm
5	Branston	3000	4800	3450
6	Barton	2250	4800	3583.5
7	Alexander	6750	1335	6450

Unhiding Rows and Columns

You can unhide rows and columns with the **Format→Row→Unhide** command and the **Format→Row→Unhide** command. Before unhiding rows, you must select row(s) above and below the hidden rows. Likewise, you must select column(s) on the left and right of hidden columns before issuing the Unhide command.

To unhide Column D, you must first select Columns C and E.

	A	C	E	G
1		Centron Cellular		
2				
3		Region 1		
4	Sales Rep	Jan Comm	Feb Comm	Mar Comm
5	Branston	3000	4800	3450
6	Barton	2250	4800	3583.5
7	Alexander	6750	1335	6450

You could unhide Columns B, D, and F with a single command by selecting Columns A–G and then issuing the Unhide command.

Hands-On 16.11 Hide and Unhide Rows and Columns

1. Follow these steps to hide Columns B, D, and F.

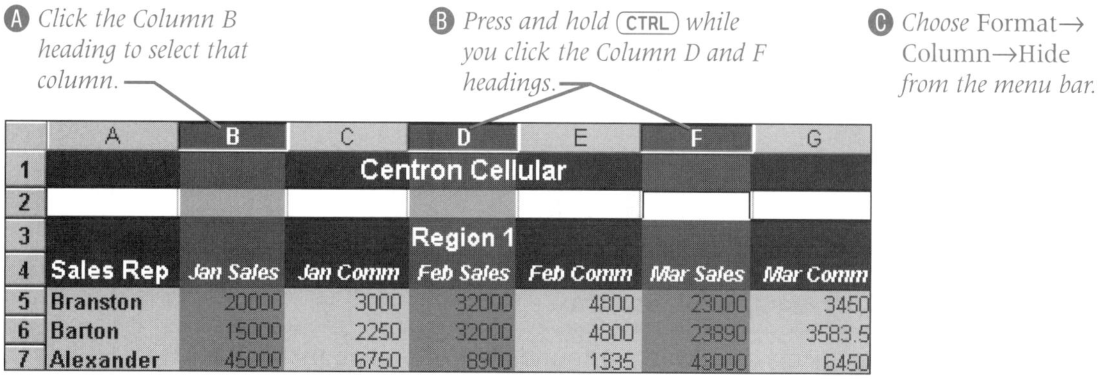

A Click the Column B heading to select that column.
B Press and hold CTRL while you click the Column D and F headings.
C Choose Format→Column→Hide from the menu bar.
A B C D E F G
Centron Cellular
Region 1
Sales Rep Jan Sales Jan Comm Feb Sales Feb Comm Mar Sales Mar Comm
Branston 20000 3000 32000 4800 23000 3450
Barton 15000 2250 32000 4800 23890 3583.5
Alexander 45000 6750 8900 1335 43000 6450

2. Follow these steps to unhide Columns B, D, and F.

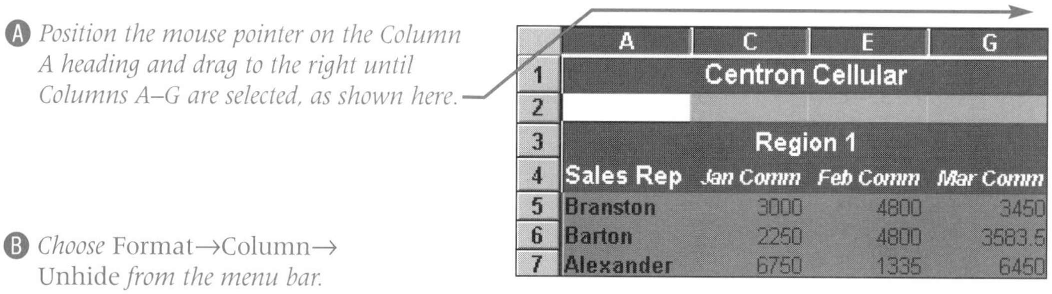

A Position the mouse pointer on the Column A heading and drag to the right until Columns A–G are selected, as shown here.
B Choose Format→Column→Unhide from the menu bar.
A C E G
Centron Cellular
Region 1
Sales Rep Jan Comm Feb Comm Mar Comm
Branston 3000 4800 3450
Barton 2250 4800 3583.5
Alexander 6750 1335 6450

3. Click Undo to hide the columns again.
   Imagine that you are only interested in the overall results of the Centron Cellular sales force—not the performance of the individual sales reps.
4. Select Rows 5–9 by dragging the mouse down over the row headings.
5. Choose **Format→Row→Hide** to hide the rows.
6. Hide the rows for the individual sales reps in Region 2.
7. Feel free to experiment with any of the topics you have learned in this lesson.
8. Save the workbook when you have finished experimenting, and then close the workbook.

Concepts Review

True/False Questions

1. The Office Assistant's speech balloon has a Search box that lets you search for Help topics. TRUE FALSE
2. AutoCorrect entries are expanded when (SPACE BAR) is tapped or when the entry is completed. TRUE FALSE
3. You must accept an AutoComplete entry that Excel proposes. TRUE FALSE
4. MIN and MAX are examples of functions. TRUE FALSE
5. A function's arguments are always surrounded by quotation marks " ". TRUE FALSE
6. You can paste a copied formula into multiple cells with one Paste command. TRUE FALSE
7. The maximum zoom percentage is 200%. TRUE FALSE
8. Values in hidden rows and columns cannot be referenced by formulas in visible rows and columns. TRUE FALSE

Multiple-Choice Questions

1. Which command displays the AutoCorrect dialog box?
   a. Format→AutoCorrect
   b. Tools→AutoCorrect
   c. Edit→AutoCorrect
   d. None of the above
2. Which command is used to display the AutoFormat dialog box?
   a. Tools→AutoFormat
   b. Format→AutoFormat
   c. Format→Cells
   d. None of the above
3. What is the maximum number of cut or copied items that can be placed on the Office Clipboard?
   a. 3
   b. 6
   c. 12
   d. 18
4. Which of the following methods of moving entries displays a pop-up menu when the mouse button is released?
   a. Cut and Paste
   b. Drag and Drop
   c. Right Drag and Drop
   d. All of these

Skill Builders

Skill Builder 16.1 Use Copy and Paste

1. Open the workbook named Skill Builder 16.1.
2. Select the range A1:E2.
3. Click the Copy button.
4. Click Cell A10, and click the Paste button.
5. Change the year 1999 in the pasted heading to 1998.
6. Select the city names and the Total and Average headings in the range A3:A8.
7. Click Copy, click Cell A12, and then click Paste.
8. Use AutoSum to compute the totals in Rows 7 and 16.
9. Click Cell B8, and enter the function **=AVERAGE(B3:B6)**.
10. Use Copy and Paste to copy the formula with the AVERAGE function across Rows 8 and 17.
    You can safely copy this formula to both Rows 8 and 17 because the range in the function includes four cells (B3:B6). The formulas in Rows 8 and 17 both require AVERAGE functions that average four cells.
11. Click Cell B20, and enter the formula **=B7-B16**.
12. Copy this formula across Row 20.
13. Enter a formula in Cell B21 that computes the difference between the averages for 1999 and 1998, and then copy the formula across Row 20.
    Your completed worksheet should match the following example.
14. Save the changes to the workbook, and then close the workbook.

	A	B	C	D	E
1	Quality Greeting Cards - 1999 Customer Complaints				
2		Christmas	Easter	Valentines	Thanksgiving
3	Boston	27	43	14	34
4	Los Angeles	31	47	19	39
5	New York	35	51	24	44
6	St. Louis	39	55	29	49
7	Total	132	196	86	166
8	Average	33	49	21.5	41.5
9					
10	Quality Greeting Cards - 1998 Customer Complaints				
11		Christmas	Easter	Valentines	Thanksgiving
12	Boston	19	31	16	24
13	Los Angeles	22	34	18	26
14	New York	25	37	20	28
15	St. Louis	28	40	22	30
16	Total	94	142	76	108
17	Average	23.5	35.5	19	27
18					
19	Differences Between 1999 and 1998				
20	Totals	38	54	10	58
21	Averages	9.5	13.5	2.5	14.5

Skill Builder 16.2 Use AutoFormat

In this exercise, you will open a workbook on your exercise diskette. You will use AutoFormat to apply an attractive format to the worksheet.

Use AutoFormat

1. Open the workbook named Skill Builder 16.2.
2. Select the range A1:E16, which includes all active cells in the worksheet.
3. Choose **Format→AutoFormat** from the menu bar.
4. Scroll through the list, choose the **List 2** style, and click **OK.**
5. Click outside the worksheet, and you will be able to see the format.
   The format looks good, although it may be nice to have a slightly larger title.
6. Click Cell A1, and increase the size to 12.
   You can always add your own formatting enhancements to a worksheet after AutoFormat has been used.
7. Save the changes to the workbook, and then close the workbook.

Skill Builder 16.3 Use Copy and Paste

1. Open the workbook named Skill Builder 16.3.
2. Select the range A3:E4, which includes all the text entries in Rows 3 and 4.
3. Click the Copy button.
4. Click Cell A10, and Paste the entries above the second set of numbers.
   Notice that the text formats (including the coloring) were copied with the text.
5. Click Cell A17 and Paste the entries above the third set of numbers.
6. Change the headings to **February** and **March** for the second and third sets of numbers.
7. Select the range A5:A8, which includes the names and Totals heading in Column A.
8. Copy the selection, and then Paste it to Cells A12 and A19.
9. Copy the formulas from the totals row below the first set of numbers, and Paste them below the second and third sets of numbers.
10. Save the changes to the workbook, and then close the workbook.

Assessments

Assessment 16.1

1. Use the following guidelines to create the worksheet shown below.

- The beginning balance, purchases, and payments numbers in the range B5:D9 should be typed into the cells. Don't type the numbers shown in Rows 10, 11, and 12 or Columns E and F. In a moment, you will be instructed to create those formulas.
- Use formulas to calculate the interest charge in Column E and the new balance in Column F. The formulas are as follows:

  Interest Charge = 1.5% * (Beginning Balance – Payments)

  New Balance = Beginning Balance + Purchases – Payments + Interest Charge

  Notice that you must use parentheses in the Interest Charge formula to change the order of calculations. You want Excel to subtract the payments from the beginning balance and then multiply the result by 1.5%. Also, don't type the words *Beginning Balance,* etc. in the formulas. You should use the appropriate cell references in the formulas.
- Format Rows 5, 10, 11, and 12 with the Currency formatting shown below.
- Format the title row and header rows as shown.
- Calculate the totals in Row 10.
- Use the MAX and MIN functions to calculate the highest and lowest numbers in Rows 11 and 12.
- Print the worksheet when you have finished.
- Save the workbook as **Assessment 16.1,** and then close the workbook.

	A	B	C	D	E	F
1	Bill's Hot Tubs - Accounts Receivable Report					
2						
3		**Beginning**			**Interest**	
4	**Customer**	**Balance**	**Purchases**	**Payments**	**Charge**	**New Balance**
5	Zelton	$2,000	$2,300	$1,000	$15	$3,315
6	Ranier	2450	1000	2450	0	1000
7	Worthington	5400	2190	3000	36	4626
8	Alonzo	3400	500	3400	0	500
9	Barton	100	3400	100	0	3400
10	***Totals***	***$13,350***	***$9,390***	***$9,950***	***$51***	***$12,841***
11	***Highest***	***$5,400***	***$3,400***	***$3,400***	***$36***	***$4,626***
12	***Lowest***	***$100***	***$500***	***$100***	***$0***	***$500***

Assessment 16.2

1. Use the following guidelines to create the worksheet shown below.

   - Enter all the numbers and text as shown. Use the Copy and Paste or Drag and Drop techniques to copy the text or numbers whenever possible. For example, all three of the Wilson family children were given the same allowances in all four years. Therefore, you can enter the data in Row 5 and then copy Row 5 to Rows 10 and 15.
   - Use Increase Indent to indent the allowance, saved, and interest earned entries in Column A, as shown.
   - Calculate the interest earned with the formula **Interest Earned = Saved * Interest Rate.** Use the interest rates shown in the following rate table. You will notice that the interest rates change from year to year.

1996	**1997**	**1998**	**1999**
3.5%	4.5%	6.5%	6.5%

   - Widen the columns as necessary, and format the worksheet with bold, italics, and the Currency format as shown.

2. Your completed worksheet should match the example shown below.

3. Print the workbook, save it as **Assessment 16.2,** and then close it.

	A	B	C	D	E	F
1	Wilson Family Allowances					
2						
3		1996	1997	1998	1999	Total Interest
4	Jason					
5	Allowance	260	300	300	340	
6	Saved	120	110	200	220	
7	***Interest Earned***	***$ 4.20***	***$ 4.95***	***$ 13.00***	***$ 14.30***	***$ 36.45***
8						
9	Cindy					
10	Allowance	260	300	300	340	
11	Saved	120	110	200	220	
12	***Interest Earned***	***$ 4.20***	***$ 4.95***	***$ 13.00***	***$ 14.30***	***$ 36.45***
13						
14	Betty					
15	Allowance	260	300	300	340	
16	Saved	130	290	280	310	
17	***Interest Earned***	***$ 4.55***	***$ 13.05***	***$ 18.20***	***$ 20.15***	***$ 55.95***
18						
19	**Total Family Interest 1996 - 1999**					**$ 128.85**

Assessment 16.3

1. Open the workbook named **Assessment 16.3.**
2. Use the **Classic 3** AutoFormat style to format the worksheet as shown below.
3. Print the workbook, save the changes, and then close the workbook.

	A	B	C	D	E	F	G
1	Diane's Café - Employee Hourly Time Log						
2							
3	Employee	*Wednesday*	*Thursday*	*Friday*	*Saturday*	*Sunday*	*Totals*
4	Mary Johnson	6.5		5	6.5	4	22
5	Cliff Packard	4	6	6.5	6.5	4	27
6	Helen Martinez	4	6	6.5	6.5		23
7	Sarah Stonestown		4	4	4		12
8	Totals	14.5	16	22	23.5	8	84

LESSON 17—Excel

Creating an Impact with Charts

In this lesson, you will use Excel's Chart Wizard to create various types of charts. Charting is an important skill to have when using worksheets because comparisons, trends, and other relationships are often conveyed more effectively with charts. You will use the Chart Wizard to create bar charts, column charts, line charts, and pie charts. In addition, you will learn how to edit and format chart objects.

In This Lesson

Case Study

Cynthia Robbins is the founder and CEO of AutoSoft—a rapidly growing software development company. Cynthia has asked her sales manager, Gary Roberts, to prepare several charts depicting revenue for the 1999 fiscal year. Cynthia wants charts that compare sales in the various quarters, the growth trend throughout the year, and the contributions of each sales rep to the total company sales. Gary uses Excel's Chart Wizard to produce impressive charts that meet Cynthia's high standards.

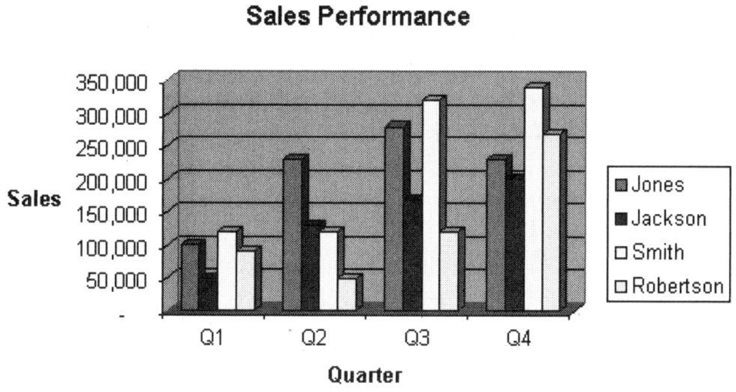
Sales Performance
350,000
300,000
250,000
200,000
150,000
100,000
50,000
-
Sales
Jones
Jackson
Smith
Robertson
Q1
Q2
Q3
Q4
Quarter

A column chart

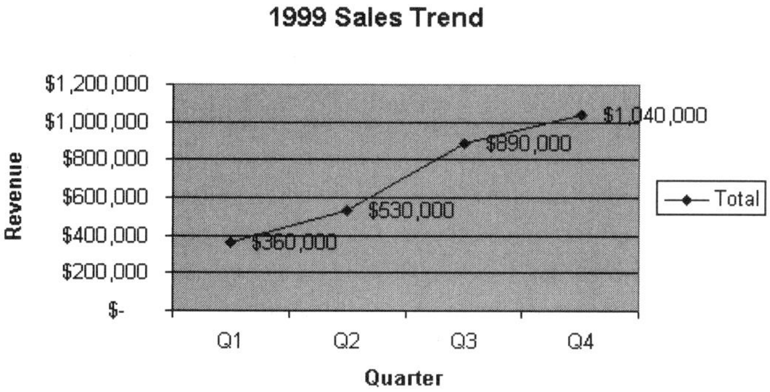
1999 Sales Trend
$1,200,000
$1,000,000
$800,000
$600,000
$400,000
$200,000
$-
Revenue
$360,000
$530,000
$890,000
$1,040,000
Total
Q1
Q2
Q3
Q4
Quarter

A line chart

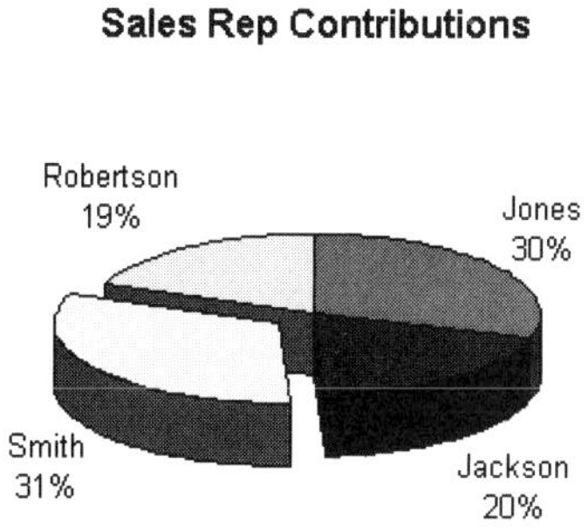
Sales Rep Contributions
Robertson
19%
Jones
30%
Smith
31%
Jackson
20%

A pie chart

Managing Worksheets

WARNING! *You cannot undo a deleted worksheet.*

Excel displays three worksheets in a new workbook. You can insert new worksheets up to a maximum of 255 sheets per workbook. Each worksheet is identified by a tab located at the bottom of the sheet. You can rename, insert, delete, move, and copy worksheets.

Quick Reference

MANAGING WORKSHEETS

Task	Procedure
Activate worksheet.	Click the desired worksheet tab.
Rename worksheet.	Double-click the worksheet tab, type a new name, and tap ENTER.
Insert worksheet.	Click anywhere in the desired worksheet and choose **Insert→Worksheet**. The new worksheet is inserted to the left of the current sheet.
Delete worksheet.	Click anywhere in the desired worksheet, choose **Edit→Delete Sheet,** and click **OK.**
Move worksheet.	Drag the worksheet tab to the desired position in the worksheet order.
Copy worksheet.	Choose **Edit→Move** or **Copy Sheet,** choose the desired position in the Before sheet box, click the **Create a copy box,** and click **OK.**

Hands-On 17.1 Experiment with Worksheets

1. Open the workbook named **Hands-On Lesson 17.**
2. Follow these steps to rename Sheet1.

TIP! *You can click anywhere in the worksheet to complete the name change.*

A *Double-click the* Sheet1 *tab at the bottom of the worksheet. The name* Sheet1 *will become selected.*

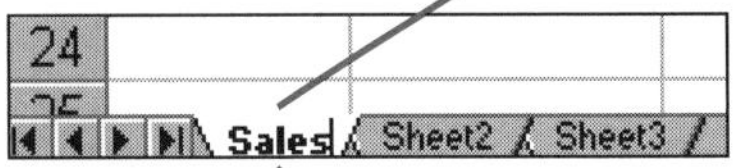

24
Sales
Sheet2
Sheet3

B *Type the name* **Sales** *as shown here.*

C *Tap* ENTER *to complete the name change.*

3. Follow these steps to move the sheet.

A *Position the mouse pointer on the* Sales *sheet tab.*

B *Drag the tab to the right of the* Sheet3 *tab, as shown here.*

C *Release the mouse button to complete the move.*

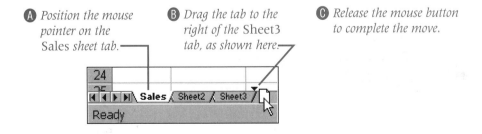

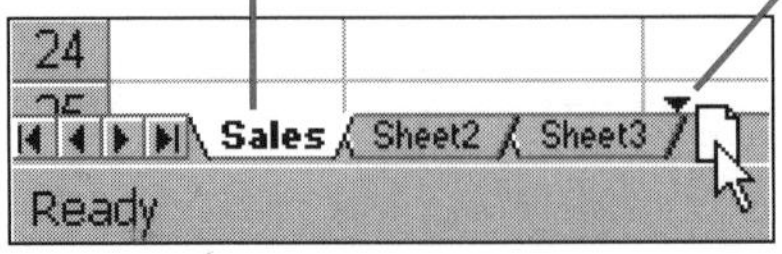

24
Sales
Sheet2
Sheet3
Ready

4. Now drag the Sales sheet back to the first position in the sheet order.
5. Click the Sheet3 tab and choose **Edit→Delete Sheet** from the menu bar.
6. Click **OK** to complete the deletion.
7. Try clicking Undo , and notice that the sheet cannot be restored.
   Worksheets are permanently deleted when you issue the ***Edit→Delete Sheet*** *command. The only way to recover a deleted sheet is to close the workbook without saving, and then reopen the workbook.*
8. Choose **Insert→Worksheet** from the menu bar.
   A new sheet will be inserted to the left of the current sheet.
9. Drag the new sheet to the right of Sheet2, and rename it Sheet3.
10. Click the **Sales** sheet tab, and continue with the next topic.

Chart Concepts

It is often easier to interpret numerical data if it is presented in a chart. Excel lets you create and modify a variety of charts. Excel provides 14 major chart types. Each chart type also has several subtypes from which you can choose. Excel literally has a chart for every occasion.

Chart Placement

You can embed a chart in a worksheet so that it appears alongside the worksheet data. You can also place a chart on a separate worksheet. This prevents the chart from cluttering the worksheet containing the data. Regardless of their placement, charts are always linked to the data from which they were created. Charts are automatically updated when worksheet data changes.

Chart Types

Each chart type represents data in a different manner. You can present the same data in completely different ways by changing the chart type. For this reason, you should always use the chart type that most effectively represents your data.

User-Defined Charts

Excel lets you create and save customized charts to meet your particular needs. For example, you could create a customized chart containing the name of your company and your company color(s) in the background. You could save the chart and then use it as the basis for all new charts of that type.

Creating Charts with the Chart Wizard

Excel's Chart Wizard  guides you through each step of chart creation. You can also edit and enhance a chart after it has been created. The first, and arguably the most important step in creating a chart, is to sclect the data you want included in the chart. Many beginners find this step to be the most difficult because they are unsure how Excel will interpret the selected data. You will receive plenty of practice selecting data in this lesson.

Column Charts and Bar Charts

Column charts compare values (numbers) using vertical bars. Bar charts compare values using horizontal bars. Each column or bar represents a value from the worksheet. Column charts and bar charts are most useful for comparing sets of values.

Category Axis and Value Axis

The horizontal line that forms the base of a column chart or bar chart is called the *category axis*. The category axis typically measures units of time such as days, months, or quarters. The vertical line on the left side of a column chart or bar chart is known as the *value axis*. The value axis typically measures values such as dollars. Most chart types (including column charts and bar charts) have a category and value axis. The following illustrations show the column chart you will create in the next few exercises. The illustrations show the objects that are present on most column charts and the corresponding data that was used to create the chart. Take a few minutes to study these illustrations carefully.

The chart below was created using the selected data shown here. Notice the Total *row was not included in the selection. The column chart compares the sales numbers for the individual quarters, but it does not include the total sales from Row 9.*

	A	B	C	D	E
1	Autosoft 1999 Quarterly Sales				
2					
3		Q1	Q2	Q3	Q4
4	Jones	100,000	230,000	280,000	230,000
5	Jackson	50,000	130,000	170,000	200,000
6	Smith	120,000	120,000	320,000	340,000
7	Robertson	90,000	50,000	120,000	270,000
8					
9	Total	$ 360,000	$ 530,000	$ 890,000	$ 1,040,000

This is the vertical value axis. The numbering scale (0–350,000) was created by Excel after it determined the range of values that were included in the chart.

*Notice the chart includes a chart title (*Sales Performance*), a value axis title (*Sales*), and a category axis title (*Quarter*). The Chart Wizard lets you specify the titles when you create the chart.*

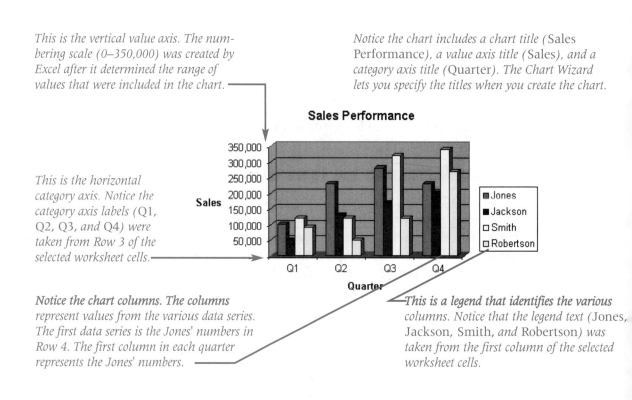

*This is the horizontal category axis. Notice the category axis labels (*Q1, Q2, Q3, *and* Q4*) were taken from Row 3 of the selected worksheet cells.*

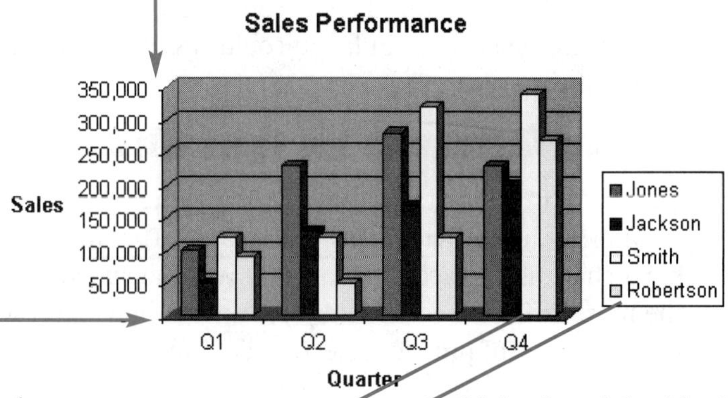

Sales Performance
350,000
300,000
250,000
200,000
150,000
100,000
50,000
Sales
Q1
Q2
Q3
Q4
Quarter
Jones
Jackson
Smith
Robertson

Notice the chart columns. The columns represent values from the various data series. The first data series is the Jones' numbers in Row 4. The first column in each quarter represents the Jones' numbers.

*This is a legend that identifies the various columns. Notice that the legend text (*Jones, Jackson, Smith, *and* Robertson*) was taken from the first column of the selected worksheet cells.*

Hands-On 17.2 Create Two Charts

The Hands-On Lesson 17 workbook should still be open from the previous exercise.

Create a Column Chart on a Separate Chart Sheet

1. Select the range **A3:E7** as shown on the previous page.
2. Click the **Chart Wizard** button on the Standard toolbar.
   The Chart Wizard dialog box will appear.
3. Follow these steps to explore the dialog box.

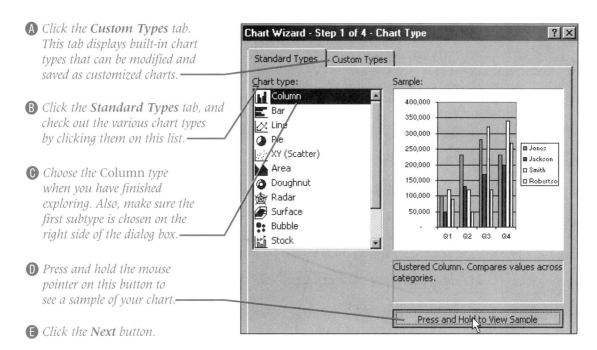

Ⓐ *Click the **Custom Types** tab. This tab displays built-in chart types that can be modified and saved as customized charts.*

Ⓑ *Click the **Standard Types** tab, and check out the various chart types by clicking them on this list.*

Ⓒ *Choose the* Column *type when you have finished exploring. Also, make sure the first subtype is chosen on the right side of the dialog box.*

Ⓓ *Press and hold the mouse pointer on this button to see a sample of your chart.*

Ⓔ *Click the **Next** button.*

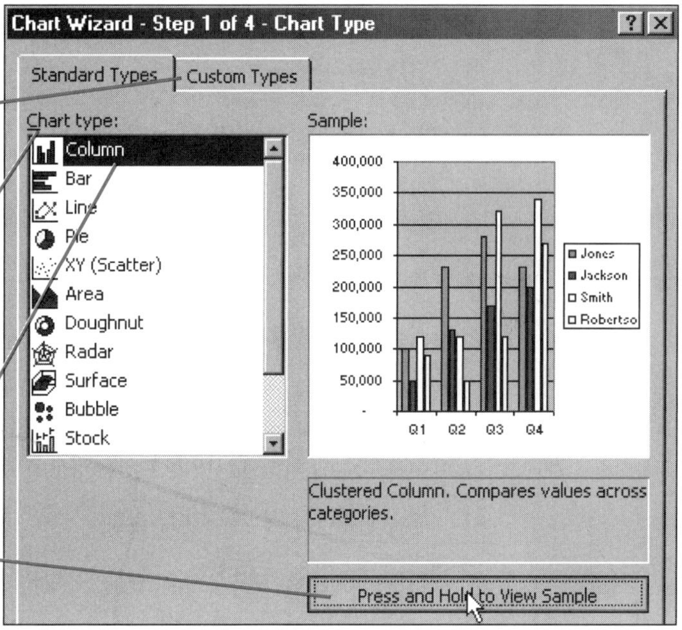

Chart Wizard - Step 1 of 4 - Chart Type
Standard Types
Custom Types
Chart type:
Column
Bar
Line
Pie
XY (Scatter)
Area
Doughnut
Radar
Surface
Bubble
Stock
Sample:
400,000
350,000
300,000
250,000
200,000
150,000
100,000
50,000
-
Q1
Q2
Q3
Q4
Jones
Jackson
Smith
Robertso
Clustered Column. Compares values across categories.
Press and Hold to View Sample

The Chart Wizard—Step 2 of 4 *box will appear. This box lets you choose a different range of cells. Notice that the range in the dialog box is =Sales!$A$3:$E$7. Sales is the worksheet name, and the dollar signs indicate that these are absolute cell references. For now, just ignore the dollar signs, and think of the range as A3:E7.*

4. The range Sales!$A$3:$E$7 is correct, so click the **Next** button.
   The Step 3 box contains 6 tabs that let you set various chart options. You will explore these options in the next few steps.
5. Click the **Titles** tab and note the three available titles.
   You will add titles to a chart in the next exercise.
6. Click the **Axes** tab.
   The options on the Axes tab let you hide the labels on the category axis and value axis. You will almost always want to leave these options set to the default settings.
7. Click the **Gridlines** tab.
   Gridlines help identify the values in the chart. Your chart should have major gridlines for the value axis displayed. The gridlines are the horizontal lines across the chart.
8. Feel free to click the various gridlines boxes and notice how they appear in the Preview window.

9. Click the **Legend** tab.
   Notice the legend on the right side of the Preview window. The legend identifies the various columns. For example, the columns for Jones are identified by a color that also appears in the legend.
10. Remove the check from the Show legend box, and the legend will vanish.
11. Click the **Show legend** box to redisplay the legend.
12. Click the **Data Labels** tab.
    Data labels display the values from the worksheet on top of the columns.
13. Click the **Show value** option to display values at the top of each column.
    The numbers will be very crowded in the Preview window.
14. Click the **Show Label** option, and then click the **None** option to remove the data labels.
15. Click the **Data Table** tab.
16. Click the **Show data table** check box, and a table will appear below the Preview chart.
17. Take a moment to check out the data table, then remove the check from the Show data table box.
18. Click the **Next** button, and the Step 4 of 4 box will appear.
19. Click the **As new sheet** option.
    This option instructs Excel to create the chart on a separate chart sheet.
20. Click the **Finish** button.
    Look at the sheet tabs, and notice that the chart has been created on a new sheet named Chart1.
21. Double-click the **Chart1** sheet tab.
22. Type the new name `Column Chart`, and tap (ENTER) to complete the name change.

Create an Embedded 3-D Column Chart

23. Click the **Sales** sheet tab. The range A3:E7 should still be selected.
24. Click the **Chart Wizard**  button.
25. Choose the fourth column chart subtype, as shown to the right.
    This subtype is known as a clustered column with a 3-D visual effect.

26. Click the **Next** button, then click **Next** again on the Step 2 of 4 box.

27. Click the **Titles** tab, and follow these steps in the Step 3 of 4 box.

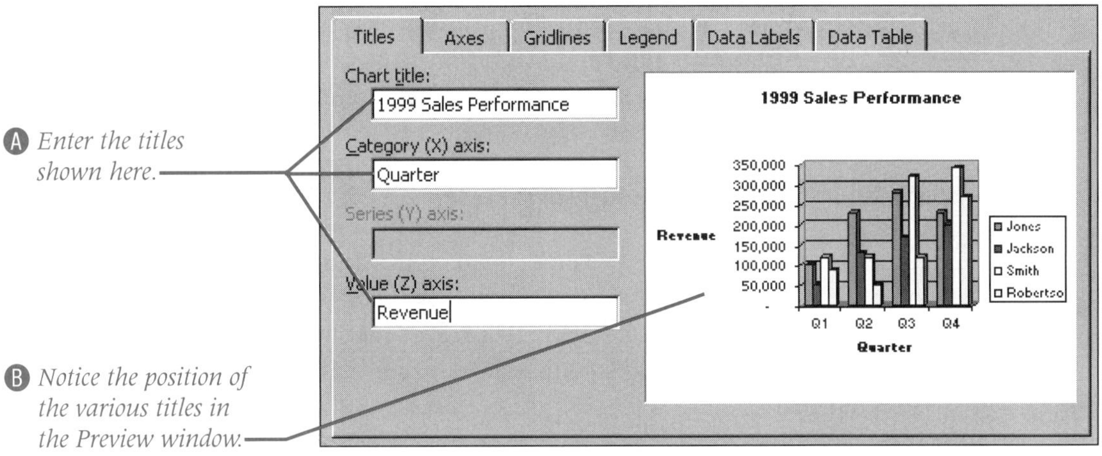
A Enter the titles shown here.
B Notice the position of the various titles in the Preview window.
Titles
Axes
Gridlines
Legend
Data Labels
Data Table
Chart title:
1999 Sales Performance
Category (X) axis:
Quarter
Series (Y) axis:
Value (Z) axis:
Revenue
1999 Sales Performance
Revenue
350,000
300,000
250,000
200,000
150,000
100,000
50,000
Q1
Q2
Q3
Q4
Quarter
Jones
Jackson
Smith
Robertso

28. Click the **Next** button.

29. Leave the chart location set to **As object in** on the Step 4 of 4 box and click **Finish.**
Excel will embed the chart in your worksheet. The Chart toolbar will most likely appear as well.

Previewing and Printing Charts

You can use the Print Preview and Print buttons to preview or print charts. If a chart is on a separate chart sheet, you must first activate it by clicking the sheet tab. If a chart is embedded, you must first select the chart before clicking the Print Preview or Print buttons.

Hands-On 17.3 Use Print Preview and Print a Chart

1. Click anywhere in the worksheet to deselect the chart.
2. Click the Print Preview button.
Notice that both the worksheet and part or all of the embedded chart are displayed.
3. Click the **Close** button on the Print Preview toolbar.
4. Click in the blank area near one of the corners of the chart.
Black squares known as sizing handles should appear on the corners and edges of the chart. Sizing handles indicate that the chart or one of the chart objects is selected.
5. Click the Print Preview button, and only the chart should be displayed.
At this point, you could print the chart by using the Print button on the Print Preview toolbar. However, you will close the chart and then print it on the separate chart sheet.
6. Click the **Close** button on the Print Preview toolbar.
7. Click the **Column Chart** worksheet tab to activate that worksheet.
8. Click the Print Preview button, and notice that the chart is displayed.
You don't need to select a chart prior to printing if it is on a separate chart sheet.

(Continued on the next page)

9. Close the **Print Preview** window, and then click the Print button.

10. Retrieve your printout from the printer.
Your chart will be printed in shades of gray unless you have a color printer.

Moving and Sizing Embedded Charts

You can easily move and size embedded charts and other objects. You must select a chart or other object before you can move, size, or modify the object. To select a chart, you click anywhere in the Chart Area. The Chart Area is the blank area just inside the border of the chart where no other objects are present. Small squares called sizing handles appear on the corners and four sides of a selected chart.

Task	Procedure
Move an embedded chart.	Drag the selected chart to a new location.
Change the chart size.	Drag any sizing handle.
Change the size while maintaining original proportions.	Press (SHIFT) while dragging a corner-sizing handle.

Hands-On 17.4 Move and Size the Embedded Chart

1. Click the **Sales** worksheet tab to activate that worksheet.
2. Click anywhere outside of the chart to deselect the chart.
The sizing handles will vanish.
3. Use the Zoom Control to zoom to 50% of normal.
This will give you plenty of room to move and size the chart.
4. Follow these steps to move and size the chart.

Ⓐ *Click in the Chart Area (the blank area inside of the chart border), and the sizing handles will reappear.*

Ⓑ *Position the mouse pointer in the Chart Area, and drag the chart to a new location.*

Ⓒ *Point to a corner-sizing-handle, and the Adjust pointer will appear.*

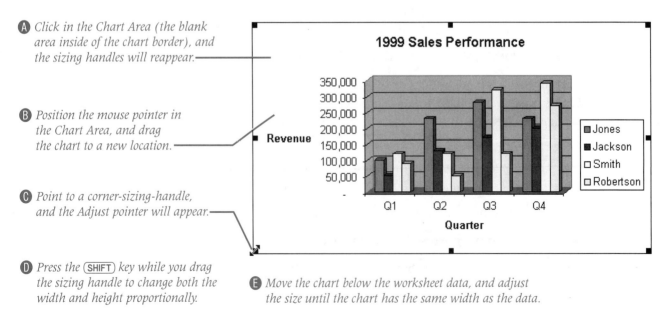

Ⓓ *Press the (SHIFT) key while you drag the sizing handle to change both the width and height proportionally.*

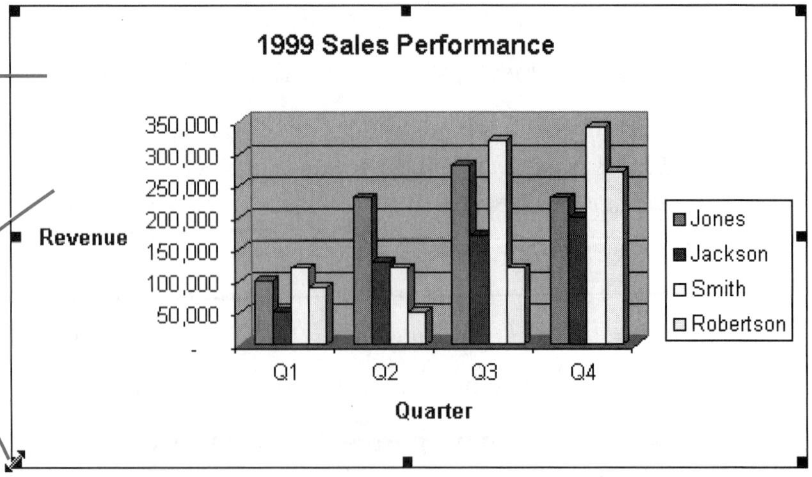
1999 Sales Performance
Revenue
350,000
300,000
250,000
200,000
150,000
100,000
50,000
-
Q1
Q2
Q3
Q4
Quarter
Jones
Jackson
Smith
Robertson

Ⓔ *Move the chart below the worksheet data, and adjust the size until the chart has the same width as the data.*

5. Click anywhere outside of the chart to deselect it, then zoom to 100%.
6. Take a moment to study your chart and the worksheet data that was used to create it.
   Make sure you understand the relationship between the columns and the worksheet data.
7. Click Cell **B4.**
8. Enter the number **300000** (five zeros) and watch the first column in the chart rise.
   Charts are linked to the worksheet data. They always reflect changes in the data even if they are placed in a separate chart sheet.
9. Click Cell **B4** again, and enter the number **1000000** (six zeros).
   Notice that 1000000 is much larger than the other numbers in the worksheet. Notice how the other columns are very small, and it is difficult to determine their values in the chart. The large number changes the scale of the value axis so much that it makes the chart difficult to interpret.
10. Click Cell **B4** again, and enter the number **100000** (five zeros).
11. Save the changes, and continue with the next topic.

Line Charts

Line charts are most useful for comparing trends over a period of time. For example, line charts are often used to show stock market activity where the upward or downward trend is important. Like column charts, line charts also have a category axis and value axis. Line charts also use the same or similar objects as column charts. The illustration below shows a line chart depicting the trend in quarterly sales throughout the year. Take a moment to study the illustration and the accompanying worksheet.

The chart below was created using the selected data shown here. Notice that the data is in two separate ranges. You will use the CTRL *key to select these non-contiguous ranges. This will let you chart just the totals for each quarter, and the Q1–Q4 labels.*

3		Q1	Q2	Q3	Q4
4	Jones	100,000	230,000	280,000	230,000
5	Jackson	50,000	130,000	170,000	200,000
6	Smith	120,000	120,000	320,000	340,000
7	Robertson	90,000	50,000	120,000	270,000
8					
9	Total	$ 360,000	$ 530,000	$ 890,000	$ 1,040,000

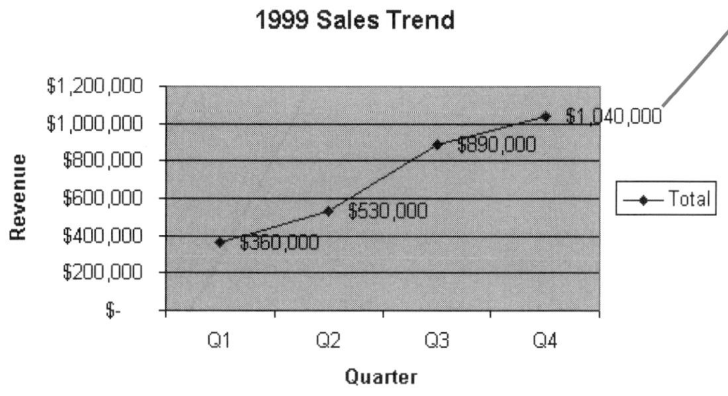
1999 Sales Trend
$1,200,000
$1,000,000
$800,000
$600,000
$400,000
$200,000
$-
Revenue
$1,040,000
$890,000
$530,000
$360,000
Total
Q1
Q2
Q3
Q4
Quarter

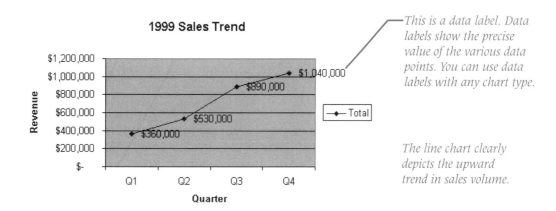

This is a data label. Data labels show the precise value of the various data points. You can use data labels with any chart type.

The line chart clearly depicts the upward trend in sales volume.

Hands-On 17.5 Create a Line Chart

In this exercise, you will create a line chart in the Sales sheet. When you are finished, the Sales sheet will contain the data and both the column and line charts.

Shrink and Move the Column Chart

1. Click in the chart area of the column chart, and sizing handles will appear on the chart border.
2. Press the SHIFT key while dragging a corner-sizing handle until the chart is very small (approximately 1″ high).
   Pressing SHIFT while sizing the chart maintains the proportions. You will increase the size of the chart later in this exercise.
3. Position the mouse pointer in the chart area, and drag the chart to the top-right corner of the screen (just to the right of the worksheet data).
4. Click outside the chart to deselect it.

Create the Line Chart

5. Follow these steps to select the data for the line chart.

3		Q1	Q2	Q3	Q4
4	Jones	100,000	230,000	280,000	230,000
5	Jackson	50,000	130,000	170,000	200,000
6	Smith	120,000	120,000	320,000	340,000
7	Robertson	90,000	50,000	120,000	270,000
8					
9	Total	$ 360,000	$ 530,000	$ 890,000	$ 1,040,000

Ⓐ *Select the range A3:E3.*

Ⓑ *Press the CTRL key while you select the range A9:E9. Both ranges should be selected.*

6. Click the Chart Wizard button.
7. Choose Line from the Chart type list, and choose the fourth subtype, as shown to the right.

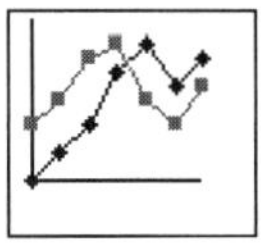

8. Click **Next** twice to display the Step 3 of 4 box.
9. If necessary, click the **Titles** tab on the Step 3 of 4 box.

10. Enter the titles in the Step 3 of 4 box as shown below.
When you have completed entering the titles, your sample chart should match the chart shown in the following illustration.

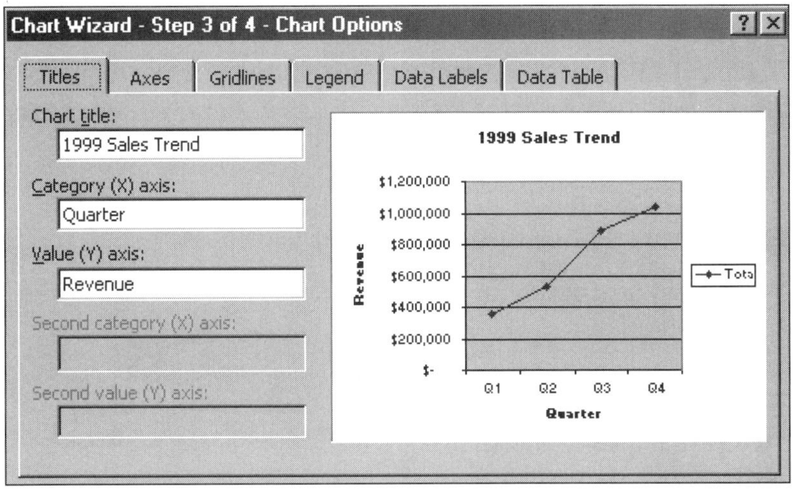

Chart Wizard - Step 3 of 4 - Chart Options
Titles
Axes
Gridlines
Legend
Data Labels
Data Table
Chart title:
1999 Sales Trend
Category (X) axis:
Quarter
Value (Y) axis:
Revenue
Second category (X) axis:
Second value (Y) axis:
1999 Sales Trend
$1,200,000
$1,000,000
$800,000
$600,000
$400,000
$200,000
$-
Revenue
Q1
Q2
Q3
Q4
Quarter
Tota

11. Click the **Finish** button.
There was no need to click Next on the Step 4 of 4 box because we want the chart embedded in the current worksheet. You can click Finish at any step in the Chart Wizard.

12. Take a few moments to examine your chart. In particular, notice the relationship between the data and the points on the line.

Pie Charts

Pie charts are useful for comparing parts of a whole. For example, pie charts are often used in budgets to show how the budget is allocated. You typically select two sets of data when creating a pie chart. You select the values to be represented by the pie slices and labels to identify the slices. The following illustration shows a worksheet and accompanying 3-D pie chart. Notice that the worksheet has a total column. You will create the total column in the next exercise.

3		Q1	Q2	Q3	Q4	Total
4	Jones	100,000	230,000	280,000	230,000	840,000
5	Jackson	50,000	130,000	170,000	200,000	550,000
6	Smith	120,000	120,000	320,000	340,000	900,000
7	Robertson	90,000	50,000	120,000	270,000	530,000

The names in Column A will become labels on the pie slices. The numbers in Column F will determine the size of the slices.

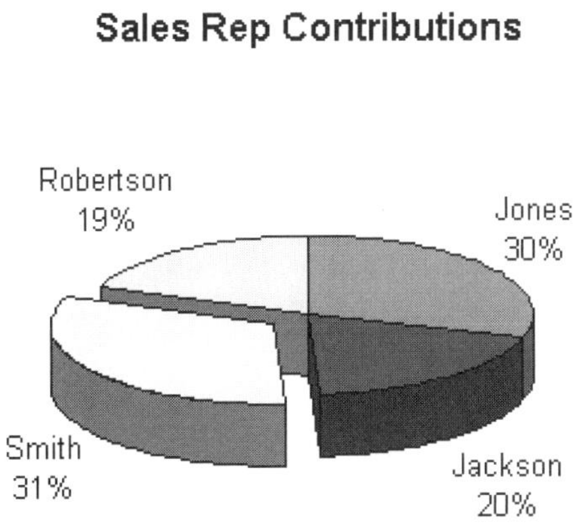

Sales Rep Contributions
Robertson
19%
Jones
30%
Smith
31%
Jackson
20%

Excel calculates the percentages based upon the numbers you select. Notice that the Smith slice is "exploded" out from the pie.

Hands-On 17.6 Create a Pie Chart on a Separate Chart Sheet

1. Click Cell **F3,** and enter the word **`Total`** (you may need to move the column chart or line chart).
2. Select the range F4:F7, and use **AutoSum** Σ to compute the totals for Column F.
   The totals calculate the total annual sales for each sales rep. Your totals should match those shown in the preceding illustration.
3. Select the ranges A4:A7 and F4:F7 as shown in the preceding illustration (you will need to use the CTRL key when selecting the second range).
4. Click the **Chart Wizard** button.
5. Choose Pie from the Chart type list, and choose the second subtype as shown to the right.

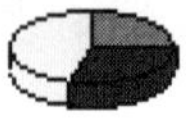

6. Click **Next** twice to display the Step 3 of 4 box.
7. If necessary, click the **Titles** tab on the Step 3 of 4 box.
8. Type **`Sales Rep Contributions`** as the Chart title.
9. Click the **Legend** tab, and remove the check from the Show legend box.
   The legend won't be needed because you will add data labels in the next step.
10. Click the **Data Labels** tab, and choose the **Show label and percent** option.
    Each pie slice should have the sales rep name and percentage of the total sales displayed.
11. Click **Next** to display the Step 4 of 4 box.
12. Choose the **As new sheet** option, and type the name **`Pie Chart`** in the As new sheet box.
13. Click the **Finish** button.
    Notice that the chart has been created on a separate sheet, and that the name Pie Chart has been assigned to the new sheet. The sheet was named Pie Chart because you typed this name in the As new sheet box in Step 12.
14. Save the changes to your workbook, and continue with the next topic.

Modifying Charts

You can modify any chart object after the chart has been created. For example, you can add or remove objects, such as legends or data labels. You can change the size, font, and color of titles. You can even move an embedded chart to a separate chart sheet and vice versa.

Using the Chart Wizard to Modify Charts

You can change the setup of a chart using the Chart Wizard. Simply click the desired embedded chart, or click a separate chart sheet, and then click the Chart Wizard button. You can move through all four screens in the Chart Wizard, choosing options as you do when a chart is first created.

The Chart Menu

When you activate a separate chart sheet or click an embedded chart, a Chart option appears on the menu bar. The first four options on the Chart menu display the same screens that appear in the Chart Wizard. You can add, remove, or modify chart objects using the desired screen(s) and change the chart location from embedded to separate sheet and vice versa. The 3-D View option on the Chart menu is useful for changing the elevation and rotation of pie charts.

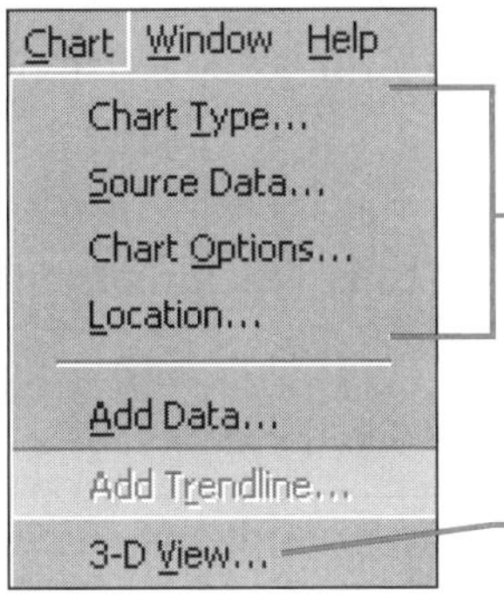

Chart Window Help
Chart Type...
Source Data...
Chart Options...
Location...
Add Data...
Add Trendline...
3-D View...

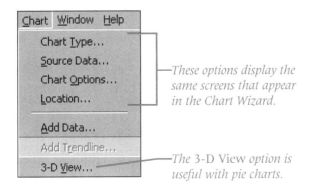

These options display the same screens that appear in the Chart Wizard.

The 3-D View option is useful with pie charts.

Hands-On 17.7 Use the Chart Wizard and the Chart Menu

Move the Line Chart to a Separate Sheet

1. Click the **Sales** sheet tab.
2. Click in the chart area of the line chart, and sizing handles should appear on the chart borders.
   Notice that the Chart option now appears on the menu bar because a chart is selected.
3. Choose **Chart→Location** from the menu bar.
   Notice that the dialog box that appears is the same dialog box that appears in the fourth step of the Chart Wizard.
4. Choose the **As new sheet** option, and type **`Line Chart`** in the As new sheet box.
5. Click **OK** to move the chart to a separate chart sheet.
   Notice that the Chart option is available on the menu bar even though the chart is not selected. The Chart option is always available in chart sheets.
6. Choose **Chart→Location** from the menu bar.
7. Choose the **As object in** option and choose **Sales** from the drop-down list of sheet names.
8. Click **OK** to move the chart back into the Sales sheet as an embedded chart.
9. Now move the chart back to a separate chart sheet named Line Chart as you did in steps 2 through 5.

Add Data Labels to the Column Chart

10. Click the **Sales** sheet tab.
11. Click in the chart area of the column chart to select the chart.
12. Now drag the chart below the worksheet data.

(Continued on the next page)

13. Press the (SHIFT) key while dragging a corner-sizing handle until the chart is as wide as the worksheet data. If necessary, adjust the chart position until it is just below the data.
14. Click the Chart Wizard button.
15. Click **Next** twice, and then click the **Data Labels** tab.
    Notice that the same screens appear as when you created a new chart.
16. Choose the **Show value** option, and click the **Finish** button.
    Excel displays data labels at the top of each column. The data labels display the actual values from the worksheet. Notice, however, that the data labels are too crowded. Data labels aren't really appropriate in this column chart because they crowd the chart.
17. Make sure the chart is still selected, and choose **Chart→Chart Options** from the menu bar.
    Notice that this is the same screen that appears in Step 3 of the Chart Wizard.
18. Choose **None** on the Data Labels tab, and click **OK** to remove the data labels.
19. Feel free to experiment with the Chart menu and the Chart Wizard, and then continue with the next topic.

Chart Objects

Charts are composed of various objects. For example, the legends, titles, and columns are all types of objects. You must select an object before you can perform an action on that object. You can select an object by clicking it with the mouse. Once an object is selected, you can delete, move, size, and format the object. You delete a selected object by tapping the (DELETE) key. You move a selected object by dragging it with the mouse. You change the size of a selected object by dragging a sizing handle.

Formatting Chart Objects

You can use buttons on the Formatting toolbar to format titles and other objects containing text. You can also use the Fill Color button on the Formatting toolbar to apply fill colors and fill effects to selected objects.

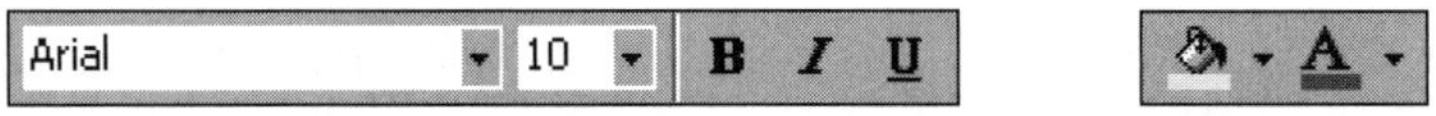
Arial
10
B I U
A

These buttons on the Formatting toolbar can be used to format text objects and add fill colors to objects.

Hands-On 17.8 Format Titles, and Fill the Chart Area

Change Text in the Titles

1. Click the chart title in the column chart, and it will become selected.
2. Click the mouse pointer just in front of the word Performance in the title.
   The flashing insertion point should be just in front of the word Performance.
3. Type the word **Rep** and tap the (SPACE BAR) to make the title "1999 Sales Rep Performance."
4. Click the "Revenue" title (the title on the left side of the chart), and it will become selected.

5. Now select the word **Revenue** within the title box by double-clicking the word.
6. Type the replacement word **`Sales`**.

Format the Titles

7. Click the **Chart Title** ("1999 Sales Rep Performance").
8. Click the Font Color  drop-down button on the Formatting toolbar, and choose a blue color.
9. Format the "Sales" and "Quarter" titles with the same blue color.

Apply a Fill Color to the Chart Area

10. Click the chart area to select the entire chart.
11. Click the Fill Color  drop-down button on the Formatting toolbar, and choose a light fill color.
    The entire chart area should be filled.
12. Feel free to experiment with the formatting techniques discussed in this exercise.

The Chart Toolbar

The Chart toolbar appears when a chart sheet is active, or when an embedded chart is selected. The Chart toolbar is used primarily for formatting chart objects. You can use the **View→Toolbars→Chart** command to display the Chart toolbar if it does not automatically appear.

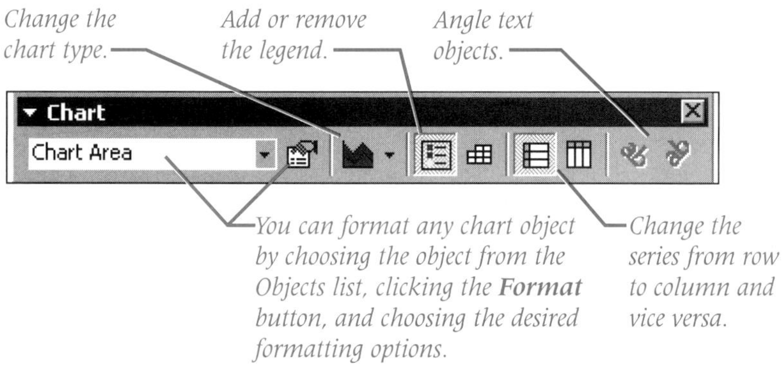
Change the chart type.
Add or remove the legend.
Angle text objects.
Chart
Chart Area
You can format any chart object by choosing the object from the Objects list, clicking the Format button, and choosing the desired formatting options.
Change the series from row to column and vice versa.

Hands-On 17.9 Use the Chart Toolbar

Change the Orientation of the Sales Title

1. Choose **View→Toolbars** from the menu bar.
2. If the Chart option is already checked, close the menu by clicking in the worksheet. Otherwise, choose Chart and the Chart toolbar will appear.
   The Chart toolbar may be anchored above the worksheet, or it may float in the worksheet area.
3. Click the "Sales" title on the left side of the chart.
   All of the buttons on the Chart toolbar should now be available.

(Continued on the next page)

4. Follow these steps to display a formatting box for the title.

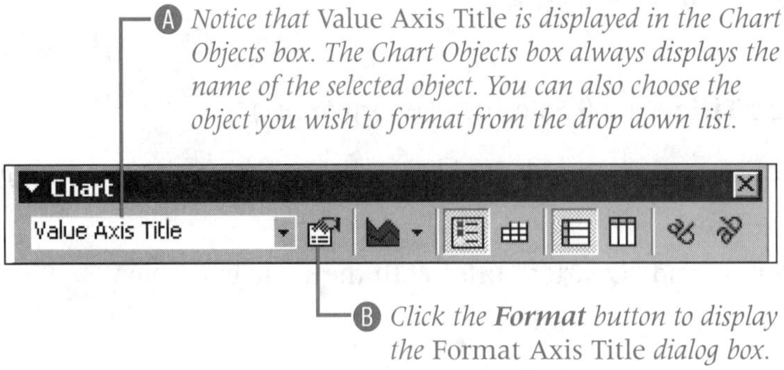
A Notice that Value Axis Title is displayed in the Chart Objects box. The Chart Objects box always displays the name of the selected object. You can also choose the object you wish to format from the drop down list.
Chart
Value Axis Title
B Click the **Format** button to display the Format Axis Title dialog box.

5. Click the various dialog box tabs, and notice that you can format the title text, apply a font color, and set other formatting options.

6. Click the **Alignment** tab.

7. Follow these steps to change the orientation to vertical.

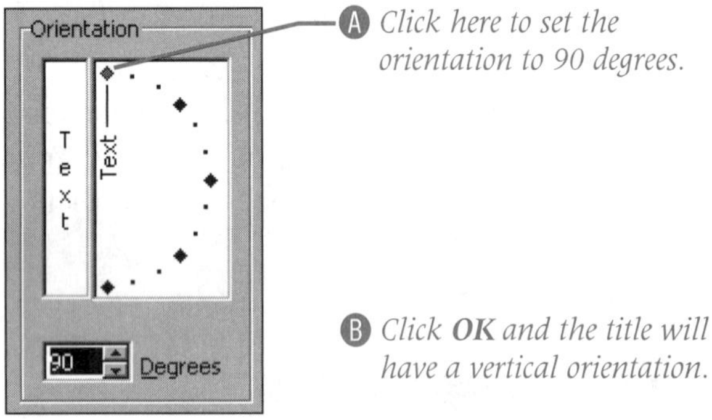
Orientation
Text
Text
90
Degrees
A Click here to set the orientation to 90 degrees.
B Click **OK** and the title will have a vertical orientation.

Experiment with the Chart Toolbar

8. Click in the chart area to select the entire chart.

9. Follow these steps to explore the Chart toolbar.

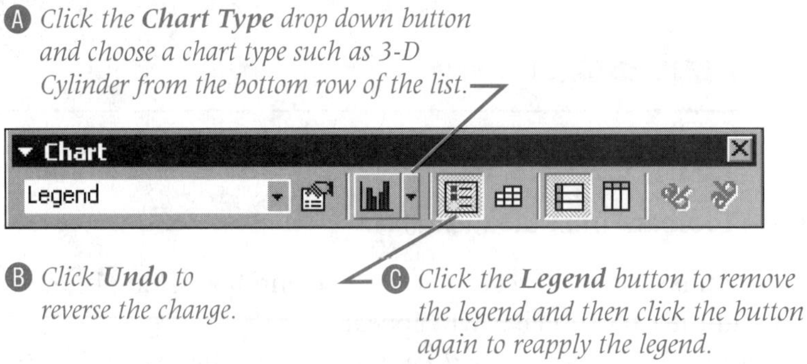
A Click the **Chart Type** drop down button and choose a chart type such as 3-D Cylinder from the bottom row of the list.
Chart
Legend
B Click **Undo** to reverse the change.
C Click the **Legend** button to remove the legend and then click the button again to reapply the legend.

10. Feel free to experiment with the options on the Chart toolbar.

Exploding Pie Slices

You can make a pie slice stand out from the rest of a pie chart by *exploding* the slice. An exploded slice is pulled out from the rest of the pie. You can also explode all pie slices, thus breaking the pie into individual pieces.

Quick Reference

EXPLODING PIE CHARTS	
Explode one slice.	■ Click once to select the entire pie. ■ Click the slice you wish to explode. ■ Drag the slice out from the pie.
Explode all slices.	■ Click once to select the pie. ■ Drag any slice (without clicking first), and all slices will separate.
Restore an exploded slice or an exploded pie.	■ Select the entire pie, and drag any exploded slice back into the pie.

Hands-On 17.10 Explode Pie Slices

Explode the Smith Slice

1. Click the **Pie Chart** worksheet tab to activate the sheet.
2. Click in the chart area to make sure the pie is not selected.
3. Click anywhere on the pie, and the entire pie will become selected.
4. Now click once on the Smith slice to select just that slice.
5. Follow this step to explode the Smith slice.

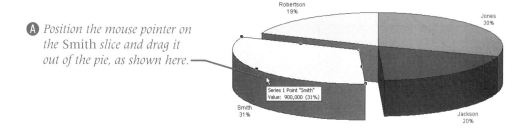

Ⓐ *Position the mouse pointer on the* Smith *slice and drag it out of the pie, as shown here.*

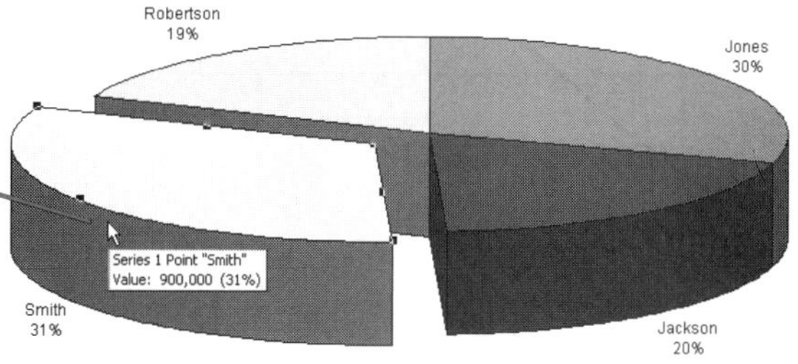
Robertson
19%
Jones
30%
Series 1 Point "Smith"
Value: 900,000 (31%)
Smith
31%
Jackson
20%

Explode All Slices

6. Drag the Smith slice back until the pie is whole again.
7. Click outside of the pie to deselect it.
8. Click anywhere on the pie, and the entire pie will become selected.
9. Drag any slice out of the pie, and all of the slices will explode.
10. Reverse the explosion by dragging any slice back to the center of the pie.
11. Now explode just the Smith slice again.

Changing the Rotation and Elevation of Pie Charts

You can rotate a pie chart to bring an important slice into view. Likewise, you can change the elevation to make an important slice more noticeable. You change the rotation and elevation using options on the 3-D View dialog box. The 3-D View dialog box is displayed with the **Chart→3-D View** command.

Hands-On 17.11 Change the Rotation and Elevation

1. Click outside of the pie, and then click the pie to make sure the entire pie is selected.
2. Choose **Chart→3-D View** from the menu bar.
3. Follow these steps to adjust the rotation and elevation.

*Ⓐ Click this button until the elevation is set to 25 in the **Elevation** box.*

*Ⓑ Click this button until the rotation is set to 320 in the **Rotation** box.*

*Ⓒ Click **OK**, and notice how the rotation and elevation change the view.*

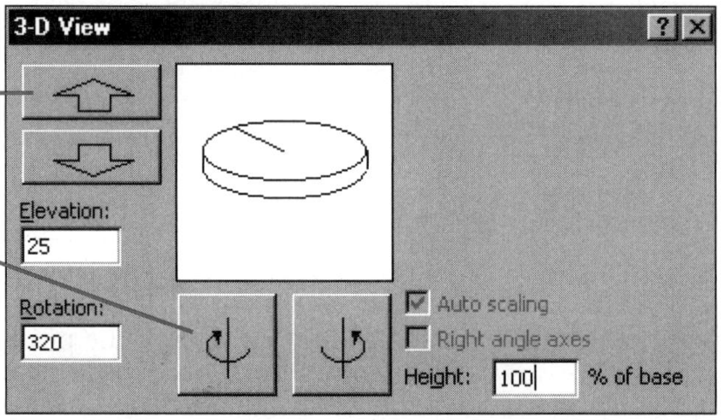
3-D View
Elevation:
25
Rotation:
320
Auto scaling
Right angle axes
Height:
100
% of base

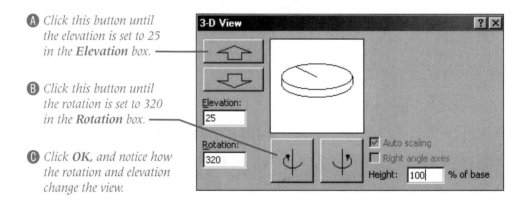

4. Feel free to experiment with any of the topics you have learned in this lesson.
5. Save your workbook when you have finished, close the workbook, and continue with the end-of-lesson questions and exercises.

Concepts Review

True/False Questions

1. You can rename a worksheet by double-clicking the sheet tab and typing the new name.	TRUE	FALSE
2. Embedded charts are updated when the worksheet data changes.	TRUE	FALSE
3. Charts on separate chart sheets are not updated when the worksheet data changes.	TRUE	FALSE
4. Column charts are most useful for comparing the parts of a whole.	TRUE	FALSE
5. Column charts have a category and value axis.	TRUE	FALSE
6. The Chart Wizard can only be used to create embedded charts.	TRUE	FALSE
7. The Chart Wizard is used to explode pie slices.	TRUE	FALSE
8. You must select a chart before you can move or resize it.	TRUE	FALSE

Multiple-Choice Questions

1. Which procedure would you use to change the position of a worksheet in the sheet order?
   a. Double-click the sheet tab, and drag the tab to the desired location.
   b. Click the sheet tab, and choose Edit→Move sheet from the menu bar.
   c. Drag the sheet tab to the desired location.
   d. None of the above

2. Which command would you use to move an embedded chart to a separate sheet?
   a. Edit→Move chart
   b. Chart→Location
   c. Chart→Move
   d. This cannot be done.

3. Which chart would be best for showing a trend over a period of time?
   a. Line
   b. Bar
   c. Column
   d. Pie

4. Which technique can be used to insert data labels after a chart has been created?
   a. Select the chart, and click the Data Labels button on the Chart toolbar.
   b. Select the chart, and choose the Insert→Data Labels command.
   c. Select the chart, choose Chart→Chart Options, click the Data Labels tab, and choose the desired data labels format.
   d. Data labels cannot be inserted after a chart has been created.

Skill Builders

Skill Builder 17.1 Use Help

In this exercise, you will use Excel's Help feature to get a description of the various chart types.

1. Start a New Workbook .
2. Use the Office Assistant to search for the phrase *chart types.*
3. Choose **Examples of chart types** from the Assistant's search results.
4. Click the graphic that appears in the Help window to display a help topic on Examples of chart types.
5. Click the various chart types on the left side of the dialog box to see a detailed description in the right side of the dialog box.
6. Close all Help windows when you have finished.
7. Click in the worksheet to dismiss the Assistant's speech balloon.

Skill Builder 17.2 Create a Column Chart

In this exercise, you will create a column chart to display student enrollments at a university.

Expand a Series

1. Open the workbook named Skill Builder 17.2.
   Notice that the enrollment data has been completed in Column B, but the years have not been completed in Column A. Notice the first two years (1983 and 1984) form the beginning of the series 1983–1999. The best way to expand this series is with the fill handle.
2. Select Cells A4 and A5.
3. Drag the fill handle down to Row 20 to expand the series.
4. Left align the years in Column A.

Create the Chart

5. Select the range A3:B20.
   This range includes the enrollment data, and the Year and Total Enrollment headings.
6. Click the Chart Wizard button.
7. Choose the Column chart type and the first subtype.
8. Click **Next** to display the Step 2 of 4 box.
   Take a moment to study the Step 2 dialog box, and you will notice a problem. Excel is interpreting the years 1983–1999 as numbers. The numbers are appearing as a data series in the chart. The years are the short columns to the left of the tall, thin enrollment data columns. The years should actually be displayed as labels on the horizontal category axis. You will correct this in the next few steps.
9. Click the **Series** tab on the dialog box.
   The Series tab lets you modify the data series that are plotted in the chart.

10. Follow these steps to remove the years from the series and to add the years as Category (X) axis labels.

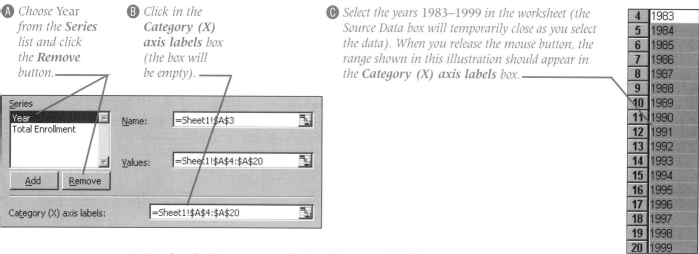

Ⓐ *Choose Year from the* ***Series*** *list and click the* ***Remove*** *button.*

Ⓑ *Click in the* ***Category (X) axis labels*** *box (the box will be empty).*

Ⓒ *Select the years 1983–1999 in the worksheet (the Source Data box will temporarily close as you select the data). When you release the mouse button, the range shown in this illustration should appear in the* ***Category (X) axis labels*** *box.*

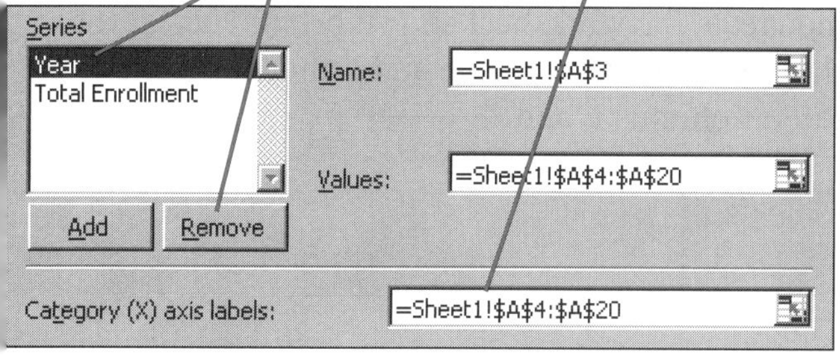

Series
Year
Total Enrollment
Add
Remove
Name:
=Sheet1!$A$3
Values:
=Sheet1!$A$4:$A$20
Category (X) axis labels:
=Sheet1!$A$4:$A$20

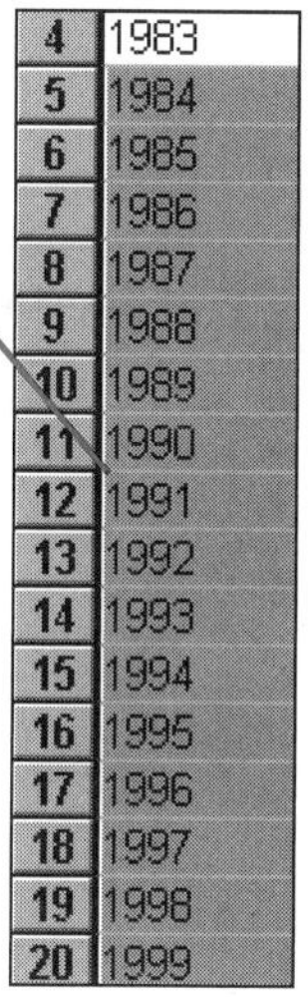

4 1983
5 1984
6 1985
7 1986
8 1987
9 1988
10 1989
11 1990
12 1991
13 1992
14 1993
15 1994
16 1995
17 1996
18 1997
19 1998
20 1999

Notice that the dates are now displayed in an angled fashion on the Category axis.

11. Click **Next** to continue with Step 3 of 4.
12. Click the **Titles** tab, and type the title **`Student Enrollments`** in the Chart title box.
13. Click the **Legend** tab, and remove the legend.
14. Click **Finish** to complete the chart.
    Take a few moments to study your worksheet and chart. Make sure you understand the relationship between the worksheet data and the chart.

Convert the Chart to a Line Chart

Suppose you are interested in seeing only the trend in enrollments as opposed to the enrollments in individual years. You can easily convert this chart to a line chart.

15. Make sure the chart is selected.
16. Choose **Chart→Chart Type** from the menu bar.
17. Choose Line as the Chart type, and choose the fourth subtype.
18. Click **OK** to convert the chart to a line chart with data markers.

Format the Chart Title

19. Click the Student Enrollments chart title.
20. Use the Font Color button to format the title with a color.
21. Feel free to format the chart and title in any other way you desire.
22. Save the changes, and then close the workbook.

Skill Builder 17.3 Create a Doughnut Chart

In this exercise, you will create a chart for Holy Doughnuts. The chart will show the contributions of various types of doughnuts to the total sales volume for two different years. What type of chart will you use? Why, a doughnut chart, what else! Like pie charts, doughnut charts are useful for comparing parts of a whole. However, doughnut charts can contain more than one data series. Each ring in a doughnut chart represents a data series.

Set Up the Worksheet

1. If necessary, start a New Workbook, and create the worksheet shown below. Format the numbers in Column C as Comma style with 0 decimals. Also, merge and center the Units Sold heading over Cells B3 and C3 and AutoFit Columns B and C.

	A	B	C	D	E
1	**Holy Doughnuts Volume Comparison**				
2					
3		**Units Sold**			
4	**Type of Doughnut**	**1998**	**1999**		
5	Creme Filled	12,000	14,500		
6	Frosted	10,500	9,000		
7	Nut Covered	2,300	2,500		
8	Glazed	7,000	8,200		
9	Old Fashioned	4,500	4,300		

Create the Chart

Doughnut charts function much like pie charts because they are used to compare parts of a whole. Therefore, the data is selected in a manner similar to pie charts.

2. Select the data in the range A4:C9.
3. Click the Chart Wizard button.
4. Choose Doughnut as the Chart type, and choose the first subtype.
5. Click **Next** twice to display the Step 3 of 4 box.
6. Click the **Titles** tab, and enter the Chart title **`Doughnut Sales: 1998 vs. 1999`**.
7. Click the **Data Labels** tab, and choose the Show percent option.
8. Click the **Finish** button to create an embedded chart.

Format the Percent Labels

9. Click any of the percent labels in the outer ring of the doughnut, and all percentages for the series will be selected.

10. Use the Font Color button on the Formatting toolbar to choose a high-contrast color such as red or white.
This will differentiate the numbers in the outer ring from those in the inner ring. Notice that the doughnut chart does not provide a title or label to identify the rings as 1998 or 1999. This is a deficiency that can only be overcome by using a textbox and arrows or lines to label the rings.

11. Save the workbook with the name **Skill Builder 17.3**, and then close the workbook.

Skill Builder 17.4 Create Pie Charts

In this exercise, you will create four pie charts to illustrate employee expenses for Hollywood Productions—a motion-picture production company. The pie charts will show how employee costs are divided between departments, and how each department's employee costs are allocated. You will create each chart on a separate chart sheet.

Create the Company Chart

1. Open the workbook named Skill Builder 17.4.
2. Follow these steps to select the required data.

3		Marketing	Production	Finance
4	Salaries	3,400,000	4,500,000	1,200,000
5	Benefits	1,292,000	1,980,000	336,000
6	Travel	1,700,000	1,500,000	120,000
7	**Total**	**$ 6,392,000**	**$ 7,980,000**	**$ 1,656,000**

Ⓐ *Use the mouse to select the range B3:D3, as shown here.*

Ⓑ *Press the CTRL key while you select the range B7:D7.*

3. Click the Chart Wizard button, and create the pie chart shown to the right on a separate chart sheet.
Make sure the chart type, title, and labels match the chart shown here. Also, notice that the chart does not include a legend.

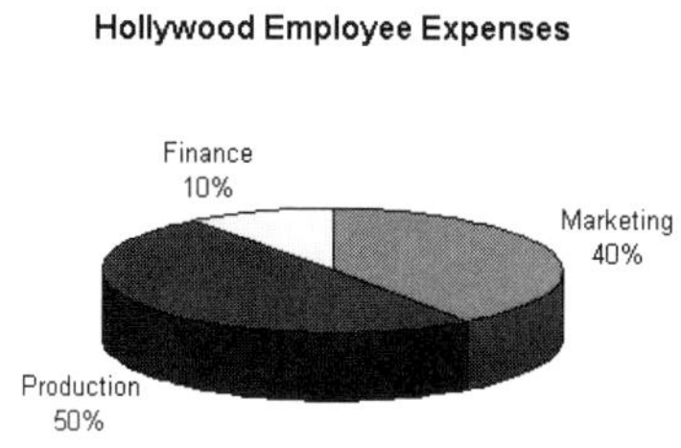

Hollywood Employee Expenses
Finance
10%
Marketing
40%
Production
50%

4. Double-click the Chart1 sheet tab, and change the sheet name to `Hollywood Chart`.
Notice that you can use long names when naming sheets.
5. Rename Sheet1 as `Employee Expense Data`.

(Continued on the next page)

Create a Pie Chart for the Marketing Department

6. Select the range shown below.

3		Marketing	Production	Finance
4	Salaries	3,400,000	4,500,000	1,200,000
5	Benefits	1,292,000	1,980,000	336,000
6	Travel	1,700,000	1,500,000	120,000
7	**Total**	**$ 6,392,000**	**$ 7,980,000**	**$ 1,656,000**

7. Click the Chart Wizard button, and create a pie chart on a separate chart sheet. Use the same chart type and labels as in the previous chart, but use the title "Marketing Employee Costs."

8. Rename the sheet as **`Marketing Chart`**.

9. Click the Employee Expense Data sheet tab to return to that sheet.

Create Pie Charts for the Production and Finance Departments

10. Use the techniques in this exercise to create the same style pie charts for the Production and Finance departments. Create each chart on a separate chart sheet. Use the chart titles and sheet names shown in the table below. Select data for the Production department chart as shown to the right. You will need to decide how to select the data for the Finance department (although that should be an easy decision to make).

3		Marketing	Production	Finance
4	Salaries	3,400,000	4,500,000	1,200,000
5	Benefits	1,292,000	1,980,000	336,000
6	Travel	1,700,000	1,500,000	120,000
7	**Total**	**$ 6,392,000**	**$ 7,980,000**	**$ 1,656,000**

Chart	Use This Title	Use This Sheet Name
Production	Production Employee Costs	Production Chart
Finance	Finance Employee Costs	Finance Chart

11. Follow these steps to move the Employee Expense Data sheet tab.

Ⓐ *If necessary, scroll to the right using the tab scrolling buttons until the **Employee Expense Data** tab is visible.*

Hollywood Chart
Marketing Chart
Production Chart
Finance Chart
Employee Expense Data
Ready

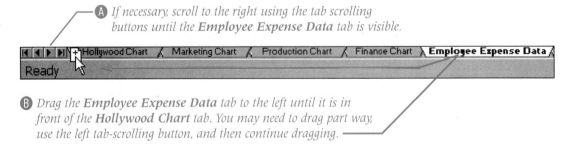

Ⓑ *Drag the **Employee Expense Data** tab to the left until it is in front of the **Hollywood Chart** tab. You may need to drag part way, use the left tab-scrolling button, and then continue dragging.*

Explode Pie Slices and Increase Elevation

12. Click the Hollywood Chart tab to activate it.
13. Click once on the pie, pause, and then click the Production slice (the largest slice).
14. Drag the slice out slightly to explode it.
15. Choose **Chart→3-D View** from the menu bar.
16. Increase the Elevation  to 25, and click **OK.**
17. Click the **Marketing Chart** sheet tab.
18. Explode the Salaries slice (the largest slice), and increase the Elevation to 25.
19. Explode the largest slice, and increase the Elevation to 25 for the Production and Finance charts.
    Take a few moments to click the various sheet tabs and check out your charts. Feel free to format and enhance your charts in any way.
20. Save the changes, and then close the workbook.

Skill Builder 17.5 Create a Pie Chart

In this exercise, you will create a pie chart that shows the budget allocation for a school district.

1. Open the workbook named Skill Builder 17.5.
2. Select the data shown below.

4	Facilities	3,500,000
5	Employee Costs	4,500,000
6	Transportation	540,000
7	Students	2,300,000
8	Equipment	1,200,000

3. Use the Chart Wizard  to create the embedded pie chart shown to the right. Make sure to include the chart title and data labels, remove the legend, and increase the elevation as shown.
4. Save the changes, and then close the workbook.

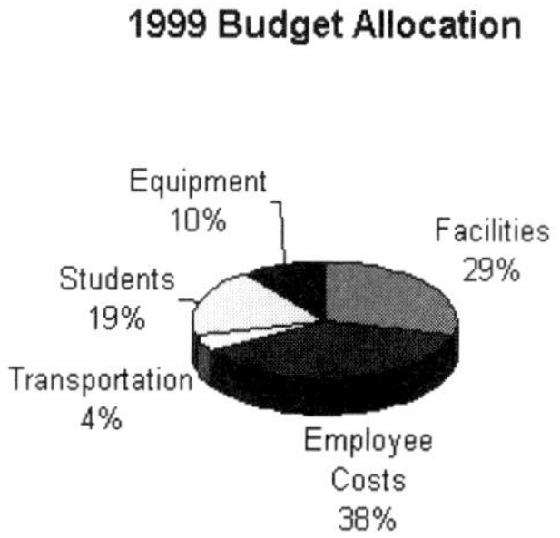
1999 Budget Allocation
Equipment 10%
Facilities 29%
Students 19%
Transportation 4%
Employee Costs 38%

Assessments

Assessment 17.1 Create a Line Chart

1. Start a New Workbook, and create the following worksheet.

	A	B	C	D
1	SysTech Stock Performance			
2	March 1998 Through February 1999			
3				
4	Date	Stock Price		
5	3/1/98	78		
6	4/1/98	82.6		
7	5/1/98	83		
8	6/1/98	78.6		
9	7/1/98	72		
10	8/1/98	62		
11	9/1/98	65.8		
12	10/1/98	72.6		
13	11/1/98	85		
14	12/1/98	86		
15	1/1/98	90		
16	2/1/98	92		

2. Use the worksheet data to create the following chart on a separate chart sheet. Make sure you set up the data labels and title as shown.

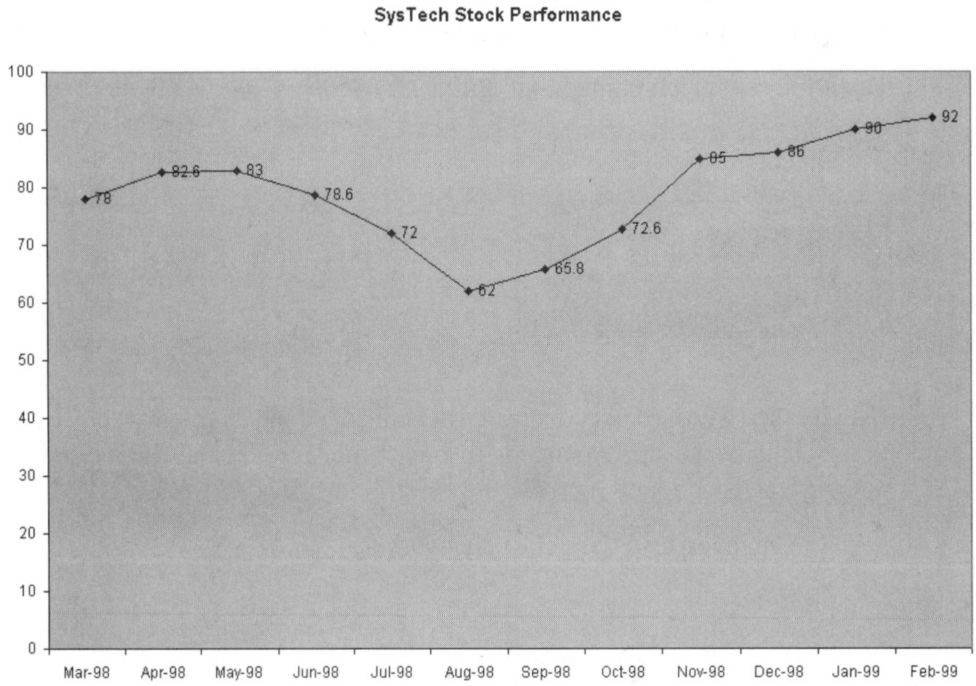
SysTech Stock Performance
100
90
80
70
60
50
40
30
20
10
0
78
82.6
83
78.6
72
62
65.8
72.6
85
86
90
92
Mar-98
Apr-98
May-98
Jun-98
Jul-98
Aug-98
Sep-98
Oct-98
Nov-98
Dec-98
Jan-99
Feb-99

3. Rename the Chart1 sheet as **`Stock Performance`**.

4. Rename the Sheet1 sheet as **`Supporting Data`**.

5. Print both the worksheet and chart.

6. Save the workbook with the name **Assessment 17.1,** then close the workbook.

Assessment 17.2 Create an Embedded Column Chart

1. Create the worksheet and embedded column chart shown below. Notice the column chart is two-dimensional. The differences in Row 6 are simply the budget numbers minus the spent numbers. Notice that the negative differences dip below the X-axis in the chart. Adjust the position and size of the embedded chart as shown.

	A	B	C	D	E	F	G	H
1	Personal Budget Analysis (January 99 - June 99)							
2								
3		Jan	Feb	Mar	Apr	May	Jun	
4	Budget	5000	5500	5000	5300	5300	5500	
5	Spent	4500	6000	4750	6200	4900	5500	
6	Difference	500	-500	250	-900	400	0	
7								

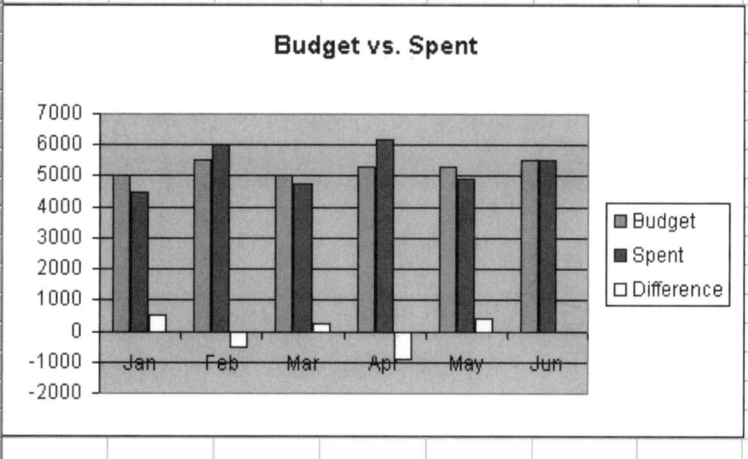

Budget vs. Spent
7000
6000
5000
4000
3000
2000
1000
0
-1000
-2000
Jan
Feb
Mar
Apr
May
Jun
Budget
Spent
Difference

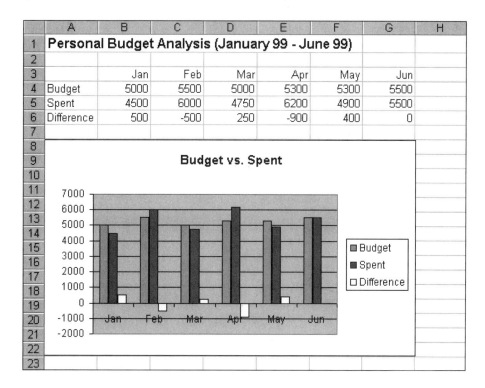

2. Print the worksheet and embedded chart on a single page.

3. Save the workbook with the name **Assessment 17.2,** then close the workbook.

LESSON 18—Web Integration

Posting an Online Workbook

Office 2000 is designed to make integration with the Web easier than ever before. For example, most Office 2000 application programs let you save your work in Web page (HTML) format. Posting information as a Web page makes it easier for others to access it whenever they need to. You can also bring together pieces of work created with several different programs into a single Office 2000 file. In this integration lesson, you will combine information from members of a project team into a single Excel workbook. Then you will post the workbook to the Web, where every project team member can access the information over the Internet.

In This Lesson

Case Study

Deion is a Print Production Manager in Los Angeles with the Acme Trading Company, an import-export firm. His primary role is to coordinate the efforts of his production team to get various publications ready for print. The production team members are scattered geographically. For example, there is a copy editor in Oregon and a graphic artist in Boston. Each team member is an expert, and they can all work smoothly together over the Internet. Deion is about mid-way through a project to produce Acme's annual report. He wants all of the production team members to know the status of the project. So he decides to assemble information about the production tasks and the schedule into an Excel workbook, then post the workbook to the Web so that everyone can review it.

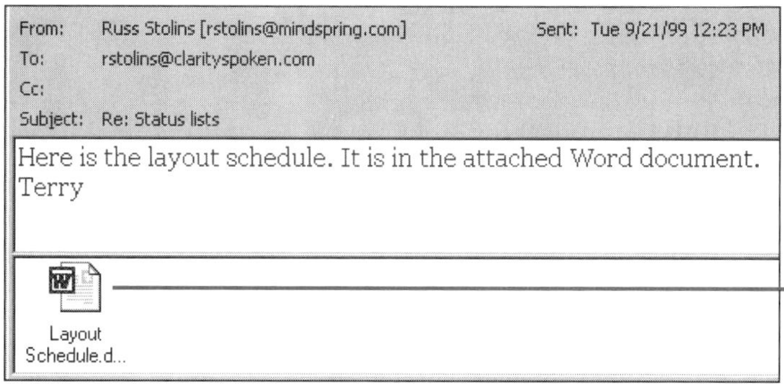
From: Russ Stolins [rstolins@mindspring.com]
Sent: Tue 9/21/99 12:23 PM
To: rstolins@clarityspoken.com
Cc:
Subject: Re: Status lists
Here is the layout schedule. It is in the attached Word document.
Terry
Layout Schedule.d...

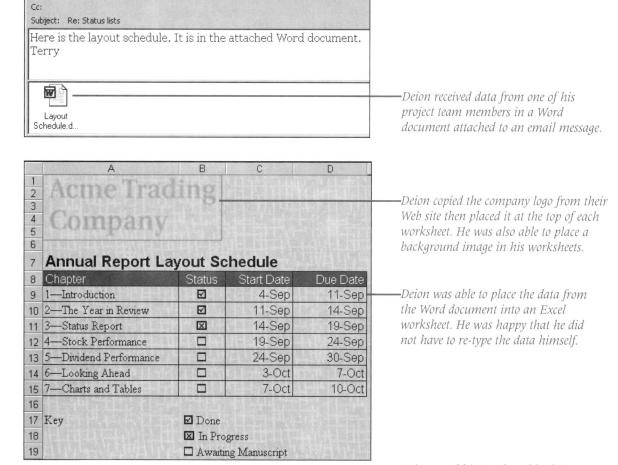

Deion received data from one of his project team members in a Word document attached to an email message.

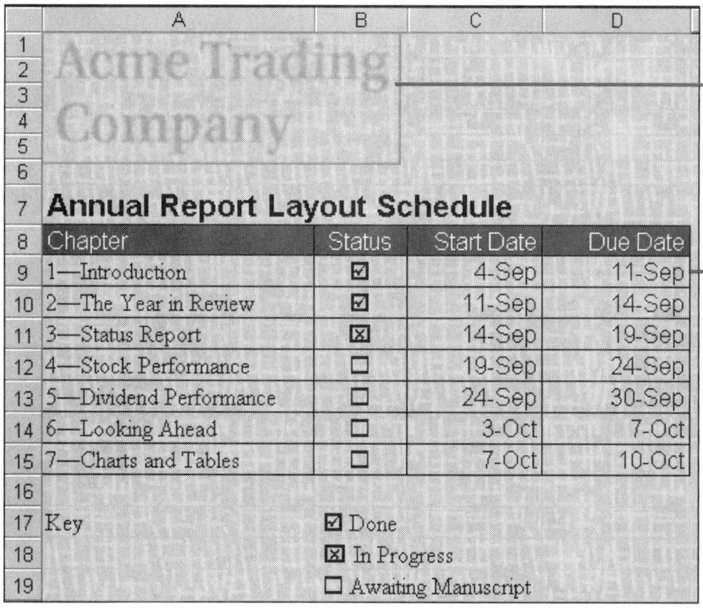
Acme Trading Company
Annual Report Layout Schedule
Chapter
Status
Start Date
Due Date
1—Introduction 4-Sep 11-Sep
2—The Year in Review 11-Sep 14-Sep
3—Status Report 14-Sep 19-Sep
4—Stock Performance 19-Sep 24-Sep
5—Dividend Performance 24-Sep 30-Sep
6—Looking Ahead 3-Oct 7-Oct
7—Charts and Tables 7-Oct 10-Oct
Key
Done
In Progress
Awaiting Manuscript

Deion copied the company logo from their Web site then placed it at the top of each worksheet. He was also able to place a background image in his worksheets.

Deion was able to place the data from the Word document into an Excel worksheet. He was happy that he did not have to re-type the data himself.

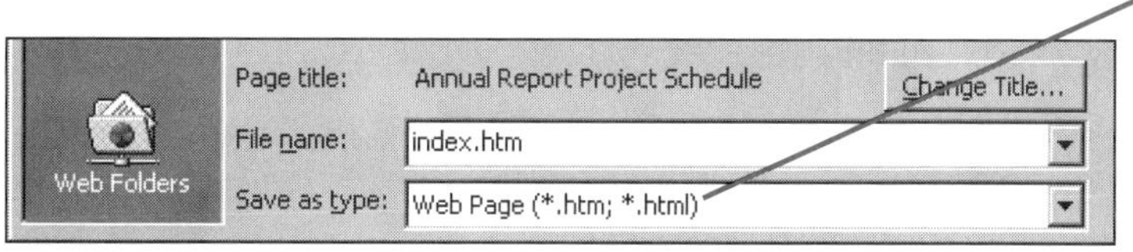
Web Folders
Page title: Annual Report Project Schedule
Change Title...
File name: index.htm
Save as type: Web Page (*.htm; *.html)

Deion saved his Excel workbook into a Web Folder as a Web page. The Web folder immediately sent his workbook to the company Web server. Now all of Deion's project team members can view the project schedule over the Web.

Obtaining and Organizing the Information

It is always a good idea to set up one or more folders for special projects. This helps you find any files related to the project and prevents their being mixed in with other files. By creating a shortcut and Favorite to the project folder, you will save yourself time searching for it later. The following Hands-On exercise will give you additional practice with these tasks.

Hands-On 18.1 Set Up a Project Folder

Before you begin: *You may want to review the topics on creating project folders, shortcuts on the Desktop, and Favorites to folders before you begin this exercise. They appear in the lesson* Internet Integration: Online Collaboration. *The following instructions will assume you are familiar with these tasks.*

1. Open a My Computer window, and display the contents of your floppy disk.

NOTE! *If Windows opens a new My Computer window for the 3½* Floppy (A:) *drive, use Step 2 of Hands-On Exercise 13.1 on page 380 to switch off the display of individual windows.*

2. Choose **File→New→Folder** from the menu bar.
3. Name the folder **`Annual Report`**.
4. If necessary, **restore** the My Computer window so that the Desktop is visible.
5. Using the *right* (not the left) mouse button, *drag* the **Annual Report** folder onto the Desktop, and then choose **Create Shortcut(s) Here** from the pop-up menu.
6. Close the My Computer window.
7. Start Excel; then click the Open button on the toolbar.
8. Follow these steps to create a Favorite for the Annual Report folder.

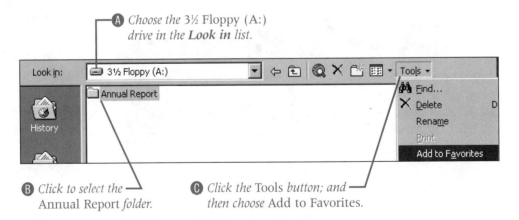

Ⓐ *Choose the 3½* Floppy (A:) *drive in the* **Look in** *list.*

Look in:
3½ Floppy (A:)
Tools
Annual Report
History
Find...
Delete
Rename
Print
Add to Favorites

Ⓑ *Click to select the* Annual Report *folder.*

Ⓒ *Click the* Tools *button; and then choose* Add to Favorites.

The folder is added to the Favorites *list. A Favorite is a navigation tool in Windows that lets you quickly navigate to Web pages, folders, and files.*

9. Click the **Favorites** button on the left side of the dialog box. Scroll down the Favorites list, if necessary, until the **Annual Report** *Favorite* is visible.
You may see some additional Annual Report Favorites with a number in parenthesis. These are additional Favorites to the Annual Report folder that were created by previous students. Since they are unnecessary, you may delete them in the next step.

10. If you see a Favorite named **Annual Report (2)** follow the steps below; otherwise skip to Step 11:

- Click to select **Annual Report (2).**
- Click the Delete button on the dialog box to delete the Favorite. Click **Yes** if You are asked to confirm the deletion.
- *Delete* any other **Annual Report Favorites** with a number in parentheses after the name.

11. Double-click on **Annual Report** in the Favorites list.
The empty folder is displayed in the dialog box. As you can see, the Favorite lets you navigate to the folder quickly, without needing to work your way through the various disk drives and folders that a folder might lie within.

12. Click **Cancel** to close the dialog box.
This will not cause you to lose the Favorite you just created in Step 8.

13. Minimize the Excel window.

Saving Images on Web Pages

Sometimes you may come upon a Web page with an interesting image that you want to save. You can save images from Web pages as individual image files on your computer. You can also copy and paste images on a Web page into other programs. For example, you might want to use a photo from a travel Web site of the spot you've picked out for a vacation. You could copy the photo and paste it into a letter or an email message. There are two ways you can save Web images:

- *Save* the image as a file on a hard drive or floppy disk by giving a *right-click*, and then choosing the **Save Picture As** command.
- *Copy* the image to the clipboard, and then *paste* it into your work in another application program.

Copyright

Just because you can save parts or all of a Web page doesn't make it your property. You can make only limited use of what you copy from most Web sites. Here are a few tips on copyright and Web page content:

- Never place the content on a commercial Web site without permission.
- In general, what you copy from another Web site should be for your personal use, not for distribution.

NOTE! *Since Deion is going to copy an image from Acme's own Web site, he does not need to worry about copyright in this case.*

Quick Reference

SAVING A WEB IMAGE

Task	Procedure
Save an image from a Web page.	■ *Right-click* the image on the Web page; then select **Save Picture As** from the pop-up menu. ■ You can also *drag* and *drop* an image from its Web page to a folder or disk displayed in a My Computer or Exploring window.
Copy and paste an image from a Web page.	■ *Right-click* on the image you wish to copy. ■ Choose **Copy** from the pop-up menu. ■ Activate the program into which you wish to paste the image. ■ Click the insertion point where you wish to paste the image; then choose **Edit→Paste** from the menu bar.

Hands-On 18.2 Save a Logo from a Web Page

In this exercise, you will navigate to a page on Acme's Web site and save the logo on that page for later use in an Excel workbook.

1. Start **Internet Explorer** from its icon on the Desktop or the Quick Launch toolbar.

Internet Explorer

2. Follow these steps to navigate to the Acme Trading Co. Web page.

Address
http://www.offtowork.com/oe/lesson18
Acme Trading Co.
Welcome to the

Ⓐ *Click in the* ***Address*** *bar, and type the following URL:* **`www.offtowork.com/oe/lesson18`**

Ⓑ *Click the* Acme Trading Co. *button.*

A simulated Acme Trading Company home page will be displayed.

3. Follow these steps to save the company logo on this page as a file:

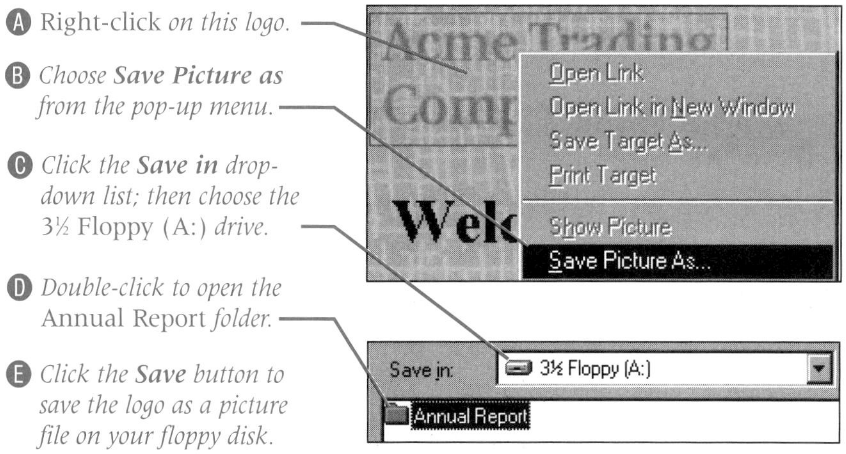

A Right-click *on this logo.*
B *Choose* ***Save Picture as*** *from the pop-up menu.*
C *Click the* ***Save in*** *drop-down list; then choose the* 3½ Floppy (A:) *drive.*
D *Double-click to open the* Annual Report *folder.*
E *Click the* ***Save*** *button to save the logo as a picture file on your floppy disk.*
Acme Trading
Comp
Welc
Open Link
Open Link in New Window
Save Target As...
Print Target
Show Picture
Save Picture As...
Save in:
3½ Floppy (A:)
Annual Report

4. Click the **Background Tile Image** hyperlink at the bottom of the Welcome page.
   The Internet Explorer window will display a small image that serves as the background to this page. By repeating this small image many times, Internet Explorer can display a colorful background without needing to use a large image. You will use this same image as the background of your worksheet pages later in this lesson.
5. *Right-click* anywhere on the image; choose **Save Picture As** from the menu bar; then click the **Save** button.
   The tile image is saved to the Annual Report folder on your floppy disk.
6. Click the **Back** button on the Internet Explorer toolbar to return to the *Welcome* Web page; then click the **Back** button again to return to the *Lesson 18* Web page.
7. Minimize the Internet Explorer window.

Saving Attachment Files

You learned how to save attachments to email messages in another lesson. Attachments can be any type of file. In the following exercise, you will save a Word document and a Notepad file from two different email messages.

Hands-On 18.3 Save Email Attachments

Before you begin, *if you do not have access to email in the computer lab, you should skip directly to the* Save Files Off the Web Page *section (Step 14) near the end of this exercise.*

Send an Email Message

1. Use **Start→Programs→Microsoft Outlook** to start the *Outlook 2000* application.

Inbox

2. Click the **Inbox** button on the Outlook bar at the left side of the window to display the Inbox view.
3. Click the New Mail 
New
button at the left side of the Outlook toolbar to create a new email message.
4. Taking care to separate them with a *semicolon* (;), type the following email addresses in the *To:* line: **terry@offtowork.com; jchan@offtowork.com**
5. Tap the TAB key until the insertion point is blinking on the **subject line.** Type the following subject: **Status lists**.
6. Tap the TAB key to jump to the body of the message; then type the following message:

```
Hello Terry and Jackie:

Please send me your latest project status list by
email. It should list the various chapters of the
annual report, the date work is scheduled to begin,
and the date each chapter is due. I will publish
your list on the Web so other production workers
can follow our schedule.

Regards,

[Your Name]
```

7. Click the **Send** button to send your message.
8. Click the Send/Receive 
Send/Receive
button on the Outlook toolbar to check for responses to your message. Keep checking every minute until you have received a reply from both Terry and Jacqueline; then go on to the next step.

Save the Attachment Files

9. *Double-click* to open the message from **terry@offtowork.com.** Read over the message; then follow these steps to save the attachment in the *Annual Report* folder:

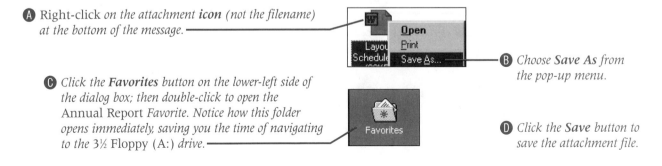

Ⓐ Right-click *on the attachment* ***icon*** *(not the filename) at the bottom of the message.*

Open
Print
Save As...

Ⓑ *Choose* ***Save As*** *from the pop-up menu.*

Ⓒ *Click the* ***Favorites*** *button on the lower-left side of the dialog box; then double-click to open the* Annual Report *Favorite. Notice how this folder opens immediately, saving you the time of navigating to the* 3½ Floppy (A:) *drive.*

Favorites

Ⓓ *Click the* ***Save*** *button to save the attachment file.*

10. Close the message from Terry; then double-click to open the message from **jchan@offtowork.com**.
Notice that the attachment at the bottom of this message has a different icon from the one you saw in the message from Terry. This is because Jacqueline sent you a file in a text *file format rather than a Word document.*

11. *Right-click* on the attachment file icon at the bottom of the message; then choose **Save As** from the pop-up menu. Click the **Save** button to save this file in the **Annual Report** folder.

12. Close the message from Jacqueline.

13. Close the Outlook window.
You can skip the next section of this exercise and continue reading the next topic.

Save the Files Off the Web Page

If you do not have access to email in the computer lab, you should use this alternative process to save the files from Terry Sanchez and Jacqueline Chan off of a Web page.

14. Restore the **Internet Explorer** window by clicking its button on the Windows Taskbar.
You should see the Lesson 18 *Web page that you left open in Hands-On Exercise 18.2.*

15. Follow these steps to save the first document file:

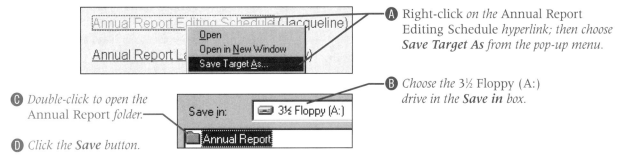

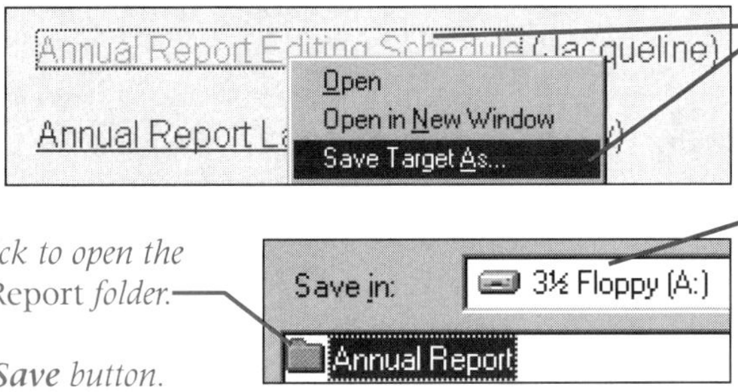

Open
Open in New Window
Save Target As...
Save in:
3½ Floppy (A:)
Annual Report

Ⓐ Right-click *on the* Annual Report Editing Schedule *hyperlink; then choose* ***Save Target As*** *from the pop-up menu.*

Ⓑ *Choose the* 3½ Floppy (A:) *drive in the* ***Save in*** *box.*

Ⓒ *Double-click to open the* Annual Report *folder.*

Ⓓ *Click the* ***Save*** *button.*

Internet Explorer will display a dialog box showing the progress of copying the file from the Web page to your floppy disk.

16. Click the **Close** button on the *Download Complete* dialog box.

17. Right-click on the **Annual Report Layout Schedule** hyperlink, and choose **Save Target As** from the pop-up menu; then save the file to the Annual Report folder on your floppy disk. Click the **Close** button on the *Download Complete* dialog box.

18. Minimize the Internet Explorer program.

Integrating Multiple Data Sources

File Formats

A file format is a technique for storing data in a computer file. Most application programs use a specific file format to save anything you create in that program. For example, Word has its own *document* format, Excel has its own *workbook* format, and Web pages are saved in HTML format. The format an application program normally uses to save files is called its *native* file format.

Converters

A *converter* is a small program that lets an application program open and save files that are not in its native file format. The Office 2000 applications come with a variety of converters that are installed automatically. You can also install additional converters that may become available as new file formats are introduced. For example, when a new version of an application program is released, it usually introduces a new native file format.

Example

You decide to place an image on an Excel worksheet. You use the **Insert→Picture→From File** command. Excel displays any image files for which it has an installed converter. When you choose an image file to insert and click **OK,** Excel uses the appropriate converter to read the file and place it in the worksheet.

Project Data Sources

In this lesson, you will work with the following types of data sources:

- A Word document
- A Notepad text-only document
- Two images
- An Excel worksheet saved as a Web page

Hands-On 18.4 Import Data from Other Data Sources

In this exercise, you will insert the Acme Trading Company *logo at the top of each workbook page.* Then you will insert text from the two documents into the workbook.

Add the Logo to the Top of Each Worksheet Page

1. *Restore* the **Excel** window by clicking its button on the Windows Taskbar.
2. Click in Cell **A1** on the first worksheet; then choose **Insert→Picture→From File** from the menu bar.
3. Click the **Favorites** button on the left side of the dialog box; then double-click on the **Annual Report** Favorite.
4. Double-click to insert the **logo** (or **logo.jpg**) file.
   The logo is immediately placed at the top-left corner of the worksheet.
5. Click the Copy button on the toolbar.

6. Click the **Sheet 2** tab at the bottom of the workbook window.
7. Make sure the highlight is in Cell **A1;** then click the Paste button on the toolbar.
As you may recall from an earlier lesson, the clipboard will retain the most recently copied or cut item until you copy or cut a new item. Thus, you can paste the logo onto multiple pages after you give the Copy command.
8. Click the **Sheet 3** tab, and paste the logo into Cell **A1** of that worksheet.

Rename the Worksheets

Deion renames the worksheets to make the workbook easier to navigate. He also deletes any surplus worksheets that are not needed.

9. Double-click the **Sheet 1** tab, and change the name to **`Editing Schedule`**, and tap (ENTER).
   - Change the **Sheet 2** tab to **`Layout Schedule`**, and tap (ENTER).
   - Change the **Sheet 3** tab to **`Production Schedule`**, and tap (ENTER).
10. Click the Save button; then save the workbook in the *Annual Report* folder on your floppy disk with the name **`Status`**.

Add Plain Text to a Worksheet

Jacqueline uses a very basic program to create short documents. There is no formatting in the document she sent. You will copy and paste the text from her document onto a worksheet, and then clean it up and format the text.

11. Minimize the Excel window.
12. *Double-click* on the **Shortcut to Annual Report** icon on the Desktop.
A My Computer window will appear to display the contents of your Annual Report folder. Shortcuts like this can save you time navigating through the disk drives to locate a specific folder.
13. Double-click on the **editing** (or **editing.txt**) file.
Windows will probably open the file in the Notepad applet. Notepad is a simple text editor that comes with Windows. Notice that the columns are neatly aligned in this document.
14. Choose **Edit→Select All** from the menu bar; then use (CTRL)+C to copy the document to the clipboard.
15. Close the Notepad window. Click **No** if you are asked if you wish to save the document.
Even though you have closed the Notepad window, everything you copied in Step 14 is still on the Windows clipboard.
16. **Restore** the Excel window by clicking its button on the Windows Taskbar.
17. Click the tab for the **Editing Schedule** Worksheet; then click on Cell **A7,** and use (CTRL)+V to *Paste* the text data onto the worksheet.
Notice that the once-neat columns on the right are now crooked. This is because Jacqueline used the (TAB) key to align her columns. But if an item did not align, she pressed (TAB) again to move it over. When you placed the text into Excel, each tab character in the document shifted the text over one column on the worksheet. Now you need to clean up the text so that it is easy to read.

(Continued on the next page)

18. Use Drag and Drop to align the data in the worksheet as shown below. You will need to adjust the width of some columns.

7	Annual Report Editing Schedule		
8			
9	Chapter	Due Date	Status
10	1 Introduction	3-Sep	Done
11	2 The Year in Review	10-Sep	Editing
12	3 Status Report	14-Sep	Late 2 Days
13	4 Stock Performance	18-Sep	On schedule
14	5 Dividend Performance	23-Sep	On schedule
15	6 Looking Ahead	2-Oct	Late 1 Day
16	7 Charts and Tables	6-Oct	On schedule

19. After the data has been aligned, add *bold* formatting to the headings in *Row 9* and the heading in *Cell A7*. Format the column headings so that they stand out. Add any other formatting that you think will make the table more readable.

20. Click the Save button to save the Workbook.
It's always a good idea to issue the Save command after you have completed five or ten minutes worth of work. If the computer should freeze unexpectedly (crash), all of your work up to the most recent Save command is safely stored on the floppy disk.

Importing Data with Drag and Drop

You can drag and drop data between other applications and an Excel workbook. For example, you can drag and drop a table or text from a Word document onto an Excel worksheet. You simply select the data to be imported, then drag and drop it to the desired worksheet. When you use the drag-and-drop technique, the data is deleted (cut) from the original document. However, if you do not save the changes to the original document when you close it, the data you dragged and dropped will be retained in the original document.

Tiled Backgrounds on Worksheets

Excel lets you place an image in the background of any worksheet. If the image is smaller than the viewable area of the worksheet, it will be *tiled* (repeated) to fill the entire worksheet window. In the next Hands-On exercise, you will tile the small background image you saved from the Acme home page earlier in this lesson.

Quick Reference

HOW TO ASSIGN A BACKGROUND IMAGE TO A WORKSHEET

Task	Procedure
Place a tiled background image on a worksheet.	■ Display the worksheet you wish to assign a background image. ■ Choose **Format→Sheet→Background** from the menu bar. ■ Choose a background image; then click **Insert.**

Repeating Your Most Recent Command

From the Keyboard

(F4) to repeat your most recent command.

There may be times when you need to apply the same command at several places in a workbook. For example, you may give a format cell command that you wish to repeat on cells in a different worksheet. Excel lets you repeat your most recent command by tapping the (F4) function key on the keyboard. Just as you can paste the same item from the clipboard repeatedly, you can continue using the (F4) function key to repeat the same command until you issue a different command.

Hands-On 18.5 Import Data with Drag and Drop

In this exercise, you will open a Word file and then drag and drop data from the file onto an Excel worksheet. You will also drag-and-drop data from a Web page.

Add Word Text to a Worksheet

Terry used Word to compose her status list. You will copy and paste from her Word document into her page in the workbook.

1. *Restore* the **A:\Annual Report** window by clicking its button on the Windows Taskbar.
2. Double-click on the **layout** (or **layout.doc**) file in the *Annual Report* folder.
   Windows will start Microsoft Word to display the document. Before copying this information, you will need to minimize the My Computer window.
3. Follow these steps to minimize the My Computer window.

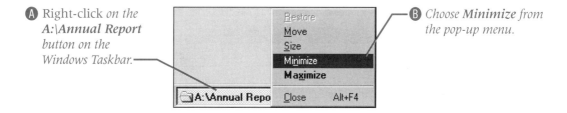

Ⓐ Right-click *on the* ***A:\Annual Report*** *button on the* Windows Taskbar.

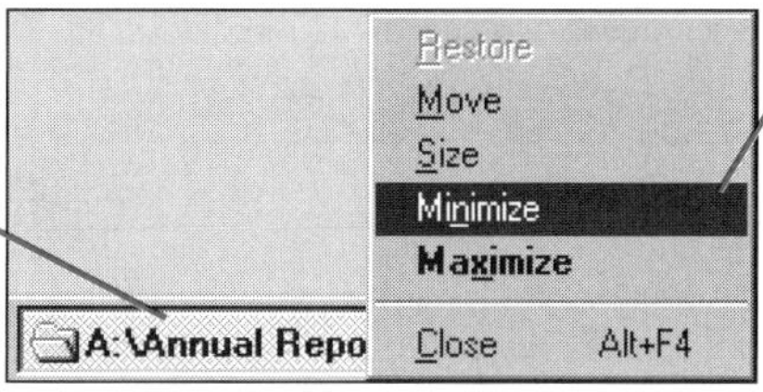
Restore
Move
Size
Minimize
Maximize
A:\Annual Repo
Close Alt+F4

Ⓑ *Choose* ***Minimize*** *from the pop-up menu.*

4. Follow these steps to display the Word and Excel windows side-by-side.

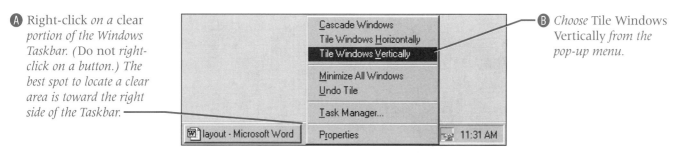

Ⓐ Right-click *on a* clear *portion of the Windows Taskbar.* (Do not *right-click on a button.) The best spot to locate a clear area is toward the right side of the Taskbar.*

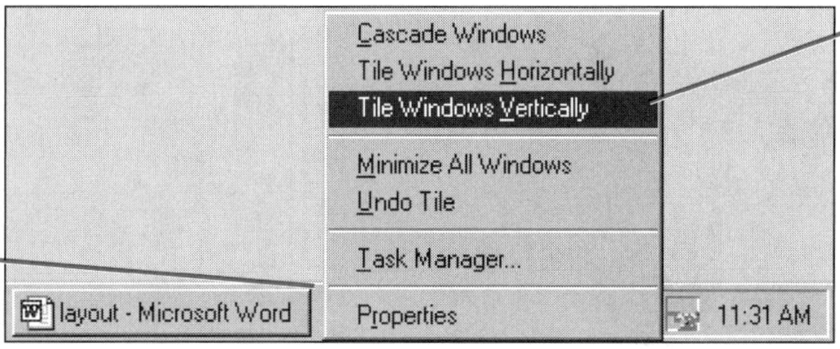
Cascade Windows
Tile Windows Horizontally
Tile Windows Vertically
Minimize All Windows
Undo Tile
Task Manager...
layout - Microsoft Word
Properties
11:31 AM

Ⓑ *Choose* Tile Windows Vertically *from the pop-up menu.*

Now the two program windows are side-by-side. This will make it easy to drag and drop the data from Word into Excel.

5. Click the tab for the **Layout Schedule** worksheet at the bottom of the Workbook window.
   Terry used Word's table feature to create a well-formatted table. Let's see if this formatting gets copied into Excel.

(Continued on the next page)

6. Follow these steps to drag and drop the layout schedule from the Word document onto the Excel worksheet.

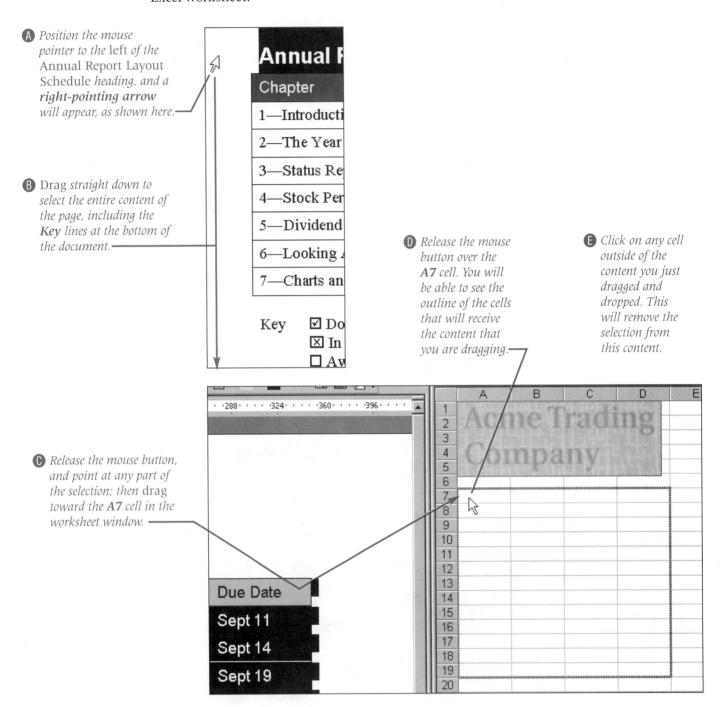

Ⓐ *Position the mouse pointer to the left of the* Annual Report Layout Schedule *heading, and a* ***right-pointing arrow*** *will appear, as shown here.*

Ⓑ Drag *straight down to select the entire content of the page, including the* ***Key*** *lines at the bottom of the document.*

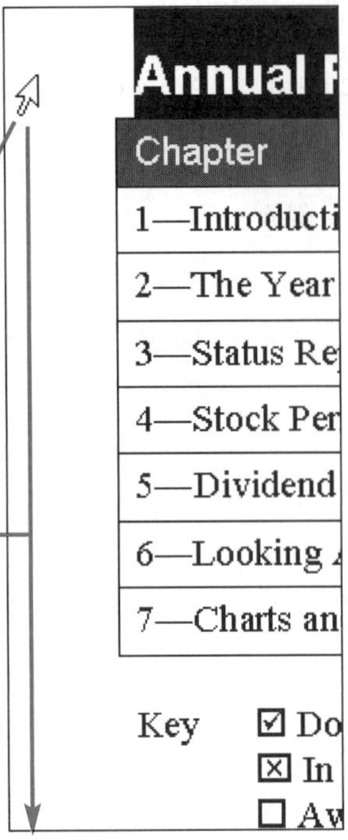

Annual R
Chapter
1—Introducti
2—The Year
3—Status Re
4—Stock Per
5—Dividend
6—Looking
7—Charts an
Key
Do
In
Av

Ⓓ *Release the mouse button over the* ***A7*** *cell. You will be able to see the outline of the cells that will receive the content that you are dragging.*

Ⓔ *Click on any cell outside of the content you just dragged and dropped. This will remove the selection from this content.*

Ⓒ *Release the mouse button, and point at any part of the selection; then drag toward the* ***A7*** *cell in the worksheet window.*

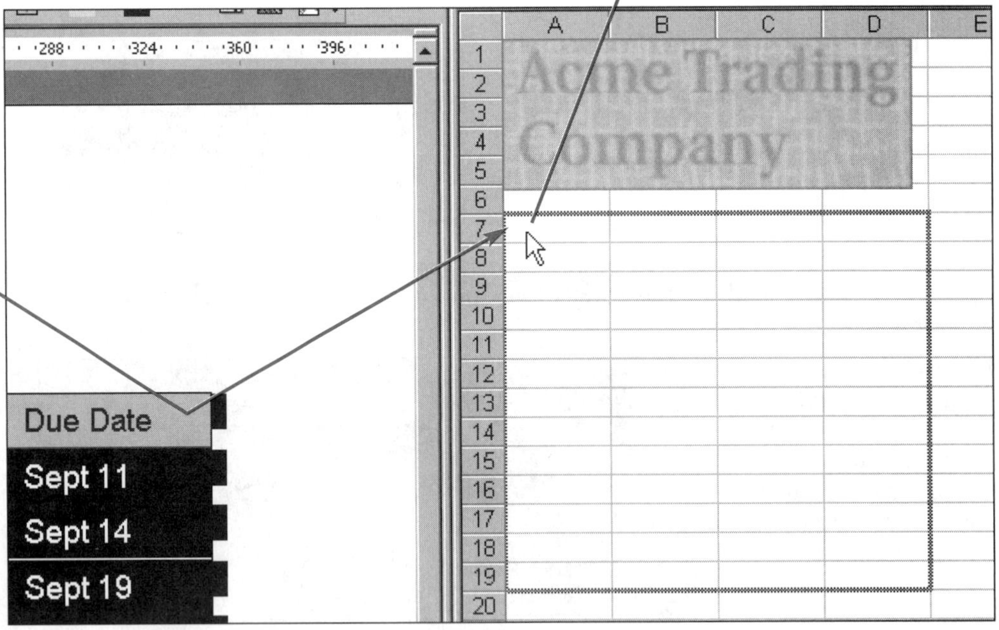

288
324
360
396
Due Date
Sept 11
Sept 14
Sept 19
A
B
C
D
E
Acme Trading Company
1
2
3
4
5
6
7
8
9
10
11
12
13
14
15
16
17
18
19
20

The selected content from the Word document is pasted onto the worksheet. Notice that this content has disappeared from the Word document.

7. Close ☒ the *Word* window. Click **No** when you are asked to save changes to the document.
This will prevent the loss of the content that you just dragged and dropped. The next time you open this document, all of the content will reappear.

8. Maximize ☐ the *Excel* window.
Thanks to Excel's Word filter, the formatting was essentially carried over into the Excel worksheet. However, the column widths did not fare as well. Let's fix that.

9. Follow these steps to clean up the Word table:

Ⓐ *Double-click this column boundary to AutoFit Column A. Notice that the column expands too wide due to the heading in Cell **A10**.*

Ⓑ *Drag to adjust Column A to fit the text in the body of the table as shown here.*

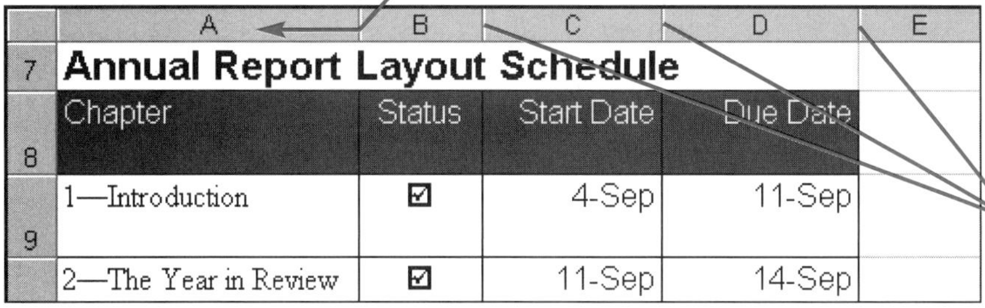

A
B
C
D
E
7 Annual Report Layout Schedule
Chapter
Status
Start Date
Due Date
8
1—Introduction
4-Sep
11-Sep
9
2—The Year in Review
11-Sep
14-Sep

Ⓒ *Drag to adjust the remaining columns to fit the data in each column as shown here.*

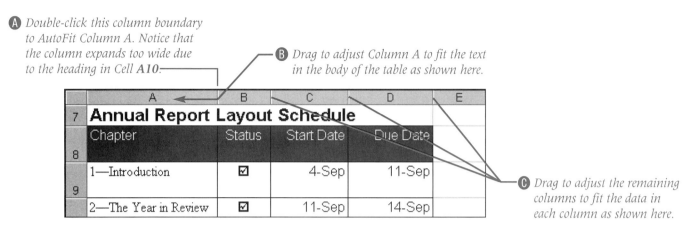

10. Drag on the *headings* to select Columns **C** and **D** as shown at right.

B
C
D

11. Click the Align Right button on the toolbar.
    Now the columns look good, and the height of the rows has been adjusted as well.
12. Click the Save button on the toolbar.

Add the Production Schedule

Now you will finish working on the new workbook by adding Deion's worksheet.

13. Click the **Production Schedule** worksheet tab; then click on Cell **A7.**
14. Restore the **Internet Explorer** window by clicking its button on the Windows Taskbar.
15. Click the **Non-Interactive** button on the **Lesson 18** window.
    This page displays an Excel worksheet that has been saved as a Web page without any interactive features. You will learn more about the interactive option later in this lesson.
16. *Right-click* on a clear area of the Windows Taskbar; then choose **Tile Windows Vertically** from the pop-up menu.
17. Follow these steps to drag and drop data from the Internet Explorer window onto the Excel worksheet.

Ⓒ *Release the mouse button when the insertion point is over Cell **A7** and you will see a **rectangle** that represents the content being dragged, as shown here.*

Ⓑ Point *at any part of the selection, then drag toward Cell **A7** in the Excel window.*

Ⓐ Drag *down and to the right to select the table in the Internet Explorer window.*

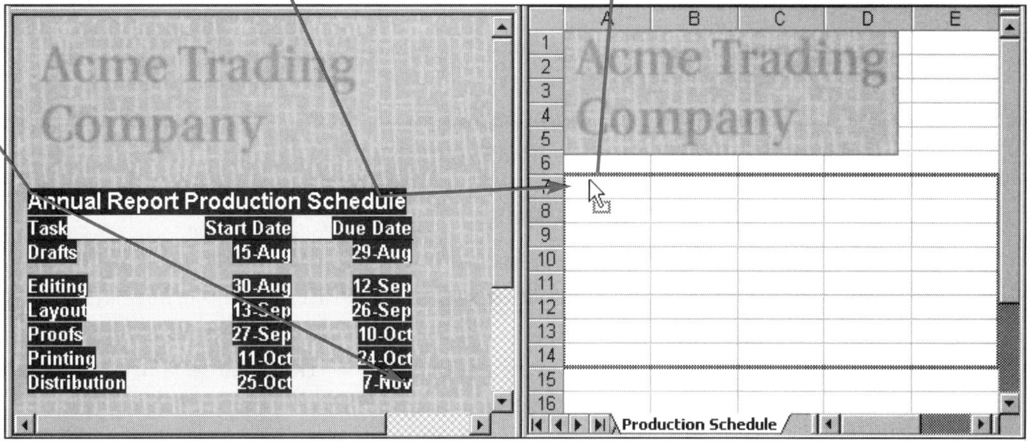

Acme Trading Company
Annual Report Production Schedule
Task
Start Date
Due Date
Drafts
15-Aug
29-Aug
Editing
30-Aug
12-Sep
Layout
13-Sep
26-Sep
Proofs
27-Sep
10-Oct
Printing
11-Oct
24-Oct
Distribution
25-Oct
7-Nov
A
B
C
D
E
Acme Trading Company
Production Schedule

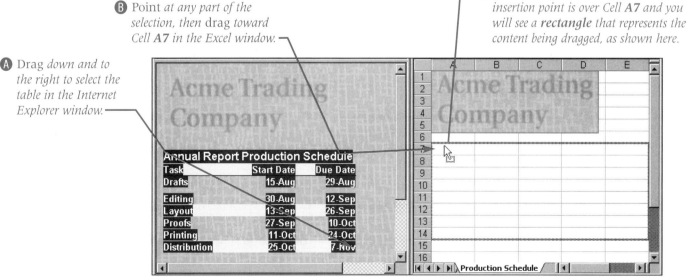

(Continued on the next page)

18. Minimize the *Internet Explorer* window; then Maximize the *Excel* window.

19. Adjust the row and column widths until the table is similar to the example shown below. Adjust the formatting of the labels and shading if you like.

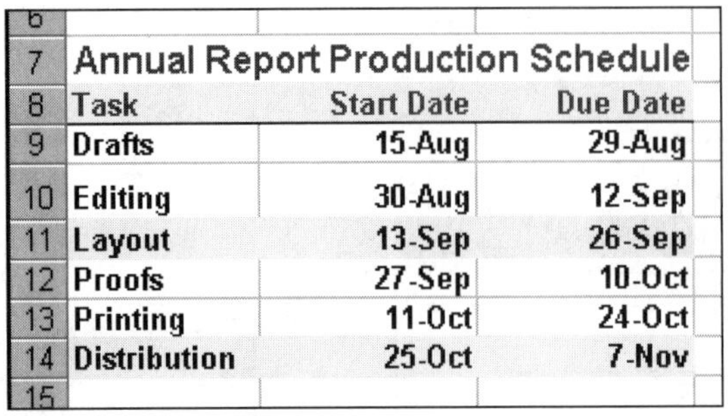

6			
7	Annual Report Production Schedule		
8	Task	Start Date	Due Date
9	Drafts	15-Aug	29-Aug
10	Editing	30-Aug	12-Sep
11	Layout	13-Sep	26-Sep
12	Proofs	27-Sep	10-Oct
13	Printing	11-Oct	24-Oct
14	Distribution	25-Oct	7-Nov
15			

20. Click the Save button on the toolbar.

Add a Background Image

When you save the worksheet as a Web page, it will look more attractive if there is some color on the page. You will now add the background image you copied from the Web page earlier in the lesson to the background of each worksheet.

21. Choose **Format→Sheet→Background** from the menu bar.

22. Double-click to choose the **tile** (or **tile.jpg**) file as the background image.
Just as you saw on the Web page in an earlier exercise, the tile image is repeated to cover the entire Excel worksheet.

23. Click the **Layout Schedule** tab at the bottom of the workbook window; then tap the (F4) function key to repeat the previous command.
The background is set for Sheet 2. Excel will keep repeating your most recent command each time you tap the (F4) function key.

24. Click the **Editing Schedule** tab; then tap the (F4) function key.

25. Click the Save button on the toolbar.
Leave the Workbook open; you will continue to use it.

Converting Workbooks to Other File Formats

In the previous topic, you learned that the native file format is how an application normally saves files. But what if you want to save a file in a different (non-native) file format? This is called *exporting*. In order to export your work to a different file format, Excel must use a conversion filter to convert the workbook file into the new format.

Limitations of File Formats

Some file formats will not be able to save all of the information in the workbook file. For example, a *tab delimited* file won't be able to save data on multiple worksheets or any text formatting. Excel will warn you about any features, formatting, or data you might lose in the new file format. If you save to a non-Excel file format, your original workbook file is always kept intact. The converted workbook is saved to different file.

Example

You have a co-worker who still uses an older version of Lotus 1-2-3 as her spreadsheet program. You want to send her information from an Excel workbook. You open the workbook normally in Excel and use the Save As command to choose a different file format (export) and save it. Then you send the exported file to your co-worker. You end up with two different copies of the workbook, each in a different format.

Quick Reference

HOW TO EXPORT A FILE

Task	Procedure
Export a Workbook to a different file format.	■ Open the workbook in Excel; then choose **File→Save As** from the menu bar. ■ Click on the **Save As Type** box; choose the desired file format; then click **Save.** ■ Read any warnings Excel displays about the potential for lost formatting and/or worksheets in the new file; then click **OK** or **Cancel.**

Hands-On 18.6 Export the Excel Workbook

In this exercise, you will save the workbook in a different file format.

1. Click the **Production Schedule** worksheet tab.
2. Click the Help button on the Excel toolbar if you do not see the *Office Assistant.* The animated Office Assistant on your computer may appear different from the example shown here.

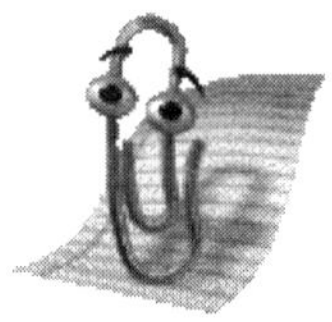

3. Choose **File→Save As** from the menu bar.
4. Follow these steps to save the file with a different file format.

Ⓐ *Click at the end of the **File name** box; then add* **`(tab delimited)`** *to the end of the filename, as shown here.*

Ⓑ *Click the **Save as type** drop-down list button. Scroll up and down the list to review the available file formats. Every format type in this list has a corresponding converter that was installed along with Excel. It is possible to install additional converters later if they are needed.*

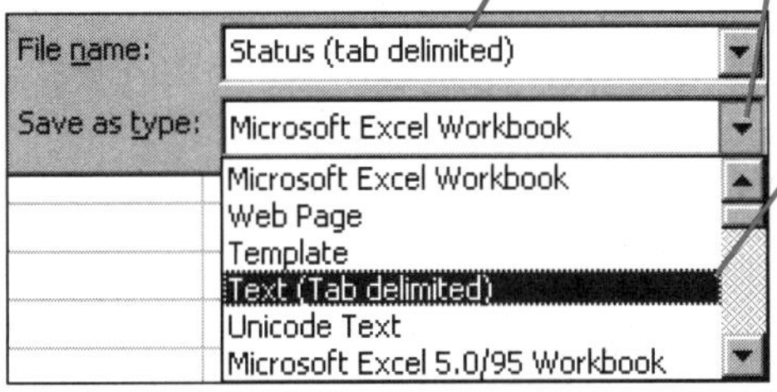
File name:
Status (tab delimited)
Save as type:
Microsoft Excel Workbook
Microsoft Excel Workbook
Web Page
Template
Text (Tab delimited)
Unicode Text
Microsoft Excel 5.0/95 Workbook

Ⓒ *Choose the **Text (Tab Delimited)** format near the top of the list.*

Ⓓ *Click the **Save** button to complete the command.*

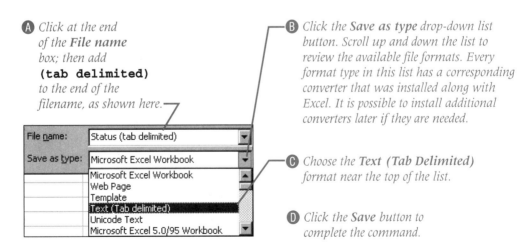

Excel will warn you that the Text file format cannot save data on multiple worksheets. For this example, that's OK. However, if you needed to save all of the data in this workbook, you would either place all of the data onto a single worksheet before you save the workbook, or you would have to save each worksheet individually. For now, you will save just the data on the Production Schedule worksheet.

(Continued on the next page)

5. Click **OK** to accept the fact that only the currently active worksheet will be saved to the new file.
Excel will prompt you that some data and/or formatting could be lost when you save to this file format. You are given the choice of preserving the features of the workbook, or aborting the save and saving the file in Excel's native file format.

6. Click **Help** near the bottom-left corner of the Office Assistant Speech Balloon.
The primary Help window will appear to display information on file formatting that is not transferred when you convert a file.

7. If necessary, *scroll down* near the bottom of the Help window; then click the Text (Tab Delimited) (*.txt) hyperlink. Look over the first two paragraphs of information on converting a worksheet to this format.
This Help information can aid you in choosing the correct file format, or in foreseeing the types of formatting that would be lost.

8. Close the **Help** window.

9. Click **Yes** to accept saving to the newly selected file format and the loss of formatting.

10. Close the **Excel** window. Click **No** if you are asked to save changes to the Status (tab delimited) workbook.

View the Worksheet File in Its New Format

11. Click the **A:\Annual Report** button on the Taskbar to restore that window.

12. Double-click the **Status (tab delimited)** file.
The file will be displayed in the Notepad applet. Notice that all of your formatting has been stripped away. Notice also that the columns no longer line up neatly. You would need to "clean up" the alignment of the columns in this Notepad file just as you had to clean up the Editing Schedule file that you copied into the Workbook earlier.

13. Close the **Notepad** window.

14. Make sure that the *Status (tab delimited)* file is selected in the My Computer window; then tap the DELETE key on the keyboard. Click **Yes** if you are asked to confirm the deletion.

Saving an Excel Workbook for the Web

Like most of the Office 2000 applications, Excel is designed to post information to the Web whenever you need this capability. You no longer need to send a file individually to each person participating in a project. Now you can simply post the workbook to the Web. When someone needs the information, they can save the Web page or copy and paste individual cells from the online workbook.

Publishing Compared to Saving as Web Page

When you save an Excel workbook for viewing on the Web you have two basic options. Each option has benefits and limitations.

- **Save as Web Page—**This save option lets you save the entire workbook in Web (HTML) format with a single command. *Save as Web Page* lets users navigate among the worksheets with the familiar tabs at the bottom of the window. However, a workbook saved as a Web page cannot offer any of the interactive features available with the other formats.

- **Publish—**This save option allows you to save only one worksheet (or a range of cells on one worksheet) at a time. You should use the *Publish* option when you want to offer *interactivity* features with a worksheet (see *Allowing Interactivity* on the next page. For example, users can enter new data into a worksheet, and then save it, or they can view a pivot table online.

Web Page Preview

In previous lessons you have used the Print Preview command to see how an Excel workbook will appear in print. Excel also makes it easy to see what the workbook will look like when you post it to the Web. The **File→Web Page Preview** command launches your Web browser and displays the workbook exactly as it will appear on the Web.

Quick Reference

HOW TO SAVE A WORKBOOK AS A WEB PAGE

Task	Procedure
Save an entire workbook so that it may be viewed on the Web.	■ Open the Workbook in Excel. ■ Choose **File→Save As Web Page** from the menu bar. ■ If desired, click the **Change Title** button to type the title that will appear in the Web browser when the workbook is displayed over the Web. ■ Choose a **destination** for the Web page. This can be a folder on a disk drive or a Web folder (see *Publishing with Web Folders* on page 550). ■ Click **Save** to save the workbook in Web page format.
Preview a workbook in your Web browser.	■ Choose **File→Web Page Preview** from the menu bar.

Deion decides to publish the worksheets of his workbook to the Web. This will allow each project team member to view each other's schedules and keep abreast of any delays or rushes that may affect their own work.

Hands-On 18.7 Save the Workbook as a Web Page

In this exercise, you will use Web Page Preview, and then save the workbook as a Web page.

Preview the Workbook as a Web Page

1. Double-click the **Status** workbook file in the My Computer window.
2. Choose **File→Web Page Preview** from the menu bar.
   Excel will start Internet Explorer *or your default Web browser program. The page is displayed just as it would appear if it were viewed over the Web. Notice that the worksheet tabs at the bottom of the browser window are similar to the tabs at the bottom of every Excel workbook window.*
3. If necessary, Maximize the Internet Explorer window.
4. Click each of the worksheet tabs at the bottom of the Internet Explorer window to view the three worksheets.
   There's really not much difference between viewing the workbook in a Web browser and viewing it in an Excel window. About the only things missing are the gridlines.

(Continued on the next page)

5. Close ☒ the **Internet Explorer** window.
   You are back to viewing the Excel window.

Save the Workbook as a Web Page

Now you will save the workbook as a Web page on your floppy disk. Later, you will learn how to save the Workbook as a Web page on the World Wide Web.

6. Choose **File→Save As Web Page** from the menu bar.
7. Click the **Change Title** button near the lower-right corner of the dialog box; then type the title: **`Annual Report Production`**, and click **OK.**
   This command sets the title that displays when your workbook is viewed in a Web browser.
8. Click the Save button.
   There will be a pause as the workbook is converted to Web page (HTML) format and all of the necessary data is saved to your floppy disk.

Open the Web Page

9. Minimize the Excel window.
   The Annual Report window should now be active.
10. Choose **View→Large Icons** from the menu bar.
11. Choose **View→Arrange Icons→By Name** from the menu bar.
    Notice that there are now two files named Status; *one for each version of the file that you have saved as shown below.*

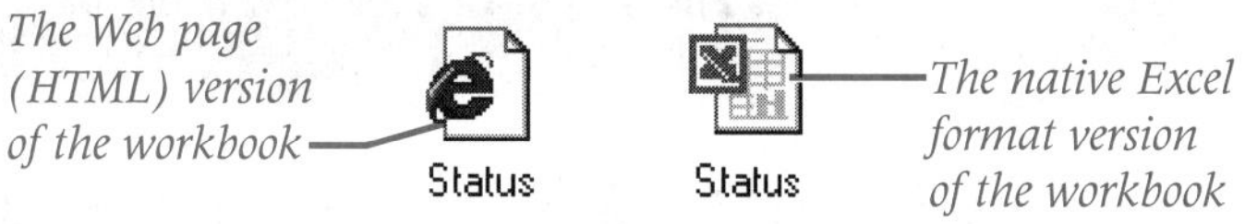
The Web page (HTML) version of the workbook
Status
Status
The native Excel format version of the workbook

12. Double-click the **Status** icon for the **Web page** version of your workbook.
    Internet Explorer (or another browser program) will start to display the workbook.
13. Click each of the worksheet tabs at the bottom of the Internet Explorer window to verify that the workbook was successfully converted to Web page format.
    The worksheets should appear as they did when you viewed the workbook with the Web Page Preview *command earlier in this exercise. Leave the Internet Explorer window open.*

Allowing Interactivity

It is also possible to save an individual worksheet with interactive capabilities. This means that users viewing the worksheet in their Web browser can enter, format, and analyze data. For example, a user could enter data in the worksheet, and any formulas that use the data would work also to display any new calculations.

TIP! *In order to view an interactive worksheet on a Web page, the viewer must be running* Internet Explorer version 4.01 or later *and also have installed the* Microsoft Office Web Components.

Quick Reference

HOW TO SAVE AN INTERACTIVE WORKSHEET

Task	Procedure
Save a Worksheet so that others can interact with its data in an Internet Explorer window.	■ Display the worksheet in the workbook window. ■ Choose **File→Save as Web Page** from the menu bar. ■ Click the **Selection: Sheet** option in the dialog box; then make sure that the *Add interactivity* box is checked. ■ Make sure that the filename and Web Page title settings are correct; then click the **Save** button.

Lost Formatting on Interactive Worksheets

When you save an interactive worksheet as a Web page, not all of the features and formatting of the worksheet will be retained. For example, any *images, pattern fills,* and *comments* on worksheets are **not** saved when the workbook is saved as an interactive Web page. Some formatting, such as font settings and color fills, will still display correctly. Excel's online help lists the functionality that is lost or retained when you save your workbook as a Web page. You may also need to experiment and make sure all of the necessary elements of the workbook are visible in Web page format.

Hands-On 18.8 Use an Interactive Web Worksheet

In this exercise, you will navigate to a worksheet that has been saved to support interactivity. The worksheet uses formulas to calculate dates. You will change the date in a cell and observe the new dates on the Web worksheet.

1. Type the Web address of the lesson Web page in the Address box of the Internet Explorer toolbar: **`www.offtowork.com/oe/lesson18`**.
2. Click the **Interactive** button.
   This page displays the part of the production schedule worksheet that contains data. You can save an interactive worksheet that only contains selected cells. Notice that the graphics are missing from this worksheet. This is one limitation of interactive worksheets.
3. Follow these steps to enter new data into the worksheet.

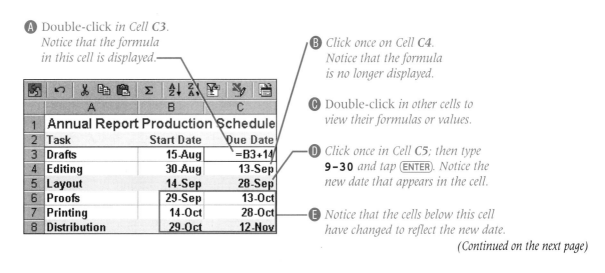

Ⓐ Double-click *in Cell* ***C3****. Notice that the formula in this cell is displayed.*

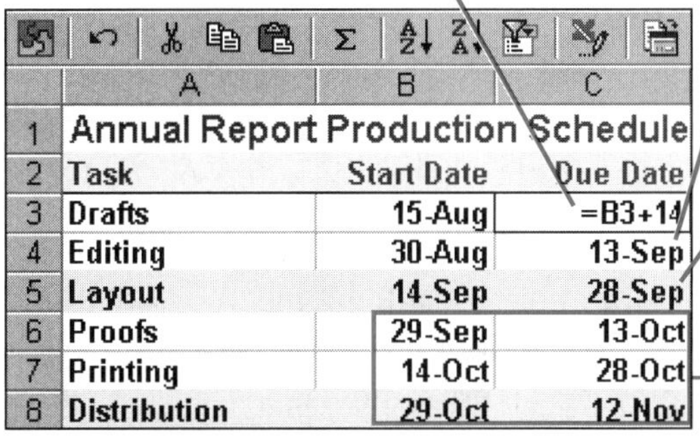

A
B
C
1 Annual Report Production Schedule
2 Task Start Date Due Date
3 Drafts 15-Aug =B3+14
4 Editing 30-Aug 13-Sep
5 Layout 14-Sep 28-Sep
6 Proofs 29-Sep 13-Oct
7 Printing 14-Oct 28-Oct
8 Distribution 29-Oct 12-Nov

Ⓑ *Click once on Cell* ***C4****. Notice that the formula is no longer displayed.*

Ⓒ Double-click *in other cells to view their formulas or values.*

Ⓓ *Click once in Cell* ***C5****; then type* **9-30** *and tap* ENTER*. Notice the new date that appears in the cell.*

Ⓔ *Notice that the cells below this cell have changed to reflect the new date.*

(Continued on the next page)

4. Click in Cell **C6;** then type **10-16** as the new date for this cell and tap the (ENTER) key.
   Cells in rows 7 and 8 will change to reflect the new date.
5. Minimize the Internet Explorer window.

Thus far, your workbook has been saved as a Web page, but by itself this does not make the page available over the Internet. In order for others to view the workbook over the Internet, you must *publish* the page to a *Web server.* You will learn how to do this in the next topic.

Publishing with Web Folders

In order for others to view your Web pages over the Internet or an intranet, the pages must be *hosted* on a Web server. The act of placing your Web pages into a folder on a Web server is called *publishing* the pages. Most *Internet service providers* (ISPs) provide their subscribers with at least a megabyte or more of free Web space. Many ISPs offer a variety of hosting plans and services to meet the needs of individuals, small businesses, and large corporations.

Publishing Methods

You can choose from several methods to publish your Web pages to a Web server. The method you choose depends on the capabilities of the ISP or corporate network system that hosts the Web site. Some of the easiest methods are listed in the following table.

Method	When to Use It
Web folders	Use this method if your operating system supports Web folders. Windows 95, 98, NT 4.0, and Windows 2000 all support the use of Web folders to publish Web pages.
Via FTP (File Transfer Protocol)	Use this method when there is no automated method to publish the pages. An FTP utility allows you to manually send your pages to the folder/directory in the hosting service system that will serve your pages.
ISP-provided utilities	Use this method when the ISP that hosts the Web site provides a special utility for publishing your Web pages.

Naming Web Pages

When you create your own Web pages, you should pay careful attention to their names. Many Web servers run on an operating system called UNIX that has rules for naming files that differ from Windows. The following points will help you name the workbook files that you publish to the Web so that they are compatible with most Web server systems:

- **Never use spaces in the filenames of Web pages and graphics—**UNIX systems do not allow spaces in filenames. To help you conform to this rule, FrontPage Express automatically names your page files with the first eight letters of the Web page name.
- **Give the primary page on your Web site the name *index.htm*—**If someone browses to your folder with the URL, but does not type a filename, most Web servers will display the index.htm page automatically. If you do not have an index.htm page on your Web site, someone browsing your site may get an error message.

- **Try not to use uppercase letters in filenames—**Web page filenames are case-sensitive. On UNIX servers for example, *MyHomePage.htm* and *myhomepage.htm* represent different filenames. If you consistently use lowercase letters in the filenames for Web pages and graphics on your Web site, it is less likely that those browsing your site will receive an error message.

Linking the Workbook to a Web Page

When you post a workbook to the Web, you may want to include one or more hyperlinks to help users navigate to other Web pages. As is the case with other Office 2000 applications, Excel lets you insert hyperlinks wherever you need them.

Quick Reference

HOW TO INSERT A HYPERLINK ONTO A WORKSHEET

Task	Procedure
Insert a hyperlink to another Web page onto a worksheet	■ Display the worksheet that will contain the hyperlink. ■ Click in the cell that will contain the hyperlink. ■ Click the Insert Hyperlink button on the toolbar. ■ Fill in the dialog box, and click **OK.**

Hands-On 18.9 Insert Hyperlinks on Worksheets

In this exercise, you will insert a hyperlink to the Acme home page and then copy the hyperlink to the other worksheets in the workbook.

Insert the Hyperlink

1. *Rest*ore the **Excel** window by clicking its button on the Windows Taskbar.
2. Click the **Editing Schedule** worksheet tab.
3. Click Cell **A20;** then click the Insert Hyperlink button on the toolbar.
   The Insert Hyperlink dialog box will appear. This dialog box offers several different methods to place a hyperlink. You will use one of the easiest methods in this exercise.
4. Click the **Web Page** button on the right side of the dialog box.
   The Internet Explorer browser window will appear.
5. Follow these steps to navigate to the Acme Trading Co. Web page.

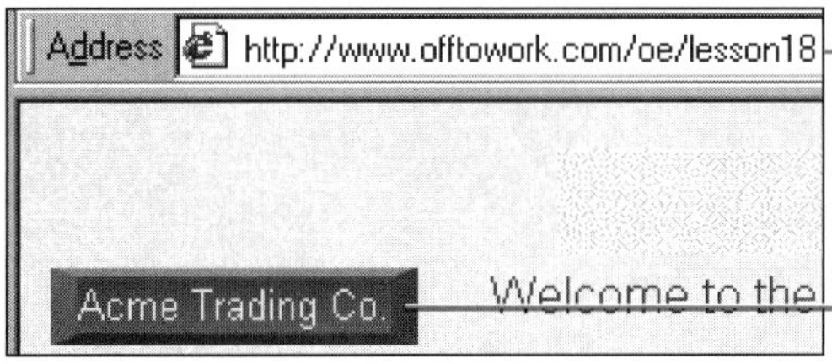

Address
http://www.offtowork.com/oe/lesson18
Acme Trading Co.
Welcome to the

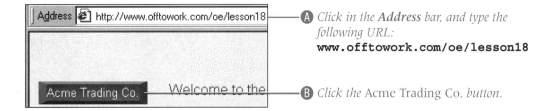

Ⓐ *Click in the* ***Address*** *bar, and type the following URL:* **www.offtowork.com/oe/lesson18**

Ⓑ *Click the* Acme Trading Co. *button.*

The simulated Acme Trading Company home page will be displayed. Notice the Web address (URL) in the address bar.

6. Click the **Excel** button on the Windows Taskbar to make it the active window.
   You are back to viewing the Insert Hyperlink dialog box.

(Continued on the next page)

7. Follow these steps to finish inserting the hyperlink.

(A) *Select the existing text in the **Text to display** box, then type* **`Return to the Acme home page`**.

(B) *Notice that the Web page address is now displayed in the dialog box.*

(C) *Click **OK** to insert the new hyperlink.*

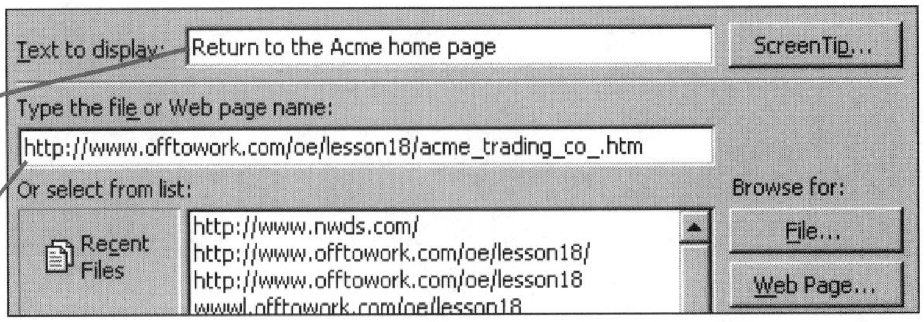

Text to display:
Return to the Acme home page
ScreenTip...
Type the file or Web page name:
http://www.offtowork.com/oe/lesson18/acme_trading_co_.htm
Or select from list:
Browse for:
Recent Files
http://www.nwds.com/
http://www.offtowork.com/oe/lesson18/
http://www.offtowork.com/oe/lesson18
File...
Web Page...

8. Point (don't click) over the new hyperlink you just created.
   Notice how the mouse pointer changes to a small hand. This indicates that the cell is functioning as a hyperlink. Excel will also display a ScreenTip with the Web address (URL) of the linked Web page.

Paste the Hyperlink

Cut
Copy

9. *Right-click* on the new hyperlink; then choose **Copy** from the pop-up menu as shown at right. If you give a normal click (left-click) by mistake, click the **Back** button on the left side of the toolbar, and you will return to the worksheet view.
10. Click the **Layout Schedule** tab, click in Cell **A20,** and then click the Paste button on the toolbar.
    The hyperlink you copied in Step 9 is pasted in the cell.
11. Click the **Production Schedule** tab, click in Cell **A16,** and then click the Paste button on the toolbar.
12. Click the Save button on the toolbar.

Test the Hyperlink

13. Point on the hyperlink you just pasted until the pointer looks like a hand; then click.
    An Internet Explorer window will appear to display the Acme home page. This may be a new window, or it may be a transformation of your Excel window.
14. Click the Back button to return to the worksheet.
    The Internet Explorer window transforms back into an Excel window. Leave the Excel window open.

Using Web Folders

Web Folders

Web folders allow you to publish Web pages and graphics with drag-and-drop ease. A Web folder is a folder on the computer that is directly associated with a folder on a Web server system. When you move or copy files to a Web folder, the files are automatically copied to the associated folder on the Web server system. Deleting files from a Web folder causes them to be deleted from their associated Web server folder.

Quick Reference

SAVE A WORKBOOK TO A WEB FOLDER

Task	Procedure
Publish to a Web site with a Web folder.	■ Choose **File→Save** as Web Page from the menu bar. ■ Click the **Web Folders** button on the left side of the dialog box, or click the *My Network Places* button if you are running Windows 2000. ■ Double-click to open the desired Web folder. ■ Complete the Save command as normal.
Delete files from a Web site with a Web folder.	■ Open a *My Computer* or *Exploring* window; then open the *Web folders* folder or *My Network Places* if you are running Windows 2000. ■ Open the Web folder from which you wish to delete files. Select any files you wish to delete; then click the **Delete** button on the toolbar.

Hands-On 18.10 Publish the Workbook

In this exercise, you will save your workbook in Web page format to a Web folder. You will then navigate to the URL (Web address) for the Web folder to view your files over the Internet or your school's intranet.

Before you Begin, *ask your instructor for the Web folder name, user name, and password you will use to access the appropriate Web folder. Complete these items of information on the lines below:*

Web Folder Name: ______________________

User Name: ______________________ (optional)

Password: ______________________ (optional)

Publish to a Web Folder

1. Choose **File→Save as Web Page** from the menu bar.
   Before you save the workbook, you will check the properties of your Web folder. You will copy the Web address of the folder's associated Web site so that you can paste it into the Internet Explorer address bar later in this exercise.
2. Follow these steps to copy the Web address of the Web server associated with your Web folder.

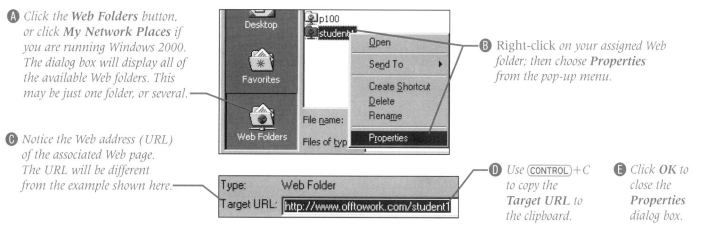

A *Click the **Web Folders** button, or click **My Network Places** if you are running Windows 2000. The dialog box will display all of the available Web folders. This may be just one folder, or several.*

Desktop
Favorites
Web Folders
p100
student1
Open
Send To
Create Shortcut
Delete
Rename
Properties
File name:
Files of typ
Type: Web Folder
Target URL: http://www.offtowork.com/student1

B Right-click *on your assigned Web folder; then choose **Properties** from the pop-up menu.*

C *Notice the Web address (URL) of the associated Web page. The URL will be different from the example shown here.*

D *Use* CONTROL+*C to copy the **Target URL** to the clipboard.*

E *Click **OK** to close the **Properties** dialog box.*

Now that you have copied the Web address for your Web page, you are ready to save your workbook to the Web folder so it can be viewed over the Internet.

(Continued on the next page)

3. Follow these steps to save the workbook to a Web folder.

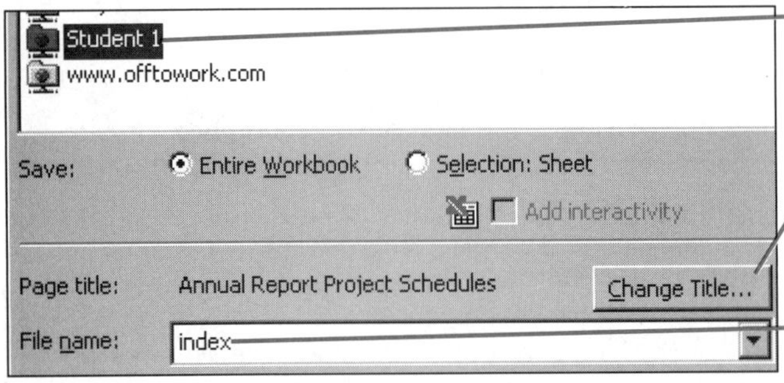

Student 1
www.offtowork.com
Save:
Entire Workbook
Selection: Sheet
Add interactivity
Page title:
Annual Report Project Schedules
Change Title...
File name:
index

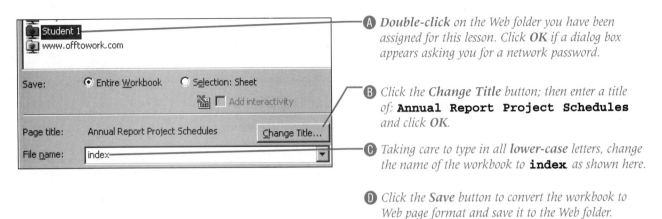

Ⓐ ***Double-click*** *on the Web folder you have been assigned for this lesson. Click* ***OK*** *if a dialog box appears asking you for a network password.*

Ⓑ *Click the* ***Change Title*** *button; then enter a title of:* **`Annual Report Project Schedules`** *and click* ***OK****.*

Ⓒ *Taking care to type in all* ***lower-case*** *letters, change the name of the workbook to* **`index`***, as shown here.*

Ⓓ *Click the* ***Save*** *button to convert the workbook to Web page format and save it to the Web folder. Click* ***Yes*** *if you are asked to replace an existing file.*

A Transferring File *dialog box will appear to show the progress of the transfer as the workbook is transmitted to the associated Web server folder. Your workbook is now hosted on the Internet!*

Display the Workbook Over the Internet

4. After the Transferring File window disappears, Minimize the Excel window.

Address
http:\\www.offtowork.com\student1

5. Click in the **Address bar** of the Internet Explorer window to select the existing URL. Use CTRL+V to paste the Web folder's URL as shown below; then tap the ENTER key to navigate to the URL.
   Your workbook will be displayed in the Internet Explorer window.

6. Click on the Return to the Acme home page hyperlink at the bottom of one of your worksheets.
   This should navigate you directly to the Acme home page.

7. Click the Back button on the Internet Explorer toolbar to return to your workbook.
   Leave the Internet Explorer window open.

NOTE! *After you have completed this exercise, feel free to tell others the URL of your Web workbook. Your workbook will be displayed until another student uses this computer to perform a Hands-On exercise with this Web folder.*

Saving a Workbook from the Web

When you save a workbook to the Web in a *non-interactive* Web page format, some features of the workbook are not available. For example, the formulas in the workbook will not work from within the Web browser window. However, all of the data in your workbook (including formulas and comments) are still stored in the Web page version. If you load the Web page version of the workbook back into Excel, you can restore the file to the native Excel format. Once this has been done, the formulas and other interactive features of the workbook are available again. The process of taking an Excel workbook from workbook (native) format to Web page (HTML) format then back again to workbook format is called a *round trip*. This process is shown in the diagram on the next page.

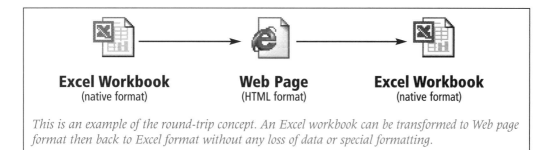

Excel Workbook (native format) | **Web Page** (HTML format) | **Excel Workbook** (native format)

This is an example of the round-trip concept. An Excel workbook can be transformed to Web page format then back to Excel format without any loss of data or special formatting.

Quick Reference

CONVERT A WEB FORMAT WORKBOOK BACK TO NATIVE FORMAT

Task	Procedure
Save an Excel workbook that is posted on the Web.	■ Open the workbook in Internet Explorer. ■ Click the **Edit** button on the Internet Explorer toolbar; then choose *Microsoft Excel* from the drop-down list. ■ Click **OK** if you are asked for a network password. ■ After the file has loaded in Excel, choose **File→Save As** from the menu bar. ■ Change the Save as type to *Microsoft Excel Workbook* format and click **OK**.

Hands-On 18.11 Perform a Round Trip with an Excel Workbook

In this exercise, you will load the Web page version of your workbook into Excel; then save it as a normal Excel workbook.

1. Make sure that the Web page version of your workbook is still displayed in the Internet Explorer window.

NOTE! *If you were unable to perform* Hands-On Exercise 18.10, *double-click the shortcut on the Desktop to your* Annual Report *folder; then follow* Steps 10–12 *of Hands-On exercise* 18.7 *on page 548 to open the Web page version of your workbook.*

2. Follow these steps to load the Web page version workbook into Excel.

Print
Edit
Discuss
NYTimes
Links
Edit with Microsoft FrontPage
Edit with Windows Notepad
Edit with Microsoft Excel for Windows

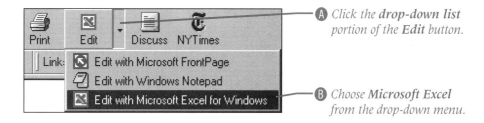

Ⓐ *Click the* ***drop-down list*** *portion of the* ***Edit*** *button.*

Ⓑ *Choose* ***Microsoft Excel*** *from the drop-down menu.*

You may receive a prompt that some files for this Web page are not in the expected location. This is a security feature to help you avoid files that might contain a computer virus. Since you created this file yourself, there is no need to worry.

3. Click **Yes** if you receive a notification that some files on this Web page are not in the expected location.

(Continued on the next page)

4. Click **OK** if you receive a prompt to enter a Web folder password.

5. Click the various worksheet tabs to confirm that the Web page was loaded successfully from the Web site.

6. Choose **File→Save As** from the menu bar.

7. Follow these steps to finish saving the workbook in Excel format.

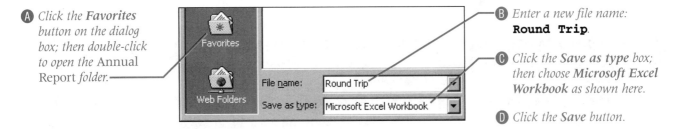

Ⓐ *Click the* ***Favorites*** *button on the dialog box; then double-click to open the* Annual Report *folder.*

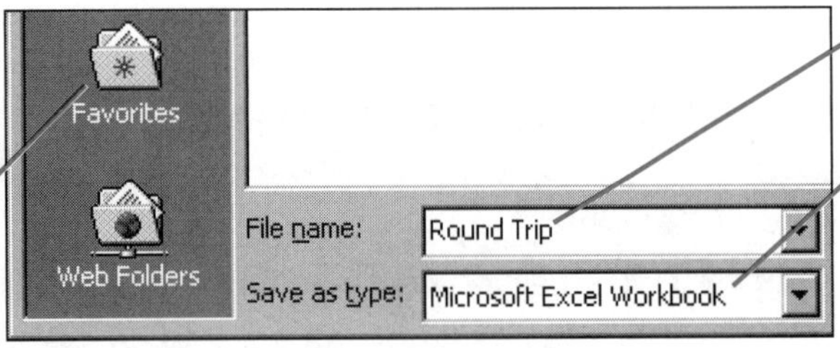

Favorites
Web Folders
File name:
Round Trip
Save as type:
Microsoft Excel Workbook

Ⓑ *Enter a new file name:* **`Round Trip`**.

Ⓒ *Click the* ***Save as type*** *box; then choose* ***Microsoft Excel Workbook*** *as shown here.*

Ⓓ *Click the* ***Save*** *button.*

8. Choose **File→Save As** from the menu bar.
   Notice that the Save as type *box now reads Microsoft Excel Workbook. This indicates that you have successfully converted the workbook from the Web page format to the native Excel format (a round trip).*

9. Click the **Cancel** button to close the dialog box.

10. Close ☒ the Excel, Internet Explorer, and any open My Computer windows.

11. Drag the **Annual Report** shortcut to the *Recycle Bin* on the Desktop. Click **Yes** if you are asked to confirm the deletion.

Concepts Review

True/False Questions

1.	Importing is the process of bringing in data from a non-native file format.	TRUE	FALSE
2.	Exporting is the process of saving data in a non-native file format.	TRUE	FALSE
3.	You can place an image in the background of a worksheet.	TRUE	FALSE
4.	An attachment file can only contain a Web page.	TRUE	FALSE
5.	You can always use any picture you save from the Web for any type of project.	TRUE	FALSE
6.	A file format is a technique for saving data.	TRUE	FALSE
7.	All of the features of a worksheet can be saved in Web page format.	TRUE	FALSE
8.	You publish a workbook by saving it to the hard drive.	TRUE	FALSE
9.	Publishing and saving a workbook are identical processes.	TRUE	FALSE
10.	Interactivity lets users modify a worksheet while viewing it in Internet Explorer.	TRUE	FALSE

Multiple-Choice Questions

1. Which statement best describes an attachment to email?
   a. An attachment is really an email message.
   b. An attachment is a file that arrives as part of an email message.
   c. An attachment is an Excel file that may be viewed over the Internet.
   d. None of the above

2. Which of the following represent an export of a workbook?
   a. A workbook that has been saved with just one worksheet per file
   b. A workbook that has been sent to a user in another country
   c. A workbook that has been saved as a text-only file
   d. All of the above

3. Which of the following statements best describes a Web folder?
   a. A Web folder copies any files you drag into it over to a Web server.
   b. A Web folder is the name for any folder on a Web site.
   c. A Web folder is created automatically when you subscribe to an Internet Service Provider (ISP).
   d. All of the above

4. Which of the statements below best describes a round trip?
   a. You convert an Excel workbook that was in Web page format back to its native format.
   b. You send an Excel workbook to someone as an attachment to email and then receive it back with revisions.
   c. You copy and paste data into an Excel workbook from a text file and then convert the workbook into a text (tab delimited) format.
   d. None of the above

UNIT 6

Access 2000

Proper data management is a prerequisite for the success of every organization. Modern businesses can live or die based on their ability to analyze data and make decisions from that information. Access 2000 provides database management tools that are useful to nearly every organization. It can be used to set up customized databases for a department or an entire organization. Access lets you query databases for the information you need and then generate reports. In this unit, you will learn everything you need to set up and use an effective Access database system. You will even learn how to output Access information to Excel for further analysis.

LESSON 19—Access

Creating Tables and Entering Data

In this lesson, you will begin developing a database for the Pinnacle Pet Care clinic. You will set up two Access tables and enter data in them. All data in an Access database is stored in tables. You will learn how to change the structure of tables and edit records within a database. You will also learn how to widen table columns, change the margins and page orientation, and print the contents of tables. The Pinnacle Pet Care database will continue to be developed in later lessons.

In This Lesson

Case Study

Al Smith is a veterinarian and owner of the Pinnacle Pet Care clinic. Al recently contracted with Penny Johnson—a freelance programmer and Microsoft Access database developer—to develop an order entry system using Access 2000. Al wants to improve customer service by giving the office staff instant access to customer account information. Al chose Access as the database tool because of the customization capabilities of Access and its integration with other Office applications. Al hopes Access and the other Office applications will make Pinnacle Pet Care's customer service as excellent as the care provided to pets.

You can use forms to enter data into tables and to display records.

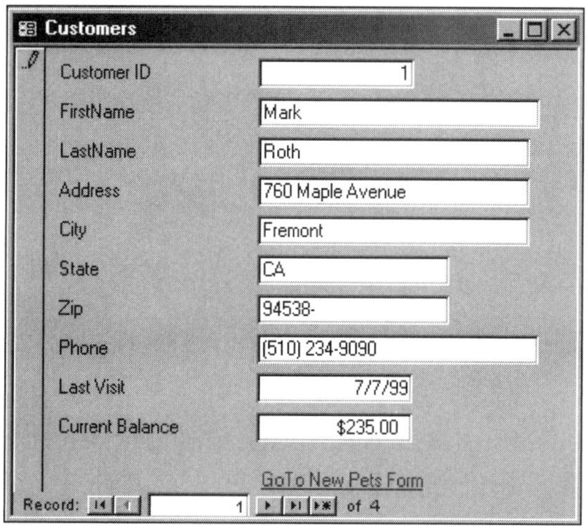

Customers
Customer ID
1
FirstName
Mark
LastName
Roth
Address
760 Maple Avenue
City
Fremont
State
CA
Zip
94538-
Phone
(510) 234-9090
Last Visit
7/7/99
Current Balance
$235.00
GoTo New Pets Form
Record:
1
of 4

In Access, all data is stored in tables.

Customer ID	FirstName	LastName	Address	City	State	Zip	Phone	Last Visit	Current Balance
1	Mark	Roth	760 Maple Avenue	Fremont	CA	94538-	(510) 234-9090	7/7/99	$235.00
2	Tony	Simpson	312 York Lane	Richmond	CA	94804-	(510) 238-2233	9/7/99	$185.00
3	Jason	Jones	2233 Crystal Street	San Mateo	CA	94403-	(415) 312-2312	7/15/99	$48.00
4	Jacob	Samuels	2300 North Pratt Str	Atlanta	GA	30309-	(404) 367-8002	10/8/99	$250.50

You can create reports using data from your tables.

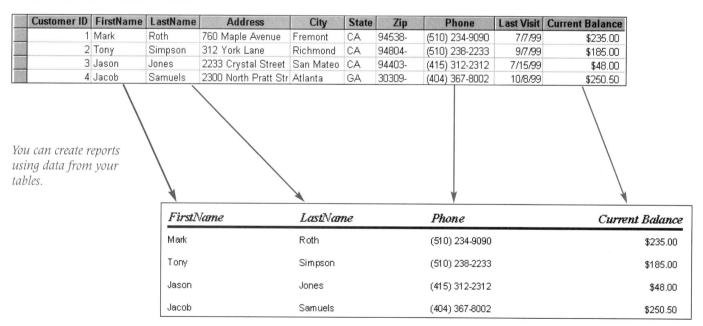

FirstName	*LastName*	*Phone*	*Current Balance*
Mark	Roth	(510) 234-9090	$235.00
Tony	Simpson	(510) 238-2233	$185.00
Jason	Jones	(415) 312-2312	$48.00
Jacob	Samuels	(404) 367-8002	$250.50

What Is Microsoft Access?

Microsoft Access is a relational database management system that lets you store, organize, and manage information. Access is a powerful and flexible program that can handle virtually any data management task. For example, you can use Access to keep a simple contact list, or you can develop a full-featured order entry and database management system. Access gives anyone with a personal computer the ability to organize and manage data in a sophisticated manner.

Access is an integral part of the Office 2000 suite of software tools. Access plays a pivotal role in Office 2000 because it is the data storage and management tool. You can share Access data with Word, Excel, PowerPoint, and Outlook. For example, you can merge a Word form letter with an Access database to produce a mass mailing. You can also export Access data to Excel, and then use the calculating and charting capabilities of Excel to analyze the data.

Starting Access

The method you use to start Access depends upon whether you intend to create a new database or use an existing database. If you intend to create a new database, then use one of the following methods to start Access. Once the Access program has started, you can begin working in the new workbook that appears.

- Click the Start button and choose Microsoft Access from the Programs menu.
- Click the Microsoft Access button on the Quick Launch toolbar (located near the Taskbar).
- Click the Start button, choose New Office Document, choose the General tab, and double-click the Blank Database icon.

Once Access is started, you can create a new database by choosing the Blank Access database radio button and clicking OK. Access will prompt you to save the new database and give it a name.

Use one of the following methods if you intend to open an existing Access database. Once the Access program has started, the desired database will open in a window.

- Navigate to the desired database using Windows Explorer or My Computer and double-click the database.
- Click the Start button and point to Documents. You can choose the desired database from the Documents list. The Documents list displays the most recently used Office documents.

Hands-On 19.1 Start Access

1. Start your computer, and the Windows desktop will appear.
2. Click the Start button, and choose **Programs.**
3. Choose Microsoft Access from the Programs menu.
   Access will start, and the Access window will appear. If this is the first time Access has been started on your computer, the Office Assistant will appear at the lower right corner of the screen. Choose Start Using Microsoft Access *from the Assistant's message box if that option is available.*

Creating a New Database

You can create a new Access database from scratch, or you can use Access's Database Wizard to help you build a database. The dialog box that appears when Access is started gives you both choices.

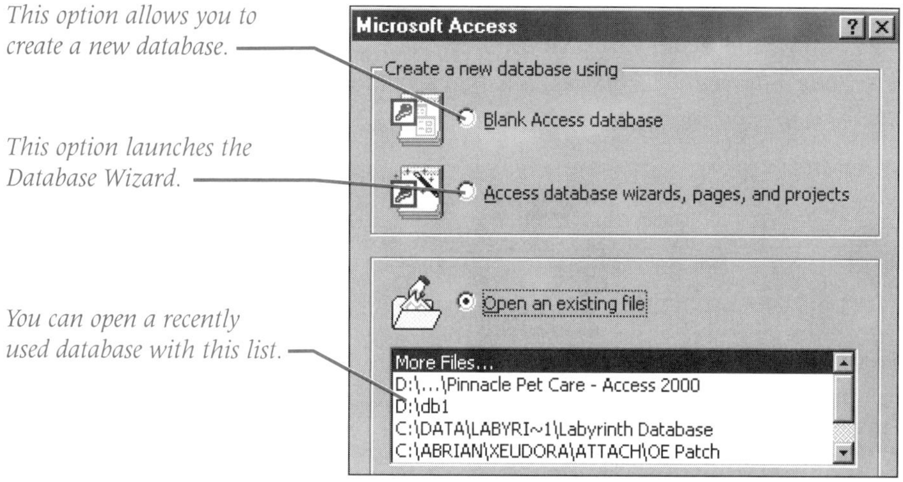
This option allows you to create a new database.
This option launches the Database Wizard.
You can open a recently used database with this list.
Microsoft Access
Create a new database using
Blank Access database
Access database wizards, pages, and projects
Open an existing file
More Files...
D:\...\Pinnacle Pet Care - Access 2000
D:\db1
C:\DATA\LABYRI~1\Labyrinth Database
C:\ABRIAN\XEUDORA\ATTACH\OE Patch

The Database Wizard

The Database Wizard lets you choose one of Access's built-in database templates as the basis for your new database. The Database Wizard takes you step-by-step through a series of screens that let you customize a built-in template to suit your needs. The resulting database is often sufficient to meet the needs of individuals and some small businesses and organizations. A database created with the wizard can also be used as a foundation from which a more sophisticated database can be developed.

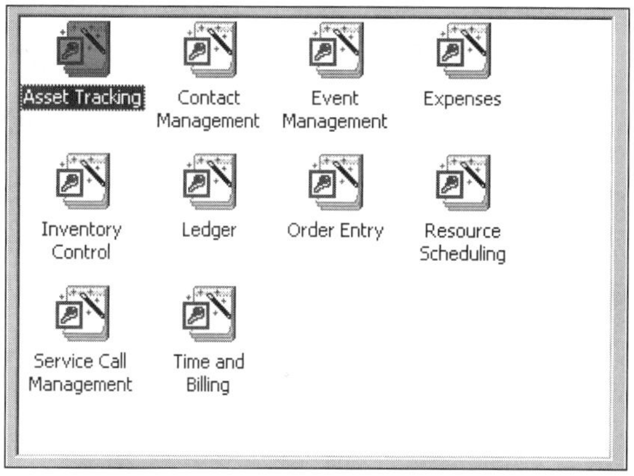
Asset Tracking
Contact Management
Event Management
Expenses
Inventory Control
Ledger
Order Entry
Resource Scheduling
Service Call Management
Time and Billing

Built-in database templates.

Design View

You can also start with a blank database and add objects to your database as needed. An Access database is composed of various objects, including tables, queries, forms, and reports. Each object type can be created from scratch using a Design view for the particular type of object. Access also provides Wizards to help you set up individual objects. You will use both of these techniques as you develop the Pinnacle Pet Care database throughout this course.

Determining Data Inputs and Outputs

The first step in designing any database system is to determine the necessary data inputs and data outputs. Examples of data inputs include the name, address, telephone number, and email address of customers or contacts. Once the required data inputs are determined, the database can be designed to accommodate the inputs and store the required data. Likewise, the required data outputs must be determined before reports and other objects can be designed.

Hands-On 19.2 Create a Blank Database

The Microsoft Access dialog box should still be displayed in the Access window from the previous exercise.

1. Click the **Blank Access database** radio button, and click **OK.**
2. Follow these steps to save the new database to your exercise diskette.
   Your instructor will provide you with a diskette or have you save your database somewhere on the hard disk of your computer system.

Ⓐ *Click here, and choose the disk drive with your exercise diskette. It is most likely the 3½ Floppy (A:).*

Ⓑ *Notice that Access proposes a name such as db1 in the **File name** box.*

Ⓒ *Type the name* **`Pinnacle Pet Care`**, *and it will replace the proposed name. (If you switched disk drives, then you may need to click in the **File name** box, delete the name in the box with the* DELETE *or* BACKSPACE *keys, and then type the new name.*

Ⓓ *Click the **Create** button.*

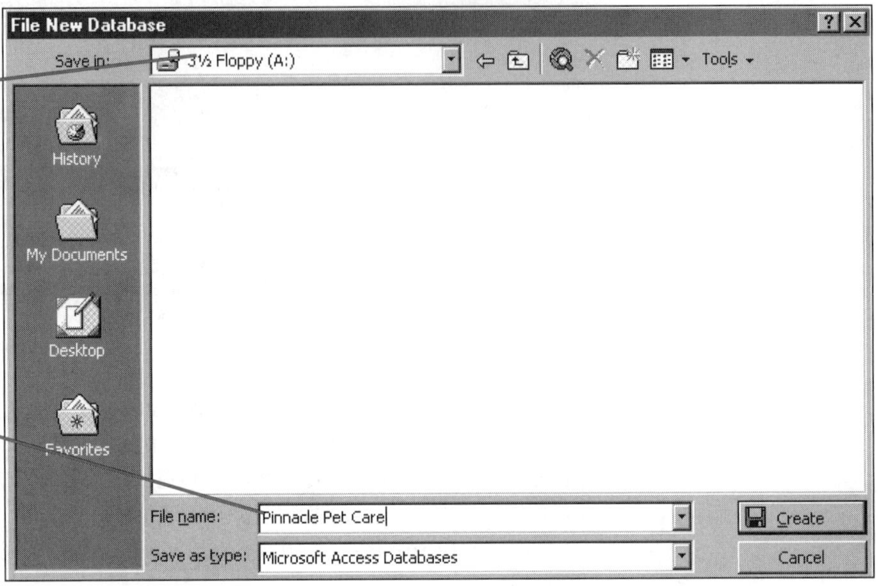

File New Database
Save in:
3½ Floppy (A:)
Tools
History
My Documents
Desktop
Favorites
File name:
Pinnacle Pet Care
Save as type:
Microsoft Access Databases
Create
Cancel

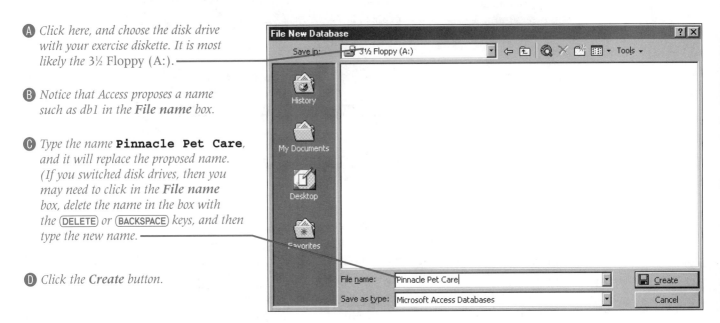

3. Follow these steps to explore the Access database window.

Ⓐ *Notice the various object buttons displayed on the **Objects** bar. An Access database is composed of objects. You can create new objects in Design view or with Wizards by choosing one of the Create options displayed in the window. Objects you create are also displayed in the database window.*

Ⓑ *Try clicking the various object buttons.*

Ⓒ *Click the **Tables** button when you have finished.*

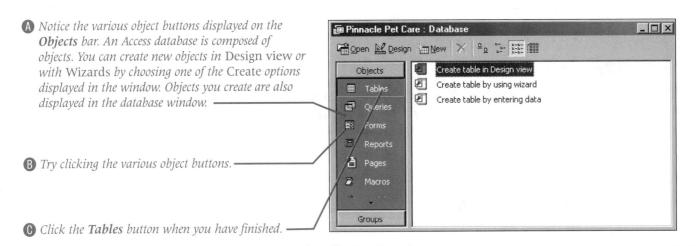

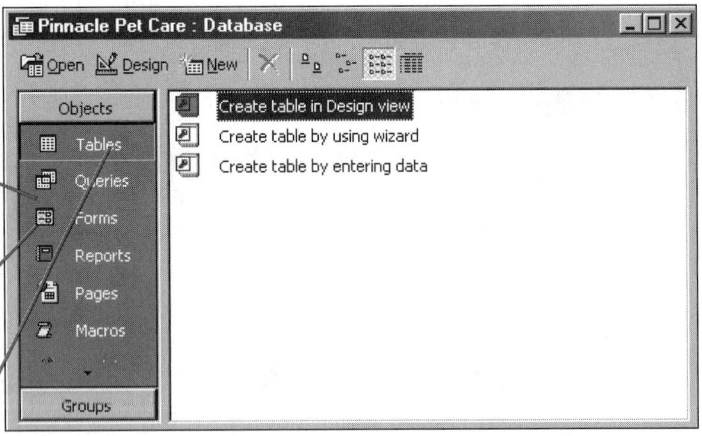

Pinnacle Pet Care : Database
Open
Design
New
Objects
Tables
Queries
Forms
Reports
Pages
Macros
Groups
Create table in Design view
Create table by using wizard
Create table by entering data

Access Tables

In Access, data is stored in tables. Tables organize data so that it can easily be output at a later time. A simple database may have one or two tables, while a sophisticated database may have dozens or even hundreds of tables. A separate table is used for each type of related data. For example, your Pinnacle Pet Care database will initially have a table for customers and a table for pets.

Records

Tables are composed of rows, and each row is known as a record. For example, your Pinnacle Pet Care database will have a Customer table that stores all of the customer information. Each row of the Customer table will contain data for one customer.

Fields

Each record is divided into fields. A record can have many fields. For example, the Customers table will have fields for the Customer ID, name, address, telephone number, etc. In Access, each column in a table is a field. Take a few moments to study the following illustration which shows the first two tables that you will create in the Pinnacle Pet Care database.

*The **Customers** table contains one record for each customer. All data for a customer is stored in one row of the **Customers** table.*

The records are composed of fields.

Customer ID	FirstName	LastName	Address	City	State	Zip	Phone	Last Visit	Current Balance
1	Mark	Roth	760 Maple Avenue	Fremont	CA	94538-	(510) 234-9090	7/7/99	$235.00
2	Tony	Simpson	312 York Lane	Richmond	CA	94804-	(510) 238-2233	9/7/99	$185.00
3	Jason	Jones	2233 Crystal Street	San Mateo	CA	94403-	(415) 312-2312	7/15/99	$48.00
4	Jacob	Samuels	2300 North Pratt Str	Atlanta	GA	30309-	(404) 367-8002	10/8/99	$250.50

Pet ID	Pet Name	Pet Type	Breed	Sex	Color	Date of Birth	Last Visit	Expenditures	Number of Visits	Customer ID
CT02	Max	Cat	Unknown	Male	White	1/7/86	9/7/99	$1,450.55	20	2
CT16	Stripes	Cat	Tortoise shell	Male	Black and brown	10/8/90	7/15/99	$450.00	9	3
CT92	Tony	Cat	Unknown	Male	Brown with black stripes	4/3/97	7/7/99	$145.00	6	1
DG12	Wolfy	Dog	German Shepherd	Male	Brown	6/6/91	7/15/99	$450.00	7	3
DG13	Dillon	Dog	Mutt	Male	Black	10/5/94	7/7/99	$150.55	3	1
DG24	Ben	Dog	Terrier	Male	Black	6/1/92	10/8/99	$480.00	3	4
DG25	Spike	Dog	Chow	Male	Brown	4/3/84	10/8/99	$890.00	12	4
RB23	Bugs	Rabbit	Jack	Unknown	Brown	6/7/95	9/7/99	$600.50	4	2

*Notice that the Customer ID field appears in both the **Customers** and **Pets** tables. Eventually, this field will be used to establish a relationship between the two tables. Establishing relationships between tables is what gives Access and other relational database systems their power and flexibility.*

Table Structure

In Access, you can set up tables in Design view or with the Table Wizard. In Design view, you specify the field names, the data type of each field, and any other parameters as needed. Design view lets you precisely determine the characteristics of each field. The Table Wizard automates the process of creating a table by letting you choose from a set of predefined fields. The Table Wizard lacks the flexibility of Design view; however, it is often useful for beginning Access users. Besides, you can always switch to Design view to modify a table that has been set up with the Table Wizard. Access gives you complete control in setting up and modifying tables and other Access objects.

Field Names

Each field in an Access table is identified by a unique name. The name can be up to 64 characters in length and can contain letters, numbers, spaces, and most punctuation marks. Field names cannot contain periods, exclamation marks, or square brackets [ ]. Some examples of field names from the Pinnacle Pet Care Customers table are Firstname, Lastname, Address, City, State, and Zip.

Data Types

Each field is assigned a data type that determines the type of data the field may contain. Common data types are text, number, currency, and date.

- **Text—**Text fields can contain any type of characters. The default size of text fields is 50 characters; however, you can increase or decrease the size as desired.
- **Number—**Number fields can only contain numbers. Number fields can be used in calculations. You should use the Text data type if a field will contain a combination of text and numbers.
- **Currency—**Currency fields can be used in calculations. Access formats the numbers in a currency field with dollar signs, commas, decimal points, and digits following the decimal point.
- **Date—**Date fields contain dates. Dates can also be used in calculations. For example, you could subtract two dates to determine the number of days between the dates.

Field Properties

Each data type has several field properties that can be used to customize the field. For example, you can change the Field Size property for text fields to increase or decrease the maximum number of characters allowed in the field. The field properties can be modified for each field in a table when the table is displayed in Design view.

Quick Reference

SETTING UP TABLES IN DESIGN VIEW

- Click the Tables button on the Objects bar in the Access Database window.
- Double-click the **Create table in Design view** option.
- Type a field name in the Field Name column of the table that appears.
- Choose a Data Type for the new field and type a description if desired.
- If necessary, modify the field properties at the bottom of the dialog box.
- Repeat the previous three steps for all desired fields.
- Close the table and give it a name when you have finished.

Hands-On 19.3 Set up a Table in Design View

In this exercise, you will begin setting up the Pets table for the Pinnacle Pet Care database.

Define Text Fields

1. Follow these steps to display a new table in Design view.

Ⓐ *Make sure the **Tables** button is chosen on the **Objects** bar.*

Ⓑ *Double-click the* Create table in Design view *option.*

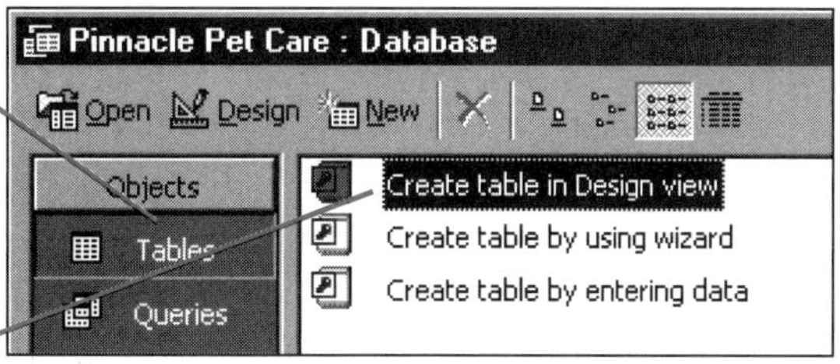

Pinnacle Pet Care : Database
Open
Design
New
Objects
Tables
Queries
Create table in Design view
Create table by using wizard
Create table by entering data

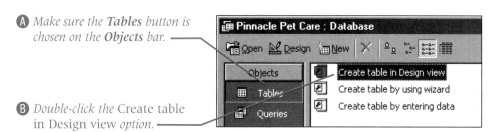

2. If necessary, maximize both the Access program window and the table design window within the Access window.

3. Follow these steps to define a text field.

Ⓐ *Type* **`Pet ID`** *as the field name.*

Ⓑ *Tap the* TAB *key to move to the **Data Type** box. Notice the Data Type is set to* Text*. This is the correct setting because the Pet ID will be composed of letters and numbers. The Text data type is used if the field contains text or a combination of text and numbers.*

Ⓒ *Tap the* TAB *key to move to the **Description** box and type the description shown here. You will learn about primary keys later in this lesson.*

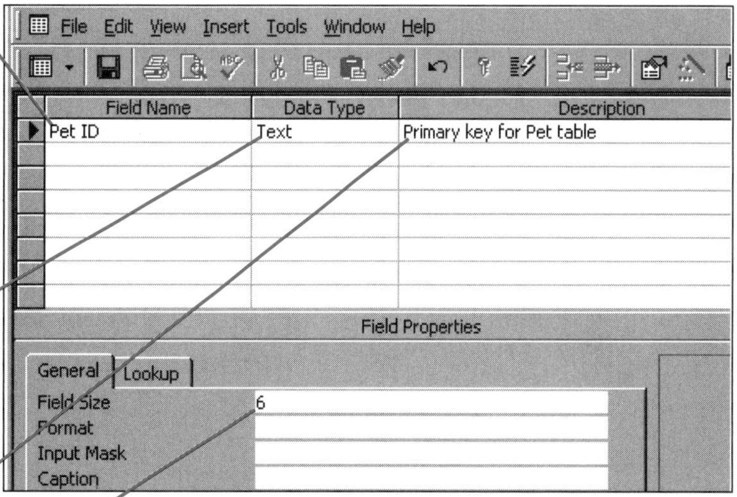

File Edit View Insert Tools Window Help
Field Name
Data Type
Description
Pet ID
Text
Primary key for Pet table
Field Properties
General
Lookup
Field Size
6
Format
Input Mask
Caption

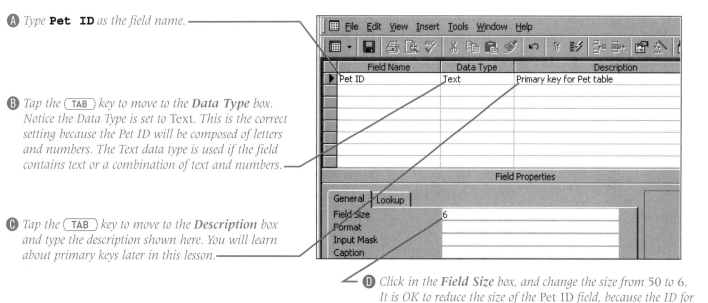

Ⓓ *Click in the **Field Size** box, and change the size from 50 to 6. It is OK to reduce the size of the* Pet ID *field, because the ID for each pet will contain a maximum of six characters. The **Field Properties** section of the dialog box reflects the properties of the current field (*Pet ID*). You will learn more about these properties as you progress through this course.*

You have just defined a field in your database. You will enter data into this field and other fields later in this lesson. You will use a data entry mode known as Datasheet view to enter the data. Currently, you are working in Design view, which allows you to define a table. The Text field type that you chose for the Pet ID field will allow you to enter any type of data in the field. However, the Pet ID for each pet will be restricted to six characters.

(Continued on the next page)

4. Follow these steps to define another text field.

Ⓐ *Click in the next* ***Field Name*** *box, and type* **`Pet Name`**. *The* Pet Name *field will contain the names of the pets.*

Ⓑ *Tap the* TAB *key, and* Text *will appear as the default* ***Data Type.*** *Leave the Data Type set to Text, and do not enter a description for this field. Descriptions are optional and are only used when necessary.*

Ⓒ *Click in the* ***Field Size*** *box, and change the size to* 30 *as shown here.*

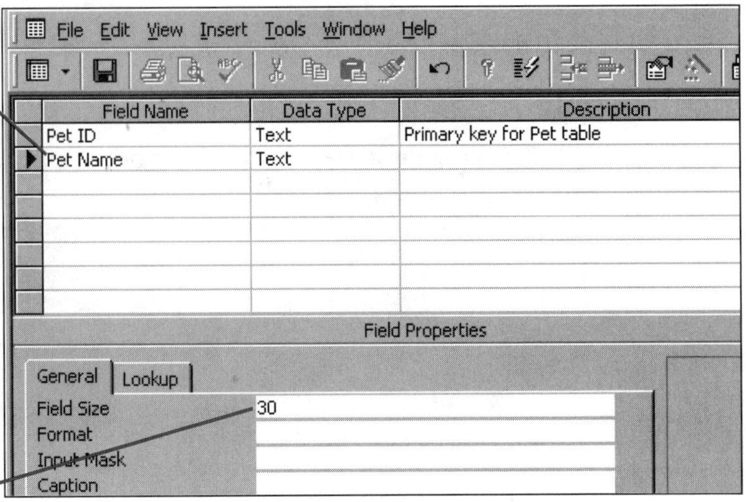

File Edit View Insert Tools Window Help
Field Name
Data Type
Description
Pet ID
Text
Primary key for Pet table
Pet Name
Text
Field Properties
General
Lookup
Field Size
30
Format
Input Mask
Caption

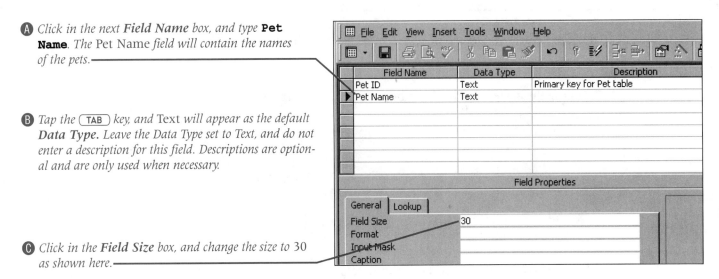

5. Follow the steps in the preceding illustration to create the next four fields, as shown in the following illustration. Set the Field Size to 30 for all of the fields except the Gender field. Set the size of the Gender field to 10.

Field Name	Data Type	Description
Pet ID	Text	Primary key for Pet table
Pet Name	Text	
Pet Type	Text	
Breed	Text	
Gender	Text	
Color	Text	

Define Date Fields

In the next few steps, you will define two fields that will eventually contain dates. You will set the Data Type to Date for these fields. Setting the Data Type to Date is useful because Access will identify the contents of the fields as dates. Dates can be used in calculations. For example, you could have Access calculate the number of days an account is past due by subtracting the invoice date from the current date.

6. Follow these steps to define a date field.

Ⓐ *Click in the next* ***Field Name*** *box, and type* **`Date of Birth`**.

Ⓑ *Tap the* TAB *key, and click the drop-down button in the* ***Data Type*** *box. A list of data types will appear, as shown here.*

Ⓒ *Choose* Date/Time *from the drop-down list.*

Ⓓ *Notice the* ***Field Properties*** *section does not contain a Field Size box. You cannot set the field size for date fields. The options on the Field Properties list change for each data type.*

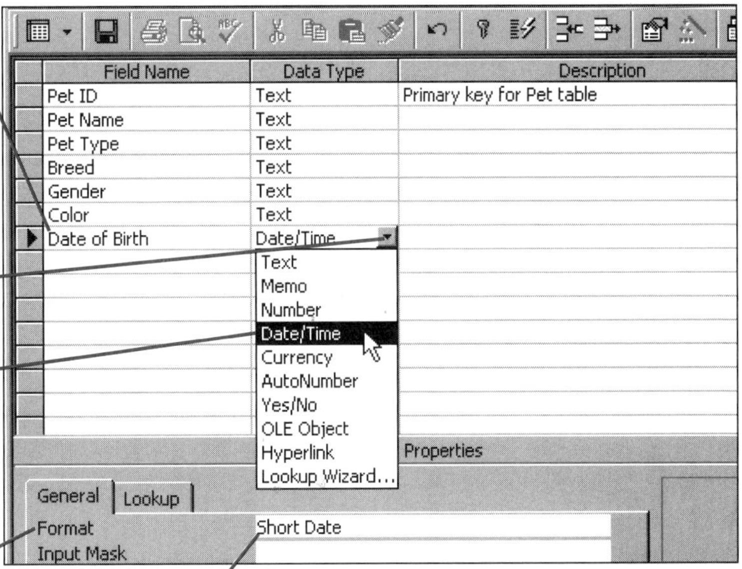

Field Name
Data Type
Description
Pet ID
Text
Primary key for Pet table
Pet Name
Text
Pet Type
Text
Breed
Text
Gender
Text
Color
Text
Date of Birth
Date/Time
Text
Memo
Number
Date/Time
Currency
AutoNumber
Yes/No
OLE Object
Hyperlink
Lookup Wizard...
Properties
General
Lookup
Format
Short Date
Input Mask

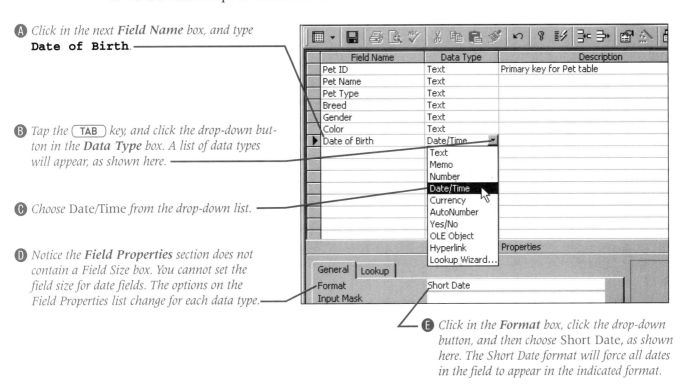

Ⓔ *Click in the* ***Format*** *box, click the drop-down button, and then choose* Short Date, *as shown here. The Short Date format will force all dates in the field to appear in the indicated format.*

7. Now define another date field named **`Last Visit`**, as shown in the following illustration. Set the Format to Short Date, as shown at the bottom of the illustration.

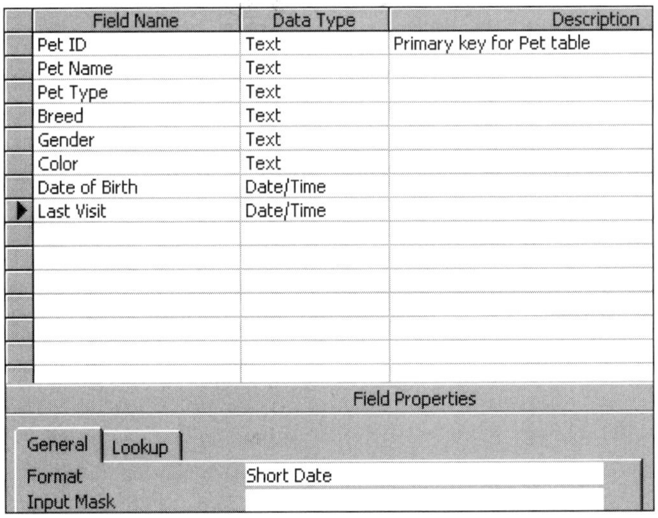

Field Name
Data Type
Description
Pet ID
Text
Primary key for Pet table
Pet Name
Text
Pet Type
Text
Breed
Text
Gender
Text
Color
Text
Date of Birth
Date/Time
Last Visit
Date/Time
Field Properties
General
Lookup
Format
Short Date
Input Mask

(Continued on the next page)

Define Currency and Number Fields

In the next few steps, you will define two more fields. You will set the Data Type to Currency for one of the fields and Number for the other. Currency and number fields can be used in calculations. Furthermore, fields that are formatted with the Currency data type will display a dollar sign, a decimal point, and decimals whenever you enter data into the fields.

8. Follow this step to define the Expenditures and Number of Visits fields.

Ⓐ *Define the* Expenditures *and* Number of Visits *fields as shown here. Set the Data Types as shown, and enter the descriptions as shown. Leave the Field Properties at the bottom of the dialog box set to the default settings. Number fields normally have a* **Field Size** *of* Long Integer *as shown here. Keep in mind that choosing* **Field Properties** *can be an involved process that often requires extensive knowledge of Access.*

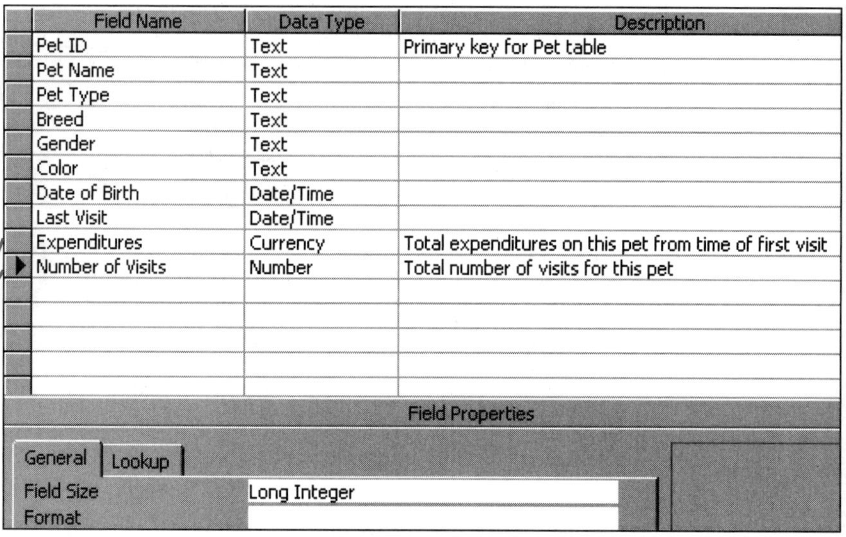

Field Name
Data Type
Description
Pet ID
Text
Primary key for Pet table
Pet Name
Text
Pet Type
Text
Breed
Text
Gender
Text
Color
Text
Date of Birth
Date/Time
Last Visit
Date/Time
Expenditures
Currency
Total expenditures on this pet from time of first visit
Number of Visits
Number
Total number of visits for this pet
Field Properties
General
Lookup
Field Size
Long Integer
Format

9. Now continue with the next topic; you will define a primary key for the table.

Primary Keys

Every Access table must have one field defined as the primary key. The primary key field uniquely identifies each record in the table. For this reason, each record must have a unique entry in the primary key field. Most tables use numbers or codes in the primary key field. For example, the Pet ID field will be the primary key in the Pets table. A unique Pet ID will identify each pet. In table Design view, you specify a primary key by clicking in the desired field and clicking the Primary Key button on the Access toolbar. Access will also prompt you to choose a primary key field if you close a table that has not been assigned a primary key.

Hands-On 19.4 Choose a Primary Key

1. Follow these steps to choose a primary key.

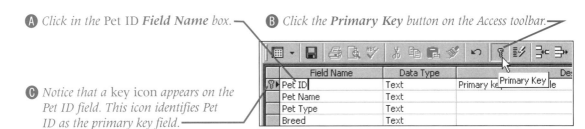

Ⓐ *Click in the* Pet ID ***Field Name*** *box.*

Ⓑ *Click the* ***Primary Key*** *button on the Access toolbar.*

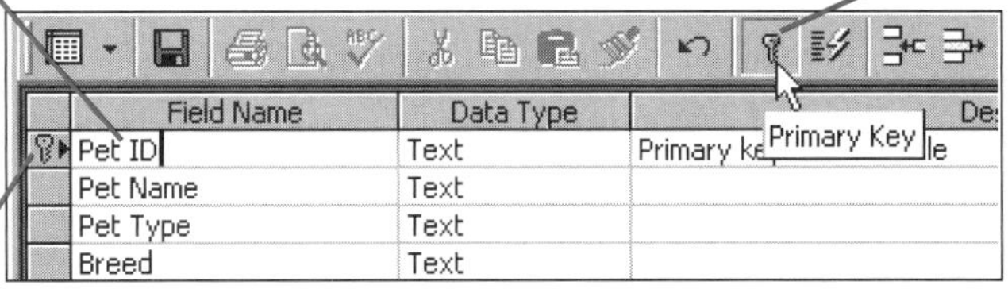

Field Name
Data Type
De
Pet ID
Pet Name
Pet Type
Breed
Text
Text
Text
Text
Primary Key

Ⓒ *Notice that a key icon appears on the Pet ID field. This icon identifies Pet ID as the primary key field.*

Saving Database Objects

An Access database is a "container" that holds tables and other types of objects. The entire database is saved as a single file onto a hard disk or diskette. However, you must also save the objects within the database. Database objects are assigned names when they are saved. This allows you to identify the objects at a later time. A database object name can be up to 64 characters in length and may contain letters, numbers, spaces, and other types of characters.

From the Keyboard

CTRL+S to save an open object

You save an open object by clicking the Save button on the Access toolbar. Access will also prompt you to save an object if you attempt to close the object without saving the changes.

Hands-On 19.5 Save the Table

1. Click the Save button on the Access toolbar.
2. Type the name **Pets** in the Save As box, and click OK.
3. Follow these steps to close the table.

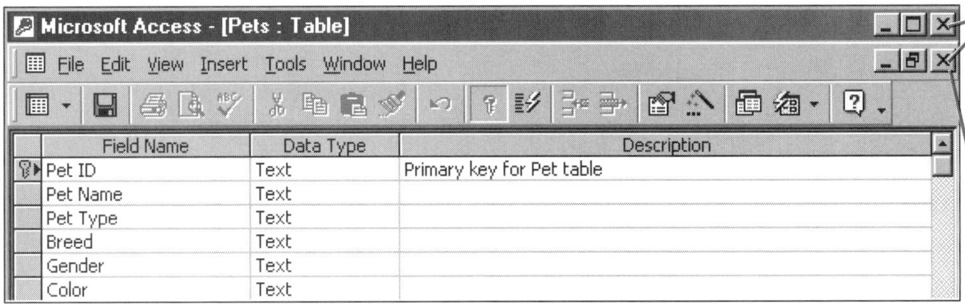

Microsoft Access - [Pets : Table]
File Edit View Insert Tools Window Help
Field Name
Data Type
Description
Pet ID
Text
Primary key for Pet table
Pet Name
Text
Pet Type
Text
Breed
Text
Gender
Text
Color
Text

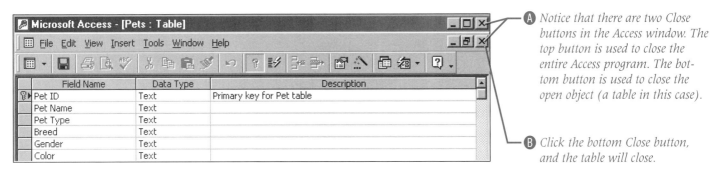

Ⓐ *Notice that there are two Close buttons in the Access window. The top button is used to close the entire Access program. The bottom button is used to close the open object (a table in this case).*

Ⓑ *Click the bottom Close button, and the table will close.*

A "Pets icon" will appear in the Tables section of the Access window. You have completed the process of setting up a table. At this point, you could set up additional tables or other types of objects. However, you will enter data into the Pets table in the next exercise. To accomplish this, you will use Datasheet view.

Selecting Objects with the Objects Bar

From the Keyboard

ENTER to open a selected object
CTRL+ENTER to open a selected object in Design view

The Access Database window provides access to all database objects. You can select any object by clicking the appropriate objects button and then clicking the desired object. Once you select an object, you can open the object or display it in Design view.

*You can open a selected object by double-clicking it or clicking the **Open** button.*

*You use this button to display a selected object in **Design** view.*

You select an object by clicking an object button and then choosing the desired object.

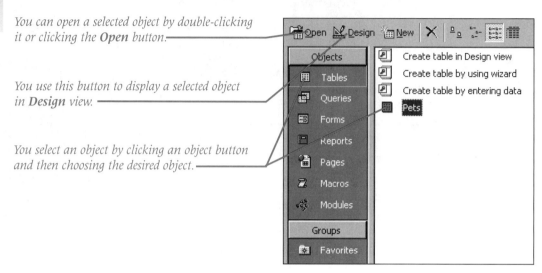

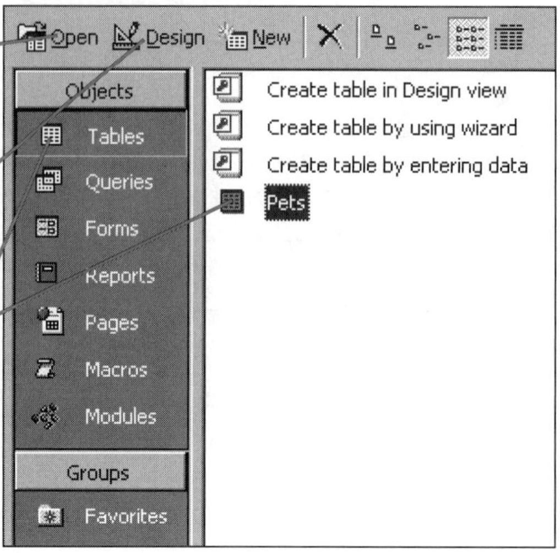
Open
Design
New
Objects
Tables
Queries
Forms
Reports
Pages
Macros
Modules
Groups
Favorites
Create table in Design view
Create table by using wizard
Create table by entering data
Pets

Datasheet View

In the previous exercises, you used Design view to set up the Pets table. Design view lets you set up or modify the structure of tables. However, to enter data into a table, you must display the table in Datasheet view. You can open a table in Datasheet view from the Access Database window as discussed in the previous topic.

Hands-On 19.6 Enter Data

1. Follow these steps to open the Pets table in Datasheet view.

Ⓐ *Make sure the **Tables** button is chosen, and click the Pets table icon.*

Ⓑ *Click the **Open** button. You could also have opened the Pets table by double-clicking the Pets icon.*

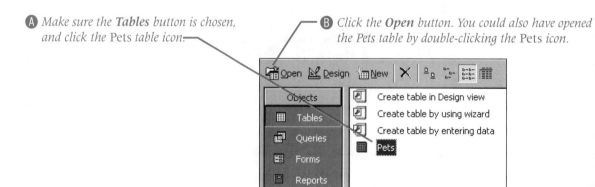

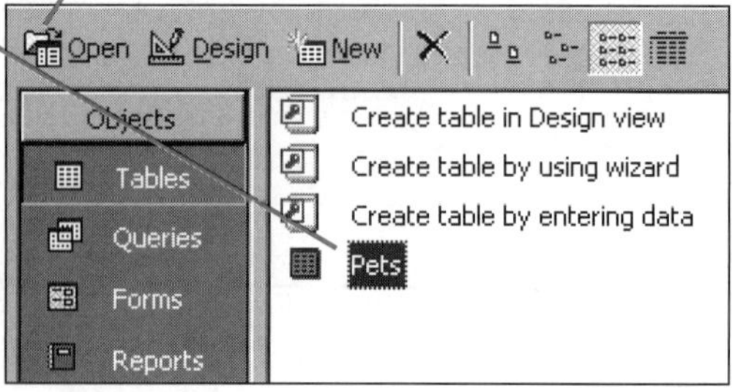
Open
Design
New
Objects
Tables
Queries
Forms
Reports
Create table in Design view
Create table by using wizard
Create table by entering data
Pets

2. Follow these steps to explore the Datasheet view window.
Keep in mind that your window may have different dimensions than shown here.

(A) Notice that many of the toolbar buttons are different from those in the Design view window.

(B) Notice that the field names are displayed as column headings.

(C) Data is entered into the rows (although you will only see one row at this point). Each row is a record. For example, each row will contain all of the data for one pet. You use the TAB *key to move the insertion point from one field to the next within a row (or you can click in the desired row or field).*

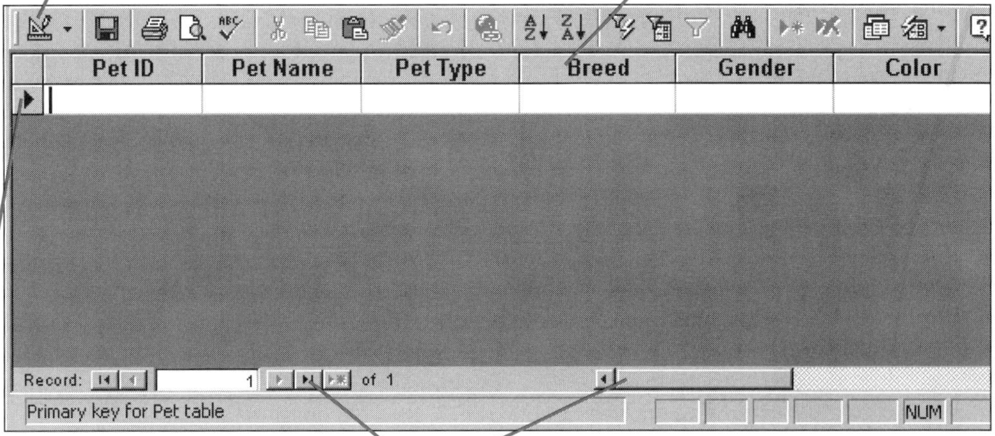

Pet ID
Pet Name
Pet Type
Breed
Gender
Color
Record: 1 of 1
Primary key for Pet table
NUM

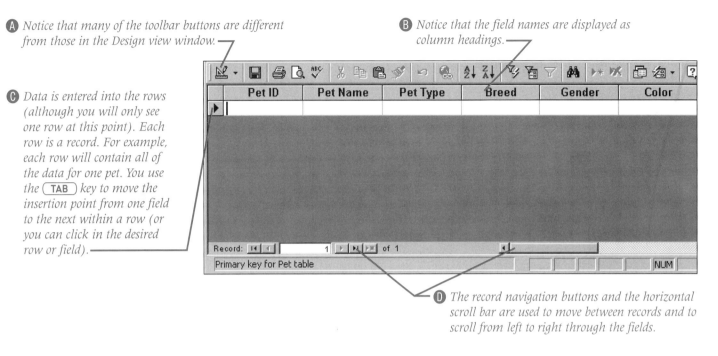

(D) The record navigation buttons and the horizontal scroll bar are used to move between records and to scroll from left to right through the fields.

3. Follow these steps to begin entering a record.

(A) Type **DG12** *as the Pet ID, and Access will add a new row in preparation for the next record.*

(B) Tap the TAB *key to move to the next field and type the pet name* **Wolfy**.

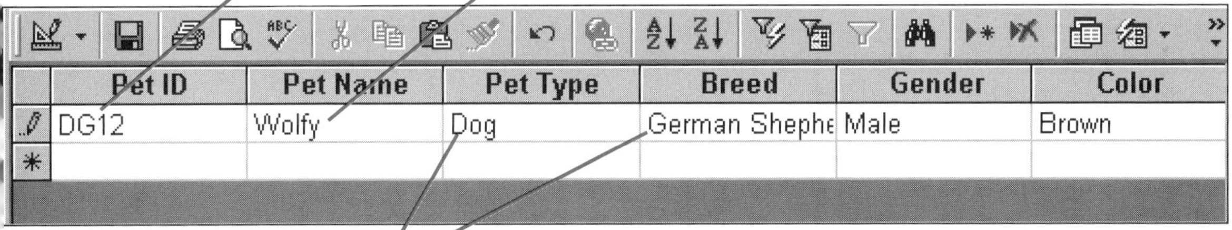

Pet ID
Pet Name
Pet Type
Breed
Gender
Color
DG12
Wolfy
Dog
German Shephe
Male
Brown

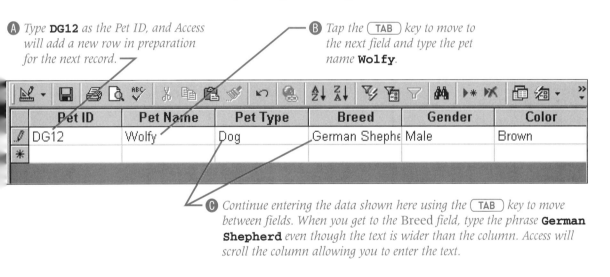

(C) Continue entering the data shown here using the TAB *key to move between fields. When you get to the Breed field, type the phrase* **German Shepherd** *even though the text is wider than the column. Access will scroll the column allowing you to enter the text.*

4. Follow this step to display the remaining fields.

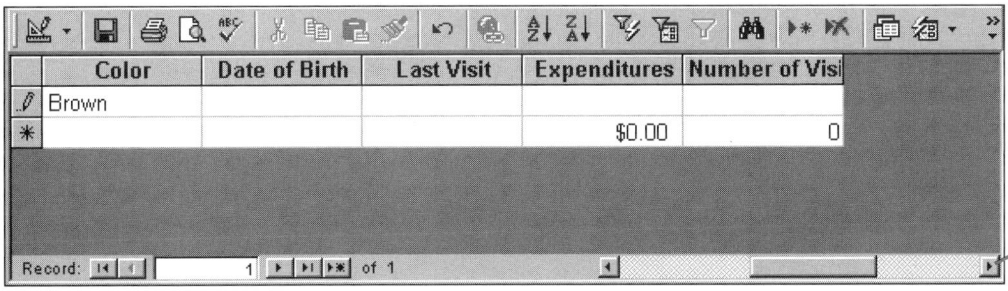

Color
Date of Birth
Last Visit
Expenditures
Number of Visi
Brown
$0.00
0
Record: 1 of 1

(A) If necessary, use the horizontal scroll bar to scroll to the right until the fields shown here are visible.

(Continued on the next page)

5. Follow these steps to enter data in the remaining fields.

A *Make sure the insertion point is in the* Date of Birth *field, and type* **6/6/91**. *Access will display an error message if you enter a number (or text) that is not a valid date. For this reason, you must use the forward slashes (/) while entering dates, or enter dates using another valid date format such as 6-Jun-91.*

B *Tap the* TAB *key, and enter* **7/15/99** *in the* Last Visit *field.*

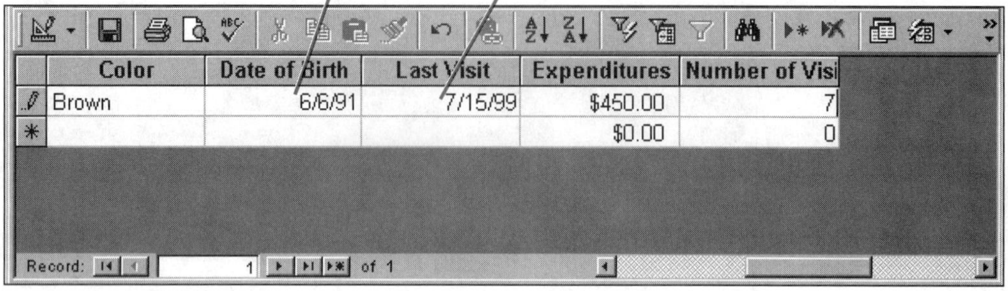

Color
Date of Birth
Last Visit
Expenditures
Number of Visi
Brown
6/6/91
7/15/99
$450.00
7
$0.00
0
Record:
1
of 1

C *Tap the* TAB *key, and type* **450** *in the* Expenditures *field. Tap* TAB *again, and Access will format the number with a dollar sign ($), a decimal place, and two zeros to the right of the decimal. Access formats the number this way because you chose the Currency format for this field when you set up the table.*

D *Type* **7** *in the* Number of Visits *field, and then tap* TAB *to move to the* Pet ID *field in the next record.*

Also notice that Access right-aligned the dates and numbers in the last four fields. Access always right-aligns entries that can be used in calculations.

6. Follow these guidelines to enter the records shown below into the table.
   - Use the TAB key to move between fields.
   - Make sure you use forward slashes / when entering the dates.
   - **Do not** type dollar signs when entering numbers in the Expenditures field. However, **do** type a decimal point followed by the indicated decimals.

Pet ID	Pet Name	Pet Type	Breed	Gender	Color	Date of Birth	Last Visit	Expenditures	Number of Visits
DG13	Dillon	Dog	Mutt	Male	Black	10/5/94	7/7/99	150.55	3
CT89	Puffy	Cat	Siamese	Female	White with patches	12/12/96	7/7/99	30.00	1
RB23	Bugs	Rabbit	Jack	Unknown	Brown	6/7/95	9/7/99	600.50	4
CT02	Max	Cat	Unknown	Male	White	1/7/86	9/7/99	1450.55	20
CT16	Stripes	Cat	Tortoise shell	Male	Black and brown	10/8/90	7/15/99	450.00	9

7. Check your data carefully to make sure it is error-free. Accuracy is extremely important when entering data.

8. When you have finished checking your work, choose **File→Close** from the menu bar.
Access will close the table, and the Database window will be displayed. You can close objects with either the File→Close command or by clicking the Close button (as you did in an earlier exercise). Notice that Access did not prompt you to save the table. Access automatically saves data entered into a table.

Changing the Structure of a Table

You can change the structure of a table after it has been set up. For example, you may need to change the size or name of a field or add a new field. Structural changes are made to a table in Design view.

Impact on Data

You must be careful when changing the structure of a table, especially if data has already been entered. For example, imagine that a field has a length of 30 and you have already entered records into the table. If you reduce the field length to 20, you may delete up to 10 characters from some records. Access will usually provide a warning message if you attempt to make a change that has the potential of destroying data in a field.

Switching Between Object Views

The Datasheet View button appears on the left end of the Access toolbar whenever you are in Design view. You can switch from Design view to Datasheet view by clicking the Datasheet View button.

Likewise, the Design View button appears on the left end of the Access toolbar when you are in Datasheet view. You can switch to Design view by clicking the Design View button.

Setting the Default Value of Fields

NOTE!

Only set a default value if the field will have that value 50% or more of the time.

Access lets you set default values for fields. The default value is automatically entered in new records when you enter data in Datasheet view. This can be convenient if a field is typically set to a certain value. For example, you will set the default value of the Number of Visits field to 1. Pets will be entered into the database when they make their first visit to the clinic. By setting the Number of Visits field to 1, you will be able to skip over the Number of Visits field when entering data for a new pet. In Design view, default values are set in the Field Properties area at the bottom of the dialog box.

Hands-On 19.7 Change Table Structure

Change a Field's Properties

1. Click the Pets icon in the Access window, and then click the Design button on the Database toolbar. The Database toolbar is located just above the Objects bar.
   The Pets table will open in Design view.
2. Follow these steps to change the default value for the Number of Visits field.

Ⓐ *Click anywhere in the* Number of Visits *row (you may need to scroll down).*

Ⓑ *Change the default value to* **1**.

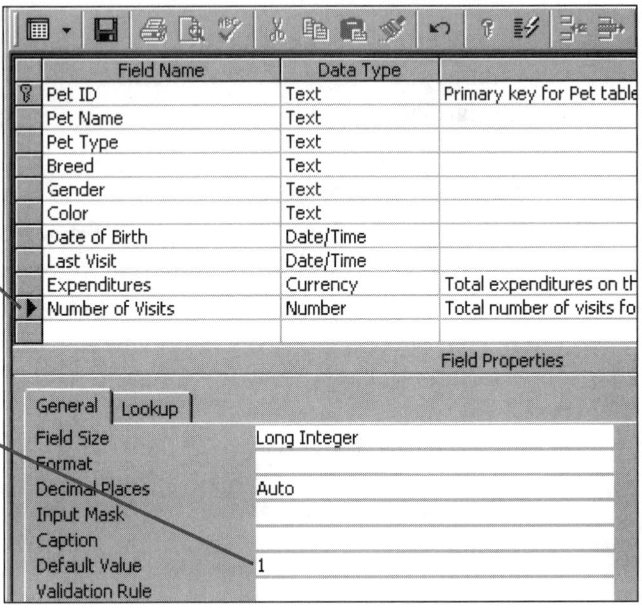

Field Name
Data Type
Pet ID
Text
Primary key for Pet table
Pet Name
Text
Pet Type
Text
Breed
Text
Gender
Text
Color
Text
Date of Birth
Date/Time
Last Visit
Date/Time
Expenditures
Currency
Total expenditures on th
Number of Visits
Number
Total number of visits fo
Field Properties
General
Lookup
Field Size
Long Integer
Format
Decimal Places
Auto
Input Mask
Caption
Default Value
1
Validation Rule

Add a Field

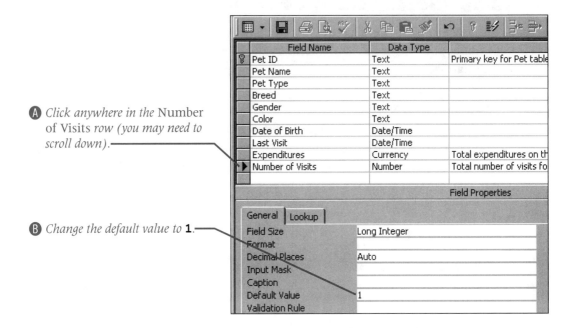

In the next few steps, you will add a Customer ID field to the table. The Customer ID field will eventually link the Pets table to a Customers table.

3. Follow these steps to add the Customer ID field.

Ⓐ *Click in the box below* Number of Visits, *and type the name* **`Customer ID`**. *Make sure you include a space between Customer and ID. The space is necessary because the name will eventually need to match the name in the Customers table.*

Ⓑ *Set the* ***Data Type*** *to* Number.

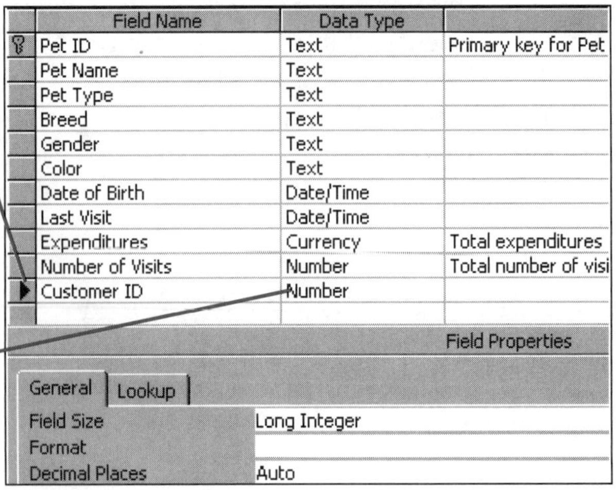

Field Name
Data Type
Pet ID
Text
Primary key for Pet
Pet Name
Text
Pet Type
Text
Breed
Text
Gender
Text
Color
Text
Date of Birth
Date/Time
Last Visit
Date/Time
Expenditures
Currency
Total expenditures
Number of Visits
Number
Total number of visi
Customer ID
Number
Field Properties
General
Lookup
Field Size
Long Integer
Format
Decimal Places
Auto

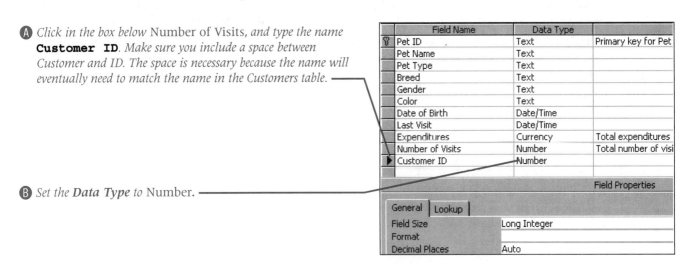

Ⓒ *Take a moment to check the spelling of every field name. Make sure the spelling is correct and matches the spelling of the field names in this illustration. It is important that the field names be spelled correctly because they will be used in other objects throughout this course.*

Switch Views and Add Customer IDs

Automatic ALPHA ORDER

4. Click the Datasheet View button on the left end of the Access toolbar, and then click the **Yes** button when the Office Assistant asks if you want to save the table.
Notice that the order of the records has changed in the table. The records should now be sorted in alphabetical order based upon the primary key field. The records were sorted when you closed the table and then reopened it. One of the benefits of choosing a primary key field (such as Pet ID) is that Access will sort the records based upon the primary key field.
5. Now add the Customer IDs shown below into the table. Make sure you enter the correct Customer ID in each record. You may need to scroll to the left and right in the table to ensure that the correct Customer ID has been entered for each Pet ID. As you can see from this example, it can be difficult to add data to records after changing the structure of a table. For this reason, you should spend as much time as necessary designing and planning a database to minimize the number of changes that are required.

Pet ID	Pet Name	Pet Type	Breed	Gender	Color	Date of Birth	Last Visit	Expenditures	Number of Visits	Customer ID
CT02	Max	Cat	Unknown	Male	White	1/7/86	9/7/99	$1,450.55	20	2
CT16	Stripes	Cat	Tortoise shell	Male	Black and brown	10/8/90	7/15/99	$450.00	9	3
CT89	Puffy	Cat	Siamese	Female	White with patches	12/12/96	7/7/99	$30.00	1	1
DG12	Wolfy	Dog	German Shepherd	Male	Brown	6/6/91	7/15/99	$450.00	7	3
DG13	Dillon	Dog	Mutt	Male	Black	10/5/94	7/7/99	$150.55	3	1
RB23	Bugs	Rabbit	Jack	Unknown	Brown	6/7/95	9/7/99	$600.50	4	2

Make sure each Pet ID *has the correct* Customer ID.

6. Leave the table in Datasheet view, and continue with the next topic.
You will add a record and make other changes in the next exercise.

Record Management

In Datasheet view, the Access toolbar has several buttons that let you manage records. The following quick reference table defines three of these buttons.

Quick Reference

RECORD MANAGEMENT BUTTONS

Button	Function
Find	Lets you locate a record by searching for a word or phrase. The Replace option lets you replace a word or phrase with another word or phrase.
New Record	Adds a new record at the end of the table.
Delete Record	Deletes the current record.

Navigating Within a Table

In Datasheet view, a record navigation bar appears at the bottom of the Access program window. The following illustration defines the buttons on the navigation bar.

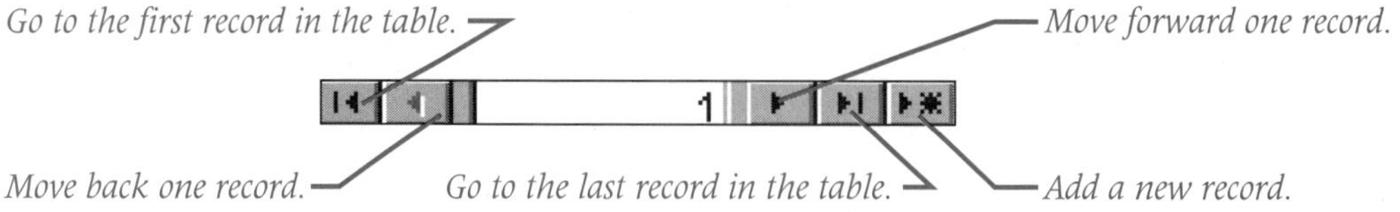
Go to the first record in the table.
Move forward one record.
1
Move back one record.
Go to the last record in the table.
Add a new record.

Notice the Back One Record button is "ghosted out" in this illustration. This is because the insertion point is in the first record as shown in the center of the navigation bar. In other words, there is no record to move back to.

Hands-On 19.8 Manage Records

The Pets table should be in Datasheet view from the previous exercise.

Add a Record

1. Click the New Record button on the Access toolbar.
   The insertion point will move to a new record at the end of the table.
2. Enter the following data into the new record.

Pet ID	Pet Name	Pet Type	Breed	Gender	Color	Date of Birth	Last Visit	Expenditures	Number of Visits	Customer ID
CT92	Tony	Cat	Unknown	Male	Brown with black stripes	4/3/97	7/7/99	145	6	1

Navigate to Records

3. Follow these steps to navigate to various records.

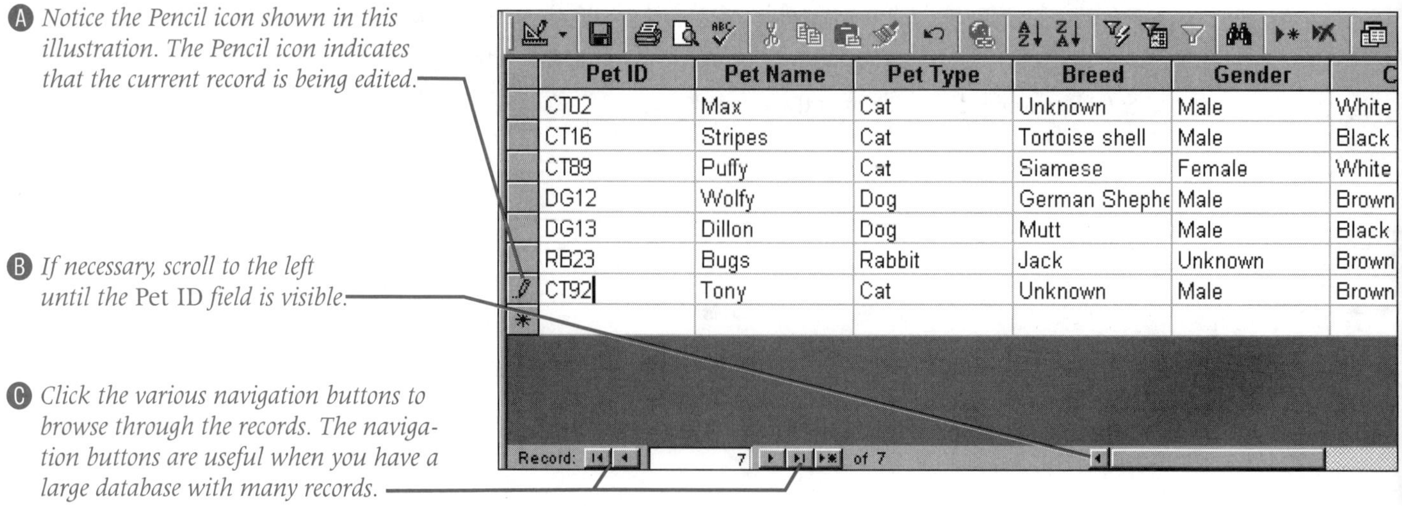
A Notice the Pencil icon shown in this illustration. The Pencil icon indicates that the current record is being edited.
B If necessary, scroll to the left until the Pet ID field is visible.
C Click the various navigation buttons to browse through the records. The navigation buttons are useful when you have a large database with many records.
Pet ID
Pet Name
Pet Type
Breed
Gender
CT02 Max Cat Unknown Male White
CT16 Stripes Cat Tortoise shell Male Black
CT89 Puffy Cat Siamese Female White
DG12 Wolfy Dog German Shephe Male Brown
DG13 Dillon Dog Mutt Male Black
RB23 Bugs Rabbit Jack Unknown Brown
CT92 Tony Cat Unknown Male Brown
Record: 7 of 7

Delete a Record

4. Follow these steps to delete a record.

Ⓐ *Click the record selector box (square box) to the left of the CT89 record to select the entire record. The vertical column of boxes to the left of the records is called the Selection bar.*

Ⓑ *Click the **Delete Record** button on the Access toolbar.*

Ⓒ *Click the **Yes** button on the warning box that appears to confirm the deletion.*

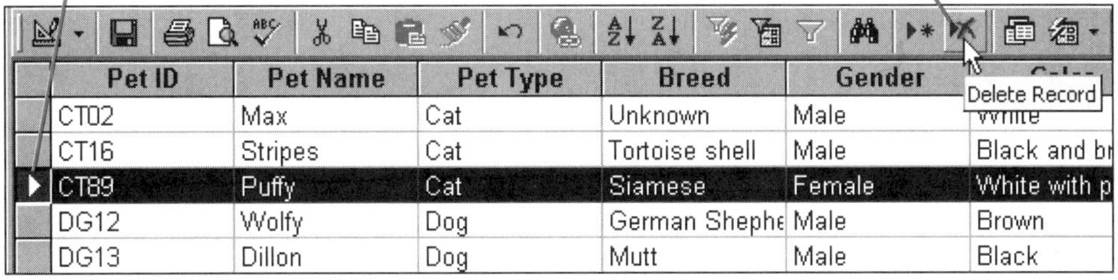

Pet ID
Pet Name
Pet Type
Breed
Gender
Delete Record
CT02
Max
Cat
Unknown
Male
CT16
Stripes
Cat
Tortoise shell
Male
Black and br
CT89
Puffy
Cat
Siamese
Female
White with p
DG12
Wolfy
Dog
German Shephe
Male
Brown
DG13
Dillon
Dog
Mutt
Male
Black

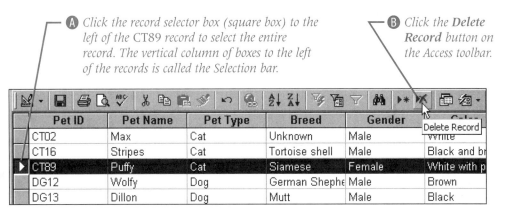

In the preceding steps, you selected the CT89 record prior to deleting it. You could actually have deleted the record by clicking anywhere in the CT89 row and then clicking the Delete Record button. The Selection bar is most useful when you want to delete several records. You can select several records by dragging the mouse down the Selection bar.

Find Records

5. Click on any Pet ID in the Pet ID column.
   In the following steps, you will search for Pet IDs. You must position the insertion point somewhere in the column that you wish to search through prior to initiating the search.
6. Click the Find button on the Access toolbar.
7. Follow these steps to conduct the search.

Ⓐ *Type* **ct92** *in the **Find What** box.*

Ⓑ *Notice that the **Look In** field indicates that you are searching for a Pet ID. In a large database, narrowing the search to a particular field can speed up the search.*

Ⓒ *If the **More** button is available, click it to display additional options. The More button will turn into a **Less** button, as shown here.*

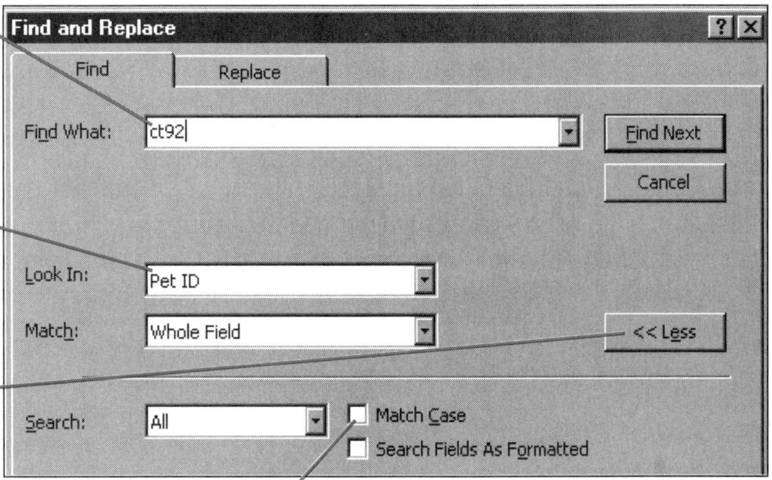

Find and Replace
Find
Replace
Find What:
ct92
Find Next
Cancel
Look In:
Pet ID
Match:
Whole Field
<< Less
Search:
All
Match Case
Search Fields As Formatted

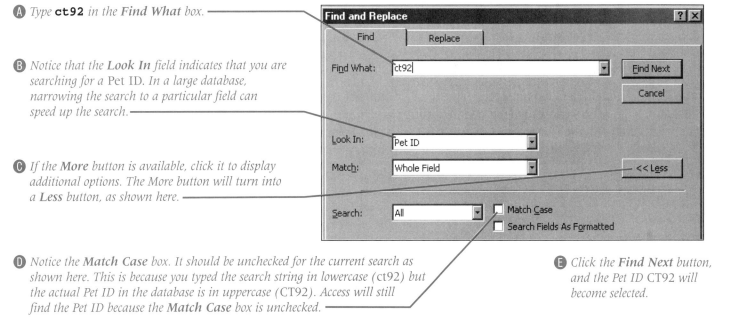

Ⓓ *Notice the **Match Case** box. It should be unchecked for the current search as shown here. This is because you typed the search string in lowercase (ct92) but the actual Pet ID in the database is in uppercase (CT92). Access will still find the Pet ID because the **Match Case** box is unchecked.*

Ⓔ *Click the **Find Next** button, and the Pet ID CT92 will become selected.*

8. Use the preceding steps to find Pet ID **DG12.**
   Keep in mind that the Find feature is most useful when you have a large database and the item you are searching for is not visible on the screen.

(Continued on the next page)

Check Out the Replace Option

9. Click the **Replace** tab at the top of the dialog box.
10. Notice that a Replace With box and several replace buttons appear.
    You can use the Replace options to replace data in a table. For example, you could enter a word or phrase in the Find What box, type a replacement word or phrase in the Replace With box, and click the Replace All button to make the replacement in all records of the table.
11. Click the **Cancel** button to close the dialog box.
12. Leave the table open in Datasheet view, and continue with the next topic.

Cut, Copy, and Paste

Cut, Copy, and Paste are available in all Office 2000 applications. With Cut, Copy, and Paste you can move or copy data from one table cell to another. Copying data can be useful especially when a cell's contents are lengthy. You can even use Cut, Copy, and Paste to move or copy entire rows and columns. In addition, Copy and Paste can be used to copy objects in the Database window.

Quick Reference

CUT, COPY, AND PASTE

Command	Discussion	Procedure
Cut	The Cut command removes entries from table cells and places them on the Office clipboard.	Click the Cut button or press CTRL+X.
Copy	The Copy command also places entries on the Office clipboard, but it leaves a copy of the entries in the original table cells.	Click the Copy button or press CTRL+C.
Paste	The Paste command pastes entries from the Office clipboard to table cells.	Click the Paste button or press CTRL+V.

The Office 2000 Clipboard

NOTE! *Use the View→Toolbars→Clipboard command to display the Clipboard toolbar.*

Office 2000 introduces a new clipboard that can hold up to 12 cut or copied items. The Clipboard toolbar uses icons to display cut or copied items. You can paste any item by choosing it from the Clipboard toolbar. You can paste all items from the toolbar by clicking the Paste All button. The items are pasted in the order in which they were cut or copied to the toolbar.

Clipboard (2 of 12)
Paste All
Breed German Shepherd

*This **Clipboard** toolbar has had two items copied to it. The Clipboard can hold items from all Office programs.*

When you point at an item, a ScreenTip pops up. When you click an item, it is pasted into the table.

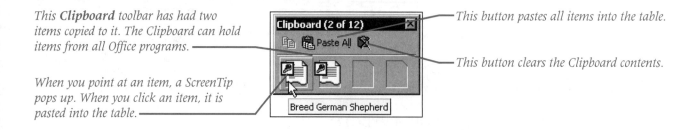

This button pastes all items into the table.

This button clears the Clipboard contents.

Hands-On 19.9 Use Copy and Paste

In this exercise, you will use Copy and Paste to assist you in entering a new record.

1. Click the New Record button on the Access toolbar to add a new record to the table.
2. Follow these steps to enter data and to copy and paste data.

Ⓐ *Type* **DG14** *in the* Pet ID *field, type* **Fetch** *in the* Pet Name *field, and type* **Dog** *as the* Pet Type, *as shown here.*

Ⓑ *Position the mouse pointer on the left edge of the* Breed *cell for* Wolfy *the dog, and the pointer will have a thick cross shape as shown here.*

Ⓒ *Click the mouse button to select the text in the Breed cell. You could also have selected the text by dragging over the cell's contents.*

Pet ID	Pet Name	Pet Type	Breed
CT02	Max	Cat	Unknown
CT16	Stripes	Cat	Tortoise shell
DG12	Wolfy	Dog	German Shephe
DG13	Dillon	Dog	Mutt
RB23	Bugs	Rabbit	Jack
CT92	Tony	Cat	Unknown
DG14	Fetch	Dog	

Ⓓ *Click the* **Copy** *button on the Access toolbar.*

Ⓔ *Position the mouse pointer on the left edge of the* Breed *cell for the new record, and click when the thick cross appears. The entire blank cell will be selected.*

Ⓕ *Click the Paste button on the Access toolbar. The phrase* German Shepherd *will be pasted into the cell.*

3. Type **Male** in the Gender field.
4. Use Copy and Paste to copy the color information from the "Stripes the cat" record to the new record for "Fetch the dog."
5. Complete the new record by entering the data shown below.

Date of Birth	Last Visit	Expenditures	Number of Visits	Customer ID
6/12/96	9/10/99	345.00	3	3

Printing Tables

It is very important that you enter data accurately. There are few things more upsetting to customers and other business contacts than misspelling their names and discovering careless data entry errors. For this reason, it is important to check your data for accuracy after it has been entered. Perhaps the best way to check data accuracy is to print out the contents of your tables. Proofreading hard copy (paper printout) is usually the best way to spot errors.

From the Keyboard
CTRL+P to display the Print dialog box

The Print button on the Access toolbar sends the entire contents of a table open in Datasheet view to the current printer. You must display the Print dialog box if you want to change printers, adjust the number of copies to be printed, or to set other printing options. You display the Print dialog box with the **File→Print** command. The illustration on the following page highlights the most frequently used options available in the Print dialog box.

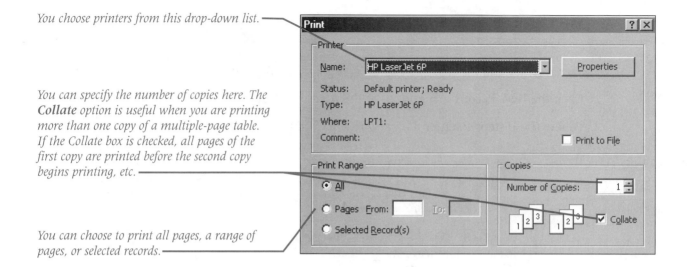

You choose printers from this drop-down list.

You can specify the number of copies here. The ***Collate*** *option is useful when you are printing more than one copy of a multiple-page table. If the Collate box is checked, all pages of the first copy are printed before the second copy begins printing, etc.*

You can choose to print all pages, a range of pages, or selected records.

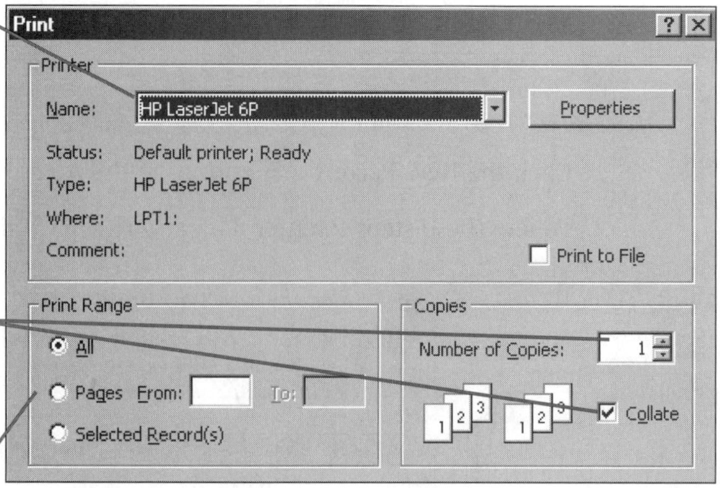

Print
Printer
Name:
HP LaserJet 6P
Properties
Status:
Default printer; Ready
Type:
HP LaserJet 6P
Where:
LPT1:
Comment:
Print to File
Print Range
All
Pages
From:
To:
Selected Record(s)
Copies
Number of Copies:
1
Collate

Print Preview

The Print Preview button on the Access toolbar displays the Print Preview window. Print Preview lets you see exactly how a table will look when it is printed. Print Preview can save time, paper, and wear-and-tear on your printer. Print Preview is especially useful when printing a table with a large number of records. It is always wise to preview a large table before sending it to the printer. When you display the Print Preview window, the Access toolbar is replaced by the Print Preview toolbar.

Hands-On 19.10 Use Print Preview

1. Click the Print Preview button on the Access toolbar.
2. Zoom in by clicking anywhere on the table.
3. Zoom out by clicking anywhere on the table.
   Notice that only six of the table's columns are visible in the Print Preview window. It is a good thing that you used Print Preview before printing the table. You will hold off on printing the table until you change the page orientation and margins.
4. Click the **Close** button on the Print Preview toolbar to exit without printing.

Adjusting Column Widths

You may need to adjust table column widths in order to see the entire contents of table cells on a printout. In Datasheet view, you can use several techniques to adjust column widths, as described in the following table.

Quick Reference

ADJUSTING COLUMN WIDTHS

Adjustment Technique	Procedure
Manually adjust column widths.	Drag the border between two column headings.
AutoFit a column to fit the widest entry in the column.	Double-click the border between two column headings, or choose Format→Column Width, and click the Best Fit button.
Set a precise column width.	Choose Format→Column Width, and enter the desired width.
Set column widths to the default standard width.	Choose Format→Column Width, check the Standard Width box, and click OK.

Hands-On 19.11 Adjust Column Widths

1. Follow these steps to manually adjust the width of the Pet ID column.

(A) *Position the mouse pointer on the border between the* Pet ID *and* Pet Name *column headings, and the Adjust pointer will appear.*

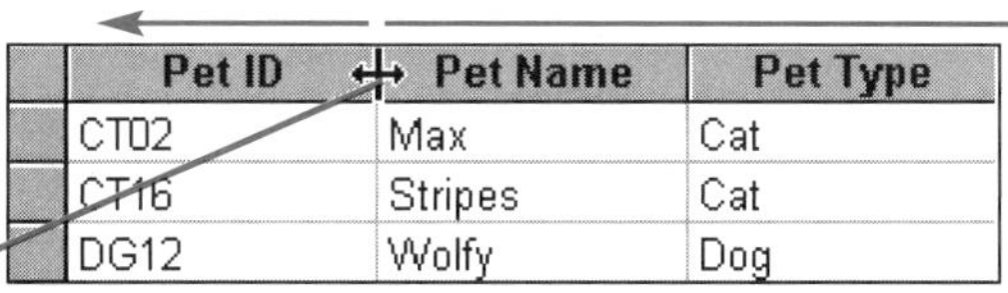
Pet ID
Pet Name
Pet Type
CT02
Max
Cat
CT16
Stripes
Cat
DG12
Wolfy
Dog

(B) *Drag the border to the left until the* Pet ID *column is just wide enough to display the column heading (*Pet ID*).*

2. Follow this step to AutoFit a column to the width of the column heading.

(A) *Position the mouse pointer on the border between the* Pet Name *and* Pet Type *columns, and double-click when the adjust pointer appears. This technique can be tricky, so keep trying until the* Pet Name *column shrinks to the width of the heading. If the column has entries wider than the heading, then the width will adjust to fit the widest entry in the column.*

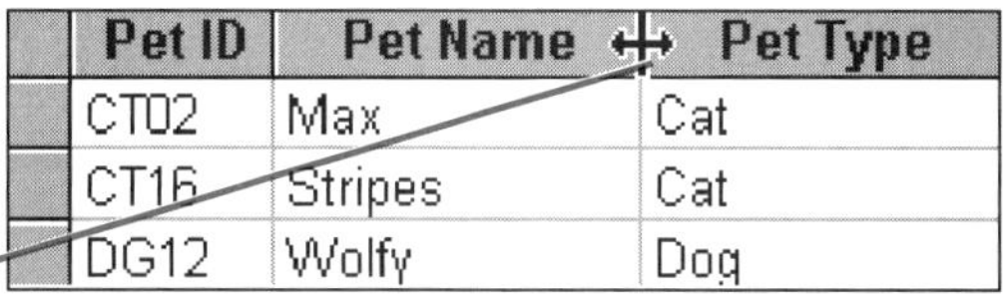
Pet ID
Pet Name
Pet Type
CT02
Max
Cat
CT16
Stripes
Cat
DG12
Wolfy
Dog

3. Follow these steps to AutoFit the width of all columns.

(A) *Position the mouse pointer on the* Pet ID *column heading, and press and hold the left mouse button. The column selection pointer will appear, as shown here.*

(B) *Drag the mouse over all 11 column headings in the table so that all columns are selected.*

(C) *Choose* ***Format→Column Width*** *from the menu bar and click the* ***Best Fit*** *button.*

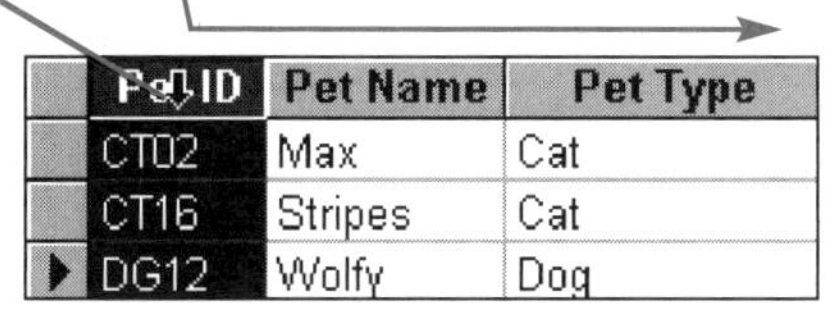
Pet ID
Pet Name
Pet Type
CT02
Max
Cat
CT16
Stripes
Cat
DG12
Wolfy
Dog

4. Click anywhere in the table to deselect the columns.
5. Scroll to the left, and notice that all column widths fit the widest entry (or heading) in the columns.

Margins and Page Orientation

Many tables are quite wide and may not fit on a single printed page. Fortunately, most printers can print text vertically in **portrait** orientation or horizontally in **landscape** orientation. Landscape orientation may allow a wide table (such as the Pets table) to print on a single page. You set the orientation of a page by issuing the **File→Page Setup** command, clicking the Page tab, and choosing the desired orientation. The margins can also be adjusted in the Page Setup dialog box.

Hands-On 19.12 Set Page Orientation and Margins, and Print

1. Choose **File→Page Setup** from the Access menu bar.
2. Make sure the Margins tab is active, and set all four margins to **0.25″** (that's 0.25 not 25).
3. Click the **Page** tab, and choose the **Landscape** option.
4. Click **OK** to complete the changes.
5. Click the Print Preview button on the Access toolbar.
6. If necessary, zoom in by clicking anywhere on the table. Scroll left or right to view all columns in the table.
   Notice that the page orientation is now horizontal (landscape). All columns should be visible on the page.
7. Print the table by clicking the Print button on the Print Preview toolbar.
8. Click the **Close** button on the Print Preview toolbar when you have finished.
9. Now close the table by choosing **File→Close** from the Access menu bar.
10. Click the **Yes** button when Access asks if you want to save the changes.
    In the next topic, you will set up another table using the Table Wizard.

The Table Wizard

Access provides a Table Wizard to help you set up common tables. The Table Wizard provides a variety of sample tables and sample fields for each table. You can choose the sample fields to include in a table and the Wizard will then build the table for you. In the next exercise, you will use the Table Wizard to set up a Customers table. Thus, you will have experience setting up tables in Design view and with the Table Wizard. In the future, you can use whichever method you prefer.

To start the Table Wizard, you click the New button on the Access Database toolbar, and choose Table Wizard from the New Table box. You can also double-click the **Create table by using wizard** option that appears in the Tables section of the Access Database window.

Hands-On 19.13 Use the Table Wizard

Use the Table Wizard to Create a New Table

1. Click the New button on the Access Database toolbar (located just above the Objects bar).
2. Choose **Table Wizard,** and click **OK.**
3. Use the following steps to begin setting up a table.

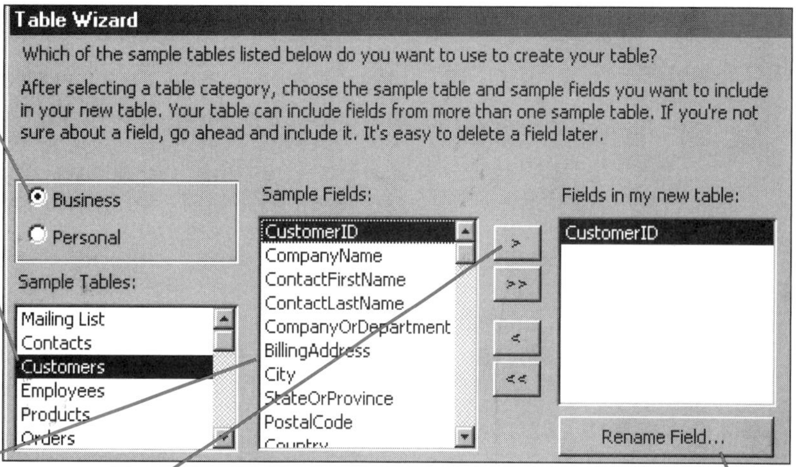

Table Wizard
Which of the sample tables listed below do you want to use to create your table?
After selecting a table category, choose the sample table and sample fields you want to include in your new table. Your table can include fields from more than one sample table. If you're not sure about a field, go ahead and include it. It's easy to delete a field later.
Business
Personal
Sample Tables:
Mailing List
Contacts
Customers
Employees
Products
Orders
Sample Fields:
CustomerID
CompanyName
ContactFirstName
ContactLastName
CompanyOrDepartment
BillingAddress
City
StateOrProvince
PostalCode
Fields in my new table:
CustomerID
Rename Field...

Ⓐ *Make sure the **Business** category is chosen. The **Wizard** provides sample tables for both business and personal use.*

Ⓑ *Choose the* Customers *sample table.*

Ⓒ *Notice the list of **Sample Fields** for the Customers table. Each sample table contains a different set of sample fields.*

Ⓓ *Make sure the* CustomerID *field is selected in the **Sample Fields** list; then click this Add button. The* CustomerID *field will move to the* Fields in my new table *list, as shown here.*

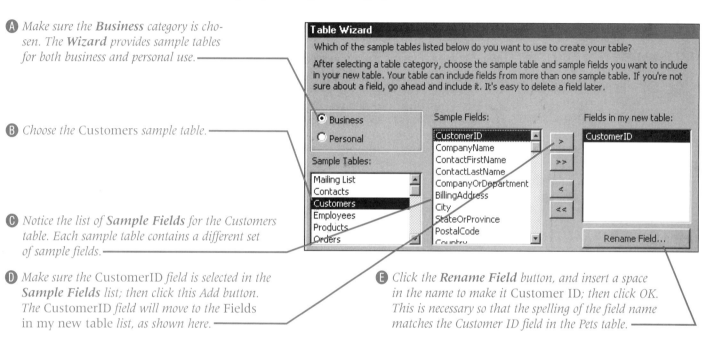

Ⓔ *Click the **Rename Field** button, and insert a space in the name to make it* Customer ID; *then click OK. This is necessary so that the spelling of the field name matches the Customer ID field in the Pets table.*

4. Now add the **ContactFirstName**, **ContactLastname**, **BillingAddress**, **City**, **StateOrProvince**, **PostalCode**, and **PhoneNumber** fields by choosing them one at a time and clicking the Add button. Change the names of the fields as you add them, as shown in the following table.

Change this Field Name . . .	to This Name
ContactFirstName	Firstname
ContactLastName	Lastname
BillingAddress	Address
City	Leave as is
StateOrProvince	State
PostalCode	Zip
PhoneNumber	Phone

(Continued on the next page)

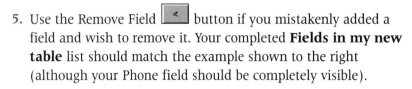

5. Use the Remove Field button if you mistakenly added a field and wish to remove it. Your completed **Fields in my new table** list should match the example shown to the right (although your Phone field should be completely visible).

Fields in my new table:
Customer ID
Firstname
Lastname
Address
City
State
Zip
Phone

6. Click the Next button at the bottom of the dialog box.
The next screen will propose the table name Customers and offer to set the primary key for you.
7. Leave the options set as they are by clicking the **Next** button.
The next screen will ask you about relationships between tables.
8. Leave the option set to **not related to Pets** by clicking the **Next** button.
The next screen will ask how you wish to display the completed table.
9. Choose the **Modify the table design** option and click the **Finish** button.
Access will create the table for you, and display it in Design view.

Modify the Table Structure

You may find Access wizards most useful for setting up tables and other objects. Once objects are set up, you can modify them to suit your particular needs. In the next few steps, you will use this approach by modifying the structure of the Customers table.

10. Follow these steps to explore the table you just created.

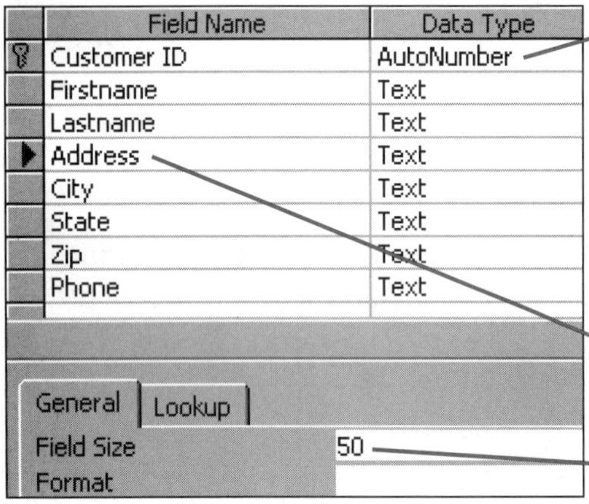
Field Name
Data Type
Customer ID
AutoNumber
Firstname
Text
Lastname
Text
Address
Text
City
Text
State
Text
Zip
Text
Phone
Text
General
Lookup
Field Size
50
Format

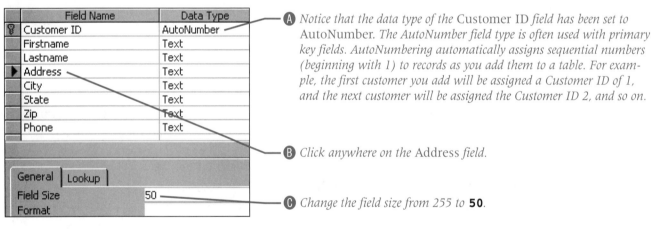

Ⓐ *Notice that the data type of the* Customer ID *field has been set to* AutoNumber. *The AutoNumber field type is often used with primary key fields. AutoNumbering automatically assigns sequential numbers (beginning with 1) to records as you add them to a table. For example, the first customer you add will be assigned a Customer ID of 1, and the next customer will be assigned the Customer ID 2, and so on.*

Ⓑ *Click anywhere on the* Address *field.*

Ⓒ *Change the field size from 255 to* **50**.

11. Follow these steps to change the default value of the State field.

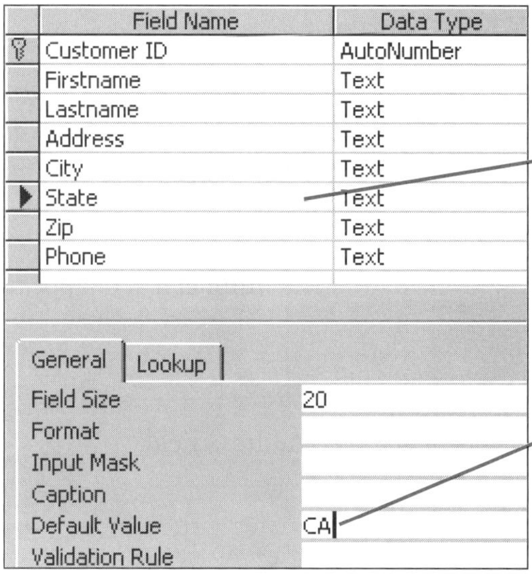

Field Name
Data Type
Customer ID
AutoNumber
Firstname
Text
Lastname
Text
Address
Text
City
Text
State
Text
Zip
Text
Phone
Text
General
Lookup
Field Size
20
Format
Input Mask
Caption
Default Value
CA
Validation Rule

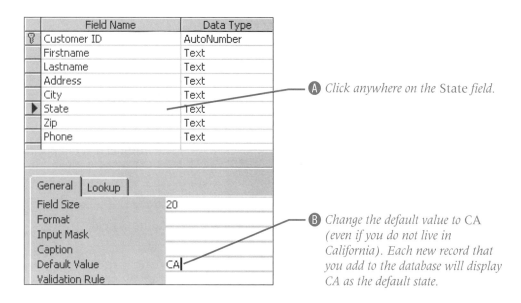

Ⓐ *Click anywhere on the* State *field.*

Ⓑ *Change the default value to* CA *(even if you do not live in California). Each new record that you add to the database will display* CA *as the default state.*

12. Follow these steps to check out the Input Mask property for the phone field.

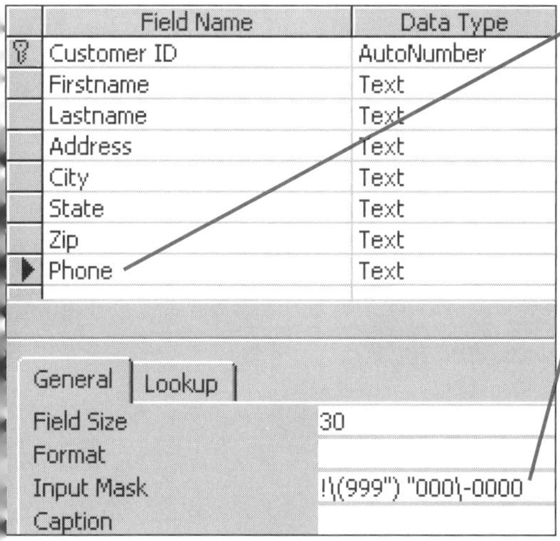

Field Name
Data Type
Customer ID
AutoNumber
Firstname
Text
Lastname
Text
Address
Text
City
Text
State
Text
Zip
Text
Phone
Text
General
Lookup
Field Size
30
Format
Input Mask
!\(999") "000\-0000
Caption

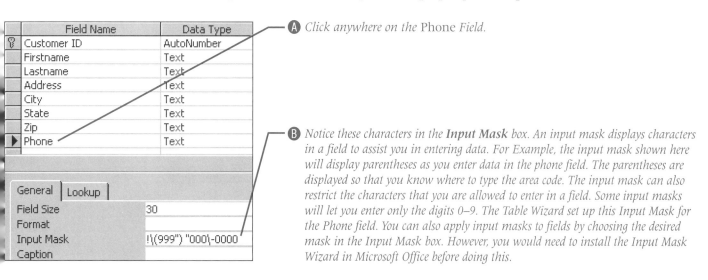

Ⓐ *Click anywhere on the* Phone *Field.*

Ⓑ *Notice these characters in the* **Input Mask** *box. An input mask displays characters in a field to assist you in entering data. For Example, the input mask shown here will display parentheses as you enter data in the phone field. The parentheses are displayed so that you know where to type the area code. The input mask can also restrict the characters that you are allowed to enter in a field. Some input masks will let you enter only the digits 0–9. The Table Wizard set up this Input Mask for the Phone field. You can also apply input masks to fields by choosing the desired mask in the Input Mask box. However, you would need to install the Input Mask Wizard in Microsoft Office before doing this.*

Add new Fields

13. Follow these steps to insert a new date field.

Ⓐ *Click below the Phone field, and type* **`Last Visit`**.

Ⓑ *Click in the Data Type box, and choose* Date/Time *from the drop down list.*

Ⓒ *Choose* Short Date *as the format.*

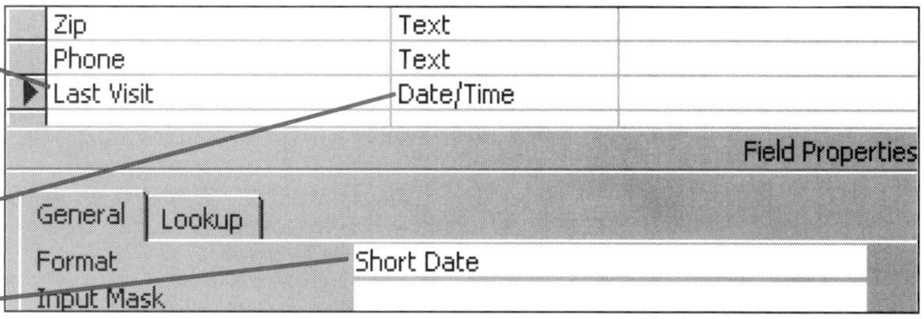

Zip
Text
Phone
Text
Last Visit
Date/Time
Field Properties
General
Lookup
Format
Short Date
Input Mask

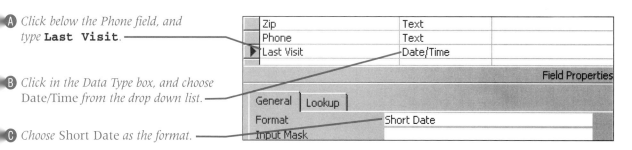

14. Now add a field named **Current Balance**, and set the Data Type to **Currency**.
At this point, you have finished setting up the Customers table. In the next steps you will add data to the table.

(Continued on the next page)

Add Data to the Table

15. Click the Datasheet View button on the Access toolbar.
16. Click **Yes** when Access asks if you wish to save the table.
    Notice the word (AutoNumber) is selected in the first empty record. This field is formatted with the AutoNumber data type so you will bypass it in the next step. Access will automatically assign the number 1 to the record when you begin entering data in the Firstname field.
17. Tap the TAB key to bypass the Customer ID field.
18. Type the name **Mark** in the Firstname field, and the number 1 will appear in the Customer ID field.
19. Tap TAB, and type **Roth** in the Lastname field.
20. Tap TAB, and type **760 Maple Avenue** in the Address field.
21. Tap TAB, and type **Fremont** in the City field.
22. Tap TAB, and notice that the State field is set to CA.
    This is because you set CA as the default value for this field.
23. Tap TAB to bypass the State field (CA is correct) and type **94538** in the Zip field.
    You will notice that a hyphen appears to the right of the digits. This is because the Zip field has also been formatted with an input mask. The input mask inserts a hyphen between the first five and last four digits (if you use nine digits).
24. Tap TAB to bypass the last four digits of the zip code.
25. Type the area code **510** in the Phone field, and the input mask will surround the number with parenthesis.
26. Complete the phone number by typing **2349090**.
    Access will format the number by inserting a hyphen between the 4 and the 9.
27. Tap TAB, and type **7/7/99** in the Last Visit field.
28. Tap TAB, and type **235** in the Current Balance field.
29. Now add the following two records to the table.
    The AutoNumber feature will insert numbers in the Customer ID field, so just tap TAB when you reach that field. Also, do not type parenthesis in the phone numbers because the input mask will automatically apply parenthesis for you.

Customer ID	Firstname	Lastname	Address	City	State	Zip	Phone	Last Visit	Current Balance
2	Tony	Simpson	312 York Lane	Richmond	CA	94804	(510) 238-2233	9/7/99	185
3	Jason	Jones	2233 Crystal Street	San Mateo	CA	94403	(415) 312-2312	7/15/99	48

Print the Table

30. Adjust the width of all columns to fit the widest entry/heading in the columns. You can accomplish this by double-clicking the borders between the column headings. You can also select all of the columns by dragging the mouse pointer across the column headings and then double-clicking the border between the column headings of any two selected columns. Finally, you can also select all columns and use the **Format→Column Width** command, and then click the **Best Fit** button.
31. Use the **File→Page Setup** command to set all four margins to 0.5″.
32. Notice that the Print Headings box is checked on the Margins tab.
    In a moment when you preview the table printout, you will notice a header and footer appear at the top and bottom of the page. The Print Headings box displays the header and footer. The Table Wizard turned on this option.
33. Set the orientation to **Landscape** using the Page tab in the Page Setup dialog box, and click **OK.**
34. Use Print Preview to preview the table, and then print the table if desired.
35. Close Print Preview, and feel free to experiment with any of the topics that you have learned in this lesson.
36. Close the table when you have finished experimenting, and save any changes.
37. Close Access by choosing **File→Exit** from the Access menu bar.
38. Now continue with the end-of-lesson questions and exercises on the following pages.

Concepts Review

True/False Questions

1. An Access database can have a maximum of 1 table.	TRUE	FALSE
2. Datasheet view is used to set up the structure of tables.	TRUE	FALSE
3. If you are in Design view and you want to switch to Datasheet view, you must close the table and reopen it in Datasheet view.	TRUE	FALSE
4. A database is like a container because it can hold several types of objects, including tables.	TRUE	FALSE
5. Changing the structure of a table will never result in lost data.	TRUE	FALSE
6. The page orientation can be changed with the File→Print command.	TRUE	FALSE
7. Portrait orientation causes a table to print horizontally on a page.	TRUE	FALSE
8. The Table Wizard is used to automate data entry in a table.	TRUE	FALSE

Multiple Choice Questions

1. What is the maximum number of characters that a field name may contain?
   a. 8
   b. 32
   c. 64
   d. 255

2. What is the first step that you should take if you want to delete a record?
   a. Click in the desired record, or select the record.
   b. Click the Delete Record button on the toolbar.
   c. Narrow the column width.
   d. Delete all text from the cells.

3. Which of the following commands is used to change the page orientation?
   a. File→Print
   b. File→Page Setup
   c. Format→Page Orientation
   d. Format→Print Preview

4. What happens when you double-click the border between two column headings in Datasheet view?
   a. The table is closed.
   b. The column width is set to the default column width.
   c. A new column is inserted.
   d. The column width is AutoFit to the widest entry.

Skill Builders

Skill Builder 19.1 Set Up a Table in Design View

In this exercise, you will set up a new database for the Tropical Getaways travel company. Tropical Getaways is an exciting new travel company that specializes in inexpensive vacations to tropical locations worldwide. You have been asked to set up a database to track clients and trips. In this exercise, you will create the first table for the database.

1. Start Access, choose the **Blank Access** database option, and click **OK.**
2. Assign the name **Tropical Getaways** to your new database, and save it on your exercise diskette.
   The Tables object list should be displayed in the Access Database window.
3. Double-click the **Create table in Design view** option to begin setting up a new table in Design view.
4. Type **`Customer ID`** as the first field name, and tap the TAB key.
5. Click the drop-down button in the Data Type box, and choose **AutoNumber**.
   Access will automatically assign sequential Customer IDs when you enter data in this table.
6. Click the Primary Key button on the toolbar to make Customer ID the primary key.
7. Set up the remainder of this table using the field names, data types, and options shown in the following table. Keep in mind that you have already set up the Customer ID field.

Field Name	Data Type	Field Size	Primary Key	Description
Customer ID	AutoNumber		Yes	
Firstname	Text	30		
Lastname	Text	30		
Address	Text	50		
City	Text	30		
State	Text	2		
Zip	Text	5		
Profile	Text	20		The profile indicates the category of trips the customer prefers

8. When you have finished, click the Datasheet View button on the Access toolbar.
9. Click **Yes** when Access asks if you wish to save the table.

(Continued on the next page)

10. Type the name **Customers**, click **OK**, and then enter the following four records. The Customer ID numbers should be entered automatically because Customer ID has an AutoNumber data type.

Customer ID	Firstname	Lastname	Address	City	State	Zip	Profile
1	Debbie	Thomas	450 Crestwood Lane	Austin	TX	78752	Adventure
2	Wilma	Boyd	855 State Street	Richmond	NY	12954	Leisure
3	Ted	Wilkins	900 C Street	Fort Worth	TX	76104	Adventure
4	Alice	Simpson	2450 Ridge Road	Fort Worth	TX	76105	Family

11. When you have finished, choose **File→Close** from the Access menu bar to close the table. *Access automatically saves the data you entered. You will set up another table in the next Skill Builder exercise.*

Skill Builder 19.2 Set Up a Table in Design View

In this exercise, you will set up another table for the Tropical Getaways database.

1. Double-click the **Create table in Design view** option to begin setting up a new table in Design view.
2. Set up the table using the following structure.

Field Name	Data Type	Field Size/Format	Primary Key	Description
Trip ID	Text	8	Yes	Four- to eight-character unique identifier for each trip
Customer ID	Number	Long Integer		ID number from Customers table
Destination	Text	50		
Category	Text	30		All trips have a category such as Adventure, Leisure etc.
Departure Date	Date/Time	Short Date		
Return Date	Date/Time	Short Date		
Cost	Currency			

3. Switch to Datasheet, view and save the table as **Trips**.

4. Enter the following data into the Trips table. Do not type the dollar signs and commas when entering the Cost numbers. Access will add the dollar signs and commas for you because you chose the Currency data type when setting up the Cost field.

Trip ID	Customer ID	Destination	Category	Departure Date	Return Date	Cost
Adv01	1	Kenyan Safari	Adventure	8/5/97	9/4/97	$6,600
Lei01	2	Caribbean Cruise	Leisure	9/19/98	9/28/98	$2,390
Adv02	1	Amazon Jungle Trek	Adventure	8/7/98	9/14/98	$7,765
Fam01	4	Orlando	Family	3/4/99	3/10/99	$3,400

5. Close the Trips table when you have finished.
   The Tables objects list should now display both the Customers and Trips table icons. In the next exercise, you will print the Customers table.

Skill Builder 19.3 Print the Table

The Tropical Getaways database should be open, and the Customers and Trips tables should be visible in the Access Database window.

1. Double-click the **Customers** table to open it in Datasheet view.
   You can always open a table in Datasheet view by double-clicking it.
2. Adjust the widths of all columns to display the widest entries in the columns.
3. Use the Print Preview  button to preview the table.
4. Zoom in on the table by clicking anywhere on it.
5. Feel free to print the table and check your data for accuracy.
6. Close Print Preview when you have finished.
7. Close the table and choose **Yes** when Access asks if you want to save the changes.
8. Now open the **Trips** table, and adjust the column widths to fit the widest entries in the columns.
9. Print the table, and check your data for accuracy.
10. Close the table, and save the changes when you have finished.
11. Exit from Access by choosing **File→Exit** from the menu bar.

Assessment

Assessment 19.1 Create a Table

In this assessment, you will begin creating a database for Classic Cars. Classic Cars is an organization devoted to tracking, categorizing, and preserving classic automobiles. You will begin by creating tables to track collectors and cars.

1. Start Access, and create a new database named **`Classic Cars`**.
2. Create a new table with the following structure.

Field Name	Data Type	Field Size	Primary Key	Description
Collector ID	AutoNumber	Yes	Yes	
Firstname	Text	30		
Lastname	Text	30		
Address	Text	50		
City	Text	30		
State	Text	2		
Zip	Text	5		
Era of Interest	Text	20		This field identifies the time period that the collector is most interested in
Collection Size	Number	Long Integer		Number of cars in collection

3. Enter the following records into the table, and name the table **`Collectors`**.

Collector ID	Firstname	Lastname	Address	City	State	Zip	Era of Interest	Collection size
1	Cindy	Johnson	4220 Edward Street	Northlake	IL	60164	1950's	42
2	Tammy	Olson	1200 Big Pine Drive	Moses Lake	WA	98837	1960's	6
3	Ed	Larkson	2300 Watson Street	Cainesville	OH	43701	Early 1900's	34
4	Bob	Barker	6340 Palm Drive	Rockridge	FL	32955	1950's	7

4. AutoFit the width of all columns to fit the largest entry/heading in the columns.
5. Use Print Preview to preview the table. If necessary, switch the orientation to landscape and reduce the margins until the table fits on one page.
6. Print the table.

7. Close the table when you have finished, and save any changes that you have made.

8. Create another new table with the following structure.

Field Name	Data Type	Field Size/ Format	Primary Key	Description
Car ID	Text	15	Yes	Up to 15 characters to uniquely identify each car
Collector ID	Number	Long Integer		ID number from Collectors table
Year	Text	20		
Make	Text	30		
Model	Text	50		
Color	Text	30		
Condition	Text	30		
Value	Currency			Estimated value

9. Enter the following records into the table and name the table **`Cars`**.

Car ID	Collector ID	Year	Make	Model	Color	Condition	Value
CJ01	1	58	Chevrolet	Corvette	Red and white	Mint	$65,000
TO05	2	62	Chevrolet	Corvette	Blue	Excellent	$30,000
CJ22	1	59	Ford	Thunderbird	Tan	Good	$20,000
BB03	4	58	Chevrolet	Corvette	Black	Excellent	$35,000

10. AutoFit the width of all columns to fit the largest entry/heading in the columns.

11. Use Print Preview to preview the table.

12. Print the table.

13. Close the table when you have finished, and save any changes that you have made.

14. Exit from Access when you have finished.

LESSON 20—Access

Forms and Reports

In this lesson, you will enhance the Pinnacle Pet Care database with forms and reports. You will create forms that will make it easy to view, enter, and edit data in the Customers and Pets tables. You will also create reports to present your data in a variety of ways.

In This Lesson

Case Study

Most of the employees at Pinnacle Pet Care have little computer experience and even less experience using Microsoft Access. For this reason, Penny Johnson must make it easy for employees to enter and extract data from the database. Penny decides to set up data entry forms that let employees enter customer information and pet information. Penny also works closely with her employees to determine the types of reports they require. Penny realizes that her employees require an outstanding customer balance report that includes the customer names and telephone numbers. Another report will list the expenditures and number of visits for each pet. This report will be sorted by expenditures so that the customers spending the most on their pets will appear at the top of the report.

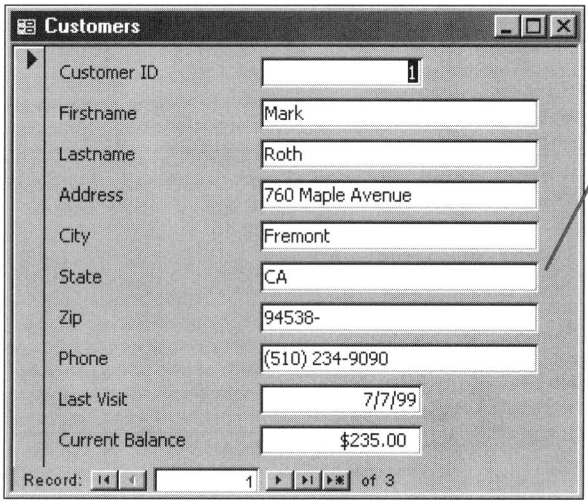
Customers
Customer ID
1
Firstname
Mark
Lastname
Roth
Address
760 Maple Avenue
City
Fremont
State
CA
Zip
94538-
Phone
(510) 234-9090
Last Visit
7/7/99
Current Balance
$235.00
Record: 1 of 3

*Form for **Customers** table*

Outstanding balances report for customers

Outstanding Balances

Firstname	*Lastname*	*Phone*	*Current Balance*
Mark	Roth	(510) 234-9090	$235.00
Tony	Simpson	(510) 238-2233	$185.00
Jason	Jones	(415) 312-2312	$48.00
Jacob	Samuels	(404) 367-8002	$250.50

The Office Assistant

Microsoft Access
You must first save the table.
Do you want to save the table now?
Yes
No
Office Assistant

The Office Assistant is an interactive Help tool available in all Office 2000 applications. The Assistant monitors your activities and provides tips, suggestions, and alert messages whenever it assumes you need assistance. For example, the Assistant may display a **speech balloon** asking if you want to save a table when you switch from table Design view to Datasheet view.

Using the Assistant to Get Help

The Assistant's speech balloon contains a search box where you can enter phrases and questions. When you click the Search button, the Assistant interprets the phrase or question in the search box and displays a list of topics relating to the search box text. When you click a topic, Access displays a Help window providing you with detailed help information.

Controlling the Assistant

You can control all aspects of the Assistant. For example, you may not want the Assistant to display a tip of the day, or you may want to turn the Assistant off. You set options for the Assistant in the Office Assistant dialog box. The following Quick Reference table outlines various methods of controlling the Assistant.

Quick Reference

CONTROLLING THE OFFICE ASSISTANT

Task	Procedure
Display the Assistant's speech balloon (four different methods).	■ Click anywhere on the Assistant. ■ Press F1. ■ Click the Help button on the Standard toolbar. ■ Choose Microsoft Access Help from the Help menu.
Close the speech balloon.	Click anywhere in the Access window or tap ESC.
Display Office Assistant dialog box.	Display the speech balloon, and click the Options button.
Change animated character.	Display the Office Assistant dialog box, click the Gallery tab, use the Next button to browse the available characters, choose a character, and click OK.
Temporarily hide the Assistant.	Choose Help→Hide the Office Assistant, or right-click the Assistant, and choose Hide from the pop-up menu.
Turn Assistant off completely.	Display the Office Assistant dialog box and uncheck the Use the Office Assistant box.
Unhide the Assistant, or turn the Assistant back on.	Choose Help→Show the Office Assistant.

Forms

In the previous lesson, you learned that an Access database is composed of various objects. A form is a type of object that lets you view, edit, and enter data. The benefit of a form is that it allows you to focus on a single record in the database. This is in contrast to Datasheet view where you are able to view many records at the same time. The following illustration shows a form for the Customers table in the Pinnacle Pet Care database.

Notice that the form displays one complete record from the database. Forms let you focus on a single customer, pet, etc.

*Fields such as **Phone, Last Visit,** and **Current Balance** are automatically formatted with symbols (as they are in Datasheet view).*

The form also contains navigation buttons to let you browse through the database.

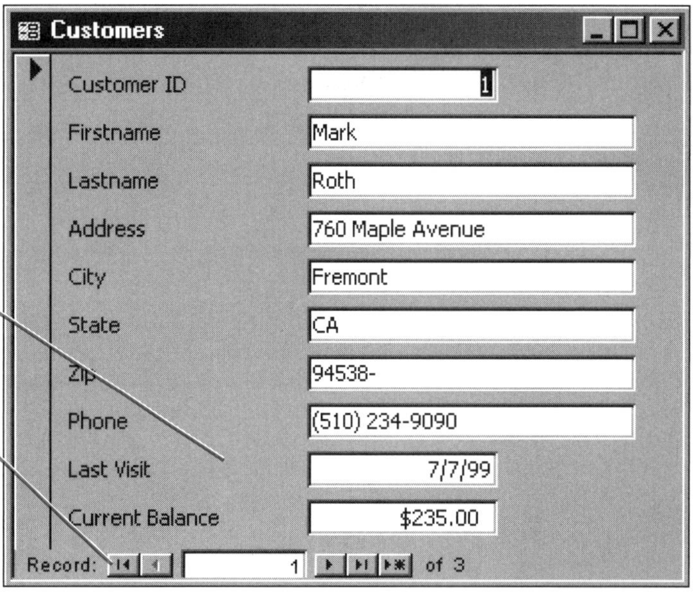
Customers
Customer ID
1
Firstname
Mark
Lastname
Roth
Address
760 Maple Avenue
City
Fremont
State
CA
Zip
94538-
Phone
(510) 234-9090
Last Visit
7/7/99
Current Balance
$235.00
Record:
1
of 3

Creating Forms with AutoForm

You can use AutoForm to automatically create simple forms. AutoForm creates a form that displays all fields from a particular table. The form in the preceding illustration was created from the Customers table using AutoForm. More complex forms can be created using form Design view or with the Form Wizard.

Quick Reference

CREATING FORMS WITH AUTOFORM

- Choose the desired table in the Access Database window.
- Click the New Object drop-down button near the right end of the Access toolbar.
- Choose AutoForm from the drop-down list.
- Close the form when you have finished using it, and assign it a name.

Hands-On 20.1 Use AutoForm

In this exercise, you will open the Pinnacle Pet Care database from your exercise diskette. You will continue to enhance the Pinnacle Pet Care database throughout this course. If you have not satisfactorily completed the Hands-On exercises in the previous lesson, then ask your instructor to copy the file named Pinnacle Pet Care - Lesson 20 to your exercise diskette. This file provides the Pinnacle Pet Care database in the state it should be in after completing Lesson 19. If necessary, your instructor can provide you with files to give you a fresh starting point whenever you begin a new lesson in this book.

1. Start Access, and follow this step to open the Pinnacle Pet Care database.

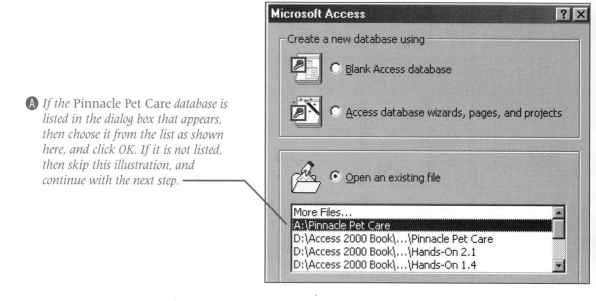

Ⓐ *If the* Pinnacle Pet Care *database is listed in the dialog box that appears, then choose it from the list as shown here, and click OK. If it is not listed, then skip this illustration, and continue with the next step.*

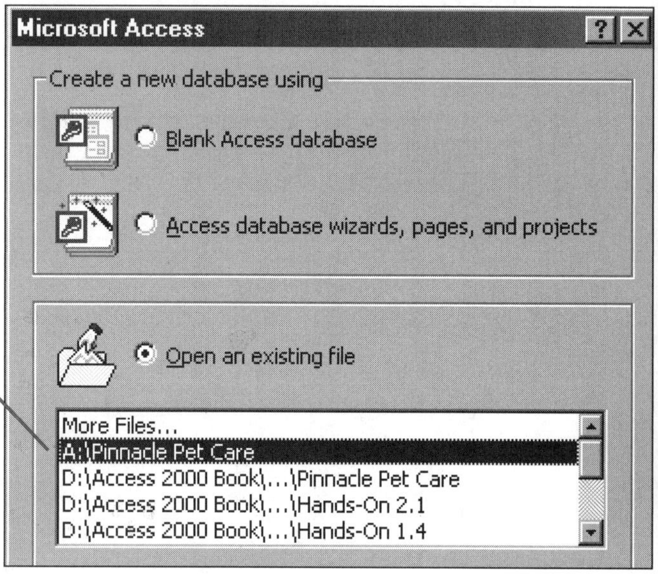
Microsoft Access
Create a new database using
Blank Access database
Access database wizards, pages, and projects
Open an existing file
More Files...
A:\Pinnacle Pet Care
D:\Access 2000 Book\...\Pinnacle Pet Care
D:\Access 2000 Book\...\Hands-On 2.1
D:\Access 2000 Book\...\Hands-On 1.4

2. If the Pinnacle Pet Care database was not listed as shown above, then click the **Cancel** button on the dialog box, click the **Open** button on the Access toolbar, navigate to your exercise diskette, and open the Pinnacle Pet Care file.

3. Follow these steps to create a form for the Customers table.

Ⓐ *Choose the* Customers *table from the list of tables. You must choose the desired table before creating a form.*

Ⓑ *Click the drop-down button on the* **New Object** *button, and choose* AutoForm*, as shown.*

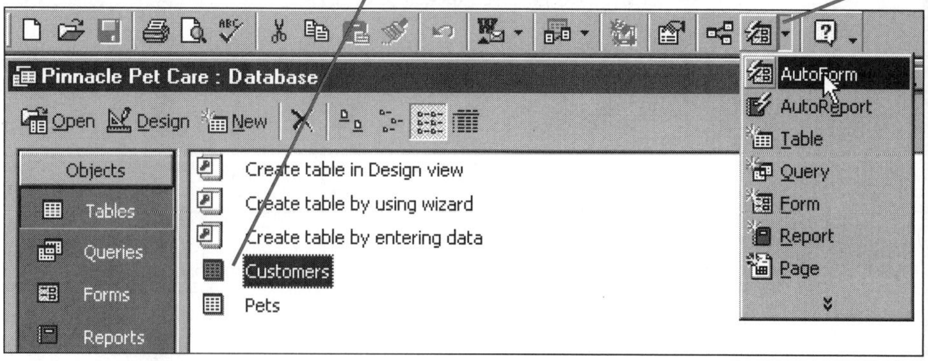
Pinnacle Pet Care : Database
Open
Design
New
Objects
Tables
Queries
Forms
Reports
Create table in Design view
Create table by using wizard
Create table by entering data
Customers
Pets
AutoForm
AutoReport
Table
Query
Form
Report
Page

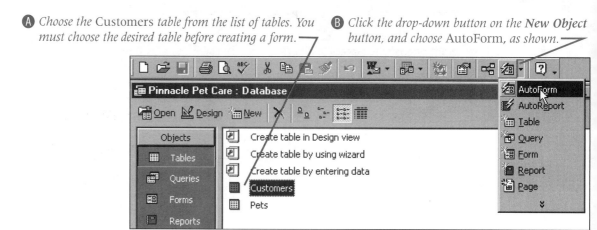

Access will create the form, and the Mark Roth record will be displayed. This is because the Mark Roth record is the first record in the table.

Entering Data and Navigating Records in Forms

Forms are used for viewing and entering data one record at a time. When you enter data using a form, the data is stored in the underlying table that the form is based upon. Forms also make it easy to navigate to various records. The navigation bar at the bottom of a form lets you navigate to records in the underlying table. The form navigation bar has the same buttons that appear on the navigation bar in Datasheet view.

Go to the first record in the table. *Move forward one record.*

1

Move back one record. *Go to the last record in the table.* *Add a new record.*

Hands-On 20.2 Enter Data and Navigate

1. Follow these steps to prepare to enter a new record.

Ⓐ *Click the **New Record** button, and a new record will appear, as shown here.*

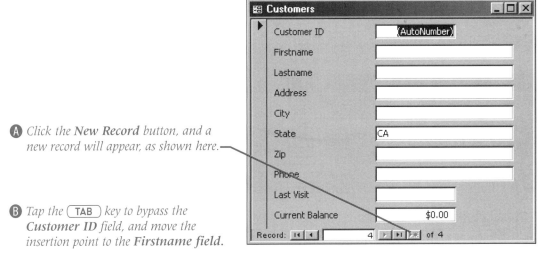

Ⓑ *Tap the* TAB *key to bypass the **Customer ID** field, and move the insertion point to the **Firstname field.***

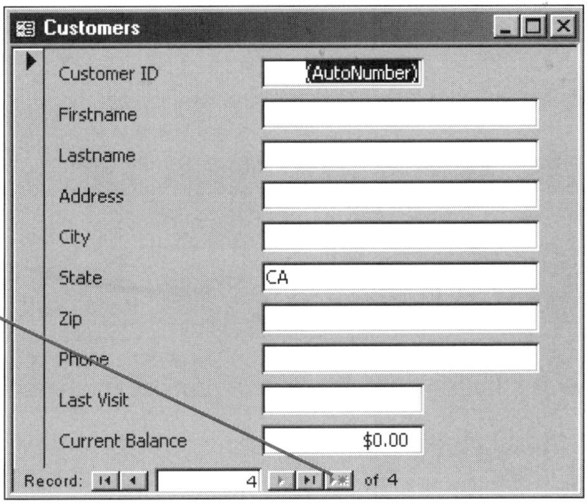

Customers
Customer ID
(AutoNumber)
Firstname
Lastname
Address
City
State
CA
Zip
Phone
Last Visit
Current Balance
$0.00
Record:
4
of 4

(Continued on the next page)

2. Follow this step to enter the data.

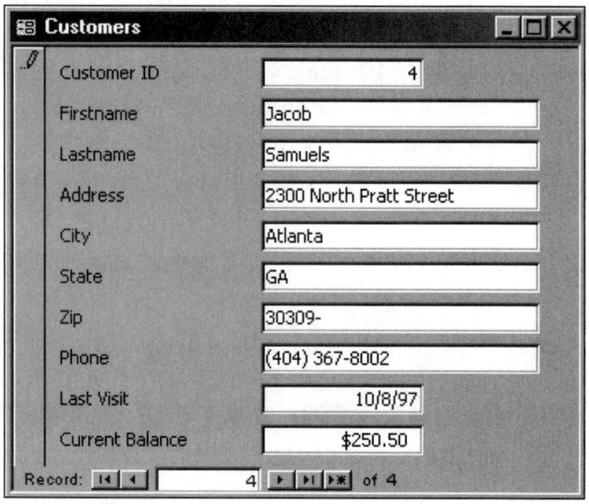

Customers
Customer ID
4
Firstname
Jacob
Lastname
Samuels
Address
2300 North Pratt Street
City
Atlanta
State
GA
Zip
30309-
Phone
(404) 367-8002
Last Visit
10/8/97
Current Balance
$250.50
Record: 4 of 4

Ⓐ *Enter the data shown here using the* TAB *key to move from one field to the next. Notice that you must change the entry in the* ***State*** *field from CA to GA. You can always change the default value for a record by typing a new value. You set the default value to CA when you created the table in the previous lesson. Also, the dollar sign will not appear in the* ***Current Balance*** *field until you go to another field or record after typing the entry in the Current Balance field.*

In the next few steps, you will close the form and assign a name to it. You name forms as you name tables and all other database objects.

3. Follow this step to close the form.

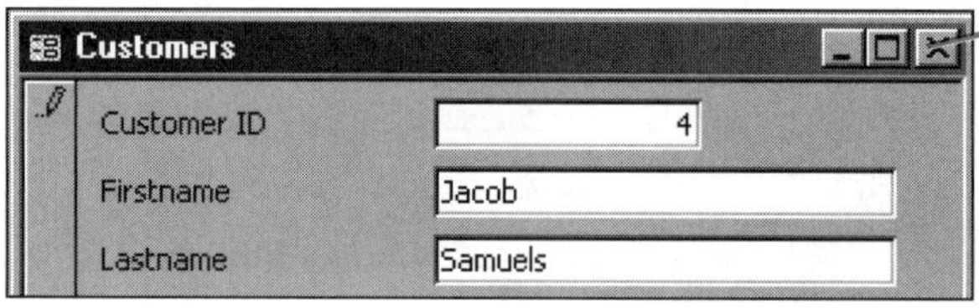

Customers
Customer ID
4
Firstname
Jacob
Lastname
Samuels

Ⓐ *Click the Close button on the form, and Access will ask if you want to save the form.*

4. Click the **Yes** button, and Access will propose the name Customers.

5. Click **OK** to accept the proposed name.

6. Follow these steps to confirm that the form has been created and to reopen the form.

Ⓐ *Click the* ***Forms*** *button on the* ***Objects*** *bar, and the* **Customers** *icon will be visible as shown here.*

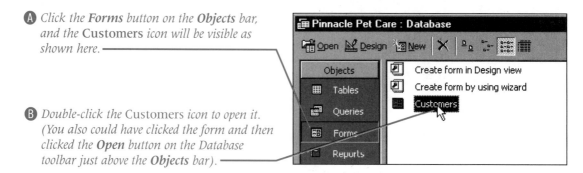

Ⓑ *Double-click the* Customers *icon to open it. (You also could have clicked the form and then clicked the* ***Open*** *button on the Database toolbar just above the* ***Objects*** *bar).*

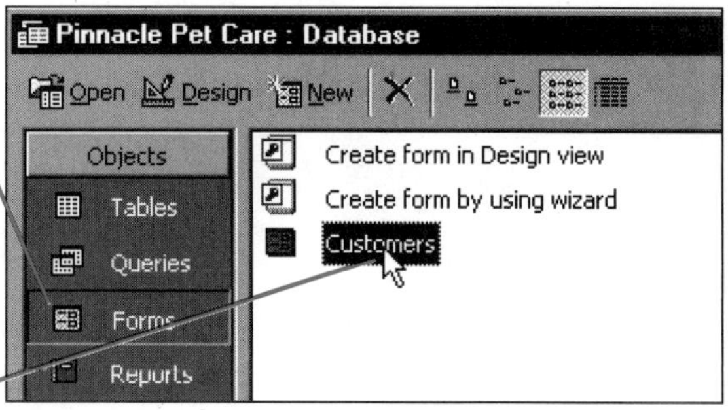

Pinnacle Pet Care : Database
Open
Design
New
Objects
Tables
Queries
Forms
Reports
Create form in Design view
Create form by using wizard
Customers

7. Use the navigation bar at the bottom of the form to browse through the records.
Notice that the Jacob Samuels record you just added is visible as the last record. The data you entered for Jacob Samuels has been entered into the Customers table.

8. Now close the Customers form again by clicking its Close ☒ button.

Deleting and Editing Records with Forms

The Delete Record button on the Access toolbar deletes the current record displayed in a form. The record is deleted from the underlying table. You can also use a form to edit data in an underlying table. Keep in mind that you must first navigate to a record before you can edit the data or delete the record.

Hands-On 20.3 Create a New Form and Work with Records

1. Follow these steps to create a new form for the Pets table.

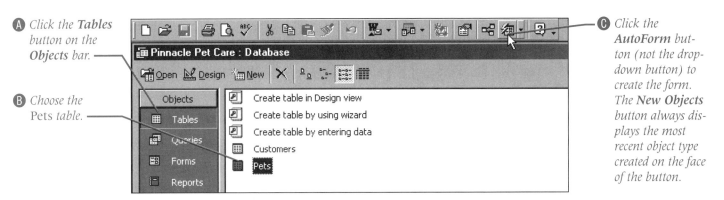

Ⓐ *Click the* ***Tables*** *button on the* ***Objects*** *bar.*

Ⓑ *Choose the* Pets *table.*

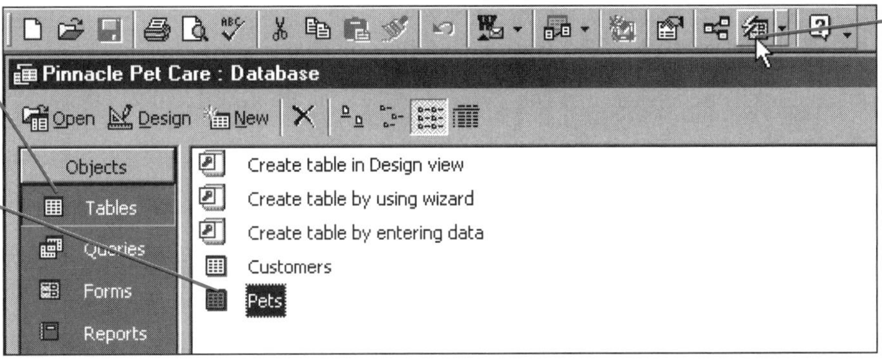

Pinnacle Pet Care : Database
Open
Design
New
Objects
Tables
Queries
Forms
Reports
Create table in Design view
Create table by using wizard
Create table by entering data
Customers
Pets

Ⓒ *Click the* ***AutoForm*** *button (not the drop-down button) to create the form. The* ***New Objects*** *button always displays the most recent object type created on the face of the button.*

Notice that the new form is based upon the fields in the Pets table.

2. Click the New Record button on the navigation bar at the bottom of the form.
3. Enter the following records, stopping at the Breed field for Slinky the Snake.

Pet ID	Pet Name	Pet Type	Breed	Gender	Color	Date of Birth	Last Visit	Expenditures	Number of Visits	Customer ID
DG24	Ben	Dog	Terrier	Male	Black	6/1/92	10/8/99	480	3	4
DG25	Spike	Dog	Chow	Male	Brown	4/3/84	10/8/99	890	12	4
SN01	Slinky	Snake								

4. It turns out that snakes are not welcome in the Pinnacle Pet Care clinic, so click the Delete Record button on the Access toolbar.
5. Click **Yes** to confirm the deletion of Slinky the Snake.
6. Use the navigation bar to navigate backwards through the records, and notice that the Ben the dog record and the Spike the dog record are still there.
7. Click the Close button on the form.
8. Click **Yes** when Access asks if you want to save the form.
9. Click **OK** on the Save As box to accept the name Pets.
Both the Customers and Pets form icons should be visible in the Database window.

Printing Forms

You can print the records in a table by clicking the Print button from an open form. Access will print a copy of the form with displayed data for each record in the database. This technique can be useful if there are a large number of fields in a table. Printing a datasheet with a large number of fields is often difficult because the fields can't be displayed on a single page. A form, however, will often fit on a single page. On the other hand, printing forms may not be wise if the table has a large number of records. Forms typically take a large amount of space on the printed page, and you will use a lot of paper if you print a table with many records.

Hands-On 20.4 Preview the Pets Form

1. Click the **Forms** button on the Objects bar.
2. Double-click the Pets icon in the Forms section of the database window.
3. Click the Print Preview button on the Access toolbar.
4. If necessary, maximize the Print Preview window.
5. Click anywhere on the page in the Print Preview window to zoom in.
   Notice that a copy of the form is displayed for each record in the Pets table.
6. Use the navigation bar at the bottom of the Print Preview window to browse through the pages.
   As you can see, printing data via a form may require a lot of paper.
7. Close the Print Preview window without printing.
8. Click the Restore button near the top right corner of the window to restore the Pets form (not the Access program window).
9. Click the Close button on the Pets form.

Reports

You can create reports to present data in a printed format. You can specify the fields to include in reports and you can format reports using built-in report styles. In the next exercise, you will create the report shown below. Notice that the report lists just four fields from the Customers table.

Outstanding Balances

Firstname	*Lastname*	*Phone*	*Current Balance*
Mark	Roth	(510) 234-9090	$235.00
Tony	Simpson	(510) 238-2233	$185.00
Jason	Jones	(415) 312-2312	$48.00
Jacob	Samuels	(404) 367-8002	$250.50

Complexity of Reports

In this lesson, you will use the Report Wizard to create simple reports. However, Access reports can be quite complex. For example, reports can include calculated fields that sum up columns of numbers and grouping levels to organize records in logical groups.

AutoReport and the Report Wizard

In the previous exercises, you used AutoForm to create forms. AutoForm creates a form using all fields from a table. This is acceptable, because you will normally want all fields from a table on a form. Reports, on the other hand, usually require a subset of a table's fields. For example, the report shown in the previous illustration uses just four fields from the Customers table. AutoReport has limited use because it inserts all fields from a table into a report. Fortunately, Access provides a Report Wizard that gives you flexibility when setting up reports. The Report Wizard lets you choose the fields to include in the report. The Report Wizard also lets you specify various formatting options.

Quick Reference

USING THE REPORT WIZARD

- Click the **Reports** button on the Objects bar in the Database window.
- Double-click the **Create report by using wizard** option. You can also click the New button on the Access Database toolbar and choose Report Wizard from the dialog box.
- Choose the desired table or query that you wish to base the report on from the Tables/Queries list, and click **OK.**
- Follow the Report Wizard steps to create the desired report.

Previewing and Printing Reports

The Preview button appears on the Access Database toolbar whenever the Reports button is pressed on the Objects bar and a report is chosen. You can open the report in Print Preview mode by clicking the Preview button. The Print Preview window functions the same way with reports as it does with other objects.

From the Keyboard

CTRL+P to display Print dialog box

The Print button can be used to print reports directly from the Database window. The Print button also appears on the Print Preview toolbar when a report is chosen. You can print all pages of a report by clicking the Print button. You must use the **File→Print** command to display the Print dialog box if you want to print a range of pages or set other print options.

Hands-On 20.5 Use the Report Wizard

1. Follow these steps to launch the Report Wizard.

Ⓐ *Click the* ***Reports*** *button on the Objects bar.*

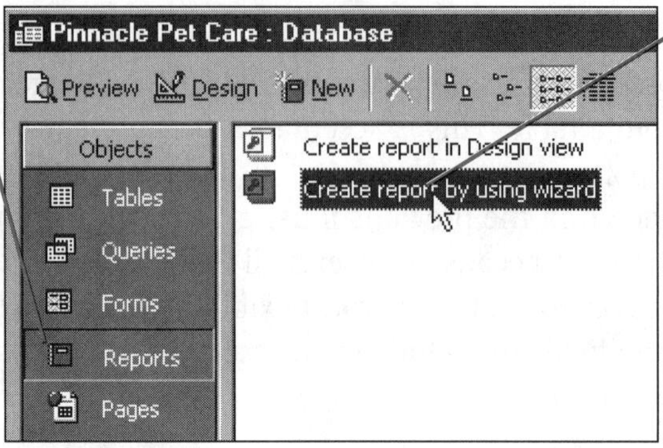
Pinnacle Pet Care : Database
Preview
Design
New
Objects
Tables
Queries
Forms
Reports
Pages
Create report in Design view
Create report by using wizard

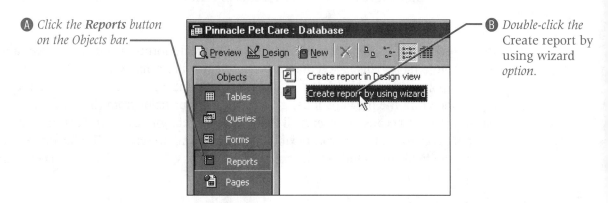

Ⓑ *Double-click the* Create report by using wizard *option.*

2. Follow these steps to choose the Customers table as the basis for the report and to add the Firstname field to the Selected Fields list.

Ⓐ *Make sure* Customers *is chosen from the* ***Tables/Queries*** *list.*

Ⓑ *Choose* Firstname *from the* ***Available Fields*** *list.*

Ⓒ *Click the* ***Add Field*** *button.*

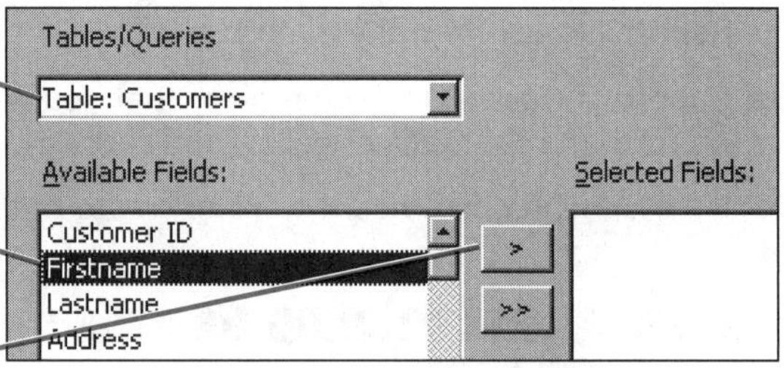
Tables/Queries
Table: Customers
Available Fields:
Selected Fields:
Customer ID
Firstname
Lastname
Address
>
>>

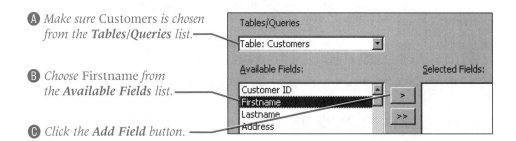

3. Now add the **Lastname**, **Phone**, and **Current Balance** fields. The completed Selected Fields list is shown to the right.

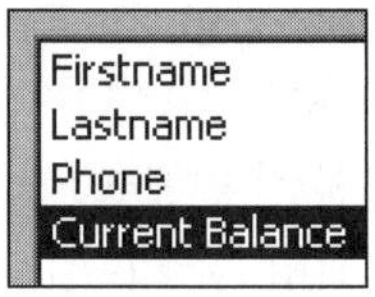
Firstname
Lastname
Phone
Current Balance

4. Click **Next** to display the Grouping Levels screen.
5. Click **Next** to bypass the Grouping Levels screen and display the Sort Order screen.
6. Click **Next** to bypass the Sort Order screen and display the Layout screen. Make sure the layout options are set as shown on the next page.

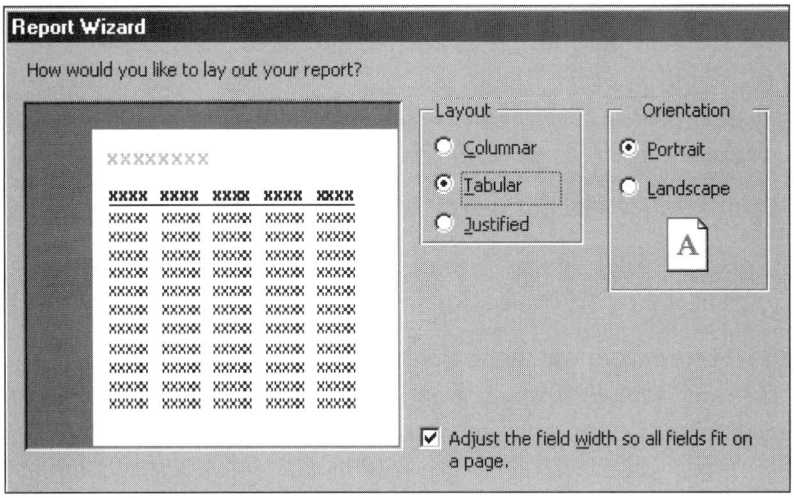
Report Wizard
How would you like to lay out your report?
Layout
Columnar
Tabular
Justified
Orientation
Portrait
Landscape
A
Adjust the field width so all fields fit on a page.

7. Click **Next** to display the Style screen.
8. Choose **Corporate**, click **Next**, and follow these steps to set the final report options.

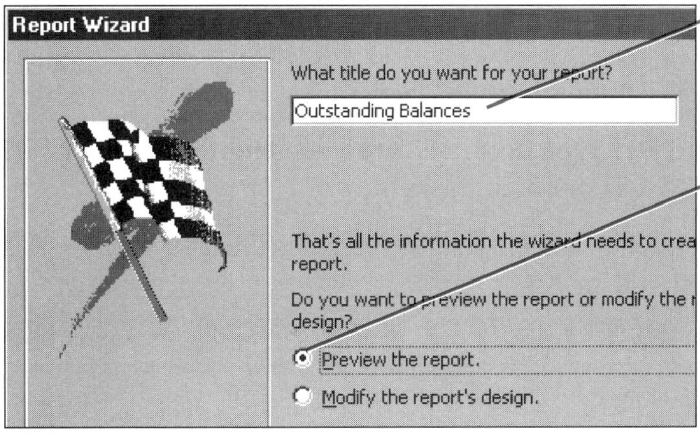
Report Wizard
What title do you want for your report?
Outstanding Balances
That's all the information the wizard needs to crea
report.
Do you want to preview the report or modify the r
design?
Preview the report.
Modify the report's design.

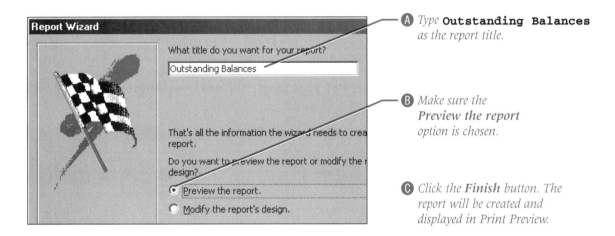

Ⓐ *Type* **`Outstanding Balances`** *as the report title.*

Ⓑ *Make sure the* ***Preview the report*** *option is chosen.*

Ⓒ *Click the* ***Finish*** *button. The report will be created and displayed in Print Preview.*

9. If necessary, maximize the Print Preview window by clicking its **Maximize** ☐ button.
10. Zoom in or out on the report by clicking the mouse pointer anywhere on it.
    The top section of your report should match the following example (although the sort order may be different). You will sort reports in the Skill Builder exercises.

Outstanding Balances

Firstname	*Lastname*	*Phone*	*Current Balance*
Mark	Roth	(510) 234-9090	$235.00
Tony	Simpson	(510) 238-2233	$185.00
Jason	Jones	(415) 312-2312	$48.00
Jacob	Samuels	(404) 367-8002	$250.50

(Continued on the next page)

11. Click the Design View button on the left end of the Print Preview toolbar.
The report will display in Design view with a report header, page header, detail section, etc. In Design view, you can change the position of objects, add and remove objects, and change the properties of objects. However, you won't work in Design view at this time.
12. Click the Print Preview button on the left end of the toolbar to switch back to Print Preview.
13. Feel free to print the report by clicking the Print button on the Print Preview toolbar.
14. Choose **File→Close** from the menu bar to close the report.
The Report will automatically be assigned the name Outstanding Balances, and an Outstanding Balances icon will appear in the Reports section of the database window. As you can see from this example, creating simple reports is quite easy if you use the Report Wizard. Now continue with the next exercise, where you will create a report to accompany the Pets table.

Hands-On 20.6 Create a Report for the Pets Table

1. Make sure the Reports button is pressed on the Objects bar, and double-click the **Create report by using wizard** option.

Selected Fields:
Pet Name
Pet Type
Expenditures
Number of Visits

2. Choose the **Pets** table from the Tables/Queries list.
3. Add the **Pet Name**, **Pet Type**, **Expenditures**, and **Number of Visits** fields to the Selected Fields list as shown at the right.
4. Click the **Finish** button to accept all of the remaining default settings, and the completed report shown below will appear.
Once again, the sort order may be different than shown here.

Pets

Pet Name	*Pet Type*	*Expenditures*	*Number of Visits*
Wolfy	Dog	$450.00	7
Dillon	Dog	$150.55	3
Bugs	Rabbit	$600.50	4
Max	Cat	$1,450.55	20
Stripes	Cat	$450.00	9
Tony	Cat	$145.00	6
Fetch	Dog	$345.00	3
Ben	Dog	$480.00	3
Spike	Dog	$890.00	12

5. Notice the alignment of the fields within the columns.
Fields have the same left or right alignment in a report as they do in the table the report is based on.
6. Close the report with the **File→Close** command.
The Reports section should now have an Outstanding Balance report and a Pets report.

Copying Objects

From the Keyboard

CTRL+C to copy
CTRL+V to paste

You can copy tables, forms, reports, and other types of objects. Objects can be copied and then pasted into the same database, to a different database, or to other applications. Copying an object to the same database can be useful if you intend to modify the object. By making a copy, you will have a backup of the object in case you damage the original. You copy objects with the **Copy** and **Paste** buttons on the Access toolbar.

Deleting Objects

From the Keyboard

DELETE to delete selected object

Objects can also be deleted from an Access database. However, you must be careful when deleting objects because they are permanently deleted from the database. Deleting objects can be useful, especially when using Wizards and tools like AutoForm. If you make a mistake or are unhappy with the results that one of these automated tools produces, you can delete the object and start over. You delete an object by choosing the desired object in the database window and issuing the **Edit→Delete** command.

Hands-On 20.7 Copy a Report, and Then Delete the Copy

Copy the Report

1. Choose the Pets icon in the Reports section of the database window.
2. Click the Copy button on the Access toolbar.
3. Click the Paste button on the toolbar, and the Paste As box will appear.
4. Type the name **`Copy of Pets`** in the Paste As box, and click **OK.**
   The Copy of Pets report will appear in the Reports section.
5. Double-click the **Copy of Pets** report, and it will open.
   Notice that this report is identical to the Pets report.
6. Close the report with the **File→Close** command.

Delete the Report

7. Make sure the Copy of Pets report is chosen.
8. Choose **Edit→Delete** from the menu bar.
9. Click **Yes** to confirm the deletion.
   Keep in mind that you can delete a report (or other object) whenever you want to "get a fresh start." This technique is useful when using wizards and other automated tools. You may need to use this technique in the Skill Builder and Assessment exercises on the following pages. You will create several reports in these exercises that are more complex than the reports you just created. If you make a mistake, remember to delete the report and recreate it with the Report Wizard.
10. Close the Pinnacle Pet Care database with the **File→Close** command.

Concepts Review

True/False Questions

1. Forms can be used to enter data in tables. TRUE FALSE
2. The main benefit of forms is that they allow you to view several records simultaneously. TRUE FALSE
3. The navigation buttons at the bottom of a form can be used to move between records. TRUE FALSE
4. Forms do not display currency symbols $ and other formatting characters. TRUE FALSE
5. AutoForm creates a form for the table that is selected in the Tables section of the Access window. TRUE FALSE
6. The Report Wizard lets you choose the fields that you wish to include in a report. TRUE FALSE
7. Reports can be printed. TRUE FALSE
8. The Report Wizard lets you choose portrait or landscape orientations. TRUE FALSE

Multiple-Choice Questions

1. Which of the following statements is/are accurate?
   a. Forms can be used to enter records into a table.
   b. Forms can be used to browse through the records in a table.
   c. Forms let you focus on one record at a time.
   d. All of the above

2. Which of the following commands can you issue through the navigation buttons on a form?
   a. Add a new record.
   b. Delete a record.
   c. Change the size of a field.
   d. All of the above

3. Which of the following statements is true?
   a. The Report Wizard lets you choose portrait or landscape orientations.
   b. The Report Wizard lets you choose the fields to include in a report.
   c. The Report Wizard lets you choose a title for the report.
   d. All of the above

4. The Report Wizard is initiated from which section of the database window?
   a. The Tables section
   b. The Reports section
   c. The Forms section
   d. Any of the above

Skill Builders

Skill Builder 20.1 Create Forms

The Access window should be open from the previous exercise, and all databases should be closed. In this exercise, you will open the Tropical Getaways database from your exercise diskette. You will continue to enhance this database as you progress through the Skill Builder exercises in this course. If you did not accurately complete the Skill Builder exercises in the previous lesson, then ask your instructor to copy the file named Tropical Getaways—Lesson 20 to your exercise diskette. This file provides the Tropical Getaways database as it should be after completing Lesson 19.

Create a Form for the Customers Table

1. Click the Open button on the Access toolbar, navigate to your diskette, and open the **Tropical Getaways** database.
2. Make sure the Tables button is pressed on the Objects bar.
3. Choose the Customers table, click the New Object drop-down button, and choose AutoForm.
Access will create the form shown below. The form uses all of the fields in the Customers table.

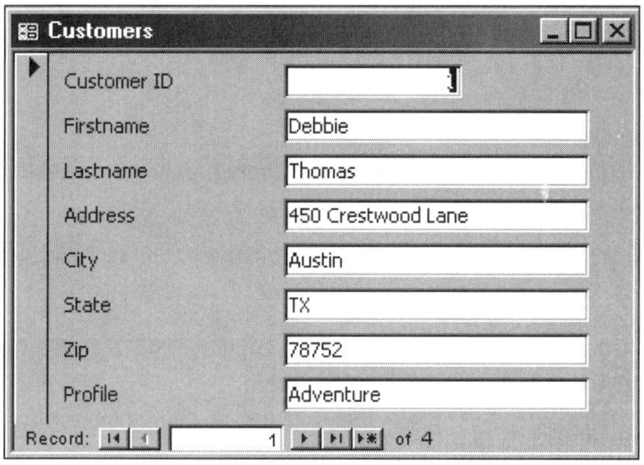

Customers
Customer ID
Firstname
Debbie
Lastname
Thomas
Address
450 Crestwood Lane
City
Austin
State
TX
Zip
78752
Profile
Adventure
Record:
1
of 4

4. Click the New Record button on the form's navigation bar, and add the following records.

Customer ID	Firstname	Lastname	Address	City	State	Zip	Profile
5	Victor	Thomas	2311 Wilmont Street	Danvers	MA	01923	Adventure
6	Lisa	Simms	100 Westside Drive	Batavia	NY	14020	Leisure
7	Ted	Carter	250 Smith Street	Charlton	MA	01507	Family

5. Click the Close button on the form, and choose **Yes** when Access asks you to save the form.
6. Click **OK** to accept the proposed name Customers.

(Continued on the next page)

Create a Form for the Trips Table

7. Use AutoForm to create a form for the Trips table.
8. Use the form to add the following records to the Trips table.

TripID	Customer ID	Destination	Category	Departure Date	Return Date	Cost
Adv03	1	Swiss Alps	Adventure	10/10/98	11/5/98	$3,500
Adv04	5	Rocky Mountains	Adventure	5/6/99	5/22/99	$2,190
Adv05	5	Baja California	Adventure	8/8/99	8/18/99	$2,900
Lei02	6	Hawaii	Leisure	2/5/99	2/15/99	$4,500
Fam02	7	Hawaii	Family	3/7/99	3/15/99	$5,300

9. Close the form, and save it with the proposed name Trips.
   Leave the Tropical Getaways database open. You will continue to use it in the next exercise.

Skill Builder 20.2 Create Reports

In this Skill Builder exercise, you will create reports for the Tropical Getaways database. You will use the sort option in the Report Wizard to sort the records in the reports.

Create a Customer Profiles Report

1. Click the Reports button on the Objects bar.
2. Double-click the **Create report by using wizard** option.
3. Choose **Customers** from the Tables/Queries list.
4. Add the **Firstname**, **Lastname**, **State**, and **Profile** fields to the Selected Fields list.
5. Click the **Next** button twice to display the Sorting screen.
6. Click the drop-down button on the first sorting box, and choose **State** as shown to the right.

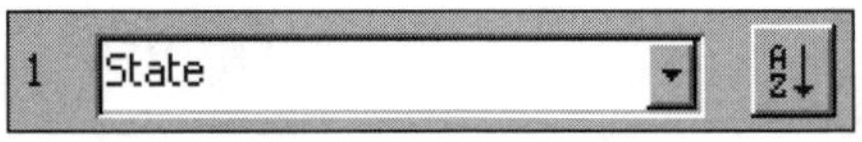
1
State

   This will group all records with the same state together in the report. Notice that you could set additional sort options. For example, imagine that you had a large database and you wanted the records sorted first by state and then by zip code within the states. In that situation, you would set the second sort key to zip code.
7. Click the **Next** button twice to display the Report Style screen.
8. Choose the **Soft Gray** style and click **Next.**
9. Type the name `Customer Profiles by State` in the title box of the last screen.

10. Click the **Finish** button to complete the report.

The completed report is shown below. Notice that the State field appears first in the report, and the records for each state are grouped together. The State field appears first because you sorted on that field.

Customer Profiles by State

State	Firstname	Lastname	Profile
MA	Ted	Carter	Family
MA	Victor	Thomas	Adventure
NY	Wilma	Boyd	Leisure
NY	Lisa	Simms	Leisure
TX	Alice	Simpson	Family
TX	Ted	Wilkins	Adventure
TX	Debbie	Thomas	Adventure

11. Close the report when you have finished viewing it.

Access will automatically name the report Customer Profiles by State.

Create a Report for the Trips Table

12. Now create the report shown below for the Trips table. You will need to start the Report Wizard and choose the appropriate fields from the Trips table. Also, sort the report on the Category field, choose the Soft Gray style, and use the report title Trips by Category.

Trips by Category

Category	Destination	Cost
Adventure	Baja California	$2,900.00
Adventure	Rocky Mountains	$2,190.00
Adventure	Swiss Alps	$3,500.00
Adventure	Amazon Jungle Trek	$7,765.00
Adventure	Kenyan Safari	$6,600.00
Family	Hawaii	$5,300.00
Family	Orlando	$3,400.00
Leisure	Hawaii	$4,500.00
Leisure	Caribbean Cruise	$2,390.00

(Continued on the next page)

13. Close the report when you have finished viewing it.
   Your Tropical Getaways database should now have two reports: Customer Profiles by State *and* Trips by Category.
14. Use the **File→Close** command to close the database. The Access program window should remain open.

Assessment

Assessment 20.1 Create Forms and Reports

1. Open the Classic Cars database.
   You began setting up this database in the assessments in the previous lesson.
2. Use AutoForm to create the form shown below for the Collectors table.

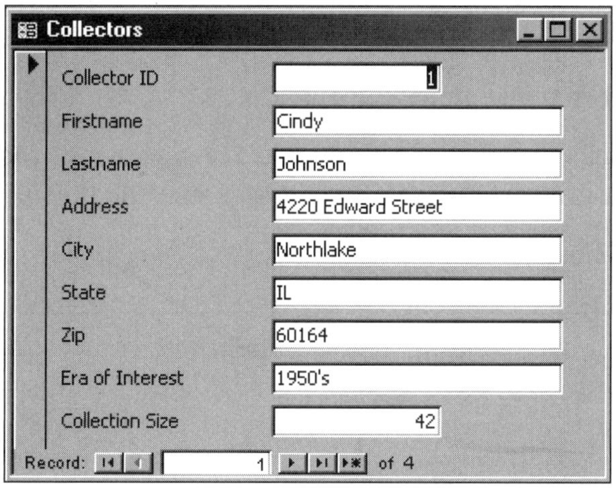
Collectors
Collector ID
1
Firstname
Cindy
Lastname
Johnson
Address
4220 Edward Street
City
Northlake
State
IL
Zip
60164
Era of Interest
1950's
Collection Size
42
Record:
1
of 4

3. Use the form to enter the following new record into the Collectors table.

Collector ID	Firstname	Lastname	Address	City	State	Zip	Era of Interest	Collection Size
5	Jake	Johnson	840 Edgewood Drive	Arcadia	FL	33821	1920s	3

4. Close the form, and save it with the proposed name *Collectors.*
5. Use AutoForm to create the form shown below for the *Cars* table.

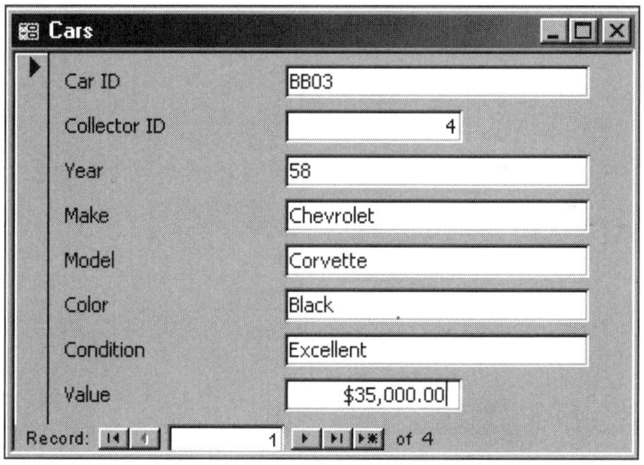
Cars
Car ID
BB03
Collector ID
4
Year
58
Make
Chevrolet
Model
Corvette
Color
Black
Condition
Excellent
Value
$35,000.00
Record:
1
of 4

(Continued on the next page)

6. Use the form to enter the following new records into the table.

Car ID	Collector ID	Year	Make	Model	Color	Condition	Value
CJ04	1	48	Packard	Custom Eight Sedan	White	Fair	$15,000
JJ01	5	27	Ford	Model A	Black	Mint	$75,000
BB04	4	57	Chevrolet	Corvette	Red	Excellent	$42,000

7. Close the form, and save it with the proposed name *Cars.*

8. Create the report shown below for the Collectors table. The report sorts the records by the Era of Interest field, and it uses the Compact style. Also notice the title is Era of Interest.

9. Print the report, and then close it.

Era of Interest

Era of Interest	Firstname	Lastname	Collection Size
1920's	Jake	Johnson	3
1950's	Bob	Barker	7
1950's	Cindy	Johnson	42
1960's	Tammy	Olson	6
Early 1900's	Ed	Larkson	34

10. Create the report shown below for the Cars table. When adding the fields in the first Report Wizard screen, you will need to add them in the order shown on the report. For example, add the Model field first, the Year field second, the Condition field third, etc. This report is sorted on the Model field, and it uses the Compact style.

Models Report

Model	Year	Condition	Color	Value
Corvette	57	Excellent	Red	$42,000.00
Corvette	58	Excellent	Black	$35,000.00
Corvette	62	Excellent	Blue	$30,000.00
Corvette	58	Mint	Red and white	$65,000.00
Custom Eight Sedan	48	Fair	White	$15,000.00
Model A	27	Mint	Black	$75,000.00
Thunderbird	59	Good	Tan	$20,000.00

11. Print the report, and then close it.

12. Close the Classic Cars database when you have finished, and continue with the next lesson.

LESSON 21—Access

Getting Answers with Queries

In this lesson, you will learn how to set up and use queries. Queries are an essential part of any Access database. Queries allow you to extract and combine data from tables. You will learn how to specify criteria in queries to extract only the records you desire. You will create calculated fields, work with statistical functions, and sort and group query results.

In This Lesson

Case Study

The staff at Pinnacle Pet Care has used their new database for some time, and now they want answers to a variety of questions. For example,

- What is the current balance of each customer in California?
- Which customers have a current balance that is greater than $200?
- Which customers in California have a current balance that is greater than $200?
- What is the average amount of money that customers spend on cats and dogs?

Penny Johnson sets up queries in the Pinnacle Pet Care database to answer these questions. The following illustration shows a query, the Customers table, and the resulting recordset.

Field:	Firstname	Lastname	Phone	Current Balance
Table:	Customers	Customers	Customers	Customers
Sort:				Descending
Show:	☑	☑	☑	☑
Criteria:				>200

A query contains fields and criteria that are used to select records from a table.

Customer ID	Firstname	Lastname	Address	City	State	Zip	Phone	Last Visit	Current Balance
1	Mark	Roth	760 Maple Avenue	Fremont	CA	94538-	(510) 234-9090	7/7/99	$235.00
2	Tony	Simpson	312 York Lane	Richmond	CA	94804-	(510) 238-2233	9/7/99	$185.00
3	Jason	Jones	2233 Crystal Street	San Mateo	CA	94403-	(415) 312-2312	7/15/99	$48.00
4	Jacob	Samuels	2300 North Pratt Str	Atlanta	GA	30309-	(404) 367-8002	10/8/99	$250.50

Firstname	Lastname	Phone	Current Balance
Jacob	Samuels	(404) 367-8002	$250.50
Mark	Roth	(510) 234-9090	$235.00

Access produces a recordset when the query is run.

What Are Queries?

Queries are an essential part of any Access database. Most people use queries to get answers to questions and to extract data from one or more tables. When you run a query, Access creates a temporary table using the fields and criteria you specify in the query. The temporary table is known as a **recordset.** The recordset is composed of data from one or more tables in your database. A query's recordset can even be used as the basis for forms and reports. Thus, queries give you the ability to produce forms and reports using data from multiple tables.

Select Queries

Select queries are the most common type of query. Select queries let you selectively extract data from one or more tables in a database. When designing select queries, you specify the fields that you wish to include in the recordset. You can also specify **criteria** that are used to select records from the table(s) in your database. The following illustration shows the Customers table from the Pinnacle Pet Care database and the resulting recordset. Take a few moments to study the illustration.

Customer ID	Firstname	Lastname	Address	City	State	Zip	Phone	Last Visit	Current Balance
1	Mark	Roth	760 Maple Avenue	Fremont	CA	94538-	(510) 234-9090	7/7/99	$235.00
2	Tony	Simpson	312 York Lane	Richmond	CA	94804-	(510) 238-2233	9/7/99	$185.00
3	Jason	Jones	2233 Crystal Street	San Mateo	CA	94403-	(415) 312-2312	7/15/99	$48.00
4	Jacob	Samuels	2300 North Pratt Str	Atlanta	GA	30309-	(404) 367-8002	10/8/99	$250.50

Firstname	Lastname	Phone	Current Balance
Jacob	Samuels	(404) 367-8002	$250.50
Mark	Roth	(510) 234-9090	$235.00

A query is run that instructs Access to only choose the Firstname, Lastname, Phone, and Current Balance fields from the Customers table for those customers with a Current Balance > $200.

The query produces the recordset shown here. Notice that the recordset only includes the specified fields for customers with a Current Balance > $200.

Setting Up Queries

You can use the **Query Wizard** to assist you in setting up queries, or you can set them up yourself using the **query design grid.** The design grid gives you complete flexibility in determining the fields, criteria, and other options that you wish to use in the query. The following Quick Reference table describes how to display the Query window and how to add tables to the query. You must add table(s) to the Query window so that you can use the desired fields from the table(s) in the query.

Quick Reference

ADDING TABLES TO THE QUERY WINDOW

- Open the desired database, and make sure the Queries button is pressed on the Objects bar.
- Double-click the Create query in Design view option.
- Choose a table that you want the query to extract data from in the Show Table box, and click Add.
- Add any other tables from which you wish to extract data.
- Click the Close button on the Show Table box.

Hands-On 21.1 Set Up a Query

In this exercise, you will begin setting up a query. You will display the Query window, and you will add the Customers table in the Pinnacle Pet Care database to the Query window.

Display the Query window

1. Start Access, and open the **Pinnacle Pet Care** database.
2. Click the **Queries** button on the Objects bar.
3. Double-click the **Create query in Design view** option.
   The Query window will appear, and the Show Table dialog box will be displayed. The Show Table dialog box lets you choose the table(s) that you wish to use in the query. In this exercise, you will add just the Customers table to the Query window.
4. Choose **Customers,** and click the **Add** button.
   A Customers field list will appear above the design grid. The field names in the list are taken from the Customers table. In a moment, you will use the Customers field list to add fields to the query.

TIP! *You can also double-click the table name.*

5. Click the **Close** button on the Show Table dialog box.
   You won't be using the Pets table in this exercise.

Set Up the Window

6. Make sure that the Access window is maximized and that the Query window is maximized within the Access window.
7. Follow these steps to adjust the size of the design grid and the Customers field list.

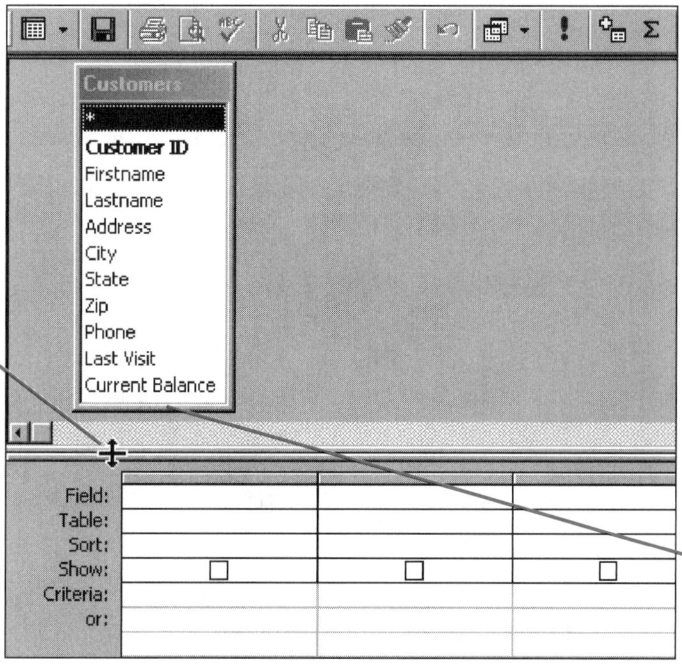

Customers
*
Customer ID
Firstname
Lastname
Address
City
State
Zip
Phone
Last Visit
Current Balance
Field:
Table:
Sort:
Show:
Criteria:
or:

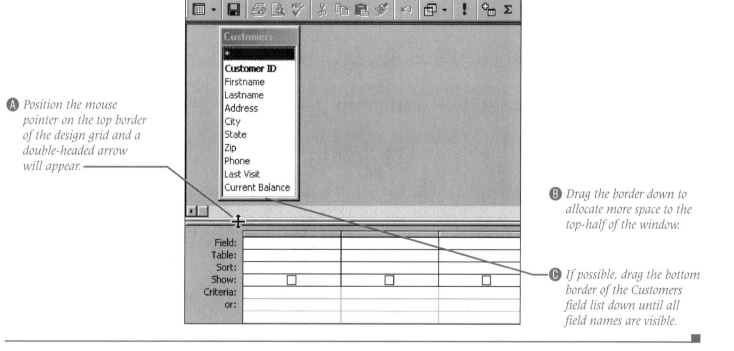

Ⓐ *Position the mouse pointer on the top border of the design grid and a double-headed arrow will appear.*

Ⓑ *Drag the border down to allocate more space to the top-half of the window.*

Ⓒ *If possible, drag the bottom border of the Customers field list down until all field names are visible.*

The Query Design Grid

The design grid appears when you begin setting up a new query. The design grid lets you specify the fields to include in the query. You can also use the design grid to specify criteria and other parameters that affect the query recordset. The following illustration displays the design grid and the recordset for the sample query shown. You will develop the query shown in the illustration as you progress through the next few exercises.

The Table row indicates the table from which each field is taken. In this example, all fields are taken from the Customers table.

*Fields such as **Firstname, Lastname, Phone,** and* Current Balance *are added to the columns of the design grid. These fields will be displayed in the recordset.*

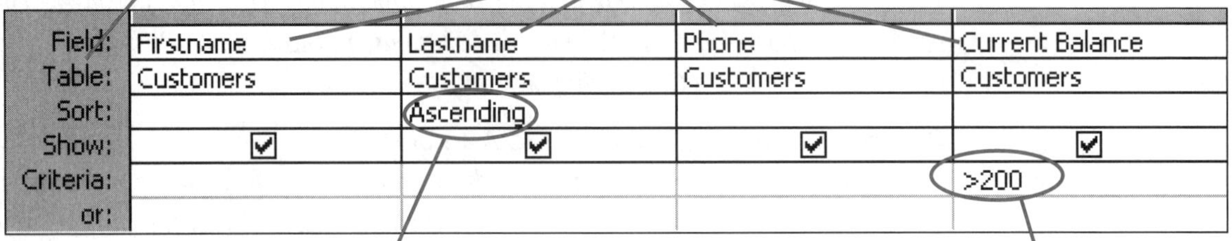

Field:
Table:
Sort:
Show:
Criteria:
or:
Firstname
Customers
Lastname
Customers
Ascending
Phone
Customers
Current Balance
Customers
>200

*The **Sort** row lets you specify one or more fields for sorting the selected records. In this example, the recordset will be sorted in Ascending order (A–Z) by the* Lastname *field.*

You can use criteria to select records from the table(s). In this example, only customer records with a Current Balance *greater than* $200 *will be selected.*

The recordset includes customer records with a Current Balance greater than $200. Only the fields specified in the query appear in the recordset.

Firstname	Lastname	Phone	Current Balance
Mark	Roth	(510) 234-9090	$235.00
Jacob	Samuels	(404) 367-8002	$250.50

Adding Fields to the Design Grid

The first step in defining a query is to add fields to the design grid. The fields you add to the design grid will appear in the recordset. Once you have added fields to the design grid, you can specify sorting options, criteria, and other options that affect the recordset. The following Quick Reference table describes the techniques you can use to add fields to the design grid.

Quick Reference

ADDING FIELDS TO THE QUERY DESIGN GRID

Technique	Description
Double-click	You can add a single field to the design grid by double-clicking the desired field in the field list.
Drop-down list	You can add a single field by clicking in a field cell, clicking the drop-down button that appears, and then choosing the desired field from the drop-down menu.
Drag	You can add a single field or multiple fields to the design grid by dragging them from a field list to the desired cell in the design grid. You can select multiple fields prior to dragging by pressing and holding the CTRL key while clicking the desired field names in the field list.
All fields	You can add all fields to the design grid by double-clicking the asterisk * symbol at the top of the desired field list.

Hands-On 21.2 Add Fields to the Design Grid

1. Follow these steps to add the Firstname field to the design grid.

Ⓐ *Double-click the* Firstname *field in the field list and it will appear in the first cell of the design grid.*

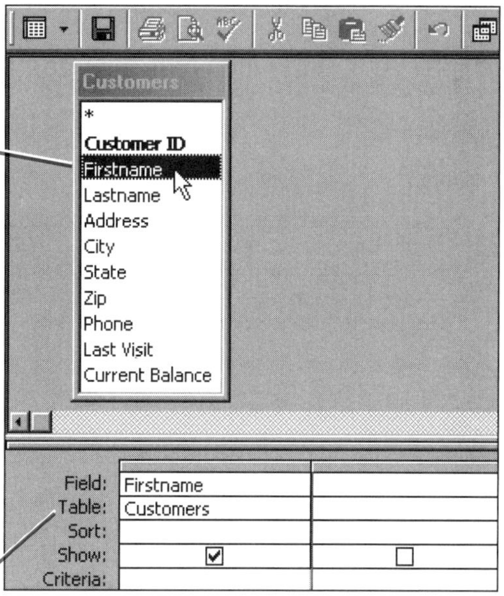

Customers
*
Customer ID
Firstname
Lastname
Address
City
State
Zip
Phone
Last Visit
Current Balance
Field: Firstname
Table: Customers
Sort:
Show:
Criteria:

Ⓑ *Notice the* ***Table*** *row specifies that the field is taken from the Customers table. Knowing which table the field is taken from can be important especially when the same field name is used in more than one table.*

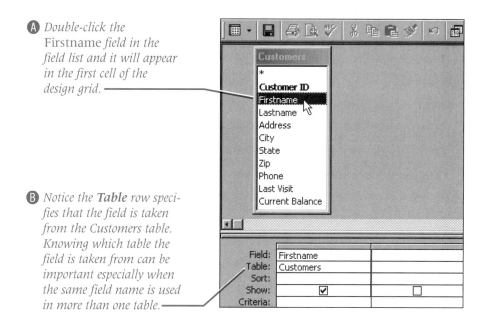

2. Now add the *Lastname, Phone,* and *Current Balance* fields to the design grid by double-clicking them on the field name list. The design grid should match the following illustration when you have finished adding the fields.

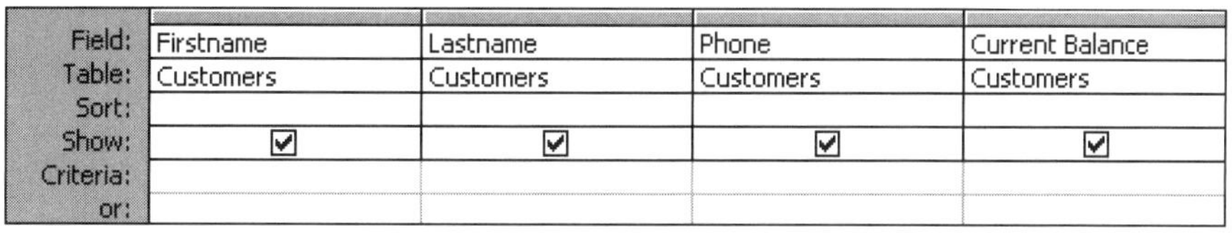

Field: Firstname Lastname Phone Current Balance
Table: Customers Customers Customers Customers
Sort:
Show:
Criteria:
or:

Removing Fields from the Design Grid

You can remove fields from the design grid by clicking in the desired column and choosing **Edit→Delete Columns** from the menu bar. You may need to remove fields from time to time as you develop queries. Remember to use this technique if you make a mistake and add an incorrect field to the design grid.

Hands-On 21.3 Delete a Field

1. Click anywhere in the Current Balance column in the design grid.
2. Choose **Edit→Delete Columns** from the menu bar, and the field will be removed.
3. Follow these steps to reinsert the Current Balance field using the drop-down list technique.

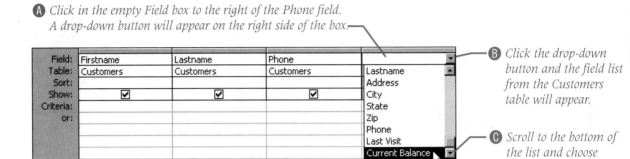

Ⓐ *Click in the empty Field box to the right of the Phone field. A drop-down button will appear on the right side of the box.*

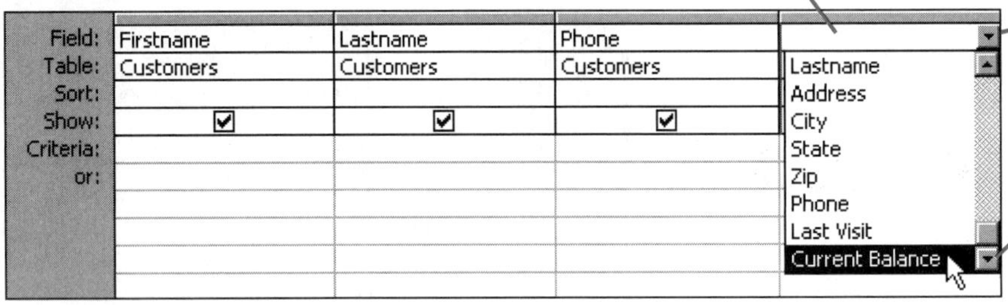
Field:
Table:
Sort:
Show:
Criteria:
or:
Firstname
Customers
Lastname
Customers
Phone
Customers
Lastname
Address
City
State
Zip
Phone
Last Visit
Current Balance

Ⓑ *Click the drop-down button and the field list from the Customers table will appear.*

Ⓒ *Scroll to the bottom of the list and choose Current Balance.*

The Current Balance field should be returned to the grid. As you can see, there are several ways to add fields to the design grid. Once again, feel free to remove fields from the design grid whenever you make a mistake or wish to change the order of the fields in the grid.

Running Queries

You can run a query by clicking the Run button on the Access toolbar. When you run a select query, Access selects records and fields from tables in your database and displays the recordset. You can navigate through the recordset or print it if desired. The recordset will always reflect the current data stored in the database.

Editing Data In a Recordset

When you run a select query, the recordset is connected to the underlying table(s) that the query is based upon. If you edit data in the recordset, then the data in the underlying tables is changed as well. However, most select queries are only used for viewing selective data.

Hands-On 21.4 Run the Query

1. Click the Run button on the Access toolbar.
   The query will run, and the recordset shown below will appear. Keep in mind that your query is quite basic. This query simply displays four fields from each record in the Customers table.

Firstname	Lastname	Phone	Current Balance
Mark	Roth	(510) 234-9090	$235.00
Tony	Simpson	(510) 238-2233	$185.00
Jason	Jones	(415) 312-2312	$48.00
Jacob	Samuels	(404) 367-8002	$250.50

2. Now continue with the next topic, where you will learn how to sort the query results.

Sorting the Query Results

You can instruct Access to sort the rows in a recordset using one or more fields as sort keys. For example, you may want to view the recordset with the largest current balances displayed first. You sort recordsets by setting the sort box to Ascending or Descending for one or more fields in the design grid. If you set the sort box for more than one field, then the first field is used as the primary sort key, followed by the next field, and so on.

Hands-On 21.5 Sort the Results

The recordset should be displayed from the previous exercise.

1. Notice that the records in the recordset do not appear to be sorted in any particular order.
   However, the records are actually sorted on the Customer ID field, which is the primary key for the Customers table. In the next few steps, you will set the sort key for the Lastname field in the design grid. You will run the query again, and the recordset will be sorted by last name with the Jones record first, followed by the Roth record, and so on.
2. Click the Design View button on the left end of the Access toolbar.
   The design grid will reappear. You can always use the view button to switch back and forth between the recordset and the design grid.
3. Follow these steps to set a sort key.

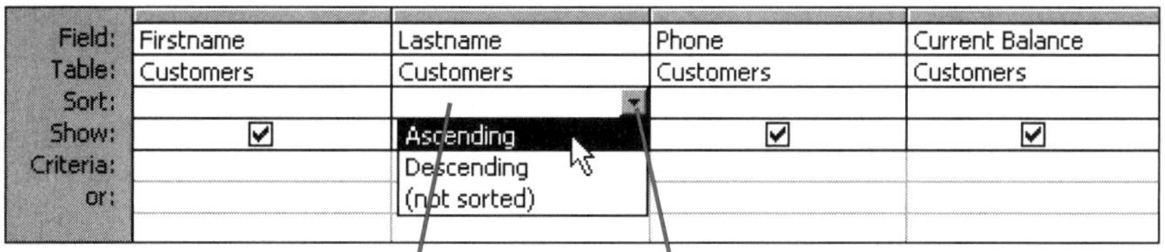
Field: Firstname Lastname Phone Current Balance
Table: Customers Customers Customers Customers
Sort:
Show:
Criteria:
or:
Ascending
Descending
(not sorted)

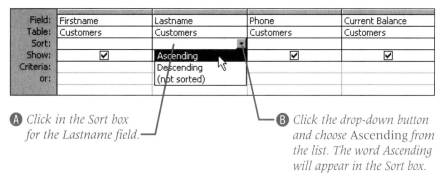

Ⓐ *Click in the Sort box for the Lastname field.*

Ⓑ *Click the drop-down button and choose Ascending from the list. The word Ascending will appear in the Sort box.*

(Continued on the next page)

4. Click the Run button, and the recordset shown below will appear.
Notice that the records are sorted by the Lastname field.

Firstname	Lastname	Phone	Current Balance
Jason	Jones	(415) 312-2312	$48.00
Mark	Roth	(510) 234-9090	$235.00
Jacob	Samuels	(404) 367-8002	$250.50
Tony	Simpson	(510) 238-2233	$185.00

5. Click the Design View button to display the design grid.
6. Follow these steps to remove the Lastname sort key and to set the sort order to descending based upon the Outstanding Balance field.

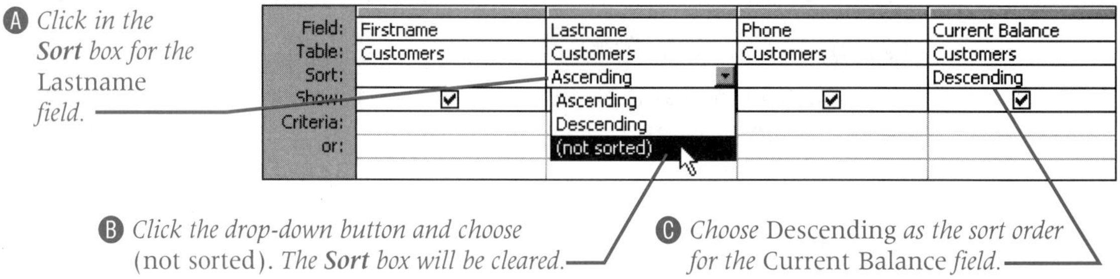
A Click in the Sort box for the Lastname field.
Field: Firstname Lastname Phone Current Balance
Table: Customers Customers Customers Customers
Sort: Ascending Descending
Show:
Criteria:
or:
Ascending
Descending
(not sorted)
B Click the drop-down button and choose (not sorted). The Sort box will be cleared.
C Choose Descending as the sort order for the Current Balance field.

7. Click the Run button, and the recordset shown below will appear.
Notice that the records with the largest Current Balance are displayed first.

Firstname	Lastname	Phone	Current Balance
Jacob	Samuels	(404) 367-8002	$250.50
Mark	Roth	(510) 234-9090	$235.00
Tony	Simpson	(510) 238-2233	$185.00
Jason	Jones	(415) 312-2312	$48.00

8. Click the Design View button to display the design grid.

Using Criteria to Select Records

One of the most important benefits of queries is that you can select specific records by specifying **criteria.** This gives you the ability to select the precise data you desire from a database. For example, you may want to know how many customers have an outstanding balance that is greater than $200. Or, perhaps you are interested in viewing only those records where the state is equal to CA (California). These and other questions are easily answered by specifying criteria in the query design grid.

Equality Criteria

You can use *equality criteria* to choose only those records where a field has a specific value. For example, you may want to display only those records where the state field is equal to CA. You accomplish this by entering the value that you want the field to equal in the Criteria row of the design grid. The following illustration shows how this is accomplished.

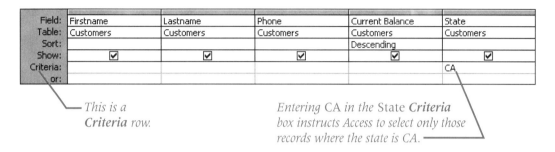

Field:	Firstname	Lastname	Phone	Current Balance	State
Table:	Customers	Customers	Customers	Customers	Customers
Sort:				Descending	
Show:	☑	☑	☑	☑	☑
Criteria:					CA
or:					

This is a ***Criteria*** *row.*

Entering CA *in the* State ***Criteria*** *box instructs Access to select only those records where the state is CA.*

As expected, only records where the state is CA *appear in the recordset.*

Firstname	Lastname	Phone	Current Balance	State
Mark	Roth	(510) 234-9090	$235.00	CA
Tony	Simpson	(510) 238-2233	$185.00	CA
Jason	Jones	(415) 312-2312	$48.00	CA

Comparison Criteria

You can use the comparison operators > (greater than), < (less than), >= (greater than or equal), <= (less than or equal), and NOT (not equal) when specifying criteria. Access will select only those records matching the criteria. For example, placing the criterion >200 in the Current Balance field instructs Access to select only records where the Current Balance is greater than 200.

The Show Check Box

The Show row in the design grid contains a check box ☑ for each field. You can prevent a field from displaying in the recordset by removing the check from the Show box. This can be useful in many situations. For example, in the preceding illustration, the State field is used to select only records where the state is equal to CA. The State field must be present in the design grid in order to specify this criteria. However, you may not want the State field to be displayed in the recordset. You could prevent the State field from being displayed in the recordset by removing the check from the State field in the design grid.

Hands-On 21.6 Use Criteria

The design grid should be displayed from the previous exercise.

Use an Equality Criterion

1. Double-click the **State** field on the Customers field list to add the field to the design grid.
   The State field should be in the fifth column of the design grid.
2. Follow these steps to set an equality criterion for the State field.

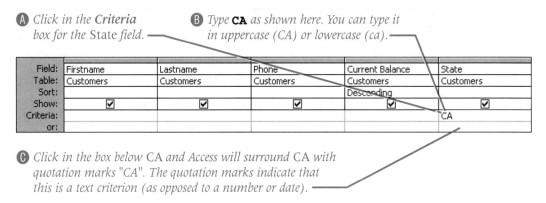

   Ⓐ *Click in the **Criteria** box for the State field.*

   Ⓑ *Type **CA** as shown here. You can type it in uppercase (CA) or lowercase (ca).*

Field:	Firstname	Lastname	Phone	Current Balance	State
Table:	Customers	Customers	Customers	Customers	Customers
Sort:				Descending	
Show:	☑	☑	☑	☑	☑
Criteria:					CA
or:					

   Ⓒ *Click in the box below CA and Access will surround CA with quotation marks "CA". The quotation marks indicate that this is a text criterion (as opposed to a number or date).*

3. Click the Run button.
   The three records with the State field equal to CA should appear in the recordset.
4. Click the Design View button to display the design grid.

Use Comparison Criteria

5. Follow these steps to create a "greater than" comparison criterion for the Current Balance field.

Field:	Firstname	Lastname	Phone	Current Balance	State
Table:	Customers	Customers	Customers	Customers	Customers
Sort:				Descending	
Show:	☑	☑	☑	☑	☑
Criteria:				>200	

   Ⓐ *Click in the **Criteria** box for the Current Balance field and type **>200**.*

   Ⓑ *Click in the **Criteria** box for the State field and delete the "CA" criterion.*

6. Click the Run button, to produce the recordset shown below.
   Notice that the current balance is greater than $200 for each record.

Firstname	Lastname	Phone	Current Balance	State
Jacob	Samuels	(404) 367-8002	$250.50	GA
Mark	Roth	(510) 234-9090	$235.00	CA

7. Click the Design View button again to display the design grid.
8. Change the >200 criterion to **<200** and run the query again.
   Only records with current balances less than $200 will appear in the recordset.

Uncheck the Show box

In the next few steps, you will prevent the State field from appearing in the recordset by removing the check from the Show box.

9. Click the Design View button to display the design grid.
10. Follow these steps to set up the query.

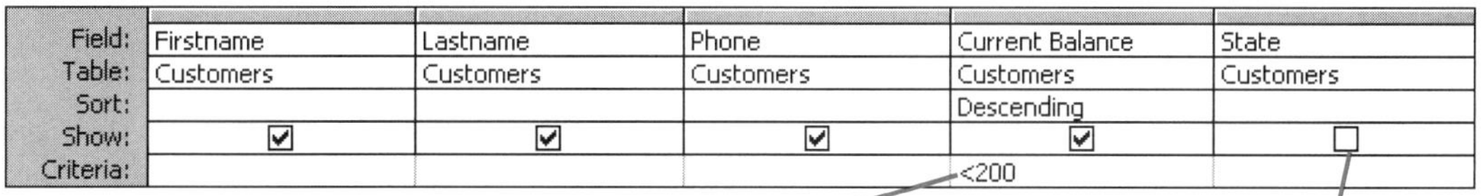

Field: Firstname | Lastname | Phone | Current Balance | State
Table: Customers | Customers | Customers | Customers | Customers
Sort: Descending
Show:
Criteria: <200

Ⓐ *Make sure the* Current Balance *criterion is set to <200.*

Ⓑ *Click the* **Show** *check box for the* State *field to remove the check.*

11. Click the Run button and the State field will be removed from the recordset.
12. Take 10 minutes to experiment with the query you have been using. Try entering various criteria and perhaps adding and removing fields from the design grid. Continue with the next topic when you have finished experimenting.

Clearing the Design Grid

You can clear all entries from the design grid with the **Edit→Clear Grid** command. This command can be used to give you a "fresh start" when working in the design grid.

Hands-On 21.7 Clear the Grid and Add All Fields

1. If necessary, click the Design View button to display the design grid.
2. Choose **Edit→Clear Grid** to remove all fields from the grid.
3. Follow these steps to add all fields from the Customers table to the design grid.

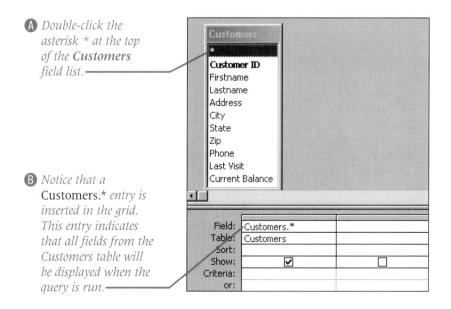

Ⓐ *Double-click the asterisk * at the top of the* **Customers** *field list.*

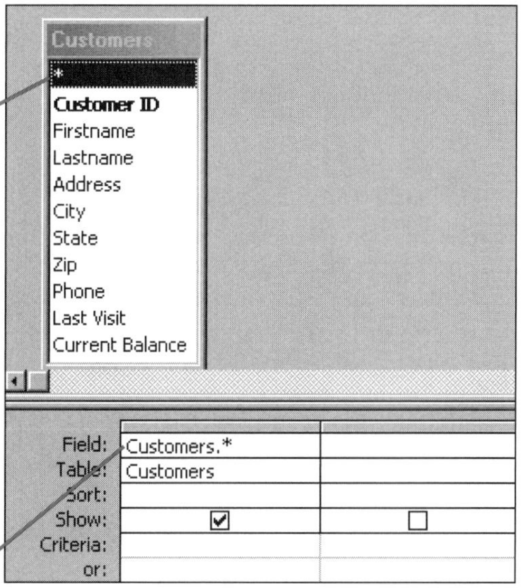

Customers
*
Customer ID
Firstname
Lastname
Address
City
State
Zip
Phone
Last Visit
Current Balance
Field: Customers.*
Table: Customers
Sort:
Show:
Criteria:
or:

Ⓑ *Notice that a* Customers.* *entry is inserted in the grid. This entry indicates that all fields from the Customers table will be displayed when the query is run.*

(Continued on the next page)

4. Click the Run button. All records from the Customers table should appear in the recordset.

Use a Criterion to Select the Records

In the next few steps, you will add the Current Balance field to the design grid and specify a criterion for that field.

5. Click the Design View button to display the design grid.
6. Follow these steps to add the Current Balance field to the grid and to specify a criterion.

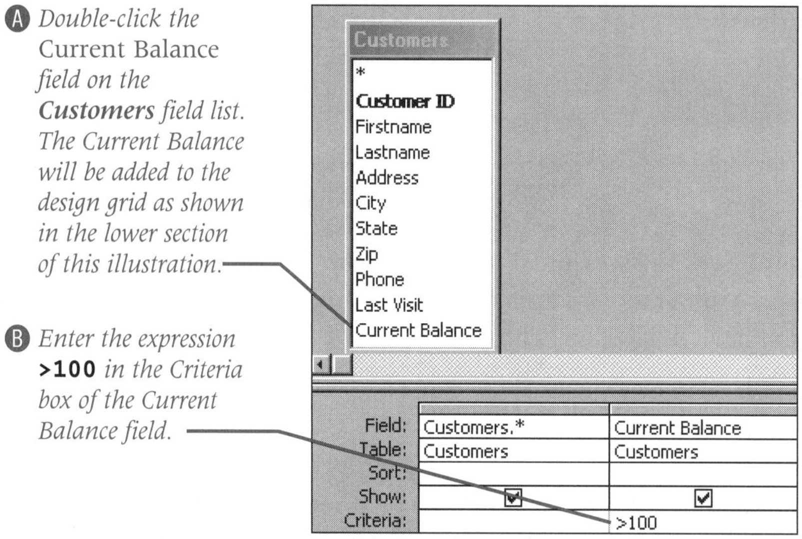

A Double-click the Current Balance field on the Customers field list. The Current Balance will be added to the design grid as shown in the lower section of this illustration.
B Enter the expression >100 in the Criteria box of the Current Balance field.
Customers
*
Customer ID
Firstname
Lastname
Address
City
State
Zip
Phone
Last Visit
Current Balance
Field:
Table:
Sort:
Show:
Criteria:
Customers.*
Customers
Current Balance
Customers
>100

7. Run the query to produce the recordset shown in the following illustration.
Notice that the last two columns of the recordset contain a Customers.Current Balance *field and a* Field0 *field. This unusual nomenclature was used because the Current Balance field was included twice in the query design grid. It was included once as part of the Customers.* entry and again as a separate field in the second column. Access cannot display the same field name twice in a table or recordset, therefore, Access changed the names of the column headings in the recordset. You will correct this by removing the check from the Show box in the next few steps.*

Customer ID	Firstname	Lastname	Address	City	State	Zip	Phone	Last Visit	Customers.Currei	Field0
1	Mark	Roth	760 Maple Avenue	Fremont	CA	94538-	(510) 234-9090	7/7/99	$235.00	$235.00
2	Tony	Simpson	312 York Lane	Richmond	CA	94804-	(510) 238-2233	9/7/99	$185.00	$185.00
4	Jacob	Samuels	2300 North Pratt Str	Atlanta	GA	30309-	(404) 367-8002	10/8/97	$250.50	$250.50

8. Switch to Design View, and remove the check from the Show box of the Current Balance field. The design grid should match the example to the right.

Field:	Customers.*	Current Balance
Table:	Customers	Customers
Sort:		
Show:	☑	☐
Criteria:		>100

9. Run the query; only one Current Balance field will be visible.
The >100 criterion in the Current Balance field selects the appropriate records. However, the field is not displayed in the recordset because the Show box is unchecked.
10. Choose **File→Close** from the menu bar, and click the **Yes** button to save the query.
11. Type the name **`Current Balance`** in the Save As box, and click **OK.**

Compound Criteria

Thus far, you have worked with relatively simple queries containing one criterion. However, you will sometimes need to use more than one criterion. Criteria that are composed of two or more criteria are known as *compound criteria.* There are two types of compound criteria: *AND* criteria and *OR* criteria.

AND Criteria

AND criteria let you select records based on logical AND expressions. In the next exercise, you will use AND criteria to select records in the Pets table. For example, you will use an AND expression to select all records where the pet type is dog *and* the number of visits is greater than 5. With AND criteria, Access will only select records when all of the criteria are true.

OR Criteria

OR criteria allow you to select records based on logical OR expressions. For example, you will use an OR expression to select all records where the pet type is dog *or* the pet type is cat. With OR criteria, Access will select records if any of the criteria are true.

Setting up Compound Criteria

You set up compound criteria in the design grid. AND criteria are set up by placing two or more criterion in different fields within the same Criteria row. OR criteria are set up by placing two or more criteria on different rows within the design grid. The following illustration shows the compound criteria you will set up in the next exercise.

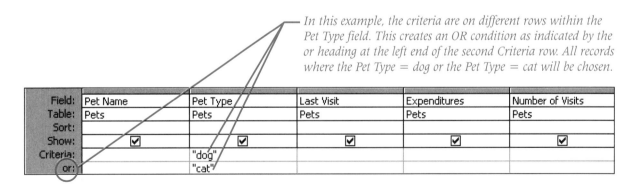

Field:	Pet Name	Pet Type	Last Visit	Expenditures	Number of Visits
Table:	Pets	Pets	Pets	Pets	Pets
Sort:					
Show:	☑	☑	☑	☑	☑
Criteria:		"dog"			>5

In this example, the criterion "dog" *and* >5 *are on the same* ***Criteria*** *row. This creates an AND condition. Only records where the* Pet Type *is* dog *and the* Number of Visits > 5 *will be chosen.*

In this example, the criteria are on different rows within the Pet Type field. This creates an OR condition as indicated by the or heading at the left end of the second Criteria row. All records where the Pet Type = dog or the Pet Type = cat will be chosen.

Field:	Pet Name	Pet Type	Last Visit	Expenditures	Number of Visits
Table:	Pets	Pets	Pets	Pets	Pets
Sort:					
Show:	☑	☑	☑	☑	☑
Criteria:		"dog"			
or:		"cat"			

Hands-On 21.8 Use Compound Criteria

In this exercise, you will set up a new query using the Pets table from the Pinnacle Pet Care database. You will use compound criteria to query the database in various ways.

Set Up the Query Window

1. Make sure the queries are displayed in the Database window.
2. Double-click the **Create query in Design view** option.
3. Choose **Pets** from the Show Table box, and click the **Add** button.
4. Click the **Close** button on the Show Table dialog box.
5. If necessary, maximize the query window. Also, you may want to adjust the size of the design grid and the Pets field list to allow you to see the entire content of the Pets field list. You used this technique in the first exercise in this lesson with the Customers field list.

Create an AND Criterion

6. Double-click the **Pet Name**, **Pet Type**, **Last Visit**, **Expenditures**, and **Number of Visits** fields on the Pets field list to add those fields to the design grid.
7. Enter the criteria shown below into the Pet Type and Number of Visits boxes in the Criteria row.

Field:	Pet Name	Pet Type	Last Visit	Expenditures	Number of Visits
Table:	Pets	Pets	Pets	Pets	Pets
Sort:					
Show:	☑	☑	☑	☑	☑
Criteria:		"dog"			>5

8. Click the Run button to produce the following recordset.
Notice that each record has Dog as the Pet Type and that the Number of Visits is greater than 5.

Pet Name	Pet Type	Last Visit	Expenditures	Number of Visits
Wolfy	Dog	7/15/99	$450.00	7
Spike	Dog	10/8/99	$890.00	12

Create an OR Criterion

9. Switch to Design View, and remove the >5 criterion from the Number of Visits criteria box.
10. Add the cat criterion to the row below the dog criterion as shown below. It isn't necessary to type the quotation marks shown in the illustration. Access will add the quotation marks as soon as you click outside of the field after typing the criterion.

TIP! *When using OR criteria, you can use as many rows as necessary. Each row that you add creates one more condition in the OR expression.*

Field:	Pet Name	Pet Type	Last Visit	Expenditures	Number of Visits
Table:	Pets	Pets	Pets	Pets	Pets
Sort:					
Show:	☑	☑	☑	☑	☑
Criteria:		"dog"			
or:		"cat"			

11. Click the Run button to produce the following recordset (although the sort order may be different than shown here).
Notice that all records have a Pet Type of Dog or Cat.

Pet Name	Pet Type	Last Visit	Expenditures	Number of Visits
Wolfy	Dog	7/15/99	$450.00	7
Dillon	Dog	7/7/99	$150.55	3
Max	Cat	9/7/99	$1,450.55	20
Stripes	Cat	7/15/99	$450.00	9
Tony	Cat	7/7/99	$145.00	6
Fetch	Dog	9/10/99	$345.00	3
Ben	Dog	10/8/99	$480.00	3
Spike	Dog	10/8/99	$890.00	12

Use a Combination of AND and OR Compound Criteria

12. Switch to Design View, but do not change the "dog" and "cat" criteria.

13. Add the >5 criteria to the Number of Visits field as shown below.
This compound criteria will choose all records where the Pet Type is dog and *the Number of Visits is greater than 5* or *the Pet Type is cat* and *the Number of Visits is greater than 5.*

Field:	Pet Name	Pet Type	Last Visit	Expenditures	Number of Visits
Table:	Pets	Pets	Pets	Pets	Pets
Sort:					
Show:	☑	☑	☑	☑	☑
Criteria:		"dog"			>5
or:		"cat"			>5

14. Click the Run button to produce the following recordset.

Pet Name	Pet Type	Last Visit	Expenditures	Number of Visits
Wolfy	Dog	7/15/99	$450.00	7
Max	Cat	9/7/99	$1,450.55	20
Stripes	Cat	7/15/99	$450.00	9
Tony	Cat	7/7/99	$145.00	6
Spike	Dog	10/8/99	$890.00	12

15. Switch to Design view and take 10 minutes to experiment with compound criteria.
Be creative; query the Pets table for answers to any questions that may come to mind.

16. When you have finished experimenting, choose **File→Close** from the menu bar, and click the **Yes** button when Access asks if you want to save the query.

17. Type the name **`Compound Criteria`** in the Save As box, and click **OK.**

Calculated Fields

Access lets you create *calculated fields* within queries. Calculated fields perform calculations using values from other fields within the query or from fields in the underlying table(s). For example, in the next exercise, you will set up a new query that will be based upon the Pets table. The Pets table contains an Expenditures field that represents the total expenditures for a particular pet. The Pets table also contains a Number of Visits field that represents the total number of visits by the pet. You will create a calculated field within the query named Expenditures Per Visit. The Expenditures Per Visit will be calculated as the Expenditures divided by the Number of Visits. The following illustration shows the design grid with the Pet Name and Pet Type fields and the Expenditures Per Visit calculated field.

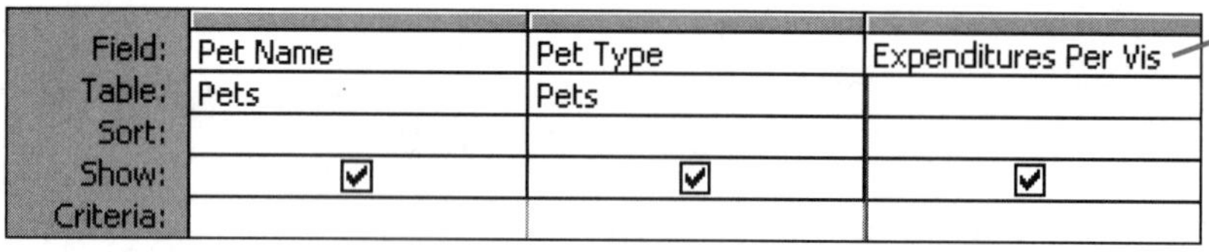
Field:
Table:
Sort:
Show:
Criteria:
Pet Name
Pets
Pet Type
Pets
Expenditures Per Vis

Expenditures Per Visit *is a calculated field, and it is too wide to be completely visible in the cell. The complete content of the cell is* Expenditures Per Visit: [Expenditures]/[Number of Visits].

The following illustration discusses the syntax that must be used with calculated fields.

A descriptive name for the calculated field is entered into an empty field cell. You can use spaces in the name.

A colon : must follow the name. The colon identifies the field as a calculated field.

*An expression follows the colon. The expression can include field names, numbers, and operators such as +, -, *, and /. The various parts of the expression are surrounded with square brackets.*

Expenditures Per Visit: [Expenditures]/[Number of Visits]

The Zoom Dialog Box

Calculated field expressions can be quite long and complex. For this reason, you may not be able to see the entire expression as you enter it in a cell. Fortunately, Access provides a Zoom command that displays a Zoom dialog box. When you enter the desired expression into the Zoom dialog box, you can see the entire expression as it is entered. In the following exercise, you will use the Zoom dialog box to enter an expression. You display the Zoom dialog box by right-clicking the cell where the expression will be entered and choosing Zoom from the pop-up menu.

Hands-On 21.9 Create a Calculated Field

The Queries section of the Database window should be displayed from the previous exercise.

1. Create a new query in Design view, and add the **Pets** table to the query.
2. Close the **Show Tables** dialog box.
3. Add the **Pet Name** and **Pet Type** fields to the design grid.

4. Follow these steps to display the Zoom dialog box.

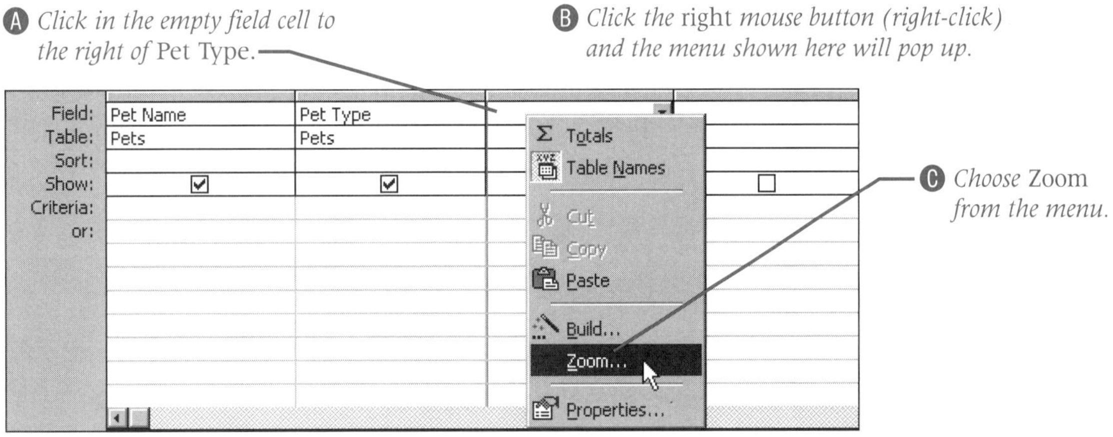
A Click in the empty field cell to the right of Pet Type.
B Click the right mouse button (right-click) and the menu shown here will pop up.
C Choose Zoom from the menu.
Field:
Table:
Sort:
Show:
Criteria:
or:
Pet Name
Pets
Pet Type
Pets
Totals
Table Names
Cut
Copy
Paste
Build...
Zoom...
Properties...

5. Enter the calculated field expression shown in the following illustration into the Zoom box. Make sure you enter the expression exactly as shown. In particular, make sure you use a colon : (not a semicolon ;), correctly spell the field names, use the correct open and closed brackets [ ], and use the forward slash / symbol to represent division. Access is leniant when it comes to spaces, so you can omit the spaces that come after the colon and before and after the forward slash / if you desire.

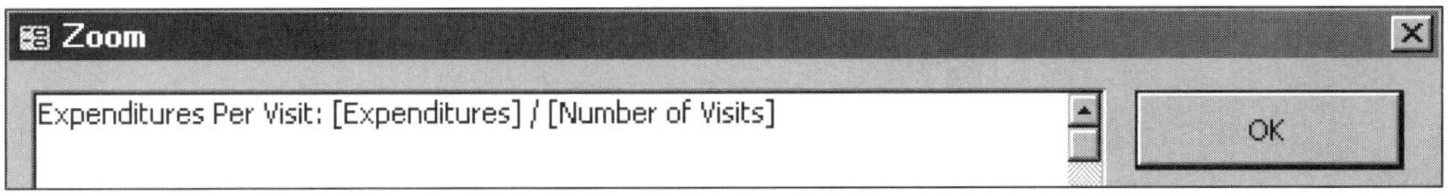
Zoom
Expenditures Per Visit: [Expenditures] / [Number of Visits]
OK

6. Click **OK** to insert the expression in the field.

7. Use the ← and → keys on your keyboard to scroll through the expression within the cell. Make sure the syntax is correct as shown above. If necessary, you can edit the expression within the cell or redisplay the Zoom dialog box and make any necessary changes.

8. Click the Run button to produce the following recordset.
The numbers shown in the Expenditures Per Visit field represent the average expenditure for each pet on each visit. Notice the excessive number of decimal places that are displayed in the calculated field. In the next exercise, you will reduce the number of displayed decimal places by changing one of the properties of the Expenditures Per Visit field.

Pet Name	Pet Type	Expenditures P
Max	Cat	72.5275
Stripes	Cat	50
Tony	Cat	24.1666666667
Wolfy	Dog	64.2857142857
Dillon	Dog	50.1833333333
Fetch	Dog	115
Ben	Dog	160
Spike	Dog	74.1666666667
Bugs	Rabbit	150.125

9. Switch to Design View, and continue with the next topic.

Modifying Query Properties

The Properties button on the Access toolbar displays the Properties dialog box. You can use the Properties dialog box to change the properties of any Access object, including fields within queries. Properties can affect the appearance and format of objects. For example, in the following exercise, you will set the Format property of the Expenditures Per Visit field to Currency. The Currency format will reduce the number of displayed decimal places in the recordset.

Hands-On 21.10 Set the Format Property

The query design grid should be displayed from the previous exercise.

1. Click in the **Expenditures Per Visit** box, and then click the Properties button on the toolbar.
   The Field Properties dialog box will appear.
2. Follow these steps to set the format of this field to Currency.
   When the query is run, the Currency format will display a dollar sign and two decimal places in the Expenditures Per Visit field.

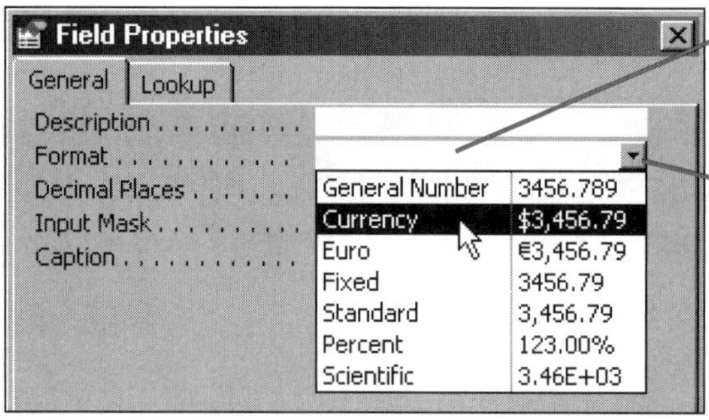

Field Properties
General
Lookup
Description
Format
Decimal Places
Input Mask
Caption
General Number 3456.789
Currency $3,456.79
Euro €3,456.79
Fixed 3456.79
Standard 3,456.79
Percent 123.00%
Scientific 3.46E+03

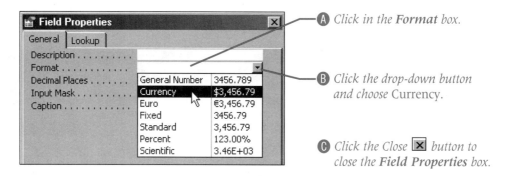

Ⓐ *Click in the **Format** box.*

Ⓑ *Click the drop-down button and choose* Currency.

Ⓒ *Click the Close button to close the **Field Properties** box.*

3. Click the Run button.
   The numbers in the Expenditures Per Visit field should now be formatted with the Currency format, which includes a dollar sign and two decimal places.
4. Switch to Design View.

Insert a Criterion

5. Click in the Criteria box for the Pet Type field, and type **dog** as shown below.

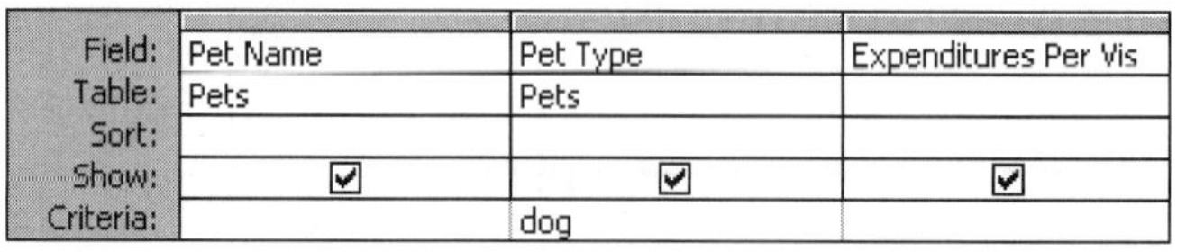

Field: Pet Name | Pet Type | Expenditures Per Vis
Table: Pets | Pets
Sort:
Show:
Criteria: dog

6. Click the Run button.
   The Pet Name, Pet Type, and Expenditures Per Visit will be displayed for records where the Pet Type is Dog. As you can see, Access allows you to combine criteria, calculated fields, and other parameters within a query.
7. Choose **File→Close** to close the query, and save it as **Expenditures Per Visit.**

Statistical Functions

Access provides built-in statistical functions for calculating statistical information within a query. The built-in statistical functions include SUM (summation), AVG (average), MIN (minimum), MAX (maximum), COUNT, VAR (variance), FIRST, and LAST. For example, you could use the AVG function to compute the average expenditures on pets, or you may want to use the COUNT function to count the number of dogs that attend the Pinnacle Pet Care clinic.

The Total Row

To use the statistical functions, you must first click the **Totals** button to display a Total row in the query design grid. Once the Total row is displayed, you can choose statistical function(s) for the desired field(s) in the query. Queries that use statistical functions will normally have just one or two fields.

*Statistical functions are entered in the **Total** row of the query design grid.*

Field:	Expenditures
Table:	Pets
Total:	Avg
Sort:	
Show:	☑
Criteria:	

Hands-On 21.11 Use Statistical Functions

1. Set up a new query in Design view, and add the **Pets** table to the query.
2. Close the Show Tables dialog box.
3. Add the **Expenditures** field to the design grid.
4. Click the Totals [Σ] button on the toolbar, and a Total row will appear below the Table row.
   The Total row lets you choose statistical functions and set grouping for fields. You will learn about grouping later in this lesson.
5. Follow these steps to choose the Average function for the Expenditures field.

Field:	Expenditures
Table:	Pets
Total:	Avg
Sort:	
Show:	☑
Criteria:	

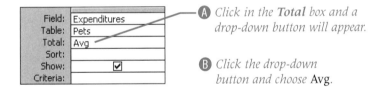

Ⓐ *Click in the **Total** box and a drop-down button will appear.*

Ⓑ *Click the drop-down button and choose* Avg.

   When you run the query, Access will determine the average expenditure for all pets. Access will display a single cell in the recordset containing the result of the average calculation.

6. Click the Run [!] button.
   The result should be $551.29. In other words, each pet has been responsible for an average of $551.29 in revenue.
7. Switch to Design View, and click in the **Totals** box that currently contains the Avg function.
8. Click the drop-down button, scroll to the top of the list, and choose **Sum.**
9. Run [!] the query again. This time the result should be $4,961.60.
   This number represents the summation of the expenditures for all pets.
10. Switch to Design View, and continue with the next topic.

Using Criteria with Statistical Functions

You can combine criteria with statistical functions to refine your statistical calculations. For example, imagine you are interested in determining the total expenditures for dogs at Pinnacle Pet Care. The answer can be found by summing the Expenditures of all records where the Pet Type is dog. The following illustration shows how this is expressed in the design grid.

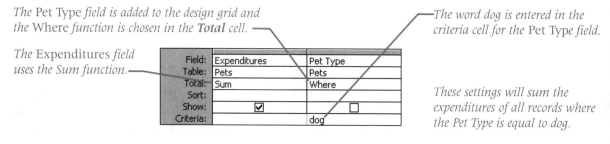

The Pet Type *field is added to the design grid and the* Where *function is chosen in the* ***Total*** *cell.*

The word dog is entered in the criteria cell for the Pet Type *field.*

The Expenditures *field uses the Sum function.*

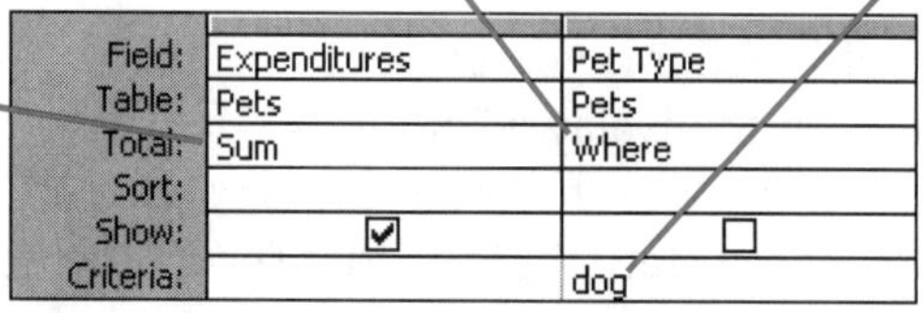

Field:
Table:
Total:
Sort:
Show:
Criteria:
Expenditures
Pets
Sum
Pet Type
Pets
Where
dog

These settings will sum the expenditures of all records where the Pet Type is equal to dog.

Hands-On 21.12 Use Criteria with Statistical Functions

1. Double-click the **Pet Type** field on the Pets field list to add it to the design grid.
2. Follow these steps to specify criteria for the Pet Type field.

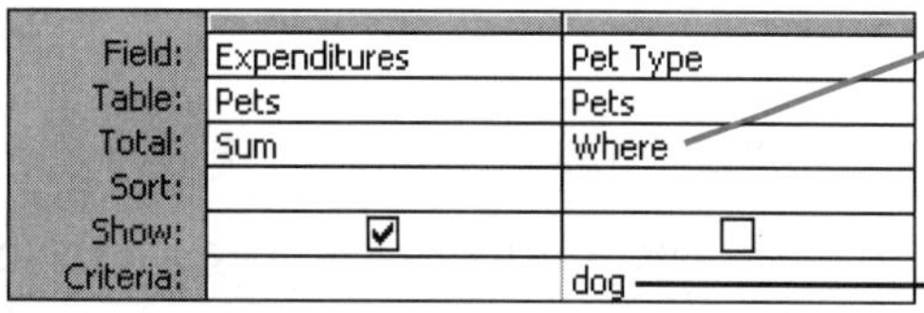

Field:
Table:
Total:
Sort:
Show:
Criteria:
Expenditures
Pets
Sum
Pet Type
Pets
Where
dog

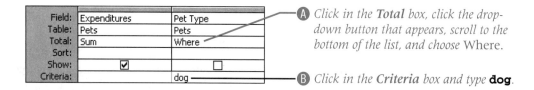

Ⓐ *Click in the* ***Total*** *box, click the drop-down button that appears, scroll to the bottom of the list, and choose* Where.

Ⓑ *Click in the* ***Criteria*** *box and type* **dog**.

3. Run the query. The result should be $2,315.55.
   This number represents the total expenditures on dogs.
4. Switch back to Design view, and continue with the last topic.

Using Grouping with Statistical Functions

The Total row in the design grid has a Group By option that can be used in conjunction with statistical functions. If you choose Group By for a field and run the query, then Access will group all records together that have the same value in the Group By field. For example, if the Pet Type field is set to Group By, then all records that have cat as the pet type will be in one group. Likewise, all records with a pet type of dog will be in another group. If you are performing a statistical calculation as well, then the statistical calculation will be performed on each group. For example, if you use the Sum function to calculate the expenditures for the groups mentioned above, then the total expenditures for cats will be calculated, as will the total expenditures for dogs.

Hands-On 21.13 Use the Group By setting

1. Follow these steps to set grouping for the Pet Type field.

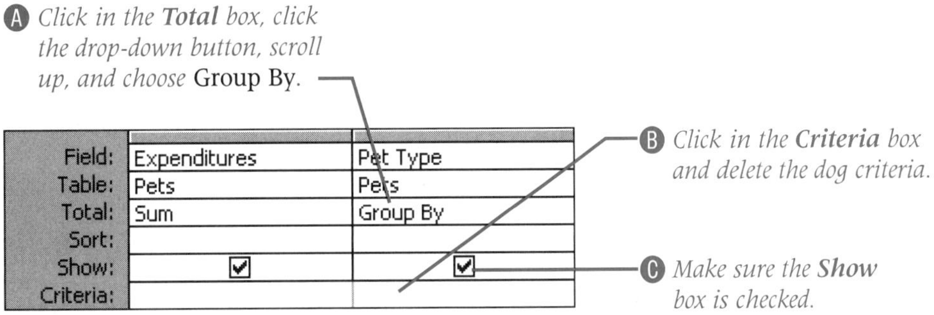
A Click in the Total box, click the drop-down button, scroll up, and choose Group By.
B Click in the Criteria box and delete the dog criteria.
C Make sure the Show box is checked.
Field:
Table:
Total:
Sort:
Show:
Criteria:
Expenditures
Pets
Sum
Pet Type
Pets
Group By

2. Run the query to produce the following recordset.
   The recordset displays the total expenditures for each pet type.

SumOfExpend	Pet Type
$2,045.55	Cat
$2,315.55	Dog
$600.50	Rabbit

3. Switch back to Design view.
4. Practice using all of the querying techniques you have learned in this lesson.
5. When you have finished practicing, close the query, and save it as **Expenditures by Pet Type.**
6. Now use the **File→Close** command again to close the Pinnacle Pet Care database.
7. Continue with the end-of-lesson questions and exercises on the following pages.

Concepts Review

True/False Questions

1. Criteria determine the records that are selected by a query. TRUE FALSE
2. The query design grid is where you define a query. TRUE FALSE
3. You can add fields to the design grid by double-clicking the desired fields on the field list(s) above the design grid. TRUE FALSE
4. You can add all fields to the design grid by double-clicking any field in the field list. TRUE FALSE
5. Changing data in the recordset has no impact on the underlying data in the table(s) that the query is based upon. TRUE FALSE
6. You must type criteria in the same case (uppercase or lowercase) as the data in the tables you are querying or Access will not select the desired records. TRUE FALSE
7. If a field has been entered into the design grid, then there is no way to prevent the field from appearing in the recordset. TRUE FALSE
8. The two types of compound criteria are Sum and Avg. TRUE FALSE

Multiple-Choice Questions

1. Which of the following commands can be used to remove fields from the design grid?
   a. Field→Remove
   b. Edit→Delete Columns
   c. Edit→Delete Rows
   d. File→Delete Columns

2. Which of the following symbols is used to represent greater than in query criteria?
   a. <
   b. >
   c. <=
   d. >=

3. Which of the following commands is used to clear the design grid?
   a. File→Clear All
   b. File→Clear Grid
   c. Edit→Clear Grid
   d. The grid cannot be cleared.

4. Which symbol(s) must be placed after the field name when creating a calculated field?
   a. A colon :
   b. A semicolon ;
   c. Parenthesis ( )
   d. Brackets [ ]

Skill Builders

Skill Builder 21.1 Use Comparison Criteria and Compound Criteria

In this exercise, you will use comparison criteria and compound criteria to query the Customers table in the Tropical Getaways database.

1. Open the Tropical Getaways database on your exercise diskette, and click the **Queries** button on the Objects bar.
2. Double-click the **Create query in Design view** option.
3. Choose **Customers** in the Show Table box, and click the **Add** button.
4. Click the **Close** button to close the Show Table dialog box.
5. If necessary, maximize the Query window, and adjust the height of the design grid and the Customers field list box.
6. Add the **Firstname**, **Lastname**, and **Profile** fields to the design grid by double-clicking them on the Customers field list.
7. Type the word **`adventure`** in the Criteria box of the Profile field as shown below.

Field:	Firstname	Lastname	Profile
Table:	Customers	Customers	Customers
Sort:			
Show:	☑	☑	☑
Criteria:			adventure

8. Run the query. Only records with the Adventure profile will be displayed, as shown below.

Firstname	Lastname	Profile
Debbie	Thomas	Adventure
Ted	Wilkins	Adventure
Victor	Thomas	Adventure

9. Switch back to Design view.
10. Add the **State** field to the design grid.
11. Set the criteria for the State field to **TX** and the sort order of the Lastname field to **Ascending** as shown below.

Field:	Firstname	Lastname	Profile	State
Table:	Customers	Customers	Customers	Customers
Sort:		Ascending		
Show:	☑	☑	☑	☑
Criteria:			"adventure"	TX

12. Run the query. Only records where the profile is Adventure *and* the state is TX will be displayed, as shown below.

Firstname	Lastname	Profile	State
Debbie	Thomas	Adventure	TX
Ted	Wilkins	Adventure	TX

13. Close the query, and save it as **Adventure Profiles.**

Skill Builder 21.2 Nest Calculated Fields

In this exercise, you will use calculated fields in the Tropical Getaways database.

1. Set up a new query in Design view, and add the Trips table to the query.
2. Close the Show Tables dialog box.
3. Add the **Destination**, **Category**, and **Cost** fields to the design grid.
4. Set the Sort box for the Category field to **Ascending.**
5. Follow these steps to display the Zoom box for a new calculated field.

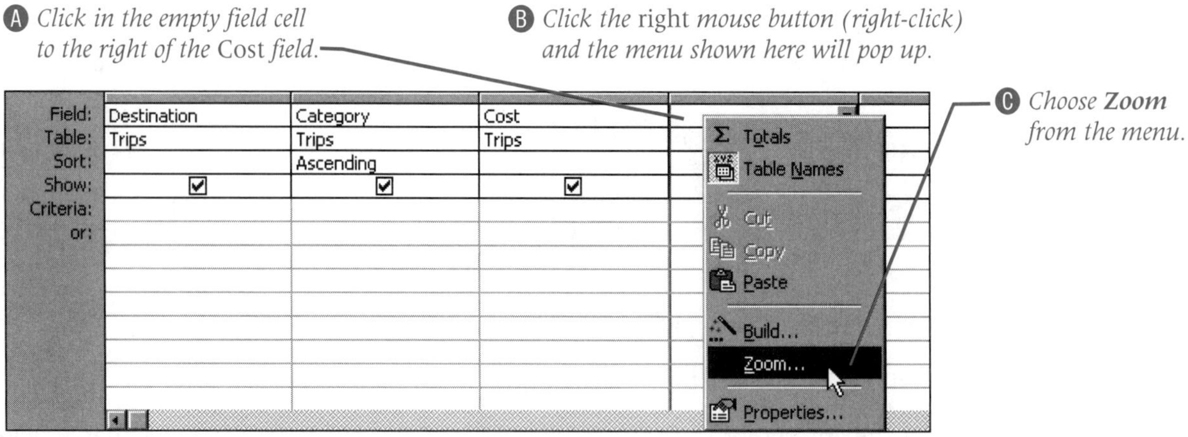
A Click in the empty field cell to the right of the Cost field.
B Click the right mouse button (right-click) and the menu shown here will pop up.
C Choose Zoom from the menu.
Field: Destination Category Cost
Table: Trips Trips Trips
Sort: Ascending
Show:
Criteria:
or:
Totals
Table Names
Cut
Copy
Paste
Build...
Zoom...
Properties...

6. Enter the expression shown below into the Zoom box. Make sure you type the expression exactly as shown, including the colon after the word *Duration.*
   When you run the query, this expression will calculate the duration of each trip. You can perform calculations using dates in Access and Excel.

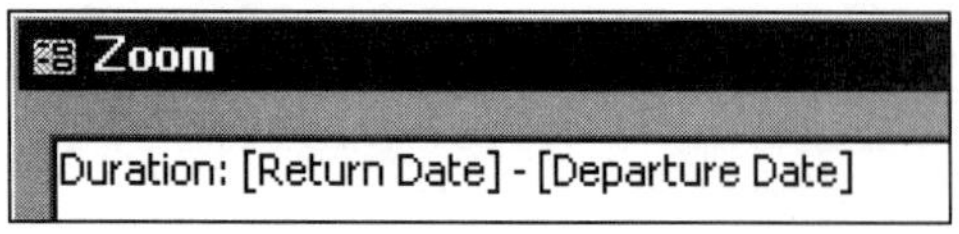
Zoom
Duration: [Return Date] - [Departure Date]

7. Click **OK.** If necessary, use the left arrow and right arrow keys on your keyboard to check your new calculated field for errors. Correct any errors that you find.

8. Run the query to produce the following recordset.

Destination	Category	Cost	Duration
Baja California	Adventure	$2,900.00	10
Rocky Mountains	Adventure	$2,190.00	16
Swiss Alps	Adventure	$3,500.00	26
Amazon Jungle Trek	Adventure	$7,765.00	38
Kenyan Safari	Adventure	$6,600.00	30
Hawaii	Family	$5,300.00	8
Orlando	Family	$3,400.00	6
Hawaii	Leisure	$4,500.00	10
Caribbean Cruise	Leisure	$2,390.00	9

In the next few steps, you will add another calculated field that calculates the average daily cost of each trip. The average daily cost will be calculated as the Cost / Duration. This new calculated field will use the Duration calculated field as part of the calculation. Access allows you to "nest" calculated fields in this manner.

9. Switch to Design view.

10. Right-click in the empty cell to the right of the Duration cell, and choose **Zoom** from the pop-up menu.

11. Enter the following expression into the Zoom box.

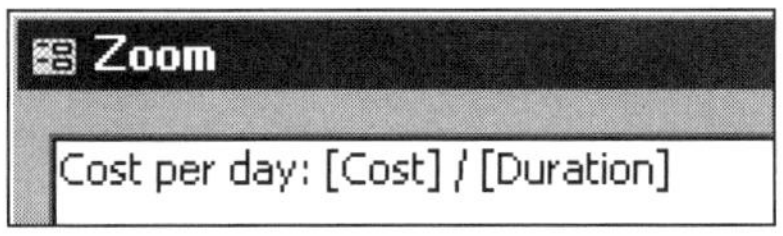
Zoom
Cost per day: [Cost] / [Duration]

12. Click **OK** to insert the Cost per day calculated field into the cell.

13. Run the query to produce the following recordset.
Notice that the Cost per day numbers are not formatted with the Currency format. You will correct this in the next few steps.

Destination	Category	Cost	Duration	Cost per day
Baja California	Adventure	$2,900.00	10	290
Rocky Mountains	Adventure	$2,190.00	16	136.875
Swiss Alps	Adventure	$3,500.00	26	134.615384615
Amazon Jungle Trek	Adventure	$7,765.00	38	204.342105263
Kenyan Safari	Adventure	$6,600.00	30	220
Hawaii	Family	$5,300.00	8	662.5
Orlando	Family	$3,400.00	6	566.666666667
Hawaii	Leisure	$4,500.00	10	450
Caribbean Cruise	Leisure	$2,390.00	9	265.555555556

(Continued on the next page)

14. Switch to Design view.
15. Right-click on the Cost per day field, and choose **Properties** from the pop-up menu.
16. Click in the Format box, click the drop-down button, and choose **Currency.**
17. Close the Properties box.
18. Run the query. The Cost per day numbers should be formatted as Currency with two decimal places.
19. Close the query, and save it as **Cost per day.**

Skill Builder 21.3 Use Statistical Functions

In this exercise, you will create a query to perform statistical calculations in the Tropical Getaways database.

1. Create a new query that uses the Trips table.
2. Add the **Cost** field to the design grid.
3. Display the Total row by clicking the Totals button on the toolbar.
4. Choose the **Avg** function in the Total box, as shown below.

Field:	Cost
Table:	Trips
Total:	Avg
Sort:	
Show:	☑
Criteria:	

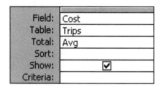

5. Run the query. The average cost of a trip should be calculated as $4,282.78.
6. Switch to Design view.
7. Add the **Category** field to the design grid.
   The Total box will automatically be set to Group By as shown below. When you run the query, the Avg function in the Cost field will calculate the average cost for each category of trip.

Field:	Cost	Category
Table:	Trips	Trips
Total:	Avg	Group By
Sort:		
Show:	☑	☑
Criteria:		

8. Run the query to produce the following recordset.

	AvgOfCost	Category
	$4,591.00	Adventure
	$4,350.00	Family
▶	$3,445.00	Leisure

9. Close the query, and save it as **Cost by Category.**
10. Close the Tropical Getaways database.

Assessment

Assessment 21.1 Create Queries

1. Open the **Classic Cars** database.
2. Create a new query, and add the **Collectors** table to the query.
3. Set up the query to produce the recordset shown below. Notice that this query simply chooses the indicated fields and sorts the records in descending order by Collection Size.

Firstname	Lastname	Era of Interest	Collection Size
Cindy	Johnson	1950's	42
Ed	Larkson	Early 1900's	34
Bob	Barker	1950's	7
Tammy	Olson	1960's	6
Jake	Johnson	1920's	3

4. Run the query, print the recordset, close the query, and save it as **Collection Sizes.**
5. Create a new query, and add the **Cars** table to the query.
6. Set up the query to produce the recordset shown below. Notice that this query only selects records where the model is **Corvette** and the condition is **Excellent.** The query also sorts the records by Value, with the largest values appearing first.

Make	Model	Year	Color	Condition	Value
Chevrolet	Corvette	57	Red	Excellent	$42,000.00
Chevrolet	Corvette	58	Black	Excellent	$35,000.00
Chevrolet	Corvette	62	Blue	Excellent	$30,000.00

7. Run the query, print the recordset, close the query, and save it as **Excellent Corvettes.**
8. Create a new query, and add the **Cars** table to the query.
9. Set up the query to produce the recordset shown in the following illustration. Notice that this query calculates the average value of each group of models. In other words, the query groups the records on the Model field and then calculates the average value of each group. The query also sorts the records by Value, with the largest values appearing first.

Model	AvgOfValue
Model A	$75,000.00
Corvette	$43,000.00
Thunderbird	$20,000.00
Custom Eight Sedan	$15,000.00

10. Run the query, and then adjust the width of the Model column as shown in the preceding illustration to fit the widest entry in the column. You can accomplish this by double-clicking the border between the Model and AvgOfValue column headings.

11. Print the recordset, close the query, and save it as **Average Value of Model Groups.**

12. Close the Classic Cars database when you have finished, and exit from Access.

LESSON 22—Integration

Analyzing Access Data with Excel

Access provides sophisticated data-storage capabilities in Office 2000. Excel gives you powerful tools for analyzing data. When you combine the two tools, you have both a powerful database system and a powerful tool to analyze data in limitless ways. In this lesson, you will use Access 2000's OfficeLinks feature to extract data from the Pinnacle Pet Care database and analyze it with Excel.

In This Lesson

Case Study

It's the end of the year, and Al Smith wants to make important business decisions to steer Pinnacle Pet Care into the next millennium. Al wants to expand the services at Pinnacle Pet Care for the types of pets that are most profitable to his fledgling enterprise. He decides to query his Access database to find the average expenditures per visit for each pet type. He uses Access to generate the query results and then sends the data to Excel. Once the data is in Excel, Al effortlessly creates a pie chart that clearly displays the results of the Access query.

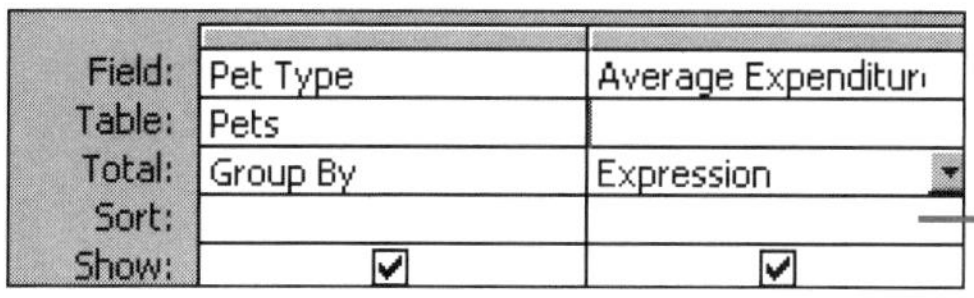
Field: Pet Type | Average Expenditur
Table: Pets
Total: Group By | Expression
Sort:
Show:

When this Access query is run, the output is sent to Excel, where a pie chart is used to analyze and compare the results.

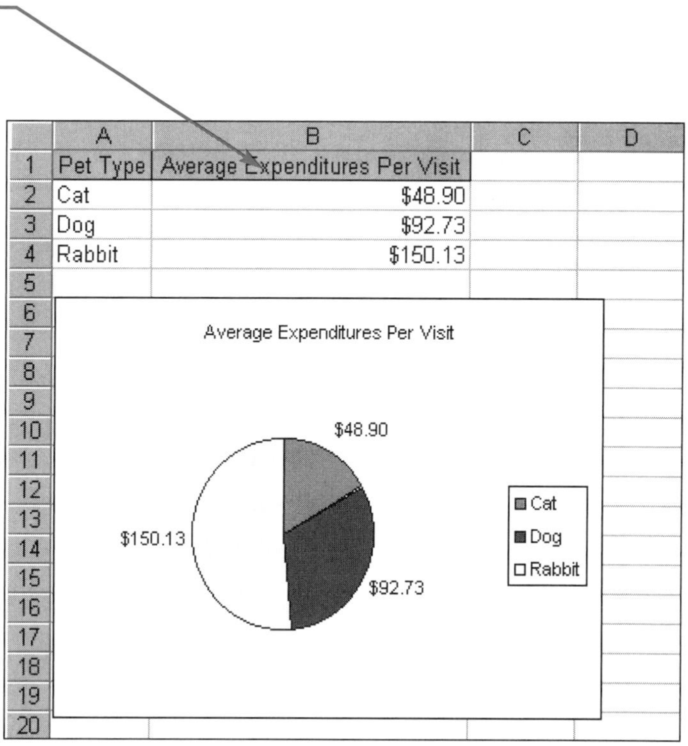
A B C D
1 Pet Type Average Expenditures Per Visit
2 Cat $48.90
3 Dog $92.73
4 Rabbit $150.13
Average Expenditures Per Visit
$48.90
$150.13
$92.73
Cat
Dog
Rabbit

Outputting from Access to Excel

The true power of Office 2000 lies in the integration of its various programs. Access provides the database and storage capabilities in Office 2000. Access also provides excellent tools for querying a database and generating reports. However, there are times when more sophisticated analysis of data is required. For example, you may need to perform complex calculations on Access data or create charts from Access data. The best approach in these situations is to output the data to Excel and use the analyzing and charting capabilities of Excel.

Using the Excel OfficeLink with Access

The Access toolbar contains an OfficeLinks button that lets you easily output data from Access to Word and Excel. The Excel OfficeLinks button is available whenever a table or query is highlighted in the Access database window. When you click the Excel OfficeLink button, Access opens the highlighted table or runs the highlighted query. Access then opens the Excel program and copies the table data or query results to Excel. You can then use Excel to analyze the data. Changes that are made to the data in Excel have no impact on the original Access data.

Hands-On 22.1 Set Up a Query

In this exercise, you will set up a new query in the Pinnacle Pet Care database. The new query will contain a calculated field that computes the average expenditures per visit for each pet type.

Display the Query Window

1. Start Access, and open the Pinnacle Pet Care database.
2. Click the **Queries** button on the Objects bar.
3. Double-click the **Create query in Design view** option.
4. Add the Pets table to the query window and then close the Show Table dialog box.
5. Double-click the **Pet Type** field in the Pets field list to add that field to the design grid.

Create a Calculated Field

6. Follow these steps to display the Zoom dialog box.

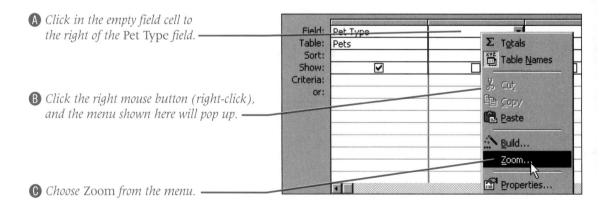

Ⓐ *Click in the empty field cell to the right of the* Pet Type *field.*

Ⓑ *Click the right mouse button (right-click), and the menu shown here will pop up.*

Ⓒ *Choose* Zoom *from the menu.*

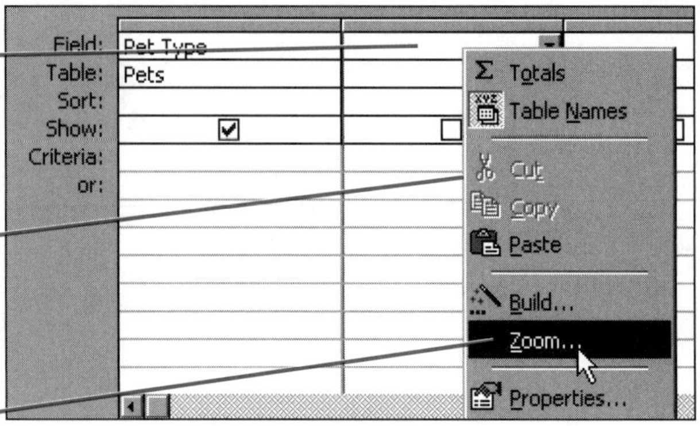
Field:
Pet Type
Table:
Pets
Sort:
Show:
Criteria:
or:
Totals
Table Names
Cut
Copy
Paste
Build...
Zoom...
Properties...

7. Enter the calculated field expression shown below into the Zoom box. Make sure you enter the expression exactly as shown. In particular, make sure you use a colon : (not a semicolon ;), correctly spell the field names, use the correct open and closed parentheses ( ) and brackets [ ], and use the forward slash / symbol to represent division. This expression will eventually calculate the average expenditures per visit for each pet type.

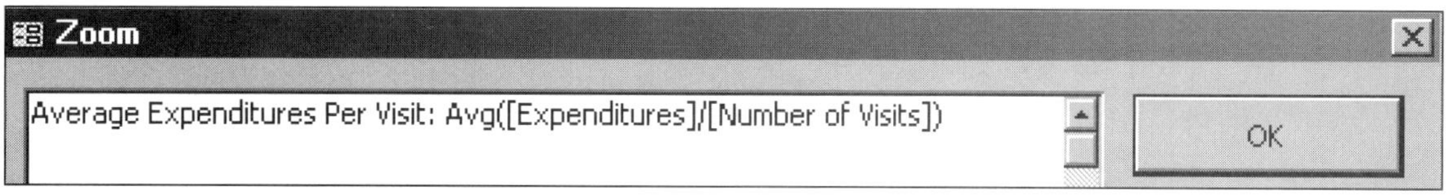
Zoom
Average Expenditures Per Visit: Avg([Expenditures]/[Number of Visits])
OK

8. Click **OK** to insert the expression in the field.

9. Use the left arrow and right arrow keys on your keyboard to scroll through the expression within the cell. Make sure the syntax is correct as shown above. If necessary, you can edit the expression within the cell or redisplay the Zoom dialog box and make any necessary changes.

Add Grouping to the Pet Type Field

10. Click the Totals button on the toolbar, and a Total row will appear below the Table row. *The Total boxes will be set to Group By for both the Pet Type field and the calculated field.*

11. Follow these steps to set the Total box to Expression for the calculated field.

Field:	Pet Type	Average Expenditur
Table:	Pets	
Total:	Group By	Expression
Sort:		
Show:	☑	☑

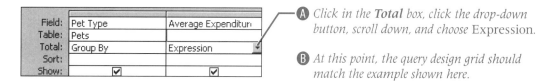

Ⓐ *Click in the **Total** box, click the drop-down button, scroll down, and choose* Expression.

Ⓑ *At this point, the query design grid should match the example shown here.*

These settings will group the records by Pet Type and calculate the average expenditures per visit for each group. In other words, the average expenditures per visit will be calculated for dogs, cats, and other pet types.

12. If necessary, click the Properties button on the Access toolbar to display the Field Properties dialog box.

13. Click in the Format box, click the drop-down button, scroll down, and choose Currency. *When the query is run, the resulting numbers will be formatted with dollar signs and two decimals.*

14. Click the Run button to run the query. The results shown to the right should appear.

Pet Type	Average Expe
Cat	$48.90
Dog	$92.73
Rabbit	$150.13

15. Close the query by clicking the Close button at the top-right corner of the query window.

16. Click the **Yes** button when Access asks if you want to save the query.

17. Type the name **`Average Expenditures per Visit by Pet Type`** in the Save As box, and click **OK.**

(Continued on the next page)

Output the Query Results to Excel

18. Follow these steps to output the query results to Excel.

Ⓐ *Choose the* Average Expenditures per Visit by Pet Type *query in the database window.*

Ⓑ *Click the OfficeLinks drop-down button and choose* Analyze It with MS Excel.

Open
Design
New
Merge It with MS Word
Publish It with MS Word
Analyze It with MS Excel
Objects
Tables
Queries
Forms
Create query in Design view
Create query by using wizard
Average Expenditure per Visit by Pet Type
Compound Criteria
Current Balance

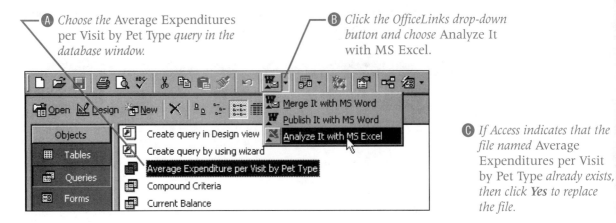

Ⓒ *If Access indicates that the file named* Average Expenditures per Visit by Pet Type *already exists, then click* ***Yes*** *to replace the file.*

Excel will start, and the query results will appear in the Excel window as shown below. Access actually creates an Excel file on the hard disk of your computer system when you output the query. This is why Access may have asked if you wanted to replace the file named Average Expenditures per Visit by Pet Type.

19. Follow this step to widen Column B in the Excel worksheet.

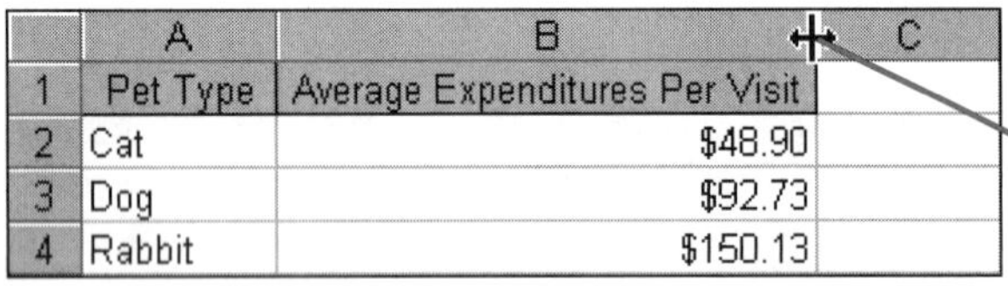

A
B
C
1 Pet Type | Average Expenditures Per Visit
2 Cat | $48.90
3 Dog | $92.73
4 Rabbit | $150.13

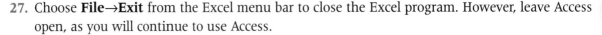

Ⓐ *Double-click the border between the columns headed B and C to widen ColumnB, as shown here.*

Create a Pie Chart

20. Select the range A1:B4.
    This range includes the two heading cells and the data in Rows 2, 3, and 4.
21. Click the Chart Wizard button.
22. Choose the Pie chart type and the first subtype.
23. Click the **Next** button twice, and the Step 3 of 4 box will appear.
24. Click the **Data Labels** tab, and choose the Show value option.
    When the chart is created, each pie slice will have the average expenditures per visit displayed next to the slice.
25. Click the **Finish** button, and the chart will appear in the worksheet as shown to the right.

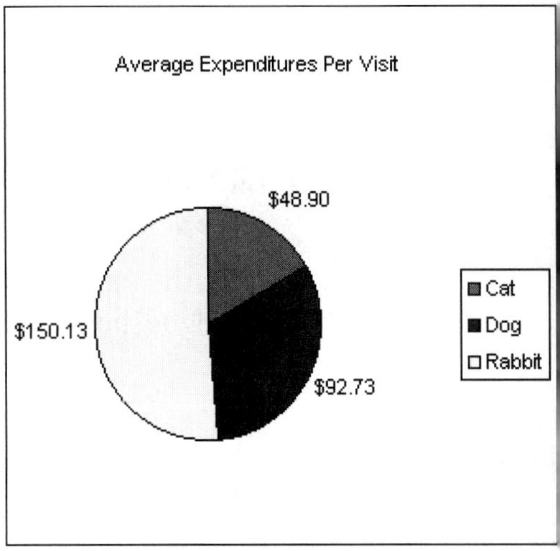

Average Expenditures Per Visit
$48.90
$150.13
$92.73
Cat
Dog
Rabbit

26. Save the worksheet to your exercise diskette as **Hands-On Lesson 22.**
27. Choose **File→Exit** from the Excel menu bar to close the Excel program. However, leave Access open, as you will continue to use Access.

Output an Entire Table to Excel

28. Click the **Tables** button on the Access Objects bar.

29. Notice that the OfficeLinks button now has the Excel icon on the face of the button.
This is because Excel was the last OfficeLink that you used.

30. Choose the Pets table in the database window, and click the OfficeLinks button.
Excel will start, and Access will output the entire Pets table to Excel. If Access asks you to save the file, then click Yes to replace the existing pets.xls file.

31. Type **`Total Expenditures`** in Cell A11, which should be the first empty cell in Column A.

32. If the text wraps within Cell A11, then use the **Format→Cells** command to display the Format Cells dialog box. Click the Alignment tab, and uncheck the Wrap Text box.

33. Click Cell I11, which should be the first empty cell in the Expenditures column.

34. Click the AutoSum button, and tap (ENTER) to calculate the total expenditures.

35. Feel free to create other totals or to chart any of the data.

36. Save the workbook as **Hands-On Lesson 22—Part 2.**

37. Close the workbook when you have finished.

38. Use the **File→Exit** command to close both Excel and Access.

Concepts Review

True/False Questions

1. Office 2000 lets you output data from Access to Excel. TRUE FALSE
2. Only query results can be output from Access to Excel. TRUE FALSE
3. Data that you output to Excel remains linked to the original Access data. TRUE FALSE

Multiple-Choice Questions

1. Which of the following buttons is the OfficeLinks button?
   a. 
   b. 
   c. 
   d. None of the above

2. What must you do prior to clicking the OfficeLinks button?
   a. Choose the desired table or query in the database window.
   b. Open the desired table or run the desired query.
   c. Print the desired table or query results.
   d. None of the above

UNIT 7

PowerPoint 2000

Presenting to groups can be a daunting experience for most people. Fortunately, proper preparation and excellent presentation tools can help you meet the challenges of speaking to groups. PowerPoint 2000 lets you create professional presentations that will impress even the most critical audiences. PowerPoint makes it easy to set up, organize, animate, and deliver professional presentations. By the end of this unit, you will be able to create dynamic presentations with professional formatting, graphics, and special effects such as sound and animation.

LESSON 23—PowerPoint

Creating and Delivering a Presentation

In this lesson, you will begin developing a PowerPoint presentation for the Pinnacle Pet Care pet clinic. As you develop your presentation, you will learn basic techniques, such as adding slides to a presentation using AutoLayouts. You will format slides using bulleted lists, text formats, and paragraph formats. You will learn how to navigate through a presentation and deliver a presentation using transparencies and an electronic slide show. The Pinnacle Pet Care presentation will continue to be developed in later lessons.

In This Lesson

Case Study

Al Smith, owner of Pinnacle Pet Care, needs to make a presentation to a large group at the annual Pet World trade show. Al wants to introduce Pinnacle to the trade show attendees and entice them with a promotional offer. Al decides to use PowerPoint to develop and deliver his presentation. The presentation will be delivered using a laptop PC attached to a video projection system. Al chose PowerPoint because it is easy to learn and seamlessly integrates with his other Office 2000 applications. Al's dynamic speaking abilities together with PowerPoint's presentation capabilities are a powerful combination certain to win over the trade show attendees.

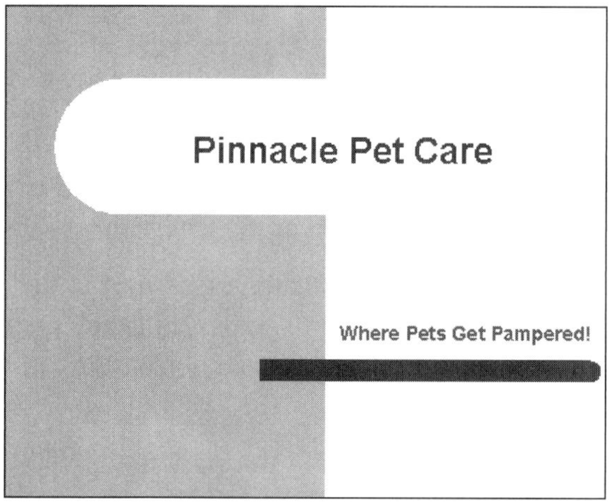
Pinnacle Pet Care
Where Pets Get Pampered!

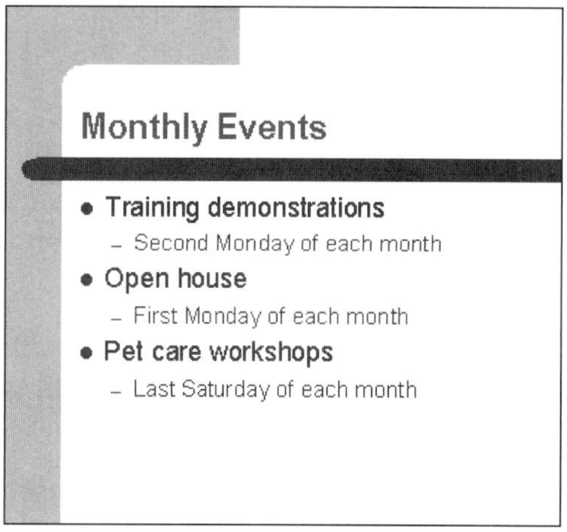
Monthly Events
Training demonstrations
Second Monday of each month
Open house
First Monday of each month
Pet care workshops
Last Saturday of each month

Slides from the Pinnacle Pet Care Presentation

Presenting PowerPoint

PowerPoint 2000 is a presentation graphics program that allows you to easily develop dynamic presentations. Whether you are developing a one-on-one presentation for your supervisor or a sophisticated presentation for a large group, PowerPoint provides the tools to make your presentation a success. PowerPoint lets you output your presentation on transparencies for use with an overhead projector, on 35mm slides for more formal presentations, and using a projection device directly from your PC. With PowerPoint 2000, you can even create virtual presentations for delivery on the Internet or an Intranet (a network within an organization).

PowerPoint provides powerful tools that let you concentrate on the content of your presentation instead of the design details. With PowerPoint's built-in design templates, you can rapidly create highly effective professional presentations. PowerPoint makes it easy to organize your ideas, create, edit, and deliver your presentations with precision and control.

Presentation Design Tips

Have you ever heard the expression, "It isn't what you say, it's how you say it"? This old adage remains true even when designing high-tech PowerPoint presentations. The design of your presentation will effect your audience's perception of you and the amount of information they retain. Use the following helpful hints to design effective PowerPoint presentations.

- **Keep it short**—Long presentations tend to lose the audience. Most audiences are lost after just 20 to 30 minutes. Keep your presentation focused and to the point. You can always lengthen your presentation by opening it up to questions after you have finished speaking.
- **Amount of information**—Avoid placing too much information on one slide. Too many words or pictures can distract your audience. If a slide has too much information, then try turning it into two or three slides.
- **Use bullets**—Many PowerPoint slides are set up with bullets. A typical slide should have between three and six bullets. Keep your bulleted phrases as short as possible. If you have too many bullets on a slide, then break the bullets into two columns or create a second slide.
- **Animation and special effects**—PowerPoint lets you use animation and special effects in presentations. Keep in mind that animation and special effects should draw attention to your important points. Don't get carried away with these tools and use them as entertainment. This may be enjoyable, but your audience may miss your point.

Presentation Tips

The manner in which you deliver your presentation is also important. You want the audience to focus on the presentation instead of focusing on you. Use the following helpful hints to deliver effective presentations.

- **Maintain a moderate pace**—Speaking too fast will exhaust your audience, and speaking too slow may put them to sleep. Therefore, you should try to maintain a moderate pace.
- **Pauses are important**—Try pausing for five to ten seconds after making important points. This will let your audience rest and give them time to absorb what you have said.

- **Stay still**—Avoid excessive movement while presenting. Movement can be distracting because your audience's attention is drawn to your movements instead of your presentation. Excessive movement may be OK for high-energy, motivational presentations but it is a bad approach for most business presentations. The best way to avoid this is to face your audience or maintain a slight angle towards your audience. Avoid moving your feet or rocking on your feet. Move freely from the waist up, including your arms and hands. Using your body language to make points is good technique, provided you are not "running around the room" while presenting.
- **Speak to your audience**—Always face your audience while speaking. Many presenters speak while facing a white board or projection screen. Your points will definitely be missed if you turn your back to your audience while speaking.

Starting PowerPoint

The method you use to start PowerPoint and other Office programs depends in large part upon whether you intend to create a new presentation or use an existing presentation. If you intend to create a new presentation, then use one of the following methods to start PowerPoint.

- Click the **Start** button, and choose Microsoft PowerPoint from the Programs menu.
- Click the Microsoft PowerPoint  button on the Quick Launch toolbar (located near the Taskbar).
- Click the **Start** button, choose New Office Document, choose the General tab, and double-click the Blank Presentation icon.

Use one of these methods if you intend to open an existing PowerPoint presentation.

- Start PowerPoint, and choose *Open an existing presentation* from the PowerPoint dialog box. Choose the desired presentation from the list of recently used presentations, and click **OK.** If your presentation is not on the list, then click **Cancel** on the PowerPoint dialog box, click the **Open** button, and navigate to the desired presentation.
- Navigate to the desired presentation using Windows Explorer or My Computer, and double-click the presentation file.

The following illustration describes the options in the PowerPoint dialog box that appears when PowerPoint is started.

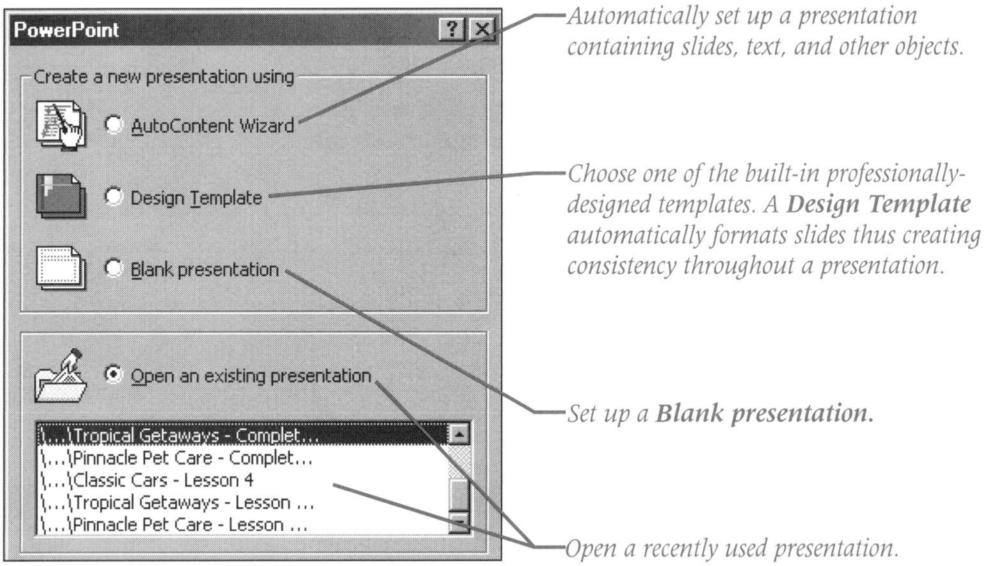
PowerPoint
Create a new presentation using
AutoContent Wizard
Design Template
Blank presentation
Open an existing presentation
\...\Tropical Getaways - Complet...
\...\Pinnacle Pet Care - Complet...
\...\Classic Cars - Lesson 4
\...\Tropical Getaways - Lesson ...
\...\Pinnacle Pet Care - Lesson ...
Automatically set up a presentation containing slides, text, and other objects.
Choose one of the built-in professionally-designed templates. A Design Template automatically formats slides thus creating consistency throughout a presentation.
Set up a Blank presentation.
Open a recently used presentation.

Using Design Templates

You can use PowerPoint's built-in design templates as the basis for presentations. Design templates provide a consistent background, color scheme, and design for the slides in a presentation. Design templates also position placeholders on slides for titles, text, bulleted lists, graphics, and other objects. By using design templates, you can literally fill in the blanks as you create your presentation. You choose a design template from the New Presentation dialog box. The New Presentation dialog box is displayed when you choose Design template from the PowerPoint dialog box as shown in the preceding illustration. You can also display the New Presentation dialog box at anytime by choosing **File→New** from the PowerPoint menu bar.

Hands-On 23.1 Start PowerPoint, and Set Up a New Presentation

1. Start your computer, and the Windows Desktop will be displayed.
2. Click the Start button, and choose Programs.
3. Choose Microsoft PowerPoint from the Programs menu.
4. Choose Design Template from the PowerPoint dialog box, and click **OK.**
   The New Presentation dialog box will appear with the Design Templates tab visible.
5. Follow these steps to explore the dialog box and choose a design template.

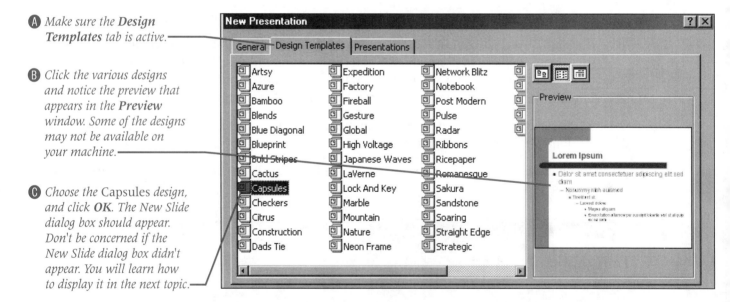

Ⓐ *Make sure the **Design Templates** tab is active.*

Ⓑ *Click the various designs and notice the preview that appears in the **Preview** window. Some of the designs may not be available on your machine.*

Ⓒ *Choose the* Capsules *design, and click **OK**. The New Slide dialog box should appear. Don't be concerned if the New Slide dialog box didn't appear. You will learn how to display it in the next topic.*

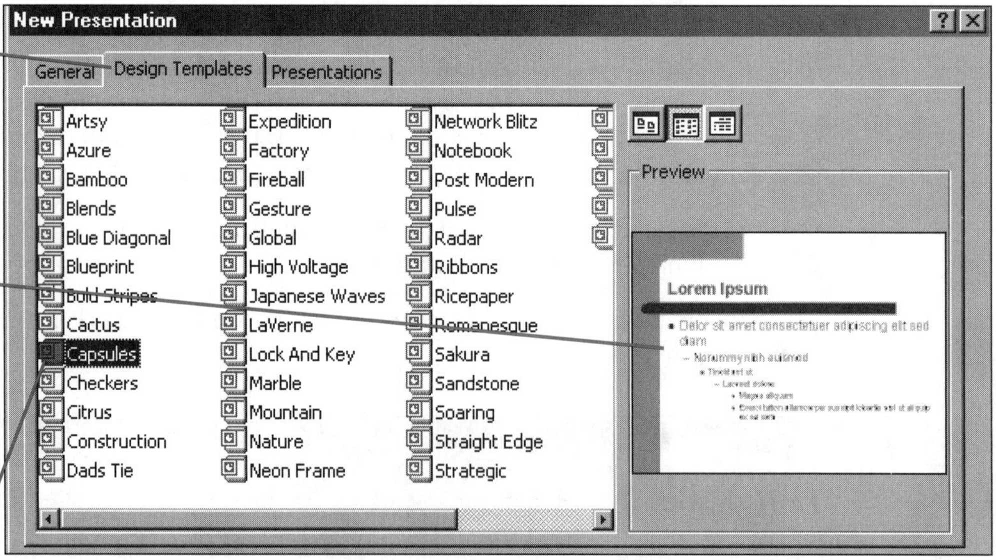
New Presentation
General
Design Templates
Presentations
Artsy
Azure
Bamboo
Blends
Blue Diagonal
Blueprint
Bold Stripes
Cactus
Capsules
Checkers
Citrus
Construction
Dads Tie
Expedition
Factory
Fireball
Gesture
Global
High Voltage
Japanese Waves
LaVerne
Lock And Key
Marble
Mountain
Nature
Neon Frame
Network Blitz
Notebook
Post Modern
Pulse
Radar
Ribbons
Ricepaper
Romanesque
Sakura
Sandstone
Soaring
Straight Edge
Strategic
Preview
Lorem Ipsum

The New Slide dialog box lets you choose an AutoLayout style for each slide in your presentation. You will use AutoLayouts throughout this lesson as you build your presentation slide-by-slide.

6. Continue with the next topic, where you will learn more about slides. You will choose a slide from the New Slide dialog box in the next exercise.

Working with Slides

PowerPoint presentations are composed of slides. Slides are composed of various objects such as titles, bulleted lists, and graphics. If your presentation is based upon one of the built-in design templates, then the slides you use will be preformatted to give your presentation a consistent background, color scheme, and design.

Adding New Slides

The New Slide button on PowerPoint's Standard toolbar displays the New Slide dialog box. The New Slide dialog box lets you choose from a variety of predefined layouts known as **AutoLayouts.** AutoLayouts include placeholders for text, bulleted lists, pictures, charts, and other objects. If your presentation is based upon a design template, then the AutoLayouts format slides match the color scheme and formats defined in the template. You can also add a new slide by clicking the **Common Tasks** button on the Standard toolbar and choosing New Slide. The new slide is placed after the current slide in the presentation.

From the Keyboard

CTRL+M to display New Slide box

Types of Slides

Most presentations are composed of the same types of slides. For example, almost every presentation has a title slide, a closing slide, and one or more slides with text, bulleted lists, charts, graphics, and other objects. The following illustration identifies the AutoLayouts available in the New Slide dialog box.

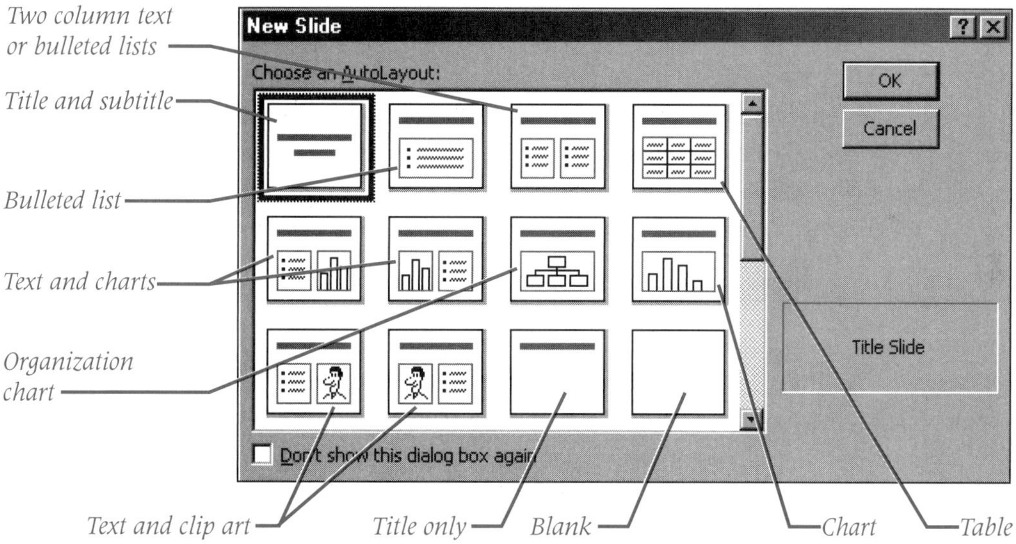

Two column text or bulleted lists
Title and subtitle
Bulleted list
Text and charts
Organization chart
New Slide
Choose an AutoLayout:
OK
Cancel
Title Slide
Don't show this dialog box again
Text and clip art
Title only
Blank
Chart
Table

Hands-On 23.2 Add Slides

In this exercise, you will add a title slide and bulleted list slide to the presentation.

Add a Title Slide

1. If the New Slide dialog box is not displayed, then click the New Slide button on the Standard toolbar to display the box.
2. Choose the Title Slide layout (the first layout), and click **OK.**

(Continued on the next page)

3. Follow these steps to explore the PowerPoint window and to enter a title and subtitle.

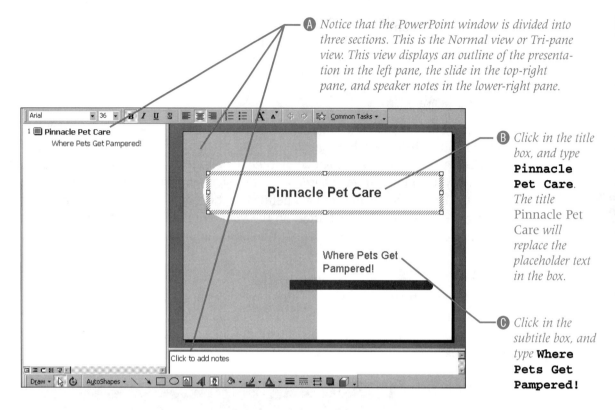

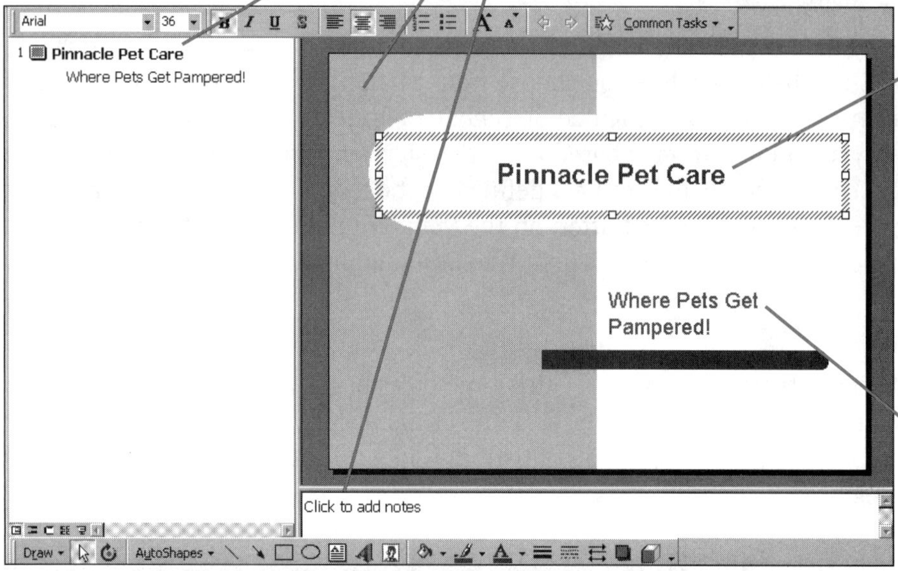
Arial
36
Common Tasks
1 Pinnacle Pet Care
Where Pets Get Pampered!
Pinnacle Pet Care
Where Pets Get Pampered!
Click to add notes
Draw
AutoShapes

A *Notice that the PowerPoint window is divided into three sections. This is the Normal view or Tri-pane view. This view displays an outline of the presentation in the left pane, the slide in the top-right pane, and speaker notes in the lower-right pane.*

B *Click in the title box, and type* **`Pinnacle Pet Care`**. *The title* Pinnacle Pet Care *will replace the placeholder text in the box.*

C *Click in the subtitle box, and type* **`Where Pets Get Pampered!`**

Notice that the subtitle text wraps in the box creating a second line. You will adjust the font size in a later exercise to enable the text to fit on a single line. Also, notice the color scheme, design elements, and the position and style of the title and subtitle boxes. The Capsules design template sets up all of these design elements for you.

Add Another Slide

4. Click the Common Tasks button on PowerPoint's Formatting toolbar, and choose **New Slide.**
The New Slide dialog box appears. This is the same dialog box that appeared when you first choose the Capsules design template. Also, the second AutoLayout should automatically be highlighted.

5. Click the **OK** button to add a new slide using the second AutoLayout style.
Notice that the outline on the left side of the window shows two slides. The outline displays the title and subtitle of the title slide.

6. Click in the title box of the new slide, and type **`Monthly Events`**.

7. Continue with the next topic, where you will learn about AutoNumber Bulleted Lists.

AutoNumber Bulleted List Slides

PowerPoint makes it effortless to create bulleted lists. In fact, many of the AutoLayout slides (such as the slide you just added to your presentation) already have placeholders for bulleted lists. In PowerPoint, these AutoNumber bulleted lists can have up to five levels. The illustration on the following page shows the completed Monthly Events slide.

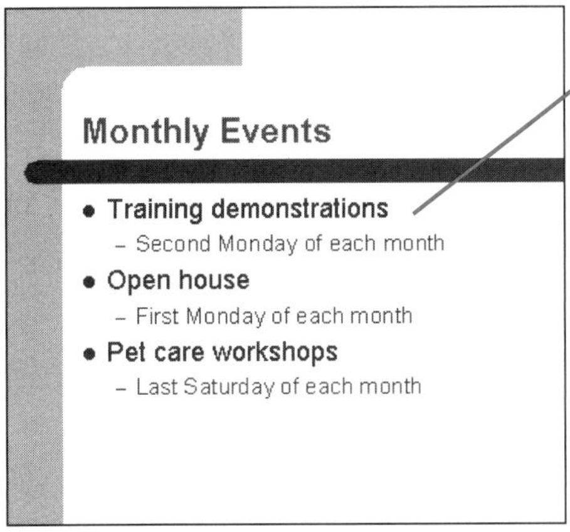
Monthly Events
• Training demonstrations
– Second Monday of each month
• Open house
– First Monday of each month
• Pet care workshops
– Last Saturday of each month

This bulleted list has two levels. A large dot is used for first-level paragraphs, and a hyphen is used for second-level paragraphs.

Working with Bulleted Lists

If your presentation is based upon a design template, then the template automatically formats each paragraph in a bulleted list. The format impacts the bullet style, indentation level, font type, and font size for each bulleted paragraph. The following Quick Reference table describes the various techniques that can be used with bulleted lists.

Quick Reference

BULLETED LISTS

Task	Procedure
Turn bullets on and off.	Select the desired paragraph(s), and click the Bullets button on the Formatting toolbar.
Promote paragraphs.	Select the desired paragraph(s), and click the Promote button on the Formatting toolbar. Promoting reduces a paragraph's indentation level and changes the bullet character. If the bullet is already at the first level, then promoting creates a new slide with the bullet text used as the title of the slide.
Demote paragraphs.	Select the desired paragraph(s), and click the Demote button on the Formatting toolbar. Demoting increases a paragraph's indentation level and changes the bullet character.

Hands-On 23.3 Create a Bulleted List

Type the List

1. Click in the bulleted list box.
2. Type the phrase **`Training demonstrations`**, and tap ENTER.
   PowerPoint formats the new paragraph with the same large bullet. Paragraph formats are carried to new paragraphs when you tap the ENTER *key.*
3. Complete the list shown to the right by typing the indicated text and tapping ENTER at the end of each paragraph. However, do not tap ENTER after the last paragraph.
   You will demote several of the list items in the next few steps.

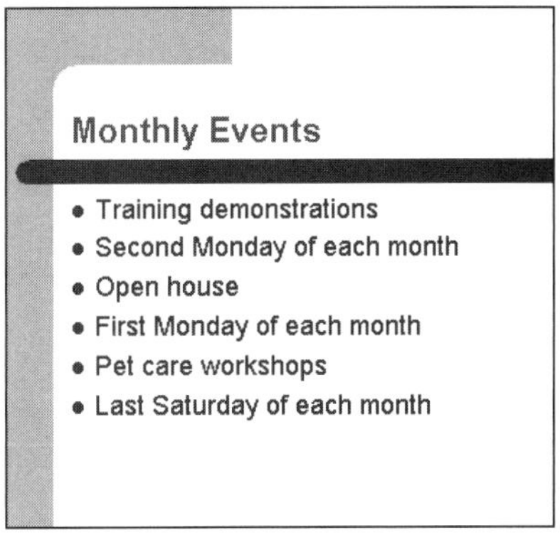
Monthly Events
• Training demonstrations
• Second Monday of each month
• Open house
• First Monday of each month
• Pet care workshops
• Last Saturday of each month

(Continued on the next page)

Demote Several Paragraphs

The most efficient way to create multilevel bulleted lists is to first type the entire list (as you did in the previous step). Once all of the text has been typed, you can promote and demote paragraphs as desired.

4. Click anywhere on the second bulleted paragraph (Second Monday of each month).
   The flashing insertion point should be positioned on the paragraph text.
5. Click the Bullets button on the Formatting toolbar.
   The Bullets button will no longer be recessed, and the bullet will be removed from the paragraph. You can always use this technique to remove bullets from paragraphs.
6. Click the Bullets button again to reapply the bullet.
7. Click the Demote button on the Formatting toolbar.
   The paragraph will be indented, and the bullet style will change to a hyphen. Demoting a paragraph makes the paragraph subordinate to the preceding paragraph.
8. Click the Demote button several more times.
   The bullet style will change, and the indent will increase each time you click the button. Also, the font size and font style will change with each demotion. These formats are determined by the Capsule design template, which the presentation is based upon.
9. Promote the paragraph until it is at the second indentation level with the hyphen bullet style.
10. Click anywhere on the fourth paragraph (First Monday of each month).
11. Demote the paragraph once.
12. Demote the last paragraph (Last Saturday of each month).
13. Click outside the bulleted list box to view the completed slide.
    Notice that the hierarchical structure of your presentation is displayed in the Outline pane on the left side of the window.

Moving Between Slides in Tri-Pane View

In Tri-pane view, you can develop a presentation by adding new slides and typing text in the slides. This is the technique you have used thus far. You can also add new slides by typing text directly in the outline pane. You will use this technique later in this lesson.

The Previous Slide and Next Slide buttons on the vertical scroll bar can be used to move between slides in Tri-pane view. You can also navigate to a slide by dragging the scroll box on the vertical scroll bar. Finally, you can display a slide in the slide pane of Tri-pane view by clicking the desired slide's text in the outline pane.

Hands-On 23.4 Add Another Bulleted Slide, and Move Between Slides

Add a Slide

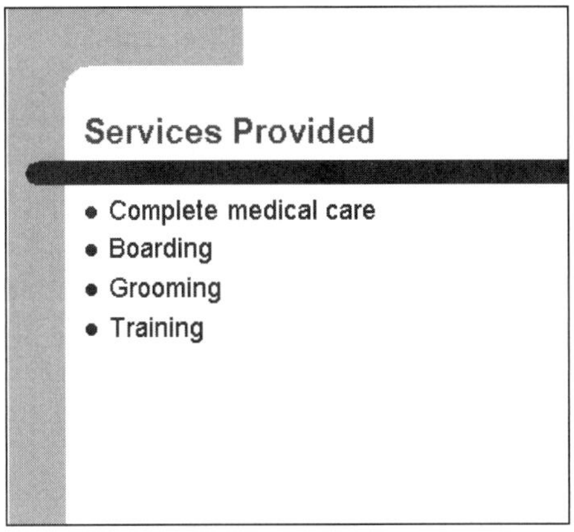
Services Provided
• Complete medical care
• Boarding
• Grooming
• Training

1. Click the Common Tasks button, and choose New Slide.
2. Make sure the second AutoLayout style is chosen, and click **OK.**
3. Click the Title box, and type the phrase **`Services Provided`**.
4. Click the bulleted list box, and type the four bulleted paragraphs shown to the right.

Move Between Slides

5. Click the Previous Slide button (near the bottom of the vertical scroll bar) to display the Monthly Events slide.
6. Click the Previous Slide button again to view the title slide.
7. Click the Next Slide twice to move to the Services Provided slide.
8. Click on the title *Pinnacle Pet Care* in the outline pane to display the title slide.
9. Click on any text for the *Services Provided* slide in the outline pane to display that slide.
10. Feel free to browse through your slides and make any editing changes as necessary.
    You can edit slides at anytime while working in Tri-pane view.

Saving a Presentation

From the Keyboard

CTRL+S for Save

The Save button on the Standard toolbar initiates the Save command. If the presentation had previously been saved, then PowerPoint replaces the previous version with the new edited version. If the presentation had never been saved, then PowerPoint displays the Save As dialog box. The Save As dialog box lets you specify a name and storage location for the presentation. You can also use the Save As dialog box to make a copy of a presentation by saving it under a new name or to a different location. You can use filenames containing as many as 255 characters.

Hands-On 23.5 Save the Presentation

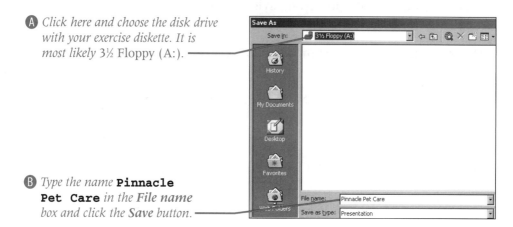

1. Click the Save button on the Standard toolbar.
2. Follow these steps to save the presentation to your exercise diskette.
   If necessary, obtain a 3½" diskette, and insert it in the diskette drive.

Ⓐ *Click here and choose the disk drive with your exercise diskette. It is most likely* 3½ Floppy (A:).

Ⓑ *Type the name* **`Pinnacle Pet Care`** *in the* ***File name*** *box and click the* ***Save*** *button.*

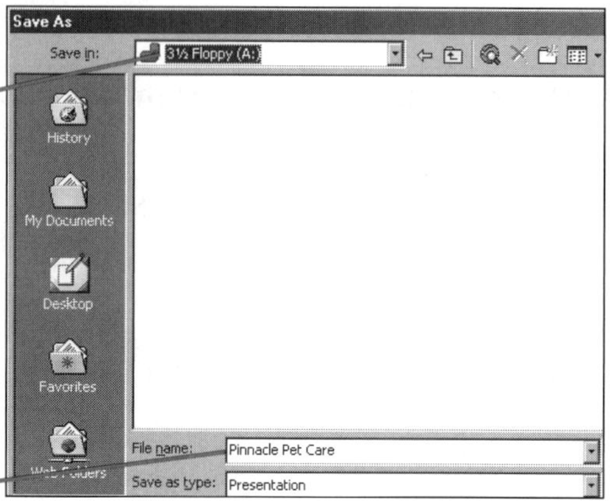

Save As
Save in:
3½ Floppy (A:)
History
My Documents
Desktop
Favorites
File name:
Pinnacle Pet Care
Save as type:
Presentation

Moving and Copying Text and Objects

You can move and copy text and objects using Drag and Drop or Cut, Copy, and Paste. It is usually most efficient to use Drag and Drop if you are moving or copying within a slide or to another slide that is visible on the screen. Drag and Drop is also quite effective for rearranging slides in the Outline pane and for moving or copying text between slides in the Outline pane. Cut, Copy, and Paste are most efficient when moving or copying to another slide or location not visible on the current screen.

Quick Reference

MOVING AND COPYING

Technique	Discussion
Drag and Drop	■ Select the desired text or click an object such as a placeholder box.
	■ Drag the text or object to the desired location. Press the CTRL key while dragging if you wish to copy.
Right Drag and Drop	■ Select the desired text, or click an object such as a placeholder box.
	■ Use the right mouse button to drag the text or object to the desired location.
	■ Release the mouse button at the desired location, and choose, Move Here, Copy Here, or Cancel from the pop-up menu.
Cut, Copy, and Paste	■ Select the desired text, or click an object such as a placeholder box.
	■ Click the Cut button, or press CTRL+X to cut the item and place it on the Windows clipboard. Click the Copy button, or press CTRL+C to copy the object to the clipboard.
	■ Navigate to the desired slide, and click at the location where you want to paste.
	■ Click the Paste button, or press CTRL+V to paste the item.

Hands-On 23.6 Add a Slide, Change the Slide Layout, and Move Paragraphs

In this exercise, you will add a new slide to the presentation. You will enter a bulleted list into the new slide. Then you will change the AutoLayout for the new slide and rearrange the paragraphs in the bulleted list. You can always change the AutoLayout for a slide after the slide has been created.

Add the Slide

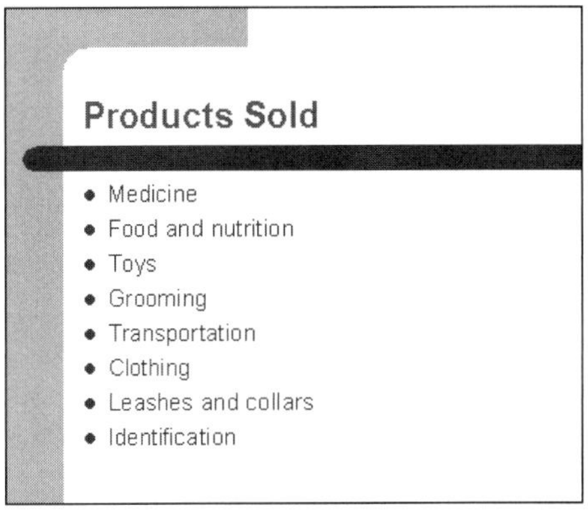

Products Sold
Medicine
Food and nutrition
Toys
Grooming
Transportation
Clothing
Leashes and collars
Identification

1. Make sure the Services Provided slide is visible in the presentation.
   New slides are always added after the slide that is visible in Tri-pane view.
2. Click the Common Tasks button, and choose New Slide.
3. Make sure the second AutoLayout style is chosen, and click **OK.**
4. Click the Title box, and type the phrase **`Products Sold`**.
5. Click the bulleted list box, and type the bulleted paragraphs shown above.
   When you begin typing the last bullet, PowerPoint will reformat all of the paragraphs with a smaller font size. PowerPoint does this to allow the bullets to fit in the box. A long list of bulleted paragraphs may appear cluttered and overwhelming to an audience. For this reason, it is usually best to limit the number of bullets in a column to four or five. Another strategy that can be employed is to break the list into two columns. In the next few steps, you will use this technique by choosing a different AutoLayout for the slide. You can change the AutoLayout of a slide after the slide has been created.
6. Click the Common Tasks button, and choose **Slide Layout.**
7. Choose the third AutoLayout (2-column text), and click the **Apply** button.
   PowerPoint will display a second bulleted list box to the right of the first box.
8. Follow these steps to move the last four bulleted paragraphs to the second box.

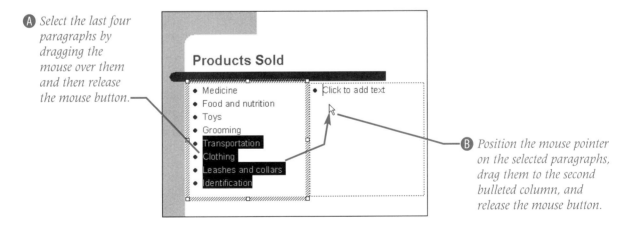

Ⓐ *Select the last four paragraphs by dragging the mouse over them and then release the mouse button.*

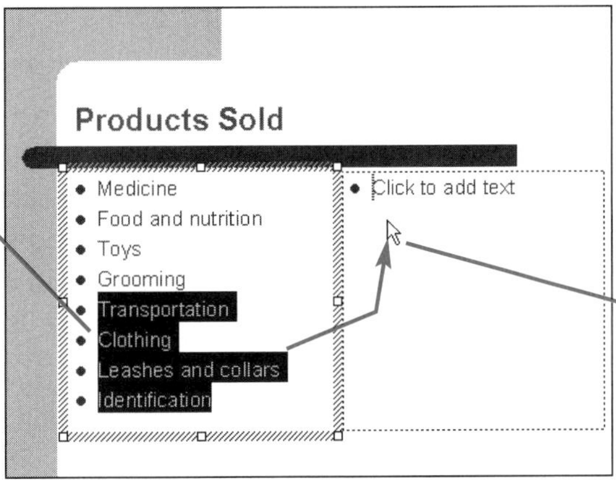

Products Sold
Medicine
Food and nutrition
Toys
Grooming
Transportation
Clothing
Leashes and collars
Identification
Click to add text

Ⓑ *Position the mouse pointer on the selected paragraphs, drag them to the second bulleted column, and release the mouse button.*

The last four bulleted paragraphs should now be in the second box.

9. Click the Save button to save the changes to your presentation.

Formatting Paragraphs

From the Keyboard

CTRL+B for Bold
CTRL+U for Underline
CTRL+I for Italics

You can format text within a placeholder box by selecting the desired text and using buttons on the Formatting toolbar. You can format all text within a placeholder by first selecting the placeholder and then applying the desired formats. You select a placeholder by clicking it once and then clicking any border on the placeholder. The following illustration explains the buttons on PowerPoint's Formatting toolbar that can be used to format text.

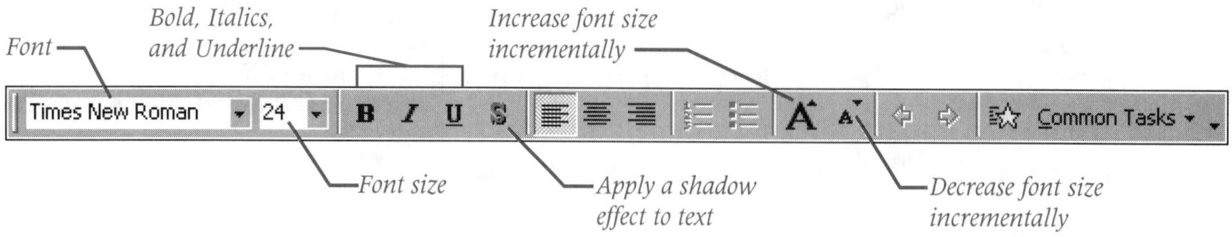

Font
Bold, Italics, and Underline
Increase font size incrementally
Times New Roman
24
Common Tasks
Font size
Apply a shadow effect to text
Decrease font size incrementally

Hands-On 23.7 Change Font Size

Use the Font Size Buttons

1. Navigate to the title slide, and notice that the subtitle wraps within the box.
   The slide will look better if the subtitle does not wrap. Also, it may look good to have the title just a little larger.
2. Follow these steps to select the subtitle placeholder box.

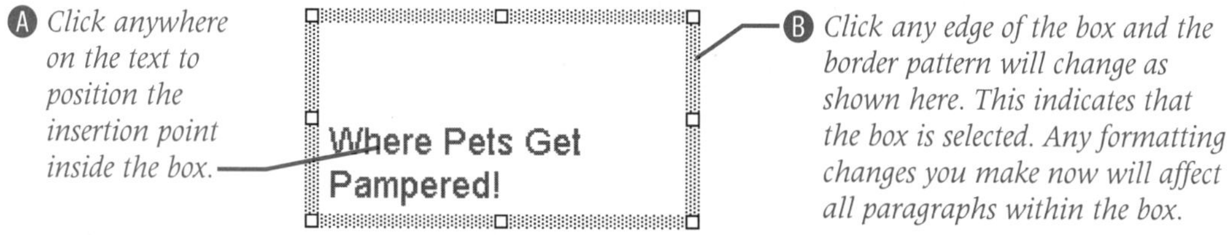

A Click anywhere on the text to position the insertion point inside the box.
Where Pets Get Pampered!
B Click any edge of the box and the border pattern will change as shown here. This indicates that the box is selected. Any formatting changes you make now will affect all paragraphs within the box.

3. Notice that the **Font Size** box [28] is currently set to 28.
   The Capsules design template applied this font size to the subtitle.
4. Click the Decrease Font Size button to reduce the size to 24.
5. The subtitle still wraps within the box, so click the Decrease Font Size button again.
   The subtitle should fit within the box, but now it is a little too small. The font size buttons let you easily increase or decrease the font size; however, they increment the size by four points. Fortunately, you can use the font size box to set the font size with precision.

Continue to Format the Subtitle

6. Click in the **Font Size** box [20], type **22**, and tap ENTER.
   Now the text is a little larger, and it fits within the box. However, it is still a little difficult to read, so you will apply bold formatting.
7. Click the Bold button.
   Now the text is easily visible, but the bold format has caused it to wrap within the box.

8. Follow these steps to widen the box slightly.

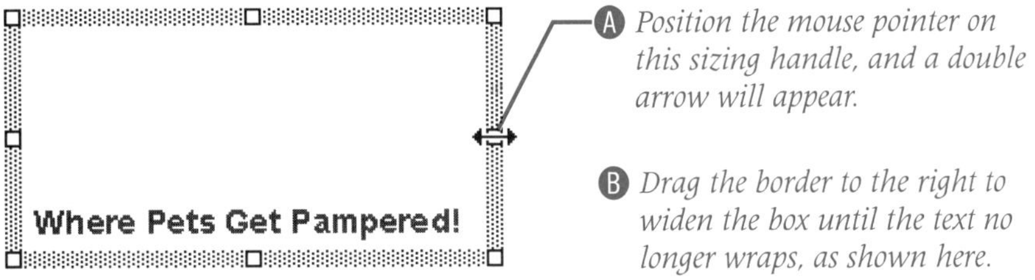
Where Pets Get Pampered!
A Position the mouse pointer on this sizing handle, and a double arrow will appear.
B Drag the border to the right to widen the box until the text no longer wraps, as shown here.

You can always change the size of a placeholder box using this technique. You can also move a box by dragging it to a different location on a slide.

Format the Title

9. Click in the title box (not the subtitle), and then click a border of the box.
10. Click the Increase Font Size button once to increase the size to 40.

Line Spacing and Paragraph Spacing

The **Format→Line Spacing** command displays the Line Spacing dialog box. Line spacing determines the amount of space within paragraphs and between paragraphs. The Line Spacing dialog box also lets you set the paragraph spacing before and after. The paragraph spacing settings let you increase the space before and after paragraphs, but they do not change the line spacing within paragraphs. These settings are useful if text is wrapping within a placeholder box and you want to change the spacing between paragraphs but not within the wrapped lines.

Hands-On 23.8 Work with Line Spacing and Paragraph Spacing

In this exercise, you will insert a new slide. Also, you will adjust the paragraph spacing to increase the amount of space between the bullets.

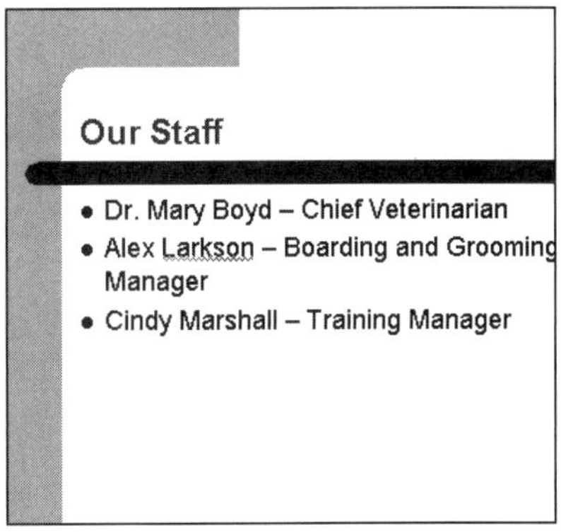
Our Staff
• Dr. Mary Boyd – Chief Veterinarian
• Alex Larkson – Boarding and Grooming Manager
• Cindy Marshall – Training Manager

1. Navigate to the last slide in the presentation (Products Sold).
2. Add a new slide using the second AutoLayout style.
3. Click the Title box, and type the title **`Our Staff`**.
4. Click in the bulleted list box, and type the three bulleted paragraphs shown to the right.
Notice that the second bullet paragraph wraps to a second line. PowerPoint automatically wraps lines as you type. In this slide, the lines are long, which gives the slide a cluttered appearance. Try to avoid wrapped lines when creating slides. In the next few steps, you will eliminate the wrapping by reducing the font size of the text. You will also increase the paragraph spacing *to "open up" the slide. Increasing the spacing will also help balance the slide, since it has just three bullets. Finally, notice that PowerPoint's Spelling-As-You-Type feature has put a wavy red line under the name Larkson. You can correct or ignore a word marked with a wavy red underline by right clicking the word and choosing a replacement word or* Ignore All *from the pop-up menu.*
5. Click a border on the bulleted list box.

(Continued on the next page)

6. Click in the Font Size box, type **26**, and tap (ENTER).
   The text should be small enough now so that the second line no longer wraps in the box.
7. Choose **Format→Line Spacing** from the menu bar.
8. Follow these steps to set the Before paragraph spacing.

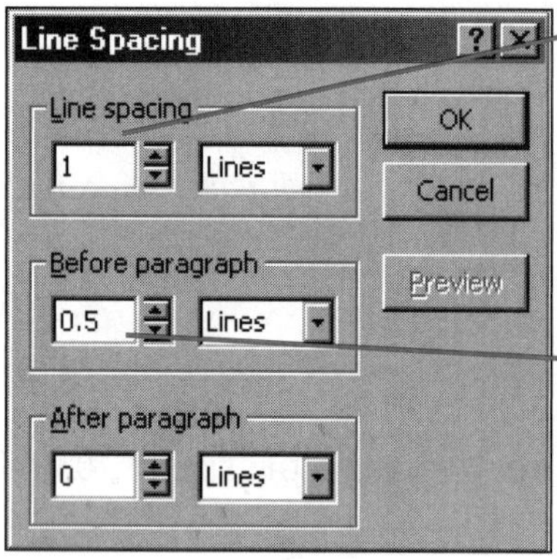

Line Spacing
Line spacing
1
Lines
OK
Cancel
Before paragraph
0.5
Lines
Preview
After paragraph
0
Lines

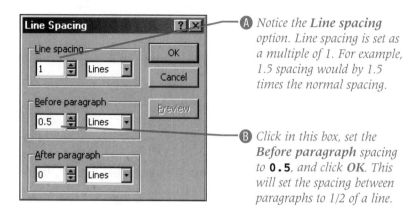

Ⓐ *Notice the **Line spacing** option. Line spacing is set as a multiple of 1. For example, 1.5 spacing would by 1.5 times the normal spacing.*

Ⓑ *Click in this box, set the **Before paragraph** spacing to **0.5**, and click **OK**. This will set the spacing between paragraphs to 1/2 of a line.*

Notice how the change has "opened up" the slide by creating more spacing between the paragraphs.

9. Click the Save button to save the changes to your presentation.

PowerPoint Views

Thus far, you have worked in Normal view, or Tri-pane view as it is often called. Tri-pane view is actually a combination of three views: Slide view, Outline view, and Notes Page view. In addition to these three views, PowerPoint has several other views that are useful for developing and delivering presentations. You can switch views by clicking buttons on the View bar, which is located on the left end of the horizontal scroll bar. You can also switch views by choosing the desired view from the View menu. The various PowerPoint views are described in the following Quick Reference table.

Quick Reference

POWERPOINT VIEWS

View	Purpose
Slide	Slide view lets you view and focus on one slide at a time.
Outline	Outline view lets you view an outline of your presentation. Outline view is particularly useful for organizing and restructuring a presentation.
Notes Page	Notes Page view lets you develop speaker notes to accompany the presentation.
Normal	Normal or Tri-pane view combines Slide view, Outline view, and Notes Page view.
Slide Sorter	Slide Sorter view displays all slides in the presentation. In Slide Sorter view, you can rearrange slides by dragging the desired slide(s) to different positions within the presentation.
Slide Show	The Slide Show button lets you run the presentation.

Hands-On 23.9 Explore the Various Views

1. Locate the View bar on the left end of the horizontal scrollbar.
   The first view (Normal) should be pushed in.
2. Click the Outline View button (the second button).
   Notice that the majority of the window is allocated to the outline.
3. Click the Slide View button (the third button) to explore Slide view.
4. Click the Slide Sorter View button (the fourth button).

   Notice how a thumbnail of each slide is displayed. Slide Sorter view is useful for sorting or rearranging slides.
5. Notice the last button Slide Show (but don't click it).
   You use the Slide Show button to run an electronic slide show. You will run your slide show later in this lesson.
6. Click the Outline View button (the second button) to return to Outline view.
   You will use Outline view in the next exercise.

Using Outlines

Several of the PowerPoint views display outlines of the presentation. Outline view can be quite useful for developing your ideas and the overall structure of a presentation. You can add slides to a presentation in Outline view, and you can easily rearrange slides and restructure your presentation. You switch to Outline view by choosing **View→Outline** or by clicking the Outline view button on the left end of the horizontal scrollbar.

The outline, current slide, and notes are visible in Outline view. However, a larger portion of the window is allocated to the outline.

The Outlining toolbar also appears in Outline view. The buttons on the Outlining toolbar are discussed in the next illustration.

The Outline button on the View bar switches you to Outline view.

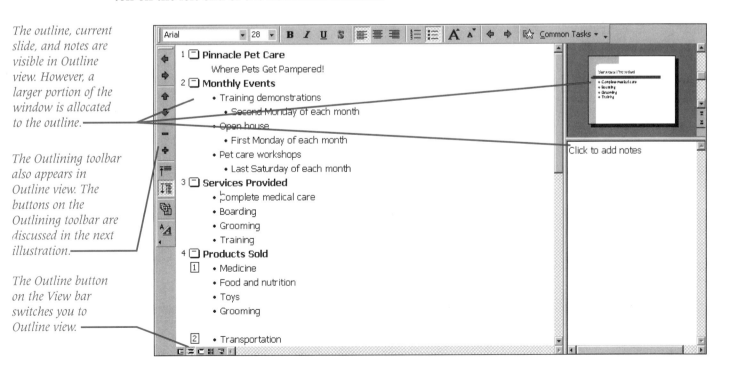

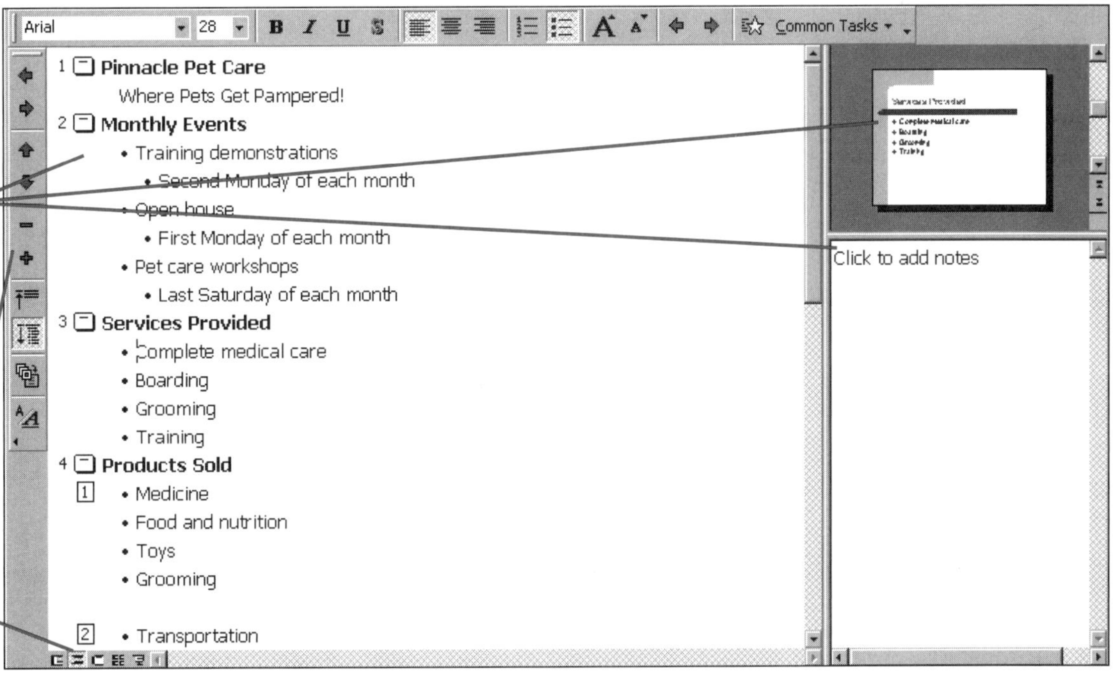

Arial
28
Common Tasks
1 Pinnacle Pet Care
Where Pets Get Pampered!
2 Monthly Events
• Training demonstrations
• Second Monday of each month
• Open house
• First Monday of each month
• Pet care workshops
• Last Saturday of each month
3 Services Provided
• Complete medical care
• Boarding
• Grooming
• Training
4 Products Sold
• Medicine
• Food and nutrition
• Toys
• Grooming
• Transportation
Click to add notes

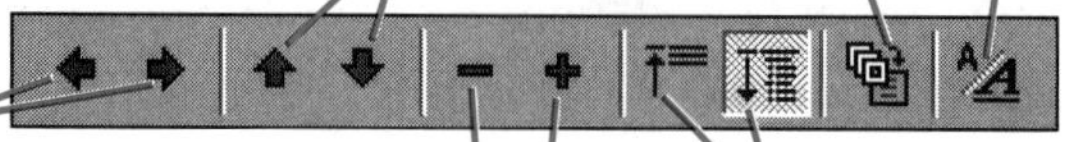
The **Promote** and **Demote** buttons let you promote or demote titles and bullets. For example, promoting a first-level bullet would create a new slide. The promoted bullet text would become the title of the new slide.
The **Move Up** and **Move Down** buttons let you rearrange bullets and entire slides.
The **Summary Slide** button lets you create summary slides.
This button is used to display or hide text formatting.
The **Expand** and **Collapse** buttons let you display (expand) additional levels and hide (collapse) levels. For example, you may want to collapse (hide) all bullets so that only the slide titles are displayed.
The **Collapse All** button displays only the slide titles. The **Expand All** button displays all levels.

Quick Reference

WORKING WITH OUTLINES

Task	Procedure
Select text in an outline.	Drag over the desired text.
Select an entire slide.	Click the slide icon.
Select a bulleted item and all of its subitems.	Click the bullet.
Add a new slide.	Promote a bulleted paragraph, or press CTRL+ENTER when the insertion point is in a bulleted paragraph.

Hands-On 23.10 Add Slides

1. Follow these steps to add a new slide while in Outline view.

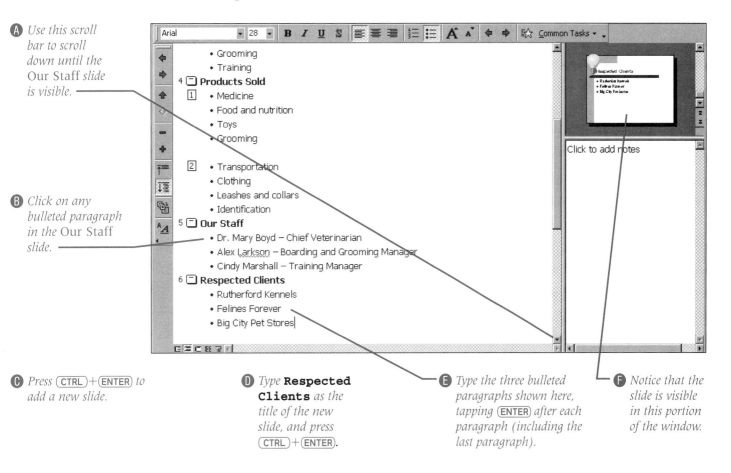

Ⓐ *Use this scroll bar to scroll down until the* Our Staff *slide is visible.*

Ⓑ *Click on any bulleted paragraph in the* Our Staff *slide.*

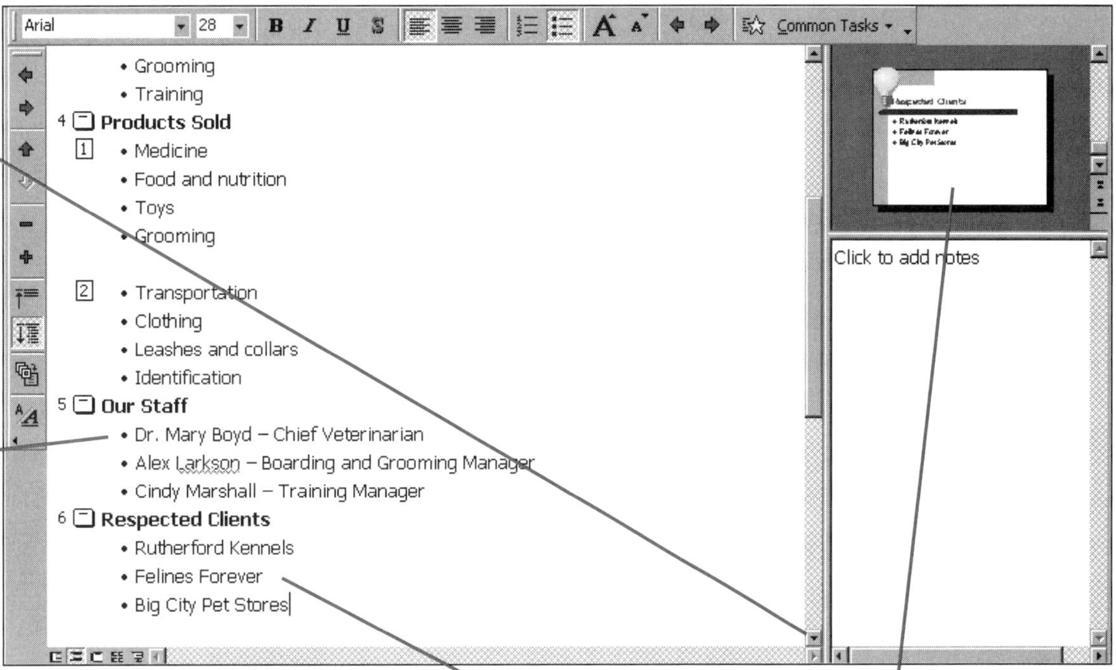

Arial
28
Common Tasks
• Grooming
• Training
4 Products Sold
1 • Medicine
• Food and nutrition
• Toys
• Grooming
2 • Transportation
• Clothing
• Leashes and collars
• Identification
5 Our Staff
• Dr. Mary Boyd – Chief Veterinarian
• Alex Larkson – Boarding and Grooming Manager
• Cindy Marshall – Training Manager
6 Respected Clients
• Rutherford Kennels
• Felines Forever
• Big City Pet Stores
Click to add notes

Ⓒ *Press* (CTRL)+(ENTER) *to add a new slide.*

Ⓓ *Type* **`Respected Clients`** *as the title of the new slide, and press* (CTRL)+(ENTER).

Ⓔ *Type the three bulleted paragraphs shown here, tapping* (ENTER) *after each paragraph (including the last paragraph).*

Ⓕ *Notice that the slide is visible in this portion of the window.*

As you can see, the (CTRL)+(ENTER) *keystroke combination adds a bullet to the current slide if the insertion point is on the title when you press the keystrokes. This keystroke combination adds a new slide if you are on a bullet when you issue the keystrokes.*

2. At this point, you should have a new bulleted paragraph below the Big City Pet Stores paragraph. If you don't, then tap (ENTER) to add the paragraph.

Add Two New Slides

3. Make sure the insertion point is on the blank bulleted paragraph.

4. Click the Promote [button] button on the Outlining toolbar. If the Outlining toolbar is not visible, then choose **View→Toolbars→Outlining** to display it.
   The bulleted paragraph will be promoted to a new slide.

5. Type **`Welcome-Aboard Special`**, and tap (ENTER).
   Notice that tapping (ENTER) *created a new slide. You must use the* (CTRL)+(ENTER) *keystroke combination to add a bulleted paragraph after a title slide. However, you will fix this by demoting the new slide in the next step.*

(Continued on the next page)

6. Click the Demote button on the Outlining toolbar.
The new slide should now be a bullet under the Welcome-Aboard Special title.

7. Complete the new slide as shown to the right, tapping ENTER after each paragraph (including the last paragraph).

7 **Welcome-Aboard Special**
- 25% discount on boarding
- Free grooming (dog or cat)
- 10% discount on products
- Valid until July 30

8. Promote the new paragraph that follows the *Valid until July 30* paragraph.

9. Complete the new slide as shown to the right. Do not tap ENTER after the last bullet in this slide, since it is the closing slide.
You will format this closing slide in a later exercise.

8 **Pinnacle Pet Care**
- Call
- (510) 235-7788
- Or
- Visit our Web site at
- Pinnaclepets@globelink.com

Use Buttons On the Outlining Toolbar

10. Follow these steps to explore Outline view.

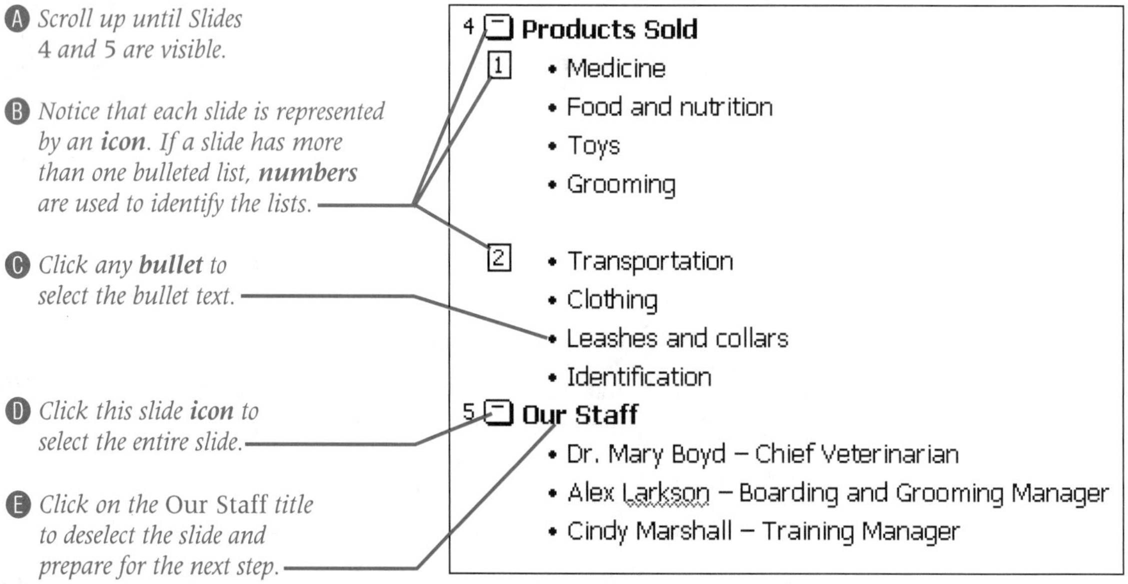
A Scroll up until Slides 4 and 5 are visible.
B Notice that each slide is represented by an icon. If a slide has more than one bulleted list, numbers are used to identify the lists.
C Click any bullet to select the bullet text.
D Click this slide icon to select the entire slide.
E Click on the Our Staff title to deselect the slide and prepare for the next step.
4 Products Sold
1
• Medicine
• Food and nutrition
• Toys
• Grooming
2
• Transportation
• Clothing
• Leashes and collars
• Identification
5 Our Staff
• Dr. Mary Boyd – Chief Veterinarian
• Alex Larkson – Boarding and Grooming Manager
• Cindy Marshall – Training Manager

11. Click the Collapse button on the Outlining toolbar.
The Collapse button collapses the bulleted paragraphs beneath the title.

12. Click the Expand button to redisplay the bulleted paragraphs.

13. Click the Collapse All button to display only the slide icons and titles of each slide.

14. Click the Expand All button to expand all of the slides.

Move a Slide

The easiest way to move a slide in Outline view is to first collapse all slides. Then you can click on the desired slide title and use the Move Up and/or Move Down buttons on the Outlining toolbar.

15. Click the Collapse All button.
16. If necessary, scroll up until all slides are visible.
17. Click on the Respected Clients title, and then click the Move Down button.
    The Respected Clients title should now appear below the Welcome-Aboard special title.
18. Click the Expand All button.
19. If necessary, scroll down, and notice that the subordinate paragraphs (the bullets) below the Respected Clients title were moved along with the title. In other words, the entire slide was moved.

Delete the Slide

20. If necessary, click the Respected Clients slide icon to select the entire slide.
21. Tap the DELETE key on the keyboard to delete the slide.
22. Now continue with the next topic and exercise, where you will format the closing slide.

Changing Paragraph Alignment

You use the Align Left , Center and Align Right buttons on the Formatting toolbar to change the alignment of paragraphs. The desired paragraphs or the text box containing the paragraphs must be selected before issuing the command.

Hands-On 23.11 Format the Closing Slide, and Use Slide Sorter View

Format the Closing Slide

1. Click the Slide View button on the View bar at the left end of the horizontal scroll bar.
   Slide View allocates most of the window space to the current slide.
2. If necessary, navigate to the closing slide at the end of the presentation.
3. Click in the bulleted list box, and then click a border of the box.
4. Click the Bullets button on the Formatting toolbar to remove bullets from the paragraphs.
5. Click the Center button on the Formatting toolbar to center the paragraphs within the box.
6. Choose **Format→Line Spacing** from the menu bar.
7. Set the Line Spacing to **1.2**, and click **OK.**
   This will increase the space between the paragraphs.
8. Select the entire telephone number by dragging the mouse pointer over the text.

(Continued on the next page)

9. Click the Increase Font Size button to increase the size to 32.

10. Now increase the size of the last line (the Web site URL) to 32.

Arrange Slides in Slide Sorter View

11. Click the **Slide Sorter View** button on the View bar at the left end of the horizontal scroll bar.

12. Follow these steps to move a slide.

Ⓐ *Notice the Slide Sorter toolbar that appears. This toolbar lets you create transitions between slides and other types of special effects. However, you won't use these options at this time.*

Ⓑ *If necessary, click this drop-down button, and change the zoom percentage until all seven slides are visible. Don't be concerned if your slides have a different arrangement than shown in this illustration.*

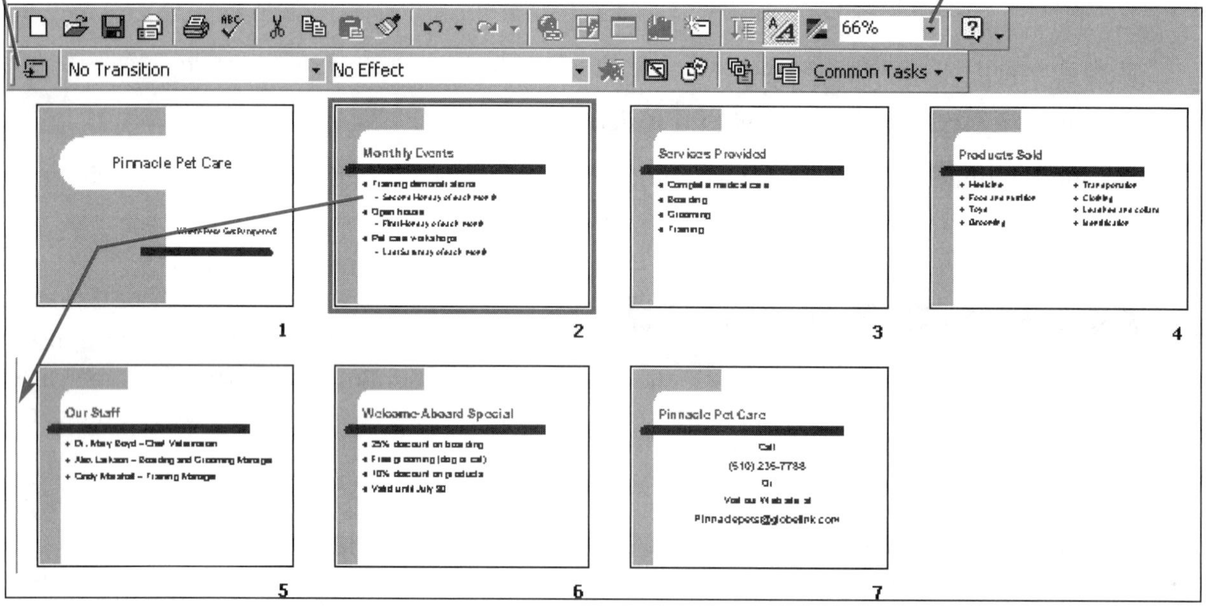

66%
No Transition
No Effect
Common Tasks
Pinnacle Pet Care
Monthly Events
Services Provided
Products Sold
Our Staff
Welcome Aboard Special
Pinnacle Pet Care
1
2
3
4
5
6
7

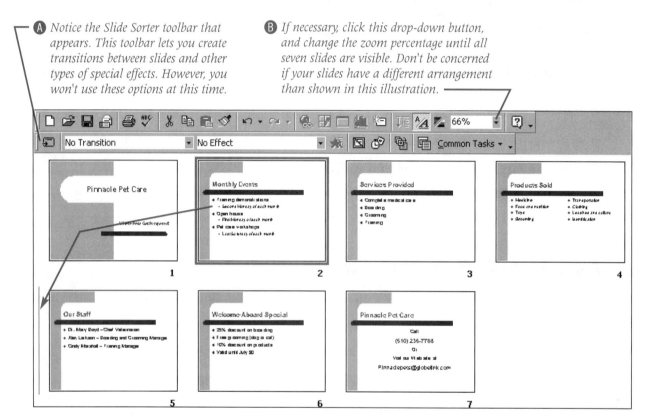

Ⓒ *Drag the Monthly Events slide to the left of the Our Staff slide, and a large vertical bar will indicate the eventual position of the slide. Don't be concerned if the Our Staff slide is in a different row or column than shown here.*

Ⓓ *Release the mouse button, and the Monthly Events slide will become the fourth slide.*

13. Click the **Normal View** button on the View bar to return to Tri-pane view.

Speaker Notes

For most people, presenting to groups can be an intimidating experience. In fact, studies have shown that speaking in front of a group is the greatest fear of most people. Adequate preparation is an important step that you can take to overcome your anxieties. PowerPoint helps you prepare for presentations by developing speaker notes. You can create speaker notes for any slide in your presentation. You can print speaker notes along with the accompanying slides. Speaker notes can help you deliver effective, anxiety-free presentations. Speaker notes are entered in the notes pane of Tri-pane view, or you can use the **View→Notes Page** command to switch to Notes view.

Hands-On 23.12 Add Speaker Notes

1. Choose **View→Notes Page** from the menu bar.
   PowerPoint will display a full screen view that includes the current slide and the notes area. However, notice that the phrase Click to add text *in the notes area is difficult to read.*
2. Adjust the zoom control percentage on the Formatting toolbar to 100%.
3. Navigate to the title slide at the top of the presentation.
4. If necessary, scroll down until the phrase *Click to add text* is visible on the title slide.
5. Click on the phrase *Click to add text,* and type **`Don't forget to thank the following people:`** as the replacement phrase.
6. Tap ENTER to move the insertion point to the next line.
7. Click the Bullets button on the formatting toolbar.
8. Type the names and titles shown to the right, tapping ENTER after each line.

   > Don't forget to thank the following people:
   > •Pet World Trade Show Organizing Committee
   > •Donald Johnson – Pet World Vendor Committee
   > •Tanisha Smith – Vendor Support

9. Scroll down through the presentation until you reach the Services Provided slide.
10. Click the phrase *Click to add text,* and type the speaker note shown to the right.

    > Mention the 1999 Pet World magazine article ranking us as the most comprehensive pet care facility.

11. Scroll down to the Products Sold slide, and add the speaker note shown to the right.

    > Once again, mention the Pet World magazine article.

12. Scroll down to the Our Staff slide, and add the speaker notes shown to the right.
    At this point, four slides in your presentation should contain speaker notes. Later in this lesson, you will print the speaker notes.

    > •Seven other staff members
    > •Combined experience is 63 years

13. Click the Slide Sorter View button on the View bar to return to Slide Sorter view.

Printing Presentations

PowerPoint lets you print presentations in a variety of formats. For example, you can choose options that let you print on paper, overhead transparencies, or 35mm slides.

Grayscale Preview

TIP! *Choose **View→Slide Miniature** to display a small color version of the slide next to the gray shade version.*

The Grayscale Preview button on the Standard toolbar displays slides in shades of gray. This view can be useful if you intend to print your slides using a black-and-white laser printer or an ink jet printer. This is often done during the development and testing phase of a presentation. In addition, PowerPoint lets you print speaker notes and audience handouts, which are usually printed in black and white.

If you press the SHIFT key and click the Grayscale Preview button, then PowerPoint displays the slides in pure black and white (without gray shades). However, you will probably find that this technique has limited use especially if your presentation is based upon a design template. The fill colors in design templates won't print if the black-and-white option is chosen. The fill colors will print in various shades of gray if the grayscale print option is enabled.

Hands-On 23.13 Use Grayscale Preview

1. Make sure the view is set to Slide Sorter with all seven slides displayed.
2. Click the Grayscale Preview button on the Standard toolbar.
3. Click the Slide View button on the view bar.
   Notice that you can switch views while Grayscale Preview is active.
4. Choose **View→Slide Miniature** from the menu bar.
   A small color version of the slide appears. This allows you to compare the color version with the grayscale version.
5. Scroll through the presentation, and notice how the gray shades are applied to the various slides.
6. Click the Grayscale Preview button to turn off Grayscale Preview.
7. Now press the SHIFT key while you click the Grayscale Preview button.
   PowerPoint displays the slide only in black and white. Notice how the colored areas on the slide miniature do not appear on the black-and-white slide.
8. Choose **View→Slide Miniature** to close the slide miniature.
9. Click the Grayscale Preview button to return to Slide View.

Page Setup Options

The **File→Page Setup** command displays the Page Setup dialog box. You choose options on the Page Setup dialog box to set the format, size, and orientation of slides prior to printing. The illustration on the following page describes the options on the Page Setup dialog box.

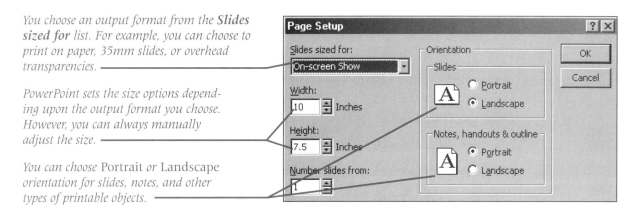

You choose an output format from the ***Slides sized for*** *list. For example, you can choose to print on paper, 35mm slides, or overhead transparencies.*

PowerPoint sets the size options depending upon the output format you choose. However, you can always manually adjust the size.

You can choose Portrait *or* Landscape *orientation for slides, notes, and other types of printable objects.*

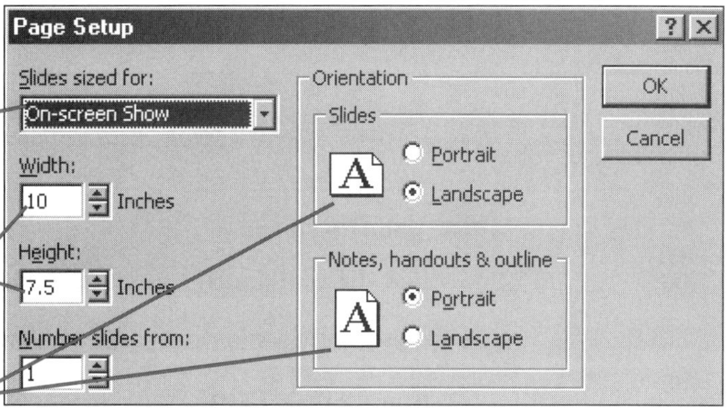

Page Setup
Slides sized for:
On-screen Show
Width:
10
Inches
Height:
7.5
Inches
Number slides from:
1
Orientation
Slides
Portrait
Landscape
Notes, handouts & outline
Portrait
Landscape
OK
Cancel

Printing Transparencies

You can deliver a presentation using transparencies and an overhead projector. Many laser printers and ink-jet printers let you create transparencies by printing directly onto transparency film. You can print onto transparency film in grayshades, black and white, or in color. Prior to printing transparencies, you should use the Page Setup dialog box to choose Overhead from the *Slides sized for* list. This will size the slides to 10 inches wide by 7.5 inches high—the correct size for transparencies.

Print Dialog Box

From the Keyboard

CTRL+P to display Print dialog box

The Print button on the Standard toolbar sends the entire presentation to the current printer. You must display the Print dialog box if you want to change printers, specify the number of copies to be printed, print selected slides, and choose other printer output options. The Print dialog box is displayed with the **File→Print** command. You can set various options in the Print dialog box as shown in the following illustration.

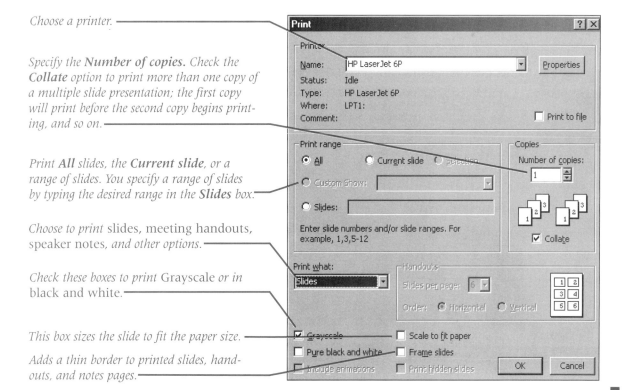

Choose a printer.

Specify the ***Number of copies.*** *Check the* ***Collate*** *option to print more than one copy of a multiple slide presentation; the first copy will print before the second copy begins printing, and so on.*

Print ***All*** *slides, the* ***Current slide****, or a range of slides. You specify a range of slides by typing the desired range in the* ***Slides*** *box.*

Choose to print slides, meeting handouts, speaker notes, *and other options.*

Check these boxes to print Grayscale *or in* black and white.

This box sizes the slide to fit the paper size.

Adds a thin border to printed slides, handouts, and notes pages.

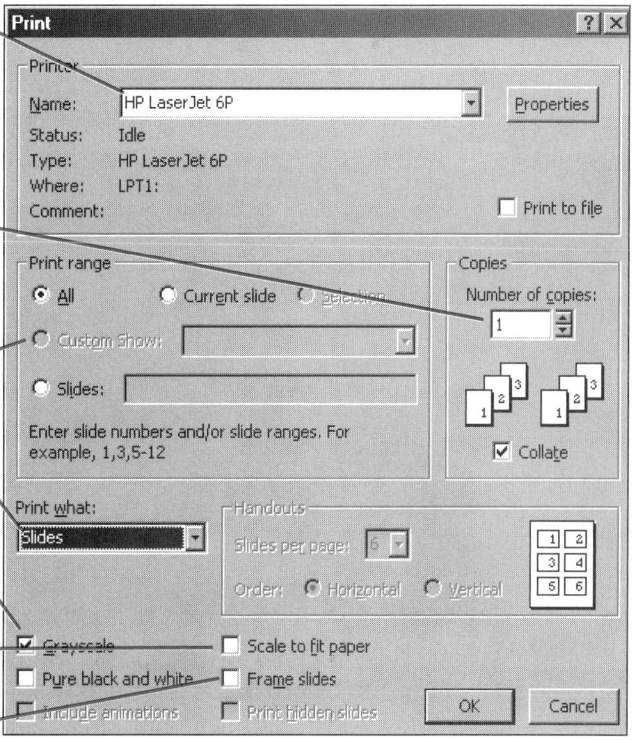

Print
Printer
Name:
HP LaserJet 6P
Properties
Status:
Idle
Type:
HP LaserJet 6P
Where:
LPT1:
Comment:
Print to file
Print range
All
Current slide
Selection
Custom Show:
Slides:
Enter slide numbers and/or slide ranges. For example, 1,3,5-12
Copies
Number of copies:
1
Collate
Print what:
Slides
Handouts
Slides per page:
6
Order:
Horizontal
Vertical
Grayscale
Scale to fit paper
Pure black and white
Frame slides
Include animations
Print hidden slides
OK
Cancel

Hands-On 23.14 Print Slides and Speaker Notes

In this exercise, you will print the title slide in your presentation with and without speaker notes. This will show you how to set the various Print dialog box options, and it will help conserve paper and printing time.

Print the Title Slide

1. Click the Slide Sorter View button to return to Slide Sorter view.
2. Click the title slide in the Slide Sorter view.
3. Choose **File→Print** from the menu bar.
4. Set the print range to Current slide.
5. Make sure the Print what option is set to Slides and the Grayscale box is checked.
6. Click **OK** to print just the title slide.

Print the Title Slide with Speaker Notes

7. Choose **File→Print** from the menu bar.
8. Set the Print what option to Notes Pages.
9. Set the print range to Current slide, and click **OK.**
   The speaker notes will be printed below the title slide on a single page.

Delivering an Electronic Slide Show

The Slide Show button on the View bar lets you initiate an electronic slide show. You can deliver a slide show using just a personal computer, or you can attach a projection device to your PC for presentations to large groups. The following table describes the options available for starting, delivering, and ending a slide show.

Quick Reference

DELIVERING A SLIDE SHOW

Task	Procedure
Start a slide show from any slide.	From Slide Sorter view, click the desired slide, and then click the Slide Show button. From Slide view, navigate to the desired slide, and then click the Slide Show button.
Advance to next slide.	Click anywhere on the current slide, or tap PGDN, N (for Next), ENTER, or SPACE BAR.
Return to previous slide.	Tap PGUP, P (for Previous), or BACKSPACE.
End a slide show.	Tap the ESC key.

Using the Pop-up Menu

From the Keyboard

SHIFT+F10 to display pop-up menu

The Pop-up Menu Button appears at the bottom-left corner of the screen during a slide show. You can click the pop-up button to display a menu of commands. The menu includes commands for navigating among slides, ending the slide show, and other useful functions.

Hands-On 23.15 Run the Slide Show

Your presentation should be displayed in Slide Sorter view from the previous exercise.

1. Click the title slide in the Slide Sorter window.
   You will start your presentation by displaying the Title slide.
2. Click the Slide Show button on the View bar.
   PowerPoint will display your title slide in a full-screen view. All toolbars and other screen objects will be hidden from view.
3. Click the mouse pointer anywhere on the screen to move to the next slide.
4. Continue to click anywhere on the screen until the closing slide appears (the slide with the phone number and Web site URL).
5. Click the closing slide, and the slide show will end.
6. Click the fourth slide in Slide Sorter View, and then click the Slide Show button.
   You can start a presentation on any slide.
7. Tap the (PGDN) key several times, and then tap (PGUP) several times. Use the keys near the main keyboard (not the keys on the numeric keypad).
   PowerPoint displays the next or previous slide each time you tap these keys.
8. Click the Pop-up Menu button at the bottom-left corner of the window.
   Notice that the pop-up menu has options to go to the Next and Previous slides and to end the slide show. The pop-up menu also lets you use a Pen tool to draw on the slide and make other enhancements. In the next step, you will use the Go option on the pop-up menu to go to a specific slide.
9. Choose **Go→By Title→Welcome-Aboard Special** from the pop-up menu.
   PowerPoint will display the Welcome-Aboard Special slide. You can always use this technique to rapidly navigate to a specific slide.
10. Right-click (click with the right mouse button) anywhere on the current slide to display the pop-up menu.
11. Choose **Go→Slide Navigator** from the pop-up menu.
12. Choose the **Products Sold** slide from the Slide Navigator box, and click the **Go To** button.
    As you can see, there are many ways to navigate slides in an electronic slide show.
13. Click the Pop-up Menu button, and choose End Show from the menu.
14. Feel free to practice running your electronic slide show.
15. When you have finished, click the Save button to save the changes to your presentation.
16. Choose **File→Close** from the menu bar to close the presentation.

Concepts Review

True/False Questions

1. Design templates give presentations a consistent format and appearance.	TRUE	FALSE
2. The New Slide box has a special AutoLayout just for title slides.	TRUE	FALSE
3. AutoLayouts are predefined layouts for slides.	TRUE	FALSE
4. A slide's AutoLayout cannot be changed once the slide has been created.	TRUE	FALSE
5. Each slide in a PowerPoint presentation is saved as a separate file.	TRUE	FALSE
6. The horizontal alignment of paragraphs cannot be changed.	TRUE	FALSE
7. Slide view is most useful for organizing and rearranging a presentation.	TRUE	FALSE
8. Slide Sorter view is most useful for focusing on the development of a single slide.	TRUE	FALSE
9. You start a presentation by clicking the Slide Show  button.	TRUE	FALSE
10. While delivering an electronic presentation, you can display a pop-up menu by clicking the left mouse button anywhere on a slide.	TRUE	FALSE

Multiple-Choice Questions

1. Which of the following techniques can be used to add a new slide to a presentation?
   a. Click the New Slide  button on PowerPoint's toolbar.
   b. Choose New Slide from the Common Tasks menu.
   c. Both a and b
   d. None of the above

2. Which technique can be used to turn off bullets for a single paragraph?
   a. Click on the desired paragraph and click the Bullets button.
   b. Click on the desired paragraph and tap the (DELETE) key.
   c. Click the placeholder box that contains the bulleted paragraph and click the Bullets button.
   d. None of the above

3. Which of the following buttons is used to promote a bulleted paragraph?
   a. 
   b. 
   c. 
   d. 

4. Which of the following techniques can be used to move to the next slide in an electronic slide show?
   a. Click anywhere on the current slide.
   b. Tap the (PGDN) key on the keyboard.
   c. Right-click the current slide, and choose Next from the pop-up menu.
   d. All of the above

Skill Builders

Skill Builder 23.1 Set Up a Presentation

In this exercise, you will set up a presentation for the Tropical Getaways travel service. The managers at Tropical Getaways need to deliver a presentation to audiences of up to 40 people. The presentation will be used for marketing purposes to sell potential customers a tropical getaway to paradise.

Set Up the Title Slide

1. If the PowerPoint window is still displayed from the previous exercise, then choose **File→New** to start a new presentation. If PowerPoint is not currently running, then start the program, choose Design Template from the PowerPoint dialog box, and click **OK.**
2. If necessary, click the Design Templates tab in the New Presentation dialog box.
3. Choose the Nature design, and click **OK.**
4. Click **OK** on the New Slide dialog box to set up the title slide.
5. Click the Title box, and type the title **`Tropical Getaways`**.
6. Click the subtitle box, and type the phrase **`Adventures in Paradise`**.

Set Up Another Slide

7. Click the [Common Tasks ▾] button, and choose New Slide.
8. Choose the third AutoLayout (2 column text), and click **OK.**
9. Click the Title box, and type the phrase **`Most Popular Destinations`**.
10. Add the paragraphs shown to the right in the bulleted list boxes.

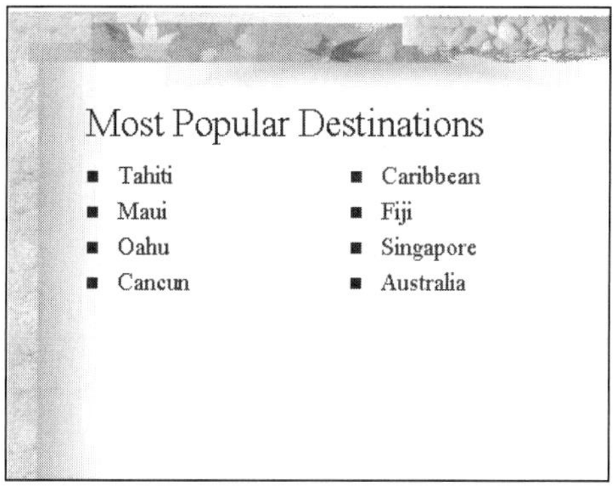

Most Popular Destinations
Tahiti
Maui
Oahu
Cancun
Caribbean
Fiji
Singapore
Australia

Set Up the Remaining Slides

11. Add another slide using the third AutoLayout.
12. Enter the phrase **`Complete Packages`** in the title box.
13. Enter the phrase **`Packages Include`** in the first bulleted list box.
14. Tap (ENTER) once, and click the **Demote Bullet** button.
15. Type the word **`Airfare`**, and tap (ENTER).
16. Complete the slide as shown to the right.

Complete Packages
Packages Include
Airfare
Lodging
Rental car
Activities
Low Prices
3 days from $599
5 days from $799
7 days from $999

(Continued on the next page)

17. Add a new slide to your presentation using the second AutoLayout.

18. Enter the title and bulleted lists into your new slide as shown to the right. You will need to demote the bulleted paragraphs under the headings Package 1 and Package 2. Also, notice that there is a large space above the Package 2 heading. You can create this space by tapping (ENTER) twice after typing the bulleted paragraph with the text $429 per person.

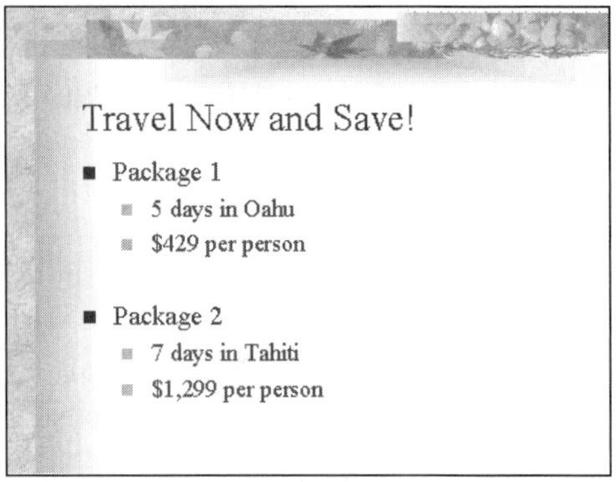
Travel Now and Save!
Package 1
5 days in Oahu
$429 per person
Package 2
7 days in Tahiti
$1,299 per person

19. Add the following slides to your presentation using the second AutoLayout style for both slides. You will need to remove the bullets from the bulleted list box in the second slide and center the paragraphs. Also, you will need to push the paragraph with the text Donna Givens down by tapping (ENTER) twice.

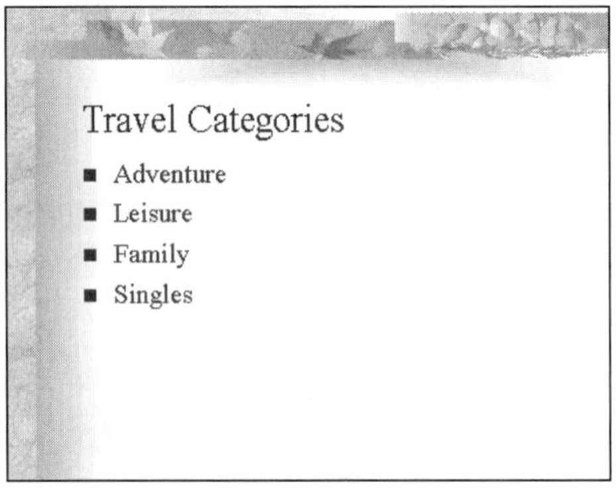
Travel Categories
Adventure
Leisure
Family
Singles

Tropical Getaways
Donna Givens
(310) 544-8870

Add Speaker Notes

20. Choose **View→Notes Page** from the menu bar.

21. Navigate to the title slide at the top of the presentation.

22. Adjust the zoom control percentage on the Standard toolbar to 100%.

23. If necessary, scroll down until the phrase *Click to add text* is visible on the title slide.

24. Click on the phrase *Click to add text,* and type **`Welcome the employees to their new travel service`** as the replacement phrase.

25. Tap (ENTER), and type **`Thank Glenda Johnson—Director of Human Resources`**.

26. Navigate to the Most Popular Destinations slide, and type the note **`Employees get a 35% discount on all destinations on the Popular Destinations list`**.

27. Navigate to the Travel Now and Save slide.

28. Click on the phrase *Click to add text* in the speaker notes box.

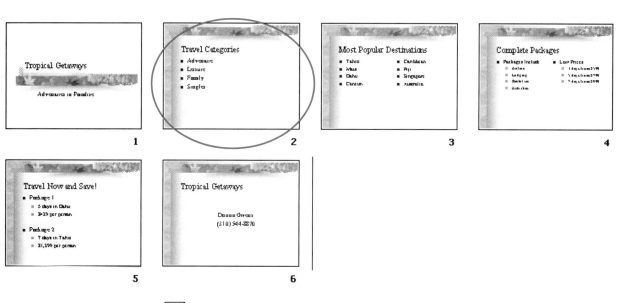

29. Click the Bullets button and enter the speaker notes shown to the right.

> •12 preferred discount packages available to employees.
> •No time limit on preferred discount packages.
> •Limit of two packages per employee per year.

30. Click the Save button, and save the presentation to your exercise diskette with the name **`Tropical Getaways`**.

Skill Builder 23.2 Rearrange Slides

In this exercise, you will reposition one of the slides in the Tropical Getaways presentation.

1. Click the Slide Sorter button on the View bar to switch to Slide Sorter view.
2. Drag the Travel Categories slide from Position 5, and drop it in Position 2 as shown below.

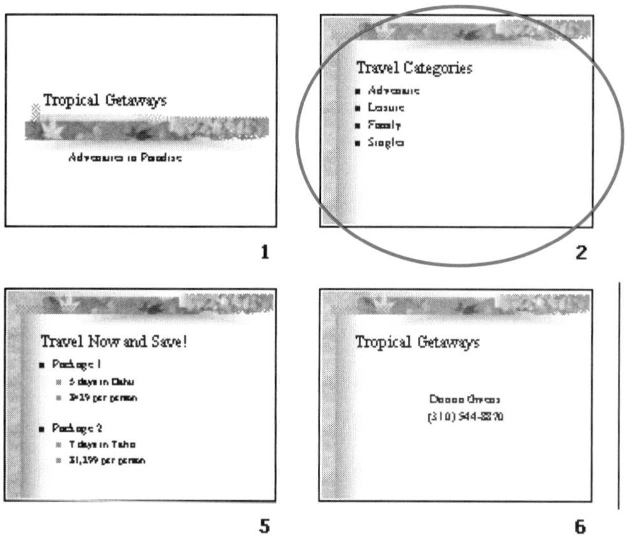
Tropical Getaways
1
Travel Categories
2
Most Popular Destinations
3
Complete Packages
4
Travel Now and Save!
5
Tropical Getaways
6

3. Save the change, and continue with the next exercise.

Skill Builder 23.3 Deliver an Electronic Presentation

1. Click the first slide in the presentation, and then click the Slide Show button.
2. Click each slide in the presentation until the presentation is complete.
3. Start the presentation again.
4. Click the Pop-up Menu button at the bottom-left corner of the slide.
5. Choose **Go→By Title→Travel Now and Save** to go to the Travel Now and Save slide.
6. Use the Pop-up Menu button to end the slide show.
7. Choose **File→Close** from the menu bar to close the presentation. Click the **Yes** button if PowerPoint asks you to save the changes.

Assessment

Assessment 23.1 Set Up a Presentation

In this assessment, you will set up a presentation for Classic Cars. Classic Cars is an organization devoted to tracking, categorizing, and preserving classic automobiles. The presentation will be given to members of the Classic Cars organization at the annual Classic Cars convention.

1. Choose **File→New** and click the Design Templates tab in the New Presentation box.
   You use the File→New command to display the New Presentation box from within PowerPoint.
2. Choose the Dads Tie design, and click **OK.**
3. Add the five slides shown below to your presentation, and make the following adjustments.
   - Increase the line spacing to 1.3 for the bulleted paragraphs on the *Seminar Topics* and *Collections on Display* slides.
   - Use the Title AutoLayout style for both the first and last slides. You will need to reduce the font size of the title on the closing slide to allow it to fit within the placeholder.

Classic Cars
1999 Convention Highlights

Seminar Topics
Restoration Techniques
Preservation Techniques
Locating Vehicles
Success Stories
Winning Competitions

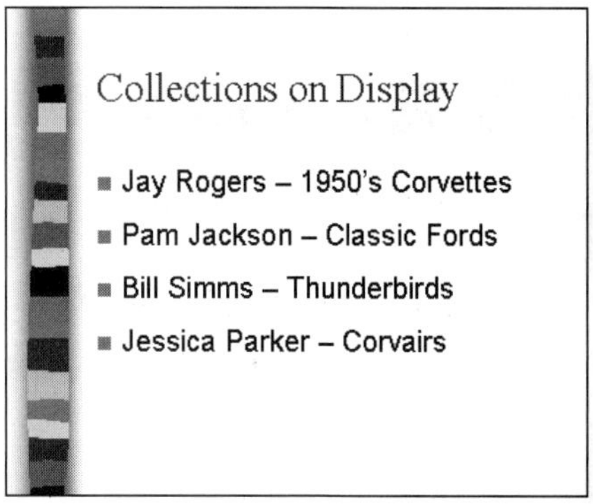
Collections on Display
Jay Rogers – 1950's Corvettes
Pam Jackson – Classic Fords
Bill Simms – Thunderbirds
Jessica Parker – Corvairs

Door Prizes
Car Care Items
– Gift certificates
– Floor mats
– Waxes and polishes
– Magazines
Entertainment
– Las Vegas vacation
– Sporting events
– Movie tickets
– Dinners

The 1999 Convention
Enjoy the Ride

4. Add the following speaker notes to the presentation. Use the Bullets button to place bullets in front of each note.

Slide	Speaker Notes
Classic Cars (title slide)	■ Thank the organizing committee.
	■ Welcome new members.
Collections on Display	■ Thank collectors.
	■ Most valuable collection of classic cars in one location
	■ 110 cars in mint condition
Door Prizes	■ No individual limits on winning
	■ Mention the secret grand prize.

5. Use the Grayscale Preview button to view your presentation.

6. Print the Notes Pages in your presentation using the Grayscale option on the Print dialog box. *This will print each slide and its accompanying notes on a single page.*

7. Save your presentation with the name **Classic Cars.**

8. Use the **File→Exit** command to exit from PowerPoint.

LESSON 24—PowerPoint

Clip Art, Transitions, and Animation

In this lesson, you will enhance the Pinnacle Pet Care presentation that you created in the previous lesson. You will use clip art to add interest to the presentation. You will also create transitions between slides and use animation to "bring the presentation to life."

In This Lesson

Case Study

After watching several of his competitors present at the Pet World trade show, Al Smith realizes that his slide show is not very exciting. Al is a talented speaker, and he needs a slide show that reflects the enthusiasm and energy level of his presentation style. Al decides to "liven up" his presentation with clip art and the powerful animation tools available in PowerPoint 2000. Al injects just the right amount of special effects to make his presentation interesting while allowing his audience to focus on the content of his presentation.

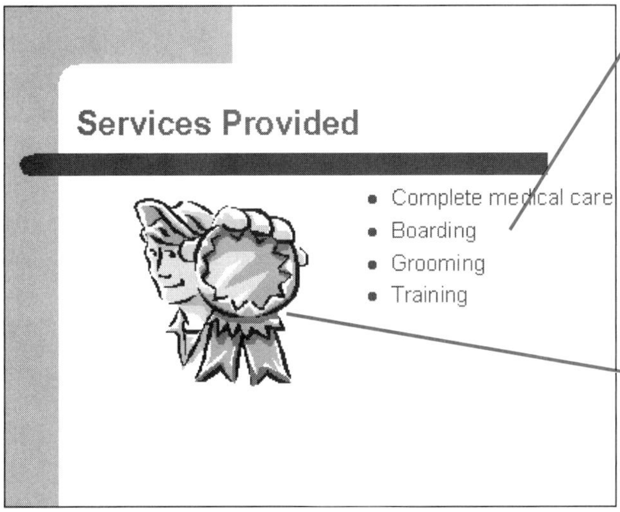
Services Provided
Complete medical care
Boarding
Grooming
Training

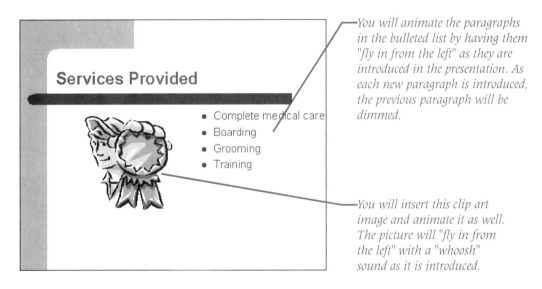

You will animate the paragraphs in the bulleted list by having them "fly in from the left" as they are introduced in the presentation. As each new paragraph is introduced, the previous paragraph will be dimmed.

You will insert this clip art image and animate it as well. The picture will "fly in from the left" with a "whoosh" sound as it is introduced.

The Office Assistant

The Office Assistant is an interactive Help tool available in all Office 2000 applications. The Assistant monitors your activities and provides tips, suggestions, and alert messages whenever it assumes you need assistance. For example, the Assistant will frequently display a light bulb icon in a slide when it has a tip. You can display the tip by clicking the light bulb. The Assistant also displays a search box where you can type questions.

What would you like to do?
How can I insert bullets?
Options
Search

The Assistant's search box

Using the Assistant to Get Help

The Assistant's speech balloon contains a search box where you can enter phrases and questions. When you click the Search button, the Assistant interprets the phrase or question in the search box and displays a list of topics relating to the search box text. When you click a topic, PowerPoint displays a Help window providing you with detailed help information.

Controlling the Assistant

You can control all aspects of the Assistant. For example, you may not want the Assistant to display a tip of the day, or you may want to turn the Assistant off. You set options for the Assistant in the Office Assistant dialog box. The following Quick Reference table summarizes various methods of controlling the Assistant.

Quick Reference

CONTROLLING THE OFFICE ASSISTANT

Task	Procedure
Display the Assistant's speech balloon (four . different methods)	■ Click anywhere on the Assistant. ■ Press (F1). ■ Click the Help button on the Standard toolbar. ■ Choose Microsoft PowerPoint Help from the Help menu.
Close the speech balloon.	Click anywhere in the PowerPoint window, or tap (ESC).
Display the Office Assistant dialog box.	Display the speech balloon, and click the **Options** button.
Change an animated character.	Display the Office Assistant dialog box, click the Gallery tab, use the Next button to browse the available characters, choose a character, and click **OK.**
Temporarily hide the Assistant.	Choose **Help→Hide** the Office Assistant, or right-click the Assistant, and choose Hide from the pop-up menu.
Turn Assistant off completely.	Display the Office Assistant dialog box, and uncheck the Use the Office Assistant box.
Unhide the Assistant or turn the Assistant back on.	Choose **Help→Show** the Office Assistant.

Inserting Graphics

PowerPoint 2000 lets you insert a variety of graphics in your presentations. You can use the clip art that is provided with Office 2000, or you can insert your own graphics such as a company logo or a scanned picture. You insert graphics while working in Slide view.

Clip Art AutoLayouts

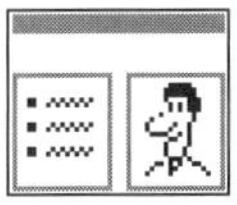

PowerPoint has two AutoLayout slides that simplify the task of inserting clip art. The AutoLayout slides contain placeholders for clip art. Clip art is automatically adjusted to the size of a placeholder box when it is inserted. You can actually insert clip art anywhere on a slide. However, the AutoLayout slides simplify the process by positioning and sizing the clip art.

The Office 2000 Clip Gallery

The Insert Clip Art  button on the Drawing toolbar displays the Clip Gallery. The Clip Gallery has been redesigned in Office 2000 to make it easier to locate and manage clip art and pictures. The Clip Gallery organizes clip art into categories such as business, animals, and Academic. The Clip Gallery can also be displayed with the **Insert→Picture→Clip Art** command. In addition, the Insert Clip Art button appears in the clip art placeholder on slides with a clip art AutoLayout. You can display the Clip Gallery by double-clicking the button on the slide.

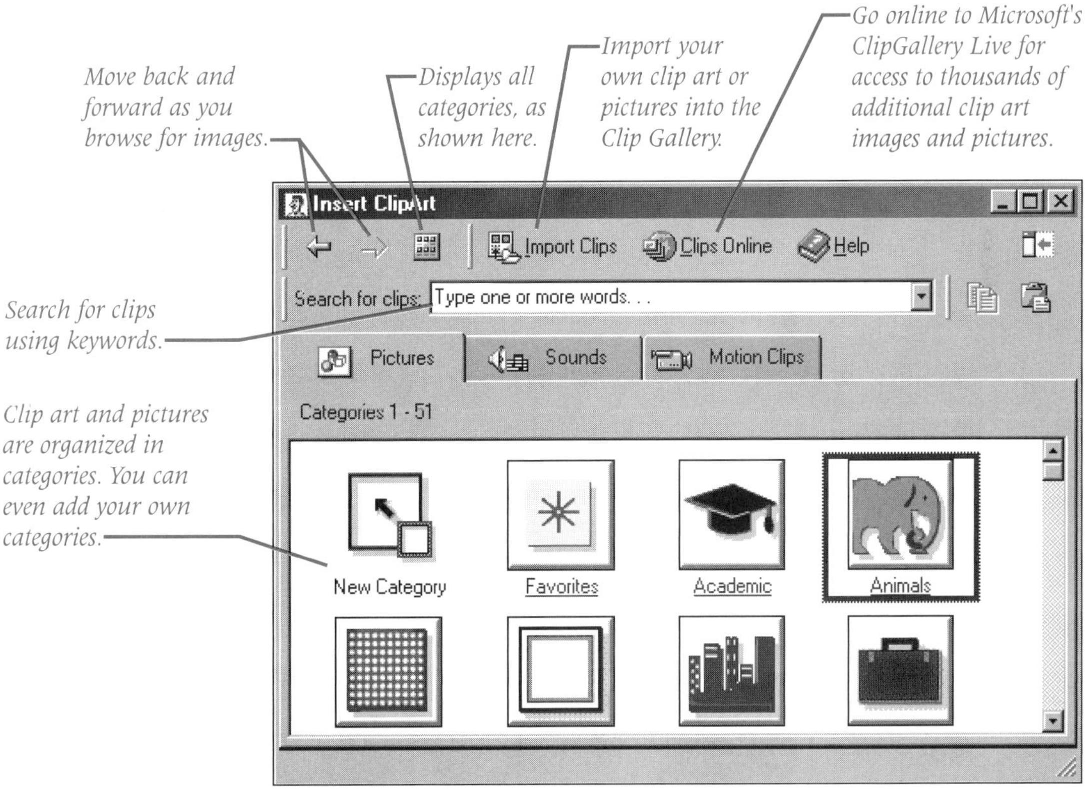
Move back and forward as you browse for images.
Displays all categories, as shown here.
Import your own clip art or pictures into the Clip Gallery.
Go online to Microsoft's ClipGallery Live for access to thousands of additional clip art images and pictures.
Search for clips using keywords.
Clip art and pictures are organized in categories. You can even add your own categories.
Insert ClipArt
Import Clips
Clips Online
Help
Search for clips:
Type one or more words. . .
Pictures
Sounds
Motion Clips
Categories 1 - 51
New Category
Favorites
Academic
Animals

Hands-On 24.1 Insert Clip Art

In this exercise, you will open the Pinnacle Pet Care presentation from your exercise diskette. You will enhance the presentation throughout this lesson. If you have not satisfactorily completed the Hands-On exercises in the previous lesson, then ask your instructor to copy the file named Pinnacle Pet Care—Lesson 24 to your exercise diskette. This file provides the Pinnacle Pet Care presentation in the state it should be in after completing Lesson 23. If necessary, your instructor can provide you with files to give you a fresh starting point whenever you begin a new lesson in this book.

Open the Presentation

1. Start PowerPoint, and the PowerPoint dialog box will appear.
2. Choose the **Open an existing presentation** option, and click **OK** to display the Open dialog box. There is no need to choose a presentation from the list of recently used presentations.
3. Navigate to your exercise diskette, choose the Pinnacle Pet Care presentation, and click the **Open** button.

Insert Clip Art On the Title Slide

4. Click the Slide view button on the View bar.
5. If necessary, navigate to the top of the presentation to display the title slide.
6. Follow these steps to display the Clip Gallery.

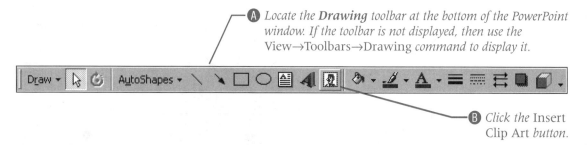

Ⓐ *Locate the* ***Drawing*** *toolbar at the bottom of the PowerPoint window. If the toolbar is not displayed, then use the* View→Toolbars→Drawing *command to display it.*

Draw
AutoShapes

Ⓑ *Click the* Insert Clip Art *button.*

7. Click the **Academic** category to display clips related to academia.
8. Follow these steps to preview a clip.

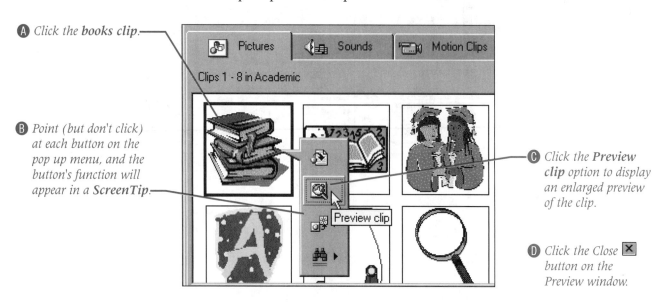

Ⓐ *Click the* ***books clip.***

Ⓑ *Point (but don't click) at each button on the pop up menu, and the button's function will appear in a* ***ScreenTip.***

Pictures
Sounds
Motion Clips
Clips 1 - 8 in Academic
Preview clip

Ⓒ *Click the* ***Preview clip*** *option to display an enlarged preview of the clip.*

Ⓓ *Click the Close button on the Preview window.*

9. Follow these steps to navigate in the Clip Gallery and search for a clip.

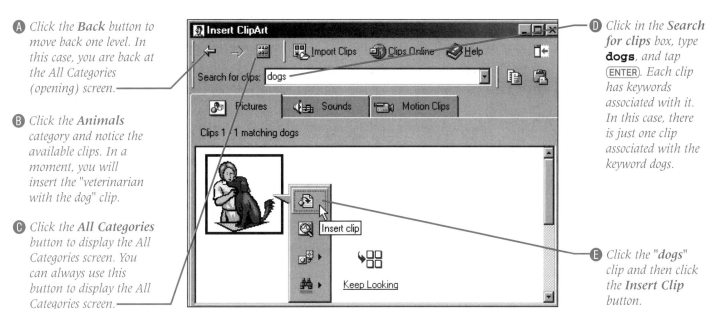

A *Click the **Back** button to move back one level. In this case, you are back at the All Categories (opening) screen.*

B *Click the **Animals** category and notice the available clips. In a moment, you will insert the "veterinarian with the dog" clip.*

C *Click the **All Categories** button to display the All Categories screen. You can always use this button to display the All Categories screen.*

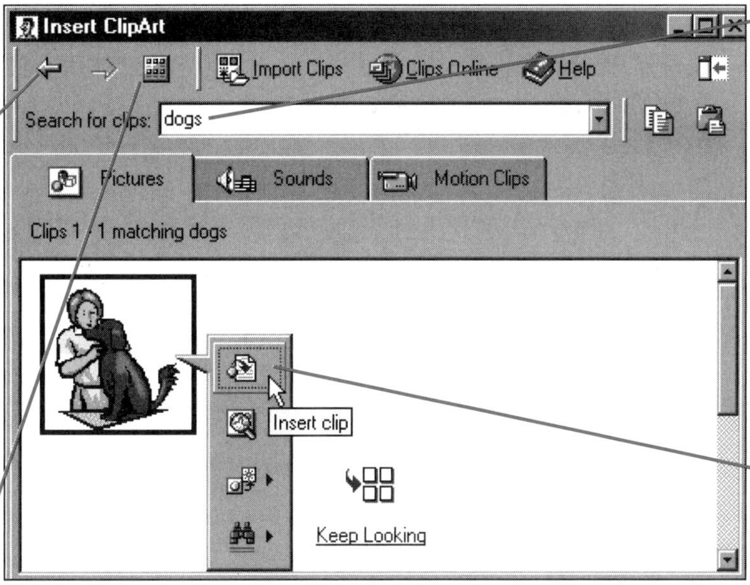

Insert ClipArt
Import Clips
Clips Online
Help
Search for clips: dogs
Pictures
Sounds
Motion Clips
Clips 1 - 1 matching dogs
Insert clip
Keep Looking

D *Click in the **Search for clips** box, type* **dogs***, and tap* (ENTER)*. Each clip has keywords associated with it. In this case, there is just one clip associated with the keyword dogs.*

E *Click the "**dogs**" clip and then click the **Insert Clip** button.*

10. Click the Close ☒ button on the Clip Gallery.

As you can see, the "dogs" picture floats on the slide. In the next exercise, you will position the picture and adjust its size.

Selecting, Moving, and Sizing Pictures

From the Keyboard

Tap arrow keys to move picture

You must select pictures and other objects before you can move or size them. The easiest way to select an object is to click anywhere on the object. Small squares called sizing handles appear on the corners and four sides of a selected object. You can change the size of a picture by dragging a sizing handle. If you drag a corner-sizing handle, then the height and width change proportionately, thus maintaining the original picture proportions.

The Format Picture Dialog Box

You can set the size and position of a picture with precision using options on the Format Picture dialog box. You can display the Format Picture dialog box by right-clicking the picture and choosing Format Picture from the menu. You can also choose **Format→Picture** from the menu bar or click the Format Picture button on the Picture toolbar that appears whenever a picture is selected. These techniques work with all PowerPoint objects, including placeholders for titles and bulleted lists. The following illustrations describe the size and position options on the Format Picture dialog box.

*The **Size** tab lets you specify the width and height in inches, or you can scale the original width and height by a percentage. If the **Lock aspect ratio** box is checked, you can adjust either the width or height and PowerPoint will determine the other measurement (width or height) to ensure the object retains its the original proportions.*

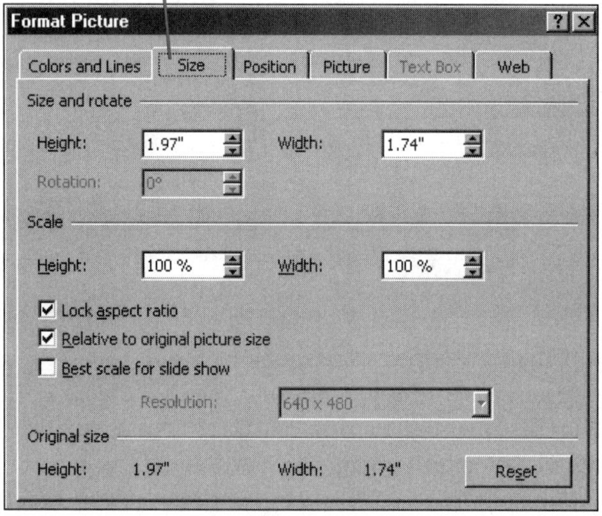
Format Picture
Colors and Lines
Size
Position
Picture
Text Box
Web
Size and rotate
Height:
1.97"
Width:
1.74"
Rotation:
0°
Scale
Height:
100 %
Width:
100 %
Lock aspect ratio
Relative to original picture size
Best scale for slide show
Resolution:
640 x 480
Original size
Height:
1.97"
Width:
1.74"
Reset

*The **Position** tab lets you specify a precise horizontal and vertical position for the picture.*

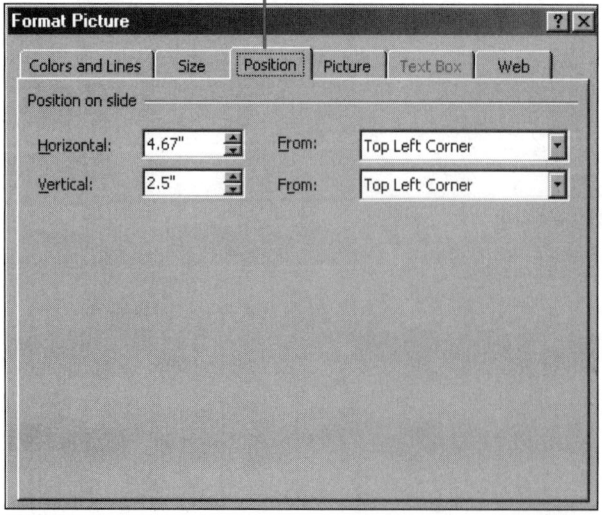
Format Picture
Colors and Lines
Size
Position
Picture
Text Box
Web
Position on slide
Horizontal:
4.67"
From:
Top Left Corner
Vertical:
2.5"
From:
Top Left Corner

Hands-On 24.2 Size and Move the Picture

1. Follow these steps to size and move the picture with the mouse.

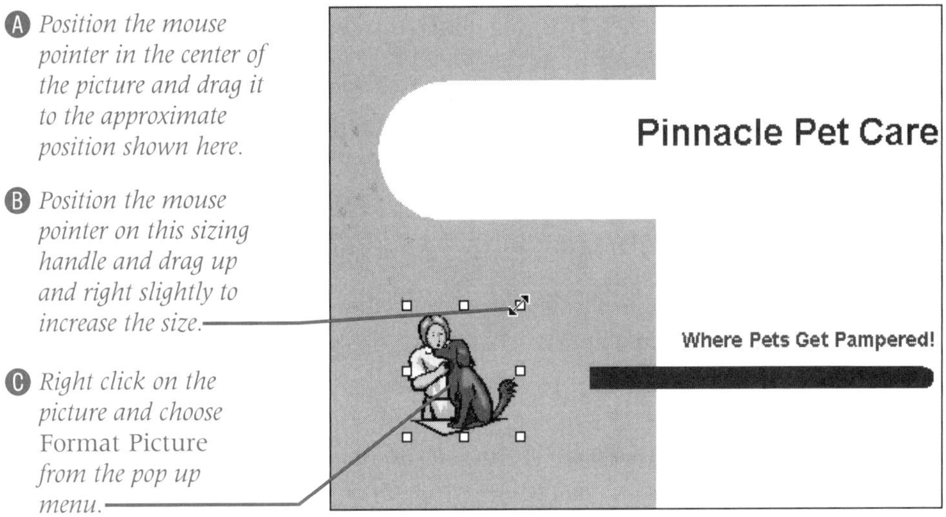
A Position the mouse pointer in the center of the picture and drag it to the approximate position shown here.
B Position the mouse pointer on this sizing handle and drag up and right slightly to increase the size.
C Right click on the picture and choose Format Picture from the pop up menu.
Pinnacle Pet Care
Where Pets Get Pampered!

2. Click the **Size** tab in the Format Picture dialog box.
3. Set the height to **`2.2"`**, and make sure the Lock aspect ratio box is checked.
4. Click in the Width box, and notice that PowerPoint adjusts the width for you, thus maintaining the original picture proportions.
5. Notice that the Scaling has been set to 112%.
   You can also adjust the height by specifying the Scaling percentage. For example, setting the scaling to 200% would double the size of the original picture.
6. Click the **Position** tab on the dialog box.
7. Set the Horizontal position to 1″ from the Top Left Corner and the Vertical position to 4.3″ from the Top Left Corner.
8. Click **OK,** and your graphic should have the size and position shown to the right.

Pinnacle Pet Care
Where Pets Get Pampered!

(Continued on the next page)

Insert Clip Art on Another Slide

In the next few steps, you will insert clip art on the Services Provided slide. First, you will change the AutoLayout for the slide to a clip art layout. You will then insert the clip art into the clip art placeholder box.

9. Navigate to the Services Provided slide (the second slide in the presentation).
10. Click the Common Tasks button, and choose Slide Layout.

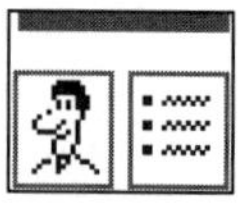

11. Choose the clip art AutoLayout shown to the right, and click the Apply button.
    Notice that the bulleted list moves to the right side of the slide, and the clip art placeholder appears on the left side. Also notice that an icon and text instructing you to double-click appear in the middle of the clip art placeholder box. You can use this icon to display the Clip Gallery from within a clip art placeholder box.
12. Double-click the Add Clip Art icon in the placeholder box to display the Clip Gallery.
13. Scroll down through the categories, and choose the Special Occasions category
14. Click the **Awards** image (it should be the first image), and click the Insert Clip button.
    The Clip Gallery closed automatically because you are working with a clip art AutoLayout. In the first exercise, you had to close the box after inserting the clip art on the title slide because you were not inserting into a clip art AutoLayout.

Size the Image

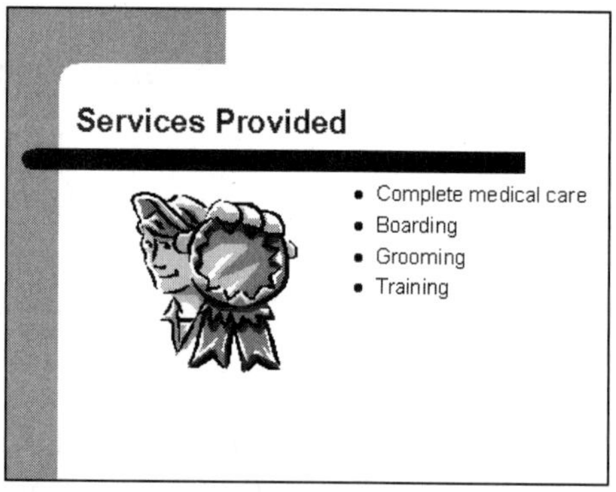

Services Provided
Complete medical care
Boarding
Grooming
Training

15. Right-click the image you just inserted, and choose Format Picture from the pop-up menu.
16. Click the **Size** tab in the Format Picture dialog box.
17. Set the height scaling option to 75%, and click **OK.**
18. Use the mouse to adjust the position of the image as shown to the right.
19. Save the changes to your presentation, and continue with the next topic.

Transitions

PowerPoint lets you create transitions between slides in electronic slide shows. For example, the Dissolve transition causes the current slide to slowly dissolve before the next slide is introduced. Transitions can be interesting for the audience, and they help create distinct break points between slides. There are over 40 transitions available in PowerPoint 2000.

Setting Up Transitions in Slide Sorter View

Slide Sorter view is the best view to use when setting up transitions. This is because transitions are often applied to multiple slides. Transitions are applied to entire slide(s), not to individual objects within slides. Later in this lesson, you will apply custom animation effects to individual objects within slides. Another reason for using Slide Sorter view when setting up transitions is that the Slide Sorter toolbar contains a button and drop-down list to help you apply transitions. The transition controls on the Slide Sorter toolbar are defined in the following illustration.

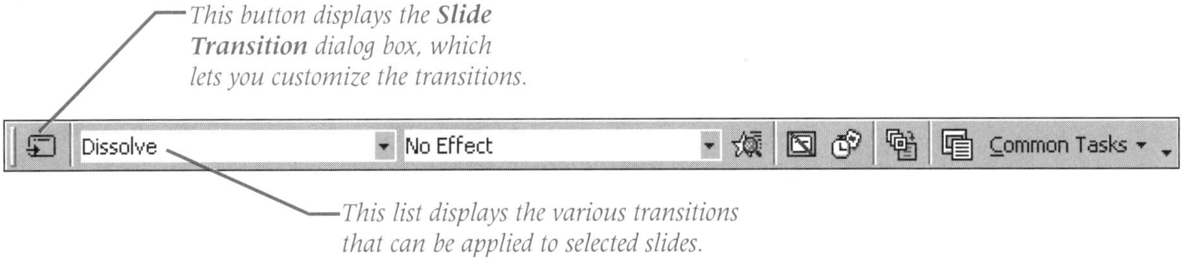
This button displays the **Slide Transition** dialog box, which lets you customize the transitions.
Dissolve
No Effect
Common Tasks
This list displays the various transitions that can be applied to selected slides.

Selecting Multiple Slides in Slide Sorter View

Transitions and other effects are applied to the selected slide(s) in Slide Sorter view. You select a single slide by simply clicking the desired slide. You can select multiple slides by pressing and holding the CTRL key while clicking the desired slides. You can select a range of slides by clicking the first slide, pressing SHIFT, and clicking the last slide. All slides between the two slides will be selected.

Hands-On 24.3 Create Transitions

In this exercise, you will apply the Dissolve transition to all slides except for the title slide. Later in this lesson, you will create a more dramatic effect for the title slide.

1. Click the Slide Sorter View button on the View bar.
2. Follow these steps to select multiple slides, and to choose a transition effect.

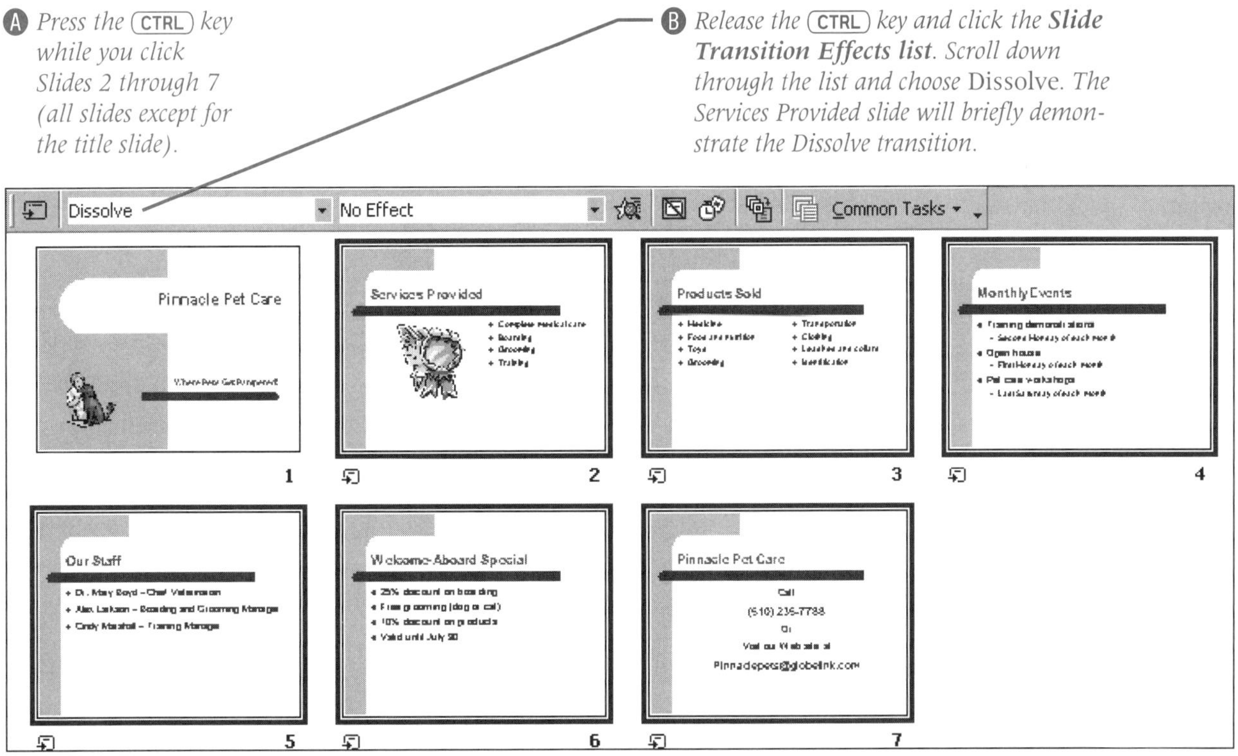
A Press the CTRL key while you click Slides 2 through 7 (all slides except for the title slide).
B Release the CTRL key and click the **Slide Transition Effects list**. Scroll down through the list and choose Dissolve. The Services Provided slide will briefly demonstrate the Dissolve transition.
Dissolve
No Effect
Common Tasks
Pinnacle Pet Care
Services Provided
Products Sold
Monthly Events
Our Staff
Welcome Aboard Special
Pinnacle Pet Care
(510) 236-7788
1
2
3
4
5
6
7

Notice that each of the selected slides has a transition effect icon just below the slide. This icon indicates that a transition effect has been applied to the slide.

(Continued on the next page)

Run the Presentation

3. Click the title slide.
   At this point, only the title slide should be selected. In the next step, you will run the presentation. Selecting the title slide will force the presentation to begin with that slide.
4. Click the Slide Show button on the View bar.
   The title slide will appear without a transition. The title slide would have opened with the Dissolve transition if you had applied the transition to it.
5. Click the mouse button, and the title slide will dissolve into the Services Provided slide.
6. Continue to click the mouse button until the presentation is complete, and the Slide Sorter window reappears.

Customize the Transition Effects

7. Select Slides 2 through 7 as you did earlier in this exercise.
8. Click the Slide Transition button on the left end of the Slide Sorter toolbar.
   The Slide Transition dialog box appears. This dialog box lets you customize transition effects.
9. Follow these steps to modify the transition effect and to explore the dialog box.

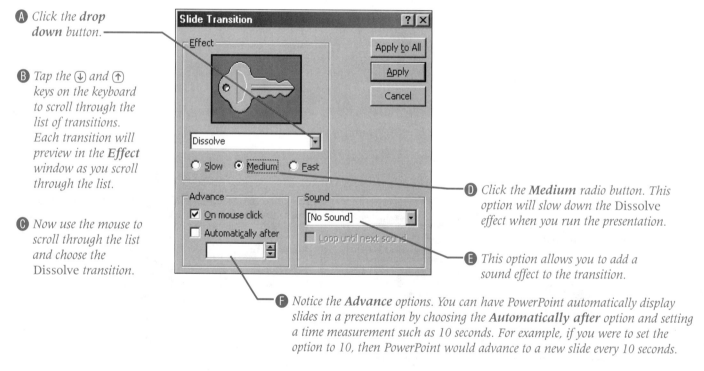

Ⓐ *Click the **drop down** button.*

Ⓑ *Tap the ↓ and ↑ keys on the keyboard to scroll through the list of transitions. Each transition will preview in the **Effect** window as you scroll through the list.*

Ⓒ *Now use the mouse to scroll through the list and choose the* Dissolve *transition.*

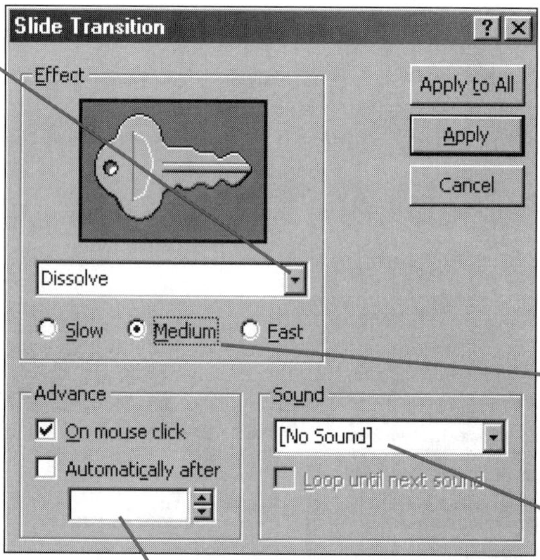
Slide Transition
Effect
Apply to All
Apply
Cancel
Dissolve
Slow
Medium
Fast
Advance
On mouse click
Automatically after
Sound
[No Sound]
Loop until next sound

Ⓓ *Click the **Medium** radio button. This option will slow down the* Dissolve *effect when you run the presentation.*

Ⓔ *This option allows you to add a sound effect to the transition.*

Ⓕ *Notice the **Advance** options. You can have PowerPoint automatically display slides in a presentation by choosing the **Automatically after** option and setting a time measurement such as 10 seconds. For example, if you were to set the option to 10, then PowerPoint would advance to a new slide every 10 seconds.*

10. Click the **Apply** (not Apply to All) button to apply the Medium Dissolve effect to the selected slides.
    If you had clicked the Apply to All button, then the effect would have been applied to all slides, including the title slide.
11. Click the title slide, and then click the Slide Show button to begin the slide show.
12. Click the mouse button repeatedly until the slide show is complete.
13. Feel free to experiment with the transition effects.
14. Save the changes, and continue with the next topic.

Animating Text Objects

PowerPoint lets you animate text and other objects in a presentation. Text objects include subtitles and bulleted paragraphs. For example, the Fly From Left effect introduces bulleted paragraphs by "flying them in" from the left side of the screen. With the Fly From Left effect, a new bulleted paragraph is introduced each time you click the mouse button. This allows you to deliver your presentation bullet-by-bullet.

Using the Text Preset Animation Options

The Slide Sorter toolbar contains a Text Preset Animation drop-down list as shown in the following illustration. This list displays the most common types of animation that are applied to text objects. When you apply animation using this list, the animation affects all text objects on the selected slide(s). You can also apply animation effects to individual paragraphs within a slide by using the Custom Animation dialog box. You will learn about custom animation in the next topic.

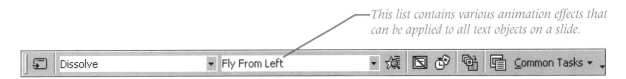

This list contains various animation effects that can be applied to all text objects on a slide.

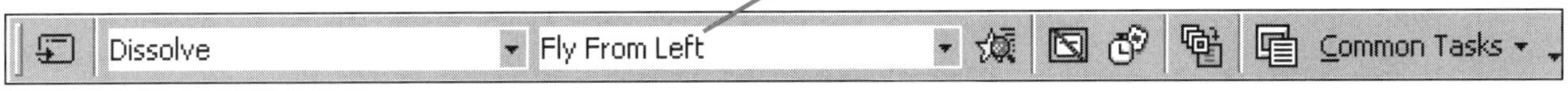
Dissolve
Fly From Left
Common Tasks

Hands-On 24.4 Add Text Animation

1. If necessary, click the Slide Sorter button to switch to Slide Sorter view.
2. Click the title slide, and follow this step to choose the Spiral effect for the title slide.

(A) Click in this box and choose the Spiral *text animation effect.*

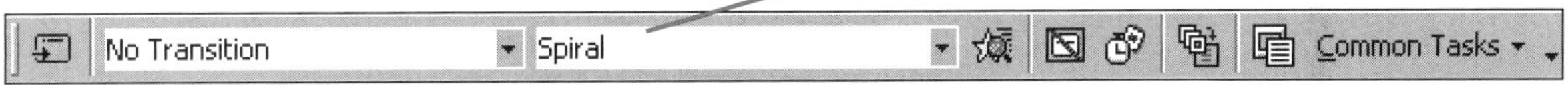
No Transition
Spiral
Common Tasks

Notice that the title slide has a text animation effect icon just below the slide. This icon indicates that a text animation effect has been applied to the slide.

3. Click the Slide Show button to begin the slide show.
   The title slide will appear without displaying the Where Pets Get Pampered! subtitle.
4. Click the mouse button, and the subtitle will spiral into view.
   Later in this lesson, you will add additional enhancements to this effect.
5. Right-click anywhere on the presentation, and choose End Show from the pop-up menu.
   The Slide Sorter screen should reappear.
6. Select the second slide by clicking anywhere on it.
7. Press CTRL while you click Slides 3 through 6.
   All slides should be selected except for the title slide and the closing slide.

(Continued on the next page)

8. Choose the Fly From Left text animation effect as shown below.

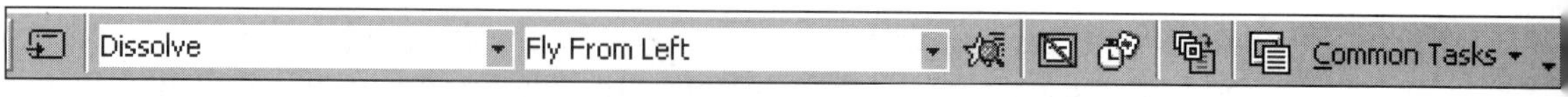
Dissolve
Fly From Left
Common Tasks

9. Click the title slide, and then click the Slide Show button to begin the slide show.
10. Click the mouse button to introduce the *Where Pets Get Pampered!* subtitle.
11. Click the mouse again to transition to the Services Provided slide.
The Dissolve transition will still be in effect.
12. Click the mouse again, and the clip art should "fly in" from the left.
13. Click again to introduce the first bullet.
14. Continue to click, and the next three bullets will be introduced.
15. Continue clicking until you have completed the entire presentation.
Each bulleted paragraph should be introduced sequentially, and the Dissolve transition will occur between slides.
16. Continue with the next topic when you have finished.

Custom Animation

The Custom Animation dialog box lets you create animation effects for individual objects within slides. You can animate clip art, text, and other types of objects. You can also add sound effects to animated objects and control the order and timing of the animation sequence.

Applying Custom Animation to Objects

Custom Animation is applied to individual objects on slides. For this reason, you must be in Slide view or Tri-pane view before you can display the custom animation dialog box. These views let you select individual objects on slides. The easiest way to display the Custom Animation dialog box is to right-click the selected object(s) and choose Custom Animation from the pop-up menu.

Custom Animation Effects

You use the Effects tab in the Custom Animation dialog box to apply effects to objects. For example, you can make pictures fly onto the screen or swirl (as you did with the subtitle on the title slide). You can also apply other effects, such as dimming or hiding an object, after its animation is complete.

Hands-On 24.5 Apply Custom Animation Effects

In this exercise, you will animate the title slide.

Animate the Picture

1. If necessary, end the slide show, and click the Slide View button.
2. Navigate to the title slide, and click the "dog" picture.
3. Now right-click the selected picture, and choose Custom Animation from the menu.

4. Follow these steps to set the effect options for the picture.

Ⓐ *Click the* ***Effects*** *tab and notice that* Picture frame 3 *(the "dogs" picture) is highlighted. The animation settings you make in Step B will be applied to the picture.*

Ⓑ *Set the* ***entry animation*** *to* Crawl From Top.

Ⓒ *Notice the* ***After animation*** box. *You can hide an object after its animation is complete or change its color. You will use this option in a later exercise to dim bulleted paragraphs as new paragraphs are introduced.*

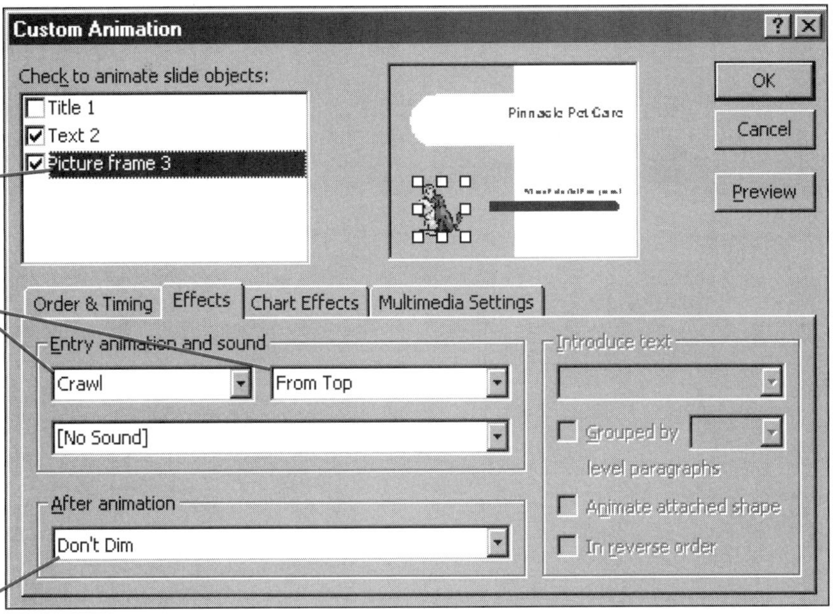

Custom Animation
Check to animate slide objects:
Title 1
Text 2
Picture frame 3
Pinnacle Pet Care
OK
Cancel
Preview
Order & Timing
Effects
Chart Effects
Multimedia Settings
Entry animation and sound
Crawl
From Top
[No Sound]
After animation
Don't Dim
Introduce text
Grouped by
level paragraphs
Animate attached shape
In reverse order

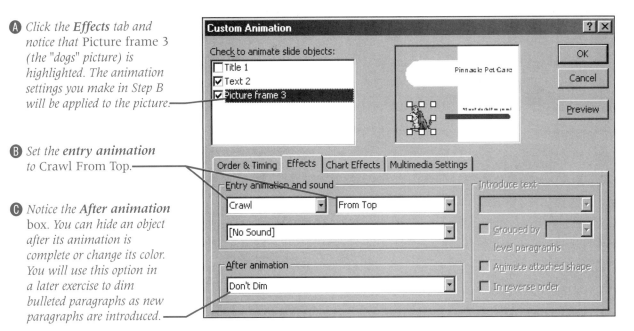

Animate the Subtitle

5. Follow these steps to set the sound effect for the subtitle.

Ⓐ *Choose* Text 2 *(subtitle) from this list. The animation effects you choose will be applied to the subtitle.*

Ⓑ *Choose* Whoosh *from the sound list. Notice the Spiral entry animation is in effect from an earlier exercise.*

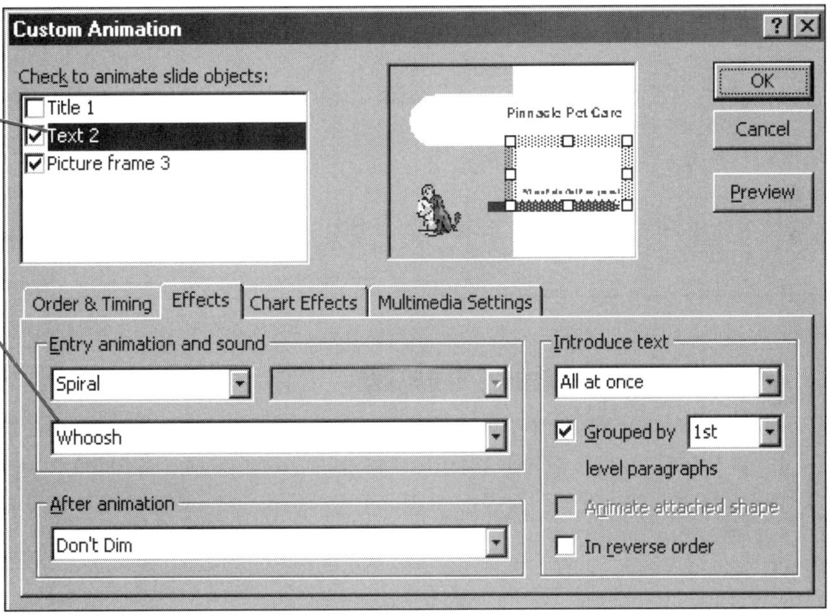

Custom Animation
Check to animate slide objects:
Title 1
Text 2
Picture frame 3
Pinnacle Pet Care
OK
Cancel
Preview
Order & Timing
Effects
Chart Effects
Multimedia Settings
Entry animation and sound
Spiral
Whoosh
After animation
Don't Dim
Introduce text
All at once
Grouped by
1st
level paragraphs
Animate attached shape
In reverse order

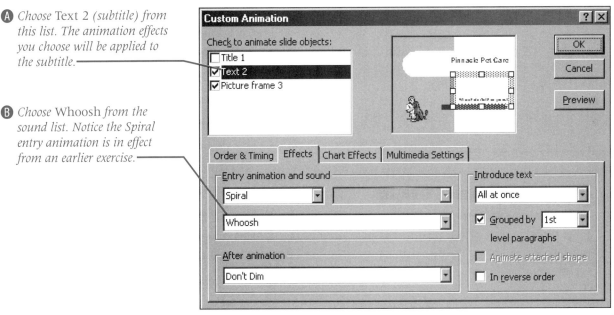

(Continued on the next page)

6. Follow these steps to set the order and timing options.

Ⓐ *Click the* ***Order & Timing*** *tab.*

Ⓑ *Choose* Picture frame 3 *in this list and click the* ***Move up*** *button. This instructs PowerPoint to animate the picture before the subtitle.*

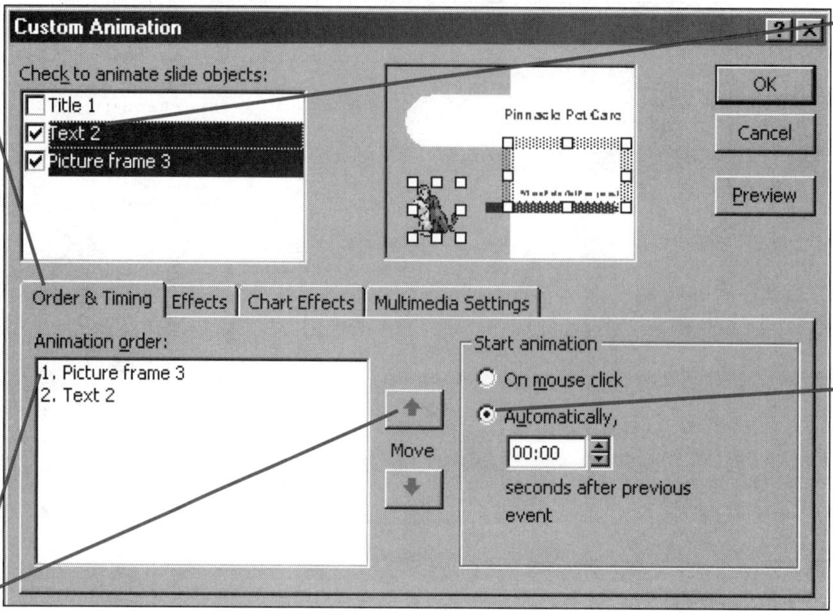

Custom Animation
Check to animate slide objects:
Title 1
Text 2
Picture frame 3
OK
Cancel
Preview
Order & Timing
Effects
Chart Effects
Multimedia Settings
Animation order:
1. Picture frame 3
2. Text 2
Move
Start animation
On mouse click
Automatically,
00:00
seconds after previous event

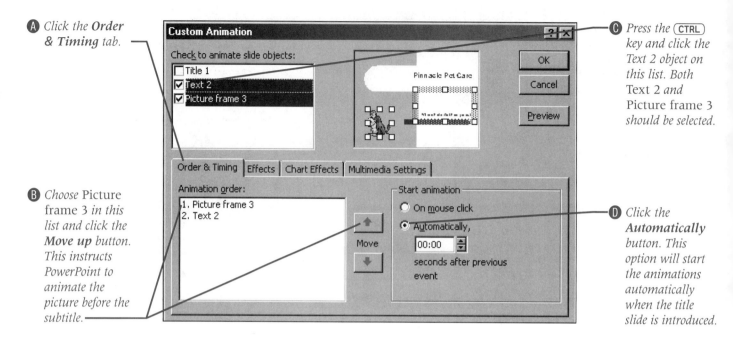

Ⓒ *Press the* (CTRL) *key and click the* Text 2 *object on this list. Both* Text 2 *and* Picture frame 3 *should be selected.*

Ⓓ *Click the* ***Automatically*** *button. This option will start the animations automatically when the title slide is introduced.*

7. Click **OK** to complete the custom animation settings.
8. Click the Slide Show button to begin the presentation.
   The picture will automatically crawl from the top of the screen. When it is in position, the subtitle will spiral into view with a whoosh sound (if your computer system is equipped with speakers).
9. Click several times until the animation is complete on the second slide (Services Provided).
   Notice that the picture "flies from the left" before the bullets are introduced. In the next exercise, you will change the order of animation to make the picture appear last.
10. Point to the bottom left corner of the screen, click the Pop-Up Menu button, and choose End Show.

Dimming and Hiding Objects

It is important to keep the audience focused on the current topic as it is being discussed. PowerPoint can help you by dimming bulleted paragraphs as new bullets are introduced. You can dim bulleted paragraphs by setting the After animation setting on the Effects tab of the Custom Animation dialog box.

Hands-On 24.6 Dim Bullets, and Animate Other Slides

1. Navigate to the Services Provided slide.
2. Right-click anywhere on the bulleted list, and choose Custom Animation from the menu.

3. Follow these steps to set the After animation option.

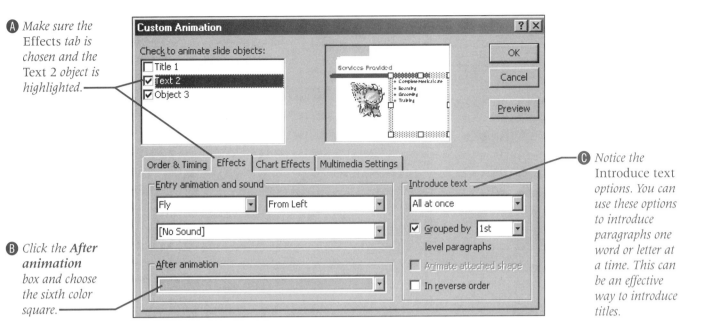

Ⓐ *Make sure the* Effects *tab is chosen and the* Text 2 *object is highlighted.*

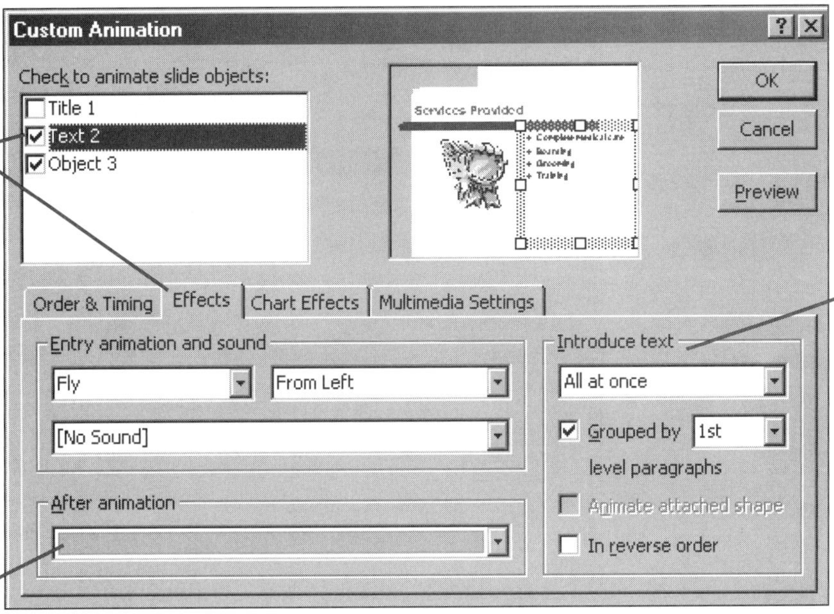
Custom Animation
Check to animate slide objects:
Title 1
Text 2
Object 3
Services Provided
OK
Cancel
Preview
Order & Timing
Effects
Chart Effects
Multimedia Settings
Entry animation and sound
Fly
From Left
[No Sound]
After animation
Introduce text
All at once
Grouped by
1st
level paragraphs
Animate attached shape
In reverse order

Ⓑ *Click the* ***After animation*** *box and choose the sixth color square.*

Ⓒ *Notice the* Introduce text *options. You can use these options to introduce paragraphs one word or letter at a time. This can be an effective way to introduce titles.*

4. Click the **Order & Timing** tab.
5. Choose Object 3 in the Animation order list, and click the Move down button.
   This will cause the picture to be introduced after the bullets. Currently, the picture is introduced first.
6. Click **OK** to complete the animation settings.
7. Make sure the Services Provided slide is the current slide, and click the Slide Show button to begin the presentation.
8. Click several times until all of the bullets and the picture have been introduced.
   Notice the dimming effect used on the bullets.
9. End the slide show, and navigate through the presentation, setting the After animation setting for each of the remaining slides except for the closing slide. To do this, simply navigate to the desired slide, display the Custom Animation dialog box, set the After animation option as you did in the previous steps, and click OK. There is no need to set the animation order or timing for the remaining slides. You are simply trying to dim the bulleted paragraphs as they are introduced. Also, make sure you set the After animation option for both bulleted lists on the Products Sold slide.

Animate the Closing Slide

10. Navigate to the closing slide.
11. Right-click the subtitle box with the telephone number, and choose Custom Animation.

(Continued on the next page)

12. Follow these steps to set the animation options.

Ⓐ *Make sure the* Text 2 *box is checked.*

Ⓑ *Set the* ***Entry animation*** *to* Zoom In From Screen Center *as shown here.*

Ⓒ *Set the* ***sound effect*** *to* Whoosh.

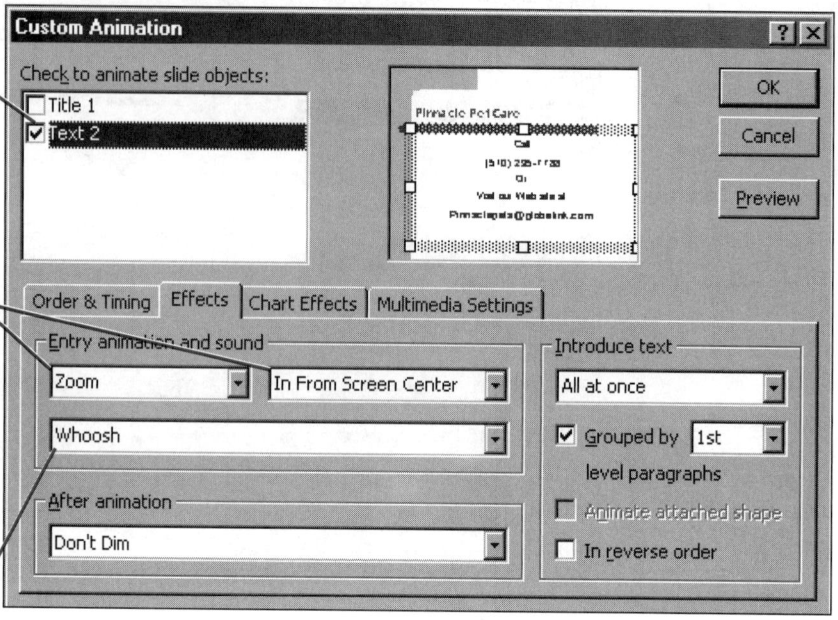
Custom Animation
Check to animate slide objects:
Title 1
Text 2
OK
Cancel
Preview
Order & Timing
Effects
Chart Effects
Multimedia Settings
Entry animation and sound
Zoom
In From Screen Center
Whoosh
After animation
Don't Dim
Introduce text
All at once
Grouped by
1st
level paragraphs
Animate attached shape
In reverse order

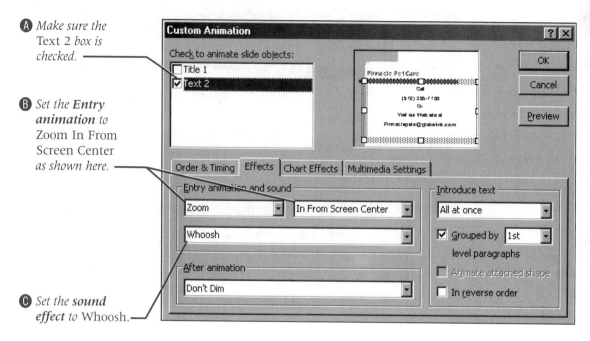

13. Click the **Order & Timing** tab.

14. Set the Start Animation option to Automatically, and click **OK.**

15. Navigate to the title slide, and click the Slide Show button.

16. Work through the presentation until it is complete.

17. Feel free to modify your presentation, and experiment with clip art, transitions, and animation.

18. Save the change to your presentation, and then close the presentation.

Concepts Review

True/False Questions

1.	Clip art can be inserted while working in Slide Sorter view.	TRUE	FALSE
2.	The Clip Gallery can be displayed by clicking the clip art icon in an AutoLayout box.	TRUE	FALSE
3.	Transitions are applied to individual objects on slides.	TRUE	FALSE
4.	Slide Sorter view is the best view to use when setting up transitions.	TRUE	FALSE
5.	You can apply a transition to multiple slides while using Slide Sorter view.	TRUE	FALSE
6.	The Slide Sorter toolbar lets you apply both transitions and text effects.	TRUE	FALSE
7.	Text objects cannot be animated.	TRUE	FALSE
8.	Clicking the mouse can initiate animation steps and transitions.	TRUE	FALSE
9.	Customized animations are applied to entire slides.	TRUE	FALSE
10.	The Clip Gallery organizes and categorizes clip art.	TRUE	FALSE

Multiple-Choice Questions

1. Which of the following keys is used to select multiple slides in Slide Sorter view?
   a. ALT
   b. HOME
   c. CTRL
   d. ENTER

2. Which of the following techniques can be used to display the Custom Animation dialog box?
   a. Right-click an open part of a slide while working in Slide view.
   b. Right-click an object while working in Slide view.
   c. Both a and b
   d. None of these

3. Which of the following effects can be controlled through the Custom Animation dialog box?
   a. Timing
   b. Sound
   c. Entry
   d. All of these

4. Which of the following buttons can be used to display the Slide Transition dialog box?
   a. 
   b. 
   c. 
   d. None of these

Skill Builders

Skill Builder 24.1 Insert Clip Art

In this exercise, you will add clip art to the Tropical Getaways presentation that was developed in the previous lesson. If you did not accurately complete the Skill Builder exercises in the previous lesson, then ask your instructor to copy the file named Tropical Getaways—Lesson 24 to your exercise diskette. This file provides the Tropical Getaways presentation, as it should be after completing Lesson 23.

1. Open the Tropical Getaways presentation.
2. If necessary, click the Slide View button to switch to Slide view.
3. Navigate to the Travel Categories slide.
4. Click the Common Tasks button, and choose Slide Layout.
5. Choose the Text and Clip Art AutoLayout, and click the **Apply** button.

6. Double-click the Insert Clip Art icon in the placeholder box to display the Clip Gallery.
7. Choose the Sports and Leisure category, and insert the tennis player clip as shown in the slide to the right. Your Travel Categories slide should now match the slide shown to the right.

Travel Categories
Adventure
Leisure
Family
Singles

8. Navigate to the Travel Now and Save slide.
9. Change the slide layout to Text and Clip Art (as you did for the Travel Categories slide).
10. Follow these steps to insert, size, and move a picture.

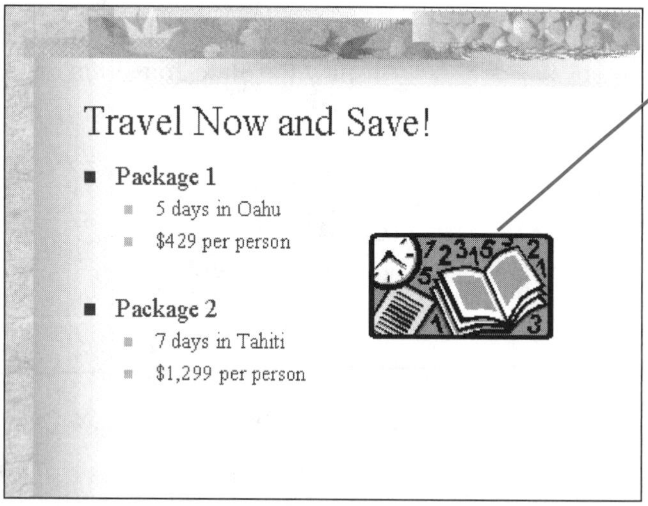

Travel Now and Save!
Package 1
5 days in Oahu
$429 per person
Package 2
7 days in Tahiti
$1,299 per person

Ⓐ *Insert this picture. It is located in the Business category.*

Ⓑ *Reduce the size of the picture by dragging a corner-sizing handle, and then drag the picture to the position shown here.*

11. Save the changes to your presentation, and continue with the next exercise.

Skill Builder 24.2 Set Up Transitions

In this exercise, you will set up transitions in the Tropical Getaways presentation.

1. Click the Slide Sorter view button on the View bar.
2. Use the CTRL key and the mouse to select Slides 2 through 6.
3. Choose the Cover Down transition effect from the Slide Sorter toolbar as shown below.

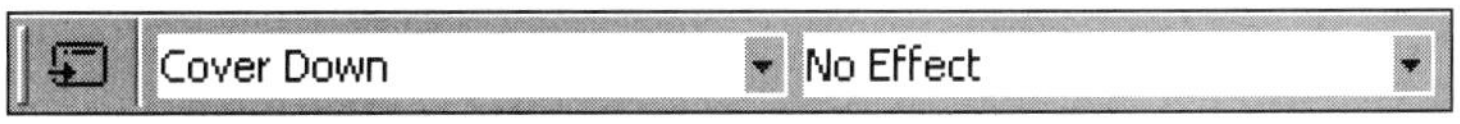
Cover Down
No Effect

4. Save the changes, and continue with the next exercise.

Skill Builder 24.3 Apply Text Animation

In this exercise, you will add preset text animation using the Slide Sorter toolbar.

1. Click the title slide, and choose the Swivel text animation.

No Transition
Swivel

2. Select Slides 2 through 5, and choose the Fly From Bottom-Right text animation.
3. Click the last slide, and choose the Zoom in From Screen Center text animation.
4. Click the title slide, and then click the Slide Show button on the View bar.
5. Click repeatedly until the presentation is complete.

Skill Builder 24.4 Apply Custom Animation

Animate the Title Slide

1. Click the Slide view button on the View bar.
2. If necessary, navigate to the title slide.
3. Right-click the subtitle Adventures in Paradise, and choose Custom Animation from the pop-up menu.
4. Choose the Whoosh sound to accompany the swivel effect.
5. Click the **Order & Timing** tab, and choose Automatically for the Start animation setting.
6. Click **OK** to complete the settings.
   These settings will cause the subtitle to automatically swivel and "whoosh" into view when the presentation begins.

Animate the Travel Categories Slide

7. Navigate to the Travel Categories slide.
8. Right-click the Tennis Player picture, and choose Custom Animation from the pop-up menu.
9. Choose the Whoosh sound.
10. Choose Text 2 from the objects list.
    The bulleted list box will appear to be selected in the preview window.
11. Choose a color from the After animation list.
    The bulleted paragraphs will change to this color as new bullets are introduced.
12. Choose Object 3 from the objects list.
13. Click the **Order & Timing** tab, and set the Start animation setting to Automatically.
14. Choose Object 3 in the Animation order box, and click the Move Down button. The Text 2 object should now be the first object in the Animation order.
    These settings will cause the picture to whoosh into view immediately after the last bullet is introduced.
15. Click **OK** to complete the settings.

Animate the Most Popular Destinations Slide

16. Navigate to the Most Popular Destinations slide.
17. Right-click the first bulleted list box, and choose Custom Animation from the pop-up menu.
18. Press the CTRL key, and click Text 3 on the objects list.
    Both Text 2 and Text 3 should be selected on the list.
19. Choose a color from the After animation list.
    The bulleted paragraphs will change to this color as new bullets are introduced.
20. Click the **Order & Timing** tab.

21. Choose Text 3 in the Animation order box, and click the Move Down [button icon] button. The Text 2 object should now be the first object in the Animation order.
These settings will allow the first bulleted list to be introduced, followed by the second bulleted list.

22. Click **OK** to complete the settings.

Animate the Complete Packages Slide

23. Navigate to the Complete Packages slide.

24. Right-click anywhere on the Packages Include subtitle, and choose Custom Animation from the pop-up menu.

25. Follow these steps to set custom animation.

Ⓐ *Press the* CTRL *key and click the* Text 3 *item. Both the* Text 2 *and* Text 3 *items should be selected, as shown here. Any effects that you set will be applied to both objects.*

Ⓑ *Click the* **Grouped by** *drop-down button and choose* 2nd. *If this option were set to* 1st, *then the* Level 1 *bullet and all* Level 2 *bullets under that bullet would fly onto the screen as a group. By choosing* 2nd, *the* Level 2 *bullets will fly onto the screen individually each time you click the mouse.*

Ⓒ *Choose a color from the* ***After animation*** *list.*

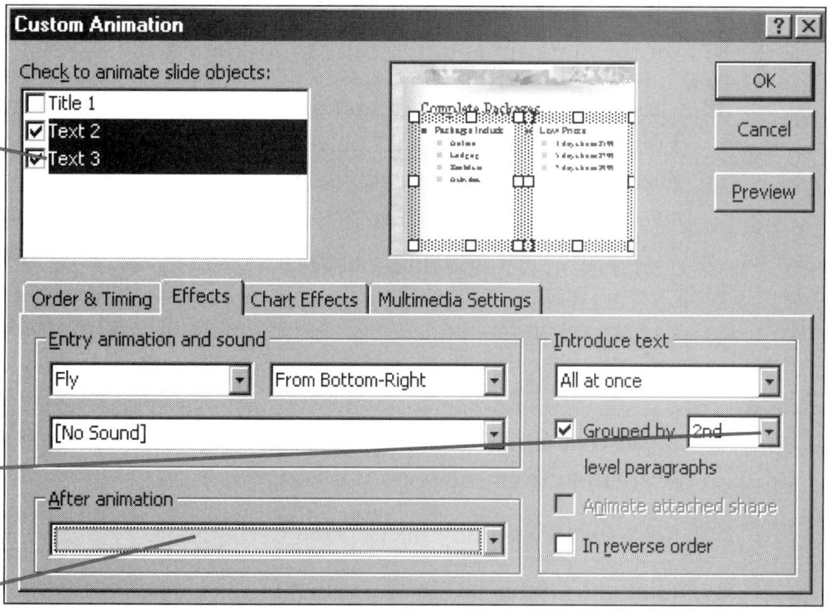
Custom Animation
Check to animate slide objects:
Title 1
Text 2
Text 3
OK
Cancel
Preview
Order & Timing
Effects
Chart Effects
Multimedia Settings
Entry animation and sound
Fly
From Bottom-Right
[No Sound]
After animation
Introduce text
All at once
Grouped by
2nd
level paragraphs
Animate attached shape
In reverse order

26. Click the **Order & Timing** tab.

27. Choose Text 3 in the Animation order box, and click the Move Down [button icon] button. The Text 2 object should now be the first object in the Animation order.
These settings will allow the first bulleted list to be introduced, followed by the second bulleted list.

28. Click **OK** to complete the settings.

29. Navigate to the title slide, and run the presentation. Continue clicking until you reach the Complete Packages slide. Continue clicking, and notice how the second-level bullets are introduced one at a time.

30. Right-click on the current slide, and choose End Show from the pop-up menu.

(Continued on the next page)

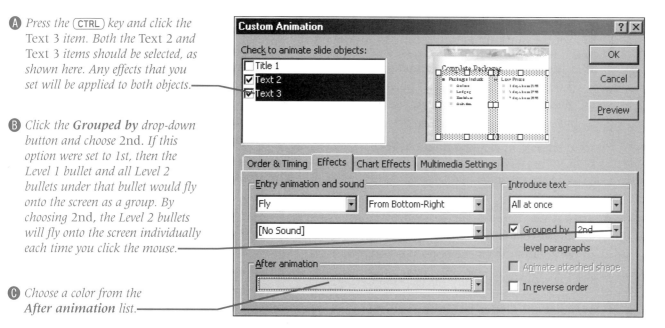

Animate the Travel Now and Save Slide

31. Navigate to the Travel Now and Save slide.
    Notice that this slide also has two bullet levels. You will leave the Grouped by option set to 1st for this slide, which will let the first- and second-level bullets fly onto the slide as a group.
32. Right-click anywhere on the picture and choose Custom Animation.
33. Set the Entry animation for the picture to spiral and the sound to Whoosh.
34. Choose Text 2 from the objects list.
    The bulleted list box will appear to be selected in the preview window.
35. Choose a color from the After animation list.
36. Click the **Order & Timing** tab, and choose Object 3 from the objects list.
    The picture will appear to be selected in the preview window.
37. Set the Start animation setting to Automatically.
38. Choose Object 3 in the Animation order box, and click the Move Down button. The Text 2 object should be the first object in the Animation order.
    These settings will cause the picture to spiral onto the slide with a "whoosh" immediately after the second bullet group is introduced.
39. Click **OK** to complete the settings.

Animate the Closing Slide

40. Navigate to the closing slide.
41. Right-click anywhere on the subtitle box with the name Donna Givens, and choose Custom Animation from the pop-up menu.
42. Set the entry sound effect option to Camera.
43. Click the **Order & Timing** tab, and set the Start animation setting to Automatically.
44. Click **OK** to complete the settings.

Run the Presentation

45. Navigate to the title slide, and run through the entire presentation.
46. Feel free to experiment with any of the special effects you have learned.
    It is important to have a systematic plan when developing presentations. In these Skill Builder exercises, you first added clip art to the presentation. Next, transitions and text effects that affected all bullets were added. Finally, custom animation was added to individual objects on the slides. This approach allows you to build a presentation layer-by-layer. You should use a similar approach when developing your own presentations.
47. Save the changes to your presentation, and then close the presentation.

Assessment

Assessment 24.1 Add Animation Effects

In this assessment, you will add animation effects to the Classic Cars presentation that was developed in the previous lesson.

1. Open the Classic Cars presentation on your exercise diskette.

Add Clip Art

2. Add clip art to the second slide as shown to the right. You can locate the picture by doing a search for the keyword car. You will need to change the slide layout for the slide and insert the picture in the placeholder box of the new layout. Reduce the size of the picture after inserting it, and adjust the position as shown. You will also need to reduce the font size of the bulleted paragraphs so that they no longer wrap.

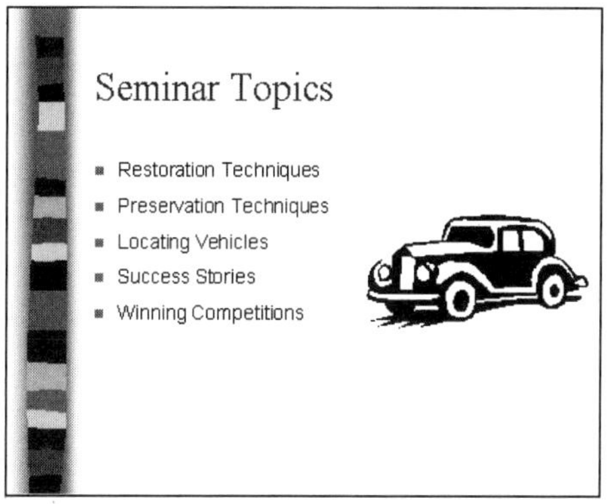

Seminar Topics
Restoration Techniques
Preservation Techniques
Locating Vehicles
Success Stories
Winning Competitions

3. Navigate to the closing slide, and change the subtitle from Enjoy the Ride to **Enjoy the Road Ahead**.
4. Add clip art to the last slide as shown to the right. There is no need to change the slide layout. Simply insert the picture, and size and position it as shown. The picture can be found in the Transportation category.

The 1999 Convention
Enjoy the Road Ahead

Add Transitions and Text Animation

5. Apply the Split Vertical Out transition to Slides 2 through 5.
6. Apply the Fly From Right text effect to Slides 2 through 4.

(Continued on the next page)

Animate the Title Slide

7. Animate the subtitle on the title slide to Fly From Left.
8. Use the Drive By sound effect to accompany the Fly From Left effect.
9. Set the timing to automatic so that the animation occurs as soon as the presentation is started.

Animate the Seminar Topics Slide

10. Navigate to the Seminar Topics slide, and animate the picture by having it Fly From Bottom-Left.
11. Use the Whoosh sound effect to accompany the Fly From Bottom-Left effect.
12. If necessary, set the animation order so that the picture is the first object animated.
13. Set the timing to Automatic so that the picture automatically whooshes into view when the slide is introduced.
14. Set the After animation setting for the bulleted list so that each bullet changes color (or dims) as each new bullet is introduced.

Animate the Third and Fourth Slides

15. Navigate to the Collections on Display slide.
16. Set the bulleted paragraphs to change color (or dim) as each new bullet is introduced.
17. Navigate to the Door Prizes slide.
18. Display the Custom Animation dialog box and change the Group by level to 2nd so that the 2nd level bulleted paragraphs fly onto the slide one at a time. You will need to do this for both the Text 2 and Text 3 objects.
19. Set the bulleted paragraphs to change color (or dim) as each new bullet is introduced.
20. Change the Animation order so that Text 2 is introduced before Text 3.

Animate the Closing Slide

21. Animate the picture on the closing slide by having it Crawl From Left.

22. Set the timing to automatic so that the picture automatically crawls into view when the slide is introduced.

Run the Presentation

23. Run your presentation when you have finished.

24. Save the changes to the presentation and then close the presentation.

LESSON 25—Integration

Excel and PowerPoint

Office 2000 provides a variety of techniques that let you exchange data between applications. The object linking and embedding (OLE) capabilities of Office 2000 let you create data links between applications. For example, in this lesson, you will place an Excel chart in a PowerPoint presentation. The chart will automatically be updated whenever the source data in the Excel workbook is changed.

In This Lesson

Case Study

Al Smith needs to develop a presentation for the Loan Committee at Bay View Bank. Under Al's guidance, Pinnacle Pet Care has done so well that Al wants to open two new branch locations. Al prepares a PowerPoint presentation for the Loan Committee. An important part of the presentation is a chart that depicts the financial projections for the next five years.

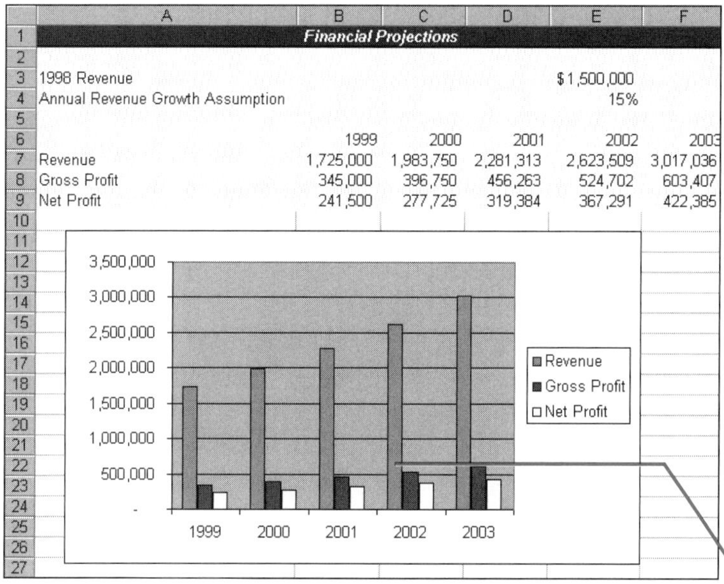

Financial Projections
1998 Revenue $1,500,000
Annual Revenue Growth Assumption 15%
1999 2000 2001 2002 2003
Revenue 1,725,000 1,983,750 2,281,313 2,623,509 3,017,036
Gross Profit 345,000 396,750 456,263 524,702 603,407
Net Profit 241,500 277,725 319,384 367,291 422,385
3,500,000
3,000,000
2,500,000
2,000,000
1,500,000
1,000,000
500,000
Revenue
Gross Profit
Net Profit
1999 2000 2001 2002 2003

The Excel chart is pasted into a PowerPoint slide, and a link is established. Any changes made to the worksheet data are reflected in the PowerPoint chart.

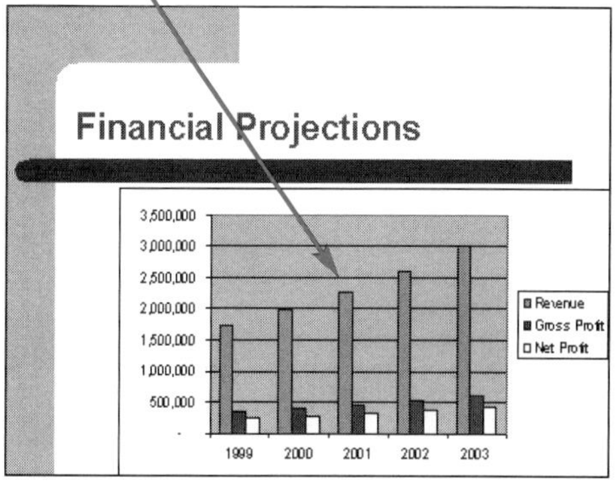

Financial Projections

Object Linking and Embedding

Office 2000 provides a variety of tools and techniques to let you exchange data between applications. Object Linking and Embedding (OLE) lets you create links between **source** documents and **destination** documents. For example, you may want an Excel chart to appear in a PowerPoint presentation. If the Excel chart is linked to the PowerPoint presentation, then changes made to the Excel data are automatically reflected in the PowerPoint chart.

The Paste Special Command

You use the **Edit→Paste Special** command to establish object linking and embedding. To establish object linking, you first select the text, chart, or other object that you wish to link to the destination document. Then you switch to the destination document, issue the **Edit→Paste Special** command, and choose the Paste link option. Changes made in the source document are then reflected in the destination document.

Inserting Excel Charts in PowerPoint Presentations

PowerPoint 2000 has several AutoLayouts with placeholder boxes for charts. You can create charts in PowerPoint, or you can create them in Excel. If you create a chart in Excel, you can use Copy and Paste or Copy and Paste Special to insert the chart in a PowerPoint presentation. Creating charts in Excel lets you take advantage of Excel's powerful analysis and charting capabilities. If you link the chart to your PowerPoint presentation, changes made to the Excel data are automatically reflected in the PowerPoint chart.

Hands-On 25.1 Create an Excel Worksheet

1. Start Excel, and enter the data shown below into a new worksheet. Make sure you enter the data in the same cells shown in the following worksheet.

	A	B	C	D	E	F
1	Financial Projections					
2						
3	1998 Revenue				$1,500,000	
4	Annual Revenue Growth Assumption				15%	
5						
6		1999	2000	2001	2002	2003
7	Revenue					
8	Gross Profit					
9	Net Profit					

2. Save the workbook to your exercise diskette as **Hands-On Lesson 25.**

Create the Revenue Formulas

3. Click Cell B7.
   You will enter a formula in Cell B7 that calculates the 1999 revenue as the 1998 revenue plus 15%.
4. Enter the formula **`=E3*(1+E4)`**.
   Notice that this formula adds the growth assumption (15%) in Cell E4 to the number 1. This number is then multiplied by the value in Cell E3. The result should be 1,725,000. The benefit of referencing Cells E3 and E4 in the formula is that you can now change the values in those cells and the projected revenue in Cell B7 will be recalculated.

5. Click Cell C7, and enter the formula **`=B7*(1+E4)`**.
The result should be 1,983,750.

6. Now enter the formulas **`=C7*(1+E4)`** in Cell D7, **`=D7*(1+E4)`** in Cell E7, and **`=E7*(1+E4)`** in Cell F7.
At this point, Row 7 in your worksheet should have the following formula results.

6		1999	2000	2001	2002	2003
7	Revenue	1725000	1983750	2281313	2623509.38	3017036

Calculate the Gross Profit and Net Profit

7. Click Cell B8, and enter the formula **`=B7*.2`**.
This formula assumes that the profit margin will be 20%.

8. Use the fill handle to copy the formula across the row to Cells C8:F8.

9. Click Cell B9, and enter the formula **`=B8*.7`**.

10. Use the fill handle to copy the formula across the row.

11. Select all cells in the range B7:F9.

12. Click the Comma Style button, and then decrease the decimals to 0.

13. Select the range A1:F9, choose **Format→AutoFormat** from the menu bar, and apply the AutoFormat of your choice. The example shown below uses the Colorful 2 format.
At this point, your worksheet should match the following worksheet.

	A	B	C	D	E	F
1	***Financial Projections***					
2						
3	1998 Revenue				$1,500,000	
4	Annual Revenue Growth Assumption				15%	
5						
6		1999	2000	2001	2002	2003
7	Revenue	1,725,000	1,983,750	2,281,313	2,623,509	3,017,036
8	Gross Profit	345,000	396,750	456,263	524,702	603,407
9	Net Profit	241,500	277,725	319,384	367,291	422,385

Chart the Data

14. Select the range A6:F9. This range includes all of the data in Rows 6 through 9.

15. Click the Chart Wizard button.
The Chart Wizard—Step 1 of 4 box will appear.

(Continued on the next page)

16. Click the **Finish** button to accept all of the default chart settings, and Excel will create the chart as shown below.

	A	B	C	D	E	F
1	*Financial Projections*					
2						
3	1998 Revenue				$1,500,000	
4	Annual Revenue Growth Assumption				15%	
5						
6		1999	2000	2001	2002	2003
7	Revenue	1,725,000	1,983,750	2,281,313	2,623,509	3,017,036
8	Gross Profit	345,000	396,750	456,263	524,702	603,407
9	Net Profit	241,500	277,725	319,384	367,291	422,385

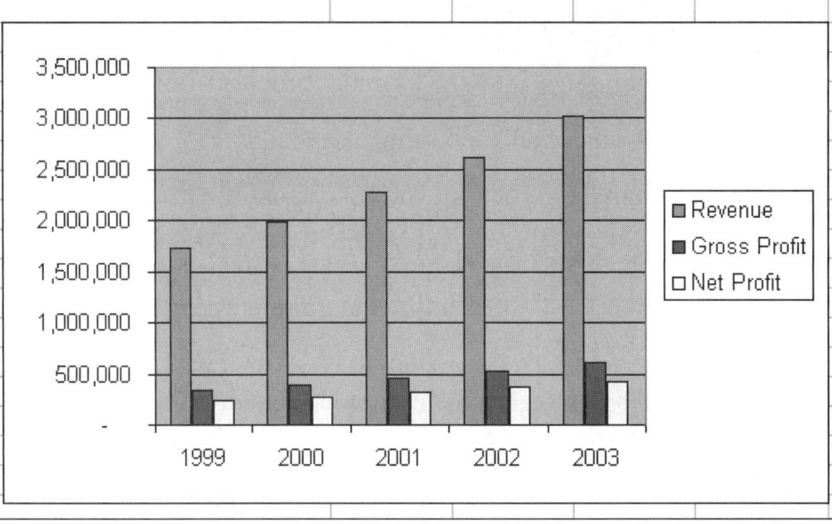
3,500,000
3,000,000
2,500,000
2,000,000
1,500,000
1,000,000
500,000
-
1999
2000
2001
2002
2003
Revenue
Gross Profit
Net Profit

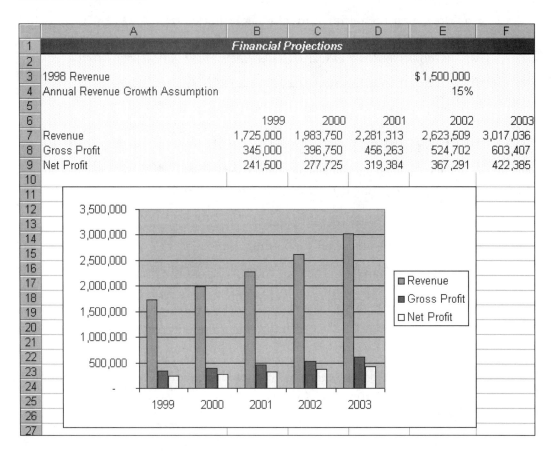

Play What-If Analysis

17. Click Cell E4, and enter the number 20%.
    All formulas in the worksheet should recalculate, and the chart should be updated. All of the formulas were recalculated because they depend upon Cell E4.

18. Change the number in Cell E4 back to 15%.

19. Save the changes to your workbook.

Set Up the PowerPoint Presentation

20. Start PowerPoint, and the PowerPoint dialog box will appear.

21. Choose Design Template, and click **OK.**

22. Choose the Capsules design, and click **OK.**

23. Add the following three slides to your new presentation.

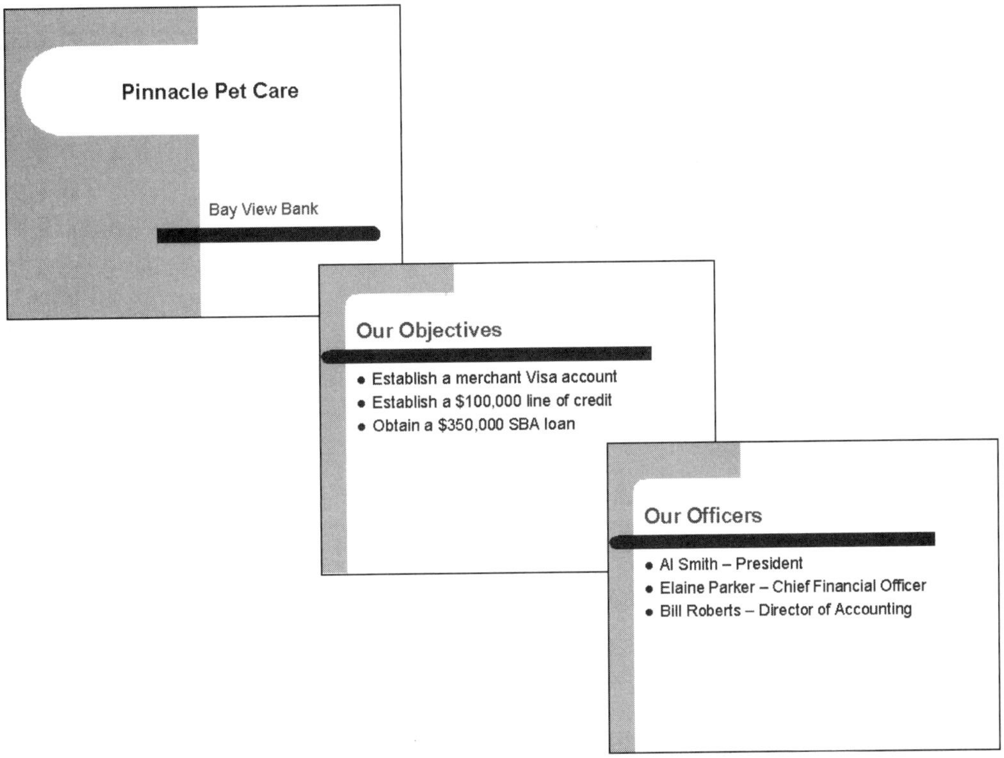

Pinnacle Pet Care
Bay View Bank
Our Objectives
• Establish a merchant Visa account
• Establish a $100,000 line of credit
• Obtain a $350,000 SBA loan
Our Officers
• Al Smith – President
• Elaine Parker – Chief Financial Officer
• Bill Roberts – Director of Accounting

24. Save the presentation as **Hands-On Lesson 25.**

Add a Chart Slide

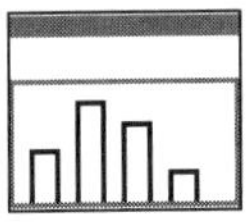

25. Click the  button, and choose New Slide.

26. Choose the Chart AutoLayout as shown to the right, and click **OK.**

27. Click the title box of the new slide, and enter the title `Financial Projections`.
You could create a chart directly in PowerPoint by double-clicking the chart icon in the chart placeholder box. However, you will copy and paste the chart from Excel. This way, you can keep your financial data in Excel and continue to use Excel's powerful analysis capabilities.

Copy and Paste the Chart

28. Switch to Excel by clicking the Microsoft Excel button on the Windows Taskbar.

29. Click on a blank area of the chart, and sizing handles will appear on the outer border of the chart.

30. Click the Copy  button on the Excel toolbar.

31. Switch to PowerPoint by clicking the Microsoft PowerPoint button on the Taskbar.

32. Click anywhere on the chart placeholder box on the Financial Projections slide, and the box will become selected.
In the next few steps, you will paste the chart into the PowerPoint presentation using the Paste Special command. This will establish a link between the chart in the Excel worksheet and the PowerPoint presentation. The link will automatically update the chart in PowerPoint whenever the Excel data changes. You could simply paste the chart using the Paste button; however, it would not be linked to the Excel data.

(Continued on the next page)

33. Choose **Edit→Paste** Special to display the Paste Special dialog box.

34. Choose the Paste link option, and click **OK.**
The chart will appear in the PowerPoint slide.

35. Notice that the numbers range from approximately 1,500,000 to 3,000,000.
These numbers will change when you update the Excel worksheet in the next few steps.

Change the Data in Excel

36. Switch to Excel by clicking the Microsoft Excel button on the Taskbar.

37. Click Cell E4, and change the number to 50%.
Notice how the Excel worksheet recalculates all of the formulas, and the Excel chart is updated.

38. Switch to PowerPoint by clicking the Microsoft PowerPoint button on the Taskbar.
The PowerPoint chart should reflect the same changes that occurred in the Excel chart. Once again, this is because the chart is linked to the Excel worksheet.

Complete the PowerPoint Presentation

39. Add the following new slide to your PowerPoint presentation.

40. Feel free to add clip art, transitions, and animation to your presentation.

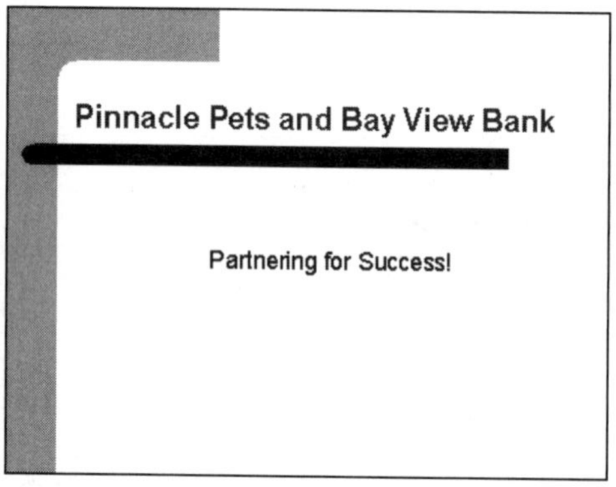
Pinnacle Pets and Bay View Bank
Partnering for Success!

41. Run your presentation, and make any other changes as desired.

42. When you have finished, save the changes to your presentation.

43. Choose **File→Exit** to exit from PowerPoint.

44. Save the changes to your Excel workbook, and then close the Excel program.

Concepts Review

True/False Questions

1. Charts can be created in PowerPoint without the need for Excel.	TRUE	FALSE
2. Excel charts that are inserted in PowerPoint presentations are always linked to the source data in the Excel workbook.	TRUE	FALSE
3. If a PowerPoint chart is linked to data in an Excel workbook, then changes in the worksheet data are reflected in the PowerPoint chart.	TRUE	FALSE

Multiple-Choice Questions

1. Which command is used to display the Paste Special dialog box?
   a. Insert→Paste Special
   b. Edit→Paste Special
   c. File→Paste Special
   d. Format→Paste Special

2. Object linking and embedding occurs between
   a. two source documents.
   b. two destination documents.
   c. a source document and a destination document.
   d. None of these

Index

A

D

E

F

I

J

K

L

M

N

O

P

Q

R

S

T

U

V

W

Z